THE FINEST SOLID MAHOGANY ENGLISH 18TH CENTURY ANTIQUE REPLICA DINING TABLE IN THE WORLD

BRITISH ANTIQUE REPLICA Masterpieces are Guaranteed for 50 YEARS

Tables 'Made to Measure' to seat from 4 to 40 people, hand polished and colour matched to your own collection.

Over fifty dining tables on display in our showrooms made by master craftsmen to a standard unsurpassed in the last century together with 100 styles of Chairs, also Sideboards, Desks, Filing Cabinets, Cocktail Cabinets, TV & Video Cabinets, Settees, Sofas, Chesterfields, Looking Glasses & Fine Large Oil Paintings. All available in three separate ranges to suit all life styles & income groups.

Visit the factory & superstore showrooms to see the world's largest display of English Antique Replica Furniture and *objets d'art*, visit www.1760.com or phone for brochure.

BRITISH ANTIQUE REPLICAS

22 SCHOOL CLOSE, QUEEN ELIZABETH AVE., BURGESS HILL
(BETWEEN GATWICK & BRIGHTON) WEST SUSSEX RH15 9RX

Mon-Sat 9am-5.30pm   Tel: 01444 245577   www.1760.com

MILLER'S

antiques

2004

MILLER'S

antiques

ELIZABETH NORFOLK *GENERAL EDITOR*

2004
VOLUME XXV

MILLER'S ANTIQUES PRICE GUIDE 2004

Created and designed by
Miller's
The Cellars, High Street
Tenterden, Kent, TN30 6BN
Tel: 01580 766411
Fax: 01580 766100

General Editor: Elizabeth Norfolk
Managing Editor: Valerie Lewis
Production Co-ordinator: Kari Reeves
Editorial Co-ordinator: Deborah Wanstall
Editorial Assistants: Rosemary Cooke, Joanna Hill, Maureen Horner
Production Assistants: Caroline Bugeja, Gillian Charles, Helen Clarkson, Ethne Tragett
Advertising Executive: Jill Jackson
Advertising Assistants: Emma Gillingham, Carol Woodcock
Advertising Co-ordinator & Administrator: Melinda Williams
Designer: Philip Hannath
Advertisement Designer: Simon Cook
Indexer: Hilary Bird
Production: Sarah Rogers
Jacket Design: Victoria Bevan
Additional Photographers: Ian Booth, Gareth Gooch, David Mereweather,
Dennis O'Reilly, Robin Saker, Steve Tanner

First published in Great Britain in 2003
by Miller's, a division of Mitchell Beazley,
imprints of Octopus Publishing Group Ltd,
2–4 Heron Quays, London E14 4JP

© 2003 Octopus Publishing Group Ltd

A CIP catalogue record for this book is
available from the British Library

ISBN 1 84000 831 8

Colour origination: 1.13, Whitstable, Kent
Lab 35, Milton Keynes, Bucks
Printed and bound: Rotolito Lombarda, Italy

Front cover illustrations:
A George III silver cruet, by John Delmester, London (TSC).
A Moss Agate beaker, c1960.
A brass cigarette case, c1730–50.

Half title illustration:
A silver cigarette case, Continental, 1898 (C).

Contents illustration:
A Meissen cup and saucer, with a view of Venice, c1850.

11

14

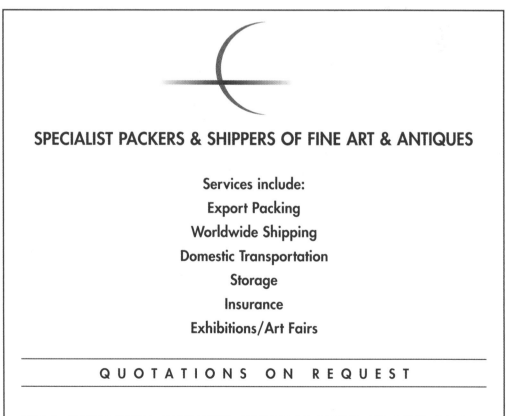

Dates	British Monarch	British Period	French Period
1558–1603	Elizabeth I	Elizabethan	Renaissance
1603–1625	James I	Jacobean	
1625–1649	Charles I	Carolean	Louis XIII (1610–1643)
1649–1660	Commonwealth	Cromwellian	Louis XIV (1643–1715)
1660–1685	Charles II	Restoration	
1685–1689	James II	Restoration	
1689–1694	William & Mary	William & Mary	
1694–1702	William III	William III	
1702–1714	Anne	Queen Anne	
1714–1727	George I	Early Georgian	Régence (1715–1723)
1727–1760	George II	Early Georgian	Louis XV (1723–1774)
1760–1811	George III	Late Georgian	Louis XVI (1774–1793) Directoire (1793–1799) Empire (1799–1815)
1812–1820	George III	Regency	Restauration Charles X (1815–1830)
1820–1830	George IV	Regency	
1830–1837	William IV	William IV	Louis Philippe (1830–1848) 2nd Empire Napoleon III (1848–1870) 3rd Republic (1871–1940)
1837–1901	Victoria	Victorian	
1901–1910	Edward VII	Edwardian	

German Period	U.S. Period	Style	Woods
Renaissance	Early Colonial	Gothic	Oak Period (to c1670)
		Baroque (c1620–1700)	
Renaissance/ Baroque (c1650–1700)			Walnut period (c1670–1735)
	William & Mary		
	Dutch Colonial	Rococo (c1695–1760)	
Baroque (c1700–1730)	Queen Anne		
Rococo (c1730–1760)	Chippendale (from 1750)		Early mahogany period (c1735–1770)
Neo–classicism (c1760–1800)	Early Federal (1790–1810)	Neo–classical (c1755–1805)	Late mahogany period (c1770–1810)
Empire (c1800–1815)	American Directoire (1798–1804)	Empire (c1799–1815)	
	American Empire (1804–1815)		
Biedermeier (c1815–1848)	Late Federal (1810–1830)	Regency (c1812–1830)	
Revivale (c1830–1880)	Victorian	Eclectic (c1830–1880)	
Jugendstil (c1880–1920)		Arts & Crafts (c1880–1900)	
	Art Nouveau (c1900–1920)	Art Nouveau (c1900–1920)	

contents

Acknowledgments

The publishers would like to acknowledge the great assistance given by our consultants. We would also like to extend our thanks to all auction houses and their press offices, as well as dealers and collectors, who have assisted us in the production of this book.

FURNITURE:	Edward Reily Collins, Hallidays, The Old College, High Street, Dorchester-on-Thames, Oxfordshire OX10 7HL
CAMPAIGN FURNITURE:	Sean Clarke, Christopher Clarke Antiques, The Fosse Way, Stow-on-the-Wold, Gloucestershire GL54 1JS
	Information on care and restoration of furniture supplied by Billy Cook, High Trees House, Savernake Forest, Nr Marlborough, Wiltshire SN8 4NE
OAK & COUNTRY FURNITURE:	Paul Hopwell, 30 High Street, West Haddon, Northamptonshire NN6 7AP
POTTERY:	John Axford, Woolley & Wallis, 51–61 Castle Street, Salisbury, Wiltshire SP1 3SU
LUSTREWARE:	Ian Sharp, 23 Front Street, Tynemouth, Tyne & Wear NE30 4DX
PORCELAIN:	John Sandon, Bonhams, 101 New Bond Street, London W1Y 0AS
ASIAN CERAMICS:	Peter Wain, Anglesey
GLASS:	Andy McConnell decanterman@freezone.co.uk
SILVER & SILVER PLATE:	Nicholas Shaw, Virginia Cottage, Lombard Street, Petworth, West Sussex GU28 0AG
CLOCKS:	Michael Turner, Sotheby's Olympia, Hammersmith Road, London W14 8UX
BAROMETERS:	Kym Walker, Weather House Antiques, Foster Clough, Hebden Bridge, West Yorkshire HX7 5QZ
DECORATIVE ARTS:	Eric Knowles, Bonhams, 101 New Bond Street, London W1Y 0AS
TWENTIETH-CENTURY DESIGN:	Jeremy Morrison, Sotheby's Olympia, Hammersmith Road, London W14 8UX
RUGS & CARPETS:	Richard Purdon, 158 The Hill, Burford, Oxfordshire OX18 4QY
ASIAN WORKS OF ART:	Peter Wain, Anglesey
BOXES:	Alan & Kathy Stacey, PO Box 2771, Yeovil, Somerset BA22 7DZ
ANTIQUITIES:	Peter A. Clayton FSA, Seaby Antiquities, 14 Old Bond Street, London W1X 4JL
TRIBAL ART:	Fiona McKinnon, Elms Lester, 1–3–5 Flitcroft Street, Soho, London WC2H 8DH
TOYS:	Glenn Butler, Wallis & Wallis, West Street Auction Galleries, Lewes, East Sussex BN7 2NJ
ROCK & POP:	Paul Wane & Jason Cornthwaite, Tracks, PO Box 117, Chorley, Lancashire PR6 0UU
SCIENTIFIC INSTRUMENTS & MARINE:	Jon Baddeley, Bonhams, 65–69 Lots Road, Chelsea, London SW10 0RN
MILITARIA:	John Wright, Q & C Militaria, 22 Suffolk Road, Cheltenham, Gloucestershire GL50 2AQ

How to use this book

In order to find a particular item, consult the contents list on page 19 to find the main heading – for example, Silver. Having located your area of interest, you will find that larger sections have been sub-divided. If you are looking for a particular factory, designer or craftsman, consult the index which starts on page 804.

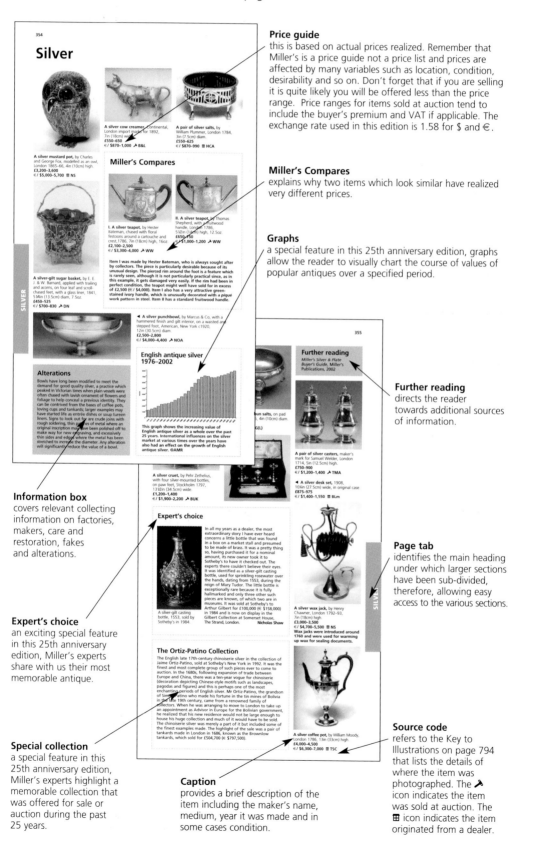

Price guide
this is based on actual prices realized. Remember that Miller's is a price guide not a price list and prices are affected by many variables such as location, condition, desirability and so on. Don't forget that if you are selling it is quite likely you will be offered less than the price range. Price ranges for items sold at auction tend to include the buyer's premium and VAT if applicable. The exchange rate used in this edition is 1.58 for $ and €.

Miller's Compares
explains why two items which look similar have realized very different prices.

Graphs
a special feature in this 25th anniversary edition, graphs allow the reader to visually chart the course of values of popular antiques over a specified period.

Further reading
directs the reader towards additional sources of information.

Page tab
identifies the main heading under which larger sections have been sub-divided, therefore, allowing easy access to the various sections.

Source code
refers to the Key to Illustrations on page 794 that lists the details of where the item was photographed. The ✗ icon indicates the item was sold at auction. The ⊞ icon indicates the item originated from a dealer.

Caption
provides a brief description of the item including the maker's name, medium, year it was made and in some cases condition.

Special collection
a special feature in this 25th anniversary edition, Miller's experts highlight a memorable collection that was offered for sale or auction during the past 25 years.

Expert's choice
an exciting special feature in this 25th anniversary edition, Miller's experts share with us their most memorable antique.

Information box
covers relevant collecting information on factories, makers, care and restoration, fakes and alterations.

BACA

BRITISH ANTIQUES AND COLLECTABLES AWARDS

presented by

Celebrating the Winners of BACA 2003

The fourth annual Awards Ceremony took place on 24 June 2003 at The Dorchester, Park Lane, London. After a champagne reception, the 300+ guests enjoyed a 3-course meal and, after eagerly awaiting the presentation ceremony, learned of the winners for the first time during the evening. Eric Knowles, Chairman of BACA, presented each winner with a certificate on stage.

The evening was a tremendous occasion continuing on into the early hours with guests and winners alike sharing in the celebrations.

Congratulations to all the short-listed nominees and winners!

Eric Knowles with guest, Michael Aspel

PROUDLY SPONSORED BY

The BACA Winners...

CATEGORY 1
General Antiques Dealer

UK: NORTH OF M62
Haughey Antiques
Kirkby Stephen, Cumbria

M62 SOUTH, TO M4 / M25
The Country Seat
Huntercombe, Manor Barn,
Henley-on-Thames

LONDON (INSIDE M25)
Gordon Watson
50 Fulham Road, London

SOUTH AND SOUTH-WEST OF ENGLAND
Lennox Cato Antiques
1 The Square, Edenbridge

CATEGORY 2
Specialist Antiques Dealers

FURNITURE
Adams Antiques
Churches Mansion, Hospital Street,
Nantwich

COLLECTABLES
sponsored by
The Girl Can't Help It
Alfies Antique Market, Marylebone,
London

SILVER & PLATE
Sanda Lipton
Elliot House, 28A Devonshire Street,
London

PRINTS
Elizabeth Harvey-Lee
1 West Cottages, Middle Aston Road,
North Aston, Oxfordshire

WATERCOLOUR
Chris Beetles Ltd
10 Ryder Street, St James, London

CERAMICS
Simon Spero
109 Kensington Church Street,
London

GLASS
Mallet & Son (Antiques Ltd)
129 Mount Street, London

JEWELLERY
Joseph H. Bonnar
72 Thistle Street, Edinburgh

CATEGORY 3
Auction Houses

UK: NORTH OF M62
Bonhams Auctioneers
17a East Parade, Leeds

M62 SOUTH, TO M4 / M25
Bonhams Auctioneers
Knowle, Solihull

INSIDE M25
Sotheby's Auctions
34–35 New Bond Street, London

SOUTH AND SOUTH-WEST OF ENGLAND
Woolley & Wallis
51–61 Castle Street, Salisbury

CATEGORY 4
Associated Awards

AON AWARD FOR AUCTIONEER OF THE YEAR
sponsored by
David Lay
Penzance Auction Rooms, Alverton, Penzance

BEST ANTIQUES CENTRE
The Swan at Tetsworth
High Street, Tetsworth, Oxfordshire

ANTIQUES ON THE INTERNET
www.welshantiques.com

BBC HOMES AND ANTIQUES MAGAZINE AWARD FOR BEST ANTIQUES SHOPPING STREET

sponsored by

High Street, Burford, Oxfordshire

ANTIQUES TRADE GAZETTE AWARD FOR IN-HOUSE EXHIBITION

Antiques Trade
GAZETTE
THE ANTIQUES TRADE WEEKLY

sponsored by
Christopher Clarke Antiques
"Campaign Furniture"

Introduction

I t is interesting to reflect on the many conversations I have had with dealers and collectors about lucky finds. Tales of barns that revealed Chinese export porcelain packed in cider barrels or the Gillows sideboard pulled out of the bonfire in the fading light of a past and distant 5 November.

There was, according to those involved in what purported to be the antique trade of post-war Britain, no shortage of 'kit'. The biggest problem, for most people, was once bought, who on earth to sell it to. Such a dilemma would be considered unthinkable today, although at the time of writing plenty of dealers involved in brown furniture might well be able to identify with their predecessors operating in a Britain that apparently had never had it so good.

It is a sobering exercise to look back on the many changes witnessed by those of us who have spent 25 years and more engrossed in this fascinating business. This has been a period dominated by such diverse personalities as Elton John whose sale back in 1988 is reviewed on page 474, or the Hunt brothers, who were determined to gain control of the silver bullion market, which saw the price of silver soar to £34 (€/ $54) per ounce only then to plummet to £7 (€/ $11).

Today many children find it simply impossible to imagine how anyone managed to live a life without a personal computer and display visible horror at the prospect of life without the precious mobile phone or Playstation II. Twenty five years ago the antiques scene was not too dissimilar to that of today. What has encroached into the business during the interim years has been the 'collectable'. Its emergence has been part and parcel of the ever growing parameter of a business intent on filling the void left by the more standard areas of antiques, many of which have become noticeably depleted in volume. This expansion has resulted in a wide variety of new markets in which can be included Rock and Pop memorabilia, post-war design, contemporary ceramics and many more.

Another significant area of expansion has been the veritable growth of reference books, specialist magazines and periodicals resulting in many a bookcase overflowing. The thirst for knowledge has also been quenched by the media in response to the public's escalating interest in all things antique.

The ball started rolling way back in the days of black and white television with the arrival of the first 'antique superstar', a certain Mr Arthur Negus. It was Arthur who set about demystifying the antique business on his not to be missed Sunday afternoon programme *Going for a Song* – revised in the mid-1990s to feature yours truly and much lamented after

almost 400 programmes second time around. At the time of writing we find ourselves with wall-to-wall television antiques programmes, the majority of which place a decided emphasis towards 'value' and suggest a business where you can 'get rich quick'. Oh, if only it were quite so simple.

The quantum leap in technology has without question altered the structure of trading patterns. The arrival of the worldwide web and the internet auction site was greeted with trumpets sounding in much the same way as the thousands of dotcoms, but now many of these have been and gone in what can only be described as a techno rationalization. Today the world of ebay continues to prosper alongside the traditional form of auction and the influence of the web cannot be understated. The effects of this global awareness are considered in the introductions provided by both Edward Reily Collins (Furniture) and John Sandon (Porcelain). Whereas Edward's comments focus on the practical demise of the bureau and its failure to accommodate present day computer hardware, John is quick to forewarn readers of the many pitfalls presented by buying porcelain off the web.

Despite all the remarkable advances in technology the antiques business is not immune to global wars, terrorism and life-threatening disease on either side of the Atlantic. However, in spite of the turmoil in world finance and the political upheavals in the Middle East this business has displayed a remarkable resilience.

As a result I am left to reflect on what the next 25 years might hold in store. The only thing I truly hope for is the same amount of fun that I have been lucky enough to experience in the previous quarter of a century.

Eric Knowles

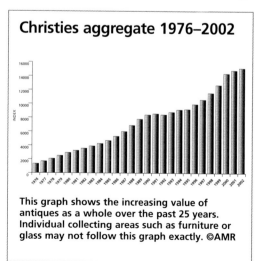

Christies aggregate 1976–2002

This graph shows the increasing value of antiques as a whole over the past 25 years. Individual collecting areas such as furniture or glass may not follow this graph exactly. ©AMR

Furniture

The 1980 edition of *Miller's Antiques Price Guide* states that increased public awareness of antiques has led to the demand for more and more information about the subject. That demand has turned into a flood as evidenced by the proliferation of television programmes, magazines and radio interviews, all dealing with antiques. One only has to compare the editorial of the 1979 *Miller's Antiques Price Guide* with this year's to notice not only the increased variety of stock but also the amount of technical information included.

Looking back over the last 25 years, the price of good mahogany furniture has fluctuated widely, due to political and economic factors as well as fashion trends. As a collector, one has to be careful to spot these trends – in 1999, for instance, a Queen Anne walnut bureau was priced at £2,700–3,300 (€/ $4,300–5,200), but in this year's Guide an almost identical piece (page 39) was priced at only £2,000–2,500 (€/ $3,200–3,500). The culprit for this decline in value is the computer, because there simply is not enough room to fit all the paraphernalia associated with the machine on a bureau. However, don't sell your bureau just yet. With

computers, like mobile phones, becoming smaller each year, the hardware will probably become so compact that they will soon fit back in the bureau again and prices will rise once more.

Although the current political and economic uncertainty may have affected the middle market for English furniture, the market for untouched furniture with provenance, good colour and patination and excellent condition, has gone from strength to strength over the last few years. As for middle range Georgian furniture we have seen similar situations in the market in 1991 and 1992, and experience shows that once the economy improves, prices increase.

If we compare period Georgian pieces with the late 19th- and early 20th-century copies that were produced in huge quantities to fill the large houses of manufacturing and trading barons, or indeed with the soulless utility furniture of today, it is plain to see that beautiful workmanship can be purchased for little more than its mass-produced imitations.

Edward Reily Collins

Beds & Cradles

A rococo painted and parcel-gilt bed, Swedish, mid-18thC, 67in (170cm) wide.
£6,000–7,500
€/ **$9,500–11,800** ⚘ S(NY)

Chippendale
- An item described as Chippendale was actually made by Thomas Chippendale.
- An item described as being Chippendale period was made during the Chippendale period but not by Thomas Chippendale.
- An item described as Chippendale-style is a later copy.

A George III mahogany tester bed, with arched canopy, drapery and twin reeded posts, 74¾in (190cm) long.
£1,200–1,400
€/ **$1,900–2,200** ⚘ S(O)

▶ **An Empire mahogany *lit en bateau*,** with folding box spring base and spring interior mattress, French, early 19thC, 93¼in (237cm) wide.
£1,700–2,000
€/ **$2,700–3,200** ⚘ S(O)

A Chippendale period stained maple and pine tester bed, posts possibly reduced in height, American, probably Massachusetts, c1780, 63½in (161.5cm) long.
£2,000–2,400
€/ **$3,200–3,800** ⚘ S(NY)

FURNITURE

A mahogany four-poster bed,
with tapering front posts and
acanthus leaf decoration, c1835,
66in (167.5cm) wide.
£8,000–9,000
€ / **$12,600–14,200** ⊞ SeH

A walnut tester bed, with drapery
hangings, Continental, 19thC,
42¼in (107.5cm) wide.
£1,700–2,000
€ / **$2,700–3,200** ⚒ S(O)

▶ **A Victorian burr-walnut-veneered
half-tester double bed,** with moulded
cornice and twin lobed hanging
pendants, fitted with side rails and
curtain hoops, the back hung with
curtains, the domed footboard with
panelled, foliate and column mouldings,
on casters, 63in (160cm) wide.
£1,800–2,000
€ / **$2,800–3,200** ⚒ FHF
**The relatively low value is due to
practical reasons. Most modern
houses do not have high enough
ceilings for such an item. However,
to make one today using such well-
matched walnut veneer would cost
at least three times this price.**

A mahogany and cane cradle, the
caned canopy top above a caned
body, on turned end supports, with
turned stretchers, on outswept feet,
19thC, 43¼in (110cm) wide.
£120–150
€ / **$190–240** ⚒ B(W)

A mahogany and cane cradle, the
arched cover with acorn finials, the
stand with ring-turned uprights,
with conforming stretchers, 19thC,
18in (45.5cm) long.
£500–600
€ / **$800–950**
⚒ GAK

▶ **A Victorian
mahogany cradle,**
c1860, 36in
(91.5cm) long.
£150–200
€ / **$250–300**
⚒ BWL

◀ **A Victorian
carved rose-
wood bed,** the
headboard with
five inset panels
surmounted by a
crest of carved
fruit, with melon
urn finials, 82in
(208.5cm) wide.
£2,800–3,200
€ / **$4,400–5,000**
⚒ JDJ

▶ **A brass
bed,** 19thC,
56in (142cm) wide.
£150–180
€ / **$250–290**
⚒ DuM
**This is missing
the side rails to
hold the base,
hence the
low price.**

FURNITURE

A Victorian mahogany half-tester bed, with serpentine-front cornice and curved footboard, 60in (152.5cm) wide.
£2,500–3,000
€/ $4,000–4,700 ⊞ SWA

A mahogany half-tester bed, c1870, 60in (152.5cm) wide.
£1,250–1,400
€/ $1,900–2,200 ⊞ NAW

A beech and walnut carved and ivory-inlaid bed, attributed to Gabriel Viardot, Paris, the headboard carved with a dragon, French, c1880, 66½in (169cm) wide.
£6,500–7,750
€/ $10,200–12,200 ↗ S(O)
Gabriel Viardot took over the family firm in rue Rambuteau from his father, Charles, in 1861. He specialized in exotic furniture and was influenced by Chinese and Vietnamese styles. Viardot was a jury member and medal winner at the 1867, 1878 and 1889 International Exhibitions in Paris.

► **A Louis XVI-style walnut bed,** with decorative carved headboard, French, c1895, 60in (152.5cm) wide.
£1,200–1,500
€/ $1,900–2,400 ⊞ SeH

A cedarwood four-poster bed, the posts with spiral-turned decoration and panelling surmounted by a fluted band canopy, with a carved scrolling headboard, Australian, New South Wales, c1845, 54¾in (139cm) wide.
£3,500–4,200
€/ $5,500–6,600 ↗ LJ

An Empire-style mahogany upholstered bed, French, c1875, 54in (137cm) wide.
£1,600–2,000
€/ $2,500–3,000 ⊞ SeH

A brass bed, c1890, 54in (137cm) wide.
£2,400–2,800
€/ $3,800–4,400 ⊞ SeH

An Empire painted bed, recovered, French, c1860, 60in (152.5cm) wide.
£2,250–2,500
€/ $3,200–3,800 ⊞ DAC

A rococo-style mahogany half-tester bed, with flame mahogany veneer, c1875, 72in (183cm) wide.
£8,000–9,000
€/ $12,600–14,200 ⊞ SeH

A Renaissance-style mahogany bed, with ormolu mounts, quarter-veneered panels and original wooden side rails, c1890, 66in (167.5cm) wide.
£1,800–2,000
€/ $2,800–4,700 ⊞ SWA

A mahogany bed, with parquetry work and ormolu decoration, French, c1895, 60in (152.5cm) wide.
£1,500–1,800
€/ $2,300–2,800 ⊞ SeH

SEVENTH HEAVEN

Genuine Antique Beds of Character and History

4' 6" Victorian Bed, circa 1890

Edwardian Inlaid Bed, circa 1910

5ft wide Cast Iron Bed, circa 1870

Choose from our unrivalled selection of genuine, fully restored antique bedsteads each with their unique design and history to create an individual bedroom of your dreams. A top quality mattress and bed base will ensure years of comfortable nights' sleep whilst our fantastic display of luxury bedding and bed linen will inspire your creative spirit.

5ft Iron Four Poster, circa 1870

5ft Cast Iron Bed, circa 1880

5ft Decorative Bed, circa 1890

For those unable to visit we provide a professional mail order service with the personal touch and rapid response via post or internet.

Browse through out current stock on-line:

www.seventh-heaven.co.uk

Louis XV style Bed, circa 1890

Chinese Style Suite, circa 1880

Pair of Single Beds, circa 1890

Free Brochure
Speedy Nation-wide Delivery.

Open 7 Days a week.
Interest Free Credit.*

Chirk Mill (MG), Chirk, Wrexham, LL14 5BU.
Tel: 01691 777622/773563   Fax: 01691 777313
e-mail: requests@seventh-heaven.co.uk

*Written quotations available on request, subject to status, on selected items only.

FURNITURE

29

FURNITURE

A Gothic-style carved walnut bed,
c1895, 60in (152.5cm) wide.
£5,000–6,000
€ / $8,000–9,500 ⊞ SeH

**A pair of Louis XVI-style carved
beechwood beds,** the headboards
upholstered in damask, the posts
modelled as arrow quivers, c1900,
42½in (108cm) wide.
£1,200–1,500
€ / $1,900–2,400 ➚ NOA

**An Edwardian brass and painted
bed,** the head with brass hoops and
rails, surmounted by ball finials,
54¼in (140.5cm) wide.
£280–350
€ / $440–550 ➚ B(W)

A brass bed, c1910,
60in (152.5cm) wide.
£1,600–1,800
€ / $2,500–2,800 ⊞ SWA

**A Louis XV-style carved and
stained beech bed,** French, 19thC,
61in (155cm) wide.
£1,600–2,000
€ / $2,500–3,200 ➚ S(O)

A painted wooden bed, with
upholstered headboard, French,
c1900, 42in (106.5cm) wide.
£1,200–1,500
€ / $1,900–2,400 ⊞ SeH

An Edwardian mahogany bed, with
inlaid stringing, 54in (137cm) wide.
£700–900
€ / $1,100–1,400 ⊞ SeH

**A Belle Epoque Louis XV boudoir-
style bed,** with lacquered finish,
French, c1910, 60in (152.5cm) wide.
£5,000–5,500
€ / $8,000–8,700 ⊞ SeH

A bedstead, the ends painted with
landscape scenes by moonlight,
Italian, c1900, 36in (91.5cm) wide.
£1,600–2,000
€ / $2,500–3,200 ⊞ SeH

A Louis XV-style walnut bed,
with original wooden side rails, with
quartered veneered panels, c1900,
60in (152.5cm) wide.
£1,300–1,500
€ / $2,000–2,400 ⊞ SWA

An Edwardian brass bed,
54in (137cm) wide.
£1,400–1,700
€ / $2,200–2,700 ⊞ SeH

A burr-walnut-veneered bed,
Italian, c1910, 72in (183cm) wide.
£5,000–6,000
€ / $8,000–9,500 ⊞ SeH

FURNITURE

Benches

A Regency mahogany hall bench, seat split, 54in (137cm) wide.
£1,500–1,800
€/ **$2,400–2,800** ⚒ B(Ba)

A mahogany hall seat, stamped 'James Winter, London', c1825, 36in (91.5cm) wide.
£6,000–7,000
€/ **$9,500–11,000** ⊞ CAT

A William IV mahogany bench, 107in (272cm) wide.
£650–800
€/ **$1,000–1,300** ⚒ S(O)

A Biedermeier softwood hall bench, the open backrest pierced with S-scrolls and stylized fleur-de-lys, the outscrolled open armrests with conforming decoration, on sabre legs, South German, mid-19thC, 74¾in (190cm) wide.
£4,000–5,000
€/ **$6,300–7,900** ⚒ S(Am)

A mahogany hall bench, with bobbin-turned decoration, c1835, 55in (139.5cm) wide.
£3,750–4,500
€/ **$6,000–7,000** ⚒ S(O)

Bonheurs du Jour

A burr-maple and rosewood-banded bonheur du jour, with step-up centre and pierced gilt-brass gallery above an arched and mirrored compartment flanked by two cupboards with Sèvres portrait panels, French, early 19thC, 39in (99cm) wide.
£2,000–2,500
€/ **$3,200–4,000** ⚒ MEA

A George III satinwood and kingwood cross-banded bonheur du jour, 32¼in (82cm) wide.
£2,200–2,750
€/ **$3,500–4,400** ⚒ S(O)

A maple and mahogany bonheur du jour, c1790, 24in (61cm) wide.
£3,000–3,500
€/ **$4,700–5,500** ⚒ S(O)

A black-japanned bonheur du jour, distressed, c1800, 20½in (52cm) wide.
£1,000–1,200
€/ **$1,600–1,900** ⚒ S(O)

◄ **A Victorian rosewood bonheur du jour,** with thuya-wood inlay and Sèvres plaques, on plain square supports and moulded plinth above turned feet, 24½in (62cm) wide.
£1,700–2,200
€/ **$2,700–3,400** ⚒ TEN

◄ **A black-lacquered papier mâché bonheur du jour,** in the style of Jennens & Bettridge, c1840, 24½in (62cm) wide.
£3,750–4,500
€/ **$6,000–7,000** ⚒ S(O)
Jennens & Bettridge were well-known papier mâché manufacturers who, in 1816, took over the Birmingham factory of H. Clay. In 1831 they invented a technique of painting onto papier mâché and later patented a type of inlay using coloured glass, mother-of-pearl, tortoiseshell and ivory. The company was active until c1864.

FURNITURE

A figured walnut bonheur du jour, the arched mirrored door enclosing a shelved cupboard, flanked by two side cupboards, crossbanded throughout and with ormolu mounts, mid-19thC, 41in (104cm) wide.
£1,500–1,800
€ / **$2,400–2,500** ⚒ TMA

A mahogany bonheur du jour, Baltic, 1850–75, 45¾in (116cm) wide.
£650–800
€ / **$1,000–1,300** ⚒ B(Ba)

A parquetry bonheur du jour, with ormolu mounts, on turned and fluted legs, French, 19thC, 31in (78.5cm) wide.
£2,500–3,200
€ / **$4,000–5,000** ⚒ G(B)

A kingwood, amboyna, satinwood and marquetry bonheur du jour, with ormolu mounts, c1880, 30in (76cm) wide.
£6,750–7,500
€ / **$10,700–12,000** ⊞ Che

A Louis XV-style kingwood and tulipwood bonheur du jour, with central mirrored door and drawer, flanked by shelves, the protruding lower part with leather inset top, above a bow-shaped frieze drawer flanked by dummy drawers, on cabriole legs with gilt-bronze foliate-cast mounts, c1880, 46½in (118cm) wide.
£2,000–2,400
€ / **$3,200–3,800** ⚒ S(Am)

A kingwood bonheur du jour, with Sèvres-style porcelain mounts, gallery possibly altered, French, c1890, 30¾in (78cm) wide.
£2,500–3,000
€ / **$4,000–4,700** ⚒ S(O)

A walnut bonheur du jour, French, 19thC, 38½in (98cm) wide.
£450–550
€ / **$700–870** ⚒ B(Ba)

◄ **A kingwood-veneered bonheur du jour,** with gilt-metal mounts and Sèvres-style porcelain plaques, the serpentine front with a blue velvet inset slide above a drawer, on cabriole legs, French, late 19thC, 30in (76cm) wide.
£3,000–3,750
€ / **$4,700–6,000** ⚒ WW

A carved walnut bonheur du jour, late 19thC, 38in (96.5cm) wide.
£2,000–2,250
€ / **$3,200–3,500** ⊞ RPh

An ebonized and parcel-gilt amboyna-veneered bonheur du jour, decorated with painted porcelain panels, the upper section with a central compartment flanked by two side cupboards, the base fitted with one long writing drawer flanked by two short drawers, late 19thC, 48½in (123cm) wide.
£2,400–3,000
€ / **$3,800–4,700** ⚒ TMA
This piece represents excellent value for money, particularly if the purchaser can regard this as an investment for 10 years or so.

A Louis XV-style mahogany, ebonized and marquetry bonheur du jour, with sliding writing surface, French, c1900, 29½in (75cm) wide.
£2,800–3,200
€ / **$4,400–5,000** ⚒ S(O)

A mahogany and inlaid bonheur du jour, the rear of the cupboard doors fitted with letter racks, the fold-over top with gilt-tooled green leather inset, c1910, 32¾in (83cm) wide.
£2,000–2,400
€ / **$3,200–3,800** ⚒ S(O)

An ebonized and amboyna bonheur du jour, with ormolu mounts, the central mirror flanked by cupboards, surmounted by a pierced-brass gallery, the base with elaborate frieze and two open shelves, with classical ceramic plaques at intervals, French, late 19thC, 55in (139.5cm) wide.
£2,800–3,500
€ / **$4,400–5,500** ⚒ JM

Items in the Furniture section have been arranged in date order within each sub-section.

Bookcases

A mahogany bookcase, with astragal-glazed doors over six drawers, c1850, 60in (152.5cm) wide.
£4,250–4,750
€/ **$6,700–7,500** ⊞ MTay

A George III mahogany bookcase, with astragal-glazed doors, 46in (117cm) wide.
£5,700–6,300
€/ **$9,000–10,000** ⊞ APO

A Regency rosewood and simulated rosewood bookcase, inlaid with satinwood bands, the moulded cornice above bead- and reel-carved frieze, the two arched astragal-glazed doors enclosing three shelves, the lower section with one long drawer and two panelled doors enclosing a shelf, on turned tapering feet, 37in (94cm) wide.
£2,000–2,500
€/ **$3,200–4,000** ⚒ B

A mahogany bookcase, the upper section with two glazed doors, c1825, 42in (106.5cm) wide.
£7,000–7,800
€/ **$11,000–12,300** ⊞ SAW

▶ **A mahogany bookcase,** the moulded cornice above open shelves and two panelled cupboards, c1840, 61in (155cm) wide.
£2,200–2,700
€/ **$3,500–4,200** ⚒ S(O)

A mahogany bookcase, the cushion-moulded cornice above two doors, the upper two-thirds glazed and with applied Gothic tracery, the lower-third panelled, on bun feet, 1825–50, 55½in (141cm) wide.
£4,500–5,700
€/ **$7,000–9,000** ⚒ NOA

Generally speaking, smaller bookcases are more valuable than larger examples as they fit more easily into modern rooms. However, it is important to check that they haven't been reduced. Look at the divisions for the shelves. The distance from the top shelf to the roof of the bookcase should be the same as that from the bottom shelf to the floor of the bookcase. Glazed bookcases were often converted from bedroom wardrobes. Check that the glazing bars have the same amount of wear and patination as the styles on the door.
Georgians had a great sense of proportion. Step back from a piece and take a good look: if it looks out of proportion, it's wrong!

A mahogany bookcase, the frieze with two drawers, probably American, New York, c1835, 43¾in (111cm) wide.
£3,500–4,200
€/ **$5,500–6,600** ⚒ S(O)

◀ **A mahogany bookcase,** the upper section with two glazed doors, the top carved with scrolls and foliage, the base with two drawers and two cupboard doors, on a plinth base, c1860, 41½in (105.5cm) wide.
£550–700
€/ **$870–1,100** ⚒ E

A Victorian Reformed Gothic oak breakfront bookcase, the foliate-carved and spindle gallery pediment over three bays of open shelves flanked by rosette-carved fluted uprights, on a plinth base, 123¾in (314.5cm) wide.
£2,200–2,750
€/ **$3,500–4,400** ⚒ Bri
Reformed Gothic was a late 19th century revivalist movement based on Arts and Crafts construction ideals but with Gothic detailing.

FURNITURE

A carved oak bookcase, with two glazed doors, possibly Welsh, c1860, 44in (112cm) wide.
£375–425
€ / $600–670 ⊞ MTay

A mahogany bookcase, stamped 'J. Stewart, Maidenhead', 1875, 48in (122cm) wide.
£1,000–1,250
€ / $1,600–1,900 ↗ L

A mahogany bookcase, the upper section with a stepped cornice above two reeded glazed doors enclosing three shelves, the lower section with two reeded drawers, above two reeded cupboard doors enclosing a shelf, on a plinth base, late 19thC, 34in (86.5cm) wide.
£750–880
€ / $1,200–1,400 ↗ PFK

A mahogany bookcase, with two glazed doors, c1860, 49in (124.5cm) wide.
£5,250–5,850
€ / $8,300–9,200 ⊞ RAN

A Renaissance revival walnut and burr-walnut bookcase, the moulded cornice over two arched glazed doors, each with original glass, on a projecting base fitted with two panelled doors enclosing four shelves, American, 1875–1900, 50in (127cm) wide.
£2,500–3,000
€ / $4,000–4,700 ↗ NOA

A Victorian oak breakfront library bookcase, with moulded dentil cornice, the three glazed doors enclosing adjustable shelves, the base with central frieze drawer above six short drawers, flanked by two cupboards, on a box base, 80in (203cm) wide.
£2,000–2,500
€ / $3,200–4,000 ↗ LVS

A mid-Victorian Gothic revival-style mahogany and ebonized bookcase, the dentil-moulded cornice above an astragal-glazed door with Gothic arches enclosing shelves, flanked by moulded uprights, on a plinth base, 22in (56cm) wide.
£1,300–1,600
€ / $2,000–2,500 ↗ B

A mahogany bookcase, American, c1900, 45in (114.5cm) wide.
£400–500
€ / $630–800 ↗ DuM

▶ **An Edwardian oak bookcase,** the glazed upper section over a base with two drawers and two cupboard doors, 49in (124.5cm) wide.
£1,100–1,200
€ / $1,700–1,900 ⊞ WiB

A Victorian mahogany-veneered bookcase, the fixed ogee cornice above arched glazed doors with horizontal bars enclosing adjustable shelves, the base with two panelled doors enclosing adjustable shelves, the sides with scroll volutes, on a plinth base, 40¾in (103.5cm) wide.
£1,400–1,750
€ / $2,200–2,700 ↗ WW

A carved oak bookcase, retailed by Hamptons, London, c1885, 52¼in (132.5cm) wide.
£3,400–3,750
€ / $5,400–6,000 ⊞ MTay

Bureau Bookcases

A George II mahogany bureau bookcase, the glazed doors enclosing shelves, folio compartments and drawers, 41¾in (106cm) wide.
£3,500–4,250
€/ **$5,500–6,700** ↗ TEN

A George III mahogany bureau bookcase, the associated top with two astragal-glazed doors, 43¼in (110cm) wide.
£1,000–1,250
€/ **$1,600–1,900** ↗ B(Ba)

A George III mahogany bureau bookcase, the associated upper section with replaced swan-neck pediment with cast-brass oval medallion terminals, the two glazed doors with wooden tracery, enclosing two shelves, the lower section with a fall-front enclosing drawers and pigeonholes, above three long drawers with Chippendale-style pierced-brass backplate bale handles, on bracket feet, some pigeonholes missing, 42in (106.5cm) wide.
£500–625
€/ **$800–1,000** ↗ PFK

A George III mahogany bureau bookcase, the associated upper section with two glazed doors enclosing adjustable shelves, the lower section with fall-front enclosing a fitted interior of a central cupboard and six drawers, 46in (117cm) wide.
£3,300–4,000
€/ **$5,200–6,300** ↗ S(O)

A bureau bookcase, associated, restored, c1800, 48½in (123cm) wide.
£4,250–4,750
€/ **$6,700–7,500** ⊞ MTay

A Sheraton period mahogany cylinder bureau bookcase, c1790, 39in (99cm) wide.
£13,000–14,500
€/ **$21,000–23,000** ⊞ Che

▶ **An Edwardian Sheraton-style mahogany bureau bookcase,** 26in (66cm) wide.
£800–1,000
€/ **$1,300–1,600** ↗ JM

English 18th-century furniture 1976–2002

This graph shows the increasing value of English furniture as a whole over the past 25 years. Individual collecting areas such as chairs or tables and from different periods may not follow this graph exactly. ©AMR

A rococo revival rosewood mechanical cylinder bureau bookcase, the upper section with a bonnet top over two conforming glazed doors, the interior with four period maple shelves, the base with mechanical cylinder top which extends the writing surface as the top opens, revealing a fitted interior with pigeonholes, on a base with a projecting drawer over two recessed cupboard doors, American, 1875–1900, 47in (119.5cm) wide.
£4,500–5,000
€/ **$7,000–8,000** ↗ NOA

◀ **A Queen Anne-style walnut bureau bookcase,** 31½in (80cm) wide.
£700–850
€/ **$1,100–1,300** ↗ S(O)

Low Bookcases

**A Regency mahogany
dwarf bookcase,**
with two drawers,
34⅜in (88.5cm) wide.
£600–750
€/ $950–1,200 ⚶ S(O)

**A mahogany open
bookcase,** the galleried
top above a waterfall
section to a rectangular
lower part, with moulded
edges, on turned legs with
brass casters, one end
of galleried top missing,
stamped 'B.B. & Co
Patent', early 19thC,
27in (68.5cm) wide.
£1,200–1,500
€/ $1,900–2,400 ⚶ WW

◄ **A pair of ebonized
and parcel-gilt open
bookcases,** each with a
shaped top and four fixed
shelves flanked by turned
pillars, on turned tapering
legs, repainted, 19thC,
21¾in (55.5cm) wide.
£1,100–1,400
€/ $1,700–2,200 ⚶ DN

**A Regency mahogany
double-sided bookcase,**
with a pierced-brass
gallery, on brass casters,
30½in (77.5cm) wide.
£2,300–2,750
€/ $3,600–4,300 ⚶ NOA

**A Victorian walnut floor-
standing open bookcase,**
on a moulded plinth base,
34in (86.5cm) wide.
£2,300–2,800
€/ $3,600–4,400 ⚶ CGC

**A late Regency mahogany
bookcase cupboard,** the
upper section with shaped
sides and two open
shelves, the lower section
with a cupboard above
an open compartment,
on splayed bracket feet,
22¾in (58cm) wide.
£1,500–2,000
€/ $2,400–3,200 ⚶ B

**A Victorian mahogany
dwarf open bookcase,**
45¼in (115cm) wide.
£420–525
€/ $650–800 ⚶ B(Ch)

Revolving Bookcases

◄ **An Edwardian walnut
revolving bookcase,**
21in (53.5cm) wide.
£420–525
€/ $650–830 ⚶ B(Ba)

**An oak revolving book-
case,** one spindle missing,
one damaged, mid-19thC,
22½in (57cm) wide.
£520–650
€/ $800–1,000 ⚶ B(Ch)

► **An Edwardian
mahogany revolving book-
case,** 23¾in (60.5cm) wide.
£520–650
€/ $800–1,000 ⚶ L

**A mahogany inlaid
revolving bookcase,**
fitted with three drawers,
c1910, 19in (48.5cm) wide.
£1,400–1,500
€/ $2,200–2,400 ⊞ MTay

**An Edwardian mahogany
revolving bookcase,** the
moulded square top over
pierced fretwork sides, the
stand with a bowed apron,
on cabriole legs and pad
feet, with a shaped
serpentine undertier,
18in (45.5cm) square.
£460–575
€/ $720–900 ⚶ EH

The revolving bookcase
was first produced
c1800, but achieved
its greatest popularity
in Edwardian times.

Secretaire Bookcases

A George III mahogany secretaire bookcase, the moulded cornice above a dentil frieze and two glazed doors enclosing shelves, the lower section with a shaped apron, on bracket feet, 44in (112cm) wide.
£2,000–2,500
€/ $3,200–4,000 ✗ CGC

A George III mahogany secretaire bookcase, in the style of Hepplewhite, with plain frieze and moulded cornice above Gothic arched glazed doors enclosing interior shelves, the base with inlaid fall-front frieze drawer and writing surface, secretaire drawers and pigeonholes above three long graduated drawers with neo-classical brass handles, on splayed bracket feet, 34in (86.5cm) wide.
£3,800–4,750
€/ $6,000–7,500 ✗ HYD

Miller's Compares

I. A late George III mahogany secretaire bookcase, the secretaire drawer fitted with pigeon-holes and satinwood-faced drawers, 42in (106.5cm) wide.
£1,400–1,800
€/ $2,200–2,800 ✗ L

II. A late George III mahogany secretaire bookcase, the upper part enclosed by a pair of glazed doors, the lower part with a fitted drawer above long drawers, 44¼in (112.5cm) wide.
£800–1,000
€/ $1,300–1,600 ✗ L

The superior quality of Item I is demonstrated by the satinwood-faced drawers inside the secretaire drawer. The wood is of a better colour and the veneering, particularly of the upper part, is more interesting than that of Item II. The design of the astragal bars and also the presence of feet on Item I give it a more elegant appearance.

A Regency mahogany secretaire bookcase, with a pair of bar-tracery glazed doors, the fall-front enclosing pigeonholes, drawers and a central cupboard, the base with panelled doors enclosing three sliding shelves, on splayed bracket feet, 50in (127cm) wide.
£3,200–4,000
€/ $5,000–6,300 ✗ DA

A Regency mahogany secretaire bookcase, with ebony stringing, on swept feet, 44in (112cm) wide.
£2,600–3,250
€/ $4,100–5,000 ✗ G(L)

◀ A Victorian walnut-veneered secretaire book-case, with adjustable shelves enclosed by two glazed doors over a fitted secretaire drawer, above an adjustable shelf enclosed by two panel doors, 50in (127cm) wide.
£1,300–1,600
€/ $2,000–2,500 ✗ WW

A Regency mahogany secretaire bookcase, with ebony stringing, the swan-neck pediment above two astragal-glazed doors, the fitted drawer above three further graduated drawers, on turned feet, 42¼in (107.5cm) wide.
£1,850–2,250
€/ $2,800–3,700 ✗ Bea

A mahogany secretaire bookcase, with ebony moulding and a fitted secretaire drawer, on a plinth base, c1840, 54in (137cm) wide.
£5,500–6,250
€/ $8,700–9,800 ⊞ RPh
The addition of the ebony moulding makes this a more desirable item.

Items in the Furniture section have been arranged in date order within each sub-section.

Boxes-on-Stands

A marquetry and laburnum oyster box, on a later stand, the hinged top enclosing a mirrored interior, c1700, 21¼in (54cm) high.
£1,700–2,000
€/ **$2,700–3,200** ✈ S(O)

An Edwardian inlaid mahogany drinks cabinet, with rising interior and galleried undertier, on square tapered legs, with brass casters, 28¾in (73cm) wide.
£950–1,200
€/ **$1,500–1,900** ✈ B&L

A mahogany sewing box-on-stand, early 20thC, 33in (84cm) high.
£720–800
€/ **$1,150–1,300** ⊞ RPh

Buckets

A late George III brass-bound mahogany peat bucket, 13in (33cm) high.
£350–450
€/ **$500–700** ✈ Bea(E)

A pair of brass-bound teak coopered buckets, c1820, 11½in (29cm) diam.
£820–900
€/ **$1,300–1,400** ✈ S(O)

A brass-bound mahogany coopered bucket, c1830, 13¾in (35cm) high.
£140–155
€/ **$220–245** ⊞ F&F

Buffets

A Louis XVI provincial mahogany and brass-mounted *console desserte*, the white marble inset top with pierced brass gallery above a frieze drawer, on turned fluted legs with undertier, the feet with turned brass sabots, 31½in (80cm) wide.
£1,200–1,500
€/ **$1,900–2,400** ✈ B
This piece originally belonged to the Rev. Lord Augustus Fitzclarence, Vicar of Mapledurham, the illegitimate son of William IV.

A William IV mahogany two-tier buffet, by James Winter & Sons, with two drawers in the apron, on reeded legs with brass casters, maker's stamp to one drawer, 43in (109cm) wide.
£1,100–1,400
€/ **$1,700–2,200** ✈ B
James Winter is listed at 101 Wardour Street, Soho, London as a furniture broker, appraiser and undertaker (1823–40). The business continued to trade until 1870 and it is unlikely that any of the furniture so marked was made by James Winter.

A Victorian mahogany two-tier buffet, with figured back, turned finial decoration and moulded edge, over a flat top with figured frieze, on baluster-turned supports with undertier below, on casters, 59¾in (152cm) wide.
£650–800
€/ **$1,000–1,300** ✈ BIG

LOCATE THE SOURCE
The source of each illustration in Miller's can be found by checking the code letters below each caption with the Key to Illustrations, pages 794–800.

Bureaux

A George III inlaid and crossbanded mahogany writing bureau, the fall-front enclosing a fitted interior, over four graduated drawers, on bracket feet, 43¼in (110cm) wide.
£600–750
€/ $950–1,200 ⚒ WilP

A Queen Anne walnut bureau, the fall-front enclosing a stepped interior of four drawers and pigeonholes flanking a central cupboard with pillar drawers and a well below, above two short and two long drawers, on later bracket feet, restored, the top later veneered, 27¼in (69cm) wide.
£2,000–2,500
€/ $3,200–4,000 ⚒ B
The fact that the top of this item was veneered at a later date is reflected in the low price.

A Chippendale-style mahogany bureau, the fall-front enclosing a writing surface and a fitted interior, the centre with an arched panelled drawer with secret compartments each side, the four oak-lined graduated and cockbeaded drawers with brass bail handles and escutcheon plates, on ogee bracket feet, c1770, 39in (99cm) wide.
£4,000–4,500
€/ $6,300–7,300 ⊞ JC
This piece attracted a higher price because of its good original condition. Untouched items with good patination will always be more sought after.

▶ **A George III mahogany bureau,** the fall-front enclosing a stepped, fitted interior, 33in (84cm) wide.
£820–1,000
€/ $1,300–2,400 ⚒ L

A George III mahogany bureau, the sloping fall-front enclosing pigeonholes above two moulded frieze drawers and a shaped apron, on shell-carved cabriole legs with pad feet, base 19thC, 26¾in (68cm) wide.
£600–750
€/ $950–1,200 ⚒ B(L)

A plum pudding mahogany bureau, with a secret drawer, late 18thC, 40in (101.5cm) wide.
£2,500–2,800
€/ $4,000–4,400 ⊞ RPh

A serpentine walnut bureau, the fall-front enclosing eight drawers and pigeonholes, German, c1770, 45in (114.5cm) wide.
£2,200–2,750
€/ $3,500–4,400 ⚒ S(O)

A mahogany tambour-top bureau, the tambour enclosing a slide with ratcheted adjustable reading slope, four small drawers and pigeonholes, c1800, 34in (86.5cm) wide.
£2,800–3,400
€/ $4,400–5,400 ⚒ S(O)

FURNITURE

A mahogany cylinder bureau,
early 19thC, 48½in (123cm) wide.
£10,000–12,500
€/ **$16,000–20,000** ⊞ W&C

A Georgian mahogany bureau,
with satinwood crossbanding,
42in (106.5cm) wide.
£2,500–2,850
€/ **$4,000–4,500** ⊞ MHA

A walnut serpentine bureau, Italian,
1800–50, 43¼in (110cm) wide.
£600–725
€/ **$950–1,150** ⚒ B(Ba)

**A marquetry cylinder
bureau,** inlaid with hunting
scenes depicting hounds
and rabbits, the interior
fitted with small drawers,
the kneehole with a drawer
flanked by two further
small drawers, on turned
fluted tapering supports,
Continental, early 19thC,
48in (122cm) wide.
£2,500–3,200
€/ **$4,000–5,000** ⚒ BWL

**A Victorian rosewood
and inlaid cylinder
bureau,** with a pierced
three-quarter gallery
above an inlaid fall-front
enclosing a leather-lined
writing slide and fitted
interior, a further frieze
drawer below, on square
tapered legs with casters,
31¼in (79cm) wide.
£1,800–2,200
€/ **$2,800–3,500** ⚒ TEN

**A Victorian mahogany
cylinder bureau,** probably
by Gillows, the single-tier
bookshelf top with three-
quarter brass gallery on,
the cylinder enclosing
satinwood-fronted drawers
and curtained pigeonholes,
with a pull-forward green
morocco leather writing
surface, each with four
graduated drawers, on
a plinth base, losses
and damage to gallery,
51½in (131cm) wide.
£3,000–3,750
€/ **$4,700–6,000** ⚒ HAM

**► An Edwardian
mahogany bureau,**
26in (66cm) wide.
£750–825
€/ **$1,200–1,300** ⊞ MHA

**A walnut and marquetry
cylinder bureau,** with
floral-inlaid fall-front over
two long drawers, on square
tapering legs, Dutch, 19thC,
34in (86.5cm) wide.
£1,000–1,250
€/ **$1,600–1,900** ⚒ G(B)

**A Victorian mahogany
cylinder bureau,** the upper
section with glazed doors,
the cylinder enclosing
drawers and pigeonholes
and a leather-lined slide,
51½in (131cm) wide.
£1,100–1,400
€/ **$1,700–2,200** ⚒ L

**A kingwood and
parquetry *bureau de
dame*,** French, c1880,
34in (86.5cm) wide.
£2,000–2,350
€/ **$3,200–3,700** ⊞ Che

**An Edwardian rosewood
cylinder bureau,** the
cylinder enclosing a bird's-
eye maple-faced interior
and a pull-out leather-lined
slide, inlaid with foliate
scrolls, 30in (76cm) wide.
£900–1,150
€/ **$1,400–1,800** ⚒ L

**An Edwardian mahogany
bureau,** the tambour front
enclosing a fitted interior
with drawers, pigeonholes,
and a pull-out leather-
inset writing surface on a
ratchet action, above two
short drawers, on ring-
turned legs, altered,
36¼in (92cm) wide.
£500–625
€/ **$800–1,000** ⚒ RbF

**► An Edwardian
mahogany satinwood-
banded *bureau de dame*,**
with floral marquetry inlay,
30¼in (77cm) wide.
£900–1,100
€/ **$1,400–1,700** ⚒ B(Ch)

FURNITURE

Cabinets

A walnut and cherrywood-banded cabinet, the ogee-moulded cornice above two doors inlaid with stylized flowerheads, decorative lines and bands, flanked on each side with strapwork panels, the sides and back with decorative lines and banding, on block feet, Austrian, mid–18thC, 74¾in (190cm) wide.
£550–700
€/ **$1,300–1,700** ➢ B

A marquetry cabinet, Dutch, early 19thC, 46in (117cm) wide.
£1,000–1,200
€/ **$1,600–1,900** ➢ S(O)

A black-japanned chinoiserie cabinet, attributed to S. Hille & Co, the top decorated with birds in flight above two doors decorated with figures in chinoiserie landscapes, with a pierced and engraved lock plate and strap hinges, above two further doors, on cabriole legs, early 20thC, 40¼in (102cm) wide.
£550–700
€/ **$870–1,100** ➢ B
The firm of Hille was founded by Salamon Hille in 1906. Their Old Street, London, workshop aimed at high-quality production with an emphasis on materials and craftsmanship. They produced furniture in a number of revivalist tastes and supplied top retailers such as Hamptons, Maples and Waring and Gillow. Chinese Chippendale-style lacquer suites were introduced around 1914, with the more exclusive pieces being produced in satinwood with lacquer panels and gold leaf decoration.

Further reading
Miller's Late Georgian to Edwardian Furniture Buyer's Guide, Miller's Publications, 2003

▶ An Edwardian mahogany and satinwood-banded coal cabinet, 15¾in (40cm) wide.
£100–125
€/ **$160–200** ➢ B(Ch)

Bedside Cabinets

◀ A George III mahogany night commode, the rising top above four false drawers opening as a cupboard, 27¾in (70.5cm) wide.
£300–375
€/ **$500–600** ➢ L

A George III mahogany tray-top commode, the shaped sides with handles, the rising front above a commode drawer, 21¼in (54cm) wide.
£700–850
€/ **$1,100–1,300** ➢ TRM

▶ A mahogany tray-top bedside cabinet, with boxwood inlay and stringing, c1790, 31in (78.5cm) wide.
£1,000–1,100
€/ **$1,600–1,700** ⊞ BMi

A mahogany tray-top cabinet, with two doors above two drawers, c1790, 22in (56cm) wide.
£2,400–2,650
€/ **$3,800–4,200** ⊞ RGa

A George III mahogany and boxwood-strung bedside cabinet, the raised shaped back with a shelf, over a tambour door with a brass handle, on square tapering legs, 16in (40.5cm) wide.
£2,300–2,800
€/ **$3,600–4,400** ➢ DN

A George III mahogany tray-top bedside cabinet, the galleried top with cut-out handles, above a door with a brass handle, on square tapering legs with a platform stretcher, 13in (33cm) wide.
£1,000–1,100
€/ **$1,600–1,700** ⊞ JC

A late George III mahogany bedside commode, with boxwood inlay and stringing, the tambour door over a commode drawer inlaid with a swag, on square section legs, 19¼in (49cm) wide.
£520–650
€/ **$800–1,000** ⚒ B(Ch)

A mahogany bedside cabinet, Dutch, early 19thC, 18½in (47cm) wide.
£250–320
€/ **$400–500** ⚒ L

A mahogany bedside cabinet, c1870, 16in (40.5cm) wide.
£525–575
€/ **$830–900** ⊞ MTay

A walnut bedside cabinet, the grey marble top over a banded drawer and fall-front compartment, on moulded cabriole legs, with undertier, French, late 19thC, 15in (38cm) wide.
£120–150
€/ **$190–240** ⚒ EH

◄ **A matched pair of Edwardian mahogany bedside cabinets,** 16in (40.5cm) wide.
£175–200
€/ **$275–300** ⊞ PaA

Restoration & repair

When the time comes to repair or restore a piece of furniture try to select a member of the British Antique Furniture Restorers' Association (BAFRA) who will be happy to provide a written quotation before work begins. It is a good idea to ask to see examples of previous restoration work or seek recommendations from a client.

Some work can be done at home, such as applying candle wax to the runners and sides of drawers to prolong their life. Other tasks will need to be done in a workshop. Every 30 or 40 years chairs need to be knocked apart and the old glue removed, before regluing and reassembly. This work should be undertaken promptly if a chair becomes loose; otherwise the chair may collapse and a standard restoration task will become a costly repair.

A walnut bedside cabinet, with marble top, on cabriole legs, French, c1885, 16in (40.5cm) wide.
£135–150
€/ **$200–240** ⊞ PaA

A pair of kingwood side cabinets, with gilt-brass galleries and mounts, c1900, 39in (99cm) high.
£1,250–1,380
€/ **$2,000–2,200** ⊞ RAN

▶ **A pair of painted bedside cabinets,** with a single shallow drawer over a double dummy drawer cupboard door, Italian, c1920, 25in (63.5cm) wide.
£1,500–1,700
€/ **$2,400–2,700** ⊞ SSW

A light oak bedside cabinet, with rosewood crossbanding, with a tambour cupboard door modelled as book spines, on tapering legs, c1900, 18in (45.5cm) wide.
£500–625
€/ **$800–1,000** ⚒ GAK

An Edwardian mahogany bedside cabinet, with satinwood banding, on casters, door stamped 'Edwards and Roberts', 16in (40.5cm) wide.
£350–400
€/ **$550–630** ⊞ RPh

FURNITURE

Bureau Cabinets

A baroque inlaid figured-walnut bureau cabinet, with serpentine front, the central door with a shaped panel enclosing a fitted interior flanked by two banks of five drawers, over a hinged fall-front and three serpentine-front drawers with gilt-metal rococo handles, on compressed bun feet, restored, German, early 18thC, 47¼in (120cm) wide.
£3,400–4,250
€/ **$5,400–6,700 ➢ Bri**

For further information on antique furniture see the full range of Miller's books at
www.millers.uk.com

A tiger maple bureau cabinet, the two panelled doors above a fall-front opening to reveal six cubbyholes and five drawers, with three graduated drawers below, brass handles and hinges replaced, American, 18thC, 36¼in (92cm) wide.
£12,000–14,000
€/ **$19,000–22,000 ➢ JDJ**

▶ **A walnut bureau bookcase,** with mirrored door, c1720, 41in (104cm) wide.
£17,500–20,000
€/ **$28,000–32,000 ⊞ Che**

▶ **A parquetry bureau cabinet,** the upper section with a serpentine cornice enclosed by two doors, with mirror cartouche outlines, the base with a sloping front above a long drawer, the central recess with a kneehole drawer, on cabriole legs with moulded scroll outlines, Italian, 18thC, 36in (91.5cm) wide.
£2,000–2,500
€/ **$3,200–4,000 ➢ L**

A mahogany bureau cabinet, north German, c1760, 43¾in (111cm) wide.
£1,100–1,400
€/ **$1,700–2,200 ➢ S(O)**

Cabinets-on-Chests

A William and Mary walnut cabinet-on-chest, fitted with a cushion frieze drawer and further drawers surrounding a central cupboard, enclosed by two doors, all with feather stringing, the base with two short and two long drawers, 47in (119.5cm) wide.
£5,500–6,500
€/ **$8,700–10,300 ➢ L**

A William and Mary walnut and featherbanded cabinet-on-chest, the ogee-moulded cornice above a cushion drawer and two burr-walnut quarter-veneered drawers enclosing a central cupboard door revealing three short drawers, the base above two long graduated drawers, on shaped bracket feet, extra height added to the feet, 43¼in (110cm) wide.
£2,300–2,800
€/ **$3,600–4,400 ➢ B**

A Queen Anne burr-walnut-veneered cabinet-on-chest, with feather-banding throughout, the cushion frieze drawer above two short and two long drawers, on later oak ball feet, 42¼in (107.5cm) wide.
£3,700–4,700
€/ **$5,800–7,400 ➢ Bea**

An Edwardian mahogany cabinet-on-chest, with satinwood and parquetry banding, moulded and dentil cornice, two brass-trimmed astragal-glazed doors enclosing shelving, the base with two short over two long drawers, on bracket feet, 43in (109cm) wide.
£650–800
€/ **$1,000–1,200 ➢ AH**

Items in the Furniture section have been arranged in date order within each sub-section.

Corner Cabinets

FURNITURE

A **japanned corner cabinet,** the door with an arched fielded reserve decorated with gilt chinoiserie, on a 19thC stand decorated en-suite, mid-18thC, 76¼in (193.5cm) high.
£650–800
€/ **$1,000–1,200** ⚒ B(S)

A **mahogany corner cupboard,** with arched doors, c1760, 27in (68.5cm) wide.
£1,500–1,650
€/ **$2,400–2,600** ⊞ F&F

A **George II walnut hanging corner cabinet,** 26¾in (68cm) wide.
£600–750
€/ **$950–1,200** ⚒ B(Ch)

A **mahogany bowfronted corner cabinet,** with block moulding and brass H-hinges, c1760, 28in (71cm) wide.
£2,700–3,000
€/ **$4,300–4,700** ⊞ ChC

A **mahogany glazed corner cupboard,** with flame veneers and boxwood stringing, c1800, 52in (132cm) wide.
£4,750–5,250
€/ **$7,500–8,300** ⊞ MTay

◄ A **George III mahogany bowfronted hanging corner cabinet,** the doors with brass H-hinges, 43in (109cm) high.
£1,100–1,400
€/ **$1,700–2,200** ⚒ BWL

A **lacquered bowfronted hanging corner cabinet,** with chinoiserie decoration, mid-18thC, 17¾in (45cm) wide.
£800–1,000
€/ **$1,300–1,600** ⚒ S(O)

A **George III mahogany hanging corner cabinet,** slight damage, 52in (132cm) high.
£600–750
€/ **$950–1,200** ⚒ RbF

A **late George II walnut bowfronted corner cabinet,** inlaid with feather stringing, 36in (91.5cm) wide.
£1,700–2,200
€/ **$2,700–3,500** ⚒ L

A **George III mahogany bowfronted corner cabinet,** enclosed by two doors inlaid with oval paterae, later inlay, 26in (66cm) wide.
£300–375
€/ **$475–600** ⚒ L

A **Victorian figured walnut corner cupboard,** enclosed by a glazed door, 26in (66cm) wide.
£300–375
€/ **$475–600** ⚒ HOLL

◄ A **Napoleon III mahogany and kingwood bowfronted corner cabinet,** the single door with a matchbook-veneer panel, on a panelled plinth base, French, 14½in (37cm) wide.
£850–1,000
€/ **$1,300–1,600** ⚒ NOA

A rosewood corner collector's cabinet, with glazed upper section, and music trays to base, on square tapering supports, stamped 'Sneider & Hanau', Frankfurt, 19thC, 42in (106.5cm) wide
£380–475
€ / **$600–750** ➤ HOLL

An Edwardian inlaid mahogany corner cabinet, with satinwood banding and boxwood stringing, 27½in (70cm) wide.
£850–1,100
€ / **$1,300–1,600** ➤ B(Ba)

An Edwardian mahogany glazed-front corner cabinet, the central bowfronted door enclosing fitted shelving, the tapering square supports joined by a solid undertier, on splayed feet, 24½in (62cm) wide.
£360–450
€ / **$580–700** ➤ GAK

A lacquered corner cupboard, c1920, 72in (183cm) high.
£1,350–1,500
€ / **$2,200–2,400** ⊞ Che

Display Cabinets

A boullework and gilt-metal-mounted dwarf cabinet, mid-19thC, 33¾in (85.5cm) wide.
£320–400
€ / **$500–630** ➤ B(Ba)

A George III mahogany display cabinet, 56in (142cm) wide.
£1,800–2,200
€ / **$2,800–3,500** ➤ S(O)

◀ **A George III mahogany display cupboard,** c1790, 45in (114.5cm) wide.
£3,200–3,500
€ / **$5,000–5,500** ⊞ Che

A Chippendale period display cabinet, the astragal-glazed doors with two panelled cupboards below, on a plinth base, c1760, 48in (122cm) wide.
£13,500–15,000
€ / **$21,000–24,000** ⊞ CAT

An ebonized mahogany two-door cabinet, with brass embellishments and velvet-lined interior, c1860, 37in (94cm) wide.
£550–625
€ / **$870–1,000** ⊞ PaA

A figured walnut credenza, with tulipwood angled crossbanding, the matchbook-veneered top with a moulded edge and wide tulipwood crossbanding with a skirting board overhang, with rounded ends and concave centre above a glazed central door enclosing a central shelf, the interior lined with raw silk, flanked by two pilasters with gilt-metal mounts to the top and base, either end with bowfronted open display shelves, on a breakfront and bow-ended plinth, c1860, 53¾in (136.5cm) wide.
£2,500–2,850
€ / **$4,000–4,500** ⊞ JC

A Victorian walnut floor-standing display cabinet, with marquetry-inlaid frieze and two glazed doors enclosing shelves, flanked by ormolu-mounted inlaid uprights, standing on a plinth base with a shaped apron, label for 'Windsor & Neate, Complete House Furnishers, Newbury', 42½in (108cm) wide.
£1,100–1,400
€ / **$1,800–2,200** ➤ CGC

FURNITURE

A Victorian walnut and floral marquetry credenza, with gilt-metal mounts and four glazed doors enclosing shelves, on a plinth base with bracket feet, 60in (152.5cm) wide.
£2,500–3,200
€/ $4,000–5,000 ✗ AH

A Victorian inlaid figured walnut breakfront side cabinet, with gilt-metal mounts, the central glazed door flanked by two curved glazed doors enclosing a red velvet-lined interior, on a plinth base and raised feet, 60in (152.5cm) wide.
£2,600–3,250
€/ $4,100–5,000 ✗ PF

A Victorian painted vitrine, on a stand, 44in (112cm) wide.
£4,200–4,700
€/ $6,600–7,400 ⊞ SAW

A line-inlaid satinwood display cabinet, with glazed door and sides, c1890, 73in (185.5cm) high.
£3,200–3,500
€/ $5,000–5,500 ⊞ JSt

A mahogany vitrine, with crossbanded panel and ormolu mounts, French, c1900, 28in (71cm) wide.
£2,000–2,200
€/ $3,200–3,500 ⊞ DAC

A walnut and bowed glass curio cabinet, American, c1900, 40in (101.5cm) wide.
£500–625
€/ $800–1,000 ✗ Dum

An Edwardian mahogany and inlaid serpentine-fronted display cabinet, by Thomas Justice & Co, Dundee, the projecting and banded cornice and plain frieze above two bowed cupboard doors, flanked by two shaped glazed cupboard doors and glazed sides, 48in (122cm) wide.
£2,000–2,500
€/ $3,200–4,000 ✗ B(Ed)

▶ **An Edwardian mahogany breakfront display cabinet,** the moulded cornice with applied vase and swag decoration, above a centre glazed door, flanked on either side by a glazed panel, each with wooden astragals and enclosing a pair of shelves, the base having a frieze with central oval paterae and bellflower swag decoration above an open shelf, on six square tapered legs with fretwork spandrels and terminating in spade feet, 55in (139.5cm) wide.
£450–565
€/ $700–870 ✗ Mit

Decorative features in detail

Acanthus

Beading

Bellflower/harebell

Fleur de lys

Lunette

Palmette

Patera

Ropework

Strapwork

Volute

An Edwardian marquetry-inlaid mahogany display cabinet, with an astragal-glazed door, on square tapered legs and spade feet, 27in (68.5cm) wide.
£320–400
€ / **$500–630** ⚒ EH

An Edwardian mahogany boxwood and ebony line-inlaid display cabinet, with dentil-moulded cornice above two astragal-glazed doors enclosing a shelved interior, over two cupboard doors decorated with cartouches, with undertier, on square tapered spade feet, 51in (129.5cm) high.
£1,000–1,250
€ / **$1,600–1,900** ⚒ G(B)

▶ **An Edwardian mahogany inlaid cabinet,** the glazed upper section with a pair of inlaid bowed doors below, 40in (101.5cm) wide.
£1,650–1,850
€ / **$2,600–3,000** ⊞ MHA

An Edwardian inlaid display cabinet, on splayed legs, 43in (109cm) wide.
£450–570
€ / **$700–900** ⚒ SWO

An Edwardian mahogany display cabinet, with glazed rounded sides, the lower part inlaid with burrwood panels, 44¾in (113.5cm) wide.
£2,400–3,000
€ / **$3,800–4,700** ⚒ L

An Edwardian mahogany display cabinet, with stringing, the moulded edged top with raised ledge back, astragal-glazed doors and glazed sides enclosing shelving, on square tapering legs with undershelf and spade feet, 24in (61cm) wide.
£520–650
€ / **$800–1,000** ⚒ AH

▶ **An Edwardian Sheraton-style mahogany display cabinet,** with boxwood line and floral marquetry inlay, moulded cornice and two glazed doors over a two-door serpentine base, on square tapering legs, 33in (84cm) wide.
£850–1,100
€ / **$1,300–1,700** ⚒ JM

A mahogany two-door display cabinet, 1920s, 62¼in (158cm) wide.
£400–500
€ / **$630–800** ⚒ SWO

◀ **A pair of Louis Martin-style glass-fronted demi-lune display cabinets,** painted, with gilt decoration, French, c1940, 67in (170cm) high.
£2,500–2,800
€ / **$4,000–4,400** ⊞ RAN

Music Cabinets

◀ **A mid-Victorian mahogany music cabinet,** 30in (76cm) wide.
£650–800
€/ $1,000–1,200 ➤ B(Ba)

A late Victorian inlaid walnut music cabinet, one foot loose, 23¼in (59cm) wide.
£500–625
€/ $800–900 ➤ B(Ch)

◀ **An Edwardian inlaid mahogany music cabinet,** 19in (48.5cm) wide.
£120–150
€/ $190–350 ➤ B(Ch)

An Edwardian inlaid mahogany music cabinet, with a glazed door over two drawers, 19in (48.5cm) wide.
£440–485
€/ $700–770 ⊞ CHAC

A pair of Edwardian mahogany music cabinets, with stringing, moulded edged top with three-quarter gallery, inlaid fluted frieze, five drawers with brass drop handles, panelled sides, on collared square tapering legs joined by shaped stretchers, label for Arthur Wilson, Pick & Co, Sheffield, 21½in (54.5cm) wide.
£500–625
€/ $800–1,000 ➤ AH

Pedestal Cabinets

A pair of satinbirch and marquetry pedestal cabinets, with ebony stringing and tulipwood banding, the inlaid tops with scrolling engraved foliage and stiff leaves to the edge, the frieze drawers above panel doors enclosing three mahogany drawers, on tapered square feet, alterations, 19thC, 20½in (52cm) wide.
£4,000–5,000
€/ $6,300–7,900 ➤ S

▶ **A bird's-eye maple pedestal cabinet,** late 19thC, 14½in (37cm) wide.
£500–625
€/ $800–1,000 ➤ B(Ba)

◀ **A Victorian mahogany pedestal cabinet,** with an inset marble top, two interior shelves, on a plinth base, marble cracked, 15in (38cm) diam.
£580–725
€/ $925–1,150 ➤ FHF

A flame mahogany pedestal cabinet, c1900, 32in (81.5cm) wide.
£1,700–2,000
€/ $2,700–3,200 ⊞ GBr

A pair of Biedermeier-style birchwood cabinets, Swedish, c1910, 15¼in (38.5cm) wide.
£2,600–3,000
€/ $4,100–4,800 ⊞ CAV

Pairs

It is not uncommon to find that pairs of pedestal cabinets are not exactly the same size. This is because they were often made at different times, the second one being ordered by the client when he could afford it, after the first one had been delivered. It was usually made from memory or perhaps copied from works day books that had not been accurately kept.

Secretaire Cabinets

A Biedermeier satinbirch *secrétaire à abattant,* possibly north German, 19thC, 29in (73.5cm) wide.
£700–850
€/ **$1,100–1,300** ✦ B(Ba)

A marquetry *secrétaire à abattant,* c1800, 24in (61cm) wide.
£4,200–4,600
€/ **$6,600–7,300** ⊞ SAW

A William and Mary walnut secretaire cabinet, the upper section with a cushion frieze drawer, the burrwood fall-front enclosing drawers and pigeonholes around a central cupboard, all with feather stringing, the associated base with three long drawers and a half sunburst to the recess and the bottom drawer, 42¾in (108.5cm) wide.
£4,200–5,000
€/ **$6,600–8,000** ✦ L

A George III mahogany secretaire cabinet, the swan-neck pediment above two fielded panelled doors enclosing four sliding trays, the base with a secretaire drawer above three graduated long drawers with brass swan-neck handles, on bracket feet, 51½in (131cm) wide.
£2,000–2,500
€/ **$3,200–4,000** ✦ GTH

▶ **A mahogany secretaire cabinet,** 19thC, 33in (84cm) wide.
£1,500–1,700
€/ **$2,300–2,700** ⊞ WAW

A mahogany secretaire side cabinet, the flap enclosing four small drawers and pigeonholes, c1835, 37in (94cm) wide.
£900–1,100
€/ **$1,400–1,700** ✦ S(O)

A satinwood and kingwood secretaire, with marble top, ormolu mounts and parquetry sides, French, c1880, 30in (76cm) wide.
£2,500–2,800
€/ **$4,000–4,400** ⊞ DAC

An Edwardian satinwood secretaire, with stringing and rosewood crossbanding, the fall-front with dummy drawers enclosing a fitted interior, over one long drawer and two doors, on splayed bracket feet, 28¼in (72cm) wide.
£2,000–2,500
€/ **$3,100–3,900** ✦ SWO

◀ **A maple secretaire cabinet,** with brass handles, American, 1930, 31in (78.5cm) wide.
£230–280
€/ **$360–440** ✦ DUM

FURNITURE

Side Cabinets

A George III mahogany D-shaped side cabinet, with crossbanded top, fitted with two frieze drawers, flanked by false drawers, 42in (106.5cm) wide.
£4,000–4,700
€ / **$6,300–7,400** ⚒ L

A mahogany side cabinet, with two doors enclosing a cellaret drawer, early 19thC, 49in (124.5cm) wide.
£580–725
€/ **$920–1,100** ⚒ L

A rosewood breakfront side cabinet, with a marble top, the central cupboard enclosed by two doors flanked by capped pillars and two further cupboards, all with gilt-metal grilled curtain doors, on a plain base, early 19thC, 71½in (181.5cm) wide.
£1,400–1,750
€ / **$2,200–2,700** ⚒ TMA

A rosewood breakfront side cabinet, with glazed tapestry doors, c1835, 56in (142cm) wide.
£3,000–3,400
€ / **$4,700–5,300** ⊞ MTay

A mahogany and marquetry side cabinet, inlaid with stringing, Dutch, c1790, 43in (109cm) wide.
£3,300–4,000
€ / **$5,200–6,300** ⚒ S(O)

A Regency mahogany chiffonier, the round cornered top over two frieze drawers and two panelled cupboards below enclosing shelves, on turned feet, 55½in (141cm) wide.
£2,000–2,400
€ / **$3,100–3,800** ⚒ TEN

A mahogany chiffonier, the shelved superstructure with three small drawers, over two drawers and two cupboard doors, c1825, 47in (119.5cm) wide.
£4,200–4,600
€ / **$6,600–7,200** ⊞ APO

▶ **A mahogany chiffonier,** with a carved back, two cushion-moulded frieze drawers, above two cupboard doors, on squat bun feet, 19thC, 40½in (103cm) wide.
£680–850
€ / **$1,100–1,300** ⚒ SWO

A mahogany side cabinet, the block-rail inlaid with satinwood, Continental, c1800, 36in (91.5cm) wide.
£5,000–5,750
€ / **$8,000–9,000** ⊞ NAW

A Regency satinwood and calamander-banded cabinet base, in the style of George Oakley, the top above two doors with re-entrant panels and scrolling ebony lines, the side pilasters applied with ebonized mounts, above shaped bracket feet painted with anthemia, evidence of a superstructure, 50¾in (129cm) wide.
£800–1,000
€ / **$1,300–1,600** ⚒ B
The firm of George Oakley (1773–1840) produced high-quality Grecian-style furniture, often using fashionable materials such as rosewood, mahogany and calamander, with inlays of satinwood, ebony and boullework.

A walnut side cabinet, with a marble top, top in two pieces, French, early 19thC, 67¼in (171cm) wide.
£600–750
€ / **$950–1,200** ⚒ B(Ch)

A walnut credenza, the moulded top above two small frieze drawers, with two panelled cupboards below, Italian, 19thC, 37½in (95.5cm) wide.
£500–625
€/ $800–1,000 ⚒ TEN

A giltwood and gesso pier cabinet, with marble top, the central door with a pastel of a muse, flanked by open shelves, French, 19thC, 44in (112cm) wide.
£900–1,100
€/ $1,400–1,700 ⚒ G(L)

A teak and marquetry side cabinet, the panel door enclosing trays, French, c1870, 30in (76cm) wide.
£700–800
€/ $1,100–1,300 ⚒ S(O)

A Victorian mahogany chiffonier, 55in (139.5cm) wide.
£1,200–1,350
€/ $1,900–2,200 ⌗ RPh

A Victorian ebonized credenza, with gilt-metal-mounts, brass inlay and cherub-mounted stiles, 62½in (159cm) wide.
£1,000–1,250
€/ $1,600–1,200 ⚒ B(Ba)

A Victorian burr-walnut credenza, the two central solid panelled doors with satinwood inlay, flanked by two quarter-round glazed doors fronted by two pairs of ebonized fluted columns with gilt-metal mounts, 72in (183cm) wide.
£3,200–4,000
€/ $5,100–6,300 ⚒ BWL

A Victorian rosewood-veneered demi-lune side cabinet, the moulded edge marble top above a moulded frieze above a central pierced fret panel, flanked by two moulded outline panel doors enclosing a shelf, on a plinth, 52¼in (132.5cm) wide.
£500–625
€ / **$800–1,000** ➤ WW

An ebonized side cabinet, in the style of Lamb of Manchester, with inlay detail, gilt work and Wedgwood plaque, c1880, 66in (167.5cm) wide.
£3,000–3,250
€ / **$4,700–5,200** ⊞ RAN

A Sheraton revival mahogany side cabinet, painted overall with flowers, musical trophies and a farm scene, the top with a reeded edge above two panelled doors enclosing shelves, on a plinth base, late 19thC, 37½in (95.5cm) wide.
£1,700–2,200
€ / **$2,700–3,500** ➤ DN

A George III-style mahogany demi-lune side cabinet, c1900, 41¼in (107.5cm) wide.
£520–650
€ / **$800–1,000** ➤ B(Ba)

A Victorian gilt-metal-mounted burr-walnut double side cabinet, the top with a gilt metal gallery above four glazed doors, the outer doors enclosing velvet-lined shelves, the projecting base of similar form, the two central doors with mirror plates, on a plinth, associated, 72in (183cm) wide.
£3,000–3,750
€ / **$4,700–6,000** ➤ PF

A pair of satinwood-veneered demi-lune commodes, with inlaid marquetry, the crossbanded top inlaid with an urn and ribbon-tied fruiting vines, above a shelf enclosed by a mahogany-banded door inlaid with an urn, flanked by oval paterae, with protruding inlaid flat pilasters on square tapering feet, minor damage, late 19thC, 49in (124.5cm) wide.
£42,000–52,000
€ / **$66,000–82,000** ➤WW
Estimated at £4,000–6,000 (€/ $6,300–9,500), these commodes, which had been owned by two different members of the same family and brought together for the sale, finally sold for £42,000 (€/ $66,300), underlining the current strength of the market for such decorative items. Although there was minor damage, the quality of the marquetry was superb, and the satinwood veneer was a further desirable factor. They are quite narrow in depth and would therefore fit comfortably in most rooms – practicality is always an important point.

A mahogany demi-lune commode cabinet, with original decorative paintwork and fitted interior with slides, c1910, 50in (127cm) wide.
£2,400–2,650
€ / **$3,800–4,200** ⊞ RAN

A Victorian walnut and inlaid breakfront credenza, with ormolu mounts, the solid centre door flanked by glazed doors, 72in (183cm) wide.
£1,500–1,800
€ / **$2,400–2,800** ➤ HOLL

An ebonized amboyna credenza, with ebony banding, ormolu moulding and mounts, with similar porcelain plaques, twin glazed side cupboards and central open shelf with double cupboard under, on turned feet, late 19thC, 72in (183cm) wide.
£2,800–3,500
€ / **$4,400–5,400** ➤ JM

A Viardot-style side cabinet, c1890, 55in (139.5cm) high.
£650–725
€ / **$1,000–1,100** ⊞ SAW

A mahogany bow-end side cabinet, in Regency style, c1920, 35in (89cm) wide.
£1,150–1,300
€ / **$1,800–2,000** ⊞ Che

FURNITURE

Cabinets-on-Stands

A Louis XVI-style mahogany cabinet-on-stand, Swedish, 1900–10, 12½in (32cm) wide.
£1,750–2,000
€/ **$2,800–3,200** ⊞ CAV

A kingwood *vernis Martin* cabinet-on-stand, with gilt-metal mounts, French, 1890, 37in (94cm) wide.
£3,200–4,000
€/ **$5,000–6,300** ➚ WW

A walnut cabinet-on-stand, the cushion frieze with a drawer, the two cupboard doors below revealing a central cupboard enclosing a drawer and ten further drawers, the later stand with two drawers, late 17thC and later, 41¾in (106cm) wide.
£2,500–3,000
€/ **$4,000–4,700** ➚ S(O)

A stained beech, mother-of-pearl and gilt-bronze side cabinet-on-stand, attributed to Gabriel Viardot, Paris, with cast mouldings, French, c1885, 30in (76cm) wide.
£1,800–2,200
€/ **$2,800–3,500** ➚ S(O)

▶ **An Edwardian satin-wood and rosewood collector's cabinet-on-stand,** with two panelled doors enclosing six drawers, on swept feet, 20in (51cm) wide.
£1,500–2,000
€/ **$2,400–3,200** ➚ G(L)

Expert's choice

A *pietra dura* cabinet, Florence, c1726, sold at Christie's on 5th July 1990.

There have been many exciting items that have come up for sale during the last 25 years, but, to me, the most memorable must be the Badminton Cabinet. I cannot think of any other piece of furniture that is so exuberant, impressive and beautifully decorative.

The cabinet is made of *pietra dura* and ebony and is mounted with ormolu. It was made in Florence c1726 for the third Duke of Beaufort. This architectural piece is of huge proportions – measuring 152in (386cm) high and 91in (23cm) wide. It is surmounted with a clock, a coat-of-arms with its Ducal coronet and, to either side, ormolu swags encrusted with semi-precious stones and the four corners mounted with ormolu figures depicting the Four Seasons. Below this is a collection of drawers centred by a cupboard door, which opens to reveal a further three purple heart and ebony drawers. The fronts of the drawers and cupboards, together with the side of the cabinet, are inlaid with the most amazing vibrantly colourful semi-precious stones with birds, some in flight around bouquets of flowers and some perched among flowers, all amazingly lifelike. To add to this already dramatic effect, the panels are edged with ormolu and bordered with amethyst quartz. The whole piece is supported on eight lapis-lazuli and red-jasper-mounted legs.

To me, the Badminton Cabinet is a piece that, once seen, can never be forgotten. It sold for £8,580,000 (€/ $13,556,400). **Edward Reily Collins**

Table Cabinets

A mahogany-veneered writing cabinet, early 19thC, 22½in (57cm) wide.
£260–325
€/ **$410–510** ➚ WW

An Edwardian bird's-eye maple and brass-bound cigar cabinet, 19¾in (50cm) wide.
£250–320
€/ **$400–500** ➚ B

A Victorian oak table collector's cabinet, the doors enclosing two banks of nine drawers, 30¼in (77cm) wide.
£220–275
€/ **$350–435** ➚ SWO

Canterburies

A six-section mahogany music canterbury, with two side drawers, c1790, 26in (66cm) wide.
£3,800–4,250
€/ $6,000–6,700 ⊞ CAT

A Regency mahogany canterbury, 19in (48.5cm) wide.
£2,200–2,400
€/ $3,200–3,800 ⊞ APO

A Victorian figured walnut canterbury, on carved turned feet and casters, 21½in (54.5cm) wide.
£1,300–1,600
€/ $2,000–2,500 ⚒ TEN

A Victorian burr-walnut-veneered canterbury, the scroll legs with brass casters, 22in (56cm) wide.
£680–850
€/ $1,100–1,300 ⚒ WW

A George III mahogany canterbury, 16½in (42cm) wide.
£520–650
€/ $825–1,000 ⚒ L

A Regency mahogany canterbury, restored, 19¾in (50cm) wide.
£750–950
€/ $1,200–1,500 ⚒ B(Ba)

A Victorian rosewood canterbury, 18in (45.5cm) high.
£1,250–1,400
€/ $2,000–2,200 ⊞ BrL

A mahogany canterbury, c1810, 20in (51cm) wide.
£2,000–2,200
€/ $3,200–3,500 ⊞ Che

A rosewood canterbury, with a single drawer, on brass casters, 19thC, 20in (51cm) wide.
£1,100–1,200
€/ $1,700–1,900 ⊞ WAW

A walnut canterbury, c1880, 19in (48.5cm) wide.
£325–360
€/ $520–600 ⊞ PaA

◀ **A Victorian walnut music canterbury,** the three divisions supported by turned pillars, above a single long drawer, on turned legs with ceramic casters, 21in (53.5cm) wide.
£400–500
€/ $630–800 ⚒ G(B)

Open Armchairs

A mahogany cockpen armchair, in the Chinese Chippendale style, the drop-in seat inset with a later solid panel, above a blind fret-carved seat rail, minor losses and faults, c1760.
£3,000–3,500
€/ **$4,700–5,500** ⚹ **BR**
During the 17th and 18th century, Europe had a fascination with the orient and Chippendale incorporated many Chinese features into his furniture using fretwork, lacquerwork, pagodas etc.

A George III mahogany open-scroll armchair, in the Chippendale style, with leather stuff-over seat, the back legs stamped with a Gothic C below a crown.
£550–700
€/ **$870–1,100** ⚹ **B(WM)**

▶ **A painted and parcel-gilt elbow chair,** with padded back and bowfronted stuff-over seat, late 18thC.
£1,200–1,500
€/ **$1,900–2,400** ⚹ **TEN**

A rococo giltwood *fauteuil en cabriolet,* the shield-shaped backrest within a moulded frame surrounded by a floral garland, with padded out-curved scrolled arms on leaf-carved supports, with a bow-shaped seat, the seat rail and cabriole legs with carved decoration, probably Spanish, c1760.
£2,300–2,700
€/ **$3,600–4,300** ⚹ **S(Am)**

A George III carved mahogany armchair, Irish.
£800–1,000
€/ **$1,300–1,600** ⚹ **S(O)**

◀ **A pair of carved walnut *fauteuils,*** with padded backs, scroll arms and stuff-over seat, one chair with insect damage, French, late 18thC.
£900–1,100
€/ **$1,400–1,700** ⚹ **JDJ**

A George III mahogany armchair.
£400–500
€/ **$630–800** ⚹ **L**

A mahogany-framed Gainsborough chair, on square legs and casters, late 18thC.
£800–1,000
€/ **$1,300–1,600** ⚹ **HOLL**

A pair of George III mahogany provincial armchairs, some restoration and later arms.
£140–175
€/ **$300–280** ⚹ **B(Ba)**

A George III mahogany and leather armchair.
£1,600–1,800
€/ **$2,500–2,800** ⚹ **APO**

FURNITURE

A pair of mahogany armchairs, the curved panelled bar back above open-pierced reeded splats with carved central paterae, the reeded arms on ring-turned vertical supports, with drop-in upholstered seats, on square tapered legs, c1810.
£2,400–2,650
€/ $3,800–4,200 ⊞ JC

A mahogany armchair, the arms with dolphin-shaped supports, c1820.
£350–420
€/ $550–670 ⚹ S(O)

A late Regency carved pollarded oak armchair, the panelled bar top-rail with moulded scroll terminals and rectangular splats, with stuff-over seat, on sabre legs and casters.
£1,700–2,200
€/ $2,700–3,500 ⚹ B(Nor)

A Georgian mahogany elbow chair, with pierced splat back, shaped top rail, scroll arms and an upholstered drop-in seat, on square chamfered supports.
£370–470
€/ $580–750 ⚹ BWL

A pair of neo-classical birch tub chairs, the curved back and sides with inlaid stringing and a central inlaid patera, the padded seat raised on splayed legs, 1800–25.
£2,500–3,250
€/ $4,000–5,500 ⚹ NOA

A pair of George IV mahogany elbow chairs, the figured swept bar backs with acanthus carving and downswept reeded arms and supports, with stuff-over seats, supported on palmette-carved and turned legs.
£900–1,100
€/ $1,400–1,700 ⚹ HAM

◄ **A simulated rosewood upholstered armchair,** with a reclining back and sliding footrest, c1835.
£350–420
€/ $550–650 ⚹ S(O)

A Regency salon armchair, with hand-painted floral decoration and upholstered seat, on turned legs.
£120–150
€/ $190–240 ⚹ WilP

A pair of Restauration armchairs, with padded backs, scrolling arms and bowed padded seats, on sabre legs, together with a similar side chair, French, 1815–30.
£1,500–2,000
€/ $2,400–3,200 ⚹ B

A rope-back carver chair, c1830.
£580–650
€/ $900–1,000 ⊞ RPh

A Regency mahogany open armchair, with leather drop-in seat.
£260–325
€/ $400–500 ⚹ B(Ba)

A mahogany open armchair, the back with five spindle splats, with flat arms and cushion seat and turned legs with brass caps and casters, 1825–50.
£1,300–1,500
€/ $2,000–2,400 ⚹ NOA

A mahogany Patent Reclining Chair, by Robert Daws, c1835.
£2,700–3,000
€/ $4,300–4,700 ⊞ ChC Robert Daws traded from 17 Margaret Street, near Oxford Circus in London, from 1820–39, when he moved to new premises in Edgware Road. He patented his 'Improved Recumbent Easy Chair' in 1827.

◄ **A William IV mahogany elbow chair.**
£650–725
€/ $1,000–1,150 ⊞ RPh

FURNITURE

A mahogany *fauteuil*, the padded back above scrolling arms, the bowed padded seat on lapetted sabre legs, French, 1830–48.
£800–975
€/ **$1,300–1,500** ✗ B

A mid-Victorian cast-iron and brass decorated rocking chair, attributed to R. W. Winfield & Co, the ringed padded back between uprights surmounted by leaf-cast terminals, the downswept padded arms and over-scrolled seat on shaped rolling rockers.
£1,800–2,250
€/ **$2,800–3,500** ✗ B
A version of this model was shown by Winfield at the Great Exhibition in 1851 and again at the London International Exhibition in 1862.
The design seemed to go against the over ornamentation that was dominant at the time.
It is thought that it may have been designed by Peter Cooper (New York, 1793–1883), who founded the Canton Iron Works in Baltimore and built the Tom Thumb, one of the earliest American locomotives, and who was to become one of the leaders of the American iron industry. The firm of Winfield was founded at Cambridge Street in Birmingham in 1829 and specialized in the production of decorative brass objects, particularly bedsteads.

► **A pair of mahogany open armchairs,** Danish, c1870.
£1,200–1,350
€/ **$1,900–2,200** ⊞ RPh

A Victorian walnut open armchair, with moulded balloon-shaped padded back and serpentine-shaped seat, on cabriole front legs and down-scroll rear legs.
£1,450–1,800
€/ **$2,300–3,000** ✗ MEA

A Victorian mahogany reclining easy chair, on brass casters.
£220–245
€/ **$350–380** ⊞ PaA

A pair of walnut Burgomaster chairs, with walnut-veneered backrest, out-curved scrolled arms on incurved supports and padded seat, on scrolled legs, alterations, Italian, 19thC.
£3,400–3,750
€/ **$5,400–6,000** ✗ S(Am)

A Victorian mahogany X-framed chair, with leather upholstery.
£800–900
€/ **$1,300–1,400** ⊞ SAW

An ebonized armchair, with curved padded backrest, padded arms and S-scrolled reeded supports carved with leaves and topped with a reeded finial, on leaf-carved turned toupie feet with casters, probably American, 19thC.
£2,300–2,750
€/ **$3,600–4,300** ✗ S(Am)

A Renaissance revival walnut open armchair, the uprights formed as caryatids, American, 1850–75.
£575–700
€/ **$900–1,100** ✗ NOA

A pierced laminated-rosewood open armchair, in the Tuthill King pattern, attributed to John Henry Belter, the high back with a crest, the serpentine front with carved rose decoration, on French-style cabriole legs on brass caster feet, 19thC.
£15,000–17,000
€/ **$24,000–27,000** ✗ JDJ
German-born John Henry Belter (1804–63) emigrated to the United States in 1833 and developed a range of sumptuously carved furniture of heavy proportions, which was intended to grace the houses of the country's *nouveau riche*. These designs are said to have given rise to the term 'a belter of a piece'. Items were seldom marked and rarely exported and therefore examples are hardly ever found outside the United States.

A walnut X-framed Savanorola armchair, the back with a grotesque and shell-carved top rail, with hide-covered padded central panel, with a padded seat, the foliate moulded legs terminating in paw feet, Italian, 19thC.
£200–250
€/ **$300–400** ✗ PF

◄ **A pair of walnut armchairs,** the padded backs flanked with acanthus-carved uprights, downswept arms with animal carved terminals and stuff-over seat with acanthus-carved apron, Continental, 19thC.
£450–550
€/ **$700–870** ✗ CGC

FURNITURE

A mahogany Gains-borough chair, with brocade upholstery, c1880.
£1,650–1,850
€ / **$2,600–3,000** ⊞ RAN

A pair of ebonized elbow chairs, by L. Hitchcock, each with a stencilled crest and back rail, the downswept arms with turned supports, the rush seat on turned legs and stretchers, stencilled 'L. Hitchcock, Hitchcocksville, Conn. Warrented', American, late 19thC.
£500–650
€ / **$800–1,000** ⚒ DN

A pair of Chippendale-style mahogany chairs, c1900.
£2,800–3,200
€ / **$4,400–5,000** ⊞ Che

▶ **An Edwardian painted satinwood elbow chair,** the caned shield back with a centre portrait splat, on shaped legs, Waring's label.
£600–725
€ / **$950–1,150** ⚒ SPF

A mahogany armchair, Continental, c1880.
£800–900
€ / **$1,300–1,400** ⊞ RPh

A walnut, ebony and bone-inlaid armchair, in the Moorish style, inlaid with flowerheads and patterns created from bone *tesserae,* the back with an ebonized swan-neck pediment above a portrait of a gentleman in 17thC costume, surmounted by an ivory-inlaid grotesque mask, flanked by further inlaid panels on an ebony ground, the downswept arms above a solid seat with a shaped apron on trestle supports, Italian, late 19thC.
£620–775
€ / **$1,000–1,200** ⚒ B

A pair of Louis XV-style walnut armchairs, recovered, c1890.
£1,600–1,800
€ / **$2,500–2,800** ⊞ DAC

A maple rocking chair, with scrolling arms and a modified curule base joined to rockers, Anglo-American, late 19thC.
£1,500–2,000
€ / **$3,500–3,200** ⚒ NOA

A pair of Biedermeier-style birchwood armchairs, Swedish, 1900–10.
£5,000–5,600
€ / **$8,000–8,800** ⊞ CAV

◀ **A pair of Louis XV-style walnut *fauteuils,*** c1930.
£1,000–1,100
€ / **$1,500–1,600** ⊞ MLL

A pair of rosewood open armchairs, inlaid with musical instruments and satinwood stringing, with upholstered seats and backs, on square tapering legs, spade feet and casters, late 19thC.
£650–820
€ / **$1,000–1,300** ⚒ RTo

A carved walnut armchair, American, c1900.
£550–700
€ / **$870–1,100** ⚒ DuM

An inlaid mahogany elbow chair, c1905.
£340–375
€ / **$550–600** ⊞ RPh

Upholstered Armchairs

A walnut wing armchair, with padded back, sides and outscrolled arms, repairs to front legs, replacement back legs, early 18thC.
£1,500–1,800
€/ **$2,400–2,800** ⚒ B

A walnut armchair, the shaped padded back, arms and seat above a walnut-veneered frieze and cabriole legs, 18thC.
£500–600
€/ **$800–1,000** ⚒ WW

A Chippendale-style cherrywood lolling chair, with serpentine top crest rail, American, Connecticut, 18thC.
£1,500–2,000
€/ **$2,400–3,200** ⚒ JDJ

A pair of stained wood upholstered armchairs, French, mid-18thC.
£800–975
€/ **$1,300–1,500** ⚒BERN

A George III mahogany chair, with stuff-over back, arms and seat.
£150–200
€/ **$240–300** ⚒ L

A mid-Georgian mahogany wing armchair, with deep button back, wings and scroll-over arms, cabriole front legs with compressed ball feet.
£850–1,100
€/ **$1,300–1,700** ⚒ PFK

A stained-wood upholstered armchair, French, mid-18thC.
£400–500
€/ **$630–800** ⚒ BERN

A late Regency simulated rosewood armchair.
£400–500
€/ **$630–800** ⚒ S(O)
Beech was often used instead of solid rosewood because it was stronger and found locally, therefore keeping down costs. The wood was then painted to simulate rosewood.

An early Victorian rose-wood-framed button-back chair, on turned legs with casters.
£450–575
€/ **$700–900** ⚒ JAd

A George III-style mahogany barrel-back wing armchair, 19thC.
£450–565
€/ **$700–900** ⚒ B(Ba)

 ◄ A Victorian mahogany spoon-back armchair, with buttoned back and padded arms and seat, on cabriole front legs.
£140–170
€/ **$220–270** ⚒ EH

FURNITURE

A Victorian walnut-framed tub chair, the buttoned back above down-swept scrolling arms and stuff-over seat, on cabriole legs with brass casters.
£400–500
€ / $630–800 ✗ CGC

A Victorian mahogany-framed armchair, on scroll-carved French-style legs and casters.
£800–900
€ / $1,300–1,400 ✗ BWL

A mid-Victorian mahogany tub chair.
£180–225
€ / $285–350 ✗ B(Ba)

A pair of button-back armchairs, on ebonized turned legs, French, c1860.
£1,000–1,200
€ / $1,600–1,900 ✗ S(O)

A pair of giltwood tub-shaped *fauteuils*, c1870.
£2,100–2,350
€ / $3,300–3,700 ⊞ RAN

A Queen Anne-style walnut-framed wing armchair, the upholstered back with out-scrolled arms, on ball-turned front legs, cut down, reupholstered, 19thC.
£420–525
€ / $950–830 ✗ B(W)

A pair of Louis XV-style walnut *fauteuils*, reupholstered, French, c1880.
£1,700–2,000
€ / $2,700–3,200 ⊞ DAC

A mahogany and leather armchair, the concave padded back and sloping arms above a bowed seat, on cabriole legs with claw-and-ball feet, 1875–1900.
£1,200–1,400
€ / $1,900–2,200 ✗ NOA

A late Victorian easy chair, on ring-turned tapering front legs with brass caps and casters.
£230–300
€ / $360–470 ✗ PFK

A button-upholstered armchair, on ebonized turned legs and ceramic casters, late 19thC.
£650–750
€ / $1,000–1,200 ✗ S(O)

A Gothic-style carved oak armchair, late 19thC.
£700–900
€ / $1,100–1,400 ✗ B(Ba)

A late Victorian mahogany-framed wing armchair, the acanthus-carved cabriole legs with ball-and-claw feet.
£270–340
€ / $425–800 ✗ B(Ch)

A giltwood wing arm-chair, with upholstered back, sides and seat, the frame carved with scrolls, on cabriole legs, late 19th–early 20thC.
£700–875
€ / $1,100–1,400 ✗ DN

A pair of walnut and leather upholstered armchairs, French, late 19thC.
£700–875
€ / $1,100–1,400 ✗ B(Ch)

A pair of Howard-style upholstered armchairs, early 20thC.
£1,800–2,250
€ / $2,800–3,500 ✗ B(Ch)

FURNITURE

Bergères

A Restauration mahogany bergère, with padded back and arms above a cushioned seat, on sabre legs, French, 1800–25.
£1,000–1,200
€/ **$1,600–1,900** ⚒ NOA

A mahogany bergère, with a reeded frame and caned back, arms and seat, on square tapering legs, with brass casters, early 19thC.
£800–1,000
€/ **$1,300–1,600** ⚒ DN

▶ **An Empire-style gilt-wood bergère,** the cove back with reeded back-rail and scroll ends, the sides and seat upholstered, the arms with carved dolphin-head supports, on squared sabre legs, French, 19thC.
£300–375
€/ **$475–600** ⚒ B&L

◀ **A William IV rosewood and caned bergère.**
£700–875
€/ **$1,100–1,400** ⚒ B(Ba)

A Regency ebonized bergère, with original decoration.
£1,250–1,400
€/ **$1,900–2,200** ⊞ CAT

A Regency mahogany bergère, with reeded frame.
£650–800
€/ **$1,000–1,300** ⚒ L

A Sheraton revival satin-wood and decorated bergère, c1890.
£2,000–2,300
€/ **$3,200–3,600** ⊞ Che

Children's Chairs

A child's mahogany high chair and table, 19thC, table 12½in (32cm) high.
£625–700
€/ **$1,000–1,100** ⊞ SDA

A child's George III mahogany chair, the arched back above a pierced vase splat, drop-in seat and moulded chamfered square legs, on a later square-legged stand, c1780.
£950–1,200
€/ **$1,500–1,900** ⚒ S(O)

A child's Georgian mahogany open arm-chair, with serpentine top-rail, pierced vase splat, rush drop-in seat, on square legs, restored.
£380–475
€/ **$600–750** ⚒ Bea

A child's mahogany high chair, with horizontal splat and drop-in seat, the turned tapering front supports and sabre back legs joined by stretchers, 19thC.
£160–200
€/ **$250–300** ⚒ FHF

▶ **A child's Victorian oak and caned bergère,** on turned supports with cross-stretcher.
£85–100
€/ **$135–160** ⚒ WilP

Safety
The children's furniture illustrated in this guide no longer complies with EC safety regulations and must not be used for its original purpose.

FURNITURE

Corner Chairs

A Chippendale-style carved and figured walnut corner chair, repairs to one leg, American, Philadelphia, 1760–80.
£2,000–2,400
€/ **$3,200–3,800** ✗ S(NY)

A George III mahogany high-back corner chair, the scrolled top-rail above pierced splats, gun barrel columns and a drop-in seat, on square legs joined by stretchers, restored.
£1,200–1,500
€/ **$1,900–2,400** ✗ B(L)

A mahogany corner armchair, altered and restored, 18thC.
£1,200–1,500
€/ **$1,900–2,400** ✗ B(Ba)

A marquetry corner armchair, Dutch, c1850.
£770–950
€/ **$1,200–1,500** ✗ S(O)

A pair of oak corner chairs, c1880.
£800–875
€/ **$1,300–1,400** ⊞ GBr

A Victorian carved oak corner chair, with a coronet and a painted leather seat.
£130–160
€/ **$200–250** ✗ SWO

A pair of Edwardian rosewood corner chairs, the top-rails and splat backs inlaid with satinwood, above stuff-over seats, on square tapering legs, with spade feet.
£450–565
€/ **$700–900** ✗ RTo

An Edwardian light mahogany corner chair, the splat back inlaid with boxwood stringing and a panel, over three open fret and carved supports, on cabriole legs joined by a cross-stretcher.
£220–270
€/ **$350–425** ✗ DA

Dining Chairs

A George I walnut dining chair, with splat back and drop-in seat, on cabriole legs carved with shell knees, on pad feet joined by an H-stretcher.
£280–350
€/ **$440–550** ✗ RTo

A walnut dining chair, with scroll top-rail, pierced waisted splat and drop-in seat, on cabriole legs with shell-carved hips and claw-and-ball feet, 18thC.
£340–425
€/ **$550–670** ✗ G(L)

A set of six George III mahogany dining chairs, after a design by Thomas Sheraton, each with a curved and overlapping cresting rail, over a diamond trellis splat with leaf-capped reeded frame, flanked by reeded tapering uprights, above a stuff-over seat, on reeded knop-turned tapering front legs, repaired.
£1,700–2,200
€/ **$2,700–3,500** ✗ B(WM)

Further reading
Miller's Antiques Encyclopedia, Miller's Publications, 1998

► **A set of eight Hepplewhite-period mahogany dining chairs,** c1790.
£10,000–11,000
€/ **$11,800–17,500** ⊞ CAT

A set of six mahogany brander-back dining chairs, including two armchairs, the goblet-shaped backs enclosing five moulded splats above drop-in seats, on square tapering legs, c1800.
£1,400–1,750
€/ **$2,200–2,800** ⚘ B(Ed)
The 'brander back' was a pattern frequently used in common chairs from the eastern counties of Scotland during the last quarter of the 18th century. These were probably made for an improved farm-house and have been given an extra fashionable lift by the curvature of their stiles – a reference to the shield-back shape seen in Hepplewhite's *Cabinet and Upholsterer's Guide* 1788.

Valuing sets of chairs

Sets of dining chairs are worth proportionally more the larger the set. For good quality 19th-century copies of Georgian chairs, for example:
2: approx 3 x price of a single
4: approx 6 x price of a single
6: approx 10 x price of a single
8: approx 16 x price of a single
10: approx 25 x price of a single
The reason that the unit price between a pair and four is the same is that the latter are difficult to sell unless looking for chairs for a card table. Pairs and sets of six or more are more desirable.

A set of four George III mahogany dining chairs.
£400–500
€/ **$630–800** ⚘ L

A set of six mahogany chairs, with gilt-metal mounts, Scandinavian, early 19thC.
£1,500–2,000
€/ **$2,400–3,200** ⚘ S(O)

A set of four rosewood dining chairs, with caned seats and squab cushions, c1810.
£1,750–2,000
€/ **$2,800–3,200** ⊞ RPh

A set of eight Regency mahogany dining chairs, including two armchairs, with gadrooned top-rails, palmette-carved crossbars, upholstered seats, on tapering turned legs, restored.
£2,400–3,000
€/ **$3,800–4,700** ⚘ Bea

A set of six mahogany dining chairs, Dutch, early 19thC.
£750–950
€/ **$1,200–1,500** ⚘ L

A pair of Regency mahogany dining chairs, the bar backs with brass inlay, cane seats, damaged.
£300–375
€/ **$475–600** ⚘ SWO

◀ **A set of eight Regency mahogany dining chairs,** with two armchairs, the bar backs above pierced shell and circle motifs, on turned tapering legs.
£1,100–1,400
€/ **$1,700–2,200** ⚘ BWL

A set of six mahogany dining chairs, the backs with moulded top-rails and single horizontal bars joined by reeded X-shaped splats, with drop-in seats, on square tapered legs joined by stretchers, early 19thC.
£650–800
€/ **$1,000–1,300** ⚘ PF

▶ **A set of six late George III mahogany dining chairs,** with boxwood stringing throughout, the backs with stick splats, above upholstered seats and tapering turned legs.
£900–1,150
€/ **$1,400–1,800** ⚘ Bea

A set of six late George III mahogany bar-back dining chairs, including two carvers.
£800–1,000
€/ **$1,300–1,600** ⚘ B(Ba)

FURNITURE

A pair of Regency Gothic-style dining chairs.
£750–850
€/ $1,200–1,300 ⊞ SAW

A set of five George IV mahogany dining chairs.
£450–575
€/ $700–900 ⚒ L

A set of eight rosewood dining chairs, with carved backs and back-rails, on turned and carved legs, c1825.
£7,000–8,000
€/ $11,000–12,500 ⊞ BERA

A pair of Biedermeier birchwood and masur birch dining chairs, Swedish, 1820–30.
£2,000–2,300
€/ $3,200–3,600 ⊞ CAV

A set of four William IV mahogany dining chairs.
£900–1,000
€/ $1,400–1,600 ⊞ DY

A set of seven William IV mahogany bar-back dining chairs.
£6,200–6,850
€/ $9,800–11,000 ⊞ RAN

A pair of William IV mahogany dining chairs, upholstered in leather.
£150–200
€/ $250–300 ⚒ B(Ba)

A set of four William IV rosewood dining chairs, the top- and centre-rails profusely carved with acanthus leaf scrolls and flowerheads, above cane seats, on reeded tapering legs.
£650–820
€/ $1,000–1,300 ⚒ RTo

A set of four William IV mahogany dining chairs.
£1,440–1,550
€/ $2,300–2,400 ⊞ RPh

A set of six William IV mahogany dining chairs, with upholstered drop-in seats, on tapered front legs.
£650–820
€/ $1,000–1,300 ⚒ WL

A set of six mahogany dining chairs, c1840.
£2,250–2,500
€/ $3,500–4,000 ⊞ DY

◄ A set of six early Victorian walnut dining chairs, restored.
£600–750
€/ $950–1,200 ⚒ B(Ba)

A set of eight rosewood dining chairs, with button-upholstered seats, c1850.
£2,500–2,800
€/ $4,000–4,400 ⊞ NoC

A set of 12 George III-style mahogany dining chairs, the arched backs with foliate-carved stick splats and gilt-brass mounts, above leather-upholstered seats, on tapering square legs, damaged, one chair distressed, 19thC.
£4,500–5,500
€/ $7,000–8,800 ⚒ Bea

A pair of Victorian inlaid walnut dining chairs.
£430–475
€/ $680–750 ⊞ RPh

A set of four Victorian walnut balloon-back dining chairs.
£500–650
€/ $800–1,000 ⚒ L

► A set of eight Victorian mahogany dining chairs, with padded leather backs and seats, on turned and fluted tapering legs.
£1,800–2,200
€/ $2,800–3,500
⚒ G(L)

A set of six Victorian mahogany dining chairs, on turned reeded supports.
£620–775
€/ $1,000–1,200 ⚒ MAR

A set of four Victorian carved rosewood balloon-back dining chairs, on French cabriole legs.
£1,000–1,250
€/ $1,600–2,000 ⚒ WilP

A set of seven mahogany lyre-back dining chairs, Continental, c1880.
£5,300–6,000
€/ $8,400–9,500 ⊞ SAW

A set of six Victorian walnut dining chairs, with scroll-moulded waisted balloon backs, the sprung serpentine seats on cabochon-moulded turned legs.
£550–700
€/ $870–1,100 ⚒ PF

A set of six Victorian mahogany dining chairs.
£400–500
€/ $630–800 ⚒ L

A set of eight late Victorian mahogany dining chairs, by Lamb of Manchester, with leather-upholstered back and seats, on cabriole legs with pad feet and ceramic casters, stamped 'Lamb, Manchester'.
£1,000–1,200
€/ $1,600–1,900 ⚒ DN

◄ A set of six Edwardian walnut dining chairs, with floral-carved top-rail and spindle back, above a stuff-over seat, on ring-turned legs.
£240–300
€/ $380–475 ⚒ AMB

FURNITURE

Hall Chairs

▶ **A pair of William IV mahogany hall chairs,** the scroll-bordered waisted backs centred with stylized carved scallop shell motifs.
£630–800
€/ $1,000–1,300
↗ Bri

A pair of George III mahogany hall chairs.
£2,200–2,400
€/ $3,500–3,800 ⊞ APO

A pair of Regency mahogany hall chairs, with shaped backs, on ring-turned leg supports.
£900–1,100
€/ $1,400–1,700 ↗ AMB

◀ **A pair of late Victorian walnut hall chairs.**
£100–140
€/ $160–220
↗ B(Ba)

A set of six early Victorian mahogany hall chairs, each with a shield-shaped back with a central painted crest, the solid serpentine seat on turned tapering legs.
£1,700–2,200
€/ $2,700–3,500 ↗ DN

A carved walnut hall chair, the back ornately decorated with a mask and scrolling and pierced foliage, the shaped solid seat with a dished centre, on trestle legs.
£220–275
€/ $350–430 ↗ WW

Library Chairs

An oak library chair, with a cane seat, c1830.
£600–725
€/ $1,000–1,150 ↗ S(O)

An oak metamorphic library chair, possibly by Gillows, c1835.
£4,700–6,000
€/ $7,500–9,500 ↗ S(O)
The top portion of this chair folds forward, converting to steps.

A William IV rosewood and simulated rosewood library chair, the shaped back, scroll arms and seat upholstered in brown leather, the arms carved with diagonal reeding and florets, on turned tapered reeded legs with brass casters.
£1,700–2,200
€/ $2,700–3,500 ↗ B&L

An early Victorian leather library chair, with button-upholstered back.
£3,000–3,400
€/ $4,700–5,400 ⊞ SAW

◀ **A pair of mahogany-framed upholstered library chairs,** the arms with painted and carved swan supports, on square tapering front legs and rear swept legs, Continental, mid-19thC.
£1,100–1,400
€/ $1,700–2,200 ↗ TMA

▶ **A mahogany library chair,** with upholstered back and seat, the arms carved with lion's heads, the front legs with claw-and-ball feet, 19thC.
£1,150–1,400
€/ $1,800–2,200 ↗ SWO

Nursing Chairs

An early Victorian rosewood nursing chair, on cabriole front legs.
£200–240
€/ $300–380 ⋏ CHTR

A Victorian walnut nursing chair.
£130–160
€/ $200–250 ⋏ B(Ba)

A Victorian rosewood nursing chair, with button-upholstered lyre-shaped back on scroll supports, with serpentine-front upholstered seat, on cabriole legs with scroll feet and china casters.
£150–200
€/ $250–300 ⋏ WW

A Victorian nursing chair, with button-upholstered back.
£170–185
€/ $270–300 ⊞ WiB

A Victorian mahogany balloon-back nursing chair.
£180–225
€/ $300–350 ⋏ B(Ba)

A walnut nursing chair, on original casters, c1860.
£680–760
€/ $1,100–1,200 ⊞ SAW

LOCATE THE SOURCE
The source of each illustration in Miller's can be found by checking the code letters below each caption with the Key to Illustrations, pages 794–800.

A walnut-framed nursing chair, late 19thC.
£180–225
€/ $290–350 ⋏ SWO

Salon Chairs

A matched set of six Victorian walnut salon chairs, with pierced wavy-ladder backs and stuff-over seats, on moulded rails and slender moulded cabriole legs with tripod feet, four chairs labelled by Marsh, Jones, Cribb & Co, and two by J. H. Cooper & Sons, Ilkley, Yorkshire.
£850–1,100
€/ $1,300–1,600 ⋏ TEN
Marsh & Jones was founded in 1865 when John Marsh and Edward Jones acquired the Leeds upholstery and cabinet making business of John Kendell & Co.

A pair of Victorian walnut-framed button-backed salon chairs, reupholstered.
£2,600–3,000
€/ $4,000–4,700 ⊞ JSt

A set of four Edwardian mahogany salon chairs, with marquetry inlay, carved backs and satinwood ground marquetry panels, the seat rails with boxwood stringing, on cabriole legs, one leg repaired.
£340–425
€/ $700–670 ⋏ HoG

◄ A set of four Louis Philippe-style mahogany salon chairs, French, early 20thC.
£130–160
€/ $200–250 ⋏ B(Ch)

Sets/pairs
Unless otherwise stated, any description which refers to 'a set' or 'a pair' includes a guide price for the entire set or the pair, even though the illustration may show only a single item.

FURNITURE

Side Chairs

A walnut high-back chair, with corresponding scrolling top-rail and stretcher, and caned back and seat, 17thC.
£200–250
€/ $300–400 🪓 G(L)

A pair of walnut side chairs, the shaped backs with solid curved central splats, above slip-in upholstered seats, within stepped and rounded frames, on cabriole front legs with corner ears and pad feet, joined by rounded stretchers, the rear legs with additional stretcher, c1720.
£1,650–1,850
€/ $2,600–3,000 ⊞ JC

A set of four marquetry and walnut side chairs, the shaped backs with vase-shaped splats inlaid with bird and flower marquetry with cupid in the cresting rail, in various stained hardwoods and ivory, above shaped drop-in seats, on cabriole legs with shoe-shaped feet, Dutch, 18thC.
£3,800–4,750
€/ $6,000–7,500 🪓 HAM

A pair of Empire mahogany chairs, Swedish, 1810–20.
£2,600–3,000
€/ $4,000–4,800 ⊞ CAV

A pair of rosewood-framed side chairs, Continental, c1870.
£700–800
€/ $1,100–1,300 ⊞ RPh

A set of four mahogany Queen Anne-style side chairs, late 19thC.
£720–800
€/ $1,100–1,300 ⊞ PaA

▶ **A set of three rose-wood and marquetry side chairs,** c1910.
£350–400
€/ $550–630 ⊞ Che

◀ **An ebonized and marquetry side chair,** by Herter Brothers, with original velvet-upholstered seat, rail stamped '4718', 1877–79.
£3,000–3,750
€/ $4,700–6,000 🪓 B
By the late 1850s, Gustav and Christian Herter were established as prominent New York furniture-makers. Their furniture covered a variety of styles and they worked on many high-profile commissions.

Miscellaneous Chairs

A rosewood tub chair, 19thC.
£350–400
€/ $550–630 ⊞ SAW

◀ **A Victorian rococo revival carved walnut sewing chair,** with brocade upholstery, on cabriole legs with casters.
£120–150
€/ $200–250 🪓 BR

▶ **A walnut prie-dieu,** 1860.
£325–360
€/ $500–570 ⊞ PaA

Chaise Longues

A rosewood chaise longue, seat cushion missing, c1825, 89in (226cm) long.
£3,500–4,200
€/ $5,500–6,650 ➤ S(O)

A rosewood chaise longue, with hide upholstery and brass inlay, c1810, 81in (205.5cm) long.
£5,000–5,650
€/ $7,900–8,900 ⊞ APO

A neo-classical painted and parcel-gilt chaise longue, Swedish, 19thC, 57in (145cm) long.
£5,000–6,250
€/ $8,000–10,000 ➤ S(NY)

An early Victorian mahogany chaise longue, the back and stuff-over arms with concentric disc terminals, the hinged seat with bedding box below, on inverted tulip-form legs with brass caps and casters, 70in (178cm) long.
£400–500
€/ $630–800 ➤ PFK

A chaise longue, on walnut baluster legs with brass caps and casters, c1860, 72in (183cm) long.
£1,800–2,200
€/ $2,850–3,475 ➤ S(O)

A late Victorian mahogany chaise longue, 73¼in (186cm) long.
£300–375
€/ $475–600 ➤ B(Ba)

A Victorian rosewood chaise longue, with sprung seat on cabriole legs with casters, 78in (198cm) long.
£600–750
€/ $950–1,185 ➤ PF

▶ **An ebonized wooden-framed chaise longue,** with pierced foliate and carved decoration, and velour upholstery, early 20thC, 70in (178cm) long.
£140–175
€/ $220–275 ➤ FHF

Chests & Coffers

A carved walnut _cassone_, with arched panels and paw feet, Italian, c1620, 53in (134.5cm) wide.
£5,200–5,800
€/ $8,200–9,200 ⊞ DJH

A mahogany blanket chest, with hinged cover and four apron drawers, c1770, 67¾in (172cm) wide.
£1,100–1,300
€/ $1,750–2,000 ➤ S(O)

A George III mahogany mule chest, on ogee bracket feet, base to bracket feet missing, 50½in (128.5cm) wide.
£700–875
€/ $1,100–1,380 ➤ DN
The mule chest has a lifting lid with drawers below and was mainly used in the 17th century and went on to develop into the chest of drawers.

FURNITURE

Chests of Drawers & Commodes

A walnut chest, with marquetry inlay of sycamore, boxwood, bog oak and holly, with two short over three long drawers, on replacement bun feet, c1690, 35in (89cm) wide.
£12,000–13,500
€/ **$19,000–21,000** ⊞ HA

A figured walnut veneered and crossbanded chest, with two short over three long drawers, on bun feet, c1710, 36in (91.5cm) wide.
£7,000–7,800
€/ **$11,000–12,300** ⊞ RGa

A walnut commode, with shaped front, the crossbanded and quartered top with double herringbone inlay, matching four long drawers with ornate brass handles, plain sides and high bracket feet, Continental, early 18thC, 34in (86.5cm) wide.
£6,250–7,500
€/ **$9,900–12,000** ⚒ JNic

A George II inlaid mahogany chest of drawers, the crossbanded and parquetry line-inlaid top above a brushing slide and four graduated drawers with later turned wood handles, on bracket feet, 26½in (67.5cm) wide.
£1,100–1,400
€/ **$1,750–2,200** ⚒ Bri

A Queen Anne inlaid walnut chest of drawers, with original cast-brass fittings, extensive damage, American, Pennsylvania, c1750, 40in (101.5cm) wide.
£11,000–13,000
€/ **$17,500–20,500** ⚒ S(NY)
American furniture termed, for example, 'Queen Anne' does not necessarily date from the actual period of Queen Anne. This is because the latest fashions took about 20 years to cross the Atlantic but the style is nevertheless of that period.

A George II walnut chest of drawers, the top with ovolo-moulded edge, over a slide and three long drawers, on bracket feet, 31½in (80cm) wide.
£4,000–4,800
€/ **$6,300–7,600** ⚒ TEN

The Parry Collection

The Parry Collection of predominantly oak and walnut furniture that was sold by Christie's on 24 April 1997 was notable for its wonderful near original condition, colour and deep rich patination. The Parrys had an exceedingly critical eye, and obviously only wanted the best. Their house must have been magnificently furnished as I do not think I have seen so many oak dressers and *cwrpwrdds* (cupboards) or magnificently patinated walnut chests of drawers in one sale. I had set my heart on two pieces in particular, both of which had unusual features and glorious colour and patination. The first, a late 18th-century north Wales oak architectural dresser was notable for its spindle gallery as well as its attractive scroll fret-carved frieze. It sold for three times my original estimate! The second, a George I burr-walnut bachelor's chest with a most unusual superstructure incorporating small drawers and a hinged writing surface, with a collection of three rows of small drawers and two further long drawers below, all with delicate herringbone inlay, sold for a staggering £265,000 (€/ $420,000). **Edward Reily Collins**

A George III mahogany bowfronted chest of drawers, with rosewood crossbanding and stringing, brass ring handles and later ogee-bracket feet, 39¼in (99.5cm) wide.
£500–600
€/ **$800–950** ⚒ AH

A walnut commode, with a marble top, Italian, c1770, 28in (71cm) wide.
£2,600–3,000
€ / **$4,100–4,750** ⊞ Che

A George III mahogany serpentine chest of drawers, the three long graduated drawers with a shaped apron, on splayed bracket feet, 43½in (110.5cm) wide.
£1,750–2,200
€ / **$2,750–3,475** ⚒ BWL

A mahogany parquetry commode, stamped with the crowned coat-of-arms of Amsterdam and J. G. of St Joseph Guild, Dutch, c1771, 23¾in (60.5cm) wide.
£3,200–3,800
€ / **$5,000–6,000** ⚒ S(Am)
In most major Dutch cities French-style marquetry furniture was produced from the 1760s onwards, both to meet public demand and to counteract the large amount of French furniture being imported. Following a complaint from the Amsterdam Guild of St Joseph, import regulations were tightened, and the remaining foreign stock was allowed to be sold only if it was stamped with the mark of the Guild of St Joseph. In the case of this commode, its French style probably led the officials to apply the stamp in the belief that it was of foreign origin.

A George III mahogany Lancashire chest, the fascia with five dummy drawers over four drawers with brass drop handles, flanked by cluster columns, on ogee bracket feet, 68in (172.5cm) wide.
£1,500–2,000
€ / **$2,370–3,170** ⚒ AH

A George III mahogany dressing chest, with a caddy top, brushing slide and four graduated long drawers, on shaped bracket feet, restored, 33in (84cm) wide.
£1,100–1,400
€ / **$1,750–2,200** ⚒ Bea

◄ **A walnut bachelor's chest of drawers,** probably Dutch, 18thC, 32in (81.5cm) wide.
£6,000–6,800
€ / **$9,500–10,700** ⊞ APO

► **A mahogany chest of drawers,** with two short and three long graduated drawers, on shaped bracket feet, c1780, 41¼in (105cm) wide.
£2,300–2,650
€ / **$3,650–4,250** ⊞ JC

◄ **A mahogany chest of drawers,** on bracket feet, c1780, 40in (101.5cm) wide.
£800–875
€ / **$1,260–1,380** ⊞ PaA

FURNITURE

A George III mahogany chest of drawers, the four long graduated drawers with foliate-cast swing handles, 34in (86.5cm) wide.
£1,750–2,200
€/ **$2,750–3,500** ➤ TMA

A mahogany bowfronted chest of drawers, the crossbanded top above five drawers, c1800, 37in (94cm) wide.
£4,000–4,500
€/ **$6,325–7,225** ⊞ RGa

A mahogany bowfronted chest of drawers, with two short and two long graduated drawers with original knob handles, above a shaped apron, on splay bracket feet, early 19thC, 35½in (90cm) wide.
£620–775
€/ **$975–1,225** ➤ DMC

A mahogany chest, the reeded top above a brushing slide and three long drawers, on bracket feet, 19thC, 36¾in (93.5cm) wide.
£800–1,000
€/ **$1,260–1,580** ➤ SWO

A mahogany bowfronted chest of drawers, c1800, 42in (106.5cm) wide.
£1,600–1,850
€/ **$2,500–3,000** ⊞ DUK

A Federal mahogany-inlaid figured birchwood bowfronted chest of drawers, sections of drawer facing later reveneered, American, New Hampshire, c1800, 42in (106.5cm) wide.
£3,200–3,800
€/ **$5,000–6,000** ➤ S(NY)

A Federal mahogany bowfronted chest of drawers, American, c1810, 44in (112cm) wide.
£9,000–10,000
€/ **$14,200–15,800** ⊞ Che

A mahogany chest of drawers, with two short and three long drawers, on ogee bracket feet, early 19thC, 53in (134.5cm) wide.
£900–1,000
€/ **$1,425–1,575** ⊞ MHA

▶ **A mahogany commode,** with three drawers, Dutch, early 19thC, 31in (78.5cm) wide.
£3,200–3,500
€/ **$5,000–5,500** ⊞ DOA

A George III mahogany chest of drawers, on bracket feet, 31in (78.5cm) wide.
£2,800–3,250
€/ **$4,400–5,300** ⊞ JSt

A mahogany Lancashire chest of drawers, the lifting top above five dummy drawers with four drawers beneath, on shaped bracket feet, c1800, 67in (170cm) wide.
£4,250–4,750
€/ **$6,750–7,500** ⊞ HA

A mahogany and crossbanded serpentine chest of drawers, the two short and three long graduated drawers with lozenge ivory escutcheons and brass knop handles, above a shaped apron and short splayed feet, c1820, 41in (104cm) wide.
£9,500–12,000
€/ **$15,000–19,000** ➤ WL
The colour and grain of the mahogany of this piece are exceptional, the top being formed of concentric bands of decreasing size, and the serpentine front has attractive crossbanding and cockbeading. This is a quality piece of furniture by a fine craftsman and is in completely original condition. A further plus factor is that it has been very well cared for over the years.

A mahogany chest of drawers,
with original handles, restored,
c1820, 41in (104cm) wide.
£1,200–1,350
€/ **$2,000–2,150** ⊞ MTay

A George IV mahogany chest,
the frieze with a Tunbridge ware
band, above two short and four
long graduated drawers with ivory
escutcheons and turned wooden
handles, on bracket feet,
41¼in (105cm) wide.
£480–600
€/ **$750–1,000** ➚ DD

**A pair of walnut and marquetry
commodes,** with marble tops,
French, c1830, 53in (134.5cm) wide.
£17,500–20,000
€/ **$27,500–31,500** ⊞ Che

**A mahogany and line-inlaid
commode,** south German, 19thC,
33½in (85cm) wide.
£500–625
€/ **$790–985** ➚ B(Ba)

**A mahogany bowfronted chest of
drawers,** c1820, 42in (106.5cm) wide.
£430–480
€/ **$675–750** ⊞ PaA

**A Sheraton-style figured maple
chest of drawers,** the two over
three graduated drawers with floral-
moulded pressed glass pulls, flanked
by turned pilasters, American,
1825–50, 43½in (110.5cm) wide.
£2,300–2,750
€/ **$3,600–4,300** ➚ NOA

A mahogany chest of drawers,
the marble top above two short and
three long panelled drawers with gilt-
metal handles, with canted sides, on
a plinth base with bun feet, French,
19thC, 39½in (100.5cm) wide.
£1,200–1,500
€/ **$1,900–2,375** ➚ DN

An Empire walnut commode,
with a marble top, French, c1820,
50in (127cm) wide.
£2,000–2,300
€/ **$3,150–3,600** ⊞ SIE

A mahogany chest of drawers, with
inlaid floral marquetry decoration,
with six long drawers, on bracket
feet, Dutch, 19thC, 37in (94cm) wide.
£3,400–4,250
€/ **$5,375–6,650** ➚ CHTR

**An early Victorian mahogany-
veneered barrel-front chest,**
with four long graduated drawers,
top cracked, 43in (109cm) wide.
£500–625
€/ **$790–985** ➚ WW

When looking at period walnut chests of drawers, look at the inside
carcass wood: if it is of pine the piece is country made, if oak it is
town made, i.e. for wealthy patrons and therefore will be better
made and more valuable. On late 18th-century chests the fashion
was for bun feet, which the Georgians often replaced with bracket
feet to 'modernize' the piece. To help tell if the chest is earlier than
Georgian, take out the bottom drawer and you should be able to
see the remains of the spigot (a round peg) from the bun foot.
• Up to c1660 drawers had bearers fixed to their sides which ran
  in grooves.
• Drawers of this period never reached the back boards – a space
  was left for ventilation.
• Up to c1770 boards in the bottom of drawers ran back to front.
  Subsequently they ran side to side. Victorian drawers tended to
  have just one bottom board.
• Beware of chests with three small drawers in the top: they are
  most certinaly the tops of chests-on-chests.

FURNITURE

A Victorian mahogany chest of drawers, with two short over three long drawers, 42in (106.5cm) wide.
£800–900
€/ **$1,260–1,420** ⊞ MHA

A flame mahogany commode, with a marble top, above four oak-lined drawers, Continental, c1850, 50in (127cm) wide.
£800–900
€/ **$1,260–1,420** ⊞ PaA

A Louis XV-style burr-walnut and walnut commode, with four graduated drawers, damaged, Dutch, 19thC, 35½in (90cm) wide.
£1,400–1,700
€/ **$2,200–2,700** ↗ S(Am)

A mahogany serpentine chest of drawers, with four long graduated drawers, on shaped bracket feet, early 20thC, 30in (76cm) wide.
£480–600
€/ **$775–950** ↗ PF

A Victorian mahogany chest of drawers, 40½in (103cm) wide.
£620–685
€/ **$980–1,000** ⊞ WiB

A neo-classical mahogany and brass commode, with two square and two long drawers, Russian, 1850–1900, 24¾in (60.5cm) wide.
£2,200–2,500
€/ **$3,475–4,000** ↗ S(Am)

A kingwood commode, with a marble top, French, c1880, 47in (119.5cm) wide.
£3,300–3,650
€/ **$5,200–5,700** ⊞ RAN

Daily care

Never lift a chest by the top as it may come away from the base, always open a drawer and lift it by the carcase. Be aware of tables with drawers which, if the table is tipped, may fall out. Prevent scratches to polished surfaces by placing felt pads under clocks, caddies etc., and by wrapping furniture in a clean blanket when transporting it. Never lock a bureau fall; if someone broke into it the damage could be greater than the value of the contents. Furniture should remain unlocked during transit as a small jolt can result in a jammed lock. Small piles of sawdust are a sign of live woodworm and a reputable company will fume the furniture for 48 hours without damaging timber or upholstery.

A late Victorian satinwood chest of drawers, with two short and three long drawers, on turned feet, 42in (106.5cm) wide.
£420–525
€/ **$650–830** ↗ DA

An Edwardian mahogany serpentine chest of drawers, with a brushing slide, 32in (81.5cm) wide.
£1,400–1,600
€/ **$2,200–2,500** ⊞ HiA

◄ **A mahogany and boxwood-strung serpentine chest of drawers,** by Maple & Co, the two short and three long graduated drawers with rosewood parquetry and brass handles, on a plinth base, early 20thC, 48in (122cm) wide.
£450–565
€/ **$700–1,050** ↗ DN

Chest-on-Chests

A figured maple chest-on-chest, with original cast-brass hardware, American, New England, c1760, 38½in (98cm) wide.
£8,000–9,500
€ / **$12,650–15,000**
⚲ **S(NY)**

A walnut chest-on-chest, with herringbone banding, the drawers with later brass handles, on bracket feet, 18thC, 41in (104cm) wide.
£2,700–3,400
€ / **$4,250–5,375** ⚲ **SWO**

A Regency mahogany bowfronted chest-on-chest, the arch roundel cornice over seven long graduated drawers with original scallop plate ring handles, on swept bracket feet, 52in (132cm) wide.
£3,800–4,750
€ / **$6,000–7,500** ⚲ **G(L)**

Miller's Compares

I. A George III mahogany chest-on-chest, the upper section with a moulded cornice above two short and three long graduated drawers, the lower section with three further long graduated drawers, on bracket feet, 38½in (98cm) wide.
£6,000–7,500
€ / **$9,500–12,000**
⚲ **CGC**

II. A George III mahogany chest-on-chest, the upper section with a moulded cornice and dentil frieze above two short and three long graduated crossbanded drawers flanked by fluted canted corners, the lower section with a brushing slide above three long graduated drawers, on bracket feet, 44in (112cm) wide.
£2,200–2,750
€ / **$3,500–4,300** ⚲ **CGC**

Item I is smaller than Item II, both in height and width, and this is always a desirable factor as houses today are generally smaller than in the past and large furniture is difficult to accommodate. Item I is also of better colour, while Item II is a little 'flat' – it may have been repolished at some stage. In addition there is an attractive patina on Item I, particularly around the handle plates and escutcheons, which would indicate that the piece hasn't been touched or restored recently. Both pieces were consigned from private sources, but Item I had been bought from a reputable local dealer in the 1950s or '60s and had not been on the market since then: another plus point. Although both items had been consigned with the same estimate, Item I is from a deceased estate and the executors did not want the piece back, so it 'took off' not only because of its superior appearance, but also perhaps in part due to sale-room psychology: the 'come and get me' estimate had the desired effect of attracting much interest, and people are usually prepared to bid a little bit further once they have decided they really want something.

▶ **A George IV mahogany chest-on-chest,** the stepped dentil cornice above a lattice frieze over two short and three long graduated drawers flanked by carved chamfered pilasters, the base with a dressing slide above three further graduated drawers, on ogee bracket feet, the drawers with brass drop handles and escutcheons, 43¼in (110cm) wide.
£1,650–2,000
€ / **$2,600–3,200** ⚲ **LJ**

For further information on antique furniture see the full range of Miller's books at
www.millers.uk.com

A George III mahogany chest-on-chest, crossbanded with stringing and parquetry banding, the moulded cornice above two short over three long drawers with gilt and embossed oval drop handles, with canted corners, the base with three further drawers, a shaped apron and splayed feet, 44¾in (113.5cm) wide.
£950–1,200
€ / **$1,500–2,000** ⚲ **AH**

A mahogany chest-on-chest, the two short and six long graduated drawers with original brass handles, on bracket feet, c1780, 74in (188cm) high.
£6,750–7,500
€ / **$10,700–11,800** ⊞ **JSt**

FURNITURE

Secretaire Chests

A burr-walnut secretaire chest, with three long drawers and raised pilasters, 19thC, 41¼in (105cm) wide.
£340–425
€ / $550–675 ✗ SWO

A late George III mahogany secretaire chest, with a central secretaire drawer flanked by two pairs of drawers, above cupboards enclosing fitted small drawers with ring handles, on bracket feet, 42in (106.5cm) wide.
£500–625
€ / $800–1,000 ✗ HOLL

A mahogany secretaire chest, with rosewood-veneered drawer fronts, the secretaire drawer with a fitted interior, above three graduated long drawers, on splay bracket feet, early 19thC, 46in (117cm) wide.
£500–625
€ / $800–1,000 ✗ CHTR

A Classical mahogany secretaire chest, the top with turreted ends above a conforming case with two shallow drawers over a secretaire drawer revealing an inset writing surface and a variety of drawers and cubbyholes, flanking a central cupboard, over three long graduated drawers, all flanked by engaged fluted pilasters, on turned bulbous feet, American, 1800–25, 49½in (125.5cm) wide.
£1,500–2,000
€ / $2,400–3,100 ✗ NOA

A Biedermeier satinbirch inverted breakfront secretaire commode, possibly Scandinavian, 19thC, 43¼in (110cm) wide.
£500–625
€ / $800–1,000 ✗ B(Ba)

A Regency mahogany secretaire chest, c1815, 43in (109cm) wide.
£1,700–2,000
€ / $2,700–3,100 ▦ Che

Chests-on-Stands

A William and Mary walnut and crossbanded chest-on-stand, the upper section with a moulded cornice above three short and three long graduated drawers, the stand with three further short drawers to the arched apron, on six turned and tapered legs joined by a curved undertier, on bun feet, with original engraved escutcheons and drop handles, stand with later components, 36in (91.5cm) wide.
£4,000–5,000
€ / $6,300–7,900 ✗ FHF

A William and Mary walnut chest-on-stand, with a cushion frieze drawer above two short and three long drawers with feather crossbanding, the stand with three short drawers to the shaped apron, on cup-and-cover-turned legs, 42in (106.5cm) wide.
£2,750–3,200
€ / $4,300–5,000 ✗ L

A William and Mary laburnum oyster-veneered and line-inlaid chest-on-stand, the moulded pediment above two short and three long graduated drawers, the stand with three further drawers above a shaped apron, on turned baluster legs and bun feet, 43¾in (111cm) wide.
£4,000–5,000
€ / $6,300–7,900 ✗ RTo

A William and Mary walnut chest-on-stand, with later legs, 40½in (103cm) wide.
£1,700–2,200
€ / **$2,700–3,500** ✒ B(Ba)

A George I walnut chest-on-stand, the burr-walnut facings with feather crossbanding, stand later, 38½in (98cm) wide.
£2,000–2,500
€ / **$3,200–4,000** ✒ L

A George II walnut chest-on-stand, stand later, 41¾in (106cm) wide.
£900–1,100
€ / **$1,400–1,750** ✒ B(Ba)

▶ **A William and Mary-style walnut and floral marquetry chest-on-stand,** the projecting top above two short and two long drawers, on an associated stand with spiral-turned legs, late 19thC, 38½in (98cm) wide.
£2,200–2,750
€ / **$3,500–4,300** ✒ BR

A Queen Anne walnut chest-on-stand, 39in (99cm) wide.
£2,700–3,500
€ / **$4,250–5,500** ✒ L

A George I walnut chest-on-stand, the drawers with feather stringing, stand later, 37in (94cm) wide.
£1,250–1,500
€ / **$2,000–2,400** ✒ L

A walnut chest-on-stand, c1750, 40in (101.5cm) wide.
£4,500–5,000
€ / **$7,000–8,000** ⊞ RPh

A Queen Anne walnut and featherbanded chest-on-stand, the later veneered top above a moulded cornice and three short and three long drawers with double ovolo mouldings, the later stand on spiral-turned oak legs, on bun feet, stretcher restored, 40¾in (103.5cm) wide.
£900–1,100
€ / **$1,450–1,750** ✒ BR

A George II walnut chest-on-stand, altered, 38¼in (97cm) wide.
£2,800–3,400
€ / **$4,400–5,400** ✒ S(O)

A carved and figured maple chest-on-stand, with original cast-brass hardware, legs later, American, Massachusetts, c1750, 38in (96.5cm) wide.
£8,000–9,500
€ / **$12,650–15,000** ✒ S(NY)

Wellington Chests

◀ **A satinbirch Wellington chest,** the upper panelled door enclosing a void interior, above four drawers, c1840, 23¾in (60.5cm) wide.
£1,100–1,400
€ / $1,750–2,200 ⚒ S(O)

A Victorian mahogany Wellington chest, with seven drawers, handles replaced, 41in (104cm) wide.
£765–850
€ / $1,200–1,350 ⊞ HiA

A mahogany Wellington chest, on a plinth base, late 19thC, 22in (56cm) wide.
£650–820
€ / $1,000–1,300 ⚒ PF

Wellington chests typically have seven drawers – one for each day of the week.

▶ **A burr-walnut Wellington-style chest,** with six drawers, on a plinth base, c1900, 41in (104cm) wide.
£530–600
€ / $850–950 ⊞ PaA

A late Victorian Wellington chest, the later mahogany top above six graduated drawers with burr-walnut-veneered fronts and wooden knob handles, locking side pilasters, on a plinth base, 22½in (57cm) wide.
£1,450–1,800
€ / $2,300–2,850 ⚒ WW

A figured walnut secretaire Wellington chest, c1850, 22in (56cm) wide.
£4,000–4,500
€ / $6,300–7,000 ⊞ Che

Clothes & Linen Presses

A mahogany dwarf linen press, c1780, 47in (119.5cm) wide.
£2,600–3,000
€ / $4,000–4,750 ⊞ Che

A Chippendale figured maple linen press, the cupboard doors enclosing three shelves, one foot facing and one door panel of a later date, American, New Jersey, c1770, 52in (132cm) wide.
£9,000–11,000
€ / $14,200–17,400 ⚒ S(NY)

A George III figured mahogany linen press, the interior with later shelves, 50½in (128.5cm) wide.
£1,300–1,600
€ / $2,000–2,500 ⚒ L

▶ **A Chippendale period mahogany linen press,** c1790, 51in (129.5cm) wide.
£4,800–5,300
€ / $7,500–8,250 ⊞ APO

FURNITURE

A George III mahogany linen press, altered, 51½in (131cm) wide.
£900–1,100
€/ **$1,400–1,750** ♪ B(Ba)

A mahogany linen press, the flared cornice above two panelled doors enclosing a brass hanging rail and slides, with later inlaid stringing and marquetry urns, the base with two long and two short drawers, on later bracket feet, 19thC, 52¼in (132.5cm) wide.

A mahogany linen press, the scrolled cornice over two panelled doors enclosing slides, drawers and twist-turned columns, c1835, 56¼in (143cm) wide.
£1,800–2,200
€/ **$2,800–3,500** ♪ SWO

A mahogany-veneered linen press, 18thC, 58in (147.5cm) wide.
£2,400–2,700
€/ **$3,750–4,250** ⊞ WAW

◀ **A George IV mahogany linen press,** the stepped moulded cresting and plain reeded frieze above a pair of single reed-moulded panelled curl-veneered doors enclosing four brushing slides, above two short and two long graduated cockbeaded drawers with turned wooden handles, on turned wooden feet, 50in (127cm) wide.
£1,000–1,250
€/ **$1,500–2,000** ♪ DD

A mahogany linen press, the flared cornice above two panelled doors enclosing a brass hanging rail and slides, with later inlaid stringing and marquetry urns, the base with two long and two short drawers, on later bracket feet, 19thC, 52¼in (132.5cm) wide.
£900–1,100
€/ **$1,400–1,700** ♪ WW

◀ **A mahogany linen press,** the two doors enclosing hanging space, above two short and three long drawers, restored, c1840, 51in (129.5cm) wide.
£2,350–2,600
€/ **$3,700–4,000** ⊞ MTay

▶ **A Victorian satinbirch linen press,** with mirrored doors, 43in (109cm) wide.
£1,350–1,500
€/ **$2,200–2,400** ⊞ MHA

A linen press, with flame mahogany panels, two doors over four drawers, c1820, 50in (127cm) wide.
£3,800–4,250
€/ **$6,000–6,750** ⊞ RPh

A mahogany linen press, the canted cornice above two panelled doors, enclosing sliding trays and hanging space, with two long drawers below, on a plinth base, 19thC, 52in (132cm) wide.
£650–820
€/ **$1,000–1,300** ♪ DMC

A black-japanned linen press, the interior with four sliding trays and three drawers, restored, c1820, 51¼in (130cm) wide.
£3,200–3,800
€/ **$5,000–6,000** ♪ S(O)

◀ **A Biedermeier-style satinwood linen press,** with rosewood, ebony and sycamore stringing, the two panelled doors over three long drawers, on square feet, north European, 19thC, 62¼in (158cm) wide.
£1,500–1,750
€/ **$2,350–2,750** ♪ AMB

A mahogany linen press, the upper section with sliding trays, possibly Irish, c1835, 52¼in (133.5cm) wide.
£530–650
€/ **$850–1,000** ♪ S(O)

An Edwardian fruitwood linen press, with maker's label 'Maple & Co', 49¼in (125cm) wide.
£320–400
€/ **$500–630** ♪ B(Ch)

Columns & Pedestals

◄ **An ebonized and gilt-bronze pedestal,** c1880, 22¾in (58cm) wide.
£1,200–1,500
€ / **$1,900–2,400** ↗ S(O)

An onyx and gilt-bronze column, late 19thC, 41in (104cm) high.
£600–700
€ / **$950–1,100** ↗ S(O)

An Empire mahogany pedestal, the marble top above an ormolu-applied frieze, joined to a lower shelf by column supports, with ormolu capitals and bases, the lower shelf centred by a marble-topped pillar, on turret feet, French, early 19thC, 14¼in (36cm) diam.
£1,650–2,000
€ / **$2,600–3,200** ↗ NOA

A pair of *brèche violette* and *verde* marble pedestals, the moulded tops on panelled tapering pilaster supports and moulded cut-corner plinth bases, 1875–1925, 47¾in (121.5cm) high.
£1,400–1,700
€ / **$2,200–2,700** ↗ B

◄ **An Edwardian Adam-style mahogany pedestal,** the *guilloche* frieze divided by carved rams' heads holding leaf swags, on a fluted base, 43in (109cm) high.
£1,400–1,700
€ / **$2,200–2,700** ↗ EH

Davenports

◄ **A Regency rosewood davenport,** on bun feet with casters, 22in (56cm) wide.
£3,200–4,000
€ / **$5,000–6,300** ↗ TEN

A rosewood davenport, mid-19thC, 22in (56cm) wide.
£1,600–1,800
€ / **$2,500–2,850** ⊞ HiA

A Victorian walnut davenport, the sloped hinged serpentine front enclosing a series of small drawers, the back with a raised stationery compartment, the lower stage with four drawers to one side and four opposing dummy drawers, the front with foliate-carved scrolled supports, on bun feet with casters, 44in (112cm) wide.
£480–600
€ / **$750–950** ↗ FHF

A Victorian mahogany davenport, the later pierced arcaded top above a leather-inset slope, lifting to reveal an interior fitted with bird's-eye maple-veneered drawers and pigeonholes, the brass lock stamped 'G. Williams, 60 Sun St' above an outline panel front with scroll support, the right side with a hinged pen drawer above four graduated drawers fitted with wooden knob handles, with opposing dummy drawers, the concave plinth on flattened bun feet with casters, writing slope cracked, 27in (68.5cm) wide.
£600–720
€ / **$950–1,100** ↗ WW

A walnut davenport, with a hinged storage compartment above a hinged writing surface, on runner feet with casters, 1850–75, 21in (53.5cm) wide.
£530–650
€ / **$850–1,000** ↗ NOA

◄ **A walnut davenport,** the leather-lined writing slope above a side drawer opposing a blind-fret panel on part-fluted and twist-turned support, lock stamped 'Bramah 24 Piccadilly', c1860, 22in (56cm) wide.
£2,200–2,500
€ / **$3,500–4,000** ↗ S(O)

FURNITURE

It is believed that in the late 18th century the firm of Gillows was commissioned to make a special desk to be used at sea in the cabin of a 'Captain Davenport'. In Gillows' Costs Book there is a sloping lid desk with a gallery, with working drawers to one side and opposing dummy drawers, captioned 'Captain Davenport Desk'.

A Victorian walnut davenport, with metamorphic stationery rack, the piano lid with a fitted sliding writing surface, four drawers to one side with opposing dummy drawers, 21¾in (55.5cm) wide.
£3,500–4,000
€/ **$5,500–6,300** ↗ BIG

◄ **A mid-Victorian rosewood 'jack in the box' davenport,** the rising top with three satinwood drawers and four pigeon-holes, the interior with two drawers and pull-out ratchet, with four real and four dummy drawers, on carved cabriole legs with bun feet, 21in (53cm) wide.
£2,200–2,750
€/ **$3,500–4,300** ↗ SPF

► **An inlaid rosewood davenport,** c1890, 20in (51cm) wide.
£875–975
€/ **$1,380–1,540** ⊞ GBr

A late Victorian rosewood and marquetry-inlaid metamorphic davenport, the tilt-action top with leather writing surface and three-quarter gallery with hinged lid, enclosing pigeonholes and a writing fitment, above a single frieze drawer and panelled fall-front enclosing two shelves, on square legs with china casters, 23¼in (59cm) wide.
£900–1,150
€/ **$1,400–1,800** ↗ BR

A banded mahogany davenport, handles replaced, c1905, 22in (56cm) wide.
£530–585
€/ **$850–925** ⊞ PaA

Daybeds

A mahogany daybed, the head- and footboards fronted by a swan's neck, joined by a highly figured front-rail, on moulded feet, French, 1825–50, 79in (200.5cm) long.
£1,200–1,500
€/ **$1,900–2,400** ↗ NOA

► **A walnut daybed,** French, c1860, 74½in (189cm) long.
£2,000–2,200
€/ **$3,200–3,500** ⊞ SIE

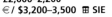
A cast-iron daybed, c1880, 72in (183cm) long.
£1,100–1,200
€/ **$1,750–2,000** ⊞ SeH

A walnut daybed, the shaped frame on scroll-carved cabriole legs, reupholstered, 19thC, 60in (152.5cm) long.
£1,700–2,000
€/ **$2,700–3,200** ⊞ JSt

► **A late Victorian mahogany-framed daybed,** with floral upholstery, 74¾in (190cm) long.
£360–450
€/ **$575–700**
↗ B(Ba)

FURNITURE

Desks

An early Georgian walnut kneehole desk, with feather and crossbanding, eight drawers and a recessed door, on bracket feet, 32in (81.5cm) wide.
£1,700–2,200
€/ **$2,680–3,500** ↗ SPF

A mahogany kneehole desk, c1740, 30in (76cm) wide.
£5,200–5,800
€/ **$8,200–9,200** ⊞ Che

A George II walnut kneehole desk, the herringbone-inlaid and crossbanded moulded top above a featherbanded long frieze drawer, shaped apron and recessed cupboard drawer, flanked by six similar short drawers, on bracket feet, restorations and alterations, 30¾in (78cm) wide.
£1,650–2,000
€/ **$2,600–3,150** ↗ CGC

A mahogany pedestal desk, the top with a reeded rim, above a central drawer, the kneehole with a recessed tambour, the pedestals each with four short drawers, one set of four being dummies forming doors, panelled to one side, on bracket feet, late 18thC, 49¼in (125cm) wide.
£1,700–2,200
€/ **$2,700–3,500** ↗ HOK

A rosewood writing desk, c1830, 45in (114.5cm) wide.
£1,750–2,000
€/ **$2,700–3,200** ⊞ RPh

A late Federal figured mahogany desk, the hinged lid opening to a well with pigeonholes, the upper right drawer inscribed 'J Button January 11th 1839 New York, Dow Beekman 1886 Middleburg N.Y.', American, c1839, 54½in (138.5cm) wide.
£2,500–3,200
€/ **$4,000–5,000** ↗ S(NY)

A Carlton House-style mahogany writing desk, the lower section with three-quarter brass gallery, eight drawers and pigeonholes, the top with leather writing surface and ratchet-adjustable slope, above a frieze drawer flanked by four further drawers, on square tapering legs with later spade feet and casters, 19thC, 54¾in (139cm) wide.
£3,250–3,750
€/ **$5,100–5,900** ↗ B

A Gothic revival walnut kneehole writing desk, with moulded tracery decoration, the gallery with a small shaped structure to each end, above an inverted breakfront moulded edge top, inset with a leather writing surface, above a frieze drawer and kneehole, flanked by six further frieze drawers, the sides and back with tracery decoration, on spirally fluted and carved legs joined by shaped X–stretchers, on bun feet, French, mid-19thC, 51¼in (130cm) wide.
£1,600–2,000
€/ **$2,500–3,200** ↗ B

A mahogany partner's desk, the reeded top with leather writing surface, over nine drawers opposed by nine further drawers, on bracket feet, 19thC, 49in (124.5cm) wide.
£2,600–3,250
€/ **$4,000–5,000** ↗ G(L)

◄ **An early Victorian mahogany desk,** the top with back-rail and rounded front corners, above two frieze drawers and two short drawers, all with wooden knob handles, flanking a central kneehole, on tapering reeded legs with brass caps and ceramic casters, 47¼in (120cm) wide.
£300–375
€/ **$475–600** ↗ PFK

A Georgian-style mahogany pedestal desk, c1860, 41in (104cm) wide.
£1,700–2,000
€/ **$2,700–3,200** ⊞ RPh

A black-lacquered lady's desk, with polychromed chinoiserie decoration, the upper section with four drawers, the lower section with a pull-out writing surface above one long frieze drawer, on turned and panelled tapering legs with ball feet, French, 1850–75, 31¼in (79.5cm) wide.
£1,100–1,400
€ / **$1,750–2,200** ⚒ NOA

A mid-Victorian mahogany pedestal desk, with solid top over a centre drawer with four drawers either side, 58in (147.5cm) wide.
£1,600–1,800
€ / **$2,500–2,850** ⊞ RPh

▶ **A Victorian mahogany escritoire,** the raised back with a gallery and moulded cornice above a triple panelled fall-front enclosing pigeonholes, drawers and a leather inset, the base with a concealed frieze drawer above two panelled doors enclosing six drawers flanking a kneehole, 49½in (125.5cm) wide.
£450–565
€ / **$700–900** ⚒ DN

◀ **A Sheraton revival satin-wood inlaid desk,** c1885, 54in (137cm) wide.
£2,600–3,000
€ / **$4,000–4,750** ⊞ Che

▶ **A Sheraton revival mahogany kidney-shaped desk,** on brass casters, late 19thC, 54in (137cm) wide.
£3,500–4,000
€ / **$5,500–6,300** ⊞ SAW

A Victorian walnut writing desk, by Maple & Co, the upper section with a rear gallery and seven drawers, the lower section with sloping writing surface, with six drawers, on turned supports, with shelves under, 54¼in (138cm) wide.
£650–820
€ / **$1,000–1,300** ⚒ WilP

A rosewood lady's writing desk, inlaid with various woods, French, c1870, 38in (96.5cm) wide.
£3,200–3,500
€ / **$5,000–5,500** ⊞ MHA

A French-style olivewood and gilt-metal-mounted kneehole writing desk, by Wright & Mansfield, with two leather-inset slides and veneering to the rear, drawer stamped 'Wright & Mansfield, 104 Bond St', c1880, 36¼in (92cm) wide.
£5,750–6,750
€ / **$9,000–10,600** ⚒ S(O)
Wright & Mansfield were one of the pre-eminent makers of furniture from about 1860–86, trading from premises in New Bond Street and exhibiting at the International Exhibition in 1862. The desk pictured here demonstrates the fashion for French furniture at this time and its association with quality. Wright & Mansfield were among a number of British cabinet makers competing for this market.

A late Victorian rosewood and satinwood marquetry writing desk, by Collinson & Lock, the marquetry possibly designed by Stephen Webb, in the Renaissance style, the stepped superstructure with pierced three-quarter gallery, with two drawers either side, above a moulded top with tooled leather writing surface and concave front with frieze drawers to each side and fluted uprights, with marquetry-panelled sides and back, on turned tapering leaf-carved and reeded legs with casters, centre drawer stamped 'Collinson & Lock, London', and numbered 109, one caster detached, 48in (122cm) wide.
£2,000–2,250
€/ **$3,100–3,500** ⚒ B

A Sheraton-style mahogany Carlton House desk, c1900, 54in (137cm) wide.
£6,000–6,600
€/ **$9,500–10,500** ⊞ Che

A mahogany semi-bowfronted kneehole writing desk, the leather-fitted top with a raised section to the rear comprising a bank of two drawers either side of a recess with pillared brass gallery, the front with a central bowfronted drawer above a kneehole, with four graduated drawers to either side, all with solid mahogany linings and ebony cockbeading, brass ring handles, locks and inset brass escutcheons, the top and sides inlaid and edged with lines and banding of ebony stringing, on eight square tapered legs with brass casters, c1910, 44¾in (113.5cm) wide.
£3,500–3,850
€/ **$5,500–6,100** ⊞ JC

A George III-style mahogany desk, stencilled 'Jewell, High Holborn', c1890, 48in (122cm) wide.
£1,200–1,500
€/ **$1,900–2,400** ⚒ B(Ba)

A rosewood and marquetry lady's desk, c1890, 39in (99cm) wide.
£3,300–3,700
€/ **$5,100–5,750** ⊞ Che

Rosewood

A South American and West Indian wood imported into Europe from the mid-18th century onwards, rosewood has a purplish-red colour with black or dark brown streaks. It was used for veneers, banding and inlays to contrast with mahogany and satinwood.

An Edwardian inlaid mahogany writing desk, by Maple & Co, 42in (106.5cm) wide.
£3,400–3,750
€/ **$5,400–5,900** ⊞ BrL

A painted satinwood Carlton House desk, 1920–30s, 52in (132cm) wide.
£17,500–20,000
€/ **$28,000–32,000** ⊞ MHA

A walnut partner's desk, with leather top, c1890, 60in (152.5cm) wide.
£2,600–3,000
€/ **$4,000–4,750** ⊞ SAW

A mahogany writing desk, the hinged top enclosing a fitted interior, c1900, 19in (48.5cm) wide.
£1,200–1,500
€/ **$1,900–2,400** ⚒ S(O)

An Edwardian mahogany lady's desk, crossbanded with stringing, the raised mirror back with broken pediment and shelf flanked by stationery compartments with gilt-metal galleries over hinged sloping lids and drawers, leather writing surface, above two frieze drawers with brass drop handles, on square tapering legs with casters, 36in (91.5cm) wide.
£900–1,100
€/ **$1,400–1,700** ⚒ AH

An oak pedestal desk, with Rexine insert top, on claw-and-ball feet, 1930s, 48½in (123cm) wide.
£260–320
€/ **$400–500** ⚒ B(Ba)

FURNITURE

Dumb Waiters

An early Victorian mahogany three-tier dumb waiter, the three graduated tiers with wavy edges, 53½in (136cm) high.
£1,500–1,800
€ / **$2,400–2,850** ⚒ B(Ba)

An early George III mahogany dumb waiter, with three graduated tiers, on a baluster column and tripod downswept legs, terminating in brass casters, 43in (109cm) high.
£1,100–1,400
€ / **$1,700–2,200** ⚒ HYD

A George III mahogany dumb waiter, with three graduated tiers, 47in (119.5cm) high.
£3,250–3,600
€ / **$5,100–5,700** ⊞ APO

A George III mahogany dumb waiter, with three dished tiers on gun barrel pillars, and a tripod cabriole base with casters, repairs, 40¼in (102cm) high.
£1,300–1,600
€ / **$2,000–2,500** ⚒ TEN

A mahogany dumb waiter, with three galleried shelves on inverted reeded columns with knopped lobed finials, on casters, c1840, 44in (112cm) high.
£1,500–1,800
€ / **$2,400–2,850** ⚒ HOK

An Empire-style mahogany and marble two-tier dumb waiter, c1890, 36in (91.5cm) high.
£1,000–1,150
€ / **$1,600–1,800** ⊞ Che

Dumb waiters were often used in pairs in large houses from the mid-18th century. When the ladies retired after dinner, the dumb waiters were placed either end of the table by the footmen and laden with drink so the gentlemen could help themselves without too much exertion and, because the staff had retired, the conversation could be more open. Hence dumb waiter!

A Georgian-style mahogany three-tier dumb waiter, early 20thC, 45in (114.5cm) high.
£1,250–1,400
€ / **$2,000–2,200** ⊞ RPh

Etagères

A walnut étagère, the glass-inset moulded top on splayed uprights above two conforming tiers, on fluted circular-section tapering legs, 19thC, 39¼in (100cm) wide.
£360–450
€ / **$575–700** ⚒ CGC

A mahogany two-tier étagère, with parcel-gilt decorated friezes, on turned supports with casters, 19thC, 16½in (42cm) wide.
£500–600
€ / **$800–950** ⚒ WW

A mahogany two-tier étagère, the galleried top with globe finials on square supports, 19thC, 16in (40.5cm) wide.
£260–320
€ / **$410–500** ⚒ WW

An ebonized three-tier étagère, with neo-classical inlay in sycamore and satinwood, c1890, 17in (43cm) wide.
£1,000–1,150
€ / **$1,600–1,800** ⊞ CGA

FURNITURE

Frames

A gilded composition frame, with plain wedge sight, moresque decoration to the frieze and D-section top edge, 19thC, 29¼ x 19½in (74.5 x 49.5cm).
£340–425
€/ **$550–670** ↗ **B(Kn)**

A gilded composition frame, 19thC, 44 x 28¼in (112 x 72cm).
£320–400
€/ **$500–650** ↗ **B(Ch)**

A gilt gesso frame, in a glazed ebonized wood surround, c1870, 30 x 23in (76 x 58.5cm).
£400–500
€/ **$630–800** ↗ **S(O)**

A giltwood frame, cornered by a cartouche- and floral-moulded design, 1875–1900, 43 x 35in (109 x 89cm).
£380–475
€/ **$600–750** ↗ **NOA**

A carved, pierced and gilded frame, Italian, 19thC, 14¼ x 12½in (36 x 32cm).
£360–450
€/ **$550–700** ↗ **B(Ch)**

A pierced, swept and gilded composition frame, Continental, 19thC, 12½ x 9in (32 x 23cm).
£220–275
€/ **$350–425** ↗ **B(Ch)**

A gilt composition frame, the moulded cartouche corner crestings with an intertwined foliate scroll with flowerheads and buds, late 19thC, aperture 27½ x 23½in (70 x 59.5cm).
£300–375
€/ **$475–600** ↗ **RTo**

A gilt composition frame, with shaped gilt-wood and composition mount, the frame with foliate rococo scroll corner crestings with a foliate spandrel towards centre crestings on two sides, late 19thC, aperture 29 x 24½in (73.5 x 62.5cm).
£300–375
€/ **$475–600** ↗ **RTo**

Hall Stands

A Victorian mahogany hall stand, the serpentine lower part with a marble top and fitted central drawer flanked by a stick stand, on carved scrolling front supports and a shaped base, requires restoration, 55in (139.5cm) wide.
£160–200
€/ **$250–315** ↗ **FHF**

A Victorian mahogany hall stand, the central support with inset mirror and lidded box with brass rings, on a shaped base with painted zinc liner, 34in (86.5cm) wide.
£300–375
€/ **$475–600** ↗ **WW**

A Gothic revival carved oak hall stand, with a hinged compartment above a cupboard door, c1880, 53½in (136cm) wide.
£1,100–1,300
€/ **$1,750–2,000** ↗ **S(O)**

A Gothic revival mahogany hall stand, the upper section with an arched top above three pierced carvings, a central arched top mirror below, with carved side columns and pierced carved brackets to the projecting upper rail, the base with a marble top and a central drawer, with pierced brackets to the canted carved arched panel supports, 19thC, 50in (127cm) wide.
£500–600
€/ **$800–950** ↗ **TRL**

Jardinières

A mahogany jardinière, with a brass liner and a swing handle, c1820, 21in (53.5cm) high.
£1,000–1,150
€/ **$1,600–1,800** ⊞ RPh

A Louis XVI-style yew wood, ebonized and boxwood marquetry jardinière table and cover, with gilt-metal mounts and a green tin liner, 19thC, 24in (61cm) wide.
£520–650
€/ **$800–1,000** ↗ B(Ch)

A carved wood pedestal jardinière, modelled as a flowering rustic trug, on carved column and root-form tripod feet, German, Black Forest, 19thC, 38in (96.5cm) high.
£400–500
€/ **$630–800** ↗ HOLL

A giltwood jardinière, the caned panels hung with floral swags, the lower part with a lattice and flowerhead frieze centred by shells, on floral-carved cabriole legs joined by an arched X-stretcher, on scroll feet, French, late 19thC, 36¾in (93.5cm) high.
£1,700–2,200
€/ **$2,700–3,500** ↗ B(O)

A satinwood-veneered *bombé* jardinière, with polychrome decoration, on cabriole legs, veneer missing, Continental, late 19thC, 15in (38cm) wide.
£300–375
€/ **$475–600** ↗ WW

◄ **A Louis XVI-style fruitwood jardinière,** the sides panelled and flanked by fluted pilasters, on tapering square legs, with metal liner, c1900, 25½in (65cm) high.
£400–500
€/ **$630–800** ↗ NOA

▶ **An Edwardian inlaid mahogany jardinière,** 36in (91.5cm) high.
£625–700
€/ **$980–1,100** ⊞ RPh

Lowboys

Miller's Compares

I. A burr-elm-veneered lowboy, the moulded fruitwood top with crossbanding, over a long frieze drawer and two small frieze drawers with line-inlaid stringing, with a shaped apron, on walnut cabriole legs, mid-18thC, 30in (76cm) wide.
£12,500–15,000
€/ **$20,000–24,000** ↗ B(O)

II. A mahogany lowboy, restored, mid-18thC, 32¼in (82cm) wide.
£680–850
€/ **$1,000–1,350** ↗ B(Ba)

A mid-Georgian walnut lowboy, 30in (76cm) wide.
£900–1,100
€/ **$1,400–1,750** ↗ L

Item I is in wonderful, untouched condition, and a little cleaning and waxing will result in a glorious colour. Item II appears to have lost all traces of original colour and finish, and is 'flat' in appearance.

A Queen Anne-style walnut lowboy, with three drawers, late 19thC, 24in (61cm) wide.
£900–1,000
€/ **$1,400–1,600** ⊞ HiA

Miniature Furniture

A late Victorian mahogany miniature half-tester bed, possibly an apprentice piece, with later bedding, 17½in (44.5cm) high.
£1,300–1,450
€/ **$2,000–2,250** ⊞ SDA

An oak and mahogany-veneered miniature waterfall bookcase, with reeded edges and two shelves, the base with a drawer with gilt-brass handle, on ball feet, 19thC, 11in (28cm) high.
£150–200
€/ **$235–315** ⚒ WW

A Victorian mahogany miniature chest, modelled as an organ case with gilt pipes and enclosing three drawers, on bun feet, 7in (18cm) high.
£200–250
€/ **$315–400** ⚒ CGC

A late Victorian rosewood miniature side cabinet, with raised mirrored back and one long drawer above a bevelled mirror-glazed single door enclosing a shelved cupboard, 12½in (32cm) wide.
£480–600
€/ **$750–950** ⚒ TMA

▶ **A walnut miniature chest of drawers,** on bun feet, c1710, 14in (35.5cm) wide.
£3,800–4,200
€/ **$6,000–6,600** ⊞ CAT
This is a very attractive piece of early date.

A Victorian mahogany miniature chest of drawers, with two short over two long drawers decorated with Tunbridge ware butterfly panels, all with brass knobs, on bun feet, 13in (33cm) wide.
£200–250
€/ **$315–400** ⚒ HoG

A mahogany miniature apprentice chest of drawers, with four long graduated drawers, on bracket feet, 19thC, 14½in (37cm) wide.
£280–350
€/ **$440–550** ⚒ B(W)

A Victorian mahogany miniature chest of drawers, the three long drawers with wooden knob handles, over a shaped apron, on integral bracket feet, 12½in (32cm) wide.
£260–325
€/ **$400–500** ⚒ PFK

A Victorian mahogany miniature chest of drawers, the three graduated drawers with glass knobs, on turned feet, 10in (25.5cm) wide.
£300–380
€/ **$475–600** ⚒ BWL

◀ **A Victorian figured and burr-walnut miniature Wellington chest,** the moulded-edge top above six drawers with fitted knob handles, with a side locking pilaster, on a plinth base, one knob missing, 15in (38cm) wide.
£600–750
€/ **$950–1,180** ⚒ WW

A mahogany miniature linen press, c1830, 11in (28cm) wide.
£3,000–3,300
€/ **$4,750–5,250** ⊞ BBo

Cheval Mirrors

A Victorian mahogany cheval mirror, mirror not attached, 37½in (95.5cm) wide.
£300–375
€/ **$475–600** ⋗ L

A George III mahogany cheval mirror, 25¼in (64cm) wide.
£360–450
€/ **$575–700** ⋗ L

A George IV mahogany cheval mirror, 31in (78.5cm) wide.
£1,350–1,500
€/ **$2,150–2,375** ⊞ WAW

A George IV mahogany cheval mirror, with a bevelled plate, on bobbin-turned supports decorated with ebonized stringing, on splay legs with brass paw feet and casters, 21in (53.5cm) wide.
£500–600
€/ **$800–950** ⋗ AG

◀ **An Edwardian mahogany cheval mirror,** with inlaid stringing, the plate on tapering supports with acorn finials, the scroll legs with brass sabots and casters, 28in (71cm) wide.
£300–375
€/ **$475–600** ⋗ WW

A Victorian mahogany cheval mirror, 35in (89cm) wide.
£600–750
€/ **$950–1,185** ⋗ B(Ba)

A beechwood *faux* bamboo cheval mirror, French, c1870, 34in (86.5cm) wide.
£670–850
€/ **$1,000–1,350** ⋗ S(O)

Dressing Table Mirrors

A walnut dressing table mirror, the arched plate with a shaped surmount, the shaped platform base with three drawers, on turned feet, early 18thC, 17in (43cm) wide.
£1,000–1,200
€/ **$1,500–2,000** ⋗ BWL

A George I walnut dressing table mirror, the base with a concave-fronted drawer, 16½in (42cm) wide.
£575–675
€/ **$900–1,000** ⋗ S(O)

A George I walnut dressing table mirror, with swing frame, the plate with a moulded border flanked by uprights surmounted by turned brass finials, above three frieze drawers, on shaped feet, one finial missing, uprights possibly later, 13¾in (35cm) wide.
£850–1,100
€/ **$1,350–1,750** ⋗ B

A mahogany dressing table mirror, c1750, 16in (40.5cm) wide.
£700–775
€/ $1,100–1,225 ⊞ RPh

A Georgian Hepplewhite-style mahogany dressing table mirror, 25in (63.5cm) wide.
£700–800
€/ $1,100–1,250 ⊞ RPh

A late George III mahogany dressing table mirror, 23¼in (59cm) wide.
£140–175
€/ $220–275 ⤴ L

A mahogany bowfronted dressing table mirror, early 19thC, 18in (45.5cm) wide.
£350–400
€/ $550–630 ⊞ RPh

A Regency maple and rosewood crossbanded dressing table mirror, 24in (61cm) wide.
£180–225
€/ $285–350 ⤴ B(Ba)

A Regency mahogany dressing table mirror, the bowfronted base with three drawers, on later bracket feet, minor restorations, 18½in (47cm) wide.
£360–450
€/ $550–700 ⤴ B(W)

A mahogany dressing table mirror, c1830, 19½in (49.5cm) wide.
£150–170
€/ $235–270 ⊞ PaA

A mahogany dressing table mirror, with two drawers, c1835, 21¾in (55.5cm) wide.
£250–300
€/ $400–475 ⤴ S(O)

Mirrors or looking glasses

Early looking glasses were made of highly polished gold, silver or bronze and set into decorative frames. Poorer people often used polished pewter, which was much less expensive. In the Middle Ages steel and crystal were used and Venetian glass began to appear. In 1663 the Duke of Buckingham established a glass house at Vauxhall, and in 1664 the importation of foreign glass was forbidden by law, which resulted in the emergence of a large home production of ever increasing sizes of plate glass.

◄ **A mid-Victorian mahogany dressing table mirror,** attributed to Gillows, with reeded scroll supports, the platform base with bun feet, 17¾in (45cm) wide.
£150–200
€/ $235–315 ⤴ B(L)
This was a standard Gillows dressing table mirror design. It was produced with or without a drawer underneath from c1829 onwards. Some also had 'tray bottoms'.

A mahogany dressing table mirror, the backplate between turned uprights, the base fitted with two short drawers, 19thC, 18½in (47cm) wide.
£150–200
€/ $235–315 ⤴ AMB

A gilded dressing table mirror, French, c1880, 23in (58.5cm) high.
£1,000–1,200
€/ $1,500–2,000 ⊞ HA

Wall Mirrors

A Queen Anne walnut-veneered cushion-framed wall mirror, with a moulded frame, alterations and restorations, 24¾ x 22½in (63 x 57cm).
£550–700
€ / **$870–1,100** ➴ B(W)

A George II giltwood wall mirror, with a bevelled plate, 26¾in (68cm) wide.
£800–1,000
€ / **$1,250–1,500** ➴ L

A George III figured mahogany and gilt-decorated fret-cut wall mirror, with a *ho-o* bird surmount and swan-neck cresting, the bevelled plate within a gilt slip, 24in (61cm) wide.
£800–1,000
€ / **$1,250–1,700** ➴ B(Pr)

▶ **A George III gilt-gesso wall mirror,** 18½in (47cm) wide.
£800–1,000
€ / **$1,250–1,580** ➴ DN

A giltwood wall mirror, with a floral- and husk-carved border, surmounted by an arched top and shaped cresting with conforming decoration, on a punched ground, with later brass candle brackets, restored, early 18thC, 19¼in (49cm) wide.
£1,400–1,750
€ / **$2,200–2,750** ➴ B(WM)

▶ **A parcel-gilt walnut wall mirror,** with a convex frame, the arched solid cresting moulded with a central shell flanked by dolphins, the base fret cut, mid-18thC, 23in (58.5cm) wide.
£600–750
€ / **$950–1,200** ➴ PF

A George II giltwood wall mirror, carved with rope-twist and egg-and-dart borders and pendant foliage, 37in (94cm) wide.
£400–500
€ / **$630–800** ➴ SWO

A George I gilt-framed wall mirror, with later bevelled plate, 18in (45.5cm) wide.
£800–1,000
€ / **$1,250–1,500** ➴ S(O)

A silvered wall mirror, the later plate within a carved and moulded frame, the border plates divided by florettes, the sides hung with Greek key leaf carvings, the apron with fluted tapering leaf-carved feet, some damage, Italian, Piedmont, 18thC, 25½in (65cm) wide.
£360–450
€ / **$550–700** ➴ B

▶ **A George III wall mirror,** the painted and parcel-gilt frame carved with bellflowers and beading, 37¼in (95.5cm) wide.
£2,000–2,500
€ / **$3,200–4,000** ➴ WW

A George II mahogany wall mirror, with a giltwood border and shaped scroll frame, 26in (66cm) wide.
£800–1,000
€ / **$1,250–1,500** ➴ JAd

A carved giltwood wall mirror, with floral and foliate decoration and floral urn surmount, the inner frame with egg-and-dart carved decoration, 18thC, 36in (91.5cm) high.
£1,000–1,250
€ / **$1,500–2,000** ➴ BWL

A George III walnut and parcel-gilt oval wall mirror, 37½in (95.5cm) high.
£340–425
€ / **$550–675** ➴ SWO

FURNITURE

A gilt-framed wall mirror, with a five-branch candleholder beneath, c1810, 39in (99cm) wide.
£2,000–2,250
€ / **$3,200–3,500** ⊞ MTay

A Federal giltwood and *verre églomisé* pier mirror, minor damage, American, New York, c1800, 46½in (118cm) high.
£11,000–14,000
€ / **$17,500–22,000** ↗ S(NY)
This is a very attractive mirror and such pieces invariably sell well in the USA.

A Regency giltwood pier mirror, the figural frieze over a bevelled plate, flanked by Egyptian-headed pilaster strips terminating in feet, 29¼in (74.5cm) wide.
£420–525
€ / **$675–825** ↗ SWO

◄ A giltwood mirror, the plate surrounded by raised intertwining palmetto- and floral-decorated frame, American, 1825–50, 34in (86.5cm) wide.
£900–1,100
€ / **$1,400–1,750** ↗ NOA

Gilt furniture

There are two types of gilding: water gilding, which has a yellow tone, and oil gilding with its distinctive deeper orange tone. Most English 18th- and 19th-century furniture was water gilded. Layers of gesso were applied to the carved wood base, then recut to define the decoration. A liquid clay base, or bole, was applied, and the gold leaf laid upon it before being burnished to achieve the final tone.

Oil gilding was less common and involved the application of an oil size to which the gold leaf was then stuck. Great care must be taken with gilt furniture. Never apply water as the gold will wash off; instead, seek the advice of a specialist gilder. Likewise, avoid hanging mirrors in bathrooms or other rooms with high humidity. To prevent damage to elaborately-carved furniture, dust lightly using a feather duster.

A pier mirror, the bevelled plate with a reeded ebonized slip, the ball-decorated cornice above a key frieze, with ribbon-tied cluster pilasters later painted, early 19thC, 26in (66cm) wide.
£300–375
€ / **$475–600** ↗ WW

A Regency ebonized and parcel-gilt mirror, with cut-glass beads, the later plate within moulded borders, Irish, 21¼in (54cm) wide.
£700–875
€ / **$1,100–1,400** ↗ B

A William IV gilt and composition convex mirror, 30¼in (77cm) diam.
£1,000–1,250
€ / **$1,500–1,900** ↗ B(Ba)

A pair of giltwood wall mirrors, with cartouche-shaped frames and pierced crest and foliate scrolls, 19thC, 13¼in (33.5cm) wide.
£600–775
€ / **$950–1,200** ↗ DN

A Regency giltwood convex girandole, gilding refreshed, 23¾in (60.5cm) wide.
£750–950
€ / **$1,200–1,500** ↗ B(Ba)

A giltwood and gesso wall mirror, the moulded frame with a later plate, the eagle surmount with a chain and ball hanging from its beak, the base with a scroll leaf and fan design, the reverse with paper label 'William Wade, Picture Frame Maker, Carver, Gilder & Printseller, No. 86 Leadenhall Street, London', early 19thC, 19in (48.5cm) wide.
£600–725
€ / **$950–1,150** ↗ WW
William Wade traded at Leadenhall Street from 1784 until after 1840.

A carved giltwood wall mirror, the plate within a scrolling foliage frame with a shell surmount, 19thC, 24½in (62cm) wide.
£550–700
€ / **$870–1,100** ↗ WW

A Louis XVI-style over-mantel mirror, French, 19thC, 42in (106.5cm) wide.
£450–575
€ / **\$700–900** ↗ L

A giltwood and gesso wall mirror, the inverted breakfront half-round and foliate pilaster frame enclosing a plate with an ebonized reeded slip, 19thC, 30in (76cm) wide.
£500–650
€ / **\$800–1,000** ↗ WW

A rococo-style giltwood wall mirror, the frame with foliate scrolls and nine small shelves, 19thC, 32in (81.5cm) wide.
£1,100–1,300
€ / **\$1,750–2,000** ↗ DN

An ebonized and gilded wall mirror, Scandinavian, 19thC, 30in (76cm) wide.
£1,500–1,700
€ / **\$2,400–2,700** ↗ S(O)

◀ **A mahogany wall mirror,** c1840, 22in (60cm) wide.
£235–260
€ / **\$370–400** ⊞ MHA

▶ **A Victorian gilt-wood wall mirror,** the bevelled plate within a ribboned frame, 36¾in (93.5cm) wide.
£340–425
€ / **\$500–675** ↗ SWO

An ebonized and silvered wood wall mirror, the bevelled plate within a moulded frame supporting two gilt-metal branches, Irish, c1860, 16½in (42cm) wide.
£400–500
€ / **\$650–800** ↗ S(O)

FURNITURE

◄ **A Victorian overmantel mirror,** with a scrolled pediment and swagged frieze, the plate flanked by architectural columns, 41in (104cm) wide.
£240–300
€/ **$380–480**
⚒ SWO

A giltwood wall mirror, the broken scroll pediment between a campana urn finial with fruiting vine and inner ribbon-tied husk border above a swagged floral spray, c1880, 30¼in (77cm) wide.
£600–750
€/ **$1,000–1,200** ⚒ WL

A rosewood overmantel mirror, with ivory inlay, c1880, 46in (117cm) wide.
£700–800
€/ **$1,100–1,250** ⊞ GBr

A gilt gesso over-mantel mirror, with ribboned top, glass with defects, late 19thC, 60¼in (153cm) wide.
£500–625
€/ **$800–1,000** ⚒ SWO

A glass and micro-mosaic wall mirror, the bevelled plate within a border of etched glass marginals and a further border of micro-mosaic flora on a gold *tesserae* ground, within a further border of etched glass marginals, Venetian, late 19thC, 30⅜in (78cm) wide.
£2,300–2,800
€/ **$3,600–4,400** ⚒ B

A George III-style giltwood and gesso overmantel mirror, with a swan-neck pediment, c1900, 54in (137cm) wide.
£700–875
€/ **$1,100–1,400** ⚒ S(O)

A mahogany, ebonized and painted mirror, the arched pediment enclosing a scantily clad winged angel, within a foliate border above the mirror plate, Baltic, 1850–1900, 25½in (65cm) wide.
£600–750
€/ **$950–1,200** ⚒ S(Am)

A giltwood overmantel mirror, French, c1880, 38in (96.5cm) wide.
£1,600–1,800
€/ **$2,500–2,850** ⊞ DAC

A Victorian gilt gesso wall mirror, the frame moulded with rococo scrolls, leaves and flowering stems, 61in (155cm) high.
£700–875
€/ **$1,100–1,375** ⚒ B(S)

A giltwood overmantel mirror, French, c1890, 34in (86.5cm) wide.
£1,450–1,600
€/ **$2,300–2,500** ⊞ DAC

A Directoire-style painted wood *trumeau*, partly constructed of antique elements, the upper oval panel painted *en grisaille* with the figure of an 18thC soldier, French, c1900, 38in (96.5cm) wide.
£750–950
€/ **$1,200–1,500** ⚒ NOA

◄ **A pair of mahogany and gilt wall mirrors,** c1920, 19in (48.5cm) wide.
£475–525
€/ **$750–825** ⊞ GBr

Ottomans

An early Victorian ottoman, the hinged woolwork top above silk-upholstered sides, on a rosewood base with bun feet, 30in (76cm) wide.
£700–850
€/ **$1,100–1,350** ✗ DN

A mahogany ottoman, upholstered in needlework, mid-19thC, 16in (40.5cm) square.
£160–180
€/ **$250–285** ⊞ HiA

A mahogany ottoman, with a deep-button, leather-padded lidded top revealing a storage space over a padded concave base, on squat bun feet, 1850–75, 21in (53.5cm) wide.
£1,200–1,500
€/ **$1,900–2,400** ✗ NOA

Screens

A painted six-fold screen, one side with an Italian landscape, the reverse with random floral motifs, Italian, 18thC, each fold 28in (71cm) wide.
£6,000–7,500
€/ **$9,500–11,750** ✗ B
This is remarkable value when compared to what one might have to pay for a framed oil painting of a similar size and date. Such pieces are often used nowadays as a less expensive alternative to oil paintings.

An embossed leather four-fold screen, painted with foliate scrolls and flowers to one side, some splits and repairs, 19thC, 72½in (184cm) wide.
£950–1,200 €/ **$1,500–1,900** ✗ DN

A late Victorian mahogany and bevelled glass three-fold screen, each fold 24in (61cm) wide.
£220–275
€/ **$350–440** ✗ BR

Fire Screens

◄ **A Chippendale-style mahogany pole screen,** panel distressed, repairs to two legs, American, Philadelphia, c1765, 56in (142cm) high.
£1,100–1,300
€/ **$1,700–2,000** ✗ S(NY)

► **A late George III mahogany pole screen,** the silkwork panel depicting a bird, the baluster-turned stem with an urn finial, the three cabriole legs with turned toes, restored, screen 11½in (29cm) wide.
£150–180
€/ **$235–285** ✗ WW

A Regency mahogany and triple-glass fire screen, decorated with roundels and with brass top corners and handle, with two fitted sliding panels and a pull-out panel, on moulded splay legs with brass terminals and casters, 42in (106.5cm) high.
£550–700
€/ **$870–1,100** ✗ MCA

A rosewood fire screen,
with barley-twist columns,
on moulded cabriole legs
with brass casters, early
19thC, 29in (73.5cm) wide.
£765–850
€ / **$1,200–1,350** ⊞ JSt

**A pair of rosewood pole
screens,** with original
needlework panels, c1835,
55in (139.5cm) high.
£3,300–3,700
€ / **$5,200–5,800** ⊞ REI

A mahogany fire screen,
with foliate carved crest
over a tapestry panel
depicting a mother and child,
the frame on cabriole legs,
19thC, 27in (68.5cm) high.
£200–250
€ / **$300–400** 🔨 G(L)

▶ **An Edwardian carved
walnut fire screen,** the
framed needlework panel
above outsplayed feet,
29½in (75cm) high.
£250–320
€ / **$400–500** 🔨 SWO

**A pair of rosewood
pole screens,** c1825,
57in (145cm) high.
£3,000–3,250
€ / **$4,750–5,200** ⊞ CAT

**An early Victorian
mahogany pole screen,**
the fabric panel in a frame
of C-scrolls and cartouches,
the pole with a carved
baluster collar, on three
out-scrolled legs, finial
missing, 54in (137cm) high.
£230–280
€ / **$360–440** 🔨 Mit

A rosewood fire screen,
with a needlework panel
depicting two girls, c1830,
28in (71cm) wide.
£450–500
€ / **$700–800** ⊞ NoC

**An early Victorian
rosewood pole
screen,** with a raised
woolwork banner, screen
17½in (44.5cm) diam.
£450–550
€ / **$700–850** 🔨 L

**An Edwardian mahogany-
framed fire screen,** with
a needlework panel in
the style of Morris & Co,
41in (104cm) high.
£160–180
€ / **$250–280** ⊞ HiA

▶ **A walnut fire screen,**
with claw feet, early 20thC,
43¼in (110cm) high.
£80–100
€ / **$125–160** 🔨 B(W)

**A William IV mahogany
pole screen,** the banner
with fleur-de-lys corners,
the floral study worked with
chenille and woolwork,
on a vase and plain turned
column with a spire finial,
62in (157.5cm) high.
£250–320
€ / **$400–500** 🔨 DD

A Victorian pole screen,
the floral needlework panel
with a moulded frame,
the turned pole on an
octagonal baluster stem,
the base with scroll feet,
18in (45.5cm) wide.
£120–150
€ / **$200–240** 🔨 WW

Settees & Sofas

A Federal mahogany sofa, central rear leg replaced, American, Philadelphia, c1800, 73½in (186.5cm) wide.
£2,400–2,750
€/ $3,800–4,300 ↗ S(NY)

A pair of mahogany-framed sofas, with acanthus-carved rails, and swept carved feet, c1815, 57in (145cm) wide.
£32,000–35,000
€/ $50,000–55,000 ⊞ HA
It is very unusual to find sofas of such compact size. Both are in excellent condition and the carving is of the highest quality, which makes them very desirable pieces.

◄ A Regency mahogany-framed sofa, the scrolling reeded arms terminating in spiral twist columns, with narrow front frieze and similar spiral-twist front supports, 57in (145cm) wide.
£500–600
€/ $800–950 ↗ TRL

► An Empire-style mahogany carved sofa, the back-rail with painted stringing and trailing leaf decoration with applied ormolu paterae, the sides carved as recumbent winged harpies with gilt wings and simulated bronze bodies, the seat-rail on square tapering legs, c1820, 73¼in (186cm) wide.
£1,800–2,250
€/ $2,850–3,500 ↗ B&L

A Regency mahogany bergère settee, possibly by Gillows, the back with paterae above a cane panel and conforming openwork band, with a cane seat below, 46in (117cm) wide.
£2,000–2,500
€/ $3,200–4,000 ↗ MEA

◄ A mahogany and upholstered sofa, part ebonized and with gilt-metal mounts, Swedish, c1830, 85½in (217cm) wide.
£1,800–2,200
€/ $2,850–3,500 ↗ S(O)

A George IV mahogany-framed sofa, with a scroll-carved top-rail and arms, on melon fluted legs, 85¾in (218cm) wide.
£950–1,200
€/ $1,500–1,900 ↗ B(Ch)

A mahogany and leather sofa, c1835, 84in (213.5cm) wide.
£5,200–5,700
€/ $8,200–9,000 ⊞ GBr

A Chippendale-style mahogany double chair-back sofa, with a foliate-embroidered seat, the back joined by splayed arms terminating in scrolls, with curved uprights above an apron, 19thC, 66in (167.5cm) wide.
£1,200–1,500
€/ $1,900–2,400 ↗ GAK

FURNITURE

A giltwood-framed canapé, French, mid-19thC, 88in (223.5cm) wide.
£6,000–6,800
€/ **$9,500–10,750** ⊞ **RAN**

An early Victorian mahogany-framed settee, the shaped back with centred carved scrolls, on turned legs, 79in (200.5cm) wide.
£380–475
€/ **$600–750** ⚒ **WW**

A leather and oak conversation seat, in the style of A. W. N. Pugin, with three seats, the leaf-carved legs with flower-carved feet, c1860, 86½in (219.5cm) wide.
£2,000–2,400
€/ **$3,200–3,800** ⚒ **S(O)**
Augustus Welby Northmore Pugin (1812–52) was commissioned, at the age of only 15, to design a set of chairs for Windsor Castle. He established his own cabinet-making firm in Hart Street, Covent Garden, (1829–31) and produced furniture in the Gothic, Elizabethan and Jacobean styles. He was also responsible for the design of all the internal decorative furniture and furnishings for the New Palace of Westminster. The leaf and flower carving on this item has similarities to carving seen in his later work.

A rosewood double-ended button-back sofa, on carved cabriole legs with casters, c1860, 70in (178cm) wide.
£3,000–3,250
€/ **$4,750–5,150** ⊞ **JSt**

The term settee, possibly a corruption of the word settle, was used from the early 17th century to describe a modified chair for two people to sit upright. From the 1760s, the term sofa (from the Ottoman *sopha*) was introduced as the settee became longer, with padded arms and back, and was deep enough to recline in comfort. Nowadays the two terms have become interchangable.

A walnut bench, the oblong padded back above a stuffed seat, the padded arms with baluster supports on turned tapering legs with beaded collars, c1860, 67in (170cm) wide.
£700–850
€/ **$1,100–1,350** ⚒ **S(O)**

A carved mahogany-framed settee, on turned and fluted legs, French, c1870, 52in (132cm) wide.
£2,500–2,850
€/ **$4,000–4,500** ⊞ **RAN**

A Victorian ebonized love seat, 41¾in (106cm) wide.
£350–450
€/ **$550–700** ⚒ **B(Ba)**

A carved giltwood-framed canapé, French, c1870, 65in (165cm) wide.
£2,400–2,650
€/ **$3,800–4,200** ⊞ **RAN**

A George III-style mahogany triple chair-back settee, c1880, 54¾in (139cm) wide.
£800–1,000
€/ **$1,250–1,600** ⚒ **S(O)**

A Louis XV-style sofa, c1885, 55in (139.5cm) wide.
£3,200–3,500
€/ **$5,000–5,500** ⊞ **Che**

FURNITURE

A Victorian mahogany-framed button-back double-ended settee, on turned legs, reupholstered, 81½in (207cm) wide.
£420–525
€ / $670–830 ➤ HoG

A Victorian walnut-framed parlour sofa, the padded back with pierced scrolling foliate surround, the padded arms on carved and scrolled supports, with serpentine stuff-over seat, on cabriole legs and casters, 73in (185.5cm) wide.
£1,100–1,400
€ / $1,750–2,200 ➤ AH

A pair of rococo-style giltwood canapés, the frames centred by a floral and foliate cartouche, Italian, 19thC, 62in (157.5cm) wide.
£7,000–7,800
€ / $11,000–12,500 ⊞ RAN

A Victorian walnut serpentine settee, with a shaped back, on turned front legs, 52in (132cm) wide.
£600–750
€ / $950–1,200 ➤ SWO

A Chippendale-style mahogany couch, c1880, 46in (117cm) wide.
£1,650–1,850
€ / $2,600–2,900 ⊞ GBr

◄ **A Victorian painted satinwood sofa,** by Gillows, 68in (172.5cm) wide.
£6,000–6,750
€ / $9,500–10,650 ⊞ SAW

A late Victorian mahogany Chesterfield sofa, button-upholstered in leather, the out-scrolled sides and serpentine seat close-nailed, on turned legs with later casters, 78¾in (200cm) wide.
£2,200–2,750
€ / $3,500–4,300 ➤ B

► **An Edwardian rosewood-framed settee,** 59in (150cm) wide.
£350–450
€ / $550–700 ➤ B(Ba)

A Louis XV-style walnut-framed settee, French, c1900, 48in (122cm) wide.
£1,000–1,150
€ / $1,600–1,800 ⊞ MLL

An Edwardian mahogany shaped-back sofa, 47in (119.5cm) wide.
£400–450
€ / $650–700 ⊞ HiA

A Georgian-style mahogany-framed sofa, the upholstered back terminating in carved scrolls, on cabriole legs with foliate-carved knees, 1920s, 62in (157.5cm) wide.
£300–375
€ / $475–600 ➤ TRL

FURNITURE

Shelves

A mahogany graduated hanging shelf, early 19thC, 24in (61cm) wide.
£330–400
€/ **$525–650** ⚲ S(O)

A mahogany four-tier graduated open bookshelf, with X-frame bracing bars, on turned feet, 19thC, 37in (94cm) wide.
£300–375
€/ **$475–600** ⚲ DMC

A mahogany hanging shelf, c1820, 18in (45.5cm) wide.
£300–335
€/ **$475–525** ⊞ F&F

A mahogany three-tier graduated hanging shelf, the shaped sides with turned paterae, on turned feet, 19thC, 33in (84cm) wide.
£340–425
€/ **$550–675** ⚲ DMC

A rosewood open wall shelf, the three serpentine shelves on moulded spiral-twist and baluster supports, some replacements, 19thC, 32in (81.5cm) wide.
£320–375
€/ **$500–600** ⚲ WW

A Victorian mahogany open shelf, the shaped scroll top above three graduated shelves and scroll supports, 24¼in (61.5cm) wide.
£320–375
€/ **$500–600** ⚲ WW

A mahogany five-tier wall shelf, with stamped patent mark, c1885, 18in (45.5cm) wide.
£400–450
€/ **$650–700** ⊞ RPh

A mahogany three-tier bowfronted wall shelf, with fretwork sides, late 19thC, 15in (38cm) wide.
£475–575
€/ **$750–900** ⚲ G(L)

Sideboards

A George III mahogany bowfronted sideboard, with a central drawer, the single side drawers with inlaid doors below, 90in (228.5cm) wide.
£4,500–5,000
€/ **$7,000–8,000** ⊞ WAW

A George III mahogany serpentine sideboard, with a single frieze drawer above a shaped apron, on boxwood-strung tapering legs with spade feet, 40½in (103cm) high.
£450–565
€/ **$700–900** ⚲ RTo

◄ **A George III mahogany sideboard,** with reeded top, above one shallow and two deep drawers, with lion mask and ring handles, some old repairs, 45in (114.5cm) wide.
£1,000–1,250
€/ **$1,600–2,000** ⚲ BWL

A George III mahogany sideboard, with line, shell and floral lozenge inlay, the upper section with sliding doors, the three central drawers flanked by two further drawers, 84in (213.5cm) wide.
£1,000–1,250
€/ **$1,600–2,000** ⚲ WilP

A George III inlaid mahogany breakfront sideboard, the central frieze drawer above a cupboard with panelled doors, all decorated with satinwood crossbanding and stringing, 61in (155cm) wide.
£1,500–1,800
€/ **$2,400–2,800** ⚲ JAd

◄ A mahogany serpentine sideboard, crossbanded in purple heart and boxwood, c1780, 44in (112cm) wide.
£11,500–13,000
€/ $18,000–20,000 ⊞ CAT

A Sheraton mahogany bowfronted sideboard, with Edwardian inlay, c1780, 54in (137cm) wide.
£8,500–9,500
€/ $13,500–15,000 ⊞ REI
The brass galleries on sideboards were for curtains, used to protect the expensive (often silk) wall coverings from being splashed when food was being served.

A mahogany serpentine pedestal sideboard, with tambour doors, c1790, 66in (167.5cm) wide.
£2,600–3,000
€/ $4,000–4,750 ⊞ Che

A Federal walnut serpentine sideboard, with tulipwood and mahogany inlay, American, North Carolina, c1800, 65¾in (167cm) wide.
£12,500–16,000
€/ $20,000–25,000 ↗ S(NY)
The sideboard was a new form introduced during the Federal period as the object for serving food in American dining rooms. It was an expensive and unusual form designed with drawers and cupboards intended for the storage of silver plate, dishes, glasses, tablecloths, bottles and other articles necessary for dining. George Hepplewhite praised the form in *The Cabinet Maker and Upholsterer's Guide* (London, 1788), noting the 'great utility of this piece of furniture has procured it a very general reception; and the conveniences it affords render a dining room incomplete without a sideboard'.

A Federal inlaid walnut sideboard, majority of inlaid collars missing, American, North Carolina, c1795, 56½in (143.5cm) wide.
£12,000–14,000
€/ $19,000–22,000 ↗ S(NY)

A mahogany bowfronted sideboard, with satinwood inlay and banding, c1790, 58in (147.5cm) wide.
£9,000–10,000
€/ $14,000–16,000 ⊞ DJH

► A late George III mahogany and satinwood-banded bowfronted sideboard, with later fitted interior, 59½in (151cm) wide.
£2,000–2,400
€/ $3,150–3,800 ↗ B(Ba)

A mahogany sideboard, the crossbanded and carved raised back with sliding fluted cupboards and centre sections, above a shaped top, over four frieze drawers, a cellaret drawer to one side and a cupboard to the other, both with lion mask handles and carved with ribbon-and-vine swags, early 19thC, 96in (244cm) wide.
£1,500–1,800
€/ $2,400–2,850 ↗ B(Ed)
This sideboard has the characteristic Scottish feature of a rear stage with sliders or sliding panels that reveal storage space for glasses. Because of its size, it can be identified as a Glasgow example. Glasgow cabinet makers began their sideboards at 84in (213.5cm) long, instead of 72in (183cm), as in Edinburgh.

FURNITURE

A Sheraton period mahogany sideboard, with boxwood stringing, the raised back enclosed by twin sliding tambour shutter doors, with three frieze drawers flanked by deep cellaret drawers, with end pot cupboard, early 19thC, 88in (223.5cm) wide.
£2,000–2,400
€/ **$3,200–3,800** ➤ DMC

A mahogany and ebonized inlaid breakfront sideboard, the crossbanded top above a central frieze drawer and a recess arcaded deep drawer, flanked by part-bowed drawers, a cupboard door and a cellaret drawer, panelled pilasters, later brass rosette ring handles, top split, early 19thC, 77½in (197cm) wide.
£1,700–2,200
€/ **$2,700–3,500** ➤ WW

A Regency mahogany bowfronted sideboard, 42in (106.5cm) wide.
£400–500
€/ **$650–800** ➤ B(Ba)

A Regency mahogany sideboard, the D-shaped top with outset tower corners, over a frieze drawer and arched apron, flanked by bowed deep drawers, one fitted as a cellaret, 60¼in (153cm) wide.
£3,200–3,750
€/ **$5,000–6,000** ➤ TEN

A Regency mahogany sideboard, the raised triangular back over a crossbanded top, the central sunk panelled frieze drawer flanked by inversely tapered pedestals, with panelled doors between fluted pilasters, enclosing shelves to one side and fitted cellaret drawers to the other, on ebonized ball feet, 72½in (184cm) wide.
£2,200–2,750
€/ **$3,500–4,300** ➤ TEN

A Regency mahogany sideboard, the crossbanded top above a bowed centre drawer with frieze drawer below, flanked by a cellaret drawer and a cupboard, 60¼in (153cm) wide.
£700–875
€/ **$1,100–1,400** ➤ GTH

A Regency mahogany breakfront sideboard, the top with a three-quarter gallery over a central frieze drawer, flanked by bowed fitted cellaret drawers with cupboards below, on ball feet, stamped 'Gillows, Lancaster', 66in (167.5cm) wide.
£2,800–3,500
€/ **$4,500–5,500** ➤ TEN

A Regency mahogany pedestal sideboard, with black line decoration, 76½in (194.5cm) wide.
£2,200–2,500
€/ **$3,500–4,000** ➤ B(Ba)

A late Regency mahogany bow-fronted sideboard, surmounted by a tubular brass curtain rail, with a long drawer above an arched apron flanked by a cupboard and a deep cellaret drawer, with a small cupboard to one side, 78in (198cm) wide.
£2,200–2,500
€/ **$3,500–4,000** ➤ B(S)

A carved mahogany rosewood sideboard, with brass mounts, the doors opening to shelves, the side fitted with retractable slides, repairs to both right feet, American, c1815, 72in (183cm) wide.
£3,000–3,500
€/ **$4,800–5,500** ➤ S(NY)

A mahogany sideboard, the frieze with three drawers, each pedestal with a hinged compartment in the top, above a drawer and cupboard, one with a cellaret drawer, c1820, 95in (241.5cm) wide.
£1,300–1,500
€/ **$2,000–2,400** ➤ S(O)

A George IV mahogany breakfront pedestal sideboard, with spiral twist and lappet-carved stiles, 68½in (174cm) wide.
£600–750
€ / $950–1,200 ↗ B(Ch)

A George IV mahogany pedestal sideboard, on a plinth base, 78¼in (199cm) wide.
£1,300–1,600
€ / $2,000–2,500 ↗ DN

A George IV Gothic-style mahogany twin pedestal sideboard, with an architectural panelled back, above a bowfronted frieze drawer, with Gothic arched panel cupboards to the pedestals, flanked by turned columns, on inverted breakfront bases, 61in (155cm) wide.
£950–1,200
€ / $1,500–2,000 ↗ HYD

A George IV mahogany bowfronted sideboard, with one short drawer, one deep drawer, and two cupboards with brass lion mask ring handles, 50in (127cm) wide.
£800–1,000
€ / $1,300–1,600 ↗ AG

▶ **A mahogany four-door sideboard,** c1865, 60in (152.5cm) wide.
£2,000–2,250
€ / $3,150–3,500 ⊞ Che

Many 18th-century sideboards have a small cupboard in one of the sides towards the back. Known as the 'pot cupboard', this is exactly what it contained. After dinner, when the ladies had retired, a butler would produce the pot (often silver) and the gentlemen would relieve themselves as it was passed around the table!

A mahogany bowfronted sideboard, the shaped top above two short drawers, flanked by two cupboard doors modelled as dummy drawers, 19thC, 54¼in (138cm) wide.
£800–1,000
€ / $1,250–1,600 ↗ CGC

FURNITURE

A Victorian carved figured mahogany mirrored-back sideboard, the shaped-top glass with foliate trail-carved crest and side uprights, over an inverted breakfront base with a central frieze drawer and twin panel-fronted cupboards, flanked by oval-panel-inset doors with fitted interiors of slides and cellaret drawer, on a plinth base, damaged, 78in (198cm) wide.
£750–950
€/ $1,200–1,500 ✗ Bri

A rosewood and satinwood crossbanded sideboard, with boxwood stringing, the top with a raised three-quarter gallery and moulded edge, above five drawers with brass handles around a kneehole, late 19thC, 46in (117cm) wide.
£800–1,000
€/ $1,300–1,600 ✗ DN

A Victorian mahogany pedestal sideboard, with an inverted break-front top, and three frieze drawers above cupboard doors, with trays, 82in (208.5cm) wide.
£425–525
€/ $675–825 ✗ SWO

An Edwardian inlaid mahogany bowfronted sideboard, 49in (124.5cm) wide.
£850–950
€/ $1,350–1,500 ⊞ MHA

A late Victorian walnut mirrored-back sideboard, with original handles and mirrors, 72in (183cm) wide.
£1,600–1,800
€/ $2,500–2,850 ⊞ SWA

▶ **An inlaid walnut sideboard,** German, 19thC, 93¾in (238cm) wide.
£900–1,100
€/ $1,400–1,750 ✗ B(Ch)

A Victorian mahogany inverted breakfront pedestal sideboard, superstructure missing, 71in (180.5cm) wide.
£280–350
€/ $450–550 ✗ B(Ba)

An Edwardian Sheraton-style mahogany inverted breakfront sideboard, with satinwood and boxwood banding and stringing, the central frieze drawer above an arched frieze and open shelf, flanked by two curved front drawers, 54in (137cm) wide.
£500–650
€/ $800–1,000 ✗ TRL

A Victorian mahogany sideboard, with a leaf-and-scroll-carved back, fitted with three frieze drawers, one pedestal with a cellaret section and a centre cupboard with panelled doors, on a plinth base, 71in (180.5cm) wide.
£900–1,100
€/ $1,400–1,750 ✗ HOLL

A pollarded oak and figured walnut mirrored-back sideboard, with copper mounts and carved panels, c1900, 78in (198cm) wide.
£2,700–3,000
€/ $4,300–4,700 ✗ S(O)

◀ **An Edwardian Sheraton-style inlaid mahogany sideboard,** 53in (134.5cm) wide.
£1,800–2,000
€/ $2,850–3,200 ⊞ RPh

An Edwardian crossbanded mahogany serpentine sideboard, 45¾in (116cm) wide.
£375–475
€/ $600–750 ✗ SWO

Items in the Furniture section have been arranged in date order.

Cake Stands

▶ **A mahogany cake stand,** the serpentine top with moulded edge, the fall-sides each revealing a base-lined dished tray, on four splayed feet, early 20thC, 29½in (75cm) high.
£100–125
€/ **$160–200** ➶ BIG

An Edwardian mahogany cake stand, with three dished plates and central carrying handle, on three splayed legs, 31½in (80cm) high.
£110–140
€/ **$175–220** ➶ FHF

A mahogany three-tier cake stand, c1890, 38in (96.5cm) high.
£380–425
€/ **$600–670** ⊞ GBr

▶ **An Edwardian mahogany three-tier cake stand,** 38in (96.5cm) high.
£600–675
€/ **$950–1,100** ⊞ RPh

An Edwardian inlaid mahogany three-tier cake stand, 38in (96.5cm) high.
£170–220
€/ **$270–350** ➶ JAd

Hat & Stick Stands

A Victorian painted-wood stick stand, with turned supports and lead-lined base, on turned feet, 61½in (156cm) wide.
£300–375
€/ **$475–600** ➶ WW

A carved walnut coat stand, with umbrella support, the base with inset drip pan, on spool feet, German, 19thC, 85¾in (218cm) high.
£5,500–7,000
€/ **$8,700–11,000** ➶ B(EA)
These Black Forest-type carved bear and tree coat stands are currently very popular, particularly with decorators in US ski resorts.

A cast-iron stick stand, attributed to Sheffield, Edwin & Theophilus Smith, in the form of a boy standing among reeds and grappling with a serpent, with removable leaf-cast drip tray, with registration design lozenge, c1866, 33in (84cm) high.
£1,500–2,000
€/ **$2,400–3,200** ➶ S

▶ **A brass-bound coopered mahogany stick stand,** with brass mask handles, late 19thC, 26in (66cm) high.
£1,300–1,500
€/ **$2,000–2,400** ➶ S(O)

A cast-iron stick stand, with pierced foliate-cast back, diamond registration mark, c1880, 33in (84cm) high.
£565–680
€/ **$900–1,100** ➶ S(O)

A cast-iron stick stand, after a design by Coalbrookdale, in the form of a begging dog supported on a pierced leaf-cast pedestal and holding a riding crop in its jaw, the removable tray cast as three leaves, on a moulded base with pierced scroll-cast supports, redecorated, late 19thC, 24in (61cm) high.
£4,300–4,750
€/ **$6,800–7,500** ➶ S

FURNITURE

Folio Stands

A mahogany folio stand, c1830, 27in (68.5cm) wide.
£2,600–3,000
€/ **$4,000–4,700** ⊞ GBr

A mahogany folio rack, the slatted two-division top on square tapering legs, early 19thC, 28in (71cm) wide.
£2,700–3,000
€/ **$4,300–4,700** ⚒ S(O)

A late Regency mahogany folio stand, 25¼in (64cm) wide.
£1,300–1,600
€/ **$2,000–2,500** ⚒ B(Ba)

A carved mahogany folio stand, c1870, 34in (86.5cm) wide.
£6,000–6,850
€/ **$9,600–10,800** ⊞ RAN

A rosewood folio stand, mid-19thC, 26½in (67.5cm) wide.
£375–475
€/ **$600–750** ⚒ S(O)

▶ **A walnut folio stand,** the moulded top on baluster supports and an undertier, c1900, 37in (9cm) wide.
£775–900
€/ **$1,100–1,400** ⚒ S(O)

A walnut folio stand, French, 19thC, 41in (104cm) wide.
£300–375
€/ **$475–600** ⚒ WW

Kettle & Urn Stands

A George III mahogany kettle stand, with an associated dished top, one leg later, 18¼in (46cm) high.
£1,400–1,600
€/ **$2,200–2,500** ⚒ S(O)

A George III mahogany urn stand, with associated triform top, on later-carved cabriole legs, 23¾in (60.5cm) high.
£550–650
€/ **$870–1,000** ⚒ S(O)

A pair of satinwood and tulipwood urn tables, with brass caps and casters, c1770, 25in (63.5cm) high.
£16,000–18,000
€/ **$25,000–28,000** ⊞ REI
Being made of satinwood and in excellent condition, these tables are particularly desirable.

A George III mahogany kettle stand, with a moulded tulipwood and crossbanded top above a moulded frieze fitted with a slide, on tapered stop-fluted legs and spade feet, top repositioned, 26¾in (68cm) high.
£3,200–3,500
€/ **$5,000–5,500** ⚒ S

Music Stands

◄ **A satinbirch duet stand,** by Erard's, London, the trellis rest with candle arms, on a fluted turned and tapering adjustable column and sabre-legged tripod, early 19thC, 48in (122cm) high.
£7,000–8,000
€ / $11,000–12,500 ↗ S(O)
The distinguished Parisian firm Erard's were in practice between 1777–1960. The business was founded by Sébastien Erard, who had been apprentice to a Parisian harpsichord maker for two years before establishing his own workshop in the rue de Bourbon. In 1786 the company expanded by opening a branch in London, and in 1789 his brother Jean-Baptiste joined as partner.

A pair of mahogany music stands, with adjustable height and inclination, on ring-turned pillars and tripod bases with hipped sabre legs, early 19thC, 29½in (75cm) minimum height.
£1,800–2,250
€ / $2,800–3,500 ↗ TEN

A mahogany tripod duet stand, the top with a pair of folding lattice-work music rests, on a turned tapered column on hipped sabre legs with scroll feet, early 19thC, 54in (137cm) high.
£400–500
€ / $630–800 ↗ PF

Plant Stands

◄ **A carved and painted limewood jardinière,** in the form of a cloth-draped surface on a carved cupid support with a carved tripod case, 19thC, 31in (78.5cm) high.
£500–600
€ / $800–950 ↗ HOLL

An arched top split-cane plant stand, after a design by George Smith, on turned legs with brass casters, c1820, 50in (127cm) wide.
£1,800–2,200
€ / $2,800–3,500 ⊞ GKe

A walnut two-tier plant stand, the marquetry-inlaid top with gilt mounts, French, late 19thC, 30in (76cm) high.
£900–1,100
€ / $1,400–1,700 ↗ SWO

Shaving Stands

◄ **A shaving stand,** by James Shoolbred, with maker's enamel plaque, c1870, 58¾in (149cm) high.
£530–635
€ / $850–900 ↗ S(O)
James Shoolbred & Co were operating from an address in Tottenham Court Road, London, during the late 19th century and were described by the *Art Journal* as 'Eminent among the most extensive cabinet makers and upholsterers in England.'

A mahogany shaving stand, minor damage, c1840, 67in (170cm) high.
£550–600
€ / $800–950 ⊞ PaA

► **An adjustable brass shaving stand,** late 19thC, 61½in (156cm) high.
£150–200
€ / $240–300 ↗ DMC

FURNITURE

Miscellaneous Stands

A George III mahogany bottle stand,
13in (33cm) square.
£600–750
€/ $950–1,200 ⚒ B(Ba)

◀ **A late Victorian mahogany luggage stand,** the slatted top on ring-turned tapering legs, one slat stamped 'W.B.Ld', 25½in (65cm) wide.
£320–400
€/ $500–630 ⚒ WW

◀ **An early Victorian oak lamp stand,** the top inlaid with burr-oak, rosewood and bird's-eye maple, on a tapering column and triform base, 56in (142cm) high.
£650–800
€/ $1,000–1,300 ⚒ SWO

A carved limewood stand, Venetian, c1870, 36in (91.5cm) high.
£700–800
€/ $1,100–1,300 ⊞ GBr

◀ **A pair of giltwood candle stands,** on a rococo base, c1910, 48in (122cm) high.
£1,250–1,385
€/ $2,000–2,200 ⊞ RAN

Steps

◀ **A set of mahogany library steps,** early 19thC, 50½in (138.5cm) high.
£650–800
€/ $1,000–1,300 ⚒ S(O)

A set of mahogany bed steps, the treads with leather insets, with two storage compartments, c1850, 26in (66cm) high.
£1,200–1,350
€/ $1,900–2,200 ⊞ GBr
The middle step concealed a chamber pot.

A set of library steps, the ring-turned support on four spiral steps, on pad feet, early 19thC, 46in (117cm) high.
£900–1,100
€/ $1,400–1,700 ⚒ B(L)

A set of mahogany bed steps, the three fabric-lined treads above ebony-strung panels, on ring-turned tapering legs, early 19thC, 26in (66cm) high.
£950–1,200
€/ $1,500–1,900 ⚒ S(O)

A Regency mahogany bed-step commode, minor alterations, 26½in (67.5cm) high.
£600–700
€/ $950–1,100 ⚒ B(Ba)

A late Victorian set of stained-wood library steps, with galleried top-rail, the top stage with storage compartment, on turned supports, 22½in (57cm) high.
£200–250
€/ $300–400 ⚒ FHF

A set of mahogany metamorphic library steps, the treads inset with tooled leather, on ring-turned legs, 19thC, 27¾in (70.5cm) high extended.
£1,100–1,400
€/ $1,700–2,200 ⚒ B(WM)
The top two steps fold down to make a leather-topped table.

Stools

A William and Mary walnut stool, the padded seat with later damask top panel, on square-section panelled tapering legs, upper capitals to legs and feet replaced, seat rails with paper label from Leamington Spa Art Gallery Treasures of Warwickshire Exhibition, July 1948, 21¼in (54cm) wide.
£1,500–2,000
€/ **$2,400–3,200** ⚒ B

A George III mahogany stool, with drop-in seat, 20in (51cm) wide.
£280–350
€/ **$440–550** ⚒ SWO

A giltwood footstool, in the style of Thomas Hope, the milled seat-rail on fluted square section end supports, on turned and tapered feet with roundel mouldings, with later button-upholstered seat, restorations and replacements, 19thC, 30¼in (77cm) wide.
£2,500–3,200
€/ **$4,000–5,000** ⚒ S

A pair of George II walnut stools, with stuff-over seats, on C-scroll-carved cabriole legs with pad feet, minor restoration, 20¾in (52.5cm) wide.
£3,200–4,000
€/ **$5,000–6,300** ⚒ B(WM)

A mahogany stool, in the style of Duncan Phyfe, the scrolling tapered seat on U-shaped supports, on inward-curved scrolling feet, American, early 19thC, 20½in (52cm) wide.
£5,000–6,000
€/ **$8,000–9,500** ⚒ B
Duncan Phyfe (1768–1854) is the best-known New York cabinet maker of the early and mid-19th century. He made use of the forms and ornament of classical Greece and Rome and gave his name to the generic term for American furniture in the neo-classical style. Phyfe-type furniture was made into the mid-19th century, with a revival in the late 19th/early 20th century.

◀ **A mahogany stool,** with spiral-twist column legs, 1860, 38in (96.5cm) wide.
£280–320
€/ **$440–500** ⊞ PaA

A George III mahogany stool, on turned legs with pad feet, 13¾in (35cm) diam.
£220–275
€/ **$350–435** ⚒ AMB

A pair of Regency upholstered footstools, 15in (38cm) wide.
£1,700–2,000
€/ **$2,700–3,200** ⊞ APO

A pair of carved oak footstools, 19thC, 34in (86.5cm) wide.
£7,500–8,500
€/ **$12,000–13,500** ⊞ CAT

◀ **A carved mahogany X-frame stool,** on casters, c1845, 21½in (54.5cm) wide.
£380–425
€/ **$600–670** ⊞ MTay

A Victorian walnut stool, the upholstered drop-in top on scrolled X-shaped supports, 21in (53.5cm) wide.
£160–220
€/ **$250–350** ⚒ TRM

FURNITURE

A Victorian carved mahogany stool, with upholstered seat and cabriole legs with satyr masks, on claw-and-ball feet, 24in (61cm) wide.
£260–325
€/ $400–500 ✗ G(L)

A Victorian rosewood stool, with drop-in seat on curved X-supports, 21½in (54.5cm) wide.
£300–375
€/ $475–600 ✗ B&L

A carved walnut stool, covered with floral tapestry, on cabriole legs, c1875, 28in (71cm) wide.
£1,150–1,300
€/ $1,800–2,000 ⊞ MTay

A pair of faded mahogany footstools, covered with floral tapestry, c1880, 15in (38cm) wide.
£200–225
€/ $300–350 ⊞ GBr

A pair of Victorian giltwood footstools, 13½in (34.5cm) wide.
£600–720
€/ $950–1,100 ✗ L

▶ **A pair of mahogany and Tunbridge ware-inlaid footstools,** with beadwork coverings, c1880, 11in (28cm) diam.
£600–675
€/ $950–1,100 ⊞ JSt

A walnut stool, with caned back, c1910, 25in (63.5cm) high.
£300–325
€/ $475–500 ⊞ RPh

Music Stools

◀ **A rosewood and brass-inlaid piano chair,** c1815.
£2,000–2,250
€/ $3,200–3,600 ⊞ Che

A Victorian walnut piano stool, by Gillows, 24in (61cm) wide.
£2,000–2,200
€/ $3,200–3,500 ⊞ SAW

For further information on antique furniture see the full range of Miller's books at
www.millers.uk.com

A Victorian mahogany and inlaid music stool, the string-inlaid frieze over out-splayed front legs, 36in (91.5cm) high.
£140–175
€/ $220–275 ✗ DA

A mahogany revolving piano stool, c1825, 20in (51cm) high.
£330–370
€/ $520–580 ⊞ GBr

◀ **An Edwardian inlaid mahogany adjustable piano stool,** 19¾in (50cm) high.
£280–350
€/ $440–550 ✗ SWO

◀ **A walnut adjustable duet stool,** on ring-turned supports and splayed feet, c1905, 34in (86.5cm) wide.
£350–450
€/ $550–700 ✗ GAK

Bedroom Suites

A mahogany bedroom suite, comprising triple wardrobe, marble-topped dressing table, pot cupboard, side chair and washstand, late 19thC.
£500–625
€/ $800–1,000 ➤ B(Ba)

A walnut four-piece bedroom suite, consisting of marble-topped chest of drawers, commode with marble top and splash-back, bed and mirror, bed shortened in height, some veneer loss, American, late 19thC, headboard 60in (152.5cm) high.
£900–1,100
€/ $1,400–1,700 ➤ JDJ

An Edwardian inlaid mahogany three-piece bedroom suite, comprising wardrobe, dressing table and bedside cupboard, wardrobe 72in (183cm) wide.
£1,000–1,250
€/ $1,600–1,900 ➤ SWO

Salon Suites

A walnut and inlaid salon suite, comprising a sofa, two side chairs, a tub chair and a nursing chair, late 19thC.
£550–700
€/ $870–1,100 ➤ B(Ba)

A painted beechwood five-piece salon suite, with cushions and cane seats, paint worn, settee with unmatched cushion, c1800, settee 50½in (128.5cm) wide.
£2,200–2,750
€/ $3,500–3,800 ➤ S(O)

▶ **A mahogany salon suite,** comprising a sofa, two elbow chairs and four dining chairs, with pierced splat backs, serpentine aprons and cabriole front legs, late 19thC.
£800–1,000
€/ $1,300–1,600 ➤ GAK

A chinoiserie green-painted and gilt three-piece bergère suite, comprising a settee and a pair of armchairs, c1920, settee 67in (170cm) wide.
£1,500–2,000
€/ $2,400–3,200 ➤ S(O)

An Edwardian mahogany-framed three-piece salon suite, comprising two tub armchairs and a sofa, on turned and reeded legs.
£750–950
€/ $1,200–1,500 ➤ B&L

An Edwardian mahogany salon suite, comprising a settee, four side chairs and two armchairs.
£600–750
€/ $950–1,200 ➤ B(Ba)

FURNITURE

Architects' Tables

▶ **A mahogany architect's table,** the adjustable top above a supported drawer, with writing slide and compartments, 18thC, 35in (89cm) wide.
£1,000–1,200
€/ **$1,600–1,900** ⚒ LAY

An early George III mahogany architect's table, the top sloping on a ratchet, the frieze with a pull-out drawer, the sides with pull-out candle slides, 34½in (87.5cm) wide.
£1,600–2,000
€/ **$2,500–3,100** ⚒ L

An early George III mahogany architect's table, with adjustable hinged top and drop flaps above a frieze drawer with brass swan-neck handle, on chamfered legs with brass toes and casters, 30in (76cm) wide.
£3,500–4,250
€/ **$5,500–6,700** ⚒ HYD

A mahogany architect's table, with ratchet top and a single drawer on turned legs, c1790, 39in (99cm) wide.
£3,800–4,300
€/ **$6,000–6,700** ⊞ SAW

▶ **A mahogany architect's table,** the ratchet and adjustable top above two frieze drawers and two side slides, on turned legs with turned feet and casters, restored, 36¼in (92cm) wide.
£1,500–1,800
€/ **$2,400–2,800** ⚒ B(W)

A Directoire mahogany architect's table, the hinged leather-inset writing surface above a frieze drawer enclosing a sliding writing surface and various compartments, with sliding padded side leaves, on tapered legs with casters, stamped 'Chapuis', 38½in (98.5cm) wide.
£14,000–16,000
€/ **$22,000–25,000** ⚒ S(Am)
Jean-Joseph Chapuis (1765–1864) from Brussels is best known for his quality mahogany furniture. In 1798 he started workshops in rue de Borgval and after his marriage moved to 264 rue de Loxum. He appeared in the *Almanachs du Commerce* until 1824 and was active until about 1830.

Bedside Tables

A pair of Louis XV-style kingwood bedside tables, with marble tops and ormolu mounts, French, c1880, 28in (71cm) wide.
£1,250–1,400
€/ **$1,900–2,200** ⊞ DAC

A mahogany drop-leaf bedside table, with undertier, late 19thC, 27¼in (69cm) wide.
£220–260
€/ **$350–400** ⚒ B(Ch)

A pair of satinwood bedside tables, with marble tops and ormolu mounts, French, c1900, 31in (78.5cm) high.
£1,000–1,150
€/ **$1,600–1,800** ⊞ BrL

A pair of Louis XV-style kingwood and marquetry bedside tables, c1920, 25in (63.5cm) high.
£1,150–1,300
€/ **$1,800–2,000** ⊞ Che

Card Tables

A George II mahogany card table, with baize-lined fold-over top, the frieze enclosing a drawer, on turned tapering legs and pad feet, 30in (76cm) wide.
£1,300–1,500
€/ **$2,000–2,350** ✗ WW

A George III mahogany card table, on brass casters, 37in (94cm) wide.
£3,000–3,400
€/ **$4,800–5,400** ⊞ APO

A George III mahogany card table, the shaped top on cabriole legs, 35in (89cm) wide.
£900–1,000
€/ **$1,400–1,600** ⊞ WAW

A late Georgian mahogany card table, 36in (91.5cm) wide.
£750–850
€/ **$1,180–1,350** ⊞ HiA

A Sheraton mahogany card table, attributed to Samuel Field McIntire, on tapering reeded legs, American, c1800, 37½in (95.5cm) wide.
£1,300–1,500
€/ **$2,000–2,350** ✗ JDJ

A George III mahogany card table, the fold-over top enclosing recessed counter wells and candle sconces, on cabriole legs with paw feet, Irish, 89in (226cm) wide.
£4,000–4,800
€/ **$6,400–7,600** ✗ JAd

A George III demi-lune satinwood card table, the tulipwood-banded fold-over top inlaid with a large shell motif, on tapered legs, 38¼in (97cm) wide.
£2,000–2,400
€/ **$3,200–3,800** ✗ G(B)

A Sheraton card table, inlaid with rosewood, c1805, 36in (91.5cm) wide.
£6,200–7,000
€/ **$9,800–11,000** ⊞ F

A brass-bound mahogany demi-lune card table, with a later suede-lined interior above a panelled frieze, on fluted, tapering legs with gilt-brass sabots, two legs replaced, Russian, early 19thC, 43¼in (110cm) wide.
£1,100–1,400
€/ **$1,750–2,200** ✗ B

A Regency zebrawood card table, the top on a scissor-action frame, the curved supports on sabre legs with brass caps and casters, 36in (91.5cm) wide.
£2,400–3,000
€/ **$3,800–4,800** ✗ TEN

FURNITURE

A Regency rosewood card table, with baize-lined fold-over top, on tapering column support with lion-paw feet, 36in (91.5cm) wide.
£400–500
€/ **$650–800** ⚒ AMB

A Sheraton-style mahogany card table, inlaid with boxwood, c1820, 36in (91.5cm) wide.
£1,250–1,400
€/ **$1,900–2,200** ⊞ DUK

A late Regency mahogany card table, on turned, tapering legs, 31¾in (80.5cm) wide.
£1,650–1,850
€/ **$2,500–3,000** ⊞ JC

A William IV rosewood card table, the fold-over top on a leaf-carved and turned column, on a quatrefoil base with lion-paw feet, 36in (91.5cm) wide.
£600–775
€/ **$950–1,200** ⚒ TMA

A William IV rosewood card table, the baize-lined fold-over top above a tablet frieze, on a tapering column with scroll and paw feet and recessed casters, one caster missing, 35¾in (91cm) wide.
£800–1,000
€/ **$1,250–1,600** ⚒ DN

A mahogany crossbanded card table, with baize-lined demi-lune top, inlaid panelled frieze, on square tapering legs and spade feet, 19thC, 37¼in (94.5cm) wide.
£750–950
€/ **$1,200–1,500** ⚒ AH

A Victorian walnut card table, the quatrefoil base above turned columns on scrolled legs with brass and porcelain casters, 54in (137cm) wide.
£1,100–1,400
€/ **$1,700–2,200** ⚒ JM

A rosewood-veneered card table, the carved, reeded column above a platform base with claw feet, 19thC, 38in (96cm) wide.
£500–600
€/ **$800–950** ⚒ HoG

A Victorian rosewood card table, the fold-over top on carved, quadripartite legs, 19thC, 36¼in (92cm) wide.
£700–875
€/ **$1,100–1,400** ⚒ SWO

A Victorian walnut card table, 36in (91.5cm) wide.
£1,100–1,250
€/ **$1,750–1,900** ⊞ NAW

A Victorian walnut card table, with a baize-lined fold-over serpentine top, on cabriole legs with scroll feet and ceramic casters, 38in (96cm) wide.
£750–850
€/ **$1,200–1,350** ⚒ CGC

A Victorian walnut card table, on a central column with carved feet, 36in (91.5cm) wide.
£600–700
€/ **$950–1,100** ⊞ WAW

A figured-walnut card table, on swept supports and cabriole legs with scrolled splay feet and casters, c1870, 36in (91.5cm) wide.
£2,700–3,000
€/ **$4,250–4,800** ⊞ JSt

A Louis XV-style ebonized boulle card table, the fold-over top inlaid with turtle shell and brass, on cabriole legs and sabots, French, late 19thC, 35¾in (91cm) wide.
£1,000–1,250
€/ **$1,600–1,900** ⋩ Gam

A red boulle and ormolu card table, with baize-lined fold-over top, with beaded borders and cherub-head mounts, on square tapering legs, 19thC, 36in (91.5cm) wide.
£700–900
€/ **$1,100–1,400** ⋩ JM

An Edwardian inlaid mahogany demi-lune card table,
30in (76cm) wide.
£1,000–1,100
€/ **$1,600–1,800** ⊞ RPh

An Edwardian mahogany envelope card table, with stringing and parquetry banding, the frieze drawer with brass handles, on square tapering legs, 21½in (54.5cm) wide.
£250–320
€/ **$400–500** ⋩ AH

A pair of George III-style mahogany demi-lune card tables, c1910, 33in (84cm) wide.
£5,250–5,850
€/ **$8,250–9,250** ⊞ RAN

Centre Tables

A rosewood centre table, with three short frieze drawers, on ring-turned baluster legs with brass mounts, Portuguese, 17thC, 53in (134.5cm) wide.
£2,000–2,500
€/ **$3,200–4,000** ⚒ L

A Louis XVI-style mahogany marquetry centre table, inlaid with later floral marquetry, on square tapering legs, Dutch, c1800, 35¼in (89.5cm) wide.
£2,500–3,000
€/ **$4,000–4,800** ⚒ S(Am)

A rosewood and ormolu centre table, attributed to Gillows of Lancaster, the top composed of mixed specimen marbles, c1810, 32in (81.5cm) wide.
£5,000–5,500
€/ **$8,000–8,700** ⊞ HA
This table was made for the Ponsonby family of Ponsonby Hall, near Kirkby Lonsdale, Cumbria.

A mahogany centre table, the dished marble top above a plain frieze, on shaped legs above a fluted acorn standard on splayed brass-inlaid legs with caps and casters, Baltic, c1825, 28in (71cm) wide.
£900–1,100
€/ **$1,500–1,800** ⚒ NOA

A flame mahogany centre table, the tilt-top on a central column, c1835, 47in (119.5cm) diam.
£2,400–2,700
€/ **$3,800–4,300** ⊞ GBr

A rosewood centre table, 19thC, 30in (76cm) wide.
£450–500
€/ **$710–790** ⚒ SWO

A rosewood centre table, with maker's label 'Thomas Mills, Bradford', c1840, 23¾in (60.5cm) wide.
£700–850
€/ **$1,100–1,350** ⚒ S(O)

A rococo revival mahogany centre table, with a fruit and floral carved frieze, on cabriole legs, American, 1850–75, 39in (99cm) wide.
£650–820
€/ **$1,000–1,300** ⚒ NOA

A marquetry serpentine centre table, with ormolu mounts, veneered in various coloured woods, the frieze enclosing one side drawer, mid-19thC, 51½in (131cm) wide.
£3,200–3,750
€/ **$5,000–5,800** ⚒ TMA

A kingwood and tulipwood marquetry centre table, with gilt-metal mounts, the frieze with a drawer, above foliate sabots, French, c1860, 45in (114.5cm) wide.
£3,200–3,500
€/ **$5,000–5,500** ⊞ JSt

A burr-walnut centre table, with boxwood inlay, c1860, 53in (134.5cm) wide.
£2,000–2,250
€/ **$3,200–3,500** ⊞ GBr

A pollarded oak centre table, 19thC, 54in (137cm) diam.
£9,000–10,000
€/ **$14,000–16,000** ⊞ SAW

Colour & patination

- These are two of the most important factors when valuing furniture
- Patination is produced by decades of waxing combined with dirt, grease and dust, all hardened by regular dusting.
- When valuing furniture, check for darker colour where the piece would be handled, i.e. chair arms, front of drawers under handles etc.
- Colour, if original, should vary from one side to the other as the side nearest the window will fade more because of the sun. If a piece has been repolished the colour will be even all over.
- On carved furniture dirt will have accumulated in the carving, producing darker patches. If repolished, there will be no contrast.

A Victorian walnut centre table, the top inlaid with satinwood and ebony, on splayed legs, with wavy block feet, 41¾in (106cm) wide.
£550–700
€/ **$870–1,100** ⚒ CGC

A walnut and ebonized centre table, by Lamb of Manchester, 19thC, 38in (96.5cm) wide.
£1,250–1,400
€/ **$1,900–2,200** ⊞ WAW

▶ **A pollarded oak centre table,** c1880, 45in (114.5cm) wide.
£1,100–1,200
€/ **$1,750–1,900** ⊞ SAW

A Victorian oak centre table, on cabriole legs, 40in (101.5cm) wide.
£700–780
€/ **$1,100–1,225** ⊞ MHA

An Edwardian satinwood crossbanded and inlaid centre table, the top radially veneered above shaped stretchers, on tapering legs and paw feet, 49¼in (125cm) wide.
£3,350–4,200
€/ **$5,200–6,650** ⚒ B(EA)
This is an example of quality Edwardian cabinet making.

Console & Pier Tables

A Louis XV carved oak console table, with a marble top, Liège, Belgium, 18thC, 23in (58.5cm) wide.
£1,800–2,250
€/ **$2,800–3,500** ⚒ BERN

A Biedermeier walnut console table, the figured top above a frieze enclosing one central drawer, joined by a mirrored back and front square columns on a lower plinth shelf, northern European, 1800–25, 39½in (100.5cm) wide.
£2,600–3,200
€/ **$4,100–5,000** ⚒ NOA

A Federal painted poplar pier table, extensively damaged, American, c1810, 35¾in (91cm) wide.
£2,800–3,200
€/ **$4,400–5,000** ⚒ S(NY)
The very poor condition of the top has badly affected the price.

A Regency carved giltwood console table, after a design by Holland & Son, with a mottled yellow ochre top on a plinth base, 54¼in (138cm) wide.
£4,500–5,500
€/ **$7,000–8,500** ⚒ Gam

A late Regency rosewood console table, with a later *verde antico* top, 29½in (75cm) wide.
£1,100–1,400
€/ **$1,700–2,200** ⚒ B(Ba)

A William IV mahogany console table, with a beaded top, on scrolled supports and paw feet, on a platform base, Irish, 48in (122cm) wide.
£1,600–2,000
€/ **$2,500–3,000** ⚒ JAd

Miller's Compares

I. A painted satinwood pier table, the crossbanded top painted with foliage, on ribbed, tapering legs, Irish, late 18thC, 39¼in (99.5cm) wide.
£13,000–16,000
€/ **$20,000–25,000** ⚒ HOK

II. A satinwood side table, the fan-inlaid top on square tapering legs, Irish, 19thC, 50in (127cm) wide.
£1,250–1,600
€/ **$1,900–2,500** ⚒ HOK

There may be only 20-odd years' difference in the date of these two tables, but Item I is smaller in size than item II and therefore of better proportion. The quality of the decoration is also far superior in Item I, but the most important factor is that it has provenance: it had once been owned by the Overend family of Airfield House, Dublin, who were keen collectors of good-quality 18th-century furniture.

A Louis XV-style gilt console table, with an onyx top, French, c1880, 54in (137cm) wide.
£1,700–2,000
€/ **$2,700–3,200** ⊞ DAC

A Victorian oak console table, with a plain top and frieze, on scroll supports and feet, 54in (137cm) wide.
£850–1,100
€/ **$1,350–1,750** ⚒ JAd

Dining Tables

> Items in the Furniture section have been arranged in date order.

A mahogany drop-leaf dining table, on turned legs with pointed pad feet, mid-18thC, 52in (132cm) extended.
£650–800
€/ $1,000–1,260 ⚲ BR

A George II mahogany drop-leaf dining table, on turned tapering legs with pad feet, 47in (119.5cm) wide.
£1,000–1,200
€/ $1,600–1,900 ⚲ JDJ

An early George III mahogany drop-leaf dining table, 48in (122cm) wide, extended.
£200–250
€/ $315–400 ⚲ L

A George III cuban mahogany drop-leaf dining table, repolished, slight restoration, 65½in (166.5cm) wide.
£1,000–1,250
€/ $1,600–1,900 ⚲ B(Ch)

A mahogany single drop-leaf dining table, the crossbanded frieze with one long drawer with brass handles, on tapering legs, early 19thC, 44½in (113cm) wide.
£800–1,000
€/ $1,300–1,600 ⚲ DD

◄ **A George III mahogany D-end dining table,** each half on four tapering legs, 47¼in (120cm) wide.
£850–1,100
€/ $1,350–1,750 ⚲ SWO

FURNITURE

A mahogany tilt-top dining table, on a turned baluster column with splay legs, 19thC, 55in (139.5cm) wide.
£1,300–1,600
€/ **$2,000–2,500** ➤ JM

A mid-Victorian mahogany wind-out extending dining table, with an additional central leaf, the extending action labelled 'Samuel Hawkins Patentee Bishopsgate, London', on carved, turned tapering legs, further leaf missing, 96in (244cm) extended.
£1,700–2,200
€/ **$2,700–3,500** ➤ PFK

A Victorian walnut extending dining table, with five extra leaves, 156in (396cm) extended.
£2,300–2,800
€/ **$3,600–4,400** ➤ B(Ba)

A Victorian mahogany concertina-action extending dining table, with two extra leaves, on turned and fluted tapering legs, 96in (244cm) extended.
£1,600–2,000
€/ **$2,500–3,200** ➤ PFK

A goncalo alves-veneered dining table, the central pedestal on four legs with brass casters, 1820–30, 54in (137cm) wide.
£5,000–6,000
€/ **$8,000–9,500** ⊞ MHA

A Victorian mahogany extending dining table, with three extra leaves, 125½in (319cm) extended.
£4,500–5,500
€/ **$7,000–8,750** ➤ SWO

A Victorian walnut extending dining table, with three extra leaves, on tapering legs, 115¾in (194cm) extended.
£1,500–2,000
€/ **$2,400–3,200** ➤ DN

A Victorian mahogany extending dining table, with three extra leaves, 103½in (263cm) extended.
£2,000–2,500
€/ **$3,200–4,000** ➤ Bea(E)

A mahogany extending banqueting table, by Crace & Co, London, with five extra leaves, with four turned and lobed legs, mid-19thC, 167½in (426cm) extended.
£8,000–10,000
€/ **$12,500–16,000** ➤ HOK
The family firm of Crace & Co was founded in the mid-18th century and rose to prominence in the 19th century. Their commissions included decorating the Royal Pavilion in Brighton for the Prince Regent, and various properties for William Waldorf Astor.

◀ **An early Victorian mahogany drop-leaf dining table,** 61½in (156cm) wide.
£450–565
€/ **$700–900** ➤ B(Ba)

A Victorian mahogany extending dining table, with two extra leaves, on cabriole legs with paw feet, 98½in (250cm) extended.
£2,500–3,200
€/ **$4,000–5,000** ➤ JAd

A Victorian mahogany dining table, with three legs on a central column, 48in (122cm) diam.
£1,250–1,400
€/ **$2,000–2,200** ⊞ MHA

A Victorian oak wind-out extending dining table, with two extra leaves and handle, on turned carved legs, 93¼in (237cm) extended.
£700–900
€/ **$1,100–1,400** ➤ B(Ch)

FURNITURE

A Victorian oak wind-out extending dining table, with one extra leaf, on turned legs, 124in (315cm) extended.
£1,100–1,200
€/ **$1,700–1,900** ⊞ PaA

Daily care
Climate can greatly affect furniture and a few simple steps can be taken to prevent damage. Avoid leaving furniture in direct strong sunlight and allow some draught into a room; a small humidifier may be beneficial if the atmosphere is particularly dry. Warped table leaves should be put in a damp atmosphere where they may straighten themselves, and card tables which develop a 'smile' will benefit from being opened overnight. If this does not work, the help of a qualified restorer will be required.

A chestnut extending dining table, with two extra leaves, French, late 19thC, 94½in (240cm) extended.
£800–1,000
€/ **$1,300–1,600** ↗ B(Ch)

A mahogany extending dining table, with one extra leaf, on carved and fluted legs, two leaves missing, early 20thC, 47¾in (121.5cm) wide.
£900–1,100
€/ **$1,400–1,700** ↗ SWO

A Regency-style mahogany dining table, early 20thC, 108¼in (275cm) wide.
£1,200–1,500
€/ **$1,900–2,400** ↗ B(Ba)

A mahogany extending dining table, with two extra leaves, on claw-and-ball feet, c1920, 94in (239cm) extended.
£3,400–3,750
€/ **$5,400–6,000** ⊞ MTay

Display Tables

A mahogany and gilt-metal-mounted vitrine table, French, 1848–70, 22in (56cm) wide.
£550–700
€/ **$870–1,100** ↗ B(Ch)

◄ A late 18thC-style giltwood and gesso display table, early 20thC, 24½in (62cm) wide.
£1,500–1,800
€/ **$2,350–2,850** ↗ S(O)

► An Edwardian mahogany display table, with a glazed top and sides, 16in (40.5cm) wide.
£315–350
€/ **$500–550** ⊞ HiA

A Louis XV-style kingwood and ormolu *bijouterie* table, French, c1880, 26in (66cm) wide.
£2,350–2,600
€/ **$3,600–4,000** ⊞ Che

An 18thC-style giltwood and gesso *bijouterie* table, late 19thC, Italian, 36¼in (92cm) wide.
£950–1,200
€/ **$1,500–1,900** ↗ S(O)

A stained hardwood and mahogany display table, with a glazed top, on carved cabriole legs, with undertier, c1900, 27in (68.5cm) wide.
£1,100–1,250
€/ **$1,750–1,900** ⊞ MTay

An Edwardian walnut vitrine table, restored, 24½in (62cm) wide.
£250–325
€/ **$400–500** ↗ B(Ba)

Dressing Tables

An early George III mahogany dressing table, the hinged and divided top with figural panels and chequered line inlay, the interior with a mirror, beaker apertures and lidded compartments, the fret-carved frieze with later lopers, legs possibly later, 26in (66cm) wide.
£1,400–1,700
€/ **$2,200–2,700** ♣ B

A mahogany bowfronted dressing table, with inlaid stringing, a frieze drawer above a kneehole and two short drawers, with later brass-plate lion mask ring handles, on tapering legs with socket feet, 19thC, 35¾in (91cm) wide.
£450–550
€/ **$700–870** ♣ WW

A Transitional rococo revival *faux* rosewood dressing table, the mirror flanked by a pair of cupboards, the base with a marble top over three drawers with pie crust moulding, on bracket feet, American, mid-19thC, 42in (106.5cm) wide.
£900–1,100
€/ **$1,400–1,700** ♣ NOA

A George III gentleman's mahogany dressing table, serpentine-shaped, with central lifting mirror above drawers and doors, on square tapering legs, 35¾in (91cm) wide.
£700–850
€/ **$1,100–1,300** ♣ SWO

A George III mahogany gentleman's travelling dressing table, with a slide and a central drawer flanked by five small drawers, on tapered legs, 19in (48.5cm) wide.
£400–450
€/ **$630–710** ♣ HOLL

▶ **A Victorian bird's-eye maple dressing table,** 59in (150cm) wide.
£400–450
€/ **$630–710** ♣ B(Ba)

A Victorian figured walnut dressing table, by Heal & Son, the mirror above four jewellery drawers and three frieze drawers, on pedestal supports with three drawers, on plinth bases, 52in (132cm) wide.
£600–700
€/ **$950–1,100** ♣ HOLL

An Empire mahogany dressing table, the mirror plate tilting between columns with engine-turned capitals, the top inset with a marble top above a long drawer, on turned legs, French, 37¾in (96cm) wide.
£750–900
€/ **$1,200–1,400** ♣ B

A satinwood kneehole dressing table, with central lifting mirror, c1825, 34in (86.5cm) wide.
£400–440
€/ **$630–700** ⊞ PaA

A Chippendale revival mahogany dressing table, c1885, 38in (96.5cm) wide.
£1,450–1,600
€/ **$2,300–2,500** ⊞ Che

◀ **A Sheraton revival satinwood, tulipwood-crossbanded and ebony-strung dressing table,** the quarter-veneered top above three drawers with brass handles, flanking a kneehole, on tapering legs with brass caps and casters, late 19thC, 36¼in (92cm) wide.
£750–900
€/ **$1,200–1,400** ⚒ DN

An Edwardian mahogany dressing table, the three mirrors above a central drawer flanked by two pairs of drawers, on turned legs with brass casters, 53in (134.5cm) wide.
£880–1,000
€/ **$1,400–1,600** ⊞ MHA

A George II-style walnut dressing table, with featherbanding, the five drawers flanking a kneehole, on shell-carved cabriole legs, early 20thC, 48in (122cm) wide.
£1,000–1,100
€/ **$1,600–1,700** ⚒ S(O)

◀ **An Edwardian inlaid mahogany dressing table,** the mirror suspended between scroll uprights, over a central well with fitted trinket drawers and an arrangement of five crossbanded drawers, on tapering legs, 48in (122cm) wide.
£400–475
€/ **$630–750** ⚒ AMB

Drop-Leaf Tables

An early George III mahogany single-leaf side table, 29in (73.5cm) wide.
£320–375
€/ **$500–590** ⚒ L

Cross Reference
See Dining Tables (pages 121–123)

A mahogany drop-leaf table, with a drawer, on turned tapering legs and pad feet, 18thC, 33in (84cm) wide.
£500–575
€/ **$790–900** ⚒ BWL

A George III mahogany drop-leaf table, 48in (122cm) wide.
£800–950
€/ **$1,300–1,500** ⚒ B(Ch)

A Renaissance revival inlaid and ebonized drop-leaf table, decorated with a central classical urn, Greek key and foliate scroll roundel within a berried-laurel diamond reserve, American, c1875, 60in (152.5cm) wide.
£10,000–12,000
€/ **$16,000–19,000** ⚒ S(NY)
The Renaissance revival became the leading fashion in America by 1860. Rather than strictly reproducing forms popular during the Renaissance, the style consisted of creative adaptations of Renaissance architectural ornament.

A mahogany drop-leaf table, inlaid with floral marquetry, the legs with inlaid fluted decoration, 19thC, 43¼in (110cm) wide.
£850–1,000
€/ **$1,300–1,600** ⚒ AMB

A mahogany double drop-leaf wake table, with boxwood stringing, on tapering legs, 19thC, Irish, 73¾in (187.5cm) wide.
£1,100–1,300
€/ **$1,700–2,000** ⚒ JAd

FURNITURE

Drum Tables

A late Regency rosewood drum table, damaged, 41in (104cm) diam.
£5,800–6,500
€/ $9,200–10,300 ⊞ WAW

A Victorian mahogany drum table, the top with leatherette inset above a frieze fitted with four real and four dummy drawers, on four fluted legs with downswept scroll feet with casters, 48in (122cm) diam.
£900–1,100
€/ $1,400–1,700 🔨 Mit

A Regency-style drum table, with a tooled-leather inset top, late 19thC, 33in (84cm) diam.
£850–1,000
€/ $1,300–1,600 🔨 B(Ch)

A Regency elm and burr-elm drum table, the crossbanded top above an arrangement of two real and two dummy drawers with turned knobs and inlaid shield-shaped escutcheons, on a baluster-turned column and downswept legs with brass caps and casters, 24in (61cm) diam.
£7,000–8,000
€/ $11,000–12,600 🔨 HYD

▶ **A mahogany drum table,** the revolving top fitted with two frieze drawers with brass knobs, the baluster-turned stem on three scroll legs, 19thC, 20½in (52cm) diam.
£350–420
€/ $550–670 🔨 WW

Games Tables

A Federal inlaid birchwood and maple games table, American, c1810, 35in (89cm) wide.
£4,500–5,000
€/ $7,000–8,000 🔨 S(NY)

▶ **A walnut games table,** with reversible bagatelle top, c1870, 29in (73.5cm) diam.
£2,500–2,750
€/ $4,000–4,400 ⊞ MTay

A Victorian walnut games table, on a turned stretcher base, 31in (78.5cm) wide.
£200–230
€/ $300–350 ⊞ PaA

◀ **A Victorian walnut serpentine fold-over and swivel-top games/ sewing table,** on turned legs, 27in (68.5cm) high.
£1,750–2,000
€/ $2,700–3,200 ⊞ BrL

An Edwardian inlaid mahogany and leather games table, 28in (71cm) wide.
£765–850
€/ $1,200–1,350 ⊞ RPh

FURNITURE

ibrary Tables

A late Regency rosewood library table, the three-quarter pierced gilt-metal gallery above a leather-inset top and gadrooned frieze, with two drawers, the turned and reeded legs with casters, 44in (112cm) wide.
€2,200–2,500
€/ $3,500–4,000 ✗ TF

A William IV mahogany library table, probably by Williams & Gibton, the moulded top above two real and two dummy drawers, on two tapering cylindrical columns and bun feet, stamped 'No. 11771', Irish, 59in (150cm) wide.
£1,500–1,750
€/ $2,400–2,750 ✗ MEA

A William IV mahogany library table, with gilt-tooled leather inset top over two short drawers with brass knobs, on baluster legs and splayed and scrolled feet, 42in (106.5cm) wide.
£1,000–1,200
€/ $1,600–1,900 ✗ MCA

A Victorian rosewood library table, the top with two shaped frieze drawers, on turned tapering and lotus-moulded column legs and moulded scroll feet with brass casters, 48in (122cm) wide.
£1,300–1,500
€/ $2,000–2,400 ✗ DD

A Victorian rosewood library table, with gilt-tooled leather inset to the crossbanded top, with two frieze drawers, on lotus-carved tapering baluster legs with brass casters, 56¾in (144cm) wide.
£2,000–2,200
€/ $3,200–3,500 ✗ Bea(E)

▶ **A Victorian mahogany library table,** 48in (122cm) wide.
£800–900
€/ $1,300–1,400 ⊞ PaA

A Victorian walnut library table, the moulded top with inlaid satinwood crossbanding, above two drawers, on turned tapering baluster columns, stamped 'Holland & Sons', 47¾in (121.5cm) wide.
£2,400–2,750
€/ $3,800–4,350 ✗ Gam

A yew wood oyster-veneered library table, the moulded top with a central medallion and crossbanded edge, above an inlaid frieze with two drawers, on turned tapering legs and pad feet, Dutch, late 19thC, 49¾in (126.5cm) wide.
£1,300–1,500
€/ $2,000–2,400 ✗ BR

A rosewood library table, with thumb-moulded edge and two frieze drawers, on baluster-turned legs, Spanish, 19thC, 57½in (146cm) wide.
£2,800–3,200
€/ $4,400–5,000 ✗ JAd

A late Victorian oak library table, with a leatherette inset top, 68¼in (173.5cm) wide.
£320–375
€/ $500–590 ✗ B(Ba)

A Gothic revival oak library table, the moulded top above three real and three dummy drawers, with blind tracery carving to all sides, the ring-turned legs on bun feet, c1900, 78in (198cm) wide.
£7,000–8,500
€/ $11,000–13,500 ✗ S

Waxing

To maintain and improve patination, furniture should be waxed once a month with a wax-based (never silicone-based) polish. Over-waxing can result in a smeared finish. Apply a thin layer of wax, leave for a short time and burnish with a soft clean cloth, remembering to follow the direction of the grain. Damage can be avoided by ensuring that belt buckles, rings and buttons are not allowed to come into contact with the furniture while cleaning. Always use place mats to protect polished surfaces from hot or cold dishes. The cold water in a vase can produced a white 'chill' mark which will need the attention of an expert. When cleaning brasses use a wadding cleaner to avoid liquid spillages to the patinated surfaces. A beautiful finish can be achieved by polishing the highlights of brass handles and leaving a natural build up of wax around the backplates and knobs.

FURNITURE

Nests of Tables

▶ **A mahogany nest of three tables,** on foliate-carved cabriole legs with pad feet, c1900, 22in (56cm) wide.
£350–425
€/ $550–670
⚘ NOA

A walnut nest of tables, the tops with raised beading, on sabre legs, c1910, 17½in (45cm) wide.
£700–775
€/ $1,100–1,200 ⊞ MTay

An oak nest of tables, with bobbin-turned legs, c1930, 17in (43cm) wide.
£170–185
€/ $270–300 ⊞ CHAC

Miller's Compares

I. A set of Regency rosewood and mahogany quartetto tables, with ebonized and boxwood stringing, on turned legs, early 19thC, the largest table 18¼in (46.5cm) wide.
£4,500–5,500
€/ $7,000–8,700 ⚘ S

II. A set of Regency figured mahogany and satinwood-crossbanded quartetto tables, on ring-turned legs, 18¼in (46.5cm) wide.
£2,400–2,750
€/ $3,800–4,350 ⚘ S(O)

Item I has all the quality points that are sought after by collectors. The set, with its well-figured veneer, ring-turned legs, bowed rear stretchers and swept trestle feet, has a more elegant appearance than Item II.

Occasional Tables

A partridgewood-veneered and boxwood-strung occasional table, with two drawers, on tapering legs, c1790, 27in (68.5cm) wide.
£2,650–3,000
€/ $4,200–4,700 ⊞ HA

▶ **A William IV occasional table,** the top veneered with a fan and alternate concentric borders of yew and rosewood, on a tapering cluster column with platform base, the bun feet with recessed brass casters, 25in (63.5cm) diam.
£4,500–5,000
€/ $7,100–7,900 ⚘ BWL

A Regency mahogany and plumwood occasional table, with baluster column and hipped sabre legs, on turned feet, base repaired, 24in (61cm) wide.
£1,000–1,100
€/ $1,600–1,700 ⚘ Bon

A Regency rosewood occasional table, with fluted tapering column and concave platform base, 21in (53.5cm) wide.
£550–700
€/ $870–1,100 ⚘ BWL

A burr-maple and purple heart-inlaid occasional table, with two drawers, on brass casters, French, c1835, 30in (76cm) wide.
£5,200–5,700
€/ $8,200–9,000 ⊞ CAT

A yew wood occasional table, with parquetry top and incised carving to the pedestal base, Irish, c1820, 23¼in (59cm) wide.
£2,000–2,200
€/ $3,200–3,500 ⚘ S(O)

A Louis XV-style kingwood and marquetry occasional table, c1880, 26in (66cm) wide.
£1,400–1,600
€/ $2,200–2,500 ⊞ Che

FURNITURE

Parquetry or marquetry?

Parquetry: inlays of variously coloured small pieces of wood veneer in geometric patterns on the carcass.
Marquetry: a decorative coloured veneer of wood and other decorative materials inlaid into furniture to form arabesque or floral patterns, and sometimes pastoral or figurative designs.

A Charles Baker's patent folding occasional table, the top with a piecrust edge, on tapering legs, c1898, 30in (76cm) diam.
£100–120
€/ **$160–190** ➤ GAK

A tulipwood-veneered parquetry occasional table, with ormolu mounts, French, 19thC, 20in (51cm) wide.
£3,250–3,600
€/ **$5,000–5,700** ⊞ REI

A painted satinwood occasional table, c1890, 33in (84cm) wide.
£3,000–3,300
€/ **$4,700–5,200** ⊞ SAW

A Gothic revival rosewood occasional table, the top with an ogee-moulded frieze, on scroll supports with scroll feet, American, 1825–50, 33in (84cm) wide.
£600–700
€/ **$950–1,100** ➤ NOA

► **A parquetry occasional table,** minor losses to veneer, Italian, 19thC, 30¼in (77cm) diam.
£1,200–1,400
€/ **$1,900–2,200** ➤ B(Ba)

Olivewood

Olivewood is a hard, close-grained wood from southern Europe and has a green-to-yellow colour with interesting black-grey marking. It was used in the mid-17th century for marquetry inlay, because its colour provided contrasting decoration to walnut, which is a darkish brown with black veining. Olivewood was also frequently seen as cross-graining on chests of drawers from the mid-17th century onwards.

A Victorian olivewood occasional/display table, the rotating three-tier superstructure on spiral-turned supports, the octagonal top with moulded edge and plain frieze, on a tapering octagonal column and scroll feet, 24½in (62cm) diam.
£1,500–1,800
€/ **$2,400–2,800** ➤ TEN

A pair of Louis XVI-style mahogany occasional tables, with pierced brass galleries enclosing variegated marble tops, each with two drawers and two candle slides to the frieze, on tapering legs with brass caps, French, c1900, 18in (45.5cm) diam.
£1,000–1,200
€/ **$1,600–1,900** ➤ NOA

► **A rosewood *guéridon* table,** with brass mounts, French, c1900, 30in (76cm) high.
£450–500
€/ **$700–800** ⊞ DAC

◄ **A Victorian rosewood occasional table,** on a tapering octagonal column and tripod base, 21¾in (55.5cm) diam.
£260–325
€/ **$400–500** ➤ CHTR

FURNITURE

Pembroke Tables

A Sheraton mahogany Pembroke table, with satinwood crossbanding, c1780, 28in (71cm) wide.
£4,700–5,200
€/ **$7,400–8,200** ⊞ REI

A George III manchineel Pembroke table, with one real and one dummy drawer, on chamfered legs with casters, 25¼in (64cm) wide.
£450–540
€/ **$700–850** ⚒ TEN

A mahogany Pembroke table, decorated with inlaid marquetry in exotic woods, late 18thC, 45in (114.5cm) wide.
£3,500–4,000
€/ **$5,500–6,300** ⊞ BMi

A Sheraton sabicu-veneered Pembroke table, with padouk crossbanding, c1790, 40in (101.5cm) wide.
£2,000–2,400
€/ **$3,200–3,800** ⊞ CAT

A George III Sheraton-style satinwood Pembroke table, the top inlaid with tulipwood banding edged with boxwood and ebony stringing, with one real and one dummy frieze drawer, on tapering legs with casters, 28in (71cm) wide.
£3,700–4,500
€/ **$5,800–7,100** ⚒ HYD

A mahogany Pembroke table, with a single drawer and tapering legs, early 19thC, 31in (78.5cm) wide.
£280–320
€/ **$440–500** ⊞ PaA

◄ **A mahogany Pembroke table,** with reeded top, on ring-turned legs with casters, early 19thC, 39in (99cm) wide.
£320–400
€/ **$500–630** ⚒ BWL

► **A mid-Victorian mahogany Pembroke table,** 36in (91.5cm) wide.
£300–325
€/ **$475–500** ⊞ WiB

A George III mahogany and crossbanded Pembroke table, with serpentine leaves, restored, c1790, 35½in (90cm) wide.
£2,400–2,800
€/ **$3,800–4,400** ⚒ S(O)

A George III satinwood Pembroke table, the crossbanded top over a single drawer, on tapering legs with socket feet, alterations, 32¼in (82cm) wide.
£750–875
€/ **$1,200–1,400** ⚒ B(W)

A mahogany Pembroke table, with one real and one dummy frieze drawer with ebonized stringing and fitted with later brass knob handles, on ring-turned legs with brass casters, 19thC, 21in (53.5cm) wide.
£350–450
€/ **$550–700** ⚒ WW

FURNITURE

Reading Tables

An early George III mahogany reading table, with ratchetted lift-up top, 29½in (75cm) wide.
£550–625
€/ $870–990 ↗ L

A late Georgian mahogany adjustable reading table, on a turned column with scroll feet, 18¼in (46.5cm) wide.
£550–700
€/ $870–1,100 ↗ WiLP

A Regency mahogany reading table, with hinged adjustable top, the trestle feet with beaded moulding, 20in (51cm) wide.
£550–625
€/ $870–990 ↗ Bea(E)

A Regency rosewood reading table, the ratchetted top over a frieze drawer, on carved scroll supports, with undertier, 21¼in (54cm) wide.
£400–475
€/ $630–750 ↗ B(EA)

◀ **A Victorian walnut adjustable reading table,** 36in (91.5cm) wide.
£3,700–4,000
€/ $5,800–6,300 ⊞ SAW

▶ **A Victorian rosewood and rosewood-veneered adjustable reading table,** 33in (84cm) wide.
£450–525
€/ $710–830 ↗ SWO

Serving Tables

A late George III neo-classical-style mahogany breakfront serving table, crossbanded and inlaid with boxwood and purplewood lines, the shaped top above a painted and parcel-gilt base, decoration later, 76¾in (195cm) wide.
£3,500–4,250
€/ $5,500–6,700 ↗ B

A mahogany serving table, with a single drawer, on carved legs, c1830, 53in (134.5cm) wide.
£1,700–2,000
€/ $2,700–3,200 ⊞ RPh

A mahogany breakfront serving table, the central drawer flanked by shallow bowed drawers, the turned baluster legs headed by reeded panels, Irish, early 19thC, 78¾in (200cm) wide.
£850–1,100
€/ $1,350–1,750 ↗ HOK

To order Miller's books in the USA please ring AOL/Time Warner on 1-800-759-0190

A George IV mahogany serving table, the rounded top above two frieze drawers, on turned and reeded tapering legs headed by bead-moulded tablets, later raised back, 72¼in (183.5cm) wide.
£1,300–1,600
€/ $2,000–2,500 ↗ Bea(E)

An early Victorian mahogany serving table, the mirror-back surmounted by a foliate cartouche and scroll supports, above a base with a central frieze drawer, flanked by foliate terminals on acanthus-scrolled legs with scroll feet, 65¾in (167cm) wide.
£1,300–1,600
€/ $2,000–2,500 ↗ JAd

A Regency-style mahogany serving table, with three frieze drawers, early 20thC, 60¼in (153cm) wide.
£1,400–1,600
€/ $2,200–2,500 ↗ S(O)

FURNITURE

Side Tables

A William and Mary walnut side table, with inlaid banded top, above a frieze drawer, on spiral-turned legs, 30in (76cm) wide.
£2,800–3,500
€/ **$4,500–5,500** ✗ BWL

A late Georgian mahogany bowfronted side table, 35¾in (91cm) wide.
£1,000–1,125
€/ **$1,500–1,750** ⊞ WiB

A mahogany side table, with a frieze drawers and shaped apron, on square chamfered legs, apron restored, early 19thC, 30¾in (78cm) wide.
£400–500
€/ **$630–800** ✗ DN

An early Victorian mahogany side table, the moulded-edge top above two frieze drawers with brass swan-neck bale handles, on turned tapering legs with brass caps and casters, 48in (122cm) wide.
£180–225
€/ **$280–350** ✗ PFK

A George III John Cobb-style side table, the serpentine top centred by a harewood marquetry panel, a geometric panel with geometric trelliswork surrounding a floral marquetry medallion, and flanked by burr-yew wood-veneered panels, the conforming frieze with a central drawer flanked by burr-maple panels, with rosewood crossbandings throughout, later drawer, some later veneers and marquetry, 45in (114.5cm) wide.
£3,500–4,200
€/ **$5,500–6,650** ✗ S(O)
The marquetry decoration to this table incorporates several elements which relate to the work of the great 18th century cabinet maker John Cobb, of St Martin's Lane, London. He was the son-in-law of the celebrated cabinet maker Giles Grendey and was in business until 1777.

A mahogany side table, with associated ormolu mounts, alterations, early 19thC, 32¼in (82cm) wide.
£420–520
€/ **$670–820** ✗ B(Ba)

A late George III mahogany serpentine side table, with a frieze drawer, on square tapering legs, 34in (86.5cm) wide.
£320–400
€/ **$500–600** ✗ G(L)

A Regency figured rosewood side table, the drop-leaf top on a tulip-carved column and quatrefoil base, 29½in (75cm) wide.
£1,000–1,250
€/ **$1,500–2,000** ✗ B(Ch)

A William IV mahogany side table, with panelled gallery back, two short drawers with turned knop handles, on ring-turned tapering legs, Irish, 44in (112cm) wide.
£1,850–2,300
€/ **$2,850–3,650** ✗ WL
Mack, Williams and Gibton was the leading firm of cabinet makers in the city of Dublin in the early 19th century. In 1806, they were appointed upholsterers and cabinet makers to the king. This table dates to between 1829–44, when, on the death of John Mack in 1829, the firm traded as Williams & Gibton. In 1844, William Gibton died and the firm traded as Williams & Sons, ceasing business in 1952.

◄ **A rosewood stretcher table,** c1840, 22in (56cm) wide.
£1,000–1,150
€/ **$1,500–1,750** ⊞ SAW

A Queen Anne-style walnut side table, the banded top above a frieze with a long drawer, on cabriole legs headed by carving, with claw-and-ball feet, mid-19thC, 30¾in (78cm) wide.
£1,800–2,200
€/ **$2,850–3,500** ⚒ NOA

A rosewood side table, with three marquetry drawers, c1880, 40in (101.5cm) wide.
£1,000–1,150
€/ **$1,500–1,800** ⊞ RPh

An inlaid mahogany side table, with two drawers, c1880, 52in (132cm) wide.
£6,200–6,850
€/ **$9,750–10,750** ⊞ RAN

A Victorian walnut and line-inlaid side table, with two drawers, on reeded turned end supports, with scroll-carved legs and casters, 42in (106.5cm) wide.
£600–770
€/ **$1,000–1,200** ⚒ E

A mahogany side table, with a single drawer, on turned tapering legs with brass casters, stamped 'Cope's Patent', 19thC, 29in (73.5cm) wide.
£1,200–1,500
€/ **$2,000–2,400** ⚒ BWL

A pair of ebony and inlaid side tables, the tops with panels depicting figures, masks and sea horses enclosed by foliage, the panels interspersed by ivory and mother-of-pearl geometric designs, with frieze drawers, the cylindrical section legs joined by pierced X-stretchers with finials, on peg feet, Italian, Milanese, 19thC, 28¾in (73cm) wide.
£3,500–4,200
€/ **$5,500–6,600** ⚒ B(Ch)

FURNITURE

Silver Tables

A George III mahogany silver table, alterations, 27½in (70cm) wide.
£3,200–3,500
€ / $5,000–5,500 ➣ S(O)

A George III mahogany silver table, with pierced gallery, 29½in (75cm) wide.
£1,200–1,500
€ / $2,000–2,400 ➣ S(O)

A George II and later Giles Grendey-style red japanned silver table, with gilded chinoiserie decoration and carved scroll brackets, on cabriole legs and pad feet, 32½in (82.5cm) wide.
£6,500–7,500
€ / $10,300–11,800 ➣ HOLL

Tables with galleried edges were designed by Chippendale in 1754 and used for displaying objects and for serving tea in the 18th century. These are often now known as silver tables. In the 19th century French-style tables with metal galleries were popular.

◄ A Georgian mahogany silver table, the top with a shallow moulded gallery, the shaped apron centred on two sides by a carved scallop shell, on scroll-moulded cabriole legs with faceted pad feet, Irish, 32in (81.5cm) wide.
£7,000–8,200
€ / $11,000–13,000 ➣ S

A Chippendale-style mahogany silver table, restored, late 19thC, 39¾in (101cm) wide.
£600–700
€ / $950–1,100 ➣ B(Ch)

Sofa Tables

A Regency Thomas Hope-style rosewood sofa table, with brass stringing and gilt-metal mounts, with one real and one dummy drawer with egg-and-dart-style gilt-metal moulding, on four carved giltwood lion-paw feet with original casters, 67in (170cm) extended.
£3,700–4,500
€ / $5,750–7,100 ➣ TF

A mahogany drop-leaf sofa table, with crossbanding, on outswept legs, c1790, 43in (109cm) wide.
£6,250–7,000
€ / $9,800–11,000 ⊞ GKe

A Regency rosewood sofa table, 37in (94cm) wide.
£2,000–2,400
€ / $3,200–3,800 ➣ L

A Regency satin-banded mahogany sofa table, with two frieze drawers, on reeded downswept legs with brass caps and casters, 36in (91.5cm) wide.
£1,200–1,500
€ / $2,000–2,400 ➣ G(L)

English Regency period
- At present Regency furniture is quite sought after as its classical style, influenced by Egyptian, Etruscan, Greek and Roman periods, complements some minimalist styles.
- Many ideas were copied from French Consulate and Empire designs.
- Some of the more exuberant pieces were inlaid with brass patterns and after c1805, ebony inlay.
- Woods most frequently used include mahogany, rosewood, simulated rosewood in the form of painted beechwood, and coromandel.
- Some of the finest Regency styles are found in pieces by Thomas Hope.

Regency mahogany sofa table, with a rosewood-crossbanded top, above two frieze drawers, on a cheval frame with a turned stretcher, the reeded scroll feet with brass toe caps and casters, 38in (96.5cm) wide.
£1,200–1,500
€/ $2,000–2,400 ⚒ BWL

A Regency George Bullock-style rosewood-veneered sofa table, the top with a crossbanded edge, the similarly inlaid frieze with two drawers, on a square baluster stem, the four hipped splayed legs with foliate-cast brass caps and casters, 22½in (57cm) wide.
£2,700–3,400
€/ $4,250–5,400 ⚒ Bea

A neo-classical walnut sofa table, the highly figured top above a single frieze drawer, on a stand with swan-neck and acanthus carving, the concave base on splayed legs with paw feet, north European, early 19thC, 35½in (90cm) wide.
£1,200–1,500
€/ $2,000–2,400 ⚒ NOA

A Victorian rosewood sofa table, with two drawers, the ring- and baluster-turned stem with gadrooned collar, on a concave platform base with scrolled feet and casters, 57in (145cm) extended.
€850–1,100
€/ $1,350–1,750 ⚒ AH

A mahogany and floral marquetry sofa table, the outswept top above a frieze drawer, on scrolling legs joined by a baluster-turned stretcher, Dutch, 19thC, 47¼in (120cm) wide.
£1,800–2,250
€/ $2,850–3,500 ⚒ B

A mahogany banded sofa table, with lyre end supports, early 20thC, 54in (137cm) wide.
£700–800
€/ $1,100–1,250 ⊞ HiA

FURNITURE

Sutherland Tables

A Victorian walnut Sutherland table, the figured drop-leaf top with a moulded border, on multi-carved cabriole legs, 29½in (75cm) wide.
£550–625
€ / $870–1,000 RbF

A mid-Victorian mahogany Sutherland table, 35¾in (91cm) wide.
£280–350
€ / $450–550 B(Ba)

A Victorian inlaid walnut Sutherland table, 34¾in (88.5cm) wide.
£550–625
€ / $870–1,000 SWO

A Victorian burr-walnut Sutherland table, 34½in (87.5cm) wide.
£500–600
€ / $800–950 L

An Edwardian mahogany double Sutherland table, each top with moulded edge, on ring-turned supports, upper table 22in (56cm) wide.
£350–450
€ / $550–700 FHF

An Edwardian inlaid mahogany Sutherland table, 24in (61cm) wide.
£200–250
€ / $300–400 SWO
Sutherland tables were introduced in the 19th century and named after the Duchess of Sutherland.

Tea Tables

A George II mahogany tea table, the fold-over top above a later frieze drawer, restored, Irish, 33½in (85cm) wide.
£1,000–1,250
€ / $1,500–2,000 B(Ch)

A mahogany tea table, c1760, 34¼in (87cm) wide.
£650–800
€ / $1,000–1,250 S(O)

A mahogany metamorphic combined tea and writing table, the double fold-over top with adjustable rising sloping writing inset and three small drawers, c1790, 35¾in (91cm) wide.
£1,500–1,800
€ / $2,400–2,850 S(O)

◀ **A Hepplewhite period mahogany serpentine tea table,** the fold-over top above a banded frieze with a single drawer, on moulded channelled square tapering legs, c1790, 36in (91.5cm) wide.
£1,100–1,400
€ / $1,750–2,200 MCA

▶ **A George III mahogany tea table,** 33¾in (85.5cm) wide.
£350–450
€ / $550–700 L

A mahogany tea table, on sabre legs, c1820, 36¼in (92cm) wide.
£800–900
€ / **$1,250–1,400** ⚘ S(O)

A Regency inlaid maple tea table, 36in (91.5cm) wide.
£3,000–3,400
€ / **$4,750–5,400** ⊞ APO

A rosewood folding tea table, on a carved and turned central column, c1820, 43in (109cm) wide.
£3,300–3,700
€ / **$5,200–6,000** ⊞ SAW

A George IV mahogany tea table, the hinged top above a plain frieze, on turned and reeded tapering legs, 36in (91.5cm) wide.
£650–800
€ / **$1,000–1,270** ⚘ AG

A mahogany tea table, the veneered fold-over top above a veneered frieze with ebony stringing, on moulded square tapering legs, early 19thC, 36in (91.5cm) wide.
£280–350
€ / **$450–550** ⚘ WW

A William IV mahogany and rosewood tea table, with crossbanding and brass inlay, 35¾in (91cm) wide.
£450–550
€ / **$700–875** ⚘ B(Ba)

Tripod Tables

An early George III mahogany tripod table, the later dished top on a birdcage support, 26½in (67.5cm) diam.
£650–775
€ / **$1,000–1,200** ⚘ L
This description means that the table had a plain circular top that was lobed and dished at a later date. The Victorians were keen on 'enhancing' furniture, and this piece would be worth more today if it had not been altered.

A George II mahogany tripod table, the drop-leaf top with three hinged flaps rising in conjunction with a swivel action, on cabriole legs with pad feet, 33in (84cm) diam.
£3,800–4,200
€ / **$6,000–6,700** ⚘ S

A George II mahogany tripod table, the tilting top with a floral-carved border, on a baluster-turned twist column and tripod downswept legs carved with acanthus leaves, on claw-and-ball feet, 22in (56cm) diam.
£3,000–3,750
€ / **$4,750–6,000** ⚘ HYD

A Chippendale period mahogany birdcage tripod table, c1750, 30in (76cm) diam.
£1,900–2,100
€ / **$3,000–3,300** ⊞ SAW

◄ **A George III carved mahogany tripod table,** the shaped snap top with a pierced baluster gallery, on a fluted tapering column, the decorated tripod splayed supports with paw feet, 29¼in (74.5cm) wide.
£2,500–3,000
€ / **$4,000–4,750** ⚘ B(EA)

◄ **A satinwood and painted tripod table,** decorated with neo-classical motifs, the rounded top on a baluster stem, the tripod with sabre legs, some later painting, c1795, 17in (43cm) wide.
£1,800–2,200
€ / **$2,850–3,500** ⚘ S(O)

FURNITURE

A George III mahogany tripod table, with tilt-top, the central barrel- and vase-turned column with cabriole legs, 31in (78.5cm) diam.
£450–550
€ / **$700–870** ⚒ **PF**

A George III mahogany tripod table, the tilt-top on a bird-cage support, the three carved legs with shaped pad feet, 26½in (67.5cm) diam.
£2,000–2,500
€ / **$3,200–4,000** ⚒ **TMA**

A George III mahogany tripod table, on a turned central column, 31in (78.5cm) diam.
£2,250–2,500
€ / **$3,500–4,000** ⊞ **APO**

A child's tripod table, the walnut tilt-top on a beech stem with oak legs, c1790, 11in (28cm) diam.
£1,250–1,400
€ / **$2,000–2,200** ⊞ **HA**
This is of the correct proportions to go with a child's chair and therefore was not made for adult use.

A Federal turned and figured mahogany tripod table, with traces of possibly original finish, cleats later, American, Massachusetts, c1800, 26¾in (68cm) wide.
£2,500–2,750
€ / **$4,000–4,400** ⚒ **S(NY)**

A Regency ebonized and decorated tripod table, the top paper-mounted with classical objects and antiquities, on a turned urn-shaped column with arched legs, 11¾in (30cm) wide.
£260–325
€ / **$400–500** ⚒ **B**

◄ **A rosewood and banded tripod table,** the tilt-top on a turned column and quadruped base, with brass terminals and casters, 19thC, 39in (99cm) diam.
£700–900
€ / **$1,100–1,400** ⚒ **E**

An early Victorian rosewood-veneered tripod table, the tilt-top inlaid with marquetry flowers within sun rays, enclosed by a border of flowers and leaf motifs, the tapering faceted stem on three floral marquetry-inlaid cabriole legs with roundels to the toes, 25in (63.5cm) wide.
£700–820
€ / **$1,100–1,300** ⚒ **WW**

An early Victorian rosewood tripod table, the veneered top on a turned stem and cabriole legs, 29in (73.5cm) high.
£830–925
€ / **$1,300–1,450** ⊞ **RPh**

Is it genuine?
To avoid fakes and marriages:
- Check underneath the top: there should be a dark shadow of approximately 1½–2in (4–5cm) in a band around the edge, caused by dirt from the fingers when the table is lifted.
- Check that the lopers (the strengthening supports found under the table top) haven't been cut back. If they have, there will be a shadow left behind that will 'run off' to the edge which indicates that the top has been reduced.
- Check that the block on the column has left a shadow where it meets the underside of the table. If there is a difference, it means that the stem and table top are not original to each other.
- Georgian tavern tables with good bold swept legs were often later carved by Victorians to enhance value. This resulted in very thin-looking legs out of balance with the column.

A walnut tripod table, the veneered top above a carved stem, c1870, 20in (51cm) diam.
£340–375
€ / **$550–600** ⊞ **MTay**

► **A George II-style mahogany tripod table,** on tapering legs with pad feet, c1900, 28in (71cm) diam.
£1,300–1,450
€ / **$2,000–2,275** ⊞ **RAN**

A marquetry tripod table, on a turned column and three flat legs, 19thC, 25½in (65cm) wide.
£320–400
€ / **$500–630** ⚒ **SWO**

Two-Tier Tables

◀ **A near pair of Victorian walnut two-tier occasional tables,** one with a square top, the other with rounded corners, on splayed legs, the undertiers with pierced galleries, stamped '1020', 22¾in (58cm) wide.
£900–1,100
€/ **$1,400–1,700** ➹ TRM

A mahogany two-tier table, with a drawer, originally a whatnot, c1830, 20in (51cm) wide.
£650–725
€/ **$1,000–1,150** ⊞ RPh

A mahogany and kingwood two-tier table, the inset marble top above a quarter-veneered stretcher shelf, on cabriole legs with sabots, French, 1850–75, 17in (43cm) diam.
£600–750
€/ **$1,000–1,200** ➹ NOA

A mahogany two-tier occasional table, c1890, 20in (51cm) wide.
£260–300
€/ **$400–475** ⊞ GBr

A mahogany and inlaid two-tier table, with a tray, c1890, 35in (89cm) wide.
£2,700–3,000
€/ **$4,250–4,750** ⊞ SAW

An inlaid walnut and kingwood two-tier table, French, late 19thC, 33in (84cm) wide.
£300–375
€/ **$475–600** ➹ SWO

▶ **An Edwardian inlaid rosewood two-tier table,** on square tapering legs, 24in (61cm) wide.
£140–175
€/ **$225–275** ➹ AMB

Work Tables

◀ **A George III satinwood work table,** by Gillows, Lancaster, with a frame for a workbasket, on square tapering legs, stamped 'Gillows, Lancaster', 19¼in (49cm) wide.
£4,500–5,500
€/ **$7,000–8,700** ➹ B(NW)
Designs for several similar tables normally described as 'work-bag tables' were drawn in Gillow's Estimate Sketch Books between 1793 and 1803. They were fitted with a frame under the drawer from which silk work bags were suspended. The escutcheon and knobs are in ivory and appear to be original. These knobs would have cost Gillows 4d each in 1798 and the lock 1s 2d. The total cost to Gillows in materials and labour for making a similar pieces (in satinwood with a mahogany top) was £2 7s 1/2d: the journeyman received one guinea. This piece too would originally have had a fitted work bag.

A Regency rosewood work table, the crossbanded ratcheted top over a side drawer and a silk-covered pull-out box, on swept legs with brass paw casters, 14¼in (36cm) wide.
£1,800–2,250
€/ **$2,850–3,550** ➹ SWO

◀ **A Regency mahogany Pembroke work table,** with dummy cupboard drawers, on square tapering legs with brass casters, 29in (73.5cm) wide.
£1,450–1,600
€/ **$2,300–2,500** ⊞ APO

◀ **A Regency mahogany Pembroke work table,** with a frieze drawer over a deep drawer with double dummy drawer front, 16in (40.5cm) wide.
£3,500–3,850
€/ **$5,500–6,000** ⊞ BERA

A Regency mahogany and inlaid workbox, the hinged lid with box stringing, enclosing an open interior above a material compartment, on a concave support with a platform base and four splayed tapering and inlaid legs with brass caps and casters, 16in (40.5cm) wide.
£1,100–1,400
€ / **$1,750–2,200** ➤ **TRM**

A mahogany Pembroke work table, with two small drawers and two opposing dummy drawers, a sliding work well, on turned and fluted legs with brass cup casters, early 19thC, 15¾in (40cm) wide.
£900–1,100
€ / **$1,400–1,700** ➤ **DMC**

An early Victorian mahogany work table, the baize-lined fold-over top above a frieze and an embroidered bag section, on column support with circular base and feet, 20in (51cm) wide.
£550–675
€ / **$870–1,000** ➤ **AMB**

A George IV mahogany bowfronted work table, with ebony stringing, the hinged top above three dummy drawers above a fitted drawer, all with turned rosewood knob handles with mother-of-pearl inlay, on ring-turned legs, 17in (43cm) wide.
£1,200–1,500
€ / **$2,000–2,400** ➤ **G(L)**

A bird's-eye maple work table, on a pedestal base, American, 19thC, 18in (45.5cm) wide.
£450–550
€ / **$710–870** ➤ **DuM**

A walnut drum work table, with gilt-bronze mounts, the galleried swivel top above a compartment with pendant piastre mounts and two apron drawers, on cabriole legs, Dutch, c1840, 12¼in (31cm) wide.
£3,000–3,500
€ / **$4,750–5,500** ➤ **S(O)**

A mahogany work table, on ring-turned tapering legs with brass casters, c1820, 29in (73.5cm) high.
£1,000–1,100
€ / **$1,600–1,750** ⊞ **JSt**

An early Victorian rosewood work table, with a fitted silk interior, 20in (51cm) wide.
£1,650–1,850
€ / **$2,600–3,000** ⊞ **RPh**

▶ **An early Victorian mahogany work table,** the moulded top over two drawers and a silk box, on turned tapering legs with brass caps and casters, 23in (58.5cm) wide.
£450–550
€ / **$700–900** ➤ **BR**

A mid-Victorian burr-walnut and marquetry work table, the moulded-edge top enclosing the original papered and satin-lined interior, on a carved socle, with carved cabriole legs and scroll feet, 18½in (47cm) wide.
£600–750
€ / **$1,000–1,200** ➤ **B**
This design is known as a 'trumpet table'.

A rosewood work table, the top inlaid with a chess board, above a frieze drawer, c1830, 18in (45.5cm) wide.
£1,500–1,650
€ / **$2,400–2,600** ⊞ **GBr**

A mahogany work table, on fret-cut trestle ends joined by turned balusters, c1840, 21in (53.5cm) wide.
£2,200–2,450
€ / **$3,500–3,900** ⊞ **RAN**

A Victorian walnut work table, the serpentine top above four drop finials, a conforming frieze drawer and separate satin-covered work slide, on pierced and scroll-carved supports, and four leaf-capped outswept legs with casters, 23¼in (59cm) wide.
£1,400–1,600
€ / **$2,200–2,500** ➤ **LJ**

FURNITURE

A walnut work and vanity table, with drawers, and a fitted interior with a mirror, c1890, 21in (53.5cm) wide.
£250–275
€ / $400–430 ⊞ PaA

▶ A Victorian mahogany work table, on a triform base, 29in (73.5cm) diam.
£800–900
€ / $1,250–1,400 ⊞ RPh
The basket is for holding balls of wool.

▶ An ebonized and parcel-gilt papier mâché work table, the serpentine hinged top with a fitted interior, on a baluster column, shaped platform and four scrolled feet, gilding rubbed, 19thC, 19in (48.5cm) wide.
£450–550
€ / $700–870 ⚒ JM

A Victorian mahogany work table, 30in (76cm) wide.
£1,200–1,325
€ / $1,900–2,100 ⊞ SAW

Papier mâché

Papier mâché, possibly first known in the Orient, but recorded in France in the mid-17th century, had reached England by 1672. Henry Clay (d.1812) patented a process of using heat to bond together sheets of prepared material (pulped paper, chalk and glue) which formed panels that could be japanned and had heat-resistant properties. These sheets were made into items of furniture, boxes, dishes and trays.

An Edwardian mahogany work table, the divided hinged top enclosing a silk-lined interior with a lift-out fitted drawer, the whole outlined with a satinwood band and boxwood stringing, on square tapering supports with spade feet, 15¾in (40cm) wide.
£500–600
€ / $800–950 ⚒ DD

A walnut sewing table, early 20thC, 36in (91.5cm) wide.
£800–900
€ / $1,250–1,450 ⊞ RPh

Writing Tables

A George II mahogany writing table, with a rising stationery compartment and ratchet adjustable writing slope, 30in (76cm) wide.
£3,500–4,500
€ / $5,500–7,000 ⚒ HYD

A George III acacia wood writing table, 30in (76cm) wide.
£3,500–4,000
€ / $5,500–6,300 ⊞ APO

◀ A George III mahogany harlequin writing table, with an adjustable writing slope, 25¾in (65.5cm) wide.
£3,000–3,500
€ / $4,750–5,500 ⚒ S(O)

▶ A George III mahogany writing table, with a divided drawer and secret drawer behind, 35¾in (91cm) wide.
£1,400–1,700
€ / $2,200–2,700 ⚒ B

A George III satinwood writing table, with an adjustable dual reading slope, 34in (86.5cm) wide.
£11,250–12,500
€ / $17,500–19,750 ⊞ CAT
The adjustable slope and the wood of which it is made makes this piece particularly desirable.

FURNITURE

A Regency amboyna writing table, with two drawers, 39in (99cm) wide.
£4,200–4,600
€/ **$6,650–7,300** ⊞ APO

A partners' mahogany writing table, c1840, 48in (122cm) wide.
£750–850
€/ **$1,200–1,350** ⊞ GBr

A Victorian walnut writing table, labelled 'Richardson of Hull', c1871, 45in (114.5cm) wide.
£4,700–5,200
€/ **$7,400–8,200** ⊞ SAW

A Victorian maple writing table, the leather-inset top above two frieze drawers, on moulded sleigh feet with brass casters, 50¾in (129cm) wide.
£700–850
€/ **$1,100–1,350** ⚒ CGC

An oak writing table, by Gillows, c1900, 36in (91.5cm) wide.
£500–565
€/ **$780–880** ⊞ WiB

A Biedermeier cherrywood writing table, the top inset with gilt-tooled leather, above a frieze with three drawers, northern European, early 19thC, 39½in (100.5cm) wide.
£1,000–1,250
€/ **$1,600–1,900** ⚒ NOA

An early Victorian mahogany writing table, the galleried top above five drawers, the kneehole with carved leaf brackets, fitted with later brass handles, 41¼in (105cm) wide.
£475–575
€/ **$750–900** ⚒ WW

A mahogany kidney-shaped writing table, French, c1880, 43in (109cm) wide.
£3,800–4,200
€/ **$6,000–6,600** ⊞ Che

A kingwood, rosewood and tulipwood writing table, the top inset with red gilt-tooled leather, on cabriole legs, French, 19thC, 66in (167.5cm) wide.
£5,500–6,500
€/ **$8,700–10,300** ⚒ HAM

A rosewood and marquetry writing table, gallery probably later, German, c1830, 41¼in (105cm) wide.
£2,800–3,200
€/ **$4,400–5,000** ⚒ S(O)

A walnut and marquetry writing table, the leather-lined top above a frieze drawer, labelled 'Edwards & Roberts', c1850, 52in (132cm) wide.
£5,300–6,250
€/ **$8,300–10,000** ⚒ S(O)
Edwards & Roberts were among the foremost English cabinet makers of the second half of the 19th century. Founded in London in 1845, the firm rapidly expanded and by 1854 was trading as 'Edwards & Roberts, Antique and Modern Cabinet Makers and Importers of Ancient Furniture'. The firm produced furniture of modern design, as well as copies of 18th- and early 19th-century English and French pieces. They also retailed a great deal of second-hand furniture, so the presence of a label does not necessarily mean that the item was actually made by the firm.

An satinwood inlaid writing table, with rosewood and mahogany bandings, lock stamped 'Deutsches 202324 Reichs-Patent' and signed, Dutch or German, early 20thC, 43¼in (110cm) wide.
£1,200–1,400
€/ **$2,000–2,200** ⚒ S(O)

◄ **A parquetry writing table,** signed 'Linke', French, c1920, 37in (94cm) wide.
£14,000–16,000
€/ **$22,000–25,000** ⊞ HA
François Linke (1855–1946) was one of the most popular French cabinet makers of his time. He specialized in copying Louis XV & XVI styles.

FURNITURE

Teapoys

A George III mahogany teapoy, the hinged cover enclosing a fitted interior, 15in (38cm) wide.
£2,000–2,200
€/ **$3,200–3,500** ⊞ RPh

A mahogany teapoy, inlaid with ebony, c1820, 29in (73.5cm) wide.
£1,500–1,700
€/ **$2,400–2,700** ⊞ BMi

A George IV mahogany teapoy, the hinged lid enclosing a fitted interior, on cast-brass paw feet with casters, 45in (114.5cm) wide.
£1,000–1,200
€/ **$1,600–1,900** ⚒ JAd

A George IV rosewood teapoy, the hinged lid enclosing two lidded lift-out caddies and a vacant recess, 14⅜in (37.5cm) wide.
£450–525
€/ **$710–830** ⚒ L

A William IV rosewood teapoy, the hinged top enclosing lidded compartments and apertures, 19¾in (50cm) wide.
£470–570
€/ **$740–900** ⚒ B(Ch)

◄ **A William IV rosewood teapoy,** the rising top enclosing two cylindrical caddies and two cut-glass bowls, the scrolled feet with recessed casters, 19¼in (49cm) wide.
£1,000–1,250
€/ **$1,600–1,900** ⚒ DN

► **A Victorian burr-walnut and walnut-veneered teapoy,** the hinged top enclosing two lidded compartments, 47¼in (120cm) high.
£675–820
€/ **$1,100–1,300** ⚒ SWO

Torchères

A carved mahogany torchère, with later gilt-brass gallery, on cabriole legs with claw-and-ball feet, c1760, 41¾in (106cm) high.
£7,000–8,500
€/ **$11,000–13,500** ⚒ S

A pair of giltwood torchères, the velvet-lined tops on open scrolled supports, labelled 'Edwards & Roberts', c1860, 34in (86.5cm) high.
£2,400–2,700
€/ **$3,800–4,300** ⚒ S(O)

A yew-veneered torchère, the top with a lift-out cover, on paw feet, 19thC, 43in (109cm) high.
£2,200–2,600
€/ **$3,500–4,000** ⚒ WW

A pair of George I-style green painted torchères, c1900, 37in (94cm) high.
£1,350–1,500
€/ **$2,000–2,400** ⊞ APO

FURNITURE

Towel Rails

A mahogany double-gate towel rail, on a stretchered platform and scroll feet, early 19thC, 33¾in (85.5cm) wide.
£280–350
€/ **$450–550** ⚒ WW

A walnut towel rail, with turned reeded supports, late 19thC, 25¾in (65.5cm) wide.
£100–120
€/ **$160–190** ⚒ SWO

A mahogany and boxwood-strung towel rail, the twin-facetted rails within a lyre-shaped support and panel sides, on splayed feet, late 19thC, 38½in (98cm) wide.
£200–240
€/ **$320–380** ⚒ BIG

Trays

A Regency period lacquer tray, on a later stand, c1810, 30in (76cm) wide.
£2,400–2,700
€/ **$3,800–4,300** ⊞ REI

A mahogany butler's tray, on a stand, 19thC, 22in (56cm) wide.
£400–450
€/ **$630–700** ⚒ S(O)

A mahogany butler's tray, on a later stand, 19thC, 30in (76cm) wide.
£180–225
€/ **$280–350** ⚒ B(Ba)

A mahogany butler's tray, with countersunk brass corners, on a later stand, 19thC, 32in (81.5cm) wide.
£765–900
€/ **$1,200–1,400** ⚒ S(O)

An ebonized tray, on a simulated walnut stand, late 19thC, 24¾in (63cm) wide.
£280–320
€/ **$440–500** ⚒ B(Ch)

A mahogany butler's tray, on a later folding stand, 19thC, 34¾in (88.5cm) wide.
£450–550
€/ **$700–850** ⚒ B(Ba)

◄ **A Sheraton revival decorated satinwood tray table,** c1900, 23in (58.5cm) diam.
£585–650
€/ **$900–1,000** ⊞ Che

► **An Edwardian satinwood tray table,** 27in (68.5cm) wide.
£400–450
€/ **$630–700** ⊞ RPh

Wall Brackets

A carved limewood and walnut wall bracket, modelled as a tapering cascade of flowers, hops, barley ears, pea-pods and a snail, surmounted by a shaped plateau with a leaf-carved edge above, 18thC, the plateau later, 15in (38cm) wide.
£1,300–1,600
€/ $2,000–2,500 ➢ TEN

A giltwood wall bracket, carved and pierced with C-scrolls and shells, 1750–1800, 13½in (34.5cm) high.
£800–950
€/ $1,250–1,500 ➢ S(O)

◄ **A pair of George III painted wall brackets,** with later decoration, 17¼in (44cm) wide.
£1,300–1,500
€/ $2,000–2,400 ➢ S(O)

A pair of giltwood and gesso wall brackets, c1830, 10¾in (27.5cm) wide.
£2,200–2,700
€/ $3,500–4,300 ➢ S(O)

A pair of gilt gesso and carved wood wall brackets, the D–shaped plateau tops with flower- and foliate-carved supports, 1850–75, 13½in (34.5cm) high.
£2,000–2,500
€/ $3,200–4,000 ➢ B

A Chinese Chippendale-style mahogany wall bracket, with a shaped frieze and pierced fret triform support, fret gallery damaged, late 19thC, 13in (33cm) wide.
£150–200
€/ $230–300 ➢ WW

A pair of carved mahogany wall brackets, in the shape of a ho-o bird on foliage, 1875–1925, 15¼in (38.5cm) high.
£340–425
€/ $550–670 ➢ SWO

Wardrobes

FURNITURE

A mahogany wardrobe, c1795, 97in (246.5cm) high.
£2,600–3,000
€ / **$4,000–4,750** ⊞ **Che**

A George IV mahogany wardrobe, the moulded cornice above a plain frieze and two drawers enclosing hanging space, modelled as two dummy cupboard doors and six short dummy drawers, above a single long drawer, on bracket feet, 61½in (156cm) wide.
£900–1,000
€ / **$1,400–1,600** ⚒ **CGC**

A George IV mahogany wardrobe, with three mirrored panelled doors

A late George III mahogany wardrobe, the scroll cresting with gilt-metal mounts, the frieze with chequered stringing, above two panelled doors, on splayed bracket feet, 50in (127cm) high.
£2,000–2,300
€ / **$3,200–3,600** ⚒ **G(L)**

An early Victorian mahogany wardrobe, the moulded cornice above six drawers, on a plinth base, 86¼in (219cm) wide.
£3,000–3,750
€ / **$4,750–6,000** ⚒ **B(L)**
The quality of the timber and construction, together with the recessed panelled frieze and rounded turned knobs, suggest the work of Gillows of Lancaster.

◄ **A mahogany wardrobe,** with three doors above two drawers, c1835, 82in (208.5cm) wide.
£1,650–1,800
€ / **$2,500–2,800** ⚒ **S(O)**

Auction or dealer?

When buying at auction, prices can be lower than those of a dealer, but a buyer's premium and VAT will be added to the hammer price. Equally, when selling at auction, commission, tax and photography charges will be deducted from the hammer price. Dealers will often restore pieces before putting them back on the market.

► **A mid-Victorian walnut wardrobe,** with two doors, 54in (137cm) wide.
£850–950
€ / **$1,350–1,500** ⊞ **HiA**

A Regency mahogany 'fiddleback' wardrobe, the two panelled doors with ebony beading, on flowerhead-carved scroll feet, 51½in (131cm) wide.
£900–1,100
€ / **$1,400–1,750** ⚒ **Bea**

An early Victorian mahogany-veneered inverted breakfront wardrobe, the central architectural pediment above six long drawers with turned wood handles, on a plinth base, 80½in (204.5cm) wide.
£550–625
€ / **$870–990** ⚒ **WW**

A figured mahogany and stencil-decorated wardrobe, the doors opening to a divided interior with a drawer, shelves and a hanging rail, minor patches and repairs to doors at hinges, American, New York, c1820, 54in (137cm) wide.
£16,000–20,000
€ / **$25,000–32,000** ⚒ **S(NY)**
The relatively small size of this wardrobe, the arcaded frieze, column supports and carved winged lion paw feet make this a perfect decorator's piece

An early Victorian mahogany inverted breakfront wardrobe, the centre with two arched panelled doors enclosing slides, flanked by panelled doors enclosing a hanging space, on a plinth base, 100¼in (254.5cm) wide.
£1,600–2,000
€ / **$2,500–3,200** ⚒ **AH**

◄ **A mahogany fitted wardrobe,** with three doors, c1860, 83in (211cm) wide.
£2,200–2,450
€ / **$3,500–3,900** ⊞ **MHA**

A late Victorian mahogany wardrobe, 55½in (141cm) wide.
£450–550
€ / **$700–870** ⚒ **B(Ba)**

FURNITURE

A Victorian lady's Biedermeier-style mahogany wardrobe/ linen cabinet, the top of convex stepped design on D-formed side quarters, the two figured mahogany doors with applied convex moulding, on squat circular feet, 45in (114.5cm) wide.
£420–520
€/ **$660–820** ➚ GAK

A Victorian mahogany wardrobe, the moulded cornice with ovolu banding, the two arched leaf-carved doors enclosing hanging space and drawers, on a plinth base, 59in (150cm) wide.
£800–950
€/ **$1,300–1,500** ➚ AH

▶ **A Victorian mahogany wardrobe,** on turned feet, 51¼in (130cm) wide.
£550–625
€/ **$870–990** ➚ JAd

◀ **A Victorian oak wardrobe/ compactum,** 82in (208.5cm) wide.
£900–1,000
€/ **$1,400–1,600** ⊞ WiB

A Victorian burr-walnut breakfront wardrobe, with a mirrored central door and two side doors, 76in (193cm) wide.
£2,000–2,300
€/ **$3,200–3,650** ⊞ RPh

A late Victorian satinbirch compactum, 107in (272cm) wide.
£280–320
€/ **$440–500** ➚ B(Ch)

A walnut and mahogany triple wardrobe, with hanging space, the single door enclosing three sliding trays above three small drawers, on a plinth base, c1900, 76½in (194cm) wide.
£420–500
€/ **$670–800** ➚ SWO

▶ **An Edwardian banded mahogany triple wardrobe,** with mirrored doors, and two hanging compartments, 72in (183cm) wide.
£765–850
€/ **$1,200–1,350** ⊞ PaA

An inlaid mahogany wardrobe, c1900, 73in (185.5cm) wide.
£3,800–4,250
€/ **$6,000–6,650** ⊞ MTay

A gentleman's walnut compactum, with two cupboard doors enclosing fitted pull-out hangers, with five graduated drawers below a cupboard door, the two lower section drawers on a plinth base, c1900, 66¼in (168.5cm) wide.
£420–520
€/ **$670–820** ➚ SWO

An Edwardian inlaid mahogany wardrobe, with mirrors, drawers and cupboards, 82in (208.5cm) wide.
£1,300–1,450
€/ **$2,000–2,300** ⊞ DUK

FURNITURE

Washstands

A George III mahogany washstand, the galleried lift-off top revealing apertures, above two cupboard doors, two frieze drawers and a deep drawer with dummy fronts, the square legs with an X-undertier, 17in (43cm) wide.
£450–550
€ / **$700–870** ⚘ WW

A mahogany washstand, the top enclosing a mirror and spaces for wash bowls, above a tambour compartment and drawer to the side, c1780, 20½in (52cm) wide.
£700–850
€ / **$1,100–1,400** ⚘ S(O)

A Regency Gillows-style mahogany washstand, the three-quarter gallery back with a shelf and applied rosette terminals to the side panels, over a marble top and single frieze drawer, on four turned reeded supports, with concave-fronted undertier and brass casters, 30¼in (77cm) wide.
£800–1,000
€ / **$1,300–1,600** ⚘ Bri

A George III mahogany enclosed washstand, with a tambour door, 22in (56cm) wide.
£1,100–1,200
€ / **$1,750–1,900** ⊞ WAW

A George III mahogany washstand, the crossbanded divided top opening to reveal a now vacant interior, fitted with a false drawer above a cupboard and two long drawers, 18in (45.5cm) wide.
£340–425
€ / **$550–675** ⚘ L

A walnut washstand, French, c1880, 32½in (82.5cm) wide.
£240–265
€ / **$380–415** ⊞ PaA

A George III mahogany enclosed washstand/ writing cabinet, the hinged top with fittings, above a slide with a baize-lined slope, and five drawers simulating nine drawers, with brass lion-mask handles, on square tapering legs with brass terminals and casters, 28in (71cm) wide.
£650–800
€ / **$1,000–1,300** ⚘ DN

A George III mahogany washstand, with a hinged splash-back, the tambour shutter door enclosing a pot cupboard, with one small drawer and two dummy drawers, 25in (63.5cm) wide.
£1,500–1,650
€ / **$2,350–2,550** ⊞ RGa

A Victorian washstand, with a marble top, 42in (106.5cm) wide.
£450–500
€ / **$700–800** ⊞ RPh

◄ **A mahogany washstand,** with a marble top, early 20thC, 41¾in (106cm) wide.
£150–180
€ / **$240–280** ⚘ B(Ba)

A George III mahogany enclosed washstand, the top rising to reveal a fitted interior with adjustable mirror and compartments with hinged covers, a slide and two small drawers under, with pierced foliate-carved corner brackets, and a shaped undertier, on straight legs, 24in (61cm) wide.
£400–475
€ / **$630–750** ⚘ E

A George III mahogany bowfronted corner washstand, the galleried back above three apertures, the central tier with a central drawer, on square outsplayed legs joined by an undertier, 22in (56cm) wide.
£300–375
€ / **$475–600** ⚘ DMC

A late Victorian/Edwardian mahogany washstand, the lift-up top with a dummy drawer enclosing a wash bowl and space for a toothbrush holder, over a single panel door, on a plinth base, 23½in (59.5cm) wide.
£100–120
€ / **$160–190** ⚘ BIG

Whatnots

A mahogany four-tier whatnot, with a drawer, c1780, 20in (51cm) wide.
£1,200–1,400
€/ **$1,900–2,200** ⚒ S(O)

A rosewood three-tier whatnot, on opposed baluster supports, a drawer to the base, on turned feet and casters, early 19thC, 16½in (42cm) wide.
£1,500–1,800
€/ **$2,400–2,850** ⚒ TEN

A rosewood three-tier whatnot, with centre drawer, c1825, 40in (101.5cm) high.
£4,200–4,600
€/ **$6,600–7,300** ⊞ F

A William IV rosewood four-tier whatnot, with a drawer to the base, 55in (139.5cm) high.
£2,400–2,650
€/ **$3,800–4,200** ⊞ MTay

A mahogany four-tier whatnot, with a fretwork galleried top, a drawer at the base, on turned legs, c1835, 55in (139.5cm) high.
£2,600–2,850
€/ **$4,100–4,500** ⊞ BERA

A rosewood three-tier whatnot, on barley-twist uprights, c1850, 15in (38cm) wide.
£2,000–2,250
€/ **$3,200–3,600** ⊞ RGa

A rosewood five-tier whatnot, with barley-twist uprights, mid-19thC, 34in (86.5cm) wide.
£600–680
€/ **$950–1,100** ⊞ HiA

A walnut four-tier whatnot, with serpentine outline and barley-twist uprights, c1850, 49in (124.5cm) high.
£1,100–1,250
€/ **$1,750–1,900** ⊞ MTay

A walnut three-tier whatnot, with ormolu mounts, c1860, 36in (91.5cm) high.
£2,200–2,400
€/ **$3,500–3,800** ⊞ SAW

▶ **A Victorian ebonized four-tier whatnot,** with burr-walnut banding, 26in (66cm) wide.
£260–300
€/ **$400–475** ⊞ PaA

A rosewood four-tier whatnot, 19thC, 19in (48.5cm) wide.
£1,000–1,150
€/ **$1,600–1,800** ⊞ SAW

A rosewood whatnot/ display cabinet, inlaid with brass stringing, with marble shelves, each tier on ring-turned supports, on short turned legs, French, c1880, 24in (61cm) wide.
£2,000–2,250
€/ **$3,200–3,500** ⊞ JC

FURNITURE

Window Seats

A mahogany window seat, c1770, 38¼in (97cm) wide.
£1,650–1,800
€/ **$2,500–2,800** ↗ S(O)

An oak window seat, on turned legs, c1870, 43in (109cm) wide.
£2,200–2,450
€/ **$3,500–3,800** ⊞ CAT

A turned and carved mahogany Sheraton-style window seat, the roll ends with turned giltwood bosses, c1900, 38in (96.5cm) wide.
£500–600
€/ **$800–950** ↗ NOA

A painted window seat, Italian, early 19thC, 28¾in (73cm) wide.
£900–1,100
€/ **$1,400–1,700** ↗ S(O)

A carved and turned oak window seat, late 19thC, 44in (112cm) wide.
£2,000–2,300
€/ **$3,200–3,600** ⊞ APO

A Regency Charles Tatham-style mahogany window seat, on rounded tapering legs, 59¾in (152cm) wide.
£3,800–4,750
€/ **$6,000–7,500** ↗ B
Charles Heathcote Tatham first published his design upon which this stool is based in his *Etchings of Ancient Ornamental Architecture* drawn from the originals in Rome and other parts of Italy during the years 1794–96. This book was tremendously popular, going into three editions by 1810, and was probably used by Thomas Hope in his *Household Furniture* of 1807.

A beechwood window seat, with carved frieze and turned legs, 1920s, 55in (140cm) wide.
£600–720
€/ **$950–1,100** ↗ SWO

◄ **An Edwardian mahogany and satinwood window seat,** on square-section legs with spade feet, 41in (104cm) wide.
£550–700
€/ **$870–1,100** ↗ B(Ch)

Wine Coolers

A Chippendale period mahogany wine cooler, with later stand, c1765, 22in (56cm) diam.
£6,000–7,000
€/ **$9,500–11,000** ⊞ REI

A late George III mahogany wine cooler, the hinged top opening to reveal a later tin liner, with brass-bound sides and carrying handles, the stand with cabriole legs and pad feet, restorations, some parts missing, 27¼in (69cm) diam.
£1,600–2,000
€/ **$2,500–3,200** ↗ B(Ch)

A George III inlaid mahogany cellaret, the legs with pierced spandrels, 21¼in (54cm) diam.
£1,200–1,500
€/ **$1,900–2,400** ↗ S(O)

Items in the Furniture section have been arranged in date order within each sub-section.

A George III mahogany cellaret, the concave-moulded and ebony-strung hinged lid enclosing an interior with nine compartments, the sides with carrying handles, on bracket feet with casters, 16¼in (41.5cm) wide.
£500–625
€ / **$800–1,000** ⚹ B&L

Ice houses

Since Roman times, beautiful wine coolers and the ice they contained were both symbols of status and wealth as a large staff was needed to make ice. In winter, vast quantities of blocks of ice were cut from the rivers or lakes on a country estate and then packed in straw in caves which would enable it to last until the summer. If there were no caves, an ice house was built with no windows, a very small door and a roof that overhung the walls to keep the sun off. This was lined with straw and then packed with ice in the winter. Many country houses still have ice houses which make very good tool sheds!

A mahogany cellaret, c1800, 20in (51cm) wide.
£1,450–1,600
€ / **$2,200–2,500** ⊞ Che

A late George III mahogany bowfronted cellaret, inlaid with boxwood stringing, 21½in (54.5cm) wide.
£200–250
€ / **$300–400** ⚹ L

A George III mahogany cellaret, outlined with satinwood and ebonized bandings, with two brass handles and an ivory escutcheon, on square tapering legs, 15in (38cm) wide.
£650–825
€ / **$1,000–1,300** ⚹ DD

A mahogany and boxwood-strung bowfronted cellaret, the lid enclosing a baize-lined interior, interior divisions missing, early 19thC, 20in (51cm) wide.
£1,000–1,250
€ / **$1,600–2,000** ⚹ DN

A mahogany butler's bowfronted cellaret, the hinged top enclosing lead-lined compartments, c1820, 38¼in (97cm) wide.
£2,500–3,000
€ / **$4,000–4,750** ⚹ S(O)

A George IV mahogany cellaret, the canted lid carved with fruit, enclosing a lead-lined interior, with lion-mask handles to either side of the base, on a moulded plinth and turned lotus-carved feet with casters, some damage, 30in (76cm) wide.
£1,400–1,700
€ / **$2,200–2,700** ⚹ TEN

A George IV mahogany sarcophagus-shaped cellaret, 36in (91.5cm) wide.
£2,600–3,000
€ / **$4,100–4,700** ⊞ WAW

◀ **A brass-bound mahogany wine cooler,** on turned tapering feet, c1835, 35¾in (91cm) wide.
£6,000–6,500
€ / **$9,500–10,500** ⚹ S(O)

A Victorian walnut wine cooler, with hinged top and brass finial and handle, 21in (53.5cm) high.
£750–900
€ / **$1,200–1,400** ⚹ BWL

FURNITURE

Campaign Furniture

An old copy of the The Army and Navy Stores' catalogue will show numerous items available at the end of the 19th century to ease the life of the soldier or traveller. Officers of the armed forces, who created the demand for this furniture were also conscious of the fashion of the day and this was reflected in the work of the cabinet makers they commissioned. Although most 18th-century campaign pieces are unattributable, designs for portable furniture are known by such recognized names as Chippendale or Sheraton. The end of the 18th century saw the rise of specialist makers of camp equipage with the names of Thomas Butler and Morgan & Sanders perhaps being the most recognized. The number of such specialists increased in the 19th century fuelled by military needs, the popularity of the Grand Tour and the increase of Europeans moving to the colonies. This demand for campaign furniture encouraged many makers to be inventive in their designs thus creating many unusual and interesting pieces.

Many of the original reasons for the popularity of campaign furniture hold true today. It is practical, versatile, and by definition very easy to move about. The fold-out bed is not a modern invention and its early 19th-century forebear is just as useful for that extra guest, although far more elegant. As you would expect, Georgian campaign furniture on the whole has a greater demand than Victorian for the same reasons that apply to antique furniture. However there are factors that break this basic rule of thumb: the ingenuity of design seen in the late 19th century is one, while a good maker's name on a piece is another. Although most furniture by Ross & Co of Dublin (see the chiffonier, cabinet, ballon-back chairs and mirror on the following pages) is typically Victorian, their name enjoys a very good reputation. They were the army's preferred suppliers in their day and have a good following among collectors. Provenance is also important and if an item's history can be traced it will have a bearing on its value.

The strength of campaign furniture in today's market can be put down to a number of reasons, some of which have already been mentioned. The recent publication of the first book on the subject, *British Campaign Furniture* by Nicholas Brawer, has increased awareness in this field and so created more collectors. However, perhaps the main reason for the renewed popularity of campaign furniture is one that is true right across the antiques world – if something is different to the norm it will be more sought after. **Sean Clarke**

A Regency mahogany and brass four-poster campaign bed, with brass plate engraved 'Butlers Patent, Catherine St', 58¾in (149cm) wide.
£2,500–3,200
€/ **$4,000–5,000** ⚱ B(Ba)

Items in the Campaign Furniture section have been arranged alphabetical order.

A mahogany campaign box, fittings missing, c1780, 6in (15cm) wide.
£25–30
€/ **$40–48** ⊞ MB

A mahogany and stained-pine campaign bookcase, the two sections joined by a piano hinge, the panelled doors enclosing three adjustable pine shelves, two short drawers with ivory knobs to one side of base, mid-19thC, 19¼in (49cm) wide.
£750–850
€/ **$1,100–1,400** ⊞ ChC

A mahogany portable campaign bookshelf, painted to resemble rosewood, early 19thC, 24in (61cm) wide.
£500–550
€/ **$800–870** ⊞ ChC
The simple but effective design of this type of campaign shelf ensured that they were made during most of the 19th century and into the 20th century. The three shelves are supported and divided by brass standards that have a steel rod running through them; this is held in place by decorative brass nuts to the top and bottom. The shelves could either be set on a surface, such as a campaign chest, or hung.

◀ **A mahogany campaign dispatch box,** the underside of the lid with a removable mahogany tablet containing a paper notepad, enclosing three divided sections for pens, mid-19thC, 9½in (24cm) wide.
£180–200
€/ **$280–320** ⊞ ChC

A mahogany and brass-bound campaign box, the hinged top centred by an inset brass plaque engraved 'A. D. B. Martinez' below a Maltese Cross surmounted by a coronet, on a later moulded stand, 19thC, 44½in (113cm) wide.
£4,000–5,000
€/ $6,300–8,000 ⚒ S

A camphorwood campaign writing box, with tambour top drawer, on a chamfered stand, 19thC, 18¾in (47.5cm) wide.
£320–400
€/ $500–600 ⚒ SWO

A mahogany campaign bureau, the fall-front enclosing a fitted interior with pigeonholes and four drawers, on a stand with square tapering legs, c1870, 27½in (70cm) wide.
£1,600–1,800
€/ $2,500–2,850 ⊞ ChC
For ease of transport the bureau section lifts off its stand. It is marked with a 'Colonel Kemp' stamp to the back of both sections, and although little is known of the Colonel it does highlight that the desk was made for military purposes.

A walnut campaign cabinet, by Ross & Co, the front and removable side mouldings of solid and veneered walnut, the sides, back and top painted black, 1850–75, 42in (106.5cm) wide.
£1,000–1,100
€/ $1,500–1,750 ⊞ ChC
The inside edge of the moulding has remnants of canvas glued to it and this, along with pinholes to the edges of each side of the cabinet, suggests that a length of material was fitted to the two mouldings to cover up the unsightly top and sides when set up. The cabinet has a Ross brass label and a paper label to the inside giving packing instructions. It can be seen from this label that it originally had a bookshelf super-structure, designed to be removed for transport. The label also gives instructions for packing four chairs and a couch into the carcass. The interior has two shelves. The bun feet unscrew for packing, and the iron fittings to the front edge of the top and bottom suggest that a protective cover would be fixed over the doors for travel.

A mahogany campaign chair, 1825–50.
£1,600–1,750
€/ $2,500–2,750 ⊞ ChC
This officer's armchair breaks down very quickly for packing. Unscrewing the arm bolts allows them to be removed and the hinged back to drop down against the back legs. The legs fold with a concertina action once the drop-in seat has been removed. The iron fittings to each leg were made to bear carrying struts to give the chair a further use.

A set of four Ross & Co walnut balloon-back campaign chairs, 1850–75.
£1,600–1,750
€/ $2,500–2,750 ⊞ ChC
This set of chairs was probably made to fit inside a chiffonier or other similar piece of cased furniture. The front legs unscrew from the seat and the back legs, which screw through the seat into the chairback, have an additional small thumb bolt to further secure them. Each piece is stamped with a number which corresponds to its position on the chair, thus ensuring that parts from one chair don't get mixed up with those from another. Two of the chairs have the brass Ross & Co label to the underside of the seat, and it is typical of the firm that not all chairs in a set would be labelled.

A Victorian mahogany campaign chest, with a hinged lid and base drawer, damaged, 22¾in (58cm) wide.
£85–110
€/ $135–175 ⚒ SWO

◄ A late George III mahogany campaign chair, with removable arms and inward-folding sides.
£500–625
€/ $800–1,000 ⚒ L

FURNITURE

A teak campaign chest of drawers, with two short over three long drawers, early 19thC, 35½in (90cm) wide.
£1,800–2,000
€/ **$2,850–3,200** ⊞ ChC
The use of teak suggests that this chest of drawers was either made or destined for use in the colonies, the oily nature of the wood being more resilient to the eastern climate. The upper section has a brass fitting to each side which houses a bolt that slides down to fix the two sections together. This system of locking the two parts of the chest together is relatively unusual, as is the fact that the base is fitted with steel threads to receive the removable feet.

A teak campaign chest, 19thC, 36in (91.5cm) wide.
£1,800–2,000
€/ **$2,850–3,200** ⊞ APO

Items in the Campaign Furniture section have been arranged in alphabetical order.

A teak campaign chest, 19thC, 39in (99cm) wide.
£2,200–2,400
€/ **$3,500–3,800** ⊞ SAW

A pine cupboard case for a campaign chest, with mahogany and satinwood door panels with brass knobs, early 19thC, 41½in (105.5cm) wide.
£1,800–2,000
€/ **$2,850–3,200** ⊞ ChC
Double cupboards such as this one, although very useable in their own right, are often associated with being made to contain a two-part chest. The Army and Navy catalogue describes them as 'Cases for Chest of Drawers'.

A mahogany campaign chest, c1870, 39in (99cm) wide.
£2,200–2,450
€/ **$3,500–3,800** ⊞ GBr

A black-painted pine campaign chest, by Hill & Millard, the upper section with iron handles and mounts, the panelled doors painted 'Captain Gerard, 23rd Regiment W. Fusiliers', late 19thC, 41½in (105.5cm) wide.
£600–750
€/ **$1,000–1,200** ⚒ HAM
Army General order 13(7) from 1879 specified that all packing cases of campaign furniture must have the owner's name and regiment marked on it. Army General order 131(D) from 1871 specified a maximum size for campaign chests of drawers of 42 x 24 x 24in (106.5 x 61 x 61cm), although there were always exceptions to the rules, especially among the wealthy officers.

A Victorian teak and brass-bound campaign chest, the fitted central secretaire drawer flanked by two short drawers, over three long drawers, on turned feet, 39in (99cm) wide.
£2,300–2,800
€/ **$3,600–4,400** ⚒ G(B)

A teak campaign secretaire chest, in two sections, the central secretaire compartment enclosing secret drawers, on detachable feet, label for Hill & Millard, London, c1878, 39in (99cm) wide.
£2,500–3,000
€/ **$4,000–4,750** ⚒ S(O)
Hill & Millard were upmarket military outfitters and trunk makers formed by John Hill and Richard Millard. In the London commercial directories from 1855 to 1865, the firm is recorded as 'military outfitters and trunk makers, 7 Duncannon St., Strand'.

A walnut campaign chiffonier, by Ross & Co, 1850–75, 44½in (113cm) wide.
£1,600–1,750
€/ **$2,500–2,750** ⊞ ChC

A brass, steel and bronze luggage stand, by Tonks of Birmingham, with X-frame supports, late 19thC, 21½in (54.5cm) wide.
£75–85
€/ $120–135 ⊞ ChC
When open, this folding rack forms a low table on which to rest a piece of luggage to raise it up to a more practical height. It also has the added advantage of keeping luggage off the ground in a country where it might be susceptible to vermin.

A mahogany campaign dining table, with two extra leaves, 1750–1800, 117in (297cm) extended.
£7,000–7,500
€/ $11,000–11,850 ⊞ ChC

A mahogany campaign Pembroke table/washstand, mid-19thC, 36¾in (93.5cm) wide.
£1,250–1,400
€/ $2,000–2,200 ⊞ ChC
The central, hinged section of the top is released by pressing a button concealed under one of the drop leaves. A mirror with adjustable angle is on the underside of the top, and the table well is fitted for a bowl, jug and soap dish, as well as having a drawer to one side. The turned table legs unscrew for carriage. These tables are sometimes referred to as 'ship tables'.

A mahogany collapsible campaign mirror, by Ross & Co, the base with a hinged three-position easel arm, maker's label, reverse of mirror plate inscribed 'March 1876', 11½in (29cm) wide.
£270–300
€/ $425–475 ⊞ ChC

A tortora wood campaign occasional table, on turned legs, New Zealand, c1860, 26in (66cm) wide.
£1,100–1,250
€/ $1,750–2,000 ⊞ ChC
Tortora wood, native to New Zealand, is a very striking timber with distinctive figuring and a colour similar to satinwood. The table was designed to fold away when not in use. A sprung ash bar underneath the top keeps the legs in place, and releasing the spring enables the legs to fold underneath the top.

A teak and brass-bound campaign trunk, c1800, 31in (78.5cm) wide.
£700–785
€/ $1,100–1,300 ⊞ GBr

▶ **A leather and iron-bound campaign trunk,** 1875–1925, 30in (76cm) wide.
£320–350
€/ $500–550 ⊞ ChC
The iron loops on the back of this trunk indicate that it was made to be strapped to a mule for transport.

A mahogany campaign card/tea table, 1790–1810, 33in (84cm) square.
£600–650
€/ $950–1,000 ⊞ ChC
The top of this table is hinged so that it can be opened out, like a standard tea table, to double its size. In order that both sides of the top are supported it is swiveled on its box to a right angle. In doing this the storage space for the turned beech legs is revealed.

A satinwood campaign writing table, c1910, 24in (61cm) wide.
£1,250–1,400
€/ $1,900–2,200 ⊞ RPh

A camphorwood campaign trunk, with brass corner brackets and carrying handles, 19thC, 41in (104cm) wide.
£300–375
€/ $475–600 ✗ HoG
Camphorwood was used in making this trunk because of its pungent smell which would discourage moths and other pests.

Oak & Country Furniture

During the last two and a half decades, we have seen the availability of good, unrestored oak furniture decline year by year. For example, 25 years ago we bought 30 good dressers a year, now it's two or three; similarly, then we bought ten good court cupboards, now it's one or two. Naturally, as the scarcity of these items increases, so does the value, a situation that attracts the forger. Almost every collection I value these days includes fake items and I am being offered more all the time. To avoid such pieces buy only from experienced specialist dealers with good reputations. If you want to see the best you must build up a relationship and keep in regular contact with them.

Recent downward trends in the stock market have created an atmosphere of unpredictability for investors. However, I think that they could do very well by investing in oak furniture which, providing they focus on the three most important criteria: condition, colour and patination, will stand them in good stead for the next 25 years. Early oak in good condition, with attractive colour and patination, is now rare and extremely desirable. Its track record speaks for itself.

The *Antiques Trade Gazette* recently reported that the housing market had outstripped furniture as an investment for the first time in 35 years; if the market begins to cool, as is now predicted, this leaves oak and country furniture looking good once again as a secure long-term investment.

Do not dismiss a piece you like because it has been restored. Bear in mind that nowadays the quality of restoration, with the use of recycled timber and the availability of original handles, hinges, etc, has enabled us to return many pieces of oak furniture back to the market place after being skillfully and sympathetically restored.

Always buy a piece because you like it, and you will enjoy it every day of your life. This way you will definitely get your money's worth. Treat the investment as the perk at the end of the day.

Paul Hopwell

Beds, Cradles & Daybeds

An oak cradle, 17thC, 36in (91.5cm) long.
£400–475
€/ **$630–750** ⚶ L

An oak cradle, 19thC and earlier, 46in (117cm) long.
£800–900
€/ **$1,250–1,450** ⊞ SeH

An oak bedstead, with a panelled tester on moulded and scroll-carved rails, the baluster front supports ending in a geometric-moulded triple-panel footboard, with shaped oak side panels, restored, German, early 18thC, footboard 61in (155cm) wide.
£4,750–5,750
€/ **$7,500–9,150** ⚶ S(O)

An oak cradle, the bonnet-shaped top over a scalloped frieze, on a rocking platform, 1725–50, 24½in (62cm) long.
£225–280
€/ **$350–450** ⚶ NOA

A carved oak daybed, with slatted base, c1880, 42in (106.5cm) wide.
£450–500
€/ **$700–800** ⊞ PaA

◄ **An oak daybed,** carved with figures and mythical beasts, late 19thC, 48in (122cm) wide.
£1,800–2,000
€/ **$2,850–3,200** ⊞ SeH

◀ **A carved chestnut bed,** with original carved side rails, Breton, c1900, 54in (137cm) wide.
£1,150–1,300
€/ **$1,750–2,000** ⊞ SWA

An oak country bed, French, c1900, 54in (137cm) wide.
£800–900
€/ **$1,250–1,400** ⊞ SeH

▶ **A carved oak bedstead,** with upholstered panels, Continental, c1900, 60in (152.5cm) wide.
£5,500–6,000
€/ **$8,750–9,500** ⊞ SeH

A country bedstead, French, c1900, 60in (152.5cm) wide.
£800–900
€/ **$1,250–1,400** ⊞ SeH

OAK & COUNTRY FURNITURE

Benches

17th-century oak benches, even if paired, seem to make only half the price of the equivalent joint stool because benches are not a convenient size for today's modern homes. They are difficult to sell, so any restoration will lower the price even further. A new top, for example, can reduce the value by 75 per cent, even for a pair. Continental benches are not as popular with the British market.

An oak bench, with a later top, 17thC, 66¼in (168.5cm) wide.
£650–775
€/ **$1,000–1,200** ⚒ SWO

▶ **A pair of fruitwood benches,** French, c1840, 94in (239cm) wide.
£1,250–1,400
€/ **$2,000–2,200** ⊞ DeG

Bookcases

A Regency oak bookcase, the moulded cornice over two Gothic arch astragal-glazed doors enclosing three adjustable shelves, the base with two panelled doors enclosing a single shelf, 50½in (128.5cm) wide.
£800–1,000
€/ **$1,250–1,500** ⚒ Bri

A Victorian Jacobean revival-style oak bookcase, the upper section with two arched shelf compartments flanked by fluted columns, the base with drawers and a cupboard, with all-over carving of human masks, scrolls and foliage, 59in (150cm) wide.
£900–1,100
€/ **$1,400–1,700** ⚒ JAd

A provincial Louis XV-style fruitwood bookcase, the two doors fitted with wire grilles, enclosing three shelves, French, 1850–75, 35½in (90cm) wide.
£830–1,000
€/ **$1,300–1,600** ⚒ NOA

An Edwardian oak bookcase, the moulded cornice above two astragal-glazed doors, the projecting base with two panelled doors, 39in (99cm) wide.
£550–650
€/ **$870–1,000** ⚒ DMC

For further information on oak and country furniture see the full range of Miller's books at
www.millers.uk.com

OAK & COUNTRY FURNITURE

Boxes

An oak writing box, with a single drawer, Low Countries, c1660, 16in (40.5cm) wide.
£700–775
€/ **$1,100–1,200** ⊞ **SEA**

A carved oak Bible box, with fitted interior and secret drawer, c1680, 23in (58.5cm) wide.
£1,400–1,550
€/ **$2,200–2,400** ⊞ **TRI**

An oak Bible box, with geometrical carving and outline, late 17thC, 21½in (54.5cm) wide.
£270–300
€/ **$425–475** ⊞ **CHAC**

An oak Bible box, the front carved with a bearded mask and scrolling flowers and foliage, 17thC, 30¾in (78cm) wide.
£240–300
€/ **$375–475** ⚒ **L**

An oak box, with iron banding, c1860, 70in (178cm) wide.
£180–200
€/ **$285–315** ⊞ **AL**

◀ **An oak candle box,** with cross-banding, c1780, 21in (53.5cm) high.
£240–265
€/ **$375–415** ⊞ **PaA**

Buffets

A provincial oak buffet, the top with canted corners and a moulded edge, above a central drawer over three cupboard doors with diamond-carved panels, on scrolling feet, Italian, 1775–1800, 62½in (159cm) wide.
£2,700–3,200
€/ **$4,250–5,000** ⚒ **NOA**

A carved oak sideboard, with a central drawer over two doors, French, mid-18thC, 41¾in (106cm) wide.
£2,400–3,000
€/ **$3,800–4,800** ⚒ **BERN**

A walnut *buffet à deux corps,* with four doors, French, Burgundy, early 19thC, 56in (142cm) wide.
£2,700–3,000
€/ **$4,250–5,000** ⊞ **MLL**

A Victorian carved oak three-tier buffet, 45in (114.5cm) wide.
£380–425
€/ **$600–670** ⊞ **PaA**

◀ **A walnut** *buffet à deux corps,* French, c1840, 59in (150cm) wide.
£3,200–3,500
€/ **$5,000–5,500** ⊞ **MHA**

A painted buffet, on knurl feet, French, 19thC, 50½in (128.5cm) wide.
£600–720
€/ **$1,000–1,150** ⚒ **B(Ba)**

Bureaux

A Queen Anne oak bureau, the fall-front enclosing a fitted interior with a well, above a frieze, with two short and two long drawers, on later bracket feet, maker's label 'John Gatehouse, Cabinet Maker, Nr. Holbourn Bridge, London', 30in (76cm) wide.
£1,700–2,200
€/ **$2,700–3,500** ↗ CHTR
John Gatehouse's trade label states that he sold '... all Sorts of Cabinet Work, viz Chests of Drawers, Book-cases, Cabinets, Scrutores; All Sorts of Glasses, Pier-Glasses, Chimney Glasses and Sconces; Also all Sorts of Joiners-Work; as Oval-Tables, Cane-Chairs etc.' He is listed in a 1695 directory of inhabitants of the parish of St Andrew, Holbourn.

An ash bureau, mid-18thC, 34in (86.5cm) wide.
£675–750
€/ **$1,000–1,200** ⊞ HiA

An oak, holly and bog oak bureau, with chequerbanded decoration, the fall-front enclosing a fitted interior with pigeonholes, drawers, a slide-concealed well, pilaster drawers and secret compartments, with original brass mounts, probably Cheshire, 1760–80, 36in (91.5cm) wide.
£6,000–7,200
€/ **$9,500–11,400** ⊞ RYA

◄ **A George III provincial oak bureau,** restored, 39in (99cm) wide.
£550–625
€/ **$870–990** ↗ B(Ba)

A George II oak bureau, the fall-front enclosing a stepped interior and a well, 32in (81.5cm) wide.
£650–750
€/ **$1,000–1,200** ↗ L

Items in the Oak & Country section have been arranged in date order within each sub-section.

A George III oak bureau, the fall-front enclosing a fitted interior, over two short and three long drawers with later brass handles and escutcheons, on bracket feet, 37½in (95.5cm) wide.
£1,100–1,300
€/ **$1,750–2,000** ↗ DN

Bureau Cabinets

Look carefully when you are buying a bureau cabinet. The top section could have been reduced and even if it is all original, check that it is well-proportioned. It will be a poor investment if extensive restoration has to be carried out.

A George III oak bureau cabinet, 33½in (85cm) wide.
£1,400–1,700
€/ **$2,200–2,700** ↗ L

► **A late George III oak bureau cabinet,** with later brass handles and escutcheons, feet possibly later, 34½in (87.5cm) wide.
£600–720
€/ **$1,000–1,150** ↗ DN

An oak bureau cabinet, c1780, 42in (106.5cm) wide.
£5,800–6,500
€/ **$9,000–10,250** ⊞ Che

Paul Hopwell Antiques

Early English Oak

Dressers, tables and chairs always in stock

A George II oak three drawer dresser base on baluster turned legs.
English   c1730

A bold George I oak single drawer
side table with barrel turned legs and
moulded 'H' stretcher.
English   c1725

A Charles II oak moulded chest
of drawers.
English   c1680

Paul Hopwell Antiques

An early
18th century
oak diaddarn.
Initials 'WE'.
Dated 1749

A Charles II oak coffer with
drawer, plank top and four carved
panelled front.
English   c1680

A Charles II oak coffer with
drawer, plank top and three
geometric moulded panels.
English   c1688

Furniture restoration service available
30 High Street, West Haddon, Northamptonshire NN6 7AP
Tel: 01788 510636   Fax: 01788 510044
Email: paulhopwell@antiqueoak.co.uk   Website: www.antiqueoak.co.uk

WE WISH TO BUY 17TH & 18TH CENTURY OAK FURNITURE

Chairs

An oak *caqueteuse* jointed armchair, with a wide seat and elbowed arms, Salisbury, 1580–1630.
£11,000–12,000
€/ **$17,500–19,000** ⊞ **KEY**
A *caqueteuse* is a type of chair with a tall back and widely splayed arms capable of accommodating the full dresses of ladies in the late 16thC.

An oak wainscot armchair, the panelled back with a moulded inset top-rail surmounted by a central fan-shaped fluted crest, the open-scrolled arms on turned supports, the moulded seat above a moulded seat-rail, on turned legs, early 17thC.
£900–1,100
€/ **$1,400–1,700** ⚒ **PF**

An oak wainscot open armchair, the ebony-inlaid top-rail above a carved panel back, with a later seat, 17thC.
£700–820
€/ **$1,100–1,300** ⚒ **AMB**

A carved oak chair, South Yorkshire, c1650.
£2,250–2,500
€/ **$3,500–4,000** ⊞ **SEA**

Wainscot chairs

Wainscot chairs have to be in good condition to reach their best price. Check the seat: if replaced the value will be reduced by half. Height is very important – low chairs reduce in value by approximately a third while those around 44in (112cm) high provide the best value. As a general rule 17th-century chairs are worth 30 per cent more than 18th-century examples.

An ash, elm and pine armchair, the cresting initialled 'IM', feet retipped, c1660.
£525–625
€/ **$850–1,000** ⚒ **S(O)**

An oak chair table, with a hinged plank table top, scroll-carved open arms, baluster ring-turned arm supports and front stretcher rail, with block-carved stretcher rails and legs, one arm damaged, 17thC.
£680–820
€/ **$1,000–1,300** ⚒ **TMA**

An elm dog-kennel dug-out armchair, with a pine seat and a painted surface, Cornwall, 1700–60.
£12,000–15,000
€/ **$19,000–24,000** ⊞ **RYA**
This chair was hewn from a single tree trunk and fitted with a plank seat. The owner has been unable to trace another example which incorporates a dog kennel.

An oak country chair, with later restorations and a pine seat, 1675–1725.
£380–425
€/ **$600–675** ⊞ **CHAC**

A black-painted maple armchair, with a rush seat, reduced in height, backrests repaired, American, New England, 1710–40.
£1,350–1,500
€/ **$2,100–2,400** ⚒ **S(NY)**

◀ **An elm commode,** with metal repairs, c1730.
£750–850
€/ **$1,180–1,300** ⊞ **TRI**

A yew wood armchair, with chequered frieze, on bobbin-turned legs, the cresting initialled and dated 'GB 1711'.
£4,200–5,000
€/ **$6,600–7,900** ⚒ **S(O)**

Robert Young Antiques

Fine Country Furniture & Folk Art

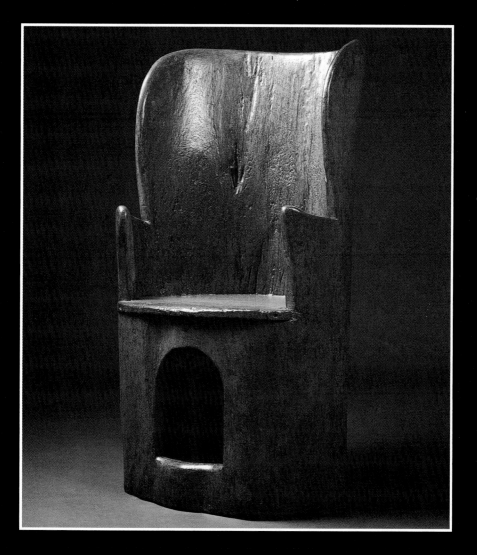

Robert and Josyane Young

68 Battersea Bridge Road, London SW11 3AG
Tel: 020 7228 7847   Fax: 020 7585 0489

ENTHUSIASTIC BUYERS OF FINE
COUNTRY FURNITURE AND FOLK ART

OAK & COUNTRY FURNITURE

A painted pine and oak primitive boarded Windsor chair, c1740.
£4,000–5,000
€ / **$6,350–7,900** ⊞ RYA

An oak country chair, with panelled back, with later alterations and restorations, mid-18thC.
£700–765
€ / **$1,100–1,900** ⊞ CHAC

A pair of Hepplewhite-style chairs, with rush seats, c1780.
£850–950
€ / **$1,300–1,500** ⊞ SEA

A yew, elm and fruitwood Windsor chair, with a pierced splat and saddle seat, on cabriole front legs, 18thC.
£1,600–1,900
€ / **$2,500–3,000** ⚒ G(L)

A fan-back Windsor armchair, both arm terminals repaired, American, Pennsylvania, late 18thC.
£2,500–2,750
€ / **$4,000–4,300** ⚒ S(NY)

An elm elbow chair, c1790.
£580–650
€ / **$900–1,000** ⊞ WELL

A painted chair, French, Provence, 18thC.
£400–450
€ / **$630–700** ⊞ SWN

A pair of painted Gustavian-style chairs, Swedish, late 18thC.
£1,500–1,650
€ / **$2,400–2,600** ⊞ CAV

◄ **An ash and elm tub chair,** East Anglian, early 19thC.
£300–360
€ / **$475–575** ⚒ S(O)

An oak lambing chair, the panelled winged back with arched top, the scrolled arms on baluster-turned supports, with a box seat and turned feet, 1775–1825.
£1,000–1,250
€ / **$1,600–2,000** ⚒ AH

An ash rocking chair, with a shaped top-rail, the high back with turned wing supports and turned twin spindle rails, with a rush seat, on turned front legs, North Country, early 19thC.
£200–240
€ / **$315–380** ⚒ TRM

Lambing chairs

Now is a good time to buy, as many lambing chairs are coming onto the market, perhaps due to the depressed state of farming. Tall chairs approximately 44in (112cm) high with large arms and big wings are the ones to look for. Chairs made in the 18th century make double their 19th-century equivalents.

An ash carver chair, with a ladder back, c1820.
£300–340
€ / **$475–550** ⊞ SWN

An elm and fruitwood Windsor elbow chair, the pierced vertical rails with central bosses, on a turned underframe, mid-19thC.
£260–320
€ / **$400–500** ⚒ BR

An oak *sugán* chair, Irish, Co Clare, c1860.
£70–80
€/ **$110–125** ⊞ **Byl**

A set of six Victorian Gothic-style oak chairs, with cane seats, repaired, c1880.
£325–360
€/ **$515–575** ⊞ **PaA**

A set of six Old Hickory-style chairs, with spindle backs and oak slat seats, American, early 20thC.
£2,800–3,200
€/ **$4,400–5,000** ⊞ **NART**

A set of six chestnut Breton chairs, each with a different carved scene on the back, c1900.
£1,200–1,300
€/ **$1,900–2,000** ⊞ **SWA**

A mahogany and elm **Darvel chair,** by Hugh Sheilds, the turned stick back with a curved top-rail and hoop elm arms, the solid seat on turned legs, Scottish, 19thC.
£300–375
€/ **$475–600** ⚲ **B(Ed)**
Hugh Sheilds was an inn keeper and wright in Newmilns, to the west of Darvel, Ayrshire. He trained with Darvel chair maker John McMath and developed his chair design, introducing elaborate stretchers for the early 19th century pattern. Darvel chairs by Hugh Sheilds usually have ten spindles (as opposed to 11 on earlier chairs) and are characteristically varnished with shellac, which gives them a distinguishing ginger colour. Like the early Darvel chairs, this example has spindles that were made using a rounding plane, not turned on a lathe. The peg housings were made using an auger, rather than a spoon bit, which accounts for the very thick seat slabs. Such a generous seat ensured that the leg sockets could be a good size without the risk of the lead screw piercing the surface of the seat. The use of mahogany for the seat is unusual; American birch seems to have been the standard timber employed for these chairs during the 19th century.

A set of four elm and ash primitive stick-back chairs, 19thC.
£1,100–1,200
€/ **$1,750–1,900** ⊞ **HiA**

A set of four ash and elm dining chairs, Irish, c1875.
£270–300
€/ **$425–475** ⊞ **Byl**

An oak, ash and sycamore stick-back chair, 1860–80.
£900–1,000
€/ **$1,400–1,600** ⊞ **SDA**

An oak wood-turner's chair, 19thC.
£320–350
€/ **$500–550** ⊞ **APO**

OAK & COUNTRY FURNITURE

Children's Chairs

A child's ash primitive stick-back Windsor armchair, c1790.
£1,150–1,275
€/ **$1,800–1,900** ⊞ **F&F**

A child's ash chair, with a later rush seat, c1825.
£450–500
€/ **$700–800** ⚒ **S(O)**

A child's armchair, with remains of original paint, Welsh, 19thC.
£400–440
€/ **$630–675** ⊞ **MFB**

A child's birchwood armchair, with a rush seat, French, c1850.
£270–300
€/ **$425–475** ⊞ **F&F**

A child's mahogany rocking commode chair, with hinged seat, 19thC.
£720–820
€/ **$1,100–1,300** ⚒ **AH**

A child's ash and elm training rocking chair, 1860–80.
£350–400
€/ **$550–630** ⊞ **SDA**

A child's oak chair, North Country, c1880.
£100–120
€/ **$160–190** ⊞ **WiB**

A child's ash and beech chair, c1900.
£120–135
€/ **$190–215** ⊞ **SDA**

Chests & Coffers

An oak chest, the hinged panelled lid enclosing a plain interior, the front with four linenfold panels and decorated lock plate, on block feet, key missing, French, 16th–17thC, 63in (160cm) wide.
£1,200–1,400
€/ **$1,900–2,200** ⚒ **S(Am)**

A walnut chip-carved coffer, with original paintwork, 1450–1500, 63in (160cm) wide.
£4,000–4,500
€/ **$6,300–7,200** ⊞ **NMA**

A panelled oak mule chest, with a carved frieze and two drawers with brass handles, c1615, 43¼in (110cm) wide.
£750–875
€/ **$1,200–1,400** ⚒ **GTH**

A storage box, with primitive decoration, early 17thC, 33in (84cm) wide.
£135–150
€/ **$215–235** ⊞ **CHAC**

A dower/mule chest, West Country, c1640, 48in (122cm) wide.
£2,500–3,000
€/ **$4,000–4,750** ⊞ **REF**

An oak chest, the triple-panelled hinged cover containing a candle box, the front carved with *guilloche* and arched ornament between panelled foliage, on square legs with block feet, cover initialled 'WL' and dated 1676, 48½in (123cm) wide.
£1,500–1,800
€/ **$2,350–2,850** ✗ WL

An oak coffer, the two-piece top with a moulded edge and original iron strap hinges, on a two-piece plain front and panelled sides, one end stile replaced, 17thC, 48½in (123cm) wide.
£350–425
€/ **$550–670** ✗ PFK

An oak coffer, with a plank top, 17thC, 52in (132cm) wide.
£450–525
€/ **$710–830** ✗ L

A carved oak coffer, the front with three architectural arched panels, with a carved frame and stiles, 17thC, 54¼in (138cm) wide.
£2,000–2,500
€/ **$3,200–4,000** ✗ SWO

An oak coffer, the domed plank lid with iron strap hinges, the panelled fascia with a lock plate, with panelled sides and moulded stiles, Continental, 17thC, 48in (122cm) wide.
£320–375
€/ **$500–590** ✗ AH

An elm chest, 17thC, 64½in (164cm) wide.
£500–550
€/ **$800–870** ✗ S(O)

An oak coffer, the hinged top with three panels above a front with a flute-moulded top-rail and two panels, iron lock, late 17thC, 48in (122cm) wide.
£900–1,100
€/ **$1,400–1,700** ✗ PF

An oak-planked coffer, late 17thC, 34in (86.5cm) wide.
£720–800
€/ **$1,150–1,250** ⊞ HiA

An oak coffer, with carved decoration, late 17thC, 56in (142cm) wide.
£1,500–1,650
€/ **$2,300–2,600** ⊞ KEY

An oak mule chest, the wire-hinged cover over a carved front with three panels over two drawers, early 18thC, 50½in (128.5cm) wide.
£1,200–1,400
€/ **$1,900–2,200** ✗ TMA

A carved cedarwood chest, carved 'ANO HOS 1710 KEG', lid now locked, Alpine, 1710, 20½in (52cm) wide.
£850–1,000
€/ **$1,350–1,580** ✗ S(O)

An oak coffer, with plank sides, late 17thC, 39½in (100.5cm) wide.
£220–250
€/ **$350–400** ✗ HOLL

◄ **An oak coffer,** c1720, 41in (104cm) wide.
£850–950
€/ **$1,350–1,500** ⊞ TDS

An oak coffer-on-stand, with four drawers, c1740, 36¾in (93.5cm) wide.
£800–1,000
€/ **$1,250–1,600** ✗ S(O)

OAK & COUNTRY FURNITURE

A Georgian fruitwood coffer, with domed lid, original handles and lock, 33in (84cm) wide.
£1,150–1,300
€/ $1,800–2,000 ⊞ APO

A carved and panelled oak coffer, 18thC, 45in (114.5cm) wide.
£500–550
€/ $800–870 ⊞ HiA

An oak coffer, the three-quarter hinged top above a plain front with a brass keyplate, on a shaped plinth, Welsh, late 18thC, 26in (66cm) wide.
£375–450
€/ $590–710 ✗ PF

An elm dowry chest, Irish, c1865, 48in (122cm) wide.
£550–600
€/ $870–950 ⊞ Byl

A George III oak and mahogany-banded mule chest, the lift-up top above four fielded panels, with two drawers below with brass escutcheons and swing handles, on shaped bracket feet, 54¼in (138cm) wide.
£350–425
€/ $550–670 ✗ M

An elm coffer, 18thC and later, 39½in (100.5cm) wide.
£160–200
€/ $250–300 ✗ B(Ba)

A painted walnut chest, the front with three fielded panels, c1830, 46in (117cm) wide.
£800–900
€/ $1,250–1,450 ⊞ DMe

An oak and iron-bound chest, c1870, 38in (96.5cm) wide.
£350–400
€/ $550–630 ⊞ GBr

◄ **A late Victorian carved oak coffer,** the front with three panels, 42in (106.5cm) wide.
£200–225
€/ $300–350 ⊞ PaA

An oak coffer, 18thC, 44in (112cm) wide.
£700–800
€/ $1,100–1,250 ⊞ MHA

An oak coffer, the front with three carved panels, on bracket feet, repaired, late 18thC, 48in (122cm) wide.
£280–320
€/ $440–500 ⊞ PaA

A leather and brass-studded marriage chest, probably Flemish or Dutch, c1830, 40in (101.5cm) wide.
£1,200–1,400
€/ $1,900–2,200 ⊞ REF

A painted elm mule chest, with dummy drawers above a single long drawer, Irish, Co Kilkenny, c1870, 44in (112cm) wide.
£1,100–1,200
€/ $1,750–1,900 ⊞ DMe

An elm six-plank coffer, 19thC, 46½in (118cm) wide.
£230–275
€/ $360–430 ✗ SWO

Chests of Drawers

An oak chest of drawers, with panelled sides, the four drawers with panelled fronts, on later bracket feet, 17thC, 41in (104cm) wide.
£650–750
€/ $1,000–1,200 ➤ E

An oak chest of drawers, with four moulded drawers, on bracket feet, early 17thC and later, 37in (94cm) wide.
£400–500
€/ $630–790 ➤ GAK

An oak chest of drawers, with four long drawers, raised on later elm bun feet, 17thC, 37½in (95.5cm) wide.
£1,300–1,500
€/ $2,000–2,400 ➤ AMB

An oak chest of drawers, on later bracket feet, late 17thC, 37¾in (96cm) wide.
£850–1,000
€/ $1,350–1,600 ➤ S(O)

A panelled oak chest of drawers, the upper section with two short and two deep inlaid drawers flanking a conforming door, the lower section with two geometrically panelled long drawers, on later bun feet, alterations, late 17thC, 44in (112cm) wide.
£1,000–1,100
€/ $1,600–1,700 ➤ Bea

An oak chest of drawers, the moulded top above four geometrically moulded drawers, with panelled ends, on stile feet, drawer linings replaced, late 17thC, 29½in (75cm) wide.
£950–1,100
€/ $1,500–1,700 ➤ HAM

An oak geometrically moulded chest of drawers, with two short and three long graduated drawers, with split-baluster pilaster spindles, with later top and panelled ends, late 17thC, 41¼in (105cm) wide.
£950–1,100
€/ $1,500–1,700 ➤ B(NW)

A carved and painted chest of three drawers, probably walnut, Italian, Piedmonte, c1740, 43in (109cm) wide.
£20,000–22,000
€/ $32,500–35,000 ⊞ RYA
This piece retains its original paint and metalwork and is of extremely good proportions.

A panelled oak and pine chest of drawers, restored, American, Massachusetts, c1700, 37½in (95.5cm) wide.
£2,200–2,500
€/ $3,500–4,000 ➤ S(NY)

LOCATE THE SOURCE

The source of each illustration in Miller's can be found by checking the code letters below each caption with the Key to Illustrations, pages 794–800.

▶ **A George III oak chest of drawers,** on ogee bracket feet, originally surmounted by a screw-press, 33in (84cm) wide.
£550–650
€/ $870–1,000 ➤ L

A George III oak and mahogany crossbanded chest of drawers, with two short and three long drawers flanked by reeded pilasters, on bracket feet, formerly the top part of a chest-on-chest, 43¾in (111cm) wide.
£470–570
€ / **$750–900** ✗ DN

◄ **A Chippendale-style figured cherrywood chest of drawers,** with original cast-brass handles, restorations to base, American, probably Connecticut, c1780, 38¼in (97cm) wide.
£1,250–1,500
€ / **$1,900–2,400** ✗ S(NY)

A provincial oak chest of drawers, in two sections, restored, 18thC, 43¾in (111cm) wide.
£280–340
€ / **$440–540** ✗ B(Ch)

An oak chest of drawers, with two short and three long geometrically moulded drawers, with panelled sides, on block feet, 18thC, 36¼in (92cm) wide.
£475–575
€ / **$750–900** ✗ B(W)

An oak bowfronted corner chest of drawers, the moulded top above two short and two long drawers, Dutch, 18thC, 29¼in (74.5cm) wide.
£5,000–6,000
€ / **$7,900–9,500** ✗ S(O)

A pair of inlaid oak commodes, Continental, c1800, 53in (134.5cm) wide.
£7,500–8,500
€ / **$11,750–13,500** ⊞ APO

OAK & COUNTRY FURNITURE

OAK & COUNTRY FURNITURE

◄ An oak chest of drawers, on ogee bracket feet, c1800, 47in (119.5cm) wide.
£550–600
€/ **$850–950** ⊞ **PaA**

A late George III provincial oak chest of drawers, with mahogany crossbanding, restorations and alterations, 43in (109cm) wide.
£320–375
€/ **$500–590** ⚒ **B(Ba)**

► A Victorian pollarded oak chest, the rounded top above a panelled frieze drawer, over two short and three long drawers, on bun feet, 44in (112cm) wide.
£550–625
€/ **$870–990** ⚒ **BR**

An elm dowry chest-on-stand, the upper section with six dummy drawers, the lower section with two short drawers over one long drawer, with brass plaque inscribed 'Margaret Coonan', Irish, Co. Kilkenny, c1840, 49in (124.5cm) wide.
£800–900
€/ **$1,250–1,400** ⊞ **HON**

Chests-on-Chests

◄ A George III oak chest-on-chest, the upper section with a moulded Greek key cornice, above two short and three long graduated cock-beaded drawers, flanked by canted corners, the base with three long graduated cock-beaded drawers, all with brass drop handles with foliate backplates, on bracket feet, 42in (106.5cm) wide.
£1,100–1,400
€/ **$1,750–2,200** ⚒ **Mit**

A mid-Georgian oak chest-on-chest, on bracket feet, with later wooden knob handles, lower section possibly shortened, 40¼in (102cm) wide.
£650–750
€/ **$1,000–1,200** ⚒ **PFK**

A George III provincial oak and mahogany chest-on-chest, restored, 45in (114.5cm) wide.
£2,000–2,250
€/ **$3,150–3,500** ⚒ **B(Ba)**

Items in the Oak & Country section have been arranged in date order within each sub-section.

Chests-on-Stands

An oak chest-on-stand, with two short and two long drawers, on a later stand, 17thC, 37½in (95.5cm) wide.
£700–820
€/ **$1,100–1,300** ⚒ **B(W)**

► A William and Mary oak chest-on-stand, alterations and restorations, 37¾in (96cm) wide.
£780–875
€/ **$1,200–1,400** ⚒ **B(Ba)**

An oak chest-on-stand, the two short and three long drawers with brass drop handles, the stand with turned legs, late 17thC, 38in (96.5cm) wide.
£2,000–2,250
€/ **$3,150–3,500** ⚒ **JNic**

A George I oak chest-on-stand, with two short and five long drawers, on later pad feet, 41¼in (105cm) wide.
£1,800–2,150
€/ **$2,850–3,400** ⚷ **SWO**

▶ **A Georgian oak chest-on-stand,** the top with a plain cornice and fluted chamfered corners, above two short and three long drawers, the base with three frieze drawers, on cabriole legs, 37¾in (96cm) wide.
£1,300–1,500
€/ **$2,000–2,400** ⚷ **B&L**

An oak and walnut-cross-banded chest-on-stand, c1740, 40¼in (102cm) wide.
£2,200–2,500
€/ **$3,500–4,000** ⚷ **S(O)**

A George III oak chest-on-stand, with two short and four long drawers, the later stand with a shaped apron, on cabriole legs, 37½in (95.5cm) wide.
£900–1,100
€/ **$1,400–1,750** ⚷ **L**

▶ **A Carolean-style oak chest-on-stand,** with geometric mitred drawer fronts, the upper section with two deep drawers, above a projecting base with a single drawer, on stile feet, c1900, 32in (81.5cm) wide.
£350–400
€/ **$550–630** ⚷ **BR**

A provincial oak chest-on-stand, on later feet, restorations, alterations, 18thC, 39½in (100.5cm) wide.
£600–700
€/ **$950–1,100** ⚷ **B(Ba)**

OAK & COUNTRY FURNITURE

Clothes & Linen Presses

A George III oak linen press, the moulded cornice with plain mahogany frieze, above two arch-panelled press doors, over two short and two long drawers, with a serpentine apron and bracket feet, 54in (137cm) wide.
£900–1,100
€/ **$1,400–1,700** ⚷ **B(W)**

▶ **An early Victorian oak linen press,** the applied reeded-edge top above slides and a cupboard enclosed by three doors with outline panels and reeded stiles, the base with two drawers, on turned feet, 68½in (174cm) wide.
£650–750
€/ **$1,000–1,200** ⚷ **WW**

A George III oak linen chest-on-stand, with brass carrying handles, 44½in (113cm) wide.
£850–1,000
€/ **$1,350–1,600** ⚷ **B(Ba)**

A George III oak linen press, 49in (124.5cm) wide.
£1,800–2,000
€/ **$2,800–3,200** ⊞ **APO**

A George III oak linen press, with later interior shelf, 54½in (138.5cm) wide.
£1,200–1,400
€/ **$1,900–2,200** ⚷ **L**

A Gothic revival oak linen press, late 19thC, 47in (119.5cm) wide.
£2,000–2,300
€/ **$3,200–3,650** ⊞ **WAW**

Cupboards

A Charles II oak cupboard, adapted from a larger piece, 35½in (90cm) wide.
£1,100–1,250
€/ $1,700–2,000 ✗ S(O)

An oak food cupboard, with wainscot-panelled door, c1690, 36in (91.5cm) wide.
£5,000–6,000
€/ $8,000–9,500 ⊞ PHA

An oak mural livery cupboard, with yew spindles, mid-17thC, 41in (104cm) wide.
£4,700–5,200
€/ $7,500–8,200 ⊞ KEY

An oak livery cupboard, the moulded-edge plank top above a lunette-carved frieze, and panelled fascia with a central door, on turned and block supports, 17thC, 38½in (98cm) wide.
£1,300–1,500
€/ $2,000–2,400 ✗ AH

◄ **An oak cupboard,** the top above a plain frieze and panelled door, enclosing shelves, flanked by ribbed pilasters, on sledge feet, restorations, Dutch, 17thC and later, 31in (78.5cm) wide.
£450–550
€/ $700–870 ✗ S(Am)

An oak cupboard, with pierced sides, 17thC, 51¾in (131.5cm) wide.
£1,500–1,800
€/ $2,400–2,850 ✗ L

An oak cabinet-on-stand, with the date 1703 carved on the doors, c1703, 42½in (108cm) wide.
£2,200–2,375
€/ $3,500–3,700 ⊞ CHAC

A carved oak cupboard, Flemish, 17thC, 58in (147.5cm) wide.
£7,000–8,000
€/ $11,000–12,500 ⊞ APO

An oak press cupboard, the carved frieze with turned pendants, above two carved cupboard doors flanking a panel, with flowerhead-centred *guilloche*-carved stiles, and foliate-carved end stiles, the lower section with a moulded top above a foliate and pokerwork frieze, with two panelled doors, the moulded end stiles extending as legs, boarded top replaced, later shelf, 17thC and later, 61in (155cm) wide.
£1,600–2,000
€/ $2,500–3,200 ✗ PFK

◄ **A Queen Anne oak cupboard,** the interior with two shaped shelves and four folio dividers, with later top and feet, formerly the upper section of a larger item, 38¼in (97cm) wide.
£600–720
€/ $950–1,150 ✗ S(O)

An elm wall-hanging corner cupboard, c1720, 33in (84cm) wide.
£1,500–1,800
€/ **$2,400–2,800** ⊞ RYA

LOCATE THE SOURCE
The source of each illustration in Miller's can be found by checking the code letters below each caption with the Key to Illustrations, pages 794–800.

▶ **An oak cupboard,** the moulded cornice above two raised and fielded panel doors, the slightly projecting base with three raised and fielded panels, on stile supports, early 18thC, 51¼in (130cm) wide.
£600–700
€/ **$950–1,100** ⚒ DD

An oak corner cupboard, the panelled door enclosing shelves, early 18thC, 30in (76cm) wide.
£280–320
€/ **$440–500** ⚒ DN

▶ **A carved elm armoire,** French, c1750, 86in (218.5cm) high.
£4,500–5,000
€/ **$7,000–8,000** ⊞ TDS

A yew wood and cherrywood armoire, French, c1760, 91in (231cm) high.
£3,500–4,000
€/ **$5,500–6,300** ⊞ TDS

An oak press cupboard, the top section with Gothic-shaped fielded panels, over a base with three drawers, Welsh, Meirionnydd, c1760, 42in (106.5cm) wide.
£5,000–6,000
€/ **$8,000–9,500** ⊞ CoA

An oak wall cupboard, with a single three-panel door, Welsh, 1760–80, 27in (68.5cm) wide.
£1,750–2,000
€/ **$2,700–3,200** ⊞ KEY

An oak hanging corner cabinet, with a moulded shaped door, 1770, 26in (66cm) wide.
£315–350
€/ **$480–550** ⊞ PaA

A mid-Georgian oak hanging cupboard, with a drawer to the base, 24in (61cm) wide.
£500–600
€/ $800–950 🔨 L

◀ **An oak and pine bread and cheese cupboard,** with three internal shelves and two drawers, the upper double doors with spindle ventilation, Welsh, Anglesey, c1780, 73½in (186.5cm) high.
£5,300–6,000
€/ $8,300–9,500
⊞ MFB

A painted chestnut armoire, c1780, 49½in (125.5cm) wide.
£1,300–1,450
€/ $2,000–2,300 ⊞ SIE

An oak livery cupboard, c1790, 51in (129.5cm) wide.
£2,250–2,500
€/ $3,500–4,000 ⊞ NoC

An oak housekeeper's cupboard, c1790, 56in (142cm) wide.
£2,800–3,250
€/ $4,400–5,000 ⊞ WELL

A George III oak and mahogany crossbanded corner cupboard, the doors with moulded panels, with inlaid ivory lock escutcheons and reeded sides, 41in (104cm) high.
£400–500
€/ $650–790 🔨 HOLL

A cherrywood armoire, with brass hinges and lock, French, 18thC, 52in (132cm) wide.
£1,500–1,700
€/ $2,400–2,700 ⊞ DUK

A provincial chestnut cabinet, the moulded cornice enclosed by a fielded panel door with a drawer below, on turned legs, with gallery base and slat foot, French, 18thC, 24½in (62cm) wide.
£250–300
€/ $400–475 🔨 TRM

◀ **An oak press cupboard,** the two doors over three short and two long drawers, late 18thC, 51in (129.5cm) wide.
£1,000–1,100
€/ $1,600–1,750 ⊞ WAW

◀ **An oak and mahogany corner cupboard,** c1790, 31in (78.5cm) wide.
£1,000–1,125
€/ $1,600–1,800 ⊞ MHA

A George III oak cupboard, the upper section with crossbanded doors, 54in (137cm) wide.
£800–950
€/ $1,250–1,500 🔨 L

◀ **A George III oak corner cupboard,** the bowfront enclosed by solid doors with mahogany crossbanding, with a shaped apron, 26¼in (66.5cm) wide.
£300–350
€/ $475–550 🔨 L

A fruitwood armoire, the door panels carved with birds, French, c1800, 51in (129.5cm) wide.
£5,500–6,200
€ / **$8,500–9,800** ⊞ HA

A George IV oak and mahogany-crossbanded cabinet-on-chest, the stepped cornice and inlaid frieze above two panelled cupboard doors enclosing three shelves, the lower section with two short and three long graduated cockbeaded drawers with ivory lozenge escutcheons, on a shaped apron and short splayed feet, probably Welsh, 48in (122cm) wide.
£1,200–1,400
€ / **$1,900–2,200** ⚒ WL

A fruitwood cupboard, with solid panel doors, French, 19thC, 44in (112cm) wide.
£300–350
€ / **$475–550** ⚒ B(Ba)

A neo-classical oak cabinet, the arched pediment carved with an urn and foliage above a plain frieze and two panelled doors flanked by columns, the lower section with three long drawers flanked by fluted pilasters, on square fluted tapering feet, Dutch, c1800, 67in (170cm) wide.
£1,500–1,800
€ / **$2,400–2,800** ⚒ S(Am)

A chestnut armoire, French, c1830, 57in (145cm) wide.
£1,450–1,600
€ / **$2,250–2,500** ⊞ GD

A Gothic-style oak side cabinet, with brass strapwork mounts and *guilloche* and roundel embossed panels, c1875, 40in (101.5cm) wide.
£1,800–2,000
€ / **$2,800–3,200** ⊞ NAW

An oak cupboard, with blind and fielded panels, the base with a fall-front and two secret drawers, Welsh, c1800, 40in (101.5cm) wide.
£7,000–8,000
€ / **$11,000–12,500** ⊞ PHA

A Louis XV provincial fruitwood armoire, the moulded cornice above two doors, with shaped panels, a scalloped apron below, on scrolled toes, French, 1800–25, 74½in (189cm) wide.
£2,300–2,750
€ / **$3,600–4,300** ⚒ NOA

A carved oak hall cupboard, the top with a carved boar's head, German, 19thC, 99in (251.5cm) high.
£1,100–1,200
€ / **$1,750–1,900** ⊞ HiA

▶ **A carved chestnut food cupboard,** Breton, c1900, 39in (99cm) wide.
£1,100–1,200
€ / **$1,750–1,900** ⊞ SWA

An oak and pine panelled food cupboard, with a moulded cornice, the two doors with pierced central panels, with two drawers and two doors below, on bracket feet, early 19thC, 42½in (108cm) wide.
£1,600–2,000
€ / **$2,500–3,200** ⚒ Bea(E)

An oak double corner cupboard, the moulded cornice above a glazed door enclosing shelves, the lower section with two arched panelled doors, with canted angles, on a shaped plinth, Welsh, mid-19thC, 37in (94cm) wide.
£900–1,100
€ / **$1,400–1,700** ⚒ PF

OAK & COUNTRY FURNITURE

Spice Cupboards

An oak spice cupboard, 17thC, 15in (38cm) wide.
£1,350–1,500
€/ $2,100–2,400 ⊞ SEA

An inlaid oak spice cupboard, the five short drawers with ring handles, c1700, 14½in (36.5cm) wide.
£320–375
€/ $500–590 ⚲ TEN

An oak wall-hanging spice cupboard, the fielded panel door enclosing a fitted interior, the drawers with paper spice labels and later handles, c1780, 22in (56cm) wide.
£1,000–1,200
€/ $1,600–1,900 ⚲ S(O)
Spices and herbs were used extensively from the Middle Ages to either add flavour to unexciting food or disguise tainted meat and game.

Desks

An oak writing desk, the fall-front enclosing an interior with a lidded well and open compartments, on turned fluted legs, c1720, 28¼in (72cm) wide.
£1,500–1,800
€/ $2,400–2,800 ⚲ S(O)

Further reading
Miller's Pine & Country Furniture Buyer's Guide, Miller's Publications, 1995

A Victorian carved oak kneehole desk, on bobbin-turned legs, 31in (78.5cm) wide.
£350–400
€/ $550–650 ⊞ PaA

▶ **A Victorian carved oak pedestal desk,** with three frieze drawers and six pedestal drawers, 48in (122cm) wide.
£300–350
€/ $475–550 ⚲ SWO

A Victorian oak writing desk, by John Taylor & Son, Edinburgh, the leather-inset top fitted with a leather inset slide, with one central drawer and four short drawers, on reeded leg with casters, one drawer stamped, Scottish, 48in (122cm) wide.
£1,000–1,250
€/ $1,600–2,000 ⚲ B(W)

Dough Bins

An elm dough bin, with a hinged plank lid, on baluster-turned and block legs and turned feet, 18thC, 36½in (92.5cm) wide.
£475–575
€/ $750–910 ⚲ AH

An elm dough bin, on turned legs, 18thC, 24in (61cm) wide.
£550–600
€/ $870–950 ⊞ SWN

A provincial fruitwood dough table, the removable planked top revealing a dough bin, on square legs, now altered to coffee table height, French, mid-19thC, 48in (122cm) wide
£700–800
€/ $1,100–1,300 ⚲ NOA

To order Miller's books in the USA please ring AOL/Time Warner on 1-800-759-0190

Dressers

A George II oak dresser, Welsh, 55½in (141cm) wide.
£4,250–5,000
€/ $6,700–7,900 ✠ S(O)

An early George III oak dresser, with a boarded rack and three frieze drawers, on low ogee bracket feet, Welsh, 73½in (186.5cm) wide.
£9,500–11,500
€/ $15,000–18,000 ✠ B(SW)

◄ An oak dresser, with original brass handles, Welsh, 1760–80, 63in (160cm) wide.
£8,750–9,750
€/ $14,000–15,500 ⊞ NMA

► A George III oak dresser, with mahogany banding and brass drop handles, 62in (157.5cm) wide.
£2,300–2,800
€/ $3,650–4,500 ✠ AH

An oak pot board dresser, Welsh, Cardiganshire, c1760, 74in (188cm) wide.
£7,000–7,800
€/ $11,000–12,500 ⊞ CoA

An oak pot board dresser, Welsh, Carmarthenshire, 1780, 72in (183cm) wide.
£8,500–9,500
€/ $13,500–15,000 ⊞ CoA

An oak dresser, with stained-pine back boards and baseboard, Welsh, c1780, 63¾in (162cm) wide.
£2,200–2,500
€/ $3,500–4,000 ✠ S(O)

n oak dresser, with a boarded rack, on square legs with a pot board base, 18thC, 53in (134.5cm) wide.
£4,000–4,750
€/ $6,300–7,500 ✠ BWL

A George III oak dresser, with associated superstructure, 64½in (164cm) wide.
£2,000–2,500
€/ $3,200–4,000 ✠ B(Ba)

OAK & COUNTRY FURNITURE

An oak dresser, the boarded rack with three shelves, above a base with three frieze drawers and three ogee arched panelled cupboards, on stile legs, rack associated, Welsh, 18thC, 58¾in (149cm) wide.
£2,000–2,500
€ / **$3,200–4,000** ⚒ B(SW)

A cherrywood dresser, the open delft rack with an ogee-moulded cornice and three shelves, with shaped sides, above a base with three short drawers flanked by two flush-panelled cupboards revealing a shelf, on a plinth base, late 18thC, 76in (193cm) wide.
£4,750–5,750
€ / **$7,500–9,100** ⚒ HAM

An oak dresser, the canopied structure with three shelves, the base with three cockbeaded frieze drawers, above three graduated cockbeaded central dummy drawers, flanked by two doors with turned wooden knob handles and inlaid bone keyplates, on bracket feet, Welsh, mid-19thC, 62in (157.5cm) wide.
£3,000–3,600
€ / **$4,750–5,750** ⚒ PF

An oak dresser, the boarded rack with a moulded cornice and plain frieze above two shelves, the lower section with three moulded drawers above two twin-fielded panelled cupboard doors, centred by a fielded panel, on extended stile supports, Denbighshire, 18thC, 60½in (153.5cm) wide.
£2,500–3,000
€ / **$4,000–4,750** ⚒ B(NW)

A fruitwood dresser, the boarded rack with a moulded cornice above four shelves, the base with three frieze drawers above two cupboards, each enclosed by a panelled door, spaced by a central panel, on shaped bracket feet, early 19thC, 75¼in (191cm) wide.
£4,000–4,800
€ / **$6,300–7,500** ⚒ B(NW)

A pear, apple and walnut dresser, French, Burgundy, 19thC, 56in (142cm) wide.
£1,500–1,700
€ / **$2,400–2,700** ⊞ MLL

An oak dresser, the delft rack with two shelves, with moulded cornice and shaped side supports, the base with ebonized cockbeading and escutcheons, the three drawers with brass drop handles, on square tapering legs, rack associated, 18thC, 59in (150cm) wide.
£1,400–1,700
€ / **$2,200–2,700** ⚒ JM

An oak dresser, the upper section with central open shelves, flanked by a glazed cupboard and a drawer on each side, the base with three drawers and two panelled doors, flanking a central 'kennel', on turned feet with turned column sides, 19thC, 62in (157.5cm) wide.
£700–840
€ / **$1,100–1,300** ⚒ E

An oak dresser, with original brass fittings, late 19thC, 60in (152.5cm) wide.
£1,250–1,400
€ / **$2,000–2,200** ⊞ SWA

Low Dressers

An oak dresser base, with three frieze drawers, c1700, 75in (190.5cm) wide.
€1,700–2,000
€/ **$2,700–3,150** ✣ BWL

A Queen Anne and later oak low dresser, with three frieze drawers, 77¼in (196cm) wide.
£1,300–1,600
€/ **$2,000–2,500** ✣ CGC

► **An oak low dresser,** the frieze with three moulded drawers, above a cupboard flanked by two drawers, with iron drop handles, early 18thC and later, 68in (172.5cm) wide.
€2,400–3,000
€/ **$3,800–4,800** ✣ AH

An oak low dresser, the two drawers with replacement brass handles, early 18thC, 54in (137cm) wide.
£2,200–2,500
€/ **$3,500–4,000** ✣ JNiC

◄ **An oak low dresser,** the three central drawers flanked by two side cupboards, early 18thC, 71½in (181.5cm) wide.
£1,000–1,200
€/ **$1,600–1,900** ✣ TMA

An oak low dresser, with original handles, Lancashire, c1760, 70in (178cm) wide.
£11,250–12,250
€/ **$17,500–19,500** ⊞ NMA
This completely original piece has cushion-moulded drawers and is a superb colour.

► **A mid-Georgian elm dresser base,** the three frieze drawers with swan-neck handles, above a shaped apron, 67¾in (172cm) wide.
€1,600–1,900
€/ **$2,500–3,000** ✣ Bri

An oak dresser base, the two drawers with original brass handles, c1780, 59in (150cm) wide.
£8,000–9,000
€/ **$12,500–14,000** ⊞ REI

◄ **A George III oak dresser base,** with 17thC components, doors reversed, restored, 75¼in (191cm) wide.
£1,400–1,700
€/ **$2,200–2,700** ✣ S(O)

Expert's choice

A farmer turned up at our workshop in the 1970s with two of the smallest Charles II geometrically-moulded oak dresser bases with turned baluster legs that I have ever seen. One was turned upside down and screwed to the other. The legs of the top one and all of the drawers had been removed. The drawer cavities were covered with chicken mesh as the piece was being used as bantam nest boxes – the drawers were being used to set potatoes.

We bought the pair for £225 (€/ $350), fitted the legs back, removed the chicken wire and droppings and fully restored them. The drawers still had their original brass furniture, and the wood had excellent colour and patina. We sold them for approximately £1,000 (€/ $1,600) each. Today those dressers would make a minimum of £18,000 (€/ $28,000).   **Paul Hopwell**

A George III oak low dresser, with three long and two short drawers over two central drawers flanked by panelled cupboard doors, with brass drop handles, 70in (178cm) wide.
£1,800–2,200
€/ **$2,800–3,500** ✣ AH

OAK & COUNTRY FURNITURE

An oak dresser base, altered and restored, 18thC, 58¾in (149cm) wide.
£550–625
€/ **$870–1,000** 🔨 B(Ba)

An oak low dresser, with three drawers over two cupboard doors and two further drawers, reduced in height, feet lacking, 18thC, 75½in (192cm) wide.
£3,000–3,500
€/ **$4,750–5,500** 🔨 TEN

An oak and mahogany-banded low dresser, with three frieze drawers above a cupboard flanked by two pairs of drawers, with brass swan-neck handles, 1775–1825, 77½in (197cm) wide.
£4,200–5,000
€/ **$6,600–8,000** 🔨 WW

An oak dresser base, with original handles and metalwork, French, c1800, 82in (208.5cm) wide.
£3,400–3,800
€/ **$5,400–6,000** ⊞ PICA

◀ **A late George III oak dresser base,** with three drawers over a central open section with pot board, flanked by two pairs of panelled doors, later alteration and additions, 36¼in (92cm) wide.
£2,200–2,800
€/ **$3,500–4,400** 🔨 BIG

Many dresser bases, potboards and cupboards started life with racks which are now missing. As a general rule only buy pieces whose proportions still seem right without a rack and which have a bold top with good moulding. Many original dresser cornices were removed and then replaced at a later date. If this is the case check that the colour and patina are a good match. Such marriages reduce the value by half.

◀ **An oak side cabinet,** the two doors and ends with Gothic tracery carving, late 19thC, 35½in (90cm) wide.
£150–180
€/ **$240–280** 🔨 SWO

Lowboys

A Georgian oak lowboy, the three cockbeaded drawers with swan-neck handles, on pad feet, 30in (76cm) wide.
£550–700
€/ **$870–1,100** 🔨 HoG

A Georgian oak lowboy, the centre drawer replaced, 29in (73.5cm) wide.
£780–875
€/ **$1,200–1,400** ⊞ RPh

An oak lowboy, the banded top above three drawers with brass handles, a shaped frieze below, the cabriole legs on spade feet, later carving to back legs, 18thC, 32in (81.5cm) wide.
£420–525
€/ **$675–825** 🔨 WW

Settles & Seats

An oak settle, the back with five panels above downcurved arms, on partially-turned legs, early 18thC, 72½in (184cm) wide.
£500–650
€/ **$800–1,000** ↗ Mit

An oak settle, the panelled back above shaped arms and a squab seat, on cabriole legs with pad feet, mid-18thC, 71¾in (182.5cm) wide.
£700–850
€/ **$1,100–1,350** ↗ DN

A Charles II oak monk's bench, the two-plank rising top above scroll arms and a solid rising seat, on turned legs with block feet, 36¾in (93.5cm) wide.
£1,000–1,250
€/ **$1,600–1,900** ↗ CGC

An oak settle, with a leather-studded seat, on turned bulbous and square block legs with hoof feet, mid-18thC, 76in (193cm) wide.
£600–750
€/ **$1,000–1,200** ↗ WL

An elm settle, with a box seat, Welsh borders, mid-18thC, 42in (106.5cm) wide.
£3,500–3,800
€/ **$5,500–6,000** ⊞ KEY

A panelled oak settle, the box seat with a removable central lid, lid formerly hinged, restored, c1780, 68in (172.5cm) wide.
£2,400–2,800
€/ **$3,800–4,400** ↗ S(O)

OAK & COUNTRY FURNITURE

An elm high-back settle, the box seat with a single door, 18thC, 42in (106.5cm) wide.
£3,200–3,600
€/ **$5,000–5,700** ⊞ NMA

An oak and fruitwood box settle, the back with eight panels above a hinged seat, with scroll-ended downswept arms, the front triple panelled, on baluster and ring-turned front legs and later ball feet, 18thC, 53½in (136cm) wide.
£2,300–2,800
€/ **$3,700–4,400** ⚒ B(NW)

A painted metamorphic settle/ table, the base with a half lid, with mortice and tenon joints, 18thC, 29½in (75cm) wide.
£1,500–1,800
€/ **$2,400–2,800** ⚒ JDJ

A turned ash and poplar Windsor settee, with rod back, initials and dates to underside of seat, some parts possibly of a later date, American, Pennsylvania, c1800, 76in (193cm) wide.
£2,400–2,800
€/ **$4,000–4,400** ⚒ S(NY)

A carved and panelled oak settle, the base is an early 18thC coffer, 19thC, 46in (117cm) wide.
£700–800
€/ **$1,100–1,250** ⊞ HiA

An oak box settle, carved with kings, queens and knights, the arms carved with lions' heads, c1880, 66in (167.5cm) wide.
£1,600–1,800
€/ **$2,500–2,800** ⊞ REF

◄ **A painted beech settee,** with a rush seat, French, c1880, 48in (122cm) wide.
£800–900
€/ **$1,250–1,450** ⊞ MLL

► **An oak metamorphic settle,** the gouge-carved panelled back above a slatted seat unfolding to create a single bed with a slatted base, late 19thC, 42½in (108cm) wide.
£350–420
€/ **$550–670** ⚒ B(Ch)

Stools

An oak box stool, with a hinged top, c1640, 15in (38cm) wide.
£4,300–4,800
€/ **$6,800–7,600** ⊞ TRI

An oak joint stool, the box seat with a hinged lid enclosing an interior formerly with divisions, faults, c1660, 16in (40.5cm) wide.
£2,000–2,200
€/ **$3,150–3,500** ⚒ S(O)

An oak joint stool, c1680, 18¼in (46.5cm) wide.
£1,100–1,300
€/ **$1,750–2,000** ⚒ S(O)

A pair of oak joint stools, 17thC, 17¼in (44cm) wide
£800–1,000
€/ **$1,250–1,600** ⚒ L

For further information on antique furniture see the full range of Miller's books at
www.millers.uk.com

An oak joint stool, the thick top bove turned legs, 1650–1700.
2,250–2,500
/ $3,500–4,000 ⊞ KEY

An oak joint stool, with an upholstered top, late 17thC, 16in (40.5cm) square.
£1,000–1,100
€/ $1,600–1,750 ⊞ SuA

An ash stool, c1780, 30in (76cm) wide.
£580–650
€/ $900–1,000 ⊞ SEA

An elm joint stool, c1780,
8in (45.5cm) high.
180–200
/ $280–315 ⊞ F&F

An elm milking stool, with ash legs, 18thC, 11in (28cm) diam.
£110–125
€/ $175–200 ⊞ CHAC

A sycamore and elm milking stool, early 19thC, 19in (48.5cm) wide.
£150–180
€/ $230–280 ⚒ S(O)

An oak stool, the stuff-over eedlework seat with brass nails, n square tapering chamfered legs, arly 19thC, 18in (45.5cm) wide.
200–250
/ $300–400 ⚒ WW

A mahogany stool, c1820,
25in (63.5cm) high.
£200–220
€/ $300–350 ⊞ F&F

An elm stool, c1860,
16in (40.5cm) wide.
£350–400
€/ $550–650 ⊞ SSW

A pair of primitive elm stools,
9thC, larger 32in (81.5cm) wide.
1,150–1,300
/ $1,800–2,000 ⊞ SAW

A beech stool, c1880,
11in (28cm) high.
£280–320
€/ $440–500 ⊞ HRQ

◀ An ash country stool, c1900,
9in (23cm) high.
£130–145
€/ $200–230 ⊞ SDA

OAK & COUNTRY FURNITURE

Tables

An oak gateleg table, c1660, 42in (106.5cm) wide.
£2,700–3,000
€/ $4,250–4,750 ⊞ SEA

A walnut side table, on turned supports and stretchers, c1670, 28in (71cm) wide.
£2,800–3,250
€/ $4,500–5,000 ⊞ WELL

An oak side table, with a single drawer, on turned legs, 17thC, 28in (71cm) wide.
£3,500–4,000
€/ $5,500–6,300 ⊞ APO

An oak occasional table, restored, 17thC, 20in (51cm) wide.
£800–1,000
€/ $1,250–1,500 ⚒ B(Ch)

Miller's Compares

I. A Charles II oak gateleg table, with a plain frieze, on bobbin-turned legs with inverted cup feet, 38½in (98cm) wide.
£950–1,200
€/ $1,500–1,900 ⚒ CGC

II. A Charles II oak drop-leaf table, with opposing frieze drawers, on bobbin-turned legs with ball feet, 38½in (98cm) wide.
£320–400
€/ $500–630 ⚒ CGC

The top of Item I belongs to the base (in other words it is not a marriage), which is always an important factor to look for, whereas the ends of the leaves of Item II have been restored and the drawers are replacements. The bobbin turning on the legs of Item I are also bolder than that of Item II, and this appeals to some buyers. Because of the repairs that have been carried out on Item II, the colour is not uniform, whereas that of Item I is richer and much more even. Item I has come from a good, private source and has been looked after over the years, which almost invariably helps to lift the price.

An oak refectory table, with a plank top on square chamfered legs, length reduced, 17thC, 71¾in (182.5cm) long.
£1,200–1,500
€/ $1,900–2,400 ⚒ SWO

An oak centre table, with silhouette legs, c1680, 27in (68.5cm) wide.
£5,500–6,500
€/ $8,700–10,250 ⊞ RYA

An oak gateleg table, c1680, 36in (91.5cm) wide.
£2,000–2,200
€/ $3,200–3,500 ⊞ DJH

◄ An elm and oak side table, with a carved frieze, on baluster-turned legs joined by moulded stretchers, 17thC, 45in (114.5cm) wide.
£600–725
€/ $1,000–1,150 ⚒ CGC

A child's oak cricket table, with turned legs, c1690, 22in (56cm) diam.
£3,500–3,850
€/ $5,500–6,000 ⊞ SuA

An oak gateleg table, with
alterations, late 17thC,
50¾in (129cm) wide.
£350–420
€ / **$550–670** ⚒ B(Ba)

n oak side table, with a long frieze
awer, on a bobbin- and block-turned
ame, late 17thC, 26in (66cm) wide.
550–650
/ **$870–1,000** ⚒ TMA

An oak gateleg table, with
baluster-turned legs, c1690,
39in (99cm) extended.
£4,500–5,500
€ / **$7,100–8,700** ⊞ RYA

◄ **An oak gateleg table,** on
bobbin-turned legs with square
feet, formerly with drawer, late
17thC, 66in (167.5cm) wide.
£750–875
€ / **$1,200–1,400** ⚒ PF

n oak refectory table, with a
anel top above a carved frieze,
n cup and cover legs, 1675–1725,
3in (160cm) long.
2,000–2,500
/ **$3,200–4,000** ⚒ JNic

A Queen Anne oak silver table,
5in (66cm) long.
1,300–1,450
/ **$2,000–2,300** ⊞ SuA

An oak gateleg table, c1710,
60in (152.5cm) wide.
£2,800–3,250
€ / **$4,400–5,000** ⊞ SEA

OAK & COUNTRY FURNITURE

An oak side table, the moulded-edge top above a frieze drawer, on turned tapered legs, early 18thC, 27in (68.5cm) wide.
£650–750
€/ **$1,000–1,200** ➤ DMC

An oak side table, with a single drawer, c1725, 35½in (90cm) wide.
£3,500–4,200
€/ **$5,500–6,600** ⊞ PHA

An oak side table, the drawer with brass escutcheons and swing handles, on turned tapering legs and pad feet, c1750, 30¼in (77cm) wide.
£650–820
€/ **$1,000–1,300** ➤ WL

An oak cricket table, early 18thC, 27in (68.5cm) diam.
£800–950
€/ **$1,250–1,500** ➤ L

An oak tripod table, with original revolving birdcage, on spider legs, bearers replaced, 1740–60, 28½in (72.5cm) diam.
£2,250–2,800
€/ **$3,500–4,500** ⊞ RYA

An oak refectory table, with three drawers, French, c1750, 79in (200.5cm) wide.
£2,250–2,500
€/ **$3,500–4,000** ⊞ DAC

An elm tavern table, on an X-frame, c1770, 52in (132cm) wide.
£2,000–2,500
€/ **$3,150–4,000** ⊞ RYA

◀ **A Georgian oak, elm and fruitwood country wine table,** 16in (40.5cm) diam.
£875–975
€/ **$1,400–1,550** ⊞ CGA

An oak gateleg table, with a single drawer and a wavy apron, on baluster turned legs with turned feet, early 18thC, 60in (152.5cm) wide.
£400–480
€/ **$630–760** ➤ PF

An oak and fruitwood country side table, the frieze drawer above a shaped apron, on turned tapering legs with pad feet, spliced leg and other repairs, mid-18thC, 27¼in (69cm) wide.
£380–450
€/ **$600–710** ➤ DN

A Georgian provincial elm and fruitwood cricket table, on three tapering splayed legs, 22½in (57cm) diam.
£650–750
€/ **$1,000–1,200** ➤ Bea(E

An oak tilt-top table, 1760–80, 30in (76cm) diam
£950–1,100
€/ **$1,500–1,750** ⊞ KEY

n oak side table, c1770, 9¾in (75.5cm) wide.
900–1,000
/ $1,400–1,600 ⚒ S(O)

A George III oak side table, 30¾in (78cm) wide.
£420–525
€ / $670–830 ⚒ L

A walnut side table, French, Alsace, c1780, 39in (99cm) wide.
£850–950
€ / $1,350–1,500 ⊞ TDS

chestnut farmhouse table, ench, c1780, 80in (203cm) long.
,000–6,500
/ $9,500–10,000 ⊞ REI

An oak table, Spanish, c1780, 24in (61cm) wide.
£420–465
€ / $675–725 ⊞ SSW

A provincial cherrywood dressing table, opening to reveal a mirror and compartments, with a writing surface and two drawers, French, 18thC, 31¼in (79.5cm) wide.
£800–950
€ / $1,250–1,500 ⚒ S(P)

n elm and pine tilt-top table, ith a painted top, c1790, 3in (58.5cm) wide.
,000–1,150
/ $1,580–1,750 ⊞ SuA

An oak-top farmhouse table, 18thC, 74½in (189cm) wide.
£1,350–1,500
€ / $2,200–2,400 ⊞ SWN

An oak cricket table, with a plank top, over a shaped apron, on three tapering legs, 18thC, 26in (66cm) diam.
£1,000–1,200
€ / $1,600–1,900 ⚒ BWL

◀ An oak cricket table, with a plank top and undertier, 18thC, 33in (84cm) diam.
£650–750
€ / $1,000–1,200 ⚒ HOLL

n oak side table, with a drawer, 8thC, 27in (68.5cm) wide.
,700–2,000
/ $2,700–3,200 ⊞ WAW

A beech and chestnut trestle table, French, 18thC, 63in (160cm) long.
£2,250–2,500
€ / $3,500–4,000 ⊞ AMS

◀ An oak cricket table, c1800, 22in (56cm) diam.
£850–950
€ / $1,350–1,500 ⊞ REF

OAK & COUNTRY FURNITURE

A painted wood folding peasant table, with original paint, c1800, 40¼in (102cm) wide.
£800–950
€/ **$1,250–1,500** ⚒ BUK(F)

An oak farmhouse table, with a partially stripped three-plank top, a frieze drawer to each end, on square tapering legs, early 19thC, 69in (175.5cm) long.
£400–475
€/ **$630–750** ⚒ PFK

An ash and pine cricket table, c1820, 22in (56cm) high.
£430–475
€/ **$675–750** ⊞ SEA

A cherrywood farmhouse table, c1830, 75in (190.5cm) long.
£2,700–3,000
€/ **$4,300–4,750** ⊞ DeG

A Louis Philippe-style provincial cherrywood side table, with a marble top, above a frieze with one drawer, on turned bulbous legs with ball feet, French, 1850–75, 31½in (80cm) wide.
£280–320
€/ **$440–500** ⚒ NOA

A Victorian carved oak refectory-style table, the plank top above a strapwork-carved front frieze, on turned and carved legs, 84¾in (215.5cm) long.
£2,200–2,700
€/ **$3,500–4,250** ⚒ B(NW)

◄ **A Victorian oak dining table,** 120in (305cm) extended.
£4,700–5,200
€/ **$7,500–8,200** ⊞ REF

An oak farmhouse table, 19thC, 66in (167.5cm) long.
£750–850
€/ **$1,200–1,350** ⊞ WAW

◄ **A fruitwood farmhouse table,** French, 19thC, 75½in (192cm) wide.
£600–700
€/ **$950–1,100** ⚒ SWO

A 17thC-style oak refectory table, with three drawers, Flemish, c1900, 70½in (179cm) wide.
£1,100–1,300
€/ **$1,750–2,000** ⚒ S(O)

An end table, the two tiers decorated with twigs, American, Adirondacks, 1875–1925, 31½in (80cm) wide.
£2,000–2,400
€/ **$3,200–3,800** ⊞ NART

Pine Furniture

eds

pine bed, German, c1890,
5in (91.5cm) wide.
280–320
/ $440–500 ⊞ HRQ

A pine bed, central European,
c1900, 39in (99cm) wide.
£450–500
€/ $700–800 ⊞ COF

A pine bed, Continental, c1900,
39in (99cm) wide.
£315–350
€/ $500–550 ⊞ COF

Bookcases

A Victorian glazed
pine bookcase,
36in (91.5cm) wide.
£330–365
€/ $520–575 ⊞ P&T

pine bookcase, with four shelves,
id-19thC, 68in (173cm) wide.
530–630
/ $840–1,000 ⚒ S(O)

A Victorian pine open bookcase, on a plinth
base, 72in (183cm) wide.
£315–350
€/ $500–550 ⊞ PaA

◄ A pine bookcase, Irish,
c1870, 47in (119.5cm) wide.
£450–500
€/ $700–790 ⊞ Byl

► A late
Victorian pine
bookcase, the
upper section
with two glazed
doors, 41in
(104cm) wide.
£720–800
€/ $1,150–1,250
⊞ P&T

A pine bookcase, the upper
section with four glazed doors,
over four panelled doors, c1890,
102in (259cm) wide.
£1,800–2,000
€/ $2,800–3,200 ⊞ TPC

◄ A pine bookcase, with two
glazed doors above two panelled
doors, c1880, 42in (106.5cm) wide.
£380–430
€/ $600–680 ⊞ DFA

A stepped pine bookcase, c1900,
46in (117cm) wide.
£70–80
€/ $110–135 ⊞ DFA

PINE FURNITURE

Boxes

A Shaker stained pine lap desk, the top drawer with a divided interior, American, early 19thC, 20¼in (51.5cm) wide.
£4,000–4,800
€/ **$6,300–7,500** ⚒ S(NY)
This desk represents a rare form made by a Shaker craftsman, a group formed in 1776 by Mother Ann Lee, a proponent of an existence focused on simplicity, purity and integrity of workmanship. This piece follows the classic elements of Shaker design philosophy taught by Mother Ann, who advised that things be made 'plain and simple...unembellished by any superfluities which add nothing to its goodness or durability'.

A carved and open fret-cut pine wall-hanging candle box, with a single drawer, Scottish, c1860, 8¾in (22cm) wide.
£320–400
€/ **$510–630** ⊞ RYA

For further information on antique furniture see the full range of Miller's books at
www.millers.uk.com

A cabinet maker's painted pine tool box, the interior with parquetry decoration and fitted with drawers and lidded compartments, the top later-decorated with a winged figure and hieroglyphics, 19thC, 36¾in (93.5cm) wide.
£250–300
€/ **$400–475** ⚒ SWO

A pine box, with inlaid decoration, c1860, 13in (33cm) wide.
£75–85
€/ **$120–135** ⊞ AL

A pine box, with a domed lid, c1880, 29in (73.5cm) wide.
£400–450
€/ **$630–700** ⊞ COF

A pine blanket box, with iron handles, c1880, 37in (94cm) wide.
£115–130
€/ **$180–200** ⊞ DFA

A pine blanket box, c1880, 30in (76cm) wide.
£100–120
€/ **$160–190** ⊞ DFA

A pine box, c1880, 23in (58.5cm) wide.
£100–115
€/ **$160–180** ⊞ AL

A pine document box, Irish, c1880, 29in (73.5cm) wide.
£110–120
€/ **$175–190** ⊞ Byl

A pine blanket box, with wooden handles, c1900, 26in (66cm) wide.
£100–120
€/ **$160–190** ⊞ HRQ

A pine box, with steel brackets, c1890, 25in (63.5cm) wide.
£90–100
€/ **$140–160** ⊞ AL

A pine box, with a domed lid, c1900, 30in (76cm) wide.
£80–90
€/ **$125–140** ⊞ HRQ

▶ A pine box, with rope handles, c1920, 13in (33cm) wide.
£80–90
€/ **$125–135** ⊞ DFA

Chairs

◄ A turned maple, pine and hickory Windsor armchair, underside of seat branded 'CMD', American, New England, c1780.
£3,000–3,500
€/ $4,750–5,500 ⚒ S(NY)

A pine country chair, Hungarian, c1880.
£45–50
€/ $70–80 ⊞ Byl

A pine country chair, Irish, c1870.
£130–145
€/ $200–230 ⊞ Byl

A carved and turned pine chair, c1880.
£55–60
€/ $85–95 ⊞ DFA

A pine chair, with original paint, c1900.
£40–45
€/ $65–70 ⊞ DFA

► A set of four pine kitchen chairs, Continental, c1910.
£200–220
€/ $300–350 ⊞ PaA

A child's pine chair, c1920.
£70–80
€/ $110–125 ⊞ AL

PINE FURNITURE

Chests & Coffers

A pine chip-carved dowry chest,
with original iron fittings, Norwegian,
c1700, 21in (53.5cm) wide.
£2,400–2,700
€/ **$3,800–4,250** ⊞ RYA

A polychrome-painted pine chest,
the panelled front now with two
hinged doors, German, 1700–50,
55¼in (140.5cm) wide.
£1,350–1,600
€/ **$2000–2,600** ↗ S(O)

A pine coffer, c1800,
80in (203cm) wide.
£240–265
€/ **$380–420** ⊞ AL

A pine marriage chest, with original
decoration, c1850, 45in (114.5cm) wide.
£265–300
€/ **$420–475** ⊞ PaA

A pine dwarf trunk, with a domed
lid, c1820, 10¾in (27.5cm) wide.
£115–130
€/ **$180–200** ⊞ CHAC

An early Victorian pine mule chest,
with a single drawer, 35in (89cm) wide.
£300–345
€/ **$475–550** ⊞ P&T

▶ **A stained pine coffer,** the
interior with lidded candle box,
late 19thC, 48in (122cm) wide.
£160–200
€/ **$250–315** ↗ SWO

A pine blanket chest, the interior
with a candle tray, with iron handles,
late 19thC, 54in (137cm) wide.
£200–240
€/ **$315–380** ↗ DA

Chests of Drawers

A Georgian pine chest of drawers,
with two short over two long
drawers, 36in (91.5cm) wide.
£500–550
€/ **$800–870** ⊞ P&T

**A painted elm and pine nest of apothecary
drawers,** c1800, 39½in (100.5cm) wide.
£2,700–3,000
€/ **$4,250–4,750** ⊞ RYA

**A pine and maple chest
of drawers,** the hinged top
opening to reveal a well
with two dummy and three
real drawers, American,
Massachusetts, 1700–30,
45in (114.5cm) wide.
£2,750–3,250
€/ **$4,300–5,000** ↗ S(O)

▶ **A pine chest of
drawers,** with two short
over three long drawers,
c1810, 40in (101.5cm) wide.
£600–670
€/ **$950–1,000** ⊞ AL

A pine chest of drawers, on bracket feet,
c1820, 40in (101.5cm) wide.
£720–800
€/ **$1,150–1,250** ⊞ COF

A pine chest of drawers, American, 19thC, 40in (101.5cm) wide.
£165–200
€/ $260–315 ⚘ DuM

A Victorian pine chest of drawers, with splashback and two short over two long drawers, with original knobs, 40in (101.5cm) wide.
£360–400
€/ $575–650 ⊞ P&T

A Victorian pine chest of drawers, with two short over two long drawers, 34in (86.5cm) wide.
£270–300
€/ $425–475 ⊞ CHAC

A Victorian painted pine chest of drawers, 41¼in (105cm) wide.
£130–160
€/ $200–250 ⚘ B(Ba)

A Victorian pine chest of drawers, with china knobs, 35in (89cm) wide.
£200–230
€/ $315–360 ⊞ PaA

A pine chest of drawers, with splashback, c1860, 36in (91.5cm) wide.
£325–360
€/ $515–570 ⊞ HRQ

A grained pine apprentice chest of drawers, mid-19thC, 11in (28cm) wide.
£160–180
€/ $250–290 ⊞ SWN

A pine chest of drawers, with original paint, Swedish, Stockholm, c1870, 46in (117cm) wide.
£2,500–3,000
€/ $4,000–4,750 ⊞ JF

Items in the Pine Furniture section have been arranged in date order.

A painted pine chest of drawers, with splashback, c1870, 37in (94cm) wide.
£850–1,000
€/ $1,350–1,600 ⚘ S(O)

A Louis-Philippe-style chest of drawers, Continental, c1870, 41in (104cm) wide.
£350–400
€/ $550–630 ⊞ HRQ

PINE FURNITURE

A pine chest of drawers, with turned pillars and original paint, c1870, 62in (157.5cm) wide.
£600–660
€/ **$950–1,000** ⊞ DMe

A pine chest of drawers, with turned decoration, c1880, 42in (106.5cm) wide.
£240–265
€/ **$380–420** ⊞ DFA

A pine chest of drawers, with turned decoration, Romanian, c1880, 50in (127cm) wide.
£270–300
€/ **$425–475** ⊞ Byl

A pine chest of six drawers, on bun feet, c1880, 39in (99cm) wide.
£450–500
€/ **$700–800** ⊞ TPC

A pine chest of drawers, with turned pillars and bun feet, c1870, 46in (117cm) wide.
£330–370
€/ **$520–580** ⊞ DMe

A stripped pine chest of drawers, with two short over three long drawers, late 19thC, 42½in (108cm) wide.
£200–240
€/ **$315–380** 🔨 B(W)

A pine chest of drawers, with two short over two long drawers, Irish, c1880, 38in (96.5cm) wide.
£240–265
€/ **$380–420** ⊞ Byl

A pine chest of drawers, c1890, 34in (86.5cm) wide.
£430–475
€/ **$680–750** ⊞ COF

◀ A pine chest of drawers, with shaped top and decoration to drawer fronts, Continental, c1890, 45in (114.5cm) wide.
£260–300
€/ **$400–475** ⊞ PaA

A pine chest of drawers, with turned decoration, eastern European, c1875, 46in (117cm) wide.
£270–300
€/ **$425–475** ⊞ Byl

A pine chest of drawers, with original handles, c1880, 30in (76cm) wide.
£320–350
€/ **$500–550** ⊞ HRQ

A pine chest of drawers, with two short over three long drawers, with original handles, c1880, 38in (96.5cm) wide.
£350–400
€/ **$550–630** ⊞ HRQ

A pitch pine four-drawer commode, with a marble top, early 20thC, 39in (99cm) wide.
£450–500
€/ **$700–800** ⊞ MHA

PINE FURNITURE

Cupboards

A painted pine corner cupboard, the glazed upper section with two shelves, the base with a fall-front enclosing an open interior above panel doors enclosing a shelf, Norwegian, 18thC, 68½in (174cm) high.
£1,300–1,500
€/ **$2,000–2,400** ⚒ B(Ed)

A fret-carved pine corner cupboard, the upper section with three shelves, the lower section with a panelled door, refinished, 1775–1800, 39in (99cm) wide.
£900–1,000
€/ **$1,400–1,600** ⚒ NOA

A pine hanging corner cupboard, with original paint, 18thC, 44in (112cm) high.
£580–650
€/ **$900–1,000** ⊞ SWN

A George III bowfronted painted pine corner cupboard, the upper section with a moulded cornice over a pair of glazed doors, the base with a pair of panelled doors, 54in (137cm) wide.
£2,400–2,800
€/ **$3,800–4,400** ⚒ HYD

A provincial pine cupboard, the arched cornice above a pair of glazed panel doors, over a further pair of doors, with later feet, French, late 18thC, 53½in (136cm) wide.
£850–1,000
€/ **$1,350–1,600** ⚒ B(Ch)

◄ **A pine butler's cupboard,** c1800, 48in (122cm) wide.
£650–750
€/ **$1,000–1,200** ⊞ TPC

A stained pine cupboard, the panelled doors opening to reveal two shelves, losses, American, New York, 1750–1800, 53½in (136cm) wide.
£5,000–6,000
€/ **$8,000–9,500** ⚒ S(NY)

A George III pine four-door corner cupboard, c1780, 42in (106.5cm) wide.
£1,125–1,250
€/ **$1,800–1,900** ⊞ HRQ

A pine corner cupboard, with original paint, late 18thC, 39in (99cm) wide.
£2,000–2,300
€/ **$3,150–3,600** ⊞ PICA

A provincial pine glazed cupboard, the lower cupboard doors opening to reveal a pair of drawers, French, 1750–75, 55½in (141cm) wide.
£1,200–1,400
€/ **$1,900–2,200** ⚒ S(O)

A pine cupboard, the doors with fielded pudding panels, Irish, c1790, 57in (145cm) wide.
£4,300–4,600
€/ **$6,800–7,300** ⊞ DMe

LOCATE THE SOURCE

The source of each illustration in Miller's can be found by checking the code letters below each caption with the Key to Illustrations, pages 794–800.

A Biedermeier pine cupboard, German, c1800, 56in (142cm) wide.
£550–600
€/ **$870–950** ⊞ HRQ

PINE FURNITURE

A painted pine cupboard, the glazed upper section over two reeded-panel doors, c1810, 97in (246.5cm) high
£4,000–5,000
€ / **$6,300–8,000** ⊞ JF

A painted pine armoire, with panelled doors, Irish, c1830, 64in (162.5cm) wide.
£7,000–8,000
€ / **$11,000–12,500** ⊞ DMe

A pine larder cupboard, with four panelled doors, c1840, 61in (155cm) wide.
£750–820
€ / **$1,200–1,300** ⊞ DFA

◄ **A pine cupboard,** with panelled sides and doors, with original paint, Irish, Co Roscommon, 1840–50, 54in (137cm) wide.
£900–1,000
€ / **$1,400–1,600** ⊞ HON

A pine linen press, the upper section with a moulded cornice over a pair of panel doors and spirally-reeded quarter columns, the base fitted with six drawers, early 19thC, 69¼in (176cm) wide.
£1,200–1,400
€ / **$1,900–2,200** ⚒ B(Pr)

A pine marriage cupboard, with painted folk art decoration, central European, dated 1835, 42in (106.5cm) wide.
£3,200–3,800
€ / **$5,000–6,000** ⊞ RYA

A pine housekeeper's cupboard, the lower section with six drawers, south Derbyshire, c1840, 65in (165cm) wide.
£1,500–1,650
€ / **$2,400–2,500** ⊞ HRQ

▶ **A pine cupboard,** the moulded cornice above a reeded frieze, over four panelled cupboard doors and two drawers, on bracket feet, 1800–25, 62in (157.5cm) wide.
£1,000–1,200
€ / **$1,600–1,900** ⚒ NOA

A stained pine corner cupboard, 19thC, 74¾in (190cm) high.
£480–540
€ / **$760–850** ⚒ SWO

A painted pine pot cupboard, with a simulated marble top, c1840, 14½in (37cm) diam.
£1,000–1,200
€ / **$1,600–1,900** ⚒ S(O)

PINE FURNITURE

A painted pine cupboard, by Mangan Bros, with two panelled doors, Irish, Co Kildare, c1840, 63in (160cm) wide.
£2,200–2,600
€ / **$3,500–4,100** ⊞ **DMe**

A pine wall cupboard, c1850, 19in (48.5cm) wide.
£100–120
€ / **$160–190** ⊞ **HRQ**

A pine cupboard, with two doors, eastern European, c1870, 36in (91.5cm) wide.
£85–95
€ / **$135–150** ⊞ **HRQ**

A pine cupboard, c1845, 25in (63.5cm) wide.
£270–300
€ / **$425–475** ⊞ **P&T**

A pine cupboard, the four doors with carved sunburst decoration, with original scumble finish, c1860, 60in (152.5cm) wide.
£900–1,000
€ / **$1,400–1,600** ⊞ **HON**

◀ **A pine cupboard,** the glazed upper section over two doors, Irish, c1865, 40in (101.5cm) wide.
£520–625
€ / **$820–990** ⊞ **Byl**

A pine step-back cupboard, with four doors, Irish, c1870, 48in (122cm) wide.
£550–600
€ / **$870–950** ⊞ **Byl**

▶ **A pine larder cupboard,** with four doors, c1870, 42in (106.5cm) wide.
£375–425
€ / **$590–670** ⊞ **DFA**

A painted pine corner cupboard, the single door over a short drawer, Dutch, mid-19thC and later, 27in (68.5cm) wide.
£550–600
€ / **$870–950** 🔨 **NOA**

A glazed pine display cupboard, Irish, c1860, 50in (127cm) wide.
£475–525
€ / **$750–830** ⊞ **DMe**

A pine panelled cupboard, the two-door upper section over one short and two long drawers and two further doors, Irish, Co Tipperary, c1850, 59in (150cm) wide.
£950–1,100
€ / **$1,500–1,750** ⊞ **HON**

A painted pine cupboard, the upper section with two glazed doors, over three central drawers and two doors, c1860, 45in (114.5cm) wide.
£500–560
€ / **$790–880** ⊞ **DFA**

◀ **A pine cupboard,** c1870, 41in (104cm) wide.
£300–330
€ / **$475–520** ⊞ **Byl**

A pine cupboard, European, c1875, 36in (91.5cm) wide.
£270–300
€ / **$420–4750** ⊞ **Byl**

A pine corner cupboard, French, c1880, 33in (84cm) wide.
£650–735
€/ **$1,000–1,150** ⊞ AL

A pine corner cupboard, with a glazed top, Irish, c1880, 45in (114.5cm) wide.
£450–500
€/ **$710–790** ⊞ Byl

◀ **A pine bedside cupboard,** c1880, 30in (76cm) high.
£115–130
€/ **$180–200** ⊞ HRQ

▶ **A pine cupboard,** the two doors enclosing a shelved interior, over two drawers, c1880, 47in (119.5cm) wide.
£300–330
€/ **$475–520** ⊞ DFA

A pine cupboard, with two panelled doors, Irish, c1880, 46in (117cm) wide.
£300–330
€/ **$475–520** ⊞ Byl

A pitch pine panelled cupboard, with four doors, Irish, Co Galway, c1880, 96in (244cm) high.
£900–980
€/ **$1,400–1,600** ⊞ HON

A pine corner cupboard, c1885, 22in (56cm) wide.
£550–600
€/ **$870–950** ⊞ COF

PINE FURNITURE

A pine cupboard, the four doors with Gothic panels, with two drawers, Irish, c1890, 40in (101.5cm) wide.
£650–720
€/ **$1,000–1,100** ⊞ Byl

A pine cupboard, with a single drawer over a panelled door, on turned bun feet, c1890, 25in (63.5cm) wide.
£150–165
€/ **$240–260** ⊞ DFA

A painted pine cupboard, with glazed upper section, American, 19thC, 38in (96.5cm) wide.
£80–100
€/ **$130–160** 🔧 DuM

► **A pine wall cupboard,** European, c1910, 24in (61cm) wide.
£225–250
€/ **$350–400** ⊞ COF

A pine cupboard, with shelf over, c1890, 14½in (37cm) wide.
£55–60
€/ **$85–95** ⊞ AL

A pine cupboard, with four doors, c1890, 51in (129.5cm) wide.
£550–625
€/ **$870–1,000** ⊞ DFA

A pine wardrobe, with an arched top, central European, c1900, 39in (99cm) wide.
£625–700
€/ **$1,000–1,100** ⊞ COF

A pine bread cupboard, eastern European, c1890, 63in (160cm) wide.
£280–320
€/ **$440–520** ⊞ PaA

A pine corner cupboard, c1890, 18in (45.5cm) wide.
£450–500
€/ **$700–800** ⊞ COF

A pine cupboard, German, c1890, 43in (109cm) wide.
£550–600
€/ **$870–950** ⊞ HRQ

A pine cupboard, with a glazed upper section, c1890, 34in (86.5cm) wide.
£420–470
€/ **$660–740** ⊞ AL

◄ **A pair of pine side cupboards,** eastern European, c1900, 32in (81.5cm) wide.
£245–270
€/ **$380–430** ⊞ PaA

A pine bedside cupboard, German, c1910, 17in (43cm) wide.
£115–130
€/ **$180–200** ⊞ HRQ

◄ **A pair of pine bedside cupboards,** central European, c1920, 28in (71cm) high.
£400–450
€/ **$630–700** ⊞ COF

DESKS & BUREAUX 203

Desks & Bureaux

A pine bureau, with fully fitted interior, c1800, 38in (96.5cm) wide.
£1,500–1,800
€/ **$2,400–2,850** ⊞ TPC

A pine bureau, Irish, Co Kilkenny, 1850–60, 41in (104cm) wide.
£750–820
€/ **$1,200–1,300** ⊞ HON

A pine bureau, c1870, 56in (142cm) wide.
£2,000–2,200
€/ **$3,200–3,500** ⊞ COF

▶ **A pine writing desk,** German, c1900, 47in (119.5cm) wide.
£500–550
€/ **$800–870** ⊞ HRQ

A pine partner's desk, c1900, 49in (124.5cm) wide.
£1,350–1,500
€/ **$2,150–2,350** ⊞ COF

◀ **A pine pedestal desk,** the moulded drawers flanked by reeded columns, original paintwork, c1900, 48in (122cm) wide.
£1,100–1,200
€/ **$1,700–1,900** ⊞ TPC

A pine pedestal desk, Continental, c1920, 51in (129.5cm) wide.
£630–700
€/ **$1,000–1,100** ⊞ HRQ

THE PINE CELLARS

ANTIQUE PINE & COUNTRY FURNITURE

39 Jewry Street, Winchester
Hampshire SO23 8RY, England
Tel: 01962 867014

Hundreds of individual pieces of antique pine and country furniture, single items or container loads can be shipped anywhere in the world at very competitive prices

Also Suppliers of Old Pine Panelled Rooms

Suppliers of Pine for 20 years

Trade Enquiries Welcomed
20,000 sq. ft. on 01962 777546

Member of The Guild of Master Craftsmen

ONE HOUR FROM LONDON

Dressers

A George III stained pine dresser, Welsh, c1800, 66in (167.5cm) wide.
£1,400–1,600
€/ **$2,200–2,500** ⚒ S(O)

A pine chicken coop dresser, cornice replaced, Irish, early 19thC, 49½in (125.5cm) wide.
£950–1,100
€/ **$1,500–1,700** ⚒ S(O)

◄ **A painted pine dresser,** with carved sunburst decoration and reeded sides, original paint, Irish, c1840, 57in (145cm) wide.
£600–660
€/ **$950–1,000** ⊞ HON

► **A pine dresser,** with two plate shelves above six frieze drawers and three doors, c1850, 82in (208.5cm) wide.
£2,500–3,000
€/ **$4,000–4,800** ⊞ TPC

A painted pine dresser, original paint, losses refreshed, c1840, 67in (170cm) wide.
£7,200–8,000
€/ **$11,500–12,500** ⊞ RYA

◄ **A painted pine *buffet à deux corps*,** French, early 19thC, 50in (127cm) wide.
£1,300–1,500
€/ **$2,000–2,400** ⊞ PICA

A painted pine dresser, original paint, Irish, c1850, 61in (155cm) wide.
£1,100–1,200
€/ **$1,700–1,900** ⊞ DMe

◄ **A painted pine dresser,** the top with fret-carved decoration and reeded corners, Irish, Co Galway, c1860, 49in (124.5cm) wide.
£750–820
€/ **$1,200–1,300** ⊞ HON

A pine dresser, Irish, c1860, 49in (124.5cm) wide.
£550–620
€/ **$870–1,000** ⊞ Byl

A pine dresser, Irish, c1860, 43in (109cm) wide.
£450–500
€/ **$700–800** ⊞ DMe

A Victorian pine dresser, with pot board base, 54in (137cm) wide.
£700–800
€/ **$1,100–1,300** ⊞ WiB

A Victorian pine dresser, restored, Irish, 81in (205.5cm) wide.
£950–1,100
€/ **$1,500–1,700** ⚒ S(O)

A pine dresser, the upper section with three doors, Welsh, c1870, 59in (150cm) wide.
£1,800–2,000
€/ **$2,800–3,200** ⊞ COF

A painted pine dresser, c1870, 51in (129.5cm) wide.
£450–500
€/ **$700–800** ⊞ DFA

A pitch pine dresser, with carved shamrock decoration above two glazed doors flanking shelves, Irish, Co Clare, c1870, 56in (142cm) wide.
£900–1,000
€/ **$1,400–1,600** ⊞ HON

A pine dresser, c1870, 51in (129.5cm) wide.
£300–330
€/ **$475–525** ⊞ DFA

A pine dresser, Irish, Co Donegal, c1870, 58in (147.5cm) wide.
£500–560
€/ **$800–880** ⊞ Byl

A pine dresser, Irish, c1870, 54in (137cm) wide.
£300–330
€/ **$475–525** ⊞ Byl

A pine dresser, c1870, 57in (145cm) wide.
£850–920
€/ **$1,350–1,450** ⊞ DMe

A pine dresser, with two glazed doors, Irish, c1875, 51in (129.5cm) wide.
£500–560
€/ **$800–880** ⊞ Byl

A pine dresser, Irish, c1875, 52in (132cm) wide.
£500–560
€/ **$800–880** ⊞ Byl

A pine dresser, with two glazed doors, eastern European, c1875, 42in (106.5cm) wide.
£450–500
€/ **$710–790** ⊞ Byl

PINE FURNITURE

A pine dresser, with glazed doors, European, c1880, 54in (137cm) wide.
£450–500
€/ **$710–790** ⊞ **Byl**

A pine dresser, c1880, 41in (106.5cm) wide.
£200–225
€/ **$315–350** ⊞ **DFA**

A pine dresser, the upper section with a glazed door over a drawer flanked by two panelled doors, the base with four drawers flanked by two panelled doors, c1880, 53in (134.5cm) wide.
£1,800–2,000
€/ **$2,900–3,200** ⊞ **COF**

A pine dresser, c1880, 40in (101.5cm) wide.
£650–750
€/ **$1,000–1,200** ⊞ **TPC**

A pine dresser, with glazed top, c1890, 47in (119.5cm) wide.
£720–800
€/ **$1,200–1,300** ⊞ **HRQ**

A pine dresser, with glazed top, Irish, c1890, 51in (129.5cm) wide.
£900–1,000
€/ **$1,400–1,600** ⊞ **P&T**

A pine dresser, with glazed top, eastern European, c1890, 42in (106.5cm) wide.
£450–500
€/ **$710–790** ⊞ **PaA**

A pine dresser, with glazed top, German, c1900, 36in (91.5cm) wide.
£630–700
€/ **$990–1,100** ⊞ **HRQ**

A pine apothecary dresser, some drawers replaced, eastern European, c1900, 62in (157.5cm) wide.
£1,500–1,700
€/ **$2,400–2,799** ⊞ **PaA**

Dresser Bases & Side Cabinets

A painted pine side cabinet,
Swedish, c1800, 42in (106.5cm) wide.
£3,500–4,000
€/ $5,500–6,500 ⊞ CAV

A George III pine dresser base,
with two doors and three drawers,
74in (188cm) wide.
£800–950
€/ $1,300–1,500 ⚒ PFK

A Victorian pine dresser base,
handles replaced, 61½in (156cm) wide.
£320–400
€/ $500–630 ⚒ B(Ba)

A pine dresser base, c1870, 44in (112cm) wide.
£165–185
€/ $260–290 ⊞ DFA

**A Victorian pine
chiffonier,** 35in (89cm) wide.
£480–550
€/ $780–870 ⊞ P&T

▶ **A pine chiffonier,** with carved splashback,
Irish, Co Galway, c1870, 50in (127cm) wide.
£325–360
€/ $515–560 ⊞ HON

PINE FURNITURE

◄ **A pine dresser base,** on turned feet, c1870, 56in (142cm) wide.
£400–450
€/ **\$630–700** ⊞ DFA

A pine side cabinet, Romanian, c1875, 47in (119.5cm) wide.
£200–230
€/ **\$300–360** ⊞ Byl

A pine chiffonier, Irish, c1875, 48in (122cm) wide.
£250–280
€/ **\$400–440** ⊞ Byl

◄ **A Victorian pine chiffonier,** handles replaced, Lincolnshire, c1880, 58in (147.5cm) wide.
£1,100–1,250
€/ **\$1,700–1,900** ⊞ COF

A pine side cabinet, with carved decoration, Continental, c1900, 43in (109cm) wide.
£475–525
€/ **\$750–830** ⊞ P&T

◄ **A pine chiffonier,** with carved decoration, Irish, c1880, 45in (114.5cm) wide.
£230–260
€/ **\$360–400** ⊞ Byl

A pine dresser base, c1900, 43in (109cm) wide.
£280–320
€/ **\$440–500** ⊞ HRQ

Dressing Chests & Tables

A pine dressing table, c1895, 36in (91.5cm) wide.
£550–600
€/ **\$870–950** ⊞ COF

A painted pine dressing chest, with mirror, c1890, 36in (91.5cm) wide.
£270–300
€/ **\$425–480** ⊞ HRQ

A pine dressing table, with mirror, c1890, 42in (107cm) wide.
£400–440
€/ **\$630–690** ⊞ AL

► **A Victorian pine dressing table,** with simulated bamboo edging and legs, 43¾in (111cm) wide.
£300–340
€/ **\$475–540** ⚒ B(W)

Ladders & Steps

◄ A Victorian pine step ladder, with patented mechanism, 69in (175.5cm) high.
£200–225
€/ **$310–350** ⊞ GBr

A pine library ladder, late 19thC, 94½in (240cm) high.
£280–320
€/ **$440–500** ➴ DN

► A stained pine folding library ladder, labelled 'J. H. Heathman, Endell St, London', late 19thC, 84in (213.5cm) high.
£800–900
€/ **$1,250–1,400** ➴ S(O)

Linen Presses

◄ A pine linen press, c1830, 83in (211cm) high.
£1,800–2,000
€/ **$2,900–3,200** ⊞ P&T

An early Victorian pine linen press, 85in (216cm) high.
£800–900
€/ **$1,260–1,500** ⊞ P&T

A Victorian pine linen press, the interior with slides, 42in (106.5cm) wide.
£1,000–1,200
€/ **$1,600–1,900** ⊞ TPC

◄ A pine linen press, c1860, 82in (208.5cm) high.
£550–650
€/ **$870–1,000** ⊞ DFA

► A Victorian pine linen press, the interior with slides, c1875, 86in (218.5cm) high.
£1,300–1,500
€/ **$2,000–2,300** ⊞ PaA

PINE FURNITURE

Settles & Settees

A painted pine settle, Welsh, c1780, 56in (142cm) wide.
£3,500–4,000
€/ **$5,500–6,400** ⊞ SEA

A pine settle, c1800, 75in (190.5cm) wide.
£500–560
€/ **$800–880** ⊞ DFA

A provincial grained pine settle, 19thC, 75in (190.5cm) wide.
£1,000–1,200
€/ **$1,600–1,900** ⚒ Bea(E)

A pair of pine settles, with winged sides, one with applied horseshoe, probably Devon, 19thC, 57½in (146cm) wide.
£6,500–8,000
€/ **$10,300–13,000** ⚒ HOK
These settles were formerly the property of the painter Jack B. Yeats (1870–1957), and as they were kept in his studios, they were frequently used as backgrounds in his illustrations.

A pine settle, with hinged box seat, Continental, 19thC, 46in (117cm) wide.
£220–240
€/ **$350–380** ⊞ HRQ

A pine settle, with carved decoration and a hinged box seat, damaged, 19thC, 63in (160cm) wide
£500–600
€/ **$790–950** ⚒ SWO

A pine settle, c1860, 48in (122cm) wide.
£270–300
€/ **$425–475** ⊞ DFA

▶ **A Victorian pine settle,** 109in (277cm) wide.
£1,000–1,100
€/ **$1,600–1,700** ⚒ S(O)

A painted pine settle, c1870, 69in (175.5cm) wide.
£1,350–1,500
€/ **$2,100–2,400** ⊞ SWN

A pine settle, Romanian, c1880, 69in (175.5cm) wide.
£300–330
€/ **$475–525** ⊞ Byl

A pine settle, with one long drawer, original paint, c1890, 70in (178cm) wide.
£400–500
€/ **$630–800** ⊞ TPC

Tables

A pine table, with a single drawer, European, early 19thC, 30in (76cm) wide.
£325–360
€/ $510–570 ⊞ HRQ

A pine cricket table, Welsh, c1800, 29in (73.5cm) diam.
€720–800
€/ $1,150–1,300 ⊞ COF

A pine cricket table, early 19thC, 33in (84cm) diam.
£475–575
€/ $750–910 ⚒ HYD

◀ **An early Victorian pine table,** with three drawers, 52in (132cm) wide.
£350–400
€/ $550–630
⊞ P&T

A painted pine drop-leaf table, Swedish, c1820, 44½in (113cm) extended.
£2,300–2,800
€/ $3,600–4,400 ⊞ RYA

An early Victorian pine table, with two drawers, Irish, 60in (152.5cm) wide.
€425–475
€/ $670–750 ⊞ P&T

◀ **A Victorian pine table,** in the Gothic revival style, 75¼in (191cm) wide.
£380–450
€/ $600–710
⚒ B(Ch)

A Victorian pine side table, by Howard & Sons, the galleried top above two frieze drawers, on turned simulated bamboo legs, 48in (122cm) wide.
£750–875
€/ $1,200–1,400
⚒ DN

PINE FURNITURE

◄ **A pine table,** with a single drawer, on cabriole legs, German, c1840, 43in (109cm) wide.
£215–240
€/ **$340–380**
⊞ HRQ

A Victorian painted pine side table, 51½in (131cm) wide.
£400–450
€/ **$630–700** ⊞ WiB

A painted pine and fruitwood games table, c1840, 18in (45.5cm) diam.
£2,300–2,800
€/ **$3,600–4,400** ⚒ RYA

A pine cricket table, c1850, 28in (71cm) diam.
£300–350
€/ **$480–550** ⊞ TPC

A Victorian pine dining table, on turned legs, c1850, 91in (231cm) wide.
£1,500–1,700
€/ **$2,400–2,700** ⊞ P&T

A pine table, on turned legs, Irish, c1865, 64in (162.5cm) wide.
£315–350
€/ **$500–550** ⊞ Byl

A pine table, on turned legs, Irish, c1870, 83in (211cm) wide.
£300–330
€/ **$475–525** ⊞ DMe

A pine table, with a painted base, c1870, 75in (190.5cm) wide.
£350–400
€/ **$550–630** ⊞ DFA

◄ **A pine table,** the column base with original paint, c1870, 46in (117cm) diam.
£260–300
€/ **$400–475**
⊞ DFA

A pine drop-leaf table, Irish, c1870, 44in (112cm) wide
£225–250
€/ **$350–400** ⊞ Byl

◀ **A pine table,** c1880, 35in (89cm) wide.
£90–100
€ / **$140–160** ⊞ DFA

▶ **A pine table,** with a central drawer, c1880, 50in (127cm) wide.
£210–230
€ / **$330–350** ⊞ Byl

For further information on antique furniture see the full range of Miller's books at **www.millers.uk.com**

A pine drop-leaf table, with one drawer, c1880, 42in (106.5cm) wide.
£280–320
€ / **$440–500** ⊞ AL

A pine side table, with shelf underneath, c1880, 32in (81.5cm) wide.
£215–235
€ / **$340–370** ⊞ AL

◀ **A pine table,** with a central drawer, c1880, 61in (155cm) wide.
£160–180
€ / **$250–280** ⊞ DFA

A pine drop-leaf table, c1880, 44in (112cm) wide.
£200–225
€ / **$315–350** ⊞ HRQ

PINE FURNITURE

A pine table, with a painted base, c1880,
48in (122cm) wide.
£145–160
€/ **$230–250 ⊞ DFA**

A pine table, on turned legs, Irish, c1880,
66in (167.5cm) wide.
£350–400
€/ **$550–630 ⊞ Byl**

A pine wine table, with fold-over top,
French, c1880, 31in (78.5cm) diam.
£480–530
€/ **$750–830 ⊞ AL**

A pine table, on six walnut legs,
Welsh, c1880, 138in (350.5cm) wide.
£1,800–2,000
€/ **$2,800–3,200 ⊞ COF**

A pitch pine drop-leaf table, Irish,
c1880, 48in (122cm) diam.
£225–250
€/ **$350–400 ⊞ Byl**

A pine drop-leaf table, on turned
legs, Irish, c1880, 48in (122cm) wide.
£200–230
€/ **$315–350 ⊞ Byl**

A pine table, with beech top,
on turned legs, c1890,
42in (106.5cm) wide.
£315–350
€/ **$500–550 ⊞ HRQ**

A pine table, with one drawer,
c1890, 41in (104cm) wide.
£280–320
€/ **$440–500 ⊞ HRQ**

A pine table, Irish, c1890, 56in (142.5cm) wide.
£350–400
€/ **$550–640 ⊞ HRQ**

A pine table, c1890, 52in (132cm) wide.
£265–330
€/ **$420–520 ⊞ TPC**

PINE FURNITURE

A **pine side table,** top replaced, c1890, 25in (63.5cm) wide.
£180–200
€/ **$285–315** ⊞ AL

A **Victorian pine table,** c1895, 72in (183cm) wide.
£535–600
€/ **$845–950** ⊞ COF

A **pine side table,** German, c1920, 24in (61cm) wide.
£100–120
€/ **$160–190** ⊞ HRQ

◄ **A Victorian pine library table,** on turned legs, 63in (160cm) wide.
£715–800
€/ **$1,125–1,300** ⊞ PaA

A **painted pine side table,** with a yew top, c1930, 36in (91.5cm) wide.
£80–90
€/ **$125–145** ⊞ DFA

PINE FURNITURE

Wardrobes

A Biedermeier-style pine wardrobe, with original lock, on turned feet, German, c1840, 60in (152.5cm) wide.
£675–750
€ / **$1,100–1,200** ⊞ HRQ

A pine wardrobe, with three doors, c1870, 79in (200.5cm) wide.
£450–500
€ / **$700–800** ⊞ DFA

A pine wardrobe, Irish, c1875, 52in (132cm) wide.
£270–300
€ / **$425–475** ⊞ Byl

A pine wardrobe, with panelled doors, Irish, c1875, 50in (127cm) wide.
£1,300–1,500
€ / **$2,000–2,400** ⊞ COF

A pine wardrobe, the interior with internal drawers and a secret compartment, German, c1880, 57in (145cm) wide.
£630–700
€ / **$990–1,100** ⊞ HRQ

A pine wardrobe, the two doors above a single drawer, German, c1880, 45in (114.5cm) wide.
£550–620
€ / **$870–980** ⊞ HRQ

A pine wardrobe, the two doors above a single drawer, c1880, 52in (132cm) wide.
£300–330
€ / **$475–525** ⊞ DFA

A pine wardrobe, c1890, 37in (94cm) wide.
£225–250
€ / **$350–400** ⊞ DFA

A Victorian gesso-decorated pine wardrobe, 40in (101.5cm) wide.
£500–600
€ / **$790–950** ⊞ TPC

◀ **A pine wardrobe,** c1900, 44in (112cm) wide.
£400–450
€/ **$630–450** ⊞ HRQ

A pine wardrobe, the two doors above a single drawer, c1900, 46in (117cm) wide.
£320–350
€/ **$510–550** ⊞ PaA

◀ **A pine wardrobe,** the three doors above two drawers, German, c1900, 68in (172.5cm) wide.
£800–900
€/ **$1,250–1,500** ⊞ HRQ

▶ **A pine wardrobe,** with decorative carving, German, c1910, 64in (162.5cm) wide.
£800–900
€/ **$1,250–1,500** ⊞ HRQ

A pine wardrobe, c1900, 36in (91.5cm) wide.
£380–435
€/ **$600–690** ⊞ AL

Washstands

A pine washstand, c1880, 35in (84cm) wide.
£235–260
€/ **$365–410** ⊞ HRQ

A pine washstand, c1820, 7in (68.5cm) wide.
300–335
/ **$475–530** ⊞ AL

A pine washstand,
c1900, 24in (61cm) wide.
£90–100
€/ **$140–160** ⊞ DFA

pine washstand, c1880, 9in (48.5cm) wide.
65–70
/ **$100–110** ⊞ Byl

PINE FURNITURE

Miscellaneous

A pair of pine bedside cabinets, eastern European, c1880, 45in (114.5cm) high.
£200–230
€ / $315–360 ⊞ Byl

▶ A painted pine grain bin, c1880, 61in (155cm) wide.
£80–90
€ / $125–140 ⊞ DFA

A pine butcher's block, with two drawers, c1880, 48in (122cm) wide.
£450–500
€ / $700–800 ⊞ DFA

A pine food safe, c1900, 20in (51cm) wide.
£100–115
€ / $160–180 ⊞ AL

A pine grain bin, c1890, 30in (76cm) wide.
£175–200
€ / $275–315 ⊞ AL

◀ A pine plate rack, Irish, Co Tipperary, c1850, 49in (124.5cm) wide.
£500–560
€ / $800–880 ⊞ HON

A pine pot rack, Romanian, c1890, 70in (178cm) wide.
£250–280
€ / $395–445 ⊞ HRQ

▶ A pine shoe bench, with two doors, Continental, c1920, 42in (106.5cm) wide.
£150–175
€ / $250–275 ⊞ COF

A pine shop counter, c1890, 42in (106.5cm) wide.
£450–500
€ / $700–800 ⊞ COF

A pine towel rail, c1890, 32in (81.5cm) wide.
£60–65
€ / $90–100 ⊞ AL

◀ A pine wall rack, 19thC, 39in (99cm) wide.
£145–160
€ / $230–250 ⊞ HRQ

Bamboo & Wicker Furniture

Victorian bamboo open bookcase, the shelves and back covered in seagrass, 39in (99cm) wide.
£320–375
/ $500–590 ✿ WW

A pair of bamboo chairs, c1890.
£240–265
€/ $380–420 ⊞ AL

A chinoiserie bamboo and lacquer writing desk, with leather top, 19thC, 35in (90cm) wide.
£900–1,000
€/ $1,400–1,600 ⊞ CoHA

◀ **A bamboo jardinière,** the sides formed by four Wedgwood tiles entitled 'Oberon', 'Peasblossom', 'Herodia' and 'Cobweb', metal-lined, late 19thC, 26in (66cm) high.
£475–565
€/ $750–890 ✿ TRM

◀ **A chinoiserie bamboo music cabinet,** with a glazed door, late 19thC, 30in (76cm) wide.
£900–1,000
€/ $1,400–1,600 ⊞ CoHA

A bamboo table, with Art Nouveau tiles, c1890, 20in (51cm) square.
£175–200
€/ $275–315 ⊞ GBr

A bamboo and lacquer table, restored, late 19thC, 21in (53.5cm) diam.
£145–160
€/ $230–250 ⊞ CoHA

bamboo wardrobe, with central mirror, c1890, 7in (94cm) wide.
£600–670
/ $950–1,100 ⊞ AL

A Victorian bamboo washstand, with a marbled top and tiled splashback, 19thC, 30in (76cm) wide.
£230–275
€/ $360–430 ✿ BWL

A Victorian bamboo and lacquer whatnot, the legs with applied gilt-metal caps, 24½in (62cm) wide.
£950–1,150
€/ $1,500–2,400 ✿ S(O)

A wicker and maple three-tier whatnot, by Haywood-Wakefield, American, c1900, 17½in (44.5cm) wide.
£1,300–1,500
€/ $2,000–2,400 ⊞ NART

Kitchenware

A bone apple corer, Welsh, 18thC, 4½in (11.5cm) wide.
£135–150
€/ $215–240 ⊞ SEA

A pair of star-shaped baking tins, c1915, 9¼in (23.5cm) diam.
£40–45 each
€/ $60–70 ⊞ MSB

▶ A sycamore butter churn, Welsh, c1840, 24in (61cm) high.
£440–490
€/ $700–780 ⊞ MFB

A sycamore butter print, c1870, 3½in (9cm) diam.
£60–65
€/ $90–100 ⊞ AL

◀ An oak and iron-bound pump-action butter churn, 19thC, 38in (96.5cm) high.
£115–125
€/ $180–195 ⊞ CHAC

A sycamore butter print, Welsh, c1880, 8in (20.5cm) wide
£200–220
€/ $315–350 ⊞ MFB

A sycamore butter wheel, c1860, 6½in (16.5cm) long.
£70–80
€/ $110–125 ⊞ SDA

▶ A wooden cider keg, West Country, c1850, 8in (20.5cm) high.
£340–380
€/ $540–600 ⊞ SEA

A Victorian coffee grinder by Peugeot Frères, French, c1880, 14in (35.5cm) high
£170–200
€/ $270–315 ⊞ PaA

A china cream pail, c1920, 9½in (24cm) high.
£550–600
€/ $870–950 ⊞ SMI

An oak cutlery box, Welsh, c1780, 13in (33cm) wide.
£400–450
€/ $630–710 ⊞ SEA

A wooden flour barrel, 1890–1920, 12in (30.5cm) diam.
£70–75
€/ $110–120 ⊞ CHAC

A set of toleware wall kitchen drawers, c1920, 14in (35.5cm) wide.
£130–150
€/ $200–240 ⊞ B&R

A brass fish slice, early 18thC, 18in (45.5cm) long.
£340–375
€/ $540–600 ⊞ SEA

goffering iron, late 19thC,
in (7.5cm) high.
80–90
/ $125–140 ⊞ WeA
Goffering irons are used to iron
cuffs and sleeves.

A brass griddle, Scottish, 19thC,
4in (10cm) diam.
£135–150
€ / $215–240 ⊞ SEA

A late Victorian silver-plated ham-bone holder, of plain baluster form
with a pierced, key-type screw,
5½in (14cm) long.
£80–100
€ / $125–160 ⚒ WW

brass straining ladle, with iron handle, c1780,
4in (61cm) long.
200–225
/ $315–350 ⊞ MFB

A pine maid's box,
c1890, 11½in (29cm) high.
£90–100
€ / $140–160 ⊞ AL

◄ **A brass and tin milk can,** c1900,
18in (45.5cm) high.
£180–200
€ / $285–315 ⊞ SMI

A cast-iron mangle, by
C. E. Sheldon, Irish, c1860,
60in (152.5cm) high.
£160–180
€ / $250–280 ⊞ HON

n Eddystone milk boiler,
1910, 7½in (19cm) high.
75–85
/ $120–135 ⊞ WeA

A brass and tin milk an, c1910, 7in (18cm) high.
80–90
/ $125–145 ⊞ WeA

Royal Doulton ceramic milk pail, c1890,
0in (25.5cm) high.
180–200
/ $285–315 ⊞ SMI

A brass milk skimmer, with steel handle, early 19thC, 21½in (54.5cm) long.
£200–220
€/ **$315–350 ⊞ WeA**

A Wilson creamware jelly mould, each face painted with fruit and flowers, impressed 'Wilson', 1790–1800, 9¾in (25cm) diam.
£3,500–4,000
€/ **$5,500–6,300 ⚒ WW**
This is a rare item.

A pewter one and a half pint ice cream mould, c1870, 6in (15cm) high.
£200–220
€/ **$315–350 ⊞ MFB**

A Purssell Cornhill copper jelly mould, 19thC, 7in (18cm) diam.
£350–400
€/ **$550–630 ⊞ SEA**

A Victorian copper jelly mould, 4in (10cm) diam.
£160–175
€/ **$250–275 ⊞ WiB**

A copper and tin jelly mould, c1880, 7in (18cm) wide.
£160–200
€/ **$250–315 ⊞ WeA**

A metal chocolate mould, in the shape of a fish, 1900–20, 13in (33cm) wide.
£70–75
€/ **$110–120 ⊞ CHAC**

A wrought-iron and brass nut cracker, c1770, 5in (12.5cm) long.
£340–375
€/ **$540–600 ⊞ SEA**

An elm oatmeal crusher, Scottish, c1880, 14in (35.5cm) long.
£80–90
€/ **$125–140 ⊞ MFB**

A tinplate oven, with an open back and super-structure to hold a clock-work spit jack, early 19thC, 48in (122cm) high.
£250–300
€/ **$400–475 ⚒ S(O)**

A brass pastry cutter, with a wooden handle, c1860, 11in (28cm) long.
£160–180
€/ **$250–285 ⊞ WeA**

▶ **An elm pestle and mortar,** 19thC, 36¼in (92cm) high.
£525–625
€/ **$830–990 ⚒ SWO**

A pair of cast-iron and brass butcher's scales, French, c1880, 26in (66cm) wide.
£180–200
€ / **$285–315** ⊞ SMI

A painted tin biscuit tin, c1900, 6½in (16.5cm) wide.
£100–120
€ / **$160–190** ⊞ SWN

An oak potato press, Romanian, c1880, 22in (56cm) wide.
£55–60
€ / **$85–95** ⊞ Byl

A Denby storage jar, c1910, 14in (35.5cm) high
£100–120
€ / **$160–190** ⊞ SMI

◄ **A copper and brass Bovril urn,** c1900, 19in (48.5cm) high.
£800–900
€ / **$1,250–1,400** ⊞ AL

A three-tier boxwood spice tower, c1810, 6in (15cm) high.
£260–300
€ / **$410–475** ⊞ F&F

A T. G. Green Streamline storage jar, c1930, 4in (10cm) high.
£65–75
€ / **$100–120** ⊞ CAL

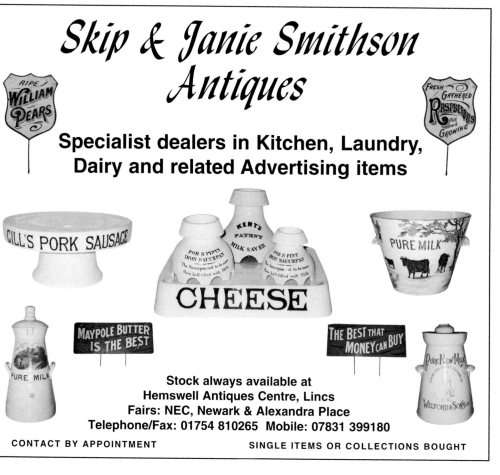

Pottery

The last year has certainly seen difficulties in the market place as a whole with many investments in share portfolios and pensions proving disastrous. Auction houses have had their fair share of turmoil, some showing huge losses. With wars in Afghanistan and now in Iraq, there is plenty of uncertainty and reasonable cause for concern about the year ahead. However, despite all this doom and gloom, the housing market remains high and the collectors' market for pottery, particularly at the top end, looks as strong as ever. Collectors and dealers are still fighting hard over rarities such as the English delft cat jug dated 1677, which recently fetched £45,000 (€/ \$71,000) at auction having been discovered lurking behind a Royal Crown Derby saucer worth about £25 (€/ \$40). The market for majolica remains good with rare game pie dishes still fetching their expected four- and five-figure sums. The majolica highlight this year was the £105,000 (€/ \$166,000) achieved for the Minton Museum Collection life-size peacocks by Paul Comolera dating from 1873.

Various other collections have appeared on the market including the sale of Staffordshire figures and animals from the Margaret Cadman Collection held at Christie's and some very fine Wood family models that were offered at Sotheby's. I have handled two collections of printed political satire pottery in the last six months and both proved sell-outs, with London specialist dealers complaining bitterly at the seemingly extortionate prices collectors and museums are willing to pay.

This in part might be accounted for by the amazing advances in communication over the last five years. With hundreds of auctioneers and thousands of dealers all posting their sale catalogues and stock online, anyone interested has easy access to anything new in the market place. It also shows that despite a difficult market with plenty of uncertainty, terrorist threats and wars, there is still a lot of enthusiasm for old pots, particularly the best pieces, from collectors across the country and around the world.

John Axford

Animals

A Staffordshire creamware model of a water buffalo, possibly Whieldon, c1755, 6in (15cm) wide.
£5,800–6,500
€/ \$9,200–10,200 ⊞ JHo
Fragments of a very similar model with a rider were found on the site of Thomas Whieldon's pottery at Fenton Vivian.

A Staffordshire salt-glazed stoneware bear baiting jug and cover, the applied clay chippings simulating fur, the snout pierced with two chain links, c1760, 10in (25.5cm) high.
£3,500–4,200
€/ \$5,500–6,600 ➢ WW
This piece was exhibited at the Northern Ceramic Society Exhibition in 1974: a useful provenance as there are many fakes of these jugs.

A pair of De Porceleyne Claeuw Dutch Delft peewit butter dishes and covers, with polychrome decoration, claw mark and numerals in blue inside covers, restored, c1765, 5½in (14cm) long.
£5,500–6,500
€/ \$8,700–10,500 ➢ S(NY)

◀ **A Ralph Wood model of a goat,** lying on a rocky base, decorated in translucent glazes, with hollow unglazed underside, 1775–85, 6½in (16.5cm) high.
£2,500–3,000
€/ \$4,000–4,800 ➢ G(L)

A tin-glazed group of a spaniel and three puppies, shaded in manganese, her tail and shaggy fur around the head and neck in bright yellow and black, the puppies with brown markings, possibly German, c1770, 9½in (24cm) wide.
£620–775
€/ \$975–1,225 ➢ B

A Ralph Wood model of a ram, c1790, 7in (18cm) wide.
£2,000–2,300
€ / **$3,200–3,600** ⊞ HOW

A Staffordshire pearlware dog whistle, lower part restored, snout chipped, c1790, 2¼in (5.5cm) high.
£900–1,100
€ / **$1,400–1,700** ⚒ S(O)

A Prattware model of a horse, possibly Staffordshire, late 18thC, 3½in (9cm) wide.
£1,100–1,200
€ / **$1,700–1,900** ⊞ JHo

A pearlware group of a cow and milkmaid, decorated in Pratt colours, the base with sponged decoration, Staffordshire or Yorkshire, minor restoration to tail, c1800, 6in (15cm) high.
£1,100–1,200
€ / **$1,750–1,900** ⊞ HOW

A Staffordshire pearlware model of a cockerel, on a rock base, decorated with polychrome enamels, c1800, 9¾in (25cm) high.
£1,600–2,000
€ / **$2,500–3,200** ⚒ G(L)

A Staffordshire model of a pointer, early 19thC, 6½in (16.5cm) wide.
£1,500–1,700
€ / **$2,400–2,700** ⊞ JHo

POTTERY

A Staffordshire model of a retriever, with light brown markings, on a green and brown rockwork base, c1820, 6½in (16.5cm) wide.
£450–550
€ / **$700–870** ⚒ F&C

A Staffordshire pearlware model of a lioness, on a shaped foliate scroll-moulded base, bocage missing, minor restoration and overpainting, 1810–15, 5½in (14cm) high.
£950–1,200
€ / **$1,500–1,900** ⚒ S(NY)

A Staffordshire model of a pug, early 19thC, 3¾in (9.5cm) high.
£500–550
€ / **$800–870** ⊞ JHo

A pair of Staffordshire pigeons, early 19thC, 3in (7.5cm) wide.
£800–880
€ / **$1,250–1,400** ⊞ JHo

A pottery model of a pig, Scottish, c1830, 6in (15cm) high.
£1,600–1,800
€ / **$2,500–2,800** ⊞ HOW

An Obadiah Sherratt-style Staffordshire bull baiting group, entitled 'Bull.Beating' and 'Now Captin Lad', modelled as a chained bull tossing a terrier over one shoulder, and being bitten on its nose by another, a man with his arms raised by the bull's hind quarters, on a flat-footed table base, minor restoration and hairline crack, c1830, 13½in (34.5cm) long.
£3,500–4,200
€ / **$5,500–6,600** ⚒ B(Kn)

A Staffordshire buff-glazed model of a lion, on a fixed stand, 19thC, 13½in (34.5cm) wide.
£650–750
€/ **$1,000–1,150** ⚒ LVS

A pair of Dutch Delft blue and white models of cows, minor glaze chips, painted A/I:H mark, 19thC, 9in (23cm) wide.
£1,500–1,800
€/ **$2,400–2,850** ⚒ S(O)

A pair of Staffordshire models of poodles, c1850, 8in (20.5cm) high.
£320–350
€/ **$500–550** ⊞ NAW
These are of good quality with separate front legs and applied sieved-clay coats. Poodles are harder to find than spaniels and therefore command a higher price, particularly when they are a good matching pair, such as these.

A pair of Staffordshire models of spaniels, c1850, 13in (33cm) high.
£450–500
€/ **$700–800** ⊞ TUN

A Staffordshire group of three dogs, c1850, 7½in (19cm) high.
£1,700–1,900
€/ **$2,700–3,000** ⊞ HOW

A glazed terracotta model of a spaniel, by James Bailey, restoration damage to ear, Canadian, Ontario, 1850s, 6¾in (17cm) high.
£1,100–1,200
€/ **$1,700–1,900** ⚒ RIT

A pair of Staffordshire models of circus ponies, c1855, 6in (15cm) high.
£800–875
€/ **$1,300–1,400** ⊞ HOW

A Staffordshire model of a hen on a nest with chicks, c1855, 7in (18cm) high.
£725–800
€/ **$1,150–1,300** ⊞ HOW

A Staffordshire model of an Afghan hound, with a figure of a girl by its side, c1860, 13in (33cm) high.
£850–950
€/ **$1,350–1,500** ⊞ ML

▶ **A pair of Staffordshire spill vases,** modelled as sporting dogs standing before trees, c1860, 10in (25.5cm) high.
£1,200–1,400
€/ **$1,900–2,200** ⊞ HOW

◀ **A pair of Staffordshire models of Dalmations,** on painted bases, tails damaged, c1860, 6½in (16.5cm) wide.
£220–260
€/ **$350–400** ⊞ BWL

A pair of Staffordshire models of Jackfield-style cats, c1860, 8in (20.5cm) high.
£775–850
€/ **$1,200–1,350** ⊞ HOW

A pair of Staffordshire models of spaniels, each holding a basket of flowers in its mouth, 1860–80, 7½in (19cm) high.
£475–565
€/ **$750–900** ⚒ TMA

A pair of Victorian Staffordshire models of spaniels, with painted features, gilt collars and chains, 8¾in (22cm) high.
£220–250
€/ **$350–400** ⚒ PF

A pair of Staffordshire models of spaniels, 1860–80, 7½in (19cm) high.
£240–265
€/ **$380–420** ⊞ CHAC

Miller's Compares

I. A pair of Staffordshire models of spaniels, c1870, 9½in (24cm) high.
£350–400
€/ **$550–630** ⊞ CHAC

II. A pair of Staffordshire models of spaniels, c1875, 9½in (24cm) high.
£220–250
€/ **$350–400** ⊞ CHAC

Item I depicts a pair of Staffordshire dogs which are commonly known as 'Disraeli spaniels' because the kiss curls on the tops of their heads are reminiscent of the hairstyle of the Victorian prime minister Benjamin Disraeli. They are only found in black and white, and are much scarcer and therefore more desirable than those without the curls, as in Item II.

A Brown-Westhead and Moore majolica group of a camel and an Arab, shape No. 1285, both seated before an open stone forming a flower holder, on a mound base, one ear of camel repaired, small chip to noseband, impressed mark, c1870, 16in (40.5cm) wide.
£2,700–3,200
€/ **$4,300–5,000** ⚒ S(O)

A Staffordshire pottery model of a King Charles spaniel, seated on a cushion, haircrack to base, 19thC, 5in (12.5cm) high.
£300–350
€/ **$475–550** ⚒ B(W)

A pair of Jackfield-style models of spaniels, c1870, 9in (23cm) high.
£380–420
€/ **$600–670** ⊞ DAN

A pottery majolica stick stand, modelled as a heron with a fish, some damage, stamped '7765/12', Continental, 19thC, 31in (78.5cm) high.
£470–565
€/ **$740–900** ⚒ SWO

▶ **A pair of Staffordshire spill vases,** modelled as spaniels, c1875, 12in (30.5cm) high.
£450–550
€/ **$710–870** ⊞ TUN

A Staffordshire model of a spaniel, with a painted face, incised initials 'WM' and 'NT' to underside, 19thC, 10¾in (27.5cm) high.
£140–160
€/ **$220–250** ⚒ SWO

POTTERY

A pair of Staffordshire pottery models of pugs, each wearing a collar with a gilt locket, one back leg reglued, late 19thC, 11in (28cm) high.
£525–625
€/ **$830–985** ⚒ **B(W)**

A Staffordshire model of a lamb, c1880, 3in (7.5cm) high.
£170–185
€/ **$270–290** ⊞ **SER**

A pair of Staffordshire spill vases, modelled as lambs beneath rustic tree trunks, minor damage, 19thC, 5in (12.5cm) high.
£380–450
€/ **$600–700** ⚒ **BWL**

A Staffordshire porcellaneous spill vase, modelled as a goat standing before a tree trunk, c1880, 4in (10cm) high.
£170–185
€/ **$270–300** ⊞ **SER**

A pair of Victorian Staffordshire models of reclining deer, 3in (7.5cm) high.
£85–100
€/ **$135–160** ⊞ **CoCo**

A Victorian Staffordshire group of a cow and calf, on a gilt-lined grassy base, horns restored, 7in (18cm) high.
£170–200
€/ **$270–315** ⚒ **PFK**

▶ **A majolica gurgler jug,** 19thC, 9¾in (25cm) high.
£105–115
€/ **$165–180** ⊞ **CHAC**
This jug makes a gurgling sound when water is poured and therefore is often known as a gurgler.

A Staffordshire model of an elephant, c1880, 8in (20.5cm) high.
£1,200–1,300
€/ **$1,900–2,000** ⊞ **HOW**

A pair of Staffordshire pottery dishes and covers, modelled as swans, 19thC, 8in (20.5cm) high.
£550–650
€/ **$870–1,000** ⚒ **SWO**

A Wedgwood majolica crocus pot and stand, modelled as a hedgehog, unmarked, late 19thC, 10½in (26.5cm) wide.
£680–820
€/ **$1,100–1,300** ⚒ **S(O)**

A pair of Staffordshire pottery models of zebras, damaged, 1875–1925, 7¾in (19.5cm) high.
£500–600
€/ **$800–950** ⚒ **RTo**

A Sarreguemines majolica tobacco box, modelled as a monkey playing a piano, piano cover and monkey's left hand missing, impressed marks, French, late 19thC, 9½in (24cm) wide.
£450–525
€/ **$700–830** ⚒ **DN**

POTTERY

Baskets

A Staffordshire pearlware blue and white basket-on-stand, printed with Grazing Rabbits pattern, within a floral border, c1820, 11½in (29cm) wide.
£850–1,000
€/ **$1,300–1,600** ➶ WL

A Wedgwood Imperial Queen's Ware reticulated basket, with rope-twist borders, the sides hung with floral garlands, on a flared foot moulded with a Vitruvian scroll, marked 'Wedgwood', c1875, 7½in (19cm) wide.
£180–225
€/ **$285–350** ➶ WW

A majolica basket, c1880, 9½in (24cm) wide.
£60–70
€/ **$95–110** ⊞ CHAC

◄ A George Jones majolica strawberry basket, moulded with blossoming strawberry plants, the base with a painted design No. 3300 111 and impressed registration lozenge, 19thC, 11¾in (30cm) wide.
£525–625
€/ **$830–990** ➶ SWO

A majolica strawberry basket, the handle modelled with strawberries, the curved body decorated with flowers, flanked by recesses for jars, impressed mark for the Victoria Pottery Co, late 19thC, 13in (33cm) wide.
£220–250
€/ **$350–400** ➶ BR

Bowls

A Hispano-Moresque lustre bowl, painted with a bird among stylized trees and foliage, minor chip and surface wear, Spanish, Valencia, 1700–50, 15in (38cm) diam.
£920–1,100
€/ **$1,450–1,750** ➶ S(O)

An English delft blue and white bowl, decorated with a bird flying over a pagoda, early 18thc, 11in (28cm) diam.
£675–750
€/ **$1,000–1,200** ⊞ KEY

A delft bowl, probably Bristol, c1730, 8¾in (22cm) diam.
£900–1,000
€/ **$1,400–1,600** ⊞ JHo

> Items in the Pottery section have been arranged in date order within each sub-section.

An Enoch Booth bowl, c1743, 7in (18cm) diam.
£4,000–4,400
€/ **$6,300–7,000** ⊞ JHo
Enoch Booth, with Thomas Astbury and Josiah Wedgwood, is associated with the invention and development of creamware. The design for this bowl is derived from Chinese blue and white porcelain.

A maiolica bowl, the top painted with a geometric pattern, cracked, rim chips, Spanish, 18thC, 12¼in (31cm) diam.
£100–120
€/ **$160–190** ➶ DN

A Neale caneware sucrier and cover, with twin handles and neo-classical-style moulding, the cover with scrolling acanthus leaves and flowers, a central fluted boss and floral knop, the base with panels containing an urn flanked by pendant husks, fine crack to flange of cover, impressed factory mark, incised 'N31', c1790, 7½in (19cm) wide.
£800–1,000
€/ **$1,250–1,600** ➶ B

POTTERY

A Staffordshire pottery pedestal bowl, printed and enamelled with figures beside a fireplace and chair, the reverse inscribed 'Love not sleep lest thou come to poverty', c1840, 3½in (9cm) diam.
£85–100
€/ **$135–160** ✕ WL

A late Victorian George Jones majolica sugar basin and milk jug, both decorated with relief-moulded flowers, the basin on three log feet, the jug with a branch handle, crack to basin, jug 3in (7.5cm) high.
£100–120
€/ **$160–190** ✕ PFK

An earthenware bowl, with everted rim and dark brown splatter glazes on a red body, hairline crack, Canadian, Quebec, 19thC, 11½in (29cm) wide.
£180–220
€/ **$280–340** ✕ RIT

A pottery bowl, c1860, 10in (25.5cm) diam.
£155–170
€/ **$245–270** ⊞ MFB

A faïence barber's bowl, polychrome-painted with floral sprays and insects, damaged, French, 19thC, 10in (25.5cm) wide.
£100–120
€/ **$160–190** ✕ EH

A Furnival Pottery punch bowl, transfer-printed and coloured with Gothic arcading, late 19thC, 19½in (49.5cm) diam.
£400–500
€/ **$630–800** ✕ S
Various Furnival partnerships produced pottery in Cobridge, Staffordshire, in the second half of the 19th century. Furnivals Ltd was in production from 1890–1968.

A Minton majolica bowl, modelled as a lily bowl above three crouching frogs, on a circular base, stem restored, dated 1865, 4½in (11.5cm) high.
£950–1,150
€/ **$1,500–1,800** ✕ B(W)

A Wedgwood majolica punch bowl, cracks, 19thC, 13½in (34.5cm) diam.
£220–250
€/ **$350–400** ✕ MAR

A Wemyss basket, painted with irises, with rope-twist handle, impressed 'Wemyss', printed retailer's mark for Thomas Goode & Co, London, early 20thC, 16in (40.5cm) long.
£2,500–3,000
€/ **$4,000–4,700** ✕ S

Buildings

A Staffordshire watch stand, modelled as a castle keep on a mound base, c1820, 8in (20.5cm) high.
£1,800–1,900
€/ **$2,800–3,000** ⊞ JHo

A Prattware money box, modelled as a house flanked by two figures, some restoration, impressed flowerhead mark, 1800–50, 5in (12.5cm) high.
£185–220
€/ **$290–350** ✕ WW

A Staffordshire porcellaneous model of a cottage, c1840, 4in (10cm) high.
£200–225
€/ **$315–350** ⊞ DAN

A Staffordshire model of Euston Station, c1855, 11in (28cm) high.
£1,200–1,400
€/ **$1,900–2,200** ⊞ HOW

Busts

A pearlware female head, with elaborate coiffure, possibly a *bonbonnière*, screw-on cover missing, 1775–1825, 3in (7.5cm) high.
£55–65
€ / $85–100 ♣ PFK

A Staffordshire bust of Alexander I of Russia, by Wood & Caldwell, c1805, 12in (30.5cm) high.
£1,500–1,650
€ / $2,400–2,600 ⊞ JHo

A Staffordshire pearlware bust of Voltaire, impressed title to reverse of pedestal, early 19thC, 6in (15cm) high.
£550–650
€ / $870–1,000 ♣ S

A Wedgwood black basalt bust of Mercury, modelled after the Antique by William Hackwood, on a waisted socle, impressed 'Wedgwood' to bust and socle, 19thC, 18½in (47cm) high.
£1,300–1,500
€ / $2,000–2,400 ♣ Bea(E)

POTTERY

Candlesticks

A Minton majolica candlestick, modelled as a putto supporting a sconce on his head, on a circular base, reglued through the ankles, impressed marks and date cypher for 1867, 7in (18cm) high.
€700–850
€ / $1,100–1,350 ♣ WW

► **A Minton majolica candlestick,** the bulbous gadrooned shaft on a shaped circular base, c1870, 7½in (19cm) high.
£500–600
€ / $800–950 ♣ B
Ex-Minton Sale. Masterpieces of Minton was the title of an auction held at Bonhams in July 2002. The sale comprised 380 pieces of pottery and porcelain from the Minton Museum Collection.

A pair of Wedgwood blue and white triton two-light candlesticks, each supporting two leaf- and scroll-moulded branches beneath foliage sconces, restored, impressed marks, painted '2129', c1876, 14¼in (36cm) high.
£650–750
€ / $1,000–1,200 ♣ S(O)

Cheese Domes

A stoneware cheese dome, with floral decoration, c1870, 11in (28cm) diam.
£100–120
€ / $160–190 ⊞ WAC

A George Jones majolica cheese dome, the textured ground moulded with briars and leafy wildflowers, pink-glazed interior, glued repair to stand, impressed mark, black script pattern No. 5223, post-1873, 7in (18cm) high.
£1,400–1,600
€ / $2,200–2,500 ♣ S(O)

A Thomas Forester & Sons majolica cheese dome, modelled with a frieze of four panels edged in bamboo, each containing a stork wading among waterlilies and bulrushes, with a bamboo handle, rim chips, glaze wear and crazing, inscribed '28', c1883, 11¼in (28.5cm) high.
£500–625
€ / $800–1,000 ♣ B

POTTERY

Cow Creamers

A Prattware-style cow creamer and cover, restored, c1800, 6¼in (16cm) long.
£450–550
€/ $700–870 ↗ S(O)

A cow creamer, probably Swansea, early 19thC, 7in (18cm) long.
£375–450
€/ $600–700 ↗ DAU

A cow creamer, North Yorkshire, early 19thC, 5¼in (13.5cm) long.
£1,000–1,100
€/ $1,600–1,750 ⊞ JHo

Dishes

A Liverpool or London delft sweetmeat dish, c1760, 8½in (21.5cm) diam.
£3,000–3,300
€/ $4,750–5,250 ⊞ JHo

A Durlach faïence dish, painted with sprays of *indianische Blumen* and scattered sprigs, minor glaze chips to rim, German, c1760, 13½in (34.5cm) wide.
£700–800
€/ $1,100–1,250 ↗ S(O)

A Rörstrand faïence dish, Swedish, 1765, 19in (48.5cm) wide.
£450–550
€/ $700–870 ↗ BUK

Three Minton majolica oyster dishes, with moulded shell decoration, marked, 1868, 9in (23cm) diam.
£700–820
€/ $1,100–1,300 ↗ SWO

A Sarreguemines double asparagus dish, French, c1880, 15in (38cm) wide.
£270–300
€/ $425–475 ⊞ MLL

A pottery dish, the exterior printed with three fish, crazing and foot chip, 19thC, 7in (18cm) diam.
£160–200
€/ $250–315 ↗ PFK
The fish are meant to represent char, which were made into a paste and stored in these vessels. The char is a fish that belongs to the *Salmonidae* family and inhabits lakes in Scotland, Ireland and Wales. It flourished years ago, but is seldom seen today.

A majolica strawberry dish, 1850–1900, 10½in (26.5cm) wide.
£75–85
€/ $120–135 ⊞ CHAC

A slip-trailed pottery dish, with two compartments, a beaded rim and integral trailing, 19thC, 11¾in (30cm) wide.
£65–75
€/ $100–115 ↗ PFK

A Wemyss quaich, painted with roses, c1900, 7in (18cm) diam.
£320–350
€/ $500–550 ⊞ RdeR

Covered Dishes

A Marieberg faïence butter dish and cover, Swedish, 1766–69, 8in (20.5cm) wide.
£1,500–1,700
€/ **$2,400–2,700** ↗ BUK

A Minton majolica game pie dish and cover, the lid with a hare, mallard and woodsnipe, the base with basketweave and oak leaves, date cypher for 1858, 14in (35.5cm) wide.
£1,000–1,200
€/ **$1,600–1,900** ↗ HOLL

A Staffordshire creamware butter dish and cover, the knop modelled as a cow, 18thC, 7in (18cm) diam.
£2,500–2,800
€/ **$4,000–4,400** ⊞ JHo

A Minton majolica game pie dish and cover, the cover surmounted by a gundog lying on a gun and a gamebag, relief decorated with a hare to the front and a pheasant to the reverse, on four moulded paw feet, impressed marks to base, c1870, 8in (20.5cm) wide.
£2,000–2,400
€/ **$3,200–3,800** ↗ B(EA)

A Mosbach faïence butter dish and cover, on a fixed stand, painted with flower sprays and scattered leaves, the cover with a pear finial, minor glaze chips to rims, CT monogram in black, German, 1775–1825, 9½in (24cm) diam.
£500–600
€/ **$800–950** ↗ S(O)

A sardine box, the lid with an applied dolphin finial and moulded with seaweed, decorated in cream with gilded detail on a puce ground, the base also embossed with seaweed or foliage within gilded rims, 19thC, 5½in (14cm) wide.
£100–120
€/ **$160–190** ↗ GAK

POTTERY

Drainers & Strainers

A London delft drainer, painted with radiating lines, rim chip, glaze worn, mid-18thC, 7in (18cm) diam.
£900–1,100
€/ **$1,400–1,700** ↗ B

A creamware strainer, c1790, 3in (7.5cm) wide.
£200–225
€/ **$315–350** ⊞ DSA

A Hicks & Meigh Ironstone drainer, c1820, 13in (33cm) wide.
£280–320
€/ **$440–500** ⊞ CoS

Further reading

Miller's Ceramics Buyers Guide,
Miller's Publications, 2000

A Spode Ironstone drainer, c1825, 15in (38cm) wide.
£360–400
€/ **$550–630** ⊞ CoS

A Minton & Hollins drainer, pattern No. 5160, over-enamelled with flowers, c1843, 12in (30.5cm) wide.
£380–420
€/ **$600–675** ⊞ CoS

A Mason's drainer, decorated with Bandana pattern, c1850, 13in (33cm) wide.
£380–420
€/ **$600–675** ⊞ CoS

Figures

A faïence figure of St Louis, standing with his right arm outstretched and his left arm raised before him, his costume painted in blue, his crown, feet and the fleur-de-lys moulded on his cape picked out in ochre, base inscribed 'Saint.Louis.,1735', minor damage, French, possibly Nevers, 15¾in (40cm) high.
£350–420
€/ **$550–660** ⚹ B

A Staffordshire figure of Iphigenia, c1790, 8½in (21.5cm) high.
£250–280
€/ **$400–440** ⊞ SER

A Staffordshire pearlware group of children, entitled 'Scuffle', modelled as a boy and two girls fighting over a hat, c1810, 6¼in (16cm) high.
£375–450
€/ **$600–700** ⚹ S(O)

A Staffordshire figure of Faith, restored, c1780, 8in (20.5cm) high.
£170–185
€/ **$270–300** ⊞ SER

A Prattware figure of a fiddler, probably Staffordshire, c1790, 7½in (19cm) high.
£1,600–1,800
€/ **$2,500–2,800** ⊞ JHo

A pair of Staffordshire Tittensor figural groups, c1810, 6in (15cm) high.
£3,200–3,500
€/ **$5,000–5,500** ⊞ JHo
Charles and John Tittensor were Staffordshire figure-makers during the late 18th century and early 19th century. Some pieces have impressed marks.

A Ralph Wood pearlware figure of a shepherd, the base decorated with sheep and birds, c1785, 8½in (21.5cm) high.
£450–500
€/ **$700–800** ⊞ JRe

A Ralph Wood pearlware figural group, entitled 'The Bird Cage', decorated with overglaze enamels, impressed No. 89, c1790, 10½in (26.5cm) high.
£900–1,000
€/ **$1,400–1,600** ⊞ JRe

▶ **A Staffordshire pearlware figure of Diana,** decorated with overglaze enamel, c1810, 11½in (29cm) high.
£450–500
€/ **$700–800** ⊞ JRe

A Wood family pearlware figure of Simon, standing before a tree stump, his arms folded, on a grassy mound base, small chips, c1785, 8¾in (22cm) high.
£1,700–2,000
€/ **$2,700–3,200** ⚹ S(O)

The Wood family of potters

Many of the most celebrated English pottery figures of the 18th century were made by members of the Wood family working in Staffordshire. The rare and extremely expensive pew groups of c1745 are often attributed to Aaron Wood (1717–85). Ralph Wood I (1715–72) and Ralph Wood II (1748–95) are famous for their skillfully modelled Toby jugs and figures with high temperature underglaze colours. Some pieces have impressed marks or an incised rebus mark of a small clump of trees.

A pair of Staffordshire creamware figures of children, decorated in enamels, c1800, 8in (20.5cm) high.
£850–950
€/ **$1,350–1,500** ⊞ JRe

◀ A Staffordshire
Walton figural group,
entitled 'Friendship',
c1820, 7½in (19cm) high.
£850–950
€ / **$1,350–1,500** ⊞ HOW

**A Staffordshire pearlware
spill vase rural group,**
of a deer, a stag, a boy
and a squirrel, c1820,
8½in (21.5cm) high.
£1,500–1,700
€ / **$2,400–2,700** ⊞ HOW

A Staffordshire inkwell,
modelled as a boy on a
dolphin, early 19thC,
5in (12.5cm) high.
£1,000–1,100
€ / **$1,600–1,750** ⊞ JHo

**A pair of pearlware figures of The
Welsh Tailor and Wife,** after Derby,
each modelled riding a goat with a
basket on their back containing infants
and kids, painted with overglaze colours,
on scroll-moulded bases, damaged,
early 19thC, 5½in (14cm) high.
£170–200
€ / **$270–315** ⤴ PF

▶ A Stafford-
shire figure of
Dr Syntax,
early 19thC,
5in (12.5cm) high.
£900–1,000
€ / **$1,400–1,600**
⊞ JHo
Dr Syntax is a
comic character
originally depicted
in a series of
drawings by the
cartoonist Thomas
Rawlinson, c1800.

**A Staffordshire pearlware
figure of an old soldier,**
decorated with over-
glaze enamels, c1820,
8in (20.5cm) high.
£2,000–2,300
€ / **$3,200–3,650** ⊞ JRe

POTTERY

A Staffordshire pearlware pastoral group, modelled as a man and a woman sitting beneath a gnarled tree stump with two lambs and an owl, damaged, 1800–50, 8in (20.5cm) high.
£200–240
€/ **$315–380** ➤ WW

A Staffordshire figural group of The Traveller, c1820, 4in (10cm) high.
£1,100–1,200
€/ **$1,750–1,900** ⊞ JHo

A Staffordshire pearlware spill vase group of a Vicar and clerk, christening a child, with three figures looking on, before a turreted castle flanked by flowering trees, the oval mound base moulded with a scroll, restored, c1825, 7in (18cm) high.
£850–975
€/ **$1,350–1,550** ➤ LFA

An Obadiah Sherratt-style pearlware group of the Battle of the Breeches, modelled as a couple fighting over a pair of breeches, a baby and a cat at their feet, damaged, 1820–30, 7½in (19cm) high.
£2,300–2,700
€/ **$3,600–4,200** ➤ S(O)

A Staffordshire pearlware group, entitled 'Petter Rising The Lame Man Acts Ch 2', c1825, 10½in (26.5cm) high.
£1,500–1,700
€/ **$2,400–2,700** ⊞ HOW

A Staffordshire figure of a female gardener, c1825, 7in (18cm) high.
£550–600
€/ **$870–950** ⊞ HOW

A Staffordshire figural group of a dancer and a musician, with a swan beneath a bridge, c1840, 7½in (19cm) high.
£155–170
€/ **$245–270** ⊞ CHAC

A pair of Staffordshire figures of royal chidren on ponies, by Thomas Parr, c1850, 9in (23cm) high.
£1,400–1,600
€/ **$2,200–2,500** ⊞ HOW

A Staffordshire figure of Garibaldi, with Liberté flag, c1850, 13in (33cm) high.
£340–375
€/ **$550–600** ⊞ ML

▶ **A Staffordshire spill vase,** modelled as Macomo and the lion, on a gilt-scroll base, c1850, 8¼in (21cm) high.
£850–1,000
€/ **$1,350–1,600** ➤ SJH

A pair of Staffordshire figures of Gringoire and Esmerelda, restored, c1850, 7in (18cm) high.
£155–170
€/ **$245–270** ⊞ CHAC

A pair of Staffordshire figures of a girl and a boy with birds, c1850, 6in (15cm) high.
£270–300
€/ **$430–470** ⊞ ACO

A pair of Staffordshire figures of a man and a woman playing musical instruments, the bases decorated with vine leaves, c1850, 13in (33cm) high.
£630–700
€/ **$1,000–1,100** ⊞ TUN

A Staffordshire figural group of a prince and princess in a carriage, c1850, 8in (20.5cm) high.
£1,100–1,200
€/ **$1,750–1,900** ⊞ HOW

A Staffordshire figure of a girl gardener, by a bridge over a stream, c1850, 7¼in (18.5cm) high.
£60–70
€/ **$95–110** ⊞ CHAC

A Staffordshire pottery spill vase group, modelled as a fortune teller, 1850–60, 10in (25.5cm) high.
£200–235
€/ **$315–375** ⊞ DAN

A Staffordshire figural group of a soldier and a sailor, c1854, 12in (30.5cm) high.
£300–325
€/ **$475–515** ⊞ SER

POTTERY

A Staffordshire pottery figure, entitled 'The First Ride', c1855, 11½in (29cm) high.
£1,800–2,000
€/ **$2,800–3,200** ⊞ HOW

A pair of Staffordshire figures, she entitled 'Sand', he entitled 'Beesums', c1855, 9in (23cm) high.
£765–850
€/ **$1,200–1,350** ⊞ ML
Most working class cottages used to have flagstone floors which would get covered in grease and dirt. The method of cleaning them would be to spread sand liberally over the floor and leave it to be walked on for two or three days to soak up the grease. It would then be swept up with besom – a broom made of twigs tied round a stick. These itinerant traders would travel together from marketplace to marketplace selling their wares.

A Staffordshire figural group of Welsh shepherds, c1855, 14in (35.5cm) high.
£400–450
€/ **$630–700** ⊞ TUN

A pair of Staffordshire figures of Scottish gardeners, wearing traditional dress, each with two pots of flowers, on a scroll-moulded base, c1860, 9¼in (23.5cm) high.
£65–80
€/ **$100–125** ⋋ TMA

◄ **A pair of Staffordshire pottery figures of a fisherman and a fisher-woman,** each holding a basket of fish, 1860–80, 13in (33cm) high.
£120–140
€/ **$190–220** ⋋ G(L)

A Staffordshire mustard pot figure, in the form of a portly gentleman, c1860, 6in (15cm) high.
£100–110
€/ **$160–175** ⊞ DHA

A pair of Staffordshire figures of a girl and a boy reading, c1860, 6in (15cm) high.
£200–220
€/ **$315–350** ⊞ SER

A Staffordshire figure, entitled 'Will Watch', 19thC, 15in (38cm) high.
£200–225
€/ **$315–355** ⊞ CHAC

For further information on antique pottery see the full range of Miller's books at
www.millers.uk.com

POTTERY

A Staffordshire group of Uncle Tom and Eva, from *Uncle Tom's Cabin*, c1860, 10in (25.5cm) high.
£300–325
€/ $475–515 ⊞ DHA

A Staffordshire figural group of a Scottish couple, seated on a clock, 19thC, 13½in (34.5cm) high.
£100–120
€/ $160–190 ⊞ CHAC

A pair of Staffordshire porcellaneous figural groups, of ladies mounted on stags, cracks, c1860, 7½in (19cm) high.
£380–450
€/ $600–700 ↗ BR

A Staffordshire figural group of a shepherdess and a sheep, c1860, 7in (18cm) high.
£60–70
€/ $95–110 ⊞ ACO

A Staffordshire figural group of a girl with a goat, c1860, 6in (15cm) high.
£140–155
€/ $220–244 ⊞ SER

A pair of Stafforshire figural groups of a boy and a girl sitting on goats, c1865, 6in (15cm) high.
£300–335
€/ $475–525 ⊞ ML

▶ A Wedgwood black basalt figural group, entitled 'Cupid Disarmed', impressed 'Wedgwood', and title to the reverse, late 19thC, 13¾in (35cm) high.
£1,750–2,100
€/ $2,800–3,300 ↗ B(WM)

A Staffordshire figural group of two musicians and a dog, 19thC, 12½in (32cm) high.
£120–135
€/ $190–215 ⊞ CHAC

A pair of Staffordshire figures of a girl and a boy with sheep, c1880, 7½in (19cm) high.
£350–400
€/ $550–630 ⊞ SER

A pair of majolica figures of women, one clutching wheat sheaves and holding a basket, the adjacent tree stump surmounted by wheat sheaves and a sickle, the other with upraised arms, the adjacent tree stump surmounted by a water jug, firing crack, 1850–1900, 21in (53.5cm) high.
£1,700–2,000
€/ $2,700–3,150 ↗ RIT

◀ A Staffordshire figure of a grape picker, 19thC, 13½in (34.5cm) high.
£120–150
€/ $190–240 ↗ L

A Staffordshire pottery spill vase figural group, of a young man holding a bird, and a young woman holding a bird's nest, standing above a bridge, on a gilt-lined base, 19thC, 13in (33cm) high.
£75–90
€/ $120–140 ↗ DMC

A Staffordshire figure, entitled 'Infant Jesus', wearing a loin cloth, leaning on a pedestal surmounted by a book, on a gilt-lined base, 19thC, 11in (28cm) high.
£750–900
€/ $1,200–1,400 ↗ SJH

Flatware

A pink lustre plate, with floral decoration, Hispano-Moresque, 16thC, 12½in (32cm) diam.
£2,000–2,200
€/ $3,150–3,200 ✗ DA

A maiolica dish, painted with a landscape and Cupid flanked by Venus and Mars embracing, and a bearded man, the reverse with a series of concentric rings and inscribed 'nonara e martto', Italian, possibly Urbino, 16thC, 9in (23cm) diam.
£3,000–3,600
€/ $4,750–5,700 ✗ Bea

A maiolica dish, painted with the Madonna and Child, restored, hair crack, Italian, Venice, 1550–1600, 9½in (24cm) diam.
£2,000–2,400
€/ $3,200–3,800 ✗ S(NY)

Items in the Pottery section have been arranged in date order within each sub-section.

An English delft charger, painted with oak leaves and cherries, late 17thC, 13¾in (35cm) diam.
£5,800–7,000
€/ $9,000–11,000 ✗ S(O)

A Dutch Delft dish, painted with a pomegranate and objects, chips to edges, late 17thC, 13¾in (35cm) diam.
£300–350
€/ $475–550 ✗ BR
This design was copied directly from Chinese kraak porcelain of 1600–40.

A faïence dish, painted with a central flowering plant flanked by the date, the rim with four similar flower sprays, German, Zittau, dated 1685, 12in (30.5cm) diam.
£725–875
€/ $1,150–1,400 ✗ S(O)

▶ **A Dutch Delft royal portrait dish,** commemorating Queen Mary, chip and crack to underside, initialled 'KM', numbered 20, 1675–1725, 13in (33cm) diam.
£1,400–1,600
€/ $2,200–2,500 ✗ TEN

Expert's choice

A delft armorial plate, 1653, sold by Woolley & Wallis on 28th November 2001.

It's the unexpected that is usually the most exciting. Recently while on a valuation I discovered hanging above a kitchen sink a delft armorial plate inscribed with initials, and, more importantly, it was dated. Dated English delftware is among the 'holy grail' of English pottery, a small number of pieces having fetched over £100,000 (€/ $158,000) at auction. On consulting Dated English Delftware, by Louis Lipski and Michael Archer (Sotheby's Publications 1984), I discovered a moulded dish with the same coat-of-arms and, like 'my' plate, dated 1653, the year Cromwell became Lord Protector of England. A footnote suggested that the arms were perhaps those of the Makers of Playing Cards Company, or the Paste Board Makers, although it seems these arms were not authorized in the 17th century. Unfortunately the plate had been broken into eight pieces and riveted back together. Had this been an equally rare piece of 18th-century Chinese porcelain, or Royal Worcester for that matter, it would have been nearly worthless, but English delft collectors are more pragmatic and realize that if they insist on perfect pieces, they would rarely buy anything at all. This was amply demonstrated when the plate was knocked down in the saleroom for £10,200 (€/ $16,000). **John Axford**

POTTERY

POTTERY

A London delft blue-dash charger, decorated with tulips and flowers growing from a mound, the reverse also tin-glazed, some restoration, c1700, 13½in (34.5cm) diam.
£2,800–3,200
€/ **$4,400–5,000** ⚒ S

A London or Bristol delft plate, c1725, 10in (25.5cm) diam.
£400–435
€/ **$630–680** ⊞ JHo

A Bristol delft plate, c1750, 12in (30.5cm) diam.
£675–750
€/ **$1,100–1,200** ⊞ SEA

Delft & delft

Delft is tin-glazed earthenware made in Holland since the 16th century, so-called from the town where so much of it was produced. From the 17th century tin-glazed earthenware was made in England using similar techniques and styles. In order to differentiate them, it is best to precede the term 'Delft' or 'Delftware' by Dutch or English. However, it has become customary for dealers and auction houses to use 'Delft' for the Dutch wares and 'delft' or 'delftware' for the English.

An English delft marriage plate, painted with cupids, the border with leaf scrolls and wheel medallions, reserving a panel with the initials 'E & EK', the reverse with repeating circles and groups of four dots, minor glaze chips and cracks, dated 1708, 8¾in (22cm) diam.
£4,000–4,750
€/ **$6,300–7,500** ⚒ B

A London delft dish, painted with a parrot seated on a ring, with rocks and flowers, rim chips, c1730, 13¾in (35cm) diam.
£525–625
€/ **$830–980** ⚒ S(O)

An English delft charger, painted centrally with flowers, rocks and a fence, within a border of repeated flower stems, mid-18thC, 13½in (34.5cm) diam.
£170–200
€/ **$270–315** ⚒ CGC

▶ **A Moustiers faïence plate,** with central coat-of-arms, within a border of garlands, painted Olery mark, French, c1750, 9¾in (25cm) diam.
£280–340
€/ **$440–550** ⚒ Bea(E)

A Dutch Delft plate, painted with a Chinese man and a bird beside a vase of flowers, the rim with diaper border and five ribbon-bound leaf vignettes, early 18thC, 9in (23cm) diam.
£225–250
€/ **$350–400** ⚒ CGC

A Bristol delft plate, decorated with a peacock between trees, c1730, 8in (20.5cm) diam.
£2,200–2,400
€/ **$3,500–3,800** ⊞ JHo

A delft dish, possibly English, painted with chinoiserie flowers in a fenced garden, chips to rim, hairline glaze cracks, mid-18thC, 13½in (34.5cm) diam.
£200–225
€/ **$315–350** ⚒ RTo

An English delft plate, painted with an exotic bird on a leafy branch, with rockwork and flowers, mid-18thC, 8¾in (22cm) diam.
£260–325
€ / **$400–500** ✎ WW

A Dutch Delft dish, painted with a vase and jardinière of flowers, the border with five foliate panels, some glaze damage to rim, mid-18thC, 12in (30.5cm) diam.
£270–320
€ / **$425–500** ✎ Bea(E)

A Dutch Delft plate, painted with a pot issuing flowers, c1750, 14in (35.5cm) diam.
£360–400
€ / **$575–625** ⊞ SEA

A Bristol delft plate, painted with a bird on a rocky pinnacle, c1760, 12in (30.5cm) diam.
£1,100–1,200
€ / **$1,700–1,790** ⊞ KEY

A set of four English delft plates, painted with a Chinese pagoda set in a landscape, c1760, 9in (23cm) diam.
£585–650
€ / **$925–1,000** ⊞ KEY

A salt-glazed plate, decorated with a Liverpool Sadler & Green printed design, c1765, 9in (23cm) diam.
£700–780
€ / **$1,100–1,200** ⊞ JHo

A Whieldon-style spongeware plate, c1765, 9in (23cm) diam.
£360–400
€ / **$575–630** ⊞ HOW

Thomas Whieldon

Thomas Whieldon (1719–95) was one of the principal 18th-century Staffordshire potters. He started a factory in 1740, making a wide range of wares, and partnered Josiah Wedgwood between 1754 and 1759. His name is most often associated with wares decorated with high-temperature underglaze colours, typically mottled green, grey, purple, yellow and brown, as well as the 'tortoiseshell ware' with sponged manganese decoration. Unfortunately for the ceramic historian his pieces were never marked.

A creamware miniature platter, the centre moulded with a lobster, with a feather-moulded edge, c1780, 4¼in (11cm) wide.
£315–375
€ / **$500–600** ✎ HAM

A pair of Wedgwood creamware soup plates, from the Earl of Shaftesbury service, painted with the full arms of Anthony Ashley Cooper, 5th Earl of Shaftesbury, impressed marks, c1786, 9¾in (25cm) diam.
£525–625
€ / **$830–900** ✎ B

An English delft plate, with floral decoration, 18thC, 9in (23cm) diam.
£400–450
€ / **$630–700** ⊞ SEA

A Bristol delft charger, painted with stylized flowers and foliage, 18thC, 13in (33cm) wide.
£1,000–1,200
€ / **$1,600–1,900** ✎ HYD

POTTERY

POTTERY

A Dutch Delft plate, painted with a vase of flowers, 18thC, 9in (23cm) diam.
£100–120
€ / **$160–190** 🔨 SWO

A Delft dish, painted with Oriental flowers within a flower and leaf border, rim chips, probably Dutch, 18thC, 12in (30.5cm) diam.
£120–150
€ / **$190–240** 🔨 TMA

A delft plate, painted with a hot air balloon above a house and garden, within a swag border, some fritting, late 18thC, 8¾in (22cm) diam.
£1,300–1,500
€ / **$2,000–2,400** 🔨 CHTR

A Swansea Pottery arcaded plate, painted with a heron, c1815, 8in (20.5cm) diam.
£1,000–1,100
€ / **$1,600–1,700** ⊞ HOW

A pearlware plate, commemorating Alderman Wood, the Lord Mayor of London, giving up his house to Queen Caroline on her arrival in London, 1820, 8in (20.5cm) diam.
£1,100–1,300
€ / **$1,700–2,000** ⊞ RdV

An enamelled plate, commemorating the coronation of Queen Victoria, the centre painted with a portrait and inscription, the border relief-moulded with stylized flowers, c1837, 6¾in (17cm) diam.
£350–420
€ / **$550–650** 🔨 DD

A child's plate, decorated with turkeys, within a moulded rim, c1840, 7½in (19cm) diam.
£145–160
€ / **$230–250** ⊞ HOW

A nursery plate, painted with flowers and the name 'Alice', mid-19thC, 5½in (14cm) diam.
£135–150
€ / **$215–240** ⊞ SWN

A spongeware cream pottery dish, by Mann & Co, Hanley, 1858–60, 14in (35.5cm) diam.
£270–300
€ / **$425–475** ⊞ MFB

A plate, printed with a view of the Philadelphia Exhibition 1876, decorated with a star device rim, 1876, 8¾in (22cm) diam.
£85–100
€ / **$130–160** 🔨 SAS

A majolica 'corn on the cob' bread platter, some chips, 19thC, 14½in (37cm) wide.
£135–150
€ / **$215–240** ⊞ CHAC

A Wemyss plate, painted with green gages, c1900, 5in (12.5cm) diam.
£270–300
€ / **$425–475** ⊞ RdeR

Flower Bricks

A London or Bristol delft flower brick, c1740, 6¼in (16cm) wide.
£1,000–1,100
€/ **$1,600–1,700** ⊞ JHo

A pair of London delft flower bricks, each side painted with a vase of flowers, rim chips, c1750, 5¾in (14.5cm) wide.
£2,000–2,400
€/ **$3,200–3,800** ⚒ S

A delft flower brick, possibly Liverpool, each side painted with a cottage, the ends painted with a bird, chips, c1760, 6in (15cm) wide.
£900–1,100
€/ **$1,400–1,700** ⚒ S(O)

Garden Seats

A majolica garden seat, modelled as a blackamoor child among bulrushes, supporting a cushion, the base on three bun feet, c1870, 17½in (44.5cm) high.
€850–1,000
€/ **$1,350–1,600** ⚒ S(NY)

▶ **A George Jones majolica garden seat,** modelled as a tripod of vine sticks roped together and hung with fruiting vines at the top, chips, with applied pad mark inscribed 'stoke-on-trent', with GJ monogram, foot chipped, c1870, 18in (45.5cm) high.
£750–900
€/ **$1,200–1,400** ⚒ B

A Minton majolica garden seat, shape No. 1219, decorated in low relief with cranes and stylized flowering foliage, incised shape No., impressed Minton mark and date cipher for 1885, 17¾in (45cm) high.
£900–1,100
€/ **$1,400–1,700** ⚒ B
Ex-Minton Sale.

Inkstands & Inkwells

A delft inkstand, probably Liverpool, each side painted with buildings, the ends with a man in a boat, c1760, in (12.5cm) wide.
800–950
€/ **$1,250–1,500** ⚒ S(O)

A stoneware inkwell, probably by Wilson, with raised sprigged decoration, c1800, 1¾in (4.5cm) high.
£225–250
€/ **$350–400** ⊞ DIA

◀ **A delft ink stand,** with twin wells with covers and a drawer to each end, painted with Chinese figures and landscapes on a scrolling ground, monogrammed AR, 19thC, 7¾in (19.5cm) wide.
£135–160
€/ **$215–250** ⚒ WW

Stoneware

'Stoneware' is a general heading for a wide range of ceramic wares which are fired at a high temperature (1200°–1400°C), so that the body becomes vitrified and impervious to liquids. Stonewares are always hard but, unlike porcelain, are seldom translucent and not usually white. The earliest stonewares were made in China in the 7th century AD as forerunners to porcelain, but it was not until the 15th century that they appear in Europe, initially in northern parts of Germany. Stonewares can be grey, red, brown, black or white and are often decorated with a salt glaze with the characteristic 'orange peel' surface. Fine and very hard red stonewares were made by Böttger at Meissen in the early 18th century and by the Elers Brothers in England, who were copying the red wares from Yixing in South China. Other centres in England include Nottingham, Derbyshire and London, while in Staffordshire fine white stonewares were produced, often decorated with vibrant coloured enamels to compete with the new porcelain trade.

Jardinières

A Victorian majolica jardinière, moulded in high relief with Chinese dragons chasing a flaming pearl among clouds, damaged, 15in (38cm) high.
£375–450
€/ $600–700 ✗ PF

▶ A Victorian pottery jardinière, on a matching stand, 34¼in (87cm) high.
£100–120
€/ $160–190 ✗ SWO

A pair of majolica jardinières, modelled as tree trunks, one cracked, 19thC, 8in (20.5cm) high.
£140–160
€/ $220–250 ✗ G(L)

A majolica jardinière, modelled as a woven basket with twin handles, with a stand of rustic twig design, 19thC, 23¾in (60.5cm) high.
£260–325
€/ $400–500 ✗ TRM

An earthenware flower pot, attributed to Dion family, with ruffled rim and base, decorated with a dark brown streaky glaze on a red body, cracks, Canadian, Quebec, 19thC, 8in (20.5cm) diam.
£160–200
€/ $250–315 ✗ RIT

A majolica jardinière, with moulded morning glory flowers and stems entwined around the side, late 19thC, 7in (18cm) high.
£200–225
€/ $315–350 ⊞ CHAC

A late Victorian Wardle majolica jardinière and stand, both with relief-moulded foliage decoration, impressed marks, 30in (76cm) high.
£220–250
€/ $350–400 ✗ PFK

A majolica jardinière and stand, French, 1850–1900, 80in (203cm) high.
£3,800–4,300
€/ $6,000–6,800 ⊞ BrL

A majolica jardinière and stand, probably by Bretby, the jardinière with lobed spirally moulded rim, the stand with balustroid stems on a spirally moulded foot, 1875–1925, 29½in (75cm) high.
£130–160
€/ $200–250 ✗ PFK

An earthenware jardinière and stand, German, c1900, 46in (117cm) high.
£630–750
€/ $990–1,200 ✗ DuM

▶ A Wemyss pottery Combe jardinière, painted with dog roses between bands, impressed 'Wemyss Ware R. H. & S.', cracks, c1900, 7in (18cm) high.
£420–500
€/ $670–800 ✗ S(O)

A Wemyss 'Rothes' flower pot, painted with four sandmartins among sponge trees, haircracks and chip, impressed Wemyss Ware, R.H. & S, early 20thC, 8in (20.5cm) high.
£500–600
€/ $790–950 ✗ S

Jars

A Dutch Delft tobacco jar, painted with two Native Americans flanking barrels of tobacco beneath festooned drapery, inscribed 'A = La Roose', damage to rim, 1675–1725, 10½in (26.5cm) high.
£900–1,100
€ / **$1,400–1,750** ➷ RTo

A Bristol or London delft jar, 1700–15, 7in (18cm) high.
£6,000–6,800
€ / **$9,500–10,750** ⊞ JHo

A Castelli maiolica apothecary jar, painted with a figure seated by a tortoise and enclosed by flowering plants, inscribed 'Flemmatico Pea1 Acqua' above larger label inscribed 'Aq. Chelid', one handle and base missing, rim repair, early 18thC, 14½in (37cm) high.
£600–700
€ / **$950–1,100** ➷ S(O)

A maiolica wet drug jar, with a spout and a loop handle, with foliate decoration and the initials 'M.B.', Italian, 18thC, 9½in (24cm) high.
£200–240
€ / **$315–380** ➷ TRM

Two Dutch Delft tobacco jars, by De Drie Klokken (The Three Bells) factory, each decorated with a jar labelled 'St Domingo' and 'Hanover', flanked by a Native American smoking, barrels and ships, 18thC, 10¼in (26cm) high.
£1,200–1,400
€ / **$1,900–2,200** ➷ Bri

A Dutch Delft tobacco jar and brass cover, painted with a flower and scrollwork medallion, inscribed 'Romano' in a reserve, marked P:C in underglaze blue, glaze wear and abrasion, 18thC, 13¼in (33.5cm) high.
£550–650
€ / **$870–1,000** ➷ S(Am)

A Minton majolica two-handled pedestal jar and cover, moulded in relief with oak leaves and acorns, date code for 1856, 11½in (29cm) high.
£720–850
€ / **$1,150–1,350** ➷ DN

A Farrar Pottery earthenware tobacco jar, by James Black, with dark brown glaze and applied relief foliage and pipes, the cover with cylindrical finial, Canadian, Quebec, 1880–1908, 8½in (21.5cm) high.
£200–240
€ / **$315–380** ➷ RIT

Jugs & Ewers

stoneware jug, German, c1580, 12in (30.5cm) high.
1,200–1,400
/ **$1,900–2,200** ⊞ SEA

A Westerwald stoneware jug, German, c1670, 8in (20.5cm) high.
£600–660
€ / **$950–1,000** ⊞ JHo

A Staffordshire solid agateware cream jug, with a shaped rim and scroll handle, on lion-paw feet, each with a lion mask at the knee, one foot repaired, 1745–55, 4in (10cm) high.
£1,400–1,600
€ / **$2,200–2,500** ➷ B

POTTERY

A Wedgwood jug, printed in Liverpool with a couple taking tea in the garden, c1765, 5in (12.5cm) high.
£170–185
€/ **$270–300** ⊞ JHo

A Neale pearlware jug, decorated with floral sprays, c1790, 7in (18cm) high.
£450–500
€/ **$700–800** ⊞ DSA

A creamware puzzle jug, with a pierced border and spout, and scroll handle, painted with sprays of flowers and inscribed and dated 1792 to the frieze and base, 18thC, 9in (23cm) high.
£900–1,100
€/ **$1,400–1,700** ↗ HYD

A Farrar's Pottery stoneware jug, buff-glazed with hand-painted cobalt floral decoration, chips to base, American, Vermont, early 19thC, 15in (38cm) high.
£160–200
€/ **$250–315** ↗ RIT

A commemorative jug, with a named portrait of 'Admiral Lord Nelson', c1805, 8in (20.5cm) high.
£1,700–1,900
€/ **$2,700–3,000** ⊞ RdV

Ironstone

'Ironstone', or 'Ironstone china', is a trade name for a hard, durable earthenware patented by Charles Mason in 1813, and which was claimed to contain slag of iron as an ingredient. Although this claim has since been proved false, nearly 200 years later clever marketing ensured 'Mason's Patent Ironstone China' is still a household name. Early examples are highly sought after by collectors and are very expensive. Other Staffordshire makers of Ironstone include Davenport, Spode, Ridgway and the Ashworth Brothers.

A Mason's Ironstone china foot-bath jug, the lobed bulbous body surmounted by a cylindrical neck with an inset angular spout, a reeded handle, and a further dragon-head-moulded handle beneath the spout, decorated with a Japanese pattern, minor faults, crown and drape mark, 1820–40, 12in (30.5cm) high.
£1,300–1,600
€/ **$2,000–2,500** ↗ DN

A pearlware Pan's head jug, decorated with colourful knots, small chips, marked 'Shorthose & Co', c1820, 6¼in (16cm) high.
£240–280
€/ **$380–440** ↗ WW

► **A pair of pottery puzzle jugs,** each with moulded decoration depicting windmills, oak trees and figures drinking, 19thC, larger 8½in (21.5cm) high.
£55–70
€/ **$85–110** ↗ TRM

A Devon slipware jug, by Fishley, with central panel of two birds, the reverse inscribed 'Beware as the potter said to the lump of clay, I'll be burnt first sauci responded the mud', below a borde of leaves, 19thC, 11½in (29cm) high.
£5,750–6,750
€/ **$9,000–10,700** ↗ SJH
Devon slipware is very collectabl and pieces by the Fishley family don't often come onto the market

A pottery Coronation jug, the body moulded with a trellis design and scrolling cartouche printed with portraits and panels of Coronation trophies, 1831, 7¼in (18.5cm) high.
£300–375
€/ $475–600 ➶ SAS

▶ **A Minton majolica Tower' jug,** the hinged cover with a jester's head finial, with Britannia metal mounts, above an entwined branch rustic handle continuing around the rim band, above a frieze of four dancing figures, finial chipped, impressed 'Mintons, 1231', rear cypher for 1881, 12½in (32cm) high.
£525–625
€/ $830–1,000 ➶ TEN

A Robert Burns stoneware mask-head jug, by Machin & Potts, moulded with scenes of merrymaking, with Tam O'Shanter to the reverse, centred by a named portrait, moulded mark and dated 1834, 8¼in (21cm) high.
£60–75
€/ $95–120 ➶ SAS

▶ **A majolica jug,** c1880, 6in (15cm) high.
£60–70
€/ $95–110 ⊞ CHAC

A Minton 'Henri Deux' ornamental ewer, by Charles Toft, the fixed overhead handle with a seated dog finial, the spout above a bearded male mask, with Renaissance-style arabesques and Celtic motifs, the foot and middle section applied with scrolls, signed 'C. Toft Minton & Co,' c1878, 10½in (26.5cm) high.
£1,600–2,000
€/ $2,500–3,200 ➶ B
Ex-Minton Sale.

◀ **A Mason's Patent Ironstone china footbath jug,** with a relief serpent mask handle to the front and a tail to the rear, 19thC, 13in (33cm) high.
£820–975
€/ $1,300–1600 ➶ SWO

A majolica pitcher, by Eureka Pottery, decorated in low relief with a fan, dragonfly, prunus and waterlily motifs, American, New Jersey, 1883–87, 7¼in (18.5cm) high.
£270–330
€/ $430–530 ➶ RIT

A graduated set of three Mason's Ironstone Hydra-shaped jugs, floral-decorated, with serpent-form handles, printed mark, 19thC, largest 6½in (16.5cm) high.
£140–160
€/ $220–250 ➶ DMC

A Wemyss ewer, possibly by Edwin Sandland, painted with dragonflies above reeds, within line borders, impressed and painted Wemyss, early 20thC, 9½in (24cm) high.
£1,000–1,200
€/ $1,600–1,900 ➶ S

POTTERY

Mugs & Tankards

A Nottingham salt-glazed stoneware mug, inscribed 'William Bomer 1723', incised with two bands of scrolling flowers, 4½in (11.5cm) high.
£2,300–2,800
€/ **$3,600–4,400** ↗ WW

A Leeds creamware mug, with moulded gadrooned borders and reeded cross-over scroll handles, with applied floral terminals, 18thC, 3¾in (9.5cm) high.
£625–750
€/ **$1,000–1,175** ↗ PFK

A delft tankard, probably London, chips, mid-18thC, 5½in (14cm) high.
£3,500–3,850
€/ **$5,500–6,000** ⊞ JHo

A Thuringian pewter-mounted faïence tankard, painted with a scrollwork cartouche enclosing a standing elephant, flanked by flowering branches, the cover inscribed 'RW' and '1745' below an inlaid portrait medallion of Louis XV, some wear and repair, maker's mark, HL monogram to base, German, mid-18thC, 9½in (24cm) high.
£750–875
€/ **$1,200–1,400** ↗ S(O)

A pearlware tankard, with a leaf-capped loop handle, painted *en grisaille* with a classical maiden seated by a tree, with gilt embellishment, base inscribed 'Swansea', 1775–1825, 5¾in (14.5cm) high.
£3,500–4,250
€/ **$5,500–6,700** ↗ AH
This mug was identified as being decorated by William Weston Young, who worked at Swansea for only four years from 1803–07. Only three such pieces have been on the market in the last ten years.

Items in the Pottery section have been arranged in date order within each sub-section.

A creamware mug, printed with two children and a dog at play, c1800, 3½in (9cm) high.
£500–550
€/ **$800–880** ⊞ DSA

A creamware Masonic mug, printed and painted with an armorial shield and emblems, and inscribed 'Richd & Thomason Rodgers, West Herrington', base crack, c1800, 5¾in (14.5cm) high.
£900–1,100
€/ **$1,400–1,700** ↗ WW

▶ **A pearlware mug,** inscribed 'My Dear Boy', above floral sprigs, chipped and cracked, c1820, 3½in (9cm) high.
£100–120
€/ **$160–190** ↗ HAM

The Rous Lench Collection

Many ceramics aficionados will agree with me that the heavyweight champion of English auctions over the last 25 years was the sale of Thomas George Burne's wonderful collection of pottery and porcelain. It was formed over many years to fill the fine 16th-century timbered house Rous Lench Court, in Worcestershire, that he was given as a 21st birthday present in 1928. The rarity of the pieces and the fantastic prices they realized is legendary and still act as a benchmark for prices well over a decade after they were sold. Following his death in 1985, his collection was sold in two parts by Sotheby's in 1986 and by Christie's in 1990. The collection included some 140 pieces of 16th–18th century English delft, among them a single candlestick dating from the Commonwealth period of 1653 which fetched £154,000 (€/ $243,000). From the non-Delft pottery a silver-mounted Tudor jug of c1550 fetched £275,000 (€/ $435,000). Quintessentially English 17th-century slipware was well represented and other pottery included fine Staffordshire white salt-glazed stonewares, Whieldon ware, Astbury figures and a charming Pew group of the type attributed to Aaron Wood dated to c1745.

The wonderful 18th-century English porcelain was among the best ever seen on the market, so for collectors of English pottery or porcelain, the two sale catalogues are simply a must for the reference library. Even in those days, 25 lots sold at over £40,000 (€/ $63,000) and one wonders about the sanity of such prices. A question easy to ask but harder to answer is 'Would these items make such high prices today?' Some pieces, although they appeared astonishingly expensive at the time, certainly would be very pricey in the sale rooms today and could quite conceivably make more, but for the most expensive pieces, it is more difficult to say. The market at that time was polarized between two extremely determined American collectors who, to the auction houses' delight, would neither compromise nor stop bidding.

John Axford

A Mason's Ironstone moulded mug, painted with flowers and foliage, with an animal mask handle, early 19thC, 6in (15cm) high.
£230–280
€ / **$350–450** ⚒ WW

A nursery mug, inscribed 'A Present for Hannah', mid-19thC, 3in (7.5cm) high.
£135–150
€ / **$215–240** ⊞ SWN

An Orange Order mug, printed and decorated with Masonic emblems, a lustre rim, restored chip, 1800–1850, 4¾in (12cm) high.
£200–250
€ / **$300–380** ⚒ WW

POTTERY

A majolica mug, decorated with birds and lillies, c1880, 4½in (11.5cm) high.
£175–200
€ / **$275–315** ⊞ CHAC

A majolica mug, decorated with a grape vine, 19thC, 4½in (11.5cm) high.
£50–60
€ / **$80–95** ⊞ CHAC

A Wemyss mug, painted by Karol Nekola with thistles, Wemyss mark to base, early 20thC, 5½in (14cm) high.
£375–450
€ / **$590–710** ⚒ DAU

Plaques

A Makkum plaque, painted with a quayside with sailing vessels and windmills, minor glaze wear, the reverse dated 1704, Dutch, 14½in (36.5cm) high.
£320–400
€ / **$500–625** ⚒ S(Am)

▶ An Enoch Wood blue jasper medallion, applied with a relief figure of Minerva, impressed 'Minerva The Goddess of Wisdom, War and Wool "Heathen Mythology" Enoch Wood Sculpsit', minor chip, c1790, 4¾in (12cm) high.
£350–425
€ / **$550–670** ⚒ B

A Pratt-style plaque, moulded with Vulcan standing at a forge, pierced for hanging, rim chips, c1800, 7½in (19cm) high.
£650–750
€ / **$1,000–1,200** ⚒ S(O)

LOCATE THE SOURCE
The source of each illustration in Miller's can be found by checking the code letters below each caption with the Key to Illustrations, pages 794–800.

A faïence wall plaque, painted with a view of Mont Saint Michel, French, late 19thC, 9 x 8in (23 x 20.5cm).
£140–175
€ / **$220–280** ⚒ SWO

A pottery wall plaque, entitled 'No Surrender', commemorating the Battle of the Boyne in 1698, late 19thC, 9in (23cm) wide.
£60–70
€ / **$95–110** ⊞ STA

POTTERY

Pot Lids

A portrait of **Wellington,** with clasped hands, Ball No. 160B, with an overglazed pot decorated with fruiting vines, c1850, 4in (10cm) diam.
£200–220
€/ **$315–350** ⚒ SAS

▶ **'The Best Card',** Ball No. 254, with a decorative border, c1860, 4in (10cm) diam.
£100–110
€/ **$160–175** ⚒ SAS

'Dressing My Lady's Hair', Ball No. 434, framed, c1880, 4in (10cm) diam.
£850–1,000
€/ **$1,350–1,600** ⚒ SAS

'Napirima, Trinidad', Ball No. 225, c1853, 4¼in (11cm) diam.
£120–140
€/ **$190–220** ⚒ SAS

'Charity', Ball No. 362, with a decorativ border, c1860, 2¾in (7cm) diam.
£220–250
€/ **$350–400** ⚒ SAS

American Dentifrice inscribed 'C.J. Peacock D. D. S. Pennsylvania College of Dental Surgery 2 West Park Terrace Scarborough', minor wear, c1880, 3½in (9cm) diam.
£280–340
€/ **$440–540** ⚒ BBR

◀ **Price & Co Alexandra Cherry Paste,** inscribed 'The Celebrated Alexandra Cherry Paste prepared by Price & Co late Price & Gosnell Perfumers to the Royal Family for the Teeth and Gums 246 Regent Street, London', wear, crazing and chips, c1880, 3½in (9cm) diam.
£350–420
€/ **$550–660** ⚒ BBR

Pots

A **delft posset pot,** painted with chinoiserie figures in a garden, early 18thC, 6in (15cm) high.
£1,300–1,600
€/ **$2,000–2,500** ⊞ KEY

▶ A **salt-glazed stoneware crock,** by W. Hart, decorated with a spotted fish, hairline crack, American, New York, mid-19thC, 11in (28cm) high.
£3,500–4,200
€/ **$5,500–6,700** ⚒ S(NY)

▶ A **delft posset pot and cover,** painted with a Chinese figure in a boat approaching a dwelling, damage to rim, mid-18thC, 9½in (24cm) wide.
£675–825
€/ **$1,000–1,300** ⚒ TEN

A **Wemyss pot,** painted with fruit, late 19thC, 3in (7.5cm) high.
£165–185
€/ **$260–290** ⊞ SER

Dessert Services

A Hicks & Meigh stone china part dessert service, comprising 13 pieces, decorated in the Imari palette with willow and peony within fenced gardens, heightened in gilt, minor faults and one dish repaired, printed factory marks to bases, early 19thC.
£820–975
€/ **$1,300–1,500** RTo

A Minton stone china part dessert service, comprising 9 pieces, decorated with Amherst Japan pattern, some damage and repair, blue-printed marks, red script pattern No. 824, c1840.
£675–820
€/ **$1,000–1,300** S(O)

A majolica dessert service, comprising 18 pieces, decorated with a waterlily and leaf pattern, two pieces chipped, 19thC.
£625–750
€/ **$980–1,185** AG

A Mason's Ironstone part dessert service, comprising 15 pieces, decorated with flowers, leaves and fruit, one dish chipped, impressed factory marks, c1820.
£3,300–4,000
€/ **$5,200–6,300** WW

A Copeland & Garrett fruit service, comprising 13 pieces, decorated with poppies and forget-me-nots, 19thC.
£100–120
€/ **$160–190** TRM

POTTERY

Dinner Services

An Ironstone dinner service, comprising 62 pieces, decorated with flowers and heightened with gilding, minor damage, impressed marks and painted pattern No. 7129, mid-19thC.
£520–625
€/ **$820–1,000** S(O)

A Victorian dinner service, comprising 77 pieces, transfer-decorated with vases of flowers within floral panelled borders, heightened with colour.
£1,900–2,200
€/ **$3,000–3,500** B(Pr)

◄ **An Ironstone dinner service,** comprising 66 pieces, 19thC.
£2,700–3,200
€/ **$4,250–5,000** JAd

A Mason's Ironstone part dinner service, comprising 75 pieces, with Oriental-style decoration, 19thC.
£925–1,100
€/ **$1,400–1,700** RTo

A Staffordshire pottery part dinner service, comprising 71 pieces, decorated in the Pekin pattern, some damage, c1880.
£725–875
€/ **$1,100–1,375** DN

POTTERY

Tea Services

A Staffordshire part tea service, pattern No. 247, comprising six pieces, decorated with stylized flowers and rockwork, c1830.
£130–160
€/ $200–250 ✗ WW

A Staffordshire drabware part tea service, comprising three pieces, applied with trailing leaves and flowers, chips and losses, incised marks, c1840.
£200–225
€/ $300–350 ✗ S(O)

▶ **A George Jones majolica Japanese-style cabaret service,** model Nos. 3450 and 3465, comprising ten pieces, damaged, marked, registration lozenges for 1875.
£9,200–11,000
€/ $14,500–17,000 ✗ B
Despite the damage to this service, George Jones is always popular and commands high prices.

Stands

A Savona faïence stand, moulded with a stand ring in the centre and a lobed rim, painted with a putto in a landscape, small chip to rim, blue tower mark, 1700–50, 7in (18cm) diam.
£320–350
€/ $500–550 ✗ S(O)

A London delft stand, with polychrome decoration, on claw feet, c1730, 5½in (14cm) diam.
£3,400–3,800
€/ $5,400–6,000 ⊞ JHo

▶ **A Wedgwood lazy Susan,** with a printed border, impressed mark, 19thC, 19in (48.5cm) diam.
£275–325
€/ $430–515 ✗ SWO

A Dublin delft tureen stand, probably by Henry Delamain, painted with Peony and Fence pattern, minor frits, blue-painted 7 to reverse, 1755–60, 22in (56cm) wide.
£2,600–3,000
€/ $4,150–4,750 ✗ S(O)

Tea Canisters

A Durlach faïence tea canister, painted with Oriental flowers in a fenced garden, the shoulder with two insects, minor glaze chips, German, c1770, 4½in (11.5cm) high.
£500–600
€/ $790–950 ✗ S(O)

A Prattware tea canister, decorated with Macaroni figures, c1790, 5½in (14cm) high.
£300–320
€/ $475–500 ⊞ KEY

A Prattware tea canister, decorated with Macaroni figures, c1790, 5½in (14cm) high.
£300–320
€/ $475–500 ⊞ KEY

ea, Coffee & Punch Pots

A Staffordshire salt-glazed miniature teapot, c1740, in (7.5cm) high.
880–980
/ $1,400–1,550 ⊞ KEY

Leeds creamware coffee pot, the d with a rose knop, with acanthus-moulded spout, the entwined handle vith leafy terminals, c1780, 0in (25.5cm) high.
620–680
/ $980–1,000 ⊞ KEY

A Staffordshire lead-glazed red ware teapot, possibly Astbury, decorated with creamware, c1760, 3½in (9cm) high.
£1,200–1,400
€/ $1,900–2,200 ⊞ JRe

A Pratt-style pearlware punch pot, decorated with floral garlands, initials to body, spout and lid chipped, 1780–90, 9½in (24cm) high.
£180–220
€/ $280–350 ⋏ SWO

A creamware teapot, attributed to William Greatbatch, with double C-scroll handle, foliate spout and pierced collar, metal cap to spout, repair to collar, c1780, 5in (12.5cm) high.
£175–200
€/ $275–325 ⋏ RIT

A Minton majolica teapot and cover, shape No. 1838, modelled as a seated chinaman wearing a kimono and trousers, holding a Noh mask, the spout issuing from its mouth, restoration and hairline crack, impressed Minton and date cypher, 1875, 5¾in (14.5cm) high.
£1,300–1,500
€/ $2,000–2,400 ⋏ B
Ex-Minton Sale.

POTTERY

Prattware

Prattware is a lightweight pottery made in Staffordshire, Scotland and the North East of England, characterized by the use of high temperature underglaze colours, typically a dirty orange, sludgey green, a rather drab blue, manganese and brown. As the colours are underglaze, they do not flake as enamel colours so often do. Named after a family of Staffordshire potters, the wares mostly date from the late 18th and early 19th centuries, and include figures, animals, relief-moulded jugs and tea canisters, Toby jugs and plaques. Later in the 19th century, the Pratt family pottery became famous for the production of colour-printed pottery pot lids.

A majolica eapot, decorated vith a bamboo nd bird design, epair to inner m, c1880, 6½in 6.5cm) high.
100–120
/ $160–190
CHAC

◀ **A jasper ware teapot,** c1890, 5in (12.5cm) high.
£70–80
€/ $110–125
⊞ CoCo

Tiles

A Dutch Delft tile, 1600–20, 4¼in (11cm) square.
£400–435
€/ **$630–700** ⊞ JHo

An English delft tile, painted in Fazackerly colours, mid-18thC, 5¼in (13.5cm) square.
£270–325
€/ **$425–500** ⚒ WW

A Liverpool delft tile, printed with the fox and cockerel from *Aesop's Fables,* c1770, 5in (12.5cm) square.
£350–400
€/ **$550–630** ⊞ RdV

A tile picture, comprising six tiles, depicting a seated cat with two mice, restored, mounted onto board, Dutch, 1770–90, 15¼in x 10in (38.5 x 25.5cm).
£1,700–1,900
€/ **$2,700–3,000** ⚒ S(Am)

A *pâte-sur-pâte* tile, by P. Ipsen, Danish, Copenhagen, c1870, 8in (20.5cm) square.
£290–320
€/ **$460–480** ⊞ KMG

A Trent Tile Co tile, signed by Isaac Broome, American, c1890, 6in (15cm) square.
£240–265
€/ **$380–420** ⊞ KMG

▶ **A tile picture,** comprising six tiles, 19thC, 11¾ x 17¼in (30 x 44cm).
£80–95
€/ **$120–150** ⚒ SWO

Toby & Character Jugs

A Staffordshire Prattware character jug, modelled as Bacchus, c1790, 12in (30.5cm) high.
£1,700–1,900
€/ **$2,700–3,000** ⊞ JRe

A Ralph Wood The Squire Toby jug, pipe missing, c1790, 11in (28cm) high.
£3,500–4,000
€/ **$5,500–6,300** ⊞ JBL
The Toby's hand has a hole to take a pipe which, was usually the first thing to break. Later moulds did not incorporate this aperture.

It is thought that Toby jugs derive their name from a humorous song written in the mid-18th century about Toby Fillpot, a fellow who was more than a little fond of his drink. Long after he had died, his body turned into clay in the ground, and an enterprising potter made it into a jug. A mezzotint was produced to accompany this song which proved very popular in Georgian Britain.

A Wood-style Toby jug, wearing a tricorn hat, holding a frothing beer cup and an empty beer jug, damaged, late 18thC, 14¼in (36cm) high.
£1,100–1,300
€/ **$1,750–2,000** ⚒ HAM

A Prattware Martha Gunn Toby jug, with a pearlware glaze, c1790, 10in (25.5cm) high.
£1,800–2,000
€/ **$2,800–3,200** ⊞ JBL
Martha Gunn, 'the Queen of the Dippers', was a celebrated Brighton character who assisted ladies in bathing in the sea, from bathing machines, in the latter half of the 18th century and early 19th century. It is said that she also bathed the Prince of Wales (later George IV).

A Staffordshire pearlware Warty Face Toby jug and cover, seated holding a foaming jug and a pipe, chips to pipe, early 19thC, 9½in (24cm) high.
£270–320
€/ **$430–500** ⚒ S(O)

A Toby jug, possibly Enoch Wood, decorated in enamels, c1820, 10in (25.5cm) high.
£450–500
€/ **$700–800** ⊞ JBL

◀ **A Staffordshire pearlware George Whitfield jug,** 1820–25, 8in (20.5cm) high.
£500–550
€/ **$800–870** ⊞ JRe
George Whitfield (1714–70) was a famous Methodist preacher and a friend of John Wesley. This Toby is often mistakenly called The Nightwatchman.

A spongeware Portobello Toby jug, c1820, 10in (25.5cm) high.
£520–585
€/ **$800–900** ⊞ JBL
This Toby's hat lifts out and can be used as a measure to drink from.

A pair of Punch and Judy character jug, c1880, 10in (25.5cm) high.
£580–650
€/ **$915–1,000** ⊞ JBL

POTTERY

POTTERY

Tureens

A Staffordshire salt-glazed tureen and cover, minor restoration, c1740, 11in (28cm) wide.
£1,000–1,100
€/ **$1,600–1,750** ⊞ JRe

A Rörstrand faïence tureen and cover, Swedish, c1758, 16½in (42cm) wide.
£1,700–2,000
€/ **$2,700–3,200** ⋟ BUK

A Mosbach faïence soup tureen and cover, the domed cover with a fruit finial, decorated with flower sprays and scattered sprigs, restored, cracked, rim chip to cover, CT monogram in manganese, German, c1780, 12½in (32cm) wide.
£375–450
€/ **$600–700** ⋟ S(O)

A Neale & Co creamware sauce tureen, the cover with a floral finial, decorated with a frilled band and flowers, chips, impressed mark, 18thC, 8¼in (21cm) wide.
£140–160
€/ **$220–250** ⋟ AG

A Leeds creamware sauce tureen and cover, the cover with a pomegranate finial, with moulded handles, late 18thC, 7in (18cm) wide.
£325–375
€/ **$500–600** ⋟ TRM

A Davenport pearlware tureen and cover, the finial modelled as a bunch of grapes, painted with flowers, chips and staining, impressed 'Davenport' above an anchor, incised 22 to foot and cover, 1810–25, 7¾in (19.5cm) wide.
£800–950
€/ **$1,300–1,500** ⋟ S(O)

◀ **A Mason's Ironstone soup tureen, cover and stand,** heightened with enamels, printed marks, 19thC, 14in (35.5cm) wide.
£350–420
€/ **$550–650** ⋟ SWO

▶ **A Victorian Ironstone tureen and cover,** transfer-printed in the Imari palette, 11in (28cm) wide.
£80–90
€/ **$120–140** ⋟ BR

Vases & Urns

A Caltagirone maiolica bottle vase, painted with flowers and scrolling foliage, chips and repairs, Italian, 17thC, 9in (23cm) high.
£650–775
€/ **$1,000–1,225** ⋟ S(O)

A Clérissy faïence tulip vase, probably by Moustier, decorated *en camaïeu* after the engravings by J. Bérain, rim chips, French, c1730, 9½in (24cm) high.
£2,000–2,200
€/ **$3,200–3,500** ⋟ S(Am)
Jean Bérain (1640–1711) was influenced by the Renaissance period and worked as a designer to the Court of Louis XIV.

A Dutch Delft vase, c1740, 11in (28cm) high.
£340–375
€/ **$550–600** ⊞ SEA

▶ **A faïence *bouquetière*,** possibly Durlach, chips and cracks, German, c1770, 6¼in (16cm) high.
£420–500
€/ **$670–800** ⋟ S(O)

A London blue and white delft vase, decorated with flowers, c1760, 8in (20.5cm) high.
£1,000–1,100
€/ **$1,600–1,700** ⊞ JHo

A Marieberg faïence vase, Swedish, 1777, 11½in (29cm) high.
£625–725
€/ $1,000–1,200 ➹ BUK

A Davenport creamware urn and cover, painted with chinoiserie figures in a garden setting, the shoulder reserved with four gilt scroll-edged cartouches of river landscapes, repeated on the cover beneath a gilt border reserved with acanthus leaves around a gilt knop, mounted with a silver spigot, restored, c1810, 22½in (57cm) high.
£3,200–3,800
€/ $5,000–6,000 ➹ S(NY)

An earthenware vase, by Simon Humberstone, with relief horizontal bands and mottled green and yellow glazes on a buff body, rim chips, Canadian, Ontario, late 19thC, 10in (25.5cm) high.
£450–500
€/ $700–800 ➹ RIT

A Wedgwood & Bentley Queensware basalt cassolet, with a reversible cover, the urn with twin scroll handles decorated with swags, raised on a basalt base, late 18thC, 11in (28cm) high.
£920–1,100
€/ $1,400–1,700 ➹ TRM
A cassolet has a reversible cover so that it can be used as either an urn or a candle holder.

A Wedgwood amphora-shaped vase, painted with a wide band depicting villages by a rustic stile with a church and a cottage in the background, a figure in a country lane approaching a cottage, the shoulders and base with gilt line decoration, 19thC, 7in (18cm) high.
£100–110
€/ $160–175 ➹ TMA

A Victorian Staffordshire pottery vase, with printed enamel and gilt decoration, 11¾in (30cm) high.
£75–90
€/ $120–140 ➹ SWO

A pair of Wedgwood and Bentley black basalt vases, with ram's head masks and loop handles, the shoulders with laurel leaf borders, covers missing, damage to one handle, impressed marks, late 18thC, 3¾in (9.5cm) high.
£380–450
€/ $600–700 ➹ S(O)

A Davenport vase, decorated with a flying bird pattern, c1820, 16in (40.5cm) high.
£780–850
€/ $1,250–1,300 ⊞ SCO

A Wedgwood jasper ware vase, decorated with paterae and floral swags hung from fluted pilasters, impressed Wedgwood mark, 1794–1800, 5in (12.5cm) high.
£375–425
€/ $600–675 ➹ WW

A Staffordshire pearlware spill vase, moulded with a clock face within a garter, flanked by royal supporters, on a table base, 1825–35, 10¼in (26cm) high.
£2,000–2,400
€/ $3,100–3,800 ➹ S(NY)

POTTERY

Miscellaneous

A Minton earthenware beer set, by Henry Stacy Marks, comprising a tray, a jug and two mugs, inscribed 'Chaucer, ye be welcome withouten any greeve', slight damage, minor restoration, dated 1873, tray 15¼in (38.5cm) wide.
£600–720
€ / **$950–1,100** ♪ B

▶ **A Wedgwood transfer-printed cup and saucer,** c1770, saucer 5in (12.5cm) diam.
£200–220
€ / **$315–350** ⊞ JHo
This was probably sent from the Wedgwood factory to Liverpool to be printed.

A Bristol pearlware thread box, with sliding cover, c1820, 7 x 3in (18 x 7.5cm) wide.
£530–585
€ / **$840–920** ⊞ DAN

A pearlware condiment set, on integral stand, c1820, 6in (15cm) high.
£250–300
€ / **$400–475** ♪ SWO

A Nottingham salt-glazed stoneware loving cup, decorated with trailing leaf and flower sprays, inscribed 'Thos Lowe 1813', rim chips, 6½in (16.5cm).
£450–550
€ / **$710–870** ♪ B

A Staffordshire Prattware pipe, c1790, 9in (23cm) long.
£800–900
€ / **$1,200–1,400** ⊞ JRe

▶ **A Marieberg faïence snuff box,** decorated with cameos, Swedish, 1758–66, 3½in (9cm) wide.
£600–720
€ / **$950–1,145** ♪ BUK

A majolica stick stand, decorated with lozenge-shaped panels of fans, within borders of flowering prunus, cracked, Continental, late 19thC, 21¾in (55.5cm) high.
£120–150
€ / **$190–240** ♪ DN

A salt-glazed stoneware cornucopia wall pocket, moulded with a cartouche of Flora carrying a cornucopia of flowers, with a rocaille border under a rim with three pierced rings, c1770, 11in (28cm) high.
£320–375
€ / **$500–590** ♪ TEN

A Leeds creamware sauce boat, moulded in the form of a shell, 1770–80, 6in (15cm) high.
£300–340
€ / **$475–540** ⊞ KEY

A Wemyss wash set, comprising ewer, basin, sponge dish and strainer, soap dish with cover and drainer, painted with cherries, minor damage, impressed marks, c1900, basin 15in (38cm) diam.
£600–720
€ / **$950–1,150** ♪ S(O)

POTTERY

Transfer-Printed Pottery

A Davenport pearlware pierced basket and stand, transfer-printed with castle views, 1825–30, 12in (30.5cm) wide.
£385–425
€ / $600–670 ⊞ DSA

► A Minton footed bowl, transfer-printed with Camel and Giraffe pattern, c1820, 11¾in (30cm) wide.
£170–200
€ / $270–315 ⚒ SWO

A Heath Pottery bowl and ewer, transfer-printed with Willow pattern, c1810, jug 8in (20.5cm) high.
£550–600
€ / $870–950 ⊞ SCO

A bowl, transfer-printed with Gun Dogs pattern, 1815–25, 7½in (19cm) diam.
£200–225
€ / $315–350 ⊞ GRe

A Spode slop bowl and cover, transfer-printed with Musicians pattern, blue printed marks, some damage, 1820–30, 13in (33cm) high.
£1,400–1,700
€ / $2,200–2,700 ⚒ B(Kn)

A Clews cheese coaster, transfer-printed with Castle pattern and fleur-de-lys, with scroll handles, on a moulded oval foot, minor damage, early 19thC, 16in (40.5cm) wide.
£1,300–1,500
€ / $2,000–2,400 ⚒ EH
The Castle pattern was popular at Spode and was copied by many other makers. It is supposed to be based on an aquatint by Merigot entitled 'The Gate of Sebastian' (1796), with the foreground taken from another aquatint, 'Ponte Molle'.

To order Miller's books in the UK please ring 01903 828800
See the full range at
www.millers.uk.com

A creamware coffee pot, transfer-printed with a pastoral landscape, 11¾in (30cm) high.
£250–320
€ / $400–500 ⚒ JAd

A Spode dessert comport, transfer-printed with The Lion in Love on the top and the Leopard and Fox on the underside, from the *Aesop's Fables* series, c1830, 6in (15cm) diam.
£500–550
€ / $790–870 ⊞ GN

An Andrew Stevenson pearlware tea bowl and saucer, transfer-printed with a rural scene, impressed mark, c1820, saucer 5in (12.5cm) diam.
£170–200
€ / $270–315 ⊞ DSA

A Copeland cup and saucer, commemorating the Arctic Expedition of 1875, transfer-printed with a polar bear within an inscribed and dated band, the reverse with three anchors fouled with inscribed ribbons, cup chipped, saucer 4in (10cm),diam.
£500–575
€ / $790–910 ⚒ SAS
The Arctic Expedition of 1875 was led by Sir George Strong Nares.

A pickle dish, transfer-printed with a chinoiserie pattern, c1820, 5in (12.5cm) wide.
£145–160
€ / $230–250 ⊞ CoCo

POTTERY

A pair of Spode dishes, transfer-printed with Flower Cross pattern, c1820, 10in (25cm) wide.
£80–100
€/ **$125–160** ⚒ **SWO**

A Minton dish and cover, transfer-printed with Pin Wheel pattern, c1820, 9½in (24cm) wide.
£135–150
€/ **$215–235** ⊞ **SCO**

A Spode egg stand, transfer-printed with Chinese Flowers pattern, c1820, 7½in (19cm) diam.
£90–100
€/ **$145–160** ⊞ **SCO**

A Spode earthenware meat dish, transfer-printed with Shooting a Leopard pattern from the Indian Sporting series, with canted corners, impressed and printed marks, c1810, 20¾in (52.5cm) wide.
£2,400–2,800
€/ **$3,800–4,400** ⚒ **RTo**

A meat dish, transfer-printed with Pashkov House, Moscow pattern, 1815–25, 21in (53.5cm) wide.
£900–1,100
€/ **$1,400–1,700** ⚒ **B(Kn)**

A Minton pearlware meat dish, transfer-printed with Benevolent Cottagers pattern, 1815–20, 15in (38cm) wide.
£500–550
€/ **$790–870** ⊞ **DSA**

An Andrew Stevenson plate, transfer-printed with a pattern from the Ornithological series, 1816–30, 6¼in (16cm) diam.
£60–65
€/ **$95–105** ⊞ **CHAC**

A Ridgway pearlware meat dish, transfer-printed with a pattern from the Angus Seats series within a landscape-panelled border, c1820, 17¾in (44cm) wide.
£260–325
€/ **$410–515** ⚒ **LFA**

A Clews plate, transfer-printed with a scene of Dr Syntax taking possession of his living, c1820, 10in (25.5cm) diam.
£325–360
€/ **$515–565** ⊞ **CoS**

For further information on Dr Syntax see page 235

A Mason plate, transfer-printed with Tyburn Turnpike pattern from the Beaded Frame series, c1820, 8in (20.5cm) diam.
£180–200
€/ **$285–315** ⊞ **GRe**

A pair of plates, transfer-printed in blue and white with Ladies of Llangollen pattern within a shaped floral border, impressed mark, probably Staffordshire, c1820, 10in (25.5cm) diam.
£420–500
€/ **$650–790** ⚒ **F&C**
The 'Ladies of Llangollen', Eleanor Butler and Sarah Ponsonby, the first sapphic couple of polite society, lived in a black and white timbered cottage, 'Plas Newydd', in North Wales.

A meat dish, transfer-printed with a view of Lancaster North East from the Antique Scenery series, 1825–35, 21½in (54.5cm) wide diam.
£800–880
€ / $1,250–1,400 ⊞ GRe

A pair of Staffordshire meat dishes, transfer-printed with a chinoiserie motif, c1825, 16in (40.5cm) wide.
£530–585
€ / $850–900 ⊞ DAN

A Copeland meat dish, transfer-printed with Horse and the Loaded Ass pattern from the *Aesop's Fables* series, 1825–50, 18in (45.5cm) wide.
£500–600
€ / $800–950 ⤴ PFK

A Ridgway stoneware meat dish, transfer-printed with Regina pattern from Asiatic Pheasants series, 1830–40, 21½in (54.5cm) wide.
£450–500
€ / $700–800 ⊞ PGO

▶ A meat dish, by Wagstaff & Brunt, transfer-printed with Belfast Views pattern, dated 1883, 13in (33cm) wide.
£135–150
€ / $215–235 ⊞ STA

◀ A meat dish, transfer-printed with Willow pattern, c1850, 17½in (44.5cm) wide.
£70–80
€ / $110–125 ⊞ CHAC

A Rogers pottery meat dish, transfer-printed with Boston State House pattern, impressed marks, 19thC, 18¾in (47.5cm) wide.
£1,000–1,200
€ / $1,580–1,900 ⤴ TMA
This dish was made for export to the American market.

A pair of Ridgway plates, transfer-printed with a floral motif, 1880–90, 10in (25.5cm) diam.
£70–80
€ / $110–125 ⊞ CHAC

A jug, transfer-printed with an Indian scene from the Parrot Border series, minor restoration, 1815–25, 12½in (32cm) high.
£300–350
€ / $475–550 ⤴ B(Kn)

A William Adams double-ended garden seat, transfer-printed with Seasons pattern showing July/August, c1830, 18½in (47cm) wide.
£2,000–2,200
€ / $3,200–3,500 ⊞ GN

POTTERY

A jug, transfer-printed with two identical Italianate scenes, impressed mark 'S', 1825–50, 9in (23cm) high.
£75–90
€/ **$120–140** ⚒ PFK

A Thomas Fell pearlware jug, transfer-printed with rural scenes, c1840, 10in (25.5cm) high.
£385–425
€/ **$600–670** ⊞ DSA

A Farmer's Arms jug, transfer-printed with Masonic symbols within a union border, inscribed 'E R Broom', dated 1841, 9½in (24cm) high.
£850–950
€/ **$1,400–1,500** ⊞ GN

A cider tankard, transfer-printed with a floral design, 1835–45, 5in (12.5cm) diam.
£115–130
€/ **$180–200** ⊞ CoCo

A mug, transfer-printed with a chinoiserie pattern and 'Hunter's Improved Soda Font London', with internal partition, 19thC, 4¼in (11cm) high.
£450–525
€/ **$710–830** ⚒ BBR

A John Meir pap feeder, transfer-printed with Willow pattern, c1830, 5in (12.5cm) wide.
£135–150
€/ **$215–235** ⊞ GN

◄ **A part dinner service,** attributed to Minton, comprising 33 pieces, transfer-printed with Royal Persian pattern, minor rim chips, impressed marks, 1825–40.
£220–250
€/ **$350–400** ⚒ DN

A Dawson's Low Ford Pottery part dinner service, comprising 79 pieces, transfer-printed with figures in a landscape, some damage, restoration, impressed marks, 1840–60.
£1,100–1,300
€/ **$1,700–2,000** ⚒ S(O)

An Elkin & Newbon part dinner service, comprising 38 pieces, transfer-printed with Botanical Beauties pattern, 19thC, meat dish 15¾in (40cm) wide.
£180–220
€/ **$284–350** ⚒ SWO

◄ **A Herculaneum pearlware teapot,** transfer-printed with a fishing scene, c1820, 5in (12.5cm) high.
£440–485
€/ **$700–770** ⊞ CoS

A toast rack, probably by William Hackwood, the dividers decorated as towers, 1825–40, 8in (20.5cm) wide.
£270–475
€/ **$425–750** ⊞ GRe

A Copeland & Garrett tureen, cover and stand, transfer-printed with Byron Group floral pattern, 1838–40, 7in (18cm) wide
£300–325
€/ **$475–515** ⊞ DSA

A John Meir waste pail and cover, transfer-printed with Laconia pattern, rim chip, printed mark, 19thC, 13½in (34.5cm) high.
£420–525
€/ **$650–800** ⚒ TMA

ustreware

he earliest lustrewares date from 13th-century Persia and were made popular again by Wedgwood at the beginning of the 19th century. Lustreware was soon produced by many other British potteries, particularly those in north east England. Pink lustre was the most popular in the early to mid-19th century, with orange or apricot appearing around 1855.

The earliest lustrewares from north east England seem to date from around 1820. Most popular of the decorative wares produced on the Rivers Wear and Tyne were the rectangular and circular wall plaques, along with the multitude of jugs, bowls, frog mugs, chamber pots etc, decorated with transfers reflecting contemporary social events. From 1794–1890, a large number of pieces were decorated with various transfers commemorating the opening of the Sunderland Bridge. It is interesting to note transfers of the Sunderland 'New Bridge' can be safely dated post-1859, as this is when the old bridge was levelled due to structural faults and then reconstucted.

The term Sunderland Ware seems to derive from the transfer decoration of the Sunderland Bridge. This term can be confusing as there were more potteries on the River Tyne producing Sunderland Ware than there were on the River Wear. The Wear potteries of Dixon & Co, Anthony Scott, Dawson & Co and Samuel Moore, excelled in lustre-decorated wares. Tyneside factories on the Tyne such as C. T. Maling, Thomas Fell, Joseph Sewell and John Carr of North Shields made equally good quality wares. The range of subjects seemed never ending: Royalty, politics, religion, murders, births, disasters were all captured.

Lustreware production peaked in the North East around 1845, but cheap imports from the Staffordshire potteries caused standards to fall and many potteries closed. Soon only a handful were left. John Carr of North Shields produced lustreware as late as c1890 until finally closing in 1918. The last pottery in the North East to produce lustreware was C. T. Maling & Sons, Newcastle. This factory was the largest and longest in production, initially manufacturing pottery at Sunderland in 1762 and finally extinguishing the last kiln in Newcastle in 1963, ending over 200 years of pottery manufacture in the north east of England.

Ian Sharp

POTTERY

A pair of Staffordshire lustreware models of spaniels, c1875, 12½in (32cm) high.
£220–245
€/ $345–385 ⊞ CHAC

◄ A pink lustre pearlware model of a grandfather clock, probably by Portobello, Scotland, c1830, 4½in (11.5cm) high.
£400–450
€/ $635–715 ⊞ RdV

A Dixon & Co pink lustre bowl, transfer-printed with the Mariners' Arms, c1830, 7in (18cm) diam.
£250–280
€/ $395–445 ⊞ IS

A Sunderland pink lustre chamber pot, the inner decorated with the head and shoulders of a figure and inscribed with a verse, the outer inscribed 'To the Wife' and 'A Present'; hairline crack, c1840, 5¼in (13.5cm) high.
£480–565
€/ $760–890 ⚒ S(O)

A puce lustre frog chamberpot, the inner decorated with head and shoulders of a figure, inscribed 'use me well, keep me clean, I will not tell what I have seen', the outer decorated with panels of verse, early 19thC, 8½in (21.5cm) high.
£500–575
€/ $790–910 ⚒ GAK

A pink lustre jug, relief-moulded with portraits of Princess Charlotte and Prince Leopold above a stiff-leaf border, with split-scroll handle, haircracks, c1816, 6in (15cm) high.
£380–430
€/ $600–680 ⚒ S

POTTERY

A lustre jug, relief-moulded with a stag hunting scene, painted in brightly coloured enamels with bands of purple lustre, slight damage, c1830, 7¼in (18.5cm) high.
£220–250
€ / **$350–400** 🔨 **F&C**

A Newcastle Pottery lustre creamware jug, decorated with the Gardener's Arms, c1830, 7in (18cm) high.
£500–550
€ / **$790–870** ⊞ **IS**
This type of decoration was once mistakenly attributed to Addison, Faulkener & Co.

A North Shields Pottery jug, decorated with a view of the Iron Bridge at Sunderland, c1840, 5½in (14cm) high.
£400–450
€ / **$635–715** ⊞ **IS**

A pink lustre jug, transfer-printed with the sailing ship *William the IV*, flanked by oval panels inscribed with verses, cracked, early 19thC, 8¼in (21cm) high.
£280–320
€ / **$440–500** 🔨 **RTo**

A Sunderland lustre jug, with decorated panels inscribed 'Ancient Order of Foresters' and 'Manchester Unity', c1830, 9in (23cm) high.
£630–700
€ / **$1,000–1,100** ⊞ **RdV**

A pink lustre Masonic jug, inscribed 'Mason's Arms', c1840, 6½in (16.5cm) high.
£800–900
€ / **$1,300–1,500** ⊞ **RdV**

A Tyneside lustre jug, inscribed 'The Mariners' Compass', the reverse with verse, c1855, 5½in (14cm) high.
£250–280
€ / **$395–445** ⊞ **IS**

◄ **A Staffordshire lustre jug,** transfer-printed and overpainted with a band seated and playing musical instruments, with printed verse 'I wish I was in Dixy Land' and 'Sally is the girl for me', 19thC, 6¼in (16cm) high.
£400–470
€ / **$630–740** 🔨 **TMA**

A Dixon & Co lustre creamware jug, transfer-printed with a view of the Cast Iron Bridge over the River Wear, Sunderland, factory mark, c1825, 6½in (16.5cm) high.
£430–480
€ / **$680–760** ⊞ **IS**

A Sunderland pink lustre jug, attributed to Dawson's, transfer-printed with inscriptions of various free trade societies, c1835, 6½in (16.5cm) high.
£400–450
€ / **$630–715** ⊞ **IS**

A lustre and enamelled jug, attributed to Anthony Scott, Southwick Pottery, decorated with a cartouche entitled 'Return to his True Love', c1850, 6½in (16.5cm) high.
£400–450
€ / **$635–715** ⊞ **IS**
This type of 'squiggle' lustre decoration is typical of Anthony Scott.

A lustre jug, attributed to Anthony Scott, Southwick Pottery, decorated with the 'Sailors Farewell' c1860, 7in (18cm) high.
£430–480
€ / **$680–760** ⊞ **IS**

A lustre jug, decorated with Masonic symbols and cartouches of Justice, Charity and Hope, c1820, 6in (15cm) high.
£675–750
€/ $1,100–1,200 ⊞ RdV

A Sunderland lustre mug, c1835, 5in (12.5cm) high.
£400–450
€/ $630–715 ⊞ HOW

► A Sunderland pink lustre frog mug, transfer-printed with a view of the Cast Iron Bridge over the River Wear, Sunderland, c1840, 4¾in (12cm) high.
£425–470
€/ $670–750 ⊞ RdV

A Northumberland Pottery lustre mug, commemorating the 1826 Northumberland election, decorated with a cartouche inscribed 'Bell and Victory', 4½in (11.5cm) high.
£675–750
€/ $1,100–1,200 ⊞ IS

A Sunderland lustre mug, decorated with a ship in full sail, and 'Peace & Plenty' legend in a cartouche, c1835, 5in (12.5cm) high.
£500–550
€/ $790–870 ⊞ HOW

A Sunderland pink lustre pearlware mug, depicting 'The Sailors' Farewell' and the 'Cast Iron Bridge', c1840, 5in (12.5cm) high.
£520–575
€/ $820–900 ⊞ RdV

POTTERY

◄ A Sunderland orange lustre frog mug, decorated with the 'Norah Creina' Steam-Yacht', and a verse, over-painted with enamel colours, minor damage to girdle, c1850, 7in (18cm) high.
£220–260
€/ $350–400 ➶ BR

◄ A Sunderland lustre jug, attributed to Anthony Scott, Southwick Pottery, decorated with a view of the New Sunderland Bridge, c1860, 5in (12.5cm) high.
£250–280
€/ $400–450 ⊞ IS

A Sunderland lustre frog mug, commemorating the Crimean War, decorated with the flags of Great Britain and France, c1855, 5in (12.5cm) high.
£440–500
€/ $700–800 ⊞ RdV

A Victorian lustre frog mug, decorated with a ship, inscribed 'Health to the sick', 5¼in (13.5cm) high.
£85–100
€/ $135–160 ➶ BIG

POTTERY

A Sunderland lustre plaque, decorated with a portrait of John Wesley, inscribed 'The best of all God is with us', c1830, 6¾ x 5¾in (17 x 14.5cm) high.
£400–450
€/ **$630–715** ⊞ RdV

A Sunderland lustre plaque, inscribed 'God Speed the Plough', c1835, 8 x 9in (20.5 x 23cm).
£430–475
€/ **$680–750** ⊞ HOW

A Sunderland lustre plaque, transfer-printed 'Thou God Seest me', indistinct impressed mark, probably Dixon, 19thC, 8in (20.5cm) wide.
£100–120
€/ **$160–190** 🔨 DAU

A lustre commemorative plate, inscribed 'Charlotte in Memoriam', c1820, 8in (20.5cm) diam.
£550–620
€/ **$870–980** ⊞ RdV

A Sunderland lustre plaque, inscribed 'The Token or Jack's Safe Return', c1830, 9½ x 8¼ in (24 x 21cm).
£430–475
€/ **$680–750** ⊞ PSA

A Sunderland lustre plaque, decorated with a ship in full sail, c1840, 8 x 9½in (20.5 x 24cm).
£430–475
€/ **$680–750** ⊞ HOW

A Tyneside pink lustre plaque, decorated with a view of the Iron Bridge over the River Wear, Sunderland, damaged, c1850, 8½in x 7½in (21.5 x 19cm).
£100–110
€/ **$160–175** ⊞ NAW

A Sunderland lustre named plate, inscribed 'Stephen Hill', impressed Dixon & Co, c1820, 7½in (19cm) diam.
£630–700
€/ **$1,000–1,100** ⊞ RdV

A Garrison Pottery pink and copper lustre plaque, decorated with a Middle Eastern scene, impressed 'Dixon, Phillips & Co', c1835, 8in (20.5cm) wide.
£340–380
€/ **$540–600** ⊞ IS

A Low Lights Pottery pink lustre plaque, by John Carr, c1845, 9½ x 8in (24 x 20.5cm).
£200–225
€/ **$315–350** ⊞ NAW

A Sunderland orange lustre script plaque, attributed to Anthony Scott, Southwick Pottery, c1865, 8½in (21.5cm) wide.
£250–275
€/ **$400–430** ⊞ IS

A pair of lustre vases, possibly St Anthony's Pottery, Newcastle-upon-Tyne, all-over decorated in variegated pink lustre, rim chip, c1815, 5¾in (14.5cm) high.
£475–565
€/ **$750–890** 🔨 B

Porcelain

M any people are frightened to collect porcelain because it feels fragile and breakable, but to a porcelain enthusiast, this very fragility makes it special. There is a real joy in owning a delicate vase that has survived unbroken through many generations. Cracks, repair or restoration make an enormous difference to the value of a piece of fine porcelain. However, over recent years, attitudes have changed and many collectors now view damage in a different light.

Bonhams' sale last year of part of the Minton Museum collection focused attention on the subject of damage, as a surprising amount of pieces offered in this sale were cracked or broken. This is because it was a reference collection of samples, retained by Minton for exhibitions and to train new decorators and many pieces had travelled the world, or been handled repeatedly in a working factory. Damaged porcelain is difficult to sell, but nevertheless, the saleroom was packed with private collectors who saw beyond the cracks and over-painting. They realized these were unique Minton pieces with a historic provenance. Broken vases sold for the same price I would expect to achieve for perfect examples without such provenance.

Collectors who cannot afford rare and historic porcelain in fine condition are often happy to buy damaged examples to have repaired. Many collectors favour 'museum-type' repairs that clean the dirt from old cracks to leave pieces looking attractive, but without extensive surface spraying. A damaged item can be transformed by careful conservation but only special pieces justify the cost of fine repair. Just remember, no matter how skilful the repair, restored porcelain will always be worth much less than perfect.

As the volume of porcelain sold on the internet increases, an alarming trend is emerging. Descriptions of damage are often woefully inadequate, cracks are frequently ignored, and a worrying amount is professionally restored. Don't take anything at face value. Before you buy, ask for a guarantee that the condition is as described. Wherever possible, though, try to buy undamaged porcelain, as this will give much more pleasure in the long term. **John Sandon**

Animals

A model of a pigeon, nesting on a basket-work base, chipped, Spanish, probably Alcora, 1775–1800, 6in (15cm) high.
£375–450
€/ $600–700 ⚘ B

A Kloster Veilsdorf group of a leopard attacking a mule, modelled by Pfränger, on a scroll-edged base, German, c1775, 8¼in (21cm) wide.
£1,100–1,300
€/ $1,700–2,000 ⚘ S(O)
This is a very rare group, but the gruesome subject may have been the reason for the modest price realized.

A Belleek spill vase, modelled as a fish, Irish, First Period, 1863–90, 7in (18cm) high.
£585–650
€/ $900–1,000 ⊞ MLa

A Minton vase, modelled as a fantail dove, c1870, 6in (15cm) high.
£275–330
€/ $430–520 ⚘ SWO

A Belleek Parian group of greyhounds, Irish, First Period, 1863–90, 8in (20.5cm) high.
£5,200–6,200
€/ $8,200–9,800 ⚘ JAd

A Moore Bros table centrepiece, modelled as two swans flanking a bulrush-moulded vase on a waterlily-moulded base, damaged, impressed 'Moore' and printed T. Goode', c1875, 12¼in (31cm) wide.
£180–200
€/ $280–315 ⚘ RTo
In good condition this group would have realized considerably more.

Expert's choice

When I was shown this porcelain cat in 1990, it was totally unrecorded. The owner thought it was delft, but I knew it was a significant piece of early English porcelain. Just a few months earlier, archaeologists digging on a site in east London had discovered one of the first porcelain factories. The few dozen broken fragments identified the products of the Limehouse porcelain manufactory. Among the shards from Limehouse, being sorted at the Museum of London, I recognized a fragment of the foot of a cat. It matched the cat I had been asked to sell. Until these shards were found, this distinctive porcelain had been incorrectly identified as Liverpool. Research continues and archaeology has many new lessons to teach collectors of porcelain. The cat realized £5,280 (€/ $8,300) in September 1991. No others have turned up since, and today it would be worth £12,000–15,000 (€/ $19,000–24,000).   **John Sandon**

A Limehouse cat, 1746–48, sold by Bonhams in September 1991.

▶ **A Chamberlain Worcester model of a cat and a kitten,** the cat painted with tabby markings, on a cushion base with gilded edge detail, minor damage, impressed 'Chamberlains', 1820–30, 2½in (6.5cm) high.
£900–1,000
€/ **$1,400–1,600** ⚒ B

A Saint Cloud soft paste snuff box, modelled as a recumbent dog, decorated with figures and houses, 1740–50, 1¾in (4.5cm) high.
£4,200–5,000
€/ **$6,600–7,900** ⚒ S(P)

▶ **A model of a tabby cat,** with puce printed retailer's mark for John Mortlock, Orchard St, London, mid-19thC, 11½in (29cm) high.
£1,500–1,800
€/ **$2,400–2,800** ⚒ S(O)

A Royal Worcester model of a swan holding a basket between its wings, mark with date code for 1901, 7¼in (18.5cm) high.
£250–280
€/ **$400–440** ⚒ SWO

A monkey band group, comprising 9 pieces, some damage, German, early 20thC, 7in (18cm) high.
£650–750
€/ **$1,000–1,200** ⚒ G(L)

Baskets

A Belleek two-strand lily of the valley basket, Irish, First Period, 1863–90, 10in (25.5cm) diam.
£1,800–2,000
€/ **$2,800–3,200** ⊞ MLa

A Bow basket, the centre painted with a floral spray, chipped foot and restoration, c1760, 11in (28cm) wide.
£220–250
€/ **$350–400** ⚒ SWO
The low price realized for this basket reflects extensive restoration.

A Coalport basket, the sides, bail handle and rim applied with flowers, the interior painted with flowers and gilt scrolls, handle repaired, 'CD' mark, c1840, 8½in (21.5cm) wide.
£170–200
€/ **$270–315** ⚒ WW
The low price realized for this basket reflects the damage.

Miller's Compares

A Worcester basket, the sides pierced with interlaced circles applied with florets at the intersections, the centre painted with Staghunt pattern, side of rim restored, c1756, 6¼in (16cm) diam.
£750–875
€/ **$1,200–1,400** ➤ B
The price reflects the damage and restoration.

I. A Worcester basket, the sides pierced with interlocking circles, applied externally with florets at the intersections, the exterior washed in yellow, the centre painted with a floral spray surrounded by smaller sprigs, the sides with further small trailing sprigs, 1763–65, 7¾in (19.5cm) diam.
£2,000–2,200
€/ **$3,200–3,500** ➤ B

II. A Worcester dessert basket, the sides pierced with overlapping circles, applied externally at the intersections with florets, the centre painted with a floral spray, with a foliate scroll border, minor wear and crack, 1758–60, 7¾in (19.5cm) diam.
£650–775
€/ **$1,000–1,200** ➤ B

These two baskets are the same size and of a similar date, but Item I is more desirable because of its yellow exterior which gives it a more attractive appearance. Item II, moreover, has a minor crack to the rim – damage will nearly always reduce an item's value, unless the item is particularly rare.

A Worcester basket, the sides pierced with interlocking circles, applied externally with florets, the centre painted with a spray of flowers and a smaller sprig, c1760, 5in (12.5cm) diam.
£1,000–1,200
€/ **$1,600–1,900** ➤ B

▶ **A Worcester basket,** the reticulated sides applied with flowerheads, the interior painted with flowers, damaged, c1765, 8in (20.5cm) diam.
£250–300
€/ **$400–500** ➤ WW
The low price achieved by this basket reflects the amount of damage it has sustained.

Bowls

◀ **A Belleek sugar bowl,** moulded with ivy leaves and berries, Irish, First Period, 1863–90, 6in (15cm) wide.
£80–100
€/ **$125–160** ➤ WW

▶ **A Belleek coral and cardium shell bowl,** Irish, Second Period, 1891–1926, 4½in (11.5cm) high.
£450–500
€/ **$700–800** ⊞ MLa

A Belleek bowl, the exterior applied with flowers below the frilled rim, on three scroll feet, minor chips and losses to flowers, black printed mark, Irish, Second Period, 1891–1926, 10in (25.5cm) diam.
£375–450
€/ **$600–700** ➤ S(O)

A Belleek Celtic fruit bowl, heightened in enamel and gilding, the interior washed in yellow, Irish, 1926–39, 10in (25.5cm) diam.
£420–500
€/ **$670–800** ➤ S(O)

PORCELAIN

A **Belleek bowl,** Irish, Third Period, 1926–46, 11in (28cm) diam.
£1,100–1,200
€/ **$1,700–1,900** ⊞ MLa

A **pair of Adolph Hamann handpainted monteiths,** each with a gilded rim and two branch handles, decorated with floral sprays, inscribed decorator's mark, German, Dresden, 1875–1925, 6in (15cm) wide.
£300–350
€/ **$475–550** ⚒ RIT

A **Sèvres bowl,** painted by Edmé-François Bouillat or Geneviève-Louise Bouillat, with three oval panels of buildings and small figures in river landscapes, including a fire scene, alternating with medallions, the border with trailing flowers above a gilt floral swag border, minor wear to gilt rim, interlaced 'LL', date code 00 and painter's mark 'y', French, dated 1791, 7in (18cm) diam.
£1,500–1,800
€/ **$2,400–2,800** ⚒ S(O)

A **Royal Worcester fruit bowl,** moulded with fruiting foliage on a basketweave ground, with pierced arcaded rim, puce mark, date code for 1890, 9½in (24cm) diam.
£80–100
€/ **$125–160** ⚒ PFK

▶ A **Bow bowl,** painted in the *famille rose* palette with flowers, leaves and rockwork, and a figure in a boat, workman's mark, 1752–53, 6½in (16.5cm) diam.
£600–700
€/ **$950–1,100** ⚒ WW

▶ An **Imperial Porcelain Manufactory bowl,** painted with floral sprays, slight wear, Russian, St Petersburg, 1855–81, 12¼in (31cm) diam.
£700–820
€/ **$1,100–1,300** ⚒ BUK

A **Royal Worcester bowl,** hand-painted by Ricketts with apples and blackberries, dated 1926, 7in (18cm) diam.
£420–500
€/ **$670–800** ⚒ B(W)

◀ A **Caughley bowl,** enamel-painted, probably by Fidelle Duvivier, with two figures in an extensive wooded river landscape, and with three similar vignettes, the interior similarly decorated, beneath a leaf-scroll and ribbon band, minor rim chip, c1790, 8¼in (21cm) diam.
£2,000–2,200
€/ **$3,200–3,500** ⚒ LFA

A **Worcester porringer,** with an ozier-moulded border below the rim, the twin rustic handles with a moulded scroll at the lower terminal, the upper terminal flanked by applied flowers, leaves and stalks, the interior printed and overpainted with *Les Garçons Chinois*, the exterior painted with scattered flower sprays, minor losses to handles, c1757, 7in (18cm) wide.
£4,500–5,200
€/ **$7,000–8,200** ⚒ B
The shape appears to be unrecorded. Related moulding is found on rare covered *écuelles* usually decorated in blue, but no similar handles have been recorded. The extensive decoration inside strongly suggests this shape was complete without a cover and that it may have served as a wine cup or quaich.

◀ A **miniature bowl-on-stand,** the bowl with gilded ram's head-handles, both painted with flowers against gilt borders, chips to pedestal base, 1815–20, bowl 3½in (9cm) diam.
£230–275
€/ **$360–430** ⚒ G(L)

PORCELAIN

Covered Bowls

A Caughley sucrier and cover, with rounded knop, decorated in gold with leaf garlands suspended from bands gilt with leaf scrolls, c1790, 4½in (11.5cm) high.
£375–450
€ / $600–700 ⚲ LFA

A Gaudy Welsh sucrier, c1840, 6in (15cm) high.
£90–100
€ / $140–160 ⊞ WAC

A pair of Grainger's Worcester reticulated bowls and covers, pierced with foliate and floret chamfered rectangles, date code for 1893, 4½in (11.5cm) diam.
£475–550
€ / $750–870 ⚲ L

For further information on antique porcelain see the full range of Miller's books at
www.millers.uk.com

A Sèvres écuelle, cover and stand, French, c1774, stand 10in (25.5cm) wide.
£1,500–1,650
€ / $2,400–2,600 ⊞ DHu

Reticulation

The art of 'reticulation' was perfected at the Royal Worcester factory. Initially Worcester craftsmen cut formal honeycomb patterns out of lightly moulded teawares. More elaborate productions copied carved ivories imported from India.

By the 1880s truly magnificent pierced vases were made in the Persian taste. The Grainger factory also made equally fine reticulated work. The holes were cut out one by one while the clay was still wet, following complicated moulded scroll-work patterns. George Owen excelled above all other craftsman, dispensing with moulded guidelines and producing unbelievable pierced patterns using hand and eye alone. His signed vases are testament to his genius and deserve the high prices they now command.

◄ **A Royal Worcester reticulated bowl and cover,** by George Owen, the cover with a pierced band of unique design, the finial surrounded by a band of applied 'pearls', a wide band of honeycomb below a border of scrolls and anthemia in raised gold, supported on a plinth by a row of gilded 'pearls', gold mark, shape No. 2521, incised 'G Owen', 1920–21, 5in (12.5cm) diam.
£10,000–12,000
€ / $16,000–19,000 ⚲ B

Boxes

◄ **A Belleek biscuit box and cover,** modelled as a straw-moulded crate bound by string, cover with retouched chip, impressed and black printed marks, Irish, First Period, 1863–90, 7¾in (20.5cm) wide.
£420–500
€ / $670–790 ⚲ S(O)

A trinket box, with Sèvres-style decoration, French, late 19thC, in (12.5cm) wide.
585–650
/ $925–1,000 ⊞ MAA

A Dresden box, with gilt-metal mounts, the lid with a hand-painted courting scene, a landscape to the base, pseudo crossed swords mark, German, late 19thC, 2in (5cm) diam.
£100–120
€ / $160–190 ⚲ SWO

A Royal Worcester reticulated casket and cover, by George Owen, the cover with a pierced boss, flanked by honeycomb panels, with pierced borders edged in raised gold, the twin handles applied with beaded rings, further bands of 'pearls' applied to the base and cover, the shoulder pierced with scrollwork and flowers picked out in gold, above a wide band alternately pierced with diamonds and circles within tall upright panels, on a scroll-moulded base and ball feet, small chip to inner rim partly refilled, gold mark, shape No. 2412, incised signature, dated 1909, 6¼in (16cm) wide.
£12,500–15,000
€ / $20,000–24,000 ⚲ B
The minor damage to this piece is reflected in the realized price.

PORCELAIN

Busts

A Copeland Parian bust of The Veiled Bride, after Raphael Monti, impressed 'R. Monti 1861 Copeland', on a socle base impressed 'Crystal Palace Art Union', 15in (38cm) high.
£3,000–3,400
€/ **$4,700–5,400** ⚘ Mit

▶ **A pair of busts of Princess Charlotte and Prince Leopold,** by J. & R. Riley, prince restored at neck, signed and dated 1819, 15¾in (40cm) high.
£4,800–5,700
€/ **$7,600–9,000** ⚘ S

A W. H. Goss Parian bust of the Earl of Derby, 1876–91, 6½in (16.5cm) high.
£165–185
€/ **$260–300** ⊞ G&CC

A Minton biscuit bust of Lord Brougham, on a glazed pedestal with gilt borders, the base titled in gilding, minor crack, 1830–40, 6in (15cm) high.
£900–1,100
€/ **$1,400–1,700** ⚘ S

For further information on antique porcelain see the full range of Miller's books at
www.millers.uk.com

A Sèvres biscuit bust of General Desaix de Veygoux, impressed 'Sèvres' and incised 'D 81.10', the base with printed circle mark and date code 'S.82', French, c1882, 16in (40.5cm) high.
£1,000–1,200
€/ **$1,600–1,900** ⚘ S(NY)
Louis Charles Antoine Desaix de Veygoux (1768–1800) was a general in the French Revolutionary Wars. He died at the Battle of Marengo in northern Italy on June 14 1800.

A Wedgwood Parian bust of Milton, after the model by E. W. Wyon, titled to the reverse, collar chip, c1860, 14¼in (36cm) high.
£250–280
€/ **$400–440** ⚘ WW

Candlesticks & Chambersticks

► **A Coalport chamberstick,** with encrusted floral decoration, c1830, 2in (5cm) high.
€660–700
€/ $1,000–1,100 ⊞ DIA

A Barr, Flight & Barr 'Music' candlestick, painted with an upright panel of Beauchief Abbey, Derbyshire, within gilded neo-classical borders applied with bands of 'pearls', some scratches and wear, script marks, c1810, 5¼in (13.5cm) high.
€375–450
€/ $600–700 ✗ B
The Flight factory invoices use the name 'Music' for sticks of this shape.

A Chamberlain Worcester taperstick, decorated with Japan pattern, No. 240, c1810, 2¾in (7cm) high.
£800–880
€/ $1,300–1,400 ⊞ DIA

A Worcester Barr, Flight & Barr chamberstick, the base painted with four shells, with a reattached gilt handle, impressed and painted marks, 1807–13, 3¼in (8.5cm) high.
£1,000–1,200
€/ $1,600–1,900 ✗ G(L)

A chamberstick, the shell-moulded base with encrusted floral decoration, c1830, 2in (5cm) high.
£550–600
€/ $870–950 ⊞ DIA

Centrepieces

A pair of Belleek centrepieces, the open clam shells on a pile of smaller shells above a water-moulded base, small chips, black printed mark, First Period, 1863–90, 5in (12.5cm) high.
€650–750
€/ $1,000–1,200 ✗ S(O)

LOCATE THE SOURCE
The source of each illustration in Miller's can be found by checking the code letters below each caption with the Key to Illustrations, pages 794–800.

► **A Belleek centrepiece,** black printed mark, Third Period, 1926–46, 12in (30.5cm) high.
€1,000–1,100
€/ $1,600–1,700 ⊞ MLa

PORCELAIN

A Berlin figural centrepiece, the centre of the bowl painted with an arrangement of flowers, supported by three biscuit putti around a parcel-gilt biscuit foliate column, on a tripartite base, restored chip to column, sceptre mark in underglaze blue, red printed 'KPM' and orb, German, c1840, 8½in (21.5cm) high.
£2,800–3,200
€/ **$4,400–5,000** ⚒ S(NY)

A John Bevington Meissen-style centrepiece, modelled as a lady and a gentleman running around a flower-encrusted column supporting a pierced basket, minor losses, marked, c1860, 18in (45.5cm) high.
£1,000–1,100
€/ **$1,600–1,800** ⚒ B(Kn)

A William Cookworthy pickle stand, the dishes modelled as three clam shells, on a tripod pedestal foot supported at the corners by three dolphins surrounded by shells, a pyramid of shells at the top forming the handle, a flower spray inside each dish, chips and restoration, 1768–73, 6¾in (17cm) high.
£1,700–2,000
€/ **$2,700–3,200** ⚒ B

◄ **A Minton** *pâte-sur-pâte* **centrepiece,** with a pieced scroll rim, the sides decorated with a medallion of a maiden and cherub, and strips decorated with neo-classical motifs, on four scroll feet, cracked, c1892, impressed and printed marks, indistinct date cypher and shape number, 16½in (42cm) wide.
£3,200–3,800
€/ **$5,000–6,000** ⚒ B
Ex-Minton Sale.

A pair of Royal Crown Derby comports, decorated in the Imari palette, pattern No. 2444, date code for 1901, 9in (23cm) diam.
£320–375
€/ **$500–600** ⚒ SWO

A Plaue centrepiece, the pierced basket encrusted with roses, on a scroll-moulded stem applied with three putti, small chips, crossed lines in underglaze blue, German, c1900, 12in (30.5cm) high.
£380–450
€/ **$600–700** ⚒ S(O)

A Spode dessert centrepiece, painted with roses, c1820, 13in (33cm) wide.
£1,600–1,800
€/ **$2,500–2,900** ⊞ DAN

A Swansea centrepiece, painted with groups of flowers, firing crack to rim and some wear, Welsh, 1814–26, 13½in (34.5cm) wide.
£2,200–2,500
€/ **$3,500–4,000** ⚒ S(O)

A centrepiece, the flower-encrusted bowl pierced with lattice panels and decorated with flowers, on a flower-encrusted stem, the base modelled as a figural group of a lady and gallant playing chess, watched by a female attendant, damaged, Continental, late 19thC, 22¾in (58cm) high.
£200–225
€/ **$315–350** ⚒ RTo

A Carl Thieme Potschappel centrepiece, applied with flowers and figures of cherubs, the interior painted with flowers, minor damage, blue marks, German, c1900, 16½in (42cm) wide.
£300–360
€/ **$475–575** ⚒ DORO

A centrepiece, the dish supported by a satyr, cracked and stained, 19thC, 9¼in (23.5cm) high.
£250–300
€/ **$400–475** ⚒ SWO

PORCELAIN

Coffee & Teapots

A Belleek teapot, decorated with horn pattern, Irish, First Period, 1863–90, 4in (10cm) high.
£720–800
€/ **$1,100–1,200** ⊞ MLa

▶ **A Belleek 'Grass' tea kettle and cover,** with a ribbon-bound handle, rubbing, black printed mark, the interior of the cover with black printed instructions for warming the pot, First Period, 1863–90, 6in (15cm) high.
£320–375
€/ **$500–600** ⋟ S(O)

◀ **A Belleek teapot,** with enamelled floral decoration, Second Period, 1891–1926, 5in (12.5cm) high.
£1,000–1,100
€/ **$1,600–1,800** ⊞ MLa

◀ **A Caughley coffee pot and cover,** the domed cover applied with a flower finial, painted in bright enamels with four Chinese 'bubblehead' figures beside an iron red fence, including a small child holding a stick, the reverse with three similar figures, small chips to cover, c1775, 7½in (19cm) high.
£1,000–1,200
€/ **$1,600–1,900** ⋟ B

A Derby teapot and stand, c1810, 6in (15cm) high.
£675–750
€/ **$1,000–1,200** ⊞ CoS

PORCELAIN

A Ludwigsburg coffee pot and cover, painted by Gottlieb Friedrich Kirschner with a large flower spray, a smaller sprig on the reverse and further scattered flowers, the domed cover with a fruit knop, the gilt-edged spout and handle moulded with rocailles and acanthus leaves, chips, wear and some restoration, crowned interlaced 'CC' monogram in underglaze blue, painter's mark 'K' in green, impressed 4 and 3, incised A, German, c1775, 8¼in (21cm) high.
£2,500–3,000
€/ **$4,000–4,800** ⚒ S(O)
Gottlieb Friedrich Kirschner (1748–89) was a painter of birds and flowers and an engraver who was active at the Ludwigsburg manufactory between about 1770 and 1787.

A Worcester teapot and cover, painted with a Chinese family, the cover with a floral knop, c1770, 5¾in (14.5cm) high.
£450–525
€/ **$700–830** ⚒ S(O)

◀ A Christian's Liverpool palm tree teapot, the fluted lid and acanthus-moulded panelled body painted in blue with formal floral groups, chips, haircrack to finial, c1770, 7¼in (18.5cm) high.
£1,300–1,500
€/ **$2,000–2,400** ⚒ LAY

A New Hall coffee jug and cover, the high-domed cover with a pine-cone knob, the spout with a shaped bridge across the widest part, small chips and cracks, 1782–85, 10¼in (26cm) high.
£3,700–4,400
€/ **$5,700–7,000** ⚒ B

A Worcester teapot, painted with floral sprays, the spout and handle with puce scrollwork, damaged, old collectors' labels to underside, 1765–68, 5in (12.5cm) high.
£90–110
€/ **$140–175** ⚒ PFK

▶ A Worcester Flight, Barr & Barr teapot, cover and stand, c1815, 8in (20.5cm) high.
£540–600
€/ **$850–950** ⊞ CoS

◀ A Worcester Flight teapot, c1790, 7in (18cm) high.
£400–450
€/ **$630–700** ⊞ DSA

A Lowestoft miniature teapot, with domed lid, the body painted with floral sprays, cracked, spout detached but present, old collector's label '445 Lowestoft' to base, c1775, 3¼in (8.5cm) high.
£1,500–1,800
€/ **$2,400–2,800** ⚒ PFK
Lowestoft miniature teawares are very rare in colours other than blue and white, hence this high price for a badly damaged piece.

A Worcester teapot and cover, painted with Conjurer pattern, the cover with a flower finial, chips to spout and finial, 1768–70, 6in (15cm) high.
£550–625
€/ **$870–990** ⚒ B

A Worcester teapot and cover, painted with panels of Chinese figures and smaller panels of landscapes, some restoration, c1770, 7in (18cm) wide.
£550–625
€/ **$870–1,000** ⚒ WW

◀ A Worcester teapot, painted with a floral pattern in the Chinese style, c1770, 5in (12.5cm) high.
£480–530
€/ **$750–830** ⊞ DSA

Coffee & Tea Services

A Copeland & Garrett part coffee and tea service, comprising 13 pieces, painted with panels of garden flowers with scroll-moulded and gilt reserves, printed mark in green, c1840.
£300–350
€/ **$475–550** ➤ Bea(E)

A Caughley part coffee and tea service, comprising 27 pieces, fluted and painted with French sprigs, some damage, c1785.
£625–725
€/ **$990–1,150** ➤ B(Kn)

An assembled Caughley tea service, comprising 25 pieces, decorated with Pagoda pattern, some damage, blue S marks, c1785.
£650–750
€/ **$1,000–1,200** ➤ B(Kn)

◄ **A Coalport John Rose part tea service,** comprising 27 pieces, painted and gilt in the Japanese style with shrubs issuing flowers, and baluster panels with C-scroll borders, minor wear, one can with restored handle, c1810.
£1,300–1,500
€/ **$2,000–2,400** ➤ DN

A Derby tea service, comprising 52 pieces, decorated in the Japanese style with flowers and foliage, c1825.
£1,100–1,200
€/ **$1,700–1,900** ➤ E

A Derby Crown Porcelain Co cabaret service, comprising 15 pieces, printed and painted with Japan pattern, haircrack to one saucer, printed and impressed factory marks, painted pattern No. 198, c1884, tray 14in (35.5cm) wide.
£500–575
€/ **$800–900** ➤ S(O)

A Royal Crown Derby coffee service, comprising 15 pieces, decorated in the Imari palette with a floral design, printed mark and various date cyphers, c1900.
£300–340
€/ **$475–550** ➤ GAK

A Hilditch part tea service, comprising 17 pieces, decorated with chinoiserie scenes, some damage, printed factory marks, c1825.
£275–325
€/ **$430–500** ➤ WW

A Fürstenberg coffee service, comprising 22 pieces, painted with various landscape vignettes including buildings and rural figures supported by scrollwork cartouches with suspended flower garlands, minor damage, painted marks, impressed numerals, German, 1770–75, coffee pot 10½in (26.5cm) high.
£1,800–2,000
€/ **$2,800–3,200** ➤ S(Am)

➤ **A Minton *pâte-sur-pâte* cabaret set,** comprising nine pieces, by Thomas Mellor, each with a panel depicting putti in different attitudes, the ground with neo-classical ornament, edged with running patterns of gilt scrolls and leaves, some restoration, impressed factory marks and date codes, one saucer with monogram 'TM', 1878–80.
£7,500–9,000
€/ **$12,000–14,000** ➤ B

PORCELAIN

A New Hall composite part tea and coffee service,
comprising 52 pieces, printed and coloured with Window
pattern, restoration and damage, painted No. 425,
1775–1825.
£1,500–1,850
€ / **$2,400–2,900** ⚒ S(O)

A Paris coffee service, comprising 13 pieces, with gilt
decoration of leaf garlands, gilding worn, coffee pot knop
repaired, French, c1820.
£650–750
€ / **$1,000–1,200** ⚒ BUK

◀ **A Staffordshire rococo revival
tea service,** comprising 41 pieces,
with gilt-enriched borders, pattern
No. 1/1698, some damage, lozenge
mark, c1845.
£80–90
€ / **$125–145** ⚒ PFK

A Sèvres-style 'jewelled' solitaire,
comprising 7 pieces, each reserved
with panels enclosing titled scenes
from medieval history, including Joan
of Arc, battle and bedside scenes,
the saucer with trophies, some
restoration and chips, pseudo-Sèvres
mark, date letters, incised marks and
blue script titles, French, late 19thC,
tray 9½in (24cm) wide.
£2,500–3,000
€ / **$4,000–4,800** ⚒ S(O)

▶ **A Swansea part tea service,**
comprising four pieces, decorated
in the Japanese Imari style with
flowers and panels, teapot stand and
plate marked 'Swansea', pattern
No. 194, Welsh, 1816–20.
£850–1,000
€ / **$1,300–1,600** ⚒ WW

A Swansea part tea service, comprising 43 pieces, painted
with flower sprigs on a spiral- and ozier-moulded ground,
minor restoration and cracks, gilt script mark, Welsh, c1820.
£2,200–2,500
€ / **$3,500–4,000** ⚒ S(O)

A Vienna coffee and tea service, comprising 20 pieces,
decorated with flowers and gilt rims, wear and damage
to one rim, c1800, coffee pot 6¼in (16cm) high.
£525–625
€ / **$830–990** ⚒ DORO

Items in the Porcelain section have been arranged in
factory order, with non-specific pieces appearing at
the end of each sub-section.

A Chamberlain Worcester tea service, comprising
36 pieces, impressed and printed marks, c1830.
£850–1,000
€ / **$1,300–1,600** ⚒ TEN

A Royal Worcester boxed coffee set, comprising
22 pieces, painted by George Johnson, with panels of
exotic birds in the 18thC-style, some damage, import
marks and date code for 1927, in a fitted box.
£625–725
€ / **$990–1,200** ⚒ DN

PORCELAIN

Clocks

A Chelsea chinoiserie-style clock case, modelled as a lady seated on the steps of a rococo pavilion, the upper section with a harebell three-tiered roof containing a clock cavity, the rear with a rocky base applied with florets, some restoration, chips and losses, red anchor mark, 1756–58, 10¼in (26cm) high.
£5,000–5,500
€ / $7,900–8,700 🔨 B

A Jacob Petit mantel clock, stand and finial, the dial set in a rococo-moulded surround, painted with two lovers in an interior, the reverse and sides painted with flower panels, surmounted by a floral cluster finial, restoration and losses, painted mark, French, mid-19thC, 28in (71cm) high.
£3,000–3,500
€ / $4,700–5,500 🔨 S(O)

A mantel clock, in a Jacob Petit-style case enriched with gilding and floral panels, with looking plate strike and silk suspension with radiating *guilloche* silvered dial, steel Breguet hands, the detachable base with a scene of Oriental fisherfolk, French, mid-19thC, 16in (40.5cm) high.
£650–750
€ / $1,000–1,200 🔨 TEN

A rococo-style mantel clock and stand, encrusted and painted with flowers, surmounted by three cherubs above an enamel dial signed 'Leroy', the two-train brass movement with anchor escapement and outside count wheel, striking on a bell, French, c1900, 15½in (39.5cm) high.
£340–400
€ / $550–630 🔨 BR

Cups

▶ **A Bow coffee cup,** painted in the *famille rose* style with a floral pattern, c1755, 2½in (6.5cm) high.
£340–380
€ / $550–590 ⊞ DSA

A Berlin coffee can and saucer, probably decorated outside the factory, painted by Charlotte Bose, with a gilt-edged panel of a shepherd tending his flock, a small town in the distance, the saucer inscribed 'Souvenir de 'année 1778', chips, impressed and incised marks, script signature, German, dated 1811.
£750–875
€ / $1,200–1,400 🔨 S(O)

A Chelsea tea bowl, painted in the Kakiemon style with scattered flowerheads, hair crack and chip, c1752, 2¾in (7cm) wide.
£425–500
€ / $$670–790 🔨 WW

A Coalport breakfast cup and saucer, from the Earl Nelson service, the border with Greek key pattern between gold bands, painted with the two crests of the *San Josef* and the *Chelengk* awarded to Admiral Lord Nelson, beneath an Earl's coronet, chip to foot rim of saucer, 1806–08, saucer 6in (15cm) diam.
£1,600–1,900
€ / $2,500–3,000 🔨 B
This rare set was commissioned by William, 1st Earl Nelson, who inherited the title following the death of his brother Horatio. A selection of pieces from this set is in the National Maritime Museum, Greenwich.

A Caughley tea bowl and saucer, painted with Target pattern, 1793–95, 2in (5cm) high.
£300–330
€ / $475–525 ⊞ DSA

A Champion Bristol coffee cup and saucer, painted with floral sprays, c1775, 2in (5cm) high.
£540–600
€ / $850–950 ⊞ DSA

PORCELAIN

Further reading

Miller's Collecting Porcelain,
Miller's Publications, 2002

◀ **A Coalport coffee can,** c1805,
2½in (6.5cm) high.
£65–75
€/ **$100–120** ⊞ JAY

**A Derby Crown Porcelain Co cup and
saucer,** c1880, 5in (12.5cm) high.
£160–175
€/ **$250–275** ⊞ CoS

King Street Derby

Derby was home to two major
porcelain factories, Royal Crown
Derby and King Street Derby. Aside
from Royal Crown Derby, another
manufactory was established across
the city in King Street. Between 1862
and 1866 the King Street works were
managed by George Stephenson and
Sampson Hancock. They were
continued by Hancock alone until 1935.
The King Street factory mark copied
the old Derby crowned D, but with
added initials SH. Most productions were
revivals of traditional Derby shapes and
patterns. This lack of originality means
that King Street Derby is generally
cheaper than Royal Crown Derby.

A Lowestoft tea bowl and saucer, printed
with Fisherman Crossing a Bridge pattern,
1775–80, 3in (7.5cm) diam.
£430–475
€/ **$680–750** ⊞ DSA

A New Hall coffee can, decorated with
pseudo Tobacco leaf pattern, pattern
No. 856, c1810, 2¼in (5.5cm) high.
£160–175
€/ **$250–275** ⊞ CoS

**A Derby King Street tea
cup and saucer,** possibly
painted by Annie Bailey
with floral sprays, painted
marks, 1900–25.
£170–200
€/ **$270–315** ⊁ DN

**A Lowestoft blue and
white tea bowl and
saucer,** painted with a
pagoda in a fenced garden,
within diaper borders, c1780.
£480–565
€/ **$750–870** ⊁ DN

**A Nymphenburg cabinet cup and
saucer,** the cup painted with a flower
bouquet on a medallion, with a
band of gilt classical urns and swags,
the handle and cup interior gilt,
impressed marks, German, c1815.
£1,200–1,400
€/ **$1,900–2,200** ⊁ S(O)

A Derby coffee cup, with a wishbone
handle, painted with a Chinese lady
seated on a rock, another lady, a
child and a dog to her left, rim chip,
c1758, 2½in (6.5cm) high.
£480–565
€/ **$750–870** ⊁ B

**A Fürstenberg chocolate cup
and *trembleuse* saucer,** the cup
modelled with a tied ribbon forming
the handle, painted with floral
bouquets, one in the shape of the
initial S, cover missing, saucer
chipped, script mark, German,
c1775, saucer 5½in (14cm) diam.
£55–65
€/ **$85–100** ⊁ BR

A New Hall coffee can, c1805,
2½in (6.5cm) high.
£85–100
€/ **$135–160** ⊞ JAY

A Paris cup and saucer, red
stamped marks, French, early 19thC,
cup 2½in (6.5cm) high.
£170–200
€/ **$270–315** ⊁ DORO

PORCELAIN

A **Schlaggenwald cup and saucer,** marked, Bohemian, 1844, cup 2¾in (7cm) high.
£180–200
€/ **$280–315** ⚒ DORO

A **Vauxhall tea bowl and saucer,** printed and overpainted with sprays of flowers and insects, a further spray to the inside base of the tea bowl, several chips and fine cracks, 1758–60, saucer 4½in (11.5cm) diam.
700–820
€/ **$1,100–1,300** ⚒ B

A **Sèvres cabinet cup and saucer,** painted by Jacques-Nicolas Sinsson with garden flowers, with gilt *faux* gadroons and foliate borders in gold and platinum, the cup with scrolling handle with biting snake terminals, fine crack to base of handle, printed mark of Charles X, painter's initials and date markings, dated 1828, saucer 6in (15cm) diam.
£1,000–1,200
€/ **$1,600–1,900** ⚒ B

A **Swansea cup,** painted with colourful flowers, with gilt border designs, small chip, marked 'Swansea', Welsh, 1814–20, 4in (10cm) high.
£1,200–1,400
€/ **$1,900–2,200** ⚒ WW

A **Worcester tea bowl,** decorated with Fruit pattern, c1780, 3¼in (8.5cm) diam.
£100–110
€/ **$160–175** ⊞ JAY

◀ A **Vienna cup and saucer,** painted mark, Austrian, 1827, saucer 6in (15cm) diam.
£750–900
€/ **$1,200–1,400** ⚒ DORO

A **Worcester tea bowl and saucer,** transfer-printed with Bat pattern, c1785, saucer 5in (12.5cm) diam.
150–165
€/ **$240–260** ⊞ WAC

A **Royal Worcester reticulated tea cup and saucer,** painted with sprays of roses alternating with pierced sections highlighted in gold, beneath pansy flowers, printed mark, 1870, saucer 4¼in (11cm) diam.
625–725
€/ **$990–1,100** ⚒ S(O)

A **Worcester reeded cup and saucer,** with floral and gilt decoration, 1780–85, 2½in (6.5cm) high.
£350–400
€/ **$550–650** ⊞ DSA

A **Worcester Flight, Barr & Barr coffee can,** c1825, 2½in (6.5cm) high.
£130–145
€/ **$200–230** ⊞ CoS

▶ A **cup and saucer,** each painted with a bird and shrub, within gilded borders, some wear to gilding, c1820, saucer 5in (12.5cm) diam.
£135–150
€/ **$210–240** ⚒ G(L)

A **Chamberlain Worcester tea cup,** painted with a view 'Doniquaik, Scotland', the name in script beneath, against a marbled gilt ground, painted mark, c1815, 2½in (6.5cm) high.
£240–275
€/ **$380–430** ⚒ G(L)

PORCELAIN

Custard Cups

A Caughley custard cup and cover, printed in blue with Willow Nankin pattern and a dagger border, 1785–90, 3in (7.5cm) high.
£420–500
€/ $670–790 ➶ B

A Marieberg set of four custard cups and covers, damage to knops, Swedish, 1769–88.
£750–900
€/ $1,200–1,400 ➶ BUK

A Chamberlain Worcester set of eight armorial custard cups and covers, painted with panels of flowers within gilt C-scroll borders, the two-handled tray set with recesses and painted with a central bunch of flowers, small restored areas, the covers with grey printed marks, c1820.
£1,700–2,000
€/ $2,700–3,200 ➶ DN

Dessert & Dinner Services

A Samuel Alcock part dessert service, comprising 25 pieces, painted with flowers, c1845.
£750–850
€/ $1,200–1,300 ➶ S(O)

A Caughley part dessert service, comprising 28 pieces, gilt with a central flower within a border of interlinked ovals, some damage and wear, c1790.
£380–450
€/ $600–700 ➶ S(O)

▶ **A Coalport part dessert service,** comprising 22 pieces, painted with fruits within geometric and fruiting vine borders, 19thC.
£850–1,000
€/ $1,350–1,600 ➶ B(Ed)

A Cauldon dessert service, comprising 29 pieces, painted with flowers, the borders with gilt floral decoration, c1910.
£1,000–1,200
€/ $1,600–1,900 ➶ B(Kn)

A Derby dinner service, comprising 49 pieces, painted with cornflowers, with gilt foliate decoration, some cracks and restoration, 1820–30, dinner plate 10in (25.5cm) diam.
£800–950
€/ $1,300–1,500 ➶ AG

A Royal Crown Derby Imari pattern dinner service, comprising 62 pieces, painted with a floriate pattern, printed and impressed marks, c1890.
£4,200–5,000
€/ $6,600–7,900 ➶ LJ

◀ **A Derby part dessert service,** comprising 41 pieces, painted with a bouquet of flowers within gilt borders, some damage and wear, marked, c1810.
£2,400–2,800
€/ $3,800–4,400 ➶ S(O)

Frank Haviland Limoges part dinner service, comprising 3 pieces, decorated with a floral pattern, retailer's mark, French, c1900, dinner plate 10in (25.5cm) diam.
£750–900
€ / **$1,200–1,400** ⚒ **NOA**

A Minton dessert service, comprising 17 pieces, each painted with a botanical specimen, one plate with small crack, impressed diamond registration marks, dated 1857.
£650–750
€ / **$1,000–1,200** ⚒ **B**
Ex-Minton Sale.

◄ **A Minton part dessert service,** comprising eight pieces, each with a hand-painted topographical scene, c1870.
£300–350
€ / **$475–550** ⚒ **SWO**

A Ridgway dessert service, comprising 21 pieces, each piece painted with a different flower species, with gilt scrolled panels and pierced borders with flower sprays, minor damage, painted pattern No. 2 over 5183, 1840–45, dessert plate 9¼in (23.5cm) diam.
£550–625
€ / **$870–990** ⚒ **BR**

► **A Royal Worcester part dessert service,** by Richard Sebright, comprising five pieces, painted with a group of fruits against a mossy ground, reserved on border with raised and flat gilding, minor damage, puce marks, 1913–19, plates 8¾in (22cm) diam.
£1,500–1,800
€ / **$2,400–2,800** ⚒ **B(NW)**

◄ **A Vienna-style dessert service,** comprising nine pieces, painted by Riemer, with gilt panels around a central Kauffman-style classical panel, titles in black script, blue enamel shield/beehive marks, late 19thC, plate 9in (23cm) diam.
£1,800–2,200
€ / **$2,800–3,500** ⚒ **TEN**

A Staffordshire dessert service, comprising 37 pieces, painted with a floral spray, within a shaped border gilded with scrolls, pattern No. 5903, cracks, 1845–50.
£1,500–1,800
€ / **$2,400–2,800** ⚒ **B(EA)**

PORCELAIN

Dishes

A Berlin dish, decorated with flower sprays within 'Königsglatt' pattern borders, German, c1785, 13in (33cm) wide.
£800–900
€ / **$1,300–1,400** ⊞ **US**

A Caughley dessert dish, painted with a floral spray to the centre and a border pattern, 1780–85, 10in (25.5cm) wide.
£470–520
€ / **$750–830** ⊞ **DSA**

A Chelsea peony dish, moulded with a large flowerhead and leaves, the stalk handle issuing a flower bud, red anchor mark, c1755, 8¾in (22cm) diam.
£1,700–2,000
€ / **$2,700–3,200** ⚒ **WW**

A Derby dish, from the Ducie service, the fluted border decorated with *faux* pearls, reserved with a panel bearing the cypher of Francis Reynolds Moreton, 3rd Baron Ducie, and a coronet within a ribboned wreath, on a low foot, minor rubbing, painted and impressed marks, c1791, 12½in (31.5cm) wide.
£800–950
€/ **$1,300–1,500** ⚒ B

A Limehouse pickle dish, moulded in the form of a scallop shell, painted with a Chinese hut by a pine tree surrounded by scroll and feather motifs, a shell flanked by two leaves at the base, the underside with floral sprays, 1746–48, 4in (10cm) diam.
£2,500–3,000
€/ **$4,000–4,700** ⚒ B

▶ **A Vauxhall dish,** the well with geometric moulding, the edge panels enclosing pierced trellis motifs, bordering smaller panels with diaper designs, some cracks and chips, 1755–58, 10in (25.5cm) diam.
£3,000–3,600
€/ **$4,700–5,700** ⚒ B

A Derby shell-shaped dessert dish, painted with a flower, *Gladiolus Cardinalis*, within gilt-line borders, slight wear, some regilding, pattern No. 197 and title in blue, c1800, 9½in (24cm) diam.
£400–475
€/ **$630–750** ⚒ B

A Sèvres dessert dish, painted with rose sprigs within a border of gilt-centred flowerheads, within a network of *oeils-de-perdrix* reserved with gilt-framed panels enclosing a single rose, French, dated 1771, 8½in (21.5cm) square.
£950–1,100
€/ **$1,500–1,700** ⚒ S(NY)

A Worcester moulded leaf dish, painted with bouquets of flowers with gilt rococo reserves, c1775, 10in (25.5cm) wide.
£700–765
€/ **$1,100–1,200** ⊞ RAV

A Chamberlain Worcester dessert dish, painted with feathers within a panel, the undulating rim gilded with foliage and scrolls, footrim chipped, c1815, 9½in (24cm) wide.
£525–625
€/ **$830–990** ⚒ G(L)

A Derby King Street dish, painted by H. S. Hancock, with sprays of flowers within a gilt border and gilt-gadrooned rim, signed, script marks, 1900–25, 11in (28cm) wide.
£1,300–1,500
€/ **$2,000–2,400** ⚒ DN

A Spode pineapple serving dish, painted with roses and forget-me-nots, the central holder raised on a moulded base, painted mark c1820, 9in (23cm) diam.
£300–350
€/ **$475–550** ⚒ TRM

A Worcester dessert dish, moulded with leafy vine branches lying on a basket, the centre and arcaded borders painted with flowers, a crack and some wear, double anchor mark, 1765–68, 12in (30.5cm) wide.
£2,000–2,200
€/ **$3,200–3,500** ⚒ B

A Royal Worcester shell-shaped dish, decorated with sprays of flowers on a blush ivory ground, No. 1274, dated 1893, 9in (23cm) wide.
£220–240
€/ **$350–380** ⚒ HYD

Figures

▶ **A pair of Bow figures of a shepherd and shepherdess,** c1765, 6in (15cm) high.
£3,200–3,500
€/ **$5,000–5,500**
⊞ DMa

▶ **A Bow figure of Juno and the eagle,** representing Air, after Etienne Le Hongre, restored, red anchor mark, c1765, 10in (25.5cm) high.
£400–475
€/ **$630–750** ⚹ WW

A pair of Belleek figures, representing Affection and Meditation, Irish, First Period, 1863–90, 14in (35.5cm) high.
5,500–6,000
/ **$8,700–9,500** ⊞ MLa
These pieces are large and rare.

A Berlin figure of Amphiaraus, German, 19thC, 9in (23cm) high.
£170–185
€/ **$270–300** ⊞ SER

▶ **A Chelsea figural scent bottle,** modelled as a bearded friar carrying a basket and a sack, on a mound painted with flower sprigs, minor chips, stopper missing, c1755, ¾in (9.5cm) high.
1,300–1,500
/ **$2,000–2,400** ⚹ B

A Chelsea figural flower holder, after a Saint Cloud original, modelled as a fish seller with a basket, seated on a rockwork base, chips and crack, red anchor mark, c1755, 9in (23cm) high.
£800–950
€/ **$1,300–1,500** ⚹ LFA

▶ **A Copeland Parian figure of Beatrice,** by E. Papworth, c1860, 22in (56cm) high.
£675–750
€/ **$1,000–1,200** ⊞ JAK

Copeland Parian figure of Night, after Raphael Monti, modelled as a woman with arms outstretched, a sleeping child at her feet, with a separate plinth base moulded in relief with a frieze of masks and putti above a Vetruvian scroll lower section, some damage, impressed and incised marks, c1862, 26in (66cm) high.
1,400–1,600
/ **$2,200–2,500** ⚹ DN

A Copeland Parian figure, after an original by Joseph Durham, entitled 'Go to Sleep', modelled as a young girl seated on a rock, wagging a finger at a dog on her lap, impressed marks for 'Copeland' and the 'Art Union of London', 1862'z,17¾in (45cm) high.
£900–1,100
€/ **$1,400–1,700** ⚹ Bea(E)

English 18th-century porcelain 1976–2002

This graph shows the increasing value of English 18th-century porcelain as a whole over the past 25 years. Individual collecting areas from different periods may not follow this graph exactly. ©AMR

PORCELAIN

◀ **A pair of Derby figures of Milton and Shakespeare,** each resting on a stack of books supported on a column, on rococo bases, 18thC, larger 12¼in (31cm) high.
£550–650
€/ $870–1,000
⚒ B(Pr)

▶ **A Derby King Street figure of Dr Syntax,** seated, with a sketch book and pencil, a pair of ducks at his feet, chip to beak of one duck, 19thC, 5¼in (13.5cm) high.
£275–325
€/ $430–515 ⚒ TMA

A Derby biscuit figural group, entitled 'Poetry', the base incised with crown and crossed batons, 216 and the mark of Isaac Farnsworth, 1775–80, 10¼in (26cm) high.
£900–1,100
€/ $1,400–1,700 ⚒ TMA

A Derby figure of a putto, minor losses, c1800, 4½in (11.5cm) high
£165–185
€/ $260–290 ⊞ SER

A pair of Derby King Street figures, c1890, 8½in (21.5cm) high.
£850–950
€/ $1,300–1,500 ⊞ DAN

A Derby King Street candle snuffer, modelled as Sarah Gamp, late 19thC, 4in (10cm) high.
£400–440
€/ $630–700 ⊞ TH
Sarah Gamp is a character in Charles Dickens's novel *Martin Chuzzlewit.*

A Frankenthal figure of a Chinese man, holding a jug in one hand and waving with the other, modelled by C. Lück, underglaze blue crowned CT mark, German, c1775, 5in (12.5cm) high.
£1,000–1,200
€/ $1,600–1,900 ⚒ DORC

A biscuit model of a peasant woman, impressed and printed marks for the Gardner factory, Russian, late 19thC, 8in (20.5cm) high.
£350–400
€/ $550–630 ⚒ WW

A W. H. Goss figure of an angel holding a stoup, 1862–86, 6in (15cm) high.
£400–450
€/ $630–700 ⊞ G&CC
This is a copy of the font at St John's Church, Barmouth, north Wales.

▶ **A Höchst figure of a boy gardener,** standing with a rake on a grassy mound, minor damage, wheel mark in blue, German, c1770, 5¼in (13.5cm) high.
£450–525
€/ $710–830 ⚒ B

A biscuit model of Spinario, after the Antique, the boy sitting removing a thorn from his foot, impressed marks for Gustavsberg, Swedish, early 20thC, 10¾in (27cm) high.
£380–450
€/ $600–700 ⚒ WW

◀ **A Le Nove figural group,** dressed in 18thC costume, on a rustic base, Italian, 18thC, 7in (18cm) high.
£1,100–1,300
€/ $1,700–2,000 ⚒ HYD

▶ **A Limbach figure of a lady,** depicting Autumn, from a set of The Seasons, wearing a wide-brimmed hat, holding a basket of grapes, the base with scrollwork, some restoration, German, c1780, 5¼in (13.5cm) high.
£950–1,100
€/ $1,500–1,700 ⚒ S(O)

A Minton Parian figure of Margaret of Anjou, dated 1851, 17in (43cm) high.
£240–275
€/ $380–430 ⚒ G(B)

◀ **A Minton Parian figural group of Una and the Lion,** the maiden seated on a lion, the base relief-moulded 'John Bell', damaged, moulded registration lozenge, impressed marks and date codes, c1860, 14¾in (37.5cm) high.
£380–450
€/ $600–700 ⚒ RTo
Una (the representation of Truth) is one of the characters in Edmund Spencer's 16th-century allegorical poem *The Faerie Queene*. She was accompanied by a lion who guarded her virtue. This was a popular image in Victorian times, since in 1838 the young Queen Victoria had been portrayed as Una on the reverse of a gold £5 coin engraved by William Wyon, the Chief Engraver at the Royal Mint. It is regarded as one of the most beautiful coins ever made.

A Minton Parian figure, entitled 'Comedy', by John Bell, c1864, 16in (40.5cm) high.
£1,100–1,200
€/ $1,700–1,900 ⊞ JAK

PORCELAIN

PORCELAIN

A Minton Parian figure of Lalage, after the model by John Bell, depicted sitting holding her knee and a floral wreath, titled and with impressed marks, c1864, 16¼in (41.5cm) high.
£650–775
€/ **$1,000–1,200** ⚘ WW

A biscuit group, probably Niderviller, modelled as four rustic figures holding flowers, around a central tree, on a rocky mound base with later gilt-metal mount, some chips and losses, French, late 18thC, 14¼in (36cm) high.
£300–350
€/ **$475–550** ⚘ DN

A Royal Dux figure of a cavalier, seated on a chair, pouring ale from a jug, raised and painted marks, Bohemian, late 19thC, 11½in (29cm) high.
£850–975
€/ **$1,350–1,50** ⚘ SJH

A pair of Royal Worcester figures of Egyptian musicians, crack to one base, dated 1886, 13in (33cm) high.
£2,100–2,300
€/ **$3,300–3,600** ⊞ MER

▶ **A pair of coloured biscuit figures,** each holding a dove for the purpose of receiving and sending a love letter, on gilt-decorated bases, French, c1875, 16in (40.5cm) high.
£400–480
€/ **$630–750** ⚘ TMA

A Vienna figural group, representing Winter, modelled as a man holding a pipe in one hand and a glass of schnapps in the other, the girl sitting at his feet holding a bottle, minor damage, Austrian, c1755, 5¼in (13.5cm) high
£750–900
€/ **$1,200–1,400** ⚘ DORC

A pair of figural scent bottles, modelled as actors, each holding a mask, with apertures in their hats, French, mid-19thC, 10¼in (26cm) high.
£250–300
€/ **$400–475** ⚘ SWO

A Royal Worcester figure of a woman, probably Cleopatra, partially draped, wearing a snake armlet, dated 1865, 9½in (24cm) high.
£650–750
€/ **$1,000–1,200** ⚘ GTH

A pair of figures, of a man and a woman, wearing 18thC costume, each with a jug beside a well, Continental, 19thC, 13¾in (35cm) high.
£280–325
€/ **$440–500** ⚘ GTH

A biscuit porcelain figural group, of a satyr with an infant satyr and a child, entwined with flower garlands, impressed 'Clodion', French, late 19thC, 9¾in (25cm) high.
£220–260
€/ **$350–400** ⚘ HOLL

Matching pairs

Most figures were sold as matching pairs, such as a male and female. When a pair was ordered, two figures were selected at random from the warehouse, and so were not necessarily a perfect match. They might have been coloured by different decorators and have different painter's marks underneath. Some pairs were totally mismatched at the time. Others were bought separately, or a companion figure may be a later replacement. Collectors take this seriously. A matching pair must comprise the two correct models with corresponding colouring, made at the same time. Ideally they should have identical marks. Matching painter's marks, while not essential, are always an advantage. A married pair, assembled later and with differences in colouring, is always worth less than a true pair.

latware

Belleek dessert plate, decorated
th a Greek pattern, Irish, Second
riod, 1891–1926, 9½in (24cm) diam.
50–400
€/ $550–630 ⊞ MLa

Chelsea plate, painted with sprays
d sprigs of flowers, within a scroll-
oulded border painted with four pairs
birds among foliage, red anchor
ark, c1755, 8½in (21.5cm) diam.
'00–850
€/ $1,100–1,300 ⚒ S(O)

Copeland cabinet plate, by
harles Ferdinand Hürten, the pierced
sketweave reticulated border
served with four panels painted
th blackberry sprays, the centre
inted with tumbling rose sprays,
corated with tooled gold, printed
ark, c1880, 9in (23cm) diam.
,500–4,200
€/ $5,500–6,500 ⚒ B

LOCATE THE SOURCE
The source of each illustration
in Miller's can be found by
checking the code letters below
each caption with the Key to
Illustrations, pages 794–800.

A Berlin cabinet plate, the centre
painted with a lady borne aloft by Time,
putti and the winds, within a tooled
gilt border of foliate scrollwork,
impressed and painted marks, German,
1817–23, 9¾in (25cm) diam.
£1,000–1,200
€/ $1,600–1,900 ⚒ S(O)

A Chelsea plate, enamel-painted in
the Hans Sloane style with a turnip,
two butterflies, flowers, a leaf and an
insect, riveted crack, red anchor mark
and No. 2, c1755, 9½in (24cm) diam.
£750–900
€/ $1,200–1,400 ⚒ LFA

A Derby plate, in the Chelsea style,
the border panels with long-tailed
birds and foliage in tooled gold,
separated by spiralling flower sprays,
the rim moulded with scrollwork,
minor wear, painted marks, c1815,
9½in (24cm) diam.
£320–375
€/ $500–600 ⚒ B

▶ **A pair of Doccia plates,** painted
with flowers, Italian, c1770,
9in (23cm) diam.
£1,200–1,300
€/ $1,900–2,000 ⊞ DAN

A Bow saucer dish, painted with
a butterfly and flower sprays,
with scattered sprigs, 1765–70,
8¼in (21cm) diam.
£550–625
€/ $870–1,000 ⚒ B

A pair of Coalport plates, painted
with bird and flower panels inside gilt
frames around a central gilt foliate
medallion, minor wear, c1820,
9¾in (25cm) diam.
£500–600
€/ $800–950 ⚒ S(O)

A Derby dessert plate, by 'Quaker'
Pegg, painted with a flower, *Passiflora
Alata*, within a plain gilt rim, painted
marks, c1815, 6in (15cm) diam.
£1,300–1,500
€/ $2,000–2,400 ⚒ B

A W. H. Goss commemorative plate, decorated with possibly a royal gravedigger carrying a spade in one hand and keys in the other, inscribed with a verse and 'July 2nd of 1594 R.S. Oetatis 98', and printed mark and registration No. for 1885–86, 9in (23cm) diam.
£140–160
€ / $220–250 ✦ GAK

A Minton cabinet plate, painted by Antonin Boullemier, with a Watteau-style scene of 'Le Bougeois Gentilhomme', depicting a cavalier fencing with two ladies, within gilt-decorated borders, painted and impressed marks, dated 1875, 9¾in (25cm) diam.
£375–450
€ / $600–700 ✦ B
Ex-Minton Sale.

▶ **A pair of Nantgarw dessert plates,** painted with flowers inside a C-scroll and foliate-moulded border, minor wear, one with impressed mark, Welsh, c1820, 8¼in (21cm) diam.
£2,200–2,500
€ / $3,500–4,000 ✦ S(O)

A Nantgarw dessert plate, probably painted in the Sims workshop, London, with a border of flower sprigs surrounding a central rose, impressed mark, Welsh, 1818–20, 9¼in (23.5cm) diam.
£1,000–1,200
€ / $1,600–1,900 ✦ B(SW)

A plate, painted by Yelizaveta Verngardovna Rosendorf on an Imperial Porcelain Factory blank, sickle mark, Russian, dated 1920, 9½in (24cm) diam.
£320–375
€ / $500–600 ✦ HYD

A Minton *pâte-sur-pâte* cabinet plate, by Alboin Birks, the pierced lobed reticulated rim moulded with shells and waves, the centre decorated with a pebble-gilt ground reserved with a *pâte-sur-pâte* panel depicting a cherub with a skipping rope, signed, printed and impressed marks, c1895, 9in (23cm) diam.
£3,000–3,500
€ / $5,000–5,500 ✦ B
Alboin Birks devised the process of moulded *pâte-sur-pâte* panels on porcelain items. These were particularly popular in the USA.

A pair of Neuberg-Gieshübl plates, both painted with finches among fruit beneath a tree trunk, within a pierced acanthus border, overlaid in gold, impressed marks, German, mid-19thC, 10in (25.5cm) diam.
£320–375
€ / $500–600 ✦ RTo

A set of four Minton plates, painted in the Chinese style with exotic birds perched on tree branche impressed marks and date ciphers, dated 1865, 9¾in (25cm) diam.
£900–1,100
€ / $1,500–1,700 ✦ B
Ex-Minton Sale.

A Nantgarw floral soup plate, with a moulded C-scroll and foliate border, impressed marks, Welsh, c1820, 9½in (24cm) diam.
£4,300–5,000
€ / $6,500–8,000 ✦ S(O)

A Nantgarw charger, with a cent spray of flowers and fruit, within a gilt mosaic border with six floral pane restored, impressed mark, Welsh, 1818–20, 21in (53.5cm) diam.
£1,700–2,000
€ / $2,700–3,200 ✦ B

A Paris cabinet plate, painted with a harbour scene, French, c183 9½in (24cm) diam.
£530–585
€ / $840–925 ⊞ DAN

Wedgwood plate, with a pierced
[bo]rder, the centre painted with cattle
[an]d signed by Henry Mitchell, brown-
[pr]inted Wedgwood mark, c1880,
[9i]n (23cm) diam.
[9]50–1,100
[€]/ $1,500–1,700 ⊞ DIA
[H]enry Mitchell was a fine painter
[o]f animals, and is best known
[fo]r his work at Minton. After
[le]aving Minton he worked for
[o]ther Staffordshire makers,
[in]cluding Doulton.

A Worcester
[pl]ate, with a
[sc]alloped edge,
[d]ecorated with
[a]d Mosaic
[p]attern, pseudo-
[o]riental mark,
[1]768, 8½in
[2]1.5cm) diam.
[4]75–575
[€]/ $750–900
⊹ HYD

◀ **A set of six Paul Delvaux**
dinner plates, in the style of Jean
Pillement, the centres decorated
with chased gilt chinoiserie figural
vignettes, one chip and wear,
French, c1900, 10in (25.5cm) diam.
£160–200
€/ $250–300 ⊹ NOA

A Swansea soup plate, from the
Lysaght service, probably painted by
Henry Morris, with a basket of flowers
to the centre, minor wear to gilding,
Welsh, c1820, 9½in (24cm) diam.
£2,200–2,500
€/ $3,500–4,000 ⊹ S(O)

▶ **A Worcester saucer dish,**
painted with a bridge and buildings,
surrounded by a border of scattered
flowers and insects, edged with a
gilt-decorated border, painted mark,
c1780, 7in (18cm) diam.
£700–820
€/ $1,100–1,300 ⊹ S(O)

◀ **A Worcester**
plate, painted
with two exotic
birds by trees,
within a gilt
border, seal
mark, c1772–75,
7½in (19cm) diam.
£400–500
€/ $630–800
⊹ CGC

◀ **A Chamberlain**
Worcester plate,
painted with the
arms and crest of
Hay, Earl of Errol,
the border with
Rich Queens
pattern, c1805,
9in (23cm) diam.
£900–1,000
€/ $1,400–1,600
⊞ DHu

PORCELAIN

A Royal Worcester plate, painted by John Stinton, the gilt rim acid-etched with neo-classical designs, minor damage, signed, puce mark, dated 1912, 10¼in (26cm) diam.
£1,000–1,200
€ / $1,600–1,900 ✎ B

A saucer, painted with a variety of shells, the border decorated with enamel, cracked, c1825, 6in (15cm) diam.
£100–120
€ / $160–190 ✎ G(L)

An anti-slavery plate, the centre painted with an African figure, the scroll-moulded border with four inscriptions, chipped, c1835, 9in (23cm) diam.
£220–260
€ / $350–400 ✎ SAS

Ice Pails & Wine Coolers

A pair of Coalport ice pails and covers, painted with sprays of flowers beneath gilt dentil-edged borders, the covers similarly decorated, on gilt paw feet on square bases, liners missing, hair-crack, c1820, 14¾in (37.5cm) diam.
£3,000–3,600
€ / $4,700–5,700 ✎ S(NY)

A pair of Derby ice pails, with liners, decorated with Imari pattern, with gilt shell-moulded handles, the covers with foliate loop handles, cover handles repaired, chips, painted marks, c1815, 12¾in (32.5cm) diam.
£800–900
€ / $1,300–1,400 ✎ S(O)

A Derby ice pail and cover, decorated with bands of flowers and leaves with gilt borders, with a scroll knop, restored, painted marks, early 19thC, 12¼in (31cm) diam.
£275–320
€ / $430–500 ✎ WW

A Derby ice pail and cover, gilded and enamelled in the Imari palette with birds, flowers and blossoming branches, with two handles, hairline crack and discolouration, painted mark, early 19thC, 9¾in (25cm) high.
£380–450
€ / $600–700 ✎ RTo

A pair of Chamberlain Worcester wine coolers, applied with fruiting vines around the rim, the body embossed with rose, shamrock and thistle sprays around painted floral sprays, the handles formed of entwined wheat sheaves, on a marbled base, restored, chips, losses and wear, 1816–20, 9in (23cm) high.
£900–1,100
€ / $1,400–1,700 ✎ B

A Nymphenburg wine cooler, painted with a flower spray and further scattered flowers, with pierced gilt-edged scrollwork handles with moulded rocaille terminals, impressed marks, German, c1765, 6¼in (16cm) high.
£750–875
€ / $1,200–1,400 ✎ S(O)

Further reading

Miller's Porcelain Antiques Checklist,
Miller's Publications, 1991

▶ **A pair of ice pails,** decorated in the Imari palette with flowers, with twin handles, the covers waisted with a high collar, c1815, 11in (28cm) high.
£900–1,100
€ / $1,400–1,700 ✎ Bri

PORCELAIN

nkstands & Inkwells

Royal Crown Derby inkwell, ecorated in the Imari palette, 1919, n (7.5cm) high.
430–470
/ **$670–750** ⊞ DIA

▶ **A Staffordshire inkwell,** decorated with a panel of peasants in a landscape, attributed to William Pollard, c1825, 3in (7.5cm) high.
£1,100–1,200
€/ **$1,700–1,900** ⊞ DIA

A Worcester Flight, Barr & Barr inkwell, painted with a panoramic landscape and three figures, the well gilded with palmettes and seaweed, the handle with a mask terminal, two chips, cover missing, 1813–40, 5½in (14cm) wide.
£1,300–1,500
€/ **$2,000–2,400** ⚒ G(L)

◀ **An inkwell,** painted with flowers, within gilt dentil borders, cover missing, early 19thC, 1½in (4cm) high.
£40–50
€/ **$60–80** ⚒ TMA

A Chamberlain inkwell, the cover surmounted by a biscuit figure of a seated classical lady writing, a gilded quillholder to her right, one side of the base painted with a view of Moxhull Hall, Warwickshire within Gothic-style gilded borders, painted marks, losses and wear, c1823, 4¾in (12cm) high.
£1,000–1,200
€/ **$1,600–1,900** ⚒ B

ardinières

Coalport jardinière nd stand, decorated with silhouette portrait of eorge III, within the gilt scription 'A Token from heltenham', with gilt ng-moulded handles, inor chips, 1805–10, ⁴in (17cm) high.
1,000–1,100
/ **$1,600–1,700** ⚒ S(O)

A Nymphenburg jardinière, with *bombé*-shaped sides, each corner with an angel's-head finial, the side panels painted with *deutsche Blumen* and flower sprays within moulded and scrolled borders, painted marks, German, early 20thC, 12¼in (31cm) wide.
£280–320
€/ **$440–520** ⚒ BR

A Worcester Flight & arr jardinière, with oulded ring handles and preading foot, painted ith feathers over a gilt et ground, reserved ithin a panel with a sprig nd foliate border, crack nd wear, incised mark, 1800, 6¼in (16cm) high.
2,200–2,600
/ **$3,500–4,000** ⚒ B

A Samson, Paris jardinière, on a raised foot, decorated in the *famille rose* style, painted mark, French, late 19thC, 19in (48cm) diam.
£450–550
€/ **$700–870** ⚒SWO

A Royal Worcester jardinière, with gilded everted rim and scroll-moulded shoulder details, painted with studies of roses, on a stepped foot, signed 'W.E. Jarman', printed and painted marks, dated 1913, 10¼in (26cm) diam.
£900–1,100
€/ **$1,400–1,700** ⚒ DD

Jugs & Ewers

A Belleek jug, Irish, First Period, 1863–90, 6in (15cm) high.
£700–800
€ / $1,100–1,300 ⊞ MLa

A Du Paquier ewer, painted with flowers, the foot with restored firing crack, Austrian, Vienna, c1735, 6in (15cm) high.
£1,600–2,000
€ / $2,500–3,200 ⚒ DORO

A Bow jug, the grooved strap handle applied with a heart at the lower terminal, decorated with three fan-shaped panels depicting Chinese river scenes, alternating with floral panels, irregular panels below the rim, replacement metal spout, base detached and restuck, c1760, 8½in (21.5cm) high.
£400–500
€ / $630–800 ⚒ B

A Lowestoft sparrow beak cream jug, polychrome-painted with Oriental figures in a garden, 1770–75, 3¼in (8.5cm) high.
£675–750
€ / $1,000–1,200 ⊞ DSA

◄ **A Sèvres jug,** with a part-fluted body, on a flared foot, printed mark, French, c1876, 4in (10cm) high.
£130–150
€ / $200–240 ⚒ WW

A Caughley mask jug, with cabbage-leaf-moulded body, decorated with Fisherman pattern, printed mark, late 18thC, 8¾in (22cm) high.
£550–650
€ / $870–1,000 ⚒ Bea

► **A New Hall 'Robin' jug,** decorated with a Chinese lady with a parasol and a boy with a kite by a fence in a garden, pattern No. 20, 1782–87, 2¾in (7cm) high.
£1,400–1,700
€ / $2,200–2,700 ⚒ B

A ewer, with a high gilt-scroll handle and tooled gilt spout, painted with a continuous frieze of various birds alternating with fruits, French or Bohemian, early 19thC, 10½in (26.5cm).
£700–850
€ / $1,100–1,300 ⚒ S(O)

A Derby jug, decorated with a pictorial vignette, handle restored, inscribed 'In Italy' to base, c1820, 4½in (11cm) high.
£140–160
€ / $220–250 ⚒ SWO

A pair of Rockingham ewer vases, painted with botanical subjects, on rococo-moulded quatrefoil bases, some damage, printed marks, c1830, 9¼in (23.5cm) high.
£3,700–4,200
€ / $5,800–6,600 ⚒ HAM

◄ **A Staffordshire mask jug,** moulded and enamelled with titled portrait busts of Brougham and Denman flanked by patriotic flowers, some restoration and cracks, c1820, 5½in (14cm) high.
£400–450
€ / $630–700 ⚒ S
Brougham and Denman were legal advisers to Queen Caroline, the estranged wife of the Prince Regent.

Rockingham

The Rockingham china works at Swinton, Yorkshire, made very individual English porcelain. Elaborate teapots and eccentric vases epitomize English taste in the 1830s. Rockingham figures and tea services bearing the factory mark of a griffin were keenly collected 100 years ago. Unfortunately, unmarked teawares from other makers were incorrectly identified as Rockingham and enormous confusion resulted. The Rockingham name is still widely misused, even though comprehensive reference books now enable collectors to recognize the real thing.

PORCELAIN

graduated set of four Staffordshire lobed jugs, ightened with gold, c1830, largest 8in (20.5cm) high. ₤50–420
/ $550–660 ➹ TMA

ese jugs are decorated with roses, thistles and amrock, known as 'Union' sprigs representing the nited Kingdom.

A Vienna jug, painted with flowers, minor restoration to edge, shield mark, c1770, 6¾in (17cm) high.
£250–300
€/ $400–475 ➹ DORO

A Worcester sparrow beak jug, transfer-printed with The Fence pattern, 1770–75, 5in (12.5cm) high.
£230–260
€/ $370–400 ⊞ WAC

Worcester cream jug, inted in the Chinese yle with figures on rraces, the gilt flower d leaf-scroll ground corated with flowers d leaves within roll borders, c1772, ¼in (9cm) high.
₤50–900
/ $1,200–1,400 ➹ LFA

A Royal Worcester jug, painted with flowers and foliage, gilt handle, clay and date mark for 1888, 9in (23cm) high.
£300–340
€/ $475–540 ➹ AG

A Grainger's Worcester jug, the panel-moulded ground decorated with relief-moulded and painted flowers, the handle decorated with a key pattern, heightened with gold, dated 1892, 8in (20.5cm) high.
£120–140
€/ $190–220 ➹ B(W)

A Factory X ewer, the ribbed body painted with flowers, the interior with a border of leaves, flowers and festoons, pattern No. 134, c1790, 5in (12.5cm) high.
£230–270
€/ $360–430 ➹ WW

Mugs & Tankards

◄ **A Bloor Derby porter mug,** painted by Daniel Lucas, hair crack, printed circular mark, c1830, 5in (12.5cm) high.
£380–440
€/ $600–700 ➹ B

Cookworthy

William Cookworthy was a chemist who discovered in Cornwall the raw materials for making hard paste porcelain. He obtained a patent in March 1768 and his factory at Plymouth commenced full production soon afterwards. Sadly, kiln losses were heavy and much Plymouth porcelain suffered from a burnt glaze. The last firing at Plymouth was in November 1770. Thanks to new backing from a fellow Quaker, Richard Champion, Cookworthy moved his factory to Bristol, where he continued as before until his retirement in 1774. Because it is so hard to distinguish the porcelain made at Plymouth from early productions at Bristol, many collectors prefer to call it Cookworthy porcelain, rather than Plymouth.

A Bow mug, painted with a floral pattern, c1760, 3½in (9cm) high.
£580–650
€/ $900–1,000 ⊞ DSA

Bristol mug, painted with a floral ray and scattered sprigs beneath laurel leaf border, minor wear gilt rim, marked, c1775, ¼in (9.5cm) high.
,000–1,200
/ $1,600–1,900 ➹ S(O)

A Cookworthy tankard, with a grooved loop handle, painted with birds among leafy trees and foliage, cracks and repairs, enamels worn, tin mark, c1770, 5¼in (13.5cm) high.
£750–875
€/ $1,200–1,400 ➹ B

PORCELAIN

A **Worcester mug,** with grooved strap handle, painted with Prunus Fence pattern, small flake to foot rim, workman's mark, 1755–60, 2½in (6.5cm) high.
£850–1,000
€/ **$1,300–1,600** ➢ Bea

▶ A **Worcester mug,** decorated in the Imari palette with exotic birds among foliage, 1753–54, 3¼in (8.5cm) high.
£27,000–32,000
€/ **$43,000–50,000** ➢ HYD
This mug is an exceptionally rare piece of early Worcester in very good condition.

◀ A **Worcester mug,** printed with the King of Prussia and emblems of war, small rim chips, dated 1757, 3½in (9cm) high.
£650–750
€/ **$1,000–1,200** ➢ G(L)

A **Worcester Flight & Barr mug,** painted in London, probably by Thomas Baxter with two boys playing shuttlecock, within a panel, the reverse with a couple walking in the grounds of a country house, a border below the rim painted with fruit, flowers, scrollwork, a bird, a butterfly and a caterpillar, slight wear to gilding, unmarked, 1802–05, 4¼in (11cm) high.
£900–1,100
€/ **$1,400–1,700** ➢ B

Plaques

A **George Jones** *pâte-sur-pâte* **plaque,** by Frederick Schenk, decorated with two nymph-like figures beside a rock pool, impressed factory mark, gilt No. 5661, c1880, 11in (28cm) diam.
£1,100–1,300
€/ **$1,700–2,000** ➢ S(O)

A **Royal Worcester plaque,** painted by John Stinton with Highland cattle grazing beside a river, hills in the distance, signed, printed mark for 1930, 4in (10cm) diam, in a gilt and swept frame.
£1,100–1,300
€/ **$1,700–2,000** ➢ M

A **pair of plaques,** one painted with flowers, berries and a dragonfly, the other with grapes, foliage and other fruit, c1830, 9½ x 8in (24 x 20.5cm), framed.
£1,100–1,300
€/ **$1,700–2,000** ➢ B(P)

A **plaque,** hand-painted with a lady wearing a feather hat within a border of ornate foliate scrolls and grotesques, German, 19thC, 13¾in (35cm) square.
£200–225
€/ **$320–350** ➢ B(W)

A **pair of plaques,** painted with Jesus Christ and Mary, set in a gilt-tooled leather travelling case, Continental, late 19thC, 5½ x 3½in (14 x 9cm).
£200–240
€/ **$320–380** ➢ G(L)

A **plaque,** decorated with a young girl with a parrot perched on her hand, some fruit to the side, German, c1880, 4in (10cm) wide.
£375–450
€/ **$600–700** ➢ HAM

ot-Pourri Jars & Vases

Spode pot-pourri jar and ver, with inner cover and t handles, decorated th cherubs and acanthus aves, pattern No. 2063, pressed mark, early thC, 9in (23cm) high.
30–275
/ $360–430 ↗ TRM

A Tournai pot-pourri vase and cover, the pierced cover with a grapevine finial, the pierced body with gilt ram's head handles, the gadrooned lower section applied with swags of fruiting vines, on a gilt-edged rocky base with a putto reclining on an urn spilling water, and a seated dog, decoration later, minor damage and putto's head restuck, French, c1765, 8in (20.5cm) high.
£300–350
€/ $475–550 ↗ S(O)
This would have been worth much more if the decoration had been contemporary.

A Royal Worcester rose pot-pourri jar and cover, by George H. Cole, the pierced cover with a gilded finial, the body with a reserved cartouche painted with garden flowers, signed 'Cole' within a C-scroll border in raised gilding, damaged, transfer-printed factory mark, date mark for 1903, 9½in (24cm) high.
£700–820
€/ $1,100–1,300 ↗ PF

A Royal Worcester pot-pourri vase and two covers, decorated with flowers, c1914, 13in (33cm) high.
£1,400–1,600
€/ $2,200–2,500 ⊞ JUP

pot-pourri vase and ver, the cover and foot erced and moulded with k leaves and acorns, t with branch handles, inted with a panel birds, the reverse th flowers, 1840s, ³⁄₄in (45cm) high.
50–750
/ $1,000–1,200 ↗ S(O)

▶ **A pair of pot-pourri vases and covers,** each with scroll side handles and four lion-paw feet, decorated with gilt vines, one handle repaired, 1826–30, 5in (12.5cm) high.
£250–300
€/ $400–475 ↗ WW

A pair of pot-pourri vases and covers, after Derby originals, painted with swags of roses, gilding worn, Continental, early 20thC, 8¾in (22cm) high.
£550–650
€/ $870–1,000 ↗ S(O)

PORCELAIN

auce & Cream Boats

◀ **A Bow sauce boat,** on three lion-paw feet, the sides painted in *famille rose* colours with peony sprays, a further spray inside the base, the rim with a diaper pattern reserved with flowerhead panels, damaged, 1752–54, 8¾in (22cm) wide.
£300–350
€/ $475–550 ↗ B

A Bow sauce boat, decorated with Desirable Residence pattern, footrim repaired, c1765, 7½in (19cm) long.
£200–225
€/ $320–350 ↗ SWO

▶ **A Penning-ton's Liverpool cream boat,** painted with floral sprays, chip to spout, c1785, 5in (12.5cm) wide.
£500–550
€/ $800–870
⊞ **DSA**

pair of Caughley cream boats, inted with the Apple Prints pattern, 80–85, 2½in (6.5cm) high.
1,100–1,300
/ $1,700–2,000 ↗ LFA

◄ A Lowestoft sauce boat, hairline crack and restoration, workman's mark to underside, c1765, 7½in (19cm) long.
£180–220
€/ **$280–340**
🔨 SWO

A Vienna sauce boat, painted with flowers, fruit and vegetables, edge and foot restored, shield mark, c1760, 9in (23cm) wide.
£160–200
€/ **$250–315** 🔨 DORO

A Worcester cream boat, rim chips, c1752, 4¼in (11cm) wide.
£2,200–2,500
€/ **$3,500–4,000** 🔨 B

► A Worcester two-handled sauce boat, painted with Two-Handled Sauceboat Landscape pattern, rim chip and haircrack, workman's mark, c1757, 7½in (19cm) wide.
£650–750
€/ **$1,000–1,200** 🔨 S(O)

The Watney Collection

The Watney collection of English porcelain sold for £2million (€/ $3million) in 1999–2000, but its value was much more than monetary. It was a working and learning collection, and as such it made a massive contribution to the study and understanding of early blue and white.

During a lifetime spent trawling the stalls of London's Portobello Road, Bernard Watney bought nearly 2,000 pieces, the majority of which were not identified. As a doctor, Bernard used his analytical approach to sort his collection into distinct groups and then investigated likely makers. Many pieces in the collection were damaged and broken in some way, but when they were auctioned after Bernard's death, the prices achieved showed that collectors valued rarity and provenance far above condition.   **John Sandon**

A pair of Worcester sauce boats, painted with a version of Little Fisherman pattern, one chipped, crescent mark, c1765, 5¼in (13.5cm) wide.
£650–750
€/ **$1,000–1,200** 🔨 Bea

Scent Bottles

PORCELAIN

A Dresden scent bottle, modelled as a cushion with a flame finial on a domed stopper, the body painted with alternating panels of figures and flowers, with moulded tasselled corners and gilt highlights, German, 19thC, 3½in (9cm) wide.
£130–150
€/ **$200–240** 🔨 AH

► A Fürstenberg gilt-metal-mounted scent flask, after a Chelsea model, the basket-moulded body reserved with a raised panel inscribed 'Eau de Senteur' hanging from a moulded gilt chain, the neck painted with a flower sprig, the foliate pierced metal stopper attached with a chain, marked, German, c1770, 3½in (9cm) high.
£600–720
€/ **$950–1,100** 🔨 S(O)

A Derby scent bottle, stopper regilded, 1830, 4in (10cm) high.
£320–350
€/ **$500–550** ⊞ CoS

► A pair of Rockingham scent bottles, encrusted with flowers and heightened with gold, the necks with raised gilt rings, the stoppers encrusted with flowers, damaged, 1830–35, 5in (12.5cm) high.
£650–750
€/ **$1,000–1,200** 🔨 TMA

► A Spode scent bottle, minor restoration, pattern No. 4650, c1825, 5in (12.5cm) high.
£260–285
€/ **$400–450** ⊞ CoS

ea Canisters

A pair of Worcester-style Samson tea canisters and covers, moulded with flutes and panels painted with buildings and flowers, one with a seal mark, the other with a cross mark, French, 1880, 4¾in (12cm) high.
£350–400
€/ **$550–630** ➶ WW

Fürstenberg tea canister and over, with moulded floral decoration, painted in puce with floral sprays within shaped gilt reserves, minor hips, finial missing, German, c1775, ¾in (12cm) high.
100–120
/ **$160–190** ➶ F&C

To order Miller's books in the UK please ring 01903 828800
See the full range at
www.millers.uk.com

A Worcester tea canister, transfer-printed and hand-coloured with figures and ruins, Knowles Boney Collection label, cracked, cover missing, c1765, 5¼in (13.5cm) high.
£320–375
€/ **$500–600** ➶ S(O)

rays

A Caughley spoon tray, decorated with a patera and leaf swags, marked, c1785, 6¾in (17cm) wide.
£160–200
€/ **$250–315** ➶ WW

Belleek tray, decorated with a ragon, Irish, First Period, 1872, 5in (38cm) diam.
3,300–3,600
/ **$5,200–5,700** ⊞ MLa

A Caughley/Coalport spoon tray, painted with Tower pattern, the fluted border with a butterfly and diaper border, c1798, 6in (15cm) wide.
£1,300–1,500
€/ **$2,000–2,400** ➶ LFA

A Minton tray, painted by Lucien Boullemier with a Bacchic putto within a Sèvres-style border of flowers and a gilt foliate rim, hairline crack, globe mark, 1900–25, 14in (35.5cm) wide.
£1,100–1,300
€/ **$1,700–2,000** ➶ DN

A Chamberlain's Worcester topographical card tray, painted with a titled view of the Houses of Parliament within a shell-encrusted border, damaged, painted factory mark and title, c1840, 11¾in (30cm) wide.
£750–900
€/ **$1,200–1,400** ➶ S(O)

Vienna cabaret tray, with a gilt nd pierced rim, the central panel ainted with Rubens' Boys and gned 'Bauer, Wien', within a assical-style border of grotesques, mall chip to one corner, impressed nd shield marks, Austrian, id-19thC, 13in (33cm) wide.
1,500–1,800
/ **$2,400–2,800** ➶ B

▶ **A Sèvres-style tray,** decorated with flowers, with a relief-moulded border heightened in gold, gilt pseudo-Sèvres mark, Bohemian, c1900, 21¼in (54cm) wide.
£320–375
€/ **$500–600** ➶ DORO

PORCELAIN

Tureens

◀ **A Derby dessert tureen, cover and stand,** painted with botanical specimen sprays within gilt leaf-band borders, each piece inscribed in blue with botanical names, blue baton marks, c1790, stand 9in (23cm) wide.
£1,600–2,000
€ / **$2,500–3,200** ↗ DN

A Bloor Derby tureen and cover, hand-painted with flowers, edged in gold, with a scrolled gilt handle, mino restoration, c1830, 10in (25.5cm) wide
£200–225
€ / **$320–350** ↗ B(W)

◀ **A Nantgarw dessert tureen with matching Swansea cover and stand** painted in London, some restoration, gilding worn, tureen impressed 'Nantgarw C.W.', stand impressed 'Swansea', 1814–23, 7½in (19cm) wide
£7,000–8,000
€ / **$11,000–12,500** ↗ S(O)
The price for this piece reflects the present strength of the Welsh porcelain market.

A Höchst tureen and cover, the cover applied with an artichoke finial, the rim moulded with the *Altbrandenstein* pattern, the body painted with flowers, some restoration, impressed initials, German, 1760–65, 10¼in (26cm) diam.
£950–1,100
€ / **$1,500–1,750** ↗ S(Am)

▶ **A pair of Spode porcelain dessert tureens, covers and stands,** painted and sprigged with flower sprays, some wear to gilding, c1815, 7in (18cm) high.
£420–500
€ / **$670–790** ↗ S(O)

A Vienna tureen and cover, heightened with gold, impressed mar and Vienna shield mark, Austrian, date mark for 1846, 6½in (16.5cm) high.
£160–200
€ / **$250–315** ↗ DORO

Vases

▶ **A pair of Chelsea vases,** on four scrolled feet, painted on both sides with birds perched on rocks and fruiting branches, surrounded by garlands of applied flowers, buds and leaves, covers possibly missing, flowers damaged, gold anchor marks, c1765, 9½in (24cm) high.
£750–900
€ / **$1,200–1,400** ↗ B

A Belleek ram's head cornucopia vase, Irish, First Period, 1863–90, 4in (10cm) high.
£850–950
€ / **$1,350–1,500** ⊞ MLa

A pair of Belleek bronze-effect vases, with cherubs, Irish, First Period, 1863–90, 12in (30.5cm) high.
£5,000–5,500
€ / **$8,000–8,700** ⊞ DeA

▶ **A garniture of Derby frill vases,** comprising a central vase and a pair of trumpet vases, minor damage, restoration, the pair of vases possibly lacking covers, patch marks, 1760–65, centre vase 11¾in (30cm) high.
£2,400–2,700
€ / **$3,800–4,300** ↗ B

PORCELAIN

Royal Crown Derby aisted vase, decorated th Imari pattern, dated 11, 5in (12.5cm) high.
40–275
/ $380–430 ⚒ SWO

Staffordshire vase, ssibly Mayer & Newbold, inted in enamels with wers and leaves within t cartouches, regilded n, 1820–25, n (12.5cm) high.
40–485
/ $680–780 ⊞ CoS

Rockingham miniature asket, with loop handle, oulded with leaves and corated with gold, on a ped base, red number, 835, 2¾in (7cm) high.
,000–1,200
/ $1,600–1,900 ⚒ LFA

A pair of Sèvres-style ses, with 'jewelled' coration, c1860, in (25.5cm) high.
,300–2,500
/ $3,600–4,000 ⊞ DHu

A pair of Jagetet Pinon vases, each gilt and silvered with a wreath medallion enclosing two birds, with scattered acorns and oak leaves, gilt dragon handles, one foot repaired, gilt painted mark, French, Tours, early 20thC, 24¾in (63cm) high.
£575–650
€ / $900–1,000 ⚒ S(O)

A Minton vase, painted with hanging game and hunting trophies, the borders with foliage and butterflies, with gilt leaf and ring handles, slight wear to border, c1850, 9½in (24cm) high.
£450–525
€ / $700–830 ⚒ B
Ex-Minton Sale.

A pair of Sèvres-style vases, with 'jewelled' decoration, one finial restored, c1880, 10in (25.5cm) high.
£3,200–3,500
€ / $5,000–5,500 ⊞ MAA

A Christian's Liverpool baluster vase, painted with a willow tree flanked by peony and bamboo, cracked, c1770, 3½in (9cm) high.
£550–650
€ / $870–1,000 ⚒ S(O)

A Minton quadruple bottle vase, painted with rural vignettes and a scene of the Houses of Parliament beneath rose festoons, the four handles extending upwards to form a crown studded with cabochons, minor damage, c1870, 8¾in (22cm) high.
£350–400
€ / $550–630 ⚒ B
Ex-Minton Sale.

A pair of Sèvres-style vases, with 'jewelled' decoration, one finial restored, c1880, 10in (25.5cm) high.
£3,200–3,500
€ / $5,000–5,500 ⊞ MAA

A Longton Hall rococo vase, painted with panels of exotic birds in landscapes and applied with flowers and foliage, on a foot painted with scattered flowers, cracks and chips, c1755, 8½in (21.5cm) high.
£900–1,100
€ / $1,400–1,700 ⚒ S(O)

A pair of Paris two-handled vases, with gilt swan handles, painted with a continuous scene of a stylized garden with fountains, trellis arbours and pots of roses, the waisted feet on marble bases, French, c1820, 13¼in (33.5cm) high.
£2,500–3,000
€ / $4,000–4,700 ⚒ S(NY)

A Spode trumpet vase, with everted gilt rim, painted with two bouquets of flowers against a gilded scale ground, with beaded borders, star crack, pattern No. 1166, painted mark, c1810, 6¼in (16cm) high.
£200–240
€ / $320–380 ⚒ G(L)

PORCELAIN

PORCELAIN

A Willets Manufacturing Co 'Belleek' vase, painted by E. Welcher, probably outside the factory, with roses beneath a gilt rim, green printed mark 'Willets Belleek' and serpent, American, dated 1904, 20¾in (52.5cm) high.
£1,600–2,000
€/ $2,500–3,200 ↗ S(NY)
The Willets Manufacturing Co of Trenton, New Jersey, was established in 1879 by brothers Joseph, Daniel and Edmund Willets. They made American Belleek from c1894–1909, Trenton having become a major centre for the production of American Belleek after china clay had been discovered there in the 1860s. Enthusiasm for these wares had been fired by the Irish Belleek factory's exhibition at the 1876 Philadelphia Exhibition.

▶ A flower vase, c1840, 8in (20.5cm) high.
£400–450
€/ $630–700 ⊞ DAN

A pair of Worcester Flight, Barr & Barr miniature vases, each painted with an exotic bird in a landscape, minor chips to gadrooned rims, puce mark, c1825, 2in (5cm) high.
£1,400–1,600
€/ $2,200–2,500 ↗ G(L)

A Locke & Co Worcester vase, with dolphin shoulder handles, hand-painted with violets and a butterfly, small rim chips, c1890, 4¼in (11cm) high.
£240–275
€/ $380–430 ↗ B(W)

A pair of Royal Worcester vases, with gilt scroll handles, painted with flowers and foliage, date code for 1895, 5¾in (14.5cm) high.
£375–425
€/ $600–670 ↗ L

A pair of Royal Worcester Hadley Ware vases, decorated with a pair of peacocks in the branches of a pine tree against a misty twilight, etchings coloured in by Reginald H. Austin, artist's signature, green factory mark, date codes, 1903, 12in (30.5cm) high.
£1,400–1,600
€/ $2,200–2,500 ↗ TEN

A pair of Grainger's Worcester vases, moulded as shells, c1900, 3in (7.5cm) high.
£130–145
€/ $200–230 ⊞ PSA

For further information on antique porcelain see the full range of Miller's books at
www.millers.uk.com

A rococo vase and cover, the cover with gilded scroll and floral ornament, twin handles, the body decorated with roses, convolvulus and other flowers, on a pierced rococo base with scrollwork and dragons, Bohemian, c1860, 23¼in (59.5cm) high.
£320–375
€/ $500–600 ↗ TRM

Wall Brackets

◀ A pair of Dresden-style mirror-back wall brackets, each with a floral painted back panel surround, with putti over a demi-lune ebonized platform, above a pierced and floral-encrusted basket support with a further putto mounted beneath, each on a velvet-covered backboard, damaged, German, late 19thC, 34¼in (87cm) high.
£1,300–1,500
€/ $2,000–2,400 ↗ Bri

A pair of Grainger's Worcester wall brackets, painted mark, c1870, 8in (20.5cm) high.
£1,000–1,200
€/ $1,600–1,900 ↗ G(B)

A Royal Worcester wall bracket, the shaped top supported by a winged cherub head, two impressed marks, c1870, 8in (20.5cm) high.
£250–300
€/ $400–475 ↗ EH

Miscellaneous

Du Paquier beaker, painted with Oriental flowers, two exotic birds in flight and insects, the interior rim with a formal border heightened with gold, foot and glaze abrasion to rim, Austrian, Vienna, c1730, 2¾in (7cm) high.
£775–900
€/ $1,200–1,400 ✗ S(Am)

A Caughley eye bath, moulded with leaf scrolls and printed with Fisherman pattern, beneath a cell diaper and pendant flowerhead border, on a scroll-moulded baluster stem and fluted foot, c1785, 2in (5cm) high.
£1,400–1,700
€/ $2,200–2,700 ✗ LFA

A *bonbonnière*, modelled as a female head wearing a mask beneath elaborately-coiffured hair, the reverse mounted with a gilt-metal cover engraved with scrolling foliage and flowers, German, possibly Thuringian, 1750–1800, 3in (7.5cm) wide.
£1,000–1,200
€/ $1,600–1,900 ✗ S(O)

Three tulip flowerheads, modelled with overlapping petals around a central aperture, one petal chipped, probably German, 1775–1800, 2¼in (5.5cm) high.
£500–600
€/ $800–950 ✗ S(O)

A Sèvres ice cup, from the Louis XVI service, painted by Philippine l'aîné with an allegory of Justice, scales in her right hand, a sceptre in her left, books by her side, enclosed by tooled *guilloche* gilding, the ground gilt with foliate scrolls and flower swags, minor damage, French, 1790, 2½in (6.5cm) high.
£2,200–2,500
€/ $3,500–4,000 ✗ B
While the majority of the Louis XVI service was sold by the French Revolutionary government in 1793 and was later acquired by George IV in 1811, it is known that several items, which appear in the records, became separated from the main service. This cup would appear to be one of these items.

needle case, handpainted with vines and a cupid at one end, German, 1760, 5in (12.5cm) long.
1,200–1,400
/ $1,900–2,200 ⊞ US

A Spode pastille burner, modelled as a cottage with a pitch roof cover, enamelled with encrusted flowers on a mound base, minor cracks, Feldspar porcelain mark, c1830, 4¾in (12cm) high.
£420–475
€/ $670–750 ✗ G(L)

A Worcester spitoon, decorated with Three Flowers pattern, c1770, 4½in (11.5cm) high.
£600–650
€/ $950–1,000 ⊞ WWW

▶ A Worcester cornucopia wall pocket, painted with insects and flower sprays, damaged, 1755–60, 10in (25.5cm) high.
£450–525
€/ $700–830 ✗ WW
Coloured Worcester cornucopia are very rare and the price of this reflects the damage.

Bristol Champions spoon, painted with owers, c1775, 4in (10cm) long.
530–700
/ $1,000–1,100 ⊞ JUP

Meissen

Meissen is Europe's oldest successful porcelain factory, the earliest pieces dating from c1710. These are known today as 'Böttger porcelain' after Johann Böttger, the alchemist who discovered the secret of making 'hard paste' porcelain to rival the valuable imports from China and Japan.

Some early Meissen directly copied Oriental prototypes, although most productions were totally original. The brilliant painter J. G. Herold specialized in chinoiserie subjects. Other enamellers painted landscapes, detailed figure subjects or the finely-executed flowers known as *deutsche Blumen*. Every piece of 18th-century Meissen was decorated to the highest possible standards. Their principal figure modeller, Johann Kändler, is best known for his harlequins and figures of street vendors. By the 19th century, such pieces had become enormously popular in Britain and the United States, and they were reissued in new colouring, every piece being carefully hand-decorated.

Recently 19th-century Meissen has rocketed in value and some pieces are nearly as valuable as 18th-century examples. Mostly, though, earlier productions are worth more, and for this reason identifying the date of manufacture is crucial. Fortunately almost every piece is clearly marked with the famous crossed swords, derived from the arms of Saxony. In the 18th century each sword was painted as a neat, straight line. During the 'Academic' period (1763–74), a dot was placed between the sword hilts, and during the 'Marcolini' period (1774–1813) a star or asterisk was painted above the hilts. Somewhat scruffy marks were used until the 1840s and then, until the early 20th century, the swords were carefully painted, each gently curved, and a 'pommel' (dark spot) placed at the tip of each hilt. From 1926 to 1939 a dot was placed between the blades of the swords. Post-WWII pieces have thin, curved swords, with no dot or pommels.

The crossed swords marks are extensively faked, for Meissen is the most widely copied porcelain. Many other makers in the Dresden area have reproduced popular Meissen shapes and patterns. It is therefore essential to distinguish between actual Meissen factory productions and 'Dresden'-style porcelain, which is always inferior. **John Sandon**

A Meissen model of an elephant, by J. J. Kändler, wearing a caparison hung with gilt tassels and gilt with florets, minor restoration, c1750, 5¾in (14.5cm) long.
£1,200–1,500
€/ $1,900–2,400 ✗ B

A Meissen model of pug dog, by J. J. Kändler, one foreleg repaired, c1750, 3in (7.5cm) long.
£1,600–2,000
€/ $2,500–3,200 ✗ S(O)

A Meissen model of a bullfinch, c1880, 3½in (9cm) high.
£300–340
€/ $475–550 ⊞ BROW

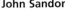

◄ **A Meissen model of an Alsatian,** No. V188, first modelled by Eric Hösel in 1927, crossed sword mark, c1928, 7¼in (18.5cm) long.
£1,200–1,300
€/ $1,900–2,000 ⊞ DAV

A Meissen model of a Bolognese terrier, damaged, blue crossed swords mark and incised numerals, 1850–1900, 9in (23cm) high.
£600–700
€/ $950–1,100 ✗ HYD

► **A Meissen beaker,** painted with *deutsche Blumen*, crossed swords mark, c1745, 3¼in (8.5cm) diam.
£240–275
€/ $380–430 ✗ WW

A Meissen trinket box, painted with a view of Albrechtsburg Castle at Meissen, crossed swords mark, c1900, 4in (10cm) diam.
£580–650
€/ $900–1,000 ⊞ DAV

PORCELAIN

◀ A Meissen *Kinderkopf* **bust of a girl,** a nosegay on her left shoulder, incised and impressed numerals, mid-19thC, 6in (15cm) high.
£600–700
€/ **$950–1,100** ⚒ TMA

▶ **A Meissen candle snuffer,** encrusted with flowers and painted with two insects, marked, c1860, 8¼in (8.5cm) high.
£200–240
€/ **$320–380** ⚒ SWO

A Meissen candlestick, c1850, 3in (7.5cm) high.
£270–300
€/ **$425–475** ⊞ DAN

◀ **A pair of Meissen candlesticks,** heightened in gold with a panel of flowers to front and back, crossed swords marks, c1870, 5½in (14cm) high.
£700–800
€/ **$1,100–1,200** ⊞ DAV

A pair of Meissen chamber sticks, modelled with miniature figures of child gardeners, c1860, 5½in (14cm) high.
£1,500–1,700
€/ **$2,400–2,700** ⊞ MAA

A Meissen tea bowl and saucer, c1735, 3in (7.5cm) diam.
£1,400–1,500
€/ **$2,200–2,400** ⊞ US

◀ **A Meissen cup and saucer,** with deep base for hot water, mid-19thC, 5in (12.5cm) high.
£1,000–1,100
€/ **$1,600–1,700** ⊞ BROW

A Meissen egg cup, painted with scattered sprigs of *deutsche Blumen*, gilt-edged rim, crossed swords mark, 1755–60, 2¼in (5.5cm) high.
£750–875
€/ **$1,200–1,400** ⚒ S(O)
The double egg cup can be used to place the egg either horizontally or vertically, depending on whether the custom is to break open its end or side, the latter being the case in Germany and Austria, the former in France and Italy.

A Meissen Comedia Dell'Arte figure of Pantaloon, by J. J. Kändler, on a floral-moulded base, c1738–40, 6in (15cm) high.
£7,000–8,200
€/ **$11,000–13,000** ⚒ EH
This is a rare earlier version of the model. The later version is slightly smaller and Pantaloon has one arm raised.

A Meissen figure of a pipe smoker, c1747, 5in (12.5cm) high.
£3,500–4,000
€/ **$5,500–6,300** ⊞ BHa

▶ A Meissen figure of a fishmonger, minor restoration, c1760, 6in (15cm) high.
£1,400–1,600
€/ **$2,200–2,500** ⚖ DORO

A Meissen figure of a boy on a hobby horse, c1860, 6½in (16.5cm) high.
£1,300–1,500
€/ **$2,000–2,400** ⊞ BROW

A Meissen figural group of child gardeners, leaves restored, crossed swords mark, c1900, 8¾in (22cm) high.
£1,100–1,300
€/ **$1,700–2,000** ⚖ DORO

A Meissen figure of a Turkish gentleman, by J. F. Eberlein, c1748, 7in (18cm) high.
£3,400–3,800
€/ **$5,400–6,000** ⊞ BHa

A Meissen flower seller, c1870, 5½in (14cm) high.
£1,200–1,400
€/ **$1,900–2,200** ⊞ BHa

A Meissen figure of a young man, c1750, 5in (12.5cm) high.
£1,400–1,500
€/ **$2,000–2,300** ⊞ MAA

A Meissen figure of a seamstress, by J. J. Kändler, holding pieces from a jacket, on a scroll-moulded base, minor chips and losses, crossed swords mark, c1760, 9in (23cm) high.
£1,600–1,800
€/ **$2,500–2,800** ⚖ S(NY)

18th-century Meissen 1976–2002

[bar chart titled "18th-century Meissen 1976–2002" with INDEX on y-axis ranging 0 to 8000 and years 1976 to 2002 on x-axis]

This graph shows the changing value of 18th-century Meissen porcelain as a whole over the past 25 years. Individual collecting areas and different periods, such as the 19th century, may not follow this graph exactly. ©AMR

A Meissen figure of a man reading, restored, 19thC, 5in (12.5cm) high.
£225–250
€/ **$350–400** ⊞ SER

A Meissen group of cherubs, carrying flowers, c1900, 6½in (16.5cm) high.
£1,800–1,900
€/ **$2,800–3,000** ⊞ MAA

◀ A pair of Meissen figures of Malabar Musicians, playing musical instruments, wearing Chinese hats and flowered clothing, on scrolled bases, damaged, crossed swords mark, 1860–80, 13in (33cm) high.
£1,200–1,400
€/ **$1,900–2,200** ⚖ JNic

A Meissen plate from the Swan service, by J. J. Kändler, the shell-moulded ground with two swans swimming among bulrushes in the centre, a crane in flight overhead, the rim painted with the arms of Brühl and Kolowrat-Krakowsky, scattered sprigs and *indianische Blumen* with a gilt-dashed rim, minor wear, crossed swords and impressed potter's mark of four radiating triangles, 1738–39, 9in (23cm) diam.
£8,500–10,000
€/ **$13,500–16,000** ⚒ S(O)
The Swan service was ordered in 1736 for the director of the factory, Count Heinrich von Brühl (1700–63). The service originally comprised over 2,200 pieces, most of which remained at the family seat, Schloss Pförten, until 1945, when Russian troops destroyed much of the service and the castle was burned to the ground.

A set of four Meissen soup plates, painted with *deutsche Blumen* within basket weave borders, one with foot rim crack, gilding worn, c1760, 8¾in (22cm) diam.
£500–600
€/ **$800–950** ⚒ BUK

A Meissen cabinet plate, the central panel painted with a scene after Boucher, depicting Venus bathing attended by a nymph, within a lobed and pierced rim moulded with panels of forget-me-nots, crossed swords mark, impressed and incised numerals, c1870, 10¼in (26cm) diam.
£2,200–2,500
€/ **$3,500–4,000** ⚒ B

A pair of Meissen plates, with enamelled floral sprays, within basket weave borders, crossed swords mark, mid-18thC, 11¾in (30cm) diam.
£350–420
€/ **$550–670** ⚒ SWO

A Meissen miniature teapot and cover, with scroll handle, painted with *deutsche Blumen* and scattered sprigs, the cover with a flower bud finial, traces of crossed swords mark, c1760, 4in (10cm) high.
£625–725
€/ **$1,000–1,200** ⚒ S(O)

A Meissen topographical vase, painted with a titled view of Pillnitz within a moulded rococo cartouche, further cartouches enclosing flowers, crossed swords mark, incised and impressed numerals, mid-19thC, 12in (30.5cm) high.
£1,600–2,000
€/ **$2,500–3,200** ⚒ RTo

► **A Meissen vase,** decorated with flowers and fruit and Watteau-style figures within a panel, c1880, 5½in (14cm) high.
£1,200–1,300
€/ **$1,900–2,000** ⊞ MAA

A Meissen vase, decorated with flowers and fruit, c1860, 10in (25.5cm) high.
£1,600–1,800
€/ **$2,500–2,800** ⊞ MAA

PORCELAIN

A Selection of Chinese Dynasties & Marks
Early Dynasties

Neolithic	10th – early 1st millennium BC	Tang Dynasty	618–907
Shang Dynasty	16th century–c1050 BC	Five Dynasties	907–960
Zhou Dynasty	c1050–221 BC	Liao Dynasty	907–1125
Warring States 480–221 BC		Song Dynasty	960–1279
		Northern Song 960–1127	
Qin Dynasty	221–206 BC	*Southern Song* 1127–1279	
Han Dynasty	206 BC–AD 220	Xixia Dynasty	1038–1227
Six Dynasties	222–589	Jin Dynasty	1115–1234
Wei Dynasty 386–557		Yuan Dynasty	1279–1368
Sui Dynasty	581–618		

Ming Dynasty Marks

Hongwu 1368–1398

Yongle 1403–1424

Xuande 1426–1435

Chenghua 1465–1487

Hongzhi 1488–1505

Zhengde 1506–1521

Jiajing 1522–1566

Longqing 1567–1572

Wanli 1573–1619

Tianqi 1621–1627

Chongzhen 1628–1644

Qing Dynasty Marks

Shunzhi 1644–1661

Kangxi 1662–1722

Yongzheng 1723–1735

Qianlong 1736–1795

Jiaqing 1796–1820

Daoguang 1821–1850

Xianfeng 1851–1861

Tongzhi 1862–1874

Guangxu 1875–1908

Xuantong 1909–1911

Hongxian 1916

Chinese Ceramics

The international demand for Chinese ceramics has, until now, ensured that prices were unaffected by localized recessions, but the global recession of the past two years has affected the market, especially for pristine, well-documented pieces in the £1,000–20,000 (€/ $1,700–32,000) price range. Large decorative pieces are still sought by interior designers but demand is slowing. The Chinese mainland market is only expanding for large, highly decorated, 19th-century items considered to be of 'Chinese taste'. The finest and rarest pieces are still in demand, however, especially as alternative investments, and academic collectors are always keen to acquire small, interesting examples of various types or kilns.

The last 25 years have seen many changes in collecting fashions and market values. The systematic looting of tombs in China, and improved 'faking' techniques, has led to a serious downturn in values of Tang and Han Dynasty excavated ceramics. Figures considered very rare 25 years ago are now commonplace, and thermoluminescence testing has become the norm. Imperial porcelains of the Qing Dynasty (1662–1911) have increased ten-fold in value due to Chinese demands, arising from a shortage of Ming and earlier Imperial works. Collectors recognized that high quality and rare objects of any period should be obtained while still available. Early 20th-century 'official wares' have sold for up to £30,000 (€/ $47,000) each.

Even in depressing times, the beauty and perfection of the best Chinese ceramics continue to attract connoisseurs and collectors. This is particularly evident with Chinese Export ceramics, where the market has slowed for routine goods but still realizes record prices for exceptional pieces.

The next 25 years will see a huge increase in the value of Imperial ceramics as the full purchasing power of mainland China takes effect. Lesser-quality tomb figures will continue to drop in price due to market saturation and lack of confidence in authenticity, and at least another five ship-wrecks of ceramics (already located) will surface, thus further diminishing a slow market.

Peter Wain

Animals

A pottery model of a boar, Tang Dynasty, 618–907, 13¼in (34cm) high.
£700–850
€/ $1,100–1,300 ➤ S(O)

A pottery model of a dog, Oxford T/L tested, Han Dynasty, 206 BC–AD 220, restored, 21in (53.5cm) high.
£1,800–2,000
€/ $2,800–3,200 ⊞ GLD

A straw-glazed pottery model of a horse, Oxford T/L tested, Sui Dynasty, 581–618, 11in (28cm) high.
£1,500–1,700
€/ $2,400–2,700 ➤ S(O)

A pottery model of a horse, Oxford T/L tested, some damage and restoration, Tang Dynasty, 618–907, 9½in (24cm) high.
£240–275
€/ $380–420 ➤ WW

A sancai-glazed model of a camel, Tang Dynasty, 618–907, 20in (51cm) high.
£3,000–3,500
€/ $4,800–5,800 ➤ B

A glazed Yueyao model of a ram, with an aperture on the forehead, Jin Dynasty, 1115–1234, 6in (15cm) high.
£2,000–2,200
€/ $3,200–3,500 ➤ S(Am)

T/L test

Oxford T/L test refers to a test certificate awarded by Oxford Authentication Ltd to those genuine pieces of ceramics which have passed their thermoluminescence test which is accurate to plus or minus 200 years.

◄ **A pair of *famille verte* models of Dogs of *Fo*,** with vases on their backs, raised on plinths, both damaged, Kangxi period, 1662–1722, 7¾in (19.5cm) high.
£150–175
€/ $240–280 ✎ WW

A glazed model of a dog, 18thC, 3in (7.5cm) high.
£300–350
€/ $475–550 ✎ L

Items in the Chinese Ceramics section have been arranged in date order within each sub-section.

A pair of *famille rose* candle holders, in the form of recumbent lions, one looking to the left, the other to the right, restored, Canton, 19thC, 7½in (19cm) wide.
£2,500–3,000
€/ $4,000–4,800 ✎ B

A pair of glazed models of cockerels, standing on rocks, one with gilt-metal base, 18thC, 6¼in (15.5cm) high.
£600–720
€/ $950–1,200 ✎ S(O)

A pair of models of cockerels, late 19thC, 9in (23cm) high.
£850–950
€/ $1,400–1,600 ⊞ AUA

Bowls

A glazed porcelain bowl, Song Dynasty, 960–1279, 9in (23cm) diam.
£1,600–1,800
€/ $2,500–2,800 ⊞ GLD

A Provincial bowl, decorated with scrolling foliage, commendation mark, 1550–75, 4¾in (12cm) diam.
£1,500–1,800
€/ $2,400–3,000 ✎ L

A Junyao stoneware tea bowl, with hare's fur glaze, Song Dynasty, 960–1279, 4¾in (12cm) diam.
£1,100–1,300
€/ $1,700–2,000 ⊞ PCA

A bowl, decorated in the centre with a crane, below *ruyi* heads and pendants, 16thC, 8½in (21.5cm) diam.
£700–820
€/ $1,100–1,300 ✎ G(L)

◄ **A Swatow bowl,** decorated with flowers and birds, late Ming Dynasty, 17thC, 9¾in (25cm) diam.
£400–500
€/ $600–720 ✎ S(O)

A Henan bowl, Jin Dynasty, 1115–1234, 4¾in (12.5cm) diam.
£2,500–3,000
€/ $4,000–4,800 ✎ B

A bowl, c1643, 8in (20.5cm) diam.
£100–125
€/ $160–200 ⊞ McP
This piece is from the Hatcher cargo, retrieved from a shipwreck that occurred in the South China Sea c1643, and named after the diver who arranged the salvage operation. The cargo consisted of predominantly blue and white wares from Jingdezhen.

A *famille verte* fluted basin,
decorated in the centre with birds,
surrounded by floral sprays, Kangxi
period, 1662–1772, 11in (28cm) diam.
£3,400–3,800
€ / **$5,400–6,000** ⊞ **G&G**

An Immortal basin, the centre painted
with an Immortal dressed in flowing
robes, standing on a dragon, within
a barbed border, Kangxi mark and
period, 1662–1772, 16¼in (41cm) diam.
£5,500–6,500
€ / **$8,600–10,200** ⚏ **S(HK)**
It is unusual to find a powder-blue
dish of this type with a large blue
and white figure design depicting
an Immortal.

A Chinese export *famille rose*
bowl, decorated with floral sprays,
1775–1825, 9in (23cm) diam.
£180–220
€ / **$280–350** ⚏ **PFK**

A bowl, European decorated with
a couple in front of a column and
trees, the exterior yellow-glazed
and incised with dragons, 19thC,
5in (12.5cm) diam.
£600–700
€ / **$950–1,100** ⚏ **G(L)**

A bowl, Kangxi mark and period,
1662–1722, 8in (20.5cm) diam.
£2,000–2,300
€ / **$3,200–3,600** ⊞ **GLD**

A blue and white bowl, from
the *Vung Tau* cargo, late 17thC,
6in (15cm) diam.
£130–145
€ / **$200–230** ⊞ **McP**
The Chinese ship the *Vung Tau*
was wrecked off the coast of
Vietnam c1696 and salvaged c1990.

A bowl, painted with eight
Immortals, Qianlong mark and
period, c1780, 10in (25.5cm) diam.
£1,300–1,500
€ / **$2,000–2,400** ⊞ **CHT**

A porcelain bowl, both the exterior
and interior decorated with figures
playing games, floral internal border,
with blue-gilt fret borders, Canton,
19thC, 13½in (34.5cm) diam.
£575–675
€ / **$900–1,000** ⚏ **DMC**

A porcelain bowl, the exterior
painted with four dragons among
cloud scrolls, the interior with a
single dragon, with everted rim,
minor flake to rim, character marks,
Kangxzi period, 1662–1772,
7¼in (18.5cm) diam.
£4,500–5,500
€ / **$7,000–8,400** ⚏ **Bea(E)**
The quality, mark and pattern
of this bowl all indicate it is an
Imperial piece, that is, made for the
Royal Court. In perfect condition
it would be worth £12,000–15,000
(€ / $18,000–24,000).

A bowl, from the Nanking cargo,
c1752, 6in (15cm) diam.
£160–185
€ / **$250–300** ⊞ **McP**
The Dutch East India Company's
ship *Geldermalsen* sank near Java
in 1751. Included in its cargo was
a particular type of Chinese blue
and white porcelain known as
Nanking, hence the name.
Although there was little in the
cargo to excite the purist collector
of Asian ceramics, the story of the
salvage attracted intense public
interest, which was reflected in
the prices achieved when the
pieces were sold at auction. Items
from this cargo still, nearly 20
years later, command a premium
over comparable pieces of
Chinese export porcelain.

A pair of *famille rose* bowls, the
sides painted with four medallions
enclosing the characters *wu fu
wan shou*, one cracked, Guangxu
mark and period, 1875–1908,
5½in (14cm) diam.
£700–850
€ / **$1,100–1,400** ⚏ **S(Am)**
The characters *wu fu wan shou*
mean five blessings for 10,000 years.

◄ **A fish bowl,** the exterior painted
with a pair of peacocks and other
birds among seasonal flowers
between diaper bands, the interior
with five goldfish and weed, Canton,
early 20thC, 14¼in (36cm) diam.
£300–350
€ / **$475–550** ⚏ **CGC**

CHINESE CERAMICS

Boxes

A Chinese export *famille rose* box and cover, painted with sprays of flowers and leaves, both rivetted, Qianlong period, 1736–95, 5½in (14cm) diam.
£250–300
€ / $400–480 ➚ LFA

A box and cover, painted with a flower medallion reserved on a scrolling butterfly ground, marks, 19thC, 12in (30.5cm) diam.
£700–850
€ / $1,100–1,300 ➚ S(O)

▶ **A blue and white box and cover,** inscribed, 1820–40, 5in (12.5cm) wide.
£60–70
€ / $95–110 ⊞ McP

A *famille rose* box and cover, the rounded sides painted with flowering branches, the top centred with a large flower, Guangxu mark and period, 1875–1908, 12¼in (31cm) diam.
£10,000–12,000
€ / $16,000–19,000 ➚ S(HK)
This box is an Imperial piece and much sought after by Chinese ceramics collectors as it is rare to find good-quality items of this period.

▶ **A *famille rose* box and cover,** decorated with boys on a terrace, 19thC, 3in (7.5cm) diam.
£160–200
€ / $250–315 ➚ G(L)

Brushpots

A brushpot, painted with figures and a horse in a landscape, c1640, 7½in (19cm) high.
£4,700–5,700
€ / $7,500–9,000 ➚ B

▶ **A *famille verte* brushpot,** painted with a long-tailed bird and prunus, rim chips, Kangxi period, 1662–1722, 5½in (14cm) high.
£600–700
€ / $950–1,100 ➚ G(L)

A brushpot, painted with scholars in a bamboo grove, above a raised narrow border, c1640, 8½in (21.5cm) diam.
£1,800–2,200
€ / $2,800–3,500 ➚ S(O)

A brushpot, painted with a large phoenix, Shunzhi/Kangxi period, 1650–70, 8in (20.5cm) diam.
£8,000–10,000
€ / $12,500–15,800 ➚ S(NY)

A *famille rose* brushpot, painted on each side with a fruiting flower branch, on bracket feet, 18thC, 5¼in (13.5cm) high.
£600–720
€ / $950–1,100 ➚ S(O)

Cups

A **stoneware offering tray,** with seven fixed cups, Six Dynasties period, 222–589, 7in (18cm) diam.
£400–500
€ / **$630–800** ⊞ **GLD**

A *famille verte* **tea bowl and saucer,** Kangxi period, 1662–1722, bowl 3in (7.5cm) diam.
£320–360
€ / **$500–570** ⊞ **McP**

A *wucai* **month cup,** painted with a white prunus tree emblematic of the 11th month, the side inscribed with a poem, Kangxi period, 1662–1722, 2¾in (6.5cm) high.
£5,200–6,200
€ / **$8,200–9,800** ⚒ **S(HK)**
A full set of 12 month cups would command a very high price.

A **footed cup,** the sides painted with boys flying a kite below a splashed border, glaze chips to rim, c1640, 4¼in (11cm) high.
£2,200–2,500
€ / **$3,500–4,000** ⚒ **B**

◄ A **tea bowl and saucer,** decorated with a huntsman, a mountainous landscape in the background, Kangxi period, 1662–1722, saucer 4¼in (11cm) diam.
£270–300
€ / **$420–500** ⊞ **GLD**

Expert's choice

The outstanding Peony Pavilion Collection sold by Christie's London, in 1989 was formed in Japan by one family over six generations. It consisted of 200 lots (approximately 1,000 pieces) of late Ming Chinese export ceramics made specifically for use in the Japanese tea ceremony. The porcelain was made during the reign periods of Tianqi and Chongzhen (1621–43) and showed an extensive range of rare designs and shapes. The latter decades of the Ming Dynasty (known as the Transitional period) was a period of some obscurity in Chinese porcelain production. It was a time of national disintegration and civil war that resulted in the disruption of ceramic production in China and loss of traditional markets. Despite local troubles these wares suggest a spirit of innovation in a search for new markets. New shapes and designs were produced, in underglaze blue and white and on-glaze enamels, reflecting Japanese taste. This resulted in an unusual mix of cultures. Many designs had never been seen in Europe before. The whole collection was a revelation. These late Ming pieces were assessed as of a little-understood period and as an insight into the contemporary neo-Confucian culture in Japan.

This collection would have been formed at very little financial cost in Japan, but it could only have been so comprehensive as a result of the inherited passion and enthusiasm of five generations.
Peter Wain

A **wine cup,** painted with two birds, one perched in a fruiting peach tree, the other in a flowering magnolia issuing from rockwork, Kangxi mark and period, 1662–1722, 1¾in (4.5cm) high.
£4,000–5,000
€ / **$6,400–7,900** ⚒ **B**

A **pair of** *famille rose* **tea bowls and saucers,** painted with a winged cherub below a multi-coloured eight-panelled border, Yongzheng period, 1723–35.
£1,400–1,600
€ / **$2,200–2,600** ⚒ **G(L)**

A **tea bowl and saucer,** Kangxi period, 1662–1722, saucer 4in (10cm) diam.
£400–450
€ / **$640–700** ⊞ **CHT**

A **tea bowl and saucer,** Dutch-decorated, Qianlong period, 1736–95, cup 4in (10cm) diam.
£160–180
€ / **$250–280** ⊞ **GLD**

CHINESE CERAMICS

A Chinese export tea bowl and saucer, c1740, 2½in high.
£235–260
€ / **$370–400** ⊞ DAN

A Mandarin palette trio, comprising tea bowl, coffee cup and saucer, c1770, saucer 5in (12.5cm) diam.
£160–180
€ / **$250–280** ⊞ DAN

A Chinese export porcelain tea bowl, painted *en grisaille* with Britannia and a reclining soldier, the reverse with Venus and Cupid seated on a cloud, the interior with a central sprig and a gilt rim, 19thC, 3in (7.5cm) diam.
£140–160
€ / **$220–250** ⚒ SWO

A pair of Chinese export tea bowls and saucers, decorated with initials within a cartouche, with C-scroll and flower borders, cracks, mid-18thC.
£200–225
€ / **$320–350** ⚒ DN

▶ **A Libation cup,** of archaic *yi* form, with coffee glaze, 19thC, 5¼in (13.5cm) diam.
£850–1,000
€ / **$1,300–1,500** ⚒ S(O)

A coffee cup, decorated with Masonic symbols, Qianlong period, 1736–95.
£750–875
€ / **$1,200–1,400** ⚒ G(L)

◀ **A tea bowl and saucer,** from the *Tek Sing* cargo, c1822, saucer 4in (10cm) diam.
£115–125
€ / **$180–200**
⊞ DAN
The *Tek Sing* sank in the Gaspar Straits in Indonesia in 1822.

Dishes

A *wucai* dish, made for the Japanese market, decorated with two elephants and their keepers near a pine tree, 1621–27, 9¾in (25cm) diam.
£2,500–3,000
€ / **$4,000–4,700** ⚒ S(Am)

A silver-mounted dish, Kangxi/ Yongzheng period, 1710–50, mounts Dutch, 19thC, 9in (23cm) diam.
£415–460
€ / **$640–720** ⊞ McP

▶ **A teapot stand,** enamel-painted in the workshop of James Giles, London, with a pair of exotic birds perched among rocks and foliage, two smaller birds flying overhead, gilt rim, minor wear, 1765–70, 5¼in (13.5cm) wide.
£1,300–1,500
€ / **$2,000–2,400** ⚒ B

A *famille rose* teapot stand, c1760, 5in (12.5cm) wide.
£260–285
€ / **$400–450** ⊞ DAN

MILLER'S CLUB

Collets House

Crane Close

Denington Road

Wellingborough

NN8 2QH

Great savings on Miller's books!

If you would like to receive our newsletter* and special offers on Miller's books, join the Miller's Club today – absolutely free. Please complete this card or visit our website.

name _____

address _____

_____

_____ postcode _____

e-mail _____

*One main newsletter a year

The Miller's Club is available to UK and ROI residents only

From time to time, this information may be passed to other carefully selected organizations. If you do not wish your name to be used, please tick this box ☐

Miller's Compares

I. A pair of Chinese Imari shell dishes, painted with radiating sprays of chrysanthemums within a geometric border, minor frits, Qianlong period, 1736–95, 7in (18cm) wide.
£1,100–1,300
€/ **$1,700–2,000** ⊞ G&G

II. A pair of shell dishes, with floral decoration, Qianlong period, 1736–95, 6½in (16.5cm) wide.
£750–850
€/ **$1,000–1,400** ⊞ G&G

These pairs of mid-18th century shell dishes were both made in Jingdezhen for the European market. Item I is decorated in the much rarer and therefore more desirable Chinese Imari palette and is worth much more than Item II which is a blue and white example.

A spoon tray, decorated with the 'Arms of Liberty' depicting John Wilkes and his opponent Lord Mansfield, c1770, 4¾in (12cm) wide.
£1,200–1,400
€/ **$1,900–2,200** ⚒ G(L)

◄ **A** *famille rose* **pedestal dish,** painted with butterflies, the exterior with roses and other flowers, Canton, Qing Dynasty, 19thC, 15in (38cm) wide.
£320–360
€/ **$500–570** ⚒ B(B)

A *famille rose* **porcelain dish,** the centre with a medallion depicting figures in a lakeside landscape, within a field of butterflies and birds among flowers, the border decorated with scrolls and swords, silvered and gilt-enriched, 19thC, 9¼in (23.5cm) square.
£160–200
€/ **$250–300** ⚒ PFK

Ewers & Kendi

A Yue ware ewer and cover, Warring States period, 480–221 BC, 8in (20.5cm) high.
£4,000–4,500
€/ **$6,300–7,000** ⊞ GLD
Yue are high-fired green wares.

A Yingqing glazed ewer and cover, with curved spout, the C-shaped handle applied with a loop, the cover and finial set with a smaller loop, Song Dynasty, 960–1279, 6in (15cm) high.
£1,700–2,000
€/ **$2,700–3,200** ⚒ S(Am)

A blue and white *kendi,* painted in underglaze blue with panels of flowers and precious objects, Wanli period, 1573–1619, 8½in (21.5cm) high.
£450–525
€/ **$700–830** ⚒ B(WM)

A *kendi,* from the Hatcher cargo, c1643, 5in (12.5cm) high.
£770–860
€/ **$1,200–1,400** ⊞ McP

◄ **A** *kendi,* painted with panelled foliage, with brass-mounted spout, early 17thC, 8in (20.5cm) high.
£350–425
€/ **$550–670** ⚒ G(L)

► **An octagonal lobed ewer,** with phoenix-head spout, decorated with peony, lotus and other flowers, cover missing, Kangxi period, 1662–1722, 8¾in (22cm) high.
£4,000–5,000
€/ **$6,300–7,900** ⚒ G(L)

Figures

A set of five pottery equestrian figures, each soldier in military attire, the saddlecloths and trappings richly painted, traces of mud encrustation, Han Dynasty, 206 BC–AD 220, 11¼in (28.5cm) high.
£5,500–6,000
€/ **$8,700–9,500** ➹ S(NY)
Various pottery figures of similar models are recorded but this is remarkable as one figure bears an impressed potter's seal. The inscription reads '*Guo nan*' (Baron Guo), which suggests that these figures were made for the tomb of a member of the Han aristocracy.

◄ **A porcelain figure of Guanyin,** decorated in blue and white, a bird perched on her left hand, damaged, Kangxi period, 1662–1722, 8¼in (21cm) high.
£280–325
€/ **$440–500** ➹ F&C

A painted pottery figure of a courtier, traces of pigment to gown, the head later, Tang Dynasty, 618–907, 41¾in (106cm) high.
£1,200–1,400
€/ **$1,900–2,200** ➹ S(O)

A glazed celadon figural group of Guanyin and an acolyte, with biscuit features, some damage, Ming Dynasty, 15thC, 10in (25.5cm) high.
£650–700
€/ **$1,000–1,100** ⊞ GLD

A Chinese export *blanc de Chine* figure, Qianlong period, 1736–95, 9½in (24cm) high.
£1,400–1,600
€/ **$2,200–2,500** ⊞ McP

A *famille rose* figure of an Immortal, restored, Qianlong period, 1736–95, 9¼in (23.5cm) high.
£320–350
€/ **$475–550** ⊞ G&G

A celadon figure, Qianlong period, c1750, 5in (12.5cm) high.
£230–260
€/ **$360–400** ⊞ McP

A *famille rose* figure of a jovial boy, kneeling, holding a pomegranate and a *ruyi* fungus, Jiaqing period, 1796–1820, 6¼in (16cm) high.
£320–350
€/ **$480–550** ➹ S(O)

◄ **A *blanc de Chine* figure of Wenzhu,** seated on a lion, holding the scroll of knowledge (*putsaka*) in his hand, minor chips, early 18thC, 7½in (19cm) wide.
£950–1,100
€/ **$1,500–1,700** ➹ TEN
Wenzhu is the Bodhisattva of Wisdom.

A pair of figures of the He-He Erxien, holding *ruyi* sceptres and other Buddhist objects, 18thC, 8in (20.5cm) high.
£250–300
€/ **$400–475** ➹ CGC
The He-He Erxien are the twin genii of mirth and harmony, and the patron deities of merchants, potters and lime burners.

Flatware

A celadon moulded dish, Northern Song Dynasty, 960–1127, 6in (15cm) diam.
£1,600–1,800
€/ **$2,500–2,800 ⊞ GLD**

A Junyao plate, with a flattened rim and covered with a thick glaze, 12th–13thC, 8¼in (21cm) diam.
£1,300–1,500
€/ **$2,000–2,400 ⋟ S(O)**

An offering dish, carved with a roundel of plum blossom encircled by the Eight Buddhist Emblems, early Ming Dynasty, 8¾in (22cm) diam.
£450–550
€/ **$700–870 ⋟ S(O)**
The Eight Buddhist Emblems or happy omens are the Chakra (wheel), the Conch Shell, the Umbrella, the Canopy, the Lotus, the Vase, the Pair of Fish and the Endless Knot.

Kraak porselein

In 1603 the Dutch captured the Portugese carrack *Santa Carterina*. Its cargo of fine porcelain, known as *kraak porselein*, was auctioned in Amsterdam amid great excitement. With the subsequent founding of the Dutch East India Company, there was a huge expansion in the export trade.

A dish, damaged, 16thC, 14in (35.5cm) diam.
£600–670
€/ **$950–1,000 ⊞ NAW**

A dish, Jiajing period, 1522–66, 14in (35.5cm) diam.
£1,100–1,300
€/ **$1,700–2,000 ⊞ GLD**

◄ **A kraak porselein** plate, Wanli period, c1600, 8in (20.5cm).
£600–700
€/ **$950–1,100 ⊞ McP**

► **A kraak porselein dish,** damaged, Wanli period, c1600, 14in (35.5cm) diam.
£675–750
€/ **$1,000–1,200 ⊞ McP**

A kraak porselein dish, the centre decorated with a hanging flower basket with trailing roots, rivetted, 1610–25, 19in (48.5cm) diam.
€2,200–2,500
€/ **$3,500–4,000 ⊞ AUA**

A kraak porselein saucer, c1620, 4in (10cm) diam.
£225–250
€/ **$350–400 ⊞ CHT**

CHINESE CERAMICS

A 'Master of the Rocks' dish, painted with a man on land and two fishermen, on an inverted foot, Shunzhi period, 1644–61, 33½in (85cm) diam.
£2,500–3,000
€/ **$4,000–4,700** ⚒ S(O)
'Master of the Rocks' is a style of blue and white painting (usually showing rocks and mountains) of the Shunzi/early Kangxi period. The quality of pieces decorated in this style is always excellent.

A famille verte octagonal saucer, the border painted with flowering plants, Kangxi period, 1662–1722, 5in (12.5cm) diam.
£250–300
€/ **$400–475** ⚒ L

A pair of Chinese Imari armorial plates, 1710–20, 8½in (21.5cm) diam.
£700–800
€/ **$1,100–1,300** ⊞ McP

A famille rose plate, decorated with a boating scene, Qianlong period, 1736–95, 14¾in (37.5cm) wide.
£800–880
€/ **$1,200–1,400** ⊞ G&G

A famille verte dish, painted with figures on a café-au-lait ground, Kangxi period, 1662–1722, 11in (28cm) diam.
£280–320
€/ **$440–500** ⊞ McP

A famille verte plate, painted with flowers on a café-au-lait ground, Kangxi period, c1700, 8in (20.5cm) diam.
£100–125
€/ **$160–200** ⊞ DAN

A plate, with six-character Chengua mark, Kangxi period, c1720, 9in (23cm) diam.
£630–700
€/ **$1,000–1,100** ⊞ CHT

A pair of Chinese export famille rose plates, enamelled with European figures in a rural landscape within gilt floral borders, the rims decorated with fruit and flower sprays, Qianlong period, 1736–95, 9in (23cm) diam.
£1,600–2,000
€/ **$2,500–3,200** ⚒ B

A famille verte dish, painted with flowers, Kangxi period, 1662–1722, 11in (28cm) diam.
£1,300–1,500
€/ **$2,000–2,400** ⊞ GLD

A Chinese Imari plate, Kangxi period, c1710, 9in (23cm) diam.
£450–500
€/ **$700–800** ⊞ CHT

A soup plate, decorated with a coat-of-arms within a spearhead border, Qianlong period, c1740, 9in (23cm) diam.
£750–875
€/ **$1,200–1,400** ⚒ G(L)

A Chinese export octagonal plate, painted with two Continental armorials in a vase-shaped cartouche, within radiating lotus petals and a scale band, c1745, 8¼in (21cm) diam.
£1,300–1,500
€/ **$2,000–2,400** ⚒ LFA
This is a very rare item.

A dish, painted with a leaping
dragon among scrolling foliage,
encircled by two further dragons,
Qianlong period, 1736–95,
5¼in (13.5cm) diam.
£3,800–4,500
€/ **$6,000–7,100** ➢ S(HK)

A glazed plate, with six-character
mark, Qianlong period, 1736–95,
9½in (24cm) diam.
£380–450
€/ **$600–700** ➢ S(O)

A *famille rose* **saucer dish,** painted
with long-tailed birds and peonies
issuing from rockwork, Qianlong
period, 1736–95, 8¾in (22cm) diam.
£170–200
€/ **$270–320** ➢ G(L)

A Chinese export plate, the centre
decorated with figures in a garden,
c1770, 8in (20.5cm) diam.
£260–300
€/ **$400–475** ⊞ DAN

The Edward T. Chow & T. Y Chao Collections

The past 25 years have seen some spectacular sales of Chinese
ceramics and works of art. Two of the most important were the
Edward T. Chow collection, sold in three sales over 1980–81 and
the T. Y. Chao collection, sold over 1986–87. Any piece from these
collections will be greatly enhanced by its provenance.

Edward Chow (b1910) worked in a gallery in Shanghai and
already had a small collection of Chinese ceramics by the age of 20.
He met, and was influenced by, many famous western collectors,
including Sir Percival David. After a brief spell in New York during
WWII, Chow settled in 1949 in Hong Kong, where most of his
collection was formed. He moved to Switzerland in 1966 and died
in 1980. Chow kept an open mind in his collecting and, following
the tenets of rarity, quality and perfection, would get just as
excited by a Daoguong period (1821–50) tea bowl as he would a
Xuande period (1426–35) stem cup.

T. Y. Chao was also a Hong Kong-based businessman with a good
eye, keen interest and the financial means to form a major collection.
His first interest was Qing Dynasty (1644–1911) Imperial porcelain,
but his interests broadened to include Chinese ceramics and fine
jades of all periods. His Ming Dynasty (1368–1644) Imperial Wares
contained an extraordinary group of early 15th-century blue and
white, which had been enhanced by purchases from the Edward
T. Chow sale.

It will be many years before a private collector can build up a
comparable collection, as so many items of this quality have now
been acquired by museums and permanent collections. **Peter Wain**

A pair of fluted saucer dishes,
painted with flowering plants issuing
from rockwork, Qianlong period,
1736–95, 10in (25.5cm) diam.
£275–325
€/ **$430–500** ➢ L

A Chinese export *famille rose*
dinner plate, of European silver
shape, minor damage, Qianlong
period, c1770, 9¼in (23.5cm) diam.
£850–1,000
€/ **$1,300–1,600** ➢ BUK

A meat plate, painted with a river
landscape within Fitzhugh-style
diaper pattern borders, minor
chips, Qianlong period, 1736–95,
18½in (47cm) wide.
£170–200
€/ **$270–320** ➢ BR
**The Fitzhugh pattern is
characterized by a border of four
split pomegranates and butterflies
and was made for the American
market, being named after the
person who first ordered it.**

A *famille rose* **meat dish,** painted
in enamels with leaves and flowers,
heightened with gilt, 18thC,
13in (33cm) wide.
£1,200–1,500
€/ **$1,900–2,400** ➢ TMA

◄ **A pair of dishes,** Jiaqing period,
1796–1820, 12in (30.5cm) wide.
£340–380
€/ **$550–600** ⊞ McP

CHINESE CERAMICS

Garden Seats

▶ **A reticulated *famille verte* garden seat,** painted with formal lotus scrolls and with moulded lion masks, between bands of *ruyi*-shaped collars decorated with lions, Kangxi period, 1662–1722, 19¾in (50cm) high.
£8,500–10,000
€/ **$14,000–16,000** ⚥ S(HK)
Surviving Kangxi garden seats are very rare – particularly decorated in 'Chinese taste' that is, not for export. This piece would appeal greatly to the Chinese mainland market.

A celadon garden seat, carved with roundels of lotus reserved on a diaper ground, cracked, Ming Dynasty, 16thC, 15¾in (40cm) high.
£2,500–3,000
€/ **$4,000–4,700** ⚥ S(Am)

▶ **A Chinese export celadon hexagonal garden seat,** with raised enamel decoration, 19thC, 18½in (47cm) high.
£200–250
€/ **$320–400** ⚥ L

A pair of garden seats, painted with birds among flowers and rockwork within borders of reticulated medallions, scholar's objects and studs, Qing Dynasty, c1900, 18in (45.5cm) high.
£1,800–2,200
€/ **$2,800–3,500** ⚥ B

Jars

A glazed jar, with applied decoration, Tang Dynasty, 618–907, 4in (10cm) high.
£1,800–2,000
€/ **$2,800–3,200** ⊞ GLD

A glazed miniature jar, the two-tone clay with an even marbled effect, Tang Dynasty, 618–907, 3½in (9cm) high.
£250–300
€/ **$400–475** ⚥ S(O)

A Junyao jar, Jin Dynasty, 1115–1234, 5¼in (13.5cm) high.
£450–500
€/ **$700–800** ⚥ S(O)

A jar, painted with four dragons chasing flaming pearls below a *ruyi*-lappet collar, minor frits, Wanli period, 1573–1619, 5¼in (13.5cm) high.
£1,600–2,000
€/ **$2,500–3,200** ⚥ B

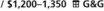

A *wucai* jar, decorated with Buddhist boys, minor damage and restoration, Chongzhen period, 1628–44, 9in (23cm) high.
£750–850
€/ **$1,200–1,350** ⊞ G&G

A baluster jar and cover, painted with three rows of landscape and garden scene panels beneath a foliate border, damaged, Kangxi period, 1662–1722, 22½in (57cm) high.
£1,000–1,200
€/ **$1,600–1,900** ⚥ Bri

pair of *wucai* jars, c1670, 6½in (16.5cm) high.
50–950
$1,350–1,500 ⊞ CHT

A lidded jar, from the *Vung Tau* cargo,
700, 6in (15cm) high.
00–450
$630–700 ⊞ McP

A jar, the panels decorated with a
musician, scholar and a lady beneath
a diaper border, leaf mark, 17thC,
7in (18cm) high.
£350–400
€/ $550–630 ⋏ DN

◄ **A streaky-glazed jar,**
of Han Dynasty bronze
form, with applied loop
handles, 19thC,
13in (33cm) high.
£350–400
€/ $550–630 ⋏ S(O)

jar, the central fluted
nd decorated with four
nels of scholars and a
arrior, with a hardwood
ver, Kangxi period,
722, 9¼in (23.5cm) high.
00–575
$800–900 ⋏ G(L)

A jar, Qianlong/Jiaqing
period, 1780–1820,
10in (20.5cm) high.
£420–460
€/ $670–725 ⊞ McP

A jar, decorated with
figures, rocks and plantains,
19thC, 15½in (39.5cm) high.
£900–1,100
€/ $1,400–1,700 ⋏ DN

◄ **A *wucai* jar and
cover,** painted with
flying horses, 19thC,
11¾in (30cm) high.
£700–800
€/ $1,100–1,300 ⋏ S(O)

**A *famille rose* jar and
ver,** painted with a
urtyard scene between
rders of gilt raised
otrusions, applied with
ock mask ring handles,
e cover with peach
ial, Canton, 19thC,
in (21cm) high.
,600–1,800
$2,500–2,800 ⋏ S(Am)

ugs

jug and cover, of European
ape, Qianlong period, c1750,
n (18cm) high.
550–620
/ $850–1,000 ⊞ McP

A sparrow beak jug, 1775–1825,
4in (10cm) high.
£170–200
€/ $270–320 ⋏ SWO

A Chinese Imari jug and cover, the
fluted body decorated with symmetrical
foliate designs, cover and handle
with original apertures for metal
mounts, 18thC, 8¾in (22cm) high.
£300–350
€/ $475–550 ⋏ S(O)

CHINESE CERAMICS

Mugs & Tankards

◄ **A tankard,** painted with lotus, peony, chrysanthemum and prunus sprays, with curved strap handle, restored, Kangxi period, 1662–1722, 4in (10cm) high.
£650–750
€/ **$1,000–1,200** ↗ B

A famille rose mug, c1760, 5in (12.5cm) high.
£400–450
€/ **$630–700** ⊞ DAN

A gilt-decorated tankard, painted with classic lotus below a pair of lions and a brocade ball, Kangxi period, 1662–1722, 4½in (11.5cm) high.
£650–750
€/ **$1,000–1,200** ↗ S(O)

A Chinese export porcelain mug, with Mandarin-style panel, c1770, 5in (12.5cm) high.
£200–235
€/ **$320–370** ⊞ DAN

A Compagnie des Indes tankard, painted in *famille rose* enamels with an urn and scattered sprigs, with entwined strap handle, Qianlong period, 1736–95, 6in (15cm) high.
£300–350
€/ **$475–550** ↗ G(B)

Items in the Chinese Ceramics section have been arranged in date order within each sub-section.

A Chinese Imari porcelain tankard, painted with flowers and vases of peacock feathers, 19thC, 6in (15cm) high.
£120–140
€/ **$190–220** ↗ AH

Tea, Chocolate & Coffee Pots

An enamelled 'Cadogan' teapot, painted with a dignitary attended by two boys, the reverse with another official and two retainers, minor damage, c1640, 5½in (14cm) high.
£6,000–7,000
€/ **$9,500–11,000** ↗ TEN
This piece is rare because of its early date.

Cadogan teapots

Earl Cadogan was the first Englishman to own a curiosity piece from China known as a 'wine pourer'. During the voyage from the east in the 18th century, these items were packed with tea to avoid damage, and therefore the British assumed these pots were used for brewing tea. Today, a Cadogan teapot refers to a type of lidless pot into which water is poured through a hole in the bottom and the pot is then quickly turned the right way up. An interior funnel prevents the water from leaking out through the hole.

A reticulated teapot and cover, painted with flowers, minor frits, Kangxi period, 1662–1722, 7in (18cm) wide.
£2,000–2,400
€/ **$3,200–3,800** ↗ G(L)

A Chinese Imari teapot, with white metal attachments, c1720, 6in (12.5cm) high.
£550–600
€/ **$870–950** ⊞ CHT

◄ **A 'Cadogan' teapot,** Qianlong period, 1736–95, 5in (12.5cm) high.
£200–220
€/ **$320–350** ⊞ McP

A famille verte teapot and cover, painted with a garden scene of birds and trees, Kangxi period, 1662–1722, 4in (10cm) high.
£600–700
€/ **$950–1,100** ↗ S(O)

CHINESE CERAMICS

◄ **A Chinese Imari chocolate pot,** painted with flowers on a terrace, crack, cover restored, early 18thC, 6¾in (17cm) high.
£200–250
€/ **$315–400** ⚒ G(L)

▶ **A Chinese export chocolate pot and cover,** reserved with four panels of peonies on a daisy meander ground, c1735, 7¼in (18.5cm) high.
£1,500–1,800
€/ **$2,400–2,800** ⚒ S(NY)

Chocolate pots can be easily identified as the handle is at right angles to the spout.

A Compagnie des Indes *famille rose* **coffee pot,** decorated with figures in a landscape, chipped, Qianlong period, 1736–95, 10¼in (26cm) high.
£400–500
€/ **$630–790** ⚒ BERN

teapot and cover, decorated in namels with tobacco leaves, 18thC, 4in (18.5cm) diam.
1,400–1,700
/ $2,200–2,700 ⚒ S(O)

A Yixing teapot and cover, with gilt-metal mounts, 18thC, 4½in (11.5cm) high.
£450–550
€/ **$700–870** ⚒ G(L)

A double teapot and covers, decorated with squirrels on grape vines, the reverse with a bird on willow trees, early 19thC, 5in (12.5cm) high.
£600–700
€/ **$950–1,100** ⚒ S(O)

Tureens

pomegranate tureen, cover and tand, painted with a continuous ndscape scene, with moulded stalk nd twig handles, the cover moulded high relief with three pomegranates, ith lobed stand, Qianlong period, 736–95, stand 9½in (24cm) diam.
3,750–4,500
/ $6,000–7,000 ⚒ B

A Chinese export tureen, decorated in *famille rose* colours with European flowers, on shell feet, slight chips to glaze, wear to enamel, Qianlong period, 1736–95, 12½in (32cm) wide.
£1,400–1,600
€/ **$2,200–2,500** ⚒ BUK

A Meissen-style tureen and cover, decorated in *famille rose* colours with floral sprays, the cover with a crown finial and the base with Prince of Wales feather handles terminating in European masks, damaged and restored, Qianlong period, 1736–95, 15in (38cm) wide.
£4,300–4,800
€/ **$6,700–7,500** ⊞ G&G

tureen and cover, decorated in amille rose colours, enamelled with nusicians and figures at leisure, racked and rivetted, Qianlong eriod, 1736–95, 14in (35.5cm) wide.
400–500
/ $630–800 ⚒ B(Kn)

A soup tureen and cover, decorated in *famille rose* colours with a pavilioned landscape, the pierced cover with a pineapple finial, with bracket handles, on a splayed foot, 18thC, 11½in (29cm) high.
£1,400–1,600
€/ **$2,200–2,500** ⚒ S(O)

A Chinese export porcelain tureen and cover, decorated with flowers, the cover with a rose knop, damaged and repaired, Qianlong period, 1736–95, 12½in (32cm) wide.
£1,000–1,200
€/ **$1,600–1,900** ⚒ BUK

Vases

A cizhou slip-painted vase, with a band of stylized foliage, a further band with lotus, between freely-drawn characters, Song/Yuan Dynasty, 13thC, 16¼in (41.5cm) high.
£1,000–1,200
€ / **$1,600–1,900** ⚹ G(L)

A meiping, painted with classical lotus on undulating leafy stems, between lappets and cloud-head borders, Ming Dynasty, 16thC, 9in (23cm) high.
£650–800
€ / **$1,000–1,300** ⚹ S(O)

A stoneware vase, Ming Dynasty, 15th–16thC, 25in (63.5cm) high.
£1,600–1,800
€ / **$2,500–2,800** ⊞ GLD

A Chinese Imari baluster vase and cover, painted with long-tailed birds on rockwork issuing peony, some cracks, finial incomplete, 17thC, 26in (66cm) high.
£1,400–1,600
€ / **$2,200–2,500** ⚹ G(L)

A vase, painted on one side of the neck with an armoured figure on horseback, a lady and a small child, a five-column poem inscribed below, rim crack, c1640, 18in (45.5cm) high.
£3,500–4,200
€ / **$5,500–6,600** ⚹ B

A vase, painted with landscapes and fishermen, Transitional period, c1640, 10in (25.5cm) high.
£2,000–2,200
€ / **$3,200–3,500** ⊞ GLD

A yen yen vase, painted and lightly moulded with prunus branches reserved around the flowerheads with a blue wash, 1662–1722, 18½in (47cm) high.
£3,500–4,000
€ / **$5,500–6,300** ⚹ G(L)
This vase is decorated with a very beautiful and rare design. Such a piece could sell for as much as £5,000–6,000, (€ / $7,900–9,500).

A gilded vase, restoration to rim, Kangxi period, early 18thC, 17in (43cm) high.
£2,700–3,000
€ / **$4,300–4,700** ⊞ GLD

A yen yen vase, Kangxi period, c1720, 9in (23cm) high.
£850–950
€ / **$1,300–1,500** ⊞ CHT

A Chinese export bottle vase, with applied foliate and pierced handles, decorated with a band of birds on flowering branches and flower sprays, Kangxi period, 1662–1722, 9¾in (25cm) high.
£2,200–2,700
€ / **$3,500–4,300** ⚹ DN

A famille verte vase, Kangxi period, 1662–1722, 9½in (24cm) high.
£425–475
€ / **$670–750** ⊞ McP

◄ **A glazed bottle vase,** with a tall neck, 18thC, 7¼in (18.5cm) high.
£500–550
€ / **$800–870** ⚹ S(O)

**flambé-glazed bottle
ase,** with moulded bands
ound the waist and
oulder, surmounted by a
bed neck with cupped
outh and lipped rim, on
spreading foot, Qianlong
eriod, 1736–95,
½in (37cm) high.
3,200–3,700
/ $5,000–6,000 ⚲ B

A ru-style baluster vase,
with canted corners, broad
shoulder and waisted neck,
restored chip, Qianlong
period, 1736–95,
13¼in (33.5cm) high.
£2,000–2,500
€/ **$3,200–4,000** ⚲ B
Ru is a thick, smooth,
greenish-blue glaze
first used in the Song
Dynasty (960–1279) on
Imperial wares from
Henan Province.

Chinese ceramics 1976–2002

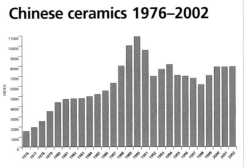

This graph shows how the value of Chinese
ceramics as a whole has fluctuated over the
past 25 years. Specific collecting areas such as
tomb figures or Imperial porcelain of the Qing
Dynasty will deviate from this graph. ©AMR

A square-section vase,
each face decorated with
watery landscapes, 1800–50,
14¼in (36cm) high.
£1,400–1,600
€/ **$2,200–2,500** ⚲ WW

baluster vase,
ecorated with landscape
nd pagoda scenes, the
verse with two boats,
8thC, 16in (40.5cm) high.
250–300
/ $400–475 ⚲ DMC

**A flambé-glazed bottle
vase,** of garlic-clove form
surmounted by a cylindrical
neck, with flambé glaze,
18thC, 13¾in (35cm) high.
£1,700–1,900
€/ **$2,700–3,000** ⚲ S(O)

A baluster vase, with a
slender neck, the incised
and enamelled decoration
depicting four figures
with vases of flowers
and butterflies, handles
damaged, Canton, 18thC,
9¼in (23.5cm) high.
£80–100
€/ **$125–160** ⚲ TMA

A flambé vase, decorated
in *famille rose* colours,
with flowers issuing
from rockwork, 19thC,
16¼in (41.5cm) high.
£650–750
€/ **$1,000–1,200** ⚲ S(O)

**pair of Transitional-style
ases,** each decorated with
fant Buddhas running
rough lotus scrolls,
ith hardwood covers
nd stands, 19thC,
0½in (26.5cm) high.
1,000–1,200
/ $1,600–1,900 ⚲ RTo

**A pair of porcelain bottle
vases,** each underglaze-
painted with dragons among
clouds and precious objects,
19thC, 25½in (65cm) high.
£800–1,000
€/ **$1,300–1,600** ⚲ Bri

**A pair of celadon-
glazed vases,** of fluted
chrysanthemum shape with
bulbous necks, applied
with stylized handles,
19thC, 8in (20.5cm) high.
£1,400–1,600
€/ **$2,200–2,500** ⚲ S(Am)

▶ **A pair of panelled vases,** decorated in enamel with
Oriental figures on a bridge and in garden landscapes,
19thC, 22in (56cm) high.
£550–650
€/ **$870–1,000** ⚲ JAd

◀ **A baluster vase and cover,** painted with scrolling floral designs, between formal borders, the cover with a dog of *Fo* finial, 19thC, 19¼in (49cm) high.
£100–125
€ / **$160–200** ✗ PFK

A *hu*-shaped vase, decorated in *famille rose* colours, painted with figures in various pursuits, with side handles, 19thC, 10¾in (27.5cm) high.
£475–575
€ / **$750–900** ✗ WW
A *hu* is a bronze vessel for ritual use.

A pair of baluster vases, with flared rims and gilt handles, painted with a travelling sage, on a ground of birds and butterflies, among floral sprays, Canton, 19thC, 8¾in (22cm) high.
£320–375
€ / **$500–600** ✗ Mit

◀ **A vase,** painted in *famille rose* colours with travellers and fishermen in a lakeside setting, the neck inscribed with a poem, the base with a seal mark, early 20thC, 8in (20.5cm) high.
£2,200–2,700
€ / **$3,500–4,300** ✗ S(HK)

A pair of vases, relief-decorated with lizards and dogs of *Fo*, buds and garden landscapes, Canton, 1875–1925, 22in (56cm) high.
£275–320
€ / **$430–500** ✗ DD

◀ **An earthenware baluster vase,** with low-relief geometric and floral decoration in enamels, impressed character mark, early 20thC, 17¼in (44cm) high.
£130–150
€ / **$200–240** ✗ AMB

Miscellaneous

A Chinese Imari fishbowl or jardinière, the interior decorated with fish, the exterior with the Three Friends of Winter, some damage, 17th–18thC, 15¼in (38.5cm) diam.
£1,000–1,200
€ / **$1,600–1,900** ✗ B(Kn)
In Chinese culture, the Three Friends of Winter are prunus (wild plum), pine and bamboo, all emblems of longevity. They are also symbolic of the qualities of a gentleman – Prunus: good looks and independence; Pine: constancy of friendship in a time of adversity; Bamboo: durability, integrity and loyalty. They are also symbolic of the three religions of China: Daoism, Buddhism and Confucianism.

A Chinese export *famille rose* tea canister and cover, c1760, 5½in (14cm) high.
£300–340
€ / **$475–500** ⊞ DAN

▶ **A *blanc-de-Chine* wine pot and cover,** applied with two writhing *chilong*, one forming the handle, the other forming the spout, the cover surmounted by a pierced coiled *chilong*, chips and star crack to base, 17thC, 5¼in (13.5cm) high.
£1,800–2,200
€ / **$2,800–3,500** ✗ B

A Kangxi wine kettle, with metal mounts to the handle, c1710, 9in (23cm) high.
£900–1,000
€ / **$1,400–1,600** ⊞ CHT

apanese Ceramics

Japanese chronology chart

Jomon (Neolithic) period	c10,000–100 BC	Muromachi (Ashikaga) period	1333–1568
Yayoi period	c200 BC–AD 200	Momoyama period	1568–1600
Tumulus (Kofun) period	200–552	Edo (Tokugawa) period	1600–1868
Asuka period	552–710	*Genroku period*	*1688–1703*
Nara period	710–794	Meiji period	1868–1911
Heian period	794–1185	Taisho period	1912–1926
Kamakura period	1185–1333	Showa period	1926–1989

Bowls

An Arita bowl, c1700–30,
½in (14cm) diam.
420–460
/ **$650–720** ⊞ McP

A Kakiemon-style bowl, with
everted iron-oxide rim, decorated
with additional enamels and gilt with
birds and flowers, marked *'kin'*,
18thC, 9½in (24cm) diam.
£775–900
€ / **$1,200–1,400** ⚒ S(O)

An Imari barber's bowl, decorated
in underglaze blue, iron-red and gold,
late 18thC, 10¾in (27.5cm) diam.
£525–625
€ / **$830–1,000** ⚒ B(WM)

A Satsuma bowl, the interior
depicting the story of The Moon
and The Moor, Meiji period, c1890,
in (12.5cm) diam.
1,400–1,500
/ **$2,200–2,400** ⊞ AUA
he Moon and The Moor relates
he story of two brothers,
asuma, the flute player and
Kidomaru, the outlaw.

A bowl, decorated in Imari palette,
three-character mark on the base,
Arita, c1900, 9½in (24cm) diam.
£950–1,100
€ / **$1,500–1,700** ⚒ BUK
**This well-known group of bowls
decorated with ships was produced
in Arita for export, c1900–10.**

Cups

◄ **An Imari tea bowl and
saucer,** damaged, c1730,
saucer 5in (12.5cm) diam.
£60–70
€ / **$95–110** ⊞ McP

> **For further
> information on**
> Eggshell porcelain
> see page 330

A cased set
of six eggshell
porcelain coffee
ans and saucers,
arly 20thC, case
5in (38cm) wide.
180–220
€ / **$280–350**
⚒ BR

Miller's Compares

**I. A pair of Kakiemon
cups,** painted with flowers
in iron-red and enamels,
18thC, 2½in (6.5cm) diam.
£1700–2,000
€ / **$2,700–3,200** ⚒ S(O)

II. A Kakiemon tea bowl,
painted in enamels with
flying birds and flowers
emerging behind rocks,
18thC, 4in (10cm) diam.
£500–600
€ / **$800–950** ⚒ S(O)

Naturally, a pair is likely to be worth more than
a single item, but Item I had the advantage
over Item II by also being of a more pleasing
shape. The decoration of Item I is also classic
Kakiemon, a plus-point with collectors. Further-
more, a footnote included with Item I referred to
a similar piece and therefore made it attributable
to one that was already well-documented.

Dishes

A pair of Kakiemon-style dishes,
1662–1722, 6in (15cm) square.
£2,200–2,500
€/ **$3,500–4,000** ⊞ McP

▶ **An Imari dish,** late 19thC,
18½in (47cm) wide.
£180–220
€/ **$280–350** ⚒ CHTR

An Imari dish, 19thC, 6in (15cm) wide.
£100–120
€/ **$160–190** ⊞ McP

An Arita map dish, decorated in
relief with a map of Japan, the sea
in a stylized fish-scale pattern, dated
1830, 12½in (32cm) wide.
£900–1,000
€/ **$1,400–1,600** ⚒ S(O)
**These dishes are decorated with
a popular pattern on imported
Japanese porcelain 1830–40. They
were a production of Arita ware
and were produced mainly by the
Kama-no-tani kiln.**

Figures

**A pair of Imari figures
of actors,** wearing robes
decorated with morning glory,
c1700, 17¾in (45cm) high.
£4,500–5,000
€/ **$7,000–7,900** ⚒ S(O)
**These export figures
are very popular with
decorators. Often damaged,
this pair appears to be
perfect and of a good size.**

◀ **An Imari
figure of a** *bijin*,
her kimono
painted with
flower branches
and meander
diaper patterns,
restoration to
foot, 19thC, 18¾in
(47.5cm) high.
£1,200–1,400
€/ **$1,900–2,200**
⚒ S(Am)

**A Satsuma group of a young
woman and her child,** with
enamel decoration, early 20thC,
5½in (14cm) high.
£475–575
€/ **$750–900** ⚒ RTo

Flatware

An Imari dish, the centre painted
with a Mandarin duck, 17th/18thC,
8½in (21.5cm) diam.
£200–240
€/ **£300–380** ⚒ G(L)

An Arita Ko-Imari-style dish, early
18thC, 5in (12.5cm) diam.
£380–420
€/ **$600–670** ⊞ McP

A map dish, moulded in relief with the
map of Japan, each of the provinces
named, with a wind dial and the signs
of the Zodiac, spurious six-character
mark, 1830–44, 18in (45.5cm) diam.
£2,500–3,000
€/ **$4,000–4,700** ⚒ S(Am)
**This map dish is rare because of
the addition of the Zodiac signs.**

charger, the underglaze blue central
on framed with an Imari panel,
ecorated with pheasants and prunus
ossoms, 19thC, 16¼in (41.5cm) diam.
160–200
/ $250–300 ⚲ BR

An Imari charger, late 19thC,
14¾in (37.5cm) diam.
£130–160
€/ $200–250 ⚲ PFK

A Fukugawa porcelain charger,
decorated in underglaze blue,
coloured enamels and gilding, with
bamboo, irises and flowering shrubs,
the reverse with sprays of flowers,
signed, Meiji period, 1868–1911,
18¾in (47.5cm) diam.
£320–375
€/ $500–600 ⚲ F&C
Fukugawa was a family of potters
in Arita with a distinctive style
of work.

◀ **A pair of chargers,** decorated with
carp, early 20thC, 18in (45.5cm) diam.
£800–900
€/ $1,300–1,400 ⚲ S(O)
Although quite late, these
chargers are very attractive and
therefore desirable to decorators
as well as collectors, which results
in this high price.

Jars

**A pair of Imari jars and
overs,** one cover restored,
1690, 15¼in (38.5cm) high.
950–1,200
/ $1,500–1,800 ⚲ BERN

An Imari jar and cover,
painted and gilt with chrysanthemum, the shoulders with
a band of floral branches,
with a bud finial, 18thC,
21in (53cm) high.
£3,500–4,000
€/ $5,300–6,300 ⚲ S(Am)

**A pair of Imari jars and
covers,** painted and gilt
with peonies and prunus,
with inner lids, 19thC,
7¾in (19.5cm) high.
£220–250
€/ $350–400 ⚲ PFK

**A Satsuma earthenware
jar,** decorated with a
procession of figures
including *samurai* and
geisha among musicians and
dancers, between bands of
dragons and formal designs
incorporating the Satsuma
mon, signed *Hosen zo*,
Meiji period, 1868–1911,
11½in (29cm) high.
£1,300–1,500
€/ $2,000–2,400 ⚲ S(O)

Koros

A koro and cover, the
knop modelled as a *shishi*,
signed 'Kinkozan', Meiji
eriod, 1868–1911,
¼in (11cm) high.
1,000–1,200
/ $1,600–1,900 ⚲ S(O)

A koro and metal cover,
painted with chrysanthemums,
signed 'Hododa', Meiji
period, 1868–1911,
4¼in (11cm) high.
£1,700–2,000
€/ $2,700–3,200 ⚲ S(O)

An Imari koro and cover,
the segmented cover with
piercing and a Dog of Fo
knop, handles glued,
19thC, 11¾in (30cm) high.
£140–160
€/ $220–250 ⚲ B(W)

**A Satsuma earthenware
koro and cover,** hand-
painted and gilded, on three
mask-form feet, signed,
c1900, 6¾in (17cm) high.
£375–450
€/ $600–700 ⚲ AMB

Tea & Coffee Services

A tea service, comprising 22 pieces, detailed in enamels and gilt with six scenes of birds in seasonal settings, signed 'Senzan', Meiji period, 1868–1911, teapot 4in (10cm) high.
£600–720
€/ $950–1,100 ⟋ S(O)

▶ **An eggshell porcelain tea service,** comprising 21 pieces, painted with battle scenes, early 20thC, tray 18¼in (46.5cm) square.
£300–350
€/ $475–550 ⟋ PFK

A cased Satsuma tea service, comprising 18 pieces, painted with Thousand Lohan pattern, with dragon handles and cover knops, signed 'Ariyama', Satsuma *mon* marks, early 20thC.
£320–375
€/ $500–600 ⟋ CGC

Eggshell porcelain

Japanese porcelain tea services, often eggshell thin, were produced in their many thousands during the period 1900–1920. Always highly decorative and of good quality, they were the most popular souvenir purchase of merchant seamen visiting the Far East. Almost every family in Europe with sea-faring traditions owns the remnants of such a service. A complete service should contain a teapot, milk jug, sugar pot, six tea cups and saucers, six side plates and two bread/cake plates. The service was sold in a fitted box. A complete undamaged boxed set is worth about £300 (€/ $475), whereas an individual tea cup and saucer is worth about £10 (€/ $15) or £15 (€/ $24) if a geisha girl can be seen through the base of the cup.

Vases

◀ **An Arita vase,** c1690, 16in (40.5cm) high.
£600–680
€/ $950–1,100 ⊞ McP

An Imari wall vase, modelled as a double gourd with applied leaves and tendrils, painted in enamels and gilt with floral designs, early 18thC, 8¼in (21cm) high.
£1,800–2,000
€/ $2,800–3,200 ⟋ S(O)

A pair of Satsuma earthenware vases, enamelled and gilt with chrysanthemum sprays, figures within landscapes to either side, painted marks, Meiji period, 1868–1911, 4¾in (12cm) high.
£80–100
€/ $125–160 ⟋ WL

▶ **A Satsuma vase,** decorated with panels of landscapes, signed 'Kinkozan', Meiji period, 1868–1911, 5in (12.5cm) high.
£2,500–2,800
€/ $4,000–4,500 ⊞ MER

A Satsuma vase, by the Kinkozan Studio, signed 'Sozan', Meiji period, 1868–1911, 4in (10cm) high.
£3,700–4,200
€/ $6,000–6,600 ⊞ MER

An Arita bottle vase, decorated with flowerhead and bamboo leaves, early 18thC, 2½in (6.5cm) high.
£350–400
€/ $550–650 ⊞ AUA

A pair of Satsuma vases, decorated with Samurai warriors and ladies, maker's mark and Satsuma *mon*, late 19thC, 14½in (37cm) high.
£400–500
€/ $630–800 ⟋ SWO

A **Satsuma earthenware vase,** with a short waisted neck, decorated with circular emblems, late 19thC, 5in (12.5cm) high.
£140–160
€ / **$220–250** ⚒ **Bea(E)**

► A **Satsuma vase,** decorated with quails, signed, impressed mark for Taizan, Meiji period, c1890, 13in (33cm) high.
£2,000–2,200
€ / **$3,200–3,500** ⊞ **AUA**

A **Kutani vase,** decorated with panels of figures and flowers, with a spreading neck and *shishi* handles, late 19thC, 10¼in (26cm) high.
£140–160
€ / **$220–250** ⚒ **WW**

◄ A **pair of Satsuma earthenware vases,** decorated with scholars, early 20thC, 10in (25.5cm) high.
£130–150
€ / **$200–240** ⚒ **SWO**

An **Imari porcelain vase,** with a flared rim, decorated with exotic birds and foliage, late 19thC, 25½in (65cm) high.
£700–850
€ / **$1,100–1,300** ⚒ **DMC**

◄ A **Satsuma vase,** decorated with three panels depicting blossoming branches, on a ground of hexagonal geometric motifs, signed 'Kinkozan', c1912, 23¼in (59cm) high.
£4,000–4,800
€ / **$6,300–7,500** ⚒ **B**

Miscellaneous

A **Satsuma earthenware belt buckle,** c1900, 1¾in (4.5cm) diam.
£80–100
€ / **$120–160** ⚒ **DuM**

A **Satsuma jardinière,** decorated with butterflies among flowers, painted signature, 1875–1925, 9¾in (25cm) high.
£320–375
€ / **$500–600** ⚒ **SWO**

A **Satsuma model of a cottage,** with hens on the roof, c1900, 7in (18cm) wide.
£1,500–1,700
€ / **$2,400–2,700** ⊞ **GLD**

An **Arita oil or vinegar jug,** from a condiment set, made for the Dutch market, 1710–20, 4in (10cm) high.
£470–520
€ / **$750–830** ⊞ **McP**

A **pair of European-decorated Arita wine flasks,** the sides printed with four chinoiserie scenes, damaged, late 17thC, 8½in (21.5cm) high.
£550–625
€ / **$870–1,000** ⚒ **TEN**

An **Arita teapot and cover,** painted with a European wooded landscape with buildings and passing travellers, damage, c1700, 4¼in (11cm) high.
£3,000–3,500
€ / **$4,700–5,500** ⚒ **B**
This is a rare piece and attractively decorated.

Glass

Exhibitions, books and the dispersal of notable collections can have marked effects on the appreciation and demand for particular categories of decorative antiques, and glass has proved no exception over the past 25 years. The publication of new literature generates an understanding, appreciation and interest among collectors that boosts demand and inflates prices. The popularity of 18th-century English drinking-glasses rose sharply after the sales of the Smith Collection in 1967–68, waned during the 1980s, rallied after the appearance in 1987 of L. M. Bickerton's *Eighteenth Century Drinking Glasses* and is currently at a new peak. Interest in British glass made between the wars, initially stimulated by an exhibition in 1987 at the Broadfield House Glass Museum, near Stourbridge, continues to grow.

The irony particular to glass is that most collectors remain narrowly focused. For example, 18th-century drinking glasses, lighting pieces, scent bottles and Victorian rock crystal and cameo are extremely sought after, and Irish pieces command prices disproportionate to English equivalents of superior quality.

However, a vast majority of old glass remains relatively cheap and available. The most obvious laggard is cut-glass, the British and Irish speciality, which remains widely neglected. Others include 18th-century jellies, syllabubs, sweetmeats and salts, most 19th-century glassware including drinking glasses, and almost all decanters. It is hard to predict whether interest in these will rise although, as wine consumption increases, decanters might be considered a hot tip for the future.

The greatest complicating factor when attempting to predict future values is the general health of the economy. For example, the financial problems that have afflicted Germany for the past decade have undermined demand for all central European antiques, including Bohemian glass.

In the coming decades 20th-century British cut glass might be expected to rise ahead of the market. Most examples bear a maker's mark, and the stark and stylized contemporary designs are well suited to modern homes. It is already fetching prices that would have been laughed at just a decade ago. **Andy McConnell**

Ale, Spirit & Wine Glasses

A *façon de Venise* winged goblet, the conical bowl over an openwork stem, the interlaced section inset with coloured spiralling threads applied with pinched ornament, the coiled tubing terminating in pincered serpent-style heads, above a baluster section and a conical foot, probably Lowlands, c1680, 7¼in (18.5cm) high.
£2,000–2,200
€/ $3,200–3,500 ⚒ S

▶ **A *latticinio* wine glass,** the bowl set on a multi-knopped stem with mereses above and below, the bowl and foot composed of *vetro a retorti* with repeated gauze cable, lace and spiral-thread ribs, the stem with *vetro a fili*, Venetian, 17thC, 5½in (14cm) high.
£1,700–2,000
€/ $2,700–3,200 ⚒ B

A baluster wine glass, the bell bowl with a solid teared base, on a plain teared stem with an annular shoulder knop and a basal knop, on a folded foot, c1725, 6¼in (16cm) high.
£1,200–1,300
€/ $1,900–2,000 ⊞ GS

A *façon de Venise* wine glass, the conical bowl over a hollow baluster stem, with a folded foot, traces of glass disease, Swedish, Kungsholm, 1675–1700, 6¾in (17cm) high.
£500–575
€/ $800–900 ⚒ BUK
Glass disease is also called 'crizzling'. It is caused by poorly prepared ingredients and results in an irreparable maze of silvery cracks in the glass

◀ **A goblet and cover,** the facet-cut bowl over a faceted knopped stem and inverted baluster section, all enclosing spiralling threads, on a conical foot with a rosette-cut base, the domed cover with a knopped finial inset with spiralling threads, Bohemian, 1720–30, 11½in (29cm) high.
£2,300–2,700
€/ $3,600–4,300 ⚒ S

The Parkington Collection

It was not long ago that interest in antique glassware was limited to up until the end of the Regency period. The sale in 1997 and 1998 at Christie's of Michael Parkington's vast glass collection helped shatter this date boundary. Parkington started by collecting 18th-century drinking glasses but gradually shifted his interest to Victorian and Edwardian cut, engraved, coloured and pressed glass. He also collected 20th-century pieces by Whitefriars, Keith Murray, Gray-Stan and Monart. The results of the sale provided benchmark prices for the public and trade, and spurred further interest in the subject.

Tales of Parkington's acquisitive fever remain legendary, with almost as many pieces jokingly said to have been housed under his floorboards as displayed on his shelves. Yet glass collecting inspired a passion within him that provided a sanctuary from his life as an international lawyer whose clients included the incarcerated Nelson Mandela. **Andy McConnell**

A Kit-Kat wine glass, with a drawn trumpet bowl, the stem with a beaded knop, on a domed foot, c1730, 7¼in (18.5cm) high.
£750–875
€/ $1,200–1,400 ⚡ LFA
These glasses are so-named because they are of a type seen in Sir Geoffrey Kneller's early 18th-century paintings of London's Kit-Kat Club.

A wine glass, with a drawn trumpet, on a plain stem, with a folded foot, c1730, 7in (18cm) high.
£160–180
€/ $250–290 ⊞ JHa

▶ **A cordial glass,** with a pan-top funnel bowl, over a multiple-series air-twist stem with a swollen central knop, c1750, 5½in (14cm) high.
£500–600
€/ $790–950 ⊞ BrW

A wine glass, the trumpet bowl with a swelling shoulder teared knop, on a plain drawn stem, with a folded conical foot, c1730, ¼in (16cm) high.
235–260
/ $370–400 ⊞ Som

A wine glass, the bell bowl with a knopped spiral air-twist stem, on a conical foot, c1750, 6½in (16.5cm) high.
£400–440
€/ $630–700 ⊞ PSA

A wine glass, the bell bowl engraved with a band of fruiting vine, on a multi-spiral air-twist stem with a vermicular collar, on a conical foot, c1750, ½in (16.5cm) high.
550–600
/ $870–950 ⊞ Som

A wine glass, with an engraved bowl above an opaque twist stem, c1750, 6in (15cm) high.
£200–225
€/ $320–350 ⊞ CHAC

GLASS

GLASS

A light baluster wine glass, the bell bowl on a swelling knop, over an inverted baluster and basal-knop stem, on a conical foot, c1750, 7¼in (18.5cm) high.
£950–1,100
€/ **$1,500–1,700** ⊞ GS

A light baluster wine glass, the trumpet bowl engraved with a band of fruiting vine, on a multi-knopped stem, on a conical foot, c1750, 7in (18cm) high.
£1,300–1,400
€/ **$2,100–2,500** ⊞ GS

A wine glass, the funnel bowl with basal fluting, on a double-knopped multi-spiral air-twist stem, c1750, 5½in (14cm) high.
£420–465
€/ **$670–730** ⊞ WMa

▶ **A Dutch-engraved light baluster goblet,** the round funnel bowl engraved with arms of four lions rampant, beneath a coronet and flanked by lion supporters, on a bobbin-knopped stem, the central knop filled with bead inclusions, on a conical foot, small chip, c1750, 7½in (19cm) high.
£2,000–2,200
€/ **$3,200–3,500** ⚒ DN

A wine glass, the honeycomb-moulded funnel bowl on a plain stem, on a conical foot, c1755, 6½in (16.5cm) high.
£600–700
€/ **$950–1,100** ⚒ S(O)

◀ **An ale flute,** the panel-moulded bowl on a double-series air-twist stem, c1760, 8in (20.5cm) high.
£1,000–1,200
€/ **$1,600–1,900** ⊞ WMa

A wine glass, the round funnel bowl engraved with a rose, two buds and a moth, on a multi-spiral air-twist double-knopped stem, c1750, 6¼in (16cm) high.
£850–950
€/ **$1,300–1,500** ⊞ BrW

An ale flute, the deep round funnel bowl on a double-series opaque-twist stem, on a conical foot, c1760, 8in (20.5cm) high.
£350–400
€/ **$550–630** ⊞ Som

A wine glass, the drawn trumpet bowl with a mult spiral air-twist composite stem and a beaded short inverted baluster, on a domed foot, c1750, 7in (18cm) high.
£775–900
€/ **$1,200–1,400** ⚒ S(O)

A wine glass, the rounded funnel bowl over an inverted baluster knop and cylindrical stem, on a domed spreading folded foot, c1755, 5¾in (14.5cm) high.
£260–300
€/ **$400–475** ⊞ PSA

A glass, the funnel bowl with a double-series opaque air-twist stem, on a conical foot, c1760, 5½in (14cm) high.
£300–330
€/ **$475–515** ⊞ PSA

A wine glass, the bowl with a swag-engraved ⬦p, on an opaque double-⬦wist stem, c1760, ⬦¾in (14.5cm) high.
400–450
€**/ $630–710 ⊞ CHAC**

A wine glass, the drawn trumpet bowl on an opaque-twist stem, c1760, 7½in (17.5cm) high.
£280–320
€**/ $440–500 ⊞ BrW**

A wine glass, with an opaque double-twist stem, c1760, 6¾in (17cm) high.
£315–350
€**/ $480–550 ⊞ CHAC**

A wine goblet, on a multi-spiral opaque-twist stem with a shoulder and base knop, c1760, 7in (18cm) high.
£800–875
€**/ $1,300–1,400 ⊞ WMa**

GLASS

▶ **A wine glass,** the bucket bowl on a double-series opaque-twist and gauze stem, with a conical foot, c1765, 5½in (14cm) high.
£265–300
€**/ $420–475 ⊞ PSA**

A wine glass, the bowl ⬦ngraved with a bird, on ⬦n air-twist stem, c1760, ⬦¾in (14.5cm) high.
360–400
€**/ $550–630 ⊞ CHAC**

A Beilby enamelled wine glass, the funnel bowl painted with fruiting vine, on a double-series opaque-twist stem, on a conical foot, c1765, 6in (15cm) high.
£1,800–2,000
€**/ $2,800–3,200 ⚒ S(O)**

A ratafia flute, the conical bowl with rib-moulding on a double-series opaque-twist stem, with a conical foot, c1765, 7¼in (18.5cm) high.
£1,200–1,400
€**/ $1,900–2,200 ⚒ S(O)**

A wine glass, the ⬦moulded bowl on a single-⬦eries opaque-twist stem, ⬦nd domed foot, c1765, ⬦in (15cm) high.
630–700
€**/ $1,000–1,100 ⊞ Del**

◀ **A wine glass,** the ogee bowl gilt-decorated in the Giles Workshop, with trailing fruiting vines, with a gilt rim, on an opaque-twist stem with two spiral threads enclosed by two corkscrew twists, on a conical foot, 1765–68, 6in (15cm) high.
£900–1,100
€**/ $1,400–1,700 ⚒ B**

A wine glass, the ogee bowl engraved 'Nunquam Non Paratus' (Never Unprepared), above a cockatrice, on a double-series opaque stem, on a conical foot, c1765, 6in (15cm) high.
£800–900
€**/ $1,300–1,400 ⊞ RAP**

GLASS

A wine glass, the ogee bowl with engraved rococo motifs, on a folded foot, 18thC, 5½in (14cm) high.
£165–185
€ / **$260–290 ⊞ PSA**

A wine glass, the bowl engraved with a thistle, on a faceted stem, c1770, 6in (15cm) high.
£320–350
€ / **$510–550 ⊞ JHa**

A wine glass, the bowl engraved with a flower and a bee, the shoulder knobbed, on a facet stem with a row of shield cuts, c1770, 5in (12.5cm) high.
£340–380
€ / **$550–600 ⊞ JHa**

A colour-twist ale flute, the tapering bowl engraved with hops and barley, the stem with spiral threads enclosing a central lace twist, on a conical foot, c1770, 7½in (19cm) high.
£3,000–3,500
€ / **$4,700–5,500 ⋌ B**
The blue spiral increases the price by at least half as much again compared to a standard white air-twist glass.

A wine glass, the bell bowl on a domed folded foot, c1770, 6¾in (17cm) high.
£250–280
€ / **$400–440 ⊞ PSA**

A wine glass, the bowl with the engraved and gilt royal monogram of Frederik V, Norwegian, c1770, 6¼in (16cm) high.
£450–550
€ / **$710–870 ⋌ BUK**

A wine glass, the deceptive rounded bowl with basal flutes, on a multi-spiral opaque-twist stem, the ply bands outside a corkscrew, c1770, 5¾in (14.5cm) high.
£2,000–2,400
€ / **$3,200–3,800 ⋌ LFA**
The deceptive bowl is more unusual than regular ones.

Neo-classical design in glass

The architect Robert Adam's return from his Grand Tour in 1758 was the prime catalyst in the decorative revolution that overthrew rococo in favour of the neo-classical style that has since remained the preferred expression of British taste. Neo-classical motifs were applied, usually in symmetrical cutting, but sometimes engraved, onto British glassware from 1765–95. James Giles applied in gold motifs such as wheel-like paterae and ox-skull *bucraniae*, taken from Roman funerary carvings, to decanter and cruet bottles. Similarly engraved pieces have also been linked to his workshop, and that of Fleet Street merchant/decorator William Parker.

A wine glass, the lipped cup bowl with faceting to the base, on a faceted stem, c1770, 5½in (14cm) high.
£220–250
€ / **$350–400 ⊞ PSA**

◀ **A Nöstetangen wine glass,** the bowl with the engraved and gilt royal monogram of Frederik V, Norwegian, c1770, 6¼in (16cm) high.

A wine glass, the diamond facet-cut bowl with an Adam-style swag and medallion, with bucrania and patera engraving, c1770, 5in (12.5cm) high.
£880–975
€ / **$1,400–1,500 ⊞ WM**

A 'Lynn' wine glass, the funnel bowl with five ribs, on a multi-spiral opaque-twist stem, with a ply band enclosing two spiral cables, c1770, 5½in (14cm) high.
£750–875
€ / **$1,200–1,400 ⋌ LFA**
'Lynn' glasses, with their distinctive grooved horizontal rings around the bowl, are so-called because it used to be thought that they were made in Kings Lynn, Norfolk.

A firing glass, the ogee bowl on a thick tapering stem and terraced foot, mid-18thC, 3½in (9cm) high.
£100–120
€/ **$160–190** ➹ PFK

A pan-topped rummer, with a petal-moulded bowl, c1800, 4½in (11.5cm) high.
£55–60
€/ **$85–95** ⊞ JHa

◀ **A rummer,** the petal-moulded bowl above a short stem, on a conical foot, c1800, 4½in (11.5cm) high.
£65–75
€/ **$100–120** ⊞ Som

An ale glass, the drawn trumpet bowl engraved with hops and barley, on a plain foot, 18thC, 6½in (16.5cm) high.
£60–70
€/ **$95–110** ⊞ JHa

A glass goblet, engraved with an armorial and scrolling foliage between bands of printies, on a hollow-knopped stem and an engraved foot, Continental, 18thC, 9¾in (25cm) high.
£280–320
€/ **$440–500** ➹ WW

A pair of Yarmouth gilt rummers, attributed to William Absolon, each bowl inscribed 'From rocks & sands & dangers free Pray God protect the ship & we', within grasses and formal star and flowers, the reverse with an anchor, below a gilt line band, above a collar and spreading foot, gilding rubbed, c1800, 5in (12.5cm) high.
£2,000–2,200
€/ **$3,200–3,500** ➹ S(O)

A rummer, engraved with a ship in full sail, dated 1819, 5in (12.5cm) high.
£315–350
€/ **$480–550** ⊞ Del

A set of six dram glasses, the ovoid bowls on single-knop stems and conical feet, c1840, 4½in (11.5cm) high.
£135–150
€/ **$215–240** ⊞ PSA

▶ **A goblet,** possibly Harrach Glasshouse or Schachtenbach, the thistle-shaped bowl and conical foot gilt with scroll and Gothic arched panels, applied with pincered trails, the clear hexagonal stem with opaque twist spirals between gilt collars, Bohemian, c1850, 11¾in (30cm) high.
£800–900
€/ **$1,300–1,400** ➹ S(O)

A Regency rummer, the bucket bowl etched with thistles and flowers, over a slice-cut and hobnail band, on a star-cut foot, 7½in (19cm) high.
£200–240
€/ **$315–380** ➹ EH

A rummer, the bucket bowl engraved with looped laurel leaves and ribbon bows, on a bladed-knop stem and conical foot, Irish, c1825, 5in (12.5cm) high.
£45–50
€/ **$70–80** ⊞ Som

GLASS

GLASS

A ruby-stained goblet, possibly by Anton Heinrich Pfeiffer, the bowl cut with eight facets, cut with a raised oval medallion and intaglio-engraved with the Virgin and Child, the reverse cut with a lens framed by fruiting vine branches, Bohemian, 1850–1900, 6¾in (17cm) high.
£800–1,000
€/ **$1,300–1,600** ✎ S

A goblet, the bowl decorated with leaves, birds and red deer, on a clear glass foot, foot damaged, Bohemian, c1860, 5in (12.5cm) high.
£350–420
€/ **$550–670** ✎ DORO

A lidded goblet, engraved with a coat-of-arms in a cartouche, Bohemian, c1860, 8¾in (22cm) high.
£275–325
€/ **$430–520** ✎ DORO

A goblet, engraved with snowdrops and ferns, c1880, 6in (15cm) high.
£100–110
€/ **$160–175** ⊞ JHa

◀ **A set of 18 roemers,** possibly Theresienthal, each with a cup-shaped bowl on a clear baluster stem with trailing and three applied raspberry prunts, Bohemian, c1880, 6¼in (16cm) high.
£575–675
€/ **$900–1,100** ✎ S(O)

Expert's choice

The Hinnenburg Goblet, c1715, sold by Sotheby's in 2000.

The Hinnenburg Goblet was made in Dresden, c1715, for Augustus the Strong, Elector of Saxony, and was listed as an 'Emperor Goblet' in a royal inventory of 1739. It was discovered by Simon Cottle of Sotheby's in the cellars of a German castle. Formed in three sections, lid, body and screwing stem/foot, it is decorated with deep swag cutting and polished engraving, and has a teared-ball knop above a hollow baluster stem. However, its greatest attribute is a series of 12 silver-gilt medallion busts of Roman Emperors inserted into its bowl. A group of Meissen red stoneware medallions with similar modelling known to be by Johann Böttger confirm a link between the ceramics and glassware produced at the Saxon court. The goblet fetched £133,500 (€/ $211,000) at Sotheby's in 2000. **Andy McConnell**

A glass goblet, decorated with a coat-of-arms, with historismus-style enamelling, the rim with a pearl border, Bohemian, c1880, 8in (20.5cm) high.
£240–300
€/ **$380–475** ✎ DORO

▶ **A glass goblet and cover,** engraved on one side with a Danish inscription, the reverse with a building in Bredgade, Copenhagen, c1880, 14in (35.5cm) high.
£1,100–1,200
€/ **$1,700–1,900** ⊞ G&G

A Murano Glass Co goblet and cover, by Dr Antonio Salviati, the funnel bowl with a partly-gilt rim, on an openwork stem with aventurine inclusions, above a conical foot with a folded rim, the domed cover with a similar openwork finial, c1880, 28¾in (73cm) high.
£3,500–4,000
€/ **$5,500–6,300** ✎ S

Beakers & Tumblers

An enamelled armorial beaker, painted with a shield and coronet, the reverse inscribed 'Vivat Joannes.V.' above stylized flowers, below a scroll border, German, Saxony, 18thC, 6¼in (16cm) high.
£775–900
€ / **$1,200–1,400** ⚖ S(O)

An alabaster glass footed beaker, decorated in the rococo style with rocailles, flowers and leaves, Bohemian, c1830, 5in (13cm) high.
£650–750
€ / **$1,000–1,200** ⚖ DORO

A coloured sulphide tumbler, by Baccarat or Val St Lambert, decorated with a central roundel containing a sulphide depicting a dove and a wreath of flowers, flanked by lobes cut with fine diamonds, the footrim facet-cut, chip under footrim, Belgian, c1850, 3½in (8.5cm) high.
£200–240
€ / **$300–380** ⚖ B

A Henrikstorp beaker, with engraved decoration of trailing foliage and a monogram, minor foot chips, Swedish, 1700–50, 3¼in (8.5cm) high.
£850–1,000
€ / **$1,300–1,600** ⚖ BUK

An Agatin or Lithyalin marbled beaker, the faceted bowl waisted towards the bottom and cut with a waistband, Bohemian, c1830, 5¼in (13.5cm) high.
£1,000–1,200
€ / **$1,600–1,900** ⚖ S

A beaker, enamel-decorated with a band of silver flowers, Bohemian, c1860, 5in (13cm) high.
£280–340
€ / **$440–550** ▦ DORO

▶ **A beaker,** painted with humorous representations of the months of the year, rim slightly damaged, German, c1900, 5½in (14cm) high.
£240–280
€ / **$380–440** ⚖ DORO

A Kosta beaker, engraved with wedding motifs of birds, a heart and stylized flowers, Swedish, 1750–1800, 8¼in (21cm) high.
£320–375
€ / **$500–600** ⚖ BUK

▶ **A footed beaker,** with enamel overlay and gilt decoration, gilt slightly rubbed, Bohemian, c1840, 5in (12.5cm) high.
£350–420
€ / **$550–670** ⚖ DORO

A transparent-enamelled spa beaker, the waisted cylindrical bowl painted with a scene within an amber-stained frame inscribed in gilding 'Brandenburgerthor. Berlin. 1825', the reverse cut with a lens, below an amber-stained band, gilt rim and star-cut base, gilding rubbed, Bohemian, 19thC, 4½in (11.5cm) high.
£775–900
€ / **$1,200–1,400** ⚖ S(O)

A beaker, with a gilt rim and gilt decoration of a huntsman in a wooded landscape with a castle, Bohemian, c1760, 3¾in (9.5cm) high.
£320–375
€ / **$500–600** ⚖ DORO

An enamelled beaker, possibly by Lobmeyr or Meyr's Neffe, the tapering bowl enamelled in *Schwartzlot* in transparent enamels, the four panels of classical maidens alternating with floral garlands entwined around torches, the border with amber flashing and a gold foliate band, Bohemian, c1900, 4½in (11.5cm) high.
£500–570
€ / **$790–900** ⚖ B
Schwartzlot means 'black lead' decoration. This is a **Historismus** piece: a reproduction of a style of decoration pioneered c1700 in Silesia/Bohemia by Ignaz Preissler (born 1670).

Bottles, Carafes & Decanters

A mallet-shaped wine bottle, applied with a string rim, with a deep pontil-scarred base, with all-over iridescent patination, 1720–30, 6½in (16.5cm) high.
£240–275
€/ **$380–440** ↗ BBR

A wine bottle, applied with a seal inscribed 'B. Greive, 1727', 6½in (16.5cm) high.
£3,000–3,500
€/ **$4,700–5,500** ↗ L
This is an unrecorded bottle. Collectors of bottles are prepared to pay substantial sums for rare items, particularly pieces of early date, such as this example. A seal, especially a dated one, can increase the price by about ten times.

A Nailsea-type globular-shaped bottle, with white flecks, with applied collar, pontil scar to the base, 1770–80, 6in (15cm) high.
£375–450
€/ **$600–700** ↗ BBR

A decanter, with cut fluting and a neo-classical engraved band, c1780, 12in (30.5cm) high.
£315–350
€/ **$500–550** ⊞ JHa

A square-section case decanter, with an engraved cartouche for 'Rum' and floral motifs, c1780, 9in (23cm) high.
£165–185
€/ **$260–290** ⊞ CHAC

A pair of club-shaped cruet bottles, 1790–1820, 5in (12.5cm) high.
£400–450
€/ **$630–700** ⊞ Del

A decanter, engraved with panels of Masonic emblems and figures, above a chequered band with drapery below, the neck with three triple-annular rings, stopper missing, one ring chipped, c1800, 8½in (21.5cm) high.
£600–700
€/ **$1,000–1,100** ↗ S(O)

A pair of Bristol blue club-shaped decanters, for rum and brandy, the club-shaped bodies decorated in gilt, gilding worn, 1790–1820, 8¾in (22cm) high.
£350–400
€/ **$550–630** ⊞ PSA

A pair of club-shaped decanters, with lozenge stoppers, c1800, 9½in (24cm) high.
£450–500
€/ **$700–800** ⊞ CHAC

A pair of glass bottles, cold-painted with titled portraits of 'Peter Floirs, Vice-Admiraal van Friesland' and 'Adriaan Bankert, Admiraal van Zeeland', over scenes of naval engagements, Dutch, early 19thC, 14¼in (36cm) high.
£1,500–1,800
€/ **$2,400–2,800** ↗ TEN

A set of three barrel-shaped spirit decanters, with original stoppers, c1830, 8½in (21.5cm) high.
£350–400
€/ **$550–650** ⊞ PSA

An engraved shaft-and-globe bottle, inscribed 'Walter Galbraith' and dated 1837 within a scroll, depicting agricultural implements including a plough, scythe, rake, fork and shovel, above a thistle and a rose, Scottish, 10¼in (26cm) high.
£375–450
€/ **$600–700** ↗ B(Ed)

GLASS

An opaline glass carafe and stand, with hand-painted floral enamelling, 1840–60, 8in (20.5cm) high.
€100–125
€ / $160–200 ➚ SWO

A claret decanter, on a star-cut base, stopper missing, small chips, 19thC, 11¾in (30cm) high.
£220–260
€ / $350–400 ➚ TMA

◄ **A pair of shaft-and-globe decanters,** cut with flutes and printies, with scale-cut necks and cut stoppers, c1860, 8¾in (22cm) high.
£170–200
€ / $270–300 ⊞ Som

A decanter, by Fritz Heckert, decorated in gilt with enamel highlights, pommel damaged, Bohemian, c1880, 9¾in (25cm) high.
£400–500
€ / $630–800 ➚ DORO
This type of decoration is known as 'Jodphur style'.

◄ **A silver-mounted decanter,** the stopper modelled as a beaker, silver hallmarked Chester 1906, 10¾in (27.5cm) high.
£150–175
€ / $230–280 ➚ FEN

A Lobmeyr decanter, engraved in the Baroque style with half figures below canopied thrones within foliate scrollwork with animals and birds, the domed stopper with a ball finial, the faceted neck with a scroll band, on a flared faceted foot, engraved mark, c1880, 10½in (26.5cm) high.
£1,800–2,000
€ / $2,800–3,200 ➚ S(O)

GLASS

GLASS

Bowls

A finger bowl, 1820,
3¾in (9.5cm) high.
£60–65
€ / $95–100 ⊞ PSA

A Stourbridge-style opalescent
glass preserve bowl, c1900,
3in (8.5cm) high.
£85–100
€ / $130–160 ⊞ GRI

◄ A cut-glass fruit bowl, with wave
rim, on a star-cut base, rim chipped,
Irish, c1790, 9¾in (25cm) high.
£350–400
€ / $550–630 ♪ G(L)

A bowl, cut with strawberry
diamonds, on a star-cut base,
1810–20, 8in (20.5cm) diam.
£100–120
€ / $160–190 ♪ TMA

A rib-moulded glass rose bowl,
with rococo-revival gilding, late
19thC, 9¼in (23.5cm) diam.
£130–160
€ / $200–250 ♪ JDJ

A lidded bowl, with blue-flashed
and gilded neo-classical decoration,
Russian, 1750–1800, 9in (23cm) diam.
£3,800–4,500
€ / $6,000–7,000 ♪ BUK

A tea caddy bowl, with a fan-cut
rim, the arched and diamond-cut
body on a star-cut foot, c1830,
4in (10cm) diam.
£145–160
€ / $230–250 ⊞ Som

Boxes

A cut-glass casket, with ormolu
mounts, the hinged cover cut with
strawberry diamonds, the body cut
with pillars and serrated vertical
bands, on a star-cut base, chipped,
French, c1830, 4¾in (12cm) high.
£450–500
€ / $700–800 ♪ S(O)

A blue-flashed casket, with gilt
decoration and engraved with scenes
of Karlsbad, Bohemian, 1840–50,
6in (15cm) wide.
£650–775
€ / $1,000–1,200 ♪ BUK

► A Moser-style cranberry glass
casket, with ormolu mounts, cold-
painted with floral and foliate
scrollwork, Bohemian, 1860–80,
4¾in (12cm) square.
£400–475
€ / $630–750 ♪ GTH

A ruby-flashed sugar box and cover,
with enamel decoration, Bohemian,
c1860, 5¼in (13.5cm) wide.
£150–180
€ / $240–280 ♪ DORO

Centrepieces

A Clichy paperweight tazza, the rims applied with a spiralling ribbon, the bowl inset with a central rose within five interlaced cane garlands alternating with a single cane, above a knopped baluster stem and domed foot, French, c1850, 4in (10cm) high.
£3,000–3,500
€/ **$4,700–5,700** ⚒ S(O)

A uranium glass table centrepiece, with gilded and enamel decoration, Bohemian, c1840, 6½in (16.5cm) high.
£400–500
€/ **$630–800** ⚒ DORO

A cut-glass épergne, the scroll arms hung with baskets and surmounted by a chevron- and diamond-cut bowl with Van Dyck-style rim, on a diamond-cut dome scalloped base, baskets matched, Continental, late 18thC, 22in (56cm) high.
€3,500–4,200
€/ **$5,500–6,500** ⚒ B

A ruby-flashed table centrepiece, decorated with rococo scrolls in enamel and gold, rim slightly damaged, Bohemian, c1860, 5¾in (14.5cm) high.
£180–220
€/ **$280–350** ⚒ DORO

An épergne, with frill rims, with four trumpet vases, on a stand, 19thC, 21in (53.5cm) high.
£160–200
€/ **$250–300** ⚒ G(L)

A Lobmeyr Persian-style tazza, the bowl inscribed with Kufic lettering within gilt scrollwork, the interior with a central medallion enclosing a stylized flower, on an annulated collar and trumpet foot, painted grid mark, c1880, 3½in (9cm) high.
£2,500–3,000
€/ **$4,000–4,700** ⚒ S(O)
This is Lobmeyr's equivalent of Heckert's 'Jodhpur style' (see Bottles, Carafes & Decanters page 341).

A table centrepiece, with a crimped rim, c1880, 4¼in (11cm) high.
£120–135
€/ **$190–215** ⊞ PSA

◄ **A late Victorian four-vase épergne,** with clear glass trailed banding, frilled opaque and overlaid rims, on a shaped dished opaque base, 14in (35.5cm) high.
£130–160
€/ **$200–250** ⚒ TMA

A four-vase épergne, on a wavy-edge bowl, c1890, 18½in (47cm) high.
£750–850
€/ **$1,200–1,300** ⊞ CB

GLASS

GLASS

◀ **An opaque glass centrepiece,** the spirally crimped dish on a plated stand pierced with vine decoration, on a beaded foot, 19thC, 11in (28cm) diam.
£65–80
€/ **$100–125**
↗ **PFK**

An épergne, with a cut-glass vase, on a gilt-metal base modelled with two birds among fruit and foliage, stamped 'Defreville', 19thC, 15⅜in (39.5cm) high.
£375–450
€/ **$600–700** ↗ **HYD**

A six-vase épergne, the vases applied with pinched trailing ornament, below fluted rims, Bohemian, late 19thC, 17¼in (44cm) high.
£900–1,000
€/ **$1,400–1,700** ↗ **S(O)**

Eight crimp-edged vases, in a silver-plated frame, c1900, 18in (45.5cm) wide.
£400–500
€/ **$630–800** ⊞ **CB**

John Walsh Walsh

The fame of Victorian Britain's leading glassworks – Richardson, Thomas Webb and Stevens & Williams – has obscured the existence of scores of others that operated principally in the Midlands, the North and North-East. They include the bizarrely named John Walsh Walsh, which produced a wide range of cut, engraved, etched, cameo, art and reproduction 'antique' glassware in Birmingham from 1850–1951. The company grew gradually to a peak during the 1930s, when it employed around 400 staff. It remains best known for its ranges designed by William 'Clyne' Farquharson.

A John Walsh Walsh ormolu-mounted épergne, with five opalescent glass bowls on a stand and a spiralling frame, early 20thC, 14¼in (36cm) wide.
£850–1,000
€/ **$1,300–1,600** ↗ **S(O)**

Flasks

A façon de Venise mottled glass barillet, the narrow aperture moulded with a folded rim and flanked by two scroll handles, French, c1700, 4¾in (12cm) wide.
£1,000–1,100
€/ **$1,600–1,700** ↗ **S(O)**

> Items in the Glass section have been arranged in date order within each sub-section.

An amber-flashed and cut-glass flask, with metal screw-stopper, Bohemian, c1860, 5¼in (13.5cm) high.
£120–140
€/ **$190–220** ↗ **SWO**

A Stourbridge Oriental-style gilt and silvered moonflask, by Thomas Webb & Sons, attributed to Jules Barbe, one side depicting two carp, one chasing an eel, the reverse with a frog among lily pads flanked by flowering grasses within stylized scroll borders, c1890, 9½in (24cm) high.
£7,200–8,000
€/ **$11,500–12,600** ↗ **S**
This rare piece is an example of outstanding craftsmanship.

Jugs & Ewers

A *milchglas* jug and cover, decorated in gold and enamels in the rococo style, the cover with a pear knop, Bohemian, c1760, 9¾in (25cm) high.
£250–300
€ / **$400–475** ↗ DORO

A glass water jug, with applied scroll handle, engraved with a monogram, the reverse dated 1798, 8¾in (22cm) high.
£600–700
€ / **$1,000–1,100** ↗ G(L)

A glass water jug, with scroll handle, decorated with Adam-style neo-classical cut motifs, on a facet-cut foot, Irish, c1810, 9¾in (25cm) high.
£400–450
€ / **$630–700** ↗ LFA
This type of decoration is typical of Irish works.

An enamelled and gilt glass ewer, by Harrachor Glasshouse, painted with floral bouquets, with a scroll handle, gilding rubbed, chipped, Bohemian, c1845, 10¼in (26cm) high.
£1,500–1,800
€ / **$2,400–2,800** ↗ S

Anglo-Bohemian Victorian engraving

Demand for engraved glassware between 1850 and 1890 created a skills shortage that drew scores of Bohemian engravers to Britain. Working principally in Edinburgh, Stourbridge and London, they developed new decorative styles that saw their traditional subject matter, such as stags in woodland, supplanted by a range of classical and naturalistic decorative themes and the development of 'rock crystal' glassware. The leading exponents included William Fritsche and Frederick Kny, who spent a combined 80 years working in Stourbridge, mostly for Thomas Webb & Sons. Kny's son Ludwig was the chief designer at Stuart Crystal between the world wars.

▶ **A glass ewer,** etched with trailing vines and baskets of flowers beneath a waisted neck with engraved arched panels, on a pedestal base, c1870, 12½in (32cm) high.
€575–675
€ / **$900–1,000** ↗ HAM

A ruby-flashed glass claret jug, by James Charles Edington, the fluted and Gothic-arch cut glass with silver vine stock handle and girdle, shaped collar and cover with vine tendril ring finial, London 1847, 11½in (29cm) high.
£3,000–3,400
€ / **$4,700–5,400** ↗ Bri

A cranberry glass water jug, with a clear scroll handle, 19thC, 8in (20.5cm) high.
£160–200
€ / **$250–300** ↗ SWO

A Lobmeyr rococo revival opalescent glass ewer and goblet, engraved and gilt with scrolling foliate rocaille round and 'jewelled' with opaque dots, chipped and cracked, monogram mark, c1880, ewer 9¾in (25cm) high.
£400–475
€ / **$630–750** ↗ DN

Champagne decanters

Champagne decanters have existed for over three centuries, generally containing a stoppered bubble or tube of glass into which crushed ice is inserted to chill their contents. In 1755, examples were priced at six shillings each, making them cheaper than their contents, which cost eight shillings a bottle. While their function may appear illogical, their use for dispensing vintage Champagnes remains recommended by connoisseurs. This is because decanting allows the taste of the Champagne to develop, reduces the number of bubbles and slightly raises its temperature to above the point at which it numbs tastebuds.

A cranberry ice glass champagne decanter and stopper, with clear handle, 19thC, 15in (38cm) high.
£140–160
€ / **$220–250** ↗ GTH

GLASS

Lustres

The term 'lustre' can be confusing as it has been applied to a number of different items over the past 300 years. They have included a chandelier (18th century), a cut-glass table centrepiece supporting a single candlestick (19th century), or a single drop suspended from a chandelier, centrepiece or candlestick (current usage).

A pair of clear glass lustres, with cut drops, 1840–50, 7¾in (19.5cm) high.
£350–400
€/ **$550–630** ✎ SWO

▶ **A pair of enamelled glass lustres,** decorated with enamelled portrait medallions of children and floral sprays with gilded foliage, beneath a scrolling, scalloped rim, hung with cut-glass prisms, on domed feet with further medallions, Bohemian, late 19thC, 11in (28cm) high.
£800–950
€/ **$1,200–1,500** ✎ RIT

A pair of glass lustres, with Albert drops, c1840, 8in (20.5cm) high.
£1,100–1,200
€/ **$1,700–1,900** ⊞ Del

Mugs & Tankards

◀ **A ruby-stained glass tankard and cover,** with pewter mounts, engraved with a stag and deer in a woodland scene, the cover engraved 'FAK' in Gothic lettering, with a rounded star-cut base, late 19thC, 7in (18cm) high.
£850–1,000
€/ **$1,300–1,600** ✎ S

A ruby-flashed and enamelled glass tankard and cover, with pewter mounts, decorated in colours and gilt with flowers, thumbpiece missing, Bohemian, c1830, 5¼in (13.5cm) high.
£220–250
€/ **$350–400** ✎ DORO

A glass mug, with a swirled body, pontil scar to base, 1775–1825, 3in (7cm) high.
£80–90
€/ **$125–145** ✎ BBR

Panels & Pictures

A reverse glass painting, depicting the Biblical story of Noah and his three sons, Ham, Sem and Japheth, inscribed, south German, 18thC, in a later ebonized and gilt frame, 16¼ x 20in (41 x 51cm).
£700–800
€/ **$1,100–1,200** ✎ S(Am)

A leaded and stained glass Historismus panel, depicting a coat-of-arms above an inscribed banner, German, 19thC, 17in (43cm) high.
£400–500
€/ **$630–800** ✎ RTo

A Victorian stained and leaded glass window, depicting a hunter against a background of trees, birds in flight and snow-covered ground, some cracks and bulging, 34 x 27½in (86.5 x 70cm), mounted in a light box.
£800–950
€/ **$1,200–1,500** ✎ JDJ

Paperweights

A Baccarat concentric millefiori paperweight, French, c1848, 2½in (6.5cm) diam.
£350–400
€/ $550–630 ⊞ DLP

A Baccarat close-pack millefiori paperweight, with 15 silhouettes, initialled 'B', French, 1848, 3½in (9cm) diam.
£8,000–9,000
€/ $12,700–14,200 ⊞ SWB

A Baccarat scattered millefiori paperweight, with a variety of canes, one inscribed 'B1848', on a tossed muslin ground, French, dated 1848, 3¼in (8.5cm) diam.
£1,000–1,200
€/ $1,600–1,900 ⚒ G(L)

A specimen flower paperweight, probably Baccarat, decorated with a pansy with central star motif, on a star-cut foot, bruised and scuffed, French, 19thC, 3in (7.5cm) diam.
£475–550
€/ $750–870 ⚒ BR

A Boston & Sandwich Glass Co poinsettia paperweight, American, c1860, 3in (7.5cm) diam.
£700–800
€/ $1,100–1,300 ⊞ DLP

A Clichy miniature paperweight, with a central rose, on a carpet ground of fine canes, French, mid-19thC, 1¾in (4.5cm) diam.
£4,000–4,800
€/ $6,300–7,500 ⚒ B

GLASS

GLASS

A Clichy rose paperweight, with a central rose, French, 1845–60, 2in (5cm) diam.
£2,200–2,400
€/ **$3,300–3,800** ⊞ SWB

A Pantin rose paperweight, French, c1878, 3in (7.5cm) diam.
£9,000–10,000
€/ **$14,000–16,000** ⊞ DLP
Pantin paperweights are arguably the finest glass paperweights ever made. They have a 3-dimensional quality and realism that is spectacular. Fewer than 20 rose weights are known to exist from this maker, one of about 200 weights documented from Pantin.

A Clichy paperweight, the central cluster within a garland design, bruise to base, French, 19thC, 3in (7.5cm) diam.
£240–275
€/ **$380–430** ⚒ G(B)

A St Louis miniature crown paperweight, the twisted *latticinio* threads alternating with lengths of twisted ribbon around a central cane, minor damage, French, mid-19thC, 2in (5cm) diam.
£220–250
€/ **$350–400** ⚒ B

A pair of scrambled paperweights, possibly Franchini, set with a variety of colourful canes, *latticinio* tubing and aventurine, pontil scar, Venetian, mid-19thC, 2½in (6.5cm) diam.
£550–650
€/ **$870–1,000** ⚒ S(O)

Further reading
Miller's Paperweights of the 19th & 20th Centuries: A Collector's Guide, Miller's Publications, 2000

A Salvador Ysart Y-cane paperweight, 1930s, 3in (7.5cm) diam.
£330–365
€/ **$520–580** ⊞ SWB

Scent Bottles

A glass scent bottle, the hinged silver top inset with Stuart crystal, c1690, 3½in (9cm) high.
£530–600
€/ **$850–950** ⊞ **LBr**

James Giles

James Giles (1718–80) has long been recognized as one of England's finest 18th-century porcelain decorators. However, it is now known that glassware amounted to around 15 per cent of his workshop output. He applied a wide range of rococo and neo-classical motifs in gold to items of table glass, including decanters and drinking glasses, and in gold and polychrome vitreous enamels to a series of small coloured and cut-glass scent or 'smelling bottles', as they were known. The latter, dated 1760–65, were often inscribed with mottoes such as 'Fidelité' and 'Toujours' and were presented between clandestine lovers.

▶ **A diamond-cut-glass scent bottle,** modelled as a horn, with engine-turned silver mount, chain and finger ring, c1850, 4in (10cm) long.
£270–300
€/ **$430–470**
⊞ **Som**

A glass scent bottle, probably James Giles, London, the front gilt with a flaming heart and tree and 'Pour vous seul', the reverse gilt with a floral spray, with a swirl-chased gold cap, c1760, 3in (7.5cm) high, in original fishskin case.
£1,400–1,600
€/ **$2,200–2,500** ⚒ **S(O)**

A cut-glass scent flask and stopper, the shoulder cut with oval facets below the three-ringed neck, on a solid foot cut with strawberry diamonds, with similarly-cut stopper, c1830, 10in (25.5cm) high.
£475–575
€/ **$750–900** ⚒ **S(O)**

GLASS

A Stourbridge glass scent bottle, with a silver top, c1870, 5in (12.5cm) high.
£500–550
€/ **$800–870** ⊞ **CoS**

▶ **A glass scent bottle,** overlaid with a plaque painted with a female portrait bust against gilded foliage, Bohemian, 19thC, 4¾in (12cm) high.
£160–200
€/ **$250–300** ⚒ **G(L)**

◀ **A Sampson Mordan scent flask and vinaigrette,** with silver-gilt mounts, London 1873, 4in (10cm) long.
£550–600
€/ **$870–1,000** ⚒ **HAM**

Sampson Mordan

Founded in 1815, Sampson Mordan & Co became one of the leading makers of late Victorian novelties, often in designs that married wood, ceramics, silver and glass. Typically, they produced a scent bottle modelled as a Champagne bottle (1869), a chased silver egg containing sewing tools (1876), a miniature barrel-shaped spirit flask (1882), an inkwell disguised as a tortoise (1881), an owl pincushion (1895) and a ceramic walnut scent bottle with silver mounts (1885). The company mark also appeared on silver-mounted claret jugs shaped as an eagle (1881) and a kangaroo (1882).

A Stourbridge cameo glass scent bottle, carved with passion flowers and leaves, with a hinged silver mount, late 19thC, 5½in (14cm) high.
£900–1,100
€/ **$1,400–1,700** ⚒ **B**

A glass scent bottle, encased in brass foliate work, Continental, 19thC, 4in (10cm) high.
£200–250
€/ **$300–400** ⚒ **SWO**

Sets & Services

▶ **A gilt part drinking set,** comprising seven pieces, decorated with scattered floral sprays, chips and minor rubbing to gilding, Continental, c1850, goblet 5¾in (14.5cm) high.
£525–625
€/ **$830–1,000** ⚲ S(O)

A glass hock decanter, with a set of six matching glasses, c1840, 14in (35.5cm) high.
£550–600
€/ **$870–950** ⊞ Del
This colour is usually attributed to Richardson's of Stourbridge and is typical of early Victorian glass.

◀ **A cut-glass service,** comprising 66 pieces, 1930s.
£200–240
€/ **$300–380** ⚲ TRM

Sweetmeat & Jelly Dishes

◀ **A pan-topped jelly glass,** with moulded panels and a scroll handle, on a domed foot, c1750, 4½in (11.5cm) high.
£250–300
€/ **$400–475** ⚲ LFA
Glasses like this, filled with colourful syllabubs, jellies and mousses were often arranged on dining tables, on a series of glass salvers, ranging from large to small, as described in Mrs Glasse's cookery book of the 1740s.

To order Miller's books in Canada please ring McArthur & Co on 1-800-387-0117. See the full range at
www.millers.uk.com

A sweetmeat glass, with a flute- and petal-cut rim, on a domed radially-moulded foot, c1760, 6in (15cm) high.
£400–450
€/ **$630–700** ⊞ Som

A sweetmeat glass, the honeycomb-moulded double-ogee bowl on an octagonal pedestal and domed foot, foot trimmed, c1760, 6½in (16.5cm) high.
£300–350
€/ **$475–550** ⚲ DN

Vases & Urns

◀ **A pair of covered glass urns,** the covers with facet-cut finials and fluted rims, the bodies with a band of fluting above a band of leaves, on square feet, Irish, c1795, 11¾in (30cm) high.
£2,000–2,200
€/ **$3,200–3,500** ⚲ HOK

▶ **An Empire-style flashed glass urn,** with Regency-style cutting, on an ormolu base, slight damage to rim, 1800–15, 16in (40.5cm) high.
£2,800–3,200
€/ **$4,400–5,000** ⚲ BUK

A pair of cut-glass covered urns, the high domed covers with lapidary-cut finials, the bodies panel-cut with diamond-cut bands, Anglo-Irish, c1800, 14½in (37cm) high.
£850–1,000
€/ **$1,300–1,600** ⚲ NOA

GLASS

An overlay glass vase, with an opaline panel enamelled with polychrome massed flowers, the body decorated with gilt flowers, Bohemian, mid-19thC, 12½in (32cm) high.
€280–320
€/ $440–500 ⚘ PFK

► A pair of glass posy vases, with gilt decoration, Continental, 1880–90, 3in (7.5cm) high.
€100–120
€/ $160–190 ⊞ GRI

A glass vase, hand-painted in enamels with panels of flowers, 19thC, 13in (33cm) high.
€200–225
€/ $300–350 ⚘ SWO

A pair of opaque glass vases, hand-painted with parrots and gilded leaf sprays, one chipped, Continental, 19thC, 15¾in (40cm) high.
€1,200–1,500
€/ $1,900–2,400 ⚘ JAd
The decoration of these vases is of superior quality and they therefore achieved a high price at auction.

An opaline glass baluster vase, possibly by Baccarat, decorated in gold and polychrome enamels, French, c1850, 14in (35.5cm) high.
£170–200
€/ $270–300 ⚘ BUK

A pair of Japonaise opaque overlay glass vases, decorated in relief with prunus blossom and flying fish beneath scroll and beaded rims, on stepped bases, the four corner feet modelled as elephants' masks, 19thC, 15in (38cm) high.
£150–180
€/ $240–280 ⚘ TMA

► A ruby-flashed glass trumpet vase, engraved with a continuous scene of deer in a forest landscape, on a domed and fluted foot with a floral band, minor damage, Bohemian, late 19thC, 18in (45.5cm) high.
£1,000–1,200
€/ $1,600–1,900 ⚘ DN
The decoration of this vase is of a very high standard.

A pair of Baccarat opaline glass vases, painted with roses and foliage within gilt borders, enamels and gilding rubbed, c1855, 19¾in (50cm) high.
£1,800–2,000
€/ $2,800–3,200 ⚘ S(O)

A pair of Thomas Webb & Sons 'Queen's Burmese Ware' glass stick vases, gilt with leaf and berry sprays in the workshop of Jules Barbe, with dimpled bases, 1885–90, 6in (15cm) high.
£240–275
€/ $380–430 ⚘ B
Burmese glass, characterized by a body colour that graduates from yellow to pale pink, was originally produced in the United States in 1886 by the Mount Washington Glass Company. In Britain that same year, this style of glass was patented by Thomas Webb & Sons under the name 'Queen's Burmese', so-called because it was favoured by Queen Victoria. This distinctive colour was created by using a combination of gold and uranium oxides, together with sodium nitrate: the glass changed colour when reheated quickly, as seen at the top of this vase. Burmese wares were mainly ornamental pieces such as vases.

A glass vase, decorated with alternate panels of enamelled flowers and diamond cutting within gilt bands, c1900, 15½in (39.5cm) high.
£400–450
€/ $630–700 ⚘ DORO

Miscellaneous

◄ **A glass carafe,** enamelled with flowers and the bear emblematic of the city of Berne, applied string-ring to neck, Swiss, c1730, 6¾in (17cm) high.
£1,100–1,300
€/ **$1,700–2,000** ⊞ **G&G**

An oval glass dish, cut with strawberry diamonds and intersecting prisms, beneath a notched rim, c1820, 11½in (29cm) wide.
£320–350
€/ **$500–550** ⊞ **Som**

A flatware set, with Bohemian millefiori glass handles, c1850.
£700–800
€/ **$1,100–1,300** ⊞ **DLP**

A frigger of a seaside town, modelled with a locomotive travelling along a bridge between two tunnels, the bay beneath with two sailing ships, the cliffs with houses and a lighthouse, on a wooden stand, beneath a glass dome, late 19thC, 19¾in (50cm) high.
£650–750
€/ **$1,000–1,200** ↗ **DN**
A frigger is a decorative or novelty glass object apparently made by glassworkers in their own time, using surplus glass that remained in the furnace pots.

A *façon de Venise* **glass inkwell,** applied with two cylindrical sconces or pen-holders with trailed and pincered ornament, scroll handle, applied flowers with ruby beads, on a wide foot with upturned rim, probably Venetian, c1800, 4in (10cm) high.
£400–450
€/ **$630–700** ↗ **S(O)**

A cranberry glass patch pot, with opaque decoration inscribed 'Firenze', c1885, 2½in (6.5cm) diam.
£180–200
€/ **$280–300** ⊞ **GRI**

◄ **A set of 24 glass rinsers,** each with a facet-cut band, minor damage, 19thC, 3½in (9cm) diam.
£650–750
€/ **$1,000–1,200** ↗ **S(O)**
These were used for rinsing wine glasses during meals, to save having to change them between different wines.

A ribbed cranberry glass salt, with colourless coronet frill, c1900, 2½in (6.5cm) diam.
£80–90
€/ **$125–145** ⊞ **GRI**

► **A toddy lifter,** the flute-cut neck with two cut rings, c1810, 5¼in (13.5cm) high.
£120–150
€/ **$190–240** ⊞ **Som**
Toddy lifters are relics of an age when punch was a staple beverage across the English-speaking world. Made in Britain and Ireland during the 18th and 19th centuries, they were used for transferring punch 'toddies' from bowl to glass without requiring a messy ladle. Generally formed as vertically stretched miniature decanters, they had holes bored in both ends. The bulbous end was immersed into a bowl of punch until full and a thumb closed the upper hole, creating a vacuum to suspend the contents. The thumb was then removed to release the measure into a waiting glass.

An amethyst glass vinaigrette, with a silver top, cut with Regency-style strawberry diamonds, 1860, 1in (2.5cm) high.
£425–475
€/ **$670–750** ⊞ **CoS**

GLASS

Silver

Around the time the first edition of *Miller's Antiques Price Guide* was published, strange things were happening in the silver world. In 1980, a small group, headed by the millionaire Hunt brothers of Texas, decided to purchase all available bullion silver to gain control of the market and act as a hedge against inflation. Prices went through the roof and peaked at £34 (€/ $54) per ounce. As a result beautiful old pieces of silver were being sold for their bullion rather than their antique value and melted down. Silver had never cost so much, and anyone who purchased at that time is unlikely to ever get their money back as within a few months the trading rules on the New York Metals Market were changed and the Federal Reserve intervened. The Hunts' game was over and immediately prices plummeted to about £7 (€/ $11) per ounce. The speculators disappeared, and so had a great deal of antique silver.

Prices were just beginning to recover when, from 1983–92, a few private individuals competed against each other to buy large, top grade silver items, thus lifting the prices for such pieces to new heights. As the best pieces became virtually impossible to afford, an enthusiastic market for middle-range English silver developed. Much was being purchased by European dealers, until the value of the pound became so strong in the early 1990s that such pieces were no longer in demand abroad. However, a market for more affordable items, 'collectables' such as card cases, snuff boxes, vinaigrettes and provincial silver began to emerge.

The picture today is that the value of English domestic silver from 1600–1840, in good condition, has appreciated above inflation, although prices for coffee pots and some later Georgian tankards have remained fairly static since, in spite of the Hunt brothers, there are still plenty of them about. Wine-related objects and collectable pieces are keenly sought after but standard items such as tea sets from c1900–50 are not selling well due to the absence of the export market.

Top range antique silver is becoming ever more rare and beyond the means of many collectors. At present the average age of the collector of antique silver is rising. It is important to attract younger blood into the field and with the large range of more affordable items available there is plenty to choose from, even for those on a limited budget. **Nicholas Shaw**

Animals

A silver mustard pot, by Charles and George Fox, modelled as an owl, London 1865–66, 4in (10cm) high.
£3,200–3,600
€/ $5,000–5,700 ⊞ NS

A silver cow creamer, Continental, London import marks for 1892, 7in (18cm) wide.
£550–650
€/ $870–1,000 ➶ B&L

A silver model of a stag, Continental, c1890, 9¾in (25cm) wide, 25oz.
£1,300–1,500
€/ $2,000–2,400 ➶ TEN

A silver jardinière, by Durgin Division of Gorham, modelled as a swan, with a removable gilt-metal flower grid, marked on base, American, c1900, 13in (33cm) wide, 54oz.
£5,000–6,000
€/ $7,900–9,500 ➶ S(NY)

A silver fish *étui*, Continental, 19thC, 5in (12.5cm) long.
£1,300–1,500
€/ $2,000–2,400 ⊞ SHa

A pair of silver pin cushions, modelled as hedgehogs, Birmingham 1904, 1¼in (3cm) wide.
£380–450
€/ $600–700 ➶ G(L)

A silver parasol handle, by W.B., modelled as a parrot's head, mounted on a parasol with a bamboo shaft, London 1910, 35in (89cm) long.
£160–200
€/ $250–320 ➶ SWO

SILVER

SILVER

Baskets

A silver bread basket, by William Plummer, engraved with the armorials of the King family within a rococo floral cartouche, below a crest and above a motto, the sides pierced with panels of scrolls, roundels, crosses and other motifs between curved beaded straps, handle missing, London 1768, 13in (33cm) wide, 17oz.
£700–800
€ / $1,100–1,300 ⚒ S(O)

A silver-gilt sugar basket, by Tudor & Leader, the pierced gallery sides below embossed paterae and husk swags with bead-edge borders, on a pedestal foot, with a glass liner, Sheffield 1776, 4¾in (12cm) high, 2.5oz.
£800–950
€ / $1,300–1,500 ⚒ B(L)

A silver basket, by Peter and Ann Bateman, with floral swag decoration and engraved initials, on a shaped base, London 1792, 6¼in (16cm) wide, 8oz.
£500–600
€ / $800–950 ⚒ RIT

A silver basket, by Jonas Nylander, decorated with a coat-of-arms, Swedish, Skara 1824, 12in (30.5cm) wide.
£1,100–1,300
€ / $1,700–2,000 ⚒ BUK

▶ **A silver-gilt sugar basket,** by E. E. J. & W. Barnard, applied with trailing oak leaves and acorns, on four leaf and scroll-chased feet, with a glass liner, London 1841, 5¼in (13.5cm) diam, 7.5oz.
£450–525
€ / $700–830 ⚒ DN

A silver cake basket, pierced and embossed with flowers, scrolls and shells, Chester 1896, 12¼in (31cm) wide, 10.5oz.
£160–200
€ / $250–320 ⚒ DN

◀ **A silver fruit basket,** by Henry Matthews, the shaped rim cast with flowers and C-scrolls above pierced and embossed sides, on a raised foot cast with flowers and scrolls, Birmingham 1903, 13¾in (35cm) wide
£750–875
€ / $1,200–1,400 ⚒ RTo

Beakers

A silver beaker, by Jean-Nicholas Saget, with a moulded girdle between applied fruiting vine decoration, engraved with an armorial, the date 1789 and inscribed below the rim and to the foot, French, Paris c1787, 4¾in (12cm) high, 5oz.
£320–380
€ / $500–600 ⚒ CGC

A silver christening mug, by John Anton Bunning, the tapering body with applied rim and friezes of engraved decoration centred by a scroll cartouche with initials, traces of gilding, maker's mark, South African, Capetown, c1790, 2½in (6.5cm) high, 2oz.
£160–200
€ / $250–320 ⚒ WW

A silver beaker, by Paul Storr, engraved with a contemporary coat-of-arms, London 1802–03, 3¾in (9.5cm) high, 4oz.
£2,500–2,800
€ / $4,000–4,400 ⊞ NS

▶ **A silver beaker,** by M. Koshov, Russian, Moscow 1875, 2¾in (7cm) high.
£160–175
€ / $250–280 ⊞ GRe

A pair of horn and silver beakers, with threaded rim, mid-19thC, 4in (10cm) high
£180–220
€ / $280–350 ⚒ TMA

Bowls

silver christening bowl, graved with initials 'MN', maker's ark PD, Channel Islands, c1700, in (14cm) wide, 3oz.
,800–2,200
/ $2,800–3,500 ⚒ **B&L**

silver quaich, by J. Hay, Scottish, inburgh 1875–76, 5in (12.5cm) wide.
,500–1,700
/ $2,400–2,700 ⊞ **NS**

silver rose bowl, with flower-oulded loop handles, on pad feet, ith a glass liner, Continental, 9thC, 17in (43cm) wide, 38oz.
800–950
/ $1,300–1,500
⚒ **AH**

A silver se bowl, with poussé, floral and rolled decoration, ndon 1902, 8¼in 1cm) diam, on ebonized stand.
150–175
/ $240–280
⚒ **WilP**

◄ **A silver rose bowl,** by F.B. & Sons, with embossed C-scroll vacant cartouches, Sheffield 1902, 8½in (21.5cm) diam.
£240–275
€/ $380–440
⚒ **DMC**

silver punchbowl, by Marcus & Co, with a hammered nish and gilt interior, on a waisted and stepped foot, merican, New York c1920, 12in (30.5cm) diam.
2,500–2,800
/ $4,000–4,400 ⚒ **NOA**

A silver bowl and cover, probably by William Darker, with a plain waisted band, London 1728, 4in (10cm) diam.
£1,800–2,200
€/ $2,800–3,500 ⚒ **HOLL**

A silver bowl, by Charles Stuart Harris, London 1886, 3¾in (9.5cm) high.
£270–300
€/ $425–470 ⊞ **GRe**

A silver bowl, possibly by Charles Townsend of Dublin, with shaped rim and chased wrythen fluting, engraved with two crests, on three shell-capped short scroll legs and hoof feet, maker's mark, Irish, c1760, 5in (12.5cm) diam.
£375–425
€/ $590–670 ⚒ **G(L)**

A silver punch bowl, by Alexander Clark, with gadrooned rim, the bowl half fluted and reeded with wrythen decoration, on a flared foot, Sheffield 1899, 11in (28cm) diam.
£750–900
€/ $1,200–1,400 ⚒ **RTo**

SILVER

Boxes

A silver counter box, by B. B. & Crescent, London c1685, 1¾in (4.5cm) high.
£800–900
€/ **$1,300–1,400** ⊞ BEX

A silver tea caddy, by Daniel Smith and Robert Sharp, with a foliate knop, the body with an engraved armorial, London 1764, 3¼in (8.5cm) wide.
£2,000–2,400
€/ **$3,200–3,800** ⋌ SWO

A silver box, with repoussé decoration of cherubs' heads, 1902, 1¾in (4.5cm) square.
£200–235
€/ **$320–370** ⊞ BLm

> Items in the Silver section have been arranged in date order within each sub-section.

Caddy Spoons

◄ **A silver caddy spoon,** by William Eley, London 181... 4½in (11.5cm) lo...
£110–120
€/ **$175–190**
⊞ GRe

A silver caddy spoon, by Henry Lias, London 1856, 4in (10cm) long.
£70–80
€/ **$110–130**
⊞ GRe

A silver caddy spoon, probably by William Marshall, with a fluted bowl and a bright-cut stem with a vacant cartouche, Scottish, Edinburgh c1800, 3¾in (9.5cm) long, 0.75oz.
£100–120
€/ **$160–190** ⋌ WW

A silver caddy spoon, by Thomas Hames, the rounded square bowl with a bright-engraved band around a central roundel of diaper-work, the plain handle with a fish-tail projection at the base, 1814, 4in (10cm) long.
£320–375
€/ **$500–600** ⋌ B

► **A silver caddy spoon,** by James Collins, with foliate engraving, Birmingham 1850, 3¼in (8.5cm) long.
£70–85
€/ **$110–135**
⋌ WW

Candlesticks & Chambersticks

► **A silver dwarf candlestick,** Sheffield 1822, 4¼in (11cm) high.
£160–200
€/ **$250–320** ⋌ SWO

◄ **A silver chamberstick,** by James Dixon & Sons, Sheffiel... 1897, 5¼in (13.5cm) wide.
£900–1,000
€/ **$1,400–1,60...**
⊞ BLm

A silver miniature candlestick, possibly by William Matthew, the stop-fluted stem on a stepped base, London 1703, 2in (5cm) high.
£500–565
€/ **$800–900** ⋌ RTo

A pair of silver candlesticks, by William Comyns, with repoussé-decorated stems, 1899, 6½in (16.5cm) high.
£900–1,000
€/ **$1,400–1,600** ⊞ CoHA

SILVER

Card Cases

A silver card case, by Nathaniel Mills, depicting St Paul's Cathedral, Birmingham 1843–44, 4in (10cm) high.
£1,300–1,500
€ / $2,000–2,400 ⊞ NS

A silver card case, by Nathaniel Mills, engraved with flowers and acanthus scrolls, on an engine-turned ground, initialled 'E.R.', Birmingham 1845, 4in (10cm) high.
£200–220
€ / $320–350 ➚ B(WM)

A silver card case, embossed with a cathedral within a floral and scroll frame, the reverse with a panel filled with a quiver, arrows and a torch, framed by foliate scrolls, late 19thC, 3½in (9cm) high, cased.
£200–225
€ / $320–350 ➚ RTo

A silver card case, by A. & J. Zimmermann, Birmingham 1902, 3¾in (9.5cm) high.
£130–145
€ / $200–230 ⊞ GRe

Insurance values

Always insure your valuable antiques for the cost of replacing them with similar items, regardless of the original price paid. Both dealers and auctioneers can provide a valuation service for a fee.

▶ **A silver card case,** by William Comyns, decorated with repoussé cherubs, London 1904, 4in (10cm) high.
£350–400
€ / $550–630 ⊞ BLm

Casters

A pair of silver casters, maker's mark for Samuel Welder, London 1714, 5in (12.5cm) high.
£750–900
€ / $1,200–1,400 ➚ TMA

A set of three silver casters, maker ES, Exeter 1727, largest 6¼in (16cm) high.
£5,000–6,000
€ / $8,000–9,500 ➚ G(L)

Expert's choice

A silver-gilt casting bottle, 1553, sold by Sotheby's in 1984.

In all my years as a dealer, the most extraordinary story I have ever heard concerns a little bottle that was found in a box on a market stall and presumed to be made of brass. It was a pretty thing so, having purchased it for a nominal amount, its new owner took it to Sotheby's to have it checked out. The experts there couldn't believe their eyes. It was identified as a silver-gilt casting bottle, used for sprinkling rosewater over the hands, dating from 1553, during the reign of Mary Tudor. The little bottle is exceptionally rare because it is fully hallmarked and only three other such pieces are known, of which two are in museums. It was sold at Sotheby's to Arthur Gilbert for £100,000 (€ / $158,000) in 1984 and is now on display in the Gilbert Collection at Somerset House, The Strand, London. **Nicholas Shaw**

◀ **A silver sugar caster,** by Haseler & Haseler, with a blue glass liner, London 1898, 7½in (19cm) high, 4oz.
£230–275
€ / $360–430 ➚ WW

▶ **A silver sugar caster,** by Charles and George Asprey, London 1904, 9in (23cm) high.
£200–235
€ / $320–370 ⊞ PGO

SILVER

Centrepieces

A silver centrepiece, by John and Joseph Angell, with pierced foliate decoration, on foliate scrolling feet, London 1843, 10in (25.5cm) high.
£450–525
€/ **$700–830** ⚲ SWO

Items in the Silver section have been arranged in date order within each sub-section.

A neo-Renaissance-style silver épergne, by HW, the central reeded stem and three arched arms supporting etched glass sweetmeat bowls on later silver sconces, on a circular base with three cast hairy-paw feet, London 1877, 17¼in (44cm) high, 57oz.
£2,200–2,500
€/ **$3,500–4,000** ⚲ WL

A Victorian silver centrepiece, with gilt interior and repoussé decoration, 19in (48.5cm) wide.
£1,700–2,000
€/ **$2,700–3,200** ⚲ JDJ

A silver centrepiece, by Gorham Manufacturing Co, with wavy embossed and pierced rim, numbered, American, Providence, Rhode Island 1901, 18¼in (46.5cm) wide, 45oz.
£1,400–1,600
€/ **$2,200–2,500** ⚲ S(NY)

A silver épergne, the baskets with glass liners, Sheffield 1909, 11½in (29cm) high.
£3,200–3,500
€/ **$5,000–5,500** ⊞ BLm

A silver épergne, the lobed central dish flanked by two similar smaller dishes, supported by scrolled branches, on a spreading base with scroll feet, Birmingham 1910, 9in (23cm) high, 56oz.
£650–750
€/ **$1,000–1,200** ⚲ G(B)

A silver centrepiece, with a glass liner, London 1911, 8½in (21.5cm) high.
£2,300–2,500
€/ **$3,600–4,000** ⊞ BLm

Chocolate, Coffee & Teapots

A silver coffee pot, by Gabriel Sleath, with later chased decoration and a crest, London 1732, 9¾in (25cm) high, 26oz.
£1,000–1,200
€/ **$1,600–1,900** ⚲ S(O)

▶ **A silver coffee jug,** by John Craig, Irish, Dublin 1772, 12in (30.5cm) high.
£4,700–5,200
€/ **$7,400–8,200** ⊞ WELD

◀ **A silver teapot,** by James Ker, Scottish, Edinburgh 1737–38, 5in (12.5cm) high.
£5,000–5,500
€/ **$8,000–8,700** ⊞ NS

A silver chocolate pot, by Pehr Zethelius, the sliding knop modeled as a flower, with ebonized handle, Swedish, Stockholm 1782, 6¾in (17cm) high.
£3,500–4,000
€/ **$5,500–6,400** ⚲ BUK

Miller's Compares

I. A silver teapot, by Hester Bateman, chased with floral festoons around a cartouche and crest, with green-stained ivory handle, London 1786, 7in (18cm) high, 16oz.
£2,100–2,500
€/ **$3,300–4,000** ✦ WW

II. A silver teapot, by Thomas Shepherd, with a fruitwood handle, London 1786, 5½in (14cm) high, 12.5oz.
£650–750
€/ **$1,000–1,200** ✦ WW

A silver coffee pot, by William Moody, London 1786, 13in (33cm) high.
£4,000–4,500
€/ **$6,300–7,000** ⊞ TSC

Item I was made by Hester Bateman, who is always sought after by collectors. The piece is particularly desirable because of its unusual design. The pierced rim around the foot is a feature which is rarely seen, although it is not particularly practical since, as in this example, it gets damaged very easily. If the rim had been in perfect condition, the teapot might well have sold for in excess of £2,500 (€/ $4,000). Item I also has a very attractive green-stained ivory handle, which is unusually decorated with a *piqué* work pattern in steel. Item II has a standard fruitwood handle.

A silver teapot, by Jabez Halsey, with a monogram in a cartouche, swags and a cluster of strawberries, with a pineapple finial, maker's mark, American, New York c1790, 6½in (16.5cm) high, 18oz.
£3,300–3,800
€/ **$5,200–6,000** ✦ S(NY)

n early Victorian silver-gilt ffee pot, by Charles Reily and eorge Storer, the body engraved ith a ducal coronet above a cypher, e spout with a hinged cover, the ndle hinged to fold, on a heater se, 6¾in (17cm) high, 16.75oz.
50–1,000
/ **$1,300–1,600** ✦ CGC

A silver coffee pot, by Giulio II Zanetti, the body decorated with bands of leaves and palmettes, the spout terminating in a bird's head, with an ebonized wood handle, Italian, Bologna c1840, 12in (30.5cm) high.
£1,400–1,600
€/ **$2,200–2,500** ✦ DORO

A silver teapot, by Martin Hall & Co, embossed with rococo-style decoration, with an eagle finial, on four scroll feet, Sheffield 1909, 7½in (19cm) high, 25.5oz.
£280–325
€/ **$440–510** ✦ BR

igar & Cigarette Cases

A silver cigar case, Birmingham 1903, 5in (12.5cm) wide.
£80–100
€/ **$125–160** ✦ G(L)

silver cigar case with a hinged d, by Nathaniel Mills, one side graved with the Crystal Palace ithin a floral and scroll frame, e reverse engraved with a foliate roll cartouche on an engine-turned nd ground, Birmingham 1850, n (12.5cm) high.
50–625
/ **$870–1,000** ✦ RTo

A silver cigarette case, with a silver-gilt interior, initialled 'MM', Russian, 19thC, 3½in (9cm) wide.
£100–120
€/ **$160–190** ✦ SWO

▶ **A silver and gold-mounted officer's cheroot case,** Russian, Moscow 1908–17, 6in (15cm) wide.
£2,500–2,800
€/ **$4,000–4,400** ⊞ SHa

Clocks & Watches

A Victorian silver heart-shaped desk timepiece, with foliate scroll engraving, 4in (10cm) high.
£120–140
€/ $190–220 ✗ G(L)

◀ **A silver-cased carriage clock,** by William Comyns, with an enamel dial and French platform movement, on four bun feet, London 1901, 3¾in (9.5cm) high.
£650–750
€/ $1,000–1,200 ✗ DMC

A silver watch, by Mappin & Webb, on a hobnail-cut glass inkwell, Birmingham c1905, 4in (10cm) wide.
£1,100–1,300
€/ $1,700–2,000 ⊞ HCA

English antique silver 1976–2002

This graph shows the increasing value of English antique silver as a whole over the past 25 years. International influences on the silver market at various times over the years have also had an effect on the growth of English antique silver. ©AMR

A silver carriage clock, with eight-day French movement, and platform lever escapement, inscribed 'Goldsmith & Silversmiths Co, Regent Street', London 1905, 3in (7.5cm) high.
£670–750
€/ $1,100–1,200 ⊞ PSA

▶ **A silver miniature longcase clock,** with an easel back, Birmingham 1912, 6¼in (16cm) high.
£140–160
€/ $220–250 ✗ SWO

Coffee & Tea Services

A silver three-piece tea service, by William Fountain, the milk jug and sugar bowl with gilt interiors and wrythen handles cast in the shape of entwined horns of plenty, all on pedestal bases with gadrooned borders, London 1805–08, 57oz.
£800–1,000
€/ $1,300–1,600 ✗ WW

▶ **A silver five-piece tea and coffee service,** by William Forbes for Ball, Tomkins & Black, the sides flat-chased with rococo cartouches and engraved with a monogram, American, New York c1845, coffee pot 10in (25.5cm) high, 100oz.
£2,000–2,400
€/ $3,200–3,800 ✗ S(NY)

A silver three-piece tea service, with half-fluted bodies, the hinged teapot lid with an embossed finial, the loop handle moulded with acanthus leaf, on bun feet, London 1822 and 1823, 36oz.
£700–850
€/ $1,100–1,300 ✗ AH

A silver four-piece tea and coffee service, by Charles Reily and George Storer, with flower-spray finials, chased with leaves and flowers, engraved with an ermine crest, with leafy S-scroll handles, on scroll panel feet, London 1840, coffee pot 10in (25.5cm) high, 87oz.
£1,300–1,500
€/ $2,000–2,400 ✗ Bri

A silver neo-classical four-piece tea and coffee service, by Edward Barnard & Sons, the teapot and coffee pot with pineapple finials, each piece decorated in relief with human masks, floral swags and leaves, chased with ribbons, swags, bellflowers and medallions, London 1868, 83oz.
£2,800–3,200
€/ $4,400–5,000 ✗ PFK

SILVER

silver five-piece tea and coffee service, by Charles
uart Harris, London 1886–87, 100oz.
,300–4,800
/ $6,800–7,600 ⊞ JC

arles Stuart Harris entered his mark in 1852 as a
poon Maker'. Later in 1896 he was described as a
ver worker. He carried on in business until 1904,
hen the firm became known as C. S. Harris & Sons Ltd.

A silver three-piece tea service, by Elkington,
Birmingham 1891, teapot 4in (10cm) high.
£1,200–1,300
€ / $1,900–2,000 ⊞ BLm

silver three-piece tea service,
Barnard Bros, London 1898,
n (7.5cm) high.
50–600
/ $870–950 ⊞ GRe

A silver and porcelain coffee set,
by Elkington & Co, with Copelands
China coffee cans and saucers, on
bun feet, one coffee can and saucer
missing, Birmingham 1899, stand
14¼in (36cm) wide.
£350–420
€ / $550–670 ⚒ RTo

A silver part tea and coffee service,
by Sebastian Garrard, the engine-
turned baluster bodies with ivory
handles, the covers with a crest in the
form of a ram's head, 1910, 124oz.
£900–1,100
€ / $1,400–1,700 ⚒ L

ondiment Pots

pair of silver bun salts, on pad
et, London 1735, 4in (10cm) diam.
00–120
/ $160–190 ⚒ G(L)

A silver novelty salt, modelled as
open sack, 1874, 2½in (6.5cm) high.
200–225
/ $315–350 ⚒ G(L)

A pair of silver salts, by
William Plummer, London 1784,
3in (7.5cm) diam.
£550–625
€ / $870–990 ⊞ HCA

silver hexagonal mustard pot,
ith associated mustard spoon,
859, 3½in (9cm) high.
200–250
/ $315–400 ⚒ SWO

A silver mustard pot, London
911, 3½in (9cm) high.
260–300
/ $400–475 ⊞ GRe

A pair of silver parcel-gilt salts, by
Henry Chawner, of pedestal design
with twin-reeded loop handles and
conforming banding, London 1796,
3in (7.5cm) high.
£300–350
€ / $470–550 ⚒ GTH

A pair of cut-glass mustard pots,
with silver mounts, Birmingham
1903, 3in (7.5cm) high.
£120–135
€ / $190–215 ⊞ BrL

A pair of silver salts, by Gorham &
Co, each with three drop ring handles
and Greek key border, on three cast
winged sphinx feet, incised '410',
American, 1913, 3½in (9cm) diam.
£200–225
€ / $315–350 ⚒ WW

Cruets

A silver cruet, by Thomas Daniell, the central beaded loop handle incorporating a pierced spacer for the eight cut-glass silver-mounted bottles, on claw-and-ball feet, London 1784, 9¾in (25cm) high.
£900–1,100
€/ **$1,400–1,700** ⚒ CGC

A silver cruet, by Pehr Zethelius, with four silver-mounted bottles, on paw feet, Stockholm 1797, 13½in (34.5cm) wide.
£1,200–1,400
€/ **$1,900–2,200** ⚒ BUK

A silver cruet, by Rebecca Emes and Edward Barnard, on anthemion-cast feet, three bottles missing, London 1827, 7½in (19cm) wide.
£250–300
€/ **$400–475** ⚒ BR

▶ **A silver condiment set,** comprising three pieces, by Barnards, London 1899, largest 4in (10cm) high.
£240–265
€/ **$380–420**
⊞ GRe

Cups & Goblets

A silver tumbler cup, the base marked 'AW, probably by Clement Reed, York 1694, 3in (7.5cm) high, 2oz.
£4,200–5,000
€/ **$6,600–8,000** ⚒ TEN

A Britannia standard silver tea cup, by VN, with a scrolled handle and a moulded base, engraved with a crest, London 1697, 2½in (6.5cm) high.
£4,200–5,000
€/ **$6,600–8,000** ⚒ TRM

A silver wine goblet, by Henry Chawner, the bell bowl engraved with a coat-of-arms, on a reel-shaped base, London 1789–90, 6½in (16.5cm) high, 9.75oz.
£1,800–2,000
€/ **$2,800–3,200** ⊞ NS

Cutlery

A silver spoon, with a fig-shaped bowl, the silver-gilt baluster terminal pricked with initials 'E P', London 1572.
£1,700–2,000
€/ **$2,700–3,200** ⚒ DN

A silver trefid spoon, by William Matthew, with a bead and reeded rat-tail, reverse of stem marked, London c1690, 8in (20.5cm) long, 2.25oz.
£275–325
€/ **$430–515** ⚒ WW

A silver tablespoon, by Jeremiah Morgan, Irish, Clonmel c1750, 8in (20.5cm) long.
£2,500–2,800
€/ **$4,000–4,400** ⊞ WELD
Items from Clonmel are very rare.

A pair of silver table spoons, by W & PC, Edinburgh 1826, 9in (23cm) long.
£80–90
€/ **$125–140** ⊞ WAC

Dishes

A pair of silver-gilt dishes, with scroll borders and trellis-pierced panels engraved with armorials, on scroll feet, 19thC, 10in (25.5cm) diam.
£625–725
€/ $1,000–1,100 ♣ G(L)

A silver bonbon dish, by Mappin & Webb, relief decorated with shells and flowerheads, with scroll-edged lattice-pierced panels, hallmarked Sheffield 1906, 10½in (26.5cm) diam, 10oz.
£120–150
€/ $190–240 ♣ PFK

A silver dish, embossed with the mask of a mastiff dog surrounded by a whip, Sheffield 1909, 4¾in (12cm) diam, 21oz.
£120–150
€/ $190–240 ♣ HOLL

◀ A set of four silver dishes, by Tiffany & Co, c1910, boxed, 5½in (14cm) wide.
£675–750
€/ $1,100–1,200
⊞ SHa

A silver bonbon dish, by H. Vale & Co, with pierced decoration, Chester 1911, 8in (20.5cm) wide.
£270–300
€/ $430–475 ⊞ CoHA

Covered Dishes

A pair of silver entrée dishes and covers, by The Goldsmiths & Silversmiths Co, crested, London 1903, 9½in (24cm) wide, 73oz.
£800–1,000
€/ $1,300–1,600 ♣ CGC

▶ A pair of silver entrée dishes and covers, by The Goldsmiths & Silversmiths Co, crested, London 1903, 9½in (24cm) wide, 73oz.

A pair of silver entrée dishes, with gadrooned rims and detachable foliate-scrolled loop handles, with chased crests, maker's mark 'J.A.', London 1777–78, 11½in (29cm) wide, 100oz.
£2,200–2,500
€/ $3,500–4,000 ♣ AH

A silver-gilt covered dish and stand, with a fruit finial, French, 19thC, 7in (18cm) wide, 16oz.
£200–250
€/ $315–400 ♣ TRM

A silver revolving breakfast dish, with a rotating lid and two removeable trays, Sheffield 1908, 13in (33cm) wide.
£550–650
€/ $870–1,000 ♣ B(W)

Dish Rings & Crosses

A silver dish cross, by Hester Bateman, with a pear-shaped lamp, London 1782, 12½in (32cm) extended, 13oz.
£1,600–1,900
€/ $2,500–3,000 ♣ S(NY)

A silver dish ring, with a glass liner, Sheffield 1907, 4in (10cm) high.
£1,300–1,400
€/ $2,000–2,200 ⊞ BLm

A silver dish ring, decorated with hounds within chased and engraved foliage, Irish, Dublin 1909, 4in (10cm) high, 15oz.
£1,800–2,200
€/ $2,800–3,500 ♣ JAd

SILVER

SILVER

Dressing Table Sets

A six-piece silver-backed dressing table set, Chester 1909, cased.
£80–100
€/ $130–160 ⚒ WilP

A silver dressing table set, Sheffield 1918, in fitted inlaid wood case, 15in (38cm) wide.
£380–425
€/ $600–670 ⊞ GRe

A silver and tortoiseshell seven-piece dressing table set, Birmingham 1920.
£650–750
€/ $1,000–1,200 ⚒ BR

Ewers & Jugs

A small coin silver creamer, by Thomas Barton Simpkins, the bulbous body with a scroll handle on three trifid feet, decorated with a crest and three inscriptions, American, 1724–1804, 3¾in (9.5cm) high.
£4,500–5,300
€/ $7,000–8,300 ⚒ JDJ

A silver cream jug, by John Bridge, London 1826, 5in (12.5cm) wide.
£270–300
€/ $430–475 ⊞ CoHA

A silver wine ewer, by Andrew Fogelberg, London 1780, 11in (28cm) high.
£1,800–2,000
€/ $2,800–3,200 ⊞ TSC

A silver water jug, by J. Mackay, with a mask spout, bracket handle and foliate finial, engraved with a coat-of-arms, Edinburgh 1840, 10½in (26.5cm) high, 33oz.
£1,400–1,600
€/ $2,200–2,500 ⚒ B(Ed)

◀ A silver pitcher, by the International Silver Co, engraved with swags and navette-shaped cartouches, with a waisted top and a C-scroll handle, American, Connecticut, c1930, 9½in (24cm) high.
£350–400
€/ $550–630 ⚒ NOA

A silver jug, engraved with two opposing shell and scroll cartouches, with a mask spout, scrolling figurative handle and a finial modelled as a cherub riding a swan, 19thC, 30in (76cm) high.
£320–375
€/ $500–600 ⚒ TMA

A silver hot water jug, with an ebony handle, 1900, 11in (28cm) high.
£270–300
€/ $430–475 ⊞ EXC

A silver cream jug, by Rebecca Emes and Edward Barnard, London 1820, 4½in (11.5cm) high.
£260–285
€/ $400–450 ⊞ PGO

A Victorian Cellini pattern Renaissance-style ewer, by John Samuel Hunt, with chased crest, gilded interior and original cork stopper, 11½in (29cm) high, 38oz.
£1,200–1,400
€/ $1,900–2,200 ⚒ AH
The Cellini pattern ewer was a standard design of claret jug made throughout the second half of the 19th century. It was so named because it was similar to a piece made by the 16th-century Italian goldsmith Benvenuto Cellini.

Figures

A silver whistle, in the form of a sailor, Continental, probably Danish, c1874, 3in (7.5cm) long.
£765–850
€/ **$1,200–1,300** ⊞ NS

◀ **A silver-gilt wager cup,** in the form of a young lady holding a swinging cup above her head, probably by Joseph Angell, London 1828, 6¾in (17cm) high, 7oz.
£4,000–4,800
€/ **$6,300–7,600** ⚒ HOLL
This piece had been stored in a bank vault for approximately 100 years and is still in mint condition.

A silver figure of a knight, with an ivory face, the armour elaborately chased, on a quatrefoil-shaped plinth, import marks for 1905, Austrian, c1900, 15¾in (40cm) high, 43oz.
£1,700–2,000
€/ **$2,700–3,200** ⚒ TEN

Flasks

◀ **A silver flask,** maker's mark JW, early 18thC, 5in (13cm) high, 5oz.
£900–1,100
€/ **$1,400–1,700** ⚒ S(O)

▶ **A silver-mounted hip flask,** by James Dixon & Sons, engraved with a crest and a motto, with a crocodile skin sleeve, Sheffield 1895, 6¾in (17cm) high.
£85–100
€/ **$135–160** ⚒ BR

A silver hip flask, Birmingham 1920, 7in (18cm) high.
£260–285
€/ **$400–450** ⊞ GRe

Frames

▶ **A silver frame,** Birmingham 1902, 8in (20.5cm) high.
£220–245
€/ **$350–380** ⊞ WAC

A silver frame, by Sothers, Orchard & Co, with lightly hammered surface, Birmingham 1907–08, 11¼in (28.5cm) high.
£675–750
€/ **$1,100–1,200** ⊞ NS

A silver frame, Birmingham 1903, 7in (18cm) high.
£160–175
€/ **$250–275** ⊞ BrL

late Victorian silver-mounted easel dressing table mirror, embossed with C-scrolls and flowers round an engraved cartouche, bevelled glass, 14½in (37cm) high.
£280–320
€/ **$440–500** ⚒ EH

A silver-gilt frame, with engine-turned decoration and Greek key border, London 1913, 4¾in (12cm) high.
£120–150
€/ **$190–240** ⚒ TMA

SILVER

Inkstands & Inkwells

▶ **A silver and copper inkstand,** by Black, Starr & Frost, the cartouche-shaped stand with applied bearskin above a pen tray, with applied border of whiplash scrolls, the cut-glass inkwell applied with a bull's head, American, New York c1905, 13½in (34.5cm) wide.
£3,000–3,500
€/ **$4,700–5,500** ⚒ S(NY)

A silver inkstand, by Messrs Angell, the raised pierced borders decorated with scrolls, shells and foliage, with two silver-mounted cut-glass inkpots and a chamber-stick and snuffer, retailer's stamp, London 1840, 13½in (34.5cm) wide, 42.5oz.
£1,500–1,800
€/ **$2,400–2,800** ⚒ E

◀ **A silver inkstand,** by William Hutton & Son, Sheffield 1908, 9in (23cm) wide.
£350–385
€/ **$550–600**
⊞ GRe

Kettles

◀ **A silver 'toy' tea kettle,** probably by David Clayton, London c1715, 3¾in (9.5cm) high.
£650–775
€/ **$1,000–1,200** ⚒ HYD

▶ **A silver tea kettle and stand,** by Pezé Pilleau, engraved with armorials and a crest within rococco cartouches below a chased shoulder of flowers and scrolls, the stand with floral aprons and shell feet, London 1751, 11½in (29cm) high, 52oz.
£1,300–1,500
€/ **$2,000–2,400** ⚒ S(O)

A silver kettle and stand, by J. T. Heath & J. H. Middleton, with fluted decoration, London 1891, 10¼in (26cm) high, 36oz.
£400–470
€/ **$630–740** ⚒ WW

Lamps

A silver storm chamber lamp, with a gadrooned base, ring handle and bayonet fitting glass shade, initialled, maker's mark HE?, London 1817, 4¾in (12cm) diam, 6.5oz.
£525–625
€/ **$830–1,000** ⚒ WW

A silver-gilt hanging lamp, in the form of an angel's head, maker's mark 'C.H.', Workmaster Alexander N. Mitin, Russian, St Petersburg 1851, 21¾in (55.5cm) long, 15oz.
£1,100–1,300
€/ **$1,700–2,000** ⚒ DORO

A silver hand lantern, by Drew & Sons, with hinged glazed cover, the back with finger grips and engraved crest and initials 1894, 4¼in (11cm) high.
£950–1,100
€/ **$1,500–1,700** ⚒ L

▶ **A silver carriage lamp,** by Frederick Perry, with hinged cover and door and sprung candle holder, 1882, 6in (15cm) high, 15oz.
£800–1,000
€/ **$1,300–1,600** ⚒ G(L)

Items in the Silver section have been arranged in date order.

SILVER

Menu Holders

parcel-gilt menu holder, Sampson Mordan & Co, modelled as a stack of four grenades, London c1881, in (5.5cm) high.
160–200
/ $250–315 ✦ WW

▶ **A pair of silver menu holders,** by Mappin & Webb, in the shape of galleons, London 1899–1900, 2in (5cm) high, 1.75oz.
£340–375
€/ $550–600 ⊞ NS

To order Miller's books in the UK please ring 01903 828800. See the full range at **www.millers.uk.com**

◀ **A set of six silver menu holders,** Chester 1913, 1½in (4cm) high.
£400–450
€/ $630–700 ⊞ EXC

Mirrors

silver toilet mirror, embossed and chased with flowers and scrolls, maker's initials for A. & J. Zimmerman, Birmingham 1886, 14in (35.5cm) high.
280–325
/ $440–515 ✦ G(L)

A silver-mounted dressing table mirror, by William Comyns, with an easel back, decorated in relief with C-scrolls, floral sprays and husks, London 1899, 12in (30.5cm) high.
£350–425
€/ $550–670 ✦ WW

A silver mirror, Chester 1900, 17in (43cm) high.
£675–750
€/ $1,100–1,200 ⊞ GRe

An Edwardian silver presentation toilet mirror, embossed with scrolls and flowerheads, with velvet backing, 20in (51cm) high.
£320–400
€/ $500–630 ✦ AH

SILVER

Mugs & Tankards

◀ **A lady's silver tankard,** by William Andrews, 1697–98, 5in (12.5cm) high.
£4,500–5,500
€/ $7,100–8,700 ⊞ NS

silver miniature christening mug, London 1855, 3in (7.5cm) high, with original case.
250–275
/ $400–440 ⊞ CoHA

A silver tankard, by John Cuthbert, with a hollow scroll handle, Irish, Dublin 1704–06, 4in (10cm) high, 7oz.
£1,100–1,300
€/ $1,700–2,000 ✦ HOK

▶ **A silver christening mug,** London 1863, 4in (10cm) high.
£315–350
€/ $500–550 ⊞ BrL

A silver tankard, by P. Muller, Russian, St Petersburg 1830, 6in (15cm) high.
£1,600–1,800
€/ $2,500–2,800 ⊞ SHa

Napkin Rings

◀ **A pair of silver napkin rings,** by E. J. & W. Barnard, chased with floral scrolls, London 1874, in an Elkington & Co box.
£180–220
€/ **$285–350** ⚷ FEN

A pair of silver napkin rings, London 1891, in box 5½in (14cm) wide.
£220–245
€/ **$350–380** ⊞ BLm

A set of four silver napkin rings, Sheffield 1899, 1¾in (4.5cm) diam.
£180–200
€/ **$285–315** ⊞ GRe

◀ **A set of four silver napkin rings,** by H. W. Ltd, with C-scroll edges and foliate-chased decoration, Birmingham 1907, in original case.
£150–175
€/ **$240–275** ⚷ PFK

Rattles

◀ **A baby's silver rattle,** by Joseph Willmore, with eight bells, coral teether and whistle, Birmingham 1807, 5in (12.5cm) long.
£575–675
€/ **$900–1,100** ⚷ G(B)

A baby's silver rattle, by Joseph Willmore, with chased decoration, four bells, coral teether and whistle, Birmingham c1825, 5in (12.5cm) long.
£275–325
€/ **$440–500** ⚷ WW

A Victorian baby's silver rattle, with six bells, ivory ring and whistle, 5in (12.5cm) long.
£330–400
€/ **$520–630** ⚷ JDJ

Salvers & Trays

A silver salver, by Samuel Reily, Irish, Cork c1795, 6in (15cm) wide.
£2,100–2,300
€/ **$3,300–3,600** ⊞ WELD

> **For more Salvers & Trays**
> see Papier Mâché page 605

A silver salver, by Walter and John Barnard, London 1892, 10in (25.5cm) diam, 16oz.
£350–400
€/ **$550–630** ⊞ GRe

A silver salver, with piecrust border and scroll feet, Sheffield 1909, 15in (38cm) diam.
£320–375
€/ **$500–600** ⚷ G(L)

SILVER

Sauce Boats

A pair of silver sauce boats, by Tiffany & Co, Director's mark for Edward Moore, American, c1870, 7in (18cm) wide.
£2,500–2,800
€/ **$4,000–4,400** ⊞ SHa

A pair of silver sauce boats, by Robert Innes, with an armorial, London 1748, 8in (20.5cm) wide.
£4,500–5,000
€/ **$7,000–8,000** ⊞ PAY

▶ **A pair of silver sauce boats,** by Charles Stuart Harris, with gadrooned rims and leaf-capped double scroll handles, London 1897, 7¾in (19.5cm) wide, 30oz.
£950–1,100
€/ **$1,500–1,700** ↗ WW

A pair of silver sauce boats, by Stewart Dawson, London 1911, 4in (10cm) high.
£600–670
€/ **$950–1,100** ⊞ GRe

Scent Bottles

A silver-mounted glass scent bottle, with hinged domed cover and stopper, Continental, 19thC, 4¼in (11cm) high.
£150–175
€/ **$240–275** ↗ TMA

▶ **A silver scent bottle,** engraved in the Kate Greenaway style with a child by a church, with hinged cover, London 1882, 2½in (6.5cm) high.
£220–280
€/ **$350–440** ↗ G(L)

A Victorian silver-mounted glass scent bottle/ vinaigrette, by Sampson Mordan & Co, with two hinged covers opening to reveal glass stoppers at one end, the other end a vinaigrette, incised maker's mark and registration lozenge, 3¾in (9.5cm) high.
£650–750
€/ **$1,000–1,200** ↗ WW

SILVER

Serving Implements

◀ **A set of six silver salt spoons,** by Joseph Willmore, in the shape of buttercups, with leaf handles, Birmingham 1827.
£375–425
€/ **$600–670** ↗ G(L)

A silver soup ladle, London 1865, 13in (33cm) long.
£250–285
€/ **$400–450** ⊞ PGO

A silver sauce ladle, by W. Eley and W. Fearn, London 1805, 7in (18cm) long.
£150–165
€/ **$240–260** ⊞ BEX

◀ **A silver punch ladle,** the finial formed as a female Egyptian term, the bowl engraved with a monogram, American, c1870, 15in (38cm) long, 9oz.
£1,400–1,600
€/ **$2,200–2,500** ↗ S(NY)

Snuff Boxes

A silver snuff box, by Joseph and John Angell, London 1846–47, 4in (10cm) wide, in a fitted case.
£6,800–7,500
€/ **$10,700–11,800** ⊞ NS
This piece is in immaculate condition and is therefore very desirable.

A silver snuff box, by Richard Lockwood, with bright-engraved diaper border, the cover with a crest, 1805, 2½in (6.5cm) wide.
£550–650
€/ **$870–1,000** ✦ B(Wm)

▶ **A silver snuff box,** with gilt interior, the top engraved with a view of the Kaiser Franz memorial, Vienna, silversmith Josef Witek, Austrian, Vienna 1846, 3¼in (8.5cm) wide, 3.5oz.
£400–475
€/ **$630–750** ✦ DORO

A silver table snuff box, by Nathaniel Mills, Birmingham 1834, 3½in (9cm) wide.
£2,400–2,700
€/ **$3,800–4,300** ⊞ BEX

A silver trompe l'oeil snuff box, engraved with warrants and trade label to simulate those on a Havana cigar box, maker's mark, Russian, Moscow 1896–1905, 3in (7.5cm) wide, 2.25oz.
£280–325
€/ **$440–515** ✦ WW

Snuffer Trays

▶ **A pair of silver snuffers and tray,** tray by John Carter, snuffers by John Baker, London 1771, tray 6½in (16.5cm) wide.
£1,100–1,300
€/ **$1,700–2,000** ⊞ GRe

A silver-gilt snuffer tray, by Johann Martin Satzger, engraved with a cypher below a coronet within flat-chased rococo decoration, German, Augsburg 1753–55, 7½in (19cm) wide, 8.75oz.
£1,200–1,400
€/ **$1,900–2,200** ✦ S(O)

◀ **A silver snuffer tray,** by John Emes, with a reeded rim, engraved frieze and vacant wreath cartouche, London 1801, 10in (25.5cm) wide, 4.5oz.
£320–400
€/ **$500–630** ✦ WW

Table Bells

▶ **A silver table bell,** the handle cast as a boy with a goblet and bottle in his hands, the bell with a cast frieze of dancers and a musician in a rural setting, import marks for London 1902, Continental, early 20thC, 5½in (14cm) high, 4.25oz.
£150–175
€/ **$140–275** ✦ GTH

A silver twist bell, Birmingham 1895, 3in (7.5cm) high.
£630–700
€/ **$1,000–1,100** ⊞ BLm

▶ **A silver-mounted table bell,** by William Comyns, with push button top and pierced sides of scrolling shamrock, London 1903, 4¼in (11cm) diam.
£475–550
€/ **$750–870** ✦ B(L)

SILVER

Tea Caddies

A silver tea caddy, by Peter, Anne and William Bateman, with wooden finial, with key, London 1805, 6¾in (17cm) wide, 16.5oz.
£1,000–1,200
€/ **$1,600–1,900** ⚒ CGC

A silver tea caddy, embossed with leaf and scroll decoration, the hinged cover with leaf and ball finial, maker's marks for John Harrison & Co, Sheffield 1852, 4¼in (11cm) high.
£320–375
€/ **$500–600** ⚒ FEN

A silver tea caddy, London 1860, 6½in (16.5cm) high.
£1,100–1,300
€/ **$1,700–2,000** ⊞ BLm

▶ **A silver tea caddy,** by West & Son, London 1908, 4in (10cm) high.
£270–300
€/ **$425–475** ⊞ GRe

A silver tea caddy, of lobed form, on lion-paw feet, Chester 1895, 5in (12.5cm) high.
£300–350
€/ **$475–550** ⚒ G(L)

LOCATE THE SOURCE
The source of each illustration in Miller's can be found by checking the code letters below each caption with the Key to Illustrations, pages 794–800.

Toast Racks

A silver toast rack, by Thomas Halford, London 1810, 6in (15cm) wide.
£430–475
€/ **$680–750** ⊞ GRe

A silver toast rack, by Paul Storr (Storr & Mortimer), London 1832, 5¼in (13.5cm) high, 11.75oz.
£1,000–1,200
€/ **$1,600–1,900** ⚒ CGC

A silver toast rack, c1890, 4in (10cm) wide.
£100–115
€/ **$160–180** ⊞ EXC

SILVER

Vesta Cases

A silver vesta case, 1894, 2in (5cm) wide.
£50–60
€/ **$80–95** ⊞ EXC

A silver table vesta/stamp case, by Samuel Jacobs, London 1894–95, 3in (7.5cm) high.
£1,500–1,700
€/ **$2,400–2,700** ⊞ NS

A silver vesta case, by W. H. Haseler, partially scroll-engraved, with inscription, Birmingham 1912, 2in (5cm) wide.
£80–100
€/ **$125–160** ⚒ WW

Vinaigrettes

A silver vinaigrette, by Joseph Taylor, in the shape of a purse, engraved with flowers and scrolls and pricked borders to simulate stitching, initialled, Birmingham 1810–15, 1in (2.5cm) wide.
£220–260
€/ **$350–400** ⚒ **WW**

A silver vinaigrette, with wire-work grille, Birmingham 1813, 1in (2.5cm) wide.
£180–220
€/ **$280–350** ⚒ **G(L)**

A silver and parcel-gilt vinaigrette, with raised foliate borders, pierced grille and suspension ring, maker's mark, Birmingham 1835, 1½in (4cm) wide, 0.75oz.
£140–170
€/ **$220–275** ⚒ **DMC**

◄ **A silver vinaigrette,** by Nathaniel Mills, depicting the Albert Memorial, Birmingham 1853, 2in (5cm) wide.
£600–675
€/ **$950–1,100** ⊞ **CoHA**

A silver vinaigrette, by George Knight, with chased floral and scrolling decoration, the hinged grille chased and pierced, Birmingham 1870, 1¾in (4.5cm) wide.
£200–225
€/ **$315–350** ⚒ **BR**

A silver novelty vinaigrette, in the shape of a shoe, 1891, 2¾in (7cm) wide.
£100–125
€/ **$160–200** ⚒ **G(L)**

◄ **A silver-mounted horn vinaigrette,** the cover with chased decoration and set with a cairngorm, with gilt interior, Edinburgh 1898, 4in (10cm) wide.
£475–550
€/ **$750–870** ⚒ **EH**

Further reading

Miller's Silver & Plate Buyer's Guide, Miller's Publications, 2002

Wax Jacks

A silver wax jack, by Gawen Nash, the spring-loaded taper holder with plain drip pan and a pierced scroll surmount on each arm, the central pole with acorn knop finial and three bird's claw-and-ball feet, London c1745, 5½in (14cm) high, 6oz.
£1,800–2,200
€/ **$2,800–3,500** ⚒ **WW**

A silver wax jack, by Joseph Lock, London 1777–78, 6in (15cm) high.
£3,000–3,500
€/ **$4,700–5,500** ⊞ **NS**

A silver wax jack, by Henry Chawner, London 1792–93, 7in (18cm) high.
£3,000–3,500
€/ **$4,700–5,500** ⊞ **NS**
Wax jacks were introduced around 1760 and were used for warming up wax for sealing documents.

SILVER

Miscellaneous

A silver desk set, Birmingham 1908, 10¾in (27.5cm) wide, in original case.
£875–975
€/ $1,400–1,550 ⊞ BLm

A silver table lighter, by Hawksworth, Eyre & Co, Sheffield 1907, 4in (10cm) high.
£260–285
€/ $400–450 ⊞ GRe

Items in the Silver Miscellaneous section have been arranged in alphabetical order.

► A pair of silver tea glass holders, by Gustav Klingert, Russian, Moscow 1896, 3½in (9cm) high.
£340–375
€/ $550–600 ⊞ SHa

A silver dish wedge, by Peter and William Bateman, London 1808–09, 6in (15cm) wide.
£1,000–1,100
€/ $1,600–1,700 ⊞ NS

A silver plate, by Paul de Lamerie, the twisted rope rim interspersed with shells and foliage, the border with the arms of the Corporation of London, London 1737, 10in (25.5cm) diam, 20oz.
£2,800–3,400
€/ $4,400–5,400 ⚒ HAM
Paul de Lamerie is among the foremost English silversmiths and his pieces are highly desirable.

A silver hot water jug, by William Eaton, with semi-fluted body and cover with shell and gadrooned borders, the spout with acanthus decoration, London 1821, 8½in (21.5cm) high, 29oz.
£250–300
€/ $400–475 ⚒ G(B)

A coin silver platter, by Newell Harding & Co, the centre engraved with a rococco cartouche with presentation inscription, on cast and applied acanthus feet, American, Boston, c1856, 13¼in (33.5cm) wide, 43oz.
£1,200–1,500
€/ $1,900–2,400 ⚒ NOA

A silver sugar urn, by Frank Knöll, chased with a band of floral decoration, the cover with a flower knop, old repairs, Austrian, Vienna 1814, 6¾in (17cm) high.
£1,500–1,800
€/ $2,400–2,800 ⚒ DORO

A silver wax holder, French, 18thC, 5in (12.5cm) long.
£150–165
€/ $240–260 ⊞ EXC

The Ortiz-Patino Collection

The English late 17th-century chinoiserie silver in the collection of Jaime Ortiz-Patino, sold at Sotheby's New York in 1992. It was the finest and most complete group of such pieces ever to come to auction. In the 1680s, following expansion of trade between Europe and China, there was a ten-year vogue for chinoiserie (decoration depicting Chinese-style motifs such as landscapes, pagodas and figures) and this is perhaps one of the most enchanting periods of English silver. Mr Ortiz-Patino, the grandson of Simon Patino who made his fortune in the tin mines of Bolivia in the late 19th century, came from a renowned family of collectors. When he was arranging to move to London to take up an appointment as Advisor in Europe for the Bolivian government, he realized that his new residence would not be large enough to house his huge collection and much of it would have to be sold. The chinoiserie silver was merely a part of it but included some of the finest examples made. The highlight of the sale was a pair of tankards made in London in 1686, known as the Brownlow tankards, which sold for £504,700 (€/ $797,500). **Nicholas Shaw**

SILVER

Silver Plate

A George III old Sheffield plate pierced cake basket, with bright-cut decoration and beaded rim, engraved with a coat-of-arms, with swing handle, on a pierced foot, 14½in (37cm) wide.
£150–175
€/ $240–275 ⚖ G(L)

A silver-plated candelabra, in the manner of Matthew Boulton, cast with rams' heads, the bases with a coursing dog crest, 19thC, 27¼in (69cm) high.
£275–325
€/ $430–515 ⚖ HOLL

A Victorian silver-plated centrepiece, by Elkington & Co, the beaded plate frame over a foliate-decorated tripod supported by three figures, on three claw feet, glass missing, 22½in (57cm) high.
£750–850
€/ $1,200–1,300 ⚖ CGC

A silver-plated cigar cutter, with a stag's head terminal, 1875–1900, 5½in (14cm) long.
£275–325
€/ $430–515 ⚖ WW

An old Sheffield plate swing-handle cake basket, with a fluted band below a gadrooned edge, engraved with a crest, c1820, 10½in (26.5cm) wide.
£200–240
€/ $315–380 ⚖ B(L)

◄ **An Edwardian silver-plated cake stand,** the pierced top with swing handle, on fluted legs, 10in (20.5cm) diam.
£40–50
€/ $65–80 ⚖ GAK

► **A pair of old Sheffield plate pillar candlesticks,** with fluted columns and Corinthian capitals, the beaded bases with ram's-head masks and swags, c1800, 12½in (32cm) high.
£450–540
€/ $700–850 ⚖ BWL

A Victorian silver-plated and glass centrepiece, 15in (38cm) high.
£1,100–1,200
€/ $1,700–1,900 ⊞ BrL

A Victorian EPNS tazza, the mother-of-pearl bowl supported by a putto standing on a rock- and seashell-cast domed base, on three dolphin and shell feet, 14½in (37cm) high.
£400–500
€/ $630–800 ⚖ GTH

A Victorian electroplated biscuit box, with engraved foliate decoration, the cover with urn-shaped finial, the pierced dish base on claw-and-ball feet, 8in (20.5cm) wide.
£150–175
€/ $240–275 ⚖ BR

> Items in the Silver Plate section have been arranged in alphabetical order.

An old Sheffield plate coffee biggin, with winged fluting and armorials, on a gadrooned foot, c1820, 8in (20.5cm) high.
£420–460
€/ $665–725 ⊞ G&G

A Victorian electroplated serving dish, of neo-classical form, with a gadrooned edge, on stylized paw feet, 13¾in (35cm) wide.
£100–125
€/ $160–200 ⚖ PFK

◀ **A silver-plated bacon dish,** late 19thC, 12in (30.5cm) wide.
£225–250
€/ $350–400 ⊞ GRe

▶ **An old Sheffield plate dish cross,** c1790, 11in (28cm) wide.
£385–430
€/ $600–680 ⊞ GRe

An old Sheffield plate dog collar, with applied moulded edges, inscribed, late 18thC, 5in (12.5cm) wide.
£650–750
€/ $1,000–1,200 ⚒ B

A Victorian silver-plated cutlery set, comprising 12 fish knives and forks and a pair of servers, in original case.
£160–200
€/ $250–315 ⚒ SWO

A Victorian Sheffield plate kettle and stand, engraved with flowers, scallop shells and scrolls beneath a cast scroll rim, with hinged cover, the stand with scrollwork feet, 15¾in (40cm) high.
£220–250
€/ $350–400 ⚒ RTo

An old Sheffield plate samovar, with lion-mask and ring handles, decorated with an heraldic shield, early 19thC, 18½in (47cm) high.
£380–450
€/ $600–700 ⚒ SWO

A silver-plated six-piece tea and coffee service, by Meriden Britannia Co, decorated with repoussé roses below a milled band of birds and flowers, American, Connecticut, c1900–17, pots 6in (15cm) high.
£200–225
€/ $315–350 ⚒ NOA

A Victorian silver-plated tea caddy, with engraved cartouches and borders, the cover with strawberry finial, with lion-mask and drop-ring handles and central internal divider, c1865, 6½in (16.5cm) wide.
£140–160
€/ $220–250 ⚒ WW

A silver-plated spoon warmer, by Benet Fink & Son, in the shape of Aladdin's lamp, c1880, 9in (23cm) wide.
€200–220
€/ $315–350 ⊞ BrL

A George III old Sheffield-plate teapot, with beaded borders, engraved coat-of-arms and ebony handle, 11¾in (30cm) wide.
£100–120
€/ $160–190 ⚒ G(L)

A Victorian silver-plated tray, with foliate border, engraved to centre, 30in (76cm) wide.
€240–275
€/ $380–430 ⚒ L

▶ **A pair of Adam-style silver-plated hot water urns,** decorated with Prince of Wales feathers, with reeded scroll handles, c1910, 23in (58.5cm) high.
£1,800–2,000
€/ $2,800–3,200 ⚒ NOA

SILVER PLATE

Wine Antiques

A painted-iron bar bottle opener, c1905, 9½in (24cm) long.
£120–140
€/ **$190–220** ⊞ JOL

A silver brandy saucepan, by William Fleming, London 1720–21, 3in (7.5cm) high.
£1,500–1,700
€/ **$2,400–2,700** ⊞ NS

A brandy saucepan and cover, by Samuel Wheatley, crested, with turned wooden handles and knop finial, London 1829, bowl 4¼in (11cm) diam, 9oz.
£550–650
€/ **$870–1,000** ⚒ WW

A silver wine coaster, by C. Clarke, with original wooden base, Irish, Dublin, c1775, 5in (12.5cm) diam.
£5,000–5,600
€/ **$8,000–9,000** ⊞ WELD

▶ **A pair of silver wine coasters,** by Matthew Boulton, with pierced sides and turned wooden bases, Birmingham 1813, 5½in (14cm) diam.
£1,200–1,400
€/ **$1,900–2,200** ⚒ BWL

A metal double pillar corkscrew, 19thC, 7in (18cm) long.
£110–120
€/ **$175–190** ⊞ JOL

A double-action corkscrew, with brush and turned base handle, the brass barrel applied with a royal coat-of-arms, 19thC, 7in (18cm) long.
£250–300
€/ **$400–475** ⚒ AH

A horn-handled corkscrew, 19thC, 4in (10cm) long.
£70–75
€/ **$110–120** ⊞ SEA

A Victorian Lunds two-part lever corkscrew, 8in (20.5cm) long.
£85–95
€/ **$135–150** ⊞ WiB

◀ **A folding pocket corkscrew,** containing eight tools, c1820, 2¾in (7cm) wide.
£80–100
€/ **$140–160** ⊞ CS

A silver and tusk corkscrew, Chester 1913, 5½in (14cm) long.
£50–60
€/ **$80–100** ⚒ TMA

> Items in the Wine Antiques section have been arranged in alphabetical order.

▶ **A coromandel decanter box,** the hinged lid releasing the gilt-brass mounted strap-work front doors, containing three spirit decanters, five glasses and a gilt-brass tray, c1870, 12½in (32cm) wide.
£650–725
€/ **$1,000–1,100** ⚒ CGC

A silver-mounted brandy decanter, with a ribbed, moulded body inscribed 'Brandy', Birmingham 1893, 6¾in (17cm) high.
£200–225
€ / $315–355 🔨 L

A Victorian oak tantalus, with silver-plated mounts and three decanters, 12½in (32cm) wide.
£240–275
€ / $380–430 🔨 SWO

A William IV cast-iron wine cooler, with ring handles and foliate motifs, 36in (91.5cm) wide.
£600–700
€ / $950–1,100 🔨 G(L)

A set of four silver-gilt wine labels, by Thomas Eley, in the shape of vine leaves, 1828, 2½in (6.5cm) wide.
£220–260
€ / $350–400 🔨 G(L)

A silver wine funnel and stand, funnel by J. Gibson, stand by Terry & Williams, Irish, Cork 1795, 5in (12.5cm) long.
£3,300–3,600
€ / $5,200–5,700 ⊞ WELD

A silver tantalus, by Frederick Elkington, with three decanters, Birmingham 1881, 14in (35.5cm) high.
£5,500–6,000
€ / $8,700–9,500 ⊞ BLm

A silver wine cooler, chased with yachts, one with enamelled gold flag, a paddle steamer, man o'war and other vessels, with cast seahorse handles, on scallop feet, possibly Martin & Hall, 1874, 10in (25.5cm) diam, 108oz.
£4,500–5,400
€ / $7,100–8,500 🔨 TEN

A pair of silver wine labels, by D. & C. Edwards, Scottish, Glasgow 1905, 1½in (4cm) wide.
£130–145
€ / $200–230 ⊞ GRe

An Edwardian stained bird's-eye maple and ebonized musical liqueur stand, the mechanism activated by opening the six doors, 9½in (24cm) high.
£500–575
€ / $790–910 🔨 SWO

A silver wine cooler, by R. & S. Hennell, engraved on either side with a crest, the everted gadrooned rim applied at intervals with shells, with drop-ring handles and wooden base, London 1808, 10½in (26.5cm) wide.
£5,000–5,500
€ / $8,000–8,700 🔨 S(O)

A set of three cast-silver wine labels, by G. C., with mask, fruiting vine and shell surrounds, 18thC, 2in (5cm) wide.
£250–300
€ / $400–475 🔨 BWL

Clocks

Any clock made before the era of mass production will have a unique tick and strike which can bring a room to life. The huge variety of timepieces produced since the 17th century means that there is always a style to suit every home, even the most minimalist contemporary setting.

English clocks by the most famous makers from the 'Golden Age' of clockmaking (1665–1725) will be expensive but it is still quite possible to find later antique clocks for three-figure sums. The longcase is perhaps the most popular domestic clock and modest 30-hour examples can be found for £1,000 (€/ $1,600) or less. There are still bargains to be found in Victorian and Edwardian chiming clocks. Housed in a variety of cases, they were all made to a very high standard with three-train fusee movements. Those with less space may prefer carriage clocks with their large choice of mechanisms from the simple timepiece to full *grande-sonnerie* striking. Cases are usually of brass with glazed panels on all sides; these are sometimes replaced with porcelain or enamel. Where a larger and more decorative clock can be accommodated it may be worth considering a French boulle bracket clock. Made in large numbers during the 18th and 19th centuries, they usually have high quality movements and the cases are works of art in themselves. Even 18th-century examples are still very reasonably priced. Beware cases that are in poor condition, as restoration of boulle can be very expensive.

The formation of the Antiquarian Horological Society in the 1950s helped lift clock collecting onto a more respectable footing, shedding the image of the eccentric. Regular, specialized clock auctions began in the 1970s, clocks previously having been included in furniture sales.

The market for antique clocks has remained surprisingly stable for many years, and new collectors are continuing to emerge, so I foresee no slowing down of demand in the next 25 years. The difficulty will be to find enough attractive or technically interesting pieces to satisfy this demand. Inevitably, prices will continue to rise, but clocks are still extremely good value when compared with other areas of the antique market.

Michael Turner

British Bracket, Mantel & Table Clocks

An ebonized table clock, by James Snelling, London, with three subsidiary dials, 18thC, 17½in (44.5cm) high.
£3,200–3,800
€/ $5,000–6,000 ⚒ E

A mahogany table clock, the brass dial with separate silvered brass chapter ring, false pendulum, date aperture and strike/silent feature to the arch, the eight-day double fusee movement with verge escapement striking and repeating the hours on a bell, on brass ogee feet, c1765, 17½in (44.5cm) high.
£11,000–13,000
€/ $17,500–21,000 ⊞ PAO

◀ **A mahogany table clock,** by Robert Cox, Christchurch, with concentric calendar, c1785, 20in (51cm) high.
£10,000–11,500
€/ $16,000–18,000 ⊞ JeF

A mahogany chiming table clock, by John Watson, London, the brass dial with twin subsidiary dials for date and strike/silent, the eight-day triple-train fusee movement with verge escapement, chiming and repeating the quarters on eight bells and the hour on a single bell, the back-plate engraved with scrolls and foliage and maker's name, the bell-top case surmounted by brass finials, the sides with gilt-brass caryatids, frets and handles, on ogee-bracket feet, c1770, 22½in (57cm) high.
£20,000–22,500
€/ $31,500–35,500 ⊞ PAO

A George III musical table clock, by James McCabe, London, the dial with silvered chapter ring with Roman numerals within foliate spandrels, three subsidiary dials, chime/silent, fast/slow and selection for seven tunes, the eight-day triple-train fusee movement with anchor escapement, striking the hours on a bell and chiming on 12 bells with pull repeat, the domed pediment surmounted by a gilt-metal ball finial and with panels of silk-backed gilt-metal sound frets, the canted corners with fluted pilasters, on four gilt-metal ogee-bracket feet, 25½in (65cm) high.
£10,000–12,000
€/ $16,000–19,000 ⚒ DN

A mahogany table clock, by William Hambly, Falmouth, the silvered dial with strike/silent and calendar ring and signed 'Willm.Hambly Falmouth', the twin fusee movement with verge escapement, striking on a bell, the backplate engraved with foliate scrolls, the moulded case with brass scale side frets and carrying handle, c1790, 18¾in (47.5cm) high.
£4,000–5,000
€/ **$6,300–8,000** ✦ B(NW)

A chinoiserie-decorated bracket clock, by Richard Laurence, Bath, with original wall bracket, the silvered dial with strike/silent dial over a Roman and Arabic chapter ring and engraved centre, the twin gut fusee movement with five knopped pillars, striking on a bell, decorated with raised gilt Chinese figures and buildings, 18thC, 29in (73.5cm) high.
£9,000–11,000
€/ **$14,200–17,400** ✦ B
Richard Laurence was working from Bath and Warminster between 1729 and 1773.

Spring-driven clocks

The coiled spring was first introduced about 1480. However, it gave poor results due to the variation in the strength of the drive it provided when fully wound up and when nearly run down. To overcome this, the fusee was invented (probably in France) which solved the problem of the uneven drive. The fusee was used throughout Germany, France and England on early portable and table clocks. As the quality of springs improved the fusee fell from use in France and Germany towards the end of the 17th century. It continued to be used in England up to the 20th century. The reluctance of English clockmakers to adapt to modern trends led to the downfall of the industry. When a fusee is fitted to a clock it is an indication of high quality.

▶ **An ebony table clock,** by George Philip Strigels, the brass dial with strike/silent dial in the arch, the eight-day twin-train fusee movement with verge escapement and bob pendulum, striking on a bell, the front and back doors with cut-brass frets on turquoise silk, on brass bracket feet, 18thC, 17¼in (44cm) high.
£4,200–5,000
€/ **$6,600–7,900** ✦ CGC

The prices realized at auction may reflect the fact that the clocks have sometimes undergone alterations to their movements, or are in unrestored condition.

A mahogany and brass-inlaid table clock, by Francis Perigal, London, the painted dial with Arabic and Roman numerals and subsidiary dials to the arch, the double fusee movement with anchor escapement, striking on a bell, with engraved backplate, the case with triple-pad top and brass scale side frets, on bracket feet, c1800, 15in (38cm) high.
£3,700–4,200
€/ **$5,800–6,600** ✦ HYD

A mahogany table clock, by James Parlett Saddleton, Kings Lynn, the silvered brass dial engraved with Roman hours and Arabic minutes, with strike/silent dial to the arch, the eight-day five-pillar double fusee movement with anchor escapement, striking the hours on a bell, the backplate engraved with an urn, foliage and flowers, the broken arch top with three brass-bordered pads and brass handle, on brass ogee-bracket feet, c1795, 17in (43cm) high.
£9,500–10,500
€/ **$15,000–16,500** ⊞ PAO
Clocks with triple-pad tops are particularly desirable.

A mahogany table clock, the painted convex dial with brass bezel, the brass backplate engraved 'Septimus Miles, London', with triple-train fusee movement, the case with fluted tapering pediment with pineapple finials, flanked by gilt-brass carrying handles, on ogee brass feet, c1800, 8¾in (22cm) high.
£2,400–2,800
€/ **$4,000–4,400** ⚲ HOK
Septimus Miles (d1847) was at 32 Ludgate St, London, between 1795 and 1829.

A partridge wood table clock, by Handley & Moore, London, the dial with Roman chapters and strike/silent feature, the eight-day double fusee movement with anchor escapement, striking and repeating the hours on a bell, the backplate with engraved border and maker's name, the engraved pendulum with calibrated rating, the case inlaid with satinwood lines, the sides with scale frets, on four brass ogee feet, c1810, 17in (43cm) high.
£6,500–7,300
€/ **$10,300–11,500** ▦ PAO

▶ **A rosewood and brass-inlaid mantel clock,** with silvered dial, the eight-day twin-chain fusee movement striking on a bell, early 19thC, 11in (28cm) high.
£4,800–5,800
€/ **$7,600–9,200** ⚲ SWO

▶ **A mahogany table clock,** the arched brass dial signed James Burton, Lincoln's Inn, with subsidiary calendar dial and strike/silent dial to the arch, the twin fusee movement with anchor escapement, striking on a bell, the unsigned backplate engraved with foliage and a basket of fruit, with brass carrying handle, on brass bracket feet, early 19thC, 19¼in (49cm) high.
£1,700–2,000
€/ **$2,700–3,200** ⚲ Bea(E)

Bracket/table clocks

Most 17th- and 18th-century English table clocks have carrying handles. A clock would have been an expensive purchase and so most households would have had only one, which would have been used downstairs during the day and carried up to the bedroom at night. These clocks often had quarter repeating work which could be set into action at will during the dark hours thereby audibly indicating the time to the nearest quarter hour. Handles continued to be fitted to the cases of later clocks but these were usually intended only to be decorative.

A mahogany and brass-inlaid mantel timepiece, by Stedman, Godalming, with convex painted dial and fusee movement, on brass ball feet, early 19thC, 15in (38cm) high.
£1,200–1,400
€/ **$1,900–2,200** ⚲ G(L)

An inlaid mahogany table clock, by Thomas Sherwood, Leeds, the repainted dial signed for the maker, the triple-chain fusee movement with tall shouldered plates with engraved shaded edge and pendulum bob, and anchor escapement, chiming on eight bells and striking the hours on another bell, the case with a caddy top, on a stepped base with ball feet, early 19thC, 26¾in (68cm) high.
£1,500–1,800
€/ **$2,400–2,700** ⚲ B
Thomas Sherwood was working from Leeds between 1801 and 1834.

LOCATE THE SOURCE
The source of each illustration in Miller's can be found by checking the code letters below each caption with the Key to Illustrations, pages 794–800.

◀ **A rosewood and brass-inlaid bracket clock,** the painted dial signed 'Burlington & Co, Lynn', the twin fusee movement striking on a gong, the caddy top surmounted by a gilt-metal pineapple finial, loop carrying handles to the sides, with rosewood bracket, early 19thC, 20in (51cm) high.
£1,000–1,200
€/ $1,600–1,900 ⚒ Bea(E)

A mahogany and brass-inlaid mantel clock, the cream dial with Roman numerals and signed 'James McCabe, Royal Exchange, London', with eight-day twin fusee movement, striking on a bell, early 19thC, 18½in (47cm) high.
£2,000–2,400
€/ $3,200–3,800 ⚒ TF

A Regency mahogany mantel clock, by Whitehurst & Son, Derby, with silvered dial and twin fusee movement, backplate and dial engraved with maker's name, finial missing, 17¼in (44cm) high.
£2,700–3,200
€/ $4,300–5,000 ⚒ SWO

A Regency bronze and ormolu mantel timepiece, by Parkinson & Frodsham, with drum case and Roman dial, the plinth with a floral swag, on matched pad feet, dial and back of movement signed, 8¼in (21cm) high.
€1,600–1,900
€/ $2,500–3,000 ⚒ G(L)

A Regency ormolu timepiece, by Viner & Co, London, with an engine-turned dial and single fusee movement, the rococo case with scroll sides, on four feet, hands missing, 8¼in (21cm) high.
£950–1,100
€/ $1,500–1,700 ⚒ B(W)

▶ **A Regency mahogany and brass-inlaid table timepiece,** with painted dial signed 'W. Tanner, Lewes', the inlaid case with acanthus ring handles, surmounted by a fir cone finial, the sides with scale frets, on brass ball feet, 17in (43cm) high.
£1,600–2,000
€/ $2,500–3,200 ⚒ BR

CLOCKS

Striking/chiming/musical clocks

Over the centuries various forms of striking and chiming have been used to announce the time audibly but the terms are often confused.
• Striking: The simplest form of striking is called passing strike. This is when the timepiece does not have a separate striking train but will trip a hammer to strike a single blow on a bell or a gong at the hour. The most usual form of sounding the time is to strike the full number of the hour and sometimes, in addition, the half-hour with a single blow. A more complicated form of striking is often used in Holland and is known as Dutch striking. The hour is sounded on a large bell and at the half hour the next hour is sounded in full on a small bell. Some early English makers used Dutch striking. Another complicated form of striking called Roman striking was used exclusively by the Knibb family of clockmakers.
• Quarter striking: Two different bells or gongs are usually employed to sound ting-tang striking at the quarters. This is sometimes known as *petite sonnerie*. The more complicated form known as *grande sonnerie* is when the hour is sounded at every quarter in addition to the quarter hour.
• Chiming: The clock plays a tuneful phrase on a number of bells or gongs at each quarter. One phrase is played at quarter past the hour, increasing to four phrases at the hour. The most usual form is the Westminster chime used on Big Ben.
• Musical: Some clocks will have a musical train, perhaps in addition to a chiming or striking train. The clock will often play quite a long tune on several bells, usually once every three hours.

CLOCKS

A Regency mahogany table clock, the convex painted dial with Roman numerals, the eight-day twin-train fusee movement with anchor escapement, striking on a bell, the brass-inlaid case surmounted by a gilt-metal acorn finial, feet missing, damaged, 24in (61cm) high.
£1,200–1,400
€ / **$1,900–2,200** 🔨 **DN**

A George IV mahogany and brass-inlaid table clock, the enamel dial with Roman numerals and inscribed 'Chas. Watts, Oxford', with eight-day fusee movement, striking on a bell, the backplate with engraved border, fruiting cornucopia plate ring handles to the sides, above pierced scale frets, on ball feet, 16in (40.5cm) high.
£1,500–1,800
€ / **$2,400–2,800** 🔨 **WW**

A mahogany mantel clock, by Arnold, London, the engraved silvered dial with strike/silent and rise and fall in the arch, the triple-train fusee movement with deadbeat escapement, wood rod pendulum and maintaining power, chiming on eight bells, the case with barley-twist columns and carved scrolls, c1840, 24¾in (63cm) high.
£2,800–3,200
€ / **$4,400–5,000** 🔨 **TEN**

A mahogany mantel timepiece, by Andrew Millar, Edinburgh, with Roman numerals and eight-day movement, the case with ebonized moulding, on pad feet, c1840, 13¾in (35cm) high.
£320–380
€ / **$500–600** 🔨 **TRM**

▶ **A rosewood mantel clock,** the lancet dial with Roman numerals and inscribed 'S. Hart - Devizes', the eight-day twin-train fusee movement with anchor escapement, striking on a bell, the pediment with radiating gadroons surmounted by a gilt-metal pineapple finial, 19thC, 12½in (32cm) high.
£2,000–2,200
€ / **$3,200–3,500** 🔨 **DN**

A table clock, made of West Indian specimen wood, with painted dial and English twin-train fusee movement, c1840, 21in (53.5cm) high.
£2,600–3,000
€ / **$4,000–4,700** ⊞ **APO**

A mahogany table clock, by E. T. Biggs, Maidenhead and Slough, the painted dial with maker's name, the double fusee movement striking on a bell, the case with carved floral decoration and metal frets to the sides and back door, feet missing, mid-19thC, 17½in (44.5cm) high.
£475–575
€ / **$750–900** 🔨 **TMA**

A rosewood mantel timepiece, by Robert Scott, London, with engraved Roman dial within an angled bezel, the single gut fusee movement with anchor escapement, the case with gadrooned top and later finial, on a stepped base and bun feet, mid-19thC, 11¾in (30cm) high.
£2,000–2,200
€ / **$3,200–3,400** 🔨 **B**

Bracket/table clocks

The term 'bracket clock' only came into general use in the 19th century. Most of the clocks that are called bracket clocks were never designed to be placed on a bracket. The British Museum is of the opinion that English 'bracket clocks' should really be known as spring clocks (as opposed to weight-driven clocks) or table clocks unless they were specifically designed to be placed on a bracket. Most 17th- and 18th-century table clocks have beautifully engraved backplates which were evidently meant to be seen. Clocks intended for display on a bracket usually have backplates that are plain except for the signature of the maker.

CLOCKS

A patinated- and gilt-bronze mantel clock, by E. H. Adams, Exeter, in the Gothic style, the silvered Roman dial with blued steel moon hands, the twin gut fusee movement with anchor escapement, striking on a bell, the case surmounted by three crocket finials over an embattlement above architectural tracery, pilasters and niches, on scrolled feet, mid-19thC, 15¾in (40cm) high.
£650–750
€ / $1,000–1,200 ✦ B(Kn)

Items in the Clock section have been arranged in date order.

A bronze-mounted oak bracket clock, by Wales & McCulloch, London, the silvered Roman dial with twin subsidiary dials for regulation and chime on eight bells/Westminster chimes selection, within a scroll-engraved mask, the triple-chain fusee movement with anchor escapement, chiming the quarters on eight bells and the hours on a gong, the case with four foliate and ball finials and lattice-decorated side panels, on lion-paw feet, on original carved bracket, gong block stamped 'JD', c1870, 36in (91.5cm) high.
£2,200–2,500
€ / $3,500–4,000 ✦ B

A walnut gallery time-piece, by Sir John Bennett, London, with signed painted dial and cast-brass bezel, the fusee and chain movement with anchor escapement, c1880, 28in (71cm) high.
£900–1,000
€ / $1,400–1,600 ✦ S(O)

A Victorian rosewood world mantel timepiece, with painted 24-hour revolving dial, the outer dial with world cities, with single fusee movement, the silvered-brass inner bezel inscribed 'A M Bezant, Hereford', 20¾in (52.5cm) high.
£950–1,100
€ / $1,500–1,700 ✦ WW

A walnut mantel clock, with Marti movement, striking on a gong, with brass mounts and cresting, on cast claw feet, late 19thC, 13½in (34.5cm) high.
£350–425
€/ **$550–670** ⚲ G(L)

◀ **A mahogany mantel clock,** with painted Roman dial signed 'Parsons, London', the twin fusee movement striking on a bell, the brass-inlaid and boxwood-strung case with brass carrying handle and brass frets, on brass bracket feet, 19thC, 14¼in (36cm) high.
£1,300–1,500
€/ **$2,000–2,400** ⚲ Bea

A rosewood gallery timepiece, the painted dial with Roman numerals and inscribed 'C. Stening, Hove', with eight-day fusee movement, the case on carved foliate scroll mouldings and a pedestal base, c1885, 13in (33cm) high, with associated wall bracket.
£300–340
€/ **$475–550** ⚲ RTo

An ebonized bracket clock, by Poole of London, the gilt-brass dial with Roman numerals and three subsidiary dials, the triple-train movement chiming on eight bells and striking on a gong, with carrying handles, on hairy paw feet, with matching gilt-brass-decorated bracket, c1890, 24in (61cm) high.
£2,000–2,200
€/ **$3,200–3,500** ⚲ HYD

For further information on antique clocks see the full range of Miller's books at **www.millers.uk.com**

A walnut-veneered table clock, retailed by Camerer, Kuss & Co, London, with eight-day quarter-striking Lenzkirch movement, pierced frets to each side, c1900, 14¼in (36cm) high.
£750–875
€/ **$1,200–1,400** ⚲ SWO

A late Victorian mahogany table clock, by Lund & Blockley, London, in late 17thC style, the brass matted dial with silvered chapter ring, the triple fusee movement with anchor escapement, chiming the quarters on eight bells and striking the hours on a gong, on foliate-cast and chased scrolled feet, 20in (51cm) high.
£2,000–2,300
€/ **$3,200–3,600** ⚲ BR

A late Victorian gilt-brass-mounted ebonized table clock, the silvered and brass dial with chime/silent and two chimes in the arch, the triple-train fusee movement with anchor escapement, chiming on eight bells and striking on a gong, on scrolling feet, 24½in (62cm) high.
£2,400–2,800
€/ **$3,800–4,400** ⚲ TEN

◀ **An oak bracket clock,** the silvered dial with brass Arabic numerals enclosing a matted centre, below silvered subsidiary strike/silent, slow/fast and chime on eight bells/Westminster chimes dials, with triple fusee movement chiming the quarters on eight bells, the spandrels and arch cast with shells and foliate decoration, with original oak bracket, early 20thC, 23¼in (59cm) high.
£1,600–1,900
€/ **$2,500–3,000** ⚲ PFK

Continental Bracket, Mantel & Table Clocks

n ormolu mantel clock, e striking movement in a se surmounted by a flower-ed vase, 1775–1800, 4in (35.5cm) high.
2,800–3,200
/ $4,400–5,000 ➚ S(NY)

An ormolu and biscuit porcelain *pendule à cercles tournants,* with revolving enamel rings and a striking movement, the temple enclosing a biscuit figure of a boy, French, 1775–1800, 15¼in (38.5cm) high.
£5,300–6,300
€/ $8,300–10,000 ➚ S(NY)

An ormolu-mounted marble mantel clock, the enamel dial with Roman hours, Arabic quarters and pierced hands, the circular movement with pinned pillars and silk suspension with outside countwheel, striking on a bell, surmounted by an eagle and four urn finials, on a shaped base with turned feet, French, late 18thC, 23¼in (59cm) high.
£2,200–2,500
€/ $3,500–4,000 ➚ B

An ormolu Empire timepiece, the enamel dial with Roman numerals and blued steel moon hands, signed 'Alibert à Paris', the replaced gilt verge watch movement signed 'Romilly, Paris', with pierced and engraved cock over baluster pillars, mounted on two griffins on a base, the plinth with cast feet, hair crack to dial, French, early 19thC, 9¾in (25cm) high.
£275–325
€/ $430–520 ➚ B(Kn)

n ormolu mantel clock, e Roman dial with pierced lt-brass hands within an ctagonal bezel, the circular ovement with bevelled wer edge, silk suspension nd outside countwheel riking on a bell, French, rly 19thC, 17in (43cm) high.
850–1,000
/ $1,300–1,600 ➚ B(Kn)

An ormolu mantel clock, modelled as Apollo and two of his nine muses, one holding a jester's doll, the other a tambourine, the eight-day bell striking movement with silk suspension, French, c1805, 17¾in (45cm) high.
£6,500–7,300
€/ $10,300–11,500 ⊞ GDO

Trade versus auctions

The apparently higher prices indicated for clocks sold by dealers than by auction can be misleading. Clocks bought at auction will not be in guaranteed working order, may need expensive restoration and may be missing keys, winders etc. Many clock dealers will be able to offer pieces from stock in guaranteed condition, and will usually provide documentation to support authenticity of the piece. In many cases a dealer will be prepared to set the clock up in your home and advise you on how to regulate it to time and to reset the strike, should it go out of sequence, as part of an after-sale service.

An ormolu clock, modelled as Pandora, the eight-day bell striking movement with silk suspension, French, c1818, 17¾in (45cm) high.
£3,800–4,300
€/ **$6,000–6,800** ⊞ GDO

A bronze and gilt-bronze mantel clock, flanked by personifications of the Arts and Sciences portrayed by two bronze cherubs as sculptor and designer, repeated in the frieze below, the dial with an engine-turned centre and Roman chapters, the movement by Pons of Paris, French, c1820, 17in (43cm) high.
£8,300–9,200
€/ **$13,000–14,500** ⊞ JIL

A patinated-bronze and verde antico marble mantel clock, modelled as Aurora lifting the veil of night, signed 'Ravrio bronzier à Paris' and 'Mesr Hr.', the eight-day bell-striking movement with silk suspension, French, c1820, 29½in (75cm) high
£16,000–18,000
€/ **$25,000–28,500** ⊞ GD
Ravrio and Mesnil worke together to produce ver fine quality clocks. This example is large and in exceptionally good original condition.

Ormolu (mercury gilding)

The earliest form of gilding usually found on clock cases is mercury gilding. This is where the bronze or brass casting is cleaned and chased and then applied with an amalgam of gold and mercury. Great skill is required to apply the correct amount of this amalgam so that the detail of the casting is not lost. The piece is then fired (this type of gilding is sometimes known as fire gilding), which causes the mercury to evaporate but leaves the gold adhering to the bronze or brass. This is then worked with fine abrasives to produce a lustrous finish. The result is called ormolu or gilt-bronze, even though the base metal is often brass. The term ormolu has come to be used more often when referring to the gilt clocks produced during the Empire period in France and the Regency period in England when the quality of the work had reached its zenith.

An ormolu and marble mantel clock, the engine-turned dial with Roman numerals, moon hands and bezel cast with flowerheads, the twin train movement with outside countwheel striking on a bell, the plinth with a relief plaque of cupids, on winged paw feet, French, c1825, 22in (56cm) high.
£3,000–3,400
€/ **$4,700–5,400** ⋌ GTH

A patinated-bronze and marble mantel clock, French, c1830, 22½in (57cm) high.
£1,800–2,000
€/ **$2,800–3,200** ⋌ S(O)

A lacquered-brass perpetual calendar mantel clock, the enamel dial with recessed centre revealing the Brocot escapement, on a calendar dial with outer four-yearly chapter enclosing subsidiaries for day, month, date and phases of the moon, the movement with twin mercury jar pendulum striking on a bell, the four-glass case with moulded brass top and stepped base, French, mid-19thC, 15in (38cm) high.
£3,500–4,000
€/ **$5,500–6,300** ⋌ B

A silver and gilt boudoir timepiece, with Swiss cylinder movement, surmounted by an enamelled figure of a violinist, flanked by two similar figures on enamelled columns, the glass cupola shade with figures and enamelled scenes, Austrian, 1825–50, 8¼in (21cm) high.
£1,700–2,000
€/ **$2,700–3,200** ⋌ TEN
This is a rare and unusual piece.

A burrwood portico mantel clock, with gilt-bronze mounts, the silvered dial with black chapters, four gilt-bronze half-bun feet, French, 1825–50, 22¼in (56.5cm) high.
£750–900
€/ **$1,200–1,400** ⋌ NOA

A Louis XV-style rococo ormolu mantel clock, th dial with enamel numerals Raingo Frères movement, with countwheel striking o a bell, cast with C-scrolls and foliage, hands missing, French, 19thC, 18in (45.5cm) high.
£750–875
€/ **$1,200–1,400** ⋌ G(L)

An ormolu mantel clock, by Raingo Frères, Paris, surmounted by figures and with hand-painted porcelain panels, French, 19thC, 11¾in (30cm) high.
£375–450
€/ **$600–700** ⚲ WilP

A mantel clock, the black marble base surmounted by a bronze statue of Columbus, French, c1870, 21in (53.5cm) high.
£1,700–2,000
€/ **$2,700–3,200** ⊞ SET

An ormolu and Sèvres porcelain clock, with eight-day Japy Frères bell-striking movement, decorated with 18thC-style portrait miniatures to the top and sides, French, c1870, 19¾in (50cm) high.
£7,500–8,700
€/ **$11,800–13,800** ⊞ GDO

patinated-metal clock, urmounted by a bronzed-pelter figure of a warrior, he enamel dial with oman numerals, half-ourly striking mechanism, rench, c1850, 6¾in (68cm) high.
600–700
/ **$950–1,100** ⚲ LCM

An ormolu and ewelled porcelain nantel clock, the dial ecorated with a courting ouple, with eight-day bell-triking movement, French, 1880, 19¾in (50cm) high.
6,000–6,800
/ **$9,500–10,700** ⊞ GDO

◄ **A tortoiseshell boulle mantel clock,** the dial with individual enamel numerals, the eight-day movement striking the hours and half-hours on a bell, with glass side panels and matching plinth, c1880, 22in (56cm) high.
£1,600–1,800
€/ **$2,500–2,800** ⊞ K&D

CLOCKS

CLOCKS

◄ A tortoiseshell boulle mantel clock, with bronze mounts, the cast dial with individual enamel numeral cartouches, the eight-day movement striking the hours and half-hours on a gong, French, c1890, 14in (35.5cm) high.
£1,100–1,300
€ / **$1,700–2,000** ⊞ K&D

An ormolu and *bleu céleste* porcelain mantel clock, with eight-day bell-striking movement, French, c1880, 17¾in (45cm) high.
£3,400–3,800
€ / **$5,400–6,000** ⊞ GDO

► A Gothic-style gold-fired mantel clock, the enamel dial covered by bevelled glass crystal, the eight-day time and bell-striking movement by Marti, French, late 19thC, 14in (35.5cm) high.
£750–820
€ / **$1,200–1,300** ⊞ SET

A gilt-brass clock, the dial with Roman numerals, sunburst emblem and brass hands, the twin-train movement with rack striking on a bell, the case surmounted by an eagle over a caddy with applied rosette, the base engraved, French, late 19thC, 15¾in (40cm) high.
£300–350
€ / **$475–550** ♪ B(Kn)

A bronzed spelter and marble mantel clock, surmounted by two female figures flanking a lyre, the enamel dial overlaid with gilt filigree mask, with Louis Boname bell-striking movement, applied with a plaque inscribed 'Harmonie par Math. Moreau', on female term feet, French, c1895, 30in (76cm) high.
£650–780
€ / **$1,000–1,200** ♪ S(O)
Moreau sculpted numerous figures which were then reproduced in spelter for clock mounts, lamps etc.

Spelter

Spelter is a soft brittle metal, much like zinc, which was used by the French from c1850 to make large numbers of inexpensive copies of bronze figures and clock cases. It casts well and accepts a gilt or a bronze patina which resembles the more expensive patinated-bronze or ormolu. Before gilding, the spelter was usually copper plated as the gold adhered better to the copper than to the spelter. When protected from the atmosphere under a glass dome these spelter clocks can look very good, but when exposed they tend to tarnish more quickly than true ormolu clocks. The value of a gilt-spelter clock, even in good condition, is about one third that of a similar ormolu clock.

► A Moorish-style gilt-brass mantel clock, the engraved silver dial with Turkish numerals, the eight-day movement with cylinder escapement, striking on a gong, the case modelled as a Moorish pavilion with crescent finial, embellished overall with cast *champlevé* decoration of equestrian figures, birds, and other creatures, French, c1895, 11½in (29cm) high.
£1,400–1,600
€ / **$2,200–2,500** ♪ S(O)

A boulle bracket clock, with gilt-metal mounts, the beaten brass dial with enamel numerals, the glazed door decorated with the three Fates, surmounted by Minerva, French, 19thC, 60in (152.5cm) high with bracket.
£2,200–2,500
€/ $3,500–4,000 ↗ CoH

▶ A gilt-brass mantel clock, the dial with Roman numerals and visible Brocot escapement, striking on a bell, with mercury pendulum, enclosed by four bevelled glass plates, French, 19thC, 15in (38cm) high.
£1,300–1,500
€/ $2,100–2,400 ↗ DD

A champlevé enamel and gilt-metal mantel clock, with brass chapter ring and circular movement striking on a bell, the domed-top case surmounted by a temple lion, with floral decorated panels and applied floral mounts, French, 19thC, 15¾in (40cm) high.
£1,000–1,200
€/ $1,600–1,900 ↗ Bea

◀ A gilt-metal and tortoiseshell-mounted mantel clock, retailed by E. White, Paris and London, the enamel dial with Roman numerals and elaborate hands, the scroll case surmounted by floral relief, on a scroll base, French, 19thC, 14½in (37cm) high.
£650–750
€/ $1,000–1,200 ↗ B(Kn)

A mantel clock, the dial with Roman numerals, on porcelain supports with ormolu mounts and flanked by ormolu cherubs, surmounted by a porcelain urn, the drum case with a bleu céleste floral ground, on turned feet, French, 19thC, 18in (45.5cm) high.
£750–850
€/ $1,200–1,400 ↗ TRM

A gilt-metal mantel clock, with enamel dial and eight-day movement striking on a bell, decorated with ribbons, on an alabaster base, French, 19thc, 12½in (32cm) high, with an ebonized stand.
£350–425
€/ $550–670 ↗ HOLL

▶ A gilt-metal and porcelain mantel clock, by Henry Marc, Paris, the case with putti, swags and painted porcelain panels, on a shaped base with a glass dome, damaged, French, 19thC, 15¾in (40cm) high.
€250–300
€/ $400–475 ↗ B(W)

A gilt-bronze and marble mantel clock, the enamel dial signed 'Biesta à Paris', with Japy Frères movement striking on a bell, the case inlaid with 18thC-style water-colours, French, c1890, 14¼in (36cm) high.
£1,000–1,200
€/ $1,600–1,900 ↗ S(O)

CLOCKS

A boulle mantel clock, with a drum movement striking on a gong, the case with gilt-metal mounts, French, late 19thC, 11¾in (30cm) high.
£300–350
€/ **$475–550** ↗ **SWO**

An oak and brass-mounted mantel clock, with silvered dial and eight-day striking movement, the caddy top with foliate handle and pierced corner brackets, on a moulded base with bracket feet, French, 19thC, 19½in (49.5cm) high.
£650–775
€/ **$1,000–1,200** ↗ **AH**

A gilt-metal and porcelain mantel clock, the dial with Roman numerals, the circular movement striking on a bell, surmounted by an urn, with porcelain columns and panels within a foliate-decorated case, stamped '32735', 19thC, 14½in (37cm) high.
£1,000–1,200
€/ **$1,600–1,900** ↗ **Bea(E)**

An Empire-style burr-wood mantel timepiece, the enamelled dial with Arabic numerals and painted floral swags, the single train Paris movement in a drum, French, late 19thC, 9¼in (23.5cm) high.
£650–750
€/ **$1,000–1,200** ↗ **PF**

A lacquered wood time-piece, by Dunhill, Paris, the enamel dial marked with maker's name, the barrelled spring movement with a lever platform escapement, the chinoiserie decoration depicting birds, figures and foliage, French, early 20thC, 5in (12.5cm) high.
£160–200
€/ **$250–320** ↗ **TMA**

An Edwardian mahogany lancet mantel timepiece, the enamel dial supporting a full plate platform escape-ment movement, inlaid with a fan patera and boxwood stringing, French, early 20thC, 9¼in (23.5cm) high.
£200–240
€/ **$320–380** ↗ **DMC**

An oak mantel clock, by Winterhalder & Hofmeier, with eight-day quarter-striking movement, German, c1910, 15in (38cm) high.
£1,200–1,400
€/ **$1,900–2,200** ⊞ **PTh**

A mahogany mantel clock, by Gustav Becker, Freiberg, No. 2,506, with Westminster chime, case refinished, German, c1925, 12¾in (32.5cm) high.
£675–750
€/ **$1,000–1,200** ⊞ **SET**

The Joseph Meraux Collection

In the autumn of 1992 my colleagues in the New York watch department were invited to inspect a collection of clocks in New Orleans. They were so overwhelmed by what they found that they telephoned me immediately and asked me to fly over. No details were given but they promised I would not be disappointed.

I shall never forget my first day at the house. After initial introductions I started to look around. There were clocks everywhere! Every piece of furniture, most of the wall space and all of the floor, apart from a narrow passage, was covered with clocks. Even the staircase had two or three clocks on every step. This was the collection of the late Joseph Meraux, who came from an affluent and influential Louisiana family. The young Joseph Meraux first attended the New Orleans auction houses with his mother, stimulating in him what was to become a lifelong interest in collecting, particularly clocks. At the end of my time there my colleagues and I had examined and listed 3,250 clocks! The range of clocks was enormous – English, French, German and of course American – and included many rare and unusual examples. The collection was rich in 19th-century automaton or mystery clocks. Our task was further complicated because the clocks had all been removed from their figures and stored separately – I spent many hours sorting through the various pieces and bringing them together again. Every room I entered brought fresh revelations, every cupboard was filled and no flat surface was left free of a clock. It was only near the end of the appraisal that I was told that there was a coach house nearby also filled with clocks and another building elsewhere in the town containing some particularly large examples. Even my huge enthusiasm for the subject began to wane!

For me one of the chief delights was to discover the enormous French 19th-century silvered-bronze figural mystery clock by Farcot, standing nearly ten feet (three metres) high, in one of the outbuildings; at first we could find only the figure but gradually tracked down the movement and the pendulum. This wonderful clock proved to be one of many highlights when the collection was sold for £1,700,000 (€/ $2,700,000) at Sotheby's New York on 28 June 1993.

I am sure there must be many other enthusiasts forming collections of clocks but I very much doubt whether I shall ever again have the privilege of working with such an extraordinary collection as that put together by Mr Meraux. **Michael Turner**

Carriage Clocks

An engraved gilt strut timepiece, by Thomas Cole, retailed by London & Ryder, c1853, 5½in (14cm) high.
£5,000–5,500
€ / **$8,000–8,700** ⊞ JeF

An engraved brass carriage clock, by Brunelot, with eight-day striking movement, French, c1870, 6½in (16.5cm) high, with original carrying case.
£1,400–1,600
€ / **$2,200–2,500** ⊞ BELL

Anglaise style

The *anglaise* style of carriage clock was designed by the French for the 'plain English taste'. The case components including the handle were all 'squared', giving quite a severe look. The *anglaise riche*-styled case was basically the same shape as the *anglaise* but had extra decoration, usually in the form of Corinthian columns, dentil mouldings and sometimes cloisonné enamelling or, more rarely, Limoges enamel panels.

An *anglaise riche* carriage clock, with royal blue chapter ring and alarm ring, the eight-day movement striking the hours and half hours on a gong, with silvered lever escapement and bimetallic balance, the case with Corinthian columns and key handle, French, c1880, 4in (10cm) high.
£1,700–1,900
€ / **$2,700–3,000** ⊞ PSA

A gilt-brass combined timepiece, barometer and calendar, the lantern case surmounted by a compass and loop handle, thermometer missing, signed 'Mohican', French, dated 1885, 9¾in (25cm) high.
£500–600
€ / **$800–950** ⚒ B(W)

A carriage clock, with enamel dial and a gilded mask, the eight-day movement striking the hours and half-hours on a gong, French, c1885, 5½in (14cm) high.
£750–850
€ / **$1,200–1,400** ⊞ K&D

A brass carriage clock, 19thC, 9in (23cm) high.
£220–250
€ / **$350–400** ⚒ SWO

A gilt-brass *mignonette* carriage clock, with an eight-day movement, French, c1890, 3¾in (9.5cm) high, with original leather travelling case.
£700–775
€ / **$1,100–1,200** ⊞ PSA

◄ **A brass carriage timepiece,** probably by Drocourt, retailed by Benson, French, c1890, 2½in (6.5cm) high.
£950–1,100
€ / **$1,500–1,700** ⊞ BELL

A gilt-brass miniature carriage timepiece, by A. Ecalle, Paris, the ivorine dial with Arabic numerals, the silvered lever escapement with a compensated bimetallic balance, the corniche case with winged term columns, French, 19thC, 3¼in (8.5cm) high.
£750–900
€/ $1,200–1,400 ♪ B(Kn)

A gilt-brass corniche-cased carriage clock, the two-train movement with platform escapement, with push repeat striking on a gong, French, late 19thC, 6¾in (17cm) high.
£330–400
€/ $520–630 ♪ BR

A carriage timepiece, the enamelled chapter ring with Arabic numerals, the case decorated with gilt-brass flowers between fluted pilasters supporting bevelled glass, French, late 19thC, 5¼in (13.5cm) high.
£240–275
€/ $380–440 ♪ CGC

A brass carriage clock, the silvered dial with Arabic numerals and paste 'jewelled' decoration, the repeat movement with lever escapement, glass broken, French, 1875–1925, 5¼in (13.5cm) high.
£400–475
€/ $630–750 ♪ AMB

Portable clocks

Portable or carriage clocks originated in Switzerland and France towards the end of the 18th century. They are usually known as *pendules d'officier* and often have complicated striking works and an alarm. The first maker to produce carriage clocks in glazed rectangular cases was Abraham Louis Breguet in the early years of the 19th century. The style evolved quickly and was taken up by other makers such as Paul Garnier and Leroy. For the next 100 years carriage clocks continued to be made by many French makers, usually in gilt-brass rectangular cases but sometimes embellished with porcelain or enamel panels. The movements vary from plain timepiece to full *grande sonnerie* with alarm.

A tortoiseshell and silver carriage timepiece, c1904, 3in (7.5cm) high.
€1,100–1,200
€/ $1,700–1,900 ⊞ BELL

A silver and enamel miniature timepiece, import marks for London 1910, 2¼in (5.5cm) high, with original case.
£1,100–1,300
€/ $1,700–2,000 ⊞ SHa

An ormolu-mounted pendule d'officier, the dial painted with ribbon-tied floral swags and Arabic numerals, the eight-day French brass movement striking on a gong, with beaded bezel, dial damaged, early 20thC, 8¾in (22cm) high.
£850–1,000
€/ $1,300–1,600 ♪ DD

A gilt-brass and marble carriage timepiece, the enamel dial signed 'Walker Ltd', the movement with lever platform escapement, French, c1910, 5¼in (13.5cm) high.
£575–675
€/ $900–1,000 ♪ S(O)

CLOCKS

Cartel Clocks

A provincial gilt-bronze cartel clock, the dial flanked by columns surmounted by rams' heads joined by a garland and surmounted by an urn, French, c1785, 32¼in (82cm) high.
£1,700–2,000
€/ **$2,700–3,200** ↗ S(P)

A carved giltwood cartel clock, with painted dial signed 'Beurling, Stockholm', decoration restored, Swedish, c1800, 35½in (90cm) high.
£2,500–2,800
€/ **$4,000–4,400** ↗ BUK
Per Henrik Beurling is recorded as working between 1783 and 1806.

The word cartel may come from the Italian *cartella*, or wall bracket. It refers to decorative, spring-driven wall clocks produced mainly in France during the second half of the 18th century. The cases are invariably made of intricately cast ormolu, and they generally have elaborate decorative features such as figures, female masks, scrolling foliage, swags and classical urns. Being of cast metal, the case is very strong, allowing makers to cast crisp, detailed decoration.

A Louis XV-style cartel clock, with convex dial, the eight-day movement striking the hours and half-hours on a bell, the rococo case with fretted panels, French, c1885, 19in (48.5cm) high.
£900–1,000
€/ **$1,400–1,600** ⊞ K&D

A Louis XVI-style gilt-metal cartel clock, signed 'Berthoud, Paris', the dial with Roman and Arabic numerals, the case surmounted by an urn and decorated with laurel swags and scrolls, French, 19thC, 26in (66cm) high.
£650–775
€/ **$1,000–1,200** ↗ B(W)
French 19th-century clocks that were made in the 18th-century style were often confusingly signed with an 18th-century maker's name – as in this instance.

◄ **An Empire-style giltwood cartel clock,** with painted dial, signed 'C. A. Lindström, Stockholm', Swedish, c1910, 35½in (90cm) high.
£2,700–3,000
€/ **$4,300–4,700** ⊞ CAV
C. A. Lindström was born in 1846 and was a clockmaker from 1889.

Electric Clocks

An electric mantel timepiece, by Matthäus Hipp, Neuchâtel, seconds hand missing, surface rust to steel work, Swiss, c1870, 26½in (67.5cm) high.
£4,500–5,000
€/ **$7,000–8,000** ↗ S(O)

◄ **An ebonized Bentley's patent electric wall regulator,** by Cash & Skilbeck, the engraved annular silvered dial with gilt moulded bezel and centre seconds, the movement visible through the centre, the escape wheel impulsed and unlocked by two gravity arms controlled by the separately suspended wood rod pendulum with cylindrical bob and brass-cased coil oscillating over a fixed steel magnet, switching device signed 'Cash & Skilbeck, Makers, Leeds', in a dust-proofed bevel-glazed case, the interior with silvered beat plaque, with transformer power supply, c1900, 65¾in (167cm) high.
£10,000–12,000
€/ **$16,000–19,000** ↗ S(O)

An electric timepiece, by Eureka Clock Co, London, the enamelled dial with Arabic numerals, with compensated balance, No. 8226, Patent No. 14614, the mahogany case with bevelled glass panels, 1906, 13½in (34.5cm) high.
£1,800–2,200
€/ **$2,800–3,500** ↗ B(Kn)

Garnitures

An ormolu and marble Greco-Egyptian revival five-piece mantel clock garniture, the concave gilt dial decorated with *faux* hieroglyphics and inscribed 'G. Servant à Paris, Medaille d'Or 1867', the eight-day movement striking on a bell, the case surmounted by a Ptolemic ormolu bust with headdress signed 'Emile-Hebert', with applied mummiform caryatids to the side pieces, on lion-paw feet, with two conforming busts on fluted Ionic pedestals applied with leafy garlands and two tazzas on conforming bases, French, c1870, clock 24in (61cm) high
£4,000–4,800
€/ $6,300–7,600 ✦ Bri

A marble and bronze clock garniture, with parcel-gilt decoration, bronze sculpture missing from clock, French, c1880, clock 17¼in (44cm) wide.
£700–800
€/ $1,100–1,300 ✦ S(O)

A clock garniture, with convex enamel dial and eight-day movement striking the hours and half-hours on a bell, the case set with bronze cherubs and ormolu mounts, on a marble base, French, c1875, 12in (30.5cm) high.
£1,800–2,000
€/ $2,800–3,200 ⊞ K&D

An ormolu-mounted alabaster clock garniture, by Marti, the eight-day spring-driven movement striking on a bell, top of clock urn removable, minor damage, French, c1880, 15in (38cm) high.
£1,400–1,600
€/ $2,200–2,500 ⊞ SET

◀ A gilt-spelter and porcelain clock garniture, the porcelain dial with Roman numerals, the eight-day movement striking on a gong, the case surmounted by two cherubs flanking a porcelain urn, supported by Corinthian columns flanked by a putto to either side, on reeded, scroll and paw feet, with a pair of matching urns, French, late 19thC, clock approx 20¾in (52.5cm) high.
£650–775
€/ $1,000–1,200 ✦ RTo

For further information on antique clocks see the full range of Miller's books at **www.millers.uk.com**

Lantern Clocks

◀ A brass lantern clock, the dial with Roman numeral chapter ring and brass hand, the twin-train short duration balance wheel movement with countwheel striking on a bell, old restorations, probably West Country, c1650, 14½in (37cm) high.
£4,000–4,800
€/ $6,300–7,600 ✦ Bri

▶ A brass lantern clock, the conventional movement with verge escapement, the external locking plate striking on the top-mounted bell, with a modern wall bracket, restored, c1720, 15in (38cm) high.
£2,300–2,600
€/ $3,600–4,000 ✦ S(O)

A lantern clock, with Winterhalder & Hofmeier eight-day ting-tang movement striking the quarters on two bells, German, c1900, 14in (35.5cm) high.
£780–870
€/ $1,200–1,350 ⊞ K&D

CLOCKS

Longcase Clocks

A William and Mary walnut longcase clock, by William Grimes, the brass dial with a silvered chapter ring, subsidiary seconds dial and date aperture, the eight-day movement striking on a bell, the hood with foliage marquetry and ebonized spiral-twist pilasters, the trunk door with bird and foliage marquetry and inset with a lenticle, on a conforming base, base reduced, 87in (221cm) high.
£25,000–30,000
€/ **$39,000–47,000** ⚒ WW
This clock sold well in excess of the auctioneer's expectations. This is probably because it is in unusually good original condition for a 300 year old clock. It has lost the back hood pillars and the original bun feet have been replaced with an apron, but the marquetry is of exceptionally fine quality. The clock looks as if it has not been touched for years, thereby adding to its desirability.

▶ **A chinoiserie-decorated longcase clock,** by Richard Martin, Northampton, with an eight-day movement, c1700, 98in (249cm) high.
£12,000–13,500
€/ **$19,000–21,000** ⊞ ALS

A walnut marquetry longcase clock, the dial with calendar aperture and seconds dial, the month-going movement with six ring-turned pillars, reversed five-wheel trains and outside countwheel, the hood formerly rising, c1690, 77¾in (197.5cm) high.
£13,500–15,000
€/ **$21,000–24,000** ⚒ S(O)

▶ **A walnut longcase clock,** by Thomas Lumpkin, London, the brass dial with a silvered Roman chapter ring, subsidiary seconds and a date aperture, with an eight-day movement, late 17thC, 87in (221cm) high.
£4,200–5,000
€/ **$6,500–7,900** ⚒ G(L)

A William III walnut marquetry longcase clock, by John Clows, London, the brass dial with subsidiary seconds, date aperture and ringed winding holes, with a long-plated eight-day, five ring, turned-pillar bell-striking movement, with an outside countwheel and anchor escapement, the case with a lenticle, the hood formerly rising, probably associated, 83in (211cm) high.
£5,000–6,000
€/ **$7,900–9,500** ⚒ B(NW)
John Clows was admitted to the Clockmakers Company in 1672, probably the date he completed his apprenticeship. He was a Warden of the company in 1713.

A walnut-veneered oak longcase clock, by Robert Sadler, London, the brass dial with a separate silvered brass chapter, seconds and date rings, the month-duration five-pillar movement with a latched centre pillar, the inside rack striking the hours on a bell, the trunk door with figured veneers and marquetry border, repeated to the base with a single plinth, c1710, 86in (218.5cm) high.
£25,000–28,500
€/ **$39,000–45,000** ⊞ PAC
This clock is in good, clean and restored condition with the added appeal of a month-running movement. It has beautiful hands and a rich, warm colour to the case. This clock was offered in full working condition.

An oak longcase clock, by William Snow I, Otley, the silvered dial with a Roman chapter ring, inscribed 'William Snow 584', a crescent-form date aperture and single hand, with 30-hour movement, hood finials missing, early 18thC, 81in (205.5cm) high.
€1,800–2,200
€/ $2,800–3,500 ♪ PFK
Thirty-hour clocks can be difficult to sell, but this clock was made by a well-documented maker who numbered most of the clocks he made. This always appeals to collectors, as it demonstrates the uniqueness of each clock and assists with dating.

A mahogany crossbanded oak longcase clock, by Jacob Massy, London, the brass dial with a Roman and Arabic chapter ring with half quarter marks, subsidiary seconds and a decorated date aperture, the associated early 18thC movement with five knopped and finned pillars, high barrels and anchor escapement, rack striking on a bell, in a 19thC case, formerly with strike/not-strike lever, 84¼in (214cm) high.
£1,300–1,500
€/ $2,000–2,400 ♪ B
This clock has a perfectly good movement and case, but they did not start life together and this is reflected in the low selling price.

Marriages

In the antiques world, a marriage is when components that did not start life together have been brought together to form a whole. This applies more frequently to longcase clocks than to any other form of antique. This is because longcase clock dials tend to be made to fairly standard sizes and so can be comfortably housed in a different case from the one for which they were intended. Check for the following clues: the style of the case and dial should complement each other, the dial should fit the aperture in the hood accurately, and the movement seatboard should sit comfortably on the case styles without too much evidence of recent alteration to the packing. Where the components are from the same period it may be regarded as a compatible marriage and may not reduce the value of the piece too much. If the movement has been changed so that there is a marriage of movement, case and dial, the value will be very much reduced.

▶ **An oak longcase clock,** by Robert Cutbush, Maidstone, the brass dial with Roman numerals, subsidiary seconds dial and date aperture, in a 19thC case, 1700–50 85in (216cm) high.
£750–875
€/ $1,200–1,400 ♪ RTo

CLOCKS

An oak longcase clock, by Thomas Deykin of Worcester, the brass and silvered dial inscribed 'Tho. Deykin Worcester No. 176', with an hourly-striking eight-day movement with five pillars, the door with a glass lenticle, replacement lock and repairs to the base, early 18thC, 80½in (204.5cm) high.
£4,200–5,000
€ / **$6,600–7,900** ⚒ FHF

A provincial stained-oak alarm lantern longcase clock, the relief-moulded brass dial with cartouche Roman numerals, iron hour hand and iron alarm hand, the brass and iron posted movement with verge escapement, with a knife-edge suspended pendulum, alarm and rack striking on a bell, French, c1730, 96½in (245cm) high.
£2,200–2,500
€ / **$3,500–4,000** ⚒ S(Am)

◄ **An oak longcase clock,** by William Avenell, Alresford, the dial with ringed winding and date apertures, with an eight-day movement, mid-18thC, 87¾in (223cm) high.
£6,800–7,500
€ / **$10,700–12,000** ⊞ ALS

An oak longcase clock, by Phillip Avenell, Farnham, the dial with ringed winding and date apertures, with an eight-day movement, a lenticle to the trunk door, early 18thC, 83in (211cm) high.
£6,700–7,500
€ / **$10,500–12,000** ⊞ ALS

A *faux* tortoiseshell-lacquer longcase clock, by Aylmer Stopes, London, the brass dial with a separate silvered-brass chapter ring with seconds and date, the arch with a strike/silent facility, with an eight-day, five-pillar movement striking the hours on a bell, the case with gold chinoiseries to the trunk door and base, c1740, 87in (221cm) high.
£8,500–9,600
€ / **$13,500–15,200** ⊞ PAO

► **An oak longcase clock,** by T. Thorpe, Colchester, the brass and silvered dial with calendar aperture, with 30-hour movement, mid-18thC, 86in (218.5cm) high.
£1,400–1,600
€ / **$2,200–2,500** ⚒ G(B)

A longcase clock, by Thomas Budgen (Bugden), Croydon, the brass dial with a silvered chapter ring, Roman numerals and Arabic five-minute intervals, the five-pillar movement with anchor escapement rack striking on a bell, c1740, 86in (218.5cm) high.
£1,800–2,200
€ / **$2,800–3,500** ⚒ GTH

Longcase clocks 1976–2002

INDEX

14000
12000
10000
8000
6000
4000
2000
0

1976 1977 1978 1979 1980 1981 1982 1983 1984 1985 1986 1987 1988 1989 1990 1991 1992 1993 1994 1995 1996 1997 1998 1999 2000 2001 2002

This graph shows the increasing value of antique Longcase clocks as a whole over the past 25 years. ©AMR

CLOCKS

A lacquered longcase clock, by E. Whittingham, London, the brass dial with a strike/silent subsidiary, recessed seconds and date aperture, signed on an applied plaque, the five-pillar movement with anchor escapement striking on a bell, hood reduced, minor damage, mid-18thC, 82in (208.5cm) high.
£1,700–2,000
€/ **$2,700–3,200** ⚒ B(Kn)
The high cost of restoring japanned or lacquered decoration has kept the price down on this London clock.

An oak longcase clock, by Joshua Harrocks, Lancaster, with an eight-day movement, the case with mahogany crossbanding, c1760, 84in (213.5cm) high.
£8,000–9,500
€/ **$12,700–15,000** ⊞ JeF

A rococo lacquered longcase clock, by Petter Ernst, Stockholm, with gilt-bronze mounts and carved decoration of acanthus leaves, rocailles and shells, with later painted decoration of flowers, trailing foliage and birds, Swedish, c1760, 90½in (230cm) high.
£8,200–10,000
€/ **$13,000–15,800** ⚒ BUK
This is a fine clock by one of Sweden's most respected makers. This is good value for money.

An oak longcase clock, by James Smythe, Saxmundham, with an eight-day movement, c1765, 86½in (219.5cm) high.
£6,800–7,500
€/ **$10,700–11,800** ⊞ ALS

A mahogany longcase clock, by Robert Hynam, London, the brass dial with seconds ring and a strike/silent facility to the arch, the eight-day movement with five pillars and deadbeat escapement, striking the hours on a bell, c1770, 95in (241.5cm) high.
£19,500–21,500
€/ **$30,000–34,000** ⊞ PAC
This is a rare clock, by the clockmaker to the Russian court at St Petersburg. This is one of the most desirable case styles, with well-figured veneers and restrained decoration to the hood.

A mahogany longcase clock, by Benjamin Martin, Manchester, the dial with a rolling moon, subsidiary seconds and date aperture, the eight-day bell-striking movement with an inside countwheel, c1770, 89in (226cm) high.
£4,200–5,000
€/ **$6,600–7,900** ⚒ B(NW)
Manchester clocks are popular and have distinctive cases.

A longcase clock, by Charles Raymond, Lideway, with an eight-day movement, and inlaid decoration of a star to trunk and base, c1770, 82in (208.5cm) high.
€7,700–8,500
€/ $12,000–13,500 ⊞ ALS

An oak longcase clock, by James Webster, Shropshire, with an engraved brass dial and single hand movement, c1770, 76in (193cm) high.
£5,800–6,500
€/ $9,000–10,300 ⊞ RYA
This clock is in good original condition and the appeal of a single hand added to its value despite its 30-hour movement. James Webster is recorded as working in Shrewsbury, Shropshire, c1770.

An oak longcase clock, by Wilson, Askrigg, the brass dial with date aperture, the hood with plain columns, blind fret frieze and moulded flat top, the case with a shaped headed door and quarter columns, c1770, 81in (205.5cm) high.
£2,000–2,400
€/ $3,200–3,800 ↗ TEN

A mahogany longcase clock, by E. Bilbie, Chew Stoke, the brass dial with a silvered Roman numeral chapter ring, subsidiary seconds dial and a calendar sector, the arch with rolling moon and tidal cycle, engraved 'High Water at Bristol Key' to the border, with a four-pillar rack and bell-striking movement, c1775, 92½in (235cm) high.
£5,000–6,000
€/ $7,900–9,500 ↗ Bri

A mahogany longcase clock, by William Mason, London, the brass dial with a separate silvered-brass chapter ring and seconds and date apertures, the arch with a rocking ship automaton, the eight-day duration five-pillar movement striking the hours on a bell, with removable pagoda top, c1775, 100in (254cm) high.
€16,500–18,500
€/ $26,000–30,000 ⊞ PAO
The rocking ship automaton in the arch is a rare feature on a London clock. It is in excellent restored condition and therefore commands a high price.

A mid-Georgian oak longcase clock, by John Porthouse I, Penrith, the dial with silvered chapter ring with Roman hours and Arabic minutes, a subsidiary calendar aperture, with an hour-striking 30-hour movement, 83½in (212cm) high.
£2,000–2,200
€/ $3,200–3,500 ↗ PFK

CLOCKS

An oak longcase clock, by E. Sagar, Skipton, the brass dial with an engraved centre and date subsidiary, c1780, 80in (203cm) high.
£1,400–1,600
€/ **$2,200–2,500** ⚒ **TEN**

A mahogany longcase clock, by William Priest, Bristol, the eight-day move-ment with moonphases and High Water at Bristol Key, c1780, 95in (241.5cm) high.
£13,500–15,000
€/ **$21,000–24,000** ⊞ **ALS**

An oak longcase clock, by Thomas Brown, Chester, the engraved dial with centresweep seconds and moonphases, the eight-day movement with deadbeat escapement, c1780, 90in (228.5cm) high.
£9,300–10,300
€/ **$14,700–16,200** ⊞ **ALS**

An oak longcase clock, by Benjamin Lockwood, Swaffham, the eight-day, five-pillar movement with strike/silent and pull hour repeat, c1780, 90in (228.5cm) high.
£6,700–7,500
€/ **$10,500–11,800** ⊞ **ALS**

The longcase clock evolved in the mid-17th century after the invention of the pendulum. Interference with the weights caused the clock to run unreliably, so they had to be protected. A short while later the long pendulum was introduced, which needed even more careful protection than the weights. From the very beginning clockmakers seized the opportunity to enhance the appeal of the clock by housing it in an attractive case. This set the trend for the next 300 years, and the design and decoration of clock cases evolved to reflect the current fashion.

A mahogany longcase clock, by Robert Fletcher, Chester, the arch with a moon feature, with an eight-day movement, c1790, 90in (228.5cm) high.
£12,500–14,000
€/ **$20,000–22,000** ⊞ **JeF**

◄ **A mahogany-veneered longcase clock,** by Thomas Lozano, London, with an eight-day movement, c1780, 101in (256.5cm) high.
£10,000–12,000
€/ **$15,800–19,000** ⊞ **JeF**

► **An oak longcase clock,** by John Turnbull, Hawick, the brass dial with silvered-brass chapter ring, seconds and date, a silvered-brass cartouche to the arch with the maker's name, the eight-day movement striking on a bell, Scottish, c1780, 90in (228.5cm) high.
£8,000–8,800
€/ **$12,700–14,000** ⊞ **PAO**

A mahogany longcase clock, by James Howden, Edinburgh, with an eight-day movement, the case with boxwood stringing, c1780, 87½in (222.5cm) high.
£9,300–10,300
€/ **$14,700–16,000** ⊞ **ALS**

An oak longcase clock, by Winstanley, Holywell, the dial with a calendar sector and inscribed 'Time is Valuable', the plated 30-hour movement with external locking plate striking on a bell, hood pillars and base replaced, c1780, 79in (200.5cm) high.
£800–900
€ / **$1,300–1,400** ⚒ S(O)
Alterations to the case kept the price to a modest level.

A flame-figured mahogany longcase clock, by James Wrigley, Manchester, the dial with rolling moon, subsidiary seconds, date aperture and arcaded minute ring, the rack and bell-striking eight-day movement with anchor escapement, c1780, 99½in (252.5cm) high.
£3,800–4,500
€ / **$6,000–7,000** ⚒ B(NW)
James Wrigley is a hitherto unrecorded maker, though it seems probable that he is descended from the Manchester clockmakers, James Wrigley and Isaac Wrigley, who died in 1697 and 1742 respectively.

◄ **A George III oak and crossbanded mahogany longcase clock,** by Jn. Bell, Garstang, with a seconds hand, calendar aperture and eight-day movement, 79in (200.5cm) high.
£1,500–1,800
€ / **$2,400–2,800** ⚒ Mit

► **A George III oak and mahogany crossbanded longcase clock,** by W. Belman, Broughton, the painted dial with Roman numerals and a calendar aperture, with a 30-hour movement, 79in (200.5cm) high.
£525–625
€ / **$830–1,000** ⚒ Mit

A stained wood longcase clock, the brass dial with a pewter chapter ring, Roman numerals, subsidiary seconds, pierced steel hands and a name shield signed,' Joa Chr Bartels Goslar' the posted movement with anchor escapement, rack quarter-striking on three bells, the case with a lenticle, on a *bombé* plinth with canted corners, on bracket feet, German, c1780, 93¾in (238cm) high.
£1,200–1,400
€ / **$1,900–2,200** ⚒ S(Am)

A George III mahogany longcase clock, by Joseph Avard, Bristol, the brass dial with a moonphase, High Tide at Bristol Key, subsidiary seconds and a date aperture, with an eight day movement, associated case, 85in (216cm) high.
£4,000–4,800
€ / **$6,300–7,600** ⚒ G(L)
The movement and case both appear to be from the Bristol area. The shaped trunk door, fancy edge to the glazed door and crisply cut mouldings and pillars are all typical of this area.

A George III banded mahogany and walnut longcase clock, by Blaylock Longtown, the brass dial with a silver chapter ring, Roman and Arabic numerals and subsidiary seconds and calendar dials, with an eight-day movement, 85in (216cm) high.
£3,500–4,200
€ / **$5,500–6,600** ⚒ G(B)

◄ **A George III mahogany longcase clock,** by James Brown, Portsmouth, the silvered arch dial with moonphase above a subsidiary seconds dial and a calendar aperture, the eight-day movement striking on a bell, 91½in (232.5cm) high.
£4,000–4,800
€/ **$6,300–7,600** ⚒ WW

► **A George III boxwood-lined mahogany longcase clock,** by Alex Duncan, Elgin, the silvered dial with subsidiary seconds dial and date aperture, the eight-day movement striking on a bell, Scottish, 84¾in (215.5cm) high.
2,800–3,200
€/ **$4,400–5,000** ⚒ B(Ed)
Scottish clocks from the late 18th century usually have attractive slim cases which fit comfortably into modern homes, thereby increasing their appeal and value.

A George III oak and crossbanded longcase clock, the brass dial with a silver chapter ring, the twin-train movement with anchor escapement striking a bell, signed 'Nath. Brown, Manchester', 83¾in (212.5cm) high.
£2,200–2,600
€/ **$3,500–4,100** ⚒ Bea(E)

A George III mahogany longcase clock, by Thomas Fayrer, Lancaster, the brass dial with subsidiary seconds dial and date aperture, with an eight-day striking movement, pediment reduced, 92½in (235cm) high.
£4,800–5,700
€/ **$7,600–9,000** ⚒ B(S)

CLOCKS

A George III mahogany longcase clock, by George Harden, Altrincham, the silvered dial with subsidiary seconds and date hands engraved with birds with painted moonphase, 89¾in (228cm) high.
£4,000–4,800
€ / **$6,300–7,600** ✗ B(S)

◄ **A George III mahogany longcase clock,** by Foot, South Brent, the painted dial with a rocking ship to the arch, Roman numerals to the chapter ring, subsidiary dial and date aperture, with a two-train eight-day movement striking on a bell, 89in (226cm) high.
£3,300–4,000
€ / **$5,200–6,300** ✗ HYD
The automaton feature in this clock helped it to make a higher than expected price.

A George III oak longcase clock, by Stephen King, Malmesbury, the break-arch dial painted with figures beside a building in a lakeside setting, above Roman and Arabic numerals, subsidiary seconds dial and date aperture, the eight-day movement striking on a bell, 79½in (202cm) high.
£800–950
€ / **$1,300–1,500** ✗ RTo

▶ **A George III mahogany and chequer-strung longcase clock,** by W. P., Whitby, the dial painted with a girl seated by the wayside, with black Roman numerals, a subsidiary seconds dial and arched calendar sector, the twin-train movement striking on a bell, 89in (226cm) high.
£3,000–3,600
€ / **$4,700–5,700** ✗ B(Nor)

A George III mahogany longcase clock, by B. Mitchell, Cockermouth, the painted dial with a date aperture, painted spandrels and cottage scene, with a 30-hour movement, the hood with a swan-neck pediment with punched brass terminals, 86in (218.5cm) high.
£2,500–3,000
€ / **$4,000–4,700** ✗ Mit

A George III mahogany-banded oak longcase clock, the dial with a date aperture, subsidiary seconds and painted Arabic numerals, with an eight-day movement, with swan neck pediment, 4in (213.5cm) high.
800–950
/ $1,300–1,500 ⚲ EH
This is a very reasonable price for an eight-day clock, but circular dials re not as popular as quare or arched ones.

A mahogany longcase clock, by John Edgecumbe, Bristol, the brass break-arch dial with a silvered Roman numeral chapter ring, subsidiary seconds dial and arch calendar aperture dial painted with a rocking ship before a castle with a flotilla beyond, inscribed 'The Nassau of Bristol' to the silvered arch border, with a four-pillar rack and bell-striking movement, hood damaged, c1785, 88½in (225cm) high.
£5,500–6,500
/ $8,700–10,300 ⚲ Bri

A George III provincial oak and walnut boxwood-strung and walnut-banded longcase clock, the engraved brass dial with a painted moonphase, the hood with a swan-neck pediment, 92½in (235cm) high.
£2,500–3,000
/ $4,000–4,700 ⚲ JAd

An oak longcase clock, by Thos. Olive, Cranbrook, with a silvered dial and 30-hour movement, the crested hood with a fretwork frieze, giltwood ball and spire finials, c1785, 81in (205.5cm) high.
£3,300–3,600
/ $5,200–5,700 ⊞ PGO

n oak longcase clock, he brass dial with silvered hapter ring, date and econds dial and signed 'William Mercer, Maidstone', he eight-day five-pillar ovement striking the ours on a bell, c1785, 2in (208.5cm) high.
3,400–3,800
/ $5,400–6,000 ⊞ K&D

A figured mahogany longcase clock, by James Tregent, London, the brass dial with Roman numerals, subsidiary strike/silent dial, seconds dial and date aperture, with an eight-day bell-striking movement, early 19thC, 87¾in (223cm) high.
£4,500–5,300
/ $7,000–8,400 ⚲ RTo

A mid-Georgian oak longcase clock, by Christopher Caygill, Askrigg, the brass dial and chapter ring with Roman hours, Arabic minutes and a date aperture, with a 30-hour movement, 80½in (204.5cm) high.
£2,000–2,400
€ / **$3,200–3,800** ⚖ **PFK**

A japanned wood longcase clock, by Henry Brunwin, London, the brass dial with a date aperture and strike/silent dial, 18thC, 48¾in (124cm) high.
£2,000–2,200
€ / **$3,200–3,500** ⚖ **S(O)**
This clock sold for a low price because the case is reduced and in need of restoration.

An oak longcase clock, by Watkin Owen, Llanrwst, the dial with subsidiary seconds and downswept date, the eight-day rack-and bell-striking movement fixed with a false plate cast 'Wilson', Welsh, c1790, 81in (205.5cm) high.
£1,700–2,000
€ / **$2,700–3,200** ⚖ **B(NW)**

An oak longcase clock, by James Kenway, Bridport, the brass dial and chapter ring with an engraved centre and date aperture, 18thC, 78¾in (200cm) high.
£1,000–1,200
€ / **$1,600–1,900** ⚖ **WW**

▶ **A mahogany longcase clock,** the brass dial with seconds dial and calendar, signed 'Chris Clarke, Dublin', top removed and replaced with blind fret cornice, Irish, 18thC, 82¾in (210cm) high.
£1,000–1,200
€ / **$1,600–1,900** ⚖ **HOK**
This clock has an altered case, hence the low price it achieved at auction.

A mahogany longcase clock, by Samuel Thorndike, Ipswich, the engraved silvered dial with strike/silent, date and seconds dial, the eight-day five-pillar movement striking the hours on a bell, c1790, 92in (233.5cm) high.
£5,200–5,700
€ / **$8,200–9,000** ⊞ **K&D**

A yew wood longcase clock, by Swift, Coltishall, with a silvered dial and eight-day striking movement, c1790, 77in (195.5cm) high
£5,000–5,500
€ / **$8,000–8,600** ⊞ **PGO**

An oak longcase clock, by John Christian, Aylsham, the brass dial with Roman and Arabic numerals, with an eight-day four-pillar bell-striking movement, the hood with a scrolling cornice, 18thC, 82¼in (209cm) high.
£1,200–1,400
€ / **$1,900–2,200** ⚖ **CGC**

CLOCKS

An oak and mahogany eight-day longcase clock, by Thomas Ogden, Halifax, the silvered brass dial with subsidiary dials for seconds and date and pierced steel hands, the engraved arch flanked by dolphin spandrels, 18thC, 89in (226cm) high.
£4,500–5,200
€/ **$7,100–8,200** ➷ M

A mahogany longcase clock, by Jas Monkhouse, Carlisle, with painted dial, a moonphase in the arch, date and seconds dials, the hood with swan-neck pediments above fluted Corinthian columns, the trunk with fluted pilasters and crossbanded inlay, late 18thC, 96in (244cm) high.
£2,200–2,500
€/ **$3,500–4,000** ➷ TMA

◄ **A mahogany longcase clock,** by Eardley Norton, London, No. 1165, the arched brass dial with a strike/silent subsidiary, a Roman and Arabic chapter ring, recessed subsidiary seconds and a date aperture, the movement with plates held by six knopped pillars, chiming the quarters on eight bells and the hours on a ninth, with deadbeat escapement and steel crutch, late 18thC, 100¼in (257cm) high.
£12,000–14,000
€/ **$19,000–22,000** ➷ B
Eardley Norton was working from 49 St John Street, Clerkenwell, London, in the mid 18th century and was free of the Clockmakers' Company from 1770–94. He was a maker of great repute of watches and complex clocks and in 1771 patented a striking mechanism. This clock has been in the vendor's family since c1870.

A *faux* tortoiseshell longcase clock, by Nicholls of Canterbury, with an eight-day movement, c1795, 81¾in (207.5cm) high.
£6,700–7,500
€/ **$10,500–11,800** ⊞ ALS

An oak longcase clock, by W. Flint, Ashford, the arched plain dial with seconds and date dials, the eight-day movement striking on a bell, the hood with brass-capped and reeded-angle pillars and typical 'Kent' cresting, with three brass finials, c1800, 85in (216cm) high.
£3,800–4,350
€/ **$6,000–7,000** ⊞ PAO

► **An oak longcase clock,** by George Suggate, Halesworth, the arched dial with Arabic chapters, seconds and date, the corners with painted shells, a painted ruin to the arch, with an eight-day bell-striking movement, c1800, 84in (213.5cm) high.
£3,500–4,000
€/ **$5,500–6,300** ⊞ PAO

A mahogany longcase clock, by Henry Gamble, Bramley, the silvered dial with moonphases in the arch, the centre with a date sector, the movement with an anchor escapement striking on a bell, late 18thC, 91¾in (233cm) high.
£2,500–2,800
€/ **$4,000–4,400** ➷ B(Kr
This is a good clock and could have realized as much as £4,000 (€/ $6,30

A mahogany longcase clock, by Samuel Kellett, Bredbury, the broken-arch dial with a rolling moon and calendar, a central painting of Faith, Hope and Charity, the eight-day rack and bell-striking movement with anchor escapement, in a flame-figured strung and crossbanded case, calendar hand missing, c1810, 86in (218.5cm) high.
£1,500–1,800
€/ $2,400–2,800 ⚒ B(NW)
The Kelletts were something of a clockmaking dynasty during the 18th and 19th centuries in Bredbury and Woodley in Cheshire. This clock could have been made by one of two Samuel Kelletts working at the time.

A mahogany longcase clock, by Whitehurst, Derby, with a silvered dial and a rack and bell-striking movement, the inlaid boxwood-strung case with break-arch hood, apron replaced, case later, c1800, 79in (200.5cm) high.
2,500–3,000
€/ $4,000–4,700 ⚒ S(O)

A mahogany longcase clock, by Lewis, Gravesend, the dial showing seconds and date, with Arabic chapters and matching brass hands, the eight-day movement striking on a bell, c1810, 87in (221cm) high.
£7,500–8,250
€/ $11,800–13,000 ⊞ PAO

A mahogany longcase clock, by A. Oliphant, Pittenweem, the round dial showing seconds and date, with matching brass hands, and eight-day bell striking movement, Scottish, c1810, 78½in (199.5cm) high.
£6,400–7,200
€/ $10,100–11,400 ⊞ PAO

CLOCKS

A pine longcase clock, with moonphase, and carved hood, Irish, c1810, 88in (223.5cm) high.
£2,000–2,200
€/ **$3,200–3,500** ⊞ HON

A late George III mahogany and line-inlaid longcase clock, by Bartley & Eggert, Bristol, the painted dial with Roman numerals, Arabic quarter-hour divisions, seconds and date subsidiary dials, the arch with an automaton of Adam and Eve in the Garden of Eden, the eight-day twin-train movement with anchor escapement and rack strike on a bell, 85¾in (218cm) high.
£3,200–3,800
€/ **$5,000–6,000** ⚘ DN
The Adam and Eve automaton feature in the arch is rare.

◄ **An oak and cross-banded longcase clock,** by T. Hadfield, Chapel, the broken-arch dial with moonphase, the eight-day rack and bell-striking movement with anchor escapement, the movement associated, early 19thC, 89¾in (228cm) high.
£1,300–1,500
€/ **$2,000–2,400** ⚘ B(NW)

► **An oak and mahogany longcase clock,** by Cordingley, Leeds, the dial with a stately home painted to the arch, with floral spandrels, Arabic chapters and two subsidiary dials, the eight-day movement striking on a bell, dial and movement possibly associated, early 19thC, 89¼in (226.5cm) high.
£950–1,100
€/ **$1,500–1,700** ⚘ B(L)

A mahogany longcase clock, by John Black, Aberdeen, the painted dial with subsidiary seconds and calendar dials, with an eight-day striking movement, Scottish, early 19thC, 88¼in (224cm) high.
£3,800–4,500
€/ **$6,000–7,000** ⚘ SWO

A mahogany longcase clock, by Thomas Blundell, Dublin, the dial with a silvered Roman chapter ring, the matted centre with ringed winding holes, calendar aperture and subsidiary seconds dial, the eight-day four-pillar movement with anchor escapement, rack striking on a bell, case and movement associated, Irish, early 19thC, 91¾in (233cm) high.
£2,500–2,800
€/ **$4,000–4,400** ⚘ B(Kr

An oak longcase clock, by Harvey, Abergavenny, the dial with Roman numerals and a calendar aperture, with a 30-hour movement, the hood with a dentil cornice, blind fret frieze and pillars, Welsh, early 19thC, 75in (190.5cm) high.
£1,000–1,200
€/ **$1,600–1,900** ⚘ PF

An oak longcase clock, by Jno Peacock, Lincoln, the arched painted dial with seconds and calendar dials, with eight-day, twin-train movement, the walnut banded hood with a swan-neck pediment surmounted by three brass globe finials, early 19thC, 78in (198cm) high.
£1,700–2,000
€/ **$2,700–3,200** ⚘ **PF**

A mahogany longcase clock, by Moseley, Neath, with enamel dial, Roman numerals, date aperture and seconds dial, the eight-day movement striking on a bell, Welsh, early 19thC, 89in (226cm) high.
£1,800–2,200
€/ **$2,800–3,500** ⚘ **B(SW)**

mahogany crossbanded ngcase clock, by G. Healer, antage, the painted dial ith Roman numerals and liate spandrels, with a 0-hour movement striking n a bell, the hood with rned columns, early 9thC, 78¾in (200cm) high.
450–525
/ **$700–800** ⚘ **DN**
his is a very reasonable rice for this clock.

An oak longcase clock, the arched painted enamel dial with Roman numerals, subsidiary seconds and calendar dials, the eight-day movement by J. Low, Arbroath, the hood with a swan-neck pediment, Scottish, early 19thC, 79in (200.5cm) high.
£1,000–1,200
€/ **$1,600–1,900** ⚘ **LVS**

n oak longcase clock, by mes Potts, Berwick, the rched dial with a painted ene of a Chinese woman nd a parasol, with a ubsidiary seconds dial, ate aperture and Arabic umerals, with an eight-day ovement, early 19thC, 0¼in (204cm) high.
650–750
/ **$1,000–1,200** ⚘ **TRM**

An inlaid mahogany longcase clock, the arched dial painted with a moonphase, with Roman numerals and seconds dial, with eight-day movement, early 19thC, 88¼in (224cm) high.
£2,200–2,600
€/ **$3,500–4,100** ⚘ **CHTR**

CLOCKS

CLOCKS

Most longcase clocks will have either an eight-day or a 30-hour movement. The latter was no problem when someone was always at home to wind the clock every day. After the invention of the railway and the car, travel became easier and more frequent, and so owners preferred to have a clock that would not run down and stop if they went away for the weekend. As both trains are driven by the same weight, the trick is to put a clothes peg on the strike fly to prevent the strike sounding, and the timekeeping side will then run for about four days on one winding. Eight-day clocks are more sought after and so tend to command higher prices. The same increase in value applies to the rarer month-going and longer-duration clocks.

An oak longcase clock, the arched dial painted with a coaching scene and signed 'Hexham', with seconds dial and arched date aperture, the eight-day four-pillar movement with a deadbeat escapement striking on a bell, early 19thC, 83in (211cm) high.
£800–1,000
€/ **$1,300–1,600** ✒ HOLL

A late George III oak and mahogany inlaid longcase clock, by William Randall, Newbury, the painted dial with Arabic numerals, subsidiary seconds and date dials, the arch with a moon-phase, the eight-day twin-train movement with rack striking on a bell, stamped 'Walker & Hughes', 83¾in (213cm) high.
£1,400–1,600
€/ **$2,200–2,500** ✒ DN

An oak longcase clock, by R. Summerhayes, Ilminster, the dial with seconds and date dials, and Arabic chapters, the eight-day movement striking on a bell, c1815, 86in (218.5cm) high.
£3,500–4,000
€/ **$5,500–6,300** ⊞ PAO

An oak and crossbanded-mahogany longcase clock, by R. Summerhayes, Ilminster, with an eight-day movement, c1820, 78in (198cm) high.
£3,800–4,300
€/ **$6,000–6,800** ⊞ ALS

◄ **A pine longcase timepiece,** by Samuel Beal, Sheffield, with original painted and grained decoration, c1820, 62in (157.5cm) high.
£4,000–4,500
€/ **$6,300–7,000** ⊞ MHA

A late Georgian oak and mahogany longcase clock, by Martin Roper, Penrith, the painted dial with Roman numerals and a crescent-form date aperture, with a 30-hour, hour striking movement, c1815, 80in (203cm) high.
£900–1,100
€/ **$1,400–1,700** ✒ PFK

◄ **A Biedermeier birchwood longcase clock,** by Ola Larsson, Solberga, Swedish, c1820, 88in (223.5cm) high.
£5,500–6,000
€/ **$8,700–9,500** ⊞ CAV
Ola Larsson (1762–1853) lived in Solberga, in the province of Skåne. He made a great variety of clocks, including longcase

THE LARGEST GRANDFATHER CLOCK SHOP IN THE UK
ANTIQUE CLOCKS

We have a high quality stock of 150 fine authentic longcases with automata, moonphase, chiming, musical, brass dial, painted dial 8-day clocks both by London and provincial makers. In addition we have music boxes, stick and banjo barometers, wall, bracket and carriage clocks.

Restoration by experienced craftsmen in our own workshops

Free delivery and setting up throughout the UK

OPEN ALL DAY MONDAY TO SATURDAY OR BY APPOINTMENT

CREDIT CARDS ACCEPTED

☆

WORLDWIDE SHIPPING

CLOCKS

Rare 8-day oval dial moonphase clock by Banister of Lichfield, 1783-95, in a fine mahogany and satinwood case

A fine 8-day arched brass dial high water at Bristol moonphase clock by John Plumley of Bristol, 1746-71, in an exceptional flame mahogany case

Styles of Stow
The Little House, Sheep Street
Stow-on-the-Wold, Gloucestershire GL54 1JS
Telephone/Fax: 01451 830455
Website: www.stylesofstow.co.uk
Email: info@stylesofstow.co.uk

WRITTEN GUARANTEE AND INSURANCE VALUATION
PROVIDED WITH EVERY PURCHASE

A George IV mahogany longcase clock, by William Roberts, Bath, the painted dial with date aperture and subsidiary seconds dial, the eight-day twin-train movement with anchor escapement and rack striking on a bell, 89in (226cm) high.
£1,800–2,200
€/ **$2,800–3,500** 🔨 **DN**

An oak and mahogany longcase clock, by Richard Griffith, Denbigh, the painted dial with date aperture subsidiary seconds ring, with an eight-day movement, with a false plate cast 'Finnemore & Son', Welsh, c1830, 88in (223.5cm) high.
£1,700–2,000
€/ **$2,700–3,200** 🔨 **B(NW)**

A mahogany longcase clock, by Dubberly, Monmouth, the enamelled dial with two subsidiary dials, flanked by spiral columns, the case on bracket supports, Welsh, c1830, 86in (218.5cm) high.
£1,700–2,000
€/ **$2,700–3,200** 🔨 **BWL**

A mahogany longcase clock, by W. Birtwell, Burnley, the arched brass dial with a moonphase, with an eight-day movement, the hood with a swan-neck cornice and baluster columns, the trunk with a Gothic arched door between cluster column corners with inlaid stringing, 19thC, 96in (244cm) high.
£2,000–2,400
€/ **$3,200–3,800** 🔨 **SWO**

An oak longcase clock, by Marshall, Greenside, the painted dial with floral corners, the arch painted with a peacock, the 30-hour plated movement with outside countwheel striking on a bell, the hood with a flat top dentil-moulded cornice, c1830, 81in (205.5cm) high.
£750–900
€/ **$1,200–1,400** 🔨 **S(O)**

An oak longcase clock, by George Stephenson, Warminster, the painted dial with date and seconds the eight-day movement striking the hours on a bell, c1830, 82in (208.5cm) high
£2,400–2,700
€/ **$3,800–4,300** ⊞ **K&D**

▶ **A mahogany longcase clock,** by Lawrence, Bristol, the brass dial with a lunar aperture with High Water at Bristol Key, the chapter ring with Roman numerals, cast corner spandrels, engraved centre panel, date aperture and second hand, with an eight-day striking movement, the case with boxwood and ebony string inlays, case c1840, movement and dial c1770, 89in (226cm) high.
£2,200–2,600
€/ **$3,500–4,100** ↗ HoG

A Biedermeier birchwood longcase clock, inscribed [s]ic volvitur aetas', (so time [e]lapses), Swedish, c1830, [8]6in (218.5cm) high.
5,000–5,600
€/ **$7,900–8,900** ⊞ CAV

A mahogany longcase clock, by Richard Roughsedge, Twickenham, the brass dial with a silvered chapter ring and subsidiary seconds dial, the hood with a finial-mounted arched moulded cornice above a glazed door, case c1835, movement c1775, 88¼in (224cm) high.
£1,700–2,000
€/ **$2,700–3,200** ↗ CGC

An early Victorian oak and mahogany-veneered longcase clock, by Pearce, Stratford, the dial painted with a pheasant, country houses and cottages, the 30-hour movement striking on a bell, 83in (211cm) high.
£500–600
€/ **$800–950** ↗ WW

CLOCKS

CLOCKS

An oak and mahogany longcase clock, by George Wilson, Appleby, the painted dial with Roman numerals, subsidiary seconds dial and date aperture, the arch painted with two sheep by a stream, with an eight-day hour-striking movement, c1845, 86in (218.5cm) high.
£800–1,000
€ / **$1,300–1,600** ↗ **PFK**

A mahogany longcase clock, by James Simm, Elgin, the dial painted with a country sporting scene in the arch, the corners with game, with seconds and date dials, the eight-day movement striking the hours on a bell, Scottish, c1850, 73in (185.5cm) high.
£5,500–6,200
€ / **$8,600–9,800** ↗ **PAO**

A mahogany longcase clock, by Dilger & Barclay, Glasgow, the painted dial with seconds and calendar dials, with a rack and gong-striking movement, Scottish, c1850, 82in (208.5cm) high.
£2,700–3,000
€ / **$4,300–4,700** ↗ **S(O)**
The bowfronted door is typical of mid-19th century Scottish clocks.

A mahogany longcase clock, the painted enamel dial with Roman and Arabic numerals, subsidiary seconds and calendar dials and an eight-day movement, with a moulded arch hood, Scottish, 19thC, 79in (200.5cm) high.
£1,100–1,300
€ / **$1,700–2,000** ↗ **LVS**

An oak and walnut longcase clock, by W. Pibus, Caister, the arch painted with ships, the spandrels with shells, the dial with Roman numerals, second dial, and calendar aperture, mid-19thC, 84in (213.5cm) high.
£1,200–1,500
€ / **$1,900–2,400** ↗ **PF**

A painted pine longcase clock, Swedish, c1850, 78in (198cm) high.
£4,000–4,500
€ / **$6,300–7,000** ⊞ **DeG**

A mahogany longcase clock, by R. Currer, Falkirk, the dial painted with studies of Thompson, Allan Ramsay, Sir Walter Scott, Cunningham and the Lass of Gowrie, with subsidiary seconds and date dials, with an eight-day movement, the trunk with a bowfronted door, turned pilasters and ogee columns, Scottish, mid-19thC, 85¾in (218cm) high.
£2,800–3,200
€/ **$4,400–5,000** ⚒ **B(Ed)**

A mahogany longcase clock, by Josh. Stromier, Glasgow, the dial with Roman numerals, subsidiary seconds and calendar dials, with an eight-day bell-striking movement, Scottish, 19thC, 78¼in (199cm) high.
£1,400–1,600
€/ **$2,200–2,500** ⚒ **AMB**

An oak and mahogany longcase clock, by Birley, Birmingham, the painted arched dial with seconds dial, date aperture and Roman numerals, with an eight-day four-pillar bell-striking movement, the hood with a swan-neck pediment and half-columns, 19thC, 87in (221cm) high.
£1,000–1,200
€/ **$1,600–1,900** ⚒ **CGC**

◀ **A grained wood *comtoise* clock,** by Duval, Beaumont-le-Roger, with an embossed gilt-brass framed enamel dial, the case graining including *faux*-marquetry and stringing, French, c1850, 88½in (225cm) high.
£1,000–1,200
€/ **$1,600–1,900** ⚒ **NOA**

A mahogany longcase clock, by Pirrie, Perth, the gilt-painted dial with seconds and subsidiary dials, the eight-day movement striking on a bell, the hood with a broken pediment with a ball finial above a brass-rimmed glazed door with anthemion-carved corners and side columns, Scottish, 19thC, 90½in (230cm) high.
£2,000–2,500
€/ **$3,200–4,000** ⚒ **B(Ed)**
The unusual appearance of this clock would be attractive to many people, and therefore it could sell for up to £3,000 (€/ $4,700).

A painted pine *comtoise* clock, French, c1860, 96in (244cm) high.
£700–800
€/ **$1,100–1,300** ⊞ **PaA**

▶ **A mahogany longcase clock,** by David Read, Ipswich, with painted dial, and eight-day bell striking movement, under an arched hood flanked by reeded columns, 19thC, 84¾in (215.5cm) high.
£1,600–2,000
€/ **$2,500–3,200** ⚒ **AMB**

◄ A mahogany longcase clock, the break-arch dial applied with a silvered Arabic numeral chapter ring, subsidiary dials for seconds, Westminster/Whittington chimes, strike/silent and chime/silent, the quarter-chiming triple-train movement with anchor escapement on eight tubular bells, striking the hour on a further bell, c1900, 102in (259cm) high.
£4,000–5,000
€ / $6,300–7,900 ➹ Bri

► A Gothic-revival mahogany longcase clock, retailed by Maple & Co, London, the shaped silvered dial with subsidiaries for chime/silent and Whittington chimes/Westminster chimes, over a Roman chapter and subsidiary seconds within engraved scrolls, the quarter-chiming movement with maintaining power and deadbeat escapement, the glazed trunk door revealing the mercury pendulum and beat scale, tubular chimes missing, late 19thC, 96½in (245cm) high.
£3,200–3,800
€ / $5,000–6,000 ➹ B
The lack of tubular bells has kept the price of this clock down.

The prices realized at auction may reflect the fact that the clocks have sometimes undergone alterations to their movements, or are in unrestored condition.

CLOCKS

A walnut-inlaid longcase clock, by Percy Webster, the brass dial with a silvered chapter ring, the four-pillar movement with anchor escapement rack striking on a bell, 1875–1925, 72½in (184cm) high.
£4,200–5,000
€ / $6,600–7,900 ➹ B

An Edwardian mahogany chiming longcase clock, the brass dial with a silvered chapter ring with Roman numerals, subsidiary seconds dial, the arch with chime/silent dial, the eight-day triple-train movement with deadbeat anchor escapement, striking and chiming the hours on coiled gongs, 85¾in (218cm) high.
£3,200–3,800
€/ **$5,000–6,000** ⚒ DN

A late Edwardian mahogany longcase clock, retailed by Mappin & Webb, London, the dial with silvered chapter ring with gilt Arabic numerals, seconds dial, chimes selector and dials to the arch, the eight-day movement chiming on eight tubular bells, the hood inlaid with floral scrolls and a central fan motif, 93in (236cm) high.
£3,500–4,200
€/ **$5,500–6,600** ⚒ AG

A George III-style longcase clock, the brass dial inscribed 'Tempus Fugit', the silvered boss and chapter ring with a leaf-engraved centre, with a triple-train chiming movement, the hood flanked by fluted pillars below a blind fret frieze and swan-neck pediment, early 20thC, 47¼in (120cm) high.
£5,000–6,000
€/ **$7,900–9,500** ⚒ B(WM)

► **A mahogany longcase clock,** retailed by Yoell, Retford, the brass arched dial with foliate spandrels, the silver chapter ring with Roman numerals and subsidiary seconds dial, the arch with a chime/silent dial, the eight-day triple-train movement with anchor escapement, striking the hour and chiming the quarters on five tubular bells, early 20thC, 92½in (235cm) high.
£2,500–3,000
€/ **$4,000–4,700** ⚒ DN

A mahogany longcase clock, the brass dial with chime/silent and Whittington/Westminster subsidiary dials above a silvered chapter ring with gilt Arabic numerals and subsidiary seconds dial, the eight-day chiming movement striking on tubular bells, early 20thC, 88¼in (224cm) high.
£2,800–3,200
€/ **$4,400–5,000** ⚒ RTo

◄ **An inlaid mahogany longcase clock,** the brass dial with a silvered chapter ring with Roman hours and Arabic minutes, silvered strike/silent ring and chapter ring, the movement striking on a gong, early 20thC, 72½in (184cm) high.
£1,300–1,500
€/ **$2,000–2,400** ⚒ PFK

An oak Jacobean-revival-style longcase clock, the dial with a silvered chapter ring and baroque-style spandrels, the German triple-train movement by Winterhalter & Hofmeier, chiming and striking on gongs, early 20thC, 77in (195.5cm) high.
£1,700–2,000
€/ **$2,700–3,200** ⚒ PFK

Novelty Clocks

A bronze cathedral clock, with spring-drive eight-day time and bell-strike movement, with gilt dial, spires and figures and silk thread suspension, the sides with blue glass panels behind the arches, French, c1820, 19in (48.5cm) high.
£4,000–4,500
€/ **$6,300–7,000** ⊞ SET

A patinated-brass novelty timepiece, modelled as a fountain with rotating glass 'water stream', the gilt dial with Roman numerals, the movement with silk suspension, pinned pillars and light bob, set in a brickwork arch with a lion's head spout issuing the rotating glass rod into a cut-glass bowl, on an ebonized stand, glass dome cracked, French, mid-19thC, 15¾in (40cm) high.
£625–725
€/ **$1,000–1,200** ⚒ B

A parasol timepiece, set with 12 enamel numeral plaques, the eight-day movement signed 'W Paris' below a crown, decorated with stylized leaves and flowers, with later tin cover and later lever escapement, French, c1900, 10½in (26.5cm) diam.
£575–675
€/ **$900–1,100** ⚒ S(O)

▶ **An Edwardian picture timepiece,** with watch-style movement, depicting Big Ben and the Houses of Parliament, mounted and framed, 16 x 12½in (40.5 x 32cm).
£160–200
€/ **$250–320** ⚒ SWO

A carved oak longcase clock, modelled as a squar[e] tower, the pressed brass di[al] with Arabic numerals and ornate hands, the weight-driven movement striking on two coiled gongs, with carved roof tiles, brickwork balconies and windows, ov[er] a porch and four sets of steps, German, Black Fore[st] c1900, 107in (272cm) hig[h].
£2,200–2,500
€/ **$3,500–4,000** ⚒ B

Expert's choice

A musical and automaton clock, late 18thC, sold by Sotheby's in October 1993.

During my time at Sotheby's I have handled some extraordinary clocks but perhaps the most astonishing was a magnificent English ormolu musical and automaton clock that had lain abandoned for nearly half a century.

The clock belonged to an elderly farmer in Wales whose mother had paid £290 (€/ $460) for it in 1946. It had never worked the whole time they owned it and now he wanted to sell it.

The first time I saw the clock it took my breath away. It was obviously English despite its richly gilded casing and fell into the category of what is sometimes known as 'sing-songs'. These are extraordinary musical and automaton clocks that were made by a number of talented London makers in the late 18th century. They were made for export to the Orient and were usually purchased by western merchants to present to the Emperors who they hoped could be persuaded by such gifts to smooth the path of commerce.

This particular clock had a richly gilded body set with brightly coloured pastes and was surmounted by a painted and silvered peacock standing in front of a chinoiserie pagoda inset on the base with glass rods simulating waterfalls.

The clock was carefully removed from the farmhouse and delivered to our London warehouse where, after some repair and oiling, it was excitedly restarted.

The peacock began its performance after more than half a century of lying silent. The organ bellows were in a poor condition and so the pipes produced no more than a wheezing sound but the bells played loudly and tunefully while the bird moved around in a most realistic way turning its head back and forth, moving its long flexible neck and displaying its beautiful tail, while the pagoda behind began to rise in the air until it was double its original height. As the music drew to a close the pagoda sank back to its previous level and the peacock concluded its performance with a small bow.

Research revealed that the clock had a documented provenance from 1835 when it was purchased in New Bond Street, London, by a wealthy landowner. The history of the clock before 1835 is not known but, although unsigned, it is likely that it was made in the workshops of the famous clockmaking entrepreneur James Cox. Ironically, the dealer who purchased it for £353,000 (€/ $558,000) in October 1993 had his premises on the same street where it had been sold in 1835. **Michael Turner**

CLOCKS

Skeleton Clocks

CLOCKS

A marble and brass skeleton mantel timepiece, the enamel dial with Roman numerals and Breguet hands, the movement with anchor escapement and silk suspended pendulum, on a marble base beneath a glass dome with later ebonized base, French, 1800–25, 9½in (24cm) high.
£400–500
€/ **$630–800** ⚖ S(Am)

A bronzed skeleton timepiece, with silvered chapter ring and Roman numerals, the pendulum movement with passing strike, the stepped lobed marble base with bun feet, c1875, 16½in (42cm) high.
£600–700
€/ **$950–1,100** ⊞ WL

Items in the Clock section have been arranged in date order within each sub-section.

A Victorian brass skeleton timepiece, with a fretted silvered Roman chapter ring, the eight-day single fusee mechanism with passing strike, four wheel crossings and anchor escapement, on a moulded mahogany plinth beneath a glass dome, 19¼in (49cm) high.
£750–875
€/ **$1,200–1,400** ⚖ BIG

A brass skeleton timepiece, with painted chapter ring and fusee movement with anchor escapement and passing strike on a bell, the pierced Gothic frame on a velvet-covered stand and similar base, beneath a cracked glass dome, c1875, 16½in (42cm) high.
£450–500
€/ **$700–800** ⚖ S(O)

Wall Clocks

For further information on antique clocks see the full range of Miller's books at **www.millers.uk.com**

A tavern clock, by Gillett & Healey, Manchester, with gilt chinoiserie decoration, late 18thC, 60in (152.5cm) high.
£14,000–16,000
€/ **$22,000–25,000** ⊞ ALS

An elmwood ship's automaton alarm *staartklok*, restored, automaton later, Dutch, Frisland, c1800, 50¾in (129.5cm) high.
£850–1,000
€/ **$1,400–1,600** ⚖ S(Am)

◀ **A rosewood wall timepiece,** with painted dial and eight-day fusee movement, inlaid with mother-of-pearl, c1830, 24in (61cm) high.
£1,100–1,300
€/ **$1,700–2,000** ⊞ SET

A mahogany wall clock,
by D. Meyer, Abingdon, the
convex dial with Roman
chapters, the eight-day
fusee movement with
shaped plates and anchor
escapement, c1835, dial
12in (30.5cm) diam.
£1,700–2,000
€/ **$2,700–3,200** ⊞ PAO

Wall clocks were the earliest form of clock as it was
necessary to provide room for the driving weights
to descend before the invention of the coiled
spring. Even after the invention of the spring, they
continued to be popular and were made with both
weight-driven and spring-driven movements.

In Europe the most common forms to be
found are:

- Britain: tavern clocks (weight-driven) and dial
  clocks (spring and fusee-driven). Both types
  originated in the 18th century and the dial
  clock continued to be made well into the
  20th century.
- France: cartel clocks were made from the
  mid-18th century. All French wall clocks were
  usually spring-driven.
- Germany: cuckoo clocks and 'postman's alarm'
  clocks. Both were usually weight-driven although
  some spring and fusee cuckoo clocks exist.
- Holland: *stoelkloks* and *staartkloks*. Both
  types were always weight-driven.

CLOCKS

◀ **An ebonized and
gilded wall clock,** Maltese,
19thC, 23¾in (60.5cm) high.
£4,000–4,500
€/ **$6,300–7,000** ⚒ B(Pr)
Maltese items are keenly
sought after by the
home market.

▶ **A mahogany drop-
dial wall timepiece,** by
Dearling, Croydon, with
eight-day fusee movement,
c1860, 20in (51cm) high.
£1,000–1,100
€/ **$1,600–1,700** ⊞ K&D

**A Biedermeier ash wall
timepiece,** the milk-glass
dial signed 'Ignaz Lutz in
Wien', the Roman numerals
within shields and enclosed
within a gilded pie-crust
bezel, the eight-day
movement with a wood
rod pendulum, Austrian,
c1845, 38¼in (97cm) high.
£5,200–5,800
€/ **$8,200–9,200** ⊞ C&A

A musical cuckoo clock, he dial with pierced horn ands, the triple-train novement playing four irs, with eagle cresting, he front with two opening oors, one with a piper, he other a cuckoo, the ront flanked by entwined ak leaves above a carved eer and hunting dog on a ockwork base, piper later, ierman, Black Forest, late 9thC, 43in (109cm) high.
1,800–2,200
/ **$2,800–3,200** ➹ HAM

A Vienna-style walnut wall clock, by Gustav Becker, with enamel dial and eight-day twin-train weight-driven striking movement, the case with fluted columns, German, late 19thC, 45¾in (116cm) high.
£350–425
€/ **$550–670** ➹ AMB

A Vienna-style walnut and ebonized wall clock, the enamelled dial with Roman numerals and subsidiary second hand, eight-day weight-driven striking movement, German, c1895, 40in (101.5cm) high.
£400–450
€/ **$630–700** ➹ Mit

A mahogany wall clock, with weight-driven movement, the case with three-finial pediment top, the trunk with column sides, German, early 20thC, 52in (132cm) long.
£320–375
€/ **$500–600** ➹ FHF

CLOCKS

American Clocks

carved and figured ralnut longcase clock, ith moon dial and repainted alendar wheel, the moon al stamped (Os)bornes Man)ufactory Birmingham, iside of backboard inscribed . Miller Wyoming, A', base moulding later, ennsylvania, c1780, 2in (233.5cm) high.
11,500–13,500
/ **$18,200–21,300** ➹ S(NY)
lany American longcase ocks have movements nd dials that were made England. Their rarity nd value lie in the custom-iade American cases.

A faux bois mirror wall clock, the painted wood dial with Roman numerals, gilt spandrels and matching diamond hands, the twin-train weight-driven movement with wooden wheels and anchor escapement, the countwheel striking on a bell, inside label 'Patent Clocks, manufactured & sold by David Dutton, Mont Vernon, N.H.', 1825–50, 35½in (90cm) high.
£600–720
€/ **$950–1,100** ➹ S(Am)

► **A carved walnut drop-dial wall clock,** the paper dial with Roman numerals, mid-19thC, 31½in (80cm) high.
£400–500
€/ **$630–800** ➹ SWO

A mahogany double decker shelf clock, by Birge, Peck & Co, Bristol, decorated with panels of Andrew Jackson and a beehive, replaced dial and tablets, case split, weights missing, Connecticut, 1830–56, 32¾in (83.5cm) high.
£250–300
€/ **$400–475** ➹ JDJ

A mahogany Gothic-style clock, by Birge & Fuller, Bristol, with painted dial, eight-day wagon-spring movement, the case with four candlesticks, losses to dial, replaced minute hand, bottom glass replaced, Connecticut, c1845, 26in (66cm) high.
£2,500–3,000
€/ **$4,000–4,700** ➹ ROSc

A rosewood shelf clock, by Atkins Clock Co, Bristol, with repainted dial and eight-day time/strike/alarm movement, restored, Connecticut, c1865, 16¾in (42.5cm) high.
£280–325
€/ **$440–520** ➹ ROSc

CLOCKS

A rosewood wall clock, by E. N. Welch, Forrestville, time and strike movement, case refinished, original label, Connecticut, c1865, 25in (63.5cm) high.
£750–825
€/ **$1,200–1,300** ⊞ **SET**

▶ **A mahogany trunk dial wall clock,** the painted dial signed for 'T Hyde, Sleaford', with open-spring bell striking movement signed 'E. N. Welch, Forestville, Connecticut, USA', the case with carved ears and inset with a lenticle, rim and glass missing, c1890, 21¼in (54cm) high.
£550–600
€/ **$870–950** ⚒ **S(O)**

A miniature tin mantel clock, the enamelled chapter ring dial with gilt centre, winding mechanism operated by the rear panel, stamped 'Pat.April 23rd 1878', late 19thC, 2¼in (5.5cm) diam, in original tin case.
£160–200
€/ **$250–320** ⚒ **FHF**

A spelter shelf clock, by Seth Thomas Sons & Co, with 14-day spring-driven movement striking on a bell, some repainting, 1865–79, 17in (43cm) high.
£750–820
€/ **$1,200–1,300** ⊞ **SET**

▶ **A mahogany trunk dial wall clock,** [see text above]

A Greek revival-style enamel-painted wood mantel clock, by Gilbert, chiming on rods, some repainting, dated 1913, 12in (30.5cm) high.
£280–320
€/ **$440–500** ⊞ **SET**

◀ **An oak wall clock,** Jupiter, by Seth Thomas Clock Co, with moon dial and eight-day weight-driven-movement striking on a bell, restored, c1910, 59in (150cm) high.
£5,000–6,000
€/ **$7,900–9,500** ⚒ **ROSc**

A rosewood shelf clock, Oriental, by E. Ingraham & Co, Bristol, with eight-day time and strike movement, case refinished, some veneer loss, Connecticut, c1878, 18in (45.5cm) high.
£600–720
€/ **$950–1,200** ⚒ **ROSc**

A painted wood regulator, c1890, 36in (91.5cm) high.
£80–100
€/ **$125–160** ⚒ **DuM**

An oak regulator wall timepiece, Observatory, by William L. Gilbert Clock Co, with eight-day movement, minor damage, c1910, 37in (94cm) high.
£300–350
€/ **$475–550** ⚒ **ROSc**

An oak school regulator, by Seth Thomas Clock Co, with eight-day spring-driven time and strike movement, original label, c1890, 24in (61cm) high.
£500–565
€/ **$800–900** ⊞ **SET**

A stained pine wall clock, with painted dial, and eight-day movement striking on a bell, late 19thC, 21½in (54.5cm) high.
£200–225
€/ **$320–350** ⚒ **DA**

A mahogany miniature banjo timepiece, by Waltham Clock Co, with eight-day lever movement and Waltham's 'car clock' stem wind movement, some replacements and repairs, c1930, 21in (53.5cm) high
£270–320
€/ **$430–500** ⚒ **ROSc**

British Regulators

An early Victorian mahogany regulator, the painted dial with an outer ring with Arabic five-minute divisions and centre sweep hand, subsidiary seconds and hour dials, inscribed and dated 'W W Kent 1837', the single-train movement with deadbeat escapement, 73¼in (186cm) high.
€3,000–3,400
€/ $4,700–5,400 ⚒ DN

A mahogany longcase regulator, by William Barr, Edinburgh, the painted dial with subsidiary hour and seconds dials, the movement with deadbeat escapement and maintaining power, a glass reverse-painted pendulum bob, c1859, 76in (193cm) high.
£5,800–6,500
€/ $9,200–10,200 ⊞ K&D

A mahogany regulator, by Jenkins, Merthyr, with mercury pendulum, restored, c1860, 83in (211cm) high.
£7,500–8,500
€/ $11,900–13,400 ⊞ KHW

A mahogany-veneered regulator, the silvered dial with subsidiary seconds and hour dials, inscribed 'John Garden, Aberdeen', the single-train movement with deadbeat escapement, Scottish, 19thC, 82¼in (209cm) high.
£3,200–3,800
€/ $5,000–6,000 ⚒ WW

CLOCKS

CLOCKS

◄ **An oak longcase regulator,** by William Maule, Coldstream, with engraved and signed silvered dial, weight-driven movement and deadbeat escapement, maintaining power, five-spoke wheels and minute hand counterweight, separately suspended steel rod pendulum, c1860, 75½in (192cm) high.
£3,300–4,000
€/ \$5,200–6,300
⚒ **S(O)**

A mahogany table regulator, by Pewsey, London, with signed silvered dial, maintaining power and double-wheeled deadbeat escapement to twin jar mercury pendulum, the case with a glazed front door with dependent pierced cresting, 1850–1900, 22½in (57cm) high.
£4,000–4,800
€/ \$6,300–7,600 ⚒ **B**

Regulators

A true regulator is a timepiece without strike or chime which will run so accurately (usually within a second or two a week) that other clocks can be regulated by it. A regulator will be weight driven and have some sort of compensated pendulum and a deadbeat escapement. The movement (mechanism) will be as simple as possible, and because of this the dials are distinctive, with an outer minutes ring enclosing separate seconds and hours dials. This is to eliminate additional wheel work behind the dial that would be needed if both hour and minute hands were concentric as on ordinary clocks. Many clocks such as German and Austrian 'Vienna' wall clocks and French four-glass clocks are incorrectly called regulators, even though they are capable of keeping excellent time and sometimes have a form of compensated pendulum.

Continental Regulators

A gold-plated brass crystal regulator, the enamel dial with second hand, signed 'Theo B. Starr', with eight-day spring-driven time and strike movement, mercury pendulum, minor repairs, case lacquered, French, c1870, 18½in (47cm) high.
£2,500–2,800
€/ \$4,000–4,500 ⊞ **SET**
It is quite rare to have a centre seconds hand.

A walnut *grande sonnerie Laterndluhr*, by 'Rauschmann in Ofen', the enamel dial with two subsidiary dials for the calendar work, with eight-day movement striking the quarters on two bells, the case with pen and ink decoration and ebonized backboard, lift-out side doors to the hood, Austrian, c1810, 61in (155cm) high.
£55,000–60,000
€/ \$87,000–95,000 ⊞ **C&A**

A walnut *Dachluhr*, attributed to Marrenzeller, the enamel dial no longer signed, with a gilded engine-turned bezel, the movement with high-count pinions and maintaining power, the compensated gridiron pendulum with a brass bob, the fan-top six-light case with boxwood stringing, Austrian, c1845, 66in (167.5cm) high.
£32,000–36,000
€/ \$50,000–56,000 ⊞ **C&A**

A rosewood and brass-inlaid mantel regulator, the two-piece enamel dial with Roman numerals, the centre signed 'Planté Sr De Lagrave A Paris', gilt Breguet hands, the movement with visible Brocot escapement stamped 'Noël A Robins A Paris 5528', the countwheels striking on a bell, heavy gridiron pendulum, French, mid-19thC, 22¾in (58cm) high.
£2,200–2,500
€/ \$3,500–4,000 ⚒ **S(Am)**

▶ **A four-glass regulator,** with Roman calibrated dial, the Japy Frères eight-day movement rack striking on a bell, with mercurial pendulum, the geometric case with flat top and moulded edge and bevelled glass sides, French, 1875–1925, 12½in (32cm) high.
£450–525
€/ \$700–830 ⚒ **BIG**

Watches
Pocket Watches

A silver mock triple-case pendulum verge watch, the full plate movement with Egyptian pillars, with later single steel hand, pendant and bow, maker's mark 'WE', signed 'Quare, London', late 17thC, 2¼in (5.5cm) diam.
£3,500–4,000
€/ $5,500–6,300 ⊞ PT

A gilt-metal pair-cased verge watch, with six-hour dial, subsidiary seconds and calendar work, with full plate movement, in a polished case, seconds hand missing, 1675–1725, 2¼in (5.5cm) diam.
£2,200–2,500
€/ $3,500–4,000 ⚒ B

A silver pair-cased watch, by William van der Hegge, Amsterdam, No. 73, the dial with date aperture, with pierced and engraved balance bridge, casemaker's mark 'CLP', Dutch, c1750, 2¼in (5.5cm) diam.
£600–720
€/ $950–1,100 ⚒ S(Am)

A gilt-metal verge watch, the full plate movement signed 'Gibb, Rotterdam', in a consular case covered with shagreen, 1750–1800, 2in (5cm) diam.
£825–1,000
€/ $1,300–1,600 ⚒ S(Am)

A gold-cased pocket watch, by Vauchez, Paris, No 7411, with enamel dial and diamond-set hands, the case with a border of brilliants, the reverse with an enamel portrait of a girl, 18thC, 1½in (4cm) diam.
£600–700
€/ $950–1,100 ⚒ L

A silver and tortoiseshell triple-case verge pocket watch, the movement signed 'C. Fly, London, No. 4211', the white enamel dial with gilt hands, hallmarked London 1761, 2¼in (5.5cm) diam.
£1,400–1,600
€/ $2,200–2,500 ⚒ GH

A repoussé silver air-cased pendant alarm timepiece, by Phillip Jacob Bickelman, the dial with secondary chapter ring and alarm dial, movement signed, inner case marked 'JB', outer case with remnants of stained shagreen, Austrian, mid-18thC, dial 5in (12.5cm) diam.
£3,000–3,400
€/ $4,700–5,400 ⚒ HOLL

A skeletonized gold verge watch, with stone-set silver hands and full plate fusee movement, enamel dial restored, signed 'Thuilly à Genève', Swiss, c1780, 1½in (4cm) wide.
£1,800–2,000
€/ $2,800–3,200 ⊞ PT

A gilt and underpainted horn pair-cased verge watch, by Arther Dodge, Goudhurst, No. 1773, signed, with later hands, 1780, 2in (5cm) diam.
£640–750
€/ $1,000–1,200 ⚒ S(O)

A gold and enamel consular-cased verge watch, by L'Epaute, Paris, with gilt full plate quarter-repeating movement, signed, the frame set with paste decoration, French, c1790, 1¾in (4.5cm) diam.
£1,200–1,400
€/ $1,900–2,200 ⚒ S(G)

A gold consular-cased verge watch, by L'Epine Horologers du Roy, minute hand later, with presentation case and winding key, French, c1790, 1½in (4cm) diam.
£800–900
€/ $1,300–1,400 ⚒ S(O)

A gilt and enamel verge watch, the silver regulator dial with gilt indicator, Arabic numerals and gold hands, the case with restored polychrome enamel pastoral scene, signed 'Breguet, Paris', French, c1800, 2¼in (5.5cm) diam.
£2,700–3,000
€/ $4,300–4,700 ⊞ PT

A gold pocket watch, the enamel dial signed 'Ls. Duchêne Compagnie', the painted reverse depicting Ganymede with an eagle, Swiss, late 18thC.
£3,000–3,800
€/ **$4,700–6,000** ⚒ G(B)

An 18ct gold lever watch, by Smith & Gamble, Dublin, No. 2005, with three-colour gold dial, in an engine-turned case, with associated guard chain and fob, Irish, early 19thC.
£700–820
€/ **$1,100–1,300** ⚒ B(Kn)

An 18ct Massey gold five-lever pocket watch, the gold dial with three-colour gold border and applied gold Roman numerals, with Harrison's maintaining power, hallmarked Chester 1822, 2¼in (5.5cm) diam.
£1,100–1,200
€/ **$1,700–1,900** ⊞ PT

An 18ct gold pocket watch, the fusee movement by Charles Harden, London, No. 6164, with chased and engine-turned decoration, 1823, 1¾in (4.5cm) diam.
£500–550
€/ **$800–870** ⚒ L

An 18ct gold lever pocket watch, with full plate gilt keywind fusee movement and Harrison's maintaining power, the engine-turned case with chased and engraved bezels, maker's mark 'WW', London 1825, 1¾in (4.5cm) diam, in a blue morocco-covered travelling case.
£1,000–1,200
€/ **$1,600–1,900** ⊞ PT

A gilt-metal cylinder stopwatch, by Thomas Earnshaw, London, No. 2671, in a consular case, the inner marked with initials 'TC', the outer case containing five watch papers dated from 1844–67 and a further example with a printed image of George III and a Thomas Earnshaw watch paper, early 19thC, 2in (5cm) diam.
£850–1,000
€/ **$1,300–1,600** ⚒ B

An 18ct gold open-faced pocket watch, by Charles Frodsham, London, No. 03964, the enamel dial with subsidiary seconds, the three-quarter plate gilt movement with lever escapement, London 1873, 2¼in (5.5cm) diam.
£1,900–2,300
€/ **$3,000–3,600** ⚒ S(NY)

◄ **An 18ct gold Victorian pocket watch,** the dial and case with engraved floral decoration, 1½in (4cm) diam.
£170–200
€/ **$270–315** ⚒ L

A diamond fob watch, by Le Roy & Fils, with an opalescent enamel dial surrounded by a border of brilliant-cut diamonds, the reverse engraved with a monogram and date, suspended on a silver and gold brooch set with diamonds, the chain set with rose-cut diamond accents, French, c1880.
£1,700–2,000
€/ **$2,700–3,200** ⚒ HAM

An 18ct pink-gold hunting-cased keyless cylinder watch, by Patek Philippe, No. 67074, the dial with Roman numerals, the back engraved with a coat-of-arms surmounted by a coronet, with a photocopied letter from Patek Philippe, dial with hair cracks, case now with wristwatch lugs, Swiss, 1881, 1⅛in (3cm) diam.
£900–1,100
€/ **$1,400–1,700** ⚒ S(O)

A 14ct gold keyless pocket watch, by Waltham, the case with engraved flowers and filigree patterns to the front edge, the reverse engraved with a stag, American, 1893.
£350–385
€/ **$550–600** ⊞ Bns

▶ **An 18ct gold open-faced watch,** by Breguet, No. 513, with a gilt lever movement, bi-metallic compensation balance, spiral balance with overcoil, wolf's tooth winding, and gold cuvette, French, 1889, 1¾in (4.5cm) diam, with certificate and leather box.
£1,500–1,800
€/ **$2,400–2,800** ⚒ S(NY)

An 18ct gold half-hunter-cased keyless lever watch, by George Orm & Son, No. 7708, the enamel dial with subsidiary seconds, the case reverse with an engraved entwined monogram, London 1898, 2in (5cm) diam.
£565–675
€/ $900–1,000 S(O)

An 18ct gold half-hunter watch, by M. F. Dent, No. 33028, with a secondary dial and crown wind, an engraved crest to the reverse of the case, Sheffield 1904, with original box.
£700–850
€/ $1,100–1,300 HOLL

A gunmetal watch, the gilt dial with rotating rings for minutes and hours, surmounted by a radiated cross, with a gilt lever movement, c1900, 2in (5cm) diam.
£850–1,000
€/ $1,300–1,600 S(Am)

▶ An 18ct gold open-face pocket watch, by Longines, No. 910503, the enamel dial with subsidiary seconds dial, the keyless 15-jewel movement with monometallic balance and flat balance spring, the engine-turned case with an engraved shield, Swiss, c1910.
£200–240
€/ $315–380 DN

A gold-mounted fob watch, the engine-turned gilt dial with pearl-set Roman chapters, the case set with half pearls, the surmount formed as a pearl-set shell, c1900.
£3,200–3,800
€/ $5,100–6,000 B(Ed)

◀ A diamond-set platinum pendant fob watch, c1910, 1in (2.5cm) diam.
£7,000–8,000
€/ $11,100–12,700 NBL

A silver pocket watch, the enamel dial with triple calendar and moonphase, in an engine-turned case, London 1917.
£400–450
€/ $630–710 DD

◀ A silver and enamel crucifix watch, with an enamel dial, and keywind gilt going barrel bar movement, Swiss, c1930, 3¼in (8.5cm) long.
£450–500
€/ $700–800 PT

Wristwatches

An Arbu moonphase calendar chronograph self-winding wristwatch, with an automatic movement, in a stainless steel case with push-button adjusters, Swiss, 1950s, 1¼in (3cm) diam.
£525–585
€ / **$830–920** ⊞ Bns

A Breitling Datora chronograph wristwatch, Swiss, c1953.
£900–1,000
€ / **$1,400–1,600** ⊞ HARP

A Le Coultre Master Mariner automatic wristwatch, with lapis-effect dial symbolizing the stars and the solar system and raised hour markers symbolizing planets, Swiss, c1955, with original box.
£1,400–1,500
€ / **$2,200–2,400** ⊞ HARP

A Baume & Mercier 18ct pink-gold triple date chronometer wristwatch, with registers and moonphase, subsidiary dials and seconds, minutes and hour recording, Swiss, c1950, 1½in (4cm) diam.
£6,300–7,000
€ / **$10,000–11,000** ⊞ AGR

A Cartier stainless steel wristwatch, with Girard Perregeux movement, French, 1945.
£630–700
€ / **$1,000–1,100** ⊞ HARP

A Longines silver wristwatch, Swiss, 1920s.
£580–650
€ / **$900–1,000** ⊞ TEM

◀ **A Longines stainless steel wristwatch,** the silvered dial with subsidiary seconds, with a nickel lever movement, Swiss, c1935, 1½in (3.5cm) long.
£350–400
€ / **$550–630**
⚒ S(Am)

A J. W. Benson 9ct gold wristwatch, with enamel dial and hands, hallmarked, 1933.
£450–500
€ / **$700–790** ⊞ HARP

An Eska Watch Co 18ct gold automatic centre seconds wristwatch, the cloisonné dial depicting two sailing ships, with applied faceted square and baton numerals, the cushion-form case with a faceted bezel, dial cracked, Swiss, c1955, 1¼in (3cm) wide.
£3,000–3,300
€ / **$4,700–5,200** ⚒ S(G)

A Longines 9ct gold wristwatch, with an enamel dial, Swiss, 1920s.
£550–625
€ / **$870–1,000** ⊞ TEM

▶ **A Movado steel wristwatch,** with day, date and month apertures, Swiss, 1950s.
£800–900
€ / **$1,300–1,400** ⊞ TEM

A Breitling 18ct gold triple-date chronograph wristwatch, Swiss, 1940s.
£3,200–3,600
€ / **$5,000–5,700** ⊞ TEM

An International Watch Co 18ct gold wristwatch, Swiss, 1950s.
£1,100–1,300
€ / **$1,700–2,000** ⊞ TEM

A Longines silver wristwatch, Swiss, 1930s.
£420–465
€ / **$670–730** ⊞ TEM

An Omega wristwatch, Swiss, 1930s.
£800–900
€ / $1,300–1,400   ⊞ TEM

An Omega steel three-dial chronograph wristwatch, Swiss, 1950s.
£1,800–2,000
€ / $2,800–3,200   ⊞ TEM

A Rolex 9ct gold wristwatch, No. 759142, the dial with luminous numerals and subsidiary seconds, with a nickel-finished movement, Swiss, 1918, 1¼in (3.5cm) diam.
£1,000–1,200
€ / $1,600–1,800   ⚒ B

An Omega 9ct gold wristwatch, Swiss, 1930s.
£870–970
€ / $1,300–1,500   ⊞ TEM

A Patek Philippe 18ct gold wristwatch, No. 638548, movement No. 901606, the silvered dial with subsidiary seconds, the polished case with downturned lugs, Swiss, 1940s, 1in (2.5cm) square.
£1,700–2,000
€ / $2,700–3,200   ⚒ B

A silver Rolex wristwatch, with an enamel dial, Swiss, 1920s.
£750–825
€ / $1,200–1,300   ⊞ TEM

◄ A Rolex half-hunter wristwatch, Swiss, 1920s.
£1,500–1,700
€ / $2,400–2,700   ⊞ TEM

An Omega 18ct gold wristwatch, the silvered dial with subsidiary seconds, the case with a curved back, Swiss, c1935, 1½in (4cm) long.
£650–770
€ / $1,000–1,200   ⚒ S(G)

A Pierce stainless steel chronograph wristwatch, the silvered dial with subsidiary seconds and dials for running seconds and minutes, c1940.
£190–230
€ / $300–360   ⚒ DN

An Omega stainless steel military wristwatch, the black dial with subsidiary seconds, luminous hands and marked with the King's arrow, Swiss, c1945, 1½in (3.5cm) diam.
£350–390
€ / $550–630   ⊞ Bns
The King's arrow indicates that this watch has been issued to the British Army.

WATCHES

A Rolex 9ct white-gold and diamond wristwatch, with a prima manual wind movement, the case set with 28 brilliant-cut diamonds, on a stainless steel band, c1930.
£300–360
€ / $470–570 ➹ LJ

A Rolex Prince stainless steel wristwatch, the brushed-steel dial with subsidiary seconds, Swiss, 1930s.
£2,400–2,800
€ / $3,800–4,400 ➹ AH

◀ **A Rolex Oyster Perpetual chronometer steel wristwatch,** Swiss, c1953, 1¼in (3cm) diam.
£470–560
€ / $740–880 ➹ BR

A Tiffany 14ct gold curved tank wristwatch, 1930s.
£1,300–1,500
€ / $2,100–2,400 ⊞ TEM

A silver hunter wristwatch, the dial with subsidiary seconds, early 20thC.
£140–160
€ / $220–250 ➹ G(L)

A Vacheron & Constantin gold, enamel and diamond-set bracelet watch, No. 360685, the bezel set with diamonds, with similarly decorated central lugs, Swiss, c1915, 1in (2.5cm) diam.
£1,400–1,600
€ / $2,200–2,500 ➹ S(O)

A cocktail watch, the diamond-set bezel with French-cut soapphire accents, c1925.
£200–225
€ / $320–350 ➹ HAM

A Rolex 9ct gold wristwatch, the dial with subsidiary seconds, Swiss, c1935.
£420–500
€ / $660–790 ➹ WW

A Tiffany 18ct gold wristwatch, 1920s.
£500–565
€ / $800–900 ⊞ TEM

A Zenith stainless steel top-wind wristwatch, with subsidiary seconds, Swiss, c1948.
£450–500
€ / $700–800 ⊞ HARP

A platinum square-cut diamond watch, c1925, ¾in (2cm) wide.
£1,800–2,000
€ / $2,800–3,200 ⊞ WIM

A Rolex Oyster 9ct gold wristwatch, the dial with outer seconds track and subsidiary seconds, with a 15-jewel movement, 1935, 1¼in (3cm) diam.
£420–500
€ / $660–790 ➹ B(Kn)

A diamond wristwatch, with a blue stone cabochon winding button on a white metal mesh bracelet, c1920
£650–820
€ / $1,000–1,300 ➹ WW

An Art Deco platinum diamond-set cocktail watch, the case with full diamond-set bezel, shoulder and lugs, each with a larger baguettte-cut diamond and seven circula faceted diamonds, on a 9ct twin row Brazilian link bracelet, 1930s, ½in (1.5cm) diam, with box
£1,100–1,300
€ / $1,700–2,000 ⊞ Bns

WATCHES

Barometers

Stick Barometers

A George III mahogany stick barometer, with arched silver dial inscribed 'G. Adams, Fleet Street', above a thermometer with vernier scale and hinged brass door, 37in (94cm) high.
£6,000–6,800
€/ $9,500–10,700 ➹ WW
It is less common to find stick barometers with brass doors. Always expect to pay more for examples that have this feature.

A mahogany stick barometer, by Burton, London, with silvered-brass plate and oval cistern cover, c1790, 36in (91.5cm) high.
£2,300–2,600
€/ $3,600–4,100 ⊞ AW

A mahogany stick barometer, by Jacob Abraham, Bath, the silvered plate with mercury thermometer, c1820, 36in (91.5cm) high.
£3,800–4,300
€/ $6,000–6,800 ⊞ PAO

A mahogany bowfronted stick barometer, by Dollond, London, with caddy top and ebonized cistern cover, c1830, 38in (96.5cm) high.
£6,000–7,500
€/ $9,500–11,500 ⊞ RAY

A mahogany bowfronted stick barometer, by Ramsden, London, the silvered scale with Ramsden's improved double pointer, c1800, 38in (96.5cm) high.
£10,000–12,000
€/ $15,800–19,000 ➹ TEN

A mahogany stick barometer, by Alex Trotter, Jedburgh, the decorated plates with hand-set pointer, with oval cistern cover, Scottish, c1800, 35¾in (91cm) high.
£1,300–1,500
€/ $2,000–2,400 ➹ S(O)

◀ **An oak stick barometer,** by H. Pascoe, Penzance, with ivory registers, 19thC, 35¾in (91cm) high.
£800–950
€/ **$1,300–1,500** ⚒ AH

A cast-iron-fronted stick barometer, with paper register inscribed 'J.W. Smith Stowe, VT', American, Vermont, 19thC, 37in (94cm) high.
£525–625
€/ **$830–980** ⚒ SWO

A mahogany stick barometer, by John Hay, Aberdeen, Scottish, c1850, 37in (94cm) high.
£1,800–2,000
€/ **$2,800–3,200** ⊞ TRI

◀ **A mahogany stick barometer,** by Cox, London, c1850, 37in (94cm) high.
£2,000–2,200
€/ **$3,200–3,500** ⊞ TRI

▶ **A mahogany stick barometer,** by Louis Pedrone, Liverpool, with signed silvered-brass register plates, c1850, 37in (94cm) high.
£5,500–6,000
€/ **$8,700–9,500** ⊞ AW

Always expect to pay more for a stick barometer than a wheel barometer of the same period. This is because fewer stick barometers were made and also demand for them today is higher. It is easy to understand when you realize that nowadays houses are smaller and it is easier to find space for an item that takes up only a few inches of space. Most stick barometers are only 4–6in (10–15cm) wide.

The popularity of the wheel barometer grew in the early 19th century because it was easier to read. The dial feature of a wheel barometer magnifies the inch scale, so smaller changes became more noticeable. The stick barometer measures the length of the mercury column in inches and so minor changes are less noticeable. An average wheel barometer has an 8in (20.5cm) dial size, fitted with a cabinet which is 10in (25.5cm) in diameter.

A mahogany stick barometer, signed 'NTE Opticien, Brussels', with glass print dial, slight damage, Belgian, mid-19thC, 42½in (108cm) high
£1,500–1,700
€/ **$2,400–2,700** ⚒ S(Am

A Victorian oak stick barometer, by J. Amadio, London, with ivory scales, 42¼in (107cm) high.
£600–720
€ / $950–1,100 ➹ Bea

A mahogany bowfronted stick barometer, by Dollond, London, with silvered-brass plate and inset thermometer, c1870, 38½in (98cm) high.
£3,500–4,000
€ / $5,500–6,300 ⊞ AW

A Victorian burr-walnut stick barometer, by J. B. Dancer, Manchester, with ivory plates, vernier scale and thermometer, 38in (98cm) high.
£1,300–1,500
€ / $2,000–2,400 ➹ WW

An oak Admiral Fitzroy barometer, c1880, 46in (117cm) high.
£1,600–1,800
€ / $2,500–2,800 ⊞ RAY

A Victorian oak Admiral Fitzroy storm barometer, by Negretti & Zambra, London, with signed ceramic plates, 41½in (105.5cm) high.
£1,800–2,200
€ / $2,800–3,500 ➹ WW

An ebonized wood stick barometer, by R. Beckmann, with signed silvered plates, losses, German, 1850–1900, 36½in (93cm) high.
£450–550
€ / $720–870 ➹ S(Am)

BAROMETERS

An oak Admiral Fitzroy Polytechnic barometer, by Joseph Davis, London, with signed silvered scale, two adjustable pointers for 'yesterday' and 'today' and Centigrade and Fahrenheit thermometers, c1885, 67in (170cm) high.
£2,200–2,500
€/ **$3,500–4,000** ↗ S(O)

Polytechnic barometers

Barometers of this style are interesting as they combine the advantages of the banjo barometer dial (which gives an expanded reading), with the scale and visibility of the stick barometer. The dial, instead of having the enlarged inch scale, has weather observations printed on the outer rim. These are broken into winter and summer readings, and are a modification of Fitzroy's observations. The majority of Polytechnic barometers have printed silvered-card dials, a few were made with white pottery dials and fewer still are of engraved silvered brass, the latter being the most expensive.

▶ **A mahogany stick barometer,** by Curry & Paxton, London, early 20thC, 36in (91.5cm) high.
£1,700–2,000
€/ **$2,700–3,200** ⊞ AW

◀ **An oak Admiral Fitzroy storm barometer,** c1890, 40in (101.2cm) high.
£800–900
€/ **$1,300–1,400** ⊞ AB

Wheel Barometers

A George III mahogany wheel barometer, by J. Wilson, London, with silvered dial and register above, chevron stringing, 46¾in (119cm) high.
£5,500–6,200
€/ **$8,700–9,800** ↗ WW

An inlaid mahogany wheel barometer, by R. Baker, Tamworth, with silvered-brass scale, c1800, 39in (99cm) high.
£1,600–1,800
€/ **$2,500–2,800** ⊞ PAO

An inlaid mahogany wheel barometer, by John Corti, London, with chequer stringing, c1800, 37in (94cm) high.
£2,400–2,800
€/ **$3,800–4,400** ⊞ AW

A mahogany and shell-inlaid wheel barometer, by Gough, London, with silvered register scale, alcohol thermometer and hygrometer, needs restoration, early 19thC, 38in (96.5cm) high.
£1,300–1,500
€/ **$2,100–2,400** ↗ TMA

A *verre églomisé* wheel barometer, the gilt, blue and white dial within gilt, green and red egg-and-dart border, French, c1800, 36¾in (93cm) high.
£2,000–2,200
€/ **$3,200–3,500** ⚒ S(Am)

A mahogany wheel barometer, by C. Camozzi, Buckingham, with dry/damp dial, thermometer and verge clock movement by Davidson, London, c1820, 46in (117cm) high.
€850–1,000
€/ **$1,300–1,600** ⚒ L&E

A mahogany wheel barometer, by G. Kalabergo, Banbury, with silvered-brass scale, thermometer, hygrometer and spirit level, c1830, dial 8in (20.5cm) diam.
£850–950
€/ **$1,300–1,500** ⊞ PAO

A mahogany and shell-inlaid wheel barometer, by Uago, Glasgow, with silvered dial, and alcohol thermometer, Scottish, early 19thC, 38¼in (97cm) high.
£420–500
€/ **$660–790** ⚒ B(L)

A mahogany and tulipwood crossbanded wheel barometer, by G. & C. Dixey, c1830, 43in (109cm) high.
£2,000–2,400
€/ **$3,500–3,800** ⊞ TRI

◄ **A mahogany wheel barometer,** by G. Kalabergo, Banbury, with silvered-brass scale, thermometer, hygrometer and spirit level, c1830, dial 8in (20.5cm) diam.

A crossbanded satinwood wheel barometer, by Lione Somalvico & Co, London, c1810, dial 12in (30.5cm) diam.
£3,500–4,000
€/ **$5,500–6,300** ⊞ RAY

A Regency satinwood and line-inlaid wheel barometer, by J. Predary, Manchester, with silvered dial and hygrometer, thermometer and spirit level, 40¾in (103.5cm) high.
£1,800–2,200
€/ **$2,800–3,500** ⚒ DN

BAROMETERS

◄ **A mahogany wheel barometer,** by L. Martinelli & Son, London, with silvered-brass dial, thermometer, hygrometer and spirit level, c1840m dial 14in (35.5cm) diam.
£2,500–2,800
€ / **$4,000–4,400** ⊞ PAO

A mahogany wheel barometer, with silvered dial, alcohol thermometer, hygrometer and spirit level inscribed 'Songuini Llandilo', Welsh, 19thC, 37¾in (96cm) high.
£275–325
€ / **$430–515** ➤ B(SW)

A Louis XV-style giltwood and gesso barometer, the paper dial signed 'Molteno et Baroni, Paris', French, 19thC, 43¼in (110cm) high.
£2,000–2,200
€ / **$3,200–3,500** ➤ S(O)

▶ **A mahogany wheel barometer,** by Dring & Fage, London, with silvered dial, thermometer, spirit level and replaced hygrometer, mid-19thC, 42¼in (107.5cm) high.
£650–750
€ / **$1,000–1,200** ➤ B(Kn)

A mahogany wheel barometer, with silvered-brass scale, the thermometer mounted in a removable box, with hygrometer, spirit level and mirror, c1840, 38in (96.5cm) high.
£750–850
€ / **$1,200–1,400** ⊞ PAO

An early Victorian mahogany wheel barometer, by A. Luvate, Preston, with silvered dial, hygrometer, alcohol thermometer, spirit level and mirror, replaced swan-neck pediment, 42½in (108cm) high.
£280–320
€ / **$440–500** ➤ PFK

A mahogany wheel barometer, by Richard Howse, Marlborough, with silvered-brass scale, the thermometer mounted in a removable box, with hygrometer, spirit level and mirror, c1845, dial 8in (20.5cm) diam.
£875–975
€ / **$1,400–1,500** ⊞ PAO

A mahogany boxwood-strung wheel barometer, with silvered dial, thermometer, hygrometer, mirror and spirit level, signed 'G. Riva & Co, Glasgow', Scottish, mid-19thC, 43½in (110cm).
£400–500
€ / **$630–800** ➤ Bea

▶ **A Victorian wheel barometer,** by Samuel Solomon, Devizes, with silvered dial, thermometer, hygrometer, spirit level and mirror, 38¾in (98.5cm) high.
£380–450
€ / **$620–700** ➤ WW

▶ **A Victorian mother-of-pearl and brass inlaid rosewood wheel thermometer,** with silvered dial, 40¼in (102cm) high.
£900–1,100
€/ **$1,400–1,600** ⚒ AH
This barometer has a very fine quality case and a lot of time has been spent on the cabinet-work. However, in today's market this style does not fit easily into modern homes because of the perceived fussiness of the casework. The inlay is of finely-cut mother-of-pearl interlaced with a tracery of brass. It required great expertise to complete such work. When fashions change, however, barometers of this quality will command high prices.

An oak and stained beech barometer, the painted glass dial signed 'Malizard', French, late 19thC, 35½in (90cm) high.
£420–500
€/ **$660–800** ⚒ S(O)

▶ **A mahogany wheel barometer,** by Row, Alton, with silvered dial and thermometer, late 19thC, 38½in (98cm) high.
£380–450
€/ **$620–700** ⚒ DN

A black- and gilt-japanned and mother-of-pearl wheel barometer, by Wheeler, London, with silvered dial and thermometer, the case with chinoiserie-style decoration, thermometer damaged, c1850, 42in (106.5cm) high.
£500–600
€/ **$800–950** ⚒ S(O)

The prices realized at auction may reflect the fact that the barometers have sometimes undergone alterations to their mechanisms, or are in unrestored condition.

Aneroid Barometers

◀ **A gilt-brass aneroid barometer and thermometer,** the dial signed F. L. West, London, on a spelter stand in the shape of a girl on a foliate base, 1860–80, 7in (18cm) high.
£160–175
€/ **$250–275**
⚒ B(Kn)

A brass-cased aneroid barometer and thermometer, by Negretti & Zambra, London, with silvered dial and applied curved thermometer, c1860, 4¾in (12.5cm) diam, in velvet-lined glazed oak case.
£800–900
€/ **$1,300–1,400** ⚒ S(O)

▶ **An ormolu-cased aneroid barometer,** with white enamel dial signed 'Torricelli', French, 19thC, dial 13in (33cm) high.
£575–600
€/ **$900–1,100** ⚒ EH

An oak-cased aneroid barometer, by Negretti & Zambra, c1910, 20in (51cm) high.
£800–900
€/ **$1,300–1,400** ⊞ RTW

A late Victorian aneroid barometer, in an oak case, carved with sea scrolls and scallop shells, 38in (96.5cm) high.
£275–325
€/ **$430–515** ⚒ EH

Items in the Barometers section have been arranged in date order within each sub-section.

BAROMETERS

Barographs

A mahogany-cased aneroid barograph, with single chart drawer, early 20thC, 14½in (37cm) wide.
£700–820
€ / $1,100–1,300 ⚒ GAK

A mahogany-cased barograph, by Oscar Erickson, Helsinki, with Russian marks on open barometer dial, Finnish, c1910, 14in (35.5cm) wide.
£1,300–1,400
€ / $2,000–2,200 ⊞ RTW

An oak-cased barograph, retailed by J. Lizars, Glasgow, the recording drum signed 'Gluck Co Ltd', with bevelled glass cover and a single chart drawer, early 20thC, 9in (23cm) high.
£650–775
€ / $1,000–1,200 ⚒ S(O)

A mahogany-cased barograph, retailed by Alner Coe & Co, Chicago, with bevelled glass cover and chart drawer, c1910, 14in (35.5cm) wide.
£1,600–1,800
€ / $2,500–2,800 ⊞ RTW

An oak-cased barograph, with bevelled glass cover and chart drawer, c1910, 14in (35.5cm) wide.
£900–1,000
€ / $1,400–1,600 ⊞ RTW

An oak-cased barograph, by Callaghan & Co, London, with bevelled glass cover and chart drawer, c1920, 15in (38cm) wide.
£1,000–1,100
€ / $1,600–1,700 ⊞ RTW

Further reading

Miller's Collecting Science & Technology, Miller's Publications, 2001

▶ A mahogany-cased barograph, by Short & Mason, c1920, 14in (35.5cm) wide.
£630–700
€ / $1,000–1,100 ⊞ RTW

◀ A mahogany-cased weighted barograph, by Jules Richard, French, c1925, 15in (38cm) wide.
£2,700–3,000
€ / $4,300–4,800 ⊞ RTW
This is known as a micro-barograph. The large clock drum enables an expanded reading between 28–31in (71cm–78.5cm) range, therefore small changes become more noticeable

An oak-cased 'Regency' barograph, by Negretti & Zambra, London, with bevelled glass cover and chart drawer, c1925, 16in (40.5cm) wide.
£600–700
€ / $950–1,100 ⚒ PF

BAROMETERS

Decorative Arts

t's not when policeman start to appear younger but when your bookcase becomes too small to cope with all your *Miller's Antiques Price Guides* that you know you are getting older in our business. A quarter of a century is a significant milestone for any enterprise and having worked for at least as many years in a premier London auction house have witnessed many ups and downs in the Decorative Arts world. Interest first focused on this period in the mid- to late 1970s, the age of flairs, punk and John Travolta gyrating to the strains of *Saturday Night Fever*. This was an age devoid of mobile phones and personal computers, populated by people limited to watching three TV channels and holding fondue parties. Although predicted then by many of the antiques old guard as merely a passing fad, where those who should know better were bound to get their fingers burnt, the following for all things Nouveau and Deco continues to grow.

So who and what have been the big movers? Starting Stateside, Tiffany lamps continue to hold the premier position with Newcomb College Pottery attracting huge interest and serious money in more recent years. Glass by Gallé, Daum and Lalique has maintained an international following although the heady prices paid in the late 1980s took a steep dive during the early '90s. In Britain the rarity of works by Charles Rennie Mackintosh, in tandem with a growing international appreciation, has ensured a constant demand and prices in excess of £1 million (€/ $1.6 million) for his more important furniture. British art pottery, particularly the work of William de Morgan and the Martin Brothers, now attracts international buyers with deep pockets. Factory-decorated pieces by Clarice Cliff have also been pursued by a growing army of fanatics prepared to pay £12,000 (€/ $19,000) and more for a rare Age of Jazz figure, whereas Susie Cooper, although discovered several years ago by the Japanese, has yet to find a real following in the United States.

As for the future, two names to watch out for might be glassmaker John Ditchfield and silversmith Stuart Devlin.   **Eric Knowles**

Aesthetic Movement Ceramics

A Burmantofts Anglo-Persian-style vase, attributed to Louis Kramer, artist's monogram 'KL' and impressed marks, 1880s, 14¾in (37.5cm) high.
£6,500–7,500
€/ $10,300–11,700   ↗ TEN

A Wileman & Co cabaret set, comprising eight pieces, c1889.
£100–120
€/ $160–190   ↗ BR

A Minton porcelain vase, possibly designed by Christopher Dresser, in the style of Chinese cloisonné, on three gilt legs, impressed and puce printed marks, c1873, 7½in (19cm) diam.
£800–950
€/ $1,200–1,500   ↗ S(O)

A Victorian aesthetic-style planter, the brass frame inset with four Minton ceramic tiles depicting figures emblematic of the seasons, signed 'Moyr Smith', 9½in (24cm) square.
£520–620
€/ $830–980   ↗ PFK

A Pinder & Bourne vase, the gold-blocked sides reserved with chrysanthemum mon, monogrammed 'F**A**R**', impressed mark, 1879, 14½in (37cm) wide.
£700–820
€/ $1,100–1,300   ↗ TEN

A Victorian majolica Japanese-style jug, c1880, 7½in (19cm) high.
£350–385
€/ $550–600   ⊞ CHAC

DECORATIVE ARTS

Aesthetic Movement Furniture

A pitch pine three-piece bedroom suite, comprising a triple wardrobe, dressing table and pot cupboard, with ebony stringing and geometric designs, c1880, wardrobe 89¼in (226.5cm) high.
£470–570
€ / **$750–900** ⚒ PFK

An ebonized satinwood and parcel-gilt credenza, in the style of Jackson & Graham, the later top above a sgraffito-decorated frieze, the glazed door flanked by six bevelled panels enclosing a velvet-lined interior, flanked by cupboards centred by Pre-Raphaelite-style oil paintings of women wearing classical dress, on a later plinth base with shaped bracket feet, reconstructed from a larger side cabinet, c1880, 81¼in (206.5cm) wide.
£2,500–3,000
€ / **$4,000–4,700** ⚒ B

A brass cabinet, with applied embossed panels and pierced side panels, c1880, 21in (53.5cm) wide.
£400–500
€ / **$630–790** ⚒ S(O)

A corner cabinet, by Gillows, 19thC, 56in (142cm) high.
£1,600–1,800
€ / **$2,500–2,800** ⊞ APO

An oak rocking chair, with lion-head and floral leather decoration, c1880.
£720–800
€ / **$1,100–1,300** ⊞ TDG

▶ **A pair of inlaid walnut side chairs,** attributed to Herter Brothers, American, c1870.
£2,800–3,200
€ / **$4,400–5,000** ⚒ S(NY)

A late Victorian seat, the padded fan back on turned ebonized supports with a central burr-walnut-veneered panel, centred by a jasper ware-style plaque, on turned and veneered legs with casters, 41½in (105.5cm) wide.
£170–200
€ / **$270–320** ⚒ WW

A pair of Japanese-style lacquered bedside cup-boards, by Howard & Son, 1880–90, 18in (45.5cm) wide.
£4,000–4,400
€ / **$6,300–7,000** ⊞ GKe

Items in the Aesthetic Movement sections have been arranged in alphabetical order.

An ebonized, gilt and polychrome-decorated hanging cupboard, the top with a shelf and sloping carved sides, above two panel doors with stylized flowers and bees, applied ornamental strapwork hinges, enclosing a shelf, c1875, 19¼in (49cm) wide.
£525–625
€ / **$830–990** ⚒ B

A mahogany and inlaid sideboard, possibly by Heal's, with engraved escutcheons, c1885, 55½in (141cm) high.
£2,000–2,200
€ / **$3,200–3,500** ⚒ B
This piece reflects the influence of the Aesthetic style in its decoration and has details inspired by the leading designers of the time. The superstructure with this type of pierced fret is a feature evident on other Heal's designs from the 1880s.

► **A walnut writing table,** the leather-lined top above two drawers, c1880, 45in (114.5cm) wide.
£1,500–1,800
€/ **$2,400–2,800** ➢ S(O)

A Victorian inlaid oak sideboard, the frieze with ebonized 'studs', the drawers with original brass handles, previously with a mirror back or similar, 72in (183cm) wide.
400–500
€/ **$630–800** ➢ PFK

An ebonized table, the moulded-edge top inlaid with calamander, on casters, late 19thC, 28½in (72.5cm) high.
7,500–8,800
€/ **$12,000–14,000** ➢ DN
This piece carries the stamp of Lamb of Manchester, who were successful during the second half of the 19th century. It was found in the dairy of a local farmhouse, and despite being in need of restoration, it still fetched an impressive price.

An occasional table, in the style of E. W. Godwin, the underside with hand-written label 'Stansfield', late 19thC, 20in (51cm) wide.
£2,200–2,500
€/ **$3,500–4,000** ➢ S(O)
The fact that this table sold for such a high price indicates that it was indeed considered to have been designed by E. W. Godwin.

A gilt centre table, with shelf and spindle-and-ball design, American, late 19thC, 31in (78.5cm) high.
£5,000–5,500
€/ **$8,000–8,700** ⊞ NART

> **For further information on** tables see pages 114–142

Aesthetic Movement Metalware

A silver sugar bowl, cream jug and sugar tongs, by Henry Lias and James Wakely, London 1883–84, jug 2in (5cm) high, 6oz.
£1,100–1,200
€/ **$1,700–1,800** ⊞ NS

A Gorham Manufacturing Co silver and mixed metal Japanese-style bowl, the spot-hammered surface applied with maple leaves in copper and brass, marked and numbered, American, Providence, 1879, 11in (28cm) diam.
€4,500–5,300
€/ **$7,000–8,500** ➢ S(NY)
This bowl is an example of Gorham interpreting a Tiffany Japanese-style design by Edward C. Moore.

A brass kettle, with repoussé decoration, c1890, 9in (23cm) high.
£200–220
€/ **$300–350** ⊞ RUSK

◄ **A Barbour Silver Co silver hot water urn,** decorated with engraved arabesque panels, with gadrooned bone handles, on a pierced galleried foot and a detachable tripod base with gadrooned bone feet joined by a stretcher, the burner by Gorham Corporation and dated 1883, American, Hartford, c1885, 13in (33cm) high.
£750–900
€/ **$1,200–1,400** ➢ NOA

Further reading

Miller's Art Nouveau & Art Deco Buyer's Guide, Miller's Publications, 2001

Arts & Crafts Ceramics

An American Encaustic Tiling Co tile, depicting a fable, c1920, 6in (15cm) square.
£115–125
€/ **$180–200** ⊞ KMG

A Burmantofts jardinière and stand, 1890–1910, 45in (114.5cm) high.
£1,000–1,100
€/ **$1,600–1,700** ⊞ ASA

A Rookwood floor vase, decorated by Charles Stewart Todd with a grape-vine and fruit, beneath a matt glaze, impressed marks, American, c1915, 17¾in (45cm) high.
£2,000–2,200
€/ **$3,200–3,500** ⚒ JAA

An Ashworth vase, c1900, 9½in (24cm) high.
£110–125
€/ **$175–200** ⊞ DSG

A Burmantofts jardinière, c1900, 13in (33cm) high.
£520–580
€/ **$820–900** ⊞ AFD

A Denby tube-lined tobacco jar, decorated with Festoon pattern, rim damaged, presser missing, c1925, 4in (10cm) high.
£130–145
€/ **$200–230** ⊞ KES

A Van Briggle plate, decorated with a multi-toned matt glaze, incised marks, American, 1907–12, 6in (15cm) diam.
£320–400
€/ **$500–630** ⚒ TREA

An Ault vase, moulded with six anthemia, on a lotus base, c1905, 7in (18cm) diam.
£350–385
€/ **$550–600** ⊞ HUN

A William De Morgan pottery vase, decorated with a running crackle glaze, restored, Sands End mark, c1888, 9in (23cm) high.
£400–450
€/ **$630–700** ⊞ RUSK

A Foley *intarsio* vase, c1890, 11in (28cm) high.
£900–1,000
€/ **$1,400–1,600** ⊞ RH
Foley (1892–1925) became the trade name for Wileman & Co, which was known as Shelley from 1925. The name derived from their premises, The Foley, at Longton, Staffordshire. Their Art Nouveau wares included a range of earthenware, designed and decorated by Frederick Rhead, using a dramatic form of underglaze decoration known as *intarsio*.

A jardinière, by William Baron, with moulded loop additions, incised marks, c1900, 11½in (29cm) diam.
£230–275
€/ **$360–430** ⚒ RbF

A William De Morgan lustre vase, possibly by Halsey Ricardo, impressed Sands End mark, painted initials 'HR', slightly misfired 1888–97, 10in (25.5cm) high.
£2,200–2,600
€/ **$3,500–4,000** ⚒ RTo

A Vodrey pottery vase, with beaded decoration, c1885, 5¾in (14.5cm) high.
£320–375
€/ **$500–600** ⚒ JAd
Frederick Vodrey (1845–97) was born in Tunstall, Staffordshire, where his father worked in the pottery industry. His mother moved c1860 to Dublin, where she opened a retail china and glass business, which Frederick took over in 1865. By 1880 the business had expanded to include an art pottery factory, a relatively new departure in Ireland. Frederick acted as designer while his brother Thomas was mould-maker. Like many other ceramicists of his time, Frederick became interested in recreating the forms and glazes of 17th-century Chinese pottery. His work is considered unique within the history of Irish ceramic design and won awards at all the exhibitions in Ireland in the 1880s.

Arts & Crafts Clocks

An oak mantel clock, with a pewter face and Swiss eight-day movement, retailed by Liberty & Co, platform replaced, c1900, 12in (30.5cm) high.
£1,800–2,000
€/ **$2,800–3,200** ⊞ **AFD**

An ebonized wood and painted tile mantel clock, possibly by Lewis F. Day, the tile face enclosed by four corner tiles painted with flora and the captions 'Childhood', 'Manhood', 'Age' and 'Death', c1880, 16½in (42cm) high.
£1,700–2,000
€/ **$2,700–3,200** ⋗ **B**

A brass and copper clock garniture, c1890, clock 13in (33cm) high.
£1,400–1,600
€/ **$2,200–2,500** ⊞ **ASP**

▶ **A copper mantel clock,** in the style of George Walton, hammered in relief with harebells, early 20thC, 15¼in (38.5cm) wide.
£750–900
€/ **$1,200–1,400** ⋗ **GH**

Arts & Crafts Furniture

An oak bookcase, with stamped copper hinges, c1885, 46in (117cm) wide.
£2,000–2,300
€/ **$3,200–3,600** ⋗ **WilP**

An oak open bookcase, c1890, 48in (122cm) high.
£300–325
€/ **$475–515** ⊞ **GBr**

A copper-mounted oak bedroom suite, by Shapland & Petter, comprising a triple wardrobe and dressing table, c1905, dressing table 48in (122cm) wide.
£950–1,100
€/ **$1,500–1,700** ⋗ **B**

An oak bookcase, the frieze applied with a legend, the two leaded glazed doors with patinated metal furniture below, c1900, 76½in (194.5cm) high.
£1,200–1,500
€/ **$1,900–2,400** ⋗ **Bri**

A mahogany secretaire cabinet, c1890, 59in (150cm) high.
£630–700
€/ **$1,000–1,100** ⊞ **GBr**

◀ **An oak cabinet,** the doors enclosing three sliding trays and hanging space, late 19thC, 22¾in (58cm) wide.
£600–700
€/ **$950–1,100** ⋗ **S(O)**

An inlaid mahogany display cabinet, by Shapland & Petter, c1900, 50in (127cm) wide.
£4,500–5,000
€/ **$7,000–8,000** ⊞ **ASP**

An oak open armchair, possibly by Liberty & Co, the ladderback with shaped splats between tapering uprights surmounted by ball finials, the leather-studded seat on ring-turned legs joined by stretchers supporting square-section uprights, c1900.
£500–600
€/ **$800–950** ⋗ **B**

A beechwood and walnut coffer,
by Jolliffe, with gesso decoration,
with the motto 'Safe Bind, Safe Find',
the interior with paper label giving
details of student and school, 1899,
45¼in (115cm) wide.
£4,000–4,500
€ / **$6,300–5,500** ✦ S(O)
It is probable that Jolliffe was a
student at the Kensington School of
Art and that this is an exam piece.

A Cotswold School oak hall stand,
c1870, 41in (104cm) wide.
£1,400–1,600
€ / **$2,200–2,500** ⊞ APO

A silver-plated mirror, c1900,
24in (61cm) wide.
£500–550
€ / **$800–870** ⊞ TDG

An oak Sutherland table, c1890,
28in (71cm) wide.
£300–345
€ / **$475–550** ⊞ GBr

A hall cupboard, attributed
to Shapland & Petter, c1890,
32in (81.5cm) wide.
£1,200–1,400
€ / **$1,900–2,200** ⊞ GBr

**A Keswick School of Industrial
Art copper mirror,** c1900,
17in (43cm) wide.
£1,200–1,300
€ / **$1,900–2,000** ⊞ SHa

An oak occasional table, the copper
top with an engraved design, above
a shaped frieze, on splayed tapering
legs, c1900, 57in (145cm) wide.
£100–125
€ / **$160–200** ✦ BWL

◄ **An oak dining table,** by Gustav
Stickley, No. 934-E, with two extra
leaves, branded 'Als/ik/kan' with
remnants of paper label, American,
c1902, 76in (193cm) extended.
£6,000–7,200
€ / **$9,500–11,500** ✦ S(NY)

An embossed copper fire surround
with cast-iron grate, the copper panel
decorated with stars and moons on
a brick-effect ground, the moulded
grate hood with a stylized forest
view, flora and sunburst motifs,
c1895, 54¼in (138cm) wide.
£2,400–2,800
€ / **$3,800–4,400** ✦ B

A brass wall mirror, set with
Ruskin pottery roundels, c1915,
20in (51cm) wide.
£400–450
€ / **$630–700** ⊞ WAC

A Liberty & Co oak sideboard,
the top section with a glazed door,
c1900, 70in (178cm) wide.
£1,100–1,300
€ / **$1,700–2,000** ✦ SWO

A Glasgow School oak side table,
c1905, 26in (66cm) wide.
£225–275
€ / **$360–430** ⊞ PVD

DECORATIVE ARTS

Arts & Crafts Jewellery

A silver buckle, London 1904, 3in (7.5cm) wide.
£500–550
€ / **$800–870** ⊞ SHa

▶ **A Guild of Handicraft silver hat pin,** by Bertha Lilian Goff, c1890, 8in (20.5cm) long.
£170–185
€ / **$270–300** ⊞ ANO

A necklace, with moonstones and a cornelian pendant, c1890, pendant 2in (5cm) long.
£475–525
€ / **$750–830** ⊞ ANO

A necklace, after a design by Archibald Knox, the chain with arrow-shaped pendants, interspersed with blister pearls and turquoise, c1910, 15¾in (40cm) long.
£800–950
€ / **$1,200–1,500** ⤴ B

A silver pendant, probably to a design by George Gaskin, the openwork panel set with blister pearls and chrysoprase, with a drop and similar smaller panels, c1905.
£750–875
€ / **$1,200–1,400** ⤴ TEN

A silver and enamel pendant, by Charles Horner, 1908, 2in (5cm) long.
£225–250
€ / **$350–400** ⊞ RGA

A silver and enamel pendant, by Charles Horner, 1909, 2½in (6.5cm) long.
£225–250
€ / **$350–400** ⊞ RGA

▶ **A white-metal and enamel pendant,** by Murrle Bennet, stamped, on a chain, c1910, pendant 2½in (6.5cm) long.
£700–820
€ / **$1,100–1,300** ⤴ B

Arts & Crafts Lighting

A pair of W. A. S. Benson brass wall lights, with spiral tendrils projecting from double-leaf supports and turned wall plates, with Powell bell-shaped vaseline glass shades, unmarked, c1900, 15in (38cm) long.
£4,800–5,300
€ / **$7,600–8,400** ⊞ HUN

> **For further information on**
> W. A. S. Benson see page 456

A copper and brass three-light chandelier, attributed to W. A. S. Benson, with three opalescent glass shades patterned with foliage, 26in (66cm) high.
£3,500–4,000
€ / **$5,500–6,300** ⤴ S(O)

◀ **A W. A. S. Benson brass and copper two-part chandelier,** with curved tendrils and eight opaline glass shades, c1900, 49¼in (125cm) long.
£650–750
€ / **$1,000–1,200** ⤴ B

A brass five-light chandelier, in the style of W. A. S. Benson, with shaped opalescent glass shades, early 20thC, 25½in (65cm) high.
£4,500–5,000
€/ **$7,000–8,000** ✦ S(O)

A cast-brass wall lantern, with original etched tube, signed 'Osler', c1900, 15in (38cm) long.
£520–580
€/ **$830–900** ⊞ JeH

A copper hanging lantern, with original amethyst glass, c1900, 20in (51cm) high.
£1,100–1,200
€/ **$1,700–1,900** ⊞ ASP

Always check that electric lighting conforms to the current safety regulations before using.

A Glasgow School brass lantern, with coloured glass panes, 1890–1900, 11in (28cm) high.
£450–500
€/ **$700–800** ⊞ JeH

An Arts & Crafts hall lantern, hand-painted with birds, 13in (33cm) high.
£720–800
€/ **$1,100–1,300** ⊞ OLA

A pair of brass candelabra, c1890, 26in (66cm) high.
£700–800
€/ **$1,100–1,200** ⊞ ASP

An Edwardian etched glass ceiling bowl, by Farraday & Son, with brass fittings and interlocking brass chain, marked 'F&S', 9in (23cm) diam.
£130–145
€/ **$200–230** ⊞ JeH

▶ **A copper hallway light,** c1900, 16in (40.5cm) high.
£580–650
€/ **$900–1,000** ⊞ OLA

▶ **A patinated wrought-iron, copper and mica floor lamp,** by Sam Stoltz, the standard modelled as a vine-wrapped tree trunk with a cluster of wrought-iron roots, with a copper band cut with dolphins and tropical fish, the shade with a cut-copper swamp scene of herons, a deer and a cougar in a palm tree, American, c1930, 76in (193cm) high.
£3,800–4,200
€/ **$6,000–6,600** ✦ NOA
Sam Stoltz was a talented and imaginative artist, architect, contractor and landscape designer. He and his wife relocated from Chicago to Orlando, Florida in 1925 to take advantage of the sunny weather and the real estate boom. Stoltz's first designs were homes in the suburbs of Chicago – bungalows reflecting the influence of Frank Lloyd Wright's prairie style. His fascination with birds and fauna led him to embellish his houses with depictions of herons, flamingos, pelicans, cardinals, doves, fish, deer and even monkeys, painted on plaster and glass, sculpted in plaster relief and stucco, as well as in wrought iron. He remained active until 1946 and died in 1952, aged 76.

A hammered iron newel post lamp, 1900–10, 34in (86.5cm) high.
£350–400
€/ **$550–630** ⊞ EAL

DECORATIVE ARTS

Arts & Crafts Metalware

A Keswick School of Industrial Art silver twin-handled cauldron bowl, design attributed to Harold Stabler, with embossed floral decoration, with presentation inscription, Birmingham 1899, 15½in (39.5cm) wide, 30oz.
£1,700–2,000
€ / **$2,700–3,200** ➹ B(NW)

A Newlyn embossed copper rose bowl, on a detachable base with three splayed feet, stamped, early 20thC, 8½in (21.5cm) diam.
£470–570
€ / **$750–900** ➹ S(O)

A pair of brass candlesticks, c1870, 8in (20.5cm) high.
£340–375
€ / **$550–600**
⊞ SHa

A Keswick School of Industrial Art copper charger, early 20thC, 19½in (49.5cm) diam.
£350–420
€ / **$550–670** ➹ BR

A Newlyn copper bowl, c1900, 13in (33cm) diam.
£1,300–1,500
€ / **$2,100–2,500** ⊞ SHa

An embossed copper box, the lid embossed 'Lilly' the underside marked 'V.M. 1908', 7¼in (18.5cm) wide.
£330–400
€ / **$530–630** ➹ S(O)

A pair of Newlyn-style copper chambersticks, decorated with fish, c1900, 8in (20.5cm) diam.
£350–425
€ / **$550–670** ➹ G(L)

◄ **A pair of copper candlesticks**, in the style of Margaret Gilmour, Scottish, c1900, 11in (28cm) high.
£250–280
€ / **$400–440** ⊞ AFD

A copper charger, No. 2399, by John Pearson, the centre with a galleon, the border with leaping dolphin-like fish, signed and dated 1898, 20in (51cm) diam.
£2,300–2,600
€ / **$3,600–4,100** ➹ G(L)

▶ **A pair of copper and brass chenets**, early 20thC, 17¾in (45cm) high.
£330–400
€ / **$530–630** ➹ S(O)

A Guild of Handicraft silver bowl, from a design by Charles Robert Ashbee, the beaten bowl with wirework hoop handle set with a cabochon, London 1901, 8in (20.5cm) wide, with a matching butter spoon.
£3,200–4,000
€ / **$5,000–6,300** ➹ Bea

A pair of copper and iron candlesticks, 1880–1900, 6½in (16.5cm) high.
£100–120
€ / **$160–190** ⊞ AFD

A Birmingham Guild of Handicraft copper casket, c1910, 10in (25.5cm) wide.
£450–500
€ / **$700–800** ⊞ DAD

A Newlyn copper charger, c1890, 14½in (37cm) diam.
£765–850
€ / **$1,200–1,400** ⊞ SHa

copper coal box/log bin, c1900,
7in (43cm) wide.
270–300
/ $430–475 ⊞ ASP

A brass coal bucket, 1900–10,
17in (43cm) high.
£115–130
€/ $180–200 ⊞ EAL

**An A. E. Jones silver three-piece
coffee set**, comprising a coffee pot,
a cream jug and a sugar bowl, the
coffee pot decorated with two bands
of flowerheads to the girdle and
collar, the hinged domed cover with
a wooden finial and scroll handle,
Birmingham 1918, coffee pot
8in (20.5cm) high.
£300–360
€/ $475–575 ⚒ CGC

Hukin & Heath cruet stand, by
christopher Dresser, modelled as five
onjoined wells centred by a handle,
narked, 1879, 5½in (14cm) high.
900–1,000
/ $1,400–1,600 ⚒ S(O)

**A Duchess of Sutherland's Cripples
Guild of Handicraft silver dish
and cover**, with hammered design,
based on a French *écuelle*, c1910,
7in (18cm) wide.
£700–800
€/ $1,100–1,300 ⊞ DAD

A brass footman, c1902,
21in (53.5cm) wide.
£325–360
€/ $500–560 ⊞ ASP

► An Arts & Crafts W.
A. S. Benson brass kettle-
n-stand, with burner and
aw feet, on original tray,
1in (28cm) high.
450–500
/ $700–800 ⊞ HUN

Duchess of Sutherland's Cripples Guild of Handicrafts

The Guild was set up by Millicent, Duchess of
Sutherland (1867–1955) in Trentham, Stoke-
on-Trent, to assist crippled children who had
suffered from pneumoconiosis, or lead
poisoning, in the local north Staffordshire
pottery industry.
   The Guild produced art metal from 1902. The
ouput was primarily copper and silvered-copper.
Other crafts included silver, enamels and pottery
in silver mounts. The majority of silver wares
tend to be influenced by late 17th- and early
18th-century designs. All appear to have been
submitted to the Birmingham assay office and
bear the maker's mark of MS for Millicent
Sutherland. The silver plate and copper wares
were stamped with the letters DSCG beneath
a coronet. The artist/designer Francis Arthur
Edwardes was responsible for teaching
metalwork, and the products were retailed until
1922, both locally and through a shop at 13–14
New Bond Street, London.

DECORATIVE ARTS

An A. E. Jones silver-gilt porringer and cover, Birmingham 1906, 6in (15cm) high.
£1,600–1,750
€/ **$2,500–2,700** ⊞ SHa

A silver and enamel spoon, by Connell, London 1906, 7in (18cm) long.
£500–550
€/ **$800–900** ⊞ SHa

◄ **A Duchess of Sutherland's Cripples Guild of Handicrafts silver-plated samovar,** with two ivory bar handles, c1910, 20in (51cm) high.
£350–400
€/ **$550–630** ⊞ DAD

A silver spoon, by H. G. Murphy, London 1935, 8in (20.5cm) long.
£500–550
€/ **$800–900** ⊞ SHa

A silver four-piece tea service, comprising a teapot, stand, open sugar bowl and milk jug, the teapot with a domed hinged lid, ebonized finial and loop side handle, with beaten decoration, on three feet, the three-handled sugar bowl with trefoil leaf loop terminals, maker's mark for Charles Edwards, London 1917, 30oz
£600–700
€/ **$950–1,100** ⚒ B(W)

William Arthur Smith Benson (1854–1924)

W. A. S. Benson is recognized today as being perhaps the most important English designer and architect producing commercial metalware and lighting. Benson helped to establish the Art Workers' Guild in 1883 and the Arts and Crafts Exhibition Society in 1888. Production at his Hammersmith workshop commenced in 1880 with emphasis on copper and brass, although silver wares were also produced. In 1896, following the death of William Morris, Benson became a director of Morris & Co. Unlike Morris, Benson embraced the use of machines, and his metalwork designs were produced by various mechanical processes. His silver ware was shown at the Paris Exhibition of 1900 and retailed through the Maison de l'Art Nouveau of Samuel Bing. The Hammersmith workshops eventually closed in 1920.

An Arts & Crafts W. A. S. Benson copper two-gallon thermos, with folding loop handle, 22in (56cm) high.
£570–635
€/ **$900–1,000** ⊞ HUN

A Newlyn copper tray, c1900, 28in (71cm) wide.
£450–500
€/ **$700–800** ⊞ WAC

◄ **A hammered copper tray,** with birds among trailing foliage, 1900–10, 22in (56cm) wide.
£135–150
€/ **$220–240** ⊞ EAL

A brass and copper wall sconce, c1915, 15in (38cm) high.
£150–165
€/ **$240–260** ⊞ WAC

A brass trivet, c1900, 13in (33cm) long.
£250–280
€/ **$400–450** ⊞ AFD

A Hukin & Heath silver-plated tureen, No. M-057 A, by Christopher Dresser, with hardwood handles, on tripod legs, PODR mark, 1880, 12in (30.5cm) wide.
£2,200–2,500
€/ **$3,500–4,000** ⚒ S(O)

Doulton

Royal Doulton beaker, commemorating the Diamond Jubilee of Queen Victoria, 1897, ...n (10cm) high.
200–225
/ **$320–360** ⊞ H&G

Royal Doulton ewer, 1905, 6in (15cm) high.
175–200
/ **$275–315** ⊞ PGO

◀ **A Royal Doulton model of a bird of prey on a rock,** No. 145, with circle mark lion and crown, 1917–36, 8¾in (22cm) high.
£550–650
€/ **$870–1,000**
➤ BBR

A Royal Doulton De Luxe coffee set, with printed and painted marks, 1940s, coffee pot 8¼in (21cm) high.
£150–175
€/ **$240–280** ➤ SWO

Three Doulton Lambeth salt-glazed stoneware finials, by Gilbert Bayes, some damage and repair, 1920–30, 13in (33cm) high.
£950–1,100
€/ **$1,500–1,700** ➤ S(O)

◀ **A Doulton Lambeth jardinière,** by Frank Butler, c1878, 6½in (16.5cm) high.
£2,000–2,400
€/ **$3,200–3,800** ⊞ JE

DECORATIVE ARTS

A Royal Doulton plate, by David Dewsberry, decorated with a floral bouquet and raised gilding, 1906, 9½in (24cm) high.
£780–850
€ / $1,200–1,300 ⊞ DIA

▶ A Doulton Kelmscott toilet set, c1900, largest 12in (30.5cm) high.
£800–900
€ / $1,300–1,400 ⊞ ASP

A pair of Royal Doulton vases, the necks with tube-lined cartouches, c1910, 8in (20.5cm) high.
£200–225
€ / $320–350 ⊞ LBr

A pair of Doulton vases, by George Tinworth, all-over-decorated with a scrolling foliate motif, incised artist's monogram and impressed factory marks, c1900, 7½in (19cm) high.
£800–1,000
€ / $1,300–1,600 ⚒ G(L)

A Royal Doulton vase, by Eliza Simmance, c1910, 11in (28cm) high.
£600–700
€ / $950–1,100 ⊞ JE

▶ A Royal Doulton Art Nouveau vase, 1920s, 5½in (14cm) high.
£120–135
€ / $190–215 ⊞ PGO

A Royal Doulton vase, by Eliza Simmance, with stylized Art Nouveau designs, rim restored, c1910, 15in (38cm) high.
£220–250
€ / $350–400 ⚒ SWO

A Royal Doulton Titanian Ware vase, by F. Henri, c1920, 6in (15cm) high.
£900–1,000
€ / $1,400–1,600 ⊞ JE
Titanian Ware, produced from 1915–30, used titanium oxide in the glaze to give a blue colouration, ranging in tone from pale grey to dark royal blue. It was used to provide a background for fine porcelain pieces decorated by artists such as Harry Allen and F. Henri.

◀ A pair of Doulton Lambeth pots, with silve plated rims, on a silver-plated stand stamped H.B., with a sifter spoon and ladle, 19thC, pots 3¼in (8.5cm) diam.
£250–300
€ / $400–470 ⚒ SWO

A Doulton Lambeth tyg by Mark V. Marshall, with floral decoration, c1900, 6in (15cm) high.
£420–500
€ / $660–800 ⚒ G(L)

A royal Doulton Lambet stoneware vase, by Hannah Barlow and Florenc Roberts, with an incised scene of sheep grazing, 1905, 15in (38cm) high.
£2,100–2,400
€ / $3,300–3,800 ⊞ GA

A Royal Doulton flambé vase, with a printed factor mark and painted HN monogram, c1930, 7in (18cm) high.
£470–565
€ / $720–900 ⚒ S(O)

Martin Brothers

A Martin Brothers stoneware bowl, with six applied flowerhead roundels beneath a metal mount and handles, incised marks, 1895, 11in (28cm) diam.
£770–900
€ / $1,200–1,400 ➚ S(O)

A Martin Brothers stoneware bird jar cover, small chip to beak, incised marks, 1882, 3¾in (9.5cm) high.
£900–1,000
€ / $1,400–1,600 ➚ S(O)

A Martin Brothers stoneware jardinière, modelled with a Celtic-style inter-linked band pierced and modelled with overlapping fins, incised and impressed marks, rim crack and chip, 1873, 8¼in (21cm) high.
£500–600
€ / $800–950 ➚ LFA

◄ **A Martin Brothers stoneware jug,** with incised decoration, neck damaged and repaired, incised marks, 1885, 8½in (21.5cm) high.
£700–850
€ / $1,100–1,300 ➚ S(O)

► **A Martin Brothers pottery jug,** maker's signature to base, 1887, 9in (23cm) high.
£1,400–1,600
€ / $2,200–2,500 ➚ L

A pair of Martin Brothers stoneware wall brackets, one modelled with an owl and a book, the other with a pelican, impressed marks, one chipped, c1877, 5½in (14cm) high.
£1,100–1,300
€ / $1,700–2,000 ➚ L&E

Moorcroft

A Moorcroft bowl, decorated with Pomegranate pattern, 1913–25, 4½in (11.5cm) high.
£265–300
€ / $420–475 ⊞ PGO

A Moorcroft jam pot, decorated with Moonlit Blue landscape pattern, with a plated cover, rim chip, impressed marks, c1925, 8½in (21.5cm) diam.
£380–450
€ / $600–700 ➚ PFK

A Moorcroft Macintyre jug, c1904, 7in (18cm) high.
£450–500
€ / $700–800 ⊞ MPC

A pair of Moorcroft Macintyre vases, the necks with panelled gilt scale, the bodies decorated with Art Nouveau poppies, printed marks, c1900, 6¼in (16cm) high.
£1,600–2,000
€/ **$2,500–3,200** ⚒ TEN

A Moorcroft Macintyre vase, c1904, 9in (23cm) high.
£850–950
€/ **$1,300–1,500** ⊞ MPC

A Moorcroft Macintyre Florian ware vase, decorated with Rose Garland pattern, printed marks and signature, c1907, 7¾in (20cm) high.
£1,500–1,800
€/ **$2,400–2,800** ⚒ SWO

A Moorcroft vase, decorated with Hazeldene pattern, signed, impressed marks, c1914, 9in (23cm) high.
£2,700–3,000
€/ **$4,300–4,700** ⊞ PGO

Pomegranate pattern

William Moorcroft's Pomegranate pattern proved one of the pottery's best-selling designs from the moment it was introduced in 1913. The earliest examples can be recognized by the use of a relatively thin cobalt blue that results in large areas of underlying buff pottery being exposed. Later examples from the 1920s and 1930s show a preference for dark cobalt blue glaze.

A pair of Moorcroft baluster vases, decorated with Pomegranate pattern, one damaged, painted signature and impressed factory mark, c1916, 8in (20.5cm) high.
£320–375
€/ **$500–600** ⚒ PF

A Moorcroft pottery vase, decorated with Leaves and Fruit pattern, impressed and painted marks and paper label, c1919, 5½in (14cm) high.
£850–1,000
€/ **$1,300–1,600** ⚒ TMA

▶ **A Moorcroft flambé vase,** decorated with Eventide pattern, signed, 1925, 10in (25.5cm) high.
£3,000–3,500
€/ **$4,700–5,500** ⊞ GAA

A Moorcroft vase, decorated with Pomegranate pattern, c1925, 4½in (11cm) high.
£350–400
€/ **$550–650** ⊞ PGO
This shape of vase is seldom seen.

A Moorcroft salt-glazed vase, decorated with Leaf and Grape pattern, impressed mark, signed, c1928, 9½in (24cm) high.
£400–475
€/ **$630–750** ⚒ PF

A Moorcroft baluster vase, decorated with Moonlit Blue pattern, signed, 1930, 12½in (32cm) high.
£3,500–4,000
€/ **$5,500–6,300** ⚒ B

A Moorcroft pottery salt-glazed vase, decorated with Leaf and Berry pattern, impressed marks and facsimile signature, painted signature, 1930s, 9in (23cm) high.
£950–1,100
€/ **$1,500–1,700** ⚒ S(O)

A Moorcroft pottery vase, tube-lined with fish among blooms, impressed marks and painted signature, c1935, 5¾in (14.5cm) high.
£850–1,000
€/ **$1,300–1,600** ⚒ Bea

Art Nouveau Ceramics

A Berlin porcelain exhibition vase, decorated by Theodor Hermann Schmuz-Baudiss, No. 2073 M.15m, impressed 7218, German, c1904, 18¾in (47.5cm) high.
£3,000–3,500
€/ $4,750–5,500 ♠ S(NY)
Theodor Hermann Schmuz-Baudiss (1859–1942) served as a director of the underglaze department at the Königliche Porzellanmanufaktur (KPM) in Berlin from 1902–08. He was artistic director from 1908–25, the period of the firm's most innovative production. Schmuz-Baudiss developed his own unique technique of underglaze painting, creating organically shaped ceramic vessels ornamented with naturalistic and fantasy imagery articulated in subtle tones of underglaze. According to the consignor, this vase was exhibited at the St Louis Exposition of 1904.

A Minton Secessionist jardinière, sprig-moulded with stylized foliage, c1910, 10½in (26.5cm) diam.
£200–225
€/ $320–350 ♠ G(L)

A Boch Frères vase, decorated with copper, silver and metallic glazes, Belgian, c1900, 12in (30.5cm) high.
£350–400
€/ $550–630 ⊞ DSG
The Belgian ceramics firm Boch Frères (established in 1841) was a branch of the German company Villeroy & Boch.

A Meissen *pâte-sur-pâte* vase, by Rudolf Hentschel, heightened with gilt, crossed-swords mark, impressed R151 20, c1898, 4in (10cm) high.
£1,200–1,400
€/ $1,900–2,200 ♠ S(O)

A Minton earthenware Secessionist stick stand, slip-trailed with stylized flowering stems, printed 'Mintons Ltd no. 62', dated 1920, 22¾in (58cm) high.
£1,700–2,000
€/ $2,700–3,200 ♠ B
Ex-Minton sale.

A Della Robbia pottery vase, decorated with bluebells and leaves, c1900, 10in (25.5cm) high.
£450–500
€/ $700–800 ⊞ RUSK
The Della Robbia Pottery produced ceramics at Birkenhead from 1894–1906, using the work of the 15th-century Florentine artist Luca Della Robbia as their inspiration.

A ceramic wall mirror, by Rudolf Ditmar, the frame with raised floral and geometric decoration, factory stamp and number, Czechoslovakian, Znaim, 1900–10, 25½in (65cm) high.
£1,300–1,500
€/ $2,000–2,400 ♠ DORO

A Foley Old Chelsea vase, c1890, 6½in (16.5cm) high.
£400–450
€/ $630–700 ⊞ RH

A terracotta plaque, by Alphonse Mucha, Czechoslovakian, c1900, 16in (40.5cm) diam.
£3,200–4,000
€ / $5,100–6,300 ⊞ ASP

A pair of Rookwood earthenware figural vases, with impressed mark, American, 1918, 17in (43cm) high.
£2,700–3,000
€ / $4,300–4,700 ↗ S(NY)

A Newcomb College Pottery vase, by Joseph Meyer, decorated by Desiree Roman with carved oak trees, marked to underside, American, 1906, 3in (7.5cm) high.
£5,000–5,400
€ / $8,000–8,500 ⊞ CaF

A Royal Dux porcelain bonbon dish, surmounted with a figure, Bohemian, c1915, 7in (18cm) high.
£450–500
€ / $700–800 ⊞ ASP

◀ **A Villeroy & Boch Mettlach Stoneware wall charger,** German, c1890, 15in (38cm) diam.
£850–950
€ / $1,300–1,500 ⊞ ANO

A Pilkington's Royal Lancastrian vase and cover, by Richard Joyce, the cover with a fish knop, the body relief-moulded and decorated with silver and iridescent lustre with carp swimming, painted and impressed marks, date code for 1913, 9in (23cm) high.
£3,000–3,500
€ / $4,750–5,500 ↗ WW
The value of Pilkington's Royal Lancastrian pottery is dependent upon the degree of control exhibited by the iridescent glaze. Lustrewares could prove notoriously problematic, and a uniform lustre was often the exception rather than the rule. The example shown here displays near perfection, which ensured that it would be keenly contested when offered at auction. The fish knop on the domed cover completed a splendid design that owes much to the influence of Japanese metalwork of the same period.

A Purmurend floor vase, painted with stylized flowers and foliage, painted marks, Dutch, c1900, 24½in (62cm) high.
£4,200–5,000
€ / $6,600–7,900 ↗ B(NW)

A Rozenburg earthenware pot and cover, decorated with stylized floral motifs, painted and incised marks, Dutch, 1896, 6in (15cm) high.
£1,000–1,100
€ / $1,600–1,700 ↗ S(Am)

Items in the Art Nouveau Ceramics section have been arranged alphabetically in factory order.

A Wardle jardinière-on-stand, with tube-lined decoration, c1910, 27in (68.5cm) high.
£450–500
€ / $700–800 ⊞ ASP

A Sicardo Ware lustre vase, by Samuel A. Weller, decorated by Jacques Sicard, small chip to rim, painted and impressed marks, American, Ohio, c1905, 7in (18cm) high.
£350–400
€ / $550–630 ↗ S(O)

▶ **A porcelain bonbon dish,** by Wahliss, Austrian, c1900, 6in (15cm) diam.
£160–200
€ / $250–320 ⊞ ASP

A bisque planter, Austrian, c1910, 9in (23cm) wide.
£180–200
€ / $285–320 ⊞ ASP

Art Nouveau Clocks

▶ A bronze mantel clock, attributed to Jacob van den Bosch, the architectural case with a domed top supported by rows of columns, on a marble base, Dutch, c1915, 15¾in (40cm) high.
£2,000–2,200
€/ **$3,200–3,500** ↗ S(Am)

An Arnhem Faïence Factory earthenware clock garniture, the clock and two vases decorated with stylized flowers, stamped and painted marks, Dutch, c1920, 14in (35.5cm) high.
£2,000–2,400
€/ **$3,200–3,800** ↗ S(Am)

A copper and enamel mantel clock, attributed to George Walton, retailer's mark for Goodyers, London, c1900, 13¼in (34cm) wide.
£1,700–2,000
€/ **$2,700–3,200** ↗ B

A Liberty & Co Tudric pewter mantel clock, decorated with ivy leaves and tendrils, with Lenzkirch movement, damaged, late 19thC, 8in (20.5cm) high.
£2,000–2,400
€/ **$3,200–3,800** ↗ TMA

A Liberty & Co Tudric pewter mantel clock, by Archibald Knox, the enamelled-copper dial with Roman numerals, with Lenzkirch movement, c1900, 7¾in (19.5cm) high.
£1,700–2,000
€/ **$2,700–3,200** ↗ G(L)

▶ A silvered-brass and enamelled mantel timepiece, possibly by George Walton, early 20thC, 8¼in (21cm) high.
£1,800–2,000
€/ **$2,800–3,200** ↗ S(O)

A brass mantel clock, by J. K. C. Sneltjes, with key and pendulum, surface worn, stamped monogram, Dutch, Haarlem, c1910, 12¼in (31cm) high.
£1,300–1,500
€/ **$2,000–2,400** ↗ S(Am)

A silvered-metal table clock, by Wolkenstein & Glückselig, with vertical beaded bands and raised floral decoration, clockwork not functional, impressed factory stamp, Austrian, Vienna, c1915, 7¾in (19.5cm) high.
£700–850
€/ **$1,100–1,350** ↗ DORO

A mahogany mantel clock, late 19thC, 10in (25.5cm) high.
£170–200
€/ **$270–320** ↗ GAK

An ebonized hardwood and silver mantel clock, the French drum timepiece movement with a modern lever platform escapement, the front panel hallmarked Birmingham 1909, 12in (30.5cm) high.
£250–300
€/ **$400–475** ↗ TMA

◀ An oak mantel clock, with electroplated mounts and dial, the eight-day movement striking on a visible bell, above an opaque streaked glass panel, a presentation inscription below, c1911, 14½in (37cm) high.
£475–550
€/ **$750–870** ↗ DD

Art Nouveau Figures & Busts

A bronze figure, entitled 'L'Otage', by Emmanuel Villanis, signed, French, Paris, 1895, 38½in (98cm) high.
£7,000–8,000
€/ **$11,000–13,000** ⊞ MI

A bronze vase, by Charles Korschann, applied with the figure of a young woman, French, c1900, 7in (18cm) high.
£1,000–1,100
€/ **$1,600–1,700** ⊞ MI

A gilt-bronze figure of The Metamorphosis of Daphne, by Raoul Larche, signed, French, 1900, 12¼in (31cm) high.
£3,000–3,400
€/ **$4,700–5,800** ⊞ MI

A Goldscheider terra-cotta bust of a young woman, inscribed, maker's marks, c1900, 26in (66cm) high.
£1,600–1,800
€/ **$2,500–2,800** ⚒ S(O)

A marble and bronze portrait bust, by Schumacher, on a marble base, French, c1900, 7in (18cm) high.
£400–450
€/ **$630–700** ⊞ HUM

◀ **A bronze figure,** by R. Varenne, signed, French, Paris, c1900, 9in (23cm) high.
£800–880
€/ **$1,300–1,400** ⊞ MI

A Goldscheider terracotta bust, Austrian, Vienna, c1900, 24in (61cm) high.
£1,500–1,800
€/ **$2,400–2,800** ⊞ ASP

A bronze paperweight, Austrian, c1900, 5in (12.5cm) long.
£350–400
€/ **$550–630** ⊞ ANO

A porcelain bust, by Pursol, probably Bohemian, c1910, 19in (48.5cm) high.
£1,400–1,600
€/ **$2,200–2,00** ⊞ ASP

◄ **A Royal Dux centrepiece,** decorated in shot enamels, applied pink triangle, impressed marks, minor damage, early 20thC, 16in (40.5cm) high.
£1,100–1,300
€/ **$1,700–2,000** ⚒ S(O)

► **A pair of spelter fairies,** by Auguste Moreau, entitled 'L'Aurore' and 'Le Crépuscule', French, c1910, 9in (23cm) high.
£450–550
€/ **$700–870** ⊞ ASP

► **A Wiener Keramik figure of Girl with Roses,** by Michael Powolny, impressed marks, c1910, 11½in (29cm) high.
£4,500–5,500
€/ **$7,000–8,700** ⚒ DORO

A terracotta bust, signed Barranti Pos, Italian, c1910, 15in (38cm) high.
£450–500
€/ **$700–800** ⊞ ASP

A Goldscheider terracotta bust, Austrian, c1915, 26in (66cm) high.
£2,000–2,200
€/ **$3,200–3,500** ⊞ ASP

Art Nouveau Furniture

An inlaid mahogany cabinet, by Wylie & Lochhead, design No. 6868/4004, c1900, 51¼in (130cm) wide.
£2,500–2,800
€/ $4,000–4,400 ⚒ S(O)

An inlaid mahogany cabinet, with a mirror-backed open shelf above a central door inlaid with mother-of-pearl and coloured woods, flanked by open shelves, trade label for Robson & Sons, Newcastle-upon-Tyne, c1905, 52¾in (134cm) wide.
£2,200–2,500
€/ $3,500–4,000 ⚒ TEN

▶ **A mahogany display cabinet,** c1915, 50in (127cm) wide.
£1,800–2,000
€/ $2,800–3,200 ⊞ ASP

A Secessionist walnut secretaire cabinet, the fall-front enclosing a fitted interior, over four drawers, Austrian, c1912, 39½in (100.5cm) wide.
£370–450
€/ $580–700 ⚒ B

A Liberty-style mahogany cabinet, c1900, 36in (91.5cm) wide.
£5,800–6,500
€/ $9,200–10,300 ⊞ SAW

An oak cabinet, Dutch, c1900, 55¼in (140.5cm) wide.
£2,800–3,200
€/ $4,400–5,000 ⚒ S(O)

A bentwood rocking chair, by Thonet, Austrian, late 19thC.
£500–550
€/ $800–870 ⊞ APO

A walnut, ebony-strung and chequerbanded cabinet, attributed to August Ungethum, possibly to designs by Gustav Klimt, the glazed doors with copper glazing bars, two with copper medallion portraits of Apollo and Athene by Georg Klimt, c1900, 60¾in (154.5cm) wide.
£5,500–6,500
€/ $8,700–10,300 ⚒ B
Ungethum was one of the foremost firms in Vienna in the early years of the 20th century. Many prominent designers including Hoffman and Moser commissioned them to produce their work, and the Wiener Werkstätte were later to become heavily involved with the firm. Other labelled furniture bearing Georg Klimt's panels have been recorded. Georg Klimt was the brother of Gustav and remains best known for producing the work of others, rather than for his own designs.

An inlaid mahogany armchair, c1905.
£520–580
€/ $820–900 ⊞ APO

▶ **A stained beech chair,** with replaced canework seat, restored, probably Austrian, Vienna, 1900–10.
£520–620
€/ $820–980 ⚒ DORO

A rosewood marquetry cabinet, by Louis Majorelle, c1900, 35in (89cm) wide.
£5,600–6,200
€/ $8,800–9,800 ⊞ APO

An oak, walnut and walnut-veneered display cabinet, by Louis Majorelle, signed, with marquetry decoration, some wear, French, 1905–10, 27¼in (69cm) wide.
£7,500–8,800
€/ $11,800–14,000 ⚒ DORO

An oak armchair, by Carlo Bugatti, decorated with copper, pewter and nets, parchment seat, Italian, c1900.
£4,800–6,000
€/ **$7,600–9,500** ⚒ DORO

A mother-of-pearl inlaid ebonized wood side chair, designed by Carlo Bugatti, decorated with hammered copper and parchment seat, Italian, c1900.
£5,000–6,000
€/ **$8,000–9,500** ⚒ S(Am)

An Otto Wagner bentwood armchair, by Thonet, after a design by Marcel Kammerer, with a caned seat, Austrian, c1912.
£1,500–1,800
€/ **$2,400–2,800** ⚒ B

An oak, pine and mahogany-veneered chest-of-drawers, by John Moffet & Son, Carlisle, c1900, 15in (38cm) wide.
£1,200–1,500
€/ **$1,900–2,400** ⊞ ASP

A hammered iron and copper fire screen, c1870, 33in (84cm) high.
£160–200
€/ **$250–315** ⊞ EAL

A mahogany double fire screen, with hand-painted decoration, c1900, 36in (91.5cm) wide.
£320–400
€/ **$510–630** ⊞ ASP

A fruitwood marquetry hall stand, c1900, 46in (117cm) wide.
£3,500–4,200
€/ **$5,500–6,600** ⚒ S(NY)

A bentwood hat and coat stand, design attributed to Joseph Hoffmamn, Austrian, early 20thC, 79½in (202cm) high.
£1,000–1,100
€/ **$1,600–1,700** ⚒ S(O)

Henri van de Velde (1863–1957)

Henri van de Velde initially studied art in Antwerp and Brussels, later turning to architecture and designing several important buildings in Germany. In 1894 he designed his own home near Brussels, including the contents. His early furniture displays medieval influences, but within a short period of time his work began to incorporate the flowing lines that were to eventually emerge as a distinct interpretation of Art Nouveau. His contribution to the 1897 Dresden Exhibition of Arts and Crafts established his reputation as an important designer of international acclaim and led to a significant number of commissions in Germany. His early furniture tended to make use of native woods such as beech and oak, but after 1900 he began to seek out more exotic woods imported from Africa.

His approach to design shows strong similarities to that of Charles Rennie Mackintosh. Like him, his furniture would often be designed for a specific room but when viewed out of the intended setting could appear distinctly odd. Also like Mackintosh, van de Velde designed furniture with a white-painted finish. An all-rounder, he also turned his attention to ceramics, metalwork, jewellery, textiles, wallpaper and book and magazine illustrations.

A sycamore dressing mirror, by Henri van de Velde, Belgian, c1905, 31½in (80cm) wide.
£4,300–5,200
€/ **$6,800–8,200** ⚒ S

A stained beechwood adjustable hall mirror, probably by Thonet, with bevelled glass, restored, Austrian, Vienna, c1910, 64¼in (163cm) high.
£1,800–2,200
€/ **$2,800–3,500** ⚒ DORO

An oak settle, the back carved with a stylized foliate panel flanked by inset embossed copper panels, with hinged seat, c1910, 50¼in (127.5cm) wide.
£750–875
€/ **$1,200–1,400** ⚒ Bri

An oak sofa, the apron decorated with incised scrollwork, German, c1905, 41in (104cm) wide.
£850–1,000
€/ **$1,300–1,600** ⚒ B

▶ **A fruitwood stool,** with caned seat, minor damage, American, early 20thC, 20in (51cm) high.
£1,200–1,400
€/ **$1,900–2,200** ⚒ S(Am)

A pair of mahogany side tables, inlaid with lilies, c1900, 30in (76cm) wide.
£800–950
€/ **$1,300–1,500** ⚒ G(L)

An oak, beechwood and marquetry folding occasional table, by Emile Gallé, the top inlaid with a thistle and the Cross of Lorraine, on a pierced scrollwork base, signed, French, early 20thC, 28in (71cm) wide.
£6,000–6,600
€/ **$9,500–10,500** ⚒ S

A carved mahogany mirror-back sideboard, by Shapland & Petter, decorated with glass panels overlaid with copper, c1900, 54in (137cm) wide.
£2,700–3,000
€/ **$4,300–4,700** ⊞ ASP

A fruitwood and bronze two-tier lily pad table, by Louis Majorelle, French, c1900, 17½in (44.5cm) wide.
£4,500–5,000
€/ **$7,000–8,000** ⚒ S(NY)

▶ **A walnut, satin-wood and marquetry occasional table,** attributed to Louis Majorelle, the top inlaid with trailing branches and leaves, French, c1910, 25½in (65cm) diam.
£2,500–3,000
€/ **$4,000–4,700** ⚒ B

An oak mirror-back sideboard, with label for Gullachsen & Son, Newcastle-on-Tyne, c1900, 67in (170cm) wide.
£250–300
€/ **$400–475** ⚒ B(Ch)

A beechwood salon table, by Thonet, No. 1, with veneered top, repaired, designed pre-1888, 32½in (82.5cm) wide.
£750–875
€/ **$1,100–1,400** ⚒ DORO

A pair of Gaudi-style cast-iron tables, with marble tops, c1900, 19¾in (50cm) diam.
£1,700–2,000
€/ **$3,700–3,200** ⚒ S(Am)

Art Nouveau Glass

A Burgun, Schverer & Co glass vase, polychrome-decorated with raised flowers, fleurs-de-lys and central monogram 'AM' with a cross, on a matted textured ground, gold signature with thistle, Cross of Lorraine, French, 1897–1903, 15¾in (40cm) high.
£3,000–3,300
€/ **$4,700–5,200** ↗ DORO

The Lorraine glass-making firm of Burgun, Schverer & Co was established in 1711 and is still operating today under the name Verrerie de Meisenthal. Emile Gallé served a three-year apprenticeship with the company during the late 1860s, and in 1885 they entered into a contract to produce glass for Gallé's own company. Burgun, Schverer & Co are known for their cameo wares with decoration influenced by the local flora, and decorative techniques included acid cutting, foil inclusions, gilding and the use of overlay.

A Cristal Parisiana silver-gilt-mounted glass vase, the flattened body carved on each side with formalized narcissi against a textured bronzed ground, the pierced mounts cast with waterlilies, bulrushes and leaves, etched mark, French, c1900, 8½in (21.5cm) high.
£850–950
€/ **$1,300–1,500** ↗ S

A Daum cameo glass vase, the frosted glass enamelled and etched with fuchsia, signed, Cross of Lorraine, French, c1900, 5in (12.5cm) high.
£1,500–1,800
€/ **$2,400–2,800** ↗ S(O)

An Emile Gallé opalescent cameo glass dish, carved and etched with wild poppies, incised signature, French, c1900, 16in (40.5cm) wide.
£5,000–5,500
€/ **$8,000–8,700** ↗ S(O)

A Daum cameo glass vase, decorated with a polychrome wooded landscape, signed, Cross of Lorraine, French, c1900, 5in (12.5cm) high.
£1,200–1,400
€/ **$1,900–2,200** ↗ HOLL

A Daum cameo glass coupe, decorated in high relief with blackberries, engraved mark, Cross of Lorraine, 1912, 6¼in (16cm) high.
£8,500–10,000
€/ **$13,500–15,800** ↗ S(P)

A Daum glass vase, acid-etched and carved with pendant flowers, French, c1900, 3in (7.5cm) high.
£1,100–1,300
€/ **$1,700–2,000** ⊞ OND

A Daum cameo glass vase, acid-etched and carved with roses and foliage, signed, Cross of Lorraine, French, early 20thC, 7¼in (18.5cm) high.
£750–875
€/ **$1,200–1,400** ↗ SWO

A Emile Gallé cameo glass vase, with overlaid decoration of leaves and berries, French, c1900, 7in (18cm) high.
£1,000–1,100
€/ **$1,600–1,700** ⊞ ASA

An Emile Gallé cameo glass vase, with acid-etched floral decoration, French, c1900, 14in (35.5cm) high.
£1,100–1,300
€/ **$1,700–2,000** ⊞ OND

An Emile Gallé cameo glass vase, acid-etched with a wooded mountain scene, engraved signature, French, c1900, 8in (20.5cm) high.
£1,700–2,000
€/ **$2,700–3,200** ⚒ B

An Emile Gallé vase, with enamelled and acid-etched decoration, the flowerheads with applied cabochons, French, c1900, 8in (20.5cm) high.
£1,900–2,100
€/ **$3,000–3,300** ⊞ AFD

Miller's Compares

I. An Emile Gallé cameo glass vase, carved with waterlilies and leaves, cameo mark, French, early 20thC, 7½in (19cm) high.
£1,300–1,500
€/ **$2,000–2,400** ⚒ S

II. An Emile Gallé marqueterie-sur-verre and verre parlant cameo glas vase, inscribed 'Bonheur Bon an Bon Siècle Gallé', c1900, 5½in (14cm) high.
£5,700–6,300
€/ **$9,000–10,000** ⚒ S(NY)

Item II is 2in (5cm) smaller and less interesting in form than Item I, but has the advantage of the *marqueterie-sur-verre* technique whereby molten glass is carefully embedded into the heated surface to form a flowerhead or leaf design, and as a *vase parlant* is able to speak for itself through its hand-carved inscription. Item I is a standard, industrially-produced vase with overlay and acid carving. Although the decoration is well detailed and polished, it is ultimately less desirable.

A Legras glass vase, enamelled and acid-etched with thistles, signed, French, c1900, 18in (45.5cm) high.
£2,700–3,000
€/ **$4,300–4,800** ⚒ S(Am)

A Legras glass vase, enamelled and acid-cut with full-blown poppies, painted signature, French, early 20thC, 13¾in (35cm) high.
£700–800
€/ **$1,100–1,300** ⚒ S(O)

A Loetz Papillon vase, with all-over iridescent dappling, Austrian, c1890, 6½in (16.5cm) high.
£600–680
€/ **$950–1,000** ⊞ AFD

A Loetz iridescent glass vase, decorated with cyclamen, Austrian, c1900, 5¼in (13.5cm) high.
£1,300–1,500
€/ **$2,000–2,400** ⚒ S(P)

A Loetz iridescent glass vase, with applied silver decoration, ground out inscribed pontil mark, Austrian, c1900, 8¾in (22cm) high.
£3,000–3,500
€/ **$4,700–5,500** ⚒ DORO

A Loetz iridescent glass vase, decorated with applied raised threads, Austrian, c1900, 9½in (24cm) high.
£1,000–1,200
€/ **$1,600–1,900** ⚒ DORO

◄ **A Loetz goose-neck lustre vase,** Austrian, c1900, 9½in (24cm) high.
£1,200–1,400
€/ **$1,900–2,200** ⚒ S

A hock glass, designed by Otto Prutscher, early 20thC, 8½in (21.5cm) high.
£2,800–3,200
€/ **$4,400–5,000** ⊞ ALiN
Otto Prutscher (Austrian, 1880–1949) designed many pieces for the Wiener Werkstätte.

A Tiffany Favrile glass vase, American, 1899–1920, 5½in (14cm) high.
£1,500–1,800
€/ **$2,400–2,800** ⋌ S(NY)

A silver-mounted iridescent glass vase, the pierced overlay incorporating wave, flower and strapwork motifs, probably Austrian, c1905, 7in (18cm) high.
£2,000–2,200
€/ **$3,200–3,500** ⋌ S

A glass dish, in a silver-plated mount, c1900, 6in (15cm) diam.
£430–475
€/ **$680–750** ⊞ SHa

A glass vase, c1900, 4½in (11.5cm) high.
£250–275
€/ **$400–430** ⊞ SHa

A Tiffany Favrile glass dresser box, American, c1910, 5¾in (14.5cm) wide.
£380–450
€/ **$600–700** ⋌ DuM

A pair of iridescent glass vases, Bohemian, with silver mounts hallmarked London 1906, 7½in (19cm) high.
£100–125
€/ **$160–200** ⋌ PFK

▶ **A bronze and glass vase,** French, c1900, 6in (15cm) high.
£450–550
€/ **$710–870** ⊞ ASP

A glass vase, c1900, 10in (25.5cm) diam.
£430–475
€/ **$680–750** ⊞ SHa

A Tiffany Favrile bowl and plate, American, 1890–1910, plate 7in (18cm) diam.
£750–900
€/ **$1,200–1,400** ⊞ ASA

A Tiffany three-piece glass desk set, comprising a stationery rack, stamp box and paperweight, glass missing from paperweight, stamped, American, early 20thC, rack 12½in (32cm) wide.
£1,700–2,000
€/ **$2,700–3,200** ⋌ S(O)
Popular during the first two decades of the 20th century as 'Wedding Gift Tiffany', desk sets can be found in 15 various designs including Grape-Vine (above), Pine-Needle, Venetian, American Indian, Louis XVI, Chinese and Adam. The minimum number of pieces deemed to form a set was nine and would include blotter ends, inkstand, pen tray, paper rack, paper knife, rocker blotter, memo pad holder, stamp or utility box and calendar. However, all the pieces were priced and sold individually, and therefore a set can comprise any number of pieces.

Art Nouveau Jewellery

A 9ct gold bracelet, set with turquoise and blister pearls, c1905, 6in (15cm) long.
£600–680
€/ **$950–1,000** ⊞ ANO

A 15ct gold brooch, set with a turquoise, c1890, 3in (7.5cm) wide.
£400–450
€/ **$630–700** ⊞ ANO

An enamelled brooch, modelled as a lady's head, flowers in her hair, c1890, 1in (2.5cm) wide.
£1,000–1,100
€/ **$1,600–1,700** ⊞ NBL

An enamelled triple-leaf brooch, set with pearls, Russian, c1890, 1¼in (3cm) wide.
£1,200–1,400
€/ **$1,900–2,200** ⊞ NBL

A 15ct gold brooch, set with a citrine and two diamonds, within a seed pearl border, above a pearl drop, c1900.
£280–325
€/ **$440–515** ↗ BWL

A silver brooch, set with a cabochon, German, 1900–05, 1¼in (3cm) wide.
£270–300
€/ **$430–475** ⊞ ANO

A Wiener Werkstätte silver brooch, by Koloman Moser, set with a turquoise within an openwork setting of foliage and rods, the reverse with monogram 'KM', rose mark, Diana's head mark and assay mark, Austrian, designed 1906, 1¾in (4.5cm) high.
£3,800–4,500
€/ **$6,000–7,000** ↗ DORO

A Child & Child pendant necklace, attributed to Edward Burne-Jones, the enamelled wing motif set with a baroque pearl, above two pearl drops, the gold link chain set with six further pearls at intervals, c1900, in a green leather fitted case.
£2,000–2,400
€/ **$3,200–3,800** ↗ G(L)

A 9ct gold Liberty & Co pendant, set with a turquoise, 1900–05, 1¼in (3cm) high.
£450–500
€/ **$700–800** ⊞ ANO

A silver and *plique-à-jour* enamel pendant, by Theodor Fahrner, c1900, 1½in (4cm) high.
£600–680
€/ **$950–1,000** ⊞ ANO

◀ **A silver, marcasite and ivory pendant,** by Theodor Fahrner, with enamel and chrysoprase stone, German, c1910, 2in (5cm) long.
£720–800
€/ **$1,100–1,300** ⊞ RGA
The German jeweller Theodor Fahrner (1868–1928) produced large quantities of fine jewellery in an abstract Art Nouveau style.

▶ **A silver and carved ivory pendant,** German, c1910, 1½in (4cm) high.
£225–250
€/ **$350–400** ⊞ RGA

Art Nouveau Lighting

A Daum cameo glass *plafonnier*, etched with hazel leaves and nuts, cameo mark, Cross of Lorraine, French, c1900, 15½in (39.5cm) diam, with twisted hanging cords and metal hooks.
£2,200–2,500
€ / $3,500–4,000 ➤ S(O)

A leaded glass and bronze table lamp, attributed to Duffner & Kimberly, with finial, impressed 'D', American, c1910, 22½in (57cm) high.
£5,300–6,000
€ / $8,300–9,500 ➤ S(NY)

A Limoges enamel lamp base, by Camille Fauré, French, c1910, 6¼in (16cm) high.
£1,200–1,300
€ / $1,900–2,000 ⊞ ANO

A Muller Frères cameo glass lamp, acid-etched with anemones, signed, c1900, 22¾in (58cm) high.
£5,000–6,000
€ / $8,000–9,500 ➤ B

A silvered-metal and shell Nautilus lamp, in the style of Gustav Gurschner, the hinged shade held by twin rods terminating in a counterweight, stamped mark, German, early 20thC, 10¾in (27.5cm) high.
£4,500–5,000
€ / $7,000–8,000 ➤ S(O)

Items in the Art Nouveau Lighting section have been arranged alphabetically by maker, with non-specific pieces appearing at the end.

DECORATIVE ARTS

A Tiffany Favrile glass shade, decorated with acorns, impressed mark, American, 1899–1928, 16in (40.5cm) diam.
£5,000–6,000
€/ **$8,000–9,500** ⚒ S(NY)

A Tiffany Favrile glass and bronze Nautilus lamp, impressed mark, American, 1899–1920, 13¼in (33.5cm) high.
£9,000–11,000
€/ **$14,200–17,400** ⚒ S(NY)

A Tiffany bronze student lamp, rope coil decoration applied around the oil reservoir and base, with iridescent glass shade, converted for electricity, American, c1910, 28¾in (73cm) high.
£2,800–3,300
€/ **$4,400–5,200** ⚒ B

A patinated-metal and mottled glass two-light table lamp, modelled with two grotesque winged beasts holding pendant lamp shades in their mouths, the body with embossed bronze patinated sides and mounted with leaded glass, c1900, 25in (63.5cm) high.
£3,000–3,300
€/ **$4,700–5,200** ⚒ S(O)

A table lamp, with a leaded glass shade decorated with wistaria, on a reeded patinated-metal stem and arabesque-cast base, c1900, 29½in (75cm) high.
£9,000–10,000
€/ **$14,000–16,000** ⚒ S

Always check that electric lighting conforms to the current safety regulations before using.

A spelter lamp, by E. Villanis, modelled as Fleur de Bohème, French, c1900, 38in (96.5cm) high.
£900–1,000
€/ **$1,400–1,600** ⊞ ASP

▶ **A brass 'downer' gas lantern,** with on/off pulls and leaded lights with stylized tulip decoration, early 20thC, 35in (89cm) high.
£300–350
€/ **$475–550** ⚒ TMA

A brass six-arm chandelier with replacement etched-glass bell shades, Continental, 1910–20, 23in (58.5cm) diam.
£550–600
€/ **$870–950** ⊞ JeH

The Elton John Collection

Elton John unleashed his collection of Decorative Arts onto the world stage at Sotheby's in September 1988. The biggest prices in the four-volume catalogue – now a collector's item in its own right – are to be found in the one devoted to Art Nouveau and Art Deco. Elton John was by no means the only major player in this field: the competition could be tough when up against the likes of Rod Stewart, Joan Collins, Michael Caine and Barbra Streisand. Elton gathered together the best that money could buy and although he purchased from the top dealers he had the distinct advantage of buying on a rising market. More importantly, his decision to sell proved most astute as by the early 1990s the market began to falter in tandem with the Japanese economy and French art glass in particular proved a significant casualty. However, in 1988 the art market was bathed in sunshine. There was plenty of the 'feel good' factor and, as far as the London scene was concerned, no shortage of people with 'loadsamoney'. Elton's collection attracted plenty of bidding from overseas dealers and collectors with several of the top prices paid by American and Japanese buyers.

The sculpture section was led by two bronze and ivory figures by Demêtre Chiparus, with 'The Temple Dancer' enticing a bid of £33,000 (€/ $52,000) and another exotic dancer titled 'Yambo' achieving £48,400 (€/ $76,000). Two Tiffany leaded glass table lamps saw plenty of transatlantic competition with a 'Peacock' lamp selling for £37,400 (€/ $59,000) and a miniature 'Wistaria' lamp secured for £36,300 (€/ $57,000). The most sought-after piece of glass was a Daum internally decorated, applied and carved glass vase which soared to £56,100 (€/ $89,000). The pieces which achieved the highest prices, however, were a McCulloch carpet, designed by John Henry Dearle and woven at the Merton Abbey workshops of Morris & Co, which sold for £71,000 (€/ $112,000) and a salon suite dating from c1925, designed by Raoul Dufy and covered in highly decorative Aubusson tapestries which achieved £90,200 (€/ $143,000). Both pieces were functional as well as decorative, although at these prices one wonders if their new owners were afraid to walk or sit on them! **Eric Knowles**

Art Nouveau Metalware

A WMF silver-plated fruit bowl, with glass liner, c1910, 9in (23cm) diam.
£180–200
€ / $285–315 ⊞ TDG

A silver-plated trinket box, with enamel-inset lid and Secessionist design, Continental, early 20thC, 4in (10cm) wide.
£100–120
€ / $160–190 ⚒ G(L)

A silver box, by Horton & Allday, 1904, 4in (10cm) wide.
£450–500
€ / $700–800 ⊞ ANO

A silver leaf-shaped centrepiece, by Georg Jensen, decorated with berries, Danish, Copenhagen c1915, 4in (10cm) wide.
£400–500
€ / $630–800 ⚒ BUK

A silver cigarette case, by Kate Harris, London c1904, 4in (10cm) wide.
£380–425
€ / $600–675 ⊞ ANO

A copper box, with liner and back stop, c1915, 17in (43cm) wide.
£160–180
€ / $250–280 ⊞ ASP

Items in the Art Nouveau Metalware section have been arranged in alphabetical order.

A pair of Mappin & Webb silver and enamel candlesticks, London 1910–11, 9in (23cm) high.
£4,000–4,500
€ / $6,300–7,000 ⊞ NS

A WMF pewter centrepiece, with glass liner, stamped, German, early 20thC, 13½in (34.5cm) wide.
£650–720
€ / $1,000–1,200 ⚒ S(O)

A Liberty & Co pewter biscuit box, decorated with three rows of stylized plant leaves, the cover with twin lug handle, stamped 'English Pewter 0194', c1900, 5½in (14cm) high.
£380–450
€ / $600–700 ⚒ G(L)

A silver and cut-glass trinket box, Birmingham 1903, 4in (10cm) wide.
£120–135
€ / $190–215 ⊞ BrL

A silver centrepiece, with moulded edge, twin foliate scroll and tendril handles and indented bead decoration, presentation inscription, Sheffield 1907, 17¾in (45cm) wide, 58oz.
£750–900
€ / $1,200–1,400 ⚒ TRM

A silver lidded jug, with floral decoration in relief, the knop modelled as a bust, gilt interior, master's mark 'MT', Russian, Moscow c1900, 9in (23cm) high.
£330–400
€ / $520–630 ⚒ DORO

A Liberty & Co pewter crumb tray, by Archibald Knox, c1910, 10in (25.5cm) wide.
£250–280
€ / **$400–440** ⊞ AFD

A Liberty & Co Tudric pewter three-handled dish, with stylized foliate decoration, c1900, 6in (15cm) wide.
£280–325
€ / **$440–500** ⚒ TMA

▶ **A Gorham Manufacturing Co silver three-handled presentation cup,** retailed by Spaulding & Co, Chicago, chased with strapwork enclosing trefoils, etched on one side with a stag, the reverse with presentation inscription, marked and numbered, American, Providence, 1901, 12½in (32cm) high.
£1,400–1,600
€ / **$2,200–2,500** ⚒ S(NY)

▶ **A WMF pewter dish,** German, c1904, 10in (25.5cm) wide.
£850–950
€ / **$1,300–1,500**
⊞ SHa

A silver frame, Sheffield 1902, 13in (33cm) high.
£380–430
€ / **$600–680** ⊞ BrL

A silver photograph frame, with repoussé decoration of a woman picking apples, Birmingham 1904, 9½in (24cm) high.
£320–375
€ / **$500–600** ⚒ L

A silver double inkstand, by Omar Ramsden and Alwyn Carr, the two lids mounted with wirework and hardstone finials, over hammered sides, a floral cartouche with monogram, the flared base with a penholder inscribed 'Omar Ramsden et Alwyn Carr Me Fecerunt', London 1905, 7¾in (19.5cm) wide, 15.5oz.
£3,200–3,800
€ / **$5,000–6,000** ⚒ G(L)

An Orivit gilt-metal-mounted pottery jardinière, the mounts cast and pierced as waves and bubbles, mounts stamped, German, 7¼in (18.5cm) high.
£1,300–1,500
€ / **$2,000–2,400** ⚒ S

▶ **A Liberty & Co Tudric pewter and glass claret jug,** decorated with pomegranate motifs, c1907, 7in (18cm) high.
£270–330
€ / **$430–520** ⚒ G(L)

A WMF copper lidded jug, cast in low relief with stylized foliage, cast brass handle, stamped mark and numeral, German, early 20thC, 12in (30.5cm) high.
£275–325
€ / **$430–520** ⚒ GH

◀ **A silver-plated ladle,** American, 1900–05, 6in (15cm) long.
£110–125
€ / **$175–200** ⊞ ANO

A Tiffany Japanese-style silver easel mirror, the spot-hammered surface etched with tentacle monogram 'NKS', pierced easel and serpent-form loop finial, marked and numbered, American, c1881, 8½in (21.5cm) high.
£1,800–2,200
€ / **$2,800–3,500** ⚒ S(NY)

A silver christening mug, embossed with stylized leaf devices and applied with a scroll handle, maker's mark 'GW', Sheffield 1903, 3½in (9cm) high.
£120–140
€/ $190–220 ➤ BR

A Liberty & Co cased set of six teaspoons and sugar tongs, each with a pierced scrolling terminal, decorated with an enamel plaque, Birmingham 1907.
£750–875
€/ $1,200–1,400 ➤ B(NW)

A Liberty & Co Tudric pewter four-piece tea and coffee service, by Archibald Knox, c1900, 8in (20.5cm) high.
£675–750
€/ $1,000–1,200 ⊞ WAC

A Connell pewter four-piece tea service, comprising water jug, teapot, sugar basin and milk jug, stamped marks, early 20thC.
£170–200
€/ $270–320 ➤ GH

▶ **A Liberty & Co Tudric pewter tankard,** 1900, 9in (23cm) high.
£800–900
€/ $1,300–1,400 ⊞ AFD

A pair of Liberty Cymric silver and enamelled spoons, 1890–1910, 7in (18cm) long.
£800–900
€/ $1,300–1,400 ⊞ ASA

◀ **A pottery tea canister,** with pierced silver overlay, Chester 1904, 4½in (11.5cm) high.
£585–650
€/ $920–1,000 ⊞ SHa

A bronze vase, by Julien Caussé, cast with overlapping leaves, two of which form the handles, further leaves ending in an opening flower bud, signed, French, c1900, 13in (33cm) high.
£300–350
€/ $475–550 ➤ B

◀ **A Limoges enamel vase,** by Camille Fauré, with landscape decoration, French, c1900, 7in (18cm) high.
£850–950
€/ $1,400–1,500 ⊞ ANO

◀ **A Tiffany silver vase,** attributed to Paulding Farnham, etched with scrolling foliate strapwork, engraved monogram 'EH', looped tendril handles, beaded knop and base, marked and numbered, American, c1896, 14¾in (37.5cm) high.
£4,500–5,300
€/ $7,000–8,400 ➤ S(NY)

A gilt-bronze vase, by M. Paignant, the two handles surmounted by locusts and cast foliage, signed, Jollet & Cie foundry seal, on a marble plinth, French, c1900, 8in (20.5cm) high.
£2,000–2,200
€/ $3,200–3,500 ➤ S

A Liberty & Co Tudric pewter vase, with original glass liner, c1900, 8¾in (22cm) high.
£675–750
€/ $1,000–1,200 ⊞ SHa

Art Deco Ceramics

A Carlton Ware Chevrons cigarette box and cover, with matching pin tray, each with silver lustre highlights, the box with pearlescent interior, pattern number 3657, minor wear, 1930s, box 6in (15cm) wide.
£300–360
€/ $475–570 🔨 S(O)

A Carter, Stabler & Adams bowl, designed by Truda Carter, c1930, 10in (25.5cm) diam.
£350–400
€/ $550–630 ⊞ HarC

A Carter, Stabler & Adams vase, pattern GM, shape 979, impressed marks, c1930, 8¾in (22cm) high.
£300–350
€/ $475–550 🔨 GH

A Carter, Stabler & Adams vase, 1920–30, 7in (18cm) high.
£200–225
€/ $315–350 ⊞ PGO

A Clew's Chameleonware lidded vase, 1930s, 7½in (19cm) high.
£130–150
€/ $200–240 🔨 WiLP

A Crown Devon lustre vase, c1930, 7½in (19cm) high.
£315–350
€/ $500–550 ⊞ RH

A Carlton Ware jug, moulded and painted with Spring Flower pattern, 1930s, 10in (25.5cm) high.
£180–200
€/ $285–315 ⊞ PSA

A Claude Coquerel earthenware vase, signed and monogrammed, c1940, 17in (43cm) high.
£2,000–2,400
€/ $3,200–3,800 🔨 S(NY)

A Crown Devon jug, decorated with Floral pattern, c1925, 12in (30.5cm) high.
£180–200
€/ $285–315 ⊞ TDG

A Carter, Stabler & Adams vase, designed by Truda Adams, painted by Mary Brown with Blue Bird pattern, maker's marks, c1930, 6½in (16.5cm) high.
£130–150
€/ $200–240 🔨 HoG
Although these wares are invariably referred to as Poole Pottery these days, the company was founded in Poole, Dorset, in 1873 as Carter & Co, and adopted the combined names of its partners, Carter, Stabler & Adams, upon its expansion in 1921. It was not until 1963 that the trade name of Poole Pottery emerged.

LOCATE THE SOURCE
The source of each illustration in Miller's can be found by checking the code letters below each caption with the Key to Illustrations, pages 794–800.

A Gouda Kurba vase, Dutch, c1929, 9½in (24cm) high.
£180–200
€/ $285–315 ⊞ DSG

A Hancock Coronaware bowl, decorated with Springtime pattern, signed 'F. X. Abraham', c1925, 12¼in (31cm) diam.
£240–265
€ / **$380–420** ⊞ PIC

A Moravian Pottery & Tile Works tile, Florence Nightingale's lamp, American, c1920, 4in (10cm) square.
£45–50
€ / **$70–80** ⊞ KMG

A Myott fan vase, c1930, 9in (23cm) high.
£270–300
€ / **$425–475** ⊞ RH

A Newcomb College Pottery plaque, decorated by Sadie Irvine with butterflies, marked, with paper label, American, c1926, 5½in (14cm) diam.
£4,000–4,500
€ / **$6,300–7,000** ⊞ CaF

Newcomb College Pottery (American 1895–1941)

The pottery at Newcomb College, New Orleans, has produced some of the rarest and most valuable American art pottery. Operated mainly by women, the distinctive hand-thrown wares were hand-decorated with incised patterns of local flora and fauna highlighted in polychrome slip. Early pieces have a high glaze, while post-1910 wares usually have a semi-matt finish. Larger items are the most collectable, as well as those featuring landscape decoration or pieces decorated by the better artists such as Mary Sheerer, or the founder, Jospeh Meyer.

▶ **A Pilkington's Royal Lancastrian kylix,** c1920, 10in (25.5cm) diam.
£135–150
€ / **$215–240** ⊞ RUSK

A Newcomb College Pottery vase, decorated by Anna Francis Simpson with egrets against tree trunks, American, c1930, 7¼in (18.5cm) high.
£8,500–9,000
€ / **$13,500–15,00** ⊞ CaF

A Pilkington's Royal Lancastrian lustre vase, by William Salter Mycock, 1930s, 7in (18cm) high.
£1,100–1,200
€ / **$1,700–1,900** ⊞ ASA

◀ **A Shelley Harmony ginger jar,** with drip decoration, c1930, 5in (12.5cm) high.
£135–150
€ / **$215–240** ⊞ BEV

A Roseville Pottery wistaria vase, American, 1933, 8½in (21.5cm) high.
£750–900
€ / **$1,200–1,400** ⚒ SPG

A Royal Winton vase, decorated with Flame pattern, c1930, 8in (20.5cm) high.
£145–160
€ / **$230–250** ⊞ RH

A Shelley part coffee service, comprising coffee pot and lid, milk jug, sugar bowl, five cups and six saucers, some damage, c1930.
£650–750
€ / **$1,000–1,200** ⚒ B(W)

Shelley Eve shape trio, decorated with
daisy pattern, 1934, cup 3in (7.5cm) high.
160–180
/ **$250–285** ⊞ BEV

Wiener Werkstätte earthenware bowl,
decorated with stylized birds and flowers, glaze
chips, impressed mark and number 336, painted
mark 8, Austrian, 1920s, 5in (12.5cm) diam.
300–360
/ **$474–570** ⚒ S(Am)

A Shelley Queen Anne shape trio,
decorated with Blue Iris pattern,
c1930, plate 6in (5cm) square.
£80–90
/ **$125–140** ⊞ HarC

**A Wedgwood Fairyland lustre
bowl,** c1930, 8in (205cm) diam.
£350–400
/ **$550–630** ⚒ BWL

▶ **A J. Wilkinson Tahiti Storm
vase,** designed by John Butler,
signed, c1930, 17in (43cm) high.
£1,300–1,500
/ **$2,000–2,400** ⊞ BD
John Butler, together with Fred
Ridgeway, were Wilkinson's two
top designers prior to the arrival
of Clarice Cliff in 1920.

A Shelley drip ware vase,
c1930, 7in (18cm) high.
£70–80
/ **$110–125** ⊞ RH

DECORATIVE ARTS

Clarice Cliff

A Clarice Cliff Bizarre bookend, in the shape of a seated Golly, decorated with Sunburst pattern, c1930, 6in (15cm) high.
£1,300–1,500
€ / **$2,000–2,400** ⚒ Bea

▶ **A Clarice Cliff sugar bowl and tongs,** decorated with Autumn pattern, c1930, 3½in (9cm) high.
£500–550
€ / **$800–870** ⊞ TDG

A Clarice Cliff Conical bowl, decorated with Garland pattern, c1930, 9in (23cm) diam.
£550–600
€ / **$870–950** ⊞ BD

A Clarice Cliff Bizarre bowl, decorated with Aurea pattern, c1930, 7½in (19cm) diam.
£280–320
€ / **$440–520** ⚒ SWO

A Clarice Cliff Fantasque clog, decorated with Windbells pattern, printed marks, restored 1933–34, 5½in (13.5cm) wide.
£330–400
€ / **$520–640** ⚒ S(O)

A Clarice Cliff pedestal comport, decorated with Rhodanthe pattern, 1930s, 8in (20cm) high.
£550–600
€ / **$800–950** ⊞ JOA

▶ **A Clarice Cliff jug,** decorated with Sunray pattern, printed marks, restored, c1930, 5½in (14cm) high.
£450–525
€ / **$700–830** ⚒ B

A Clarice Cliff Duck egg cup stand, with six egg cups and stand, decorated with Double V pattern, marked, c1929, cup 6¼in (16cm) diam.
£650–750
€ / **$1,000–1,200** ⚒ B

A Clarice Cliff jardinière, decorated with Delecia Iberis pattern, c1930, 11in (28cm) diam.
£200–220
€ / **$320–350** ⚒ GH

A Clarice Cliff Conical jug, decorated with Summerhouse pattern, c1930, 6½in (16.5cm) high.
£1,800–2,000
€ / **$2,800–3,200** ⊞ BD

◀ **A Clarice Cliff Bizarre plate,** produced for Brice Rogers, decorated with Tennis pattern, printed marks, 1930–31, 6¾in (17cm) diam.
£750–875
€ / **$1,200–1,400** ⚒ Bea

A Clarice Cliff Bizarre plate, decorated with Devon pattern, c1930, 8½in (21.5cm) diam.
£600–700
€ / **$950–1,100** ⚒ GH

Clarice Cliff plate, decorated with
Ilton pattern, printed marks, c1934,
in (23cm) diam.
280–320
/ $440–520 ➤ PFK

A Clarice Cliff charger, decorated
with Forest Glen pattern, printed
marks, 1935–37, 18in (45.5cm) diam.
£1,800–2,200
€/ $2,900–3,500 ➤ G(B)

A Clarice Cliff Beehive honey pot,
decorated with a geometric pattern,
signature mark, c1930,
3in (7.5cm) high.
£280–325
€/ $440–515 ➤ SWO

Clarice Cliff Bonjour jam pot,
ecorated with Melons pattern,
1930, 4½in (11.5cm) high.
720–800
/ $1,100–1,200 ⊞ BD

◀ **A Clarice
Cliff Bizarre
sandwich plate,**
decorated with
Acorn pattern,
printed marks,
1930s, 11¾in
(30cm) wide.
£280–325
€/ $440–500
➤ SWO

To order Miller's books in the USA please
ring AOL/Time Warner on 1-800-759-0190

Clarice Cliff Stamford tea set,
omprising 10 pieces, painted with
geometric pattern, c1930,
eapot 4¾in (12cm) high.
950–1,100
/ $1,500–1,700 ➤ SWO

A Clarice Cliff sandwich set, comprising
seven pieces, decorated with Applique Idyll
pattern, c1930, largest 9in (23cm) diam.
£1,700–2,000
€/ $2,700–3,200 ➤ GH

**A Clarice Cliff Conical
sugar sifter,** decorated
with a version of Rudyard
pattern, printed marks,
c1933, 5¼in (13.5cm) high.
£850–1,000
€/ $1,300–1,600 ➤ Bea

**Clarice Cliff Bizarre
vase,** decorated with Blue
Firs pattern, c1930,
4in (10cm) high.
€850–1,000
€/ $1,300–1,600 ➤ GH

**A Clarice Cliff Bizarre
vase,** decorated with
Autumn Crocus pattern,
printed and painted marks,
c1930, 8¼in (21cm) high.
£675–800
€/ $1,100–1,300 ➤ SWO

**A Clarice Cliff Fantasque
vase,** decorated with
Autumn pattern, marked,
c1930, 8in (20.5cm) high.
£600–700
€/ $950–1,100 ➤ MAR

**A Clarice Cliff Fantasque
vase,** decorated with
Autumn pattern,
printed marks, c1930,
7¾in (20cm) high.
£2,200–2,600
€/ $3,500–4,100 ➤ TEN

A Clarice Cliff Bizarre vase, decorated with Football pattern, printed marks, 1929–30, 6½in (16.5cm) high.
£2,200–2,500
€ / $3,500–4,000 ⚒ Bea

A Clarice Cliff Isis vase, produced for Lawley's, decorated with Umbrellas and Rain pattern, c1930, 9½in (24cm) high.
£2,200–2,500
€ / $3,500–4,000 ⚒ G(L)

A Clarice Cliff vase, decorated with Latona Red Roses pattern, marked, c1930, 18in (45.5cm) high.
£4,000–4,800
€ / $6,300–7,600 ⚒ B

A Clarice Cliff vase, decorated with Nasturtium pattern, c1930, 10in (25.5cm) high.
£900–1,000
€ / $1,400–1,600 ⊞ BD

A Clarice Cliff vase, decorated with Orange Battle pattern, c1930, 2in (5cm) high.
£900–1,000
€ / $1,400–1,600 ⊞ BD

A Clarice Cliff Bizarre vase, decorated with Delecia Pansies pattern, c1930, 5½in (14cm) high.
£320–375
€ / $500–600 ⚒ GH

▶ **A Clarice Cliff vase,** decorated with Orange Lily pattern, c1930, 6½in (16.5cm) diam.
£850–950
€ / $1,300–1,500
⊞ TDG

A Clarice Cliff vase, decorated with Windbells pattern, c1930, 8in (20.5cm) high.
£2,700–3,000
€ / $4,300–4,800 ⊞ BD

A Clarice Cliff vase, decorated with Delecia pattern, minor wear, c1930, 7in (18cm) high.
£300–350
€ / $475–550 ⚒ Pott

A Clarice Cliff Bizarre vase, decorated with Whisper pattern, c1930, 7¾in (19.5cm) high.
£900–1,100
€ / $1,400–1,700 ⚒ GH

A Clarice Cliff Yo vase, decorated with Delecia pattern, c1930, 6in (15.cm) high.
£1,200–1,300
€ / $1,900–2,000 ⊞ BD

◀ **A Clarice Cliff wall plaque,** decorated with Clovelly pattern, depicting cottages, poplars and a full moon, printed marks, c1930, 17½in (44.5cm) diam.
£1,800–2,200
€ / $2,800–3,500
⚒ B

A Clarice Cliff Bizarre vase, printed marks, facsimile signature, c1930, 6in (15cm).
£420–500
€ / $660–790 ⚒ PF

A Clarice Cliff Bizarre vase, decorated with Green Japan pattern, printed marks, 1933–34, 6¾in (17cm) high.
£420–500
€ / $660–790 ⚒ Bea

Susie Cooper

A Susie Cooper Patricia Rose coffee cup and saucer, c1930, 2¼in (5.5cm) high.
£80–90
€/ $125–145 ⊞ RH

A Susie Cooper coffee pot, decorated with Assyrian Motif pattern, c1963, 8in (20.5cm) high.
£100–110
€/ $160–175 ⊞ CHI

A Susie Cooper six-division entrée dish, decorated with hand-painted vegetables, on an oak tray, c1930, 19¾in (50cm) wide.
£100–120
€/ $160–1900 ➢ WiLP

► A Susie Cooper mug, with banded decoration, 1930s, 3in (7.5cm) high.
£140–160
€/ $220–250 ➢ SWO

A Susie Cooper moulded jug, with incised decoration, marks to base, 1930s, 6¾in (17cm) high.
£180–220
€/ $280–350 ➢ SWO

A Susie Cooper jug, decorated with stylized foliage, stamped, c1930, 8¾in (22cm) high.
£100–125
€/ $160–200 ➢ SWO

A Susie Cooper coffee service, comprising 16 pieces, decorated with Dresden Spray pattern, 1930s.
£140–160
€/ $220–250 ➢ PFK

A Susie Cooper dinner and tea service, comprising 63 pieces, decorated with Fern pattern, c1936.
£220–260
€/ $350–400 ➢ BR

A Susie Cooper teapot, decorated with raised enamel polka dots, c1954.
£80–90
€/ $125–145 ⊞ CHI

◄ A Susie Cooper one pint teapot, decorated with raised enamel polka dots, c1954.
£80–90
€/ $125–145 ⊞ CHI

Charlotte Rhead

A Charlotte Rhead Crown Ducal jug, decorated with flowers and stylized leaves, gilded handle, c1930, 14in (35.5cm) high.
£140–160
€/ $220–250 ➢ EH

A Charlotte Rhead Crown Ducal jug, decorated with a floral design on a mottled ground, printed marks, 1931–43, 8¼in (21cm) high.
£160–200
€/ $250–315 ➢ RIT

Charlotte Rhead was employed by several Staffordshire pottery factories before joining her father Frederick Rhead at Wood & Sons of Burslem in 1912. In 1926 she moved to Burgess & Leigh who produced Burleigh Ware and by 1937 had moved again to A. G. Richardson, makers of Crown Ducal pottery. Finally, in 1941 she worked once more for Wood's, at H. J. Wood in Burslem.

A pair of Charlotte Rhead Wood & Sons vases, decorated with stylized flowers with gilt detail, printed marks, c1915, 13in (33cm) high.
£850–1,000
€/ $1,300–1,600 ➢ WL

Art Deco Clocks

Expert's choice

I am only too ready to admit that I consider myself incredibly fortunate to have had the opportunity of handling thousands of pieces of Lalique glass and to have overseen some equally amazing sales of Lalique during my many years with Bonhams. Of all the objects I had the pleasure of auctioning, Lalique's Night and Day clock was the item I would truly have loved to have kept, being both stunning and functional. The clock makes clever use of relief and impressed moulding to achieve the tonal qualities of the male and female nude figures whose bodies arch around the central clockface.

A Night and Day clock, by R. Lalique, c1930, sold by Bonhams, 1989.

What made this clock so special was the colour – topaz, not the more usual smoky grey, but a lovely subtle topaz that changed to a vibrant dark amethyst. I've never seen another which is probably just as well for at £80,000 (€/ $126,000) the housekeeping would be under serious pressure.   **Eric Knowles**

A René Lalique frosted and polished glass mantel clock, *'Quatre Moineaux Du Japon,'* c1928, 8in (20.5cm) square
£1,400–1,500
€/ **$2,200–2,400**   ⊞ LBr

An enamelled brass electric wall clock, by Gebr. Arens, Nijmegen, maker's mark, Dutch, c1934, 11¾in (30cm) square.
£1,200–1,400
€/ **$1,900–2,200**   ⤳ S(Am)

Art Deco Figures & Busts

▶ **A patinated-bronze figure of an armed Amazon,** by M. Bouraine, signed, impressed number, French, 1925–30, 32in (81.5cm) wide.
£4,700–5,500
€/ **$7,400–8,700**   ⤳ DORO

◀ **A bronze and ivory figure of a girl,** by Dominique Alonzo, signed, French, early 20thC, 9in (23cm) high.
£900–1,100
€/ **$1,400–1,700**   ⤳ S(O)

▶ **An Art Deco bronze group of a nude girl on a leaping horse,** by L. Charles, Verbier, Paris, signed, French, 24½in (62cm) wide.
£1,300–1,500
€/ **$2,000–2,400**
⤳ TF

A gilt-bronze and carved ivory figure of a girl, by Demêtre Chiparus, entitled 'Chain Dancer', on a marble base, French, original chain missing, c1925, 10½in (26.5cm) high.
£4,500–5,200
€/ **$7,000–8,400**   ⤳ B

A pair of gilt and silvered-bronze bookends, by Noël Coulon, modelled as Native Americans, signed, French, c1930, 7¼in (18.5cm) high.
£3,000–3,300
€/ **$4,700–5,600**   ⤳ S(O)

A bronze and ivory figure of a girl, by Gerdago, on an onyx base, German, c1920, 6½in (16.5cm) high.
£4,000–4,500
€/ **$6,300–7,000**   ⊞ ASA

AUDREY STERNSHINE

A Goldscheider ceramic figure of a woman, Austrian, c1930, 11in (28cm) high.
£1,000–1,100
€ / **$1,600–1,700** ⊞ ASA

An Art Deco spelter and ivorine group of a woman and two dogs, by Georges Gori, on an onyx base, signed, French, 28in (71cm) wide.
£1,300–1,500
€ / **$2,100–2,400** ⚒ HAM

A Hagenauer bronze figure of a woman, signed and stamped to base, Austrian, 1920s, 13½in (34.5cm) high.
£2,700–3,000
€ / **$4,300–4,700** ⊞ TDG

A porcelain group of Pan and Psyche, by Hutschenreuther, German, c1920, 12½in (32cm) high.
£765–850
€ / **$1,200–1,300** ⊞ ANO

▶ **A patinated-bronze figure of Diana,** by Pierre Le Faguays, stamped mark, initialled, French, c1930, 25¾in (65.5cm) high.
£3,700–4,200
€ / **$5,800–6,600** ⚒ S

A gilt and silver-patinated bronze group, by Alexander Kéléty, entitled 'Hunter with Two Gazelles', on a marble base, French, c1930, 19¾in (50cm) high.
£1,400–1,600
€ / **$2,200–2,500** ⚒ S(P)

A René Lalique frosted glass figure, entitled 'Sirène', French, c1930, 4in (10cm) high.
£1,300–1,500
€ / **$2,100–2,400** ⊞ OND

◀ **A patinated-bronze figure of a naked woman,** by Lorenzl, on an onyx base, signed, 1920s–30s, 11¾in (30cm) high.
£1,100–1,300
€ / **$1,700–2,000** ⚒ BUK

A plaster figure of a woman, by Melani, French, c1930, 24in (61cm) wide.
£240–270
€ / **$380–425** ⊞ ASP

▶ **A silvered- and patinated-bronze figure,** by Paul Philippe, entitled 'The Bather', on an onyx base, signed, some damage, 1920s, French, 11in (28cm) high.
£1,300–1,500
€ / **$2,100–2,400** ⚒ G(L)
Paul Philippe was born in Poland but studied in France under Antonin Larroux. He exhibited with success in the Paris salons in the inter-war period.

A bronze and ivory figure, by Ferdinand Preiss, entitled 'Sunshine Girl', German, c1920, 9½in (24cm) high.
£11,000–12,000
€ / **$17,000–19,000** ⊞ ASA

A pair of patinated-bronze bookends, by Paul Silvestre, modelled as two young fauns, signed, French, c1930, 8½in (21.5cm) high.
£1,800–2,000
€ / **$2,800–3,200** ⊞ MI

gilt-bronze group of a woman nd a greyhound, by Raymond on Rivoire, on a marble base, ench, c1925, 15¼in (38.5cm) high.
5,300–6,000
/ **$8,400–9,500** ⚖ S(NY)

▶ **A porcelain figure of a female nude,** by Wallendorf, German, c1935, 10in (25.5cm) high.
£180–200
€ / **$285–315** ⊞ ASP

◀ **A bronze figural table lamp,** in the form of a young woman supporting a coloured glass globe, on a marble base, c1930, 15½in (39.5cm) high.
£420–500
€ / **$660–790**
⚖ G(B)

A carved wood bust of a woman, French, c1915, 15in (38cm) high.
£450–550
€ / **$710–870** ⊞ ASP

patinated-bronze figure f a female nude, by Felix Veiss, on a marble base, igned, Austrian, 1920s–30s, 4½in (62cm) high.
1,300–1,500
/ **$2,000–2,400** ⚖ BUK

A spelter group of a young girl and a dog, on a marble base, French, c1930, 21in (53.5cm) wide.
£400–450
€ / **$630–700** ⊞ ASP

▶ **A silver-plated figural rophy,** in the form of a ancing lady, c1932, 2¼in (31cm) high.
450–550
/ **$700–870** ⚖ CHTR

Art Deco Furniture

▶ **A pair of sycamore open bookcases,** with block-decorated back-rails above three bays, c1930, 72½in (184cm) wide.
£2,000–2,400
€ / **$3,200–3,800** ⚖ B

A silvered-wood bench, American, :1930, 42in (106.5cm) wide.
3,700–4,300
/ **$5,800–6,000** ⚖ S(NY)

▶ **A walnut bookcase,** c1930, 20in (51cm) wide.
£265–300
€ / **$415–475** ⊞ GBr

A pair of birchwood bedside cabinets, Swedish, 1920–30, 22¼in (56.5cm) high.
£2,700–3,000
€ / **$4,300–4,800** ⊞ CAV

A Bird Iles walnut cocktail cabinet, with a pair of doors enclosing a lead-lined cellaret and curved end door with interior shutters, c1934, 66in (167.5cm) wide.
£230–275
€/ **$365–430** ✦ B
Jack Bird Iles (1902–85) was one of a group of exclusive designers that included Betty Joel, Syrie Maugham and Sibyl Colefax. They worked in Mayfair and the West End of London between the wars to cater for the taste of many of London's wealthiest inhabitants. Bird Iles was one of the architects of the Dreamland Cinema in Margate, a fine example of a high Art Deco building, and he also provided the interior for the dressing rooms at Elstree Studios. WWII effectively brought an end to Bird Iles' furniture production business due to the shortage of luxury materials and the introduction of purchase tax. However, he continued to work as a decorator into the 1960s.

To order Miller's books in the UK please ring 01903 828800.
See the full range at
www.millers.uk.com

An oak cabinet, the four doors flanked by silvered and painted fretwork panels, above four drawers, c1930, 42in (107cm) wide.
£320–380
€/ **$500–600** ✦ B

A rosewood secretaire cabinet, the leather-lined fall-front decorated with an ebonized woman's head, with a maple interior, French, c1925, 55in (139.5cm) high.
£4,500–5,000
€/ **$7,000–8,000** ⊞ TDG

An André Groult giltwood bergère, with beaded trim, French, c1920.
£10,000–11,000
€/ **$15,800–17,000**
⊞ NART
André Groult (1884–1967) was an interior decorator and furniture designer whose designs were mainly executed by craftsmen working in his atelier in Paris. His designs invariably demonstrate his preference for curves.

A Süe & Mare rosewood and marquetry side cabinet, the top wit protruding corners above a frieze drawer, over a pair of doors with shaped panels of stylized floral marquetry enclosing a divided interior French, c1925, 26½in (67cm) wide.
£2,200–2,500
€/ **$3,500–4,000** ✦ B
Louis Süe and André Mare, both already established French designers, joined in partnership to set up their *Compagnie des Arts Français* in 1919. It soon became known as Süe et Mare. They produced furniture, both in wood and wrought-iron, that epitomized the opulence of the French high Art Deco style. They also designed co-ordinated interiors, using a large team of prominent designers such as Maurice Marinot.

A burr-walnut armchair, in the style of Pierre Chareau, French, 1920s
£2,000–2,400
€/ **$3,200–3,800** ✦ S(Am)

A mahogany and maple salon chair, 1930s.
£400–450
€/ **$630–700** ⊞ BDA

A set of four oak chairs, 1930s.
£520–575
€/ **$820–900** ⊞ SAT

An oak rocking chair, c1930.
£170–220
€/ **$270–350** ✦ WiLP

pair of side chairs, by Jacques dnet, French, 1940s.
2,200–2,500
/ $3,500–4,000 ⚹ **S(O)**

A wrought-iron reclining chair, upholstered in silk Illusion fabric by Jim Thompson, French, 1940s.
£1,000–1,200
€ / $1,600–1,900 ⚹ **S(Am)**

A Hague School oak kneehole desk and chair, by C. Alons, the top lined with linoleum above a central drawer, flanked by two doors opening to shelves and drawers, the reverse with open shelves, with matching chair, Dutch, c1928, 59in (150cm) wide.
£1,500–1,800
€ / $2,400–2,800 ⚹ **S(Am)**

◄ **A mahogany dining room suite,** by Jacob van den Bosch, comprising a table, two armchairs and four chairs, Dutch, c1920, table 84in (213.5cm) extended.
£1,200–1,400
€ / $1,900–2,200 ⚹ **S(Am)**

A bird's-eye maple and walnut dining room suite, comprising a table, two open armchairs and four chairs, with associated sideboard, c1935, table 72½in (184cm) wide.
£3,500–4,200
€ / $5,500–6,600 ⚹ **B**

An Epstein burr-walnut dining room suite, comprising a dining table, six chairs, a sideboard and a cocktail cabinet, c1938, table 77½in (197cm) wide.
£9,000–10,000
€ / $14,000–16,000 ⚹ **S(O)**

A dressing table, the oval mirror above a central bow-front section with frieze drawer, flanked by pedestal end sections with moulded mirror fronts enclosing shelves and fitted drawers, c1925, 50½in (128cm) wide.
£420–500
€ / $660–790 ⚹ **B**

An amboyna-veneered and inlaid dressing table, the tapered mirror flanked by frosted illuminating panels and by pedestal cupboards enclosing shelves, on ivorine feet, c1930, 58¾in (149cm) wide.
550–650
€ / $870–1,000 ⚹ **S(O)**

◄ **A William Arthur Chase marquetry inlaid wall mirror,** made for the Rowley Gallery, with a circular glazed panel entitled 'On a bat's wing I do fly', stamped, 1920s, 22¾in (57.5cm) high.
£380–420
€ / $620–740 ⚹ **S(O)**

A silvered-bronze wall mirror, above a geometric mount with stylized an, c1930, 24¾in (63cm) wide.
600–700
€ / $950–1,100 ⚹ **S(O)**

A mirror, with crystal and peach-coloured glass, 1930s, 27in (68.5cm) wide.
£215–235
€ / $340–370 ⊞ **SAT**

A four-fold screen, painted by Stuart Scott Somerville in oil on canvas with ornamental birds amid flowering vases, signed and dated 1928, 90in (348cm) wide.
£3,300–4,000
€/ **$5,200–6,300** B(EA)

An elm fire screen, 1930s, 25in (63.5cm) high.
£150–165
€/ **$240–260** SAT

A rosewood and silvered-metal table, attributed to Jules Leleu, French, c1925, 31½in (80cm) diam.
£4,700–5,500
€/ **$7,400–8,700** S(NY)

A painted centre table, by Paul Jouve, the hardstone top above four acanthus scroll supports, French, c1940, 62¼in (158cm) wide.
£1,300–1,500
€/ **$2,000–2,400** S(Am)

▶ **An oak-lined walnut wardrobe,** c1920, 63in (160cm) wide.
£780–875
€/ **$1,200–1,400** WiB

An Edwin Hardy Amies needlework four-fold screen, stitched with Oriental style-flowers, trees and a figure, 1930s, 74in (188cm) wide.
£200–225
€/ **$315–350** BIG

▶ **A pine shelf,** hand decorated, c1925, 28in (71cm) wide.
£125–140
€/ **$200–220** SAT

A Heal & Son ebonized and painted sideboard, the design attributed to Ambrose Heal, c1918, 60in (152.5cm) wide.
£2,800–3,200
€/ **$4,400–5,000** S(O)

A beech pedestal table, in the style of Emile Jacques Ruhlmann, French, 1920s, 19½in (49.5cm) diam.
£2,200–2,500
€/ **$3,400–4,000** S(Am)

A pair of Jean Hanau *verre églomisé* **four-panel screens,** decorated with stylized figures within hinged black-lacquered frames, French, 1930s, each screen 48¾in (123.5cm) squa
£2,700–3,300
€/ **$4,300–5,200** S(O)

A mahogany and brass sofa, attributed to André Arbus, French, c1940, 57in (145cm) wide
£12,500–14,000
€/ **$20,000–22,000** NART

A Bird Iles glass and tubular-copper occasional table, the top with an etched band, on bent tubular supports with a glass undertier, c1928, 30in (76cm) diam.
£750–875
€/ **$1,200–1,400**
 B

▶ **A zebra wood and Macassar ebony wardrobe,** attributed to Richter for the Bath Cabinet Makers, c1930, 77in (195.5cm) high.
£3,000–3,300
€/ **$4,700–5,200**
 TDG

Art Deco Glass

A Charder cameo glass tazza, etched with chestnuts, on an applied foot, cameo mark, French, 1926–33, 13½in (34.5cm) diam.
£1,200–1,400
€/ $1,900–2,200 ⚘ S(Am)

A Daum acid-cut glass bowl,
French, c1930, 8in (20.5cm) diam.
£550–620
€/ $870–980 ⊞ AFD

A Daum glass vase, by Louis Majorelle, with wrought-iron mounts, French, c1920, 12in (30.5cm) high.
£800–900
€/ $1,200–1,400 ⊞ AFD

◀ **A Daum glass vase,** acid-etched with horizontal bands, marked, Cross of Lorraine, French, c1930, 10in (25.5cm) high.
£2,200–2,500
€/ $3,500–4,000 ⚘ S(O)

A Daum glass vase, acid-etched with foliate decoration, French, c1930, 13in (33cm) high.
£3,400–3,800
€/ $5,400–6,000 ⊞ GoW

A cameo glass vase, by Degué, French, c1920, 14in (35.5cm) diam.
£1,900–2,100
€/ $3,000–3,300 ⊞ AFD

A Wiener Werkstätte glass centrepiece, by Josef Hoffmann, small rim chip, acid-etched monogram 'WW', Austrian, designed c1917, 6¾in (17cm) high.
£1,700–2,000
€/ $2,700–3,200 ⚘ DORO

A René Lalique opalescent glass bowl, 'Martigues', No. 377, the underside relief-moulded with swimming fish, nick to rim, moulded mark, wheel cut 'France', designed 1920, 14¼in (36cm) diam.
£1,700–2,000
€/ $2,700–3,200 ⚘ B

A René Lalique glass bowl, 'Volubilis', No. 383, the underside moulded with three convolvulus flowers, their centres forming three feet, engraved mark and numeral, French, after 1921, 8¼in (21cm) diam.
£800–930
€/ $1,200–1,300 ⚘ S

◀ **A René Lalique glass vase,** 'Avallon', No. 986, relief-moulded with birds among berried branches, marked, French, pre-1945, 5¾in (14.5cm) high.
£1,300–1,500
€/ $2,000–2,400 ⚘ SWO

▶ **A René Lalique glass vase,** 'Gui', French, c1930, 7in (18cm) high.
£1,000–1,100
€/ $1,600–1,800 ⊞ OND

◀ **A Le Verre Français cameo glass vase,** 'Clochettes', etched with geometrical motifs and stylized flowers, engraved mark, French, c1925, 17¾in (45cm) high.
£2,400–2,700
€/ **$4,000–4,300** ⚲ S(Am)

A Legras enamelled glass vase, French, c1920, 9½in (24cm) high.
£1,000–1,100
€/ **$1,600–1,800** ⊞ AFD

A Le Verre Français cameo glass vase, decorated with stylized rosettes, cameo mark and engraved mark, c1920, 8in (20.5cm) high.
£800–950
€/ **$1,200–1,500** ⚲ S(P)

An Orrefors glass vase, by V. Lindstrand, Swedish, c1929, 7½in (19cm) high.
£585–650
€/ **$930–1,000** ⊞ SHa

A Loetz glass bowl, by Michael Powolny, Austrian, c1918, 7½in (19cm) diam.
£700–780
€/ **$1,100–1,300** ⊞ AFD
Michael Powolny (1871–1954) was principally a ceramics decorator and co-founded Wiener Keramik in 1905 with Bertold Löffler.

A glass vase, by Maurice Marinot, with internal decoration, inscribed, French, c1925, 5¾in (14.5cm) high.
£4,500–5,400
€/ **$7,000–8,500** ⚲ S(NY)
Maurice Marinot (1882–1960), a trained technician, chemist and painter, became fascinated with glass when he visited the glassworks of his friends Eugène and Gabriel Viard. At first he designed glassware that the Viard brothers executed, but later he made his own glass. His pieces were all hand-made without the use of mass-production moulded techniques. Many have a clear grey or pale yellow tint. He was not prolific and therefore his work is relatively hard to find.

An Orrefors glass ice bucket, with sterling silver mounts, Swedish, c1920, 10in (25.5cm) high.
£1,100–1,300
€/ **$1,700–2,000** ⊞ SHa

◀ **A mottled glass vase,** signed 'Schneider', French, c1930, 10in (25.5cm) high.
£1,500–1,700
€/ **$2,400–2,700** ⊞ TDG

A Tiffany Favrile glass vase, inscribed, c1915, 3½in (9cm) high.
£3,800–4,500
€/ **$6,000–7,000** ⚲ S(NY)

An Almeric Walter *pâte-de-verre* figural inkwell, designed by Henri Bergé, French, c1925, 4¾in (12cm) wide.
£3,800–4,500
€/ **$6,000–7,000** ⚲ S(NY)

A glass cocktail shaker, with silver-gilt mounts, the body with vertical cuts above four rows of banding, the integral gilt strainer beneath a domed cover with hammered finish, mounts marked, probably American, 1920s, 7½in (19cm) high.
£450–500
€/ **$700–800** ⚲ S(O)

Art Deco Jewellery

A platinum and diamond link bracelet, French, c1925, 7½in (19cm) long.
£5,200–5,800
€ / **$8,200–9,200** ⊞ WIM

A 14ct rose-gold, diamond, ruby and emerald bracelet, the three geometric saw-pierced panels set with later brilliant-cut diamonds and interspaced with two rows of calibre-cut rubies, set between alternating diamond and ruby panels, with sliding clasp and safety chain, c1940, 6½in (16.5cm) long.
£2,000–2,400
€ / **$3,200–3,800** ⚒ LJ

◄ **A René Lalique frosted glass brooch,** 'Deux Figurines et Masque' in a gilt-metal mount, stamped, French, c1913, 1¾in (4.5cm) diam.
£2,200–2,400
€ / **$3,500–3,800** ⊞ AFD

An emerald and diamond brooch, c1935, in a fitted case by Collingwoods.
£7,500–9,000
€ / **$11,900–14,200** ⚒ WW

◄ **A ruby- and diamond-set dress clip,** with a scroll design, 1940s.
£500–600
€ / **$800–950** ⚒ G(L)

A René Lalique pendant, 'Libellulles', moulded in low relief with two overlapping dragonflies, chipped, intaglio mark, French, designed 1920, 2in (5cm) wide.
£200–225
€ / **$315–355** ⚒ B

► **An Egyptian-revival enamelled silver pendant,** set with moonstones, turquoise, emeralds and mother-of-pearl, c1920, 3½in (9cm) high.
£585–650
€ / **$920–1,000** ⊞ ANO

A sterling silver necklace and earrings, by Fischel and Nessler, American, 1920s, earrings 3in (7.5cm) long.
£400–450
€ / **$630–700** ⊞ RGA

A Fahrner silver, marcasite and amazonite necklace, by Gustav Braendle Forth, stamped marks, German, 1920s.
£2,000–2,200
€ / **$3,200–3,500** ⚒ S(Am)

A silver and paste necklace, French, 1920s, 23in (58.5cm) long.
£315–350
€ / **$500–550** ⊞ RGA

► **A white metal ring,** set with a light blue stone, the shank with pierced and engraved shoulders, marked 'PT', 1920s.
£200–225
€ / **$315–350** ⚒ PFK

A platinum cockerel pendant, with enamelled head, set with diamonds and a cabochon sapphire, c1930, 1in (2.5cm) wide.
£1,700–1,900
€ / **$2,700–3,000** ⊞ NBL

Art Deco Lighting

A bronzed-brass table lamp, 'Machine Age', by Norman Bel-Geddes, American, 1930s, 12¼in (31cm) high.
£475–550
€/ $750–870 ✗ DORO

A Crown Devon and chrome table lamp, the base modelled with a porcelain figure of a female dancer wearing a flower dress, with original shade, c1930, 15¾in (40cm) high.
£400–475
€/ $630–750 ✗ SWO

A René Lalique frosted and polished glass chandelier, the underside moulded with leafy branches, hanging cords with matching suspension blocks, moulded mark, French, designed 1924, 13½in (34.5cm) diam.
£2,200–2,500
€/ $3,500–4,000 ✗ B

A Giso glass and metal ceiling lamp, model No. 3051, by Willem Hendrik Gispen, the stepped shade suspended from a nickel-plated metal ceiling cap supporting two satin glass discs, Dutch, c1930, 23¾in (60.5cm) diam, with original invoices.
£2,200–2,600
€/ $3,500–4,100 ✗ S(Am)

A patinated-spelter hanging light, by Max le Verrier, signed, French, c1930, shade 13in (33cm) square.
£950–1,100
€/ $1,500–1,700 ✗ S(O)

◀ **A Silas Snider & Co patinated-bronze lamp,** 'Family Group', by Concetta Scaravaglione, American, New York, 1945, 32in (81.5cm) high.
£3,000–3,600
€/ $4,700–5,700 ✗ S(NY)
Silas Snider & Co produced a line of patinated-bronze limited edition lamps designed by sculptors. They were retailed by Abraham Strauss, among other prestigious department stores.

A pair of alabaster wall lights, French, c1925, 16in (40.5cm) wide.
£1,100–1,300
€/ $1,700–2,000 ⊞ TLG

A Wiener Werkstätte ceramic table lamp, by Vally Wieselthier, with original paper shade, monogrammed 'WW', Austrian, c1928, 16½in (42cm) high.
£2,000–2,400
€/ $3,200–3,800 ✗ DORO

LOCATE THE SOURCE
The source of each illustration in Miller's can be found by checking the code letters below each caption with the Key to Illustrations, pages 794–800.

A chrome and Bakelite desk lamp, with swivel shade, c1920, 10in (25.5cm) wide.
£570–635
€/ $900–1,000 ⊞ NART

A pair of onyx lamps, on stepped marble bases, French, c1930, 10½in (26.5cm) high.
£850–1,000
€/ $1,300–1,600 ✗ S(P)

Art Deco Metalware

A Hagenauer silvered-bronze bell, Austrian, c1930, 3¾in (9.5cm) high.
£265–300
€/ $420–480 ⊞ ANO

A Blanckensee & Son silver coffee pot, Birmingham 1923, 8in (20.5cm) high.
£225–250
€/ $350–400 ⊞ WAC

Georg Jensen silver jug, by Sigvard Bernadotte, Danish, Copenhagen, designed 1938, 6in (15cm) high.
£2,400–2,800
€/ $3,800–4,400 ✗ BUK

A silver rose bowl, with cast decoration and swing handles, 1940, 6¼in (16cm) diam.
£180–220
€/ $280–350 ✗ SWO

A pewter dish, with glass liner, c1920, 9in (23cm) wide.
£800–900
€/ $1,200–1,400 ⊞ ASP

◀ A pair of patinated-pewter candlesticks, by Just, Danish, c1920, 8in (20.5cm) high.
£850–950
€/ $1,300–1,500 ⊞ SHa

▶ A pair of silver candlesticks, Birmingham 1924, 8¼in (21cm) high.
£250–300
€/ $400–475 ✗ HoG

A silvered-metal pierced grille, by Harold Stabler, a distance post inscribed 'HPC VIII', 1932, mounted on a fabric-covered frame, 5½in (14cm) wide.
£850–1,000
€/ $1,400–1,600 ✗ S(O)
Harold Stabler (1872–1945) was one of the central figures of the Arts and Crafts movement. He become head of the Keswick School of Industrial Art in 1898, and later joined R. Llewellyn Rathbone in the metalwork department of the Liverpool Art School. After moving to London he was head of the John Cass Technical Institute Art School between 1907 and 1937. Associated for many years with Poole Pottery with his wife Phoebe, he was also a founding member of the Design and Industrial Association in 1915. He was commissioned by the London Passenger Transport Board to design tiles and other fittings for London Underground stations. This piece is a casting of an iron grille installed at Turnpike Lane underground station in 1932.

A Blanckensee & Son silver bowl, Birmingham 1936, 4¼in (11cm) diam.
£950–1,100
€/ $1,500–1,700 ✗ S(O)

A Georg Jensen silver centre bowl, designed by Hans Hansen, Danish, 1930s, 7¾in (19.5cm) diam.
£5,500–6,200
€/ $8,700–9,800 ⊞ KK

A pair of silver candlesticks, Birmingham 1924, 8¼in (21cm) high.

A nickel and steel fire grate, American, 1930s, 27in (68.5cm) wide.
£7,500–9,000
€/ $11,900–14,200 ✗ S(NY)

A Cartier silver cocktail mixing jug and spoon, American, New York c1930, 7in (18cm) high.
£700–800
€/ $1,100–1,300 ✗ S(O)

A silver pitcher, by Carl Poul Petersen, with hammered body and blossom-capped C-scroll handle, Canadian, Montreal, mid-20thC, 9in (23cm) high, 19.5oz.
£2,200–2,500
€ / $3,500–3,800 ➤ RIT

A set of six Adie Bros silver menu holders, each openwork clip depicting one of a variety of game and other birds, Birmingham 1928, 1¼in (3cm) high, 5.25oz.
£500–600
€ / $800–950 ➤ CGC

A Cartier 18ct gold vanity case, c1920, 3½in (9cm) high.
£7,800–8,800
€ / $12,300–14,000 ⊞ SHa

◀ **A Wiener Werkstätte gilt-metal vase,** by Josef Hoffmann, the bowl hand-hammered in a twisted fluted design, stamped marks, Austrian, c1922, 4¾in (12cm) high.
£1,600–1,800
€ / $2,500–2,800 ➤ S

▶ **A** *dinanderie* **vase,** with silvered geometric design, signed 'Richmain, France', c1930, 10in (25.5cm) high.
£1,200–1,400
€ / $1,900–2,200 ⊞ GoW
Dinanderie **is work in non-precious metals.**

A four-piece tea and coffee service, with ebonized handles and finials, Sheffield 1938, 1940 and 1942.
£230–275
€ / $360–430 ➤ WilP

Art Deco Carpets, Rugs & Textiles

An Amsterdam School carpet, by J. Gidding for KVT, Rotterdam, polychrome-decorated with a Tuschinsky-style pattern, Dutch, c1920, 157½ x 115½in (400 x 293.5cm).
£3,200–3,500
€ / $5,000–5,500 ➤ S(Am)

A carpet, by Paul Follot, the central panel decorated with concentric circles and leaves, within an abstract border, woven mark, repair to one corner, French, c1925, 84¼ x 108in (214 x 274.5cm).
£1,200–1,500
€ / $1,900–2,400 ➤ S

◀ **A carpet,** by Ashley Havinden, woven monogram, c1930, 97½ x 78½in (247.5 x 199.5cm).
£5,300–5,800
€ / $8,300–9,200 ➤ S(NY)

▶ **A carpet,** by Paule Leleu, woven mark, French, 1940s, 98 x 137in (249 x 348cm).
£5,000–6,000
€ / $8,000–9,500 ➤ S(NY)

A rug, by Ben Nicholson, c1930, 44 x 38in (112 x 96.5cm).
£3,000–3,600
€ / $4,700–5,700 ➤ S(O)

Twentieth-Century Design

The Modern Movement, an international movement in architecture and design that emerged in Europe in the early 20th century, was, at its core, concerned with breaking down the barriers between technology and society so that high quality pieces could be produced for the masses. In some ways, this was eventually brought about because new materials were developed, such as tubular steel, plywood and polyurethane foam, which gave a new freedom of expression to designers and quicker and less costly methods of production to manufacturers. Nowadays it is common to find white walls and wooden floors complemented by carefully chosen objects from a wide range of disciplines rather than one overriding theme. This change in style has had enormous impact on the market and 20th-century design as a whole is becoming ever more popular and fashionable. The continuous evolution in style and public perception have helped to fuel demand and an acceptance of a 'look' in interior decoration that previously would have been regarded as the taste of a minority.

Always try to buy pieces by known designers. While good quality contemporary pieces by well known designers are rarely inexpensive to buy new, their price on the secondary market can be very reasonable. There follows a period of perhaps 20 to 30 years after design and production when such pieces are uappreciated, after which they tend to be re-evaluated and re-incorporated into popular style. Certain pieces, such as Alvar Aalto's Model No. 60 stool which was designed in 1932, have become iconic and versions of this are now readily available in high street shops. As well as being aware of the designer, you should also buy pieces from the right (usually earliest) edition. For example, the classic Lounge Chair and Ottoman designed by Charles Eames in 1956 was originally made by Herman Miller in the USA and early examples fetch £4,000 (€/ $6,300) or more, whereas the editions produced in Europe by Vitra in the 1980s or later will be worth as little as £1,500 (€/ $2,400), as they can still be bought new for around £2,500 (€/ $4,000). Finally, as with all antiques, condition is all important. Many of the new materials of the 20th century are delicate. For example, some of the early foams used in upholstery have degraded over the last 30 years and are now crumbling beneath their covers. This cannot be restored and so extreme caution should be exercised when looking at such pieces.

Jeremy Morrison and Sarah O'Brien

Ceramics

A Ruskin Pottery high-fired flambé vase, c1920, 7in (18cm) high.
£1,200–1,400
€/ $1,900–2,200 ⊞ DSG

A Bernard Leach earthenware tea set, comprising 15 pieces, impressed 'BL' and St Ives seals, minor chips, c1923, milk jug 3½in (9cm) high.
£2,500–2,800
€/ $4,000–4,400 ↗ B

An Oxshott Pottery pitcher, c1925, 9in (23cm) high.
£145–160
€/ $230–250 ⊞ DSG

A Ruskin Pottery high-fired bowl, impressed mark, dated 1925, 12½in (32cm) diam.
£4,500–5,300
€/ $7,000–8,400 ↗ B(O)

A Foley tea service, comprising seven pieces, designed by Dame Laura Knight, decorated with Dove pattern, hairline crack, factory marks, signed, c1930, teapot 4in (10cm) high.
£280–325
€/ $440–500 ↗ B

◀ **A Ruskin Pottery lustre glaze jar and cover,** c1926, 10in (25.5cm) high.
£600–680
€/ $950–1,100 ⊞ AFD

Items in the Twentieth-Century Design section have been arranged in date order within each sub-section.

TWENTIETH-CENTURY DESIGN

The Albert E. Wade Collection

There are few collectors with as much enthusiasm and energy for their subject as Albert Wade, who identified British art pottery as an interesting collecting area when it was still shunned by many.

From the late 1960s he bought regularly from auctions, markets and in particular Austin's of Peckham, which, during the post–WWII period, was one of the biggest antiques emporia in Europe. It was relatively easy to acquire such pieces because many large Victorian homes in south London were being broken up, and while their furniture was keenly sought, much of the later pottery was overlooked.

Initially, very little was written on the subject of Art Pottery and so collecting it was a far more instinctive occupation than it is today. These days there are many well-researched books on the subject and illustrations of pots from Albert Wade's collection feature heavily in those relating to Moorcroft and Ruskin.

The sale of Wade's collection at Sotheby's Olympia, in two auctions in 2002 included over 2000 items in more than 800 lots and realized over £1,000,000 (€/ $1,580,000). It included the largest collection of Ruskin pottery to have come onto the market in living memory. Among the highlights was a spectacular Chinese-inspired vase dated 1905, which sold for £19,387 (€/ $30,600). This vase was previously in the famous Harriman Judd Collection which Sotheby's sold in a series of sales in New York in 2001. The reason for this extraordinary price was the very fine markings within the glaze, which was notoriously difficult to control in the kiln when the piece was being fired. Other vases of this size, shape and with less exciting glazes were fetching around £3,000 (€/ $4,700) in the UK. **Jeremy Morrison**

A Ruskin Pottery crystalline tazza, c1930, 8¼in (21cm) diam.
£550–600
€/ $870–950 ⊞ DSG

A stoneware tile, by Bernard Leach, impressed marks, c1935, 4in (10cm) square, set in an oak frame.
£280–320
€/ $440–500 ⚲ Bea(E)

A Wedgwood bowl, by Keith Murray, signed, c1935, 6½in (16.5cm) diam.
£600–725
€/ $950–1,100 ⚲ B(W)
Murray's black basalt wares are the rarest of all his products.

A stoneware footed bowl, by Charles Vyse, with figured tenmoku glaze, incised 'CV', hairline crack, dated 1939, 5¼in (13.5cm) diam.
£400–500
€/ $630–800 ⚲ B
Tenmoku is a high temperature felds-pathic glaze deeply stained with iron oxide. The process originated in China during the Tang Dynasty.

A pottery bowl, by Waylande Gregory, with sgraffito leaf decoration, the interior gilded, signed, American, mid-20thC, 9in (23cm) diam.
£400–500
€/ $630–800 ⚲ RIT

A Leach Pottery coffee pot, decorated with a mottled glaze, c1950, 9in (23cm) high.
£75–85
€/ $120–130 ⊞ RUSK

A Midwinter Stylecraft cruet-on-stand, by Hugh Casson, decorated with Riviera pattern, c1954, 9in (23cm) wide.
£85–100
€/ $130–160 ⊞ CHI

▶ **A Madoura pottery jug,** by Pablo Picasso, impressed and inscribed marks, c1955, 12¼in (31cm) high.
£2,000–2,400
€/ $3,200–3,800 ⚲ WW

A Gertrud and Otto Natzler ceramic bowl, with volcanic glaze, signed, American, c1956, 8in (20.5cm) diam.
£3,200–3,500
€/ $5,000–5,500 ⚲ BB(L)

A Midwinter tray, designed by Jessie Tait, decorated with Mosaic pattern, c1960, 22½in (57cm) wide.
£150–165
€/ **$240–260** ⊞ CHI

◀ **A Hornsea Pottery vase,** 1960s, 6in (15cm) high.
£40–45
€/ **$64–70**
⊞ LUNA

A Rörstrand bottle vase, Swedish, c1960, 6in (15cm) high.
£145–160
€/ **$230–250** ⊞ DSG

A Poole Pottery vase, by Robert Jefferson, c1960, 9in (23cm) high.
£630–700
€/ **$1,000–1,100** ⊞ HarC
Robert Jefferson was head of design at Poole between 1958 and 1966.

A Poole Pottery Delphis dish, 1960s, 17in (43cm) wide.
£100–120
€/ **$160–190** ⊞ CHI

A stoneware charger, by Bryan Newman, impressed marks, c1969, 18in (45.5cm) diam.
£150–175
€/ **$240–280** ➷ GH

A stoneware cup, by Shoji Hamada, with wax resist floral designs, c1962, 3½in (8.5cm) high.
£750–875
€/ **$1,200–1,400** ➷ B

A stoneware slab bottle vase, by Bernard Leach, impressed marks, c1970, 7¾in (19.5cm) high, with original receipt and short biography.
£1,100–1,300
€/ **$1,800–2,000** ➷ Bea(E)

A stoneware vase, by Bernard Rooke, 1960s, 11in (28cm) high.
£60–65
€/ **$95–100** ⊞ MARK

A Poole Pottery charger, by Guy Sydenham, c1970, 12in (30.5cm) diam.
£430–480
€/ **$680–760** ⊞ HarC

◀ **A Poole Pottery dish,** 1970s, 18in (45.5cm) wide.
£60–70
€/ **$95–110**
⊞ LUNA

A Troika mask, painter's mark for Linda Thomas, early 1970s, 10in (25.5cm) high.
£1,000–1,100
€/ **$1,600–1,800** ⊞ TRO

A Rudy Autio stoneware figural vessel, American, c1980, 23½in (59.5cm) high.
£3,000–3,600
€/ **$4,800–5,700** ➷ S(NY)

An Elizabeth Woodman glazed earthenware Pillow pitcher impressed 'Woodman', American, c1980, 17¼in (44cm) high.
£4,500–5,500
€/ **$7,100–8,700** ➷ S(NY)

◀ **A porcelain vase,** by Janet Leach, with two lugs, impressed marks, c1980, 7¾in (19.5cm) high.
£400–500
€/ **$640–800** ➷ B

Furniture

A lacquered-steel and leather LC3 armchair, by Le Corbusier, designed 1928, re-issued by Cassina 1980s, Italian, 39½in (100.5cm) wide.
£750–900
€/ **$1,200–1,500** ✗ BUK
This design was first made by Thonet Frères, and an original would be highly valuable.

An Isokon bent plywood stool, each foot with two metal reinforcers, three reinforcers missing, designed in 1933, 17¾in (45.5cm) high.
£700–800
€/ **$1,100–1,300** ✗ S

A velvet-upholstered bentwood Devalle sofa, designed by Carlo Mollino 1939, reissued by Edition Galleria Colombari c1995, Italian, Milan.
£1,300–1,500
€/ **$2,000–2,400** ✗ DORO

A pair of Barcelona chairs, by Ludwig Mies van der Rohe, German, designed 1929.
£2,200–2,500
€/ **$3,500–4,000** ✗ S(O)
Designed by Mies van der Rohe for the German Pavilion of the 1929 Barcelona Exhibition, these examples were made c1980. An original would be worth in the region of £40,000 (€/ $63,000).

A pair of Gispen tubular steel armchairs, model No. 414, designed by W. H. Gispen, with curved black Gisolite armrests, upholstered in leatherette, Dutch, designed 1935.
£750–875
€/ **$1,200–1,400** ✗ S(Am)

A Lloyd Chrome Co Dinette table, designed c1939, American, 36½in (92.5cm) diam.
£380–450
€/ **$600–720** ✗ BB(L)

◄ **A gilt-iron and mirrored-glass coffee table,** designed by René Prou, French, c1940, 33½in (85cm) diam.
£6,800–7,600
€/ **$10,800–12,000** ⊞ NART

A birch-framed low chair, by Gerald Summers for Makers of Simple Furniture, the seat and back upholstered in vinyl, designed c1933.
£380–450
€/ **$600–700** ✗ B

A tubular steel and ebonized wood armchair, designed by S. van Ravesteyn, upholstered in velvet, Dutch, c1936.
£5,800–6,800
€/ **$9,200–10,800** ✗ S(Am)
Architect and interior designer Sybold van Ravesteyn (1899–1983) began his career as a civil engineer and in the 1920s became acquainted with and influenced by Gerrit Rietveld and other De Stijl members. In the 1930s van Ravesteyn's work took on a more frivolous appearance derived from the baroque and Louis XV styles. Despite being criticized by his more purist colleagues, van Ravesteyn's new work led to many important commissions, such as the renovation of the Tiel Fire Insurance Company, Holland, in 1936 for which he designed this eccentric curvilinear chair. Van Ravesteyn also furnished the interior of the Dutch royal yacht, for which he supplied chairs of the same design.

LOCATE THE SOURCE
The source of each illustration in Miller's can be found by checking the code letters below each caption with the Key to Illustrations, pages 794–800.

◀ **A H. Morris & Co mahogany and laminated birch Allegro chair,** by Sir Basil Spence, with foam-padded leather-covered seat, labelled 'Morris of Glasgow' and impressed number to frame, designed 1947.
£900–1,100
€/ **$1,400–1,700** ⚒ B
This design was not a commercial success as production costs were too high, with each chair taking many hours to create.

A Martyn paroba wood reception desk, by Hugh Casson, Misha Black and John Diamond, the surface covered in goat skin with a raised ebonized surround, above two banks of four drawers and a sliding shelf, with recessed brass drop handles, designed 1952, manufactured 1953, 78in (198cm) wide.
£525–625
€/ **$830–1,000** ⚒ B

A Widdicomb mahogany table, model No. 1764, by T. H. Robsjohn-Gibbings, signed and dated 1952, 48in (122cm) diam.
£2,200–2,500
€/ **$3,500–4,000** ⚒ TREA
T. H. Robsjohn-Gibbings was British-born. He set up a shop in New York's Madison Avenue in 1936 and became one of the most important decorators in the United States in the late 1930s and '40s. He successfully mixed classical elements from Ancient Greece with the Art Deco style in a modern way.

A Swedese Lamino chair, by Yngve Eckström, Swedish, 1950s.
£520–575
€/ **$820–900** ⊞ MARK

A wood four-panel screen, by Piero Fornasetti, with printed decoration of birds in an aviary on one side and musical instruments in wood-effect on the other, Italian, c1955, each panel 13¾in (35cm) wide.
£8,500–10,000
€/ **$13,400–15,800** ⚒ S(P)

TWENTIETH-CENTURY DESIGN

A set of three rosewood and hide stools, Danish, c1960, 20in (51cm) high.
£520–575
€/ **$820–900** ⊞ MARK

A G Plan teak swivel chair, 1970s.
£550–600
€/ **$870–950** ⊞ TRA

▶ **A dining table,** by Paul Evans, American, designed c1970, 94in (239cm) wide.
£2,800–3,200
€/ **$4,400–5,000** ⚒ BB(L)

Five Fritz Hansen chromed-steel Wire Furniture Programme seating elements, by Verner Panton, Danish, 1971, each section 29½in (75cm) wide.
£2,800–3,200
€/ **$4,400–5,000** ⚒ DORO
These seating elements can be combined in various ways.

A walnut low table, designed by George Nakashima, American, c1962, 100in (254cm) wide.
£8,500–10,000
€/ **$13,400–15,800** ⚒ S(NY)

A tubular steel-framed Djinn long bench stool, by Olivier Mourgue for Airborne International, fabric upholstery renewed, French, designed 1965, 49¼in (125cm) wide.
£750–875
€/ **$1,200–1,400** ⚒ DORO
The use of pieces such as this in Stanley Kubrick's *2001: A Space Odyssey* made the Djinn series arguably the most famous examples of Pop furniture design, and the first to use urethane foam upholstery over tubular steel frames. The Djinn was named by Mourgue after the Islamic mythological spirit with supernatural powers, who can take human or animal form.

A Maxalto rosewood and ebony-inlaid Africa dining suite, by Tobia and Afra Scarpa, comprising a table and eight chairs, stamped 'M', Italian, 1975, table 57in (145cm) diam.
£5,000–5,700
€/ **$8,000–9,000** ⚒ S(O)
Tobia Scarpa (b1935) was the son of the architect Carlo Scarpa and after marrying Afra Bianchin they designed furniture for Gavina from 1960. Soon afterwards they opened their own office and went on to design for a number of well known firms including B&B Italia, Knoll, Maxalto and Benetton.

◀ **A Perspex chair,** with velvet upholstery, 1970s.
£300–330
€/ **$475–525**
⊞ TWI

A Knoll rosewood and bronze wire table and four chairs, by Warren Platner, Model No 1725A, the chairs with woollen upholstery, signed, designed 1966, produced 1970s, table 48in (122cm) diam.
£1,700–2,000
€/ **$2,700–3,200** ⚒ TREA

An Arkana moulded plastic table and four chairs, after a design by Eero Saarinen, the table with rosewood-veneered top, 1960s, table 47¼in (120cm) diam.
£380–450
€/ **$600–720** ⚒ SWO
The American Eero Saarinen's (1910–61) designs used new materials and organic, often futuristic, shapes. He is perhaps best known for his Trans World Airline Terminals at John F. Kennedy Airport in New York and for the design of the Tulip chair which sold in great numbers and was copied extensively in the 1960s.

A mahogany rocking chair, by David N. Ebner, American, 1978.
£6,500–7,200
€/ **$10,200–11,400** ⚒ S(NY)

A Nuovo Alchimia/Zabro veneered side cabinet, labelled, Italian, 1985, 52in (132cm) wide.
£2,200–2,500
€/ **$3,500–4,000** ⚒ S(O)

Glass

An enamelled glass jug, designed by Dame Laura Knight for the Art in Industry Exhibition at Harrods, factory mark, designed 1934, 7in (18cm) high.
£420–500
€/ **$660–790** 🔨 B
In the wake of the Wall Street crash in 1929, British industry was facing a tough challenge. Innovative approaches to design were needed to boost sales and profits. Many critics drew comparisons with the Swedish Exhibition of 1930 which highlighted the successful co-operation between good design and manufacturing. Following a government report, several attempts were made to fuse art with industrial production. In Britain one of the more successful results was the Art in Industry Exhibition at Harrods, named 'Modern Ware for the Table'. Alongside Laura Knight, designs were provided by Vanessa Bell, Graham Sutherland, Frank Brangwyn and others. Laura Knight also designed a range of 'Circus Ware' for Clarice Cliff's Bizarre pottery range for the exhibition.

A Venini incised glass vase, signed, Italian, c1950, 16in (40.5cm) high.
£3,800–4,200
€/ **$6,000–6,600** 🏬 GoW

A Murano Filigrana glass bottle, with a dimpled side, Italian, 1950s, 13½in (34.5cm) high.
£1,000–1,100
€/ **$1,600–1,700** 🏬 KK

A Kosta green glass vase, by Vicke Lindstrand, Swedish, 1950s, 5in (12.5cm) high.
£55–60
€/ **$87–95** 🏬 MARK

An Exbor Glassworks Sommerso glass vase, attributed to Pavel Hlava, stamped, Czechoslovakian, designed 1960, produced 1970s, 10¾in (27.5cm) high.
£200–225
€/ **$320–350** 🔨 B(Kn)
Sommerso is a technique used in Venetian glass-making where one colour is cased (or submerged – hence the name) in clear glass.

A Salviati Sassi glass vase. by Luciano Gaspari, engraved 'Salviati', with paper label, Italian, designed 1960, produced c1965, 9½in (24cm) high.
£600–700
€/ **$950–1,100** 🔨 B(Kn)

A Holmegaard glass vase, by Per Lutken, Danish, 1950s–60s, 12½in (32cm) high.
£100–120
€/ **$160–190** 🏬 ORI

A Seguso Vetri d'Arte Murano glass sculpture, modelled as an ethnic mask, the front unpolished, Italian, Venice, probably 1960s, 15¼in (38.5cm) high.
£1,300–1,500
€/ **$2,000–2,400** 🔨 S(Am)

A glass sculpture, entitled 'Bronze Solar Riser', by Tom Patti, signed and dated, American, 1979, 4¾in (12cm) high.
£5,700–7,000
€/ **$9,000–11,000** 🔨 S(NY)

An Åfors glass vase, by Bertil Vallien, signed, Swedish, 1970s, 4in (10cm) high.
£45–60
€/ **$70–95** 🏬 MARK

A Misar glass vase, by Ettore Sottsass for Memphis, one handle repaired, Italian, 1982, 12¼in (31cm) high.
£1,500–1,700
€/ **$2,400–2,700** 🔨 DORO
This vase was exhibited at the Victoria & Albert Museum, London in 1982.

◀ **A glass bowl,** by Dale Chihuly, signed, American, 1989, 22¾in (58cm) diam.
£3,500–4,000
€/ **$5,500–6,300** 🔨 BUK

Jewellery

A Jensen & Wendel silver brooch/pendant, by Georg Jensen, set with lapis lazuli, on a silver chain, Danish, Copenhagen, 1945–51, 1¾in (4.5cm) diam.
£500–600
€ / **$800–950** ⚒ BUK

A rhodium pendant, on a chain, 1950s, 3½in (9cm) square.
£35–40
€ / **$55–65** ⊞ SBL

▶ **A Georg Jensen 18ct gold and moonstone brooch,** by Nana Ditzel, c1960, 3¼in (8.5cm) wide.
£3,000–3,500
€ / **$4,700–5,500**
⊞ DID

A silver bracelet, Scandinavian, c1970, 2oz.
£160–180
€ / **$250–280** ⚒ G(L)

To order Miller's books in Canada please ring McArthur & Co on 1-800-387-0117.
See the full range at **www.millers.uk.com**

A Georg Jensen silver and quartz necklet and pendant, by Torun Bülow-Hübe, maker's marks, Danish, Copenhagen, London import marks for 1974.
£300–350
€ / **$475–550** ⚒ DN

An Artcurial silver and enamel Abstraction pendant, by Sonia Delauney, on a rigid collar, French, designed 1979, pendant 2¾in (7cm) long, in original box with certificate.
£850–1,000
€ / **$1,300–1,600** ⚒ BUK

A silver torque, by Anna Strina Åberg, modelled as stylized flower motifs, with matching ring, Swedish, Nässjo, 1984–87.
£850–1,000
€ / **$1,300–1,600** ⚒ S(O)
Åberg's work is represented at the Swedish National museum and she has created pieces for the Swedish royal family.

Lighting

▶ **A chrome Anglepoise three-step lamp,** c1920.
£270–300
€ / **$425–475** ⊞ LUNA

A chrome-plated steel adjustable desk lamp, by F. Solere, with leather shade, French, 1930s, 29½in (75cm) high.
£1,000–1,200
€ / **$1,600–1,900** ⚒ S(Am)

Always check that electric lighting conforms to the current safety regulations before using.

A brass Sputnik light fixture, with decorative bulbs, 1950s, 25in (63.5cm) diam.
£420–500
€ / **$660–800** ⚒ TREA

▶ **A painted metal desk light,** by Serge Mouille, with adjustable shade, French, c1950, 31½in (80cm) high.
£2,500–2,800
€ / **$4,000–4,400** ⚒ S(O)
Serge Mouille (1922–88) studied as a silversmith and established his own studios in 1945. He designed his first prototype lamp in 1953 for the decorator and architect Jacques Adnet. In 1953 he participated in an exhibition at the Musée des Arts Décoratifs, Paris, before collaborating with Louis Sognot on lighting solutions and going on to be one of the avant-garde designers, including Jean Prouvé, whose modern designs were shown at the Steph Simon gallery, Paris, when it opened in 1956.

A gilt-metal and enamel table lamp/radio, by Jospeh Lucas, 1950s, 17¾in (45cm) high.
£60–70
€ / **$95–110** ⚒ L&E

A Poole Pottery Helmet lamp, by Guy Sydenham, c1960, 12in (30.5cm) high.
£1,300–1,500
€/ **$2,000–2,400** ⊞ HarC

A table lamp, by Bill Curry for Design Line, American, c1968, 21½in (54.5cm) high.
£250–300
€/ **$400–475** ➤ BB(L)

A brass, steel and painted-aluminium hanging light, by Gaetano Scolari, Italian, c1960, 30in (76cm) wide.
£1,100–1,300
€/ **$1,700–2,000** ➤ BB(L)

A Murano glass and aventurine *plafonnier,* Italian, Venice, c1960, 39½in (100.5cm) diam.
£3,500–4,200
€/ **$5,500–6,600** ➤ S(P)

A Troika pottery lamp base, by Lesley Illsley, marked, late 1960s, 15in (38cm) high.
£1,400–1,600
€/ **$2,200–2,500** ⊞ TRO

◄ **A polychromed-metal and laminated wood Tahiti table light,** by Ettore Sottsass for Memphis, with label, Italian, designed 1981, 24¾in (63cm) high.
£450–500
€/ **$700–800** ➤ S(O)

A chrome and glass hanging lamp, c1970, 27in (68.5cm) high.
£35–40
€/ **$55–63** ⊞ MARK

A Fase chrome lamp, Spanish, c1960, 15in (38cm) high.
£250–275
€/ **$400–440** ⊞ MARK

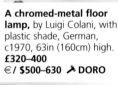

A chromed-metal floor lamp, by Luigi Colani, with plastic shade, German, c1970, 63in (160cm) high.
£320–400
€/ **$500–630** ➤ DORO

A pair of Vetri VMM glass wall lights, by Barovier & Toso, Italian, c1980, 24in (61cm) wide.
£1,300–1,500
€/ **$2,000–2,400** ➤ DORO

Metalware

A silver napkin ring, by Bernard Cuzner, Birmingham 1952, 1¾in (4.5cm) diam.
£340–375
€/ **$540–600** ⊞ SHa

A pair of gilded silver urns, by Pampaloni, Italian, Rome 1960s, 10¼in (26cm) high.
£16,000–18,000
€/ **$25,300–28,500** ⊞ KK

A bronze sculpture, by Arman, entitled 'Camera Chopped Up', signed and numbered, French, c1970, 21in (53.5cm) high.
£1,100–1,300
€/ **$1,700–2,000** ⊞ MARK

Rugs & Textiles

A tapestry-weave carpet, by Jacques Frank, French, c1950, 119 x 89in (302.5 x 226cm).
£2,700–3,000
€/ $4,300–4,700 ↗ S(O)

A wool carpet, by Paule Leleu, with woven signature, French, 1950s, 106½in (270.5cm) diam.
£5,700–6,800
€/ $9,000–10,800 ↗ S(NY)

A panel of linen Allegro fabric, by Lucienne Day for Heal Fabrics, 1952, 53¾ x 50in (135.5 x 127cm).
£850–1,000
€/ $1,300–1,600 ↗ B

A wool wall rug, after Pablo Picasso, signed 'Picasso', France, 1950s, 80¾ x 59in (205 x 150cm).
£2,000–2,400
€/ $3,200–3,800 ↗ DORO

Further reading

Miller's 20th-century Design Buyer's Guide, Miller's Publications, 2003

A wool Square Dance carpet, by Ross Litell for Unica Vaev, Danish, Copenhagen, c1960, 124½ x 90¼in (316 x 229cm).
£1,100–1,300
€/ $1,700–2,000 ↗ DORO

A pair of Sanderson & Son Sanderlin fabric Chiesa Della Salute curtains, by John Piper, 1960, 77½in x 46½in (197 x 118cm).
£380–450
€/ $600–700 ↗ B

A panel of Wave fabric, by Verner Panton for Mira-X, 1974, 47 x 59in (119.5 x 150cm).
£750–850
€/ $1,200–1,300 ⊞ MARK

A panel of cotton Top Brass fabric, by Zandra Rhodes for Heal Fabrics, c1967, 78¾ x 46¾in (200 x 119cm).
£320–400
€/ $500–630 ↗ B

A panel of Marimekko cotton Lokki fabric, by Maija Isola, signed, Finnish, 1961, 60 x 47½in (152.5 x 120.5cm)
£180–200
€/ $285–315 ↗ TREA

▶ **A jute Turquoise wall hanging,** by Alexander Calder, signed and dated, American, 1975, 56 x 78in (142 x 198cm).
£2,500–3,000
€/ $4,000–4,700 ↗ BB(L)

Lamps & Lighting
Ceiling & Wall Lights

A brass chandelier, drilled for electricity, Flemish, 18thC, 16in (40.5cm) high.
£4,500–5,400
€/ **$7,000–8,500** ⚒ S

A pair of Louis XV ormolu three-light rococo wall sconces, with integral drip pans and candle sconces, drilled for electricity, 26in (66cm) high.
£2,800–3,200
€/ **$4,400–5,100** ⚒ Bri

A pair of patinated metal one-light wall appliques, fitted for electricity, German, 1750–1800, 20½in (52cm) high.
£1,200–1,400
€/ **$1,900–2,200** ⚒ S(Am)

A tin and etched glass hall lantern, one pane damaged, Dutch, 1775–1825, 18¼in (46.5cm) high.
£300–350
€/ **$470–550** ⚒ B(Ch)

A set of four gilt-bronze wall lights, c1870, 8in (20.5cm) high.
£2,500–3,000
€/ **$4,000–4,700** ⚒ S(O)

A pair of giltwood wall appliques, 19thC, 37in (94cm) high.
£1,000–1,100
€/ **$1,600–1,700** ⚒ SWO

A child's sheet tin and waxed paper hanging night light, 19thC, 14in (35.5cm) high.
£430–475
€/ **$680–750** ⊞ SEA

A carved limewood six-light chandelier, Continental, 19thC, 36in (91.5cm) high.
£850–1,000
€/ **$1,300–1,600** ⚒ AH

A cut-glass chandelier, Swedish, 19thC, 36½in (92.5cm) high.
£2,000–2,200
€/ **$3,200–3,500** ⚒ S(O)

◄ **A pair of wall sconces,** French, c1880, 13in (33cm) high.
£500–550
€/ **$790–870** ⊞ JPr

A silvered-metal and glass lantern, Continental, 19thC, 20¼in (51.5cm) high.
£1,700–2,000
€/ **$2,700–3,200** ⚒ S(NY)

A Biedermeier hanging lantern, fitted for electricity, Austrian, Vienna, 1850–1900, 49½in (125.5cm) long.
£600–720
€/ **$950–1,100** ⚒ DORO

◄ **A gilded-brass ecclesiastical candle lamp,** French, c1890, 35in (89cm) high.
£550–600
€/ **$870–950** ⊞ EAL

A gilded-brass ceiling fitting, with etched glass shades, French, 1890–1900, 36in (91.5cm) high.
£450–500
€ / **$700–800** ⊞ **EAL**

A brass and stained glass hall lantern, 1875–1925, 10½in (26.5cm) high.
£200–240
€ / **$320–380** ⚒ **SWO**

A pair of brass phoenix two-branch candleholders, c1900, 15¾in (40cm) high.
£350–400
€ / **$550–630** ⚒ **B(Ch)**

A gilt-bronze six-branch ceiling lamp, c1900, 22in (56cm) diam.
£500–550
€ / **$790–870** ⊞ **EAL**

An oxidized brass swan-neck gas bracket, with a period glass shade, converted to electricity, c1900, 12in (30.5cm) high.
£100–110
€ / **$160–175** ⊞ **JeH**

A gilt-brass hanging lantern, fitted for electricity, 1875–1925, 64¼in (163cm) high.
£2,000–2,200
€ / **$3,200–3,500** ⚒ **S**

A pair of Louis XVI-style gilt-bronze wall lights, c1900, 21¼in (54cm) high.
£1,200–1,400
€ / **$1,900–2,200** ⚒ **S(O)**

A moulded-glass and brass pendant lamp, by Jefferson, American, c1900, 14in (35.5cm) diam.
£270–300
€ / **$430–475** ⊞ **EAL**

A gilt-bronze 12-light rococo-style chandelier, late 19thC, 33½in (85cm) high.
£650–750
€ / **$1,000–1,200** ⚒ **B**

A cut-glass eight-branch chandelier, 1875–1925, 36¼in (92cm) high.
£900–1,000
€ / **$1,400–1,600** ⚒ **S(O)**

A gilt-bronze and cut-glass chandelier, probably by Agostino Fiorentini, French, c1900, 59in (150cm) high.
£2,000–2,200
€ / **$3,200–3,500** ⚒ **S(O)**

An Edwardian copper oxide three-branch ceiling lamp, with modern shades, 16in (40.5cm) diam.
£175–200
€ / **$280–320** ⊞ **JeH**

An antler 12-light chandelier, Scottish, 1875–1925, 33¾in (85.5cm) high.
£3,200–3,800
€ / **$5,100–6,000** ⚒ **B(Ed)**

A gilt-metal ten-light chandelier, hung overall with faceted teardrop prisms, Continental, c1900, 27in (68.5cm) high.
£380–450
€ / **$600–710** ⚒ **NOA**

A silver-plated three-branch ceiling lamp, c1900, 16in (40.5cm) diam.
£630–700
€ / **$1,000–1,100** ⊞ **EAL**

A crystal pendant light, with original brass fitting, c1910, 10in (25.5cm) high
£115–130
€ / **$180–200** ⊞ **JeH**

A set of three cast-brass two-arm wall lights, c1910, 12in (30.5cm) wide.
£520–580
€/ $820–920 ⊞ JeH

A pair of pewter wall sconces, with beaded drops, rewired, early 20thC, 13in (33cm) high.
£400–450
€/ $630–710 ⊞ JPr

A brass six-light floral-painted cranberry glass electrolier, with triangular prism drops, Bohemian, early 20thC, 26in (66cm) high.
£200–240
€/ $320–380 ⋗ G(L)

A moulded glass and gilt-metal eight-light chandelier, with lustre drops and strings of beads, Italian, early 20thC, 33in (84cm) high.
£720–850
€/ $1,100–1,300 ⋗ S(O)

A gilt-metal and glass drop chandelier, early 20thC, 14½in (37cm) diam.
£230–275
€/ $360–430 ⋗ SWO

A gilt-bronze and cut-glass electrolier, early 20thC, 33½in (85cm) high.
£420–500
€/ $660–800 ⋗ B

An Edwardian gilded-brass chandelier, designed for electricity or candles, 29in (73.5cm) high.
£450–500
€/ $700–800 ⊞ EAL

An Edwardian gilt-metal and glass hall lantern, 20in (51cm) high.
£400–480
€/ $630–760 ⋗ B(Ch)

A white marble ceiling light, carved with cherubs in relief, French, c1920, 19¾in (50cm) diam.
£3,000–3,500
€/ $4,700–5,500 ⋗ S(O)

An antler chandelier, c1920, 36in (91.5cm) high.
£1,600–1,800
€/ $2,500–2,800 ⊞ DOA

A set of four gilded-bronze wall lights, French, 1920s, 16in (40.5cm) high.
£585–650
€/ $920–1,000 ⊞ JPr
three-branch are more desirable than two-branch or single-branch sconces. Pairs are proportionally worth 50 per cent more than singles and sets of four likewise worth 50 per cent more than two pairs.

A Venetian luster 16-branch chandelier, fitted for electricity, c1930, 35½in (90cm) high.
£2,000–2,400
€/ $3,200–3,800 ⋗ DORO

LAMPS & LIGHTING

Table & Standard Lamps

A gilt-bronze lamp base, by Ferdinand Barbedienne, cast with Classical female figures, signed, c1880, 20in (51cm) high.
£1,000–1,100
€ / **$1,600–1,700** ⚒ **S(O)**

A Victorian brass oil lamp, with a reeded brass column, enamelled glass reservoir and glass shade, on a stoneware plinth, 27in (68.5cm) high.
£250–280
€ / **$400–440** ⚒ **CoH**

A Victorian oil lamp, with enamelled decoration, 13in (33cm) high.
£90–100
€ / **$140–160** ⚒ **SWO**

A Victorian oil lamp, 21in (53.5cm) high.
£130–145
€ / **$200–230** ⊞ **WiB**

A porcelain lamp, in the form of an owl, with a frosted glass shade, French, late 19thC, 14in (35.5cm) high.
£220–260
€ / **$350–410** ⚒ **HOLL**

A late Victorian electroplate candlestick, now fitted as an oil lamp, with a cut crystal reservoir and an opal glass shade, 35½in (90cm) high.
£250–300
€ / **$400–475** ⚒ **BIG**

◀ **A pair of Victorian silver-plated oil lamps,** with moulded glass shades, 14½in (37cm) high.
£200–240
€ / **$320–380** ⚒ **SWO**

A pair of silver-plated spelter table lamps, modelled as cavaliers supporting opaque flame shades, late 19thC, 31in (78.5cm) high.
£320–375
€ / **$500–590** ⚒ **EH**

A gilt and patinated-bronze-mounted porcelain lamp base, with female mask head and wreath-hung handles, the girdle surmounted with a frieze of dancing Classical maidens, the pedestal with anthemion and palmette-cast mounts, late 19thC, 21in (53.5cm) high.
£420–500
€ / **$660–800** ⚒ **B**

◀ **A brass pulpit lamp,** with a cranberry shade, 19thC, 18in (45.5cm) high
£300–350
€ / **$475–550** ⚒ **GAK**

A pair of porcelain table lamps, with gilt-metal Pan-mask handles, mounts and bases, Continental, possibly Paris, 19thC, 14in (35.5cm) high.
€480–565
€ / $760–890 ➶ GAK

A pair of porcelain lamps, with later mounts, French, 19thC, 26½in (67.5cm) high.
€500–600
€ / $800–950 ➶ S(O)

An Edwardian silver-plated Corinthian column oil lamp, with a cut-glass reservoir, converted to electricity, 21in (53.5cm) high.
€280–320
€ / $440–500 ➶ BR

A metal-mounted hyacinth glass oil lamp, decorated with apple blossom and butterflies, heightened with gilt, Bohemian, 1850–1900, 19¾in (50cm) high.
£250–300
€ / $400–470 ➶ DORO

A cut-glass Corinthian column table lamp, with an ormolu terminal, 19thC, 22½in (57cm) high.
£1,300–1,500
€ / $2,100–2,400 ➶ JAd

A carved alabaster figural lampbase and shade, on a tinted base, Italian, 1920s, 29½in (75cm) high.
£650–750
€ / $1,000–1,200 ➶ B(Ch)

A brass-mounted malachite lamp stand, with an opaque glass flame globe, converted to electricity, 19thC, 30in (76cm) high.
£650–720
€ / $1,000–1,100 ➶ TMA

A cast silver-plated adjustable table lamp, c1910, 17in (43cm) high.
£135–150
€ / $220–240 ⊞ JeH

A brass table lamp, with a painted glass shade, c1920, 19in (48.5cm) high.
£135–150
€ / $215–240 ⊞ JeH

▶ **An adjustable brass desk lamp,** with an opaline shade, c1920, 16in (40.5cm) high.
£170–185
€ / $270–290 ⊞ JeH

A moulded glass and brass Banquet lamp, 19thC, 26in (66cm) high.
£800–950
€ / $1,300–1,500 ➶ BAu

A brass Pullman lamp, with an adjustable arm, 1910–20, 14in (35.5cm) high.
£90–100
€ / $140–160 ⊞ JeH

LAMPS & LIGHTING

Rugs & Carpets

◀ **A carpet,** after a Cuenca design, Spanish, 1900–25, 212 x 144in (538 x 366cm).
£2,000–2,400
€/ **$3,200–3,800** ⚒ S(O)

A needlepoint carpet, 1850–75, 92 x 91in (233.5 x 231cm).
£2,400–2,800
€/ **$3,800–4,400** ⚒ S(O)

◀ **An Aubusson carpet,** the field with stylized flowers, centred by a medallion with a scrolling vine border, French, mid-19thC, 133¾ x 118in (339.5 x 299.5cm).
£4,000–4,800
€/ **$6,300–7,600** ⚒ B(Ba)

A Donegal carpet, of Portuguese design, Irish, c1920, 203 x 135in (516 x 343cm).
£3,000–3,500
€/ **$4,700–5,500** ⚒ S(O)
The unusual design of this carpet, with its corner spandrels depicting European ships, sailors and sea monsters, is taken from a small group of 16th- or 17th-century Safavid or Moghul carpets. Carpets of this group are referred to as 'Portuguese' as their design is thought to depict the story of the death of Bahadur Shah, ruler of Gujurat, who drowned while meeting a Portuguese fleet embarked on a diplomatic mission to the Persian Gulf.

An Aubusson carpet, with part metal thread, minor reweaves and damages, French, late 19thC, 233 x 188in (592 x 478cm).
£4,500–5,000
€/ **$7,000–8,000** ⚒ S(NY)

A carpet, European, c1920, 210 x 149½in (533 x 380.5cm).
£2,000–2,200
€/ **$3,200–3,500** ⚒ B(Ch)

▶ **A rug,** minor damages and repairs, Finnish, 19thC, 70½ x 54in (179 x 137cm).
£550–650
€/ **$870–1,000** ⚒ BUK

◀ **A Bessarabian carpet,** some wear, Ukrainian, mid-19thC, 111 x 85in (282 x 216cm).
£14,000–16,000
€/ **$22,000–25,000** ⚒ WW
Bessarabian carpets are now rare. In design, they are loose copies of French carpets and were made for Russian officers and civil servants unable to afford the originals. As Russia conquered more of the Caucasus, copies of Bessarabians were made in Karabagh and elsewhere.

A Bessarabian kilim, Moldavian/ Ukrainian, c1930, 117 x 84in (297 x 213.5cm).
£900–1,000
€/ **$1,400–1,600** ⚒ S(O)

A Bergama rug, Turkish, 1875–1900,
48 x 38in (122 x 96.5cm).
£1,700–1,900
€/ **$2,700–3,000** ⊞ SAM

A Bergama rug, some wear and
small repairs, Turkish, mid-19thC,
91 x 70in (231 x 178cm).
£420–500
€/ **$800–790** 🔨 WW

A Melas rug, Turkish, mid-19thC,
72 x 48in (183 x 122cm).
£3,200–3,500
€/ **$5,000–5,500** ⊞ SAM

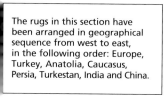

A Melas saddlebag, Turkish, c1900, 14 x 20in (35.5 x 51cm).
£675–750
€/ **$1,100–1,200** ⊞ SAM

The rugs in this section have
been arranged in geographical
sequence from west to east,
in the following order: Europe,
Turkey, Anatolia, Caucasus,
Persia, Turkestan, India and China.

▶ **An Ushak carpet,** Turkish, late
19thC, 139 x 105in (353 x 266.5cm).
£1,800–2,200
€/ **$2,800–3,500** 🔨 S(O)

An Ushak carpet, Turkish, late
19thC, 185 x 102in (470 x 259cm).
£1,800–2,000
€/ **$2,800–3,200** 🔨 S(O)

An Ushak carpet, Turkish, 1900–25,
151 x 126in (383.5 x 320cm).
£1,800–2,000
€/ **$2,800–3,200** 🔨 S(O)

▶ **An Ushak rug,** slight wear and
damage, reduced in size, Turkish,
c1900, 106 x 73in (269 x 185.5cm).
£220–250
€/ **$350–400** 🔨 WW

A Sivas carpet, central Anatolian,
c1900, 133 x 102in (338 x 259cm).
£1,000–1,200
€/ **$1,600–1,900** 🔨 S(O)

RUGS & CARPETS

A Kazak Sewan rug, southwest Caucasian, c1880, 81 x 69in (205.5 x 175.5cm).
£950–1,100
€ / **$1,500–1,700** ⚒ S(O)

A Kazak Chelaberd rug, southwest Caucasian, c1890, 93 x 65in (236 x 165cm).
£1,700–2,000
€ / **$2,700–3,200** ⚒ S(O)

A Gendje long rug, south Caucasian, c1890, 115 x 36in (292 x 91.5cm).
£950–1,100
€ / **$1,500–1,700** ⚒ S(O)

A Shahsavan salt bag, south Caucasian, Karabagh, 1875–1900, 16 x 27in (40.5 x 68.5cm).
£760–850
€ / **$1,200–1,300** ⊞ SAM

◄ **A Chondzoresk rug,** south Caucasian, Karabagh, slight wear, late 19thC, 90 x 44in (228.5 x 112cm).
£3,500–4,000
€ / **$5,500–6,300** ⚒ WW

A rug, south Caucasian, Karabagh, dated 1938, 59 x 94½in (150 x 240cm).
£650–750
€ / **$1,000–1,200** ⚒ B(Ba)

A Kazak Karatchop rug, south Caucasian, c1880, 39 x 64in (99 x 162.5cm).
£3,500–4,000
€ / **$5,500–6,300** ⚒ S(O)

◄ **A Kazak Sewan rug,** south Caucasian, c1890, 56 x 46¾in (142 x 119cm).
£1,100–1,300
€ / **$1,700–2,000** ⚒ S(O)

► **A Kazak Loripambak rug,** south Caucasian, late 19thC, 70 x 91in (178 x 231cm).
£1,100–1,300
€ / **$1,700–2,000** ⚒ S(O)

A Kazak prayer rug, south Caucasian, dated AH 1322/AD 1904, 48 x 56in (122 x 142cm).
£2,500–3,000
€/ $4,000–4,700 ➤ S(O)

A Moghan-Talish rug, south Caucasian, c1900, 95 x 50in (241.5 x 127cm).
£170–200
€/ $270–320 ➤ WW

A Kazak long rug, south Caucasian, dated AH 1320/AD 1902, 136 x 54in (345.5 x 137cm).
£700–800
€/ $1,100–1,300 ➤ S(O)

▶ A Bidjov rug, northeast Caucasian, c1890, 41 x 60in (104 x 152.5cm).
£1,400–1,600
€/ $2,200–2,500 ➤ S(O)

A Lesghi rug, northeast Caucasian, c1880, 62 x 38in (157.5 x 96.5cm).
£1,000–1,200
€/ $1,600–1,900 ➤ S(O)

A Perepedil rug, east Caucasian, late 19thC, 49 x 64in (124.5 x 162.5cm).
£2,000–2,200
€/ $3,200–3,500 ➤ S(O)

A Perepedil rug, east Caucasian, c1900, 75 x 52in (190.5 x 132cm).
£1,000–1,100
€/ $1,600–1,700 ➤ S(O)

A Perepedil rug, east Caucasian, 1900–10, 84 x 53in (213.5 x 134.5cm).
£3,500–4,000
€/ $5,500–6,300 ➤ WW

▶ A Shirvan long rug, east Caucasian, c1890, 134¼ x 70½in (341 x 179cm).
£220–250
€/ $350–400 ➤ B(Ch)

An Akstafa rug, the field with three 'Star of Islam' medallions and three pairs of stylized peacocks, filled with geometric and other symbols, enclosed by a main and two minor borders, southeast Caucasian, c1880, 91 x 55in (231 x 139.5cm).
£1,100–1,200
€/ $1,700–1,900 ⊞ DNo

RUGS & CARPETS

◄ A Bidjar *wagireh,* with leaf, floral and other foliate motifs, northwest Persian, c1880, 83½ x 62in (212 x 157.5cm).
£2,000–2,200
€ / **$3,200–3,500** ⚒ RIT

A kilim, some damage and repairs, northwest Persian, Senneh/Bidjar, c1903, 80¾ x 53¼in (205 x 135.5cm).
£200–240
€ / **$320–380** ⚒ DORO

A Shahsavan kilim, northwest Persian, c1890, 56 x 114in (142 x 289.5cm).
£550–650
€ / **$870–1,000** ⚒ S(O)

A Heriz carpet, centred by a cruciform medallion with flame palmette pendants, cornered by spandrels and framed by a rosette and palmette border, northwest Persian, c1900, 181¼ x 117⅜in (458 x 299cm).
£6,000–7,000
€ / **$9,500–11,000** ⚒ B

A Tabriz carpet, outer border missing at either end, northwest Persian, c1900, 30 x 51in (76 x 129.5cm).
£250–280
€ / **$400–440** ⊞ DNo

The rugs in this section have been arranged in geographical sequence from west to east, in the following order: Europe, Turkey, Anatolia, Caucasus, Persia, Turkestan, India and China.

A Karadja runner, northwest Persian, c1850, 171 x 43in (434 x 109cm).
£800–900
€ / **$1,300–1,400** ⚒ S(O)

A Bakhtiari carpet, west Persian, early 20thC, 127 x 155in (322.5 x 393.5cm).
£800–900
€ / **$1,300–1,400** ⚒ S(O)

A Tabriz prayer rug, damage and losses, northwest Persian, c1890, 73 x 54in (185.5 x 137cm).
£2,800–3,200
€ / **$4,400–5,000** ⚒ S(NY)

A rug, northwest Persian, mid-19thC, 57 x 39in (145 x 99cm).
£320–375
€ / **$500–600** ⚒ B(Ba)

► A Hamadan carpet, west Persian, c1920, 54 x 83in (137 x 211cm).
£1,000–1,100
€ / **$1,600–1,700** ⊞ DNo

A Lori Bakhtiari bedding bag, west Persian, 1875–1900, 39¼ x 55in (99.5 x 139.5cm).
€4,500–5,000
€ / $7,000–8,000 ⊞ SAM

The art of carpet weaving changed fundamentally during the 19th century, when its manufacture was taken over mainly by men. Previously, many carpets, if not all, were woven by women and young girls as dowry pieces and for domestic use. The designs woven were part of their ancient tradition. Once these carpets became sought after by richer nations, the art of carpet making became overtaken by commercial considerations. Most carpets manufactured during the 20th century may last 100 years, but the individuality and the artistic element has for the main part been lost.

A Malayer rug, worn, west Persian, Kurdistan, c1900, 44 x 76in (112 x 193cm).
£325–360
€ / $500–570 ⊞ DNo

A Joshagan carpet, central Persian, c1900, 163 x 125in (414 x 317.5cm).
£2,200–2,500
€ / $3,500–4,000 ➤ S(O)

A Lori *gabbeh*, west Persian, early 20thC, 47 x 31in (119.5 x 78.5cm).
£1,100–1,300
€ / $1,700–2,000 ⊞ SAM

A Mahal carpet, west Persian, c1890, 133½ x 106in (339 x 269cm).
£2,800–3,200
€ / $4,400–5,000 ➤ B(Ch)
Although this carpet is in very poor condition, it is very attractive and sympathetic restoration might increase the value.

◄ **A Sanjabi Kurds salt bag,** west Persian, Kurdistan, c1900, 14 x 26in (35.5 x 66cm).
£675–750
€ / $1,100–1,200 ⊞ SAM

A Kashgai vanity bag, southwest Persian, 1875–1900, 10in (25.5cm) square.
£250–275
€ / $400–440 ⊞ SAM

A Lori runner, west Persian, c1920, 155 x 41in (393.5 x 104cm).
£650–750
€ / $1,000–1,200 ➤ S(O)

A Sultanabad *kelleh*, west Persian, late 19thC, 123 x 59in (312.5 x 150cm).
£1,700–2,000
€ / $2,700–3,200 ➤ S(O)

LOCATE THE SOURCE

The source of each illustration in Miller's can be found by checking the code letters below each caption with the Key to Illustrations, pages 794–800.

RUGS & CARPETS

A Kamo *soffreh*, central Persian, c1900, 35½ x 34in (90 x 86.5cm).
£850–950
€ / $1,300–1,500 ⊞ SAM

◄ **A silk Kashan rug,** central Persian, c1920, 83 x 51in (211 x 129.5cm).
£1,200–1,400
€ / $1,900–2,200 ⚒ S(O)

A Belouch prayer rug, northeast Persian, c1900, 67 x 36in (170 x 91.5cm).
£1,700–1,900
€ / $2,700–3,000 ⊞ SAM

A Meshad carpet, northeast Persian, c1920, 162 x 129½in (411 x 329cm).
£850–1,000
€ / $1,300–1,600 ⚒ B(Ch)

An Afshar rug, south Persian, 1850–1900, 50 x 70in (127 x 178cm).
£3,500–3,800
€ / $5,500–6,000 ⊞ SAM

A Meshad carpet, northeast Persian, Khorasan, c1930, 101 x 126in (256.5 x 320cm).
£150–175
€ / $240–280 ⚒ WW

▶ **A flatweave,** northeast Persian, 19thC, 57 x 76in (145 x 193cm).
£2,200–2,500
€ / $3,500–4,000 ⊞ SAM

A Kirman carpet, southeast Persian, c1930, 171 x 117¼in (434 x 298cm).
£420–500
€ / $670–800 ⚒ B(Ch)

An Afshar carpet, with a rabbit and quail border, southeast Persian, c1890, 74 x 50in (183 x 127cm).
£1,100–1,300
€ / $1,700–2,000 ⊞ DNo

◄ **A Belouch vanity bag,** southeast Persian, Chakhansur, 1875–1900, 7 x 8in (18 x 20.5cm).
£125–140
€ / $200–220 ⊞ SAM

The Professor Mark Whiting & Dr Jon Thompson Collections

In the first half of the 20th century there were large numbers of Turkmen (Bokhara) weavings to be found in Great Britain, as a result of purchases by military personnel and civil servants posted to the far reaches of the British Empire in the 19th and early 20th centuries. These items included rugs, small bags and other trappings which, as they were largely inexpensive, appealed to many collectors. Dr Jon Thompson and Professor Mark Whiting in the 1960s were among the first people in the UK to take an interest in such pieces and create large collections. Their focused writing in the 1970s helped create a boom for Turkmen products, which collapsed in the early 1980s due to over-optimistic buying. Today there is still a strong interest in Turkmen weaving and the value of rarer pieces remains strong.

Whiting and Thompson both sold their collections in the 1990s. With the collapse of the Soviet Union more Turkmen pieces are appearing on the world market and it is still possible to discover interesting examples. It is an area which still provides rewards for new collectors.   **Richard Purdon**

A Yomut saddle cover, northwest Turkestani, 1850–1900, 22in (56cm) square.
£330–400
€/ **$515–630** ⚒ S(O)

A Beshir *torba*, west Turkestani, c1880, 18 x 63in (45.5 x 160cm).
£900–1,000
€/ **$1,400–1,600** ⚒ S(O)

A wedding trapping, Ersari Turkmen Tribes, west Turkestani, Beshir, mid-19thC, 16 x 51in (40.5 x 129.5cm).
£585–650
€/ **$930–1,000** ⊞ SAM

An Ersari *chuval*, southwest Turkestani, 1850–1900, 59 x 34in (150 x 86.5cm).
£575–675
€/ **$900–1,100** ⚒ S(O)

A Chodor Turkmen main carpet, north Turkestani, 1880–1900, 89 x 69in (226 x 175.5cm).
£450–525
€/ **$700–830** ⚒ WW

A Tekke carpet, west Turkestani, late 19thC, 115 x 90in (292 x 228.5cm).
£1,400–1,600
€/ **$2,200–2,500** ⚒ S(O)

◄ **A Turkmen rug,** west Turkestani, c1920, 38 x 54in (96.5 x 137cm).
£100–120
€/ **$160–190** ⚒ WW

A Tekke Turkmen saddle bag, west Turkestani, early 20thC, 19 x 34in (48.5 x 86.5cm).
£430–475
€/ **$675–750** ⊞ SAM

RUGS & CARPETS

European & Eastern rugs & carpets 1977–2002

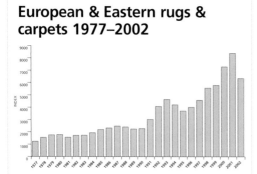

This graph shows the value of European and Eastern rugs and carpets as a whole over the past 25 years. Rugs from particular geographical areas may not follow this graph exactly. ©AMR

An Afghan *pardah*, slight wear, leather backing sewn on, north Afghani, 1900–20, 82 x 64in (208.5 x 162.5cm).
£150–170
€/ **$240–270** ⚒ WW

A *khordjin* face, Timuri tribes, west Afghani, 1850–1900, 30 x 34in (76 x 86.5cm).
£1,600–1,800
€/ **$2,500–2,800** ⊞ SAM
A *khordjin* is a double saddle bag used by nomads and villagers.

▶ **A Khotan silk pile throne rug,** the major and minor panels decorated with shrubs and medallions, enclosed by reciprocal T-borders, some wear, east Turkestani, c1870, 66 x 22in (167.5 x 56cm).
£550–600
€/ **$870–950** ⊞ DNo

A Khotan carpet, east Turkestani, c1900, 116 x 59in (294.5 x 150cm).
£1,800–2,000
€/ **$2,800–3,200** ⚒ S(O)

A rug, north Indian, late 19thC, 104 x 61in (264 x 155cm).
£2,200–2,500
€/ **$3,500–4,000** ⚒ S(O)

A carpet, one hole and one reweave, slight loss to top end, Indian, early 20thC, 136 x 98¾in (345.5 x 251cm).
£2,200–2,500
€/ **$3,500–4,000** ⚒ WW

◀ **An Amritsar rug,** north Indian, c1900, 105 x 81in (266.5 x 205.5cm).
£5,300–5,800
€/ **$8,400–9,200** ⚒ S(O)

RUGS & CARPETS

A panel from a meditation rug or a seat cover, slight wear, Chinese, Ninghsia, 1850–1900, 30in (76cm) square.
£375–450
€/ **$600–700** ↗ WW

Pricing antique rugs & carpets

The price of an antique Oriental carpet can never be set in stone, for the factors to be considered have an infinite range of subtleties which are often dependent on the mood of the market. The use of synthetic dyes, which were invented in 1858 and quickly became widely available, is the principal factor that determines value. Rugs made of synthetically dyed materials should be avoided by serious collectors.

Condition is the other major consideration. While most carpets are extremely durable, the presence of visible wear seriously devalues a carpet, especially if it is to be subjected to daily use. In valuable pieces the presence of small holes and damages is not a problem. The rarest examples can still fetch surprising sums at auction despite extensive damage and wear. However, large areas of restoration should only be undertaken with caution by a professional.

A silk and metal thread rug, the brocaded metal thread field with an overall floral lattice of flowerheads and vines, within a conforming border, Chinese, Beijing, late 19thC, 108 x 71¾in (274.5 x 182.5cm).
£2,000–2,200
€/ **$3,200–3,500** ↗ RTo

▶ **A silk and metal thread carpet,** Chinese, c1880, 142½ x 114¼in (362 x 290cm).
£750–875
€/ **$1,200–1,400** ↗ B(Ch)
The five-toed dragons on this carpet were a restricted emblem for use by the Imperial household until the dissolution of the Empire in 1914.

◀ **A silk and metal brocade rug,** inscribed 'Made for Palace of Perpetual Harmony', Chinese, possibly Beijing, late 19thC, 98 x 61in (249 x 155cm).
£6,000–7,000
€/ **$9,500–11,000** ↗ WW

A silk carpet, some pile loss, northeast Chinese, Tianjin, 1875–1925, 118 x 96in (299.5 x 244cm).
£2,000–2,400
€/ **$3,200–3,800** ↗ WW

A carpet, Chinese, c1900, 139¾ x 111½in (355 x 283cm).
£3,000–3,500
€/ **$4,700–5,500** ↗ S(O)

A pair of rugs, Chinese, early 20thC, 40 x 23¾in (101.5 x 60.5cm).
£350–420
€/ **$550–670** ↗ S(O)

◀ **A carpet,** Chinese, c1920, 164½ x 123in (418 x 312.5cm).
£950–1,100
€/ **$1,500–1,700** ↗ S(O)

Textiles
Covers & Quilts

A chintz patchwork coverlet, the patches mainly dress fabric, paper templates intact to reverse, c1845, 84½ x 89in (215 x 226cm).
£420–500
€/ **$660–790** ➤ S(O)

An embroidered linen bed cover, with Bruges lace inserts and woollen tassels, c1860, 118 x 98½in (300 x 250cm).
£550–600
€/ **$870–950** ⊞ JPr

A patchwork coverlet, possibly a 'Friendship Cloth', each square embroidered with a unique design, worked in coloured silks and cottons, with a red scallop-edged border, backed with a cotton twill, late 19thC, 104 x 82¾in (264 x 210cm).
£120–140
€/ **$190–220** ➤ B(WM)

A Princess Feather appliqué cotton quilt, with floral vine serpentine border, American, c1860, 96in (244cm) square.
£900–1,100
€/ **$1,400–1,700** ➤ COPA

A patchwork quilt, by Isabella Swales, Kepwick, with hexagonal patches in a variety of colours and with a floral-patterned border, 1862, 86 x 96in (218.5 x 244cm).
£220–250
€/ **$350–400** ➤ Mit

A cotton Bokhara susani, embroidered in silk, Uzbekistan, 19thC, 90½ x 72in (230 x 182cm).
£4,200–5,000
€/ **$6,600–7,900** ➤ B(Kn)

◀ **A patchwork quilt,** with inset cross-stitch panels, cotton back, late 19thC.
£765–850
€/ **$1,200–1,400** ⊞ JPr

A Rose Appliqué quilt, with swag and tassel borders, American, c1860, 84 x 88in (213.5 x 223.5cm).
£550–600
€/ **$870–950** ⊞ MAQ

A patchwork quilt, with wagon wheel to the centre and a crocheted border, American, dated 1884, 66in (167.6cm) square.
£750–875
€/ **$1,200–1,400** ➤ COPA

A Victorian double strip quilt, with detailed Durham stitching, 118 x 98½in (300 x 250cm).
£380–420
€/ **$600–670** ⊞ JPr

A patchwork quilt, hand-stitched in the Durham manner, early 20thC, 114¼ x 86in (290 x 260cm).
£350–400
€/ **$550–630** ⊞ JPR

A Durham quilt, hand-stitched, early 20thC, 100 x 110in (254 x 279.5cm).
£315–350
€/ **$500–550** ⊞ JPr

A child's bed sheet, with applied cut-out animals, American, c1920, 54 x 36in (137 x 91.5cm).
£380–420
€/ **$600–660** ⚒ COPA

An Aubusson mille fleurs table cover, French, c1920, 58 x 61in (147.5 x 155cm).
£3,500–4,000
€/ **$5,500–6,300** ⊞ LGU

A patchwork quilt, with squares in the form of the cross, each square depicting a psalm, American, c1930, 97 x 75in (246.5 x 190.5cm).
£850–1,000
€/ **$1,300–1,600** ⚒ COPA

A Princess Feather quilt, American, c1930, 86in (218.5cm) square.
£700–800
€/ **$1,100–1,300** ⊞ COPA

◀ **A Floral Appliqué quilt,** with rope and diamond quilting, American, c1930, 76in (193cm) square.
£350–400
€/ **$550–650** ⊞ MAQ

TEXTILES

Embroidery & Needlework

A needlework fragment, in the form of a panel of two joined pieces showing angels on a background of silver thread, 16thC, 7 x 16in (18 x 40.5cm).
£400–450
€/ **$630–700** ⊞ JPr

A silkwork picture, depicting the Sacrifice of Isaac, the figures with painted faces, slight damage, 17thC, 9¾ x 10¾in (25 x 27.5cm).
£300–350
€/ **$475–550** ⚲ TEN

A needlework landscape scene, worked in tent stitch with a shepherd and shepherdess, Dutch, mid-17thC, 5¼ x 7in (13.5 x 18cm).
£1,200–1,400
€/ **$5,400–6,400** ⚲ S(O)

A needlework panel, worked in tent stitch and stumpwork with gold and silver wirework and silk, c1660, 12½ x 17in (32 x 43cm).
£750–900
€/ **$1,200–1,400** ⚲ G(L)

A beadwork panel, depicting Adam and Eve in the Garden of Eden, on an ivory satin ground, initialled 'MS', c1660, 11½ x 14½in (29 x 37cm).
£1,700–2,000
€/ **$2,700–3,200** ⚲ S(O)

A needlework panel, depicting Elijah and the Ravens, worked in silks, wool and silver thread, early 18thC, 11¼ x 9¾in (28.5 x 25cm).
£2,000–2,200
€/ **$3,200–3,500** ⚲ F&C

Two embroidered needlework panels, one depicting a lady and her parrot and the other a parrot, worked in silk thread on satin, pen and ink details, c1700, framed, 11 x 9½in (28 x 24cm).
£4,500–5,000
€/ **$7,000–8,000** ⊞ RYA

An embroidered panel, worked in silk, Italian or Portuguese, minor damage, c1700, 69¾ x 39¾in (177 x 101cm).
£2,200–2,500
€/ **$3,500–4,000** ⚲ S(Am)

▶ **An embroidered chasuble panel,** worked in silks on a linen ground with the Annunciation, the faces of painted canvas, probably French, c1720, 56 x 31½in (142 x 80cm).
£850–950
€/ **$1,300–1,500** ⚲ S

▶ **An embroidered panel,** worked in tent stitch with wool and silk, c1740, 13in (33cm) square.
£2,000–2,200
€/ **$3,200–3,500** ⚲ S(O)

A silkwork picture, with central oil-painted and embroidered vignette of a girl and lamb, c1790, in a maple frame, 13¾ x 11½in (35 x 29cm).
£420–500
€/ **$650–800** ⚒ S(O)

A needlework panel, depicting Diana, probably from a chair-back, mounted on stretchers, damaged, c1750, 27¼ x 23¼in (69 x 59cm).
£1,500–1,700
€/ **$2,400–2,700** ⚒ SWO

A silk and wool needlework panel, French, 18thC, 7 x13in (18 x 33cm).
£315–350
€/ **$475–550** ⊞ LGU

A silkwork picture, by Sarah Brightwell, inscribed on reverse 'attributed to Mrs Potter's school', dated 16 December 1791, 16 x 19in (40.5 x 48.5cm).
£1,300–1,500
€/ **$2,100–2,400** ⊞ PSC

An embroidered silk picture, depicting a flautist and his dog, with painted hands, face and background, late 18thC, 7 x 9in (18 x 23cm), framed.
£585–650
€/ **$925–1,000** ⊞ WWo
In the late 18th and early 19th century, pictures such as this were probably issued as kits to be filled in with individual colour choices.

A silk embroidery panel, 18thC, 10¾ x 9in (27.5 x 23cm).
£200–240
€/ **$320–380** ⚒ SWO

◄ **A silk needlework picture,** French, 18thC, 23 x 18in (58.5 x 45.5cm), in original frame.
£3,000–3,300
€/ **$4,700–5,200** ⊞ LGU

A beaded bag, with original kid leather strings, early 19thC, 7in (18cm) high.
£215–240
€/ $135–380 ⊞ JPr

A silkwork and painted picture, worked in chenille, early 19thC, 15½ x 12¼in (39.5 x 31cm).
£475–565
€/ $750–900 ♪ TEN

A silkwork picture, depicting a shepherdess by a tree, early 19thC, in a *verre églomisé* frame, 11¾ x 9¾in (30 x 25cm).
£320–400
€/ $500–630 ♪ SWO

A chenille-work silk picture, depicting a wood-gatherer and his dog, early 19thC, 14¼ x 11½in (36 x 29.5cm).
£150–175
€/ $240–280 ♪ L

An embroidered picture, worked in tent stitch with a basket of flowers, on a black linen ground, early 19thC, 16½ x 21¾in (42 x 55.5cm), in a maple frame.
£420–500
€/ $670–800 ♪ S(O)

A silkwork and painted picture, depicting Mount Vernon, the sky, faces and hands painted, slight damage, American, probably New England, c1820, 15½ x 20½in (39.5 x 52cm).
£6,000–7,000
€/ $9,500–11,000 ♪ S(NY)

A silkwork picture, depicting a lady with a donkey and lion, early 19thC, 12¼ x 9½in (31 x 24cm).
£240–275
€/ $380–430 ♪ SWO

A silkwork mourning picture, with two inscriptions, repaired, American, 1800–25, 19 x 20¼in (48.5 x 51.5cm).
£4,500–5,500
€/ $7,000–8,600 ♪ S(NY)

◀ **An embroidered picture,** worked in silk with a woodsman and dogs, painted face, hands and sky, early 19thC, 22¼ x 14¼in (56.5 x 36.5cm).
£240–280
€/ $380–430 ♪ PFK

A silkwork picture, depicting a lady playing with a child, early 19thC, 6½ x 4½in (16.5 x 11.5cm), in a later frame.
£500–600
€/ $800–950 ♪ SWO

A Berlin woolwork picture, depicting a lady and two falconers in a palatial setting, 19thC, 32¼ x 26in (82 x 66cm), framed.
£80–100
€/ $125–160 ♪ PFK

A pair of silkwork banners, worked to each side with a white bird of prey, each with a wooden rail in the form of a bugle, one banner torn, 19thC, each 20in (51cm) square.
£130–150
€/ $200–240 ♪ PFK

A silkwork and painted picture, entitled 'Stella', the lady holding a wreath of fruit and flowers, c1820, 11in (28cm) high.
£220–250
€/ $350–400 ♪ HAM

A needlework picture, worked in gros point with a child dressed in tartan and her dog, a ruined castle and cottage behind, 19thC, 17¼ x 15¾in (44 x 40cm).
£375–450
€ / $600–700 ⚒ TRM

A pair of woolwork pictures, depicting a prince and princess, c1840, 18¼ x 12½in (46.5 x 32cm), in rosewood frames.
£1,100–1,200
€ / $1,700–1,900 ⚒ S(O)

A wool needlework picture, worked in gros point with a spaniel, the sky unworked, inscribed to reverse, 1842, 11¾ x 15¼in (30 x 38.5cm), in a bird's eye maple frame.
£140–160
€ / $220–250 ⚒ PFK

A Berlin woolwork picture, depicting a cat and kittens on a cushion, c1850, 10 x 14in (25.5 x 35.5cm), framed.
£180–200
€ / $285–315 ⊞ JPr

A woolwork picture, depicting a dog on a cushion, c1850, 6in (15cm) square, framed.
£225–250
€ / $350–400 ⊞ JPr

A pair of embroidered face screens, worked in petit point with flowers, with turned ivory handles, c1850, 20in (51cm) long.
£100–120
€ / $160–190 ⊞ JPr

A Victorian Berlin woolwork picture, depicting a vase of flowers, with inscription, 22 x 21½in (56 x 54.5cm), in a rosewood frame.
€320–370
€ / $500–580 ⚒ DMC

A woolwork picture, depicting a bird, c1880, 5in (12cm) wide.
£200–220
€ / $315–350 ⊞ LGU

An embroidered panel, depicting a parrot, late 19thC, 25¾ x 22in (65.5 x 56cm), framed.
€240–275
€ / $380–440 ⚒ RTo

A Victorian woolwork picture, depicting two doves on a nest, 16 x 12½in (40.5 x 32cm).
£375–450
€ / $600–700 ⚒ HYD

A crochet-edged linen tablecloth, c1900, 54in (137cm) square.
£70–80
€ / $110–125 ⊞ JuC

An 18thC-style damask panel, depicting a thistle surmounted by a crown, flanked by the Lion of Scotland, the Star and Order of St Andrew, and motto, c1900, 13½ x 11½in (34.5 x 29cm).
£500–575
€ / $800–900 ⚒ B(Ed)
This design incorporates the defiant symbols found in household linen belonging to supporters of Prince Charles Edward Stuart, manufactured in France after the Battle of Culloden, 1745–46, and widely copied.

TEXTILES

Lace

A panel of cut work, probably Italian, late 16thC, 2 x 15in (5 x 38cm).
£55–60
€/ **$87–95** ⊞ HL

A panel of needlelace, c1665, 4 x 25in (10 x 63.5cm).
£225–250
€/ **$350–400** ⊞ HL

A panel of Valenciennes costume lace, 18thC, 3½ x 44in (9 x 56cm).
£70–75
€/ **$110–120** ⊞ HL

A needlelace cloth, with carnations among tendrils and tulips, late 17thC, 56 x 20in (142 x 52cm).
£850–1,000
€/ **$1,300–1,600** ⚒ B(WM)

▶ **A panel of Alençon needlelace,** late 18thC, 3½ x 23in (9 x 58.5cm).
£50–55
€/ **$80–85** ⊞ HL

A lace sampler, by Sarah Tyzak, dated 1676, 8 x 9in (23 x 20.5cm).
£1,300–1,500
€/ **$2,000–2,400** ⚒ S(O)

A Brussels lace *pointe de gaze* Bertha collar, mid-19thC, 17in (43cm) diam.
£260–285
€/ **$400–450** ⊞ HL

A Bedfordshire lace handkerchief, mid–late 19thC, 14in (35.5cm) square.
£70–75
€/ **$110–120** ⊞ HL

A Brussels needlelace collar, c1890, 10in (25.5cm) long.
£45–50
€/ **$70–80** ⊞ JuC

A Honiton lace handkerchief, c1860, 13in (33cm) square.
£140–155
€/ **$220–250** ⊞ HL

An East Midlands lace collar, late 19thC, 14in (35.5cm) long.
£50–55
€/ **$80–87** ⊞ HL

An Edwardian Brussels lace collar, 23in (58.5cm) long.
£60–65
€/ **$95–105** ⊞ Ech

Samplers

A sampler, by Elizabeth Cooke, aged 12 years, dated 10 August 1796, 16 x 13in (40.5 x 33cm).
£850–1,100
€/ **1,300–1,700** ➤ FEN

A band sampler, by Elenor Hines, worked in silks, dated 16th October 1706, 17½in x 8in ,44 x 20.5cm, framed.
€650–750
€/ **$1,000–1,200** ➤ B(NW)

A sampler, 'The Lord is my Shepherd', 1741, 16 x 8in (40.5 x 20.5cm).
£1,350–1,500
€/ **$2,100–2,400** ⊞ HIS

A sampler, by Sarah Chamberlain, worked in silks, dated 25 October 1751, 15 x 7½in (38 x 19cm).
£1,000–1,200
€/ **$1,600–1,900** ➤ B(WM)

◀ **A needlework sampler,** by M. Jewitt, Bocking, dated 18 March 1796, 13¾in (35cm) square.
£320–375
€/ **$510–590** ➤ HAM

A sampler, worked in silks and wools, slight damage, c1800, 12½in (32cm) square.
£720–800
€/ **$1,100–1,300** ➤ B(NW)

A sampler, by Mary Vickers, dated 1st November 1800, 12 x 10in (30.5 x 25.5cm).
€360–400
€/ **$560–630** ➤ G(L)

Further reading

Miller's Samplers: How to Compare & Value, Miller's Publications, 2002

A muslin needlework sampler, depicting the Point to Point on the Delaware, American, c1800, 21 x 18¼in (53.5 x 46.5cm), framed.
£450–500
€/ **$700–800** ➤ S(NY)

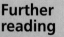

▶ **A needlework sampler,** by Jane Irwin, worked in coloured wools on cream canvas, early 19thC, 17½in (44.5cm) square, framed.
€280–320
€/ **$440–500** ➤ RTo

TEXTILES

A linen sampler, by Alice Thomson, aged eight, early 19thC, 18½ x 16½in (47 x 42cm), framed.
£720–850
€/ $1,100–1,300 ⚒ TRM

A sampler, by Polly Ballou, American, dated 1804, 12 x 10in (30.5 x 25.5cm), framed.
£315–350
€/ $500–550 ⊞ HCFA

A needlework sampler, by Martha Pound, 1811, 14¼ x 11½in (36 x 29cm).
£600–700
€/ $950–1,100 ⚒ L

A sampler, by Frances Eaton, aged ten, American, dated 1817, 15 x 13in (38 x 33cm), framed.
£800–880
€/ $1,300–1,400 ⊞ HCFA

A sampler, worked in silk, with a heart, c1803, 8 x 8½in (20.5 x 21.5cm), framed.
£900–1,000
€/ $1,400–1,600 ⊞ HIS

A sampler, by Ann Carr, aged 15, worked in silks, dated 1806, 15¼ x 13½in (39 x 34.5cm).
£5,600–6,400
€/ $8,800–10,000 ⚒ B(NW)

A needlework sampler, by Mary Anne Odem, aged ten, worked in cross-stitch in silks, dated 24 August 1812, 15½ x 11¼in (39.5 x 28.5cm), framed.
£720–850
€/ $1,100–1,300 ⚒ RTo

A needlework sampler, by Mary Lewis, 1803, 12 x 16½in (30.5 x 42cm).
£300–350
€/ $470–550 ⚒ RTo

A sampler, by Elisabeth Crane, worked in silks, dated 1807, 17¾ x 13¼in (45 x 33.5cm), framed.
£900–1,100
€/ $1,400–1,700 ⚒ B(WM)

A needlework sampler, by Jenny Stockton, aged 12, with Adam and Eve beside the Tree of Life, dated 1815, 25 x 17in (63.5 x 43cm).
£700–820
€/ $1,100–1,300 ⚒ BWL

Auction or dealer?

When buying at auction, prices can be lower than those of a dealer, but a buyer's premium and VAT will be added to the hammer price. Equally, when selling at auction, commission, tax and photography charges will be deducted from the hammer price. Dealers will often restore pieces before putting them back on the market.

A needlework sampler, by Azubah Farrow, 1817, 14½ x 11½in (36.5 x 29cm), framed.
£600–700
€/ $950–1,100 ⚲ L

A sampler, by Sarah Lewis Bayly, worked on wool with silks, dated April 1823, 12½ x 13in (31 x 33cm), in an Edwardian oak frame.
£2,200–2,500
€/ $3,500–4,000 ⚲ S(O)

A sampler, by Eliza Latham, aged eight, faded, c1830, 15 x 12½in (38 x 32cm), in a modern frame.
£800–900
€/ $1,200–1,400 ⚲ S(O)

Insurance values

Always insure your valuable antiques for the cost of replacing them with similar items, regardless of the original price paid. Both dealers and auctioneers can provide a valuation service for a fee.

A sampler, by Philinda Lamb, aged 13, American, dated 24 July 1820, 14 x 17in (35.5 x 43cm), framed.
£2,000–2,200
€/ $3,200–3,400 ⚲ COPA

A sampler, by Mary McCorrie, American, dated 1824, 16 x 13in (40.5 x 33cm), in a modern frame.
£500–560
€/ $800–880 ⊞ HCFA

An embroidered sampler, by HD, worked in silks with a map of Wales, c1830, 16½ x 13in (42 x 33cm).
£4,000–4,500
€/ $6,300–7,000 ⚲ S(O)

A needlework sampler, by Rebekah Pankhurst, dated 1830, 18¼ x 14¼in (46.5 x 36cm), in a mahogany frame.
£600–720
€/ $950–1,100 ⚲ L

A needlework sampler, by Martha Lee, dated 1823, 9 x 8in (23 x 20.5cm).
£300–350
€/ $470–550 ⚲ G(L)

A sampler, by Ruth Carpenter, American, 1826, 20 x 12in (51 x 30.5cm), framed.
£700–770
€/ $1,100–1,200 ⊞ HCFA

A sampler, by Eliza Thomas, dated 1831, 21¾ x 17¾in (55.5 x 45cm).
£1,100–1,200
€/ $1,700–1,900 ⊞ PSC

TEXTILES

A sampler, by Louisa Oldland, dated 8 March 1833, 17¼ x 13in (44 x 33cm).
£1,100–1,200
€/ **$1,700–1,800** ⚒ S(O)

A sampler, by Elizabeth Kerby, aged 13, dated 1833, 23 x 12in (58.5 x 30.5cm), framed.
£200–225
€/ **$320–360** ⚒ G(L)

A sampler, by Mary Ann White, dated 13 November 1834, 8¼ x 13in (21 x 33cm).
£450–525
€/ **$710–830** ⚒ L

A silk sampler, by Susan Wheeler, aged 11, 1835, 13in (33cm) square, framed.
£1,300–1,500
€/ **$2,100–2,400** ⊞ SEA

A sampler, by Louisa Broad, aged 11, dated 11 October 1835, 16 x 12in (41 x 30.5cm), framed.
£350–420
€/ **$550–660** ⚒ Bea(E)

◄ **A sampler,** inscribed 'MR finished April 10 1838', 16 x 12¾in (40.5 x 32.5cm), in a later frame.
£380–450
€/ **$600–710** ⚒ PF

A sampler, by Martha Parnaby, aged 10, dated 16 August 1837, 16½ x 17½in (42 x 44.5cm), in a burrwood frame.
£380–450
€/ **$600–710** ⚒ PFK

A sampler, by Rachel Walker, Ackworth School, Yorkshire, dated 1842, 6 x 9½in (15 x 24cm), framed.
£720–800
€/ **$1,100–1,200** ⊞ HIS

◄ **A school mathematical sampler,** dated 1850, 8 x 6¼in (20.5 x 16cm), framed.
£1,100–1,200
€/ **$1,700–1,900** ⊞ HIS

A sampler, by Mary Fielding, The Shepherd and Shepherdess, dated 1851, 24 x 25in (61 x 63.5cm), framed.
£1,000–1,200
€/ **$1,600–1,900** ⊞ HIS

A sampler, by Sarah Davies, aged 17, Welsh, dated 1864, 16 x 20in (40.5 x 51cm), framed.
£300–350
€/ **$470–550** ⚒ PF

A woolwork sampler, by Elisabeth Preston, dated 1852, 24in (61cm) square, mounted as a fire screen in a painted wood frame.
£280–325
€/ **$440–510** ⚒ AH

Tapestries

An Aubusson verdure tapestry, depicting a chateau and a hunting dog, tears, reweaves and restoration, French, early 18thC, 103 x 93in (262 x 236cm).
£2,200–2,500
€/ **$3,400–4,000** ⚒ S(P)

A wool and silk tapestry, depicting a hunting scene in a wooded landscape, some damage, Flemish, c1650, 110¼ x 88¼in (280 x 224cm).
£4,000–4,800
€/ **$6,300–7,600** ⚒ BUK

An armorial tapestry, with the arms of the De Los Rios of Spain, c1650, 128¾ x 115¼in (326 x 292.5cm).
£5,000–6,000
€/ **$7,800–9,500** ⚒ S(NY)

A tapestry cushion, 18thC, 10 x 19in (25.5 x 48.5cm).
£350–400
€/ **$550–630** ⊞ LGU

A tapestry cushion, woven with flowers, 18thC, 10 x 15in (25.5 x 38cm).
£200–220
€/ **$320–350** ⊞ LGU

A tapestry cushion, 18thC, 9 x 14in (23 x 35.5cm).
£200–220
€/ **$320–350** ⊞ LGU

An Aubusson tapestry cushion, woven to shape with an urn of blooms, French, late 18thC, 16 x 15½in (40.5 x 39.5cm).
£1,100–1,200
€/ **$1,700–1,900** ⚒ S(O)

A wool tapestry, depicting a woodland hunting scene, Flemish, c1800, 60 x 58½in (152.5 x 148.5cm).
£850–1,000
€/ **$1,300–1,600** ⚒ B(NW)

A tapestry cushion, with oak leaf pattern, 18thC, 14 x 10in (35.5 x 25.5cm).
£100–120
€/ **$160–190** ⊞ LGU

An Aubusson tapestry cushion, from a larger panel, French, c1880, 11 x 20in (28 x 51cm).
£350–400
€/ **$550–630** ⊞ LGU

A tapestry, depicting a 17thC Arcadian scene, Belgian, Ingelmunster, 19thC, 109 x 122in (276 x 310cm).
€1,800–2,200
€/ **$2,800–3,500** ⚒ BERN

An Aubusson verdure tapestry panel, depicting a landscape, French, late 19thC, 75 x 100in (191 x 254cm).
£1,400–1,600
€/ **$2,200–2,500** ⚒ S(O)

An Aubusson tapestry cushion, French, c1880, 11 x 17in (28 x 43cm).
£250–280
€/ **$400–440** ⊞ LGU

TEXTILES

Costume

A tapestry draw-string purse, woven with silk crosses, lined with turquoise silk, French, 1650–1700, 4in (10cm) long.
£260–300
€/ **$400–475** ⚒ S(O)

A pair of paste buckles, close set with graduated mixed cut pastes, bright-cut gold bezel, steel back, chape and tongue, c1770.
£100–120
€/ **$160–190** ⚒ WW

A lady's Jacquard woven silk sack-backed open robe, with train and matching petticoat, slight wear, c1780.
£2,500–2,800
€/ **$4,000–4,400** ⚒ B(NW)

▶ **A printed cotton bonnet,** c1860.
£50–55
€/ **$80–90** ⊞ CCO

A George III gentleman's silk embroidered waistcoat, with blue lining.
£200–240
€/ **$320–380** ⚒ BR

A Spitalfields silk dress, with woven flower decoration, 18thC.
£420–500
€/ **$660–790** ⚒ SWO

A knitted and beaded bonnet, Swiss or German, c1820.
£160–180
€/ **$250–285** ⊞ JuC

◀ **A pair of silk satin embroidered shoes,** with pink painted heels and diamanté buckles, c1880.
£70–80
€/ **$110–125** ⊞ L&L

A lace afternoon tea dress, 1890s.
£240–265
€/ **$380–420** ⊞ L&L

◀ **A silk floral panniered dress,** 1870s.
£250–275
€/ **$400–440** ⊞ L&L

A Victorian child's velvet cloak, decorated in brocade-edged silk with plants, the collar trimmed with gold thread, 28in (71cm) long.
£35–45
€/ **$55–70** ⚒ PFK

A Victorian woven silk paisley shawl, 69 x 68in (175.5 x 172.5cm).
£250–275
€/ **$400–440** ⊞ Ech

A Victorian baby's wool and silk carrying cape, with lace edging, 34in (86.5cm) long.
£85–95
€/ **$135–150** ⊞ Ech

A lace dress, with trained skirt, sequin and beaded decoration, labelled 'M. Carey and M. & A. Wall, 8 Bruton Street...London', late 19thC.
£420–500
€/ **$660–790** ⚒ Gam

A Victorian silk cape.
£220–245
€ / $340–380 ⊞ LU

An Edwardian pair of lady's leather boots.
£85–100
€ / $135–160 ⊞ Ech

A nurse's embossed and pierced belt buckle, the panels depicting cherubs' faces, Chester 1901, 5½in (14cm) wide.
£55–65
€ / $90–100 ↗ WilP

An Edwardian embroidered net blouse.
£40–45
€ / $60–70 ⊞ Ech

An Edwardian Chinese export silk shawl, Canton, 54in (137cm) square.
£150–165
€ / $235–260 ⊞ Ech

An embossed velvet and fur evening coat, 1920s.
£200–225
€ / $320–360 ↗ SWO

A Continental beaded bag, c1913, 8in (20.5cm) long.
£180–200
€ / $280–320 ⊞ JPr

A silk devoré shawl, 1920s, 48in (122cm) square.
£130–150
€ / $200–240 ⊞ Ech

An ivory satin gown, the scalloped hem applied with silver and pearlized studs, crystal beads, tasselled ties, together with underslip, French, 1925.
£450–500
€ / $700–800 ↗ S(O)
This gown was worn by debutante Susan Rawnsley when she was presented to King George V at court.
It is probably by Patou.

A black cotton dress, with all-over bead decoration, 1920s.
£450–500
€ / $700–800 ⊞ Ech

A Chanel-style printed silk chiffon dress, 1920s.
£130–145
€ / $210–230 ⊞ Ech

A flapper dress, with all-over silver beaded decoration and scalloped hem, 1920s.
£630–700
€ / $1,000–1,100 ⊞ Ech

Fans

A Chinese export ivory brisé fan, the central cartouche painted in red and gold with birds among blossom branches, above a floral border and Oriental scene, the reverse with mirrored decoration, early 18thC, 10¾in (27cm) long.
£280–320
€/ **$440–510** ⚒ B(WM)

A lacquered ivory brisé fan, painted with a banquet scene, the reverse with figures in a boat, c1720, 8½in (21.5cm) long.
£1,500–1,800
€/ **$2,400–2,800** ⊞ LDC

A fan, the leaf painted with a classical scene, French, c1730, 11in (28cm) long, with a box labelled 'Duvelleroy' and literature describing the painting.
£1,000–1,200
€/ **$1,600–1,800** ⊞ G&G

A fan, the skin leaf painted with a Biblical scene, the pierced ivory guards and sticks applied with mother-of-pearl and decorated with silver *piqué*, Italian, c1740, 10¾in (27.5cm) long.
£400–480
€/ **$630–760** ⚒ S(O)

A fan, the skin leaf painted with Venus and Adonis within a floral border, the reverse painted with a country scene, the mother-of-pearl guards and sticks pierced and carved with figures, French, c1760, 11¾in (30cm) long.
£500–600
€/ **$790–950** ⚒ S(O)

A fan, the paper leaf painted with reserves of figures in landscapes, the pierced ivory sticks painted with scrolls and zigzag shafts, the guards carved with a figure of a woman, with trailing fruit and scrolls, some wear, French, c1760, 21½in (54.5cm) wide.
£220–250
€/ **$350–400** ⚒ BR

▶ **A fan,** the paper leaf painted with figures on a terrace, c1760, 10in (25.5cm) long.
£55–70
€/ **$85–110** ⊞ VB

A fan, the paper leaf painted with a classical scene, the reverse painted with a country dance, with pierced, carved and gilded ivory guards and sticks, c1770, 10¾in (27cm) wide, with associated case.
£1,300–1,500
€/ **$2,000–2,400** ⚒ S(O)

A fan, painted with figures in a landscape, the tortoiseshell sticks pierced and gilded, French, c1770, 19in (48.5cm) wide, framed.
£420–500
€/ **$660–790** ⊞ LDC

A fan, the silk leaf painted with a parrot and doves, outlined in gold braid and trimmed with sequins, French, c1775, 19in (48.5cm) wide, framed.
£550–600
€/ **$870–950** ⊞ LDC

A fan, the leaf painted with figures in a landscape, with pierced and gilded mother-of-pearl sticks, 18thC, 18in (45.5cm) wide, framed.
£300–350
€/ **$470–550** ⚒ MEA

A pair of Chinese export ivory brisé fans, pierced with foliate roundels and shields, early 19thC, 10in (25.5cm) long, framed.
£650–750
€/ **$1,000–1,200** ⚒ S(O)

A fan, the leaf painted with musicians in a landscape, with carved, pierced and gilded horn sticks, c1820, 19in (48.5cm) wide, framed.
£360–400
€/ **$570–630** ⊞ LDC

◄ A fan, painted with a romantic scene, the reverse with putti holding garlands of flowers, with gilded mother-of-pearl sticks, French, c1840, 11in (28cm) long.
£1,000–1,200
€ / **$1,600–1,900**
✗ S(O)

A fan, the paper leaf painted with figures watching a young shepherd proposing to his lover, signed 'Goslin Maison Dorée', the reverse painted with ribbon-tied floral sprays, with pierced, carved and gilded mother-of-pearl guards and sticks, French, c1840, 11in (28cm) long.
£420–500
€ / **$660–790** ✗ S(O)

A fan, the skin leaf depicting a *fête champêtre*, signed 'Malay Dubois avernes', the pierced and carved mother-of-pearl sticks gilded in three colours, French, c1849, 10½in (26.5cm) long.
380–450
/ **$600–700** ✗ S(O)

A fan, the Chantilly leaf with tortoiseshell guards and sticks, slight damage, mid-19thC, 11in (28cm) long.
£180–200
€ / **$280–300** ⊞ HL

A fan, the leaf of Brussels needlepoint appliqué lace, Belgian, c1860, 10in (25.5cm) long.
£220–250
€ / **$350–400** ⊞ HL

A *shibayama* ivory brisé fan, one side decorated with birds among clematis, the reverse with butterflies and birds in a shrubbery, Japanese, late 19thC, 10¾in (27.5cm) wide.
£2,000–2,200
€ / **$3,200–3,500** ✗ S(O)

Chinese export brisé fan, the tortoiseshell, ivory and sandalwood sticks carved with *girures* in domestic and garden settings, the ivory guards with figures, prunus blossom and flowers, 19thC, 13in (33cm) long, with a black and gilt lacquer box.
550–650
/ **$870–1,000** ✗ TMA

A paper and wood fan, advertising Vichy, French, 1880s, 11in (28cm) long.
£90–100
€ / **$140–160** ⊞ JUJ

paper fan, advertising chocolate, French, 1880s, 10in (25.5cm) long.
90–100
/ **$140–160** ⊞ JUJ

A pair of silkwork fans, with pierced ivory handles, Chinese, early 20thC, 15¾in (40cm) long.
£65–75
€ / **$100–120** ✗ AMB

◄ An Edwardian fan, the leaf with applied decoration, with gilded wooden sticks and guards, mother-of-pearl detail on the ring, and a silk tassel finger ring, 13in (33cm) long.
£115–125
€ / **$180–200**
⊞ SAT

A lacquered ivory fan, both sides decorated in gold with swallows and plants, with the Imperial *kiku-mon* on both of the outer sticks, silver mount, Japanese, c1900, 9¾in (25cm) long, with lacquered box.
£2,500–3,000
€ / **$4,000–4,800** ✗ S(O)
This fan was an Imperial gift to the Prince of Wales (subsequently Edward VIII), in 1922. He gave it to the lacquer restorer G. Koizumi.

FANS

Jewellery
Bangles & Bracelets

An enamel bracelet, with five plaques depicting maidens, each within a turquoise and ruby-set cannetille border, the bracelet strap with a gem-set clasp, damage and losses, Swiss, c1830, 7¾in (19.5cm) long.
£600–700
€ / $950–1,100 ⚒ B(Kn)

A gold and citrine bracelet, the mixed-cut citrine with a repoussé border with circular-cut citrine accents, with a mesh bracelet, c1850, 6¾in (17cm) long.
£800–900
€ / $1,300–1,400 ⚒ S(O)

An Estruscan-style gold and lapis lazuli bangle, by Robert Philips & Sons, with applied beaded wirework and two lapis lazuli hinged panels with internal inscription '19th September 1878', with applied maker's marks, 19thC.
£3,500–4,000
€ / $5,500–6,300 ⚒ Bea

A gold, enamel, diamond and sapphire bracelet, c1880, 6½in (16.5cm) long.
£2,500–3,000
€ / $4,000–4,700 ⊞ SGr

A two-colour gold jarretière bracelet, with a beaded surround, and buckle clasp, c1890.
£280–320
€ / $440–510 ⚒ HAM

An enamel and diamond bangle and earring suite, the hinged hollow-work bangle with an enamel and rose-cut diamond detail, with a pair of ear studs en suite, minor damage, c1890, 2¼in (5.5cm) diam.
£530–630
€ / $840–1,000 ⚒ B(Kn)

A garnet-set hinged bangle, the front with a flowerhead cluster, 19thC.
£170–200
€ / $270–320 ⚒ G(L)

A 15ct gold bangle, formed to depict a musical stave, with 'Melba' set in diamonds, c1890, 2½in (6.5cm) diam.
£1,600–1,800
€ / $2,500–2,800 ⊞ NBL
This bangle was given as a present by the opera singer Dame Nellie Melba.

A late Victorian sapphire and diamond bangle, with case.
£1,000–1,200
€ / $1,600–1,900 ⚒ GTH

A hardstone bracelet, 19thC, 7½in (19cm) long, with original case by William Robb.
£550–650
€ / $870–1,000 ⚒ S(O)

◄ A gold bracelet, each link with a foliate border and cluster detail to the centre, 19thC, 6¾in (17cm) long.
£400–500
€ / $630–800 ⚒ B(Kn)

A Victorian bracelet, each link set with a turquoise stone.
£320–375
€ / $510–590 ⚲ B(O)

A Victorian 9ct gold opal and diamond-set hinged bangle, with case.
£110–130
€ / $170–210 ⚲ DMC

A Victorian gold and seed pearl-mounted bangle.
£320–375
€ / $510–590 ⚲ BIG

An Edwardian gold and amethyst bracelet,
3in (7.5cm) diam, cased.
£350–420
€ / $550–670 ⚲ B(Kn)

A 15ct gold bracelet, with double curb links, c1910,
3¾in (9.5cm) long.
£550–600
€ / $870–950 ⊞ WIM

A silver-gilt and enamel bracelet, c1910, 7½in (19cm) long.
£180–200
€ / $280–320 ⊞ SGr

A gold filigree bracelet, wrought in six sections, each
set with a pearl, c1920.
£100–115
€ / $160–180 ⚲ LCM

A Victorian 15ct gold bracelet, set with multi-coloured
gem stones, including sapphire and garnet,
2½in (6.5cm) diam.
£1,800–2,000
€ / $2,800–3,200 ⊞ WIM

A 15ct gold bracelet, c1900, 3½in (9cm) diam.
£630–700
€ / $1,000–1,100 ⊞ WIM

An Edwardian gold hinged bangle, set with a row of
alternating rubies and pearls within a rope-twist border.
£230–275
€ / $360–430 ⚲ G(L)

JEWELLERY

Brooches

A **gold brooch,** depicting Masonic devices in mother-of-pearl, enamel and gold on a blue glass ground, late 18thC, 1¼in (3cm) wide.
£230–275
€/ **$360–430** ⚒ DN

A **15ct gold-foiled amethyst Maltese cross brooch,** with cannetille work, c1830, 2in (5cm) wide.
£800–880
€/ **$1,300–1,400** ⊞ EXC

▶ A **carved bog oak brooch,** in the shape of a harp, Irish, c1870, 3in (7.5cm) long.
£90–100
€/ **$140–160** ⊞ STA

A **George III locket brooch,** set with pearls and rose-cut diamonds on a *guilloche* enamel ground, within a rose-cut diamond border, with a glazed locket compartment to the reverse, 1½in (4cm) wide.
£650–750
€/ **$1,000–1,200** ⚒ L

A **Florentine mosaic and gold brooch,** set with hardstone flowers including chalcedony, lapiz lazuli and turquoise, the frame with scrolling wirework decoration and a rope-twist border, Italian, mid-19thC, in original case.
£850–1,000
€/ **$1,300–1,600** ⚒ WW

A **15ct gold, enamel and pearl brooch,** c1890, 1in (2.5cm) wide.
£700–780
€/ **$1,100–1,200** ⊞ SGr

▶ A **Victorian 18ct gold reverse-painted crystal intaglio brooch,** depicting a fox's head, on a 15ct gold pin, ½in (1cm) diam.
£120–140
€/ **$190–220** ⚒ SWO

A **Victorian gold brooch,** set with five amethysts, with wirework decoration and a locket back.
£160–200
€/ **$250–315** ⚒ G(L)

▶ A **Vauxhall glass brooch,** formed as a floral cluster, c1800.
£170–200
€/ **$270–315** ⚒ WW

An **early Victorian garnet and seed pearl brooch,** with a glass compartment containing hair, 1in (2.5cm) wide.
£175–200
€/ **$280–320** ⚒ RIT

A **silver and gold kunzite and diamond brooch,** c1860.
£1,700–2,000
€/ **$2,700–3,200** ⚒ BUK
Kunzite is a gem variety of the mineral spodumene which fluoresces when illuminated.

A **late Victorian diamond brooch,** in the form of a Staffordshire knot, the diamonds set in silver and backed in gold.
£850–1,000
€/ **$1,300–1,600** ⚒ WL

An enamelled gold, sapphire and diamond-mounted brooch, by Carlo Guiliano, the central star sapphire within an enamelled frame surrounding old brilliant-cut diamonds and star sapphires, the pin hinge with applied maker's mark, late 19thC.
€3,500–4,000
€ / $5,500–6,300 ➤ Bea

A silver quartz-set Luckenbooth brooch, Scottish, 19thC.
€320–375
€ / $500–590 ➤ B(Ed)

A Victorian 15ct gold and turquoise brooch, 1½in (4cm) diam.
€1,000–1,100
€ / $1,600–1,700 ⊞ WIM

A porcelain and gilt-metal-mounted brooch, painted with the Madonna and child, Continental, late 19thC, 2¼in (5.5cm) long.
£100–120
€ / $160–190 ➤ BR

A Victorian gold, enamel and half-pearl brooch, with a locket reverse.
£150–175
€ / $240–275 ➤ GTH

A Victorian diamond and moonstone brooch, designed as four cherub faces with diamond-set wings below.
£4,500–5,200
€ / $7,100–8,200 ➤ HYD

◄ A 15ct gold, enamel and diamond brooch, c1900, 1in (2.5cm) diam.
£450–500
€ / $700–850 ⊞ SGr

► An Edwardian gold-mounted mother-of-pearl brooch, carved in high relief with figures of a Dutch boy and girl, with a pearl border, 1½in (4cm) diam.
£380–460
€ / $600–720 ➤ F&C

A pebble brooch, set with hardstone, 19thC.
£260–320
€ / $400–500 ➤ S

A Victorian diamond brooch, in the shape of an anchor with a rope twist, set with 33 graduated old-cut stones, 1¾in (4cm) long.
£2,000–2,400
€ / $3,200–3,800 ➤ BWL

A Victorian gold brooch and earrings set, the brooch with a raised boss centre, the earrings with tassel drops, with case.
£475–565
€ / $750–890 ➤ GAK

JEWELLERY

Cameos

A shell cameo pendant
brooch, depicting a
bacchante, in a gold frame
with beaded and rope
pattern-twist decoration,
Italian, mid-19thC, in
original fitted case.
£650–750
€/ $1,000–1,200 ⚒ WW

A mid-Victorian
sardonyx cameo brooch,
depicting a neo-classical
lady, the frame set with
ruby cabochons within a
rope-twist border, cased.
£350–420
€/ $550–660 ⚒ B(L)

A lava cameo bracelet, the cameos carved to depict
classical deities in profile, with a concealed clasp, c1860,
7in (17.5cm) long.
£300–360
€/ $475–575 ⚒ B(Kn)

A Victorian gold-framed
shell cameo brooch/
pendant, with a portrait
of a gentleman, with a
hair-panel back.
£600–700
€/ $950–1,100 ⚒ GAK

A gold-set cameo pendant,
carved with snowdrops,
the edge engraved with an
inscription, a locket containing
hair on the reverse, c1870,
¾in (2cm) long.
£300–325
€/ $475–500 ⊞ AMC

A gold-framed shell
cameo brooch, carved
with a classical scene, 19thC.
£250–300
€/ $400–475 ⚒ Bea

A lava cameo brooch,
carved with two putti,
c1880, 2in (5cm) long.
£385–460
€/ $600–720 ⚒ S(O)

A lava cameo bracelet, the panels carved with classical
busts, 19thC.
£280–325
€/ $440–500 ⚒ DN

A Victorian shell cameo brooch,
carved with Apollo, Ayrora and the
Sun, in a gold mount.
£1,200–1,400
€/ $1,900–2,200 ⚒ TEN

◄ A Victorian cameo brooch,
carved with the bust of a lady with
flowers in her hair, in a yellow-metal
and turquoise mount.
£450–525
€/ $710–830 ⚒ CHTR

A 9ct gold shell cameo brooch,
carved with a classical female
profile, late 19thC.
£230–275
€/ $360–430 ⚒ G(L)

A pair of late Victorian 15ct gold
cameo earrings, 1¾in (4.5cm) long.
£1,200–1,300
€/ $1,900–2,000 ⊞ WIM

◄ A cameo brooch, carved with
a Roman bust, set in plain gold
mount, c1900, 2¼in (5.5cm) long.
£315–350
€/ $500–550 ⊞ AMC

Cufflinks

A pair of gold cufflinks, with Essex crystal depictions of game dogs, inscribed 'Eliot Farley', late 19thC.
£1,000–1,200
€/ **$1,600–1,900** ⚲ TEN

A pair of reverse intaglio cufflinks, each depicting a dog, mounted on mother-of-pearl, c1900.
£1,600–2,000
€/ **$2,500–3,200** ⚲ S

A pair of gold and emerald cufflinks, by Mellerio, French, c1900, ½in (1cm) diam.
£800–900
€/ **$1,300–1,400** ⊞ WIM

A pair of 9ct rose-gold cufflinks, the double-faced plaques engraved with foliate designs, maker's mark SP, hallmarked Birmingham 1906.
£80–100
€/ **$130–160** ⚲ RIT

A pair of platinum and sapphire cufflinks, set with cabochon sapphires, within reeded platinum and mother-of-pearl surrounds, c1910.
£220–250
€/ **$350–400** ⚲ HAM

A pair of 18ct gold and enamel cufflinks, c1925, ½in (1cm) wide.
£720–800
€/ **$1,100–1,300** ⊞ WIM

Earrings

◀ **A pair of diamond and half-pearl pendant earrings,** c1890, with fitted case.
£800–950
€/ **$1,300–1,500** ⚲ HAM

A pair of Victorian 15ct gold earrings, set with armandine garnets, 1½in (4cm) long.
£800–900
€/ **$1,300–1,400** ⊞ WIM

A pair of Victorian gold drop earrings.
£100–120
€/ **$160–190** ⚲ L

◀ **A pair of platinum and diamond pendant earrings,** the whole set with diamonds of 23ct, and with 50 diamonds of 6.5ct, c1945.
£96,000–115,000
€/ **$152,000–182,000** ⚲ S(NY)
From the collection of Eva Peron.

A pair of black opal doublet and diamond pendant earrings, the openwork surmount millegrain-set with single and brilliant-cut diamonds, c1930, 1½in (4cm) long.
£825–1,000
€/ **$1,300–1,600** ⚲ B(Kn)

Necklaces

A paste necklace, composed of a series of stylized floral cluster sections, enclosed in silver, c1775.
£2,800–3,400
€/ **$4,400–5,400** ➶ WW

A Georgian pinchbeck chain, with a hand clasp, 46in (117cm) long.
£1,300–1,500
€/ **$2,000–2,400** ⊞ WIM

An early Victorian paste parure, comprising a necklace, two bracelets, a pair of ear pendants and a brooch, with closed back settings, in a fitted case.
£850–1,000
€/ **$1,300–1,600** ➶ B(Ed)

A 9ct gold and amethyst necklace, with cannetille work settings and chain suspensions, on a belcher-link chain, c1830.
£360–450
€/ **$575–700** ➶ B(O)

▶ **A 15ct rose-gold foil-backed amethyst necklace,** c1840, 15in (38cm) long.
£2,000–2,300
€/ **$3,200–3,600** ⊞ EXC

A gold and amethyst necklace, c1840, 13in (33cm) long.
£3,300–3,600
€/ **$5,200–5,700** ⊞ SGr

A garnet necklace, with floral bud and flower sections in foiled-back gold settings, with a detachable flower drop pendant, c1840, 17¼in (43cm) long.
£1,400–1,600
€/ **$2,200–2,500** ➶ LJ

A gold, garnet and diamond serpent necklace, the cabochon garnet serpent's head with rose-diamond eyes and nose, suspending a cabochon garnet heart, a glazed locket to the reverse, on a graduated link chain, with a fitted case, c1845.
£3,500–4,200
€/ **$5,500–6,600** ➶ WW

Items in the Jewellery section have been arranged in date order within each sub-section.

A coral demi-parure, comprising a necklace, bracelet and pendant earrings, each depicting fruiting vines, c1850.
£300–350
€/ **$475–550** ➶ TEN

A pendant necklace, the central pierced plaque with a cabochon garnet, Austro-Hungarian, c1880.
£400–480
€/ **$630–750** ➶ B(Kn)

◀ **A diamond fringe necklace,** the reeded tubular link suspending diamond-set flowerheads, mounted in silver and gold, c1880, 14¼in (36cm) long.
£2,000–2,400
€/ **$3,200–3,800** ➶ HAM

A 15ct gold half-pearl necklace, c1890, 8in (20.5cm) long, in a fitted case.
£2,000–2,300
€ / **$3,200–3,600** ⊞ **WIM**

A late Victorian coral necklace, on a box-link chain, the central three cartouches detachable, 15in (38cm) long.
£1,200–1,500
€ / **$1,900–2,400** ➤ **B(Kn)**

A Victorian garnet necklace, on a trace link chain.
£600–700
€ / **$950–1,100** ➤ **TEN**

An Edwardian peridot and seed pearl necklace, suspended from lattice work links, on a back chain.
£280–320
€ / **$440–500** ➤ **B(O)**

An Edwardian necklace, with aquamarines, pink tourmalines and seed pearls, in a fitted case.
£1,300–1,500
€ / **$2,100–2,400** ➤ **L**

▶ **A poured glass demi-parure,** comprising a neck-lace of graduated flower-heads mounted in gilt metal, and a pair of matching earclips, c1930, with two cardboard Chanel boxes.
£750–880
€ / **$1,200–1,400** ➤ **WW**

A late Victorian garnet necklace, on a trace-link chain, 18in (45.5cm) long.
£550–620
€ / **$870–980** ➤ **B(Kn)**

A Victorian seed pearl necklace, on a curb-link chain, 18in (45.5cm) long.
£650–750
€ / **$1,000–1,200** ➤ **B(Kn)**

◀ **A 14ct and 10ct two-colour gold necklace and bracelet set,** both pieces inset with small pearls and mother-of-pearl, some losses, c1900.
£200–240
€ / **$315–380** ➤ **LCM**

A Belle Epoque *sautoir*, the diamond and pearl pendant with a seed pearl tassel, and suspended from a seed pearl necklace, c1910, 17¾in (45cm) long.
£650–720
€ / **$1,000–1,100** ➤ **HAM**

A platinum, diamond and opal necklace, with a pair of earrings *en suite*, c1930.
£2,500–2,800
€ / **$4,000–4,400** ➤ **BUK**

JEWELLERY

Pendants

A silver and gold open-work pendant/brooch, of flowerhead foliate design, set with rose-cut diamonds and green paste, Spanish, 18thC, in a fitted case.
£280–320
€/ **$440–500** ⚒ **G(L)**

A gold pendant, mounted with a hair plait, with cherub motifs and gold wirework beneath a faceted crystal, 18thC.
£1,000–1,100
€/ **$1,600–1,700** ⚒ **Bea**

An amethyst, citrine and topaz pendant, with a locket back, 1790–1800, ¾in (2cm) long.
£1,200–1,300
€/ **$1,900–2,100** ⊞ **WIM**

A rose-cut diamond and enamel cross pendant/brooch, possibly French, c1840, 1¼in (3cm) long.
£1,600–1,800
€/ **$2,500–2,800** ⊞ **NBL**

A 15ct gold, diamond and garnet pendant, c1880.
£300–360
€/ **$475–570** ⚒ **LJ**

A turquoise, ruby and diamond-mounted dove pendant, on a simulated seed pearl chain, mid-19thC.
£1,200–1,400
€/ **$1,900–2,200** ⚒ **Bea**

An enamelled pendant, by A. Phillips, inset with pearls and rubies, c1860, 3in (7.5cm) long.
£5,800–6,500
€/ **$9,200–10,400** ⊞ **SGr**

◄ **A heart-shaped pendant,** set with zircons on a diamond ground, c1880, 1in (2.5cm) long.
£2,000–2,200
€/ **$3,200–3,500** ⚒ **S(O)**

An enamel, gold and pearl pendant, set within a ropework and bead surround, suspending a baroque pearl drop, c1860.
£200–220
€/ **$315–350** ⚒ **TEN**

A Victorian gold and silver rose-diamond-set pendant/brooch, the lattice design over enamel.
£700–820
€/ **$1,100–1,300** ⚒ **G(L)**

A gold locket, with a citrine in a raised claw setting, on a chased gold surround set with various hardstones, opening to reveal glazed hair compartment, Scottish, 19thC.
£460–550
€/ **$720–870** ⚒ **WW**

► **A Victorian gold and coral bead pendant,** the reverse with a plaited hair compartment, on a fancy link chain.
£180–220
€/ **$280–350** ⚒ **G(L)**

A Victorian diamond and enamel heart pendant, on a gold chain with enamel barrel spacers.
£1,800–2,200
€/ **$2,800–3,500** ⚒ **B(Ed)**

An 18ct gold-framed pendant badge, by Isaac Pothecary, with an enamel panel depicting the Tower of London below the crest of the City of London, the reverse with a presentation inscription to the Sheriff of London 1896.
£1,400–1,600
€/ **$2,200–2,500** ⚒ **CGC**

A Victorian pendant, with three cabochon garnets overlaid with a band set with diamonds, the suspension loop set with five diamonds.
£900–1,100
€ / **$1,400–1,700** ⚲ HYD

A gold, enamel, pearl and diamond pendant, in the manner of Giuliano, with a diamond and pearl drop and a cluster suspension loop, 19thC.
£6,500–7,800
€ / **$10,300–12,300** ⚲ DN

◄ **A gold pendant,** the amethyst-coloured stone set in a border of seed pearls, surrounded by a border of alternate amethysts and pearls, 1880–1910, 2½in (6.5cm) long.
£350–400
€ / **$550–630** ⚲ CGC

A reverse intaglio crystal pendant, depicting a finch among oak leaves, the reverse inset with a miniature portrait of a lady, in a gold bead and wirework frame, 19thC.
£500–600
€ / **$800–950** ⚲ G(L)

A Victorian pebble cross pendant, set with blood-stone and variegated agate, mounted in gold, engraved with flowerhead and foliate borders, Scottish.
£780–940
€ / **$1,200–1,500** ⚲ B(Ed)

A 9ct gold heart-shaped openwork pendant, set with amethysts and seed pearls, on a fine gold chain, together with a pair of similar earrings, c1900.
£170–200
€ / **$270–315** ⚲ G(L)

► **A gold and platinum pendant,** set with a carved moonstone, with diamonds and synthetic sapphires and a pearl frame, c1900.
£1,700–2,000
€ / **$2,700–3,200** ⚲ BUK

A peridot and half-pearl pendant, c1900.
£420–500
€ / **$660–790** ⚲ TEN

An amethyst and seed pearl pendant, of scrolling shield design, Continental, c1900.
£160–200
€ / **$250–315** ⚲ B(O)

An opal and diamond pendant, c1900, 2in (5cm) long.
£2,200–2,400
€ / **$3,500–3,800** ⊞ WIM

An Edwardian 9ct gold pendant, with a central amethyst and seed pearl drop, on an elongated link chain.
£100–120
€ / **$160–190** ⚲ G(L)

An Edwardian 15ct gold heart-shaped openwork pendant, set with peridots and seed pearls.
£160–200
€ / **$250–315** ⚲ G(L)

► **A 15ct gold and platinum black opal pendant,** c1910, 3in (7.5cm) long.
£1,200–1,400
€ / **$1,900–2,200** ⊞ WIM

Rings

A Claddagh ring, c1750.
£800–880
€/ $1,300–1,400 ⊞ SAY

An emerald and diamond ring, c1880.
£650–750
€/ $1,000–1,200 ✗ S(O)

An enamelled gold and garnet mourning ring, with a central skull and crossbones motif beneath a crystal, mid-18thC.
£1,400–1,600
€/ $2,200–2,500 ✗ Bea

A Victorian 18ct gold snake ring, 1in (2.5cm) diam.
£550–600
€/ $870–950 ⊞ WIM

◀ **A Victorian diamond and split-pearl engraved half-hoop ring.**
£220–250
€/ $350–400 ✗ SWO

A gold and platinum ring, set with blue enamel and decorated with the monogram of Maximilian I, with diamond encrustations, and decorated on the laterals with Imperial eagles, Austrian, 1864, with original red velvet case bearing the inscription 'Roth Jeweller of His Majesty the Emperor of Austria Vienna'.
£4,000–4,500
€/ $6,300–7,100 ✗ LCM

An opal and diamond ring, with pierced shoulders, opal cracked, c1900.
£550–620
€/ $870–980 ✗ TEN

Stick Pins

An 18ct gold stick pin, by Renée Foy for Boucheron, set with a garnet, c1875, 3½in (9cm) long.
£1,100–1,200
€/ $1,700–1,900 ⊞ WIM

A gold and diamond snake stick pin, 19thC.
£200–220
€/ $315–350 ✗ Bea

A diamond stick pin, set with a circular-cut diamond and a smaller stone, c1880, 1¾in (4.5cm) long.
£470–550
€/ $740–870 ✗ S(O)

◀ **An enamelled gold double snake stick pin,** with diamond eyes, surrounding a banded agate central stone, c1890, 3¼in (8.5cm) long.
£500–550
€/ $790–870 ⊞ ANO

A Victorian gold, diamond and opal stick pin, the central opal with a serpent surround, set throughout with old-cut diamonds, opal cracked.
£240–260
€/ $380–400 ✗ B(O)

A diamond stick pin, c1890, 2¾in (7cm) long.
£500–600
€/ $790–950 ✗ S(O)

A diamond and sapphire stick pin, the finial modelled as a fly, set with old- and rose-cut diamonds, a sapphire and red stone cabochon eyes, c1890.
£90–110
€/ $140–170 ✗ B(O)

JEWELLERY

Enamel

An enamel patch box, painted with an exotic bird, butterflies and foliage, c1900, 2in (5cm) wide.
£275–300
€/ **$430–480** ⊞ LBr

A silver-gilt and cloisonné enamel snuff box, the top decorated with birds and butterflies, the sides with foliage, Russian, St Petersburg 1908–17, 2¾in (7cm) wide.
£470–550
€/ **$740–870** ➚ WW

An enamel cosmetic box, the top painted with a couple, the base gilded with a foliate spray, French, 19thC, 2¾in (7cm) diam.
£280–320
€/ **$440–500** ➚ TMA

A silver and enamel dressing table set, Birmingham 1947, brush 10½in (26.5cm) long.
£100–120
€/ **$160–190** ➚ SWO

A pair of gilt-brass and enamel opera glasses, by Prosper Bunouste, Palais Royale, Paris, French, c1860, 4in (10.5cm) wide.
£270–300
€/ **$425–475** ⊞ HUM

A silver and cloisonné enamel tea-glass holder, maker's mark 'S.K.', Moscow 1899–1908, Russian, 4¼in (11cm) high.
£700–850
€/ **$1,100–1,300** ➚ S(O)

◄ **A Limoges-style enamel panel,** depicting a muse and her handmaidens in a sparse landscape, in a cast-bronze frame with floral trophy mantle, French, 19thC, 8in (20.5cm) high.
£340–400
€/ **$540–630** ➚ HOLL

► **A set of silver-gilt and enamel spoons,** comprising 12 teaspoons and a serving spoon, the backs enamelled with foliage on a gilded stippled ground, Russian, Moscow c1900, largest 5¾in (14.5cm) long.
£1,100–1,300
€/ **$1,700–2,000** ➚ S(NY)

A set of four silver-gilt and enamel salts, with four enamel-backed spoons, Russian, St Petersburg c1900, salts 1¾in (4.5cm) diam, with original case.
£650–780
€/ **$1,000–1,200** ➚ L

A set of six silver-gilt and cloisonné enamel coffee spoons, by Maria Semenova, Russian, Moscow 1896–1908, 4in (10cm) long.
£1,500–1,700
€/ **$2,400–2,700** ⊞ MIR

A pair of Imperial cloisonné enamel sugar tongs, 11th Artel, Russian, Moscow, 1908–1917, 4in (10cm) long.
£340–380
€/ **$540–600** ⊞ SHa

► **A Limoges enamel tray,** painted with an aristocrat surprising a servant, monogrammed 'F.C.', some damage, 19thC, 4¾in (12cm) square.
£130–160
€/ **$200–220** ➚ SWO

ENAMEL

Fabergé

◀ **A Fabergé silver-gilt and jade bell,** Moscow 1908–17, 2½in (6.5cm) high.
£2,800–3,200
€/ $4,400–5,100 ♪ DuM

A Fabergé silver and cut-glass bowl, marked 'K. Fabergé', Moscow c1910, 8¾in (22cm) wide.
£3,800–4,500
€/ $6,000–7,100 ♪ S(NY)

A Fabergé gold, silver and enamel box, workmaster Henrik Wigström, with diamond-chip cluster lip clasp, enamel chipped, marked, import marks for 1911, 2in (5cm) diam.
£550–650
€/ $870–950 ♪ SWO

A Fabergé gold, enamel and diamond brooch, marked 'K.F.', Moscow c1900, 1¼in (3cm) wide, in original holly wood box.
£10,000–12,000
€/ $15,800–19,000 ♪ S(O)

A Fabergé gold cigarette case, workmaster Henrik Wigström, the thumbpiece set with a sapphire, St Petersburg 1908–17, 4in (10cm) high.
£2,300–2,800
€/ $3,600–4,400 ♪ DORO

A Fabergé silver and enamel dish, workmaster Karl Gustav Hjalmar Armfelt, the translucent enamel over a *guilloché* ground, St Petersburg, c1890, 4in (10cm) wide.
£5,800–7,000
€/ $9,200–11,000 ♪ S(NY)

A Fabergé cane handle, workmaster Michael Perchin, the translucent enamel over engine-turned silver, the rim applied with gold, St Petersburg 1896–99, 1½in (4cm) high, in original silk-lined holly wood box.
£5,500–6,500
€/ $8,600–10,200 ♪ B

▶ **A Fabergé silver and wood frame,** workmaster Feodor Afanassiev, St Petersburg c1910, 11½in (29cm) high.
£3,500–4,000
€/ $5,500–6,300 ♪ S(NY)

A Fabergé miniature egg, gold-mounted rock crystal, the reverse intaglio-enamelled with the flower of St Nicholas, c1905, ½in (1cm) long.
£3,800–4,300
€/ $6,000–6,800 ⊞ SHa

Gold

A gold-mounted bottle, the cagework inset with diamonds, emeralds and rubies, French, c1890, 3in (7.5cm) long.
€3,500–3,600
€ / $5,500–5,600 ⊞ LBr

▶ An 18ct gold-mounted scent bottle, French, c1850, 4in (10cm) high.
€2,000–2,200
€ / $3,200–3,500 ⊞ SHa

An 18ct gold box, by Charles Rowlings and William Summer, London 1844–45, 4in (10cm) wide.
£3,500–4,000
€ / $5,500–6,300 ⊞ NS

A gold and enamel snuff box, the lid later inset with a German School portrait miniature of a young lady, maker's mark 'MS' and charge mark of Alaterre, some restoration, late 18thC, 3½in (9cm) long.
£2,800–3,200
€ / $4,400–5,100 ⚒ S(O)

A gold box, the lid centred by a medallion, the sides and base with engine-turned panels within chased foliate borders, probably German, early 19thC, 3in (7.5cm) wide.
£520–630
€ / $820–980 ⚒ S(Am)

A gold-mounted jasper snuff box, the sides and border of the lid chased with scrolling foliate decoration, c1745, 2¾in (7cm) long.
£1,300–1,500
€ / $2,000–2,400 ⚒ WW

A 9ct gold vesta case, by Joseph Walton & Co, London 1920, 1¾in (4.5cm) wide.
£160–200
€ / $250–315 ⚒ WW

A gold-mounted aventurine snuff box, Italian, c1840, 3in (7.5cm) wide.
£2,000–2,400
€ / $3,200–3,800 ⊞ G&G

A George IV-style 9ct gold engine-turned snuff box, with floral-chased borders and reeded sides, London 1929, 3¼in (8.5cm) wide.
£480–565
€ / $760–890 ⚒ DN

A gold folding telescopic monocular, with a single draw and pendant ring, c1875, 2½in (6.5cm) long, with original morocco case.
£230–275
€ / $360–430 ⚒ WW

▶ A gold-mounted bloodstone vinaigrette, the hinged lid with suspension loop and a rose-cut diamond, German, c1760, 1½in (4cm) high.
£600–700
€ / $950–1,100 ⚒ G(L)

A gold and cornelian vinaigrette, the interior with perforated grille, early 19thC, 1½in (4cm) wide.
£600–700
€ / $950–1,100 ⚒ G(L)

Asian Works of Art
Cloisonné & Enamel

A cloisonné box and cover, the top decorated with the *shou* character and stylized flowerheads, Chinese, Qianlong period, 1736–95, 2¾in (7cm) diam.
£500–550
€/ **$800–880** ⊞ G&G

A cloisonné desk set, comprising a tray, ink blotter, inkwell and cover, round pot, pen and letter opener, decorated with dragons chasing the flaming pearl, signed Laotainii Zhi, Chinese, 19thC, tray 11in (28cm) long.
£1,300–1,500
€/ **$2,100–2,400** ⊞ AUA

▶ **A cloisonné plaque,** decorated with cranes perched in flowering branches on a pink ground, Japanese, late 19thC, 19¾in x 12in (50 x 32cm).
£1,400–1,600
€/ **$2,200–2,500** ⚲ DN

A pair of cloisonné enamel vases, decorated with peonies, Japanese, late 19thC, 4¾in (12cm) high, with original padded pine box.
£100–110
€/ **$160–175** ⚲ PFK

▶ **A pair of cloisonné vases,** decorated with three panels of spring flowers and birds, Japanese, Meiji period, 1868–1911, 5in (12.5cm) high.
£650–750
€/ **$1,000–1,200** ⚲ BUK

A cloisonné jewelled and enamelled box, decorated with flowers and birds, the hinged cover centred with a diamond-set rosette, Indian, 19thC, 2¼in (5.5cm) wide.
£2,200–2,500
€/ **$3,500–4,000** ⚲ B(Kn)

A pair of cloisonné jars and covers, decorated with flowers and butterflies on a black ground, Chinese, c1880, 5in (13.5cm) high.
£200–225
€/ **$320–350** ⊞ PSA

An Imperial Canton enamel cup and saucer, in the shape of a peach, with pointed tip and branch-like handle with blossom and leaves, the interior decorated with two bats, Chinese, Yonzheng/Qianlong period, 18thC, saucer 4¾in (12cm) wide.
£3,800–4,500
€/ **$6,000–7,000** ⚲ S(HK)

A cloisonné *koro* and cover, worked in copper wire with a flock of white cranes, Japanese, Meiji period, 1868–1911, 5in (13cm) high.
£800–900
€/ **$1,300–1,400** ⚲ S(O)

A cloisonné teapot, Japanese, late 19thC, 3½in (9cm) high.
£120–140
€/ **$190–220** ⚲ DuM

A pair of cloisonné vases, decorated with wistaria flowers on a light green ground, Japanese, 19thC, 12½in (32cm) high.
£500–600
€/ **$800–960** ⚲ SWO

Glass

A Peking glass box, decorated with coloured stones, Chinese, late 19thC, 6in (15cm) wide.
£170–200
€ / **$270–320** ⚷ BWL

A reverse painting on glass, depicting the Seven Scholars of the Bamboo Grove, inscribed 'Zhu Lin Qi Xian', Chinese, 19thC, 26in (66cm) wide, in original carved wood frame.
£900–1,000
€ / **$1,400–1,600** ⚷ S(O)

A lemon glass vase, Jiaqing mark and period, 1796–1820, Chinese, 7¾in (19.5cm) high.
£4,500–5,500
€ / **$7,000–8,400** ⚷ S(NY)

Jade

A spinach jade dish, Chinese, 19thC, 9in (23cm) diam.
£900–1,000
€ / **$1,400–1,600** ⊞ GLD

A jade brushpot, carved in the form of a tree trunk, with rust-brown inclusions imitating the surface of the bark, 19thC, 5¼in (13.5cm) high.
£1,100–1,200
€ / **$1,700–1,900** ⚷ S(O)

A celadon jade brush washer, carved in the form of a curled lotus leaf, c1700, 6½in (16.5cm) wide.
£2,400–2,800
€ / **$3,800–4,400** ⚷ B

Further reading
Miller's Chinese & Japanese Antiques Buyer's Guide, Miller's Publications, 1999

▶ **A celadon jade group,** carved as two peaches with foliage and five bats, Chinese, Qianlong period, 1736–95, 4¼in (11cm) wide.
£1,700–2,000
€ / **$2,700–3,200** ⚷ L

A celadon jade vesssel, the body with eight lobes flanked by a pair of double ring handles with monster masks, Chinese, 19thC, 12¾in (32.5cm) wide.
£1,400–1,600
€ / **$2,200–2,500** ⚷ S(O)

A pale green jade bottle vase, the sides carved with prunus and rock-work, Chinese, 19thC, 4½in (11.5cm) high, with wooden stand.
£2,200–2,600
€ / **$3,500–4,100** ⚷ DN

A jade bottle vase, carved in relief with palmettes, foliage and geometric design, with ring mask handles, on carved wood fretwork stand, Chinese, late 19thC, 13in (33cm) high.
£280–340
€ / **$440–550** ⚷ SWO

ASIAN WORKS OF ART

Lacquer

A red lacquer box and cover, carved with lychee and foliage, some damage, Ming Dynasty, 1368–1644, 3in (7.5cm) high.
£1,700–2,000
€/ **$2,700–3,200** ⚒ G(L)

A lacquer box and cover, in the form of three overlapping clam shells, one decorated with autumn plants and two with landscape scenes in gold and *takamakie* and *togidashi* with details in *kirigane, aogai* and *e-nashiji,* the interior of *nashiji,* Japanese, 19thC, 5½in (14cm) wide.
£2,400–2,800
€/ **$3,800–4,400** ⚒ S(O)

A lacquer dish, signed Shomosai and Kakihan, Japanese, c1900, 5in (12.5cm) diam.
£315–350
€/ **$500–550** ⊞ G&G

▶ A Chinese export lacquer sewing box, c1860, 14½in (37cm) wide.
£850–950
€/ **$1,350–1,500** ⊞ HAA

A lacquered rattan betel box, early 20thC, 8in (20.5cm) high.
£145–160
€/ **$230–250** ⊞ QM
This type of box was used to contain a supply of betel leaves for chewing.

A lacquer offerings box, Burmese, early 20thC, 28in (71cm) high.
£340–380
€/ **$550–600** ⊞ QM

A pair of lacquer jars, decorated in gilt, Japanese, 19thC, 13in (33cm) high.
£900–1,000
€/ **$1,400–1,600** ⊞ FRY

A lacquer box, decorated with cherry blossom, pine and peony in gold and silver, Japanese, 19thC, 9in (23cm) long.
£585–650
€/ **$925–1,000** ⊞ G&G

A lacquer box, with mother-of-pearl inlaid landscape to the cover and flowers to the sides, Chinese, 19thC, 15in (38cm) wide.
£1,300–1,500
€/ **$2,000–2,400** ⚒ BWL

A lacquer box, Chinese, c1890, 7¼in (18.5cm) wide.
£225–250
€/ **$350–400** ⊞ HAA

A lacquer shrine (*Zushi*), the doors with chased gilt-metal mounts, the interior in gilt with the four armed Kannon seated on a pedestal, Japanese, 19thC, 9¾in (25cm) high.
£420–500
€/ **$670–800** ⚒ DN

A Chinese export lacquer tea caddy, on carved dragon feet, c1860, 5in (12.5cm) high.
£1,000–1,200
€ / $1,600–1,900 ⊞ HAA

A pair of *Shibayama* inlaid lacquer vases, with silver-mounted necks, one with a signed red lacquer plaque, one with missing base and damage, Japanese, Meiji period, 1868–1911, 9¼in (23.5cm) high.
£2,800–3,400
€ / $4,400–5,400 ⚒ RTo

A lacquer writing utensil box (*suzuribako*) and cover, decorated with a figure gazing at a rural landscape, the interior with figures pulling barges in a river landscape, some rubbing, Japanese, 19thC, 9in (23cm) wide.
£1,800–2,200
€ / $2,800–3,500 ⚒ DN

Metalware

A bronze basin, with phoenix and fish moulding, old wear, Chinese, Han Dynasty, 206BC–AD220, 17in (43cm) diam.
£3,500–4,000
€ / $5,500–6,300 ⊞ GLD

A bronze buffalo bell, Burmese, 19thC, 4in (10cm) diam.
£160–180
€ / $250–285 ⊞ QM

A cast bronze bell, on a pierced and carved oak stand, Japanese, late 19thC, 44in (112cm) high.
£650–725
€ / $1,000–1,200 ⚒ B(Pr)

A gold and silver-inlaid bronze belt hook (*daigou*), the shaft decorated with gold and silver sheet wire inlay, below a tapering dragon's head hook, Chinese, Warring States Period, 480–221 BC, 5½in (14cm) long.
£580–650
€ / $920–1,000 ⊞ G&G

> **For further information on**
> Metalware see pages 597–603

A cast-iron bowl, the exterior applied in high relief with the Eight Immortals between *chilong* handles, Chinese, Ming Dynasty, 16thC, 8¾in (22cm) diam.
£450–500
€ / $700–800 ⚒ S(O)

A bronze tripod censer, with phoenix-shaped handles, on three feet, Chinese, spurious Xuande mark, 19thC, 3½in (9cm) high.
£170–200
€ / $270–320 ⚒ S(O)

A brass incense burner, Indian, early 19thC, 6in (15cm) diam.
£340–375
€ / $550–600 ⊞ SEA

▶ **A silver-inlaid *huqqa* bottle,** of squat globular form, decorated with panels of flowering shrubs within geometric and foliate-patterned borders, some loss to inlay, Indian, 18th–19thC, 6¼in (16cm) high.
£250–300
€ / $400–475 ⚒ F&C

An iron tripod incense burner and cover, of compressed globular shape, cast in shallow relief with carp rising from tranquil waters, the domed cover cast and pierced with ripples, Japanese, Meiji Period, 1868–1911, 5½in (14cm) diam.
£1,600–1,900
€/ **$2,500–3,000** ⚲ B

A *Shibayama*-panelled silver *koro* and cover, inset with panels of doves, quail, crane, pheasant and other auspicious birds on a gilt ground, with upright dragon handles, finial missing, minor faults, Japanese, Meiji Period, 1868–1911, 6¼in (16cm) high.
£1,300–1,500
€/ **$2,000–2,400** ⚲ RTo

A cast iron mask of Okame, mounted on a pine board, Japanese, 18th–19thC, 8¾in (22cm) high.
£375–425
€/ **$600–670** ⚲ WW
Okame is a character from the No operas. She is the Goddess of laughter, also known as Uzume or Otafuku.

A bronze mask, Japanese, 19thC, 12in (30.5cm) high.
£300–350
€/ **$475–550** ⚲ DuM

▶ **A pair of bronze vases,** cast with dragons, Chinese, 19thC, 9¾in (25cm) high.
£220–250
€/ **$350–400** ⚲ SWO

A set of ten bronze opium weights, in the form of birds and quadrupeds, Chinese, 18th–19thC, largest 2½in (6.5cm) high.
£350–400
€/ **$550–630** ⊞ AUA

A gilt-bronze paperweight, Chinese, Han Dynasty, 206BC–AD220, 2½in (6.5cm) wide.
£2,000–2,500
€/ **$3,200–4,000** ⊞ GLD

A parcel-gilt beaker vase (*gu*), the central section and flaring foot with a pair of raised *taotie* on either side and divided by vertical flanges, the neck with four upright plaintain leaves containing stylized *taotie*, the rim and flanges inlaid with silver *leiwen* bands, Chinese, Ming Dynasty, 17thC, 13¾in (35cm) high.
£1,100–1,300
€/ **$1,700–2,000** ⚲ S(Am)

A silver vase, by Shoryusai, engraved in *shibuichi* and gold, with chrysanthemums and a meandering river, Japanese, Taisho period, 1912–26, 7in (18cm) high.
£2,000–2,200
€/ **$3,200–3,500** ⊞ AUA

A bronze vase, cast with an eagle worked in *shibuichi, shakudo* and gilt, signed, Japanese, Meiji Period, 1868–1911, 10in (25.5cm) high.
£2,500–2,800
€/ **$4,000–4,400** ⊞ LBO

A bronze vase, by Tatsuhiro Akichika, decorated in relief with two dragons struggling for possession of a glass jewel, signed and stamped with a dragonfly, Japanese, Meiji Period, 1868–1911, 13¾in (35cm) high.
£800–900
€/ **$1,300–1,400** ⚲ S(O)

A bronze *yatate*, Japanese, late 19thC, 8in (20.5cm) high.
£120–135
€/ **$190–210** ⊞ FU
A *yatate* is a case to hold a writing brush and ink and is hung from a belt.

Wood

A carved ebony box, Anglo-Indian, c1870, 9in (23cm) wide.
£135–150
€/ **$210–240** ⊞ MB

A root-wood brushpot, with a hardwood rim and fitted hardwood stand with *ruyi*-head feet, Chinese, 19thC, 5½in (14cm) high.
£700–850
€/ **$1,100–1,300** ⚒ S(O)

A bamboo carving of a bunch of grapes, by Qian Kaipang, supported on vine leaves, signed, Chinese, 18thC, 4½in (11.5cm) high.
£2,200–2,500
€/ **$3,500–4,000** ⚒ B

▶ A barbed zitan brushpot, with a plugged base, the wood flecked with vermillion, Chinese, Qing Dynasty, 18thC, 9¼in (23.5cm) high.
£7,000–8,000
€/ **$11,000–12,500** ⚒ S(HK)
Zitan is the most desirable of all the Asian woods. It is normally only obtainable in narrow strips as the tree is very small – a strip 9¼in (23.5cm) is very rare for zitan.

A pair of carved wood panels, Chinese, c1850, 15in (38cm) wide.
£120–135
€/ **$190–210** ⊞ FU

A pair of carved sycamore corbels, Chinese, c1850, 24in (61cm) high.
£1,600–1,800
€/ **$2,500–2,800** ⊞ QM

A wooden needlecase, Chinese, late 19thC, 3in (7.5cm) long.
£100–110
€/ **$160–175** ⊞ JCH

A bamboo perfume holder, pierced and carved with a man playing the *qin* within a rocky garden, a boy, a lady and her attendant looking on, with carved horn ends, Chinese, 1775–1825, 8½in (21.5cm) high.
£850–1,000
€/ **$1,300–1,600** ⚒ S(O)

A keyaki wood and bronze tobacco/cigarette box (***tabako-bon***), Japanese, c1880, 8in (20.5cm) high.
£1,800–2,000
€/ **$2,800–3,200** ⊞ AUA

▶ A wooden saddle, Mongolian, early 20thC, 18in (45.5cm) long.
£225–250
€/ **$350–400** ⊞ QM

A painted wood silk winder, probably for a wedding, Chinese, 19thC, 5½in (14cm) wide.
£40–45
€/ **$63–70** ⊞ JCH

Arms & Armour

A black-lacquered part armour, laced with silk, with sleeve armour and thigh defence, some age wear, Japanese, 1600–1750.
£1,000–1,200
€/ **$1,600–1,900** ↗ WAL

A mail shirt, of riveted and plain steel rings, minor holes, Indian, 17th–18thC.
£400–500
€/ **$630–800** ↗ B(Kn)

▶ **A lacquer suit of parade armour,** the helmet with gilt-metal covers to the flanges, two fur-covered 'ears', the *mempo* with horsehair moustache, the simulated *hishinui-do* with gilt rivets, all laced and mounted on an upright stand, Japanese, late 19thC.
£5,000–6,000
€/ **$8,000–9,500** ↗ S(O)

A bronze war helmet, the dome with a boss top above ribbing, and an arched front and back framed by riveting, Chinese, 17thC, 12¼in (31cm) high.
£400–500
€/ **$630–800** ↗ CGC

A 62-plate helmet (*Hoshi-Bachi*), with raised rivets, black lacquered peak and holder, and gilt *tehen kanemono*, *shikoro* and a few rivets missing, Japanese, 16thC.
£650–775
€/ **$1,000–1,200** ↗ WAL

An iron (*mempo*), with wrinkled cheeks, separate ear pieces, half mask and red lacquered interior, one ear piece and detachable nose missing, Japanese, Edo period, 1688–1703, 9½in (24cm) high.
£320–375
€/ **$500–600** ↗ B(Kn)

◀ **A *wakizashi* blade,** attributed to Yoshimitsu, with a rusty scabbard, Japanese, Bizen Province, 17thC, 20¼in (51.5cm) long.
£550–620
€/ **$870–980** ↗ SWO

A *shinto katana*, Japanese, c1700, 27¼in (69cm) long.
£2,000–2,200
€/ **$3,200–3,500** ↗ S(O)

A *wakizashi*, with an 18thC blade, Japanese, 19thC, 24in (61cm) long.
£3,000–3,300
€/ **$4,700–5,200** ⊞ MDL

◀ **A *kaiken*,** the guard decorated in gold lacquer with gilt-copper floral *menuki*, Japanese, 19thC, 6¾in (17cm) long.
£850–950
€/ **$1,300–1,500** ↗ S(O)

◄ **An ivory *tanto*,** carved with male and female figures within a landscape, signed in a cartouche, the fitted ivory *kozuka* carved with clouds, Japanese, Meiji Period, 1868–1911, blade 10¼in (26cm) long.
£800–1,000
€ / $1,300–1,600 ⚒ B(Kn)

A ***wakizashi*,** Japanese, c1850, 27in (68.5cm) long.
£3,400–3,800
€ / $5,400–6,000 ⊞ MDL

A ***tanto*,** Japanese, 19thC, 15in (38cm) long.
£2,400–2,700
€ / $3,800–4,200 ⊞ MDL

► **A gold-inlaid *kris*,** Indonesian, 19thC, 18¾in (47.5cm) long.
£150–165
€ / $240–260
⊞ SPA

Tsuba

◄ **A Koike Yoshiro School iron *tsuba*,** with pierced and latticed flower design, framed in brass, Japanese, c1600, 3¼in (8.5cm) diam.
£1,200–1,400
€ / $1,900–2,300 ⚒ LJ

► **An iron *tsuba*,** carved with seashells, Japanese, c1700, 3¼in (8cm) diam.
£520–570
€ / $820–900 ⚒ LJ

A brass *tsuba*, by Masayoshi, carved and inlaid with an eagle swooping towards a pierced cave with a cowering monkey, Japanese, early 19thC, 2½in (6.5cm) wide.
£1,000–1,100
€ / $1,600–1,750 ⚒ S(O)

A Choshu School iron *tsuba*, by Tomomichi, carved in relief with monkeys playing around rocks and pine trees, a waterfall on the reverse, signed, Japanese, 19thC, 3in (7.5cm) high.
£900–1,000
€ / $1,400–1,600 ⚒ S(O)

An iron *tsuba*, by Toshiyoshi, carved and pierced with breaking waves, with spray drops in inlaid silver, signed, Japanese, 19thC, 3in (7.5cm) diam.
£650–720
€ / $1,000–1,100 ⚒ S(O)

► **An iron Mokko-form *tsuba*,** by Ishiguro Masatsune, inlaid with gold *bonji* character and engraved with *karakusa*, the rim with traces of gold foil, Japanese, 19thC, 3½in (9cm) diam.
£1,200–1,400
€ / $1,900–2,200 ⚒ S(O)

◄ **A polished iron *tsuba*,** decorated in gold and silver with a tiger under a bamboo tree, signed, Japanese, 19thC, 2¼in (6cm) high.
£450–500
€ / $700–800 ⚒ LJ

Figures & Models

A grey schist figure of Buddha, halo repaired, surface mottled and encrusted, Gandharan, 2nd–3rdC AD, 18½in (47cm) high.
£2,000–2,200
€/ **$3,200–3,500**
⊞ A&O

Gandhara

Gandhara was situated in an area now covered by part of north-west India, Pakistan and Afghanistan. Alexander the Great's expedition to India in 330–325 BC was instrumental in introducing Hellenic influences into the area, but its most creative period was from 1st–3rd centuries AD, when it was visited by pilgrims and travellers from as far afield as China and Greece. Sculpture was in stone, mainly schist, although stucco was increasingly used after the 3rd century AD. Techniques and motifs from classical art are combined with Indian Buddhist iconography to produce a distinctive art form which is noted for its naturalistic modelling.

A grey schist carved model of an elephant, Gandharan, 2ndC AD, 5½in (14cm) wide.
£350–400
€/ **$550–630** ⊞ HEL

A terracotta head of a male deity, his turban decorated with crossbands of jewels, Gandharan, 4th–5thC AD, 9¼in (23.5cm) high.
£1,100–1,200
€/ **$1,700–1,900** ⚶ S

A marble head of Buddha, Chinese, c950–1100 AD, 9in (23cm) high.
£22,000–25,000
€/ **$35,000–40,000** ⊞ GRG

◄ **A terracotta tomb figure of a courtesan,** Chinese, Tang Dynasty, 618–907 AD, 9¼in (23.5cm) high.
£800–875
€/ **$1,300–1,400** ⊞ FAC

A Khmer sandstone torso of a female divinity, 11thC, 15¾in (40cm) high.
£2,700–3,000
€/ **$4,300–4,700** ⊞ LOP

► **A stucco head of a male divinity,** traces of lacquer decoration, Burmese, 14th–15thC, 8½in (21.5cm) high.
£1,100–1,200
€/ **$1,700–1,900** ⚶ S

A carved sandstone figure of Vishnu, seated and holding a mace and a trident, some losses and pitting, Indian, probably Rajasthan, c12thC, 23in (58.5cm) high.
£2,500–2,800
€/ **$4,000–4,400** ⚶ JAA

A bronze incense burner, in the form of a *shishi*, Chinese, Wanli period, 1573–1619, 7in (18cm) high.
£1,400–1,600
€/ **$2,200–2,600** ⊞ GLD

A Chieng Saen bronze torso of Buddha, Thai, 16thC, 11½in (29cm) high.
£1,600–1,800
€/ **$2,500–2,800** ⊞ LOP

A cast gilt-bronze figure of Sakyamuni, seated on a double lotus throne, the hair with traces of pigment, Tibetan, 16th–17thC, 4½in (11.5cm) high.
£1,300–1,500
€/ **$2,100–2,400** ⊞ G&G

A copper alloy head,
Laotian, 17thC,
4½in (11.5cm) high.
£850–1,000
€ / **$1,400–1,600** ⚒ S

**A bamboo carving of
the Hehe Erxian,** with the
heavenly twins standing on
a rocky outcrop, a three-
legged toad below,
Chinese, Qing Dynasty,
18thC, 11½in (29cm) high.
£3,500–4,000
€ / **$5,500–6,300** ⚒ S(NY)

A marine ivory *okimono*
of a man seated on a rock
with a child, signed, early
19thC, 8in (20.5cm) high.
£400–450
€ / **$630–700** ⊞ AMC

A pair of silver-plated figures of Buddha,
Burmese, 17thC, 4¾in (12cm) high.
£315–350
€ / **$480–550** ⊞ LOP

**A jade figure of Shou
Lao,** on a wooden stand,
slight damage, Chinese,
Qing Dynasty, 18th/19thC,
5in (12.5cm) high.
£380–450
€ / **$600–700** ⚒ BUK

**A carved coral figure of
Hotei,** his outstretched
arms clutching symbols,
Japanese, early 19thC,
6in (15cm) high.
£140–160
€ / **$220–250** ⚒ FEN
Hotei was a
Buddhist priest.

**A gilt-bronze figure of
Buddha,** Thai, 18thC,
44in (112cm) high.
£8,500–9,500
€ / **$13,300–15,000** ⊞ LOP

**A gold-splashed bronze
koro,** modelled as
Fukurukuju with his deer,
Japanese, mid-19thC,
9½in (24cm) wide.
£2,200–2,300
€ / **$3,200–3,600** ⊞ PCA
Fukurukuju is a happy
wise man/deity.

A bronze incense burner, modelled
as a horse, Chinese, 18thC,
6¼in (16cm) wide.
£420–500
€ / **$660–790** ⚒ WW

**A soapstone figure of a
deity,** in the form of a
bearded official wearing a
hat and carved flowing
robes, Chinese, 18thC,
9in (23cm) high.
£2,200–2,500
€ / **$3,500–4,000** ⚒ S

**A pair of hardwood
models of recumbent
Buddhistic lions,** minor
damage, Indonesian,
probably Balinese, 19thC,
39in (99cm) long.
£650–750
€ / **$1,000–1,200** ⚒ B

◀ **A pair of wooden
models of temple
guardian dogs,** with ivory
teeth, Chinese, c1860,
2¼in (5.5cm) wide.
£235–260
€ / **$370–400** ⊞ FU

A wooden *deva*, Burmese, 19thC, 36¼in (92cm) high.
£1,100–1,300
€/ $1,700–2,000 ⊞ LOP

A pair of wooden loom pulleys, Burmese, 19thC, 12in (30.5cm) high.
£350–400
€/ $550–630 ⊞ QM

◀ **A wooden group of monkeys holding a scroll depicting Shoki,** with inlaid mother-of-pearl eyes, signed 'Masayoshi To', Japanese, Meiji period, 1868–1911, 6½in (16.5cm) high.
£2,400–2,700
€/ $3,800–4,300 ⊞ LBO
Shoki is the ancient Chinese queller of demons.

A pair of cloisonné enamel models of cockerels, decorated with gilding, Chinese, 19thC, 9in (23cm) high.
£1,000–1,200
€/ $1,600–1,900
🔨 B&L

A bronze scroll weight, in the form of a lion dog, Chinese, 19thC, 3in (7.5cm) high.
£850–950
€/ $1,300–1,500 ⊞ AUA

A bronze figure of Ganesh, seated on a lotus-cast plinth, Indian, 19thC, 23in (58.5cm) high.
£290–320
€/ $460–500 🔨 EH

A wood and ivory *okimono*, carved as an exotic tropical bird perched on a branch, Japanese, Meiji period, 1868–1911, 15¾in (40cm) high.
£1,100–1,300
€/ $1,700–2,000 🔨 B

An enamelled silver model of a peacock, perched on a branch, Indian, probably Lucknow, c1890, 5½in (14cm) high.
£2,200–2,500
€/ $3,500–4,000 🔨 B(Kn)

An ivory *okimono* **of a man wrestling with a snake,** minor damage to snake, Japanese, Meiji period, 1868–1911, 4in (10cm) high.
£450–500
€/ $700–800 ⊞ AMC

An ivory group of artisans painting a lantern, signed 'Muneyoshi', Japanese, Meiji period, 1868–1911, 4in (10cm) wide.
£2,400–2,700
€/ $3,800–4,300 ⊞ LBO

A bronze seated figure of Jurojin, a staff in his hand, Japanese, 19thC, 5½in (14cm) high.
£100–120
€/ $160–190 🔨 WW
Jurojin is a Buddhist sage.

A carved ivory *okimono* **of a young girl,** holding an apple, three-character marks, Japanese, late 19thC, 5½in (14cm) high.
£140–160
€/ $220–250 🔨 SWO

◄ **A bronze koro,** in the form of Ebisu and his carp, Japanese, Meiji period, c1880, 10in (25.5cm) wide.
£1,100–1,300
€ / **$1,700–2,000**
⊞ PCA
Ebisu is the god of fishermen.

A carved ivory and wood figure, of a man chasing a snake from a pumpkin, with enamel and gilt decoration, signed, Japanese, 19thC, 7in (18cm) high.
£2,400–2,800
€ / **$3,800–4,400** ⚘ SWO

A carved ivory okimono, of a turbaned man riding a caparisoned camel, a water vessel at his back, on a naturalistic sandy base, Japanese, 19thC, 9in (23cm) high.
£400–500
€ / **$630–800** ⚘ PFK

A cast-bronze group of two Immortals playing Go, Japanese, late 19thC, 7in (18cm) high.
£1,600–1,800
€ / **$2,500–2,800** ⊞ PCA

A bronze figure of Buddha, Burmese, Suan States, late 19thC, 17in (43cm) high.
£770–850
€ / **$1,200–1,300** ⊞ QM

A carved ivory figure of a male entertainer, holding a baton and a disc, seated on a tree trunk, a box and mask by his feet, red seal mark, Japanese, late 19thC, 5¼in (13.5cm) high.
£900–1,100
€ / **$1,400–1,700** ⚘ AH

A carved ivory okimono of a farmer and companion, on a rustic base, red seal mark, Japanese, late 19thC, 4½in (11.5cm) high.
£750–875
€ / **$1,200–1,400** ⚘ AH

An ivory okimono of two men and a boy, signed 'Korayoki', Japanese, late 19thC, 6½in (16.5cm) high.
£1,000–1,100
€ / **$1,600–1,700** ⊞ AMC

A pair of ivory okimono, carved as maidens wearing robes and holding fans and flowers, damaged, Japanese, early 20thC, 10in (25.5cm) high.
£480–550
€ / **$750–870** ⚘ RTo

A carved and painted wooden figure of a beggar, his body decorated with henna tattoos, Indian, c1900, 20in (51cm) high, on a wooden base.
£280–320
€ / **$440–500** ⚘ PFK

A jadeite vessel, modelled as a bird with detailed plumage, a cloud collar border at the neck, archaistic scrolls at the shoulder, Chinese, c1900, 6¾in (17cm) high.
£900–1,000
€ / **$1,400–1,600** ⚘ S(O)

A carved ivory figure of a farmer and monkey, Japanese, c1900, 16¼in (41.5cm) high.
£1,400–1,600
€ / **$2,200–2,500** ⚘ TEN

◄ **A marine ivory okimono of a crab fisherman with a boy,** Japanese, c1900, 5in (12.5cm) high.
£350–400
€ / **$550–630** ⊞ AMC

Furniture

A lacquer bed, Chinese, Shanxi province, 18thC, 94in (239cm) long.
£6,300–7,000
€/ **$10,000–11,000** ⊞ QM

▶ **A lacquer cabinet,** decorated in *hiramakie* and shell inlay with scrolling peony, the interior with a shelf above a fitted drawer, old wear and damage, Japanese, early Edo period, 1620–40, 15½in (39.5cm) wide.
£2,800–3,200
€/ **$4,400–5,000** ⋏ B

An elm bench, with two drawers, late 19thC, 17in (43cm) wide.
£180–200
€/ **$285–315** ⊞ OE

A carved elm bureau, Chinese, early 20thC, 33in (84cm) wide.
£400–450
€/ **$630–700** ⊞ HiA

Chinese domestic furniture

Chinese domestic furniture has been influenced more by tradition than by fashion. Similar styles of furniture have been made over a long period using the same materials and manufacturing techniques. This can make accurate dating of the furniture very difficult.

▶ **A cabinet,** with brass fittings, Chinese, 18thC, 32in (81.5cm) wide.
£2,800–3,200
€/ **$4,400–5,000** ⊞ GRG

A Chinese export gilt and lacquer writing cabinet, decorated with figurative scenes, with two doors enclosing a pocket watch holder, two pigeonholes, a mirrored cupboard and six drawers above a portable writing box, the stand decorated with precious objects, decoration worn, mid-19thC, 28¾in (73cm) wide.
€850–1,000
€/ **$1,300–1,600** ⋏ BR

A scholar's hardwood cabinet, Chinese, c1880, 33in (84cm) wide.
£875–975
€/ **$1,400–1,500** ⊞ Che

◀ **A hardwood and *Shibayama* cabinet-on-stand,** two panels decorated with figures, the others with flowers and birds, Japanese, late 19thC, 21in (53.5cm) high.
£320–375
€/ **$500–600** ⋏ DN

A stained cherrywood cabinet, the four shelves with fretted edgings, above two drawers and two cupboard doors, bronze fittings, Chinese, c1900, 37½in (95.5cm) wide.
£400–500
€/ **$630–800** ⋏ LCM

A painted cabinet, decorated with a floral pattern, Tibetan, 19thC, 50in (127cm) wide.
£2,000–2,300
€/ **$3,200–3,600** ⊞ LOP

ASIAN WORKS OF ART

An ebony side chair, carved in low relief, on barley-twist legs, Ceylonese, mid-17thC.
£2,400–2,800
€/ **$3,800–4,400** ⚒ TMA

A lacquer money chest, with locking top panel, front feet carved with Greek key pattern, north Chinese, early 19thC, 33in (84cm) wide.
£380–420
€/ **$600–670** ⊞ OE

A George III huali wood architect's desk, the tambour top above a fitted interior and ratcheted writing surface, fitted with one long and two flanking drawers, Anglo-Asian, 36in (91.5cm) wide.
£950–1,200
€/ **$1,500–1,900** ⚒ HOLL

A rosewood plantation chair, Indian, 19thC.
£315–350
€/ **$480–560** ⊞ PAS

A painted chest, with brass fittings, decorated with a textile pattern, Tibetan, 18thC, 33in (84cm) wide.
£1,800–2,000
€/ **$2,800–3,200** ⊞ LOP

A pair of lacquer chests, with canvas covers, decorated with gilt-metal mounts and paulownia, Japanese, Meiji period, 1868–1911, 28in (71cm) wide.
£1,600–2,000
€/ **$2,500–3,200** ⚒ B

A gilt and lacquer eight-fold screen, decorated with pavilions, temples and *dhows*, within a border of opposing dragons chasing the sacred pearl, damaged, Chinese, Qianlong period, 1736–95, 90½in (230cm) wide.
£1,800–2,200
€/ **$2,800–3,500** ⚒ PFK

◄ **An embroidered screen,** with Japanese needlework worked in floss silks and couched metal threads, and European satinwood mounts, 1880s, 57½in (146cm) wide.
£950–1,100
€/ **$1,500–1,700** ⚒ S(O)

► **A hardwood screen,** with mother-of-pearl inlay, Chinese, 19thC, 41in (104cm) wide.
£270–300
€/ **$430–475** ⊞ PaA

A carved hardwood elbow chair, with pierced foliate decoration, Anglo-Indian, c19thC.
£650–750
€/ **$1,000–1,200** ⚒ SWO

A penwork chest-on-stand, decorated with figures and stylized Oriental landscapes on a foliate-carved X-frame, Indian, c1830, 35¾in (91cm) wide.
£7,000–8,000
€/ **$11,000–12,700** ⚒ S(O)

A davenport, carved with foliage, animals and figures, Indian, Bombay, c1880, 22¾in (58cm) wide.
£1,600–1,900
€/ **$2,500–3,000** ⚒ B(Kn)

A William IV padouk settee, with floral-carved back-rail, moquette back and squab, with carved vase form uprights and a floral-carved apron, on gadrooned and turned legs with brass casters, probably Indian, 74½in (189cm) wide.
£1,800–2,200
€/ **$2,800–3,500** ⚒ DMC

An ebony and satin-birch carved sideboard, with three frieze drawers and two cupboard doors enclosing shelves, probably Javanese, c1840, 68½in (174cm) wide.
£3,500–4,200
€/ **$5,500–6,600** ⚒ S(O)

A hardwood stand, with marble-inlaid top, Chinese, c1880, 25in (63.5cm) high.
£570–625
€/ **$900–1,000** ⊞ AUA

A carved wood stand, the top within a raised border, the apron relief-carved with confronting phoenix and Greek key designs, on four bracket feet, Japanese, 1875–1925, 14¼in (36cm) square.
£500–600
€/ **$800–950** ⚒ S(O)

An elm stool, with a rattan top, cloud carving on apron and corners, early 19thC, 21in (53.5cm) square.
£325–360
€/ **$515–560** ⊞ OE

A padouk and brass marquetry card table, the top inlaid with trailing vines and centred by the monogram 'E.H.H.', above a similarly inlaid frieze on detachable cabriole legs and square tapering feet, Anglo-Indian, early 19thC, 36¼in (92cm) wide.
£600–720
€/ **$950–1,100** ⚒ B

A Regency coromandel sofa table, with two drop leaves and two frieze drawers, on splayed legs with brass paw casters, Anglo-Indian, 42in (106.5cm) extended.
£3,000–3,500
€/ **$4,700–5,500** ⚒ MEA

A lacquer work table, decorated in gilt with Chinese families at leisure, on four dragon feet, gilt worn, Chinese, Canton, 19thC, 29in (73.5cm) high.
£1,800–2,200
€/ **$2,800–3,500** ⚒ B

◀ **A walnut occasional table,** with marble top and carved legs, maker's label, Indian, c1870, 15in (38cm) square.
£500–550
€/ **$800–870** ⊞ APO

A jacaranda console table, with brass mounts, Portuguese, Goa, 19thC, 51in (129.5cm) wide.
£6,000–7,000
€/ **$9,500–11,000** ⚒ S(NY)

A cherrywood nest of tables, carved with dragons and scrollwork, on square legs, Chinese, late 19thC, largest 17in (43cm) wide.
£400–475
€/ **$630–750** ⚒ JAd

◀ **A padouk pedestal,** the later rosewood crossbanded top with canted corners and brass border, the pedestal with a baluster-ribbed column and outer scrolling supports, Anglo-Indian, 19thC, 24¾in (63cm) wide.
£1,300–1,500
€/ **$2,000–2,400** ⚒ B

A carved wood washstand, with dragon decoration, Chinese, 19thC, 27½in (70cm) wide.
£1,000–1,100
€/ **$1,600–1,700** ⊞ LOP

Inro

A six-case gold lacquer *inro*, decorated in *hiramakie*, *takamakie* and *kimpun*, *nashiji* interior, signed, with attached wood *ojime* and stag antler *netsuke* pierced and carved with entwined *ruyi* fungus, Japanese, 19thC, 3¾in (9.5cm) high.
£2,300–2,500
€/ $3,600–4,000 ⊞ **G&G**

▶ **A four-case *inro*,** decorated with chrysanthemums in gold *takamakie*, inlaid mother-of-pearl and gold foil, the interior of *nashiji*, signed 'Koma Ankyo' (Yasutada), Japanese, 19thC, 3in (7.5cm) high.
£800–900
€/ $1,200–1,400 ⚒ **S(O)**

A wood three-case *inro*, by Tadakazu (Chuichi), modelled as a turtle, with head, legs and tail tucked in, the eyes of inlaid horn, signed, Japanese, 19thC, 4in (10cm) high.
£1,800–2,000
€/ $2,800–3,200 ⚒ **S(O)**

Items in the Asian Works of Art section have been arranged in date order within each sub-section.

An ivory three-case *inro*, each side with a shaped panel carved in low relief with the Seven Gods of Good Fortune, with ivory *ojime* carved with Hotei, signed 'Kosai to', Japanese, 19thC, 3½in (9cm) high.
£1,100–1,300
€/ $1,800–2,000 ⚒ **S(O)**

Netsuke

An ivory *netsuke* of a horse, Japanese, 18thC, 4½in (11.5cm) long.
£475–565
€/ $750–900 ⚒ **SWO**

An ivory *netsuke* of Daikoku with abacus, Japanese, Meiji period, 1868–1911, 1¼in (3cm) high.
£135–150
€/ $215–235 ⊞ **AMC**

▶ **A carved ivory *netsuke* of a grimacing face,** being attacked by a crab and a wasp, signed verso, Japanese, Meiji period, late 19thC, 1¾in (4.5cm) high.
£280–325
€/ $440–515 ⚒ **SWO**

▶ **A horn *netsuke* of Gama Sennin,** wearing an oak leaf cloak and carrying a toad on his shoulder, Japanese, early 19thC, 3in (7.5cm) high.
£200–220
€/ $320–350 ⊞ **AMC**
Gama Sennin is one of the Immortals. He is normally shown with a three-legged toad.

An *okimono*-style ivory *netsuke* of a group of street vendors and entertainers, in a fish basket, Japanese, Meiji period, 1868–1911, 2¼in (5.5cm) high.
£450–525
€/ $700–830 ⚒ **G(L)**

A carved ivory *netsuke* of a street vendor, signed with two characters incised on an inset red *kakihan* beneath his right sandal, Japanese, c1900, 1¾in (4.5cm) high.
£525–625
€/ $830–980 ⚒ **TEN**

A boxwood *netsuke* of two quail, possibly by Kanetomo of Nanki, Southern Kishu, with jadeite-inset eyes, on a bed of fruit bound by tendril-like leaves, the *himotoshi* formed from one leaf bearing a two-character seal mark, Japanese, Meiji period, 1868–1911, 1¾in (4.5cm) long.
£475–565
€/ $750–900 ⚒ **BR**

An ivory *netsuke* of a mask of Daikoku, Japanese, early 1900s, 1¼in (3cm) high.
£250–275
€/ $400–430 ⊞ **AMC**
Daikoku is the god of wealth.

Robes & Costume

An embroidered collar, with cloud motif, Chinese, c1880, 14in (35.5cm) diam.
£175–200
€/ **$275–320** ⊞ JCH

A man's wool coat, woven with flowerheads, darned and repaired, 19thC alterations, fabric Indian, Kashmir, c1800, construction later.
£1,200–1,400
€/ **$1,900–2,200** ⚒ S(O)

A child's hat, Chinese, late 19thC, 7in (18cm) wide.
£135–150
€/ **$215–235** ⊞ JCH

A lady's silk damask front-opening jacket, applied with brocade silk ribbons and embroidered with symbols of good fortune, Chinese, Manchu, Xianfeng period, 1851–61, 26½in (67.5cm) long.
£2,700–3,000
€/ **$4,300–4,700** ⊞ WRi

A summer court hat, damask silk over a woven bamboo frame, surmounted by a glass hat button indicating a 5th rank civil official, Chinese, Guangxu period, 1875–1908, 35½in (90cm) diam.
£1,100–1,200
€/ **$1,700–1,900** ⊞ WRi

An embroidered outer robe (chifu), couched and embroidered in gold and silver threads with coiling dragons and flaming pearls, lining missing, binding frayed, Chinese, mid-19thC.
£1,300–1,500
€/ **$2,000–2,400** ⚒ S(O)

▶ **A woman's vest (apei),** applied with 9th rank civil badges, the paradise fly catcher in couched gold threads, tasselled hem, Chinese, late 19thC.
£500–600
€/ **$800–950** ⚒ S(O)

A child's padded jacket, early 20thC, 16in (40.5cm) long.
£110–125
€/ **$175–200** ⊞ JCH

A hand-embroidered silk shawl, with silk fringing, Chinese, Canton, late 19thC, 56in (142cm) square.
£225–250
€/ **$350–400** ⊞ JPr

An embroidered damask silk skirt, with ribbon borders, Chinese, Guangxu period, 1875–1908.
£450–500
€/ **$700–800** ⊞ WRi

A dragon robe, for the Imperial Clan, decorated with clawed dragons, Chinese, c1900.
£1,200–1,400
€/ **$1,900–2,200** ⊞ JCH

◀ **A pair of child's hand-embroidered silk shoes,** Chinese, c1890, 5in (12.5cm) long.
£55–60
€/ **$85–95** ⊞ JPr

ASIAN WORKS OF ART

Snuff Bottles

An overlay glass snuff bottle, carved with prunus blossom, bamboo and pine, called The Three Friends of Winter, Chinese, 1780–1850, 2½in (6.5cm) high.
£1,400–1,600
€/ $2,200–2,500 ⊞ RHa

A nephrite snuff bottle, carved in low relief with the formalized design of a bat suspended from a ring above two peaches and lotus, Chinese, 1780–1850, 2¾in (7cm) high.
£1,400–1,600
€/ $2,200–2,500 ⊞ RHa

A translucent quartz snuff bottle, moulded with tendrils and leaves, small chip, Chinese, 19thC, 1¾in (4.5cm) high.
£340–375
€/ $550–600 ➶ G(L)

An agate snuff bottle, carved with fish among weeds, the reverse with a peach and leaf, coral stopper, Chinese, 19thC, 2in (5cm) high.
£260–300
€/ $400–475 ➶ S(O)

◀ **A silver snuff bottle,** inlaid with coral, worked in relief with squirrels eating fruit from a European bowl, with lion-mask handles at the waist, coral-inlaid stopper, Chinese, 19thC, 3in (7.5cm) high.
£350–400
€/ $550–630 ➶ S(O)

▶ **A puddingstone snuff bottle,** carved with bats and cash strings, Chinese, late 19thC, 2¾in (7cm) high.
£400–500
€/ $630–800 ➶ G(L)

An agate snuff bottle, relief-carved with figures on boats among trees and rocks, the hardstone stopper set with a white metal spatula, Chinese, late 19thC, 3in (7.5cm) high.
£380–450
€/ $600–700 ➶ BR

Textiles

A brocade altar-table front, decorated with dragons, clouds and waves, floral motifs and longevity symbols, Chinese, 18thC, 38¼in (97cm) long.
£4,500–5,000
€/ $7,000–8,000 ⊞ WRi
This was made for use in a wealthy home, probably for New Year festivities to decorate a table at which the ancestors or household gods were honoured. Among the embroidered motifs are a narcissus flower and a bat with musical chime which are characteristic of New Year decorations.

▶ **A silk brocaded patchwork coverlet,** Japanese, late Edo period, c1850, 76in (193cm) long.
£4,000–4,500
€/ $6,300–7,000 ⊞ DAW

A Chinese export embroidered coverlet, worked with birds, butterflies and bamboo, signed 'Nguyan van Lam, Brodeur a Bac Nimb', late 19thC, 55¼in (140.5cm) long.
£500–600
€/ $800–950 ➶ S(O)

A length of cotton fabric, Japanese, late 19thC, 27in (68.5cm) wide.
£200–220
€/ $320–350 ⊞ JCH

A gentleman's silk fan case, embroidered with silk thread in a geometric design, losses to thread, Chinese, Guangxu period, 19thC, 12¼in (31cm) long.
£400–450
€/ $630–700 ⊞ WRi
The geometric design is based on the complex weaves of ancient silks.

A silk fan case, embroidered with symbols representing The Five Blessings, Chinese, Guangxu period, 1875–1908, 11in (28cm) long.
£180–200
€/ $285–325 ⊞ JCH
The Five Blessings are health, wealth, a long life, the love of virtue and the hope of a natural death.

A silk fragrance pouch, Chinese, late 19thC, 3in (7.5cm) long.
£90–100
€/ $140–160 ⊞ JCH

A thanka, embroidered with four-clawed dragons, Tibetan, 18thC, 16in (40.5cm) long.
£430–475
€/ $680–750 ⊞ JCH
A thanka is a Tibetan representation of divinities. They are used on the walls of temples or shrines as a subject for meditation.

An embroidered panel, depicting an elephant with flowers, Chinese, early 20thC, 33in (84cm) long.
£200–225
€/ $315–350 ⊞ JCH

An embroidered silk panel, with central stylized flowering plants, within rosette borders, Indian, Gujerat, 19thC, 64¼ x 35in (166 x 89cm), mounted.
£800–950
€/ $1,300–1,500 ➘ B(Kn)

An embroidered panel, decorated with five bats representing The Five Blessings, Chinese, early 20thC, 20in (51cm) wide.
£1,100–1,300
€/ $1,700–2,000 ⊞ JCH

A silk-embroidered rank badge bag, Chinese, late 19thC, 11in (28cm) square.
£100–120
€/ $160–190 ⊞ JPr

A hand-embroidered panel, from an apron skirt, Chinese, c1890, 8 x 12in (20.5 x 30.5cm).
£270–300
€/ $430–475 ⊞ AUA

A silk-embroidered panel, Indian, late 19thC, 86¾ x 51¼in (220.5 x 130cm).
£650–720
€/ $1,000–1,100 ➘ S(O)

A purse, decorated with a butterfly and multicoloured tasselling, Chinese, 19thC, 9¾in (25cm) long.
£320–350
€/ $500–550 ⊞ WRi

▶ **A 4th rank badge,** with appliqué cloud goose surrounded by the eight Buddhist symbols, Chinese, c1890, 12 x 11in (30.5 x 28cm).
£475–525
€/ $750–830 ⊞ AUA

◀ **A satin wall hanging,** couched and embroidered in gold threads and silks with Immortals, grotesque figures and beauties in a garden, Chinese, late 19thC, 115¾ x 88½in (294 x 225cm).
£1,000–1,100
€/ $1,600–1,700 ➘ S(O)

Islamic Works of Art

Arms & Armour

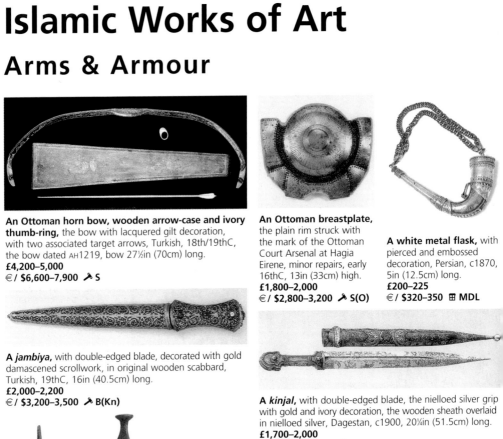

An Ottoman horn bow, wooden arrow-case and ivory thumb-ring, the bow with lacquered gilt decoration, with two associated target arrows, Turkish, 18th/19thC, the bow dated AH1219, bow 27½in (70cm) long.
£4,200–5,000
€/ **$6,600–7,900** ⚔ **S**

An Ottoman breastplate, the plain rim struck with the mark of the Ottoman Court Arsenal at Hagia Eirene, minor repairs, early 16thC, 13in (33cm) high.
£1,800–2,000
€/ **$2,800–3,200** ⚔ **S(O)**

A white metal flask, with pierced and embossed decoration, Persian, c1870, 5in (12.5cm) long.
£200–225
€/ **$320–350** ⊞ **MDL**

A *jambiya*, with double-edged blade, decorated with gold damascened scrollwork, in original wooden scabbard, Turkish, 19thC, 16in (40.5cm) long.
£2,000–2,200
€/ **$3,200–3,500** ⚔ **B(Kn)**

A *kinjal*, with double-edged blade, the nielloed silver grip with gold and ivory decoration, the wooden sheath overlaid in nielloed silver, Dagestan, c1900, 20¼in (51.5cm) long.
£1,700–2,000
€/ **$2,600–3,200** ⚔ **Herm**

◄ **A Mogul *tulwar*,** the iron hilt with traces of silver overlay and brown patina, early 17thC, blade 30½in (77.5cm) long, with the wooden carcass of the scabbard.
£385–425
€/ **$600–700** ⊞ **FAC**

Ceramics

An Ilkhanid *lajvardina* pottery bottle, decorated with a phoenix in flight, flowers and scrolls, Persian, 14thC, 8½in (21.5cm) diam.
£2,200–2,500
€/ **$3,500–4,000** ⚔ **B(Kn)**

A pottery bowl, with incised sgraffito decoration of an abstract bird, Persian, 10th–12thC, 7in (18cm) diam.
£250–275
€/ **$400–440** ⊞ **CrF**

A Tophane terracotta coffee set, with impressed and gilt decoration and inscriptions, Turkish, dated 1887, ewer 6¼in (16cm) high.
£1,600–2,000
€/ **$2,500–3,200** ⚔ **B(Kn)**

◄ **An Iznik pottery dish,** with sloping rim, decorated with a hyacinth flanked by roses and a tulip, Turkish, late 16thC, 12in (30.5cm) diam.
£2,200–2,500
€/ **$3,500–4,000** ⚔ **B(Kn)**

LOCATE THE SOURCE
The source of each illustration in Miller's can be found by checking the code letters below each caption with the Key to Illustrations, pages 794–800.

An Iznik pottery dish, with sloping rim, decorated and gilt with a *saz* leaf, tulips and roses, Turkish, 17thC, 12in (30.5cm) diam.
£1,300–1,500
€/ **$2,100–2,400** ➤ B(Kn)

A Kubachi pottery dish, the central rosette enclosing floral and foliate motifs, Persian, 17thC, 13¼in (33.5cm) diam.
£7,500–8,500
€/ **$12,000–13,500** ➤ S

A pottery dish, decorated with Kufic script and characters, Turkish, 18thC, 14¼in (36cm) diam.
£180–200
€/ **$280–320** ➤ BR

A *kalian* or *kendi*, decorated with four panels of Oriental birds in gardens, chips to footrim, Persian, 17thC, 7in (18cm) high.
£1,400–1,600
€/ **$2,200–2,500** ➤ TEN

A Kashan lustre-decorated cruciform tile, decorated with palmettes on a ground of scrolls, Persian, 13thC, 8½in (21.5cm) wide.
£250–300
€/ **$400–480** ➤ S(O)

▶ **A pair of tiles,** each painted with two exotic birds, roses, foliage and other flowers, Persian, 19thC, 13¼ x 9¾in (34 x 24.5cm).
£200–220
€/ **$315–350** ➤ CGC

A Timurid carved pottery border tile, with a band of trefoils, central Asian, late 14thC, 9½in (24cm) long.
£800–950
€/ **$1,300–1,500** ➤ B(Kn)

Furniture

◀ **A pair of mahogany side chairs,** inlaid with mother-of-pearl, each with a bulbous spindle back above a Moorish arch, on turned feet, North African, c1900.
£1,000–1,200
€/ **$1,600–1,900** ➤ NOA

A walnut and shell-inlaid coffer, Syrian, Damascus, 19thC, 56¾in (144cm) wide.
£800–900
€/ **$1,300–1,400** ➤ S(O)

An Ottoman serpentine-fronted miniature commode, inlaid with mother-of-pearl, ebony, ivory and bone, Syrian, c1900, 11in (28cm) wide.
£1,000–1,200
€/ **$1,600–1,900** ⊞ CAT

An Ottoman velvet screen, Turkish, 19thC, each panel 59 x 23½in (150 x 60cm).
£3,500–4,200
€/ **$5,500–6,600** ➤ B(Kn)

A suite of inlaid Damascus-style furniture, early 20thC, davenport 24in (61cm) wide.
£1,800–2,200
€/ **$2,800–3,500** ➤ S(O)

Glass

A wheel-cut glass bottle, cut with seven circles in relief, Persian, c9thC, 3¾in (9.5cm) high.
£1,000–1,100
€ / **$1,600–1,700** ⚒ B(Kn)

A wheel-cut glass bowl, cut with four rows of indented panels forming a honeycomb design, Persian, c9thC, 4¼in (11cm) diam.
£850–1,000
€ / **$1,300–1,600** ⚒ B(Kn)

A glass flask, with mould-blown decoration of interconnecting circle and dot motifs, Persian, 10th–12thC, 3½in (9cm) high.
£1,600–2,000
€ / **$2,200–3,200** ⚒ S

Manuscripts & Paintings

▶ **An Ottoman illuminated Qur'an,** 410 leaves, contemporary gold tooled and stamped leather binding, Turkish, 18thC, 6 x 4in (15 x 10cm).
£1,700–2,000
€ / **$2,700–3,200**
⚒ B(Kn)

An Arabic illuminated Qur'an, 338 leaves, Turkish, Constantinople, repaired and rebacked, dated 1671, 10¾ x 6¾in (27.5 x 17cm).
£4,200–5,000
€ / **$6,600–7,900** ⚒ S

A miniature painting from a copy of the Sinbadnama, opaque watercolour, ink and gilding on paper, Persian, early 16thC, 2½ x 4¾in (6.5 x 12cm).
£260–300
€ / **$400–470** ⚒ S(O)

▶ **An Arabic manuscript on paper,** the Psalms of David according to the Coptic Church, 237 leaves, Morocco binding, Egyptian, dated 1784, 5½ x 4in (14 x 10cm).
£3,000–3,500
€ / **$4,700–5,500** ⚒ S

Jewellery

A pair of Qajar enamelled and gold earrings, fringed with seed pearls and glass beads, the hooks set with rubies, Persian, 19thC, 2¼in (6cm) long.
£1,600–2,000
€ / **$2,500–3,200** ⚒ B(Kn)

An enamelled gold pendant, set with emeralds, rubies and sapphires, Moroccan, 19thC, 2in (5cm) diam.
£3,200–3,800
€ / **$5,100–6,000** ⚒ S

◀ **A Kazak necklace,** set with precious stones, Persian, 19thC.
£400–450
€ / **$630–710** ⚒ S

Metalware

A Safavid tinned copper basin, decorated with a band of calligraphy, on a narrow stem foot, Persian, 17thC, 14½in (36.5cm) diam.
£650–750
€ / **$1,000–1,200** B(Kn)

A Timurid bronze bowl, with incised calligraphic decoration, Persian, late 15thC, 5¾in (14.5cm) diam.
£1,800–2,200
€ / **$2,800–3,500** S

◄ **A silver box and cover,** chased with a cartouche and repeating floral motifs around the sides, Persian, 19thC, 3in (7.5cm) diam.
£100–120
€ / **$160–190** WW

A bronze jug, with bird finial, Persian, damaged, 12thC, 9½in (24cm) high.
£400–480
€ / **$630–760** SWO

Textiles

A silk brocade panel, Persian, 16th–17thC, 8in (20.5cm) square.
£85–100
€ / **$135–160** JCH

► **A textile fragment of Safavid design,** Persian, 19thC, 45¾ x 27in (116 x 69cm).
£350–400
€ / **$550–630** S(O)

An embroidered hanging, worked in cotton on a felted wool ground, slight wear, Persia, Rasht, c1900, 95 x 63in (241.5 x 160cm).
£350–420
€ / **$550–660** WW

Miscellaneous

◄ **An Ottoman leather quiver,** embroidered in silver wrapped around a silk core with a roundel containing a large flowerhead, Turkish, c1680, 17in (43cm) long.
£1,700–2,000
€ / **$2,700–3,300** B(Kn)

> Items in the Miscellaneous section have been arranged in alphabetical order.

A wooden manuscript box, inlaid with bone and coloured woods, Near Eastern, early 19thC, 8¾ x 6¼in (22.5 x 16cm).
£240–275
€ / **$380–430** DN

► **An Ottoman tombstone,** carved with inscriptions, probably Turkish, c1821, 44in (112cm) high.
£700–850
€ / **$1,100–1,300** S(O)

ISLAMIC WORKS OF ART

Architectural Antiques

Iron

A Regency painted-iron garden bench, the back with interlaced splats with downswept arms and slatted seat, 50in (127cm) wide.
£750–900
€/ **$1,200–1,400** ➶ **L&E**

A cast-iron garden bench, the back pierced with fern leaves, Irish, c1840, 74in (188cm) wide.
£1,000–1,200
€/ **$1,600–1,900** ⊞ **HON**

> Items in the Architectural Antiques section have been arranged in alphabetical order.

A cast-iron boot scraper, c1880, 13in (33cm) high.
£110–120
€/ **$170–190** ⊞ **SMI**

A Victorian cast-iron clock face, c1880, 72in (183cm) diam.
£2,000–2,200
€/ **$3,200–3,500** ➶ **WilP**
This clock face came from the Town Hall, Dunstable, Bedfordshire.

A cast-iron royal coat-of-arms, late 19thC, 23in (58.5cm) high.
£900–1,000
€/ **$1,400–1,500** ⊞ **SWN**

A pair of cast-iron door stops, cast as Punch & Judy, Punch dressed as Julius Caesar, c1860, 12in (30.5cm) high.
£500–560
€/ **$800–880** ⊞ **MFB**

A cast-iron door stop, c1870, 8in (20.5cm) high.
£55–60
€/ **$85–95** ⊞ **GBr**

A cast-iron lion-mask down-pipe cover, early 19thC, 10in (25.5cm) high.
£580–650
€/ **$920–1,000** ⊞ **ChC**

A cast-iron fan light, with coloured glass, minor damage, 19thC, 38in (96.5cm) wide.
£1,100–1,200
€/ **$1,700–1,900** ⊞ **WRe**

▶ **A suite of painted cast-iron garden furniture,** comprising five pieces, 19thC, largest 50in (127cm) wide
£3,800–4,500
€/ **$6,000–7,100**
➶ **HOK**

A cast-iron fountain, by Handyside Foundry, Derby, on a stepped square base, c1860, 42in (106.5cm) high.
£1,800–2,000
€/ **$2,800–3,200** ➶ S(S)

A Victorian enamelled cast-iron drinking fountain, with brass tap, 37in (94cm) high.
£240–260
€/ **$380–420** ⊞ WRe

► A wrought-iron garden gate, with scroll decoration and spiked cresting rail, late 19thC, 53½in (136cm) high.
£700–820
€/ **$1,100–1,300** ➶ BR

◄ A cast-iron grid, 1920s, 17in (43.5cm) square.
£85–95
€/ **$135–150** ⊞ WRe

A cast-iron mask, c1840, 14in (35.5cm) high.
£580–650
€/ **$920–1,200** ⊞ RGe

A cast-iron planter, decorated with pierced and trailing foxgloves, zinc liner, 1850–1900, 53in (134.5cm) diam.
£1,000–1,200
€/ **$1,600–1,900** ➶ S(S)

A cast-iron radiator, French, restored, c1900, 61in (155cm) long.
£1,300–1,500
€/ **$2,100–2,400** ⊞C&R

◄ A cast- and wrought-iron stove, moulded with a flowering urn and bellflower, Greek key and figural decoration, northern European, c1800, 76in (193cm) high.
£2,000–2,400
€/ **$3,200–3,800** ➶ S(O)

An iron laundry stove, by Thevenot Frères, French, Paris, c1900, 36in (91.5cm) high.
£500–600
€/ **$790–950** ⊞ B&R
This stove would have been used for heating flat irons.

◄ A cast-iron and enamel conservatory stove, 19thC, 27¼in (69cm) high.
£140–160
€/ **$220–250** ➶ SWO

A painted cast-iron and enamel stove, by S. D. F., pierced with strapwork and anthemia, early 20thC, 37¾in (96cm) high.
£300–350
€/ **$475–550** ✗ DD

A Victorian cast-iron garden urn, with mask handles on a square plinth, 56¾in (144cm) high.
£1,100–1,300
€/ **$1,700–2,000** ✗ SWO

A pair of Falkirk Foundry cast-iron urns, lobed and reeded, with scroll handles, 1850–1900, 24in (61cm) high.
£900–1,100
€/ **$1,400–1,700** ✗ S(S)

An iron garden urn, in the shape of a basket, early 20thC, 35½in (90cm) high.
£650–750
€/ **$1,000–1,200** ✗ SWO

◄ **A Victorian cast-iron umbrella stand,** diamond registration mark, pre-1880, 29in (73.5cm) high,
£350–385
€/ **$550–600** ⊞ RPh

A pair of painted cast-iron urns, the part-ribbed bodies with flared egg-and-dart rims, 19thC, 42in (106.5cm) high.
£1,000–1,200
€/ **$1,600–1,900** ✗ WW

A pair of cast-iron garden urns, the fluted bodies with scroll handles, labelled 'Corneau Alfred, à Charleville, No 2', French, c1900, 19¼in (49cm) high.
£240–280
€/ **$380–440** ✗ DMC

Sets/pairs

Unless otherwise stated, any description which refers to 'a set' or 'a pair' includes a guide price for the entire set or the pair, even though the illustration may show only a single item.

Bronze

A bronze church bell, by Newcome, 1614, 38in (96.5cm) high.
£2,000–2,500
€/ **$3,200–4,000** ⊞ WEL

A pair of bronze sphinxes, early 20thC, 35in (89cm) high.
£2,000–2,400
€/ **$3,200–3,800** ✗ JAd

A bronze sundial plate, the dial inscribed with the arms of Cornwall and 'Sol est Lux et Gloria Mundi, Newton Camborne', with pierced gnomon on a coiled serpent, c1900, 14in (35.5cm) diam.
£1,100–1,300
€/ **$1,700–2,000** ✗ S(S)

Lead

A length of lead water-pump housing, c1850, 40in (101.5cm) high.
£180–200
€/ **$280–320** ⊞ WRe

A lead figure of Mercury, by Crowther, c1900, 42in (106.5cm) high.
£1,100–1,200
€/ **$1,700–1,900** ⚒ OLA

A lead figure of a Neapolitan fisher boy, 1900–50, 28in (71cm) high.
£1,700–2,000
€/ **$2,700–3,200** ⚒ S(S)

A lead cistern, the front decorated with strapwork and figures of Neptune, with ownership initials, bronze tap, dated 1764, 44in (112cm) wide.
£8,000–9,500
€/ **$12,600–15,000** ⚒ S(S)

Marble

A pair of Verona marble garden chairs, in the shape of Etruscan thrones flanked by winged lions, the backs centred with a *stemma nobilare*, Italian, 18thC, 33in (84cm) high.
£33,000–40,000
€/ **$52,000–63,000** ⊞ W&C
These hand-carved seats are extremely impressive and pieces of such age rarely survive to the 21st century.

A veined marble column, with moulded decoration, late 19thC, 48in (122cm) high.
£550–650
€/ **$870–1,000** ⚒ SWO

A marble figure of a putto, 19thC, 43½in (110.5cm) high.
£2,200–2,500
€/ **$3,500–4,000** ⚒ LVS

A marble figure, 19thC, 47in (119.5cm) high.
£1,100–1,200
€/ **$1,700–1,900** ⊞ PAS

A carved marble basket of flowers, French, 19thC, 17in (43cm) wide.
£1,000–1,200
€/ **$1,600–1,900** ⚒ S(S)

A carved marble font, slight damage, probably late 17thC, 23½in (59.5cm) wide.
£650–780
€/ **$1,000–1,200** ⚒ S(S)

Four Victorian marble planters, in the shape of stylized water lilies, 14¼in (36cm) wide.
£2,500–3,000
€/ **$4,000–4,700** ⚒ B(S)

Stone

A carved sandstone
birdbath, early 20thC,
29in (74cm) high.
£400–480
€/ $630–760 ⚒ S(S)

A granite mill stone,
19thC, 41in (104cm) diam.
£720–800
€/ $1,100–1,300 ⊞ WRe

A neo-classical-style
variegated stone garden
pedestal, on a circular plinth,
c1900, 34in (86.5cm) high.
£400–450
€/ $630–710 ⚒ NOA

▶ A carved Caen stone
planter, French, 19thC,
29in (73cm) wide.
£1,000–1,200
€/ $1,600–1,900 ⚒ S(S)

A pair of carved stone baskets of fruit, early
20thC, 22in (56cm) high.
£3,000–3,600
€/ $4,800–5,700 ⚒ S(S)

Two sandstone gate-post finials, with
medial bands, 19thC, 12in (30.5cm) high.
£180–220
€/ $280–350 ⚒ PFK

A pair of stone panels, each carved in relief
with a bird of paradise with a serpent in its
beak, c1900, 34½in (87.5cm) high.
£1,800–2,200
€/ $2,800–3,500 ⚒ S(S)

A carved Bath stone date plaque, 1905,
23in (58.5cm) wide.
£110–120
€/ $175–190 ⊞ WRe

A pair of carved stone gate-post
finials, modelled as pineapples,
c1800, 40in (101.5cm) high.
£1,000–1,200
€/ $1,600–1,900 ⚒ S(S)

A Coade stone keystone, carved with
the head of a girl, stamped 'Coade,
London 1793', 10½in (26.5cm) high.
£1,300–1,500
€/ $2,100–2,400 ⚒ S(S)
Eleanor Coade opened her
Lambeth factory for ceramic
artificial stone in 1769. Two years
later she appointed the sculptor
John Bacon as its manager. She
was employed by the leading
late 18th-century architects. From
about 1777 she began creating
engraved designs and by 1784
had designed over 700 items.
In 1799 the firm became Coade
& Sealey, but reverted to the
original name in 1821. The
London 1774 Building Act
reduced exterior woodwork to
the absolute minimum to make
housing as incombustible as
possible, and the Lambeth
factory was able to supply a
great variety of fireproof
decoration for house fronts.

A Bourgogne stone planter,
late 19thC, 34in (86.5cm) wide.
£1,500–1,700
€/ $2,400–2,800 ⚒ S(S)

Terracotta

A Victorian terracotta chimney pot, 31in (78.5cm) high.
£90–100
€ / $140–160 ⊞ WRe

A Victorian terracotta chimney pot, 29in (73.5cm) high.
£45–50
€ / $70–80 ⊞ WRe

A terracotta chimney pot, 1920s, 28in (71cm) high.
£70–80
€ / $110–130 ⊞ WRe

A Victorian terracotta cock's comb finial, 22in (56cm) high.
£60–70
€ / $95–125 ⊞ WRe

A Victorian terracotta roof finial, 22in (56cm) high.
£55–60
€ / $85–95 ⊞ WRe

A Victorian terracotta garden ornament, in the form of two cherubs, slight damage, 17in (43cm) high.
£200–220
€ / $315–350 ↗ TMA

A cast-terracotta jardinière stand, by Withnall, Lancashire, early 20thC, 27½in (70cm) high.
£220–250
€ / $350–400 ↗ G(L)

A terracotta sundial pedestal, attributed to Compton, with later iron armillary sphere, early 20thC, 63in (160cm) high.
£1,400–1,600
€ / $2,200–2,500 ↗ S(S)

A Compton terracotta pot, early 20thC, 19in (48.5cm) high.
£550–620
€ / $870–980 ↗ S(S)

A Di Signa terracotta planter, moulded with cherubs and putti, early 20thC, 37½in (95.5cm) diam.
£500–600
€ / $790–950 ↗ S(S)

A terracotta roundel, modelled with a dog's head, late 19thC, 20in (51cm) diam.
£650–750
€ / $1,000–1,200 ↗ S(S)

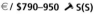

A matt-glazed terracotta unitile, decorated with a scarab, American, c1918, 16in (40.5cm) wide.
£480–575
€ / $760–900 ⊞ KMG

◄ A pair of Victorian Doulton terracotta urns, with egg-and-dart rim, 25in (63.5cm) high.
£500–600
€ / $790–950 ↗ JAd

Wood

A pair of wooden garden benches, c1900,
48in (122cm) wide.
£2,000–2,300
€/ **$3,200–3,600** ⊞ CAT

► A carved and painted wooden column,
spiral-carved with grapevines, Italian, c1900,
40in (101.5cm) high.
£170–200
€/ **$270–315** ⚒ NOA

A pair of pine and composition figural
corbels, 19thC, 11¾in (30cm) high.
£400–480
€/ **$630–760** ⚒ SWO

A carved wood
architectural frame,
1675–1725, some damage,
43¼in (110cm) high.
£1,400–1,600
€/ **$2,200–2,500** ⚒ S(O)

► A pair of carved oak
panels, French, 16thC,
21in (53.5cm) wide.
£580–650
€/ **$920–1,000** ⊞ SEA

A pair of oak Gothic carved panels, 16thC,
17in (43cm) high.
£1,000–1,100
€/ **$1,600–1,700** ⊞ KEY

A carved oak panel, 16thC,
13in (33cm) square.
£430–480
€/ **$680–760** ⊞ KEY

A carved and painted
wood pelmet, the fringed
drapery suspended from a
central tassel-hung bow
with two floral and shell
wreaths, decorated with
fruit and flowers, the
fringed tails with tassel
terminals, damaged, 19thC,
70½in (179cm) wide.
£2,400–2,800
€/ **$3,800–4,400** ⚒ B

A pair of carved and painted limewood swags,
French, c1880, 20in (51cm) wide.
£400–450
€/ **$630–700** ⊞ HUM

A polychrome-painted
cluster of wood palm
trees, with trailing leaves
and fruit and a carved olive
tree, northern European,
19thC, 88in (224cm) high.
£1,700–2,000
€/ **$2,700–3,200** ⚒ S(S)
This group was
probably part of the
background for a large
nativity scene.

Bathroom Fittings

A Victorian basin, with brass taps and decorative cast-iron bracket, 30in (76cm) wide.
£1,700–1,900
€ / **$2,700–3,000** ⊞ **WRe**

A Victorian basin, with brass taps and cast-iron brackets, 25in (63.5cm) wide.
£1,400–1,600
€ / **$2,200–2,500** ⊞ **WRe**

A pedestal basin, restored, c1900, 34in (86.5cm) wide.
£2,300–2,500
€ / **$3,600–4,000** ⊞ **C&R**

A Shelvas basin, with floral decoration, c1907, 22in (56cm) wide.
£900–1,000
€ / **$1,400–1,600** ⊞ **WRe**

To order Miller's books in the UK please ring 01903 828800.
See the full range at
www.millers.uk.com

An Edwardian Doulton & Co corner basin, with reconditioned nickel-plated taps and waste, 18in (45.5cm) wide.
£630–700
€ / **$1,000–1,100** ⊞ **WRe**

A pedestal basin, c1900, 27in (68.5cm) wide.
£1,300–1,500
€ / **$2,100–2,200** ⊞ **C&R**

A Shanks & Co pedestal basin, reconditioned, 1930s, 24in (61cm) wide.
£400–450
€/ **$630–700** ⊞ **WRe**

A Shanks & Co canopy bath, c1895, 87in (221cm) high.
£12,000–14,000
€/ **$19,000–22,000** ⊞ **C&R**

A zinc-lined copper bath, with two lift rings on one side, c1900, 69in (175.5cm) long.
£2,800–3,200
€/ **$4,400–5,100** 🔨 **NOA**

An iron bath on wheels, French, c1900, 64in (162.5cm) long.
£1,300–1,500
€/ **$2,100–2,400** ⊞ **C&R**

A Shanks & Co cast-iron bath and shower unit, restored, c1900, 85in (216cm) high.
£11,000–12,000
€/ **$17,400–19,000** ⊞ **C&R**

> For further information on Architectural Antiques see the full range of Miller's books at
> **www.millers.uk.com**

A John Bolding stone bath, c1900, 70in (178cm) long.
£3,500–4,000
€/ **$5,500–6,400** ⊞ **C&R**

A tenement bath, with brass fittings, Scottish, 1920–30, 67in (170cm) long.
£3,500–4,000
€/ **$5,500–6,400** ⊞ **WRe**

A copper geyser, c1900, 41¾in (106cm) high.
£450–500
€/ **$720–780** ⊞ **C&R**

► **A Household Closet lavatory pan,** with revolving trap pan, c1895, 17in (43cm) high.
£900–1,000
€/ **$1,400–1,600** ⊞ **WRe**

◄ **An Oeneas lavatory pan,** decorated with English Countryside pattern, c1880, 17in (43.5cm) high.
£1,300–1,400
€/ **$2,000–2,200** ⊞ **WRe**

A Puritas lavatory pan, decorated with a floral pattern, concealed trap, 1891–93, 16in (40.5cm) high.
£900–1,000
€/ **$1,400–1,600** ⊞ **OLA**

A mahogany low-level cistern, c1900, 21in (53.5cm) wide.
£450–500
€/ $720–800 ⊞ C&R

A Victorian Sanitas salt-glazed stoneware lavatory pan, 17in (43cm) high.
£550–600
€/ $870–950 ⊞ WRe

A Victorian Adams & Co lavatory pan and cistern, with wooden seat.
£550–600
€/ $870–950 ⊞ OLA

► An Oeneas lavatory pan, basin and pine washstand, c1900, stand 41in (104cm) wide.
£6,300–7,000
€/ $10,000–11,000 ⊞ C&R

A Doulton Lambeth Patent combination lavatory pan, c1900, 16in (40.5cm) high.
£1,800–2,000
€/ $2,800–3,200 ⊞ C&R

A pair of brass taps, in the form of swan's necks, c1720, 8in (20.5cm) high.
£585–650
€/ $925–1,000 ⊞ RGe

A pair of Kula polished brass bath filler taps, French, c1900, 11in (28cm) wide.
£900–1,000
€/ $1,400–1,600 ⊞ C&R

◄ A nickel-plated double towel rail, French, c1900, 23¾in (60.5cm) long.
£130–150
€/ $200–220 ⊞ C&R

A Victorian nickel-plated towel rail and radiator, c1900, 44½in (113cm) wide.
£800–1,000
€/ $1,300–1,600 ⊞ C&R

► A nickel-plated shower mixer and stand pipe, reconditioned, 1930s, 40in (101.5cm) high.
£800–1,000
€/ $1,300–1,600 ⊞ WRe

A Minton bathroom set, comprising towel rail brackets, wall shelf, a pair of hooks and a double hook, probably by John Wadsworth, hairline to shelf rim, c1930, shelf 12¼in (31cm) long.
£220–250
€/ $350–400 ⚒ B
Ex-Minton sale.

Bell Pulls

A pair of Regency mahogany and gilt-metal bell pulls, 6in (15cm) high.
£220–250
€/ $350–400 🔨 SWO

A brass servants' bell pull, in the form of a lion, early 19thC,
5in (12.5cm) high.
£850–950
€/ $1,300–1,500 ⊞ ChC

A Victorian brass bell pull, c1860,
9in (23cm) high.
£260–300
€/ $410–475 ⊞ Penn

A brass interior bell push, c1870,
5in (13cm) diam.
£55–60
€/ £85–95 ⊞ Penn

◄ A brass and ceramic bell pull,
c1890, 5in (12.5cm) high
£60–70
€/ $95–110 ⊞ Penn

Doors & Door Furniture

◄ A carved pine door, with peep-hole panel, German, early 19thC,
76in (193cm) high.
£350–400
€/ $550–640 ⊞ HRQ

An Edwardian pine nine-panel front door,
36in (91.5cm) high.
£270–300
€/ $430–480 ⊞ WRe

A wrought-iron door knocker, c1770,
7in (18cm) wide.
£180–200
€/ $280–320 ⊞ SEA

A pair of oak and pencil-work panelled doors,
19thC, 87¾in (223cm) high.
£2,000–2,200
€/ $3,200–3,500 🔨 S(O)

◄ A Kenrick & Sons door knocker and letter plate, registered No 429,
c1890, 8in (20.5cm) wide.
£160–180
€/ $250–280 ⊞ OLA

An iron door knocker,
c1850, 7½in (19cm) wide.
£110–120
€/ $175–190 ⊞ Penn

◄ A pair of brass handles,
c1890, 9in (23cm) long.
£50–55
€/ $80–85 ⊞ Penn

Fireplaces

A carved pine fire surround, mid-18thC, 70in (178cm) wide.
£5,000–5,500
€ / **$7,900–8,700** ⊞ WRe

A George III inlaid marble fire surround, the frieze centred by a carved tablet, the jambs with fluted banding, 72in (183cm) wide.
£14,000–16,000
€ / **$22,000–25,000** ⚒ JAd

A George III pine fire surround, the frieze moulded with key and swag decoration, 58¾in (149cm) wide.
£2,200–2,500
€ / **$3,500–4,000** ⚒ CGC

A George III carved pine fire surround, 70½in (179cm) wide.
£650–750
€ / **$1,000–1,200** ⚒ SWO

A neo-classical-style black marble and alabaster fire surround, the end blocks decorated with blue john roundels, c1830, 67¾in (172cm) wide.
£10,000–11,000
€ / **$15,800–17,400** ⊞ W&C

A marble fire surround, decorated with pomegranates, c1860, 52¾in (134cm) wide.
£9,000–10,000
€ / **$14,200–15,800** ⊞ W&C

◀ **A carrara marble fire surround,** c1870, 78in (198cm) wide.
£2,500–2,800
€ / **$4,000–4,400** ⊞ ASH

A carved pine and gesso fire surround, c1880, 56in (143cm) wide.
£2,200–2,500
€ / **$3,500–3,800** ⊞ WRe

▶ **A cast-iron and tiled fire surround,** c1880, 40in (101.5cm) wide.
£1,200–1,300
€ / **$1,900–2,000** ⊞ WRe

A George III-style carved pine and gesso fire surround, 19thC, 56¼in (143cm) wide.
£1,000–1,200
€/ **$1,600–1,900** ➤ S(O)

A fire surround, early 20thC, 72½in (184cm) wide.
£100–120
€/ **$160–190** ➤ B(Ba)

A cast-iron hob register grate, early 19thC, 30in (76.5cm) wide.
£500–550
€/ **$800–870** ⊞ WRe

A Victorian cast-iron and tiled fire grate, the jambs decorated with white-glazed Minton tiles, 36in (91.5cm) wide.
£300–350
€/ **$475–550** ➤ FHF

A Victorian painted wood and composition fire surround, with egg-and-dart decoration, the frieze centred with a mask, 84in (214.5cm) wide.
£2,200–2,500
€/ **$3,500–4,000** ➤ B(Ch)

A cast-iron fire grate, early 19thC, 36in (91.5cm) wide.
£850–950
€/ **$1,300–1,500** ⊞ WRe

A cast-iron hob register grate, c1820, 32in (81.5cm) wide.
£550–600
€/ **$870–950** ⊞ WRe

A Victorian cast-iron and brass fire grate, late 19thC, 33in (84cm) wide.
£700–850
€/ **$1,100–1,300** ➤ S(O)

A pine fire surround, Irish, c1880, 51in (129.5cm) wide.
£220–240
€/ **$340–380** ⊞ Byl

A cast-iron hob grate, early 19thC, 28in (71cm) wide.
£315–350
€/ **$500–550** ⊞ WRe

A silvered-brass fire grate, 19thC, 30½in (77.5cm) wide.
£2,400–2,800
€/ **$3,800–4,400** ➤ WW

LOCATE THE SOURCE
The source of each illustration in Miller's can be found by checking the code letters below each caption with the Key to Illustrations, pages 794–800.

A polished steel fire grate, c1900, 21¾in (55.5cm) wide.
£850–1,000
€/ **$1,300–1,600** ➤ S(O)

Fireplace Accessories

A pair of wrought-iron andirons, French, c1770, 30in (76.5cm) high.
£630–700
€/ **$980–1,100** ⊞ SEA

A pair of Federal polished steel andirons, American, c1800, 23½in (69.5cm) wide.
£1,200–1,400
€/ **$1,900–2,200** ⋊ JDJ

A set of mahogany and brass peat bellows, 19thC, 26½in (67.5cm) long.
£170–200
€/ **$270–315** ⋊ SWO

A set of walnut, gilt and gesso fire bellows, with 17thC-style armorial decoration and scroll and scallop shell grips, 19thC, 25in (63.5cm) long.
£550–650
€/ **$870–1,000** ⋊ G(B)

A walnut and brass coal scuttle, 1880–1900, 13¾in (35cm) high.
£130–150
€/ **$200–240** ⋊ SWO

A Victorian _tôle peinte_ coal scuttle, the hinged bucket with a _verre églomisé_ shield, on a cast-metal base, 48in (122cm) high.
£320–380
€/ **$500–600** ⋊ DN

◄ **A copper coal scuttle,** c1910, 18in (45.5cm) high.
£220–245
€/ **$350–380** ⊞ WAC

A brass and wire mesh nursery fender, with drying rail, early 19thC, 56¼in (143cm) wide.
£1,000–1,200
€/ **$1,600–1,900** ⋊ HOK

◄ **A George III brass fender,** 56¼in (143cm) wide.
£600–700
€/ **$950–1,100** ⋊ S(O)

A cast-iron fender, early 19thC, 44in (112cm) wide.
£140–160
€/ **$220–250** ⋊ L

An armorial cast-iron fireback, 17thC, 19½in (49.5cm) high
£280–320
€/ **$440–600** ⋊ F&C

► **A set of steel fire irons,** early 19thC, with associated handles, 29½in (75cm) long.
£770–920
€/ **$1,200–1,500** ⋊ S(O)

A Victorian cast-iron double trivet, 22in (56cm) wide.
£160–175
€/ **$250–275** ⊞ RPh

Sculpture

A limestone corbel head of a queen, modelled with flowing hair beneath a crown, French, 15thC, 6¾in (17cm) high.
£700–950
€ / **$1,100–1,500** ⚒ S

An alabaster group of a reclining figure contemplating a skull, Italian, Naples, 17thC, 9in (23cm) wide.
£425–500
€ / **$670–790** ⚒ S(O)

An ivory group of the Virgin and Child, head of the Virgin replaced, losses, north German, c1230, 3in (7.5cm) high.
£1,500–1,800
€ / **$2,400–2,800** ⚒ S(NY)

A carved boxwood head of a Doge, wearing a cape, north Italian, c1600, 6in (15cm) high.
£900–1,100
€ / **$1,400–1,700** ⚒ G(L)

A limewood figure of a Roman soldier, with gilt and polychrome decoration, the head with curly hair, wearing a mantle over a cuirass, damaged, arms missing, south German, c1700, 17½in (44.5cm) high.
£900–1,000
€ / **$1,400–1,600** ⚒ S(Am)

An ivory figure of Ecco Homo, minor defects, Italian, 17thC, 6¾in (17cm) high.
£1,100–1,200
€ / **$1,700–1,900** ⊞ G&G

An ivory statue of Mary Magdalene, holding an urn, a skull at her feet, on a felt plinth, Flemish, 17thC, statue 3½in (9cm) high.
£530–635
€ / **$840–1,000** ⚒ S(O)

A carved boxwood figure of Christ, 18thC, 18in (45.5cm) high.
£800–1,000
€ / **$1,300–1,600** ⚒ SWO

A pair of bronze busts of Henry IV of Navarre and the Duc de Sully, Henry IV with curled hair and a beard and wearing a lace ruff and the order of the Saint Esprit, the other wearing a lace ruff and with a sash draped across his armour, on gilt-bronze and marble half columns, 18thC, 10¼in (26cm) high.
£800–1,000
€ / **$1,300–1,600** ⚒ B

A terracotta figure of the Virgin and Child, attributed to Walter Pompe, 18thC, 22in (56cm) high.
£1,800–2,200
€ / **$2,800–3,500** ⚒ BERN

An ivory figure of a gardener, resting while smoking his pipe, on an ivory plinth with allegorical masks, Austrian, early 19thC, 12½in (32cm) high.
£4,000–4,500
€ / **$6,300–7,000** ⊞ LBO

A parcel-gilt stained-terracotta figure of a priest with the Christ Child, French, early 19thC, 27½in (70cm) high.
£500–500
€/ **$790–950** ⚒ BERN

A pair of bronze figures of putti, one holding a sickle and a bunch of grapes, the other holding a sheaf of corn, on Siena marble bases, French, 19thC, 8½in (21.5cm) high.
£850–1,000
€/ **$1,300–1,600** ⚒ TEN

An alabaster group of a seated man holding the hand of a maiden, by E. Fiaschi, signed, Italian, 19thC, 33in (84cm) high.
£1,500–1,800
€/ **$2,400–2,800** ⚒ G(B)

A marble bust of a girl, by William Calder Marshall, ARA, signed, nose restored, dated 1849, 21¼in (54cm) high.
£1,200–1,300
€/ **$1,900–2,100** ⚒ S(O)

A patinated-bronze allegorical figure of a woman, 19thC, 11in (28cm) high.
£220–250
€/ **$350–400** ⚒ TMA

A marble bust of a woman, by Pietro Magni, signed, Italian, Milan, c1871, 29½in (75cm) high.
£2,200–2,500
€/ **$3,500–4,000** ⚒ S(NY)

A patinated-bronze group of a girl with a putto and young Bacchus, by Adrien Fourdrin, on a marble base, signed, stamped, dated 1854, 20½in (52cm) high.
£1,300–1,500
€/ **$2,100–2,400** ⚒ BERN

An ivory figure of St George slaying the Dragon, on a later oak base, 19thC, 6¾in (17cm) high.
£400–480
€/ **$630–700** ⚒ S(Am)

A marble figure of a young girl reading a book, signed 'Antonio Bartone', Italian, 19thC, 39in (99cm) high.
£25,000–28,000
€/ **$40,000–44,000** ⊞ CAT
This sculpture is of a good size and by a well-known maker.

A cast bronze figure of Edmund Burke, by J. H. Foley, RA, wearing 18thC costume, base inscribed 'Elkington & Co. Founders & J. H. Foley, RA, London', c1865, 20in (51cm) high.
£2,200–2,500
€/ **$3,500–4,000** ⚒ WL

A bronze figure of The Crouching Venus, after the Antique, on a marble plinth, 19thC, 11½in (29cm) high.
£750–875
€/ **$1,200–1,400** ⚒ Mit

A bronze figure of a gentleman, seated beside a vice, c1880, 15in (38cm) high.
£700–850
€/ **$1,100–1,300** ⚒ BWL

SCULPTURE

A carved and gilt American eagle, perched on a rocky outcrop, 19thC, 28in (71cm) wide.
£4,000–4,800
€/ **$6,300–7,600** ✗ S(NY)

A terracotta group of two seated peasants, Italian, 19thC, 10¼in (26cm) high.
£280–320
€/ **$440–500** ✗ BERN

A bronze figure of a woman, by Charles Veeck, French, 19thC, 11¾in (30cm) high.
£1,900–2,100
€/ **$3,000–3,300** ⊞ G&H

A model of bassett hounds, by Emmanuel Frerniet, entitled 'Ravageot et Ravagerote', c1880, 5½in (14cm) high.
£2,700–3,000
€/ **$4,300–4,700** ⊞ BHa

A Renaissance-style alabaster bust of Laura, by A. Parello, with gilt decoration, signed and titled, Italian, c1880, 20in (51cm) high.
£2,200–2,400
€/ **$3,200–3,800** ✗ S(O)

A bronze figure of a mounted jockey, by J. Willis Good, on a marble base with presentation plaque dated 1884, signed and dated 1895, 12¼in (31cm) high.
£4,500–5,200
€/ **$7,100–8,200** ✗ B(L)

A bronze figure of a woman holding a harp, by Georges Coudray, French, late 19thC, 17¼in (44cm) high.
£4,000–4,400
€/ **$6,300–7,000** ⊞ G&H

A carved marble bust of a maiden, by F. Junck, her hair in ringlets and a plait, with a floral bandeau, wearing a wrap-over dress, on an ebonized stepped base, carved signature, Continental, late 19thC, 15½in (39.5cm) high.
£500–600
€/ **$790–950** ✗ RTo

◄ **An alabaster bust of a woman,** Italian School, socle missing, c1890, 19in (48.5cm) high.
£1,600–1,800
€/ **$2,500–2,800** ✗ S(O)

◄ **A bronze bust of a female,** by Jef Lambeaux, signed and dated 1885, 19¾in (50cm) high.
£900–1,100
€/ **$1,400–1,700** ✗ BERN

A bronzed figure of a hound, gnawing a bone, signed 'H. Fouques 1895', 15in (38cm) high.
£500–575
€/ **$790–900** ✗ L

► **A bronze group of two pointers,** by Eglantine Lemaître, entitled 'Au Coup de Fusil', signed, foundry stamp, c1890, 17¼in (44cm) wide.
£3,000–3,400
€/ **$4,700–5,400** ✗ SWO

A bronze model of a whippet, after Pierre-Jules Mène, signed, late 19thC, 6in (15cm) high.
£100–120
€/ **$160–190** ⚒ G(L)

A cold-painted bronze figure of a boy lying on the ground, wearing a fez, Austrian, late 19thC, 5¼in (13.5cm) long.
£500–580
€/ **$790–920** ⚒ RTo

A naïve carved and painted wood group of a bear and cub, late 19thC, 51¼in (130cm) high.
£1,600–1,800
€/ **$2,500–2,800** ⚒ S(O)

A pair of bronze figures of Diana and Hermes, signed, late 19thC, 14¼in (36cm) high.
£1,500–1,800
€/ **$2,400–2,800** ⚒ BERN

A bronze group of a peasant couple in a sled pulled by horses, by Evgeny Alexandrovich Lanceray, signed, Shtange foundry stamp, Russian, late 19thC, 21in (53.5cm) wide.
£2,200–2,500
€/ **$3,500–4,000** ⚒ S(NY)

A bronze figure of a seated lady, wearing classical robes, on a low stool with a lyre, signed 'J. Pradier Susse fecit', on a marbleized wooden base, late 19thC, 10¼in (26cm) high.
£400–475
€/ **$630–750** ⚒ B&L

A terracotta model of a pug dog, with curled tail and incised coat, collar and glass eyes, repaired, late 19thC, 12½in (32cm) high.
£700–850
€/ **$1,100–1,300** ⚒ B(W)

To order Miller's books in the UK please ring 01903 828800.
See the full range at
www.millers.uk.com

A marble figure of Ida, by Balleux, on a marble base, signed, French, late 19thC, 19¾in (50cm) wide.
£850–1,000
€/ **$1,300–1,600** ⚒ S(O)

A bronze figure of a warrior, by Eugène Marioton, French, late 19thC, 14¼in (36cm) high.
£2,100–2,300
€/ **$3,300–3,600** ⊞ G&H

A pair of bronze figures of Mars and Minerva, on marble bases, Italian, 1875–1925, 12¼in (31cm) high.
£800–900
€/ **$1,300–1,400** ⚒ S(O)

A bronze group of two men racing a sail-assisted canoe, by Edouard Drouot, French, c1900, 24in (61cm) wide.
£1,300–1,500
€/ **$2,100–2,400** ⊞ RGa

A cold-painted bronze model of a kingfisher, stamped with Bergman seal, beak possibly bent, Austrian, c1900, 6½in (16.5cm) long.
£240–275
€/ **$380–430** ✦ G(L)

A model of birds sitting in the branch of a tree, by G. Rischmann, signed, German or Austrian, c1900, 11½in (29cm) high.
£850–950
€/ **$1,300–1,500** ⊞ BeF

An ivory and gilt-bronze bust of L'Amour, after the model by Agathon Léonard, inscribed, Paris, numbered 80, c1900, 9¼in (23.5cm) high.
£1,700–2,000
€/ **$2,700–3,200** ✦ Mit
Agathon Léonard (1841–1923) was the pseudonym for Van Weydeveld, a Belgiam artist who moved to France early in his career. He was made a *Chevalier of the Légion d'Honneur* in 1900.

A zinc figure of a woman, stamped 'J. W. Fiske 99 Chambers St, New York', American, c1900, 51in (129.5cm) high.
£3,000–3,400
€/ **$4,700–5,400** ✦ S(NY)

A pair of painted bronze busts of Native Americans, by Franz Bergman, on ebonized plinth bases, impressed seal and numerals, Austrian, c1900, taller 8in (20.5cm) high.
£1,000–1,200
€/ **$1,600–1,900** ✦ S(O)

A marble figure of Cupid, by M. Pownall, examining a heart with a magnifying glass, other hearts scattered at his feet, on a naturalistic base, hand restored, signed and dated 1908, 10¾in (27.5cm) high.
£900–1,100
€/ **$1,400–1,700** ✦ B

A bronze group of a WWI soldier leading three horses, by Gilbert William Bayes, on a marble base, signed and dated 1915, 10¼in (26cm) wide.
£1,100–1,300
€/ **$1,700–2,100** ✦ S(O)

Paris was considered the home of sculpture in the 19th century and attracted sculptors from all over Europe and the USA. They studied, for the most part, at the Ecole des Beaux Arts and exhibited at the salons, which upheld strong classical traditions. Selected works were displayed at one of the prestigious annual salon exhibitions. As these were attended by important government and institutional purchasers, sculptors were dependent on the commissioning powers of these people for their economic survival. The salons therefore, exercised considerable control over artistic output, which resulted in works displaying a strong classical influence for most of the century.

A bronze figure of Rembrandt van Rijn, by Huib Luns, signed and inscribed, Dutch, early 20thC, 13¾in (35cm) high, with a framed etching of a copy of the drawing.
£800–900
€/ **$1,300–1,400** ✦ S(Am)

◄ **A bronze group of Orpheus and Cerberus,** by Charles Raoul Verlet, signed and inscribed 'F Barbedienne', underside stamped '/925', French, c1900, 32¼in (82cm) high.
£3,100–3,700
€/ **$4,900–5,800** ✦ B

A bronze bust of a Classical man, by Professor O. Poertzel, on a marble plinth, German, early 20thC, 10¾in (27.5cm) high.
£650–720
€/ **$1,000–1,100** ✦ S(O)

A bronze figure of a soldier, by Georges Colin, entitled 'Pour la Patrie', the soldier standing on a raft, using his rifle as a rudder, on an ebonized wood base, signed, early 20thC, 33½in (85cm) high.
£1,600–2,000
€/ **$2,500–3,200** ✦ S(Am)

Metalware

Brass

A brass bell, modelled as a pig, c1850, 7in (18cm) wide.
£1,200–1,300
€/ **$1,900–2,000** ⊞ RGe

A pair of brass candlesticks, c1750, 8in (20.5cm) high.
£620–680
€/ **$980–1,000** ⊞ SEA

A brass and steel servant's bell, c1900, 8½in (21.5cm) diam.
£90–100
€/ **$140–160** ⊞ Penn

A brass ash bucket, Dutch, c1780, 11in (28cm) high.
£525–575
€/ **$830–900** ⊞ SEA

▶ **A Victorian gilt-brass casket,** with applied pierced panels, the interior velvet lined, inscribed 'T. A Simpson & Co, 154 Regent St, W', with swing handles, 8¾in (22cm) wide.
£700–820
€/ **$1,100–1,300** ⚒ WW

A pair of Regency gilt-metal candlesticks, on triform bases, with later drip pans, 10in (25.5cm) high.
£220–250
€/ **$350–400** ⚒ B(Ba)

A Georgian brass coffee pot, with engraved crest, traces of silvering, fruit-wood handle, pseudo-hallmarks to rim, early 18thC, 10in (25.5cm) high.
£2,300–2,800
€/ **$3,600–4,400** ⚒ S(O)
This coffee pot has a spout cast in two halves instead of being made in sheet metal.

◀ **A Victorian cast brass doorstop,** modelled as a pineapple, lead weighted, 13¾in (35cm) high.
£200–220
€/ **$315–350** ⚒ WW

METALWARE

METALWARE

A brass iron, Dutch, 19thC, 8in (20.5cm) wide.
£70–80
€ / $110–130 🔨 DuM

A set of gilt-brass and porcelain letter scales, by S. Mordan & Co, London, c1870, 8in (20.5cm) wide.
£530–630
€ / $840–980 🔨 S(O)

A brass kettle, Dutch, mid-18thC, 12in (30.5cm) high.
£230–255
€ / $360–400 ⊞ SEA

◀ **A brass lamp,** Dutch, c1795, 13in (33cm) high.
£430–475
€ / $680–750 ⊞ SEA

▶ **A brass vinaigrette,** the sides engraved with a hunting scene, the lift-off cover revealing an inner top pierced with the arms of Hanow, Prussian, early 17thC, 1¾in (4.5cm) high.
£1,100–1,200
€ / $1,600–1,900 🔨 S(O)

Bronze

A bronze rumbler bell, 18thC, 4in (10cm) diam.
£340–375
€ / $550–600 ⊞ SEA
A rumbler bell is one that contains a small hard object which rattles, and was formerly often used on horses' harnesses.

A leather and gilt-bronze dress box, engraved with royal inscription and decorated with an escutcheon and applied cast bust of Prince Albert on the cover, c1850, 11½in (29cm) diam.
£1,000–1,200
€ / $1,600–1,900 🔨 S(O)
This box formerly belonged to H.R.H. Prince Albert.

◀ **A pair of Empire-style bronze and ormolu candlesticks,** the bowls of the campana nozzles cast with leaves above anthemion motifs, on ribbed columns, on three paw feet and bronze tripartite plinth, 19thC, 12¾in (32.5cm) high.
£650–750
€ / $1,000–1,200 🔨 CGC

A pair of gilt-bronze two-light candelabra, each foliate-decorated nozzle supported by similarly-decorated arms on a naturalistic base, French, early 19thC, 12½in (32cm) high.
£700–820
€ / $1,100–1,300 🔨 B(Nor)

A gilt-bronze Palais Royal four-piece desk stand, the taper inset with jasper and malachite cabochons, on ball feet, 19thC, 8¼in (21cm) wide.
£160–200
€ / $250–320 🔨 SWO

◀ **A pair of Renaissance-style patinated-bronze ewers,** with putto's head and serpent handles, cast with classical scenes of Venus and her attendants seated on two dolphins, the reverse with scrolls of birds, dogs and mythical beasts, on cast pedestals and marble circular bases, French, late 19thC, 19in (48.5cm) high.
£750–900
€/ **$1,200–1,400** ↗ B

A bronze grisset, c1750, 12in (30.5cm) wide.
£1,800–2,000
€/ **$2,800–3,200** ⊞ SEA

A gilt-bronze and silvered inkstand, with twin-lidded wells and central glass open well, mid-19thC, 11¾in (30cm) wide.
£330–360
€/ **$520–560** ↗ S(O)

A bronze mortar, bearing Charles I's coat-of-arms, c1640, 6in (15cm) high.
£1,800–2,000
€/ **$2,800–3,200** ⊞ SEA

A gilt-bronze inkwell, with relief foliage, on griffon supports, the cover cast as two horses, mid-19thC, 9¾in (25cm) high.
£580–700
€/ **$900–1,100** ↗ S(O)

A pair of Regency gilt-bronze mantel lustres, the cast foliate urn nozzles with undulating drip pans and leafy collars hung with later cut-glass prism drops, on scrolling arms centred by a fruiting finial before a model of a greyhound, on a marble plinth, 11¾in (30cm) high.
£1,300–1,500
€/ **$2,000–2,400** ↗ B

For further information on Kitchenware see pages 220–223

▶ **A bronze skillet,** Dutch, 16thC, 4in (10cm) high.
£880–980
€/ **$1,400–1,500** ⊞ SEA

A gilt-bronze vase and cover, by Pierre Jules Mêne, cast with hunting scenes, associated finial, French, c1849, 15in (38cm) high.
£400–480
€/ **$630–750** ↗ S(O)

A pair of gilt-bronze and patinated models of the Albani vase, each with a fruiting vine rim above a frieze of male masks, on a fluted foot and marble base on lion-paw feet, 19thC, 8¼in (21cm) high.
£2,800–3,200
€/ **$4,400–5,000** ↗ B

A pair of bronze vases, with foliate-decorated rims, one cast with cattle and a ploughing scene, the other with chariot and horse racing scenes, with copper liners, 19thC, 14¼in (36cm) high.
£700–850
€/ **$1,100–1,300** ↗ Bea

Copper

◄ **A copper chocolate pot,** c1850, 11in (28cm) high.
£400–440
€/ $630–700 ⊞ MFB

A copper two-handled fish kettle, with lid, stamped 'P-S', 19thC, 19in (48.5cm) long.
£70–85
€/ $110–135 ➹ PFK

A copper and wrought-iron-mounted kettle, French, c1900, 24in (61cm) diam.
£435–520
€/ $690–790 ➹ NOA

◄ **A copper 4-gallon measure,** c1875, 18in (45.5cm) high.
£250–280
€/ $400–440 ⊞ Byl

► **A copper weathervane,** the moulded horse on a double-sphere rod with directionals, American, probably New England, c1875, 65in (165cm) high.
£6,500–7,500
€/ $10,300–11,800 ➹ S(NY)

Iron

► **A painted cast-iron offertory box,** c1850, 24in (61cm) high.
£1,600–2,000
€/ $2,500–3,200 ⊞ RYA
This poor house money box was designed to collect money for the needy. Offerings were inserted through the slots in the tower above the dome.

A cast-iron bell, in the shape of a pig, with wind-up mechanism, c1860, 7in (18cm) wide.
£1,200–1,400
€/ $1,900–2,200 ⊞ RGe

A wrought-iron candle holder and rush nip, c1750, 9in (23cm) high.
£430–480
€/ $680–750 ⊞ SEA

A cast-iron door stop, by Carron, Stirlingshire and Falkirk Foundries, modelled as the Scottish freedom fighter William Wallace, c1890, 13in (33cm) high.
£150–165
€/ $230–260 ⊞ RPh

A set of wrought-iron hanging hooks, Italian, c1770, 22in (56cm) long.
£1,200–1,400
€/ $1,900–2,200 ⊞ SEA

METALWARE

A pair of cast-iron mantel horses, polychrome painted, c1870, 10in (25.5cm) high.
£400–500
€/ **$630–800** ⊞ RYA

An iron pipe kiln, mid-19thC, 14in (35.5cm) long.
£315–350
€/ **$500–550** ⊞ KEY

An iron and zinc weathercock, with traces of original paint, probably French, c1890, 35in (89cm) long.
£1,400–1,600
€/ **$2,200–2,500** ⊞ RYA

Ormolu

An ormolu box, the centre inset with a painted portrait miniature, signed 'Theo', late 19thC, 4¼in (11cm) wide.
£500–580
€/ **$790–920** ⋏ SWO

Two ormolu two-light candelabra, with leaf-and rosette-scrolled arms, tapered half-reeded columns, on anthemion-applied columns, on square bases, larger 13¼in (33.5cm) high.
£1,000–1,200
€/ **$1,600–1,900** ⋏ DN

An ormolu, malachite and carnelian-mounted desk set, comprising an ink stand, pen wipe, taper stick and a pounce tazza, each engraved with foliate scrolls and set with cabochons, Russian, mid-19thC, ink stand 4in (10cm) long.
£4,000–4,800
€/ **$6,300–7,600** ⋏ BR

> Items in the Metalware section have been arranged in alphabetical order within each sub-section.

A late George III ormolu inkstand, in the style of Thomas Weeks, on a marble base, 5¾in (14.5cm) wide.
£700–820
€/ **$1,100–1,300** ⋏ WW

▶ **An Empire-style ormolu inkstand,** the back gallery with central cartouche, fitted with two ink wells with hinged lids, French, 19thC, 9in (23cm) wide.
£200–240
€/ **$315–380** ⋏ BR

Pewter

◀ **A pewter flask,** with cover, stamped 'C. Hertzger', early 18thC, 10in (25.5cm) high.
£200–220
€/ **$320–350** ⊞ KEY

A pewter lamp, Dutch, 18thC, 11in (28cm) high.
£80–100
€/ **$125–160** ⋏ DuM

A pewter *Hannukah* lamp, with lion finials supporting a flagon and a lamp, German, c1800, 7¾in (19.5cm) wide.
£1,500–1,800
€/ **$2,400–2,800** ⋏ S(O)

METALWARE

A pewter quart measure, with brass rim, c1860, 6in (15cm) high.
£220–245
€/ **$350–380** ⊞ **MFB**

A pewter pepper pot, c1850, 4¾in (12cm) high.
£45–50
€/ **$70–80** ⊞ **MFB**

A pewter salt, c1870, 3in (7.5cm) diam.
£75–85
€/ **$120–135** ⊞ **SEA**

◄ **A glass and pewter scent bottle,** c1900, 7in (18cm) high.
£75–85
€/ **$120–135** ⊞ **WAC**

A silver-plated pewter tureen, by C. Saur, Stockholm, Swedish, c1776, 15¼in (39cm) wide.
£1,400–1,700
€/ **$2,200–2,700** ⚒ **BUK**

Toleware

A toleware box, with painted decoration, slight wear, 19thC, 9in (23cm) wide.
£280–320
€/ **$440–500** ⚒ **JDJ**

A toleware tray, painted with a Georgian domestic scene, twin handles, early 19thC, 28½in (72.5cm) wide.
£550–650
€/ **$870–1,000** ⚒ **BIG**

A toleware tobacco box, the hinged lid painted with a scene of soldiers returning from a defeated army, 19thC, 3in (7.5cm) wide.
£120–140
€/ **$190–220** ⚒ **TMA**

LOCATE THE SOURCE

The source of each illustration in Miller's can be found by checking the code letters below each caption with the Key to Illustrations, pages 794–800.

An Edwardian japanned toleware smoker's companion, inscribed in gilt 'H & S 1804', and 'H & S 1904', 10in (25.5cm) high.
£380–450
€/ **$600–710** ⚒ **PF**

A pair of toleware vases, painted with scenes of everyday life and portraits, some damage, early 19thC, 8¾in (22.5cm) high.
£2,000–2,400
€/ **$3,200–3,800** ⚒ **S(P)**

Miscellaneous

A lead tobacco box, with negro head finial, 19thC, 6¾in (17cm) wide.
£250–300
€/ $400–475 ⚒ SWO

A metal dog collar, 15thC–16thC, 5in (12.5cm) diam.
£500–550
€/ $790–870 ⊞ GGv

◀ A Victorian gilt-metal canary cage, with ebonized finial, 24in (61cm) high.
£130–160
€/ $200–250 ⚒ DA

◀ A steel key, late 17thC, 5in (12.5cm) long.
£1,100–1,200
€/ $1,700–1,900 ⊞ KEY

▶ A Victorian gilt-metal paper clip, modelled as a greyhound's head with inset glass eyes, 19thC, 6in (15cm) long.
£280–340
€/ $440–520 ⚒ SWO

A painted tin letter rack, c1850, 11in (28cm) wide.
£225–250
€/ $350–400 ⊞ SWN

A pinchbeck paperweight, in high relief and gilding with soldiers carousing in a baronial hall, with blue-cloth covered base, mid-19thC, 3¼in (8cm) diam.
£850–1,000
€/ $1,300–1,600 ⚒ S(O)

A pair of steel scissors, with engraved decoration, in a pierced engraved case, late 17thC, 3¼in (8.5cm) wide.
£480–550
€/ $760–870 ⚒ G(L)

▶ A patinated and cold-painted spelter vase, in the style of Louis Hottot, modelled as a reclining camel, French, c1880, 15¾in (40cm) high.
£900–1,100
€/ $1,400–1,800 ⚒ S(Am)
The French sculptor Louis Hottot (1829–1905) specialized in Oriental subjects.

A gilt metal tape measure, in the form of a coronation coach, 19thC, 2in (5cm) high.
£130–150
€/ $200–240 ⚒ AMB

◀ A painted tin tray, worn, 19thC, 30¾in (78cm) wide.
£100–120
€/ $160–190 ⚒ SWO

METALWARE

Leather

A gilt-tooled leather Cumberland wrestling belt, stamped 'Newton Hero 1836', 54½in (138.5cm) long including the brass buckle.
£700–820
€/ **$1,100–1,300** ⚒ PFK

A gilt-tooled leather blotter, decorated with a Cardinal's coat-of-arms within floral patterned borders, the spine inscribed 'Pont Roma Pt III', Italian, 18thC, 17 x 12in (43 x 30.5cm).
£360–430
€/ **$570–700** ⚒ G(L)

A leather blotter, by Asprey & Co, with a gilt metal lockplate, enclosing inkwells, ivory paper knife and stamp divisions, with key, 19thC, 9½ x 12in (24 x 30.5cm).
£220–250
€/ **$350–400** ⚒ G(L)

A leather box, Italian, 17thC, 10in (25.5cm) wide.
£850–950
€/ **$1,300–1,500** ⊞ SEA

A leather sewing box, decorated with panels of Dickensian scenes, each signed 'C. Schaub, London, June 4th 1873', 9in (23cm) wide.
£200–240
€/ **$315–380** ⚒ SWO

An embossed leather casket, with an iron hasp, interior restored, Spanish, 17thC, 19¾in (50cm) wide.
£380–420
€/ **$600–650** ⚒ S(O)

A brass-studded leather chest, with a domed hinged top, c1740, 48¾in (124cm) wide.
£850–1,000
€/ **$1,300–1,600** ⚒ S(O)

A brass-studded leather-covered chest, the domed top dated 1668 and initialled 'J.H.', 17thC, 42in (106.5cm) wide.
£1,300–1,500
€/ **$2,000–2,400** ⚒ CGC

A Spanish-style brass-studded leather-upholstered trunk, with iron carrying handles, on runner feet, Spanish, c1900, 35in (89cm) wide.
£700–830
€/ **$1,100–1,300** ⚒ NOA

A leather dog collar, 1890–1910, 6in (15cm) diam.
£85–95
€/ **$135–150** ⊞ GGv

A leather and brass dog collar, French, late 19thC, 5¾in (14.5cm) diam.
£200–225
€/ **$320–350** ⊞ GGv

A George IV painted leather fire bucket, with a swing handle, decorated with a crowned 'J.C.' cypher, 11½in (29cm) diam.
£75–90
€/ **$120–140** ⚒ G(L)

An Edwardian leather letter holder, with embossed vine leaf decoration, 8in (20.5cm) wide.
£35–40
€/ **$55–65** ⊞ HO

A leather writing and toiletry travel case, the locked flaps enclosing ivory handled tools, some contents replaced, stamped, late 19thC, 8½in (21.5cm) wide
£135–150
€/ **$215–240** ⊞ ChC

Papier Mâché

A papier mâché box, by the Lukutin Manufactory, the lid painted with a landowner and serfs, early 19thC, ¾in (9.5cm) diam.
£530–630
€ / $830–1,000 ↗ S(O)

A papier mâché gaming box, parcel-gilt and inlaid with mother-of-pearl, the interior with four card-deck boxes and a games pieces box en suite, late 19thC, 14¼in (36cm) wide.
£500–570
€ / $800–900 ↗ NOA

A papier mâché tray, by B. Walton & Co, stamped, 19thC, 26in (66cm) diam.
£280–320
€ / $440–500 ↗ BWL

A Victorian papier mâché and mother-of-pearl inlaid tea caddy, by Lane of Birmingham, with two divisions, painted with floral decoration, 8in (20.5cm) wide.
£170–200
€ / $270–315 ↗ G(B)

A Victorian papier mâché 'Question Box', the sides painted with figures by a cottage, 6½in (16.5cm) wide.
£180–220
€ / $285–350 ↗ G(L)

A Regency papier mâché two-handled tray, by Clay, London, the border decorated in gilt with trailing leaves, flowers, moths and butterflies, applied with a pair of C-shaped ormolu handles, some warping and damage, 27½in (70cm) square.
£400–480
€ / $630–710 ↗ BR

A papier mâché tray, painted in enamels with a floral bouquet, 19thC, 31in (78.5cm) wide.
£520–620
€ / $820–980 ↗ BWL

A Victorian papier mâché tea caddy, with a hand-painted peacock and floral design, 9¾in (25cm) wide.
£400–480
€ / $630–710 ↗ WilP

▶ A pair of Regency papier mâché bottle stands, gilt-decorated with shells and scrolling foliage, 5in (12.5cm) diam.
£280–320
€ / $440–500 ↗ L&E

A papier mâché painted snuff box, by Stobwasser, the lid with a portrait of William IV, the reverse inscribed 'William IV King of Great Britain', damaged, 19thC, 4in (10cm) diam.
£500–600
€ / $800–950 ↗ SWO

A papier mâché and lacquered tray, decorated with figures in a pagoda garden landscape, heightened with gilt, 19thC, 32in (81.5cm) wide.
£1,200–1,500
€ / $1,900–2,400 ↗ Bea

A Victorian papier mâché tray, the centre painted with figures fishing in a mountainous landscape, within a gilt-heightened shell and foliate-decorated scalloped border, 21½in (54.5cm) wide.
£950–1,100
€ / $1,500–1,700 ↗ RIT

Treen

A carved birchwood ale hen, with traces of original paint, Scandinavian, c1780, 8in (20.5cm) wide.
£650–800
€/ **$1,000–1,300** ⊞ **RYA**

A carved oak book lectern, constructed from a single board and carved with fluted scrolls, petals and roundels, with a later heart-shaped metal hook nailed to the right hand edge, 17thC, 13in (33cm) wide.
£2,500–3,000
€/ **$4,000–4,700** ✂ **TEN**

An oak boot jack, 19thC, 39½in (100cm) high.
£140–160
€/ **$220–250** ✂ **S(O)**

An elm feeding bowl with handle, turned from one piece of wood, c1850, 9in (23cm) diam.
£170–200
€/ **$270–320** ⊞ **MFB**

A dug-out birchwood ale bowl, Scandinavian, c1790, 18in (45.5cm) wide.
£650–800
€/ **$1,000–1,300** ⊞ **RYA**

A Georgian oak book press, 13in (33cm) wide.
£320–360
€/ **$500–570** ⊞ **KEY**

A turned elm bowl, c1780, 10in (25.5cm) diam.
£100–115
€/ **$160–180** ⊞ **F&F**

A sycamore dairy bowl, c1880, 10in (25.5cm) diam.
£140–160
€/ **$220–250** ⊞ **SMI**

▶ **A burr-elm box,** the lid carved in relief with portrait busts of Voltaire and Rousseau, interior slightly damaged, French, early 19thC, 3¼in (8.5cm) diam.
£400–450
€/ **$630–700** ✂ **G(L)**

A beech bird scarer, initialled TF, 19thC, 10in (25.5cm) wide.
£180–200
€/ **$280–320** ⊞ **SEA**

A Regency rosewood bookstand, the gallery with turned supports, on bun feet, 19¼in (49cm) wide.
£200–275
€/ **$360–430** ✂ **AMB**

A bowl, dug out from a root, Welsh, 18thC, 8in (20.5cm) high.
£500–550
€/ **$800–880** ⊞ **SEA**

A painted and decorated maple bowl, with moulded rim, probably Shaker, American, 19thC, 24in (61cm) diam.
£3,000–3,300
€/ **$4,700–5,200** ✂ **S(NY)**

A George III oak candle box, 18in (45.5cm) high.
£300–350
€/ $475–550 ⊞ NoC

A lignum vitae candlestick, c1660, 12in (30.5cm) high.
£675–750
€/ $1,000–1,200 ⊞ SEA

A carved mahogany and wrought-iron pricket candlestick, with bone ball feet, mid-19thC, 9in (23cm) high.
£260–300
€/ $410–475 ↗ NOA
Pricket sticks were used to light gentlemen's after-dinner cigars.

A turned lignum vitae adjustable candelabrum, the campana-shaped holders on a bobbin- and reel-turned support, the screw stem on a circular base, damaged, 19thC, 16½in (42cm) high.
£160–200
€/ $250–315 ↗ WW

Items in the Treen section have been arranged in alphabetical order.

A pair of Black Forest carved wood candlesticks, in the form of trees with acorns and leaves, each with a bird on the base, German, c1900, 7½in (19cm) high.
€170–200
€/ $270–315 ↗ DMC

A pair of mahogany open barley-twist candlesticks, on turned bases, c1900, 14in (35.5cm) high.
£250–300
€/ $400–475 ↗ SWO

A Continental carved and decorated pine centrepiece, holding carved apples, c1880, 6in (15cm) diam.
£230–270
€/ $360–430 ⊞ RYA

A mahogany, oak and inlaid cheese coaster, c1800, 16in (41cm) wide.
£350–400
€/ $550–630 ↗ S(O)

A George III mahogany cheese cradle, the central ring-turned handle and parallel edges with reeded roundel terminals, 14½in (36.5cm) wide.
£650–780
€/ $1,000–1,200 ↗ CGC

An elm costrel, c1790, 10in (25.5cm) wide.
£315–350
€/ $500–550 ⊞ SEA

A sycamore lace crimper and board, c1850, 6in (15cm) square.
£45–50
€/ $70–80 ⊞ SEA

▶ **A walnut pedestal grater and cover,** carved with leaves, early 19thC, 3in (7.5cm) high.
£80–100
€/ $125–160 ↗ G(L)

TREEN

A mahogany 'lazy susan', c1900, 21in (53cm) diam.
£220–250
€/ **$350–400** ⚒ SWO

A hand-carved wood photograph frame, dated 1932, 17in (43cm) wide.
£380–420
€/ **$600–670** ⊞ WAC

An oak piggin, c1850, 18in (45.5cm) diam.
£315–350
€/ **$500–550** ⊞ SEA

A sycamore rushlight, with twin wood nips, late 19thC, 14¼in (36cm) high.
£240–280
€/ **$380–440** ⚒ S(O)

A carved bog oak letter opener, Irish, c1860, 10in (25.5cm) long.
£90–100
€/ **$140–160** ⊞ STA

A boxwood nutcracker, 19thC, 5in (12.5cm) long.
£220–250
€/ **$350–400** ⊞ SEA

A church warden's thorn pipe, 19thC, 11in (28cm) long.
£335–375
€/ **$530–600** ⊞ SEA

A birch pounce pot, c1790, 5in (12.5cm) high.
£420–460
€/ **$660–720** ⊞ SEA

A laburnum pounce pot, c1800, 5in (12.5cm) high.
£425–475
€/ **$670–750** ⊞ SEA

◀ **A walnut mould,** in the form of a rabbit, late 19thC, 19in (48.5cm) high.
£900–1,000
€/ **$1,400–1,600** ⊞ ChC
This mould was used to make a papier mâché model of a rabbit. The papier mâché was built up around the mould and then cut off to make the model.

A pitch pine salt, Scottish, c1820, 4in (10cm) high.
£350–400
€/ **$550–630** ⊞ SEA

A child's carved maple rattle, dated 1852, 6in (15cm) long.
£700–775
€/ **$1,100–1,200** ⊞ SEA

A sycamore snuff box, in the form of a frog, c1800, 5¼in (13.5cm) long.
£530–630
€/ $850–1,000 ➤ S(O)

A mahogany snuff shoe, with brass inlay and hinged cover, dated 1870, 4in (10cm) long.
£420–500
€/ $660–790 ➤ BWL

A fruitwood snuff box, in the form of a butterfly, the cover with mother-of-pearl and ebonized inlay, c1900, 4in (10cm) wide.
£1,300–1,500
€/ $2,000–2,400 ➤ S(O)

TREEN

◄ A carved love spoon, Welsh, early 19thC, 12in (30.5cm) long.
£1,000–1,200
€/ $1,600–1,900 ⊞ SEA

A sycamore tazza, c1780, 7in (18cm) diam.
£450–500
€/ $700–800 ⊞ SEA

A carved burr-birchwood peg tankard, Norwegian, c1780, 12in (30.5cm) high.
£900–1,000
€/ $1,400–1,700 ⊞ RYA

An Edwardian mahogany tray, with shaped gallery and brass handles, inlaid with marquetry, 25¾in (65.5cm) wide.
£160–200
€/ $250–315 ➤ SWO

A pearwood tea caddy, with iron hinge and escutcheon, traces of foil lining and blush decoration, c1800, 6½in (16.5cm) high.
£4,200–5,000
€/ $6,600–7,900 ➤ GH

An Edwardian mahogany drinks tray, with two open brass handles, inlaid with a marquetry shell with foliage and stringing, 22¾in (58cm) wide.
£160–200
€/ $250–315 ➤ WW

A carved birch vessel, with a copper rim, Baltic or Norwegian, early 19thC, 13½in (34cm) diam.
£380–420
€/ $600–660 ➤ S(O)
This vessel may have been a boat baler.

► A carved olivewood flared-footed vase, Italian, early 19thC, 19in (48.5cm) high.
£900–1,100
€/ $1,400–1,700 ➤ NOA

◄ A turned mahogany wig or bonnet stand, c1820, 14in (35.5cm) high.
£80–90
€/ $125–140 ⊞ F&F

Further reading

Miller's Antiques Under £1000, Miller's Publications, 2003

An oak and beech wool winder and counter, c1660, 24in (61cm) high.
£450–500
€/ $700–800 ⊞ SEA

Tunbridge Ware

A Victorian Tunbridge ware rosewood book rack, decorated with two views of a castle, 13in (33cm) long.
£170–200
€/ **$270–315** ✦ G(L)

A Tunbridge ware box, by H. Hollamby, decorated with a view of the Pantiles, Tunbridge Wells, c1880, 9½in (24cm) wide.
£2,000–2,300
€/ **$3,200–3,600** ⊞ PGO

A Victorian Tunbridge ware-banded walnut jewellery box, 11¾in (30cm) wide.
£240–280
€/ **$380–440** ✦ WilP

To order Miller's books in the USA please ring AOL/Time Warner on 1-800-759-0190

A Regency Tunbridge ware white-wood work box, decorated with a coloured engraving of Upton Cottage near Broadstairs, on a simulated rosewood ground with dog's tooth cross-banding, some repair, 4¼in (11cm) wide.
£150–175
€/ **$240–275** ✦ BR

A Tunbridge ware box, the hinged lid decorated with a central panel of figures before a tower, some wear, early 19thC, 6¼in (16cm) high.
£200–220
€/ **$315–350** ✦ SWO

A Tunbridge ware burr-walnut glove box, the cover with a tesserae panel flanked by lozenges, 19thC, 8¾in (22cm) long.
£170–200
€/ **$270–320** ✦ BR

A Tunbridge ware coromandel cotton reel box, the lid with a tesserae bouquet within geometric crossbanding, the sides with running rose banding, enclosing a removable stand with five brass reel pins, 19thC, 6½in (16.5cm) long.
£420–500
€/ **$670–800** ✦ BR

A lady's Tunbridge ware writing box, decorated with a view of Tonbridge Castle, c1875, 11in (28cm) wide.
£1,300–1,500
€/ **$2,100–2,400** ⊞ HAA

▶ **A Tunbridge ware rosewood magnifying glass,** 19thC, 6in (15cm) long.
£350–420
€/ **$550–660** ✦ TMA

A Tunbridge ware box, with floral mosaic decoration, c1810, 4in (10cm) wide.
£100–110
€/ **$160–175** ⊞ AMH

A Tunbridge ware rosewood box, with mosaic inlay, 19thC, 3½in (9cm) wide.
£70–80
€/ **$110–125** ⊞ MB

A Tunbridge ware maple stationery box, by Henry Hollamby, the top with a tesserae rose spray within tesserae crossbanding, the sides with a rose and scroll border, maker's paper label to underside, with key, 19thC, 6¼in (16cm) wide.
£700–820
€/ **$1,100–1,300** ✦ BR

A Tunbridge ware desk stand, with three lidded compartments and a cut-glass bottle, applied label of Edmund Nye, Tunbridge Wells, 19thC, 11¾in (30cm) wide.
£230–275
€/ **$360–430** ✦ SWO

A Tunbridge ware picture, restored, 1810–80, 9¼ x 7¼in (23.5 x 18.5cm).
£1,300–1,500
€/ $2,100–2,400 ⊞ PGO

▶ **A Tunbridge ware rosewood and stickware-inlaid pin dish,** c1840, 4in (10cm) diam.
£65–70
€/ $100–110 ⊞ MB

A Tunbridge ware whitewood sewing clamp, the body painted with stylized leaves and printed with a view of Brighton Pavilion, early 19thC, 7½in (19cm) high.
£320–380
€/ $500–600 ➤ BR

A Tunbridge ware picture, attributed to Henry Hollamby, depicting a view of The Pantiles, in a tesserae frame, 19thC, 7 x 9in (18 x 23cm).
£600–700
€/ $950–1,100 ➤ BR

A Tunbridge ware pin cushion, with one drawer, mid-19thC, 8in (20.5cm) wide.
£530–585
€/ $830–930 ⊞ PGO

A Tunbridge ware sovereign holder, in the shape of a ball, c1860, 1¾in (4.5cm) diam.
£300–350
€/ $475–550 ➤ VB

◀ **A Tunbridge ware tea caddy,** c1880, 8½in (21.5cm) wide.
£440–485
€/ $700–770 ⊞ PrB

A Tunbridge ware rosewood wine table, possibly by Wise, the top with marble, half square and Van Dyke borders, damage, 1840–50, 20in (51cm) square.
£2,000–2,400
€/ $3,200–3,800 ➤ BR

▶ **A Tunbridge ware rosewood combination thermometer stand and compass,** the ivory scale signed 'H. Hollamby, Tunbridge Wells', between two tesserae-banded sides, late 19thC, 5in (12.5cm) high.
£475–565
€/ $750–900 ➤ BR

A Victorian Tunbridge ware desk thermometer, by H. Hollamby, Tunbridge Wells, supported by two columns on a base, 5in (12.5cm) high.
£200–220
€/ $315–350 ➤ WW

TUNBRIDGE WARE

Boxes

The popularity of antique boxes has risen steadily over the past 25 years, and prices therefore have been affected rather dramatically. Without doubt the largest increases have occurred in tea caddies, especially tortoiseshell, ivory and turned fruit-shaped examples. English and Continental finely painted caddies have also proved to be favourites. However, stationery boxes, games compendiums, sewing/work boxes, snuff boxes and stamp boxes have also seen significant rises in value. These have the additional benefit that they can still be used for their original intended purpose.

While we do not doubt that antique boxes will remain popular, prospective buyers should be aware of the possible pitfalls of purchasing such items. One should look out for outright fakes, badly or over-restored boxes as well as altered or adorned pieces.

The fake caddy in particular has become prolific and can be found at auctions, fairs and unfortunately, even vetted shows. Currently there are a number of Dutch-style tortoiseshell caddies in circulation which are actually made of plastic tortoiseshell veneered onto a plywood carcass. They have no lock or escutcheon and the interior is lined with modern baize. We have seen such examples on dealers' stands dated as c1850 as well as offered at auction. Other commonly faked caddies include inlaid oval and octagonal examples in the George III style and various fruitwood pieces, particularly the melon-shaped. A slightly more clever deception is the making of a tortoiseshell-embossed caddy using panels of an embossed tortoiseshell visiting card case which have been veneered onto the front of the carcass of the caddy. Genuine examples of this type always have embossed panels on all four sides.

Poor restoration is certainly not acceptable. Antique boxes that have been stripped and repolished have the least chance of a return on one's investment. All too often the trade papers read 'this box would have fetched considerably more if it had not been badly or over restored.'

The market for antique boxes is still strong. Americans and Europeans alike appreciate the value of good quality antique boxes and are always keen buyers. We feel that in the short term price increases will probably be smaller than in the past ten years. However, while one should never advocate the buying of antiques purely for investment, the fact is that if one buys well, bearing in mind the salient points mentioned here then a return to some extent should be expected.

Alan and Kathy Stacey

A chinoiserie lacquer lace box, c1700, 21in (53.5cm) wide.
£950–1,100
€/ **$1,500–1,800** ⊞ TWh

A mahogany tea caddy, fitted with three lidded containers, c1770, 9in (23cm) wide.
£700–750
€/ **$1,100–1,200** ⊞ AKS

A mahogany tea caddy, the top with barber's pole inlay, the interior with three sections, lock missing, some faults, c1780, 10¼in (26cm) wide.
£400–475
€/ **$630–750** ⋏ BR

The Robert Harman Collection

The Robert Harman Collection of tea caddies was sold at Sotheby's London in November 1999. Comprising some 40 lots, this collection offered a wide and varied selection, including some rare examples.

Arguably the tour de force was a George III marquetry caddy, the front panel of which was modelled with an architectural view of a house façade. This sold for £28,750 (€/ $45,000), although the highest price achieved was approximately £34,500 (€/ $55,000) for a Regency ivory, tortoiseshell and polychrome japanned caddy. A wonderful pair of George III painted caddies, in the manner of Henry Clay, and in good original condition, sold for £21,850 (€/ $35,000).

Many of the more standard offerings sold above market value, aided no doubt by the added attraction of being offered in a collection. There was a handful of unsold lots, including an attractive ivory and gold-mounted decagonal caddy, c1790. This possibly failed because of the high reserve and severe cracking to some of its ivory panels.

The long-term investment on many of these caddies will be positive, with the added benefit of owning such beautiful objects.

Alan Stacey

A George III mahogany knife box, outlined with holly stringing, the divided interior inlaid with ebony and boxwood, 9in (23cm) wide.
£1,100–1,300
€/ **$1,700–2,000** ⊞ JC

A mahogany tea caddy, the top with bail handle attached to a silver-plated back plate engraved with a battle scene and inscribed 'Gibraltar Sept. 13th 1782', the escutcheon similarly engraved, the interior previously fitted with three sections, 18thC, 10in (25.5cm) wide.
£250–300
€ / **$400–480** ✗ M
The plate and escutcheon engravings commemorate the last attack of the Great Siege of Gibraltar by the Combined Fleet of France and Spain on 13 September 1782.

An ivory box, the top inset with a silhouette, c1790, 4in (10cm) wide.
£1,600–1,800
€ / **$2,500–3,000** ⊞ SHa

A harewood tea caddy, with floral marquetry, c1790, 4½in (11.5cm) high.
£1,400–1,600
€ / **$2,200–2,600** ⊞ HAA

A sycamore and marquetry-inlaid jewellery box, German, c1800, 6¾in (17cm) wide.
£80–100
€ / **$125–150** ✗ BR

A tortoiseshell miniature travel writing set, decorated with silver piqué, c1800, 1½in (4cm) high.
£1,100–1,200
€ / **$1,700–1,900** ⊞ HAA

An inlaid mahogany and fruitwood-edged tea caddy, c1800, 7in (18cm) wide.
£270–300
€ / **$430–470** ⊞ MB

▶ **A stained straw-work box,** decorated with figures in relief, c1800, 2¼in (5.5cm) diam.
£230–270
€ / **$360–430** ✗ G(L)

BOXES

A George III mahogany crossbanded tea caddy, inlaid with stars, the interior now with three lidded containers, 10in (25.5cm) wide.
£275–325
€/ **$435–520** ⚒ L

A Mauchline and penwork tea caddy, the top with a scene of Loch Lomond, the interior with two canisters, Scottish, early 19thC, 9¾in (25cm) wide.
£700–820
€/ **$1,100–1,300** ⚒ B(Ed)

A painted and incised compass-drawn box, American, Pennsylvania, early 19thC, 7in (18cm) wide.
£5,000–5,500
€/ **$8,000–8,700** ⚒ S(NY)

◄ **A Regency penwork and fruit-wood desk box,** the interior lined with marbelized Florentine papers, 12½in (32cm) wide.
£620–700
€/ **$980–1,100** ⚒ NOA

A Regency rosewood tea caddy, with four canisters, a bowl and later spoons, 17in (43cm) wide.
£2,200–2,500
€/ **$3,500–4,200** ⊞ Penn

A Regency mahogany tea caddy, inlaid with satinwood and rosewood, the interior with a bowl and two lidded compartments, 13in (33cm) wide.
£600–700
€/ **$950–1,100** ⚒ B(L)

A Regency ebony-banded rosewood tea caddy, with two lidded canisters and a glass bowl, 14in (35.5cm) wide.
£320–375
€/ **$500–600** ⚒ AH

► **A Regency penwork tea caddy,** decorated with chinoiserie scenes within vine borders, 8¼in (21cm) wide.
£800–900
€/ **$1,300–1,400** ⚒ S(O)

◄ **A rosewood tea caddy,** on brass ball feet, c1820, 8in (20.5cm) wide.
£220–250
€/ **$350–400** ⊞ MB

► **A tortoise-shell tea caddy,** with mother-of-pearl appliqué decoration, c1820, 6½in (16.5cm) high.
£3,800–4,200
€/ **$6,000–6,600** ⊞ HAA

An oyster-veneered yew wood box, the lift-out four-division tray possibly associated, c1820, 13in (33cm) wide.
£1,300–1,500
€ / $2,000–2,400 🏹 S(O)

A George IV mahogany and brass-bound box, the lid engraved with a crest, the lock stamped 'Bramah Piccadilly', 12in (30.5cm) wide.
£800–900
€ / $1,300–1,400 🏹 S(O)

◄ A tortoiseshell box, the lid inset with an ivory-mounted bronze portrait of Peter the Great, c1820, 2½in (6.5cm) diam.
£180–200
€ / $285–340 🏱 MB

A Regency tortoiseshell tea caddy, with ivory banding and pewter stringing, c1825, 5in (13cm) wide.
£3,600–4,000
€ / $5,700–6,300 🏱 AKS

A rosewood inlaid work box, with a named cartouche to the inside of the lid 'Maria Borgen', c1825, 12in (30.5cm) wide.
€340–380
€ / $540–600 🏱 STA

► A Mauchline snuff box, the lid painted with a scene entitled 'The Blessing', the sides and base painted with a tartan pattern, Scottish, early 19thC, 3½in (9cm) wide.
£320–400
€ / $500–600 🏹 B(Ed)

BOXES

A sycamore and penwork tea caddy, Belgian, c1830, 4½in (11.5cm) wide.
£1,800–2,000
€ / **$2,800–3,400** ⊞ AKS

A burr-walnut writing box, with brass fretwork, c1850, 10in (25.5cm) wide.
£270–300
€ / **$425–475** ⊞ MB

A gilt-brass-mounted burrwood jewel casket, by Halstaff & Hannaford, London, with velvet-lined fitted interior, the fall-front reveals a spring-action jewel drawer and a secret morocco-upholstered slide, 1850–75, 12¾in (32.5cm) wide.
£1,300–1,500
€ / **$2,100–2,400** ↗ NOA

A marquetry-inlaid kingwood and holly wood jewel casket, lined with satin, 1850–75, 12in (30.5cm) wide.
£900–1,000
€ / **$1,400–1,700** ↗ NOA

▶ **An olivewood stationery box,** 19thC, 9in (23cm) wide.
£380–450
€ / **$600–700** ↗ WilP

A William IV rosewood and brass-inlaid tea caddy, with fitted interior, 14¾in (37.5cm) wide.
£400–475
€ / **$630–750** ↗ SWO

A Victorian figured-walnut writing slope, the lid with inscribed silver plaque enclosing boxwood compartments behind a removable rosewood-veneered dipped pen tray and two ink bottles, the original hide-covered writing surface above a bird's-eye maple-lined compartment and a side drawer, 18¾in (47.5cm) wide.
£1,200–1,300
€ / **$1,800–2,000** ⊞ JC

▶ **A tea caddy,** with ivory-faced interior and translucent top, Dutch, c1850, 4½in (11.5cm) wide.
£1,600–1,800
€ / **$2,500–2,800** ⊞ AKS

A William IV mahogany tea caddy, with fitted interior, 16in (40.5cm) wide.
£250–300
€ / **$400–475** ↗ TMA

A silver-mounted ivory *aide memoire*, c1850, 5in (12.5cm) wide.
£80–90
€ / **$125–140** ⊞ MB

Tortoiseshell boxes

Check for the following faults when buying tortoiseshell tea caddies and boxes:
- the presence of plastic filler used for repair (often coloured, so check carefully) at the extremities, eg pagoda corners, plinths, etc.
- poorly-cut-in patches of tortoiseshell on damaged areas.
- damage around the hinge area, both on the tortoiseshell and on the inner ivory edgings.
- missing or incorrect feet, escutcheons, cartouches, finials and interior knobs.
- orange-peel effect on the shell caused by French polishing, lacquering or incorrect burnishing.
- excessive carcass movement with particular regard to 'smiling' (when the lid does not fit close to the base).
- the caddy is either brand new or reveneered onto an old wooden carcass.

A buyer may still decide to purchase a box with some of these faults evident but damage or restoration should be reflected in the price.

An ivory trinket box, the lid carved with lions, 19thC, 4¾in (12cm) wide.
£180–220
€ / **$285–350** ↗ WilP

A mother-of-pearl jewellery box, with ivory edging and silver feet, c1860, 5in (12.5cm) wide.
£330–370
€/ **$520–620 ⊞ AKS**

A shell-decorated box, c1860, 7in (18cm) wide.
£175–200
€/ **$280–340 ⊞ F&F**

A horn snuff box, French, 19thC, 5in (12.5cm) wide.
£315–350
€/ **$500–550 ⊞ SEA**

An arbutus wood box, inlaid with a view of Muckross Abbey, Killarney, Irish, c1866, 9in (23cm) square.
£350–400
€/ **$550–630 ⊞ STA**

A brass-banded olivewood box, c1870, 10in (25.5cm) wide.
£215–235
€/ **$340–370 ⊞ MB**

An ebonized letter box, inlaid with mother-of-pearl and tulipwood, with rosewood fitted interior, French, c1870, 16in (40.5cm) wide.
£900–1,000
€/ **$1,400–1,700 ⊞ MB**

A burr-holly wood writing slope, inlaid with mother-of-pearl, nickel silver, malachite, agate and marble, Austrian, c1870, 13in (33cm) wide.
£320–350
€/ **$500–550 ⊞ MB**

A Victorian brass-banded oak scent casket, bottles damaged, French, c1870, 8in (20.5cm) wide.
£270–300
€/ **$425–450 ⊞ MB**

An Imperial lacquer box, by Vichnaikov, Russian, c1880, 6¼in (16cm) wide.
£585–650
€/ **$920–1,000 ⊞ SHa**

BOXES

A micro-mosaic and ormolu jewel case, the lid and sides inset with scenes of Rome, with buttoned silk interior, Italian, 19thC, 5in (12.5cm) wide.
£3,800–4,500
€/ **$6,000–7,200** ⚒ TRM

Age & patina

Wooden tea caddies and boxes often suffer from the over-zealous use of paint stripper and wire wool. In a few short minutes hundreds of years of age are wiped away, together with a high percentage of the value of the piece. Any box that has been subject to this treatment must be avoided. Only buy boxes with good original patination. This will enhance the object's beauty, integrity and value.

A lacquer dressing table box, the lid hand-painted with a courting couple, small cracks, late 19thC, 4in (10cm) diam.
£160–200
€/ **$250–300** ⚒ SWO

A tortoiseshell and silver casket, by G.F., with embossed mounts of lion's masks, putti and flowers, 1901, 7½in (19cm) wide.
£1,700–2,000
€/ **$2,700–3,200** ⚒ L

A Victorian mother-of-pearl tea caddy, with two interior lidded compartments, 5½in (14cm) wide.
£400–480
€/ **$630–750** ⚒ BWL

A Victorian figured-walnut and rosewood writing/work box, with fitted lift-out tray, the front opens to form a slope with two velvet-lined flaps enclosing compartments, 12in (30.5cm) wide.
£240–275
€/ **$380–440** ⚒ PF

A pietra dura and ebony jewellery box, inset with a hardstone panel depicting a flower, Italian, late 19thC, 10in (25.5cm) wide.
£380–450
€/ **$600–720** ⚒ BR

A Victorian rosewood and mother-of-pearl inlaid tea caddy, with fitted interior, 14½in (37cm) wide.
£320–400
€/ **$500–630** ⚒ DMC

A Victorian tortoiseshell manicure set, with six unmarked silver fittings, damaged, 6½in (16.5cm) wide.
£200–240
€/ **$320–380** ⚒ IM

A late Victorian stained and carved wood letter box, the fall-front with pierced aperture and inscribed 'Letters', minor damage, 11¾in (30cm) wide.
£200–220
€/ **$320–350** ⚒ TRM

An oak stationery box, the fall-front opening to reveal a writing surface and fitted interior, c1900, 16in (40.5cm) wide.
£400–480
€/ **$630–750** ⚒ NOA

◄ **An Edwardian mahogany writing cabinet,** the fitted interior with drop-down fascia, with brass handles, labelled 'Dimlock & Son, Norwich', 12¼in (31cm) wide.
£370–450
€/ **$580–700** ⚒ AH

BOXES

Music

Cylinder Musical Boxes

A cylinder musical box, playing eight airs, with two layers of circular engraved bells, in a burr-walnut case, mid-19thC, 22¾in (58cm) wide.
£1,500–1,800
€/ **$2,400–2,800** ➢ **L&E**

A cylinder musical box, by Paillard, playing eight airs, with matching table and extra cylinders, Swiss, c1880, 43in (109cm) wide.
£7,000–8,000
€/ **$11,000–12,700** ⊞ **GWe**

▶ **A cylinder musical box,** by Ami Riveric, playing eight airs, with original tune sheet and finish to case, movement restored, c1880, 14in (35.5cm) wide.
£1,300–1,500
€/ **$2,000–2,400** ⊞ **PGO**

◀ **A tremolo cylinder musical box,** by Nicole Frères, the 15in (38cm) cylinder playing 12 airs, indicator with fast/slow lever, in a burr-walnut and burr-maple-veneered case, with tune sheet, Swiss, c1880, 30in (76cm) wide.
£3,000–3,600
€/ **$4,700–5,700** ➢ **S(O)**

A cylinder musical box, by Nicole Frères, playing eight airs, restored, Swiss, c1865, 21in (53.5cm) wide.
£3,400–3,800
€/ **$5,400–6,000** ⊞ **KHW**

A cylinder musical box, by M. M. & Co, the double main spring barrel playing 12 airs, in a repolished buffet case, movement overhauled, Swiss, c1895, 30in (76cm) wide.
£4,700–5,200
€/ **$7,400–8,200** ⊞ **PGO**

A cylinder musical box, by L'Epée, with individually played bells, reconditioned, French, c1895, 22in (56cm) wide.
£3,000–3,900
€/ **$4,700–6,200** ⊞ **KHW**

A late Victorian cylinder musical box, by National, playing six airs, in a *faux* coromandel case, 14¼in (36cm) wide.
£240–280
€/ **$380–440** ➢ **SWO**

MUSIC

Disc Musical Boxes

A Symphonion disc musical box, with eight discs, contained in a walnut case, late 19thC, discs 7½in (19cm) diam.
£350–400
€/ **$550–630** ↗ SWO

A Symphonion disc musical box, contained in a rosewood case, with associated discs, German, 19thC, 10in (25.5cm) wide.
£260–315
€/ **$400–480** ↗ SWO

A Polyphon 19⅝in coin-operated disc musical box, with 13 discs, with twin-comb mechanism, contained in a walnut case with glazed door and pierced foliate frets flanked by turned pilasters, the base with a frieze drawer and side winding handle, German, c1900.
£4,000–4,800
€/ **$6,300–7,600** ↗ S(O)

▶ **A Polyphon disc musical box,** with original disc, movement serviced, German, c1900, disc 8¼in (21cm) diam.
£1,300–1,500
€/ **$2,000–2,400** ⊞ PGO

A Symphonion 11⅞in disc musical box, contained in a walnut-veneered case, German, c1895, 19in (48.5cm) wide.
£2,000–2,400
€/ **$3,200–3,800** ⊞ GWe

A Polyphon disc musical box, with nine discs, contained in a floral transfer-decorated case with offset lithograph to interior of lid, German, late 19thC, 8in (20.5cm) wide.
£420–500
€/ **$660–790** ↗ AMB

A Symphonion disc musical box, with ten 12in (30.5cm) discs, contained in a wooden case with rococo decoration, German, c1900, 18in (45.5cm) wide.
£5,000–5,500
€/ **$7,900–8,600** ⊞ KHW

An Ariston organette, by Paul Ehrlich, Leipzig, with 13in (33cm) card discs and 24 notes, German, c1895, 16in (40.5cm) wide.
£1,800–2,000
€/ **$2,800–3,200** ⊞ KHW

A Polyphon disc musical box, 'The Dandy Fifth', with ten 19⅜in (49.5cm) discs, contained in a walnut-veneered case, restored, German, Leipzig, c1898, 50in (127cm) high.
£8,700–9,500
€/ **$13,700–15,000** ⊞ KHW

A Symphonion 11⅞in disc musical box, contained in a carved wood case, the interior of the lid with a silk picture, German, c1900, 18in (45.5cm) wide.
£4,500–5,000
€/ **$7,000–8,000** ⊞ GWe

▶ **A Monopol disc musical box,** with ten 7¼in (18.5cm) discs, contained in an ebonized fruitwood cabinet, unrestored, German, c1905, 12in (30.5cm) square.
£1,600–1,800
€/ **$2,500–2,800** ⊞ KHW

A Britannia disc musical box, by B. H. Abrahams, with ten discs, contained in a smoker's cabinet with original finish, movement overhauled, Swiss, St Croix, c1900, 21in (53.5cm) high.
£2,000–2,200
€/ **$3,200–3,500** ⊞ PGO

A Polyphon disc musical box, with 12 bells and 14½in (37cm) disc, restored, German, c1900, 19in (48.5cm) wide.
£5,000–5,500
€/ **$7,900–8,700** ⊞ KHW

Mechanical Music

◀ **An ivory musical box,** c1890, 6½in (16.5cm) wide.
£770–850
€ / $1,200–1,300
⊞ HAA

A musical animated scene, with a ship, windmill and soldiers, beneath a glass dome, French, 19thC, 21in (53.5cm) high.
£1,800–2,000
€ / $2,800–3,200 ⊞ AUTO

A singing bird in a cage automaton, with clockwork mechanism, French, c1880, 20in (51cm) high.
£4,000–4,500
€ / $6,300–7,100 ⊞ AUTO

◀ **A hurdy-gurdy,** inlaid with ebony and ivory inked design, the finial surmounted by a male head, labelled, body stamped with maker's details, French, 1873.
£1,000–1,200
€ / $1,600–1,900 ⚒ B

▶ **A Serinette miniature barrel organ,** by Thibouville-Lamy, Mirecourt, with ten notes, French, c1850, 10in (25.5cm) wide.
£1,800–2,000
€ / $2,800–3,200 ⊞ KHW
This would have been used to teach singing birds popular tunes.

▶ **A hand-cranked parlour barrel organ,** by Preston, London, the 18in (45.5cm) barrel playing ten airs, the mahogany case with hinged lid revealing hand-written tune sheets for five barrels, the base with hinged side panel enclosing two further pinned barrels, stop panel signed, early 19thC, 57½in (146cm) high.
£1,700–2,000
€ / $2,700–3,200 ⚒ S(O)

Gramophones

A Victor Monarch gramophone, with exhibition soundbox, brass and black-painted witch's hat horn with Nipper transfer, the oak case with fluted corner pillars and maker's label, 1910, 13in (33cm) square.
£380–440
€ / $600–700 ⚒ B(WM)

An HMV gramophone, in a mahogany case, c1926, 37in (94cm) high.
£270–300
€ / $425–475 ⊞ GM

◀ **A concert gramophone,** by E. M. Ginn, with papier mâché horn, the oak cabinet with later electric turntable, c1925, 21¼in (54cm) wide.
£950–1,100
€ / $1,500–1,700 ⚒ S(O)

MUSIC

Musical Instruments

◀ **A cello,** by Ludovicus Guersan, Paris, labelled, restorations, French, 1766, length of back 28in (71cm).
£8,500–10,000
€ / **$13,500–15,800** ↗ B

An English School cello, minor restorations, c1820, length of back 29¼in (74.5cm).
£3,500–4,200
€ / **$5,500–6,600** ↗ B

◀ **A cello,** labelled 'Nicolaus Amatus...', probably Dutch, early 19thC, length of back 29¼in (74.5cm).
£6,000–7,000
€ / **$9,500–11,000** ↗ GH

A cello, by Sebastian Dallinger, Vienna, stamped, Austrian, 1786, length of back 29¾in (75.5cm).
£6,500–7,500
€ / **$10,300–11,800** ↗ B

A cello, by Simon Kriner, Mittenwald, labelled, fingerboard stamped 'W. E. Hill & Sons, Reg No. 79606', c1812, length of back 29¾in (75.5cm).
£3,000–3,600
€ / **$4,700–5,700** ↗ B

A walnut and parcel-gilt triple-strung concert harp, brass plate inscribed in Welsh and English 'Eisteddfod, Llandovery May 1872, 1st Prize', Welsh, 19thC, 78in (198cm) high.
£1,000–1,200
€ / **$1,600–1,900** ↗ PF

A cello, attributed to Lockey Hill, London, minor blemishes, manuscript label, fingerboard numbered 'P705', c1820, length of back 29in (73.5cm).
£9,500–11,000
€ / **$15,000–17,400** ↗ B

A Simatone steel-bodied guitar, by Simon Beuscher, stamped, 1953.
£850–1,000
€ / **$1,300–1,600** ↗ B

◀ **A carved giltwood, brass and maple harp,** by Francis Serouet, London, signed, 1800–25, 68in (172.5cm) high.
£3,500–4,000
€ / **$5,500–6,300** ↗ NOA

▶ **A salon harp,** by Sebastian Eraros & Pierre, London, with Gothic-style decoration above a column mounted with five carved angels playing musical instruments, on winged beast feet, late 19thC, 69in (175.5cm) high.
£2,400–2,800
€ / **$3,800–4,400** ↗ HYD

► **An ophicleide,** by J. Pask, London, minor damage, engraved maker's shield, 1800–50, 39½in (100.5cm) long, with two modern photographs reproducing early newspaper cuttings.
£900–1,100
€/ **$1,400–1,600** ✗ F&C
The ophicleide (keyed serpent) was invented by the Frenchman Halary in 1817. One of the most celebrated ophicleide parts is that in Mendelssohn's 'A Midsummer Night's Dream'. In Victorian times it was a popular instrument in brass bands and orchestras, the pre-cursor of the tuba.

A mandolin, by F. D. E. Mureda, Italian, Naples, dated 1898, with case and sheet music.
£140–160
€/ **$220–250** ✗ SWO

Items in the Musical Instruments section have been arranged in alphabetical order.

A carved walnut piano, by Wetzels, with ivory inlay, 31 panels depicting various scenes from classical literature, two depicting Classical nudes, on winged lion pedestals, some losses, paper label inscribed 'No. 800/31', French, c1810, 48in (122cm) wide.
£2,000–2,400
€/ **$3,200–3,800** ✗ JAA

A mahogany and inlaid square piano, by Wasterman & Co, early 19thC, 71¾in (182.5cm) wide.
£380–450
€/ **$600–710** ✗ SWO

A Regency mahogany piano, with satinwood banding and chequer stringing, inscribed 'New Patent, Willm Phillips...London', the three frieze drawers with later handles, 67in (170cm) wide.
£550–620
€/ **$870–980** ✗ WW

A Regency mahogany and rosewood-banded piano, by John Broadwood & Sons, with ebony inlay, the front interior in satinwood, on lion-paw feet, inscribed, 42in (106.5cm) wide.
£12,000–14,000
€/ **$19,000–22,000** ✗ MEA

A flame-mahogany grand piano, by Boisselot et Fils, Marseille, with boxwood inlay stringing, restored, French, c1835, 60in (152.5cm) long.
£20,000–23,000
€/ **$31,500–36,000** ⊞ PPC

A walnut and gilt-bronze upright piano, by Erard, London, with marquetry decoration, signed and dated 1856, 59½in (151cm) wide.
£4,200–5,000
€/ **$6,600–7,900** ✗ S(O)

A rosewood and mahogany square piano, by Clementi & Co, with crossbanding, brass inlay and gilt-metal mounts, 19thC, 68½in (174cm) wide.
£550–620
€/ **$870–980** ✗ AH

MUSIC

A burr-walnut grand piano,
by J. Kuhse, Dresden, German,
1875–1900, 59½in (151cm) wide.
£1,300–1,500
€/ **$2,000–2,400** ⚒ **NOA**

An ebonized grand piano, by Pleyel,
Paris, with chinoiserie decoration,
restored, 1886, 75in (190.5cm) long.
£25,000–28,000
€/ **$39,500–44,000** ⊞ **PPC**

An ebonized grand piano, by
Irmler, c1895, 66in (167.5cm) wide.
£700–800
€/ **$1,100–1,300** ⊞ **PEx**

A mahogany grand piano, by
Bösendorfer, Austrian, Vienna, 1901,
67in (170cm) long.
£2,800–3,300
€/ **$4,400–5,200** ⚒ **S(Am)**

A tulipwood piano, by W. Knabe,
American, 1876, 85in (216cm) wide.
£5,500–6,000
€/ **$8,700–9,500** ⚒ **LCM**

A rosewood grand piano, by
Steinway, c1890, 88in (223.5cm) long.
£8,000–10,000
€/ **$12,600–15,800** ⊞ **PEx**

**An Adam revival-style
satinwood and inlaid grand
piano,** by C. Bechstein, c1900,
59in (150cm) wide.
£8,500–10,000
€/ **$13,400–15,800** ⚒ **S(O)**

A mahogany baby grand piano,
by Steck, c1930, 54in (137cm) wide.
£1,000–1,200
€/ **$1,600–1,900** ⊞ **PEx**

▶ **A black-lacquered grand piano,**
by Werlein, New Orleans, American,
c1975, 68in (172.5cm) long, with
matching stool.
£2,000–2,200
€/ **$3,200–3,500** ⚒ **NOA**

**A rosewood concert grand
piano,** by Steinway, 1886,
108in (274.5cm) wide.
£12,000–14,000
€/ **$19,000–22,000** ⊞ **PEx**

A rosewood grand piano, by John
Brinsmead, c1892, 72in (183cm) wide.
£400–500
€/ **$630–790** ⊞ **PEx**

A carved mahogany grand piano, by
Bechstein, c1900, 72in (183cm) wide.
£7,000–9,000
€/ **$11,000–14,000** ⊞ **PEx**

A violin, attributed to Antonio Stradivari, Cremona, labelled, Italian, 1679, length of back 14in (35.5cm).
£230,000–270,000
€/ **$360,000–425,000** ⚹ B

A violin, neck straightened, base bar repaired, 1775–1825, length of back 14in (35.5cm).
£350–420
€/ **$550–660** ⚹ RTo

A violin, labelled 'Sympertus Niggell Lauten und Geigen Macher in Fussen 1777', length of back 14in (35.5cm), with case.
£1,500–1,800
€/ **$2,400–2,800** ⚹ GH

A violin, c1800, length of back 14in (35.5cm).
£3,500–4,200
€/ **$5,500–6,600** ⚹ B

A School of Guadagnini viola, enlarged, labelled, Italian, c1800, length of back 16¼in (41.5cm), with case.
£15,000–18,000
€/ **$24,000–28,000** ⚹ B

A violin, by Matthew Hardie, Edinburgh, fingerboard numbered 'G180', c1810, length of back 14in (35.5cm).
£3,000–3,500
€/ **$4,700–5,500** ⚹ B

▶ **A Turin School violin,** labelled 'Joannes Franciscus Pressenda...Taurini...1836?', length of back 14in (35.5cm), with case.
£15,000–18,000
€/ **$23,700–28,500** ⚹ B

A mahogany violin and bow, some damage, the interior with a hand-written label 'Saul Malcor?, 1807', 23in (58.5cm) long, in matched case with canvas cover.
£320–380
€/ **$500–600** ⚹ FHF

A violin, of the school of J. B. Vuillaume, Paris, labelled, French, c1840, length of back 14in (35.5cm)
£8,000–9,500
€/ **$12,600–15,000** ⚹ B

A violin, by C. A. Maucotel, Paris, labelled, French, 1855, length of back 14in (35.5cm).
£7,000–8,500
€/ **$11,000–13,500** ⚲ B

A violin, attributed to Carolus Joseph Dvorak, Prague, labelled, Czechoslovakian, 1928, length of back 14in (35.5cm), with case.
£3,000–3,500
€/ **$4,700–5,500** ⚲ B

▶ **A violin,** by Paul Kaul, Paris, labelled, French, 1945, length of back 14½in (37cm), with case.
£4,200–5,000
€/ **$6,600–7,900** ⚲ B

A violin, slight damage, strings missing, marked 'A la Ville de Cremonne/D.Nicolas ainé' and 'par hipplite Boedier, musicien...le 30 mars 1878', 24in (61cm) long, with case and two bows.
£580–680
€/ **$920–1,100** ⚲ FHF

A violin, by Richard Weichold, Dresden, labelled, German, 1899, length of back 14in (35.5cm).
£3,800–4,500
€/ **$6,000–7,100** ⚲ B

A violin, by Alfonso della Corte, Napoli, labelled, fingerboard numbered '1067', Italian, 1883, length of back 14in (35.5cm), with case.
£7,500–9,000
€/ **$11,800–14,200** ⚲ B

◀ **A violin,** by A. Poller, Vienna, labelled, Austrian, 1912, length of back 14in (35.5cm).
£4,500–5,200
€/ **$7,100–8,200** ⚲ B

Icons

An icon of the Virgin of Vladimir, with a silver oklad, Russian, 15thC, 12¼ x 10½in (31 x 26.5cm).
£7,700–8,500
€/ **$12,200–13,500** ⊞ TeG

An icon of St Parasceva, Byzantine, 15thC, 8¾ x 7in (22.5 x 18cm).
£5,500–6,000
€/ **$8,700–9,500** ⊞ RKa

An icon of the Mother of God of Tenderness, Eleousa, Cretan, late 15thC, 10in (25.5cm) square.
£16,000–18,000
€/ **$25,000–28,000** ⊞ RKa

An icon of Metropolitan Alexei of Moscow, Russian, 16thC, 12¼ x 9¾in (31 x 25cm).
£3,500–3,800
€/ **$5,500–6,000** ⊞ TeG

▶ **A roundel icon of the Mother of God,** 'Platyera', Greek, 17thC, 8⅝in (22cm) diam.
£1,300–1,500
€/ **$2,000–2,400** ⊞ TeG

An icon of the Vladimir Mother of God, the halos embellished with *faux* gemstones, Russian, c1650, 11¾ x 9¼in (30 x 23.5cm).
£950–1,100
€/ **$1,500–1,700** ⚒ JAA

An icon of Christ Washing the Feet of His Disciples, on a gold ground, within an 18thC Venetian frame, Ionian Islands, 17thC, 15¼ x 14in (38.5 x 35.5cm).
£6,500–7,800
€/ **$10,300–12,300** ⚒ S(O)

An icon of St Markari, Russian, c1700, 14¼ x 12¾in (36 x 32.5cm).
£1,600–1,800
€/ **$2,500–2,800** ⊞ TeG

An icon of the Enthroned Saviour, Greek, 17thC, 17¼ x 11in (44 x 28cm).
£12,000–14,000
€/ **$19,000–22,000** ⚒ S(O)

◀ **An icon of the Akhtuirskaya Mother of God,** the borders overlaid with a repoussé silver oklad, with an ornate silver halo, Cyrillic maker's marks for Yaroslav Frolov, Moscow, the icon with a fragment of the signature of Ivanov, Russian, c1780, 14 x 12in (35.5 x 30.5cm).
£1,000–1,200
€/ **$1,600–1,900** ⚒ JAA

A brass icon of St John the
Evangelist, Russian, 18thC,
4 x 2¼in (10 x 5.5cm).
£350–380
€/ $550–600 ⊞ RKa

An icon of the Resurrection and
Descent into Hell, Anastasis, Russian,
late 18thC, 14 x 11¾in (35.5 x 30cm).
£2,200–2,500
€/ $3,500–4,000 ⊞ RKa

An icon of the Kazan Mother of
God, set within a gilt-metal mount
composed of elements from an
earlier panel, the veil decorated with
seed pearls, turquoises and pastes,
later oklad, Russian, 18thC,
12½ x 10¾in (32 x 27.5cm).
£1,100–1,300
€/ $1,700–2,100 ⚒ S(O)

An icon of the Saviour, Russian,
late 18thC, 11¾ x 9½in (30 x 24cm).
£1,300–1,500
€/ $2,000–2,400 ⊞ TeG

An icon of St Demetrius, Russian,
c1800, 15¾ x 14¼in (40 x 36cm).
£3,200–3,500
€/ $5,000–5,500 ⊞ TeG

An icon of St Nicholas the
Wonderworker, Russian, 18thC,
34¾ x 26½in (88.5 x 67.5cm).
£4,500–5,000
€/ $7,000–7,900 ⊞ TeG

An icon of the Virgin in St Anna's
Sanctuary, Bulgarian, c1800,
18½ x 16¾in (47 x 42.5cm).
£1,300–1,400
€/ $2,000–2,200 ⊞ RKa

◀ An icon of the Shui-Smolensk
Odigitria Mother of God, overlaid
with an oklad sewn with mother-
of-pearl beads, Russian, c1800,
13 x 11in (33 x 28cm).
£1,700–2,000
€/ $2,700–3,200 ⚒ JAA

An icon of the Three-handed Mother
of God, overlaid with an oklad sewn
with coloured beads and pastes,
Russian, c1801, 13 x 11½in (33 x 29cm).
£2,000–2,400
€/ $3,200–3,800 ⚒ JAA

◀ A painted icon of the Holy
Venerable Paul of Thebes, Russian,
c1875, 8¾ x 6½in (22 x 16.5cm).
£375–450
€/ $600–700 ⚒ JAA

ICONS

◀ An icon of the Madonna and
An icon of the Madonna and Child, the silver frame and enamel-mounted oklad with gilt highlights, moulded clothing and an enamelled halo, hallmarked 'A.C1896', Russian, 12¼ x 10¾in (31 x 27.5cm).
£875–1,000
€/ **$1,400–1,600** ➚ JDJ

A painted icon of St Theodosiy, Bishop, Russian, c1890, 10½ x 9in (26.5 x 23cm).
£375–450
€/ **$600–700** ➚ JAA

An icon of the Sign Mother of God, Russian, c1900, 12½ x 10¾in (32 x 27.5cm).
£600–720
€/ **$950–1,100** ➚ JAA

An icon of Christ Pantocrator, Russian, late 19thC, 8½ x 6½in (21.5 x 16.5cm).
£220–280
€/ **$350–440** ➚ WW

An icon of the Mother of God, set in a silver oklad, each figure with crowns set with coloured stones, the borders of the oklad decorated with strapwork and Cyrillic inscriptions, workmaster's mark and initials 'D.I.', Russian, mid-19thC, 10¼ x 8½in (26 x 21.5cm).
£2,200–2,600
€/ **$3,500–4,100** ➚ LAY

An icon of the Kazan Mother of God, set with a silver and *cloisonné* enamel oklad, maker's mark 'S.G.', Russian, Moscow, late 19thC, 10½ x 9in (26.5 x 23cm).
£1,200–1,400
€/ **$1,900–2,200** ➚ S(O)

An icon of St Nicholas, with scenes from his life, Russian, 19thC, 14 x 12¼in (35.5 x 31cm).
£2,500–2,800
€/ **$4,000–4,400** ⊞ RKa

An icon of Saints Afanasi and Kyril, Russian, 19thC, 12¼ x 9¾in (31 x 25cm).
£1,300–1,500
€/ **$2,000–2,400** ⊞ TeG

▶ **An icon of the Archangel Gabriel,** Russian, 19thC, 12 x 10in (30.5 x 25.5cm).
£1,300–1,500
€/ **$2,000–2,400** ⊞ TeG

An icon of the Archangel Michael Voyevoda, Russian, 19thC, 12¼ x 10½in (31 x 26.5cm).
£3,200–3,500
€/ **$5,100–5,500** ⊞ TeG

An icon of the Virgin of Vladimir,
Russian, 19thC, 12¼ x 11in (31 x 28cm).
£800–900
€/ **$1,300–1,400** ⊞ TeG

**An icon of the Calendar for the
Month of June,** Russian, 19thC,
12¼ x 10¼in (31 x 26cm).
£1,600–1,800
€/ **$2,500–2,800** ⊞ TeG

**An icon of the Mother of God
of the Sign,** Russian, 19thC,
12¼ x 10¼in (31 x 26cm).
£1,300–1,500
€/ **$2,000–2,400** ⊞ RKa

**An icon of the Four Metropolitans
of Moscow,** Russian, 19thC,
7 x 5¾in (18 x 14.5cm).
£850–950
€/ **$1,300–1,500** ⊞ TeG

An icon of Hodigitria, with a
silver oklad, Russian, 19thC,
7¼ x 6in (18.5 x 15cm).
£550–600
€/ **$870–950** ⊞ TeG

An icon of the Saints of Vologda,
Russian, 19thC, 14 x 12in
(35.5 x 30.5cm).
£900–1,100
€/ **$1,400–1,700** ↗ S(NY)

**An icon of Christ
Pantocrator,** Russian, 19thC,
15 x 12¼in (38 x 31cm).
£450–550
€/ **$700–870** ↗ JDJ

**An icon of the Council of
the Archangel Michael,**
Russian, 19thC, 15¾ x 12½in
(40 x 32cm).
£220–260
€/ **$350–400** ↗ JDJ

An icon, depicting an
elderly male saint, with
silver-coloured metal oklad,
stamped, Russian, 1875–1925,
4¼ x 3½in (11 x 9cm).
£120–140
€/ **$190–220** ↗ GTH

**An embossed and pierced
silver icon,** marked,
Russian, 1875–1925,
8¾ x 7in (22 x 18cm).
£100–120
€/ **$160–190** ↗ SWO

◄ **An icon of St Seraphim of Sarov,**
overlaid with an engraved silver-gilt oklad
with applied *cloisonné* halo and corners,
hallmarked, Cyrillic maker's mark 'S.G.',
probably Sergiy Gupkin, Russian, Moscow,
c1903, 23 x 18in (58.5 x 45.5cm),
in a carved custom-fitted *kiot*.
£1,800–2,200
€/ **$2,800–3,500** ↗ JAA

▶ **An icon of the Fiery Ascension
of the Prophet Elijah,** inscribed,
Russian, dated 1922, 14 x 12in
(35.5 x 30.5cm).
£400–480
€/ **$630–760** ↗ JAA

Portrait Miniatures

A pair of portrait miniatures of a lady and gentleman, Spanish School, oil on copper, c1600, 3in (7.5cm) high, in modern giltwood frames.
£700–820
€/ **$1,100–1,300** ⚒ S(O)

A portrait miniature of a lady, in Renaissance costume, on ivory, named on reverse 'Mary Stuart', late 16thC, 3⅓in (8.5cm) high.
£330–400
€/ **$520–630** ⚒ TMA

A portrait miniature of a gentleman, by Susan Penelope Rosse, on vellum, late 17thC, 1½in (4cm) high.
£3,250–3,750
€/ **$5,000–6,000** ⊞ SHa

A portrait miniature of a gentleman, wearing armour, 17thC, 3in (8cm) high, in a damaged leather case.
£2,000–2,400
€/ **$3,200–3,800** ⚒ Bea(E)

A portrait miniature of Sir Gerald Aylmer, 6th Bt of Donadea, inscribed on reverse, c1726, 1¾in (4.5cm) high, in a papier mâché frame.
£1,700–2,000
€/ **$2,700–3,200** ⚒ TEN

A portrait miniature of a gentleman, by Nathaniel Hone, watercolour on ivory, monogrammed and dated 1763, 1½in (4cm) high, mounted in a gold-mounted carton pierre snuff box.
£1,400–1,600
€/ **$2,200–2,500** ⚒ G(L)

◄ **A portrait miniature of a lady,** by C. F. Zincke, on enamel, monogram on reverse, c1730, 2in (5cm) high, in a gold frame.
£3,000–3,300
€/ **$4,700–5,200** ⊞ BHa

► **A portrait miniature of a lady,** by Gervase Spencer, gold bracelet clasp mount, signed and dated 1748, 1½in (4cm) high.
£500–600
€/ **$790–950** ⚒ B

A portrait miniature of a lady, by Charles Dixon, hair panel on reverse, c1750, 2in (5cm) high, in a gold locket frame.
£3,000–3,400
€/ **$4,700–5,400** ⊞ BHa

A portrait miniature of a lady, by Richard Cosway, c1780, 2in (5cm) high, in a gold bracelet clasp frame.
£2,200–2,500
€/ **$3,500–4,000** ⊞ BHa

◄ **A portrait miniature of a lady,** signed with initial V, c1780, 1½in (3.5cm) high, in a gold frame.
£450–520
€/ **$710–820** ⚒ B

A portrait miniature of a gentleman, on ivory, c1790, 4½in (11.5cm) high, in a gold bracelet clasp frame.
£1,300–1,500
€/ **$2,100–2,400** ⚒ WL

A portrait miniature of an officer, probably of the 12th Light Dragoons, by William Denton, the reverse glazed to reveal a gold monogram 'ML' on plaited hair, signed and dated 1794, 2½in (6.5cm) high.
£1,500–1,800
€/ **$2,400–2,800** ⚒ B

► **A Georgian portrait miniature of a lady,** 1¾in (4.5cm) high, in a white metal foliate and scroll frame set with old-cut diamonds.
£1,800–2,000
€/ **$2,800–3,200** ⚒ DMC

A portrait miniature of a lady, by Hurter, on ivory, Swiss, c1790, 3in (7.5cm) high, in a gold frame.
£850–950
€/ **$1,300–1,500** ⊞ SHa

► **A portrait miniature of a lady,** watercolour on ivory, c1800, 4in (10cm) high.
£180–200
€/ **$275–300** ⊞ PSC

A portrait miniature of a lady, by J. T. Mitchell, signed and dated 1798, 2¾in (7cm) high, in a gold frame.
£450–500
€/ **$700–800** ⚒ B

◄ **A portrait miniature of a boy,** by Henry Eldridge, c1790, 2¾in (7cm) high, the frame with plaited two-coloured hair surround.
£3,500–4,000
€/ **$5,400–6,300** ⊞ BHa

A portrait miniature of a gentleman, by Henry Bone, RA, signed with monogram and dated 1793, 2¼in (5.5cm) high, in a gilt-metal frame.
£600–700
€/ **$950–1,100** ⚒ B

A portrait miniature of a lady, English School, watercolour on ivory, 18thC, 2in (5cm) high, in a gold locket frame.
£380–450
€/ **$600–710** ⚒ G(L)

A portrait miniature of Admiral Foot, by C. Hayter, the reverse with interwoven hair panel, c1800, 3½in (9cm) wide, in a gold locket frame.
£3,500–4,000
€/ **$5,500–6,300** ⊞ BHa

PORTRAIT MINIATURES

A portrait miniature of a gentleman, on ivory, c1800, 3½in (9cm) high.
£2,000–2,200
€/ **$3,200–3,500** ⊞ SHa

A portrait miniature of a lady, said to be Jane Barlow, English School, early 19thC, 1½in (4cm) high, in a gold frame with hair-plait back.
£320–380
€/ **$510–600** ⊀ Bea(E)

A portrait miniature of a gentleman, on ivory, English School, early 19thC, 3¼in (8cm) high.
£280–340
€/ **$440–540** ⊀ B(S)

A portrait miniature of a staff officer, English School, the enamelled back set with a lock of hair, early 19thC, 2¾in (7cm) high, in a gilt-metal frame.
£450–475
€/ **$710–750** ⊀ Bea(E)

A portrait miniature of a gentleman, on ivory, English School, early 19thC, 2¾in (7cm) high, in a papier mâché frame.
£1,000–1,200
€/ **$1,600–1,900** ⊀ AH

A portrait miniature of John Noble, engraved with his name and dates, early 19thC, 1¾in (4.5cm) high, in a later 9ct gold frame, with leather case.
£200–220
€/ **$320–350** ⊀ BR

A portrait miniature of a gentleman, attributed to Richard Bull, the reverse with a blue glass border and gold-mounted aperture with seed pearl monogram 'CH' surrounded by hair adorned with pearls, Irish, c1800, 3in (7.5cm) high, in a gold frame.
£650–750
€/ **$1,000–1,200** ⊀ B

A portrait miniature of J. G. Muirhead, on ivory, Continental School, the convex glass panel back enclosing an enamelled inscribed plaque, early 19thC, 2¾in (7cm) high, in a gilt-metal frame.
£300–350
€/ **$475–550** ⊀ BR

► **A portrait miniature of the Marquess of Thomand,** by Henry Bone, enamel on copper, inscribed and dated 1808, 5½in (14cm) high, in a gilded frame.
£3,300–4,000
€/ **$5,200–6,300** ⊀ BWL

A portrait miniature of a gentleman, said to be William Steenbergen, attributed to Lawrence Sully, c1800, 2¾in (7cm) high.
£800–950
€/ **$1,300–1,500** ⊀ S(NY)

PORTRAIT MINIATURES

A portrait miniature of Anne Barnes, watercolour on ivory, 1810, 4in (10cm) high.
£200–220
€/ **$320–350** ⊞ PSC

A portrait miniature of a gentleman, attributed to J. J. Gillespie, c1815, 5in (12.5cm) high.
£250–275
€/ **$400–440** ⊞ PSC

A portrait miniature of a lady, attributed to Johann Heusinger, German, signed and dated 1820, 3½in (9cm) high, in a gilded carved wood frame.
£500–600
€/ **$790–950** ⚒ B

A portrait miniature of a lady, on ivory, French, 1820, 3¼in (8.5cm) high, in a gold frame.
£3,400–3,800
€/ **$5,400–6,000** ⊞ SHa

▶ **A portrait miniature of a girl,** on ivory, English School, c1835, 4¼in (11cm) high.
£480–550
€/ **$760–870** ⚒ L

A portrait miniature of a Russian officer, by René Louis Letronne, French, signed and dated 1825, 7½in (19cm) high, in a veneered wood frame.
£1,800–2,000
€/ **$2,800–3,200** ⚒ S(O)

A portrait miniature of an officer, by Louis Gross, signed, c1830, Austrian, Vienna, 3in (7.5cm) high.
£3,200–3,500
€/ **$5,000–5,500** ⊞ BHa

A portrait miniature of Archibald Cochrane, aged 19, by J. V. Dupont, enamel, painted in Geneva, 1837, 2in (5cm) high.
£1,700–1,900
€/ **$2,700–3,000** ⊞ BHa

A portrait miniature of Mrs William Donald, by T. Carlyle, signed, inscribed and dated 1833, 4in (10cm) high.
£400–480
€/ **$630–760** ⚒ TEN

◀ **A portrait miniature of a gentleman,** watercolour on ivory, 19thC, 2in (5cm) high.
£120–140
€/ **$190–220** ⚒ G(L)

A portrait miniature of a lady, watercolour on ivory, c1840, 5¼in (13.5cm) high, in original carved wood frame.
£250–275
€ / **$400–440** ⊞ PSC

A portrait miniature of a lady, French School, c1840, 2½in (6.5cm) high, in a gilt locket frame.
£1,700–1,900
€ / **$2,700–3,000** ⊞ BHa

A portrait miniature of an officer, in 18thC uniform, English School, pinchbeck bracelet clasp mount with plaited hair bracelet, mid-19thC, 1½in (4cm) high.
£400–480
€ / **$630–760** ⚒ B

A Victorian portrait miniature of Richard Doughty, inscribed 'born 26th May 1850, aged one year and four months', lock of hair to reverse, 2¾in (7cm) high, in a yellow metal frame.
£330–400
€ / **$520–630** ⚒ BR

A portrait miniature of a lady, by John Thomas Gullick, on ivory, inscribed on reverse, c1865, 5¼in (13cm) high, in a gilt frame.
£380–450
€ / **$600–710** ⚒ SWO

A portrait miniature of a gentleman, wearing a Masonic chain, watercolour on ivory, c1880, 5¼in (13cm) high.
£175–200
€ / **$280–315** ⊞ PSC

A portrait miniature of a lady, 19thC, 3¼in (8.5cm) high.
£200–220
€ / **$320–350** ⚒ WW

A portrait miniature of a lady, on ivory, 19thC, 4¼in (11cm) high.
£480–550
€ / **$760–870** ⚒ DMC

◄ **A portrait miniature of a French lady,** on ivory, 19thC, 3½in (9cm) high, in original gilt acanthus leaf-scroll frame.
£380–450
€ / **$600–710** ⚒ BWL

► **A portrait miniature of a gentleman in uniform,** on ivory, early 20thC, 2¾in (7cm) high, in a silver and white enamel frame, hallmarked London 1910.
£200–220
€ / **$320–350** ⚒ DMC

A portrait miniature of a gentleman and a lady, on ivory, 19thC, 2½in (6.5cm) diam.
£500–600
€ / **$790–950** ⚒ DuM

Silhouettes

A silhouette of a gentleman, by Richard Jorden, painted on glass, c1780, 4in (10cm) high, in a hammered brass frame.
£240–275
€/ **\$380–430** 🔨 G(L)

A silhouette of a lady and gentleman taking tea, painted on card, c1784, 11 x 15in (28 x 38cm).
£6,000–7,000
€/ **\$9,500–11,000** 🔨 G(L)

A silhouette of a lady, by Miss Mary Lightfoot, painted on card, c1785, 3¾in (9.5cm) high, in a papier mâché frame.
£380–450
€/ **\$600–710** 🔨 B

A silhouette of an officer, wearing a Tarleton helmet, English School, painted on flat glass backed with silk, c1800, 6in (15cm) high, in a hammered brass frame.
£500–600
€/ **\$790–950** 🔨 B

A silhouette of Lady Marland's child, by J. Watkins, painted on paper, signed, early 19thC, 4¼in (11cm) high, in an ormolu and papier mâché frame.
£520–620
€/ **\$820–980** 🔨 G(L)

Two black ink silhouettes, inscribed 'Thomas Tooi' and 'Teeterree', c1818, larger 2¾in (7cm) high.
£2,800–3,200
€/ **\$4,400–5,100** 🔨 F&C

A silhouette of a gentleman, by Michael Rowed, painted on card, c1820, 3in (7.5cm) high.
£160–175
€/ **\$250–275** ⊞ PSC

A silhouette of HRH The Duke of Sussex, by W. Mason, painted on card, c1826, 3¼in (8.5cm) high, in a papier mâché frame.
£520–620
€/ **\$820–980** 🔨 G(L)

◀ **A silhouette of a young boy,** painted on card, 19thC, 2½in (6.5cm) high, in a maple frame.
£130–150
€/ **\$200–240** 🔨 AH

A set of four silhouettes of the children of the 1st Earl of Cottenham, by J. Gapp, cut-outs on card, inscribed and dated 1830, 6½in (16.5cm) high, in maple frames.
£1,400–1,600
€/ **\$2,200–2,500** 🔨 B

◀ **A Victorian silhouette of Mrs Raymond,** 10 x 8in (25.5 x 20.5cm).
£380–450
€/ **\$600–710** 🔨 WW

Artists' Materials

A wooden easel, c1900, 70in (178cm) high.
£55–60
€ / **$85–95** ⊞ AL

► An oak adjustable studio easel, by Robertson & Co, with triple-screw mechanism and handle, on trestle supports, labelled, late 19thC, 25½in (65cm) wide.
£1,500–1,800
€ / **$2,400–2,800** ➶ B(WM)

A satinwood marquetry easel, the broken pediment centred by a medallion, above a frieze inlaid with garlands, c1900, 75½in (192cm) high.
£3,000–3,500
€ / **$4,700–5,400** ➶ S(Am)

A Victorian giltwood easel, decorated with floral swags, surmounted by a pierced rococo shell and leaf pediment, 92in (233.5cm) high.
£1,800–2,200
€ / **$2,800–3,200** ➶ HYD

◄ A Victorian mahogany paint box, the compartmented interior and one long drawer partially fitted with original contents, 10in (25.5cm) wide.
£30–40
€ / **$47–63** ➶ G(L)

A Regency mahogany paint box, trade label for Rowney & Forster, with fitted interior, 8¾in (22cm) wide.
£230–275
€ / **$360–430** ➶ WW

◄ An artist's mahogany table, each side with a baize-lined slide, c1790, 20in (51cm) wide.
£950–1,100
€ / **$1,500–1,700** ➶ S(O)

Items in the Artists' Materials section have been arranged in alphabetical order.

An artist's satinwood table, banded with purpleheart and strung with boxwood and ebony, with a removable ledge and a pair of candleslides to the side, the frieze drawer enclosing a fitted compartment, on turned tapering legs, brass cappings and casters, c1800, 22½in (57cm) wide.
£22,000–25,000
€ / **$34,700–40,000** ➶ S

► An artist's mahogany travelling box, with velvet-lined folding easel slope over a box with one long drawer, early 19thC, 11in (28cm) wide.
£200–240
€ / **$315–380** ➶ TMA

Antiquities

A terracotta bowl, with an upturned rim, the interior red burnished, Egyptian, Pre-Dynastic, c4000–3000 BC, 9½in (24cm) diam.
£700–820
€ / **$1,100–1,300** ⚒ B(Kn)

A ceramic storage jar, the shoulder decorated with a stylized wave pattern, cracked, Egyptian, c3000 BC, 23½in (59.5cm) high.
£1,200–1,400
€ / **$1,900–2,200** ⚒ S(Am)

The items in this section have been arranged chronologically in sequence of civilizations, namely Egyptian, Near Eastern, Greek, Roman, Byzantine, western European, British, Anglo-Saxon and Medieval.

An Abydos ware flagon, Jordan/Israel area, c3000BC, 12in (30.5cm) high.
£230–270
€ / **$360–430** ⊞ AnAr
Abydos wares were found in the royal tombs of the 1st and 2nd Dynasties at Abydos, Middle Egypt. They were an import from the Jordan/Israel area.

A painted wooden head of a man, wearing a wig of short tiered curls, Egyptian, 6th Dynasty, 2360–2195 BC, 5¼in (13.5cm) high.
£600–700
€ / **$950–1,100** ⚒ S

◀ **A wooden headrest,** carved in three sections, Egyptian, probably 18th Dynasty, 1540–1292 BC, 2½in (6.5cm) high.
£3,000–3,500
€ / **$4,750–5,500** ⚒ S(NY)

Egyptian gods

The pantheon of the gods of ancient Egypt is enormous. Legend had it that the gods lived and ruled in Egypt long before the arrival of man. The Greek historian Herodotus (c450 BC), wrote that most animals were sacred to the Egyptians, and the practice of representing many of the gods as humans with animal or birds' heads was abhorrent to the Classical world.

Many of the human-headed gods can be recognized by the hieroglyphic symbol on their heads. For instance, Isis has a small throne and Serkhet, the scorpion goddess, has a small scorpion on her head. There were also several sacred family trinities: the major one being Osiris, god of the dead, his wife Isis and their son Horus. Other family trinities were particularly venerated in different parts of the country.

Representations of the various gods occur in all materials and sizes, those most often seen being the small faïence images, pierced for suspension, that served as protective amulets. Common among bronze statuettes are standing figures of Osiris, and seated figures of Isis nursing her son Horus. Many gods are still obscure and not easily identified.

A bronze figure of Anubis, including the top part of the attached column from the standard, Egyptian, Late Dynastic Period, 6th–4thC, 1¾in (4.5cm) high.
£115–125
€ / **$180–200** ⊞ ANG
This figure represents Anubis (Wepwawet), the 'Opener of the Ways', the jackal god of embalming, and Protector of Osiris. It is standing with characteristically sloping back legs which is how the creature is portrayed on standards carried before the Pharaoh in processions.

A bronze figure of Osiris, Egyptian, 26th Dynasty, c664–525 BC, 9½in (24cm) high.
£2,400–2,800
€ / **$3,800–4,400** ⚒ B(Kn)

◀ **A gesso-painted wooden sarcophagus fragment,** showing an ape-headed mummiform deity seated, small piercing in the bottom right-hand corner, on a black velvet mount, Egyptian, post-300 BC, 9½in (24cm) high.
£340–375
€ / **$550–600** ⊞ ANG
The representation is of the god Hapi, one of the Four Sons of Horus. He guarded the lungs of the deceased.

Gesso

Gesso is a plaster made of whiting and glue. It was used on a large scale from the 18th Dynasty for applying to wood as a ground for painting and gilding. Later it was used for mummy masks and coffins made of cartonnage. Cartonnage consists of layers of linen and gesso.

A carved limestone eye idol, of stylized form, Mesopotamian, Tell Brak, c3000 BC, 2in (5cm) high.
£550–600
€/ **$870–950** ⊞ HEL

A stone jar, the shoulder carved with a rope-twist band of decoration interspersed with four pierced miniature lugs, one lug chipped, Mesopotamian, 3000–2000 BC, 4¾in (12cm) high.
£750–875
€/ **$1,200–1,400** 🔨 B(Kn)

A pottery cuneiform trade or taxation pierced docket, inscribed 'City of Uruk', repeated twice, Mesopotamian, 2500–2200 BC, 1½in (3.5cm) high.
£400–450
€/ **$630–700** ⊞ HEL

A stone vessel, in the form of a crouching frog with a deep cavity on the back, Greater Syria, first half of 2nd millennium BC, 4¼in (11cm) wide.
£3,800–4,200
€/ **$6,000–6,600** 🔨 S(NY)

◀ **A clay cuneiform tablet,** with ten lines of Babylonian on the obverse and reverse, some damage and repair, Old Babylonian, 1900–1700 BC, 1¾in (4.5cm) high.
£260–285
€/ **$400–450** ⊞ A&O
These tablets were a type of balance sheet for products from a large economic organization.

▶ **A bronze dagger,** the flanged hilt with a finger grip, a narrow guard and an elongated blade, with a 4in (10cm) section of the original wooden hilt, Ancient Iran, c1250–950 BC, 16½in (42cm) long.
£400–450
€/ **$630–700**
⊞ A&O

A pottery model of a wagon, with incised decoration, Syrian, 2nd–1st millennium BC, 10½in (26.5cm) high.
£1,100–1,200
€/ **$1,700–1,900** 🔨 S(O)

A bronze bowl, Persian, Luristan, c1200–1000 BC, 6in (15cm) diam.
£230–270
€/ **$360–430** ⊞ AnAr

A pair of gold earrings, the ends with twisted gold wire decoration, Eastern Anatolia, Urartu, c800 BC, ½in (1cm) diam.
£250–275
€/ **$400–440** ⊞ A&O

A burnished pottery jug, Phoenician, 8th–7thC BC, 5in (13cm) high.
£200–220
€/ **$315–350** ⊞ HEL

A gypsum carved head of a god or king, Achaemenid, 5thC BC, 3in (8cm) high.
£200–220
€/ **$315–350** ⊞ HEL

The Desmond Morris Collection

Desmond Morris, zoologist, anthropologist, television personality and broadcaster, was 'hooked' on the art of Bronze Age Cyprus the moment he walked into Room Two of the Cyprus Museum in Nicosia. He bought his first Cypriot piece in 1967 and, over the next nine years, formed a magnificent collection of over 1,100 pieces. The culmination of his dedication was his publication of the collection, *The Art of Ancient Cyprus* (1985), a magnificently illustrated and researched study that has become a seminal reference work.

Having achieved his objective, Dr Morris decided to sell the collection. He hoped that it could be kept together, perhaps bought by a museum or institution as there was no doubt that the collection was the finest of its kind outside Cyprus. Many of the pieces had provenance and origins from other major collections, some formed over 100 years ago. Not able to keep such a large collection intact, Dr Morris put the most important pieces into auction in November 2001. Many of the major pieces, notably the so-called 'Scenic Compositions', were hotly pursued in the saleroom, going high above estimate, with the Getty Museum in Malibu, California, a major purchaser. **Peter Clayton**

A pottery footed cup, the sides painted with two undulating lines and concentric circles inside, Minoan or Mycenaean, c15th–14thC BC, 4¾in (12cm) diam.
£550–600
€/ **$870–950** ⚶ S

◄ **A pottery aryballos,** in the form of a vessel contained inside a greave open at the back, an incised contour line on the inner calf, alternating red and black tongues on the disk rim, tongues on the shoulder, a palmette below, restored, Greek, Rhodes, first half of the 6thC BC, 5½in (14cm) high.
£5,300–5,800
€/ **$8,500–9,200** ⚶ S(NY)

A terracotta flagon, with painted geometric decoration, Cyprus, early Iron Age, c1200 BC, 10in (25.5cm) high.
£320–400
€/ **$500–630** ⊞ AnAr

A pottery cup, painted with a geometric design, Cypriot, early Iron Age, 1050–650 BC, 4¾in (12cm) diam.
£270–300
€/ **$430–475** ⊞ HEL

◄ **A core-formed glass alabastron,** the applied handles with spurs, neck and rim missing, some iridescence, Greek, c6th–5thC BC, 4½in (11.5cm) high.
£650–750
€/ **$1,000–1,200** ⚶ B(Kn)

A pottery nestoris, painted with palmette and lotus motifs, the flat handles with rotelles, Apulian, Messapian, 5th–4thC BC, 11½in (29cm) high.
£700–800
€/ **$1,100–1,300** ⚶ S

A terracotta figure, of a lady offerant wearing a polos headdress, Greek, 5thC BC, 12in (30.5cm) high.
£1,000–1,200
€/ **$1,600–1,900** ⊞ AnAr

A Red Figure kantharos, depicting the head of a Lady of Fashion, Magna Graecia, 4thC BC, 8½in (21.5cm) high.
£1,000–1,200
€/ **$1,600–1,900** ⊞ AnAr

◄ **A gold wreath,** composed of 11 sheet-gold myrtle leaves, connecting wire missing, Greek, c4th–3rdC BC, 8¼in (21cm) diam.
£3,200–3,500
€/ **$5,000–5,500** ⚶ S(NY)

A terracotta fragment, depicting a male with a kantharos, Greek, 4th/3rdC BC, 4½in (11.5cm) high.
£130–160
€/ **$200–250** ⊞ AnAr

A carved marble foot, wearing a sandal, Roman, 1stC AD, 6in (15cm) long.
£1,500–1,700
€/ **$2,400–2,700** ⊞ HEL

A marble fragment from a sarcophagus, carved with the muse Polyhymnia facing to the right and holding a scroll, a theatre mask at her feet, Roman, c200 AD, 30in (76cm) high.
£5,000–5,500
€/ **$7,900–8,700** ⚒ S
Polyhymnia, muse of Sacred Poetry and of Mime, is often shown veiled, with a pensive look on her face. She is the seventh of the nine muses of Ancient Greece.

A marble profile portrait of a youth, restored, Roman, c1stC AD, 5¼in (13.5cm) high.
£900–1,100
€/ **$1,400–1,700** ⚒ S(Am)

A bronze vessel attachment, in the form of the god Pan, Roman, Carnuntum, 2ndC AD, 2¾in (7cm) high.
£270–300
€/ **$430–475** ⊞ ANG
This is a complete figure with a semi-circular attachment for fitting to the outside rim of a situla (table vessel).

A marble relief fragment from a sarcophagus, carved with the head of Dionysos, his right arm raised above his head, Roman, c3rdC AD, 6¾in (17cm) high.
£1,500–1,700
€/ **$2,400–2,700** ⚒ S

◀ **A bronze chest fitting,** cast and chased in the form of a lion's head, with a loop handle, remains of three iron fixing nails or studs, repair to two stud holes, Roman Syria or Near East, c2ndC AD, 5¼in (13.5cm) diam.
£350–400
€/ **$550–650** ⊞ ANG

A bronze fitting, in the form of a bacchante, probably from a tripod leg, set on an integral ridged base, with L-shaped attachment bar to her back, both arms missing from the elbows, mounted, Roman, c2ndC AD, 4½in (11.5cm) high.
£850–950
€/ **$1,350–1,500** ⊞ A&O

A bronze grotesque figure of a male, standing on one leg, on a wooden display stand, Roman, 2ndC AD, 3¼in (8.5cm) high.
£175–200
€/ **$275–320** ⊞ ANG

A bronze lamp, the handle plate in the form of Medusa's head, the calyx pierced for attachment of the missing lid, Roman, 1st–2ndC AD, 7in (18cm) long.
£2,700–3,000
€ / **$4,300–4,800** ➢ S(NY)

A bronze lamp, in the form of a wild sow, with the nozzle between her tusks, the coiled tail forming the handle, Roman or Byzantine, c4thC AD, 6in (15cm) long.
£1,300–1,500
€ / **$2,000–2,400** ➢ S(NY)

ANTIQUITIES

Roman lamps

Roman pottery lamps are among the most collectable of Roman antiquities. Examples from the 1st and 2nd century AD often have a scene represented on the discus (the top) depicting aspects of daily life: gladiators fighting, chariot racing, actors, harbours, buildings, and quite highly prized (and priced) erotic encounters. Many gods are represented, both classical and 'oriental', the latter including the Egyptian Anubis and Isis, and Cybele, Mother Goddess of Asia Minor. The base of the lamp often carries an impressed maker's mark so the factory can often be identified.

The red-fired pottery lamps of Christian Roman North Africa often have Biblical scenes, such as the Sacrifice of Isaac, the Children in the Fiery Furnace or, extremely rare, Christ surrounded by the heads of the twelve disciples. Other Christian symbols include the Chi-Rho monogram (the first two letters of Christ's name in Greek), a Christogram cross, a fish, or a chalice with doves. Some very rare lamps have a seven-branched candlestick, the Jewish menorah.

Many 1st-century AD lamps made in Italy are found in North Africa, where they were imported before local lamp factories were established there. These operated mainly between AD 350 and 425, when the Vandalic invasions destroyed most of them.

Collecting Roman lamps can be very rewarding because of their variety. It is possible to concentrate on a single theme, such as animals, ships, gods etc, or perhaps study the maker's marks to give the collection a more personal touch.

A terracotta oil lamp, the discus decorated with an actor wearing a comic theatre mask, the base with maker's name L. M. Adiec, Roman, early 2ndC AD, 5in (12.5cm) long.
£215–240
€ / **$340–380** ⊞ A&O
Lucius Munetus Adiectus was a central Italian manufacturer who exported much of his products to Roman North Africa.

LOCATE THE SOURCE
The source of each illustration in Miller's can be found by checking the code letters below each caption with the Key to Illustrations, pages 794–800.

A redware oil lamp, decorated with the Chi-Rho symbol of Christianity, the edge of the discus with decorative geometric symbols, Roman North Africa, c350–420 AD, 5¾in (14.5cm) long.
£215–240
€ / **$340–380** ⊞ A&O

A glass double balsamarium, with applied glass handles, one handle damaged, Roman, c3rd–4thC AD, 4½in (11.5cm) high.
£320–375
€ / **$500–600** ➢ B(Kn)

A glass jar, with an everted mouth, Roman, 4thC AD, 5in (12.5cm) high.
£160–200
€ / **$250–315** ⊞ AnAr

A silver ring, the carnelian intaglio carved with a stylized eagle, Roman, c2nd–3rdC AD.
£200–225
€ / **$315–350** ⊞ A&O

A glass amphora, with trail decoration around the neck, the handles applied with trailed glass extending to the rim, Roman, c4thC AD, 9in (23cm) high.
£900–1,100
€ / **$1,400–1,700** ➢ B(Kn)

A gold finger ring, mounted with a garnet cabochon, Roman, c2nd–4thC AD.
£3,000–3,500
€ / **$4,700–5,500** ➢ WW

A limestone reliquary shrine, the entablatures carved in relief with guilloche and other motifs, Byzantine, c6thC AD, 6¼in (16cm) high.
£4,500–5,000
€ / **$7,000–7,900** ⚒ S(NY)

◄ **A bronze fibula,** the pin with a poppy-head terminal, the bow with a coiled loop at either end and twisted central section, Italic, c9th–8thC BC, 10in (25.5cm) long.
£275–325
€ / **$430–515** ⚒ B(Kn)

A twisted silver torq, Celtic, c4th–3rdC BC, 7in (18cm) diam.
£800–1,000
€ / **$1,300–1,600** ⚒ B(Kn)

A bronze figure of a discus thrower, on a wooden stand, right leg missing, Italic, 4thC BC, 3in (7.5cm) high.
£175–200
€ / **$275–320** ⊞ ANG

A Celtic silver coiled arm bracelet, with serpent terminals, Thracian, c1stC BC, 4¾in (12cm) long.
£250–275
€ / **$400–440** ⊞ ANG

A Migdale-type copper-alloy flat axe, Humberside, early Bronze Age, c1800 BC, 4½in (11.5cm) wide.
£260–285
€ / **$410–450** ⊞ A&O

A bronze cauldron handle, the attachments formed as a pair of hands incised with knuckle and fingernail details, the wrist area decorated with a meander and dot pattern, mounted, Celtic, c4th–1stC BC, 8½in (21.5cm) wide.
£550–650
€ / **$870–1,000** ⚒ B(Kn)

▶ **A bronze spearhead,** the hollow socle pierced on either side, the hipped leaf-shaped blade with medial rib, mounted, Bronze Age, c1200–800 BC, 10½in (26.5cm) long.
£800–950
€ / **$1,300–1,500** ⚒ B(Kn)

A bronze openwork buckle, in the form of a sphinx, pin and backplate missing, British, Norfolk, late 2nd–early 3rdC AD, 1¾in (4.5cm) wide.
£130–145
€ / **$200–230** ⊞ ANG
This is a rare piece and, until now, unknown in Britain.

A bronze cosmetic grinding set, the boat-shaped mortar with knobbed terminals, with suspension loops, the pestle with a swan-neck loop, Norfolk, c1stC BC, mortar 3in (7.5cm) wide.
£350–385
€ / **$550–600** ⊞ A&O

A rabbit brooch, complete with pin, Romano-British, c1st–2ndC AD, ¾in (2cm) wide.
£100–120
€ / **$160–190** ⊞ A&O

A bronze vesica seal, with central decorative fleur-de-lys, and inscription 'S'LETICIE FIL WILL GISSO', c14thC, 1¾in (4.5cm) high.
£80–90
€ / **$125–145** ⊞ A&O
This seal would have been for personal use.

Pre-Columbian Art

A standing terracotta figure, Ecuador, Manabi, 500 BC–AD 500, 9¾in (25cm) high.
£220–250
€/ **$350–400** ⚒ BERN

A Mezcala stone figure, Mexican, Late Pre-Classic 300–100 BC, 4in (10cm) high.
£300–325
€/ **$475–515** ⊞ A&O

A female terracotta flat figure, on a stand, Mexican, Colima, Protoclassic Period, 100 BC–AD 250, 7¾in (19.5cm) high.
£150–175
€/ **$240–280** ⚒ BERN

A painted pottery figure, the body with geometric painting, Mexican, Jalisco, c100 BC–AD 250, 10½in (26.5cm).
£350–400
€/ **$550–650** ⚒ SK

A pottery human effigy vessel, with traces of geometric devices, old repairs, Mexican, Jalisco, c150 BC–AD 250, 8in (20.5cm) high.
£225–250
€/ **$350–400** ⚒ SK

▶ **A terracotta head,** from a large hollow figure, the face with a pierced mouth showing teeth and wearing earrings, some hair and flange missing, chips and repairs, Mexican, Veracruz, AD 250–450, 13½in (34.5cm) high.
£800–950
€/ **$1,300–1,500** ⚒ S(P)

A pottery war figure, with a built-in whistle at the back, pigment details on the head, some losses, Mexican, Vera Cruz, AD 150– 250, 9½in (24cm) high.
£280–320
€/ **$440–500** ⚒ SK

◀ **A double-chambered figural vessel,** the front chamber modelled as a king wearing a crown, his mouth forming the spout, Peruvian, Chimu, AD 1000–1200, 7in (18cm) long.
£350–400
€/ **$550–650** ⊞ A&O

A terracotta vase, Mayan, Late Classic period, AD 600–900, 6¾in (17cm) high.
£450–550
€/ **$700–870** ⚒ BERN

▶ **A pottery figure,** with perforations for attachments, minor damage, Columbia, Quimbaya, AD 500–1500, 9in (23cm) high.
£320–380
€/ **$500–600** ⚒ SK

A pair of earthenware cuchimilco figures, Peruvian, Chancay, AD 1100–1400, 18½in (46.5cm) high.
£1,300–1,500
€/ **$2,100–2,400** ⚒ BERN
Cuchimilco means 'with upraised arms'.

Tribal Art

An Inuit child's pair of fur moccasins, c1880, 5in (12.5cm) long.
£160–180
€/ $250–285 ⊞ JPr

▶ **An Inuit carved green stone swimming whale,** signed and dated '81' to the underside, 20in (51cm) long.
£350–425
€/ $550–670 ✗ RIT

◀ **An Inuit model of a kayak,** with a wooden figure wearing a skin anorak, the skin cover with ivory fittings, inscribed 'White Fish Islands 1862', 21in (53.5cm) long.
£450–525
€/ $710–830 ✗ B(Kn)

A Great Lakes choker, the beaded strip attached to birch bark, with a blue silk liner, tanned hide ties, minor damage, Native American, mid-19thC, 5in (12.5cm) diam.
£1,000–1,100
€/ $1,600–1,700 ✗ SK

A pair of Eastern Sioux beaded deerskin trousers, with a silver buckle, three metal buttons, and nickel-brass catch, the outer seams with seven beaded floral panels and fringing, Native American, late 19thC, legs 38in (96.5cm) long.
£475–550
€/ $750–870 ✗ JDJ

A pair of beaded cuffs, decorated with a stylized flower motif, with fringed beaded loops, Native American, probably Plains, 19thC, 8in (20.5cm) long.
£130–150
€/ $200–240 ✗ DN

◀ **A Navajo weaving,** minor damage, some wool loss, Native American, late 19thC, 40 x 15½in (101.5 x 39.5cm).
£2,200–2,700
€/ $3,500–4,300 ✗ SK

A pair of Dakota beaded hide spirit moccasins, Native American, c1900, 10¼in (26cm) long.
£475–550
€/ $750–870 ✗ DuM
The design symbolizes an opening to the spirit world.

A pair of Southern Plains high top moccasins, with beaded feet and two double bands of beading on the upper portion of the leggings, some holes, Native American, 19thC, 20in (51cm) long.
£600–725
€/ $950–1,100 ✗ JDJ

A pair of moccasins, Native American, Iroquois, c1880.
£160–180
€/ $250–280 ⊞ JPr

A ceremonial club, with incised motifs to either side, the central section wrapped in string binding, inscribed '44-1957', South American, Surinam, 16¼in (41.5cm) long.
£2,000–2,400
€/ $3,200–3,800 ✗ S

◀ **A pair of beaded hide moccasins,** Native American, c1910, 10½in (26.5cm) long.
£230–275
€/ $360–440 ✗ DuM

TRIBAL ART

A wooden mask, minor damage, Liberian, Bassa, 9¾in (25cm) high.
£2,000–2,400
€/ **$3,200–3,800** 🔨 S(P)

An Ebrie or Baule gold pendant, African, Ivory Coast, 3¾in (9.5cm) wide.
£1,200–1,400
€/ **$1,900–2,200** 🔨 S(NY)
The eastern coast of the Ivory Coast comprises an area of lagoons. The Ebrie, while influenced stylistically by the neighbouring Akan and Baule groups, have a distinctive style of elaborate gold jewellery. Made using the lost-wax process, it is characterized by fine linear geometric-relief decoration. The nature of the lost-wax process means that each piece is unique.

A male Chiwara wooden antelope headdress, with metal strips on the brow, African, Bambara, Mali, 42in (106.5cm) high.
£200–220
€/ **$320–350** 🔨 RIT
This stylized antelope headdress would have surmounted a basketwork cap worn at agricultural festivals. Two dancers, one wearing a male Chiwara headdress, the other a female, would be disguised in fibre costumes and would perform ritual dances to promote the fertility of the soil.

A Baule or Guro wooden pipe bowl, carved as a chicken, African, Ivory Coast, 5½in (14cm) long.
£700–800
€/ **$1,100–1,300** ⊞ HUR

◀ **A Bwa wooden mask,** with polychrome decoration, African, Burkina Faso, c1885, 48in (122cm) high.
£170–200
€/ **$270–320** ⊞ ARTi
This mask was worn by the Bwa in farming rituals. The protuberance over the stylized human face evokes an abstract head of a bird.

▶ **A wooden mask,** carved as a water spirit, crowned by four men and a boat, with red pigmentation and scarification marks, African, Cirhobo, Nigeria, 1930s, 19in (48.5cm) high.
£1,000–1,100
€/ **$1,600–1,700** ⊞ GRG

A Senufo wooden loom heddle, with spool, African, Ivory Coast, 7¾in (19.5cm) high.
£330–400
€/ **$520–630** 🔨 BERN
These pulleys are designed to hold the thread in the loom and are elaborately carved with either figurative or zoomorphic decoration. They are created purely for aesthetic satisfaction and have no magical purpose.

▶ **A Fon wooden cyclopic female figure,** African, Ivory Coast, 25in (63.5cm) high.
£600–700
€/ **$950–1,100** 🔨 S(O)

A female wooden Akuaba doll, African, Ghana, Ashanti, 9¼in (23.5cm) high.
£300–360
€/ **$480–580** 🔨 BERN
The Akuaba doll is a symbol of fertility to Ghanaian women. A doll is carried either to induce conception or, in the case of a pregnant woman, to ensure the well-being of the unborn child.

A Yoruba carved wood stool, Africa, Nigeria, 14in (35.5cm) high.
£600–700
€/ **$950–1,100** 🔨 S(O)

TRIBAL ART

A pair of female Yoruba Ibeji twins, the heads of carved wood, decorated with beads and cowrie shells, African, Nigeria, 1940s, 10in (25.5cm) high.
£900–1,000
€/ $1,400–1,600 ⊞ Cas
The Yoruba, in Nigeria, have the highest rate of twin births in the world. Twins are considered a blessing to a family. If a twin died, a figure was commissioned and the mother would feed, clothe and care for it, to look after its soul and prevent it from taking the surviving twin. In the event of both twins dying, a pair of twins would be carved.

► An Azande wooden figure of a female, the head incised with a hatched grid pattern, the shoulders and torso with geometric panels of decoration, African, Democratic Republic of Congo, 37½in (95.5cm) high.
£1,000–1,200
€/ $1,600–1,900 ⚒ B(Kn)
Collected by John Hilberth, a Swedish missionary in Angola and the Congo during the 1940s.

A Kota or Fang iron and brass bird's-head knife, African, Gabon, 13in (33cm) high.
£1,400–1,600
€/ $2,200–2,500 ⊞ HUR
Taking the form of the revered hornbill, the knife was used for ceremonial purposes. It was also a prestige item which could be traded as currency as part of a bride price.

A Fang soft wood Ngil mask, African, Gabon, c1940, 16in (40.5cm) high.
£625–700
€/ $1,000–1,100 ⊞ Cas
Ngil is the judiciary association within the Fang people who policed ceremonies.

A chief's carved wood staff, African, Ovimbundu, Angola, 21¼in (54cm) high.
£2,500–3,000
€/ $4,000–4,700 ⚒ S(P)

A Ngbandi or Yakoma knife and scabbard, the knife forged from iron and copper, the scabbard made from hide and fibre, decorated with glass beads, Central African Republic, knife 14¼in (36cm) long.
£1,400–1,600
€/ $2,200–2,500 ⊞ HUR
The Ngbandi and related peoples who live along the Zaire River are among the most skillful swordsmiths of Central Africa, with a repertoire of blades ranging from long swords to curved sabres and short spatulate knives with intricate designs. Blades such as this were intended for use as weapons and also for display in ceremonies in veneration of deceased leaders.

A Kuba wooden ceremonial table, on nine chip-carved tapering legs, with a dark red patina, African, Democratic Republic of Congo, 19thC, 20in (51cm) diam.
£320–375
€/ $500–600 ⚒ F&C

A Lozi wooden double bowl, carved as a duck, African, Zambia, 1950s, 17in (43cm) long.
£150–170
€/ $240–270 ⊞ Trib

Items in the Tribal Art section have been arranged geographically from west to east.

◄ A Karamojong feather, pigment-coloured clay and human hair head-dress, African, Karamoja, Uganda, 1950–60, 10in (25.5cm) high.
£340–380
€/ $550–600 ⊞ Trib

◄ A Nyamwezi wooden figure of a female, African, Tanzania, early 20thC, 23½in (59.5cm) high.
£3,800–4,200
€/ $6,000–6,600 ⊞ Trib

TRIBAL ART

A terracotta bowl, modelled as an abstract turtle, with traces of pigment, New Guinea, Lower Sepik River, 10in (25.5cm) diam.
£600–700
€/ **$950–1,100** S(NY)

A wooden ceremonial bowl, crack to underside, Papua New Guinea, Massim region, 31in (78.5cm) diam.
£3,200–3,800
€/ **$5,000–6,000** S(P)

A wooden *gope* board, with encrusted natural earth pigments, New Guinea, Papuan Gulf, 1915, 46½in (118cm) high.
£4,300–4,600
€/ **$6,800–7,300** S

A turtleshell ceremonial spatula, with traces of white pigment, New Guinea, Milne Bay Province, 8¼in (21cm) high.
£3,000–3,500
€/ **$4,700–5,500** S(NY)
The spatulate form of this finely carved turtleshell object belies its real use. Made only on the Louisiade Archipelago and possibly only on Tagula and Wanim, these 'spatulas' were items of great value used for both display and trade. They were part of a group of very specific objects used in exchange throughout the Massim area on the south eastern part of New Guinea in a highly organized network of trade relations called *kula*.

A cane spear thrower, with a stylized carved wood figure mounted with rattan to the centre, New Guinea, north coast, 19thC, 33½in (85cm) long.
£330–360
€/ **$520–570** FAC

▶ **A carved wood figure of a female,** with traces of red ochre pigments, minor losses, crack, New Caledonian, 23in (58.5cm) high.
£5,500–6,500
€/ **$8,700–10,300** S(P)

A Tau-Tau wooden torso, the face stained with white pigment, the neck socket passing through a separately carved hollow torso, Indonesian, 29in (73.5cm) high.
£700–820
€/ **$1,100–1,300** B(Kn)

A carved wood Garuda, decorated with coloured pigments, Indonesian, Bali, 1975–95, 41in (104cm) high.
£225–250
€/ **$350–400** ARTi
Garuda is a mythical man-bird figure.

◀ **A Dyak *mandau*,** the carved antler grip with hair tufts, with a woven rattan grip over a horn base terminal, the carved wood scabbard with original pig-hide back compartment, the shoulder straps decorated with shells, Borneo, 19thC, 20in (51cm) long.
£500–550
€/ **$800–870** FAC

A wooden ceremonial kava bowl, on four tapering adzed legs, with a pendant flange pierced through for suspension, Fijian, 23in (58.5cm) diam.
£5,500–6,500
€/ **$8,700–10,300** S(P)
Kava is a milky, intoxicating drink made from the crushed root of the pepper tree. The communal drinking of kava was an integral part of religious, economic and political life throughout the Pacific. It still retains great significance in Fiji, but it is now drunk as a social custom as well as a ceremony.

TRIBAL ART

An Aboriginal wooden spear thrower, 'woomera', with carved decoration, Western Australian, 19thC, 24½in (62cm) long.
£200–240
€/ **$320–380** ↗ F&C

◄ **An Aboriginal wooden shield,** decorated with natural pigments, inscribed '1973 C.Q.', Australian, northeast Queensland, 34in (86.5cm) high.
£7,800–8,500
€/ **$12,300–13,500** ↗ S

A Maori carved wood treasure box, the fitted lid pierced at the ends for suspension and decorated with two splayed Tiki figures, the heads carved in relief, the eyes inset with *haliotis* shell, New Zealand, 24¼in (61.5cm) wide.
£2,800–3,200
€/ **$4,400–5,000** ↗ S(NY)
These boxes are called *wakahuia* and are used to store small valuables and feathers. They were usually suspended from the rafters and viewed from below, which is why the underside is so elaborately decorated.

A wooden figure of a male, the eyes inset with obsidian, inscribed '15-1957', Easter Island, 17½in (44.5cm) high.
£2,700–3,000
€/ **$4,300–4,700** ↗ S

A Maori Kauri gum portrait head, the face with moko ornament, black-painted hair, minor damage, New Zealand, 19thC, 4in (10cm) high.
£160–200
€/ **$250–320** ↗ F&C
Moko is the ceremonial tattooing of the face of Maoris. It was believed that after death elaborate facial tattoos would be a passport to the afterlife.

TRIBAL ART

Books & Book Illustrations

Henry C. Andrews, *The Botanists' Repository of New and Rare Plants*, 1797, 4°, vol 1, 64 of 72 hand-coloured engravings, contemporary blue morocco with stamped gilt decoration.
£650–750
€/ **$1,000–1,200** ⚹ DW

Basilius Besler, *Fraga Fructu Magno*, and two other strawberry plants on one plate, published by Eichstatt and Nuremberg, 1613, 19 x 15¾in (48.5 x 40cm), copper engraving with hand-colouring.
£800–950
€/ **$1,300–1,500** ⚹ BBA

The Holy Bible, printed by Christopher Barker, London, 1584, 4°, bound with Sternhold & Hopkins *Book of Psalmes*, printed by John Daye, London 1584, with woodcut borders and map, upper cover detached, lower cover missing, contemporary calf.
£1,200–1,400
€/ **$1,900–2,200** ⚹ F&C

George Ashdown Audsley, *Gems of Japanese Art and Handicraft*, 1913, 2°, 66 chromolithographed plates, bound in modern green morocco, probably by the Ashley Bindery, japanese paper endpapers and slip-case.
£700–820
€/ **$1,100–1,300** ⚹ BBA

► **The Holy Bible,** 1864, 13 x 10in (33 x 25.5cm), original gilt-tooled leather, with brass clasps.
£110–120
€/ **$175–190** ⊞ PaA

Items in the Books & Book Illustrations section have been arranged in alphabetical order by author.

Rev William Bradford, *Sketches of the Country, Character, and Costume, in Portugal and Spain, made during the Campaign, and on the Route of the British Army, in 1808 and 1809*, 1813?, 2°, 2 vols in 1, 53 hand-coloured plates, worn and covers near detached, contemporary boards.
£850–1,000
€/ **$1,300–1,600** ⚹ DW

William Beattie, *The Ports, Harbours, Watering-Places, and Coast Scenery of Great Britain*, published by George Virtue, 1842, 4°, 2 vols, engraved additional titles, portrait and 122 plates after W. H. Bartlett, maroon polished roan gilt.
£230–275
€/ **$360–430** ⚹ L

The Holy Bible, printed by Robert Barker, London, 1612, 8°, New Testament title page in cordiform cartouche within a woodcut border, bound with the 1614 *Booke of Psalmes*, inserted engraved map of Canaan, general title page missing, antique calf.
£1,500–1,800
€/ **$2,400–2,800** ⚹ S(NY)

◄ **The Holy Bible,** late 19thC, 13 x 11in (33 x 28cm), with colour illustrations and maps, leather with brass clasps.
£90–100
€/ **$140–160** ⊞ PaA

Nicholas Blake, *Minute for Murder*, published by Collins Crime Club, 1947, 7½ x 5in (19 x 12.5cm).
£160–175
€/ **$250–280** ⊞ BIB
Nicholas Blake was the pseudonym of British poet Cecil Day Lewis (1904–72). The future Poet Laureate secretly turned to crime writing in order to pay for repairs on his house, and used an assumed name in order to preserve his poetic identity. Nicholas Strangeways, his sleuth, is said to resemble his friend and fellow poet W. H. Auden.

John Browne, *The History of the Metropolitan Church of St. Peter, York,* 1847, 4°, 2 vols, 150 engraved plates, including 10 hand-coloured plates, contemporary morocco with gilt decoration.
£240–280
€/ $380–440 ➤ DW

Arabella B. Buckley, *The Fairy-Land of Science,* published by Edward Stanford, 1899, 7½ x 5in (19 x 12.5cm).
£100–110
€/ $160–175 ⊞ TDG

▶ *The Poetical Works of Thomas Campbell,* The Lansdowne Poets series, published by Frederick Warne & Co, 1870s, 7 x 5in (18 x 12.5cm).
£120–130
€/ $190–200 ⊞ TDG

William Caxton (Translator), *The History of Reynard the Foxe,* published by Kelmscott Press, 1892, 4°, one of 300 copies, original limp vellum with ties, uncut.
£1,300–1,600
€/ $2,000–2,500 ➤ BBA

◀ **Captain Charles Chapman,** *A Voyage from Southampton to Cape Town and Back, in the Union Company's Mail Steamer* Syria, published by George Berridge & Co, 1872, 8°, recased with original printed wrappers laid on.
£700–840
€/ $1,100–1,300 ➤ BBA

A. Chapuis and E. Gélis, *Le Monde des Automates,* French, 1928, 11 x 9in (28 x 23cm), 2 vols, No. 148 of 1,000.
£1,300–1,500
€/ $2,000–2,400 ⊞ AUTO

Agatha Christie, *The Body in the Library*, published by Collins Crime Club, first edition, 1942, 7½ x 5¼in (19 x 13.5cm).
£1,200–1,400
€/ **$1,900–2,200** ⊞ BIB

Arthur Conan Doyle, *The Case-Book of Sherlock Holmes*, published by John Murray, first edition, 1927, 8 x 5in (20.5 x 12.5cm).
£5,200–5,800
€/ **$8,200–9,200** ⊞ NW

For further information on antique books see the full range of Miller's books at
www.millers.uk.com

Rev Charles Lutwidge Dodgson (Lewis Carroll), *Alice's Adventures in Wonderland*, first edition, illustrated by Harry Rountree, published by Nelson, 1908, 4°, 92 colour illustrations, pictorial cloth with gilt decoration to spine and colour illustration to upper cover.
£1,100–1,200
€/ **$1,700–1,900** ⊞ JON

This Edition is limited to One Hundred and Fifty-five copies, of which One Hundred and Fifty copies are for sale.
This copy is No. ...71...

Sir Winston S. Churchill, *Marlborough His Life and Times, 1933–38*, published by Leighton-Straker, first edition, 8°, 4 vols, signed, 71 of 155 copies, contemporary gilt morocco.
£3,800–4,500
€/ **$6,000–7,000** ⚒ L

Arthur Conan Doyle, *The Hound of The Baskervilles*, published by George Newnes, first edition, 1902, 8 x 5in (20.5 x 12.5cm).
£1,300–1,500
€/ **$2,000–2,400** ⊞ NW
Only about three copies of this book are known to exist in its original dust-jacket, and only one has ever appeared at auction, selling at Sotheby's for over £80,000 (€/ $126,000) in 1998.

▶ **Dalziel Brothers (engravers),** *The Spirit of Praise*, 1867, 10in (25.5cm) high.
£120–135
€/ **$190–215** ⊞ TDG

Daphne du Maurier, *Jamaica Inn*, published by Victor Gollancz, 1936, 8 x 6in (20.5 x 15cm), signed.
£900–1,000
€/ **$1,400–1,600** ⊞ ADD

William Curtis, *Flora Londinensis*, 1777, 2°, vols 1 and 3, 288 hand-coloured engraved plates, half green-stained calf.
£3,200–3,800
€/ **$5,100–6,000** ⚒ L

Pierre Dupin, *Les Secrets de la Cuisine Comtoise*, published by E. Nourry, Paris, 1927, five wood-engraved plates, original printed wrappers.
£100–120
€/ **$160–190** ⚒ WW

Church Services, published by Oxford University Press, 1855, 6in (15cm) high, mother-of-pearl and paua shell boards.
£225–250
€/ **$350–400** ⊞ TDG

Dalziel Brothers (engravers), *Golden Thoughts from Golden Fountains*, published by F. Warne & Co, 1870, 10in (25.5cm) high.
£165–180
€/ **$260–285** ⊞ TDG

Antoine Dupinet, *Historia Plantarum, Earum Imagines, Nomenclatura, Qualitates, & Natale Solum*, published by Vidua Gabrielis Coterii, Lyon second edition, 1567, 16°, woodcut title border, several hundred woodcut illustrations, contemporary limp vellum.
£600–700
€/ **$950–1,100** ⚒ BBA

James Dwight, *Practical Lawn Tennis*, published by Harper, New York, 1893, 8°, 25 black and white plates, original gilt cloth.
£300–360
€/ **$475–570** ↗ DW

T. S. Eliot, *Old Possum's Book of Practical Cats*, published by Faber & Faber, first edition, 1939, small 4°, original cloth, dust-jacket.
£230–275
€/ **$360–430** ↗ BBA

William Faulkner, *The Sound and the Fury*, introduction by Richard Hughes, published by Chatto & Windus, first edition, 1931, 8°, original cloth and dust-jacket with opinions of Faulkner's previous novel *Soldiers' Pay* printed on the reverse.
£420–500
€/ **$660–790** ↗ DW

John Gerarde, *The Herball or Generall Historie of Plantes*, 1633, 2°, woodcut illustrations and hand-colouring, 18thC tree calf.
£2,200–2,600
€/ **$3,500–4,100** ↗ WW

Robert Graves, *Fairies and Fusiliers*, published by William Heinemann, first edition, 1917, 7 x 5in (18 x 12.5cm), with a letter to Robbie Ross.
£900–1,000
€/ **$1,400–1,600** ⊞ ADD
Robbie Ross was a writer, critic and art dealer who acted as Oscar Wildes literary executor.

▶ **Ernest Hemingway,** *A Farewell to Arms*, published by Jonathan Cape, first edition, 1929, 8 x 5½in (20.5 x 14cm).
£400–450
€/ **$630–700** ⊞ BIB

G. A. Henty, *The Young Colonists*, published by Routledge, first edition, 1885, 8°, pictorial gilt cloth.
£650–775
€/ **$1,000–1,200** ↗ DW

Richard Rivington Holmes, *Queen Victoria*, published by Boussod, Valadon & Co, London & New York, 1897, hand-coloured frontispiece and 40 plates, No. 255 of 350, contemporary morocco with royal coat-of-arms by Zaehnsdorf.
£140–160
€/ **$220–250** ➹ DN

The Poetical Works of Thomas Hood, edited by William Rossetti, illustrated by Gustav Doré, published by E. Moxon, Son & Co, first edition, 1856, 7½in (19cm) high.
£160–175
€/ **$250–280** ⊞ TDG

Rev John Hutchins, *The History and Antiquities of the County of Dorset*, first edition, 1774, 2°, 2 vols, engraved map, plates and plans, calf-backed boards.
£700–800
€/ **$1,100–1,300** ➹ L

George M. Kelson, *The Salmon Fly: How to Dress It and How to Use It*, 1895, illustrated, gilt cloth.
£320–375
€/ **$500–590** ➹ CHTR

Jessie M. King, *Mummy's Bedtime Storybook by "Marion"*, 1929, 4°, 12 full-page colour illustrations, decorated endpapers, pictorial boards, glassine dust-jacket.
£1,000–1,200
€/ **$1,500–1,900** ➹ DW

Marie Laurencin (illustrator), *The Garden Party and Other Stories*, by Katherine Mansfield, published by the Verona Press, 1939, 4°, No. 656 of 1,200, coloured plates, original decorative cloth, slip-case.
£900–1,100
€/ **$1,400–1,700** ➹ L

Hugh Lofting, *Doctor Dolittle and the Secret Lake*, published by Jonathan Cape, London, first edition, 1949, 8°, colour frontispiece, black and white illustrations after Lofting, original cloth, dust-jacket.
£40–50
€/ **$65–80** ➹ RTo

G. Marshall and L. Niceville, *The Butterflies of India, Burmah and Ceylon*, published by Calcutta Central Press, 1882–90, 3 vols, polished calf.
£400–475
€/ **$630–750** ➹ HYD

Gerrit S. Miller, Jr, *Fauna of the N. E. United States*, Albany, 1900, 62 pages, with coloured illustrations in pen and ink with watercolour and gouache, over pencil, defects, lower cover missing.
£550–650
€/ **$870–1,000** ➹ BBA

A. A. Milne, *Now We Are Six*, with illustrations by E. H. Shepard, published by Methuen, first edition, 1927, 8 x 5in (20.5 x 12.5cm), limp leather.
£225–250
€/ **$325–400** ⊞ ADD

◀ **Nancy Mitford,** *Wigs on the Green*, published by Thornton Butterworth, London, first edition, 1935, 8°, original cloth, two pages torn, dust-jacket designed by Bip Pares.
£120–140
€/ **$190–220** ➹ RTo

◀ **Kay Nielsen (illustrator),** *Red Magic: A Collection of the World's Best Fairy Tales from all Countries*, edited by Romer Wilson, published by Cape, 1930, 8°, eight colour plates and numerous black and white illustrations, original cloth.
£650–775
€/ **$1,000–1,200** ➹ DW

George Orwell, *Animal Farm,* published by Secker & Warburg, second edition, printed within a month of the first, 1945, 8 x 5in (20.5 x 12.5cm).
£175–200
€ / **$275–320** ⊞ **ADD**

Arthur Rackham (Illustrator), *Poe's Tales,* first edition, 1935, 10 x 8in (25.5 x 20.5cm), original endpapers, gilt morocco.
£350–400
€ / **$550–630** ⊞ **ADD**

Jean-François Persoz, *Introduction à l'étude de la chimie moléculaire,* published by Mathias, Lagny Frères, Beaujouan & Jourdan, Paris, Derivaux, Strasbourg, 1839, 8¼ x 5in (21 x 12.5cm), nine folding letterpress tables, one engraved plate, gilt calf.
£230–275
€ / **$360–430** ⤢ **S(NY)**

Andrew Smith, *Illustrations of the Zoology of South Africa,* 1849, 4°, 5 vols bound in three, 279 lithographed plates, mostly hand-coloured, later buckram.
£4,000–4,700
€ / **$6,300–7,400** ⤢ **DW**

Beatrix Potter, *Peter Rabbit's Painting Book,* published by F. Warne & Co, first edition, 1911, 8°, illustrated in colour with a picture of Peter Rabbit, paper-covered boards.
£2,200–2,500
€ / **$3,500–4,000** ⊞ **JON**
Because of the nature of a children's painting book, very few have survived and most known copies have been coloured or painted. At the time of publication Beatrix Potter suggested to Warne that in addition to the book itself they might sell separate sheets of the outline drawings for children to paint. This would allow them to hang their finished work and also take into account 'some particular children, as well as the parents, (who) do not like to spoil the book.' Perhaps this copy belonged to one of these 'particular' children.

Beatrix Potter, *The Tale of the Flopsy Bunnies,* published by F. Warne & Co, first edition, 1909, 16°, early issue with Notice Board in picture on p14, colour illustrations, inscription to reverse of frontispiece, original pictorial boards, original printed glassine dust-jacket.
£800–950
€ / **$1,300–1,500** ⤢ **BBA**

Margaret Tempest (Illustrator), original artwork for *Little Grey Rabbit,* watercolour, 1936, 4in (10cm) square.
£4,700–5,200
€ / **$7,500–8,200** ⊞ **BRG**

◄ **J. R. R. Tolkien,** *The Hobbit or There and Back Again,* published by Allen & Unwin, first edition, 1937, 8°, signed by the author on the half-title page, original green cloth with blue designs on the boards, dust-jacket designed by the author, in a custom-made quarter-leather clamshell box.
£90,000–100,000
€ / **$142,000–158,000** ⊞ **JON**
On a summer afternoon in the late 1920s, J. R. R. Tolkien was marking School Certificate papers. His mind began to wander, and then across the top paper in his pile he wrote, 'In a hole in the ground lived a Hobbit.' In that moment a great literary classic was born. Only 1,500 copies of the first edition were printed and they sold out within a couple of months. Tolkien was a reclusive character and avoided contact with the public. Consequently signed copies of his work are very rare. The rarely-found dust-jacket is also without damage or restoration. The combination here of an exceptionally well-preserved copy, signed by the author, makes it an extremely desirable item.

◄ **Andy Warhol,** *The Philosophy of Andy Warhol (From A to B and Back Again),* published by Harcourt Brace Jovanovich, New York, first edition, 1975, 8½ x 5¾in (21.5 x 14.5cm), inscribed and signed, dust-jacket.
£765–850
€ / **$1,200–1,500** ⊞ **ASC**

Henry Worth, *Whaling Logbook,* 1789, 12½ x 8in (32 x 20.5cm), probably original, leather binder.
£5,000–6,000
€ / **$7,900–9,500** ⤢ **JDJ**

Paul Wytsman, *Genera Avium,* Brussels, 1905–14, 4°, original printed wrappers.
£150–180
€ / **$240–285** ⤢ **DW**

Maps & Atlases
World

G. Valk, a copperplate map of
the world, original colour, Dutch,
Amsterdam, c1658, 23 x 20in
(58.5 x 51cm).
£6,500–7,200
€/ **$10,300–11,400** ⊞ JOP

LOCATE THE SOURCE
The source of each illustration
in Miller's can be found by
checking the code letters below
each caption with the Key to
Illustrations, pages 794–800.

**Mercator's Projection of the
World,** by Covens and Mortier,
1700, 15 x 19in (38 x 48.5cm).
£2,700–3,000
€/ **$4,300–4,700** ⊞ APS

J. Henry, a woodblock map of the
world, French, Paris, 1835, 19 x 13in
(48.5 x 33cm).
£540–600
€/ **$850–950** ⊞ JOP

◄ **J. H. Colton,** a map of the world,
coloured lithograph, American, 1842,
25 x 20in (63.5 x 51cm).
£450–500
€/ **$700–800** ⊞ JOP

Samuel Dunn, *Scienta terrarum et
coelorum,* from *The General Atlas,*
published by Robert Sayer, 1772,
hand-coloured engraved, printed
on four sheets, joined, 41½ x 51in
(105.4 x 129.5cm).
£3,800–4,500
€/ **$6,000–7,100** ⚒ S(NY)

**Maps of the Society for the
Diffusion of Useful Knowledge,**
two vols, 215 engraved plates, two
missing, half calf, bindings loose,
1844, 2°.
£1,500–1,800
€/ **$2,400–2,800** ⚒ CHTR

Africa

Willem Blaeu, *Africa nova descriptio,* hand-
coloured double-page engraved map, Dutch
text to verso, c1650, 16 x 21¾in (41 x 55.5cm).
£1,700–2,000
€/ **$2,700–3,200** ⚒ B

► **Herman Moll,** a map of Madagascar and
part of the east coast of Africa, 1719,
8 x 11in (20.5 x 28cm).
£80–100
€/ **$125–160** ⊞ MAG

► **F. de Wit,** a copperplate
map of Africa, coloured,
Dutch, Amsterdam, c1680,
23 x 20in (58.5 x 51cm).
£900–1,000
€/ **$1,400–1,600** ⊞ JOP

Americas

◀ **Johannes Jansson,** *America Septentrionalis*, c1640, 18½ x 21½in (47 x 55cm).
£1,400–1,700
€ / **$2,200–2,700** ➶ DW
California is shown as an island.

Willem Blaeu, a copperplate map of Bermuda, hand-coloured, 1662, 20 x 23in (51 x 58.5cm).
£2,100–2,300
€ / **$3,300–3,600** ⊞ APS

G. & L. Valk, a copperplate map of the Americas, original colour, Dutch, c1700, 24 x 20in (61 x 51cm).
£1,600–1,800
€ / **$2,500–2,800** ⊞ JOP

H. A. Chatelain, a map of the Gulf of Mexico, 1719, 18 x 22in (45.5 x 56cm).
£2,200–2,500
€ / **$3,500–4,000** ⊞ APS

Asia

John Speed, *The Kingdome of China*, hand-coloured engraved map, repaired splits, c1676, 15¾ x 20¼in (40 x 51.5cm).
£1,300–1,500
€ / **$2,000–2,400** ➶ BBA

Jan Jansson, *Sumatrae*, engraved map with original outline hand colouring, re-margined, slight damage, c1650, 16¾ x 20¾in (42.5 x 52.5cm).
£370–430
€ / **$570–680** ➶ BBA

Joan Blaeu, *Honan*, and nine other hand-coloured double-page engraved maps of provinces of China from the same atlas, c1655, 16 x 19¼in (40.5 x 49cm).
£900–1,100
€ / **$1,400–1,700** ➶ B

To order Miller's books in the UK please ring 01903 828800.
See the full range at
www.millers.uk.com

J. N. Bellin, *Carte Réduite de L'Ocean Oriental ou Mer des Indes*, hand-coloured chart of the Indian Ocean, including Sri Lanka, Madagascar and Borneo, French, 1757, 22¾ x 35¼in (58 x 89.5cm).
£500–570
€ / **$790–900** ➶ BBA

A woodblock map, depicting Mount Fuji and its environs, Japanese, late 19thC, 13¼ x 38¼in (33.5 x 97cm).
£65–75
€ / **$100–120** ➶ SWO

MAPS & ATLASES

Europe & the Middle East

Abraham Ortelius, *Flandriae Comitatus Descriptio,* hand-coloured copper engraving, printed in Antwerp by Christopher Plantin, Flemish, 1592, 18 x 22½in (45.5 x 57cm).
£2,200–2,500
€/ **$3,500–4,000** ⚒ S
Abraham Ortelius and his sisters became map illuminators and colourists following the death of their father. He was first established as an antiques dealer and from 1558 onwards he was recorded as purchasing multiple copies of maps in order to colour them whilst building up a substantial personal collection.

Joan and Willem Blaeu, *Tabula Russiae,* from the North Sea to the Caspian Sea, engraved map with original hand-colouring, Dutch, Amsterdam, c1650, 17 x 21½in (43 x 54.5cm).
£775–900
€/ **$1,200–1,400** ⚒ BBA
The Blaeu family publishing house was founded by Willem Janszoon Blaeu (1571–1638). Originally specializing in sea charts, he published his first world atlas, the *Atlantis Appendix* in 1630. Blaeu maps are renowned for the high level of care and attention given to every stage of the production, using only the best paper with the finest engraved plates and highest standard of printing.

◀ **Johann Baptist Homann,**
Regnorum Hispaniae et Portugalliae, engraved map of the Spanish peninsula, in original hand-colouring, slight damage, c1740, 19¼ x 22½in (49 x 57cm).
£420–500
€/ **$660–790** ⚒ BBA

Frederick de Wit, *Insula Malta,* engraved map of Malta and Gozo with original outline hand-colouring, c1680, 17½ x 21½in (44.5 x 55cm).
£500–600
€/ **$800–950** ⚒ BBA

John Tallis, *Switzerland,* 1850, 10 x 13in (25.5 x 33cm).
£60–65
€/ **$95–120** ⊞ MAG

Great Britain & Ireland

Christopher Saxton, a map of Devon, later hand colouring, 1575, 16¼ x 18¼in (41.5 x 46.5cm).
£80–100
€/ **$125–160** ⚒ FHF

Christopher Saxton, a map of Northamptonshire, Bedfordshire, Cambridgeshire, Huntingdonshire and Rutland, engraved and hand-coloured, paper repair, c1576, 15¾ x 20½in (40 x 52cm).
£2,200–2,500
€/ **$3,500–4,000** ⚒ DW

John Speed, *The Kingdome of Great Britaine and Ireland,* published by Basset & Chiswell, hand-coloured, double page map, inset with views of London and Edinburgh, English text to verso, c1611, 15 x 20in (38 x 51cm).
£1,700–2,000
€/ **$2,700–3,200** ⚒ B(B)

◀ **Christopher Saxton,** *North Riding of Yorkshire,* engraved by Hole, 1610, 8 x 14in (20.5 x 35.5cm).
£330–370
€/ **$520–600**
⊞ APS

John Speed, *The Isle of Man,* hand-coloured in outline, 1610, 15¼ x 20in (39 x 51cm).
£200–240
€/ **$320–380** ⚒ WilP

John Speed, *England, Wales, Scotland and Ireland Described and Abridged with ye Historie Relation of Things Worthy Mention from a Farr Larger Volume...*, engraved title, 63 maps, 1627, oblong 8°, reversed calf.
£2,000–2,200
€/ **$3,200–3,500** 🔨 B(B)

Joannes Jansson, *Scotland*, 1646, 16 x 22in (40.5 x 56cm).
£1,400–1,600
€/ **$2,200–2,500** ⊞ APS

John Ogilby, a strip road map of Oxford to Bristol, 1675, 13 x 18in (33 x 45.5cm).
£350–400
€/ **$550–630** ⊞ MAG

Robert Morden, *Cumberland*, 1695, 15 x 17in (38 x 43cm).
£250–280
€/ **$400–440** ⊞ APS

Joan Blaeu, *Great Britain*, hand-coloured, heightened with gold, Spanish text to verso, c1640, 16½ x 21in (42 x 53cm).
£1,400–1,600
€/ **$2,200–2,500** 🔨 DW

▶ **Joan Blaeu,** *Annandale*, hand-coloured, 1663, 16½ x 20in (42 x 51cm).
£70–80
€/ **$110–130** 🔨 TRM

P. Stent, a copperplate map of England and Wales, coloured, 1662–67, 20 x 16in (51 x 40.5cm).
£1,600–1,800
€/ **$2,500–2,800** ⊞ JOP

John Speed, *Buckinghamshire*, 1676, 16 x 21in (40.5 x 53.5cm).
£1,200–1,300
€/ **$1,900–2,000** ⊞ APS

◀ **John Speed,** *The Kingdome of England*, 1676, 17 x 22in (43 x 56cm).
£1,800–2,000
€/ **$2,800–3,200** ⊞ APS

Claes Janszoon Visscher, *Ireland*, 1695, 24 x 19in (61 x 48.5cm).
£2,700–3,000
€/ **$4,300–4,800** ⊞ APS

Joan Blaeu, *Cambridgeshire*, 1645, 20 x 33in (51 x 84cm).
£900–1,000
€/ **$1,400–1,600** ⊞ APS

John Speed, *Suffolk*, hand-coloured copper engraving, c1676, 20 x 15½in (39.5 x 51.5cm).
£450–525
€/ **$700–830** 🔨 B(EA)

Robert Morden, *Oxfordshire*, c1695, 14 x 16in (35.5 x 40.5cm).
£220–250
€/ **$350–400** ⊞ SAT

John Ogilby, a strip road map of London to Newhaven, 1695, 14 x 17in (35.5 x 43cm).
£400–450
€/ **$630–700** ⊞ APS

◀ **Thomas Cox,** *The East and West Parts of the Thames from Magna Britannica*, 1724, 15 x 9in (38 x 23cm).
£450–500
€/ **$720–800**
⊞ SAT

Thomas Martyn, *A New and Accurate Map of the County of Cornwall*, inset with the Isles of Scilly, 1816, 57 x 71in (145 x 180cm), framed.
£1,200–1,400
€/ **$1,900–2,200** ⚘ B(Pr)

▶ **W. R. Gardner,** *Plan of the County of Westmorland*, in four sections from survey taken in 1823, contemporary colouring, London, 1828, 28 x 32in (71 x 81.5cm).
£300–360
€/ **$475–570** ⚘ PFK

C. & J. Greenwood, *Map of the County of Essex*, original colour, steelplate, 1831, 17 x 24in (43 x 61cm).
£250–280
€/ **$400–440** ⊞ JOP

J. & C. Walker, *British Atlas, Comprising Separate Maps of Every County in England*, engraved title and 47 maps, hand-coloured in outline, dated March 1, 1837, large 4°, upper cover detached.
£400–480
€/ **$630–760** ⚘ L

◀ **Thomas Moule,** *Kent*, 1845, 8 x 10in (20.5 x 25.5cm).
£200–220
€/ **$320–350** ⊞ APS

Town & City Plans

S. Munster, town plan of Amsterdam, coloured woodblock, Swiss, 1544–50, 16 x 11in (40.5 x 28cm).
£470–520
€/ **$750–820** ⊞ JOP

Georg Braun and Franz Hogenberg, a town plan of Cambridge, 1575, 16 x 21in (40.5 x 53.5cm).
£1,300–1,500
€/ **$2,100–2,400** ⊞ APS

Georg Braun and Franz Hogenberg, a town plan of Brightstowe, c1581, 13¾ x 17¼in (35 x 44cm).
£350–420
€/ **$550–660** ⚘ DW

John Speed, *Midle-Sex described with the most famous Cities of London and Westminster*, hand-coloured engraved map, printed by George Humble 1610, but 1627 or later, 15 x 20in (38 x 50.5cm).
£400–450
€/ **$630–700** ⚘ B

Sebastian Munster, *Londen oder Lunden*, a woodcut map of London, German text to verso, repaired tear, c1628, 12½ x 16½in (32 x 42cm).
£900–1,000
€/ **$1,400–1,600** ⚘ BBA

Joan Blaeu, *Bruxella*, hand-coloured copper engraving of Brussels, Amsterdam, 1649, 20 x 24in (51 x 61cm).
£2,200–2,500
€/ **$3,500–4,000** ⚘ S

Dolls
Selected Makers

An Alt, Beck & Gottschalck bisque-headed doll, with fixed glass eyes, closed mouth and stuffed cloth body, bisque arms, later wig, German, c1890, 29½in (75cm) high.
£800–1,000
€/ **$1,300–1,600** ⊞ YC

An Alt, Beck & Gottschalck bisque-headed doll, with weighted eyes and open mouth, five-piece composition body, impressed '1361 50', German, 1912, 22in (56cm) high.
£330–400
€/ **$520–630** ↗ VEC

▶ **A Bru Jeune Empress Eugénie bisque-headed doll,** with glass eyes, closed mouth and plaited wig, gusset-jointed kid leather body, silk shirt and muslin jacket, marked 'E' on head and left shoulder, French, c1875, 15½in (39.5cm) high.
£2,100–2,500
€/ **$3,300–4,000** ⊞ THE

A Bähr & Pröschild bisque-headed character doll, with open mouth, two teeth and glass eyes, original Sonneburg composition jointed body, new wig, body partially repainted, marked '204', German, c1910, 16½in (42cm) high.
£345–415
€/ **$540–660** ⊞ THE

A Belton Bru-style doll, with composition body, German, c1880, 10in (25.5cm) high.
£1,000–1,100
€/ **$1,500–1,700** ⊞ BaN

A DEP bisque-headed doll, with weighted glass eyes, fully-jointed composition body, produced for the French market, German, c1910, 18in (45.5cm) high, in original box.
£350–420
€/ **$550–670** ↗ B(Ch)

A Bru Jeune bisque-headed doll, with original mohair wig and composition Girard body, two original outfits, French, c1890, 21in (53.5cm) high, in original labelled box.
£10,000–11,000
€/ **$15,800–17,400** ⊞ Beb

An Ernest Descamps bisque-headed *bébé* doll, with fixed paperweight eyes and open mouth, a double-jointed composition body, incised 'E.9.D', re-made clothing, c1900, 19in (48.5cm) high.
£1,200–1,400
€/ **$1,900–2,200** ⊞ YC

A Cuno & Otto Dressel bisque-headed Poppy doll, with glass eyes and closed mouth, composition arms and stuffed cotton body, German, c1912, 9¾in (25cm) high.
£160–200
€/ **$250–320** ⊞ YC

▶ **An EFFanBEE character doll,** by Dewees Cochran, 'Anne-Shirley', with sleeping eyes, closed mouth and blonde wig, composition body, marked, hairline cracks to thigh, American, 1930s, 21in (53.5cm) high.
£525–625
€/ **$830–1,000** ↗ SK(B)

DOLLS

A Fleischmann & Bloedel Eden bébé doll, with original wig, French, 1890s, 24in (61cm) high.
£1,800–2,000
€/ **$2,800–3,200** ⊞ BaN

A bisque-headed doll, attributed to François Gaultier, with glass eyes, closed mouth, blonde wig and leather body, wearing a silk gown, marked '3', French, c1875, 16in (40.5cm) high.
£1,400–1,700
€/ **$2,200–2,700** ⊞ THE

Gebrüder Heubach (German 1820–c1945) & Ernst Heubach (German 1887–1930)

These two companies which both operated from the German state of Thuringia are often confused for each other but are unconnected.

Gebrüder Heubach were based near Wallendorf, and initially produced figurines and bisque dolls' heads, but by 1905 the firm was registered as making entire dolls. Above all they are renowned for the variety of their bisque-headed character dolls. Among the firm's other products were small bisque figurines, known as 'piano babies', and mantelpiece figures.

Ernst Heubach of Koppelsdorf made a range of more affordable bisque dolls including characters, babies and jointed girl dolls. Body types varied and included jointed, bent-limb and baby. Ernst's daughter Beatrix married the son of the famous doll manufacturer Armand Marseille, also of Koppelsdorf, and in 1919 the two factories merged to become the Koppelsdorf Porcelain Factory.

A François Gaultier bisque-headed bébé doll, with weighted eyes, closed mouth and blonde wig, eight-ball articulated wood and composition body, impressed 'F 6 G', French, c1880, 16in (40.5cm) high, with assorted original clothing.
£3,200–3,800
€/ **$5,000–6,000** ➶ SK(B)

A Heinrich Handwerck bisque-headed doll, with sleeping glass eyes, open mouth and double-jointed composition body, incised 'GG', wearing a later wig and clothes, German, c1910, 21in (53cm) high.
£450–500
€/ **$700–800** ⊞ YC

A Julius Hering bisque-headed doll, with sleeping eyes, open mouth and composition hands and feet, stamped 'Victoria, J.H.', flag symbol, German, 1875–1925, 24½in (62cm) high.
£140–170
€/ **$220–260** ➶ DMC

An Ernst Heubach bisque-headed doll, with bisque lower arms and kid and cloth body, marked 'Hch 6/0 H' with horseshoe, German, late 19thC, 17in (43cm) high.
£160–200
€/ **$250–315** ➶ JDJ

An Ernst Heubach bisque-headed doll, model No. 320, with sleeping eyes, open mouth and jointed baby body, German, c1920, 25¼in (64cm) high.
£180–220
€/ **$280–350** ⊞ YC

An Ernst Heubach bisque-headed doll, mould 350, with sleeping eyes and composition body, German, c1925, 10in (25.5cm) high.
£250–275
€/ **$400–440** ⊞ BaN

A Gebrüder Heubach bisque-headed doll, with intaglio eyes, open/closed mouth, two teeth, and five-piece curved limb composition body, sprung squeaker not working, chipped, arms restrung and one repaired, German, c1912, 6¼in (16cm) high.
£280–320
€/ **$440–510** ➶ VEC

A Gebrüder Heubach bisque-headed character doll, with sleeping eyes, closed mouth and double-jointed toddler body, original wig, wearing a modern sailor outfit, German, c1912, 14¼in (36cm) high.
£1,100–1,200
€/ **$1,700–1,900** ⊞ YC

A Gebrüder Heubach bisque-headed doll, with sleeping eyes, blonde hair and composition body, German, early 20thC, 13in (33cm) high, with original black and white photograph of a boy with the doll.
£160–200
€ / **$250–315** ✗ TMA

A Jumeau bisque-headed *bébé* doll, with brown paperweight eyes, closed mouth and composition body, incised mark 'Déposé Jumeau', French, 1880s, 27in (68.5cm) high, with the doll's own doll.
£3,800–4,500
€ / **$6,000–7,200** ✗ SK(B)

A Jumeau bisque-headed doll, with paperweight eyes, closed mouth and brown wig-over-cork pate, wood and composition fully-jointed body, repainted limbs, marked, French, c1886, 22in (56cm) high.
£2,400–2,900
€ / **$3,800–4,600** ⊞ THE

A Gebrüder Heubach bisque-headed doll, with intaglio eyes, blonde sculpted hair and wood and composition ball-jointed body, wearing a corduroy suit, a shirt and leather shoes, marked '5896 Germany', c1915, 11in (28cm) high.
£260–300
€ / **$410–475** ⊞ THE

A Jumeau bisque-headed *bébé* doll, French, c1885, 21in (53.5cm) high.
£3,000–3,500
€ / **$4,700–5,500** ⊞ Beb

A Tête Jumeau bisque-headed doll, head and body stamped, c1890, 20in (51cm) high.
£1,300–1,500
€ / **$2,100–2,400** ⊞ BaN

A Gebrüder Heubach Piano Baby doll, with moulded and painted hair, closed mouth, broken finger, stamped with trademark and marked 'Dep', German, c1915, 4in (10cm) high.
£85–100
€ / **$130–160** ⊞ THE

A Jumeau bisque-headed *bébé* doll, with paperweight eyes and composition body, French, 1885–90, 25in (63.5cm) high.
£2,700–3,000
€ / **$4,200–4,800** ⊞ Beb

A Jumeau bisque-headed doll, with fixed glass eyes, open mouth and fully-jointed composition body, hairline cracks, French, c1910, 20in (51cm) high.
£600–700
€ / **$950–1,100** ✗ B(Ch)

A Jumeau *bébé* doll, with paperweight eyes, French, c1880, 32in (81.5cm) high.
£7,200–8,000
€ / **$11,400–12,600** ⊞ Beb

A Jumeau bisque-headed doll, with glass paperweight eyes, closed mouth and double-jointed composition body, marked 'Déposé Tête Jumeau - B.T.E. S.D. G.D.', French, c1885, 15in (38cm) high.
£3,000–3,500
€ / **$4,800–5,500** ⊞ YC

A Kämmer & Reinhardt bisque-headed character doll, 'Gretchen', with painted features, original wig and double-jointed composition body, later dress, German, c1908, 19¾in (50cm) high.
£3,600–4,500
€ / **$5,700–7,000** ⊞ YC

DOLLS

A pair of Marion Kaulitz Munich Art dolls, with painted composition heads and closed mouths, on fully-jointed composition bodies, German, c1911, 13in (33cm) high.
£1,000–1,200
€ / **$1,600–1,900** ⚲ B(Ch)

A J. D. Kestner bisque-headed doll, with weighted eyes, wood and composition ball-jointed body, chips, impressed '192 9', German, c1910, 20in (51cm) high.
£450–525
€ / **$710–830** ⚲ VEC

A J. D. Kestner bisque-headed Oriental character baby doll, with brown glass sleeping eyes, black wig and composition body, wearing Chinese silk costume, some damage, impressed 'Made in Germany 243 JDK', German, 1920s, head circumference 10in (25.5cm).
£520–620
€ / **$830–980** ⚲ SK(B)

A Kämmer & Reinhardt bisque-headed character doll, No. 115/A, with sleeping eyes and closed mouth, double-jointed composition toddler body, German, c1910, 13½in (34.5cm) high.
£1,800–2,000
€ / **$2,800–3,200** ⊞ YC

A J. D. Kestner Excelsior bisque-headed doll, with weighted glass eyes, open mouth, upper teeth and fully-jointed wood and composition body, incised, stamped 'Excelsior D.R.P, no 70685', German, c1910, 21in (53.5cm) high.
£420–500
€ / **$660–800** ⚲ B(Ch)

◄ **A Buddy Lee composition doll,** with a painted face, five-piece body, wearing denim dungarees labelled 'Lee-Union Made', American, c1922, 12in (30.5cm) high.
£185–225
€ / **$290–360** ⊞ THE

A J. D. Kestner bisque-headed character doll, 'Hilda', with sleeping eyes, open mouth and composition body, original clothes, incised mark, German, c1910, 11½in (29cm) high.
£1,600–2,000
€ / **$2,500–3,200** ⊞ YC

A J. D. Kestner bisque-headed baby doll, with sleeping eyes, open mouth and painted hair, marked 'JDK, Made in-14- Germany', wearing baby clothes, early 20thC, 18in (45.5cm) high.
£275–330
€ / **$430–520** ⚲ JDJ

A J. D. Kestner bisque-headed doll, with weighted glass eyes, open mouth and wig, a wood and composition ball-jointed body, impressed 'J.D.K. 260 63 71', minor chip, German, c1916, 25½in (65cm) high.
£550–625
€ / **$870–990** ⚲ VEC

A J. D. Kestner bisque-headed character doll, No. 239, with sleeping eyes, open mouth, double-jointed composition body, original clothing, new wig, German, c1910, 19in (48.5cm) high.
£500–600
€ / **$790–950** ⊞ YC

Condition

The condition is absolutely vital when assessing the value of an antique. Damaged pieces on the whole appreciate much less than perfect examples. However a rare desirable piece may command a high price even when damaged.

A Käthe Kruse cloth doll, with painted eyes, wearing original school uniform, German, c1930, 20in (51cm) high.
£1,200–1,400
€ / **$1,900–2,200** ⚲ B(Ch)

A Käthe Kruse Du Mein sand baby doll, with magnesite head, painted eyes and closed mouth, foam-filled body covered with stockinet, stamped on right foot, German, c1940, 21in (53.5cm) high.
£1,300–1,500
€ / **$2,100–2,400** ↗ B(Ch)

A Lenci felt character doll, with painted eyes, closed mouth and a blonde mohair wig, jointed neck and limbs, wearing a sailor's outfit, Italian, 1930s, 22½in (57cm) high.
£1,400–1,700
€ / **$2,200–2,700** ↗ SK(B)

A Käthe Kruse cloth doll, with painted face, moulded ears, jointed at hips, marked '120437', German, c1940, 18in (45.5cm) high.
£600–700
€ / **$950–1,100** ↗ B(Ch)

An Armand Marseille bisque-headed doll, mould 390, with cloth body and composition arms, original wig, 1890s, 26in (66cm) high.
£430–470
€ / **$680–750** ⊞ BaN

A Käthe Kruse doll, 'Little German child', with hard plastic head, painted eyes and short wig, cloth body, German, c1950, 18in (45.5cm) high.
£450–525
€ / **$710–830** ↗ B(Ch)

An Armand Marseille bisque-headed doll, mould 390, German, c1900, 34in (86.5cm) high.
£580–650
€ / **$920–1,000** ⊞ BaN

▶ **An Armand Marseille Dream Baby doll,** with sleeping eyes, composition hands and cloth body, hands repainted, German, early 20thC, 16in (40.5cm) high.
£100–120
€ / **$160–190** ↗ JDJ

A Lenci cloth doll, with painted features, curly mohair wig, swivel neck and jointed shoulders and hips, Italian, c1930, 17in (43cm) high.
£300–350
€ / **$475–550** ↗ B(Ch)

An Armand Marseille bisque-headed doll, mould 370, the kid body with jointed limbs, impressed mark, early 20thC, 15¾in (40cm) high.
£220–250
€ / **$350–400** ↗ PFK

DOLLS

An Armand Marseille bisque-headed doll, mould 390, with sleeping eyes, marked, c1900, 22in (56cm) high.
£90–110
€ / **$140–170** ↗ JDJ

An Armand Marseille bisque-headed doll, mould 390, with glass eyes, new wig, one leg broken, marked, c1900, 27in (68.5cm) high.
£145–160
€ / **$230–250** ↗ JDJ

An Armand Marseille bisque baby doll, mould 351, with painted hair, some damage, marked, early 20thC, 20in (51cm) high.
£425–475
€ / **$670–750** ↗ JDJ

◄ **An Armand Marseille bisque-headed Googly doll,** mould 323, with sleeping eyes, closed mouth, composition toddler body, new clothes, German, c1912, 10¼in (26cm) high.
£900–1,100
€/ **$1,400–1,700** ⊞ YC

An Armand Marseille doll, mould 390, fully jointed, wearing a fairy costume, marked, German, early 20thC, 16in (40.5cm) high, with original Kalitu Production ticket.
£220–260
€/ **$350–400** ⚒ BWL

A Kewpie bisque doll, signed by Rose O'Neill, American, c1915, 6in (15cm) high.
£300–350
€/ **$475–550** ⊞ THE

A Kewpie bisque doll, 'The Traveller', incised Rose O'Neill, American, c1915, 6in (15cm) high.
£345–400
€/ **$545–630** ⊞ THE

A Bye-Lo doll, with sleeping eyes, cloth body and celluloid hands, marked 'Grace Putnam', early 20thC, 14in (35.5cm) high.
£125–150
€/ **$200–240** ⚒ JDJ

► **A Franz Schmidt bisque-headed doll,** with sleeping glass eyes and jointed composition toddler body, original wig, c1912, 21in (53.5cm) high.
£400–500
€/ **$630–800** ⊞ YC

A poured wax doll, possibly by Pierotti, c1870, 30in (76cm) high.
£2,700–3,000
€/ **$4,300–4,800** ⊞ Beb

An S. F. B. J. bisque-headed doll, with weighted brown eyes and a wood and composition body, impressed '301 7', French, c1910, 20in (51cm) high.
£130–150
€/ **$210–240** ⚒ VEC

A Simon & Halbig bisque-shoulder-headed doll, with fixed glass eyes, wig with plaited bun, on a twill-over-wood jointed body, wearing original striped dress, one thumb broken, German, c1870, 10½in (26.5cm) high, in original box with trousseau.
£2,000–2,400
€/ **$3,200–3,800** ⚒ B(Ch)

An S. F. B. J. bisque-headed doll, with weighted blue glass eyes, open mouth and moulded teeth, fully-jointed composition body, hairline crack to head, French, c1910, 31in (78.5cm) high.
£380–450
€/ **$600–710** ⚒ B(Ch)

Further reading

Miller's Antiques & Collectables: The Facts At Your Fingertips, Miller's Publications, 2000

A Simon & Halbig bisque doll, wearing an antique outfit, German, c1890, 14in (35.5cm) high.
£500–600
€/ **$870–950** ⊞ Beb

A Simon & Halbig bisque doll, with weighted eyes, wood and composition ball-jointed body, impressed 'S & H 1079 DEP 11', cracked, German, c1892, 22¾in (58cm) high.
£150–175
€/ **$240–275** ✗ VEC

A Simon & Halbig bisque-headed doll, mould 1009, with glass sleeping eyes, double-jointed wood and composition body, wearing original outfit, produced for the French market, German, c1895, 20½in (52cm) high.
£600–700
€/ **$950–1,100** ⊞ YC

▶ **A Simon & Halbig bisque-headed doll,** mould 1249, 'Santa', with sleeping glass eyes, on a double-jointed composition body, wearing original baby clothes, German, c1905, 15in (38cm) high.
£550–600
€/ **$870–950**
⊞ YC

A Simon & Halbig bisque-headed doll, German, c1910, 27in (68.5cm) high.
£750–850
€/ **$1,200–1,300** ⊞ BaN

A Simon & Halbig/Kämmer & Reinhardt bisque-shoulder-headed doll, with weighted glass eyes, original wig on a cloth body, bisque lower arms, wearing regional costume, German, c1910, 16in (40.5cm) high, in original card box, lid missing.
£320–375
€/ **$510–590** ✗ B(Ch)

A Simon & Halbig bisque-headed doll, with sleeping glass eyes, wig and amber-tinted composition ball-jointed body, wearing silk costume, marked 'Simon&Halbig-Germany-1329-5', repainted arms and legs, German, c1900, 18in (45.5cm) high.
£760–900
€/ **$1,200–1,400** ⊞ THE

A Simon & Halbig bisque-headed doll, with sleeping eyes, on jointed body, wearing original costume, impressed 'S and H 1078 Simon and Halbig 6', German, c1910, 14½in (37cm) high.
£360–430
€/ **$580–680** ✗ BWL

◀ **A Jules Steiner bisque-headed doll,** with glass paperweight eyes, on a double-jointed composition body, wearing original costume, marked 'Steiner Paris', French, c1890, 21¼in (54cm) high.
£3,500–4,000
€/ **$5,500–6,200** ⊞ YC

▶ **A Walther & Sohn bisque-headed doll,** with googly sleeping eyes, composition bent-limb body, marked '208.121', German, c1920, 7in (18cm) high.
£280–320
€/ **$440–510**
✗ AH

Auction or dealer?

When buying at auction, prices can be lower than those of a dealer, but a buyer's premium and VAT will be added to the hammer price. Equally, when selling at auction, commission, tax and photography charges will be deducted from the hammer price. Dealers will often restore pieces before putting them back on the market.

DOLLS

Unknown Makers

A wooden doll, with painted features and peg-jointed body, one arm and leg possible replacements, American, early 19thC, 5¼in (13.5cm) high.
£240–300
€/ **$380–475** ⚡ SK(B)
This doll was found in New England and a note with her states 'this doll was the plaything of Eliza Thornton, sister of Lydia Thornton Cram'.

A poured wax doll, with fixed eyes, cloth body with wax lower arms and legs, head repaired, c1870, 28in (71cm) high.
£1,500–1,700
€/ **$2,400–2,800** ⊞ BaN

A late Victorian bisque-headed doll, with jointed composition body, 23¾in (60.5cm) high.
£140–160
€/ **$220–250** ⚡ SWO

▶ **A doll,** with fixed glass eyes, open mouth with applied teeth and moulded hair, on a jointed composition body, French, c1910, 20in (51cm) high.
£1,400–1,600
€/ **$2,200–2,500** ⚡ AH

A wax doll, with painted eyes, closed mouth, with composition lower legs, original dress and apron, c1860, 6in (15cm) high.
£350–380
€/ **$550–600** ⚡ SK(B)

A bisque shoulder-headed fashion doll, made for Simmone, with glass eyes and closed mouth, stuffed kid body, original wig and dress, c1880, 16½in (42cm) high.
£1,600–1,800
€/ **$2,500–2,800** ⊞ YC

A poured wax shoulder-headed doll, with fixed eyes, cloth body and wax-over-composition lower arms and legs, cracks, damage, c1860, 23in (58.5cm) high.
£160–200
€/ **$250–320** ⚡ VEC

A bisque-headed doll, with paperweight eyes and closed mouth, pierced ears with original earrings, jointed composition body, marked 'M10', French, c1890, 22¾in (58cm) high.
£2,200–2,500
€/ **$3,500–4,000** ⚡ Bri

A bisque Googly doll, c1910, 6in (15cm) high.
£550–650
€/ **$870–1,000** ⊞ Beb

▶ **A doll,** with painted features, cloth body with composition arms, French, c1930, 12½in (32cm) high.
£65–75
€/ **$100–120** ⊞ YC

A china-headed doll, 'Grape Lady', with blue painted eyes, and a cluster of iridescent cobalt blue grapes beneath white ruffled gold snood, cloth body with china limbs, wearing original beige silk and wool dress, German, 1860s, 17in (43cm) high.
£1,300–1,500
€/ **$2,000–2,400** ⚡ SK(B)

A wax doll, with closed mouth, curly wig, 19thC, 22in (56cm) high.
£260–320
€/ **$410–500** ⚡ SWO

A wax-over-composition doll, with fixed glass eyes and cloth body, 19thC, 16in (40.5cm) high.
£145–160
€/ **$230–250** ⊞ BaN

Dolls' Houses

A painted wooden dolls' house, with a painted tiled roof, the front opening to reveal six rooms, hallway and staircase, mid-19thC, 38in (97cm) wide.
£1,000–1,200
€ / **$1,600–2,000** ⚹ B(Ch)

A painted wooden dolls' house, the front opening in two sections to reveal four rooms, c1860, 30in (76cm) wide.
£480–570
€ / **$760–900** ⚹ B(Ch)

A wooden dolls' house, with four furnished rooms, c1870, 29in (73.5cm) wide.
£3,200–3,500
€ / **$5,000–5,500** ⊞ Beb

A wooden dolls' house, damaged, late 19thC, 29in (73.5cm) wide.
£400–500
€ / **$600–800** ⚹ S(O)

A Moritz Göttschalk painted wooden dolls' house, with single opening front revealing two rooms, with original wallpaper and floor coverings, German, c1900, 11in (28cm) wide.
£600–700
€ / **$950–1,100** ⚹ B(Ch)

A painted wooden dolls' house, with lift-off front and side opening, dated 1914, 23¾in (60.5cm) wide.
£350–420
€ / **$550–650** ⚹ S(O)

A wooden dolls' house, rendered in white stucco, the front opening in two sections to reveal four rooms, hallway, staircase and landing, all with original floor coverings and fireplaces, 1920s, 36in (91.5cm) wide.
£130–160
€ / **$210–250** ⚹ B(Ch)

A Tri-ang mock-Tudor wooden dolls' house, 'Albert Cottage', No. 77, the exterior painted with flowers to the walls, the front opening in two sections to reveal four rooms, hall, staircase and built-in garage with double doors, 1930s, 33½in (85cm) wide.
£200–240
€ / **$320–380** ⚹ WAL

An 'Amersham' dolls' house, with cream-painted exterior and *faux* slate roof, the front opening to reveal two rooms with fitted fireplace, late 1930s, base 16½in (42cm) square.
£80–100
€ / **$125–160** ⚹ WAL

◄ **A Tri-ang wooden dolls' house,** 'Fashionable Tudor House', No. 93, the exterior painted cream with flowers to the walls and half-timbered gables, the front opening in four sections to reveal five rooms, hall and staircase, built-in garage with opening double doors, with original wall and floor coverings and electric lighting, with furniture and many accessories, c1950, 47in (119.5cm) wide.
£800–950
€ / **$1,300–1,500** ⚹ B(Ch)

Teddy Bears

A Chad Valley curly mohair teddy bear, with glass eyes and rexine pads, labelled, 1940s, 14in (35.5cm) high.
£270–300
€/ $430–480 ⊞ BBe

A Clemens teddy bear, German, 1940s, 18in (45.5cm) high.
£400–450
€/ $630–700 ⊞ Beb
This teddy bear comes from a collection formed by the Volpps, an American couple who wrote many story books with teddy bears as the main characters.

◀ **A Dean's Tru-to-Life mohair teddy bear,** designed by Sylvia Wilgoss, with rubber nose, feet and pads, labelled, early 1950s, 22in (56cm) high.
£2,200–2,500
€/ $3,500–4,000 ⊞ BBe

A Chad Valley Magna mohair teddy bear, with glass eyes and cotton pads, labelled, 1950s, 12in (30.5cm) high.
£350–400
€/ $550–630 ⊞ BBe

A Farnell mohair teddy bear, replaced glass eyes, head sewn on, repaired, worn, 1920s, 15in (38cm) high.
£800–950
€/ $1,300–1,500 ⋋ VEC

A Merrythought teddy bear, with glass eyes and original cotton pads, wishbone button in one ear, labelled, 1930s, 18in (45.5cm) high.
£315–350
€/ $500–550 ⊞ BBe

A Dean's Rag Book mohair mouse-eared teddy bear, pads require restoration, 1930s, 16in (40.5cm) high.
£550–600
€/ $870–950 ⊞ BBe

A Joy Toys mohair teddy bear, with glass eyes, Australian, 1940s, 14in (35.5cm) high.
£260–300
€/ $400–480 ⊞ BBe

A Merrythought mohair teddy bear, with glass eyes and cotton paw feet, labelled, 1930s–40s, 15in (38cm) high.
£350–400
€/ $550–630 ⊞ BBe

Further reading

Miller's Teddy Bears: A Complete Collector's Guide, Miller's Publications, 2001

A Merrythought Cheeky mohair teddy bear, with plastic eyes, 1960, 24in (61cm) high.
£675–750
€/ **$1,100–1,200** ⊞ BBe
Merrythought's Cheeky design was first registered in 1957. Sought-after by collectors today, it was a very popular bear in the late '50s and early '60s and was produced in a number of sizes and versions. Identifying features include bells inside the ears and the Merrythought label sewn to the foot. Over the years felt pads often became worn and were replaced so labels can be missing.

▶ **A Steiff plush teddy bear,** with glass eyes and cotton pads, German, 1940s, 16in (40.5cm) high.
£1,300–1,500
€/ **$2,000–2,400** ⊞ BBe

A Steiff plush teddy bear, with black boot-button eyes, centrally-stitched snout, hump back and button in ear, German, c1908, 22½in (57cm) high.
£2,200–2,500
€/ **$3,500–4,000** ⚹ TEN

A Steiff mohair teddy bear, with boot-button eyes, fully jointed, some wear, German, c1908, 15½in (39.5cm) high.
£1,200–1,400
€/ **$1,900–2,200** ⚹ VEC

A Steiff plush teddy bear, with button eyes, jointed limbs and button to ear, straw-filled, German, c1910, 12in (30.5cm) high.
£1,400–1,600
€/ **$2,200–2,500** ⚹ AH

A Tara Toys plush teddy bear, with jointed limbs, Irish, c1950, 18in (45.5cm) high.
£100–120
€/ **$160–190** ⚹ G(L)

A mohair teddy bear, with glass eyes and felt pads, 1920s, 15in (38cm) high.
£350–400
€/ **$550–630** ⊞ BBe

Soft Toys

A **Wendy Boston mohair dog nightdress case,** with plastic eyes, leather collar and original label, 1950s, 16in (40.5cm) long.
£60–65
€/ **$95–100** ⊞ BBe

▶ A **Chad Valley cloth golly,** with cardboard label 'By Appointment to HM Queen Elizabeth the Queen Mother', small hole to back of head, one felt nostril missing, late 1950s–early 1960s, 24in (61cm) high.
£140–160
€/ **$220–250** ⚒ VEC

▶ A **Chad Valley velvet Bonzo dog,** with painted features, swivel head and jointed limbs, card-lined feet, original collar with button attached, c1920, 10¼in (26cm) high.
£280–325
€/ **$440–510** ⚒ DA

A **Schuco mohair Yes/No monkey,** German, 1920s, 4¾in (12cm) high.
£145–170
€/ **$230–270** ⚒ JDJ

A **Schuco Goofy,** German, 1950s, 14in (35.5cm) high.
£160–180
€/ **$250–280** ⚒ TQA

A **Steiff mohair giraffe,** with original buttons, ear tag, squeaker boot and button eyes, German, 1950s, 11in (28cm) high.
£60–65
€/ **$95–100** ⊞ BBe

A **velvet Mickey Mouse,** slightly worn, some repair, c1930, 9in (23cm) high.
£140–160
€/ **$220–250** ⚒ DA

A **plush miniature monkey,** with tin face, jointed head and limbs, early 20thC, 2¼in (5.5cm) high.
£75–90
€/ **$120–140** ⚒ SWO

A **felt Mickey and Minnie Mouse,** after 1945, 13½in (34.5cm) high.
£35–40
€/ **$55–65** ⚒ G(L)

Further reading

Miller's Soft Toys: A Collector's Guide, Miller's Publications, 2000

◀ A **cloth lion,** with glass eyes, 1950s, 12in (30.5cm) high.
£27–30
€/ **$40–45** ⊞ YC

▶ A **Soo puppet,** from *Sooty & Sweep*, 1950s, 9in (23cm) high.
£10–15
€/ **$16–24** ⊞ CCO

A **fur monkey,** with glass eyes, c1960, 14in (35.5cm) high.
£22–25
€/ **$35–40** ⊞ YC

Toys

Over the many years that I have been involved in the antiques business I have found that collectors of toys generally fall into four main categories. I always advise the 'Pure Investor' to select an area to collect, research it inside out, find the rarest pieces and purchase the best examples one can afford. This will usually ensure that the items will command the best possible prices when they come to be sold at a later date. The 'Serious Collector' is looking for excellent condition and knows his subject. He also enjoys the fun of the hunt, the pure delight of arriving home from the auction or fair with the piece that has eluded him for so many months, and which is then lovingly placed in the cabinet. The 'Hobbyist' collects for the sheer joy of it and all one requires is an example of the type. Nothing has to be perfect and indeed, the fact that in years gone by a youngster has had fun with it just adds to its attraction and therefore a mint, boxed example is not necessary. The 'Limited Edition Collector' collects mainly modern models, perhaps the many series representing vehicles used in television programmes and films. These collectors should bear in mind that in the long term these items are unlikely to be a good investment, since once the craze for collecting a particular range of models has passed, the value often falls quickly.

Modern limited editions should not be confused, however, with early television- and film-related vehicles, which have become increasingly popular over the last 25 years. For example, in the 1960s Corgi and Dinky produced a range which included the *Man From U.N.C.L.E.* Oldsmobile, the James Bond Aston Martin DB5, and various *Captain Scarlet* vehicles, among others. These are very sought after today and can command extremely high prices, particularly in comparison to many other die-cast vehicles of the same period. They have proved to be an excellent investment: as an example, a mint, boxed Corgi James Bond Toyota 2000 GT which cost £18 (€/ $28) in c1980 would now cost about £375 (€/ $590). This, I feel, is mainly due to the role that film and television plays in our lives today.

Reruns on the television of the old classics such as James Bond films, *Doctor Who*, *Thunderbirds* and the like awaken feelings of nostalgia in adults who can now afford to collect toys which remind them of perhaps more carefree days. The field is immense and encompasses die-cast, tinplate and even plastic examples. The hobby is driven by a worldwide audience which is no doubt helping to push up prices.

Glenn Butler

Aeroplanes

A Dinky Toys Imperial Airways airliner, 1930s, 4in (10cm) long.
£120–135
€/ **$190–215** ⊞ CBB

A Dinky Toys Short Shetland Flying Boat, 1940s, 7in (18cm) long.
£250–280
€/ **$400–440** ⊞ CBB

▶ **A Schuco 1030 Micro Jet,** German, 1950s, with box, 5½in (14cm) square.
£40–50
€/ **$63–80** ⋟ TQA

A Fanfare Models aircraft hanger, with pilot, ground crew, mechanics and RAF personnel, and a copy of a Britain's Autogyro, c1930, 23in (58.5cm) wide.
£160–200
€/ **$250–320** ⋟ VEC

A Schuco 1031 Micro Jet, German, 1950s, with box, 5in (12.5cm) square.
£40–45
€/ **$63–70** ⋟ TQA

◀ **A tinplate bi-plane,** c1930, 18in (45.5cm) wide.
£200–220
€/ **$315–350** ⋟ VEC

Boats

◄ **A Bing clockwork battleship,** one secondary turret missing, German, c1920, 20in (51cm) wide.
£1,000–1,200
€/ **$1,600–1,900**
▲ B(Ch)

A Bing tinplate clockwork U boat, with detachable flag, 1930s, 13½in (34.5cm) wide.
£475–550
€/ **$750–870** ▲ WAL

A Schuco 3003 clockwork police boat, German, 1950s, 5in (12.5cm) wide.
£100–125
€/ **$160–200** ▲ TQA

Tinplate

The term tinplate covers a vast range of items, including boats, trains, cars, buses, automata and space ships. If your budget is relatively small – under £150 (€/ $240) – then the 1960s to 1970s is the best period to focus on. Battery-powered examples made in Japan, China, and some eastern European countries are plentiful. If you are looking to spend more, you should collect earlier items as far back as the Victorian era, where in many cases a great deal has to be spent to secure these childhood playthings.

The rules for investment buying are: buy the best examples you can find; make sure the action works; check that battery-powered examples do not show signs of battery leakage, and look for pieces in original packaging.

◄ **A Schuco clockwork 3006 Pitt boat,** German, 1950s, 11in (28cm) wide.
£100–125
€/ **$160–200** ▲ TQA

► **A motor boat,** the spirit-fired brass boiler with oscillating engine, Japanese, 1930s, 10in (25.5cm) wide.
£140–160
€/ **$220–250** ▲ HoG

Mechanical Toys

► **A Fontaine Fox clockwork painted tin trolley car,** 'Toonerville Trolley', with driver, American, 1920s, 5in (12.5cm) high.
£420–500
€/ **$660–800** ▲ BAu

A Brimtoy Pocketoy 9/501 clockwork steamroller, 1950s, 4in (10cm) wide, boxed.
£60–65
€/ **$95–105** ⊞ GTM

A JR 21 Toys Thunderbird 1, with friction motor, c1966, 8in (20.5cm) wide, boxed.
£90–100
€/ **$140–160** ⊞ GTM

► **A Lambert musical automaton of a Spanish dancer,** clothes replaced, French, c1895, 21in (53.5cm) high.
£2,700–3,000
€/ **$4,300–4,700** ⊞ KHW

A Rock Valley Toys battery-operated bubble-blowing monkey, Japanese, 1950s, 11in (28cm) high.
£125–140
€/ **$200–230** ⊞ CBB

TOYS

◄ **A pair of Schuco felt-covered tinplate clockwork pigs,** one plays a fiddle, the other a drum, German, 1920–30, 4½in (11.5 cm) high.
£300–360
€/ **$475–575** 🗡 **F&C**

An automaton walking pig, possibly by Roullet et Decamps, covered with skin, French, c1900, 11in (28cm) long.
£765–850
€/ **$1,200–1,300** ⊞ **BaN**

▶ **A flock-covered papier mâché bulldog,** with bark and nodding head, French, c1900, 21in (53.5cm) long.
£1,000–1,100
€/ **$1,600–1,700** ⊞ **AUTO**

A clockwork toy of two dancing dolls, with bisque heads, c1930, 8in (20.5cm) high.
£585–650
€/ **$925–1,000** ⊞ **AUTO**

A tinplate clockwork swan, Japanese, 1950s, 7in (18cm) long, boxed.
£115–130
€/ **$180–200** ⊞ **CBB**

◄ **A tinplate battery-operated X-7 Flying Saucer,** Japanese, 1960s, 8in (20.5cm) diam.
£175–200
€/ **$275–315** ⊞ **GTM**

Money Boxes

A cast-iron Bulldog Bank money box, with glass eyes, losses, American, dated 1880, 7¾in (19.5cm) high.
£200–225
€/ **$315–350** 🗡 **HAM**

A cast-iron money box, in the form of a golly, c1910, 6½in (16.5cm) high.
£360–400
€/ **$570–630** ⊞ **MFB**

◄ **A cast-iron mechanical money box,** the dog performs a trick, American, c1930, 9in (23cm) wide.
£360–400
€/ **$570–630**
⊞ **HAL**

TOYS

Noah's Arks

▶ **A painted Noah's Ark,** with seven figures and 39 animals, German, mid-19thC, 6¼in (16cm) wide.
£1,600–1,800
€/ $2,500–2,800 ⚒ SK(B)

A painted pine Noah's Ark, with a collection of painted pine and composition figures and animals, losses and damage, Swiss, mid-19thC, 18½in (47cm) wide.
£600–720
€/ $950–1,100 ⚒ BR

◀ **A painted wooden Noah's Ark,** with five figures and approximately 65 animals, slight damage, German, late 19thC, 28in (71cm) wide, together with a quantity of wooden farmyard fencing, trees and animals.
£1,400–1,600
€/ $2,200–2,500 ⚒ VEC

Rocking Horses

A Victorian rocking horse, on traditional rocker base, restored, 80in (203cm) long.
£1,400–1,600
€/ $2,200–2,500 ⚒ JM

A carved- and painted-wood rocking horse, c1900, 51¼in (130cm) long.
£350–400
€/ $550–630 ⚒ SWO

A carved- and painted-wood rocking horse, with horsehair mane and tail, original leather bridle and saddle, on a safety stand, marked for Henry's, Winchester, c1880, 44in (122cm) high.
£700–800
€/ $1,100–1,300 ⚒ B(Ch)

An F. Ayres ponyskin rocking horse, with horsehair mane and tail, original leather bridle, saddle and metal stirrups, on a safety rocker, minor losses, c1900, 53in (134.5cm) high.
£600–700
€/ $950–1,100 ⚒ B(Ch)

◀ **A rocking horse,** with hair mane and leather saddle, on a pine stand, restored, early 20thC, 48in (122cm) wide.
£800–950
€/ $1,300–1,500 ⚒ EH

An F. Ayres painted rocking horse, on a trestle base, restored by Stevenson Bros, c1890, 39½in (100.5cm) high.
£1,100–1,300
€/ $1,700–2,000 ⚒ BR

A rocking horse, with padded body and wooden base, possibly eastern European, early 20thC, 34¼in (87cm) wide.
£220–250
€/ $350–400 ⚒ SWO

An F. Ayres carved and painted rocking horse, with horsehair mane and tail, remains of leather bridle and saddle, with leg rest for side saddle, on safety rockers, embossed Ayres signature, c1920, 47in (119.5cm) high.
£1,100–1,300
€/ $1,700–2,000 ⚒ B(Ch)

TOYS

Soldiers

◀ **A Britains set of Germanic 16th Lancers,** comprising nine figures including officer and trumpeter, with moveable arms and twistable pennons, in associated box, losses, 1893.
£2,000–2,400
€ / **$3,200–3,800** ⚒ B(Ch)

A Britains set of Egyptian Camel Corps, set No. 48, with wire tails and removable riders, in original box, 1899.
£550–650
€ / **$870–1,000** ⚒ B(Ch)

A Britains set of 21st Lancers, set No. 94, comprising four mounted Lancers and a mounted officer, minor damage, 1901, boxed.
£400–475
€ / **$630–750** ⚒ VEC

A Britains Middlesex Regiment, set No. 76, comprising eight figures, 1903.
£180–220
€ / **$285–350** ⚒ B(Ch)

▶ **A Britains set of US Infantry,** comprising 10 marching infantrymen, 1906.
£250–300
€ / **$400–475** ⚒ VEC

Three Britains American mounted soldiers, from set No. 149, 1907–16.
£550–650
€ / **$870–1,000** ⚒ VEC

A Britains Mountain Artillery group, set No. 28, comprising six gunners, a mounted officer, four mules and dismantled R. A. gun, 1910.
£160–200
€ / **$250–315** ⚒ VEC

◀ **A Britains USA Aviation Display set,** set No. 336, comprising 16 figures of aviators and marching privates, boxed, 1929.
£600–725
€ / **$950–1,100** ⚒ VEC

A Britains Royal Horse Artillery group, set No. 318, with artillerymen mounted on standing horses, mounted officer and fumed metal limber and gun, standing artillery men missing, 1930.
£850–1,000
€ / **$1,300–1,600** ⚒ B(Ch)
This is a rare set, because boys wanted the horse cantering or trotting – standing still was in effect dull.

A Britains set of Royal Navy Bluejackets and Whitejackets, set No. 254, comprising nine figures including Petty Officer, some retouching to paint, 1935.
£100–125
€ / **$160–200** ⚒ B(Ch)

▶ **A Britains set of Royal Welch Fusiliers,** set No. 2124, with officer and goat mascot, in original box, 1958.
£140–160
€ / **$220–250** ⚒ B(Ch)

TOYS

Trains

A Bassett-Lowke gauge 0 live steam 4–6–0 Enterprise locomotive and tender, 6285, c1935, together with other items including original Bassett-Lowke bill of sale, spare wick and spring, filler, two cans of rocket oil and two cans of cylinder oil.
£500–575
€/ **$800–900** ⤳ AH

A Bassett-Lowke gauge 0 electric 0–6–0 tank locomotive, RN 68211, in BR livery, 1950s, boxed.
£320–375
€/ **$500–600** ⤳ B(Ch)

A Bing plastic signal box, restored, 1930s, 10in (25.5cm) high.
£40–45
€/ **$65–70** ⊞ WOS

A Fleischmann gauge H0 D.B. 4–6–2 mainline heavy duty locomotive and tender, German, 1950s.
£90–100
€/ **$140–160** ⊞ WOS

An American Flyer gauge 0 electric train, roof repainted, c1935, 21in (53.5cm) long.
£175–200
€/ **$275–315** ⊞ WOS

Gauges

Trains of various gauges are one of the most popular collecting fields within the toy and model world. Z and N gauge are the very small pieces normally purchased to run rather than collect, ideal for when space is at a premium. 0 and 00 are the two gauges mainly collected by people looking to invest and also run.

Frank Hornby's products, the 0 and Dublo series, are much sought after. Bassett-Lowke, Bing, Märklin, and other well-known manufacturers also have a very strong following. If you have a budget of about £350 (€/ $500) you will be able to buy many examples of these gauges.

The rarer ones can cost as much as £1,000 (€/ $1,600) or more. The rules for investment buying are: buy the best example you can find; watch for professionally restored examples as these can sometimes be passed off as mint originals; check the wheels are not later replacements; look for dents/creases that have been removed; check the condition of the clockwork or electric motor, and take a key to test the clockwork mechanism. A reputable vendor will not mind you doing this.

◀ A Bing gauge 0 live steam 0–4–0 locomotive and tender, finished in black with red lining, early 20thC.
£320–400
€/ **$510–630** ⤳ LAY

A Karl Bub tinplate gauge 0 clockwork 4–4–0 locomotive, RN 1632, with six-wheel tender and two bogie carriages with opening doors and side-hinged roof, minor damage, German, early 20thC.
£550–650
€/ **$870–1,000** ⤳ WAL

▶ A Carette gauge 1 eight-wheeled carriage, with opening doors, German, c1910.
£270–300
€/ **$425–475** ⊞ WOS

A Hornby gauge 0 Pullman coach, c1930, boxed.
£135–150
€/ **$215–240** ⊞ GTM

A Hornby gauge 0 No. 2 corridor brake end coach,
with opening windows, compensating bogies with
reduced Mansell wheels, mid-1930s.
£230–275
€ / **$365–440** ⚒ **WAL**

**A Hornby gauge 0 clockwork 0–4–0 No. 1 Tank
locomotive,** c1937.
£38–42
€ / **$60–65** ⊞ **VJ**

A Hornby two-rail BR diesel locomotive, 1950s.
£65–75
€ / **$100–120** ⊞ **WOS**

A Hornby gauge 0 tinplate station, electric lights not
original, bulbs missing, 1950s, 32in (81.5cm) wide.
£75–85
€ / **$120–135** ⊞ **WOS**

A Hornby Dublo LMS passenger train set, comprising
4–6–2 Duchess of Atholl locomotive and tender, track,
controller, spanner and oil, repaired, with original
box, 1950s.
£280–325
€ / **$440–520** ⚒ **VEC**

**A Leeds Model Co gauge 0 Brighton Belle Pullman
coach,** Hazel, minor wear, 1930s.
£100–120
€ / **$160–190** ⚒ **WAL**

▶ **A Hornby
gauge 0 E2E
engine shed,**
with two three-
rail roads, details
to one side only,
mid-1930s.
£370–425
€ / **$585–670**
⚒ **WAL**

**A Hornby Dublo gauge 00 LMR 8F electric freight
locomotive and tender,** 1958–61, with original box.
£115–125
€ / **$180–200** ⊞ **GTM**

Colour variations

Two frequently asked questions are: why are
cars produced in different colourways? why is
one more valuable than the other?

One answer is that at the end of a working
week, quite often at the end of a month, the
supply of paint on a particular production line
might have run out. Rather than stop production,
a similar paint would be requisitioned from
another line and painters would continue until
the shift ended. Maybe only a few hundred toys
would have been made in the new unrecorded
colour. Another scenario is that a company
would commission a limited number in their
own livery for promotional purposes. Values for
these limited pieces can be greatly in excess of
those for normal production pieces.

**A Hornby gauge 0 clockwork 4–4–2 No. 2 Special
Tank locomotive,** No. 6, 1930s.
£280–325
€ / **$440–500** ⚒ **VEC**

**A Lionel electric 2–6–2 streamlined locomotive
and tender,** with three-rail pickup, American, 1930s.
18in (45.5cm) long.
£150–165
€ / **$240–260** ⊞ **WOS**

A Lionel gauge 0 electric locomotive, No. 1668.E, and four tinplate rolling stock, with track, marked, American, mid-20thC.
£80–100
€ / \$125–160 ➹ SWO

A Märklin four-wheeled crane truck, No. 1668, German, 1930s.
£170–200
€ / \$270–300 ➹ VEC

▶ **A Rivarossi gauge H0 plastic station 5511,** Italian, c1965, 21in (54cm) long, boxed.
£60–65
€ / \$95–100 ⊞ WOS

A Tri-ang Hornby Minic RMD motorail set, comprising Dock Authority diesel shunter, rail transporter, Aston Martin, track and hand controller, c1967, boxed.
£250–300
€ / \$400–475 ➹ VEC

A Tri-ang RS29 Local Passenger train set, comprising 4–6–0 B12 locomotive and tender, two Mark I coaches and track, c1964, boxed.
£80–100
€ / \$125–160 ➹ VEC

A pair of Wrenn gauge 00 Pullman coaches, The Brighton Belle, 1970s.
£160–175
€ / \$250–275 ⊞ WOS

▶ **A Märklin gauge H0 Swiss railway Bo–Bo twin pantograph mainline locomotive,** German, 1950s, boxed.
£200–225
€ / \$315–350 ⊞ WOS

A Milbro gauge 0 bogie passenger coach, RN 8173, third class, corridor, 1930s.
£110–130
€ / \$170–200 ➹ WAL

TOYS

Vehicles

A Corgi Toys Green Hornet car, 1960s, 5in (12.5cm) long, boxed.
£315–350
€/ **$500–550** ⊞ HAL

A Britains Napier Bluebird record car, c1937, 4in (10cm) long, boxed.
£180–220
€/ **$285–350** ⚒ IM

A Chad Valley diecast clockwork Wee Kin cable layer toy, 1949–53, 4½in (11.5cm) long.
£80–90
€/ **$125–140** ⊞ GTM

◄ **A Crescent Toys D-type Jaguar,** No. 1292, 1957–60, 4in (10cm) long, boxed.
£115–130
€/ **$180–200** ⊞ CBB

► **A Dinky Toys tinplate petrol filling station,** No. 48, 1930s, in original box.
£350–420
€/ **$550–670** ⚒ WAL

► **A Dinky Toys MG Magic Midget,** No. 11, 1930s.
£230–275
€/ **$360–430** ⚒ B(Ch)

Dinky Toys

Frank Hornby launched his brand new Modelled Miniatures range of lead diecast toys in 1931. He could not have known that some 70 years later millions of pounds would still be spent every year on them by collectors worldwide. In 1934 they became known as Dinky Toys apparently after a visit to his grand-mother one Sunday afternoon; Hornby showed her one of his new range to be used along side his 0 gauge railway. 'What a dinky toy that is,' she is supposed to have said, and the name stuck. Over 1000 different toys and vehicles were produced until the factory closed in 1979.

Pre-WWII Dinky Toys have thin axles with smooth wheel hubs, unlike the post-war Dinkys. Watch for metal fatigue on these early examples. This is not an issue with the very early vehicles which were made of lead. Look at any prospective purchase carefully: many Dinkys have been restored; some so well you might be fooled into thinking that they are unrestored examples. Check for traces of the original paint in hard-to-get-at areas, see if the wheels have been taken off, and if parts have been replaced.

► **A Jo Hill Co land speed record car,** c1929, 5½in (14cm) long.
£175–200
€/ **$275–315** ⊞ CBB

A Kingsbury fire engine, American, 1930s, 32in (81.5cm) long.
£220–250
€/ **$350–400** ⚒ VEC

The Bob Ewers Collection

During the last 18 years many toy collections have gone through the system, but only a few come to mind as being special. One of those was owned by a man named Bob Ewers.

Bob's collection was different because for over 40 years he nurtured a passion for collecting Matchbox Series Vehicles made by Moko Lesney. There were 75 vehicles in the series, and every few years the range would change as the series was updated. The boxes were also changed as time progressed. Bob would collect each series as it came out, but would then find as many wheel, colour and export variations as he could. In those days these were regarded simply as toys, and no major value could be put to his growing collection. Only in later years, when the hobby grew to become a major player in the collecting world, did the reward come home. Sadly Bob died just before his collection was sold in 2001, and therefore did not get to see the two auctions needed to sell his hobby, which totalled over £54,000 (€/ $85,300).   **Glenn Butler**

A Mettoys BOAC van, c1953, 6in (15cm) long.
£100–110
€/ **$160–170** ⊞ GTM

▶ **A Moko Lesney Matchbox American Ford station wagon,** No. 31, boxed.
£300–350
€/ **$475–550** ⚲ VEC

A Schuco battery-operated dump truck, No. 6077, German, 1950s, 10in (25.5cm) long.
£380–450
€/ **$600–700** ⚲ TQA

◀ **A Schuco tinplate clockwork Examico 4001 car,** German, 1940s, 6in (15cm) long.
£135–150
€/ **$220–240** ⊞ HAL

◀ **A Tri-ang Minic police car,** c1948, 5in (12.5cm) long.
£63–70
€/ **$100–110** ⊞ HAL

A Tri-ang double decker bus, c1950, 7in (18cm) long, boxed.
£230–255
€/ **$360–400** ⊞ CBB
The harlequin box is scarce.

◀ **A Victory Industries battery-operated Triumph TR2,** early 1960s, 9in (23cm) long, boxed.
£225–250
€/ **$350–400** ⊞ UCO

TOYS

Miscellaneous

Items in the Toys Miscellaneous section have been arranged in alphabetical order.

► **A Tri-ang Brooklands pedal car,** c1950, 46in (117cm) long.
£765–850
€/ **$1,200–1,300** ⊞ JUN

A mahogany folding bagatelle board, with numbered arched bridge and nine balls, 19thC, 94in (239cm) wide.
£170–200
€/ **$270–315** ➤ BWL

An Edinburgh ivory chess set, c1860, king 3in (7.5cm) high.
£650–750
€/ **$1,000–1,200** ➤ CO

An olivewood games box, with roulette wheel, early 20thC, 4¼in (11cm) square.
£120–140
€/ **$190–220** ➤ TMA

◄ **A Meier tinplate 'penny toy' open landau,** with horse and driver, 1920s, 4in (10cm) long.
£280–315
€/ **$440–500** ⊞ RGa

A carved pine and gesso toy horse on wheels, with leather details, c1880, 11in (28cm) long.
£450–500
€/ **$700–800** ⊞ RYA

A cast-iron 'Nip & Tuck' toy, the painted dogs pulling on a string, c1875, 9in (23cm) wide.
£700–800
€/ **$1,100–1,300** ➤ SK(B)

A walnut-veneered Deluxe arcade pinball table, c1930, 36in (91.5cm) wide.
£900–1,000
€/ **$1,400–1,600** ⊞ ChC

◄ **A J. Jaques Squails game,** c1870, in a mahogany case 9 x 5in (23 x 12.5cm).
£135–150
€/ **$220–240** ⊞ HUM

A Pelham Puppets Duchess string puppet, with standard control and metal knee joints, pre-1955, 11¾in (30cm) high, boxed.
£200–225
€/ **$315–350** ➤ B(Ch)

◄ **An Ives Boy on a Velocipede,** with twin propulsion rods, spring motor and steering mechanism, American, 1870s, 8in (20.5cm) long.
£8,000–9,000
€/ **$12,500–14,000** ➤ SK(B)

► **A papier mâché and wood ventriloquist's dummy,** with book, photograph, case and flag, c1920, 42in (106.5cm) high.
£1,300–1,500
€/ **$2,100–2,400** ⊞ AUTO

Ephemera
Annuals & Comics

◄ **Hobbies,** issue No. 1840, published by George Newnes, with Mickey Mouse cover and cut-out Mickey and Minnie Mouse portraits insert, 1931.
£50–60
€/ **$80–95**
➤ **CBP**

Mickey Mouse Weekly, issue Nos. 48–99, complete year including Coronation with cover art by Walt Disney, Easter, Fireworks and Christmas issues, 1937.
£300–360
€/ **$470–560** ➤ **CBP**

The Beano, issue No. 46, 1939.
£150–180
€/ **$240–280** ➤ **CBP**

◄ **Young Marvelman Annual,** issue No. 1, 1954.
£50–60
€/ **$80–95** ➤ **CBP**

► **Marvelman Annual,** issue No. 2, 1955.
£80–95
€/ **$125–150** ➤ **CBP**

The Dandy Monster Comic, 1950.
£380–450
€/ **$600–700** ➤ **CBP**

Detective Comics, issue No. 325, published by DC Comics, 1964, 10 x 7in (25.5 x 18cm).
£12–14
€/ **$16–20** ⊞ **CoC**

Action Comics, issue No. 265, June 1960, 10 x 7in (25.5 x 18cm).
£18–20
€/ **$25–30** ⊞ **NOS**

Viz, issue No. 1, with free ice cream, 1979.
£250–300
€/ **$400–470** ➤ **CBP**

The Amazing Spider-Man, issue No. 300, 25th Anniversary Issue, May 1988.
£35–40
€/ **$55–65** ➤ **CBP**

EPHEMERA

Autographs

J. W. von Goethe, autograph note, 1818, 1 page, 8°.
£2,400–2,800
€/ **$3,800–4,400** ✗ S
This note was probably written on a flyleaf of Goethe's copy of the French translation of *Undine*, Friedrich de la Motte Fouqué's fairytale of 1811.

Queen Alexandra, a pre-printed letter of thanks for condolences sent following the death of Edward VII, in a silver frame, on a V-shaped foliate-engraved frame, hallmarked for London 1910, 6in (15cm) wide.
£280–320
€/ **$440–500** ✗ GAK

Winston Churchill, a signed photograph, 1947, 7 x 4½in (18 x 11.5cm), framed and glazed.
£2,400–2,800
€/ **$3,800–4,400** ✗ VS

Herbert Henry Asquith, a signed letter, 1892.
£45–50
€/ **$70–80** ⊞ AEL

Edward, Prince of Wales, a signed photograph, 1915, 9 x 5in (23 x 12.5cm).
£850–950
€/ **$1,300–1,500** ⊞ AEL

▶ **Adriana Caselotti,** a signed composite image showing Caselotti as Snow White, with an image of Snow White and the Seven Dwarfs from Disney's animated cartoon, c1937, 8 x 10in (20.5 x 25.5cm).
£70–80
€/ **$110–130** ✗ VS

Yuri Gagarin, a signed photograph, wearing his Russian spacesuit, c1961, 4½ x 3½in (11.5 x 9cm).
£280–320
€/ **$440–510** ✗ VS

Robert E. Lee, signed *carte de visite*, signed on the front 'R. E. Lee' and inscribed on the back 'Miss Cummings from her friend Mary C. Lee, Lexington Jan'y 18th 1869'.
£1,300–1,500
€/ **$2,100–2,400** ✗ SK(B)

▶ **King George V,** a signed photograph, 1923, 8 x 6in (20.5 x 15cm).
£630–700
€/ **$1,000–1,100** ⊞ AEL

Theodore Rooseveldt, signed official White House card, with envelope, dated 1908.
£100–120
€/ **$160–190** ✗ DW

◀ **Walt Disney,** an autograph on an album page, 1935, 4 x 6in (10 x 15cm).
£1,500–1,800
€/ **$2,400–2,800** ✗ S(O)

Ingrid Bergman, a signed, hand-written letter of thanks, dated 15 March 1975, 11 x 16in (28 x 40.5cm).
£200–240
€/ **$315–380** ✗ CO

Cigarette Cards

Allen & Ginter, Celebrated American First Nation Chiefs, set of 50, 1888.
£1,300–1,500
€ / $2,000–2,400 ⊞ MUR

R. C. Brown & Co, one of a set of five Capadura cigar cartoon cards, issued 1876–79.
£170–200
€ / $270–315 ⚒ B

Cavanders, Cinema Stars, set of 30, 1934.
£30–35
€ / $50–55 ⊞ MUR

Hignett Bros, Greetings of the World, set of 25, 1907.
£55–63
€ / $85–100 ⊞ MUR

J. A. Pattreiouex, Builders of the British Empire, set of 50, c1929.
£60–70
€ / $95–110 ⚒ VS

◄ **John Player & Sons,** Regimental Uniforms, set of 50, 1914.
£80–90
€ / $125–145 ⊞ MUR

Godfrey Phillips, Indian Series, set of 25, c1908.
£170–200
€ / $270–315 ⚒ VS

W. D. & H. O. Wills, Beauties, set of 52, 1875–1925.
£70–80
€ / $110–130 ⚒ VS

Ogden's, Trainers, and Owners' Colours, set of 25, first series, 1925.
£45–50
€ / $70–80 ⊞ MUR

W. D. & H. O. Wills, Roses, set of 50, 1912.
£55–60
€ / $85–95 ⊞ MUR

EPHEMERA

Postcards

A souvenir postcard, of the visit of the Czar and Czarina to Paris, unused, French, 1896, 6 x 4in (15 x 10cm).
£22–25
€/ **$35–40** ⊞ S&D

Four postcards, 'Les Petites Ouvrières', by Théophile-Alexandre Steinlen, unused, c1900, 5½ x 3½in (14 x 9cm).
£140–170
€/ **$220–270** ⚲ VSP

A postcard, No. VIII, 'Enfants de la Mer', by Raphael Kirchner, c1902.
£34–38
€/ **$55–60** ⚲ VS

A pair of patriotic royalty postcards, depicting Kaiser Wilhelm II and his wife, postally used, German, c1903, 6 x 4in (15 x 10cm).
£18–20
€/ **$28–32** ⊞ S&D

Items in the Postcards section have been arranged in date order.

An L & NW Railways Co transportation photographic postcard, c1905, 6 x 4in (15 x 10cm).
£15–18
€/ **$25–28** ⊞ S&D

A postcard, depicting the flight of Paulhan in his Farman plane, from the 'Aviation' series for the *Daily Mail*, published by E. L. D., in French and English, early 20thC.
£70–85
€/ **$110–135** ⚲ VS

A Hamburg-America Line postcard, depicting the *Cleveland*, c1908, 6 x 4in (15 x 10cm).
£15–18
€/ **$25–28** ⊞ S&D

A Fry's Cocoa advertising postcard, with postal mark, c1908, 4 x 6in (10 x 15cm).
£12–14
€/ **$18–22** ⊞ S&D

A Royal Mail Steam Packet Co postcard, depicting the dining room of the *Aragon*, c1908, 4 x 6in (10 x 15cm).
£13–15
€/ **$20–23** ⊞ S&D

A postcard, depicting the launch of the *Shamrock IV*, 1914, 4 x 6in (10 x 15cm).
£20–25
€/ **$30–40** ⊞ S&D

A B & I Line postcard, depicting the SS *Lady Longford*, c1930, 4 x 6in (10 x 15cm).
£11–12
€/ **$16–19** ⊞ S&D

A postcard, depicting Wittersham Road Station, Kent, dated 1937.
£40–50
€/ **$65–80** ⚲ VS

Posters

A Napoleonic poster, printed by J. Biettell for J. Hatchard, calling for Englishmen to mobilize against the Corsican tyrant, c1800, 22 x 18in (56 x 45.5cm), framed and glazed.
£200–225
€ / **$315–360** ➚ HAM

A Red Star Line poster, 'Anvers New York', by Henri Cassiers, Belgian, 1898, 32¾ x 18½in (83 x 47cm).
£600–700
€ / **$950–1,100** ➚ VSP

A Chemins de Fer du Nord poster, by George Blott, French, Paris, 1899, 42½ x 29½in (108 x 75cm).
£430–500
€ / **$660–800** ➚ VSP

A Crawford American Cycles poster, printed by Hazell, Watson & Viney, on linen-backed paper support, damage and repairs, c1900, 58¾ x 40in (149 x 101.5cm).
£420–500
€ / **$660–790** ➚ BBA

A Teppichhaus poster, by Burkhard Mangold, printed by J. E. Wolfensberger, Zürich, 1911, 49¼ x 37½in (125 x 95.5cm).
£330–400
€ / **$540–630** ➚ VSP

▶ **A poster,** No. 132, 'Forward! Forward to Victory Enlist Now', by Lucy Kemp Welch, published by the PRC, printed by David Allen, mounted on linen, 1915, 59½ x 39in (151 x 99cm).
£850–1,000
€ / **$1,300–1,600** ➚ ONS

An LMS Railway lithographic poster, after R. T. Roussel, advertising Southend-On-Sea, printed by McCorquadale, early 20thC, 47¾ x 37¾in (121.5 x 96cm).
£500–600
€ / **$790–950** ➚ RTo

A Chemin de Fer du Nord poster, 'Nord Express', by A. M. Cassandre, printed by Hachard & Co, mounted on japanese paper, repaired tear, slight fading, 1927, 41¼ x 29¼in (105 x 74.5cm).
£4,200–5,000
€ / **$6,600–7,900** ➚ ONS

A poster, by J. Gabriel, advertising 'Cernay Cottage Hotel, Vallée de Chevreuse', on linen, French, c1930, 61¾ x 44¾in (157 x 113.5cm).
£230–280
€ / **$360–440** ➚ VSP

A Southern Electric poster, No. 4346, by Chas Pears, advertising 'Summer Services for Winter Visitors to Portsmouth, Southsea & Isle of Wight', printed by Waterlow, 1937, 50 x 40¼in (127 x 102cm).
£1,300–1,500
€ / **$2,100–2,400** ➚ ONS

▶ **A Wood-Milne Adjustable Soles advertising poster,** creases, 1930s, 19½ x 14¼in (49.5 x 36cm).
£75–90
€ / **$120–140** ➚ BBR

A foyer poster, advertising *Tondelaya* (White Cargo), with Hedy Lamarr and Walter Pidgeon, 1942, 23 x 15in (58.5 x 38cm).
£115–125
€/ **$180–200** ⊞ MARK

An Aga Radio lithographic poster, by Gunnar Brandt, printed by J. Olsen, Stockholm, creases, Swedish, 1947, 39½ x 27¼in (100.5 x 69cm).
£125–150
€/ **$200–240** ⚹ BUK

A poster, advertising Dartmouth Winter Carnival, 1947, 34 x 22in (86.5 x 56cm).
£180–220
€/ **$280–350** ⚹ SK(B)

A poster, by Cornelius van Velsen, 'See Holland', on linen, Dutch, 1948, 38 x 24½in (96.5 x 62cm).
£150–175
€/ **$240–280** ⚹ VSP

A poster, by Pablo Picasso, advertising an exhibition at the Maison De La Pensée Française, French, 1949, 28¾ x 20½in (73 x 52cm).
£165–185
€/ **$260–290** ⚹ VSP

▶ **An MGM lithographic poster,** depicting Greta Garbo, printed by J. Olsen, Stockholm, creases and tears, 1953, 39½ x 27¼in (100.5 x 69cm).
£250–300
€/ **$400–475** ⚹ BUK

An American President Lines lithographic poster, by J. Clift, advertising Bangkok, American, 1958, 34 x 23¾in (86.5 x 60.5cm).
£80–95
€/ **$130–150** ⚹ VSP

Further reading
Miller's Movie Collectibles, Miller's Publications, 2002

A United Artists film poster, advertising *The Magnificent Seven* with Yul Brynner, Eli Wallach and Steve McQueen, American, 1960, 16 x 11½in (40.5 x 29cm).
£220–250
€/ **$350–400** ⚹ CO

A Samuel Goldwyn film poster, advertising *Stronger Than Fear*, with Dana Andrews and Farley Granger, on linen-backed paper support, minor damage, 1950s, 30 x 39¾in (76 x 101cm).
£50–60
€/ **$80–95** ⚹ BBA

A foyer poster, advertising *Vénus Imperiale*, with Gina Lollobrigida, French, 1963, 15 x 23in (38 x 58.5cm).
£115–125
€/ **$180–200** ⊞ MARK

◀ **A poster,** by John Burningham, advertising coach travel, 1961, 29¾ x 20in (75.5 x 51cm).
£100–120
€/ **$160–190** ⚹ VSP

A UFA film poster, advertising *Voulez Vous Danser avec Moi?*, with Brigitte Bardot, 1965, 31½ x 23in (80 x 58.5cm).
£210–250
€/ **$330–390** ⚹ VSP

Rock & Pop

Over the last 25 years there has been a streamlining of rock and pop artists whose memorabilia people wish to acquire. The field of collecting at the high end has largely narrowed down to The Beatles, The Rolling Stones, Elvis Presley, The Who, Led Zeppelin, Pink Floyd, Buddy Holly and Bob Dylan. The gulf between these artists and others further down the scale is considerable and seemingly ever widening – although to an extent this disparity does not seem to have any basis in reason. For example, why should a good set of Beatles' signatures sell for thousands, yet a set of the Beach Boys' autographs – a band that created music of equal, or arguably superior, quality – might only realize £100 (€/ $160)? Similarly, the memorabilia of many other extremely influential artists such as Chuck Berry and Gene Vincent continues to be of low value.

The Beatles have been at the top of the league since the market in memorabilia was established c1980 and have continued to dramatically increase their points lead over their nearest rivals. This is mainly due to their immense popularity in the 1960s which is reflected today by the number of people collecting ephemera associated with them. There is a wide range to collect, as they produced more merchandise than other artists,

and putting money into Beatles collectables is seen as a sound investment. However, a significant, ever-widening gap is opening up between the price of rare, unique and personal items such as concert posters, good autographed items and clothing and that of more common pieces such as tour programmes or mass-produced novelty items.

In second place in the league table are The Rolling Stones. In the last couple of years prices of concert posters, handbills and novelty items in particular, have gained great momentum, perhaps a side effect of the rise in value of Beatles memorabilia. Interest in The Who and Pink Floyd has been very strong recently, and Led Zeppelin has also started to accelerate, having largely been overlooked for the past several years. Interestingly, collecting Elvis Presley continues to be mainly an American phenomenon.

The other striking and important trend in collecting has been that of an increasing concern among collectors over condition. It is items in excellent to mint condition that now command a price well in excess of book value while items in less than perfect condition tend to sell below estimate. This is no doubt due to the investment factor associated with Rock and Pop and this trend has also been reflected in the market for vinyl records. **Paul Wane**

John Lennon, a photograph, the reverse inscribed 'Me at Fleetwood the year I lost my trunks. In Mr Shipway's garden', late 1940s, 2¼ x 3¼in (5.5 x 8.5cm).
£2,500–3,000
€/ $4,000–4,700 ⬈ S(O)

A Fender Telecaster electric guitar, butterscotch blonde single cutaway ash body and maple neck, serial number 28637, owned by Tim Rose on which he devised the arrangement of 'Hey Joe', 1958.
£5,500–6,300
€/ $8,700–10,000 ⬈ CO
Also included is a letter from Tim Rose which reads 'I entered a bluegrass music contest in Warrenton, Virginia... I heard a song about a guy shooting his girlfriend and taking off for Mexico... I started a group with a few friends when I began doing an arrangement of that song. By now I called it 'Hey Joe'... I finally recorded it in 1966 for CBS Records. Chas Chandler heard my record at Harlow's Discotheque in New York City and took it back to London for Jimi'.

◄ **A Beatles demonstration single record,** 'Love Me Do' and 'P.S. I Love You', by Parlophone, with misspelled credit 'Lennon – McArtney', 1962, with paper sleeve.
£1,700–2,000
€/ $2,700–3,200 ⬈ B(Ch)
Only 250 demonstration singles were produced with the misspelling of 'McArtney' and distributed to the band, their management, the press and radio disc jockeys. This unique demo was the first official pressing featuring John, Paul, George and Ringo on the same single.

A Buddy Holly & The Crickets UK Tour autographed programme, signed on the back cover, 1958.
£650–750
€/ $1,000–1,200 ⬈ S(O)

A red label Beatles single record, 'Please Please Me' and 'Ask Me Why' by Parlophone, 1963, signed on the A side by the Beatles.
£2,200–2,500
€/ $3,500–4,000 ⬈ S(O)

A knitted silk tie, owned by Ringo Starr, the prize in a competition run by *The Viewer,* with a letter from the magazine and a print of the Beatles wearing similar ties, dated 15 January 1964, 24 x 32½in (61 x 82.5cm).
£700–800
€/ **$1,100–1,300** ✗ S(O)

A letter from the Border Press Agency, signed on the reverse by all four members of the Beatles in blue ballpoint, giving press authority to the manager of the ABC cinema for the Beatles' visit to Carlisle on 21 November 1963.
£3,800–4,500
€/ **$6,000–7,200** ✗ TRM

A Beatles one-sided 7in demo record, 'Wait', by Emidisc, with hand-written label, 1965.
£420–500
€/ **$660–800** ✗ CO

◀ **A silkscreen print,** 'The Rolling Stones, Red Cage', signed by the photographer Gered Mankowitz, c1966, 16 x 20in (40.5 x 51cm).
£300–350
€/ **$480–550** ✗ CO

A Nashville Teens and The Truth concert poster, the Town Hall, Liskeard, c1966, 30 x 20in (76 x 21cm).
£90–100
€/ **$140–160** ⊞ CTO

Elvis Presley, a signed Christmas card, dedicated 'To Mary from Elvis Presley' dated 1966, 8½ x 5½in (16 x 14cm).
£400–475
€/ **$640–750** ✗ CO

▶ **A Radio England souvenir programme,** for a concert featuring the Small Faces, Koobas and Dave Berry, 1966, 12 x 9in (30.5 x 23cm) with a ticket to the concert.
£45–50
€/ **$70–80** ⊞ CTO

◀ **A Martin Sharp silk-screen poster of Donovan,** 'Sunshine Superman', 1967, 30 x 20in (76 x 51cm).
£135–150
€/ **$215–240** ⊞ ASC

A programme for The Beatles North American tour, sold at US tour venues, 1966.
£140–160
€/ **$220–250** ✗ CO

A Martin Sharp silkscreen poster of Bob Dylan, 'Blowing in the Mind', 1967, 30 x 20in (76 x 51cm).
£300–325
€/ **$475–515** ⊞ ASC

Paul McCartney, a signed album page, together with an Official Beatles Fan Club membership ticket, 1960s.
£160–200
€/ **$250–320** ✗ VS

◀ **A Big Brother & The Holding Company Jack the Ripper poster,** American, 1967, 22 x 16in (56 x 41.5cm).
£180–200
€/ **$280–320** ✗ VSP

The Beatles Book, complete set of the monthly magazines, comprising 77 issues, 1960s.
£420–500
€/ **$650–800** ✗ CO

Expert's choice

The sale of the manuscript lyrics to *A Day in the Life*, the final song on The Beatles' *Sgt. Pepper's Lonely Hearts Club Band* LP, at Sotheby's, London, on 27 August 1992 was important in several respects. Firstly, in achieving a hammer price of £40,000 (€/ $63,000) plus commission, it put the hand-written lyrics of Lennon and McCartney in the same price bracket as some of the other eminent composers of the last three centuries and at the same time affirmed the importance, in relation to other composers, of the famous song-writing team from Liverpool. Secondly, in respect of the market for Beatles and pop memorabilia in general, it established manuscript lyrics of Beatles songs as the holy grail of rock 'n' roll collectables. Thirdly, the sale was significant in that it helped to establish Beatles lyrics as an important medium for investors. Fans could invest in their lyrics, enjoy owning them and at the same time watch their money grow!

Paul Wane

Jimi Hendrix, a photograph by Bruce Fleming, taken at Monterey Rock Festival, signed on the reverse by the photographer, No. 3 of an edition of 50, June 1967, 19¾ x 23¾in (50 x 60.5cm).
£280–320
€/ **$440–500** B(Ch)

A Beatles Magical Mystery Tour paper sign, September 1967, 59 x 19in (150 x 48.5cm).
£4,500–5,200
€/ **$7,000–8,200** CO
The vendor and her family were holidaying in Devon and Cornwall. Driving along a cliff top road en route for the beach, they came upon some filming and stopped to watch the proceedings. The vendor and her sister were very excited to find the Beatles there and took some photographs of them and also obtained their autographs. Their father however, sought a greater souvenir for his daughters and carefully peeled the Magical sign from the side of the bus!

A Sgt Pepper cloth badge, made to John Lennon's specifications, c1967, 3in (7.5cm) diam.
£170–200
€/ **$270–315** CO

Brian Jones, a photograph, c1967, 24 x 16in (61 x 40.5cm).
£500–600
€/ **$800–950** S(O)

A Jimi Hendrix Experience LP record, 'Are You Experienced', by Reprise, signed on the front 'Douglas – Stay Groovy Jimi Hendrix x, Love! Mitch Mitchell and Noel', 1968.
£1,400–1,600
€/ **$2,200–2,500** CO

A Great Society with Grace Slick LP record, 'Conspicuous only in its Absence', by CBS, 1968.
£45–50
€/ **$70–80** BNO

▶ **A Bill Graham poster,** advertising Eric and The Animals in concert, designed by Lee Conklin, signed by Eric Burdon, American, c1968, 20 x 14in (51 x 35.5cm).
£80–100
€/ **$130–160** CO

A Family Dog poster, advertising The Velvet Underground, Iron Butterfly and Chrome Cyrcus at the Avalon Ballroom, San Francisco, designed by Schnepf, American, June 1968, 20 x 13in (51 x 33cm).
£100–120
€/ **$160–190** ⚒ CO

A Jimi Hendrix Experience concert poster, Hallendstadion, Zurich, 30–31 May 1968, 28¼ x 19¼in (72 x 49cm).
£3,800–4,500
€/ **$6,000–7,200** ⚒ B(Ch)

An Island Artists promotional poster, for Spooky Tooth, late 1960s, 30 x 20in (76 x 51cm).
£320–375
€/ **$500–600** ⚒ CO

A Yellow Submarine film poster, by King Features, Polish, 1968, 23 x 15in (58.5 x 38cm).
£130–150
€/ **$200–240** ⚒ B(Ch)

A City Student Lyceum All Nighter promotional poster, 2–3 May 1969, 30 x 20in (76 x 51cm).
£320–375
€/ **$500–600** ⚒ CO

A Bill Graham Fillmore West concert poster, advertising Chuck Berry and Jethro Tull, designed by David Singer, signed by Ian Anderson of Jethro Tull, c1969, 14 x 20in (35.5 x 51cm).
£65–75
€/ **$100–120** ⚒ CO

◄ **A Blind Faith LP record cover,** 'Faith', by Polydor Records, an alternative UK issue for the American market, 1969.
£180–200
€/ **$280–320**
⊞ BNO

A wooden hookah pipe, owned by John Lennon, hand painted, late 1960s, 10in (25.5cm) long.
£1,700–2,000
€/ **$2,700–3,200** ⚒ CO

◄ **A fringed suede waistcoat,** owned by Elvis Presley, c1971.
£600–700
€/ **$950–1,100** ⚒ S(O)

An Isle of Wight festival programme, featuring Jimi Hendrix, The Doors, The Who and Free, 1970, 11½ x 8in (29 x 20.5cm).
£170–200
€/ **$270–315** ⚒ CO

► **A David Bowie and The Spiders from Mars single record,** 'John, I'm Only Dancing', by RCA, signed 'Love David Bowie, Mick Ronson, Trevor Boulder and Woody', 1972, 11½in (29cm) square, framed.
£400–475
€/ **$630–750** ⚒ CO

Bob Marley, photographed by Dennis Morris, a matt fibre print, 1973, 20 x 15in (51 x 38cm).
£320–375
€/ **$500–600** ⚒ CO

A reproduction Rolling Stones concert poster, for the cancelled concert at Cardiff and Pembroke castles 1973, No. 4500 of an edition of 5000, with facsimile autographs of Mick Jagger, Charlie Watts and Keith Richards, 17 x 23in (43 x 58.5cm).
£80–100
€/ **$130–160** ⚒ CO

Freddie Mercury, a photograph by Mick Rock, signed by the photographer, 1974, 48in (122cm) square.
£330–400
€/ $520–640 🏹 CO

A pair of platform boots, owned by Elton John, late 1970s.
£530–630
€/ $840–1,000 🏹 S(O)

▶ **A Sex Pistols single record,** 'God Save The Queen' and 'Did You No Wrong', signed, 1977.
£1,100–1,200
€/ $1,700–1,900 🏹 S(O)

A pistol pin charm, removed from a leather jacket owned by Sid Vicious, with original safety pin attached to a piece of paper signed and dedicated 'CBGB for Helen SID', with a bloody finger print, c1978, with a Helen Wheels and the Skeleton Crew concert flyer and a Helen Wheels business card.
£800–950
€/ $1,300–1,500 🏹 CO
Sid Vicious and Helen Wheels were friends and became 'blood brother and sister', hence the print on the paper.

A sales award for the Abba album 'Arrival', named to Anna Frid Lyngstad, 1980, 15¼ x 17in (39 x 43cm).
£1,100–1,200
€/ $1,700–1,900 🏹 S(O)
This was awarded for sales of over 100,000 copies in the Netherlands.

◀ **The Clash,** a photograph by Bob Gruen of the US Tour, signed by the photographer, 1979, 16 x 20in (40.5 x 51cm).
£330–400
€/ $520–640 🏹 CO

Scientific Instruments
Calculating Instruments

A boxwood slide rule, early 18thC, 12in (30.5cm) long.
£250–300
€/ $400–475 ⊞ TOM

A set of ivory Napiers bones, with a fixed rod, ten individual ivory rods and a three-section tablet, each punched with numerals, in an ivory case with slide cover, case damaged, late 17thC, 2in (5cm) wide.
£5,000–5,500
€/ $7,900–8,700 ➤ S(O)
Napiers bones are used to make calculations based on the logarithm system.

An ivory four-fold rule, with ironmonger's scales and presentation inscription, dated 1848, 24in (61cm) long.
£250–300
€/ $400–475 ⊞ TOM

Miller's Compares

I. A brass arithmometer, by Thomas de Colmar, with 12 digit display windows, seven smaller digit displays and six sliding indices, French, late 19thC, 18¼in (46.5cm) wide, in an oak case with engraved silvered plaque to lid.
£2,000–2,200
€/ $3,200–3,500 ➤ S(O)

II. A brass arithmometer, by C. & E. Layton, with 16 digit display windows, nine smaller windows, c1900, 23¾in (60.5cm) wide, in a mahogany case with brass carrying handles.
£1,300–1,500
€/ $2,000–2,400 ➤ S(O)

Thomas de Colmar was the inventor of this type of calculator, and therefore one made by him is more sought after. The turned ivory operating handles and original lacquer of Item I are also desirable features. Item II has ebony operating handles rather than ivory, and it is missing an opaque glass panel on the left-hand side, both factors which contribute to its lower price.

Compasses & Dials

▶ **An ivory diptych dial,** attributed to the Ducher family workshop, Nuremberg, with pin gnomon dials for Italian hours, string horizontal dial, the compass bowl decorated with four wind motifs, the scaphe dial with zodiacal symbols, two crowned snake punch marks attributed to Hans II, Hans III or Thomas Ducher, German, 1595–1645, 3in (7.5cm) wide.
£6,500–7,200
€/ $10,200–11,400 ➤ S(O)

◀ **An ivory diptych dial,** by Lienhart Miller, German, c1680, 2½in (6.5cm) wide.
£2,000–2,400
€/ $3,200–3,800 ⊞ DJH

▶ **An ivory diptych dial,** French, Dieppe, late 17thC, 2½in (6.5cm) square.
£1,600–1,800
€/ $2,500–2,800 ⊞ DJH

A bronze horizontal plate sundial, by John Troughton, the hour scale divided IIII=XII=VIII and reading to two minutes, with a projecting gnomon, signed, dated 1755, 6in (15cm) diam.
£570–675
€/ $900–1,000 ➤ S(O)

A brass astrolabe, with five plates, one drawn for the southern latitudes, Indo-Persian, mid/late 17thC, 3½in (9cm) diam.
£10,000–11,000
€/ $15,800–17,400 ➤ S(O)
Plates for southern latitudes are unusual in astrolabes otherwise designed for northern use, but are not without utility in low latitudes of the northern hemisphere. They are therefore sometimes found in instruments produced in Lahore with which school of astrolabe-making the present instrument may be linked by its style and arrangement.

A universal equinoctial dial, with later brass sight, glass broken, probably Augsburg, late 18thC, 2¼in (5.5cm) diam, with original leather-covered card case.
£600–700
€ / $950–1,100 ➶ S(O)

A magnetic sundial, by S. Porter, c1824, 2in (5cm) diam, in an ivory case with paper label to lid.
£360–425
€ / $575–675 ➶ SWO

Expert's choice

A silvered-brass mechanical equinoctial standing ring-dial, c1720, sold as part of the Time Museum Collection, New York, in December 1999.

The mechanical ring-dial by Richard Glynne, c1720, included as part of the Time Museum auction in New York in December 1999, broke barriers in two respects. Scientific instruments have had a very specialist and small following throughout the 20th century, and it took the Time Museum Collection auction to promote the esoteric field of instruments to a far wider public.

Measuring almost 24in (61cm) in height, the instrument, which tells the time accurately using sunlight and precision mechanical adjustment, has great sculptural quality combined with fine technical design and a high-quality finish. It appealed to collectors who had never bought a scientific instrument before; this stimulated the bidding to more than triple the low estimate, and achieved a hammer price of £600,000 (€ / $950,000). Not only was this a world record price for an instrument of this type, but it took the whole field of scientific instruments to a new level of appreciation. **Jon Baddeley**

▶ **A surveying compass,** by James Gregory, Birmingham, with silver dial and folding sights, c1870, in a mahogany case, 5in (12.5cm) wide.
£500–550
€ / $790–870 ⊞ WAC

Globes & Armillary Spheres

A 12in terrestrial globe, by N. Hill, 'New Globe of the Earth', on a mahogany stand with three cabriole legs, labelled 'Sold by Bennett Instrument Maker to Ye Duke of Gloucester... Henry Prince Frederick in Crown Court, St Ann's, Soho', dated 1759, 24in (61cm) high.
£4,500–5,200
€/ **$7,000–8,200** ⚒ Gam

A 16in terrestrial globe, by Smith's, with hand-coloured gores, engraved brass meridian ring, on a printed and coloured zodiac horizon, on three reeded legs joined by a signed compass, needle and glass missing, 19thC, 45in (114.5cm) high.
£3,800–4,500
€/ **$6,000–7,000** ⚒ B

A pocket terrestrial globe, by George Adams, London, in a sharkskin case, c1760, 3in (7.5cm) diam.
£6,000–6,500
€/ **$9,500–10,200** ⊞ HUM

◄ **A 1½in miniature globe,** by Johann Georg Klinger, lithographed by C. Danzinger, with original outline hand-colouring, slight surface wear and scratches, on a modern Perspex stand, German, Nuremberg, mid-19thC.
£225–275
€/ **$350–430** ⚒ BBA

Two globes, by C. Adams, Berlin, with compass, on ebonized stands, German, the terrestrial dated 1865, the celestial dated 1867, 27in (68.5cm) high.
£9,000–10,000
€/ **$14,200–15,800** ⊞ DJH

A 1½in terrestrial globe, with coloured prints of inhabitants, the hand-coloured paper gores laid onto the wooden sphere, German, 1800–25, in original card box inscribed 'The Earth and its Inhabitants', 2¼in (5.5cm) wide.
£1,300–1,500
€/ **$2,000–2,400** ⚒ S(O)

◄ **A 3in pocket terrestrial globe,** by Holbrook & Co, the hand-coloured paper gores applied to a hinged wooden sphere opening to reveal a world map with cartouche, American, c1840.
£1,300–1,500
€/ **$2,000–2,400** ⚒ S(O)

A 4in table terrestrial globe, by Lebègue, Brussels, the paper gores on a papier mâché sphere, on a gilt-brass stand with tripod base, Belgian, c1850, in original wooden case 8in (20.5cm) high.
£1,100–1,200
€/ **$1,700–1,900** ⚒ S(O)

A collapsible New Portable silk terrestrial globe, by George Philip & Son, after the original Betts patents, c1880, 15in (38cm) diam.
£340–375
€/ **$550–600** ⊞ ChC
This globe is opened and closed by an umbrella mechanism to allow for ease of transport and originally would have had a box. Although sturdy when opened, the nature of its operation no doubt led to the silk often becoming damaged, thus rendering them relatively rare.

◄ **A 3in pocket terrestrial globe,** the paper segments showing voyages by Columbus, Cook and Vancouver, with a steel axis pin, damaged, label inscribed 'A new terrestrial globe from the best authorities by J. Smith and sold by C. Smith, 172 Strand', 19thC, in a fishskin-covered case, the interior with a celestial chart.
£2,000–2,200
€/ **$3,200–3,500** ⚒ SWO

Medical & Dental

A metal amputation saw, with a wooden handle, c1820, 18in (45.5cm) long.
£400–450
€ / **$630–700** ⊞ CuS

A metal anaesthetic inhaler, c1900, 8in (20.5cm) high.
£270–300
€ / **$425–475** ⊞ CuS

◄ **A silver-plated auroscope,** c1900, in a box 4in (10cm) square.
£150–165
€ / **$240–260** ⊞ CuS

A brass spring fleam, c1820, 2¾in (7cm) long, in original case.
£220–245
€ / **$350–380** ⊞ CuS
This instrument was used for blood letting.

A figured-walnut dentist's cabinet, with original brass fittings, c1880, 33in (84cm) wide.
£3,200–3,500
€ / **$5,000–5,500** ⊞ MTay

A dental tool sterilizer, in a panelled mahogany case with nickeled-brass fittings, with a compartment with alcohol burner and steam boiler fitted to a zinc-lined copper cavity with three removable wooden slat racks, 19thC, 11¾in (30cm) wide.
£450–500
€ / **$700–790** ⚒ JAA

A display case of wax teeth, c1900, 12 x 10½in (30.5 x 26.5cm).
£250–275
€ / **$400–430** ⊞ CuS

► **A japanned metal enema pump,** French, c1850, 10in (25.5cm) high.
£265–300
€ / **$420–470** ⊞ CuS

A pair of metal forceps, c1880, 14½in (37cm) long.
£165–185
€ / **$260–300** ⊞ CuS

A mahogany medicine chest, the hinged lid with a marquetry conch shell, opening to reveal six glass bottles with stoppers, above a base drawer, early 19thC, 6½in (16.5cm) wide.
£380–450
€ / **$600–700** ⚒ WW

A magneto-electric machine, by S. Maw, Son & Thompson, c1900, 10in (25.5cm) wide.
£160–175
€ / **$250–275** ⊞ SPA

◄ **A Victorian homeopathic sample case,** comprising 60 named glass phials in an embossed leather hinged case, within a slip case, 6¼in (16cm) high.
£320–375
€ / **$500–600** ⚒ WW

A mahogany and brass-mounted medicine chest, the hinged top enclosing a fitted interior, above two drawers, early 19thC, 10in (25.5cm) wide.
£220–250
€/ $350–400 ⚒ G(L)

Medicine chests

Medicine chests were popular with the upper classes throughout the 19th century as a means to treat everyday ailments rather than having to resort to the expense of calling in the local doctor. They always accompanied the family and were therefore designed for travel. Often in brass-bound mahogany cases, the glass bottles and accessories were securely contained in fitted drawers. It is important to ensure that all the bottles fit snugly and are therefore original to the case. In the back of the case there is often a secret sliding panel that originally held poison bottles, and a drawer in the base for a pestle and mortar and a set of scales.

A mahogany medicine chest, c1860, 8½in (21.5cm) wide.
£600–675
€/ $950–1,000 ⊞ CuS

A mahogany medicine chest, with accessories including bottles and scales, late 19thC, 9½in (24cm) wide.
£400–475
€/ $630–750 ⚒ SWO

A mahogany medicine chest, with sunken brass handles, the hinged front enclosing bottle compartment and drawers, the back with a slide, 19thC, 12in (30.5cm) wide.
£750–900
€/ $1,200–1,400 ⚒ WW

A walnut-veneered homeopathic medicine chest, c1880, 8½in (21.5cm) wide.
£240–265
€/ $380–420 ⊞ CuS

◀ **A demonstration eye,** c1890, in a box 7½in (19cm) wide.
£315–350
€/ $500–550 ⊞ CuS
This would be used by students to identify diseases in the eye.

A field operating kit, in a brass-bound mahogany box, c1890, 10in (25.5cm) wide.
£330–365
€/ $520–580 ⊞ CuS

An ophthalmoscope, c1880, in original fitted case, 4½in (11.5cm) wide.
£150–165
€/ $240–260 ⊞ CuS

▶ **A metal and ivory stethoscope,** c1890, 7in (18cm) long.
£240–265
€/ $380–420 ⊞ CuS

A tooth key, with ivory handle, c1850, 6in (15cm) long.
£200–225
€/ $320–350 ⊞ CuS

A metal trepanning brace, c1860, 12in (30.5cm) long.
£450–500
€/ $700–790 ⊞ CuS

Microscopes

A brass Withering-style botanical microscope, the lens mounted with ivory and a blackened ivory stage, with tweezers and a spike, in a wooden case with instruction label to interior of lid, c1795, case 4¾in (12cm) wide.
£500–600
€/ **$800–950** ➤ S(O)

A compound Nuremberg microscope, the box-form base with an adjustable mirror, surmounted by a compound optical tube covered with paper, on a wooden base beneath a glass dome, German, 1800–25, 15in (38cm) high.
£600–700
€/ **$950–1,100** ➤ S(O)

A binocular microscope, No. 1, by Ross, in a mahogany case, with accessories, c1860, 20in (51cm) high.
£5,500–6,000
€/ **$8,700–9,500** ⊞ ETO

A Victorian brass monocular compound microscope, by R. & J. Beck, London, with rack-and-pinion focusing, a polarizing lens on a brass stand, and two brass objectives, maker's stamp, 10in (25.5cm) high, in a mahogany case with brass carrying handle.
£170–200
€/ **$270–320** ➤ PFK

A mid-Victorian brass binocular compound microscope, by Negretti & Zambra, the lacquered and gilded-brass frame with knurled adjusters, in original box with an assortment of sleeved and named objectives, case 16½in (42cm) high.
£950–1,100
€/ **$1,500–1,700** ➤ BIG

▶ **A brass compound binocular microscope,** with rack-and-pinion focusing and double nosepiece, over a fixed stage with substage condenser and plano concave mirror on a Y-shaped base, in a case with a single drawer containing accessories including a bull's-eye condenser, five eye-pieces and two objectives, late 19thC, box 16¼in (41.5cm) high.
£320–375
€/ **$500–600** ➤ B(Kn)

SCIENTIFIC INSTRUMENTS

Surveying & Drawing Instruments

▶ **A drawing instrument set,** c1740, with a silver-mounted fishskin pocket case, signed 'S. Saunders', 6½in (16.5cm) high.
£3,500–4,200
€/ **$5,500–6,600** ➤ G(L)

A George III mahogany travelling draughtsman's box, with compartmented lateral drawer, the reverse with a folio stand, 27½in (70cm) wide.
£720–850
€/ **$1,100–1,300** ➤ S(O)

An ivory parallel rule, by Baker, Holborn, London, c1870, 7in (18cm) long.
£70–80
€/ **$110–125** ⊞ ETO

A pantograph, by Universal Drafting Machine Co, American, Cleveland, Ohio, early 20thC, 35½in (90cm) long, in a fitted mahogany box with accessories.
£130–150
€/ **$200–240** ➤ SWO

A brass theodolite, by Cary, London, c1820, 17½in (44.5cm) high.
£1,100–1,200
€/ **$1,700–1,900** ⊞ PHo

Telescopes

A 1¼in table refracting telescope, by Dollond, the signed brass tube with shagreen cover, on a tapering pillar and three scrolled folding legs, mid-18thC, 7½in (19cm) high.
£2,000–2,200
€ / $3,200–3,500 ➶ S(O)

A 3in reflecting telescope, the rayskin-covered brass body with screw adjustment, on a brass pillar with folding tripod feet, French, mid-18thC, 17in (43cm) long, in an associated wooden case with Passemant trade label to interior of lid.
£2,800–3,200
€ / $4,400–5,000 ➶ S(O)

An ivory and *lignum vitae* pocket refracting telescope, with card inner tubes, probably Continental, mid-18thC, 7¼in (18.5cm) long.
£570–675
€ / $900–1,000 ➶ S(O)

A brass refracting telescope, by Jessie Ramsden, London, c1780, barrel 31in (78.5cm) long, in original box.
£2,200–2,500
€ / $3,500–4,000 ⊞ HUM

A 1½in pocket refracting telescope, by Dollond, the body covered with shagreen, signed, early 19thC, 4¾in (12cm) long.
£330–400
€ / $520–630 ➶ S(O)

A brass eight-draw telescope, by V. Somalvico & Co, London, with leather-covered body and lens cap, 19thC, 28¼in (72cm) extended.
£130–150
€ / $200–240 ➶ DMC

A brass four-draw telescope, with mahogany hand grip, on a folding tripod stand, inscribed 'Cary, London', mid-19thC, 14in (35.5cm) high.
£280–320
€ / $440–500 ➶ WW

A Victorian telescope, by J. H. Steward, London, with leather-covered body, silvered applied maker's plaque and engraved pull-out drawer, on an associated mahogany and brass stand, 46½in (118cm) extended.
£700–800
€ / $1,100–1,300 ➶ S(O)

Weights & Measures

A wooden measuring stick, with silver band and inches marked, c1850, 54in (137cm) long.
£160–175
€ / $250–275 ⊞ GBr

▶ **A set of parcel scales,** with graduated brass weights, on a platform base, 19thC.
£200–240
€ / $320–380 ➶ BWL

A folding pocket guinea balance, made and retailed by H. Bell & Co, Prescot, Lancashire, with original paper labels, without weights, early 19thC, 6in (15cm) long.
£55–65
€ / $85–100 ➶ TMA

A set of brass scales, by Avery, Birmingham, with faceted baluster stem and four weights, late 19thC, 29in (73.5cm) high.
£425–500
€ / $670–800 ➶ S(O)

A set of brass Nuremberg cup weights, German, c1780, 2in (5cm) diam.
£430–475
€ / $680–750 ⊞ RGe

Marine
Barometers

A Regency mahogany marine barometer, with vernier and mercury thermometer, brass cistern cover, inscribed 'W. Atkin, Newcastle', 38in (96.5cm) high.
£1,800–2,200
€/ **$2,800–3,500** ➹ Mit

A mahogany marine barometer, inscribed 'Spencer Browning & Co', on contemporary gimbals, c1840, 36in (91.5cm) high.
£3,400–3,800
€/ **$5,400–6,000** ⊞ AW

An early Victorian rosewood marine barometer, by I. Mackrow, London, decorated with mother-of-pearl, brass cistern, 36in (91.5cm) high.
£1,400–1,600
€/ **$2,200–2,500** ➹ HYD

A rosewood marine barometer, signed 'J. Jeacock, London', with two-day ivory plates and verniers, thermometer and brass cistern, c1850, 37¾in (96cm) high.
£2,400–2,700
€/ **$3,800–4,300** ➹ S(O)

A brass and mother-of-pearl-inlaid rosewood marine barometer, by McGregor & Co, Glasgow & Greenock, brass cistern cover, Scottish, mid-19thC, 38½in (98cm) high.
£3,500–4,200
€/ **$5,500–6,600** ➹ B

A carved walnut marine barometer, by John Graham, Liverpool, with ivory plates, c1860, 38in (96.5cm) high.
£4,500–5,000
€/ **$7,000–8,000** ⊞ AW

A mahogany marine barometer, by B. Palasca, Liverpool, with ivory plates and single vernier, thermometer and brass cistern cover, with brass gimbal wall mount, c1860, 37in (94cm) high.
£5,000–5,500
€/ **$8,000–8,700** ➹ S(O)

A brass marine barometer, by Kelvin, White & Hutton, with thermometer, iron cistern cover and gimbal wall fitting, Scottish, c1910, 36¼in (92cm) high.
£1,100–1,200
€/ **$1,700–1,900** ➹ S(O)

Chronometers & Timekeepers

A two-day freesprung marine chronometer, by John Poole, London, helical hairspring and bimetallic balance with Poole's auxiliary compensation, Earnshaw-type detent escapement with maintaining power, in a brass-inlaid mahogany case, mid-19thC, 7in (18cm) wide.
£1,200–1,400
€/ **$1,900–2,200** ✒ B
John Poole was born in 1818. He worked from various London addresses, but 57 Fenchurch Street was used between 1858–85. He established himself as a chronometer maker in 1840 and became one of the great names. He invented his own compensation, which was first applied c1850, and his ideas and movements were used by many others. He committed suicide in 1867.

A two-day marine chronometer, by D. McGregor & Co, Glasgow & Greenock, in an ebony and brass-strung case, with outer deck box, Scottish, c1870, 7in (18cm) wide.
£5,000–5,500
€/ **$8,000–8,700** ⊞ JeF

A brass and mahogany nautical mantel timepiece, French, c1890, 14in (35.5cm) high.
£1,300–1,500
€/ **$2,100–2,400** ⊞ MSh

A two-day marine chronometer, the silvered dial with subsidiaries and signed 'J. P. Dupont & Zoon, Rotterdam', movement with spotted plates, detent escapement with compensation balance and helical spring, in a mahogany box, with possibly later travelling case, c1870, 6¾in (17cm) high.
£1,400–1,700
€/ **$2,200–2,700** ✒ S(Am)

▶ **A chromed-metal chronometer deck watch,** by Hamilton Watch Co for the US Navy, 21 jewels, compensation balance, adjusted to temperatures and six positions, in a mahogany box, 1941, 2⅜in (7cm) diam.
£900–1,100
€/ **$1,400–1,700** ✒ S(Am)

An officer's of the watch clock, by Seth Thomas, striking the hours on a saucer bell, American, 1880–90, 10in (25.5cm) high.
£340–380
€/ **$550–600** ⊞ OLD

Model Ships

A fruitwood half-block model of a yacht, c1920, 20in (51cm) long.
£135–150
€/ **$220–240** ⊞ BoC

◀ **An unrigged dockyard model of a two-deck 94-gun ship of the line,** with carved bust figurehead and catheads, on a mahogany stand, minor damage, mid-19thC, 16¼in (41.5cm) long.
£600–720
€/ **$950–1,100** ✒ DN

A Victorian carved wood model of a boat, in a mahogany case, the back painted with a Mediterranean coastal scene, 26in (66cm) wide.
£320–375
€/ **$500–600** ✒ WW

◀ **A pond yacht,** with full rigging and sails, painted wood hull and metal counterweight, later additions, c1910, 68in (172.5cm) long.
£220–250
€/ **$350–400** ✒ AH

Nautical Handicrafts

An ivory-inlaid wood love token box, made by the captain of the SS *Gloster*, American, 1871, 11in (28cm) wide.
£4,000–4,800
€/ **$6,300–7,600** ➹ S(NY)
American folk art is highly collectable. Had this piece been British the price would have been much less.

An alabaster-framed reverse painting on glass, depicting an East Indiaman in Bombay harbour, early 19thC, 5½in (14cm) diam.
£250–280
€/ **$400–440** ⊞ HUM

A miniature reverse painting on glass of a frigate, the reverse inscribed 'The frigate Arenensius(?) on her maiden voyage at Plymouth S**** 24 Oct 1854, 224 tonnes R. Westfall Skipper White Star Line', c1854, 4¼in (11cm) wide, framed.
£600–720
€/ **$950–1,100** ➹ S(O)
Captain Westfall was skipper on board the frigate on her maiden voyage from Plymouth to Darwin.

A sailor's woolwork picture of a three-masted man-o-war, a paddle steamer and other vessels, with a coal store, Royal Naval buildings and a hill, possibly of Chatham, Kent, 19thC, 20 x 24in (51 x 61cm).
£6,500–7,500
€/ **$10,300–12,000** ➹ CHTR
This sold for a high price because the dyes used in such pieces were not very fast and it is therefore very unusual to get such strong colours and a very complicated design.

▶ **A sailor's woolwork picture,** 'Leisure Hours in India', c1870, 23 x 29in (58.5 x 73.5cm), framed.
£1,600–1,800
€/ **$2,500–2,800** ⊞ SWN

Woolwork pictures

Little is known about the sailor's skills with a needle and thread beyond the practical purpose of mending sails and patching clothes. However, a number of pictures made of wool, known as 'woollies', are assumed to have been made by sailors while on board ship. Their design is often quite naïve and they therefore appeal to collectors of both samplers and folk art.

Prices have risen considerably over the past few years on the strength of the American market, with fine examples fetching up to £10,000 (€/ $16,000). Collectors are looking for well-designed images of marine interest in good condition. The dye used in the wool is not fast and the pictures are liable to both fading and moth damage. Original maple frames also add to the desirability of such woolwork pictures.

A coquilla nut snuff box, carved with maritime scenes, late 19thC, 4in (10cm) wide.
£250–300
€/ **$400–475** ➹ TMA

Navigational Instruments

◀ **A teak binnacle compass,** the brass cover housing the gimple-mounted floating compass card, flanked by two iron compensation spheres, with binnacle lamp, c1920, 56¾in (144cm) high.
£530–630
€/ **$840–1,000** ➹ S(O)

A Victorian brass navigational plotting protractor, by Blackburne, 13in (33cm) long.
£75–85
€/ **$120–135** ➹ WiB

An ebony octant, by Spencer, Browning & Co, with ivory name plaque, scale and vernier, brass index arm, one set of interchangeable filters, in a wooden case, early 19thC, 11¾in (30cm) radius.
£450–550
€/ **$700–870** ➹ S(O)

MARINE

Sea Chests

◀ **An iron-bound oak sea captain's chest,** fitted with decanters and glasses, on a later stand, 18thC, 15in (38cm) high.
£550–650
€ / **$870–1,000** ⚒ E

A ship's surgeon's oak chest, with brass plaque inscribed 'Elmina R.Y.S', on a later stand, 19thC, 21¼in (54cm) wide.
£170–200
€ / **$270–320** ⚒ WilP

◀ **An elm sea chest,** the top inscribed 'The Admiral', 19thC, 38¼in (97cm) wide.
£2,500–3,000
€ / **$4,000–4,700** ⚒ S(O)

Ship's Fittings

▶ **A ship's bell,** engraved 'SS *Commissioner,* 1905, Graton' and 'Hall, Russell & Co Ltd, Aberdeen, engineers and shipbuilders', c1905, 10¾in (27.5cm) diam.
£280–325
€ / **$440–500** ⚒ SWO

▶ **A brass-bound mahogany ship's wheel,** c1860, 60in (152.5cm) diam.
£850–950
€ / **$1,300–1,500**
⊞ HON

◀ **A carved wood and gesso figurehead,** 19thC, 30½in (77.5cm) high.
£10,000–11,000
€ / **$15,800–17,400** ⚒ S(O)
Figureheads endured the brunt of the sea being mounted at the prow of the ship. Examples in good condition such as this one are therefore very rare and this is reflected in its high price.

◀ **A brass-bound mahogany ship's wheel,** 19thC, 48½in (123cm) diam.
£650–750
€ / **$1,000–1,200**
⚒ SWO

Miscellaneous

A pair of brass binoculars, by Alexandre LaFleur, Paris, with leather grips, fitted with sliding shades to the objects lens, in a velvet-lined mahogany presentation case.
£550–625
€ / **$870–1,000** ⚒ B

A White Star Line brochure, 16 pages, c1911, 6 x 8in (15 x 20.5cm).
£1,300–1,500
€ / **$2,000–2,400** ⚒ HAld

▶ **A lacquered brass three-draw telescope,** by Gome, Paris, with morocco cover and extending shade, French, 19thC, 32in (81.5cm) extended.
£65–75
€ / **$100–120** ⚒ PFK

A Marconigram, sent from the *Titanic's* rescue ship *Carpathia,* by Madeline Astor, dated 15 April 1912, 7 x 8in (18 x 20.5cm).
£11,000–13,000
€ / **$17,000–20,000** ⚒ HAld

MARINE

Admiral Lord Nelson

A diamond anchor brooch, with scrolled initials 'H' and 'N' for Horatio Nelson, mounted in silver and gold, c1801, 2½in (6.5cm) long.
£150,000–180,000
€/ **$237,000–285,000** ♦ S
Ex-Alexander Davison Collection. This brooch is believed to have been a personal gift from Nelson to Emma, Lady Hamilton. It was placed in Alexander Davison's custody after Nelson's death.

A pictorial silk embroidery, depicting Admiral Lord Nelson and Lady Hamilton, with a verse below, early 19thC, 10¾ x 13¾in (27.5 x 35cm), framed.
£750–875
€/ **$1,200–1,400** ♦ AH

▶ **A Staffordshire Nelson jug,** modelled standing beside a canon, on a titled base, 1850–75, 11¾in (30cm) high.
£400–500
€/ **$630–800** ♦ S(O)

Horatio Nelson, single page letter with integral blank leaf, signed 'Nelson & Bronte' to Philip Longmead, Mayor of Plymouth, in his secretary's hand with Nelson's signature, discussing the honour which the 'corporation of Plymouth intend to confer upon me', 4°, with envelope bearing red seal, dated 22 January 1801, with George Tetley's *Old Times and New* (London, 1904).
£1,500–1,700
€/ **$2,500–2,700** ♦ DN

The Alexander Davison Collection

This collection of Nelson memorabilia sold by Sotheby's in 2002 was doubly exciting. Not only did it include letters, jewellery, ceramics, coinage and personal effects directly relating to Admiral Lord Nelson, but the collection was also initially unknown to historians and collectors alike.

The Sotheby's jewellery expert was called in by the direct descendants of Alexander Davison to advise them of the value of some jewellery. He subsequently discovered a hoard of material that had been owned by Davison, who was Nelson's intimate friend, treasurer, prize agent and closest advisor. The two men met in 1782 in Quebec when Nelson, at 23, was a rising post-captain. Davison was eight years older and had amassed a fortune as a ship owner and government contractor through the recent American war. He remained a constant figure in Nelson's life. At Nelsons's funeral 23 years later Davison, as one of the four principal members of his household, broke his white stave of office to be placed on the coffin as it was lowered into the vault of St Paul's Cathedral.

The fabulous prices achieved at auction for sometimes quite humble pieces reflect the immense importance paid by collectors for historic pieces with impeccable provenance, and in this case, belonging to someone who is still considered one of Britain's greatest heroes. **Jon Baddeley**

MARINE

◀ **Emma Hamilton,** a signed letter to the Duke of Queensbury begging him 'for my sake for Nelsons sake for the good I have done my country...Tis Nelson asks you' – to buy Merton '...that I may live free from fear that every debt may be paid I think & hope fifteen thousand pounds will do for every thing... purchase it take it only giving me the portraits of Sir William...I wish not for more than will pay my debts', four pages, 4°, with a transcript of a letter by Emma and copy of *Baily's Biography and Iconography*, 4 September 1808.
£2,000–2,400
€/ **$3,200–3,800** ♦ B
This letter, begging Queensbury to buy 'Paradise Merton' – the house which Emma and Nelson shared and from which Nelson departed for Trafalgar – can be seen as marking the end of a dream. The letter's recipient, the Duke of Queensbury, was an immensely rich and very ancient roué, familiarly known as 'Old Q'. He was possessed of such a wide circle of female acquaintance – all desperate to inherit his vast fortune – that he was likened to the Grand Turk with his seraglio. At the time of writing, Emma was living in one of the Duke's properties, Heron Court in Richmond. Unfortunately her plea was unsuccessful. The Duke declined to buy, Merton having been valued at £12,000 (€/ $19,000) rather than the £15,000 (€/ $24,000) asked for.

A copper medal, by T. Wyon Sr, commemorating the Battle of Trafalgar, minor damage, 1805, 1¾in (4.5cm) diam.
£220–250
€/ $350–400 ✗ DNW

A silver Alexander Davison medal for the Battle of the Nile, the obverse decorated with a figure of Peace standing with an anchor, holding an olive branch and a shield with a profile portrait of Nelson, with the legend 'Europe's Hope and Britain's Glory', the reverse with a view of the engagement in Aboukir Bay, signed 'C. H. Küchler' and 'Victory of the Nile August 1. 1798' in exergue, 1¾in (4.5cm) diam.
£600–700
€/ $950–1,100 ✗ S(O)
The practice of awarding official naval campaign medals began in 1794, when captains and flag officers present at the Battle of the Glorious First of June were awarded gold medals. They were highly prized by their recipients, but with these early medals no provision was made for junior officers or men. Therefore in 1798 Alexander Davison decided to issue a 'Tribute of Regard' to mark Nelson's victory at Aboukir Bay and to reward, for the first time, every participant in the Battle of the Nile. Gold medals were presented primarily to Nelson and to captains of his fleet, while silver examples were offered to officers, copper-gilt to petty officers and bronzed-copper to seamen, marines and others. Davison's motives were not entirely philanthropic, as he was hoping with this undertaking to consolidate his position as Nelson's prize agent and was thereby currying favour with the British fleet, Royalty and, to some extent, the public at large.

A gold-mounted pine snuff box, belonging to Alexander Davison, the cover set with a gold plaque engraved 'This is made from the *Victory* main mast close to which the Immortal Nelson fell on the 21st October 1805, Alexr, Davison', c1805, 2¾in (7cm) wide.
£50,000–60,000
€/ $79,000–95,000 ✗ S
Ex-Alexander Davison Collection. Davison may have commissioned a number of similar boxes as mementos for distribution. The masts on the *Victory* were largely shot away during the action at Trafalgar, and it was to the main mast, on the middle deck, that the barrel holding Nelson's body was secured for the long passage home. After her return to England bearing Nelson's body in a barrel of spirits, HMS *Victory* was paid off to be refitted at Chatham. She served in the Baltic until 1812 when she returned to Portsmouth for an extensive refit. She later acted as the Port Admiral's flagship and was twice visited by Queen Victoria. Although she was popular to sightseers while moored in Gosport, as the 19th century wore on and memories of Trafalgar faded, she fell into disrepair, often being stripped of materials, and suffering the final indignity of being rammed and badly damaged by HMS *Neptune* in 1903. In 1922 she was eventually moved to Portsmouth, where she remains today. In the early 20th century, a 'Save the *Victory*' campaign was launched funding the major restoration of 1922–27. In 1941 she was damaged by enemy action yet again. HMS *Victory* is still in commission.

A hand-painted silk panel, portraying two escutcheons bearing the impaled arms of Lord and Lady Nelson, one of six made for the velvet pall which covered Nelson's coffin during its journey up the River Thames, and from the Admiralty to St Paul's Cathedral, London, for burial on 9 January 1806, 17 x 23in (43 x 58.5cm), framed.
£35,000–40,000
€/ $55,000–63,000 ✗ DN
Formerly the property of the Rev Alexander John Scott (1768–1840), and thence by direct descent. Scott was Chaplain to HMS *Victory* and acted as the Admiral's interpreter, Nelson being – by his own admission – a 'poor linguist'. He was also the individual who held and supported Nelson as he lay dying in the *Victory*'s cockpit. He afterwards wrote to Emma Hamilton '...what an affectionate, fascinating little fellow he was... I become stupid with grief for what I have lost...'.

Lord Nelson's green silk purse, with 13½ guineas in gold and a manuscript *Money, Coins in Lord Nelson's Pocket, Purse &c when Killed*, 1805, 11¾in (30cm) long.
£250,000–300,000
€/ $400,000–475,000 ✗ S
Ex-Alexander Davison Collection. This purse was from the Admiral's personal effects carried aboard HMS *Victory* at the Battle of Trafalgar, and at the time of his death passed to Alexander Davison.

A souvenir of the Battle of the Nile, painted alabaster and reverse-painted convex glass, depicting the stern of HMS *Vanguard*, Nelson's flag and the fleets in action, inscribed 'Adml Nelson's Victory', 18thC, 6in (15cm) diam.
£550–625
€/ $870–1,000 ✗ LAY

A silver-gilt vinaigrette, engraved with a portrait of Nelson, Birmingham 1805, 1¾in (4.5cm) wide.
£1,300–1,500
€/ $2,000–2,500 ✗ G(L)

Cameras

A Butcher's Cameo folding plate camera, c1920.
£25–30
€ / $40–48 ⊞ VCL

A Canon F-1 camera, c1970.
£180–200
€ / $285–320 ⊞ VCL

A Coronet Midget black Bakelite camera, c1935.
£70–80
€ / $110–125 ⊞ APC

A FED Type 2 camera, early Leica copy, Russian, 1935–39.
£135–150
€ / $215–240 ⊞ HEG

A Dallmeyer mahogany and brass-plate studio camera, on an adjustable stand, 1875–80.
£1,000–1,200
€ / $1,600–1,900 ⚒ B(WM)

◄ A FED camera, early Leica copy, Russian, 1930s–40s.
£90–100
€ / $140–190 ⊞ HEG

A Houghton Butcher oxidized brass Butcher's No. 6 tropical watch pocket carbide camera, with 4in anastigmatic f4.5 lens, c1920.
£130–145
€ / $210–230 ⊞ WAC

A Houghton Butcher Ensignette miniature camera, c1930.
£35–40
€ / $55–63 ⊞ VCL

A Kiev 3A Contax copy 35mm film camera, with Rangefinder and light meter, c1950.
£70–80
€ / $110–125 ⊞ HEG

A Kodak 1st Model No. 4 cartridge camera, c1900.
£90–100
€ / $140–160 ⊞ VCL

◄ A Kodak Panoramic Model A camera, c1900.
£200–220
€ / $320–350 ⊞ VCL

► A Kodak No. 2 Stereo Brownie camera, c1910.
£320–350
€ / $510–550 ⊞ APC

A Kodak Vanity Series 111 VPK camera, c1930.
£270–300
€ / $430–480 ⊞ APC

A Kodak Vanity Ensemble camera, c1930, with box.
£1,300–1,500
€ / $2,100–2,400 ⊞ APC

A Kodak Beau Brownie box camera, c1930.
£70–80
€ / $110–125 ⊞ APC

A Lumière & Cie subminiature roll-film camera, French, 1936–46.
£50–60
€ / $80–95 ⊞ HEG

A Leica II Hektor nickel camera, c1935.
£500–600
€ / $790–950 ⊞ VCL

A Nikon S camera, with a Nikkor-S f1.4/5cm lens and instructions, 1952, with original inner and outer boxes.
£550–650
€ / $870–1,000 ⚹ B(Kn)

A Steky 16mm subminiature cassette camera, minor variations, 1950–55.
£70–80
€ / $110–125 ⊞ HEG

A Thornton Pickard Triple Imperial half-plate camera, c1910.
£270–300
€ / $430–480 ⊞ APC

A Voigtlander Bessamatic 35mm SLR camera, with light meter, c1963.
£90–100
€ / $40–160 ⊞ VCL

A Vollenda horizontal folding roll-film camera, with various lenses, 1931–32.
£70–80
€ / $110–125 ⊞ HEG

◀ **A Zeiss Ikon camera,** c1940.
£50–55
€ / $80–88 ⊞ JOA

A United Optical Co Merlin camera, with black crackle finish, 1936.
£60–70
€ / $95–110 ⊞ APC

Further reading

Miller's Collecting Science & Technology, Miller's Publications, 2001

CAMERAS

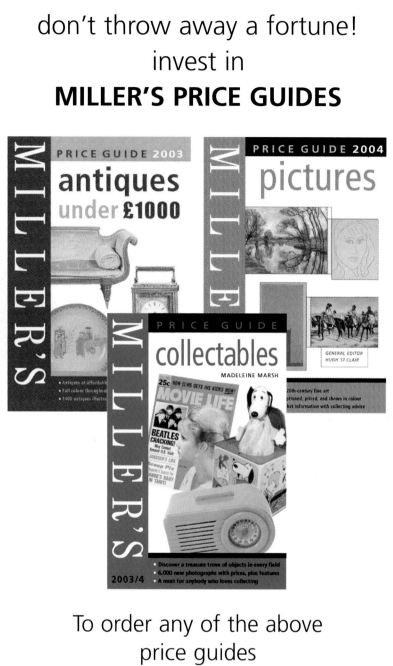

Optical Devices & Viewers

A steel and brass magic lantern and slides, with 3¼in (8.5cm) slides, oil illuminant, condenser, lens, chimney, slide carrier and carrying box with five wood-mounted circular slides, and other boxes of slides and sundries, c1880.
£200–220
€ / **$320–350** ⚲ B(WM)

A walnut-veneered stereo graphoscope, with brass and glass fittings, the single lens on brass slides and hinged double stereo lenses, fretwork card stand and adjustable support, c1875, 16in (41cm) long.
£250–300
€ / **$400–475** ⚲ BBA

A Rowsell's Patent walnut-veneered stereo graphoscope, with brass and bone fitments, filigree rest and manufacturer's name disc, with some stereocards, late 19thC, 23in (58.5cm) wide.
£280–325
€ / **$440–515** ⚲ DW

A walnut stereo grapho-scope, with decorative stringing, 5½in (14cm) lens and binocular focusing stereo lenses, built-in ebonized folding shade and mirror for glass or daguerrean views, string and pulley focusing for the easel with control knobs on each side, stamped 'Brevette SGBG', French, late 19thC, base 18½in (47cm) long.
£380–450
€ / **$600–710** ⚲ B(WM)

A burr-walnut stereoscopic viewer and cards, 19thC, 21¼in (54cm) high.
£350–420
€ / **$550–660** ⚲ SWO

A mahogany Stereo Classeur stereoscope, Le Taxiphote, the case with a moulded-edge top, fitted with two sliding drawers containing slides, late 19thC, slides 2¼ x 5¼in (5.5 x 13cm).
£480–570
€ / **$760–900** ⚲ TRM

A Richard Verascope stereo viewer, with glass slides, c1910, 4¾in (12cm) wide.
£90–100
€ / **$140–160** ⊞ APC

A rosewood Zograscope, the turned and inlaid stand flanked by brass candle sconces, 19thC, 25¼in (64cm) high.
£300–350
€ / **$475–550** ⚲ SWO

▶ **A George III mahogany Zograscope,** the mirror inlaid with diced stringing to the border and fold-over viewing glass, on an adjustable column and circular base.
£170–200
€ / **$270–315**
⚲ HOLL

A George III mahogany Zograscope, 27in (68.5cm) high.
£430–475
€ / **$680–750** ⊞ APO

Photographs

Berenice Abbott, 'Hanover Square, Manhattan', annotated by a Federal Art Project assistant in pencil and with stamped letters on reverse, American, 1936, 7½ x 9½in (19 x 24cm).
£3,800–4,500
€/ **$6,000–7,000** ⚒ S(NY)
Berenice Abbott was hired in 1935 by the Federal Art Project and the Museum of the City of New York to photograph New York as it constantly evolved and changed.

Berenice Abbott, 'West Street Row II: 217–221 West Street, Manhattan', annotated by a Federal Art Project assistant in pencil and with stamped letters on the reverse, American, 1936, 7½ x 9½in (19 x 24cm).
£3,200–3,800
€/ **$5,000–6,000** ⚒ S(NY)
This section of West Street Row, between North Moore and Franklin Streets, was razed in the 1960s. The Borough of Manhattan Community College, completed in 1980, now stands on this spot.

Ansel Adams, 'Mudhills, Arizona', plate 2 from *Portfolio V*, mounted, signed by the photographer and numbered 'V-2-97/110', No. 97 of 110, matted, American, 1947, printed later, 14¾ x 19¼in (37.5 x 49cm), framed.
£2,000–2,200
€/ **$3,200–3,500** ⚒ S(NY)

Emmy Andriesse, 'Germaine Richier', silver print, mounted on card along the upper edge, photographer's stamp 'Amstel 248 Amsterdam', Dutch, 1948, 10½ x 9¼in (26.5 x 23.5cm).
£1,000–1,100
€/ **$1,600–1,700** ⚒ S(Am)

D. F. Barry, 'Chief Gall', American, 1891, 11 x 5¾in (28 x 14.5cm).
£550–625
€/ **$870–1,000** ⚒ DuM

▶ **Brassaï,** 'Conchita with Sailors, Place d'Italie, Paris', signed, titled and numbered, French, dated 1932, printed later, 8¼ x 12in (21 x 30.5cm), framed.
£2,500–3,000
€/ **$4,000–4,700** ⚒ S(NY)

Samuel Bourne, 'Poplar Avenue, Srinagar, Kashmir', albumen print from wet collodion negative, c1865, 11½ x 9½in (29 x 24cm).
£150–200
€/ **$240–320** ⊞ RMe

Items in the Photographs section have been arranged in alphabetical order.

Bill Brandt, from a fashion series on beach wear, gelatin silver print, 1948, 10 x 12in (25.5 x 30.5cm).
£500–600
€/ **$790–950** ⊞ RMe

▶ **James Bray (Attributed),** a silver gelatin *carte de visite* photograph of Dan Kelly, Burman copy of an original, Australian, 1877–78, 3½ x 2¼in (9 x 5.5cm).
£475–550
€/ **$750–870** ⚒ LJ

European & American photography 1976–2002

(bar chart with vertical axis labeled INDEX from 1000 to 21000, horizontal axis years 1976–2002)

This graph shows the increasing value of European and American photography as a whole over the past 25 years. Individual collecting areas may not follow this graph exactly. ©AMR

Antoine Claudet, 'Portraits of a Lady and Gentleman', a pair of stereoscopic daguerreotypes, hand-coloured, gilt highlights, maker's engraved label, 1850s, in a fitted leather case with gilt stamp.
£1,100–1,200
€/ **$1,700–1,900** ⚒ BBA

Robert Doisneau, 'Créatures de Rêve', silver print, mounted on card along the upper edge, signed in ink, French, 1952, printed later, 12¼ x 10½in (31 x 26.5cm).
£1,200–1,400
€/ **$1,900–2,200** ⚒ S(Am)

Arthur Fellig (Weegee), 'Children's Performance', silver gelatin print, 1940s, 12½ x 10in (32 x 25.5cm).
£900–1,100
€/ **$1,400–1,700** ⚒ NOA

▶ **Eugene Omar Goldbeck,** 'Albert Einstein & Wife with Hopi Indians, Arizona, 1922', silver gelatin print, American, printed 1970s, 7 x 9in (18 x 23cm).
£280–320
€/ **$440–500** ⚒ NOA

Marjorie Content, 'Still Life with Calla and Spotted Leaf', signed and dated by the photographer, American, c1928, 3½ x 2¾in (9 x 7cm).
£2,200–2,500
€/ **$3,500–4,000** ⚒ S(NY)

Frantisek Drtikol, 'Portrait of L. Janácek', albumen print, mounted on card along the upper edge, Polish, c1925, 9 x 6½in (23 x 16.5cm).
£300–360
€/ **$475–575** ⚒ S(Am)

William Henry Fox Talbot, 'The Fruit Sellers', Lacock Abbey', salt print from calotype negative, c1842, in a frame 6¾ x 8¼in (17 x 21cm).
£5,000–5,500
€/ **$7,900–8,700** ⚒ S(Am)

Baron Adolf De Meyer, 'Claude Monet', signed by the photographer on the reverse, matted, 1921, 8½ x 6in (21.5 x 15cm).
£3,000–3,300
€/ **$4,700–5,200** ⚒ S(NY)

Andreas Feininger, 'New York, Downtown Manhattan from Brooklyn Bridge', silver print, titled and inscribed 'New York 1940', by the photographer, American, 1940, 13¾ x 11¼in (35 x 28.5cm).
£2,200–2,500
€/ **$3,500–4,000** ⚒ S(Am)

Francis Frith (Possibly), 'Kashmiri Policemen', albumen print, 1860–65, 7½ x 6in (19 x 15cm).
£450–500
€/ **$700–800** ⊞ RMe

Hachenberger, Bullfighters, Mexico, from a set of 30 gelatin silver prints depicting life in the country, c1930, 5 x 7in (12.5 x 18cm).
£780–850 the set
€/ **$1,200–1,300** ⊞ RMe

J. Jackson, 'Burma', a set of 16 albumen prints mounted on 12 card leaves, several signed, 1865–70, 5½ x 8¾in (14 x 22cm), in original cloth folder.
£280–325
€/ **$440–515** ↗ DW

W. E. Kilburn, a man in full military uniform with plumed hat on a table, 9th plate daguerreotype, c1850, 2½ x 1½in (6.5 x 4cm).
£200–250
€/ **$300–400** ⊞ RMe

Gustave Le Gray, 'Etude de nuages, clair-obscur', albumen print of a Normandy cloudscape from a collodion glass negative, signed, mounted on cut-down card, c1856, 11½ x 16¼in (29 x 41.5cm).
£8,500–10,000
€/ **$13,500–15,800** ↗ DW

David Octavius Hill and Robert Adamson, 'St Andrews, The College Church of St Salvator', calotype, 1845, 8½ x 6½in (21.5 x 16.5cm)
£500–600
€/ **$790–950** ⊞ HEG

Willy Kessels, 'Orchids', silver print, mounted on card along the upper edge, Belgian, c1936, 7 x 9½in (18 x 24cm).
£575–675
€/ **$900–1,000** ↗ S(Am)

Aart Klein, 'Rachmaninoff', silver print, mounted on card along the upper edge, 1936, 6½ x 9½in (16.5 x 24cm).
£1,000–1,100
€/ **$1,600–1,700** ↗ S(Am)

Hill & Adamson, Newhaven fisherman, carbon print from the original negative by Jessie Bertram, original c1845, print 1914, 7 x 5in (18 x 12.5cm).
£550–600
€/ **$870–950** ⊞ RMe

W. E. Kilburn, 'Portrait of a Gentleman', a daguerreotype, c1850, 4¼ x 3¼in (11 x 8.5cm).
£550–600
€/ **$870–950** ⊞ HEG

Joseph Lawton, Buddha, Ceylon, from an album of views and archaeological sites in Ceylon, albumen prints, c1870, 10 x 8in (25.5 x 23cm).
£2,000–2,500 album
€/ **$3,200–4,000** ⊞ RMe

◄ **Angus McBean,** 'Hepburn Desert', silver print, mounted on card, signed and dated 1951, printed 1986, 17½ x 12¾in (44.5 x 32.5cm).
£1,500–1,700
€/ **$2,400–2,700** ↗ S(Am)
This photograph is inscribed 'Audrey Hepburn's first published picture. Picked out from the chorus of the revue *Sauce* at the Cambridge Theatre 1951. One of my very few commercial jobs – The beauty which dares to come close'.

PHOTOGRAPHS

◀ **Herbert Ponting,** Captain Oates and ponies in the stable on the ship *Terra Nova*, gelatin silver contact print, 1911, 4 x 6in (10 x 15cm).
£450–500
€/ **$700–800**
⊞ RMe

Man Ray, 'Paddle Wheel of a Water Mill', silver print, mounted on card, undated, c1936, 3½ x 5½in (9 x 14cm).
£3,000–3,300
€/ **$4,700–5,200** ⚒ S(P)

André Rogi (Rosa Klein), 'Portrait of Dora Maar', contemporary silver print, semi-matt, signed and dated 1941, 11½ x 9in (29 x 23cm).
£3,700–4,200
€/ **$5,900–6,600** ⚒ S(P)

Southworth and Mawe's, 'Portrait of Robert Charles Winthrop', a daguerreotype, c1849, 6¼ x 4¾in (17 x 12cm)
£3,200–4,000
€/ **$5,000–6,300** ⊞ HEG
Robert Charles Winthrop was the Speaker of the US House of Representatives, 1838–40.

Paul Strand, 'Portrait of a Farmer, Luzzara, Italy', mounted, 1953, 4½ x 6in (11.5 x 15cm).
£2,700–3,200
€/ **$4,300–5,000** ⚒ S(NY)

Carleton E. Watkins, 'The best general view of the Yosemite Valley from the Mariposa Trail 6', albumen print, captioned and numbered on the original card mount, 1865–66, 15½ x 20½in (39.5 x 52cm).
£650–750
€/ **$1,000–1,200** ⚒ B(WM)

Johan van der Keuken, 'Ile Saint Louis, Paris', silver print, mounted on card along the upper edge, photographer's stamp, Dutch, 1956, printed later, 11½ x 15½in (29 x 39.5cm).
£1,100–1,300
€/ **$1,700–2,000** ⚒ S(Am)

T. R. Williams (attributed), a stereo daguerreotype of Queen Victoria, Prince Albert, Emperor Napoleon III and Empress Eugenie on the podium during their visit to the Crystal Palace, 20 April 1855, on a black mount with gold lining, 3 x 4in (7.5 x 10cm).
£2,500–3,000
€/ **$4,000–4,700** ⚒ B(WM)

Anon, 'Women from Sarawak', from an album of native people and views in Malaysia, Sarawak and Indonesia, albumen print, c1870, 12 x 15in (30.5 x 38cm).
£8,000–9,000 album
€/ **$12,500–14,000** ⊞ RMe

◀ **Mrs Wyatt Earp,** an anonymous photograph of her wearing a veil, c1860, 10 x 4in (25.5 x 10cm).
£3,000–3,500
€/ **$4,700–5,500** ⊞ ASP

◀ **Anon,** a mandarin's wife in court costume, 1870–80, 12 x 10in (30.5 x 25.5cm).
£650–800
€/ **$1,000–1,300** ⊞ RMe

Arms & Armour

Armour

An iron shield, the perimeter with a row of some leather remaining, some rust and spot staining, Italian, c1550, 22in (56cm) diam.
£6,750–7,500
€/ **$10,500–11,800** ⊞ FAC

An iron helmet, with brass rivets, the hinged cheek flaps with fleur-de-lys decoration, German, Berlin, 1560–70, 10½in (26.5cm) high.
£3,000–3,500
€/ **$4,800–5,400** ➴ Herm

A morion, with a high comb, with all-over chased decoration, German, c1580, 11in (28cm) high.
£2,700–3,200
€/ **$4,300–5,000** ➴ Herm

A chainmail shirt, German, 16thC, 26¾in (68cm) long.
£1,600–2,000
€/ **$2,500–3,200** ➴ Herm

A composite full armour, partly Flemish, 16thC.
£7,600–9,200
€/ **$12,000–14,500** ➴ S(O)

◀ **A cuirassier's helmet,** with a lattice visor, German, 1610–20.
£7,700–8,500
€/ **$12,200–13,400** ⊞ FAC

▶ **A close-helmet,** Italian, possibly Milanese, late 16thC, 11½in (29cm) high.
£4,000–4,800
€/ **$6,300–7,600** ➴ B(Kn)

A bright steel bridle-gauntlet, most finger scales either missing or replaced, 1575–1625, 16½in (42cm) long.
£850–1,000
€/ **$1,300–1,600** ➴ B(Kn)

▶ **A lobster-tail helmet,** European, 17thC, 11in (28cm) high.
£1,000–1,100
€/ **$1,600–1,700** ⊞ MDL

ARMS & ARMOUR

A pikeman's helmet, with moulded brim, nasal bar, plume holder missing, some damage, 17thC, 6in (15cm) high.
£220–250
€ / **$350–400** ✗ **F&C**

◄ **A composite steel pikeman's armour,** rust-patinated and polished overall, c1650.
£3,800–4,500
€ / **$6,000–7,100** ✗ **B(Kn)**

A black-and-white comb morion, one washer missing, German, 1600–25, 11½in (29cm) high.
£2,600–3,200
€ / **$4,100–5,000** ✗ **S(O)**

A chainmail shirt, Indian, c1700.
£1,000–1,200
€ / **$1,600–1,900** ⊞ **ARB**

A steel and brass backplate, French, numbered and dated 1828, 16in (40.5cm) high.
£350–400
€ / **$550–630** ⊞ **ARB**

A breastplate, French, made in August, 1876.
£250–300
€ / **$400–475** ✗ **JDJ**

Cannons

A half-pounder bronze signal mortar, on a stepped wooden carriage with brass mounts, late 18thC, barrel 9in (23cm) long.
£2,200–2,600
€ / **$3,500–4,100** ✗ **S(O)**

A bronze cannon barrel, decorated in relief with mouldings, with scroll lifting handles modelled as dolphins, on a later wheeled wooden stepped carriage, late 17thC, barrel 17½in (44.5cm) long.
£850–1,000
€ / **$1,300–1,600** ✗ **B(Kn)**

A bronze signal cannon, on a stepped teak carriage with brass mounts, 1750–1800, barrel 21in (53.5cm) long.
£2,200–2,500
€ / **$3,500–4,000** ✗ **S(O)**

LOCATE THE SOURCE
The source of each illustration in Miller's can be found by checking the code letters below each caption with the Key to Illustrations, pages 794–800.

▶ **A bronze miniature cannon,** in Flemish or German mid-16thC style, cast in relief, on a mahogany stepped carriage with quoin and four trucks, late 19th/early 20thC, barrel 16¼in (41.5cm) long.
£760–900
€ / **$1,200–1,400** ✗ **S(O)**

Edged Weapons

A left-hand dagger, with silver pellet inlay and a spirally-fluted wire-wrapped grip, c1590, 11in (28cm) long.
£5,800–6,500
€/ **$9,200–10,200** ⊞ **FAC**

A two-hand processional sword, the iron hilt with incised decoration comprising side-rings each with stylized monsters' heads and a button terminal, the quillons each with a scroll beneath and a scrolled monster-head terminal, later star-shaped pommel and wooden grip, some worming and minor damage, cover missing, German, 1575–1625, blade 58in (147.5cm) long.
£2,200–2,500
€/ **$3,500–4,000** ⚒ **B(Kn)**

A left-hand dagger, with downswept quillon and iron blade, the hilt with a conical pommel, German, c1600, 19¾in (50cm) long.
£1,700–2,000
€/ **$2,700–3,200** ⚒ **Herm**

A swept-hilt rapier, stamped 'Tomas De Ayala' within the fuller, the grip later bound with twisted steel wire, early 17thC, blade 39¾in (101cm) long.
£1,700–2,000
€/ **$2,700–3,200** ⚒ **B(Kn)**

A falchion, with a curved blade, Italian, c1620, 31in (78.5cm) long.
£3,000–3,300
€/ **$4,700–5,200** ⊞ **FAC**

A stick rapier, by Johannes Hoppe, German, Solingen, c1630, 47¼in (120cm) long.
£2,800–3,200
€/ **$4,500–5,000** ⚒ **Herm**

A rapier, with a diamond section blade, the hilt with alternating pierced and solid panels, the quillons with curled ends, engraved pommel, the wood grip with Turks' heads, grip wire missing, c1630, blade 36¼in (92cm) long.
£1,400–1,600
€/ **$2,200–2,500** ⚒ **B(L)**

A rapier, the double-edged blade stamped with illegible letters, chiselled throughout with a foliage design, later grip, rust-patinated overall, c1640, blade 37in (94cm) long.
£1,700–2,000
€/ **$2,700–3,200** ⚒ **B(Kn)**

A dish-hilted rapier, signed 'Sahagom' in the central fuller, the hilt chased with leaves against a stippled ground, replacement grip, counter guard section missing, patinated overall, c1640, blade 38½in (98cm) long.
£1,400–1,700
€/ **$2,200–2,700** ⚒ **B(L)**

A transitional rapier, chiselled with stylized faces and foliage, the grip with copper wire binding, c1650, blade 31in (78.5cm) long.
£1,600–1,800
€/ **$2,500–2,800** ⊞ **ASB**

A basket-hilted backsword, one bar from hilt missing, grip wire loose, worn overall, mid-17thC, blade 34¾in (88.5cm) long.
£1,000–1,200
€/ **$1,600–1,900** ⚒ **B(L)**

A left-hand dagger, the wood grip retaining one Turk's head, grip wire missing, rust patinated, possibly Italian, 17thC, blade 14½in (37cm) long.
£600–700
€/ **$950–1,100** ⚔ B(L)

A hanger, the gilt-brass hilt with a sculpted shell guard and stipple chased foliage, with gold within the chiselling, with an ebony pistol grip and flattened diamond-section blade, European, c1680, blade 27¼in (69cm) long.
£900–1,000
€/ **$1,400–1,600** ⊞ FAC

A brass-hilted hanger, with a curved fullered blade, the two-piece grip cast with scrolls, strapwork and foliage terminating in a stylized lion-head pommel, some wear, pitting and repair, 1650–1700, blade 26½in (67.5cm) long.
£480–575
€/ **$760–910** ⚔ B(Kn)

A silver-hilted hanger sword, with a stag horn grip, and running wolf blade, c1680, 26in (66cm) long.
£2,500–3,000
€/ **$4,000–4,700** ⊞ ARB

An iron-hilted smallsword, with plain knuckle bow and pommel, and brass wire-wrapped grip, c1740, blade 31¾in (80.5cm) long.
£750–825
€/ **$1,200–1,300** ⊞ FAC

A silver-gilt smallsword, with a hollow triangular blade, the hilt cast and chased with faceted beads, French, c1750, 31½in (80cm) long.
£2,200–2,500
€/ **$3,500–4,000** ⊞ FAC

An infantry officer's sabre for Bern Canton, the brass hilt with a lion-head pommel, double shell guard and three bar guards, the curved blade partly etched with foliage, trophies of arms and a motto, Swiss, c1750, blade 28¼in (72cm) long.
£1,400–1,500
€/ **$2,200–2,400** ⊞ FAC

A silver-hilted smallsword, with an etched trefoil blade and detailed hilt, c1770, 88in (223.5cm) long.
£1,000–1,200
€/ **$1,600–1,900** ⊞ MDL

A smallsword, the iron hilt with a faceted stylized urn-shaped pommel, slight wear and oxidation, European, 1780–1800, blade 31¾in (80.5cm) long.
£600–650
€/ **$950–1,000** ⊞ FAC

◄ **A dragoon sabre,** stamped 'S. Harvey', the steel half-basket guard with diamond pattern, flattened bun pommel and brass wire-bound fishskin-covered grip, grip restored, blade reseated, mid-18thC, curved blade 30in (76cm) long.
£2,200–2,500
€/ **$3,500–4,000** ⚔ WAL

A hunting knife, with diamond-section damascus blade, the hilt with steeled blue mounts chiselled with gilt scrolling foliage, with a ribbed ivory grip, in a velvet-covered wood scabbard with decorated steel mounts, slight wear to mounts and velvet worn, probably Russian, late 18thC, blade 10¼in (26cm) long.
£700–800
€/ **$1,100–1,300** ⚔ B(L)

A basket-hilted military backsword, wooden grip split, binding missing, some rust patination overall, Scottish, mid-18thC, blade 38½in (98cm) long.
£900–1,100
€/ **$1,400–1,700** ⚔ B(Kn)

An officer's horseman's sword, with carved ivory grip, gilt stirrup hilt with lion-head pommel, the blade engraved with blue and gilt decoration, the gilt scabbard engraved with a leaf design, American, c1800, 36in (91.5cm) long.
£2,200–2,500
€/ **$3,500–4,000** ⊞ **MDL**

A cavalry sabre, with lion-head pommel and brass hilt, the damascas-etched blade with a leather scabbard, c1800, 41in (104cm) long.
£1,500–1,700
€/ **$2,400–2,700** ⊞ **MDL**

An 1803 pattern officer's light infantry blue and gilt sword, early 19thC, 34in (86.5cm) long.
£1,100–1,200
€/ **$1,700–1,900** ⊞ **MDL**

A gilt-mounted cavalry sabre, by Brunn, the blade engraved and gilded, the gilt-brass stirrup hilt engraved, with pierced knucklebow, the leather scabbard with engraved and pierced brass mounts, c1800, 37in (94cm) long.
£2,000–2,300
€/ **$3,200–3,600** ⊞ **WSA**

A Model AN XI infantryman's shortsword briquet, with regulation one-piece brass stirrup hilt, associated brass-mounted leather scabbard, some wear, French, 1802–03, blade 23¼in (59cm) long.
£100–120
€/ **$160–190** ↗ **WAL**

A grenadier guard's hanger, the blade with regimental markings at the forte, the brass hilt with a D-form guard and ribbed grip, some staining, c1838, blade 20¾in (52.5cm) long.
£560–625
€/ **$900–1,000** ⊞ **FAC**

A cavalry trooper's sword, the hilt with remains of original blackened finish, the grip wrap and covering complete, c1843, blade 35½in (90cm) long.
£280–325
€/ **$440–520** ⊞ **FAC**

A King Ludwig Ist civil servant's sword, by Stroblberger, Munich, with finely-gilded blade, German, mid-19thC, blade 34⅞in (88.5cm) long.
£700–800
€/ **$1,100–1,300** ↗ **Herm**

◄ **An assembled Confederate presentation sword,** by Millar, Dayville, New York, the double fuller sword with dog-head pommel, iron scabbard with brass mountings and presentation inscription, slight rust, American, c1862, blade 35in (89cm) long.
£700–800
€/ **$1,100–1,300** ↗ **JDJ**

A 15th Hussars officer's sword, with gilt-brass cross quillon, ivory handle and gilt-brass scabbard, c1860, 36in (91.5cm) long.
£1,350–1,500
€/ **$2,000–2,400** ⊞ **ARB**

► **An infantry officer's sabre,** Wagner No. 150, by Weyersberg & Co, Solingen, with curved broad fullered blade, wire-wrapped sharkskin-covered grip, plated hilt, blade and scabbard, minor discolouration, Austrian, c1861, blade 32¼in (82cm) long.
£475–525
€/ **$750–830** ⊞ **FAC**

ARMS & ARMOUR

An 1834 pattern 1st life guard's NCO's dress and undress sword, No. 13748, the pierced guard applied with a brass-crowned regimental device, scrolls and border studs, plated gripstrap, stepped brass pommel and wire-bound fishskin grip, c1865, the Wilkinson blade 39in (99cm) long.
£900–1,100
€ / **$1,400–1,700** ⚔ **WAL**

A staff and field officer's sword, by Schuyler, Hartley & Graham, New York, with diamond-section double-edged blade, the guard cast with an applied sterling silver spread-winged eagle and shield beneath an American flag, the tortoiseshell-bound grip with a triple-wire wrap, the silver-plated iron scabbard with engraved brass furniture, minor losses to grip wire, hilt loose, American, 1865–75, blade 31½in (80cm) long.
£1,300–1,500
€ / **$2,000–2,400** ⚔ **JDJ**

A dirk, the straight blade decorated with a coat-of-arms, flowers and Latin inscription, the finely-carved ebony and gilt handle engraved with a reciprocal coat-of-arms, Scottish, c1874, 18½in (47cm) long.
£1,200–1,400
€ / **$1,900–2,200** ⚔ **Herm**

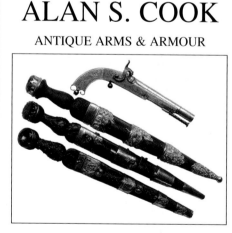

A silver-mounted dirk, with the owner's crest, the stag-horn grip with floral-engraved mounts, the scabbard with companion knife and fork, all mounted *en suite* with silver mounts, Scottish, c1880, blade 10½in (26.5cm) long.
£1,100–1,200
€ / **$1,700–1,800** ⊞ **MDL**

A Victorian Highland officer's basket-hilted broadsword, with etched blade, original liner and silk tassel, in associated nickel-plated scabbard, blade 31½in (80cm) long.
£700–800
€ / **$1,100–1,300** ⚔ **S(O)**

A Victorian bandsman's sword, of the Royal Bucks Militia Band, the one-piece brass hilt stamped 'RBM B18' on both sides, the spiral grip with lion-head pommel, the leather scabbard with engraved locket, minor rust stains, knucklechain and chape missing, leather worn and shortened, blade 24¾in (63cm) long.
£130–150
€ / **$210–240** ⚔ **WAL**

A Venezuelan officer's Prussian model 1889 pattern sword, the gilt-brass hilt with the arms of Venezuela flanked by foliage, over a motto ribbon and cornucopia above, the grip with a 'R de V' monogram, German, dated 1900, blade 31¼in (79.5cm) long.
£500–550
€ / **$800–870** ⊞ **FAC**

An infantry officer's Prussian model 1889 pattern presentation sword, the damascus blade etched with scrollwork, the outer face with presentation inscription, the hilt inscribed '1893–1911', in original blackened steel scabbard, German, c1911, blade 31½in (80cm) long.
£770–850
€ / **$1,200–1,400** ⚔ **S(O)**

ARMS & ARMOUR

Firearms

A flintlock blunderbuss, with London proof marks, rounded Brown Bess-style military lock with swan-neck cock, walnut full stock, brass mounts, ramrod missing, minor damage, c1770, 34in (86.5cm) long.
£1,200–1,400
€/ **$1,900–2,200** ↗ WAL

A George III flintlock blunderbuss, with brass-edge mahogany stock and steel tower lock, 28in (71cm) long.
£800–950
€/ **$1,300–1,500** ↗ LVS

A brass-barrelled flintlock blunderbuss, with walnut stock, inscribed 'Rigby, Dublin', nickel-plated steel action, brass rounded trigger guard fore end and butt plate, Irish, 19thC, 30in (76cm) long.
£1,500–1,800
€/ **$2,400–2,800** ↗ AH

A .577 Snider 2 band Mk III artillery carbine, by BSA, full military marks, 1866, 40in (101.5cm) long.
£1,600–1,800
€/ **$2,500–2,800** ⊞ SPA

A .75 calibre Indian pattern Brown Bess flintlock musket with bayonet, 1809 reinforced lock, bayonet marked Osborn & Grundy, introduced 1797, barrel 39in (99cm) long.
£1,100–1,300
€/ **$1,700–2,000** ↗ BWL

A .577 calibre 1853 pattern fourth model percussion rifled musket, the sighted barrel with three bands, calibrated folding adjustable back-sight, dated lock stamped 'Tower', steel ramrod, dated 1868, barrel 39¼in (99cm) long.
£660–800
€/ **$1,000–1,300** ↗ B(Kn)

A flintlock blunderbuss, by Steele, with figured-walnut full stock, three-stage brass barrel, signed lock engraved with foliage, full brass mounts, original brass-tipped wooden ramrod, lock spring replaced, c1780, 29½in (75cm) long.
£1,300–1,500
€/ **$2,000–2,400** ↗ S(O)

A Spencer Civil War repeating carbine, square base front sight and ladder rear sight, top of receiver marked, inspector's marks, stamped 'J. Russell' to buttstock, 19thC, barrel 21in (53.5cm) long.
£1,400–1,600
€/ **$2,200–2,600** ↗ JDJ

A Wanzl hinged breech SS military carbine, the full stock with steel mounts, sling swivels, breech tang stamped 'W. Mashek', plain lock stamped '863', Austrian, 1863, barrel 23¾in (60.5cm) long.
£300–360
€/ **$475–570** ↗ WAL

▶ A Derringer-style six-shot pin fire pepperbox pistol, with wooden grips, folding trigger and side gate, Continental, 19thC, 5in (12.5cm) long.
£270–300
€/ **$430–470**
⊞ MDL

A .69 calibre Pomeroy model 1821 converted musket with bayonet, Belgian-style conversion with cone in barrel, issue marks '3-F' painted on stock, lockplate and barrel tang dated 1822, barrel 42in (106.5cm) long.
£360–430
€/ **$575–675** ↗ JDJ

A flintlock pistol, with floral-carved wooden stock and engraved iron mounts, iron ramrod, engraved lock with signature 'P. Alberti', marked 'L.LA-Zarino', probably for export to eastern Europe, fore end and butt restored, Italian, 1720–30, 19¼in (49cm) long.
£1,000–1,200
€/ **$1,600–1,900** ↗ Herm

A flintlock cannon-barrelled pistol, by W. Turvey, London, the three-stage turn-off barrel with ringed muzzle, signed breech, replacement cock, c1740, barrel 5¼in (13.5cm) long.
£900–1,100
€/ **$1,400–1,700** ⚒ B(L)

A .700 calibre Saxon regulation flintlock cavalry pistol, with moulded walnut full stock and regulation brass mounts, the sighted barrel struck with 'SS' mark on the tang, left-hand lock, ramrod pipes and ramrod replacement repairs, 1760–70, 17¼in (44cm) long.
£850–950
€/ **$1,300–1,500** ⚒ S(O)

A pair of 24 bore flintlock duelling pistols, by Bennett, London, the walnut full stocks with chequered butts and ribbed finials, steel mounts including engraved French-style trigger guards with pineapple finials and single set triggers, maker's proof marks, c1795, 15in (38cm) long, cased.
£1,800–2,200
€/ **$2,800–3,500** ⚒ WAL

A pair of flintlock pistols, the walnut stock with floral carving, pierced brass mounts in relief, struck mark 'ZK' underneath, 'MW' to the side, minor restoration, German, Suhl, mid-18thC, 18¼in (46.5cm) long.
£1,700–2,000
€/ **$2,700–3,200** ⚒ Herm

A pair of silver-mounted and engraved Queen Anne-style flintlock carriage pistols, by Delany, with London proofs and foreigner's mark, the figured-walnut butts with silver wire inlay and carved with rocailles, silver furniture, signed, c1740, 12½in (32cm) long.
£3,400–3,800
€/ **$5,400–6,000** ⊞ WSA

A pair of silver-mounted brass barrel holster pistols, by Bradley, Liverpool, with Birmingham proofs, the walnut full stocks with cast and engraved silver mounts, c1765, barrels 8¼in (21cm) long.
£5,000–5,500
€/ **$7,900–8,700** ⊞ WSA

◄ **A steel flintlock belt pistol,** the lock with traces of foliate engraving, the stock with ram's-horn butt, ball trigger, part of belt hook missing, action faulty, Scottish, c1780, barrel 7¾in (19.5cm) long.
£550–625
€/ **$870–990** ⚒ B(Ed)

ARMS & ARMOUR

A percussion travelling pistol, the walnut full stock relief-carved with scrolls, the two-stage barrel with beaded mouldings, inlaid with silver scrolling tendrils, rebuilt from miquelet-lock, later ramrod, Spanish, late 18thC, 7in (18cm) long.
£700–850
€/ **$1,100–1,300** ⚔ S(O)

A Newland patent flintlock pistol, with brass plate to reinforce throat, swivel ramrod, c1800, 15in (38cm) long.
£800–900
€/ **$1,200–1,400** ⊞ SPA

A flintlock pistol, by S. Nock, with walnut full stock and brass barrel, c1800, 13½in (34.5cm) long.
£1,300–1,500
€/ **$2,100–2,400** ⊞ ARB

A double-barrel pistol, by Leech, with steel mounts, percussion lock and mahogany stock, early 19thC.
£420–500
€/ **$660–790** ⚔ G(L)

A pair of percussion pistols, by C. Freyer, Dresden, with walnut full stock and iron mounts, German, 1820–30, 15in (38cm) long.
£1,300–1,500
€/ **$2,000–2,400** ⚔ Herm

A flintlock pistol, relief-decorated in niello with military trophies, foliage and rococo moulding, Montenegrin, 18th–19thC, 15in (38cm) long.
£3,200–3,500
€/ **$5,000–5,500** ⊞ FAC

A 16 bore officer's flintlock holster pistol, by Prosser, London, the walnut full stock with chequered butt, steel mounts including engraved trigger guard with pineapple finial, swivel ramrod, c1800, 15in (38cm) long.
£850–1,000
€/ **$1,300–1,600** ⚔ WAL

A 16 bore flintlock Light Dragoon holster pistol, with walnut full stock, the barrel with tower proofs, regulation brass furniture, lock marked crown, GR cypher and 'T. Richards', with later ramrod, full stock cracked, c1800, 9in (23cm) long.
£360–440
€/ **$560–700** ⚔ WD

A pocket percussion pistol, with walnut stock engraved 'Jackson, London' and stamped 'W. P.', early 19thC, 5¾in (14.5cm) long.
£250–300
€/ **$400–475** ⚔ SWO

A .54 calibre converted Johnson 1836 model martial pistol, hammer screw replaced, the lock dated 1836, barrel 8½in (21.5cm) long.
£900–1,000
€/ **$1,400–1,600** ⚔ JDJ

A set of four bank pistols, with walnut full stocks, the twist barrels signed 'London', the engraved sidelocks signed 'Rimmer', engraved steel furniture, brass-tipped ramrods, c1840, barrels 4in (10cm) long, in a relined case with accessories.
£4,300–4,800
€/ **$6,800–7,600** ⊞ WSA

A knife pistol, the octagonal barrel with percussion nipple, slab horn sides, two knife blades and folding trigger, Continental, c1850, 7in (18cm) long, with leather holster.
£560–625
€/ **$870–985** ⊞ MDL

A pair of double-barrelled pistols, by F. P. Gastinne-Renette, with walnut grip, engraved iron butt cap and lock plates, underlever breakdown action, signed, French, Paris, c1860, 14in (35.5cm) long.
£2,400–2,800
€/ **$3,800–4,400** 🔨 Herm
F. P. Gastinne-Renette was court gunmaker to the King of Spain and Napoleon II of France.

A palm pistol, by Chicago Firearms Co, American, c1870, 5in (12.5cm) long.
£800–900
€/ **$1,200–1,400** ⊞ MDL

▶ **A Colt Navy revolver,** c1855, in a box 15in (38cm) wide.
£6,300–7,000
€/ **$10,000–11,000** ⊞ WSA

A pair of saw-handle percussion pistols, by Cole, the octagonal-twist barrels engraved 'Belfast', stocks with saw grip and horn fore end, brass-tipped ebony ramrods with embossed three-way flask, bullet mould, oil bottle and cap tin, c1850, in a brass-bound case 19in (48.5cm) wide.
£3,900–4,300
€/ **$6,200–6,800** ⊞ MDL

A Roger's patent percussion knife pistol, with Birmingham proof marks and German silver barrel, the butt with hinged German silver trap, folding trigger and two folding knife blades, one signed 'James Rogers', bullet mould and another accessory missing, mid-19thC, 6¾in (17cm) long.
£450–500
€/ **$700–790** 🔨 S(O)

A percussion salon pistol, with chequered walnut stock and grip with baluster-turned end cap, octagonal barrel, quadrant rear sight on a graduated dovetailed rail, shaped grip trigger guard, Belgian, 19thC, 17¾in (45cm) long.
£200–240
€/ **$315–380** 🔨 AH

A .44 calibre Remington model 1858 New Model army revolver, with pinched front sight, walnut grips with outline of cartouche visible and various inspector marks, brass trigger guard, American, 19thC, barrel 8in (20.5cm) long.
£1,000–1,200
€/ **$1,600–1,900** 🔨 JDJ

A percussion revolver, No. 2628, by V. Dreyse, the walnut grip with fishscale carving, signed, German, Sömmerda, c1865, 11¾in (30cm) long.
£2,800–3,200
€/ **$4,400–5,000** ⚲ **Herm**

A Colt Bisley model single-action revolver, No. 233312, case-hardened frame with rampant Colt motif and patent dates, chequered and hard rubber grips, c1875, barrel 7½in (19cm) long.
£650–750
€/ **$1,000–1,200** ⚲ **WD**

▶ **A .44 calibre percussion full stock rifle,** by J. A. Lechler, lock marked 'Josh Golcher', rear sight installed backwards, some damage, American, mid-19thC, barrel 36½in (92.5cm) long.
£450–550
€/ **$700–840** ⚲ **JDJ**

A six-shot pepperbox percussion revolver, with leaf-chased brass action, inscribed 'Boston, Wakefield', chased steel hammer and rounded trigger guard, chequered walnut grip, hinged chased steel grip cap box, 19thC, 9½in (24cm) long.
£420–500
€/ **$660–790** ⚲ **AH**

A Whitney model 1842 Mississippi rifle, the walnut stock with 'SM', 'W.A.T' and 'JH' cartouches, minor repairs, American, lock and barrel dated 1850, barrel 33in (84cm) long.
£3,200–3,800
€/ **$5,000–6,000** ⚲ **JDJ**

Polearms & Axes

A military pioneer's axe, the crescent head with spear point beak, on a wooden haft with brass ferrule and boss, 19thC, 35½in (90cm) long.
£200–240
€/ **$315–380** ⚲ **WAL**

A partisan, the crescent base with forged 'eyes', the diamond-section tapering blade with thickened elongated point, integral double-banded socket and integral cheek straps, tapering haft inlet for a base shoe now missing, French, c1630, 104in (264cm) long.
£2,100–2,300
€/ **$3,300–3,600** ⊞ **FAC**

A military camp axe, stamped 'H Macneal Gordon Highlanders', on original wooden haft, 19thC, head 7in (18cm) long.
£280–325
€/ **$440–515** ⚲ **WAL**

ARMS & ARMOUR

Militaria

Collectors of Militaria have a seemingly endless variety of fields on which to focus their interests, such as uniforms, regimental headdress, drums, regimental histories, Army, Air Force and Navy lists and, for the serious addict, even vehicles. Campaign medals are, in most cases, named around the rim or on the back with the number, rank, name and unit of the person to whom they were awarded. It is therefore possible to research the recipient's story and the campaigns in which they took part, making collecting even more interesting. Smaller items, such as military buttons and cap badges can be acquired for a modest amount and will demonstrate how a particular regiment or corps has changed since its inception. Sweetheart brooches or pins, usually a smaller version of the regimental badge, and produced by jewellers to sell to servicemen to present to their loved ones, can be found in precious metals and stones or in base metal and paste. They are a fascinating collecting area on their own and also pleasing to the eye.

Over the years collecting Militaria has proved to be a good investment as there is an enthusiastic international market and of course a limited supply of items which have survived to the present day. Some examples are: a group of eight medals awarded to a Colonel in the King's Own Yorkshire Light Infantry which sold for £85 (€/ $135) in 1973 and for £4,600 (€/ $7,300) 30 years later; a complete Trooper's uniform of the 16th Lancers, c1899 which sold for £200 (€/ $320) in 1976 and recently realized £1,100 (€/ $1,700) at auction, and a Victorian officer's helmet of the 5th Royal Irish Lancers which was worth £600 (€/ $950) in the early 1980s and revalued at over £5,000 (€/ $8,000) in 2003. It is clear that the market for Militaria is very strong at the moment, and in particular for gallantry medals, drums and cap badges.

One can never overestimate the joy for the enthusiast of adding to his collection and the golden rule is of course to always buy something because you like it, but the satisfaction of finding that there is also a financial reward at some future date can also not be denied!

John Wright

Badges

A Gordon Highlanders, 4th Donside Highland Volunteer Battalion officer's die-cast silver-plated glengarry/bonnet badge, c1893–1908.
£140–160
€/ $220–250 ✦ DNW

A Crimean War die-struck brass badge, Russian, c1853, 4½in (11.5cm) diam.
£150–175
€/ $240–280 ✦ WAL

A Royal Aberdeen Highlanders Militia other ranks' white metal glengarry badge, 1874–81.
£140–160
€/ $220–250 ✦ DNW

> To order Miller's books in the UK please ring 01903 828800.
> See the full range at
> **www.millers.uk.com**

◀ **A Victorian South Indian Railway Volunteer Rifle Corps other ranks' white metal Maltese Cross hat badge.**
£70–80
€/ $110–130 ✦ WAL

A Victorian Pretoria Volunteers Corps bronze manufacturer's sample Shako badge and helmet plate, on original card, 6 x 7in (15 x 18cm).
£550–600
€/ $870–950 ⊞ Q&C

MILITARIA

A Victorian 1st and 2nd Battalion The Buffs officer's silver-plated pouch belt badge, slight wear.
£100–120
€/ $160–190 ↗ WAL

A Victorian Engineer Volunteers other ranks' white metal glengarry badge, possibly Colonial.
£100–120
€/ $160–190 ↗ WAL

A 1st Gurkha Rifles gilt-metal puggaree badge, c1900, some staining.
£350–400
€/ $550–630 ↗ WAL

A Victorian 1st Devon Militia other ranks' brass glengarry badge.
£70–80
€/ $110–130 ↗ WAL

◄ **A Duke of Cornwall's Light Infantry silver cap badge,** hallmarked F&S, Birmingham 1910.
£170–200
€/ $270–320 ↗ WAL

Costume

A Georgian officer's field service coatee, to the rank of Major General, by 'Firmin & Westall, Strand', c1812.
£1,700–2,000
€/ $2,700–3,200 ↗ WAL

▶ **A Victorian Royal Field Artillery Staff Sergeant's uniform,** comprising pill box hat, frock, sidecap and overalls.
£550–625
€/ $870–1,000 ↗ WAL

▶ **A Victorian Bombay Volunteer Rifles Lieutenant's uniform,** comprising torrin cap, tunic, shoulder belt and waist belt, a sword knot, a pair of box spurs and a pair of shoulder cords with buttons, whistle and chains missing.
£750–900
€/ $1,200–1,400 ↗ WAL

◄ **A militia Cavalry coatee,** American, two buttons missing, c1855.
£500–600
€/ $800–950 ↗ JAd

A Lifeguard Hussars Regiment's Sergeant's coat and cap, German, 1915.
£2,000–2,200
€/ $3,200–3,500 ↗ Herm

A 20th Artillery Captain's service dress uniform, comprising peaked cap, tunic, shoulder belt and metal pouch, breeches, knee boots, waistbelt and sword, Italian, WWII.
£400–475
€/ $630–750 ↗ WAL

MILITARIA

Helmets & Headdresses

A militia officer's beaver felt bicorn dress hat, American, 1815–25.
£2,400–2,800
€ / **$3,800–4,400** ✦ JDJ

A Royal Hohenzollern-Hechinger Infantry officer's shako, German, 1820–45.
£3,500–4,000
€ / **$5,500–6,300** ✦ Herm

A Gendarmerie officer's shako, Imperial German State, 1831–37.
£2,200–2,500
€ / **$3,500–4,000** ✦ Herm

A Kingdom of the Two Sicilies 1st Batallion National Guard of Sicily helmet, Italian, 1848–60.
£1,700–2,000
€ / **$2,700–3,200** ✦ Herm

A Dragoon officer's brass and leather helmet, Swedish, c1850.
£500–570
€ / **$790–900** ⊞ MDL

◀ **A Queen's Edinburgh Rifle Volunteers officer's Shako,** c1862.
£650–780
€ / **$1,000–1,200** ✦ WAL

A Worcestershire Yeomanry Cavalry leather and white metal helmet, with horsehair plume and chin chain, c1860.
£1,700–1,900
€ / **$2,700–3,000** ⊞ MDL

An Infantry officer's model 1868 Raupenhelm, with full gilt-metal mounts, plume missing, some damage, Bavarian, c1870.
£600–675
€ / **$950–1,000** ✦ S(O)

A 1st Volunteer Batallion Border Regiment other ranks' helmet, leather missing from chin chain, c1880.
£450–500
€ / **$700–790** ⊞ MDL

A 1st/Duke of Manchester's Mounted Volunteers helmet, horsehair plume associated, back peak bent, c1865.
£1,300–1,500
€ / **$2,000–2,400** ✦ WAL

▶ **A Sherwood Foresters officer's cloth-covered helmet,** Hawkes & Co maker's stamp to the skull, c1880.
£675–750
€ / **$1,100–1,200** ⊞ MDL

MILITARIA

◄ **A Durham Light Infantry cloth-covered helmet,** stamped Hawkes & Co, c1890.
£650–725
€/ $1,000–1,100 ⊞ MDL

A Victorian 4th (Queen's Own) Hussars officer's cloth torrin cap.
£300–350
€/ $475–550 ⤠ WAL

A Victorian 4th (Queen's Own) Hussars officer's pillbox hat.
£220–250
€/ $350–400 ⤠ WAL

A Victorian 5th Royal Hussar's shako.
£800–900
€/ $1,300–1,400 ⊞ Q&C

◄ **A late Victorian 19th Hussars officer's busby,** with hat box and plume holder.
£675–750
€/ $1,100–1,200 ⊞ Q&C

▶ **A Border Regiment officer's 1878 pattern cloth-covered helmet,** sweat band and silk liner missing, with associated 1884–1901 pattern helmet plate.
£500–575
€/ $800–900 ⤠ DNW

A 1st King's Dragoon Guards officer's 1871 pattern helmet, lining missing, 1901–10.
£2,000–2,200
€/ $3,200–3,500 ⤠ S(O)

A Royal Naval bicorn hat and epaulettes, in a tin box, WWI.
£350–400
€/ $550–630 ⊞ MDL

A Prussian Infantry other ranks' leather and brass *Pickelhaube*, Berlin maker's stamp inside crown, brass peak trim missing, some wear, Imperial German, early 20thC.
£280–320
€/ $440–500 ⤠ WAL

A Grenadier's cloth and brass mitre cap, hessian liner with storekeeper's stamp dated 1910, Imperial Russian.
£2,000–2,200
€/ $3,200–3,500 ⤠ WAL

MILITARIA

Helmet Plates & Shoulder Belt Plates

A 63rd (West Suffolk) Regiment officer's gilt-copper shoulder belt plate, gilt loss, 1830–55.
£470–530
€/ $740–840 ⚒ DNW

A gilt-copper helmet plate, for a bell-top shako, c1840.
£420–465
€/ $670–720 ⊞ MDL

A gilt-copper and silver helmet plate, for a bell-top shako, c1840.
£265–300
€/ $420–475 ⊞ MDL

A 26th Regiment other ranks' brass helmet plate, one loop missing, Russian, 1854–55.
£100–120
€/ $160–190 ⚒ WAL

A Victorian 1st Middlesex Engineer Volunteers other ranks white metal helmet plate, cleaned, repairs to back.
£170–200
€/ $270–320 ⚒ WAL

A Pretoria Volunteer Rifle Corps officer's silver-plated helmet plate, with a double pole to the wagon, late 19thC.
£220–260
€/ $350–400 ⚒ WAL
The double pole to the wagon is a rare variation. The shafts of the wagon pointing downwards indicates volunteers.

Historical Medals

◄ **A silver medal,** for the Attempted Invasion of Scotland, by G. Hautsch, the obverse with a bust of Anne, the reverse with the English fleet in pursuit of the French, the coast of Scotland in the distance, the edge inscribed 'Sic Pueri Nasum Rhinocerotis Habent' (Thus Boys have the Nose of a Rhinoceros), 1708, 1½in (4cm) diam.
£340–375
€/ $550–600 ⊞ TML
The epigram on the edge comes from Martial – the attempted invasion was so ridiculous that even small boys turn their noses up at it.

A silver medal, for the Battle of Culloden, 16 April 1746, by Richard Yeo, the obverse with a bust of Cumberland, the reverse with the Duke, as Hercules, trampling on Discord and raising Britannia, edge engraved, 1746, 2in (5cm) diam.
£250–285
€/ $400–450 ⊞ TML

► **A silver medal,** for the British Army Entering Madrid, by T. and P. Wyon, the obverse with a bare-headed bust of Wellington, the reverse with a tablet of victories surmounted by shields of Britain, Portugal and Spain, enclosed by military trophies, 1812, 1¾in (4.5cm) diam.
£300–350
€/ $475–550 ⚒ DNW

LOCATE THE SOURCE
The source of each illustration in Miller's can be found by checking the code letters below each caption with the Key to Illustrations, pages 794–800.

MILITARIA

Orders & Medals

A General Service Medal, awarded to Private Robert Willis, 3rd Dragoon Guards, with Toulouse, Vittoria, Albuhera and Talavera bars, 1793–1814.
£1,700–2,000
€/ **$2,700–3,200** ⚔ **Bri**
Aged 13, Robert Willis signed up for Volunteer Service at Salisbury two days after Christmas, 1798. He rose through the ranks to Sergeant Major, holding that rank for his last ten years and 332 days. His discharge papers list his reason for leaving 'being worn out in the service' in June 1821.

A Victorian Military Service medal, awarded to Richard Charlesworth, 84th Foot, two bars, Nivelle and Nive.
£850–1,000
€/ **$1,300–1,600** ⚔ **BAL**

Miller's Compares

I. A Waterloo medal, awarded to Sergeant Richard Spencer, 2nd Battalion 95th Regiment Foot, 1815.
£2,000–2,400
€/ **$3,200–3,800** ⚔ **WAL**

II. A Hanoverian Waterloo medal, awarded to Michael Wedekind, Landwehr Battalion Alfield, 1815.
£380–450
€/ **$600–710** ⚔ **WAL**

Pictured above are two medals awarded to soldiers fighting in the Battle of Waterloo: Item I to a British soldier and Item II to a soldier of the Prussian Army who fought alongside the British. The Prussian Army was virtually an army of mercenaries, being paid for by the English Parliament, and records are almost non existent. Hanoverian Waterloo Medals were authorized by the Prince Regent on behalf of his father King George III in his capacity as Elector of Hanover. All British-issued medals were named around the rim with the recipient's name and unit, but not all German ones were. It is therefore much easier to verify a medal to a British soldier from the Regimental Medal Rolls held at the Public Records Office at Kew than it is to a member of the German Legion whose records have in most cases been lost. Value is also increased by what the Regiment did in the battle, such as in the case of Item I where the recipient's unit was in the thick of it with losses of 246 out of an original 585 men. Moreover, medals awarded to officers such as Item I command a higher price because there were fewer of them and their part in the action is well documented.

A Crimean campaign group of six, awarded to Lieutenant-Colonel Lord George Bingham, Coldstream Guards, Aide-de-Camp to the Earl of Lucan: Silver Coronation medal 1902; Coronation medal 1911; Crimea medal 1854–56, three bars; Legion of Honour Second Empire medal; Order of the Medjidie; Turkish Crimea medal, Sardinian issue.
£2,800–3,200
€/ **$4,400–5,000** ⚔ **DNW**

◀ **A silver Military Service medal,** by J. Ries, Imperial German, 1870 and 1914–18, in original case.
£850–1,000
€/ **$1,300–1,600** ⚔ **Herm**

A pair of medals, awarded to Corporal William Shaw, York & Lancaster Regiment, late 55th Foot: First China War medal, 1842, original suspension; Volunteer Force Long Service Victoria medal.
£650–750
€/ **$1,000–1,200** ⚔ **BAL**

A pair of medals, awarded to Cornet D. Gibson, Royal Scots Greys: Crimea medal 1854–56, two bars, Balaklava, Sebastopol; Turkish Crimea medal, Sardinian issue, fitted with replacement suspension.
£950–1,100
€/ **$1,500–1,700** ⚔ **Gle**

An Indian Mutiny medal, awarded to T. Ledsham, 2nd Dragoon Guards, edge knocks, one bar Lucknow 1857–58.
£320–375
€/ **$500–600** ⚔ **WAL**

MILITARIA

A group of three medals, awarded to Lieutenant-Colonel the Honorable Ranulf Allsopp, Royal Artillery & Honourable Artillery Company: Egypt & Sudan medal, 1882, one bar; Khedive's Star, 1882; Turkey, silver and enamel Order of Medjidjie 4th class breast badge, in a damaged case marked 'Metcalf of London'.
£950–1,100
€ / $1,500–1,700 ⚒ BAL

A group of three medals, awarded to Captain H. M. Birch, British South Africa Police: British South Africa Company medal 1897; British War and Victory medals, with miniatures mounted for wear.
£420–500
€ / $670–790 ⚒ L

A pair of medals, awarded to F. E. Quinton: East and West Africa medal 1892, one bar, Benin 1897; Naval LS and GC medal, Edward VII issue.
£220–250
€ / $350–400 ⚒ WAL

A group of eight medals, awarded to Captain and Group Adjutant T. J. Higgins, City of London Rifle Volunteers, late Coldstream Guards: Queens South Africa medal 1899–1902, six bars; King's South Africa medal 1901–02, two bars; 1914–15 Star; British War and Victory Medals, M.I.D. oak leaf; Army Long Service and Good Conduct, EVIIR; Army Meritorious Service Medal, G.VI.R., first issue; Serbian Cross of Karageorge, second class, with swords, dated 1914–16.
£1,000–1,200
€ / $1,600–1,900 ⚒ DNW

◄ **A pair of medals,** awarded to Lieutenant B. M. Byrne, Conn. Rang.: Africa General Service medal 1902–56, two bars; S. Nigeria, 1902–03.
£950–1,100
€ / $1,500–1,700 ⚒ BAL

The Order of St Stanislav, a gold and enamel decoration with the Stanislav coat-of-arms, Imperial Russian, c1890.
£1,100–1,300
€ / $1,700–2,000 ⊞ SHa

◄ **A group of five medals,** awarded to Private Phillip Williams, Royal Marine Light Infantry: Sierra-Leone 1898–99; 1914 Star; British War and Victory medals; George V Good Service medal.
£600–700
€ / $950–1,100 ⚒ BR

A Queen's South Africa medal, awarded to Supr A. C. Chatfield, R E, with four bars, South Africa 1902, Transvaal, OFS, Cape Colony.
£80–100
€ / $125–160 ⚒ CHTR

A Great War Military Cross and double M.S.M. group of eleven, awarded to Regimental Sergeant-Major William Lawrance, 1st Battalion, The Rifle Brigade: Military Cross, G.V.R.; Queen's South Africa medal 1899–1902, six bars; King's South Africa medal 1901–02, two bars; 1914 Star; British War and Victory medals; Defence medal; Jubilee medal 1935; Army L.S. & G.C., G.V.R., first issue; Meritorious Service medal, G.V.R., first issue; Meritorious Service medal, G.VI.R., third issue.
£3,000–3,500
€ / $4,700–5,500 ⚒ DNW

A group of six medals, awarded to Sergeant-Major G. Jakeman, 25th Sge.Bry, R.G.A.: 1914–15 Star; British War and Victory medals; Distinguished Conduct medal G.V.; Army Long Service and Good Conduct medal; Special Constabulary Long Service Medal.
£950–1,100
€ / $1,500–1,700 ⚒ G(L)

A group of ten medals, mounted as worn to a Warrent Officer, 1st Class, Royal Electrical and Mechanical Engineers: 1939–45 Star; Pacific Star; Defence Medal; War Medal; General Service Medal, one bar Malaya; British Korea; United Nations Korea; Campaign Service Medal, one bar Northern Ireland; 1977 Silver Jubilee; Regular Army Long Service and Good Conduct medal.
£540–600
€ / $850–950 ⊞ Q&C

► **A group of eight medals,** awarded to Staff Sergeant M. Antoniszewski, Polish Army Staff: Poland Cross of Valour, two bars; Monte Cassino Cross; Army Active Service Medal; Great Britain Military Medal, G.VI.R.; 1939–45 Star; Africa Star; Italy Star; Defence Medal.
£1,700–2,000
€ / $2,700–3,200 ↗ DNW

◄ **A group of nine medals,** awarded to Wing Commander T. S. Tull, Royal Air Force: Distinguished Service Order South East Asia; Commander of the British Empire; Order of the British Empire; 1939–45 Star; Burma Star; Defence Medal; 1939–45 War Medal; General Service Medal, with bar; Air Efficiency Award.
£3,250–3,600
€ / $5,100–5,700 ⊞ RMC

Pouches

► **A Victorian Royal Artillery officer's full dress shoulder belt and embroidered pouch,** with ornamental gilt buckle, tip and slide, and pouch mounts, with a velvet-lined foul weather cover.
£550–625
€ / $870–1,000 ↗ WAL

A doeskin bullet pouch, German, c1720, 14in (35.5cm) wide.
£585–650
€ / $920–1,000 ⊞ FAC

► **A British Indian Army Regiment leather pouch and belt,** c1900, 17in (43cm) long.
£80–90
€ / $125–140 ⊞ MDL

Powder Flasks & Horns

> Items in the Militaria section have been arranged in date order within each sub-section.

A powder horn, Spanish, dated 1586, 9in (23cm) long.
£1,300–1,500
€ / $2,000–2,400 ⊞ SEA

► **A musketeer's flask,** the curved wood body with iron mounts including a pierced plate, an iron belt hook to the rear, sprung cut-off and sprung cap to the tapered nozzle, four forged suspension rings, Nuremberg Town mark to top, German, c1630, 11in (28cm) long.
£850–950
€ / $1,300–1,500 ⊞ FAC

A musketeer's powder flask, the leather-covered wooden body with steel edging and scrolling corner mounts, the reverse with belt hook, the sides with suspension rings, the nozzle with spring cut-off, worn, German, 17thC, 8¼in (21cm) high.
£450–525
€ / $700–830 ↗ B(L)

MILITARIA

A flattened horn powder flask, with iron and brass wheel lock and key, minor damage, c1710, 7in (18cm) long.
£150–165
€ / $240–260 ⊞ MDL

An enamelled bronze priming flask, the centre and edge decorated with a raised geometric motif, the tapered baluster spout with sprung pivoting cap, hinged suspension rings and three rings below for tassels, Russian, 17thC, 2in (5cm) diam.
£850–950
€ / $1,300–1,500 ⊞ FAC

A powder horn, made from a stag's antler section, engraved with hook and geometric decoration, fixed spout, one iron hanging ring, ring rusted, Transylvanian, 17thC, 12½in (32cm) long.
£420–500
€ / $670–800 ⚒ WAL

▶ **A wood and leather powder flask,** Indian, c1800, 5in (12.5cm) wide.
£70–80
€ / $110–125 ⊞ ARB

A brass-mounted cowhorn powder flask, probably for Rifle Volunteers, the common brass tip with sprung lever and adjustable nozzle, brass hanging band with suspension loop, concave brass base with suspension loop, original leather charger cover and woven leather-covered suspension cords, late 18thC, 11in (28cm) long.
£350–420
€ / $550–670 ⚒ WAL

A brass and horn rifle powder flask, c1850, 12in (30.5cm) long.
£130–145
€ / $200–230 ⊞ MDL

A polished coconut powder flask, with silver mounts, the side straps with three hanging rings, charger top, c1850, 6in (15cm) long.
£350–400
€ / $550–630 ⊞ MDL

◀ **A gunner's powder flask,** with horn inspection window to each side, paint chipped, Italian, 19thC, 6¾in (17cm) long.
£300–350
€ / $475–550 ⚒ B(Kn)

Sabretaches

▶ **A Victorian Royal Artillery officer's full dress embroidered sabretache,** with a gilt-lace border, in a velvet-lined foul weather cover, some wear.
£475–550
€ / $750–870 ⚒ WAL

An East Lothian Yeomanry leather sabretache, with gilt crown above reversed VR cypher enclosed in a thistle wreath with silvered scrolls, mid-19thC, 10in (25.5cm) wide.
£570–635
€ / $900–1,000 ⊞ MDL

◀ **An 8th (The King's Royal Irish) Hussars officer's full dress leather sabretache,** the cloth-covered face with gold shamrock-pattern train lace enclosing the regimental distinctions, light cavalry crown, motto, 'VR', royal crest over the Harp & Maid battle honour scrolls from Laswarree and Hindoostan to Central India and Afghanistan, with foul weather cover, some damage, c1880.
£950–1,100
€ / $1,500–1,700 ⚒ DNW

Miscellaneous

A Victorian ambrotype of a Royal Horse Artillery mounted officer, wearing full dress with tall busby, his overalls with leather reinforcements.
£150–175
€/ $240–275 🔨 B
An ambrotype is an early type of photograph where the glass negative is backed with black varnish so that it appears as a positive image.

A 65th (2nd York North Riding) Regiment gilt-coloured belt buckle, pre-1881.
£200–240
€/ $320–380 🔨 WAL

A campaign cutlery set, in a glass, within a crocodile skin case, c1890, 4in (10cm) high.
£90–100
€/ $140–160 ⊞ MB

A carved and painted wood bust of a French cavalry officer, possibly an advertising figure, the reverse with pierced suspension lugs, and a metal ring, 19thC, 37¾in (96cm) high.
£2,200–2,500
€/ $3,500–4,000 🔨 FEN

A snare drum, the leather sliders decorated with five-pointed stars, late 19thC, with two sets of sticks and a chamois beater.
£150–180
€/ $240–280 🔨 JDJ

A 2nd Battalion The Irish Guards half shallow drum, post-WWI, 14in (35.5cm) wide.
£225–250
€/ $350–400 ⊞ Q&C

A Victorian Lord Lieutenant's full dress epaulettes, 4in (10cm) long, in a tin.
£450–500
€/ $700–800 ⊞ MDL

A Civil War 34-star flag, American, 1860–62, 53 x 65in (134.5 x 165cm).
£1,500–1,800
€/ $2,400–2,800 🔨 JDJ

A recruitment poster, depicting a Tommy with rifle, WWI, 29 x 19in (73.5 x 48.5cm).
£280–325
€/ $440–515 🔨 WAL

◄ **An Edwardian carved teak table top,** for a Royal Horse Artillery regiment, Indian, 27in (68.5cm) diam.
£350–400
€/ $550–630 ⊞ Q&C

The Potter Collection

The Potter Collection of antique drums, sold by Bosley's of Marlow on 9th June 1999, was amassed over a period of 150 years by George Potter & Co of London and Aldershot. The firm was started in the 1850s by two brothers who were ex-service musicians in the British Army. They supplied musical instruments, including regimental drums, to every regiment and corps in the British Armed Forces, as well as the British Indian Army and most of the Commonwealth forces. Many of the drums included in the sale were of great historical importance, the highlight being a bass drum that was played at the Battle of Waterloo by the Coldstream Guards, which realized £5,000 (€/ $8,000). Also on offer were miniature drums made by apprentices and used as samples by salesmen to show to prospective buyers, and plaques made from the outer wooden casing of drums which had been straightened out and framed to display the heraldry included in the decoration. The Potter Collection drums have now been scattered to the four corners of the globe so a sale such as this can never be repeated. At the time the prices achieved were very reasonable and it is likely that many pieces will have doubled in value by now.   **John Wright**

MILITARIA

Sport
Archery

◀ **A tile,** depicting an archer with bows and arrows, Dutch, 17thC, 5in (12.5cm) square.
£65–80
€/ **$100–125** ⤴ **TMA**

▶ **A walnut sporting crossbow,** with ivory inlay, German, c1750, 27in (68.5cm) long.
£3,600–4,000
€/ **$5,700–6,000** ⊞ **ARB**

A carved fruitwood crossbow, with horn inlay of shells and blossom, the butt end with a coat-of-arms and marked 'Laukol', iron mounts, German, 18thC, 24¼in (61.5cm) long.
£800–950
€/ **$1,300–1,500** ⤴ **Herm**

A 17thC-style steel and wood sporting crossbow, the engraved stock inlaid with pewter wire scrollwork, the butt with an engraved pewter stag and foliage, losses, German, 19thC, 35¾in (91cm) long.
£420–500
€/ **$630–800** ⤴ **B(Kn)**

> For further information on sporting antiques see the full range of Miller's books at **www.millers.uk.com**

An 18ct gold World Championship medal, won at Raglan Castle in 1891.
£200–240
€/ **$315–380** ⤴ **BWL**

Billiards

A copy of the printed rules for billiards, published by Solomon Erwood, London, on a card mount, repairs, framed, c1720, with a letter from the makers, Thurston & Co, dating this set of rules 'to be prior to 1730'.
£800–900
€/ **$1,300–1,400** ⤴ **S(O)**

▶ **A set of nine ivory billiard balls,** early 19thC.
£650–780
€/ **$1,000–1,200** ⤴ **S(O)**

▶ **An oak revolving cue stand,** c1890, 45in (114.5cm) high.
£1,400–1,600
€/ **$2,200–2,500** ⊞ **MSh**

> Items in the Sport section have been arranged in date order within each sub-section.

▶ **A Victorian mahogany revolving cue stand,** the top centred by a finial on a turned and ringed column, with cues and rests.
£800–950
€/ **$1,300–1,500** ⤴ **B(S)**

▶ **A painted walnut firescreen,** entitled 'When my cue comes call me', depicting a gentleman beside a billiards table, early 20thC, 31¼in (80cm) high.
£950–1,100
€/ **$1,500–1,700** ⤴ **S(O)**

SPORT

A walnut, burr-walnut and ebonized billiards table, Swedish, 1850s, 144 x 72in (366 x 183cm).
£27,000–30,000
€/ **$43,000–47,000** ⊞ WBB

A Cox & Yeoman burr-yew billiards table, 1860s, 144 x 72in (366 x 183cm).
£22,000–25,000
€/ **$34,750–38,500** ⊞ WBB

A Gillows mahogany billiards table, 1880s, 144 x 72in (366 x 183cm).
£22,000–25,000
€/ **$34,750–38,500** ⊞ WBB

▶ **An Ashcroft walnut and burr-walnut billiards table,** 1880s, 144 x 72in (366 x 183cm).
£13,000–15,000
€/ **$20,500–24,000** ⊞ WBB

A Burroughs & Watts mahogany billiards table, 1880s, 120 x 60in (305 x 152.5cm).
£4,500–5,000
€/ **$7,000–8,000** ⊞ WBB

A Riley oak billiards table, 1920s, 144 x 72in (366 x 183cm).
£4,000–4,500
€/ **$6,300–7,000** ⊞ WBB

▶ **A beech and brass billiard cue tipper,** c1900, 6½in (16.5cm) long.
£60–65
€/ **$95–100** ⊞ MSh

Bowling

A wooden ball, French, c1900, 7in (18cm) diam.
£30–35
€/ **$50–55** ⊞ TRA

A set of four *lignum vitae* **bowls,** 1920s, 5in (12.5cm) diam.
£65–70
€/ **$95–110** ⊞ MINN

A silver-mounted *lignum vitae* **bowl,** c1923, 5in (12.5cm) diam.
£45–50
€/ **$70–75** ⊞ MINN

Boxing

A colour engraving, after the original painting by Gem Ward, depicting the fight between Tom Sayers and J. C. Heenan, 19thC, 43 x 31in (109 x 78cm), framed.
£650–750
€ / $1,000–1,200 ⚒ B(NW)
This fight took place on 17 April 1860, for the championship of England and America.

A pair of child's leather boxing gloves, 1950s, 7in (18cm) long.
£45–50
€ / $70–75 ⊞ TRA

► A Wood pearlware figure of a pugilist, representing Gentleman Humphreys, restored, c1785, 8in (20.5cm) high.
£3,000–3,500
€ / $4,700–5,500 ⚒ S(O)

A pair of Staffordshire pearlware figures of Tom Cribb and Tom Molineux, 1812–15, taller 8½in (21.5cm) high.
£5,000–6,000
€ / $8,000–9,000 ⚒ S(NY)
Known as the 'Black Diamond' from his occupation as a coal porter, Tom Cribb was the foremost pugilist of his day in England, becoming champion in 1809. His most celebrated matches were fought against Tom Molineux, a freed slave from Virginia.

Jack Johnson, a signed photograph, 'From Champion Jack Johnson to Carl Brooke', c1914, 6 x 4in (15 x 10.5cm).
£1,000–1,200
€ / $1,600–1,900 ⚒ HYD

Cricket

W. G. Grace, a handwritten postcard, dated 29 April 1896.
£180–220
€ / $285–350 ⚒ B(Ch)

A photograph of the Australian cricket team, signed by 15 members, 1930, 14½ x 17in (37 x 43cm).
£350–420
€ / $550–630 ⚒ S(O)

A photograph of the Australian cricket team, signed by every member, 1934, 19¾in (50cm) square.
£850–1,000
€ / $1,300–1,600 ⚒ B(NW)

A Victorian cricket bat, by G. G. Hearne, London, 35in (89cm) long.
£135–150
€ / $215–240 ⊞ MINN

A Victorian cricket bat, by Wisden, 35in (89cm) long.
£135–150
€ / $215–240 ⊞ MINN

► A child's cricket bat, by Sandham & Strudwick, signed by the 1934 England and Australian cricket teams of the Oval Test, the reverse signed by the 1933–34 Chelsea football squad.
£650–780
€ / $1,000–1,200 ⚒ S(O)

◀ **A cricket cap worn by Australia's Ian Chappell,** sold with an invitation and menu to the Anglo-American Sporting Club Dinner, London, signed by Don Bradman, Godfrey Evans, Denis Compton, Alec Bedser and Keith Miller, 1968.
£2,300–2,700
€/ **$3,600–4,200** ⚲ S(O)
This cap was purchased at the after-dinner auction. Sir Donald Bradman was guest of honour on this occasion and it was his last official appearance in England.

W. D. & H. O. Wills, Cricketers 1908, set of 50, 1908.
£90–110
€/ **$140–175** ⚲ VS

A Fletcher & Co cream-ware commemorative mug, one side printed with a view of a cricket match at Lord's, the reverse with a view of the Oatland Stakes at Ascot, c1795, 7in (17.5cm) high.
£5,400–6,500
€/ **$8,500–10,300** ⚲ WW

A pottery dish, with a sepia portrait of Jack Hobbs, c1926, 3½in (9cm) diam.
£55–65
€/ **$85–100** ⚲ SAS
Jack Hobbs played in 61 test matches between 1907–30, and as captain in 1926 he achieved the highest score at Lords of 316 runs. He was knighted in 1953.

◀ **A late Victorian wooden novelty ink stand,** with cricket ball inkwell and stumps pen rest, 5in (12.5cm) diam.
£180–220
€/ **$280–350** ⚲ TMA

▶ **A photographic collage,** of the Canterbury Jubilee cricket match 1891, 17 x 32in (43 x 81.5cm).
£400–450
€/ **$630–700** ⊞ MSh

Equestrian

A pair of leather riding boots, with steel studs, 18thC.
£420–500
€/ **$670–790** ⚲ S(O)

◀ **A pair of leather riding boots,** with trees, 1890s.
£100–110
€/ **$160–175** ⊞ RGa

▶ **A pair of leather field boots,** with trees, c1910.
£130–145
€/ **$200–220** ⊞ SPT

An ivory box, decorated with a horse race, c1890, 9in (23cm) long.
£1,800–2,000
€/ **$2,800–3,200** ⊞ RGa

◀ **A George III silver caddy spoon,** in the shape of a jockey's cap, initialled 'I.RK.', lion passant and duty marks, c1805, 2in (5cm) wide.
£260–315
€/ **$400–480** ⚲ WW

▶ **A silver-mounted horn and wood riding crop,** monogrammed, c1900, 26in (66cm) long.
£72–80
€/ **$110–125** ⊞ RGa

◀ **A silver-mounted riding crop,** c1919, 21in (53.5cm) long.
£55–60
€/ **$90–100**
⊞ GBr

A silver-plated cruet set, by Elkington & Co, in the form of a horseshoe with riding boots, hat and riding crop-shaped spoons, c1890, 4in (10cm) high.
£1,900–2,100
€/ **$3,000–3,300** ⊞ RGa

A silver presentation cup, by Emes & Barnard, inscribed 'Northallerton Races 1835, the Duke of Leeds, the Honble Coll Arden, Stewards', the cover with an equine finial, 1825, 15¼in (39.5cm) high, 82oz.
£3,300–4,000
€/ **$5,200–6,300** ⋌ TEN

A silver trophy, inscribed 'The Pendle Forest Hunt...', London 1934, 10¾in (27.5cm) high, 24oz.
£100–120
€/ **$160–190** ⋌ SWO

An inkwell, the top in the shape of a jockey's cap, the pen rest in the shape of a saddle, late 19thC, 6in (15cm) high.
£850–930
€/ **$1,300–1,500** ⊞ RGA

A cut-glass hunting decanter, by T. J. London, with a silver top and leather case, 1893, 9in (23cm) high.
£130–150
€/ **$200–240** ⋌ FEN

A Neale & Co creamware dish, the centre decorated with a racehorse and the name 'High Flyer' on a ribbon, impressed mark, c1780, 11½in (29cm) wide.
£230–275
€/ **$360–430** ⋌ SAS

▶ **A horseshoe letter clip,** centred with a stirrup, on an oak base, late 19thC, 11in (28cm) wide.
£430–475
€/ **$680–750** ⊞ RGa

A pair of white metal Northampton Race Course member's passes, issued to Earl Spencer, c1830, 22½in (57cm) wide.
£1,200–1,400
€/ **$1,900–2,200** ⊞ TML

A Copeland & Garrett soup plate, transfer-printed with Racehorses pattern from the Field Sports series, 1846–47, 10in (25.5cm) diam.
£170–200
€/ **$270–300** ⊞ DSA

A silver tea-glass holder, repoussé-decorated with two horses' heads, Russian, Moscow, 1908–12, 4½in (11.5cm) high.
£240–280
€/ **$380–440** ⋌ S(O)

A Davies & McDonald tile, American, c1930, 8in (20.5cm) square.
£400–450
€/ **$550–650** ⊞ KMG

Fishing

SPORT

A collection of baits, including Wadhams 'Spangaloid' Clipper and Devon Minnows, with ten different Hardy baits, five Allcock 'Feathoro' Minnows and others, 1910–50, in a glazed wooden case.
£220–250
€ / $350–400 ↗ MUL

▶ **Eldridge Reeves Johnson,** *Tarpomania – The Madness of Fishing,* New York, 1908, 8°, photographic plates, inscribed and signed by the author, full green morocco with white- and gilt-inlaid tarpon, some damage.
£325–375
€ / $500–600 ↗ F&C

A Hardy 10lb trout balance, 1930s, 4in (10cm) long.
£23–25
€ / $35–40 ⊞ OTB

A leather fishing rod case, with brass fittings, 1880s, 69¼in (176cm) long.
£625–685
€ / $980–1,000 ⊞ MSh

Items in the Sport section have been arranged in alphabetical order within each sub-section.

▶ **A French reed creel,** c1900, 26¾in (68cm) wide.
£80–90
€ / $125–140
⊞ MINN

A stuffed and mounted grayling, in a bowfronted case, inscribed 'Grayling, taken by Mr T. Blatchley from the River Costa September 12th 1889, weight 2lbs 6ozs', case 24in (61cm) wide.
£700–850
€ / $1,100–1,300 ↗ AH

A stuffed and mounted dace, by J. Cooper & Sons, in a bowfronted case, inscribed in gilt 'Dace, 11 inches, 10½ozs, caught at Thetford, Sept 28th 1897, by W. Ransom, Lychnobrite Angling Society', case 16in (40.5cm) wide.
£1,800–2,200
€ / $2,800–3,200 ↗ SWO

A stuffed and mounted rudd, by J. Cooper & Sons, in a gilt-lined bowfronted case, inscribed 'Rudd 1lb 5½oz specimen 1906', with a framed copy of the 1906 minutes from the Swindon Golden Carp AA.
£725–875
€/ **$1,100–1,400** ✗ B(W)

A stuffed and mounted perch, by J. Cooper & Sons, in a bowfronted case, 1909, 18in (45.5cm) wide.
£450–500
€/ **$700–800** ⊞ OTB

A stuffed and mounted rainbow trout, by J. Cooper & Sons, in a gilt-lined bowfronted case, c1920, 29¼in (74.5cm) wide.
£850–1,000
€/ **$1,300–1,600** ✗ MUL

A stuffed and mounted pike, by A. J. Ponchard, in a bowfronted case, 1932, 45in (114.5cm) wide.
£850–950
€/ **$1,300–1,500** ⊞ MSh

▶ **A stuffed and mounted brown trout,** inscribed in gilt 'Killed by E. M. Knott, River Sense 30th May 1933, weight 2lb 11oz', case 23in (58.5cm) wide.
£450–530
€/ **$710–830** ✗ L&E

A stuffed and mounted bream, by J. Cooper & Sons, in a bowfronted case, inscribed in black and gilt 'Bream 5lbs caught by R. W. Draper Jnr, 4th Aug 1947', case 24¾in (63cm) wide.
£550–650
€/ **$870–1,000** ✗ SWO

A collection of salmon flies, in a Wheatley aluminium case, 1920s, 6in (15cm) wide.
£70–80
€/ **$110–125** ⊞ MINN

An Allcock & Co priest gaff, 1930s, 14in (35.5cm) long.
£70–80
€/ **$110–125** ⊞ MINN

▶ **A horn-cased angler's knife,** early 20thC, 4¼in (11cm) long.
£400–450
€/ **$630–700**
⊞ OTB

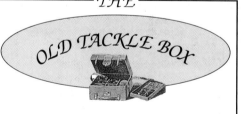

◀ **A fruitwood and brass line drier,** stamped 'Army & Navy Stores, London', c1905, 16in (40.5cm) long.
£130–150
€/ **$200–240**
✗ MUL

SPORT

A chromium-plated car mascot, inscribed 'Fly fishers' club', c1920, 5in (12.5cm) long.
£200–225
€ / **$315–350** L

A painting of a trophy fish, caught on the River Wye, inscribed 'May 6th 1913', on wood, 50½in (128.5cm) wide.
£900–1,000
€ / **$1,400–1,500** ⊞ MINN

An enamelled menu holder, by Goldsmiths & Silversmiths Co, Chester 1905, the centre panel depicting a black bass leaping, 1½in (3.5cm) diam.
£300–350
€ / **$375–550** B(W)

A folding trout net, by Millwards, with a wooden handle, measure and brass fittings, 1920s, 40in (101.5cm) long.
£105–115
€ / **$160–180** ⊞ MINN

A Jones 4in brass fly reel, with leather case, c1880.
£110–120
€ / **$170–190** ⊞ MINN

A Malloch 2¾in Sun and Planet brass and ebonite fly reel, with nickel-silver rims, fixed check, triple pillared cage, rosewood handle, brass handleplate stamped 'Patent', c1880.
£220–250
€ / **$350–400** MUL

A Hardy Hercules 4in Special Pattern Fly Reel, with raised constant check housing to front plate, waisted brass foot pierced twice, quadruple pillared cage and ivorine handle, c1890.
£220–250
€ / **$350–400** MUL

A Prickman Hercules-style 2¼in reel, with constant check, triple pillared cage, horn handle and raised brass winding plate, c1895.
£160–200
€ / **$250–315** MUL

A brass crank wind reel, probably by Reuben Heaton of Birmingham, with fixed check and transluscent amberite handle knob, 1890–1910.
£120–130
€ / **$190–200** ⊞ OTB

A J. Bernard & Son 3½in gunmetal salmon reel, c1900.
£110–120
€ / **$175–190** ⊞ MINN

An Eaton & Deller Hercules-style 2¾in brass salmon fly reel, maker's mark, c1900.
£55–60
€ / **$85–95** ⊞ OTB

A Hardy Perfect 4¼in salmon fly reel, brass rim, 1905 check, Turk's head locking nut, ivory handle and brass foot, in Hardy card box.
£400–475
€ / **$630–750** B(W)

A Hardy Perfect 4in salmon fly reel, c1906.
£675–750
€ / **$1,100–1,200** ⊞ MSh

A Farlow 4¼in Patent lever salmon fly reel, the back plate with half coin-shaped drag control, 1907–15, with original stamped block leather case.
£90–100
€ / **$145–160** ⊞ OTB

An Allcock 3½in Schooling reel, Model No. 1, perforated and brass-flanged ebonite drum, wooden core and single handle with counter balance, engraved, c1915.
£450–500
€ / **$700–800** ⊞ OTB

An Allcock Aerial 3½in centrepin reel, the six spoke drum with ventilated front and ebonite rear flange, drum removal fork and spoke tension, optional brass check button, ivorine handles and brass foot, c1915.
£400–475
€/ **$630–750** ↗ MUL

A Hardy Hardex No. 1 Mk II fixed spool reel, with chromed flier, half bail arm and brass lever spool clutch, 1930s.
£65–75
€/ **$100–110** ↗ MUL

► **A Hardy Jock Scott multiplying bait casting reel,** with line drier, oil bottle and leather-pouched reel spanner, 1938–52, in fitted teak case 6in (15cm) wide.
£720–800
€/ **$1,100–1,200** ⊞ OTB

A Hardy Duck's Foot Altex Mk I fixed spool reel, with 'turned up' body shape, spool clutch, ebonite spool and non-folding handle, stamped 'Patent Applied For', 'Mark 1', c1932.
£325–400
€/ **$500–630** ↗ MUL

◄ **A Hardy Silex 3½in multiplying reel,** first model with smooth brass foot and rim-mounted casting trigger, 1925–26 only.
£800–900
€/ **$1,300–1,400** ⊞ OTB

A Hardy Eureka 4in centrepin trotting reel, with perforated drum, telephone-shaped latch and engraved black-leaded back plate, c1930.
£155–170
€/ **$240–260** ⊞ OTB

► **A Hardy Altex No. 1 Mk II fixed spool reel,** with original leatherette case, c1940, case 6in (15cm) wide.
£80–90
€/ **$125–140** ⊞ OTB

An Eaton & Deller Hardy Uniqua-style 3in trout fly reel, with horseshoe-shaped latch and interior stamped 'D', for Walter Dingley, c1930.
£55–60
€/ **$85–95** ⊞ OTB
Walter Dingley was an ex-Hardy engineer who began his own business and made several reels in the Hardy style.

A set of brass salmon scales, 1930s, 13in (33cm) long.
£23–25
€/ **$35–40** ⊞ MINN

A selection of Hardy and Farlow line greaser and rod ferrule grease tins, 1930s–40s, largest 3in (7.5cm) diam.
£10–12
€/ **$15–18** ⊞ OTB

Football

Five James Hurst Cherry Balsam football cards, 'Play Up Oldham', featuring football players, c1900, 3in (7.5cm) high.
£170–200
€/ $270–320 ✗ BBR

An England v Scotland International cap, worn by Dicky Bond, 1906, with a print of Bond wearing an England shirt and cap.
£1,700–2,000
€/ $2,700–3,200 ✗ S(O)
Richard Bond of Preston North End, and later Bradford City, won a total of eight England caps between 1905–10. This cap was awarded to the outside-right for his appearance in the England v Scotland match at Hampden Park, 7 April 1906. Scotland won 2-1.

A Football Association representative cap, from the tour of Canada, inscribed 'F.A. England, Canada, 1931'.
£630–750
€/ $1,000–1,200 ✗ S(O)

A leather football, signed by the members of the British Isles Amateur Football team, Australia Tour 1937, and the Australian cricket team, including Don Bradman.
£280–320
€/ $440–510 ✗ SWO

A leather football, signed by the Ipswich Town squad, 1936–37 season.
£800–900
€/ $1,300–1,400 ✗ S(O)

◄ **A Scotland v England International woollen jersey,** worn by Jimmy Quinn, 1909.
£950–1,100
€/ $1,500–1,700 ✗ S(O)
Jimmy Quinn of Celtic won a total of 11 Scottish International caps between 1905–12.

A 9ct gold and enamel medal, inscribed 'Liverpool Charity Match, 1913'.
£320–375
€/ $500–600 ✗ S(O)

► **A menu card,** for a dinner relating to the Ireland v England Amateur International match, held at the Imperial Hotel, Dublin, on 15 December 1906, signed by 13 members of the England party.
£900–1,100
€/ $1,400–1,700 ✗ S(O)

A photograph of the Arsenal squad, 1888, 24 x 20in (61 x 51cm), framed.
£220–250
€/ $350–400 ✗ CO

◄ **An Arsenal team photograph,** signed by the team, c1934, 7½ x 9½in (19 x 24cm).
£450–525
€/ $710–830 ✗ S(O)

A trial match programme, between Probables and Improbables to represent Birmingham v London at Witton Road, Aston, 29th October 1877.
£2,300–2,800
€/ $3,600–4,400 ✗ S(O)

A Newcastle United v Bradford City FA Cup Final souvenir programme, contains portraits of the teams, 12 views of London and statistical information, 1911.
£3,900–4,600
€/ $6,200–7,300 ✗ S(O)

A pewter commemorative tankard, for the London F.A. v Frankfurt Inter-Cities Cup match, Wembley, 26 October 1955, with an enamelled badge bearing the crest of the London F.A., with a ruby glass base.
£480–575
€/ $760–910 ✗ S(O)
This tankard was presented to one of the Frankfurt players in the above match. This historic game was the first to be played in the competition that was the forerunner of all European football tournaments. This match was also the first game to be played under floodlights at Wembley Stadium.

A silver pocket watch, inscribed 'Presented by the Labrador Watch Company, to Mr J. Graham, Captain of the Millwall Athletic Football Club Champion Team 1st Division Southern League 1894/5', hallmarked.
£300–350
€/ $475–550 ✗ B(Ch)

A gilt-metal pocket watch, by Polito, the case decorated with a football scene, signed, Swiss, c1910.
£370–450
€/ $580–700 ✗ S(O)

Golf

A gutty ball, hand-hammered, c1860.
£530–630
€/ $840–1,000 ✗ S(O)

◄ **A Bussey automatic caddy golf bag,** c1890, 36in (91.5cm) long.
£1,400–1,600
€/ $2,200–2,600 ⊞ MSh

A silver bowl, inscribed 'Beckenham Golf Club, Captain's Prize 1943, won by Frank Bartlett', maker's mark 'H.H. & S', Birmingham, 6in (15cm) high, 11.5oz.
£85–100
€/ $135–160 ✗ BR

A J. Wilson longnose putter, c1860.
£2,300–2,500
€/ $3,600–3,800 ⊞ MSh

SPORT

A Robert Forgan & Son fruitwood-headed longnose putter, greenheart shaft, stamped, leather grip replaced, minor damage, c1885, mounted on an oak display board with inscription plaque.
£1,400–1,700
€/ $2,200–2,700 ⚘ S(O)

A Sunday golf club, with lead weight and alloy sole insert, c1900.
£230–260
€/ $360–400 ⊞ MSh

A Bradwell aluminium head driver, with gutta percha face, c1900.
£160–180
€/ $250–280 ⊞ MSh

A Slazenger driver, c1910, American, 40in (101.5cm) long.
£65–70
€/ $100–110 ⊞ MINN

An Antishank club, c1910, 38in (96.5cm) long.
£65–70
€/ $100–110 ⊞ MINN

A silver-plated figure of a golfer, by Zwick, c1920, 7in (18cm) high.
£1,200–1,300
€/ $1,900–2,000 ⊞ MSh

A Royal Doulton Kingsware dish, after C. Crombie, c1920, 4½in (11.5cm) diam.
£250–280
€/ $400–440 ⊞ MSh

Charles Crombie, The Rules of Golf Illustrated, red lettering on green cloth boards, c1905, 11¾ x 18¼in (30 x 46cm).
£340–400
€/ $540–630 ⚘ SWO

▶ A silver novelty hatpin stand/ring holder, modelled as a golf club and caddy, Birmingham 1910, 4½in (11.5cm) high.
£325–375
€/ $500–600 ⚘ G(L)

A Doulton Lambeth stoneware tyg and cover, decorated with embossed golfing scenes, with metal rim and cover, c1900, 8in (20.5cm) high.
£3,000–3,600
€/ $4,700–5,700 ⚘ S(O)

Lacrosse

A pair of Victorian leather lacrosse or hockey boots.
£75–85
€/ $120–135 ⊞ SA

A photograph, of the North of England men's lacrosse team, 1928–29, 8 x 11in (20.5 x 28cm).
£60–65
€/ $95–100 ⊞ SA

◀ A wood and leather lacrosse stick, 1920s, 49in (124.5cm) long.
£35–40
€/ $55–65 ⊞ SPT

Olympic Games

◀ **A silvered-bronze and enamel Olympic Games umpire's badge,** London, 1908.
£1,500–1,800
€/ $2,400–2,800 ⚒ S(O)

▶ **A white metal Olympic Games bearer's torch,** from the XIth Olympiad in Berlin, the handle engraved with an eagle, Olympic rings and inscribed with the route from Olympia to Berlin, 1936, 10½in (27cm) high.
£2,000–2,400
€/ $3,200–3,800 ⚒ S(O)
The tradition of the Olympic torch relay was inaugurated at the Berlin Games of 1936. The 3,422 bearers each ran 1km.

An Olympic Games bid book, leather-covered with metal and enamel emblem, with fold-out artists' impressions of proposed stadiums, and signed and sealed letters by the Governor of the State of Victoria and the Lord Mayor of Melbourne, 1956.
£420–500
€/ $670–800 ⚒ B(NW)
This book was presented to the International Olympic Committee as the successful attempt to win the 1956 games for Melbourne.

Shooting

A silver ring casket, embossed with pheasants and gun dogs, late 19thC, 3¾in (9.5cm) wide.
£140–160
€/ $220–250 ⚒ G(L)

A leather and brass cartridge magazine, c1900, 16in (40.5cm) wide.
£340–375
€/ $540–600 ⊞ MINN

A leather cartridge bag, 1920s, 9in (23cm) wide.
£55–60
€/ $85–95 ⊞ MINN

An enamel cigarette case, the hinged case decorated with a shooting scene, Continental, late 19thC, 3½in (9cm) wide.
£370–450
€/ $585–700 ⚒ AH

A Britannia metal gun oil container, by J. Dicksons & Sons, Sheffield, c1840, 3in (7.5cm) diam.
£50–60
€/ $80–90 ⊞ ARB

◀ **A copper and brass sporting powder flask,** by Hawskley, Sheffield, with a variable nozzle, c1850, 8in (20.5cm) long.
£135–150
€/ $220–240 ⊞ ARB

A Staffordshire figure of a hunter and his dog, c1820, 6in (15cm) high.
£765–850
€/ $1,200–1,300 ⊞ JHo

SPORT

A wheel-lock sporting rifle, by Martin Gummi, with swamped octagonal sighted barrel, figured hardwood full stock, iron trigger guard, with original steel-tipped ramrod, German, c1650, barrel 31½in (80cm) long.
£2,600–3,200
€/ **$4,100–5,000** ⚒ S(O)

A rifled flintlock sporting carbine, with sighted barrel signed 'Iohann Friedrich Limmer in Bamberg' and dated 1716, the butt carved with rococo ornaments, brass mounts, original brass-tipped ramrod, Bavarian, c1750, barrel 29¾in (74.5cm) long.
£1,500–1,800
€/ **$2,400–2,800** ⚒ S(O)

An SB 12 bore flintlock sporting gun, by W. Bailes, London, the barrel with London proof marks, plain walnut half stock, the wrist inlaid with silver wire foliage, steel mounts and ramrod, converted from full stock, c1800, 49¾in (126.5cm) long.
£670–800
€/ **$1,100–1,300** ⚒ WAL

A 20 bore flintlock sporting gun, with chequered walnut stock, engraved brass butt-plate and trigger guard, lock stamped 'W.S.', ramrod missing, early 19thC, 54¼in (138cm) long.
£150–180
€/ **$240–280** ⚒ F&C

A Winchester Class B double barrel shotgun, rib marked 'Winchester Repeating Arms Co (Class B) New Haven Conn. USA', the receiver engraved with arabesque pattern, double triggers and extractors, 1879–84, barrel 30in (76cm) long.
£2,600–3,000
€/ **$4,100–4,800** ⚒ JDJ

A Winchester match-grade double barrel shotgun, rib marked 'Winchester Repeating Arms Co (Match Gun) New Haven Conn. USA', the receiver engraved with a game scene, double triggers and extractors, 1879–84, barrel 29¾in (75.5cm) long.
£3,000–3,600
€/ **$4,700–5,600** ⚒ JDJ

The two Winchester shotguns (above and left) are double barrel hammer-type and breech loading, made to order in England by the Winchester Repeating Arms Co. In 1879 Winchester purchased these shotguns from several various makers to test the double-barrel breech loading shotgun market in the US. They did so well that Winchester followed with several more orders, finally designing their own pattern and placing their own name on them. Most of these were made to order by Edmond Redman of Birmingham, with several other makers also being used. These were marked 'Winchester Repeating Arms Co' on the rib and were divided into five classes, the 'Match' gun and 'A', 'B', 'C', 'D', the Match gun being the highest quality. Of approximately 10,000 of these shotguns imported by Winchester, less than 2,000 were made to their specifications and marked with their name. It is estimated that only about three per cent have survived. These shotguns come with extensive documentation and reference material and are exceedingly rare.

A pair of 50 bore percussion target pistols, by Johann Contriner, with signed sighted barrels, figured half stocks and steel mounts, ramrod missing, Austrian, Vienna, c1830, barrels 11¼in (28.5cm) long.
£1,000–1,200
€/ **$1,600–1,900** ⚒ B(Kn)

A Royal Doulton Lambeth stoneware trophy jug, Wimbledon Rifle Contest, inscribed and dated 1860–89, 5¼in (13.5cm) high.
£120–140
€/ **$190–220** ⚒ SAS

A pair of brass and rosewood calibrated powder and shot measures, c1840, 5in (12.5cm) long.
£80–90
€/ **$125–140** ⊞ ARB

▶ **An Edwardian bamboo and brass shooting stick,** 28in (71cm) high.
£115–125
€/ **$180–195** ⊞ MINN

Tennis

A sealed tin of Slazenger patent tennis balls, patent No. 103442, 27 July 1916, 8in (20.5cm) high.
£330–400
€/ **$520–630** ⚒ S(O)

A silver tennis brooch, pin missing, P.O.D.R. mark for 1880, maker's initials 'J.T.', 1¾in (4.5cm) wide.
£300–350
€/ **$475–550** ⚒ S(O)

An oak and brass dinner gong, c1890, 13½in (33cm) high.
£850–950
€/ **$1,300–1,500** ⊞ MSh

The Annals of Tennis, by Julian Marshall, c1878, 10 x 7½in (25.5 x 19cm).
£2,100–2,300
€/ **$3,300–3,600** ⊞ MSh

W. D. & H. O. Wills, Lawn Tennis, set of 25, 1931.
£150–170
€/ **$220–260** ⚒ VS

▶ **A mahogany tennis racket press,** for four rackets, with brass fittings, 1890s, 13in (33cm) wide.
£180–200
€/ **$280–320** ⊞ MSh

A History of Tennis, two volumes by E. B. Noel and J. O. M. Clark, c1924, 11¼ x 8in (28.5 x 20.5cm).
£1,300–1,400
€/ **$2,000–2,200** ⊞ MSh

▶ **A spelter figure of a tennis player,** on a marble base, c1920, 10in (25.5cm) high.
£500–550
€/ **$800–870** ⊞ MSh

A Mark Bailey tennis racket, with double stringing, 1870s.
£2,300–2,500
€/ **$3,600–4,000** ⊞ MSh

A Brouaye Real Tennis racket, with tilted head, coarse gut strings and lop-sided green morocco wedge, stamped, late 19thC.
£700–840
€/ **$1,100–1,300** ⚒ S(O)

▶ **A hazelwood Steamline junior tennis racket,** 1930s.
£580–650
€/ **$920–1,000** ⊞ MSh

A Sparke flat top tennis racket, 1880s.
£400–450
€/ **$630–700** ⊞ MSh

A Slazenger Special Design tennis racket, c1910.
£120–130
€/ **$190–200** ⊞ MSh

Glossary

Below are explanations of some of the terms that you will come across in this book.

agate ware: 18thC pottery, veined or marbled to resemble the mineral agate.

Agatin: Marbled glass intended to resemble agate, created by the use of metallic oxides.

albarello: Pottery vessel used for storing pharmaceutical ingredients.

anchor escapement: Said to have been invented c1670 by Robert Hooke or William Clement. A type of escape mechanism shaped like an anchor, which engages at precise intervals with the toothed escape wheel. The anchor permits the use of a pendulum (either long or short), and gives greater accuracy than was possible with the verge escapement.

aogai: Japanese lacquer technique.

arabesque: Scrolling foliate decoration.

associated: Term used in antiques, in which one part of an item is of the same design but not originally made for it. *See marriage.*

automaton: Any moving toy or decorative object, usually powered by a clockwork mechanism.

bezel: Ring, usually brass, surrounding the dial of a clock, and securing the glass dial cover.

Biedermeier: Style of furniture made principally in the 1820s and 1830s in Austria, Germany and parts of Scandinavia and characterized by simple, heavy Classical forms. It is named after a fictional character who symbolized the German bourgeoisie of the early 19thC.

biggin: Form of coffee percolator invented c1799 by George Biggin.

bijin: Japanese term for a beautiful woman.

bisque: French term for biscuit ware, or unglazed porcelain.

blanc-de-chine: Translucent white Chinese porcelain, unpainted and with a thick glaze, made at kilns in Dehua in the Fujian province from the Song Dynasty and copied in Europe.

blind fret carving: Fretwork either glued to, or carved upon, a solid surface and therefore unable to be seen through.

Bodhisattva: Attendant of Buddha.

boteh: Stylized design of a floral bush found on rugs, similar to a Paisley design.

bracket clock: Originally a 17thC clock which had to be set high up on a bracket because of the length of the weights; now sometimes applied to any mantel or table clock.

Britannia Standard: Higher standard of silver required between 1697 and 1720. Denoted by Britannia and a lion's head in profile on the hallmark.

bureau de dame: Writing desk of delicate appearance and designed for use by ladies. Usually raised above slender cabriole legs and with one or two external drawers.

bureau plat: French writing table with a flat top and drawers in the frieze.

cabaret set: Tea set on a tray for three or more people.

calamander: Hardwood, imported from Sri Lanka (of the same family as ebony), used in the Regency period for making small articles of furniture, as a veneer and for crossbanding.

cameo glass: Two or more layers of coloured glass in which the top layer/s are then cut or etched away to create a multi-coloured design in relief. An ancient technique popular with Art Nouveau glassmakers in the early 20thC.

cartouche: Ornate tablet or shield surrounded by scrollwork and foliage, often bearing an inscription, monogram or coat-of-arms.

cavetto: Quarter-round concave moulding.

celadon: Chinese stonewares with an opaque grey-green glaze, first made in the Song Dynasty and still made today, principally in Korea.

cellaret: Lidded container on legs designed to hold wine. The interior is often divided into sections for individual bottles.

champlevé: Enamelling on copper or bronze, similar to cloisonné, in which a glass paste is applied to the hollowed-out design, fired and ground smooth.

chapter ring: Circular ring on a clock dial on which the hours and minutes are engraved, attached or painted.

character doll: One with a naturalistic face, especially laughing, crying, pouting, etc.

chilong: Chinese mythical dragon-type lizard.

Chinese Imari: Chinese imitations of Japanese blue, red and gold painted Imari wares, made from the early 18thC.

chinoiserie: The fashion, prevailing in the late 18thC, for Chinese-style ornamentation on porcelain, wall-papers, fabrics, furniture and garden architecture.

chuval: Turkic word meaning bag.

cistern tube: Mercury tube fitted into stick barometers, the lower end of which is sealed into a boxwood cistern.

cizhou: Chinese porcelain wares characterized by bold shapes and decoration on a slip-covered body. They were named after the most important centre of production, Cixian (Cizhou), but were also produced in many different places in northern China.

clock garniture: Matching group of clock and vases or candelabra made for the mantel shelf. Often highly ornate.

cloisonné: Enamelling on metal with divisions in the design separated by lines of fine metal wire. A speciality of the Limoges region of France in the Middle Ages, and of Chinese craftsmen to the present day.

coin silver: Silver of the standard used for coinage, ie .925 or sterling.

coromandel: Imported wood from the Coromandel coast of India, of similar blackish appearance to calamander and used from c1780 for banding, and for small pieces of furniture.

countwheel: Wheel with segments cut out of the edge or with pins fitted to one face, which controls the striking of a clock. Also known as a locking plate.

cwpwrdd deuddarn: Welsh variety of the press cupboard with two tiers.

Cymric: Trade-name used by Liberty & Co for a mass-produced range of silverware inspired by Celtic art, introduced in 1899 and often incorporating enamelled pictorial plaques.

deadbeat escapement: Type of anchor escapement, possibly invented by George Graham and used in precision pendulum clocks.

Delft: Dutch tin-glazed earthenwares named after the town of Delft, the principal production centre, from the 16thC onwards. Similar pottery made in England from the late 16thC is also termed 'delft' or 'delftware'.

deutsche Blumen: Naturalistically painted flowers, either single or tied into bunches, used as a popular decorative motif on 18thC pottery and porcelain.

deva: Asian female deity.

diaper: Surface decoration composed of repeated diamonds or squares, often carved in low relief.

dog of Fo: Buddhist guardian lion.

doucai: Decoration on Chinese porcelain using five colours.

écuelle: 17th and 18thC vessel, usually of silver, but sometimes ceramic, for serving soup. Has a shallow, circular bowl, two handles and a domed cover. It often comes complete with a stand.

ensi: Rug used as a tent door by Turkoman tribes.

EPNS: Electroplated nickel silver.

escapement: Means or device which regulates the release of the power of a timepiece to its pendulum or balance.

façon de Venise: Literally 'in the Venetian Style', used to describe high quality, Venetian-influenced glassware made in Europe during the 16th–17thC.

faïence: Tin-glazed earthenwares named after the town of Faenza in Italy, but actually used to describe products made anywhere but Italy, where they are called maiolica.

famille jaune/noire/rose/verte: Chinese porcelain in which yellow, black, pink or green respectively are the predominant ground colours.

fauteuil: French open-armed drawing room chair.

fielded panel: Panel with bevelled or chamfered edges.

filigree: Lacy openwork of silver or gold thread, produced in large quantities since the end of the 19thC.

firing glass: Low drinking glass with a short, thick stem and a thick foot, used on ceremonial occasions when, after toasting, the glass would be hammered on the table to make a sound like gunfire.

flashed: Method of colouring glass that involves applying a thin layer of coloured glass to a vessel, either by painting it or dipping it into a pot of colourant. Flashed glass can also be carved to produce a less expensive version of overlay glass.

flatware (1): Collective name for flat pottery and porcelain, such as plates, dishes and saucers.

flatware (2): Cutlery.

fluted: Border that resembles a scalloped edge, used as a decoration on furniture, glass, silver and porcelain items.

frit: Powdered glass added to fine white clay to make a type of soft-paste porcelain.

fusee: 18thC clockwork invention; a cone-shaped drum, linked to the spring barrel by a length of gut or chain. The shape compensates for the declining strength of the mainspring thus ensuring constant timekeeping.

gabbeh: Word meaning 'unclipped' used to describe thick long piled rugs produced by the tribes of Fars.

gadroon: Border or ornament comprising radiating lobes of either curbed or straight form. Used from the late Elizabethan period.

girandole: Carved and gilt candle sconce incorporating a mirror.

goncalo alves: Brazilian timber sometimes mistaken for rosewood.

gope: Board presented to New Guinea warriors to commemorate an act of bravery.

grisaille: Monochrome decoration, usually grey, used on ceramics and furniture during the 18th and 19thC.

guéridon: Small circular table designed to carry some form of lighting.

guilloche: Pattern of twisting bands, spirals, double spirals or linked chains.

gül: From the Persian word for flower – usually used to describe a geometric flowerhead on a rug.

halberd: Spear fitted with a double axe.

hard paste: True porcelain made of china stone (petuntse) and kaolin; the formula was long known to, and kept secret by, Chinese potters but only discovered in the 1720s at Meissen, Germany, from where it spread to the rest of Europe and the Americas. Recognized by its hard, glossy feel.

herati: Overall repeating design of a flowerhead within a lozenge issuing small leaves. Used in descriptions of rugs.

himatoshi: Japanese term for the two cord holes in a *netsuke*.

hiramakie: Japanese term for sponged gold applied level with the surface.

hirame: Japanese lacquer decorated with gold and silver leaf.

Historismus: Late 19thC revival of medieval decorative themes.

hongmu: Type of wood used in the manufacture of Chinese furniture.

ho-o: Mythical Chinese bird, similar to a phoenix, symbolizing wisdom and energy.

huanghuali: Type of Oriental wood, much admired for its colour.

huqqa (hookah): Oriental pipe for smoking marijuana, tobacco etc, consisting of a container of water or liquid from which smoke is drawn by means of one or more flexible stems. Also known as a hubble-bubble pipe.

Hyalith: Black opaque glass, developed in Czechoslovakia by Count Bucquoy c1807. Became popular c1840, especially with gold decoration. Also made by Friedrich Egermann.

Ibeji: Nigerian cult whereby if a twin died, a wooden figure of it would be commissioned and the mother would feed, clothe and care for it, to look after it and prevent it from taking the surviving twin. If both twins died a pair would be carved.

Imari: Export Japanese porcelain of predominantly red, blue and gold decoration which, although made in Arita, is called Imari after the port from which it was shipped.

indianische Blumen: Indian flowers; painted on porcelain in the Oriental style, especially on mid-18thC Meissen.

inro: Japanese multi-compartmental medicine or seal container, carried suspended from the sash of a kimono.

ironstone: Stoneware, patented 1813 by Charles James Mason, containing ground glassy slag, a by-product of iron smelting, for extra strength.

jadeite: Type of jade, normally the best and most desirable.

Kakiemon: Family of 17thC Japanese porcelain decorators who produced wares decorated with flowers and figures on a white ground in distinctive colours: azure, yellow, turquoise and soft red. Widely imitated in Europe.

kalian cup: Part of a hookah or hubble-bubble pipe.

katana: Long Japanese sword.

kelleh: Long narrow carpets which are wider than runners.

kendi: Chinese or Japanese globular drinking vessel which is filled through the neck, the liquid being drunk through the spout.

kiku mon: Japanese stylized chrysanthemum.

kilin: Chinese mythical beast with a lion's tail, cloven hooves and the scales of a dragon.

kirigane: Decoration of rectilinear cut gold foil particles on Japanese items.

kirin: Japanese mythical beast.

knop: Knob, protuberance or swelling in the stem of a wine glass, of various forms which can be used as an aid to dating and provenance.

koro: Japanese incense burner.

kovsh: Russian vessel used for measuring drink, often highly decorated for ornamental purposes.

kozuka: Small Japanese utility knife.

kraak porselein: Dutch term for porcelain raided from Portuguese ships, used to describe the earliest Chinese export porcelain.

krater: Ancient Greek vessel for mixing water and wine in which the mouth is always the widest part.

kufic: Arabic angular script – used in rugs to refer to stylized geometric calligraphy.

kylix: Ancient Greek shallow two-handled drinking vessel.

latticinio: Fine threads of white or clear glass forming a filigree mesh effect enclosed in clear glass.

leiwen: Chinese pattern known as 'thunder pattern', used as a decorative motif, usually on bronzes.

lingzhi: Type of fungus or mushroom, used as a motif on Chinese works of art.

Lithyalin: Polished opaque glass resembling hardstones, patented by Friedrich Egermann in 1829 at his factory in Haida, northern Bohemia.

loaded: In silverware, a hollow part of a vessel, usually a candlestick, filled with pitch or sand for weight and stability.

lohan: Saintly or worthy Chinese man.

Long Eliza: Elongated female figure found on Kangxi blue and white export porcelain. The name derives from the Dutch 'lange lijsen'.

lunette: Semi-circular decorative motif popular for carved friezes in the Jacobean and Victorian periods.

made up: Piece of furniture that has been put together from parts of other pieces of furniture. See marriage.

maiolica: Tin-glazed earthenware produced in Italy from the 15thC to the present day.

majolica: Heavily-potted, moulded ware covered in transparent glazes in distinctive, often sombre colours, developed by the Minton factory in the mid-19thC.

mandau: Bornean short sword.

marriage: Joining together of two unrelated parts to form one piece of furniture. See associated and made up.

martelé: Term for silverware with a fine, hammered surface, first produced in France and later revived by the American silversmiths Gorham Manufacturing Co during the Art Nouveau period.

meiping: Chinese for cherry blossom, used to describe a tall vase with high shoulders, small neck and narrow mouth, used to display flowering branches.

menuki: Hilt ornaments for Japanese sword mountings.

merese: Flat disc of glass which links the bowl and stem, and sometimes the stem and foot, of a drinking glass.

mihrab: Prayer niche with a pointed arch; the motif which distinguishes a prayer rug from other types.

millefiori: Multi-coloured, or mosaic, glass, made since antiquity by fusing a number of coloured glass rods into a cane, and cutting off thin sections; much used to ornament paperweights.

nashiji: Multitude of gold flakes in Japanese lacquer.

nestoris: Ancient Greek pot noted for its high-reaching and sharply-angled handles.

netsuke: Japanese carved toggles made to secure sagemono (hanging things) to the obi (waist belt) from a cord; usually of ivory, lacquer, silver or wood, from the 16thC.

niello: Black metal alloy or enamel used for filling in engraved designs on silverware.

ojime: Japanese word meaning bead.

okimono: Small, finely carved Japanese ornament.

oklad: Silver or gold icon cover, applied as a tribute or in gratitude for a prayer answered. Also known as a riza or basma.

oni: Chinese devil.

ormolu: Strictly, gilded bronze but used loosely for any yellow metal. Originally used for furniture handles and mounts but, from the 18thC, for inkstands, candlesticks etc.

overlay: In cased glass, the top layer, usually engraved to reveal a different coloured layer beneath.

palmette: In rugs, a cross-section through a stylized flowerhead or fruit.

pardah: Rug which is suspended in a tent doorway.

pâte-de-verre: Translucent glass created by melting and applying powdered glass in layers or by casting it in a mould.

pâte-sur-pâte: 19thC Sèvres porcelain technique, much copied, of applying coloured clay decoration to the body before firing.

penwork: Type of decoration applied to japanned furniture, principally in England in the late 18th/early 19thC. Patterns in white japan were applied to a piece which had already been japanned black, and then the details and shading were added using black Indian ink with a fine quill pen.

pier glass: Mirror designed to be fixed to the pier, or wall, between two tall window openings, often partnered by a matching pier table. Made from the mid-17thC.

pietra dura: Italian term for hardstone, applied to a mosaic pattern of semi-precious stones and marble.

plique-à-jour: Enamelling technique in which a structure of metal strips is laid on a metal background to form enclosed areas which are then filled with transparent enamels. When the backing is removed, a transparent 'stained glass' effect is achieved.

plum pudding: Type of figuring in some veneers, produced by dark oval spots in the wood. Found particularly in mahogany.

pole screen: Small adjustable screen mounted on a pole and designed to stand in front of an open fire to shield a lady's face from the heat.

poudreuse: French dressing table.

powder flask: Device for measuring out a precise quantity of priming powder, suspended from a musketeer's belt or bandolier and often ornately decorated. Sporting flasks are often made of antler and carved with hunting scenes.

powder horn: Cow horn hollowed out, blocked at the wide end with a wooden plug and fitted with a measuring device at the narrow end, used by musketeers for dispensing a precise quantity of priming powder.

prie-dieu: Chair with a low seat and a tall back designed for prayer. Usually dating from the 19thC.

printie: Circular or oval scoop out of glass, sometimes called a lens.

prunt: Blob of glass applied to the stem of a drinking vessel both as decoration and to stop the glass from slipping in the hand.

Puritan spoon: Transitional style of silver spoon, linking early English to modern types. Similar to a slip top but with a broader stem, its name derives from its plain form.

pushti: Rug measuring approximately 3ft x 2ft.

qilin: Alternative spelling of kilin – a Chinese mythical beast.

qin: Type of Japanese harp.

quarter-veneered: Four consecutively cut, and therefore identical, pieces of veneer laid at opposite ends to each other to give a mirrored effect.

register plate: Scale of a barometer against which the mercury level is read.

regulator: Clock of great accuracy, thus sometimes used for controlling or checking other timepieces.

rocaille: Shell and rock motifs found in rococo work.

rotelles: Circular decorative 'studs' at the junction of handles on ancient pots.

rummer: 19thC English low drinking goblet.

ruyi: Chinese presentation sceptre.

sancai: Three-colour decoration on Chinese porcelain.

sang-de-boeuf: (lit. ox-blood) Bright red glaze used extensively on Chinese ceramics during the Qing Dynasty.

S.F.B.J.: Société de Fabrication de Bébés et Jouets; association of doll makers founded 1899 by the merger of Jumeau, Bru and others.

sgraffito: Form of ceramic decoration incised through a coloured slip, revealing the ground beneath.

shakudo: Japanese term for an alloy of copper and gold.

Shibayama: Lacquer applied with semi-precious stones and ivory.

shibuichi: Japanese term for an alloy of copper and silver.

shikoro: Neck guard of a Japanese helmet.

shinto: Japanese sword blades made after c1600.

shishi: Japanese mythical beast, a lion-dog.

shoulder-head: Term for a doll's head and shoulders below the neck.

shoulderplate: Area of a doll's shoulder-head below the neck.

shou symbol: Formal, artistic version of the Chinese character shou, meaning long-life.

siphon tube: U-shaped tube fitted into wheel barometers where the level of mercury in the short arm is used to record air pressure.

soffreh: Persian bread cloth.

soft paste: Artificial porcelain made with the addition of ground glass, bone-ash or soap-stone. Used by most European porcelain manufacturers during the 18thC. Recognized by its soft, soapy feel.

spadroon: Cut-and-thrust sword.

spandrel: Element of design, closing off a corner.

spelter: Zinc treated to look like bronze and much used as an inexpensive substitute in Art Nouveau appliqué ornament and Art Deco figures.

spontoon: Type of halberd often carried by junior infantry officers and senior non-commissioned officers.

strapwork: Repeated carved decoration suggesting plaited straps.

stuff-over: Descriptive of upholstered furniture where the covering extends over the frame of the seat.

stumpwork: Embroidery which incorporates distinctive areas of raised decoration, formed by padding certain areas of the design.

sugán: Twisted lengths of straw: referring to a type of Irish country chair which has a seat of this type.

susani: Central Asian hand-embroidered bridal bed-cover.

sympiesometer: Instrument that uses a gas and coloured oil to record air pressure.

takamakie: Technique used in Japanese lacquerware in which the design is built up and modelled in a mixture of lacquer and charcoal or clay dust, and then often gilded.

tanto: Japanese dagger.

Taotie: Chinese mythical animal which devours wrong-doers.

tassets: Overlapping plates in armour for the groin and thighs.

tazza: Wide but shallow bowl on a stem with a foot; ceramic and metal tazzas were made in antiquity and the form was revived by Venetian glassmakers in the 15thC. Also made in silver from the 16thC.

teapoy: Piece of furniture in the form of a tea caddy on legs, with a hinged lid opening to reveal caddies, mixing bowl and other tea drinking accessories.

tear: Tear-drop shaped air bubble in the stem of an early 18thC wine glass, from which the air-twist evolved.

term: Pillar or pedestal terminating in a carving of a human head or torso, usually armless.

tester: Wooden canopy over a bedstead supported on either two or four posts. It may extend fully over the bed, known as a full tester, or only over the bedhead half, known as a half tester.

tête-à-tête: Tea set for two people.

togidashi: Japanese lacquer technique in which further layers of lacquer are added to *hiramakie*.

thuyawood: Reddish-brown wood with distinctive small 'bird's-eye' markings, imported from Africa and used as a veneer.

timepiece: Clock that does not strike or chime.

tin glaze: Glassy opaque white glaze of tin oxide; re-introduced to Europe in the 14thC by Moorish potters; the characteristic glaze of delftware, faïence and maiolica.

toleware: Items made from tinplated sheet iron which is varnished and then decorated with brightly coloured paints.

torba: Turkmen textile bag.

touch: Maker's mark stamped on much, but not all, early English pewter. Their use was strictly controlled by the Pewterer's Company of London: early examples consist of initials, later ones are more elaborate and pictorial, sometimes including the maker's address.

trumeau: Section of wall between two openings; a pier mirror.

tsuba: Guard of a Japanese sword, usually consisting of an ornamented plate.

Tudric: Range of Celtic-inspired Art Nouveau pewter of high quality, designed for mass-production by Archibald Knox and others, and retailed through Liberty & Co.

tulipwood: Yellow-brown wood with reddish stripe, imported from Central and South America and used as a veneer and for inlay and crossbanding.

tyg: Mug with three or more handles.

verge escapement: Oldest form of escapement, found on clocks as early as 1300 and still in use in 1900. Consisting of a bar (the verge) with two flag-shaped pallets that rock in and out of the teeth of the crown or escape wheel to regulate the movement.

vernier scale: Short scale added to the traditional 3in (7.5cm) scale on stick barometers to give more precise readings than had previously been possible.

verre églomisé: Painting on glass. Often the reverse side of the glass is covered in gold or silver leaf through which a pattern is engraved and then painted black.

vesta case: Ornate flat case of silver or other metal for carrying vestas, an early form of match. Used from the mid-19thC.

vetro a fili: Type of glass decorated with threads.

vetro a retorti: Type of glass decorated with twisted threads bedded into the main body.

vitrine: French display cabinet which is often of bombé or serpentine outline and ornately decorated with marquetry and ormolu.

Vitruvian scroll: Repeated border ornament of scrolls that resemble waves.

wagireh: Knotted sampler used by rug weavers showing part of the field design and a section of the border and guard stripe.

wakizashi: Japanese sword shorter than a *katana*.

WMF: Short for Württembergische Metallwarenfabrik, a German foundry that was one of the principal producers of Art Nouveau metalware.

wucai: Type of five-colour Chinese porcelain decoration.

yen yen: Chinese term for a long-necked vase with a trumpet mouth.

Directory of Specialists

If you wish to be included in next year's directory, or if you have a change of address or telephone number, please contact Miller's Advertising Department by April 2004. We advise readers to make contact by telephone before visiting a dealer, therefore avoiding a wasted journey.

20TH CENTURY
Kent
20th Century Marks, 12 Market Square, Westerham TN16 1AW Tel: 01959 562221 Mobile: 07831 778992 lambarda@btconnect.com www.20thcenturymarks.co.uk
20thC furniture and design.

Nottinghamshire
Luna, 23 George Street, Nottingham NG1 3BH Tel: 0115 924 3267 info@luna-online.co.uk www.luna-online.co.uk
20thC objects for the home. Open Mon–Sat 10–5.30pm. Stock includes lighting, furniture, ceramics, glass, telephones, etc.

AMERICANA
USA
American West Indies Trading Co Antiques & Art, 27315 Barbuda Lane, Summerland Key, Florida 33042 Tel: 305 872 3948 awindies@att.net www.goantiques.com/members/a windiestrading
Ethnographic, Folk, Tribal, Spanish Colonial, Santos & Retablos, American Indian, Indonesian Keris, southeast Asian antiquities, orientalia, Art Deco, Floridiana.

ANTIQUE DEALERS ASSOCIATION
Oxfordshire
T.V.A.D.A., The Old College, Queen Street, Dorchester-on-Thames OX10 7HL Tel: 01865 341639 antiques@tvada.co.uk www.tvada.co.uk

Republic of Ireland
Irish Antique Dealers Association, Main Street, Adare, Co Limerick Tel: 00 353 61 396 409

ANTIQUITIES
Dorset
Ancient & Gothic, PO Box 5390, Bournemouth BH7 6XR Tel: 01202 431721
Antiquities from before 300,000 BC to about 1500 AD

USA
Hurst Gallery, 53 Mt Auburn Street, Cambridge MA 02138 Tel: 617 491 6888 manager@hurstgallery.com www.hurstgallery.com
Art of the Pacific, Africa, Asia, the Americas and the ancient world.

ARCHITECTURAL ANTIQUES
Cheshire
Nostalgia, Hollands Mill, 61 Shaw Heath, Stockport SK3 8BH Tel: 0161 477 7706 www.nostalgia-uk.com

Gloucestershire
Minchinhampton Architectural Salvage Company, Cirencester Road, Chalford, Stroud GL6 8PE Tel: 01285 760886 masco@catbrain.com www.catbrain.com
Architectural antiques, garden statuary, bespoke chimney pieces and traditional flooring. MASCo specializes in large architectural features and garden ornaments. The company also carries extensive stocks of hard and soft wood flooring as well as reclaimed building materials. Call or email for further details. Subscribers to the SALVO code. We also offer a Garden Design service.

Kent
Catchpole & Rye, Saracens Dairy, Jobbs Lane, Pluckley, Ashford TN27 0SA Tel: 01233 840840 info@crye.co.uk www.crye.co.uk

Surrey
Drummonds Architectural Antiques Ltd, The Kirkpatrick Buildings, 25 London Road (A3), Hindhead GU26 6AB Tel: 01428 609444 www.drummonds-arch.co.uk
Open 7 days.

ARMS & MILITARIA
Cheshire
Armourer – The Militaria Magazine, Published by Beaumont Publishing Ltd, 1st Floor Adelphi Mill, Bollington SK10 5JB Tel: 01625 575700 editor@armourer.co.uk www.armourer.co.uk
A bi-monthly magazine for military antique collectors and military history enthusiasts offering hundreds of contacts for buying and selling, articles on all aspects of militaria collecting plus the dates of UK militaria fairs and auctions. Available on subscription.

Gloucestershire
Q & C Militaria, 22 Suffolk Road, Cheltenham GL50 2AQ Tel: 01242 519815 Mobile: 07778 613977 qcmilitaria@btconnect.com www.qcmilitaria.com

Kent
Sporting Antiques, 10 Union Square, The Pantiles, Tunbridge Wells TN4 8HE Tel: 01892 522661
Specialist dealers in antique arms, armour, pistols – sporting and military inclusive of all accessories and tools. Books and prints. We buy and sell.

Lincolnshire
Garth Vincent, The Old Manor House, Allington, Nr Grantham NG32 2DH Tel: 01400 281358 garthvincent@aol.com www.guns.uk.com

Surrey
Alan Cook, Walton on Thames Tel: 01932 228328 Mobile: 07785 252120 antiquearms@btinternet.com www.antiquearms.co.uk
Callers by appointment.

West Street Antiques, 63 West Street, Dorking RH4 1BS Tel: 01306 883487 weststant@aol.com www.antiquearmsandarmour.com

East Sussex
Wallis & Wallis, West Street Auction Galleries, Lewes BN7 2NJ Tel: 01273 480208 auctions@wallisandwallis.co.uk www.wallisandwallis.co.uk
Auctioneers of militaria, arms and armour and medals.

Warwickshire
London Antique Arms Fairs Ltd, 15 Burbury Court, Emscote Road, Warwick CV34 5LD Tel: 01432 355416 & 01926 883665 Mobile: 07801 943983 www.antiquearmsfairsltd.co.uk

USA
Fagan Arms, Inc, Box 425, Fraser MI48026 Tel: 586 465 4637 info@faganarms.com www.faganarms.com

BAROGRAPHS
Somerset
Richard Twort Tel: 01934 641900 Mobile: 07711 939789

BAROMETERS
Berkshire
Alan Walker, Halfway Manor, Halfway, Nr Newbury RG20 8NR Tel: 01488 657670 Mobile: 07770 728397 www.alanwalker-barometers.com

Somerset
Knole Barometers, Bingham House, West Street, Somerton TA11 7PS Tel: 01458 241015 Mobile: 07785 364567 dccops@btconnect.com

Warwickshire
Summersons, 172 Emscote Road, Warwick CV34 5QN Tel: 01926 400630 clocks@summersons.com www.summersons.com
We offer a complete restoration service for antique clocks and barometers. We also undertake the following: Dial restoration, cabinetwork and French polishing, wheel cutting, one-off parts made, clock hands cut, fretwork, silvering/gilding, polishing/ lacquering, restoration parts and materials, insurance valuations, free estimates and advice. WANTED: Clocks and barometers purchased in any condition.

West Yorkshire
Weather House Antiques, Kym S. Walker, Foster Clough, Hebden Bridge HX7 5QZ Tel: 01422 882808/886961 Mobile: 07889 750711 kymwalker@btinternet.com

Wiltshire
P. A. Oxley Antique Clocks & Barometers, The Old Rectory, Cherhill, Calne SN11 8UX Tel: 01249 816227 info@paoxley.com www.british-antiqueclocks.com

USA
Medford Clock & Barometer, 3 Union Street, Medford, New Jersey 08055 Medlock@aol.com

BEDS
Wales
Seventh Heaven, Chirk Mill, Chirk, Wrexham, County Borough LL14 5BU Tel: 01691 777622/773563 requests@seventh-heaven.co.uk www.seventh-heaven.co.uk

Worcestershire
S. W. Antiques, Newlands (road), Pershore WR10 1BP Tel: 01386 555580 sw-antiques@talk21.com www.sw-antiques.co.uk

BOOKS
London
Biblion, Grays Antique Market, 1–7 Davies Mews W1K 5AB Tel: 020 7629 1374 info@biblion.com www.biblion.com www.biblionmayfair.com
Antiquarian books, maps and prints.

Middlesex
John Ives, 5 Normanhurst Drive, Twickenham TW1 1NA Tel: 020 8892 6265 jives@btconnect.com
Reference books on antiques and collecting.

Surrey
David Aldous-Cook, PO Box 413, Sutton SM3 8SZ Tel: 020 8642 4842 aldous-cook@statacom.net
Reference books on antiques and collectables.

Wiltshire
Dominic Winter Book Auctions, The Old School, Maxwell Street, Swindon SN1 5DR Tel: 01793 611340 info@dominicwinter.co.uk www.dominicwinter.co.uk

BOXES & TREEN
Berkshire
Mostly Boxes, 93 High Street, Eton, Windsor SL4 6AF Tel: 01753 858470
Open Mon–Sat 10am–6.30pm.

London
Hampton Antiques, The Crown Arcade, 119 Portobello Road W11 2DY Tel: 01604 863979 Mobile: 07779 654879 info@hamptonantiques.co.uk www.hamptonantiques.co.uk

Gerald Mathias, Antiquarius, 135–142 Kings Road, Chelsea SW3 4PW Tel: 020 7351 0484 fineantiqueboxes@geraldmathias.com www.geraldmathias.com

Somerset
Alan & Kathy Stacey Appointment only Tel: 01963 441333 Mobile: 07810 058078 info@antiqueboxes.uk.com www.antiqueboxes.uk.com
Tea caddies and fine boxes. Specialist dealers in tortoiseshell, ivory, mop, shagreen, exotic timber pieces. Professional conservation services, consultancy, valuations. Members of LAPADA and BAFRA. Each piece comes with 100% guarantee of quality and authenticity.

BRITISH ANTIQUE FURNITURE RESTORERS' ASSOCIATION
BAFRA Head Office, The Old Rectory, Warmwell, Dorchester DT2 8HQ Tel: 01305 854822 headoffice@bafra.org.uk www.bafra.org.uk

Bedfordshire
Duncan Michael Everitt, DME Restorations Ltd, 11 Church Street, Ampthill MK45 2PL Tel: 01525 405819 duncan@dmerestorations.com www.dmerestorations.com
A full restoration service of antique furniture.

Berkshire
Ben Norris & Co., Knowl Hill Farm, Knowl Hill, Kingsclere, Newbury RG20 4NY Tel: 01635 297950
Gilding, carving and architectural woodwork. Antique furniture restorer.

Cambridgeshire
Ludovic Potts, Unit 1 & 1A, Haddenham Business Park, Station Road, Ely CB6 3XD Tel: 01353 741537 mail@restorers.co.uk www.restorers.co.uk
Traditional repairs, boulle, walnut, oak, veneering, upholstery, cane, rush and gilding.

Derbyshire
Anthony Allen, The Old Wharf Workshop, Redmoor Lane, New Mills, High Peak SK22 3JL Tel: 01663 745274
Conservation and restoration of furniture, clocks and artifacts.

Devon
Tony Vernon, 15 Follett Road,
Topsham, Exeter EX3 0JP
Tel: 01392 874635
tonyvernon@antiquewood.co.uk
www.antiquewood.co.uk
*All aspects of conservation and
restoration including gilding,
carving, upholstery, veneering
and polishing. Accredited member
of BAFRA.*

Dorset
Michael Barrington, The Old
Rectory, Warmwell, Dorchester
DT2 8HQ Tel: 01305 852104
headoffice@bafra.org.uk
*The conservation and restoration
of antique and fine furniture and
clocks. Clock dials and movements,
barometers, upholstery, mechanical
music, automata and toys, antique
metalwork ferrous and non-ferrous.*

Essex
Clive Beardall, 104B High Street,
Maldon CM9 5ET Tel: 01621
857890 www.clivebeardall.co.uk
*Open Mon–Fri 8am–5.30pm,
Sat 9am–3pm.*

Brian Harris, 24 Town Street,
Thaxted CM6 2LA
Tel: 01371 832832

Gloucestershire
Alan Hessel, The Old Town
Workshop, St George's Close,
Moreton-in-Marsh GL56 0LP
Tel: 01608 650026
*Our skilled craftsmen have
restored fine furniture since 1976.
We accept commissions from
galleries and private collections.
Our specialism is from the late
17thC to early 19thC furniture.*

Hampshire
David C. E. Lewry, Wychelms, 66
Gorran Avenue, Rowner, Gosport
PO13 0NF Tel: 01329 286901
Furniture. Consultancy only.

Tankerdale Limited, Johnson's
Barns, Waterworks Road, Sheet,
Petersfield GU32 2BY Tel: 01730
233792 mail@tankerdale.co.uk
www.tankerdale.co.uk
*We offer a comprehensive
restoration and conservation
service for furniture and historic
woodwork, including carving,
gilding, marquetry, polishing,
lacquer and decorated surfaces.
Accredited by BAFRA and UKIC,
advisors to the National Trust.*

Hertfordshire
John B. Carr, Charles Perry
Restorations Ltd, Praewood Farm,
Hemel Hempstead Road, St Albans
AL3 6AA Tel: 01727 853487
cperry@praewood.freeserve.co.uk
*Specialists in restoration and
conservation of all types of
antique furniture.*

Kent
Timothy Akers, The Forge,
39 Chancery Lane, Beckenham
BR3 6NR Tel: 020 8650 9179
www.akersofantiques.com
*Longcase and bracket clocks,
cabinet-making, French polishing.*

Benedict Clegg, Rear of 20
Camden Road, Tunbridge Wells
TN1 2PT Tel: 01892 548095
All aspects of 17th–19thC furniture.

Bruce Luckhurst, Little Surrenden
Workshops, Ashford Road,
Bethersden, Ashford TN26 3BG
Tel: 01233 820589
restoration@woodwise.newnet.co.uk
www.bruceluckhurst.co.uk
*1 Year Course available, also
weekend and 5 day courses.*

Lancashire
Eric Smith Antique Restorations,
The Old Church, Park Road, Darwen
BB3 2LD Tel: 01254 776222

eric.smith@restorations.ndo.co.uk
www.ericsmithrestorations.co.uk
*Accredited member of the British
Antique Furniture Restorers
Association. Consultant to Galway
Claire Castle Galway Ireland.
Workshop is included on the
Conservation register maintained
by the United Kingdom Institute
for Conservation in London.*

Lincolnshire
Michael Czajkowski BSc,
E. Czajkowski & Son,
96 Tor O Moor Road, Woodhall
Spa LN10 6SB Tel: 01526 352895
michael.czajkowski@ntlworld.com
*Conservation and restoration of
antique furniture, clocks (dials,
movements and cases) and
barometers. Skills include: marquetry
Buhle and inlaywork; carving and
gilding; lacquerwork, re-upholstery
and upholstery conservation;
clockwork and associated
metalwork. Regular collection
service to the East Midlands and
London. Member of BAFRA and
Accredited Member United
Kingdom Institute of Conservation.*

London
Oliver Clarke Heritage
Restorations, 96 Webber Street
SE1 0QN Tel: 020 7928 3624
18th & 19thC furniture specialist.

Rodrigo Titian, Titian Studio,
32 Warple Way, Acton W3 0DJ
Tel: 020 8222 6600
enquiries@titianstudios.co.uk
www.titianstudios.co.uk
*Carving, gilding, lacquer, painted
furniture and French polishing.
Caning and rushing.*

Norfolk
Michael Dolling, Church Farm
Barns, Glandford, Holt NR25 7JR
Tel: 01263 741115 *Also at: 44
White Hart Street, East Harling
NR16 2NE. Tel: 01953 718658.*
*Restoration of antique and fine
furniture including marquetry,
carving, gilding, upholstery
and caning.*

Roderick Nigel Larwood, The Oaks,
Station Road, Larling, Norwich
NR16 2QS Tel: 01953 717937
rodlar@tinyworld.co.uk
*Restorers of fine antiques and
traditional finishers.*

Scotland
William Trist, 135 St Leonard's
Street, Edinburgh EH8 9RB
Tel: 0131 667 7775
*BAFRA. Registered with the
Museum and Galleries commission
and Historic Scotland. Restoration
and Conservation of antique
furniture. Cabinet making, desk
leathers, architectural mouldings,
French polishing, cane and rush
seating, traditional upholstery,
chairmaking, materials and fittings.
Shop with 18th and 19thC furniture.*

Shropshire
Richard Higgins Conservation,
The Old School, Longnor,
Nr Shrewsbury SY5 7PP
Tel: 01743 718162
*All fine furniture, clocks,
movements, dials and cases,
casting, plating, boulle, ivory,
tortoiseshell, gilding, lacquerwork,
carving, period upholstery.*

Somerset
Stuart Bradbury,
M. & S. Bradbury, The Barn,
Hanham Lane, Paulton, Bristol
BS39 7PF Tel: 01761 418910
enquiries@mandsbradbury.co.uk
*Antique furniture conservation
and restoration.*

Alan & Kathy Stacey Appointment
only Tel: 01963 441333
Mobile: 07810 058078

info@antiqueboxes.uk.com
www.antiqueboxes.uk.com
*Tea caddies and fine boxes.
Specialist dealers in tortoiseshell,
ivory, mop, shagreen, exotic
timber pieces. Professional
conservation services, consultancy,
valuations. Members of LAPADA
and BAFRA. Each piece comes
with 100% guarantee of quality
and authenticity.*

North Somerset
Robert P. Tandy, Lake House Barn,
Lake Farm, Colehouse lane,
Kenn, Clevedon BS21 6TQ
Tel: 01275 875014
robertptandy@hotmail.com
*Traditional antique furniture
restoration and repairs.*

Staffordshire
Stefan Herberholz, Middleton
Hall, Middleton B78 2AE
Tel: 01827 282858

Surrey
Hedgecoe & Freeland Antique
Furniture Restoration & Upholstery,
21 Burrow Hill Green, Chobham,
Woking GU24 8QP
Tel: 01276 858206/07771 953870
hedgecoefreeland@aol.com

Timothy Naylor, 24 Bridge Road,
Chertsey KT16 8JN
Tel: 01932 567129
timothy.naylor@talk21.com

West Sussex
Simon Paterson, Whitelands,
West Dean, Chichester PO18 0RL
Tel: 01243 811900
sp@hotglue.fsnet.co.uk
*Boullework, marquetry, clock case
and general restoration and repair.*

Albert Plumb, Albert Plumb
Furniture Co., Briarfield, Itchenor
Green, Chichester PO20 7DA
Tel: 01243 513700
Cabinet making and upholstery.

West Midlands
Phillip Slater, 93 Hewell Road,
Barnt Green, Birmingham B45 8NL
Tel: 0121 445 4942
Inlaywork and marquetry.

Wiltshire
William Cook, High Trees House,
Savernake Forest, Nr Marlborough
SN8 4NE Tel: 01672 512561
wcook_uk@yahoo.com

Worcestershire
Jeffrey Hall, Malvern Studios,
56 Cowleigh Road, Malvern
WR14 1QD Tel: 01684 574913

CAMERAS
Lincolnshire
Antique Photographic Co Ltd Tel:
01949 842192 alpaco47@aol.com

CERAMICS
Surrey
Julian Eade Tel: 01491 575059
Mobile: 07973 542971
*Doulton Lambeth stoneware and
Burslem wares. Royal Worcester,
Minton and Derby.*

CLOCKS
Cheshire
Coppelia Antiques, Holford Lodge,
Plumley Moor Road, Plumley
WA16 9RS Tel: 01565 722197
www.coppeliaantiques.co.uk
Open 7 days by appointment.

G. K. Hadfield, Beck Bank,
Great Salkeld, Penrith CA11 9LN
Tel: 01768 870111
gkhadfield@dial.pipex.com
www.gkhadfield-tilly.co.uk

Devon
Carnegie Paintings & Clocks, 15
Fore Street, Yealmpton, Plymouth
Pl8 2JN Tel: 01752 881170
www.paintingsandclocks.com

Musgrave Bickford Antiques,
15 East Street, Crediton EX17 3AT
Tel: 01363 775042

DIRECTORY OF SPECIALISTS

Essex
Bellhouse Antiques, Chelmsford
Tel: 01268 710415
Bellhouse.Antiques@virgin.net

It's About Time, 863 London
Road, Westcliff-on-Sea SS0 9SZ
Tel: 01702 472574
sales@antiqueclock.co.uk
www.antiqueclock.co.uk

Gloucestershire
Jeffrey Formby, The Gallery,
Orchard Cottage, East Street,
Moreton-in-Marsh GL56 0LQ
Tel: 01608 650558
www.formby-clocks.co.uk
Visitors by appointment.

The Grandfather Clock Shop,
Styles of Stow, The Little House,
Sheep Street, Stow-on-the-Wold
GL54 1JS Tel: 01451 830455
info@stylesofstow.co.uk
www.stylesofstow.co.uk
*Open all day Mon–Sat or
by appointment.*

Greater Manchester
Northern Clocks, Boothsbank
Farm, Worsley, Manchester
M28 1LL Tel: 0161 790 8414
Mobile: 07970 820258
info@northernclocks.co.uk
www.northernclocks.co.uk
*Open Thurs, Fri and Sat
10am–5pm or by appointment.*

Hampshire
Bryan Clisby Antique Clocks at
Andwells Antiques, High Street,
Hartley Wintney RG27 8NY
Tel: 01252 716436 or 842305
www.bryanclisby-antiqueclocks.co.uk

The Clock-Work-Shop
(Winchester), 6A Parchment Street,
Winchester SO23 8AT Tel: 01962
842331 Mobile: 07973 736155
www.clock-work-shop.co.uk

Kent
Campbell & Archard Ltd, Lychgate
House, Church Street, Seal
TN15 0AR Tel: 01732 761153
campbellarchard@btclick.com
www.campbellandarchard.co.uk
Open by appointment.

Gaby Gunst, 140 High Street,
Tenterden TN30 6HT
Tel: 01580 765818
Closed Sun.

The Old Clock Shop, 63 High
Street, West Malling ME19 6NA
Tel: 01732 843246
theoldclockshop@tesco.net
www.theoldclockshop.co.uk
Open Mon–Sat 9am–5pm.

Derek Roberts, 25 Shipbourne
Road, Tonbridge TN10 3DN Tel:
01732 358986 drclocks@clara.net
www.qualityantiqueclocks.com

London
The Clock Clinic Ltd, 85 Lower
Richmond Road, Putney
SW15 1EU Tel: 020 8788 1407
clockclinic@btconnect.com
www.clockclinic.com
*Open Tues–Fri 9am–6pm, Sat
9am–1pm. Closed Mon.*

Gavin Douglas Fine Antiques Ltd,
75 Portobello Road W11 2QB
Tel: 01825 723441/0207 221 1121
Mobile: 07860 680521
gavin@antique-clocks.co.uk
www.antique-clocks.co.uk

Pendulum, King House,
51 Maddox Street W1R 9LA
Tel: 020 7629 6606
www.pendulumofmayfair.co.uk

Roderick Antique Clocks,
23 Vicarage Gate W8 4AA
Tel: 020 7937 8517
rick@roderickantiqueclocks.com
www.roderickantiqueclocks.com

W. F. Turk, 355 Kingston Road,
Wimbledon Chase SW20 8JX

Tel: 020 8543 3231
www.wfturk.com

Oxfordshire
Craig Barfoot Antique Clocks,
Tudor House, East Hagbourne
OX11 9LR Tel: 01235 818968
Mobile: 07710 858158
craig.barfoot@tiscali.co.uk

Scotland
John Mann Antique Clocks, The
Clock Showroom, Canonbie,
Near Carlisle, Galloway DG14 OSY
Tel: 01873 71337/71827
Mobile: 07850 606 147
jmannclock@aol.com
www.johnmannantiqueclocks.co.uk

Somerset
Kembery Antique Clocks Ltd,
Bartlett Street Antiques Centre, 5
Bartlett Street, Bath BA1 2QZ Tel:
0117 956 5281 Mobile: 07850
623237 kembery@kdclocks.co.uk
www.kdclocks.co.uk

Staffordshire
The Essence of Time, Antique
Clocks, Unit 2, Curborough
Antiques & Craft Centre, Watery
Lane, (off Eastern Bypass), Lichfield
WS13 8ES Tel: 01543 418239
Mobile: 07944 245064
*Open Wed, Thurs, Fri, Sat and Sun
10.30am–5pm. Closed Mon–Tues.*

Surrey
Antique Clocks by Patrick Thomas,
62a West Street, Dorking RH4 1BS
Tel: 01306 743661
clockman@fsmail.net
www.antiqueclockshop.com

The Clock House, 75 Pound Street,
Carshalton SM5 3PG Tel: 020 8773
4844 Mobile: 07850 363 317
markcocklin@theclockhouse.co.uk
www.theclockhouse.co.uk
*Open Tues–Fri 9.30am–4.30pm,
Sat 9am–6pm or by appointment.*

The Clock Shop, 64 Church Street,
Weybridge KT13 8DL Tel: 01932
840407/855503
*Open Mon–Sat 10am–6pm.
Closed Wed.*

Horological Workshops,
204 Worplesdon Road, Guildford
GU2 9UY Tel: 01483 576496
enquiries@horologicalworkshops.com
www.HorologicalWorkshops.com

East Sussex
Sam Orr Antique Clocks, 34–36
High Street, Hurstpierpoint,
Nr Brighton BN6 9RG Tel: 01273
832081 Mobile: 07860 230888
clocks@samorr.co.uk
www.samorr.co.uk

Warwickshire
Summersons, 172 Emscote Road,
Warwick CV34 5QN Tel: 01926
400630 clocks@summersons.com
www.summersons.com
*We offer a complete restoration
service for antique clocks and
barometers. We also undertake
the following: Dial restoration,
cabinetwork & French polishing,
wheel cutting, one-off parts made,
clock hands cut, fretwork, silvering/
gilding, polishing/lacquering,
restoration parts and materials,
insurance valuations, free
estimates and advice. WANTED:
Clocks and barometers purchased
in any condition.*

West Midlands
Woodward Antique Clocks,
14 High Street, Tettenhall,
Wolverhampton WV6 8QT
Tel: 01902 745608

Wiltshire
P. A. Oxley Antique Clocks &
Barometers, The Old Rectory,
Cherhill, Calne SN11 8UX Tel:
01249 816227 info@paoxley.com
www.british-antiqueclocks.com

*Open Mon–Sat 9.30am–5pm.
Closed Wed or by appointment.*

Allan Smith Clocks, Amity
Cottage, 162 Beechcroft Road,
Upper Stratton, Swindon
SN2 7QE Tel: 01793 822977
Mobile: 07778 834342
allansmithclocks@lineone.net
www.allansmithantiqueclocks.co.uk

Yorkshire
Brian Loomes, Calf Haugh Farm,
Pateley Bridge HG3 5HW
Tel: 01423 711163
www.brianloomes.com
Established 37 years.

Time & Motion, 1 Beckside,
Beverley HU17 0PB
Tel: 01482 881574

Republic of Ireland
Jonathan Beech, Westport,
Co Mayo Tel: 00 353 98 28688
www.antiqueclocks-ireland.com
*Member of the Irish Antique
Dealers' Association.*

USA
Medford Clock & Barometer,
3 Union Street, Medford, New
Jersey 08055 Medlock@aol.com

R. O. Schmitt Fine Art, Box 1941,
Salem, New Hampshire 03079
Tel: 603 893 5915
bob@roschmittfinearts.com
www.antiqueclockauction.com
Specialist antique clock auctions.

Setniks In Time Again, 815 Sutter
Street, Suite 2, Folsom, California
95630 Tel: 916 985 2390 Toll Free
888 333 1715 setniks@pacbell.net
setniksintimeagain.com

COMICS
London
Comic Book Postal Auctions Ltd,
40–42 Osnaburgh Street
NW1 3ND Tel: 020 7424 0007
comicbook@compuserve.com
www.compalcomics.com

DECORATIVE ARTS
Dorset
Market Street Gallery Ltd T/A Delf
Stream Gallery, Bournemouth Tel:
07974 926137 oastman@aol.com
www.delfstreamgallery.com

Gloucestershire
Ruskin Decorative Arts, 5 Talbot
Court, Stow-on-the-Wold,
Cheltenham GL54 1DP
Tel: 01451 832254
william.anne@ruskindecarts.co.uk
*Specializing in the Decorative Arts
1860–1930. Arts and Crafts, Art
Nouveau and Art Deco items.
Cotswold School Movement
including Guild of Handicraft,
Gordon Russell and Gimson and
The Barnsleys, Heals.*

Greater Manchester
A. S. Antique Galleries, 26 Broad
Street, Pendleton, Salford
M6 5BY Tel: 0161 737 5938
Mobile: 07836 368230
as@sternshine.demon.co.uk
*Open Thurs, Fri and Sat or
by appointment.*

Kent
The Design Gallery 1850–1950,
5 The Green, Westerham
TN16 1AS Tel: 01959 561234
Mobile: 07974 322858
sales@thedesigngallery.uk.com
www.thedesigngallery.uk.com

London
Artemis Decorative Arts Ltd,
36 Kensington Church Street W8
4BX Tel: 020 7376 0377
Artemis.w8@btinternet.com
www.artemisdecorativearts.com

Crafts Nouveau, 112 Alexander
Park Road, Muswell Hill
N10 2AE Tel: 020 8444 3300
Mobile: 07958 448 380

craftsnouveau@btconnect.com
www.craftsnouveau.co.uk

Rumours, 4 The Mall, Upper
Street, Camden Passage, Islington
N1 0PD Tel: 020 7704 6549/078
36 277274 Mobile: 07831 103748
Rumdec@aol.com
Moorcroft.

Shapiro & Co., Stand 380, Gray's
Antique Market, 58 Davies Street
W1K 5LP Tel: 020 7491 2710
Fabergé.

Northamptonshire
Aspidistra Antiques, 51 High
Street, Finedon, Wellingborough
NN9 9JN Tel: 01933 680196
Mobile: 07768 071948
info@aspidistra-antiques.com
www.aspidistra-antiques.com

Scotland
decorative arts @ doune, Stand
26, Scottish Antique and Arts
Centre, By Doune, Stirling FK16
6HD Tel: 01786 461 439 or 0141
946 3571 Mobile: 07778 475 974
decorativearts.doune@btinternet.com
www.decorativearts-doune.com

Yorkshire
Muir Hewitt, Art Deco Originals,
Halifax Antiques Centre, Queens
Road Mills, Queen's Road/Gibbet
Street, Halifax HX1 4LR Tel: 01422
347377 muir.hewitt@virgin.net
www.muirhewitt.com
Clarice Cliff.

Republic of Ireland
Mitofsky Antiques, 8 Rathfarnham
Road, Terenure, Dublin 6
Tel: 00 353 1 492 0033
info@mitofskyartdeco.com
www.mitofskyartdeco.com

EPHEMERA
Nottinghamshire
T. Vennett-Smith, 11 Nottingham
Road, Gotham NG11 0HE
Tel: 0115 983 0541
info@vennett-smith.com
www.vennett-smith.com
Ephemera auctions.

**EXHIBITION & FAIR
ORGANISERS**
Devon
Trident Exhibitions, West Devon
Business Park, Tavistock PL19 9DP
Tel: 01822 614671
info@trident-exhibitions.co.uk
www.tridentexhibitions.co.uk
www.interfine.com
www.surreyantiquesfair.co.uk
www.buxtonantiquesfair.co.uk

Nottinghamshire
DMG Fairs, PO Box 100, Newark
NG24 1DJ Tel: 01636 702326
www.dmgantiquefairs.com

Warwickshire
London Antique Arms Fairs Ltd,
15 Burbury Court, Emscote Road,
Warwick CV34 5LD Tel: 01432
355416 & 01926 883665
Mobile: 07801 943983
www.antiquearmsfairsltd.co.uk

West Midlands
Antiques for Everyone Fair,
NEC House, National Exhibition
Centre, Birmingham B40 1NT
Tel: 0121 780 4141
antiques@necgroup.co.uk
www.antiquesforeveryone.co.uk

EXPORTERS
Devon
Pugh's Antiques, Pugh's Farm,
Monkton, Nr Honiton EX14 9QH
Tel: 01404 42860
sales@pughsantiques.com
www.pughsantiques.com
Open Mon–Sat.

Gloucestershire
Piano-Export, Bridge Road,
Kingswood, Bristol BS15 4FW
Tel: 0117 956 8300
Open Mon–Fri.

Nottinghamshire

Antiques Across the World, James Alexander Building, London Road/Manvers Street, Nottingham NG2 3AE Tel: 0115 979 9199 tonyrimes@btopenworld.com

Staffordshire

Acorn G.D.S. Ltd, 183 Queens Road, Penkhull, Stoke-on-Trent ST4 7LF Tel: 01538 399670 acorn@acorn-freight.co.uk www.acorn-freight.co.uk

East Sussex

International Furniture Exporters Ltd, Old Cement Works, South Heighton, Newhaven BN9 0HS Tel: 01273 611251 ife55@aol.com www.int-furniture-exporters.co.uk

The Old Mint House, High Street, Pevensey BN24 5LF Tel: 01323 762337 antiques@minthouse.co.uk www.minthouse.co.uk *Open Mon–Fri 9am–5.30pm, Sat 10.30am–4.30pm or by appointment.*

Wiltshire

North Wilts. Exporters, Farm Hill House, Brinkworth SN15 5AJ Tel: 01666 510876 Mobile: 07836 260730 mike@northwilts.demon.co.uk www.northwiltsantiqueexporters.com *Open Mon–Sat 8am–6pm or by appointment.*

FISHING
Hampshire

Evans & Partridge, Agriculture House, High Street, Stockbridge SO20 6HF Tel: 01264 810702 *Sporting auctions.*

Kent

Old Tackle Box, PO Box 55, Cranbrook TN17 3ZU Tel: 01580 713979 Mobile: 07729 278 293 tackle.box@virgin.net

London

Angling Auctions, PO Box 2095 W12 8RU Tel: 020 8749 4175/07785 281349 neil@anglingauctions.demon.co.uk

FURNITURE
Berkshire

Hill Farm Antiques, Hill Farm, Shop Lane, Leckhampstead, Nr Newbury RG20 8QG Tel: 01488 638541/638361 Mobile: 07836 503561 beesley@hillfarmantiques.demon.co.uk *Specialists in antique dining tables.*

The Old Malthouse, Hungerford RG17 0EG Tel: 01488 682209 hunwick@oldmalthouse30.freeserve.co.uk

Cumbria

Anthemion, Cartmel, Grange Over Sands LA11 6QD Tel: 015395 36295 Mobile: 07768 443757

Derbyshire

Spurrier-Smith Antiques, 28, 30, 39 Church Street, Ashbourne DE6 1AJ Tel: 01335 343669/342198/344377

Devon

Musgrave Bickford Antiques, 15 East Street, Crediton EX17 3AT Tel: 01363 775042

Pugh's Antiques, Pugh's Farm, Monkton, Nr Honiton EX14 9QH Tel: 01404 42860 sales@pughsantiques.com www.pughsantiques.com *Open Mon–Sat.*

Jane Strickland & Daughters, 71 High Street, Honiton EX14 1PW Tel: 01404 44221 JSandDaughtersUk@aol.com www.janestricklanddaughters.co.uk

Essex

F. G. Bruschweiler (Antiques) Ltd, 41–67 Lower Lambricks, Rayleigh SS6 8DA Tel: 01268 773 761/773 932 info@fgbantiques.com www.fgbantiques.com *Member of LAPADA.*

Gloucestershire

Christopher Clarke (Antiques) Ltd, The Fosseway, Stow-on-the-Wold GL54 1JS Tel: 01451 830476 cclarkeantiques@aol.com www.campaignfurniture.com *Specialists in Campaign furniture and travel items, including furniture, leather goods, luggage, boxes, candlesticks, personal items and artwork, etc. Annual exhibition.*

Hertfordshire

Collins Antiques, Corner House, Wheathampstead AL4 8AP Tel: 01582 833111

Kent

Flower House Antiques, 90 High Street, Tenterden TN30 6JB Tel: 01580 763764

Pamela Goodwin, 11 The Pantiles, Royal Tunbridge Wells TN2 5TD Tel: 01892 618200 mail@goodwinantiques.co.uk www.goodwinantiques.co.uk *Antique furniture, clocks, oil lamps, mirrors and decorative items.*

Jeroen Markies Antiques & Furniture Exchange Uk.Com, 25 High Street, Edenbridge TN8 5AB Tel: 01732 867687 jeroen@furnitureexchange.uk.com www.furnitureexchange.uk.com

Sutton Valence Antiques, North Street, Sutton Valence, Nr Maidstone ME17 3AP Tel: 01622 843333/01622 675332 svantiques@aol.com www.svantiques.co.uk

Swan Antiques, Stone Street, Cranbrook TN17 3HF0 Tel: 01580 712720

Lincolnshire

Seaview Antiques, Stanhope Road, Horncastle LN9 5DG Tel: 01507 524524 tracey@seaviewantiques.co.uk www.seaviewantiques.co.uk

London

Oola Boola Antiques London, 139–147 Kirkdale SE26 4QJ Tel: 020 8291 9999 Mobile: 07956 261252 oola.boola@telco4u.net

Middlesex

Phelps Antiques, 133–135 St Margaret's Road, Twickenham TW1 1RG Tel: 020 8892 1778/7129 antiques@phelps.co.uk www.phelps.co.uk *Mon–Fri 9am–5.30pm, Sat 9.30am–5.30pm, Sun 12am–4pm.*

Oxfordshire

Blender Antiques, Cotefield Farm, Oxford Road, Bodicote, Nr Banbury OX15 4AQ Tel: 01295 254754 blenderantiques@btopenworld.com www.blenderantiques.co.uk

The Chair Set, 18 Market Place, Woodstock OX20 1TA Tel: 01428 707301 Mobile: 07711 625 477 allanjames@thechairset.com www.thechairset.com *Specialists in sets of chairs, furniture and accessories for the dining room.*

Rupert Hitchcox Antiques, Warpsgrove, Nr Chalgrove, Oxford OX44 7RW Tel: 01865 890241 www.ruperthitchcoxantiques.co.uk

Georg S. Wissinger Antiques, Georgian House Antiques, 2, 21 & 44 West Street, Chipping Norton OX7 5EU Tel: 01608 641369

Surrey

Dorking Desk Shop, J. G. Elias Antiques Limited, 41 West Street, Dorking RH4 1BU Tel: 01306 883327/880535 info@dorkingdeskshop.co.uk www.desk.co.uk *Antique desks.*

J. Hartley Antiques Ltd, 186 High Street, Ripley GU23 6BB Tel: 01483 224318

East Sussex

The Old Mint House, High Street, Pevensey BN24 5LF Tel: 01323 762337 antiques@minthouse.co.uk www.minthouse.co.uk *Open Mon–Fri 9am–5.30pm, Sat 10.30am–4.30pm or by appointment.*

Pastorale Antiques, 15 Malling Street, Lewes BN7 2RA Tel: 01273 473259 or 01435 863044 pastorale@btinternet.com *Large showrooms. Genuine Georgian and Victorian furniture as seen in Miller's Antiques Price Guide. Also French provincial and old pine. A further 3,000 sq ft now available for serious traders. Phone for details.*

West Sussex

British Antique Replicas, 22 School Close, Queen Elizabeth Avenue, Burgess Hill RH15 9RX Tel: 01444 245577 www.1760.com *Antique replica furniture.*

Stable Antiques, Adrian Hoyle, 98a High Street, Lindfield RH16 2HP Tel: 01444 483662 Mobile: 07768 900331 ahoyle@msn.com *Regency furniture.*

Warwickshire

Apollo Antiques Ltd, The Saltisford, Birmingham Road, Warwick CV34 4TD

Tel: 01926 494746/494666 mynott@apolloantiques.com www.apolloantiques.com

Coleshill Antiques & Interiors, 12–14 High Street, Coleshill B46 1AZ Tel: 01675 467416 enquiries@coleshillantiques.com www.coleshillantiques.com *Dealers in fine antiques and exclusive interiors.*

West Midlands

Martin Taylor Antiques, 323 Tettenhall Road, Wolverhampton WV6 0JZ Tel: 01902 751166/07836 636524 enquiries@mtaylor-antiques.co.uk www.mtaylor-antiques.co.uk

Wiltshire

Cross Hayes Antiques, Units 6–8 Westbrook Farm, Draycot Cerne, Chippenham SN15 5LH Tel: 01249 720033 david@crosshayes.co.uk www.crosshayes.co.uk *Shipping furniture.*

USA

Antique Associates at West Townsend, PO Box 129W, 473 Main Street, West Townsend MA 01474 Tel: (978) 597 8084 drh@aaawt.com

Dragonflies Antiques & Decorating Center, Frank & Cathy Sykes, New England Events Mgt, PO Box 678, 24 Center Street, Wolfeboro, New Hampshire 03894 Tel: 603 569 0000 Dragonflies@metrocast.net *Also Folk Art, mahogany speed boat models, maps and antiquarian books.*

Warehouse Provence, 1120 Massachusetts Ave, (Rte 111) Boxborough, Maine MA 01719 Tel: 978 266 0200 warehouseprovence@aics.net www.warehouseprovence.com

DIRECTORY OF SPECIALISTS

GLASS

Somerset
Somervale Antiques, 6 Radstock Road, Midsomer Norton, Bath BA3 2AJ Tel: 01761 412686 Mobile: 07885 088022 ronthson@somervaleantiquesglass.co.uk
www.somervaleantiquesglass.co.uk

Staffordshire
Gordon Litherland, 25 Stapenhill Road, Burton on Trent DE15 9AE Tel: 01283 567213 Mobile: 07952 118987 pubjugs@aol.com
Bottles, breweriana and pub jugs, advertising ephemera and commemoratives.

ICONS

London
The Temple Gallery, 6 Clarendon Cross, Holland Park W11 4AP Tel: 020 7727 3809 info@templegallery.com
www.templegallery.com

IRISH ANTIQUE DEALERS ASSOCIATION

Northern Ireland
Marion Langham Limited, Claranagh, Tempo, County Fermanagh BT94 3FJ
Tel: 028 6654 1247 marion@ladymarion.co.uk
www.ladymarion.co.uk
Belleek and paperweights specialist.

Republic of Ireland
Jonathan Beech, Westport, Co Mayo Tel: 00 353 98 28688 www.antiqueclocks-ireland.com

IVORY & TORTOISESHELL

Somerset
Alan & Kathy Stacey Appointment only Tel: 01963 441333 Mobile: 07810 058078 info@antiqueboxes.uk.com
www.antiqueboxes.uk.com
Tea caddies and fine boxes. Specialist dealers in tortoiseshell, ivory, mop, shagreen, exotic timber pieces. Professional conservation services, consultancy, valuations. Members of LAPADA and BAFRA. Each piece comes with 100% guarantee of quality and authenticity.

JEWELLERY

London
Sarah Groombridge, Stand 335, Grays Market, 58 Davies Street W1K 5LP Tel: 020 7629 0225 Mobile: 07770 920277 sarah.groombridge@totalise.co.uk

Wimpole Antiques, Stand 349, Grays Antique Market, 58 Davies Street W1K 5LP Tel: 020 7499 2889 WimpoleAntiques@compuserve.com

Canada
Fiona Kenny Antiques, PO Box 11, 18 Front Street North, Thorold, Ontario Tel: 905 682 0090 merday@cogeco.ca
www.trocadero.com/merday
18th–20thC jewellery and antiques, sterling and silver plate, china and pottery, 20thC modern, collectibles and advertising.

KITCHENWARE

Gloucestershire
Bread & Roses, Durham House Antique Centre, Sheep Street, Stow on the Wold GL54 1AA
Tel: 01451 870404/01926 817342

Lincolnshire
Skip & Janie Smithson Antiques
Tel: 01754 810265
Mobile: 07831 399180
Dairy bygones, enamel wares, laundry items and advertising.

East Sussex
Ann Lingard, Ropewalk Antiques, Rye TN31 7NA Tel: 01797 223486 ann-lingard@ropewalkantiques.freeserve.co.uk

LIGHTING

Devon
The Exeter Antique Lighting Co, Cellar 15, The Quay, Exeter EX2 4AP Tel: 01392 490848 Mobile: 07702 969438 www.antiquelightingcompany.com
Antique lighting and stained glass specialists.

Somerset
Joanna Proops Antique Textiles & Lighting, 34 Belvedere, Lansdown Hill, Bath BA1 5HR Tel: 01225 310795 antiquetextiles@aol.co.uk
www.antiquetextiles.co.uk

USA
Lamps: By The Book, Inc, 514 14th West Palm Beach, Florida 33401 Tel: 561 659 1723 booklamps@msn.com
www.lampsbythebook.com
Gift lamps. Also buy leather-bound books.

MARKETS & CENTRES

Derbyshire
Chappells Antiques Centre – Bakewell, King Street, Bakewell DE45 1DZ Tel: 01629 812496 ask@chappellsantiquescentre.com
www.chappellsantiquescentre.com
30 established dealers inc BADA and LAPADA members. Quality period furniture, ceramics, silver, plate, metals, treen, clocks, barometers, books, pictures, maps, prints, textiles, kitchenalia, lighting and furnishing accessories from the 17th–20thC, scientific, pharmaceutical and sporting antiques. Open Mon–Sat 10–5pm, Sun 12–5pm. Closed Christmas Day, Boxing Day and New Year's Day. Please ring for brochure, giving location and parking information.

Matlock Antiques, Collectables & Riverside Café, 7 Dale Road, Matlock DE4 3LT
Tel: 01629 760808 bmatlockantiques@aol.com
www.matlock-antiques-collectables.cwc.net
Proprietor W. Shirley. Over 70 dealers. Open 7 days 10am–5pm including Bank Holidays. Parking available.

Devon
Colyton Antiques Centre, Dolphin Street, Colyton EX24 6LU
Tel: 01297 552339 colytonantiques@modelgarage.co.uk
www.modelgarage.co.uk

Essex
Debden Antiques, Elder Street, Debden, Saffron Walden CB11 3JY Tel: 01799 543007 info@debden-antiques.co.uk
www.debden-antiques.co.uk
Mon–Sat 10am–5.30pm, Sun and Bank Holidays 11am–4pm. 30 quality dealers in a stunning 17thC Essex barn. Large selection of 16th–20thC oak, mahogany and pine furniture, watercolours and oil paintings, rugs, ceramics, silver and jewellery. Plus garden furniture and ornaments in our lovely courtyard.

Gloucestershire
The Antiques Emporium, The Old Chapel, Long Street, Tetbury GL8 8AA Tel: 01666 505281
Open Mon–Sat 10am–5pm, Sun 1–5pm. 38 dealers. Jewellery, clocks, antiquities, books, furniture, treen, flatware, glass, china, porcelain and decorative accessories.

Gloucester Antiques Centre, The Historic Docks, 1 Severn Road, Gloucester GL1 2LE Tel: 01452 529716 www.antiques.center.com
The Gloucester Antiques Centre makes a fine day out, with antiques

and collectibles of every description. There is something for everyone, even those that are not antiques collectors will find items to decorate any home. Collectors of modern items are catered for. Open Mon–Sat 10am–5pm Sun 1pm–5pm.

Jubilee Hall Antiques Centre, Oak Street, Lechlade on Thames GL7 3AY Tel: 01367 253777 mail@jubileehall.co.uk
www.jubileehall.co.uk

Kent
Malthouse Arcade, High Street, Hythe CT21 5BW Tel: 01303 260103

Lancashire
The Antique Centre, 56 Garstang Road, Preston PR1 1NA Tel: 01772 882078 info@paulallisonantiques.co.uk
www.paulallisonantiques.co.uk
Open 7 days a week.

GB Antiques Centre, Lancaster Leisure Park, (the former Hornsea Pottery), Wyresdale Road, Lancaster LA1 3LA Tel: 01524 844734
Over 140 dealers in 40,000 sq ft of space. Showing porcelain, pottery, Art Deco, glass, books and linen. Also a large selection of mahogany, oak and pine furniture. Open 7 days a week 10am–5pm.

Kingsmill Antique Centre, Queen Street, Harle Syke, Burnley BB10 2HX Tel: 01282 431953
Open 7 days 10am–5pm, 8pm Thurs. 8,500 sq ft. Trade welcome.

Leicestershire
Oxford Street Antique Centre, 16–26 Oxford Street, Leicester LE1 5XU Tel: 0116 255 3006

Lincolnshire
Hemswell Antique Centres, Caenby Corner Estate, Hemswell Cliff, Gainsborough DN21 5TJ
Tel: 01427 668389 info@hemswell-antiques.com
www.hemswell-antiques.com
Open 7 days 10am–5pm.

London
Antiquarius Antiques Centre, 131/141 King's Road, Chelsea SW3 5ST Tel: 020 7351 5353 antique@dial.pipex.com
Open Mon–Sat 10am–6pm.

Atlantic Antiques Centres, Chenil House, 181–183 Kings Road SW3 5EB Tel: 020 7351 5353 antique@dial.pipex.com

Bond Street Antiques Centre, 124 New Bond Street W1Y 9AE
Tel: 020 7351 5353 antique@dial.pipex.com
Open Mon–Sat 10am–5.30pm.

The Mall Antiques Arcade, Camden Passage, Islington N1 Tel: 020 7351 5353 antique@dial.pipex.cpm
Open Tues, Thurs and Fri 10am–5pm, Wed 7.30am–5pm anf Sat 9am–6pm.

Nottinghamshire
Antiques Trade Space, Brunel Drive, Newark NG24 2DE
Tel: 01636 651444 info@antiquestradespace.com
www.antiquestradespace.com

Newark Antiques Warehouse Ltd, Old Kelham Road, Newark NG24 1BX Tel: 01636 674869 Mobile: 07974 429185 enquiries@newarkantiques.co.uk
www.newarkantiques.co.uk

Oxfordshire
Chipping Norton Antiques Centre, Ivy House, Middle Row, Market Place, Chipping Norton
Tel: 01608 644212

The Swan at Tetsworth, High Street, Tetsworth, Nr Thame

OX9 7AB Tel: 01844 281777 antiques@theswan.co.uk
www.theswan.co.uk
Over 80 dealers displaying 40 showrooms of quality Georgian antiques right through to Art Deco in Grade II Elizabethan Coaching Inn. Open every day 10am –6pm. 5 mins junctions 6/8 M40 motorway. Award winning restaurant. Tel 01844 281777 for brochure or visit website www.theswan.co.uk

Shropshire
Old Mill Antiques Centre, Mill Street, Low Down, Bridgnorth W15 5AG Tel: 01746 768778 www.oldmill-antiques.co.uk

East Sussex
Church Hill Antiques Centre, 6 Station Street, Lewes BN7 2DA Tel: 01273 474 842 churchhilllewes@aol.com
www.church-hill-antiques.co.uk

Hastings Antique Centre, 59–61 Norman Road, St Leonards-on-Sea TN38 0EG Tel: 01424 428561

Wales
Afonwen Craft & Antique Centre, Afonwen, Nr Caerwys, Nr Mold, Flintshire CH7 5UB Tel: 01352 720965
Open all year Tues–Sun 9.30am–5.30pm, closed Mon, open Bank Holidays. The largest centre in North Wales and the borders. 14,000 sq ft, 40 dealers. Fabulous selection of antiques, china, silver, crystal, quality collectables, fine furniture, oak, walnut, mahogany, pine from around the world. Excellent restaurant, free entrance, free large car park.

Offa's Dyke Antique Centre, 4 High Street, Knighton, Powys LD7 1AT Tel: 01547 528635/520145 *Open Mon–Sat 10am–1pm, 2pm–5pm. 12 dealers in 18th–20thC ceramics including Delft and slipware, glass, books on antiques, general antiques and collectables.*

Warwickshire
Barn Antiques Centre, Station Road, Long Marston, Nr Stratford-upon-Avon CV37 8RB Tel: 01789 721399 www.barnantique.co.uk
Huge old barn crammed full of affordable antiques. Over 13,000 sq ft and 50 established dealers. Open daily 10am–5pm, Sun 12pm–6pm. Large free car park. Licensed bistro.

Yorkshire
Cavendish Antique & Collectors Centre, 44 Stonegate, York YO1 8AS Tel: 01904 621666 www.cavendishantiques.co.uk
Open 7 days 9am–6pm. Browse at leisure. Over 70 dealers on three floors. Jewellery, silver, porcelain, glass engravings and prints, furniture, oils and watercolours, watches, collectables.

The Chapel Antiques Centre, 99 Broadfield Road, Heeley, Sheffield S8 0XQ Tel: 0114 258 8288 enquiries@antiquesinsheffield.com
www.antiquesinsheffield.com
Open 7 days, over 25 dealers displaying a wide range of antiques and collectables including specialists in clocks, Art Deco, French furniture, books, pine, fabrics, porcelain, and much more. Services: upholstery, furniture restoration, re-caning, pottery restoration, French polishing and delivery.

The Court House, 2–6 Town End Road, Ecclesfield, Sheffield S35 9YY Tel: 0114 257 0641 Mobile: 07973 409505

MEDALS

Roxburghshire
Romsey Medal Centre,
The Grapes Hotel, 16 Douglas
Square, Newcastleton TD9 0QD
Tel: 013873 75245
post@romseymedals.co.uk
www.romseymedals.co.uk

MINIATURES

Gloucestershire
Judy & Brian Harden Antiques,
PO Box 14, Bourton-on-the-Water,
Cheltenham GL54 2YR
Tel: 01451 810684
Mobile: 07831 692252
harden@portraitminiatures.co.uk
www.portraitminiatures.co.uk
Portrait miniatures.

MONEY BOXES

Yorkshire
John & Simon Haley,
89 Northgate, Halifax HX1 1XF
Tel: 01422 822148/360434
toysandbanks@aol.com

MUSICAL INSTRUMENTS

Gloucestershire
Keith Harding's World of
Mechanical Music, The Oak House,
High Street, Northleach GL54 3ET
Tel: 01451 860181
keith@mechanicalmusic.co.uk
www.mechanicalmusic.co.uk
*Mechanical music and automata,
antique and modern. Also antique
musical boxes and clocks.*

Piano-Export, Bridge Road,
Kingswood, Bristol BS15 4FW
Tel: 0117 956 8300
Open Mon–Fri.

Kent
Stephen T. P. Kember, Pamela
Goodwin, 11 The Pantiles,
Royal Tunbridge Wells TN2 5TD
Tel: 01959 574067
Mobile: 07850 358067
steve.kember@btinternet.com
www.antique-musicboxes.co.uk
*Antique cylinder and disc
musical boxes.*

Nottinghamshire
Turner Violins, 1–5 Lily Grove,
Beeston NG9 1QL
Tel: 0115 943 0333
info@turnerviolins.co.uk

OAK & COUNTRY

Cambridgeshire
Mark Seabrook Antiques,
PO Box 396, Huntingdon
PE28 0ZA Tel: 01480 861935
Mobile: 07770 721931
enquiries@markseabrook.com
www.markseabrook.com

Kent
Douglas Bryan Antiques, The
Old Bakery, St David's Bridge,
Cranbrook TN17 3HN Tel: 01580
713103 Mobile: 07774 737303
By appointment only.

London
Robert Young Antiques,
68 Battersea Bridge Road
SW11 3AG Tel: 020 7228 7847
Country furniture and Folk Art.

Northamptonshire
Paul Hopwell, 30 High Street,
West Haddon NN6 7AP Tel: 01788
510636 Mobile: 07836 505950
paulhopwell@antiqueoak.co.uk
www.antiqueoak.co.uk

Oxfordshire
Key Antiques of Chipping Norton,
11 Horsefair, Chipping Norton
OX7 5AL Tel: 01608 644992
info@keyantiques.com
www.keyantiques.com

Surrey
The Refectory, 38 West Street,
Dorking RH4 1BU Tel: 01306
742111 www.therefectory.co.uk
*Oak & Country – Refectory
table specialist.*

Anthony Welling, Broadway Barn,
High Street, Ripley GU23 6AQ
Tel: 01483 225384
ant@awelling.freeserve.co.uk

ORIENTAL

London
R & G McPherson Antiques,
40 Kensington Church Street
W8 4BX Tel: 020 7937 0812
Mobile: 07768 432 630
rmcpherson@orientalceramics.com
www.orientalceramics.com
Specialists in shipwreck ceramics.

Somerset
Lopburi Art & Antiques,
5 Saville Row, Bath BA1 2QP
Tel: 01225 322947
mail@lopburi.co.uk
www.lopburi.co.uk

USA
Mimi's Antiques, 8763 Carriage
Hills Drive, Columbia MD 21046
Tel: 410 381 6862/443 250 0930
mimisantiques@comcast.net
www.mimisantiques.com
www.trocadero.com/mimisantiques
*18th and 19thC Chinese export
porcelain, American and English
furniture, Continental porcelain,
paintings, Sterling, Oriental rugs.*

PACKERS & SHIPPERS

Dorset
Alan Transport Franklin, 26
Blackmoor Road, Ebblake Industrial
Estate, Verwood, BH31 6BB
Tel: 01202 826539

Gloucestershire
The Shipping Company, Bourton
Industrial Park, Bourton-on-the-
Water, Cheltenham GL54 2HQ
Tel: 01451 822451
enquiries@theshippingcompanyltd.
com
www.theshippingcompanyltd.com

Middlesex
Sterling Art Services, Unit 5,
Cypress Court, Harris Way,
Sunbury on Thames TW16 7EL
Tel: 01932 771442
salis@sterlingartservices.co.uk
www.sterlingartservices.co.uk

PAPERWEIGHTS

Cheshire
Sweetbriar Gallery Paperweights
Ltd, Sweetbriar House, Robin
Hood Lane, Helsby WA6 9NH
Tel: 01928 723851
Mobile: 07860 907532
sales@sweetbriar.co.uk
www.sweetbriar.co.uk

Northern Ireland
Marion Langham Limited,
Claranagh, Tempo, County
Fermanagh BT94 3FJ Tel: 028 895
41247 marion@ladymarion.co.uk
www.ladymarion.co.uk

USA
The Dunlop Collection, PO Box
6269, Statesville NC 28687
Tel: (704) 871 2626 or Toll Free
Tel: (800) 227 1996

PHOTOGRAPHS

London
Jubilee Photographica,
10 Pierrepoint Row,
Camden Passage N1 8EE
Mobile: 07860 793707
*Specialist shop and gallery
dealing in rare and collectable
photographs from the 19th and
20thC. We sell and hold a large
and constantly changing stock of
cartes de visite, stereocards,
daguerreotypes and ambrotypes,
albums of travel, topographical
and ethnic photographs, art
photographs and a range of
books on the art and history of
photography. We also have magic
lanterns and lantern slides, and
stereoscopic viewers. The shop is
open Wed–Sat 10am–4pm.*

PINE

Cornwall
Julie Strachey, Trevaskis Barn,
Gwinear Road, Nr Hayle TR27 5JQ
Tel: 01209 613750
*Antique farm and country
furniture in pine, oak, etc.
Ironwork and interesting pieces
for the garden (no repro). By
appointment. Junction 9 M40
2 miles. Established 27 years.*

Cumbria
Ben Eggleston Antiques, The
Dovecote, Long Marton, Appleby
CA16 6BJ Tel: 01768 361849
ben@beneggleston antiques.co.uk
www.beneggleston antiques.co.uk
Trade only.

Essex
English Rose Antiques,
7 Church Street, Coggeshall
CO6 1TU Tel: 01376 562683
Mobile: 07770 880790 & 0049
(0)1719 949541
englishroseantiques@hotmail.com
www.englishroseantiques.co.uk
www.Delta-Line-Trading.com
*Large selection of English and
Continental pine furniture. Open
Mon–Sun 10am–5.30pm.
Closed Wed.*

Gloucestershire
Cottage Farm Antiques,
Stratford Road, Aston Subedge,
Chipping Campden GL55 6PZ
Tel: 01386 438263
info@cottagefarmantiques.co.uk
www.cottagefarmantiques.co.uk

Hampshire
Pine Cellars, 39 Jewry Street,
Winchester SO23 8RY
Tel: 01962 777546/867014

Kent
Up Country, The Old Corn Stores,
68 St John's Road, Tunbridge
Wells TN4 9PE Tel: 01892 523341
www.upcountryantiques.co.uk

Lancashire
David Roper Antiques, Hill View
Farm, Gill Lane, Longton, Preston
PR4 4ST Tel: 01772 615366
Mobile: 07803 134851
davidroper@supanet.com
*Mostly English 18th–20thC pine
and country furniture. Trade
suppliers. No reproductions.*

Nottinghamshire
A. B. Period Pine, The Barn,
38 Main Street, Farnsfield, Newark
NG22 8EA Tel: 01623 882288
alan@abperiodpine.fsnet.co.uk
www.abperiodpine.co.uk

Harlequin Antiques,
79–81 Mansfield Road,
Daybrook, Nottingham
NG5 6BH Tel: 0115 967 4590
sales@antiquepine.net
www.antiquepine.net

Somerset
Gilbert & Dale Antiques,
The Old Chapel, Church Street,
Ilchester, Nr Yeovil BA22 8ZA
Tel: 01935 840464
Painted pine and country.

Westville House Antiques,
Westville House, Littleton,
Nr Somerton TA11 6NP
Tel: 01458 273376
Mobile: 07941 510823
antique@westville.co.uk
www.westville.co.uk

East Sussex
Ann Lingard, Ropewalk Antiques,
Rye TN31 7NA Tel: 01797 223486
ann-lingard@ropewalkantiques.
freeserve.co.uk

Graham Price, Apple Store,
Chaucer Industrial Estate,
Dittons Road, Polegate BN26 6JF
Tel: 01323 487167
www.grahampriceantiques.co.uk

Warwickshire
Pine & Things, Portobello Farm,
Campden Road, Nr Shipston-on-
Stour CV36 4PY Tel: 01608
663849 www.pinethings.co.uk

Wiltshire
North Wilts Exporters, Farm Hill
House, Brinkworth SN15 5AJ
Tel: 01666 510876
Mobile: 07836 260730
mike@northwilts.demon.co.uk
www.northwiltsantiqueexporters.com
*Open Mon–Sat 8am–6pm or
by appointment.*

Republic of Ireland
Bygones of Ireland Ltd, Lodge
Road, Westport, Co Mayo
Tel: 00 353 98 26132/25701
bygones@anu.ie
www.bygones-of-ireland.com

Delvin Farm Antiques, Gormonston,
Co Meath Tel: 00 353 1 841 2285
info@delvinfarmpine.com
john@delvinfarmpine.com
www.delvinfarmpine.com

Ireland's Own Antiques, Alpine
House, Carlow Road, Abbeyleix,
Co Laois Tel: 00 353 502 31348
*Ireland's own antiques have a fine
stock of original country furniture,
which for years has been collected
from country cottages and
mansions all over Ireland by Peter
and Daniel Meaney. Years of
experience in the art of packing
and shipping, and have many
customers. This is a well worth
while call for overseas buyers.*

PORCELAIN

Essex
Barling Porcelain Tel: 01621
890058 stuart@barling.uk.com
www.barling.uk.com

Bellhouse Antiques, Chelmsford
Tel: 01268 710415
Bellhouse.Antiques@virgin.net

Gloucestershire
Judy & Brian Harden Antiques,
PO Box 14, Bourton-on-the-Water,
Cheltenham GL54 2YR
Tel: 01451 810684
harden@meissenfigures.co.uk
www.meissenfigures.co.uk
Meissen figures.

Hampshire
The Goss & Crested China Club
& Museum, incorporating
Milestone Publications,
62 Murray Road, Horndean
PO8 9JL Tel: (023) 9259 7440
info@gosschinaclub.demon.co.uk
www.gosscrestedchina.co.uk
Goss and Crested china.

London
Diana Huntley Antiques,
8 Camden Passage, Islington
N1 8ED Tel: 020 7226 4605
diana@dianahuntleyantiques.co.uk
www.dianahuntleyantiques.co.uk

Marion Langham Limited
Tel: 020 7730 1002
marion@ladymarion.co.uk
www.ladymarion.co.uk
Belleek.

Shropshire
Harvey Antiques, Corve Villa, 30A
Corve Street, Ludlow SY8 1GB
Tel: 01584 876375
christopher-harvey@tesco.net
By appointment only.

East Sussex
Tony Horsley, PO Box 3127, Brighton
BN1 5SS Tel: 01273 550770
*Candle extinguishers, Royal
Worcester and other fine porcelain.*

Warwickshire
Coleshill Antiques & Interiors,
12–14 High Street, Coleshill
B46 1AZ Tel: 01675 467416
enquiries@coleshillantiques.com
www.coleshillantiques.com

Wiltshire
Andrew Dando, 34 Market Street,
Bradford on Avon BA15 1LL
Tel: 01225 865444
www.andrewdando.co.uk
*English, Oriental and
Continental porcelain.*

Yorkshire
The Crested China Co, Highfield,
Windmill Hill, Driffield YO25 5YP
Tel: 01377 257042
dt@thecrestedchinacompany.com
www.thecrestedchinacompany.com
Goss and Crested china.

POTTERY
Berkshire
Special Auction Services,
Kennetholme, Midgham, Reading
RG7 5UX Tel: 0118 971 2949
www.invaluable.com/sas/
*Specialist auctions of
commemoratives, pot lids and
Prattware, Fairings, Goss and
Crested, Baxter and Le Blond prints.*

Buckinghamshire
Gillian Neale Antiques, PO Box
247, Aylesbury HP20 1JZ
Tel: 01296 423754/07860 638700
gillianneale@aol.com
www.gillgiannealeantiques.co.uk
*Blue and white transfer-printed
pottery 1780–1860.*

Dorset
Greystoke Antiques, 4 Swan Yard,
(off Cheap Street), Sherborne
DT9 3AX Tel: 01935 812833
*Established 28 years. Adjacent
to town centre car park.
10am–4.30pm daily. Closed Wed.
Also blue transfer-printed pottery
1800–50. Always some 200–300
pieces in stock.*

Hampshire
Millers Antiques Ltd, Netherbrook
House, 86 Christchurch Road,
Ringwood BH24 1DR
Tel: 01425 472062
mail@millers-antiques.co.uk
www.millers-antiques.co.uk
*Majolica and Quimper,
decorative items, English and
Continental furniture.*

Kent
Serendipity, 125 High Street,
Deal CT14 6BB Tel: 01304
369165/01304 366536
dipityantiques@aol.com
Staffordshire pottery.

London
Jonathan Horne, 66 Kensington
Church Street W8 4BY
Tel: 020 7221 5658
JH@jonathanhorne.co.uk
www.jonathanhorne.co.uk
Early English pottery.

Oxfordshire
Key Antiques of Chipping Norton,
11 Horsefair, Chipping Norton
OX7 5AL Tel: 01608 644992
info@keyantiques.com
www.keyantiques.com

Surrey
Judi Bland Antiques
Tel: 01276 857576 or
01536 724145
*18th and 19thC English Toby jugs
and Bargeware.*

Tyne & Wear
Ian Sharp Antiques, 23 Front
Street, Tynemouth NE30 4DX
Tel: 0191 296 0656
iansharp@sharpantiques.demon.co.uk
www.sharpantiques.demon.co.uk
Tyneside and Wearside ceramics.

Wiltshire
Andrew Dando, 34 Market Street,
Bradford on Avon BA15 1LL
Tel: 01225 865444
www.andrewdando.co.uk
*English, Oriental and
Continental pottery.*

PUBLICATIONS
Cheshire
Armourer – The Militaria Magazine,
Published by Beaumont Publishing
Ltd, 1st Floor Adelphi Mill,
Bollington SK10 5JB Tel: 01625
575700 editor@armourer.co.uk
www.armourer.co.uk
*A bi-monthly magazine for military
antique collectors and military
history enthusiasts offering
hundreds of contacts for buying
and selling, articles on all aspects
of militaria collecting plus the
dates of UK militaria fairs and
auctions. Available on subscription.*

West Midlands
Antiques Magazine, H. P.
Publishing, 2 Hampton Court
Road, Harborne, Birmingham
B17 9AE Tel: 0121 681 8000
Subs 01562 701001
copy@antiquesmagazine.com
www.antiquesmagazine.com

RESTORATION
Northamptonshire
Leather Conservation Centre,
University College Campus,
Boughton Green Road, Moulton
Park, Northampton NN2 7AN
Tel: 01604 719766
lcc@northampton.ac.uk
*Conservation and restoration of
leather screens, wall hangings, car,
carriage and furniture upholstery,
saddlery, luggage, firemens'
helmets and much, much more.
The Centre is included in the
Register maintained by the United
Kingdom Institute for Conservation.*

ROCK & POP
Cheshire
Collector's Corner, PO Box 8,
Congleton CW12 4GD
Tel: 01260 270429
dave.popcorner@ukonline.co.uk

Lancashire
Tracks, PO Box 117, Chorley
PR6 0UU Tel: 01257 269726
sales@tracks.co.uk
Beatles and rare pop memorabilia.

London
Cooper Owen, 10 Denmark Street
WC2H 8LS Tel: 020 7240 4132
www.CooperOwen.com

RUGS & CARPETS
Gloucestershire
Samarkand Galleries, 7–8 Brewery
Yard, Sheep Street, Stow-on-the-
Wold GL54 1AA Tel: 01451
832322 mac@samarkand.co.uk
www.samarkand.co.uk
*Antique rugs from Near East and
Central Asia. Antique Nomadic
weavings. Decorative carpets. Tribal
artefacts. Unique contemporary Rugs.
Contact: Brian MacDonald FRGS.*

Scotland
Samarkand Galleries, 16 Howe
Street, Edinburgh EH3 6TD
Tel: 0131 225 2010
howe@samarkand.co.uk
www.samarkand.co.uk
*Antique rugs from Near East and
Central Asia. Antique Nomadic
weavings. Decorative carpets.
Tribal artefacts. Unique
contemporary Rugs. Contact: Brian
MacDonald FRGS.*

SCIENTIFIC INSTRUMENTS
Cheshire
Charles Tomlinson, Chester
Tel: 01244 318395
charles.tomlinson@lineone.net
www.lineone.net/~charles.tomlinson

Kent
Sporting Antiques, 10 Union
Square, The Pantiles, Tunbridge
Wells TN4 8HE Tel: 01892 522661
*Theodolites, sextants, levels,
marine and military compasses,
microscopes, telescopes and drawing
instruments. We buy and sell.*

Scotland
Early Technology, Monkton House,
Old Craighall, Musselburgh,
Midlothian EH21 8SF Tel: 0131
665 5753 Mobile: 07831 106768
michael.bennett-levy@virgin.net
www.earlytech.com
www.tvhistory.tv
Open any time by appointment.

Surrey
Eric Tombs, 62a West Street,
Dorking RH4 1BS Tel: 01306
743661 ertombs@aol.com
www.dorkingantiques.com

SERVICES
Essex
The National Clock Register
Tel: 08707 422485
www.nationalclockregister.co.uk
Clock anti-theft register.

Hampshire
Securikey Ltd, PO Box 18,
Aldershot GU12 4SL Tel: 01252
311888 enquiries@securikey.co.uk
www.securikey.co.uk
Underfloor safes.

Surrey
The Internet Fine Art Bureau,
The Elms, Alma Way, Farnham
GU9 0QN Tel: 01252 640 666
enquiries@interfine.com
www.interfine.com
*Specialist designers of websites for
the antiques and fine art trade.*

SILVER
Dorset
Greystoke Antiques, 4 Swan Yard,
(off Cheap Street), Sherborne
DT9 3AX Tel: 01935 812833
*Adjacent to town centre car park.
10am–4.30pm daily. Closed Wed.
Georgian, Victorian and later silver.*

London
Daniel Bexfield, 26 Burlington
Arcade W1J 0PU Tel: 020 7491
1720 antiques@bexfield.co.uk
www.bexfield.co.uk

Lyn Bloom & Jeffrey Neal, Vault 27,
The London Silver Vaults, Chancery
Lane WC2A 1QS Tel: 020 7242
6189 Mobile: 07768 533055
bloomvault@aol.com
www.bloomvault.com
*We stock fine quality silver items
ranging from £70 to £20,000
which includes anything from
silver napkin rings and flatware to
large centrepieces. Our speciality is
a range of over 200 antique
miniature silver toys.*

Shropshire
Harvey Antiques, Corve Villa,
30A Corve Street, Ludlow
SY8 1GB Tel: 01584 876375
christopher-harvey@tesco.net
By appointment only.

SPORTS & GAMES
Kent
Sporting Antiques, 10 Union
Square, The Pantiles, Tunbridge
Wells TN4 8HE Tel: 01892 522661
*Fishing rods, reels, trophies, books
and prints. Golf and general
antique sporting goods.*

Nottinghamshire
T. Vennett-Smith, 11 Nottingham
Road, Gotham NG11 0HE
Tel: 0115 983 0541
info@vennett-smith.com
www.vennett-smith.com
Sporting auctions.

TEDDY BEARS
Gloucestershire
Bourton Bears, Bourton-on-the-
Water Tel: 01451 821466
mel@strathspey-bed-fsnet.co.uk
www.bourtonbears.com

Oxfordshire
Teddy Bears of Witney, 99 High
Street, Witney OX28 6HY
Tel: 01993 702616/706616

TEXTILES
London
Erna Hiscock & John Shepherd,
Chelsea Galleries, 69 Portobello
Road W11 Tel: 01233 661407
Mobile: 0771 562 7273
erna@ernahiscockantiques.com
www.ernahiscockantiques.com
Antique samplers. Sat 7am–3pm.

Somerset
Joanna Proops Antique Textiles &
Lighting, 34 Belvedere, Lansdown
Hill, Bath BA1 5HR Tel: 01225
310795 antiquetextiles@aol.co.uk
www.antiquetextiles.co.uk

USA
Antique European Linens,
PO Box 789, Gulf Breeze, Florida
32562-0789 Tel: 850 432 4777
Cell 850 450 463
name@antiqueeuropeanlinens.com
www.antiqueeuropeanlinens.com
*Hungarian goose down pillows
and European duvets.*

TOYS
Berkshire
Special Auction Services,
Kennetholme, Midgham, Reading
RG7 5UX Tel: 0118 971 2949
www.invaluable.com/sas/
*Specialist auctions of toys for the
collector including Dinky, Corgi,
Matchbox, lead soldiers and
figures, tinplate and model
railways, etc.*

Kent
The Collector's Toy & Model Shop,
52 Canterbury Road, Margate
CT9 5BG Tel: 01843 232301
Mobile: 07973 232778
www.collectorstoyandmodelshop.com

East Sussex
Wallis & Wallis, West Street
Auction Galleries, Lewes BN7 2NJ
Tel: 01273 480208
grb@wallisandwallis.co.uk
www.wallisandwallis.co.uk
*Auctioneers of diecast toys, model
railways, tinplate toys and models.*

Yorkshire
John & Simon Haley,
89 Northgate, Halifax HX1 1XF
Tel: 01422 822148/360434
toysandbanks@aol.com

USA
Joyce M. Leiby, PO Box 6048,
Lancaster PA 17607
Tel: (717) 898 9113 joyclei@aol.com
*Early German Christmas Santas
and decorations, also Easter toys.*

TRIBAL ART
USA
Hurst Gallery, 53 Mt. Auburn
Street, Cambridge MA 02138
Tel: 617 491 6888
manager@hurstgallery.com
www.hurstgallery.com
*Art of the Pacific, Africa, Asia, The
Americas and the ancient world.*

TUNBRIDGE WARE
Kent
Bracketts, The Auction Hall, The
Pantiles, Tunbridge Wells TN2 5QL
Tel: 01892 544500
sales@bfaa.co.uk www.bfaa.co.uk
Tunbridge ware auctioneers.

WATCHES
Kent
Tempus, Tunbridge Wells Antique
Centre, Union Square, The
Pantiles, Tunbridge Wells
Tel: 01932 828936
tempus.watches@tinyonline.co.uk
www.tempus-watches.co.uk

London
Pieces of Time, (1–7 Davies Mews),
26 South Molton Lane W1Y 2LP
Tel: 020 7629 2422
info@antique-watch.com
www.antique-watch.com

Directory of Auctioneers

Auctioneers who hold frequent sales should contact us by April 2004 for inclusion in the next edition.

UNITED KINGDOM
Bedfordshire
W&H Peacock, 26 Newnham Street, Bedford MK40 3JR Tel: 01234 266366

Berkshire
Cameo Auctions, Kennet Holme Farm, Bath Road, Midgham, Reading RG7 5UX Tel: 01189 713772 cameo-auctioneers@lineone.net

Dreweatt Neate, Donnington Priory, Donnington, Newbury RG14 2JE Tel: 01635 553553 fineart@dreweatt-neate.co.uk www.auctions.dreweatt-neate.co.uk

Law Fine Art, Firs Cottage, Church Lane, Brimpton RG7 4TJ Tel: 0118 971 0353 info@lawfineart.co.uk www.lawfineart.co.uk

Padworth Auctions, 30 The Broadway, Thatcham RG19 3HX Tel: 01734 713772

Shiplake Fine Art, 31 Great Knollys Street, Reading RG1 7HU Tel: 01734 594748

Special Auction Services, Kennetholme, Midgham, Reading RG7 5UX Tel: 0118 971 2949 www.invaluable.com/sas/

Buckinghamshire
Amersham Auction Rooms, Station Road, Amersham HP7 0AH Tel: 01494 729292 info@amershamauctionrooms.co.uk www.amershamauctionrooms.co.uk

Bosley's, 42 West Street, Marlow SL7 2NB Tel: 01628 488188

Bourne End Auction Rooms, Station Approach, Bourne End SL8 5QH Tel: 01628 531500

Dickins Auctioneers Ltd, The Claydon Saleroom, Calvert Road, Middle Claydon, MK18 2EZ Tel: 01296 714434 info@dickens-auctioneers.com www.dickens-auctioneers.com

Cambridgeshire
Cheffins, Clifton House, Clifton Road, Cambridge CB1 7EA Tel: 01223 213343 www.cheffins.co.uk

Rowley Fine Art, The Old Bishop's Palace, Little Downham, Ely CB6 2TD Tel: 01353 699177 mail@rowleyfineart.com www.rowleyfineart.com

Willingham Auctions, 25 High Street, Willingham CB4 5ES Tel: 01954 261252 www.willinghamauctions.com
Contact Colin. Quality auctions held every three weeks. Furniture, clocks, silver, china, glass and collectables. Six different sale rooms. Cafe and extensive parking on site.

Channel Islands
Bonhams and Langlois, Westaway Chambers, 39 Don Street, St Helier, Jersey JE2 4TR Tel: 01534 722441

Cheshire
Bonhams, New House, 150 Christleton Road, Chester CH3 5TD Tel: 01244 313936 www.bonhams.com

Halls Fine Art Auctions, Booth Mansion, 30 Watergate Street, Chester CH1 2LA Tel: 01244 312300/312112

Frank R. Marshall & Co, Marshall House, Church Hill, Knutsford WA16 6DH Tel: 01565 653284

Maxwells of Wilmslow inc Dockree's, 133A Woodford Road, Woodford SK7 1QD Tel: 0161 439 5182

Wright Manley, Beeston Castle Salerooms, Tarporley CW6 9NZ Tel: 01829 262150 www.wrightmanley.co.uk

Cleveland
Vectis Auctions Ltd, Fleck Way, Thornaby, Stockton-on-Tees TS17 9JZ Tel: 01642 750616 admin@vectis.co.uk www.vectis.co.uk
Vectis Auctions Limited, one of the world's leading toy auctioneers, holding over 50 auctions yearly, with a superior internet site giving a full and up-to-date picture of the company.

Cornwall
Bonhams, Cornubia Hall, Eastcliffe Road, Par PL24 2AQ Tel: 01726 814047

Lambrays, Polmorla Walk Galleries, The Platt, Wadebridge PL27 7AE Tel: 01208 813593

W. H. Lane & Son, Jubilee House, Queen Street, Penzance TR18 2DF Tel: 01736 361447

David Lay ASVA, Auction House, Alverton, Penzance TR18 4RE Tel: 01736 361414

Martyn Rowe, The Truro Auction Centre, Triplets Business Park, Poldice Valley, Nr Chacewater, Truro TR16 5PZ Tel: 01209 822266 www.invaluable.com/martynrowe

Cumbria
Bonhams, 48 Cecil Street, Carlisle CA1 1NT Tel: 01228 542422

Kendal Auction Rooms, Sandylands Road, Kendal LA9 6ES Tel: 01539 720603 or 07713 787509 www.kendalauction.co.uk
Regular sales of antique & quality reproduction furniture held at this Lake District based auction room. Situated 10 minutes from Junction 36 or 37 of M6 motorway.

Mitchells Auction Company, The Furniture Hall, 47 Station Road, Cockermouth CA13 9PZ Tel: 01900 827800

Penrith Farmers' & Kidd's plc, Skirsgill Salerooms, Penrith CA11 0DN Tel: 01768 89078 penrith.farmers@virgin.net

Thomson, Roddick & Medcalf Ltd, Coleridge House, Shaddongate, Carlisle CA2 5TU Tel: 01228 528939

Devon
Bearnes, St Edmund's Court, Okehampton Street, Exeter EX4 1DU Tel: 01392 422800 nsaintey@bearnes.co.uk www.bearnes.co.uk

Bonhams, Dowell Street, Honiton EX14 1LX Tel: 01404 41872

Bonhams, 38/39 Southernhay East, Exeter EX1 1PE Tel: 01392 455 955

Michael J. Bowman, 6 Haccombe House, Netherton, Newton Abbot TQ12 4SJ Tel: 01626 872890

Eldreds Auctioneers & Valuers, 13–15 Ridge Park Road, Plympton, Plymouth PL7 2BS Tel: 01752 340066

Robin A. Fenner & Co, The Stannary Gallery, Drake Road, Tavistock PL19 0AX Tel: 01822 617799 sales@rafenner.com www.rafenner.com

S. J. Hales, 87 Fore Street, Bovey Tracey TQ13 9AB Tel: 01626 836684

Honiton Galleries, 205 High Street, Honiton EX14 1LQ Tel: 01404 42404 sales@honitongalleries.com www.honitongalleries.com

The Plymouth Auction Rooms, Edwin House, St John's Rd, Cattedown, Plymouth PL4 0NZ Tel: 01752 254740

Rendells, Stonepark, Ashburton TQ13 7RH Tel: 01364 653017 stonepark@rendells.co.uk www.rendells.co.uk

G. S. Shobrook & Co, 20 Western Approach, Plymouth PL1 1TG Tel: 01752 663341

John Smale & Co, 11 High Street, Barnstaple EX31 1BG Tel: 01271 42000/42916

Martin Spencer-Thomas, Bicton Street, Exmouth EX8 2SN Tel: 01395 267403

Dorset
Bonhams, Long Street Salerooms, Sherborne DT9 3BS Tel: 01935 815271

Chapman, Moore & Mugford, 9 High Street, Shaftesbury SP7 8JB Tel: 01747 852400

Charterhouse, The Long Street Salerooms, Sherborne DT9 3BS Tel: 01935 812277 enquiry@charterhouse-auctions.co.uk www.charterhouse-auctions.co.uk

Cottees of Wareham, The Market, East Street, Wareham BH20 4NR Tel: 01929 552826 www.auctionsatcottees.co.uk

Hy Duke & Son, Dorchester Fine Art Salerooms, Dorchester DT1 1QS Tel: 01305 265080

Onslow's Auctions Ltd, The Coach House, Manor Road, Stourpaine DT8 8TQ Tel: 01258 488838

Riddetts of Bournemouth, 177 Holdenhurst Road, Bournemouth BH8 8DQ Tel: 01202 555686 auctions@riddetts.co.uk www.riddetts.co.uk

Semley Auctioneers, Station Road, Semley, Shaftesbury SP7 9AN Tel: 01747 855122/855222

Essex
Ambrose, Ambrose House, Old Station Road, Loughton IG10 4PE Tel: 020 8502 3951

Leigh Auction Rooms, John Stacey & Sons, 88–90 Pall Mall, Leigh-on-Sea SS9 1RG Tel: 01702 477051

Saffron Walden Auctions, 1 Market Street, Saffron Walden CB10 1JB Tel: 01799 513281 www.saffronwaldenauctions.com
Contact Colin. Sales held every six weeks on Sunday's at 11 o'clock.

Sworders, 14 Cambridge Road, Stansted Mountfitchet CM24 8BZ Tel: 01279 817778 www.sworder.co.uk

Gloucestershire
Bristol Auction Rooms, St John's Place, Apsley Road, Clifton, Bristol BS8 2ST Tel: 0117 973 7201 www.bristolauctionrooms.com

Bruton, Knowles & Co, 111 Eastgate Street, Gloucester GL1 1PZ Tel: 01452 521267

The Cotswold Auction Company Ltd, incorporating Short Graham & Co and Hobbs and Chambers Fine Arts, The Coach House, Swan Yard, 9–13 West Market Place, Cirencester GL7 2NH Tel: 01285 642420 info@cotswoldauction.co.uk www.cotswoldauction.co.uk

Mallams, 26 Grosvenor Street, Cheltenham GL52 2SG Tel: 01242 235712

Moore, Allen & Innocent, The Salerooms, Norcote, Cirencester GL7 5RH Tel: 01285 646050 fineart@mooreallen.co.uk www.mooreallen.co.uk

Specialised Postcard Auctions,
25 Gloucester Street, Cirencester GL7 2DJ
Tel: 01285 659057

Tayler & Fletcher, London House,
High Street, Bourton-on-the-Water,
Cheltenham GL54 2AP
Tel: 01451 821666
bourton@taylerfletcher.com
www.taylerfletcher.com

Wotton Auction Rooms, Tabernacle Road,
Wotton-under-Edge GL12 7EB
Tel: 01453 844733
info@wottonauctionrooms.co.uk
www.wottonauctionrooms.co.uk

Greater Manchester
Bonhams, The Stables, 213 Ashley Road,
Hale WA15 9TB Tel: 0161 927 3822

Capes Dunn & Co, The Auction Galleries,
38 Charles Street, Off Princess Street
M1 7DB Tel: 0161 273 6060

Hampshire
Bonhams, 54 Southampton Road,
Ringwood BH24 1JD Tel: 01425 473333

Evans & Partridge, Agriculture House,
High Street, Stockbridge SO20 6HF
Tel: 01264 810702

Jacobs & Hunt, 26 Lavant Street,
Petersfield GU32 3EF Tel: 01730 233933
www.jacobsandhunt.co.uk

George Kidner, The Old School, The Square,
Pennington, Lymington SO41 8GN
Tel: 01590 670070
info@georgekidner.co.uk
www.georgekidner.co.uk

May & Son, The Old Stables,
9A Winchester Road, Andover SP10 2EG
Tel: 01264 323417
office@mayandson.com
www.mayandson.com

D. M. Nesbit & Co, Fine Art and Auction
Department, Southsea Salerooms,
7 Clarendon Road, Southsea PO5 2ED
Tel: 023 9286 4321
auctions@nesbits.co.uk
www.nesbits.co.uk

Odiham Auction Sales, Unit 4, Priors
Farm, West Green Road, Mattingley
RG27 8JU Tel: 01189 326824
auction@dircon.co.uk

Herefordshire
Brightwells Fine Art, The Fine Art
Saleroom, Ryelands Road, Leominster
HR6 8NZ Tel: 01568 611122
fineart@brightwells.com
www.brightwells.com

Morris Bricknell, Stroud House,
30 Gloucester Road, Ross-on-Wye
HR9 5LE Tel: 01989 768320
morrisbricknell@lineone.net
www.morrisbricknell.com

Nigel Ward & Co, The Border Property
Centre, Pontrilas HR2 0EH
Tel: 01981 240140
www.nigel-ward.co.uk

Williams & Watkins, Ross Auction Rooms,
Ross-on-Wye HR9 7QF
Tel: 01989 762225

Hertfordshire
Sworders, The Hertford Saleroom,
42 St Andrew Street, Hertford SG14 1JA
Tel: 01992 583508 www.sworder.co.uk

Tring Market Auctions, The Market
Premises, Brook Street, Tring HP23 5EF
Tel: 01442 826446
sales@tringmarketauctions.co.uk
www.tringmarketauctions.co.uk

Kent
Bonhams, 49 London Road, Sevenoaks
TN13 1AR Tel: 01732 740310

Bracketts, The Auction Hall, The Pantiles,
Tunbridge Wells TN2 5QL
Tel: 01892 544500
sales@bfaa.co.uk
www.bfaa.co.uk

Calcutt Maclean Standen, The Estate
Office, Stone Street, Cranbrook
TN17 3HD Tel: 01580 713828

The Canterbury Auction Galleries,
40 Station Road West, Canterbury
CT2 8AN Tel: 01227 763337
auctions@thecanterburyauctiongalleries.com
www.thecanterburyauctiongalleries.com

Mervyn Carey, Twysden Cottage,
Scullsgate, Benenden, Cranbrook
TN17 4LD Tel: 01580 240283

Gorringes, 15 The Pantiles, Tunbridge
Wells TN2 5TD Tel: 01892 619670
www.gorringes.co.uk

Ibbett Mosely, 125 High Street, Sevenoaks
TN13 1UT Tel: 01732 456731
auctions@ibbettmosely.co.uk
www.ibbettmosely.co.uk

Lambert & Foster, 102 High Street,
Tenterden TN30 6HT Tel: 01580 762083
saleroom@lambertandfoster.co.uk
www.lambertandfoster.co.uk

Wealden Auction Galleries, Desmond
Judd, 23 Hendly Drive, Cranbrook
TN17 3DY Tel: 01580 714522

Lancashire
Smythe's, 174 Victoria Road West,
Cleveleys FY5 3NE Tel: 01253 852184

Tony & Sons, 4–8 Lynwood Road,
Blackburn BB2 6HP Tel: 01254 691748

Leicestershire
William H. Brown, Warner Auction
Rooms, 16–18 Halford Street, Leicester
LE1 6AS Tel: 0116 255 9900

Gildings, 64 Roman Way, Market
Harborough LE16 7PQ Tel: 01858 410414
sales@gildings.co.uk www.gildings.co.uk

Heathcote Ball & Co, Castle Auction
Rooms, 78 St Nicholas Circle, Leicester
LE1 5NW Tel: 0116 253 6789
heathcote-ball@clara.co.uk
www.heathcote-ball.clara.co.uk

Lincolnshire
DDM Auction Rooms, Old Courts Road,
Brigg DN20 8JD Tel: 01652 650172

Thomas Mawer & Son, Dunston House,
Portland Street, Lincoln LN5 7NN
Tel: 01522 524984
mawer.thos@lineone.net

Marilyn Swain Auctions, The Old Barracks,
Sandon Road, Grantham NG31 9AS
Tel: 01476 568861

Walter's, No. 1 Mint Lane, Lincoln
LN1 1UD Tel: 01522 525454

London
Academy Auctioneers & Valuers,
Northcote House, Northcote Avenue,
Ealing W5 3UR Tel: 020 8579 7466
www.thesaurus.co.uk/academy/

Angling Auctions, PO Box 2095
W12 8RU Tel: 020 8749 4175
neil@anglingauctions.demon.co.uk

Bloomsbury Book Auctions,
3 & 4 Hardwick Street, Off Rosebery
Avenue EC1R 4RY Tel: 020 7833 2636/7
& 020 7923 6940
info@bloomsbury-book-auct.com
www.bloomsbury-book-auct.com

Bonhams, 65–69 Lots Road, Chelsea
SW10 0RN Tel: 020 7393 3900
www.bonhams.com

Bonhams, 101 New Bond Street W1S 1SR
Tel: 020 7629 6602 www.bonhams.com

Bonhams, 10 Salem Road, Bayswater
W2 4DL Tel: 020 7313 2700
www.bonhams.com

Bonhams, Montpelier Street, Knightsbridge
SW7 1HH Tel: 020 7393 3900
www.bonhams.com

Bonhams, 101 New Bond Street
W1S 1SR Tel: 020 7629 6602
www.bonhams.com

Christie, Manson & Woods Ltd,
8 King Street, St James's SW1Y 6QT
Tel: 020 7839 9060

Christie's South Kensington Ltd,
85 Old Brompton Road SW7 3LD
Tel: 020 7581 7611
christies.com

Comic Book Postal Auctions Ltd,
40–42 Osnaburgh Street NW1 3ND
Tel: 020 7424 0007
comicbook@compuserve.com
www.compalcomics.com

Cooper Owen, 10 Denmark Street
WC2H 8LS Tel: 020 7240 4132
www.CooperOwen.com

Criterion Salerooms, 53 Essex Road,
Islington N1 2BN Tel: 020 7359 5707

Dix-Noonan-Webb, 1 Old Bond Street
W1S 4PB Tel: 020 7499 5022

Glendining's (A division of Bonhams
specialising in coins & medals),
101 New Bond Street W1S 1SR
Tel: 020 7493 2445

Harmers of London, 111 Power Road,
Chiswick W4 5PY
Tel: 020 8747 6100
auctions@harmers.demon.co.uk
www.harmers.com

Lloyds International Auction Galleries,
Lloyds House, 9 Lydden Road, Earlsfield
SW18 4LT Tel: 020 8788 7777
www.lloyds-auction.co.uk

Lots Road Auctions, 71–73 Lots Road,
Chelsea SW10 0RN
Tel: 020 7351 7771
marketing@lotsroad.com
www.lotsroad.com

Morton & Eden Ltd, in association with
Sotheby's, 45 Maddox Street W1S 2PE
Tel: 020 7493 5344
info@mortonandeden.com

Proud Oriental Auctions, Proud Galleries,
5 Buckingham Street
WC2N 6BP Tel: 020 7839 4942

Rosebery's Fine Art Ltd,
74/76 Knights Hill SE27 0JD
Tel: 020 8761 2522
auctions@roseberys.co.uk

Sotheby's, 34–35 New Bond Street
W1A 2AA Tel: 020 7293 5000
www.sothebys.com

Sotheby's Olympia, Hammersmith Road
W14 8UX Tel: 020 7293 5000
www.sothebys.com

Spink & Son Ltd, 69 Southampton Road,
Bloomsbury WC1B 4ET
Tel: 020 7563 4000

Merseyside
Cato Crane & Co, Liverpool Auction
Rooms, 6 Stanhope Street,
Liverpool L8 5RF
Tel: 0151 709 5559
johncrane@cato-crane.co.uk
www.cato-crane.co.uk

Outhwaite & Litherland, Kingsway
Galleries, Fontenoy Street, Liverpool
L3 2BE Tel: 0151 236 6561

Middlesex
West Middlesex Auction Rooms,
113–114 High Street, Brentford TW8 8AT
Tel: 0208 568 9080

Norfolk
Garry M. Emms & Co Ltd, Great Yarmouth
Salerooms, Beevor Road (off South Beach
Parade), Great Yarmouth NR30 3PS
Tel: 01493 332668
g_emms@gt-yarmouth-auctions.com
www.gt-yarmouth-auctions.com

Thomas Wm Gaze & Son, Diss Auction
Rooms, Roydon Road, Diss IP22 4LN
Tel: 01379 650306
sales@dissauctionrooms.co.uk
www.twgaze.com

Horners Professional Valuers & Auctioneers, incorporating Howlett & Edrich and Jonathan Howlett, North Walsham Salerooms, Midland Road, North Walsham NR28 9JR
Tel: 01692 500603

Keys, Off Palmers Lane, Aylsham NR11 6JA Tel: 01263 733195
www.aylshamsalerooms.co.uk

Knight's, Cuckoo Cottage, Town Green, Alby, Norwich NR11 7HE
Tel: 01263 768488

Northamptonshire
Merry's Auctioneers, Northampton Auction & Sales Centre, Liliput Road, Brackmills, Northampton NN4 7BY
Tel: 01604 769990

Northern Ireland
Anderson's Auction Rooms Ltd, Unit 7, Prince Regent Business Park, Prince Regent Road, Castereagh, Belfast BT5 6QR Tel: 028 9040 1888

Northumberland
Jack Dudgeon, The New Saleroom, 76 Ravensdowne, Berwick-upon-Tweed TD15 1DQ Tel: 01289 332700
jack@jackdudgeon.co.uk
www.jackdudgeon.co.uk

Nottinghamshire
Bonhams, 57 Mansfield Road, Nottingham NG1 3PL Tel: 0115 947 4414

Arthur Johnson & Sons Ltd, The Nottingham Auction Centre, Meadow Lane, Nottingham NG2 3GY
Tel: 0115 986 9128
arthurjohnson@btconnect.com

Mellors & Kirk, The Auction House, Gregory Street, Lenton Lane, Nottingham NG7 2NL Tel: 0115 979 0000

Neales, 192 Mansfield Road, Nottingham NG1 3HU
Tel: 0115 962 4141 fineart@neales.co.uk
www.neales-auctions.com

C. B. Sheppard & Son, The Auction Galleries, Chatsworth Street, Sutton-in-Ashfield NG17 4GG Tel: 01773 872419

T. Vennett-Smith, 11 Nottingham Road, Gotham NG11 0HE Tel: 0115 983 0541
info@vennett-smith.com
www.vennett-smith.com

Oxfordshire
Bonhams, 39 Park End Street, Oxford OX1 1JD Tel: 01865 723524

Holloway's, 49 Parsons Street, Banbury OX16 5PF Tel: 01295 817777
enquiries@hollowaysauctioneers.co.uk
www.hollowaysauctioneers.co.uk

Mallams, Bocardo House, 24 St Michael's Street, Oxford OX1 2EB
Tel: 01865 241358 oxford@mallams.co.uk

Simmons & Sons, 32 Bell Street, Henley-on-Thames RG9 2BH
Tel: 01491 612810
www.simmonsandsons.com

Soames County Auctioneers, Pinnocks Farm Estates, Northmoor OX8 1AY
Tel: 01865 300626

Scotland
Bonhams, 65 George Street, Edinburgh EH2 2JL Tel: 0131 225 2266

Bonhams, 176 St Vincent Street, Glasgow G2 5SG Tel: 0141 223 8866

Christie's Scotland Ltd, 164–166 Bath Street, Glasgow G2 4TG Tel: 0141 332 8134

William Hardie Ltd, 15a Blythswood Square, Glasgow G2 4EW Tel: 0141 221 6780

Loves Auction Rooms, 52 Canal Street, Perth PH2 8LF Tel: 01738 633337

Lyon & Turnbull, 33 Broughton Place, Edinburgh EH1 3RR Tel: 0131 557 8844
john.mackie@lyonandturnbull.com

Macgregor Auctions, 56 Largo Road, St Andrews, Fife KY16 8RP
Tel: 01334 472431

Shapes Fine Art Auctioneers & Valuers, Bankhead Avenue, Sighthill, Edinburgh EH11 4BY Tel: 0131 453 3222
auctionsadmin@shapesauctioneers.co.uk
www.shapesauctioneers.co.uk

L. S. Smellie & Sons Ltd, Within the Furniture Market, Lower Auchingramont Road, Hamilton ML10 6BE
Tel: 01698 282007 or 01357 520211

Sotheby's, 112 George Street, Edinburgh EH2 4LH Tel: 0131 226 7201
www.sothebys.com

Thomson, Roddick & Medcalf Ltd, 60 Whitesands, Dumfries DG1 2RS
Tel: 01387 279879

Thomson, Roddick & Medcalf Ltd, 20 Murray Street, Annan DG12 6EG
Tel: 01461 202575

Thomson, Roddick & Medcalf Ltd, 43/4 Hardengreen Business Park, Eskbank, Edinburgh EH22 3NX Tel: 0131 454 9090

Shropshire
Halls Fine Art Auctions, Welsh Bridge, Shrewsbury SY3 8LA Tel: 01743 231212

McCartneys, Ox Pasture, Overture Road, Ludlow SY8 4AA Tel: 01584 872251

Mullock & Madeley, The Old Shippon, Wall-under-Heywood, Church Stretton SY6 7DS Tel: 01694 771771
auctions@mullockmadeley.co.uk
www.mullockmadeley.co.uk

Nock Deighton, Livestock & Auction Centre, Tasley, Bridgnorth WV16 4QR
Tel: 01746 762666

Welsh Bridge Salerooms, Welsh Bridge, Shrewsbury SY3 8LH Tel: 01743 231212

Somerset
Aldridges, Newark House, 26–45 Cheltenham Street, Bath BA2 3EX
Tel: 01225 462830

Bonhams, 1 Old King Street, Bath BA1 2JT Tel: 01225 788 988

Clevedon Salerooms, The Auction Centre, Kenn Road, Kenn, Clevedon, Bristol BS21 6TT Tel: 01934 830111
clevedon.salerooms@blueyonder.co.uk
www.clevedon-salerooms.com

Gardiner Houlgate, The Bath Auction Rooms, 9 Leafield Way, Corsham, Nr Bath SN13 9SW Tel: 01225 812912
gardiner-houlgate.co.uk
www.invaluable.com/gardiner-houlgate

Greenslade Taylor Hunt Fine Art, Magdelene House, Church Square, Taunton TA1 1SB Tel: 01823 332525

Lawrence Fine Art Auctioneers, South Street, Crewkerne TA18 8AB Tel: 01460 73041

Tamlyn & Son, 56 High Street, Bridgwater TA6 3BN Tel: 01278 458241

Staffordshire
Louis Taylor Auctioneers & Valuers, Britannia House, 10 Town Road, Hanley, Stoke-on-Trent ST1 2QG
Tel: 01782 214111

Potteries Specialist Auctions, 271 Waterloo Road, Cobridge, Stoke-on-Trent ST6 3HR
Tel: 01782 286622

Wintertons Ltd, Lichfield Auction Centre, Fradley Park, Lichfield WS13 8NF
Tel: 01543 263256
enquiries@wintertons.co.uk
www.wintertons.co.uk

Suffolk
Abbotts Auction Rooms, Campsea Ashe, Woodbridge IP13 0PS
Tel: 01728 746323

Boardman Fine Art Auctioneers, Station Road Corner, Haverhill CB9 0EY
Tel: 01440 730414

Bonhams, 32 Boss Hall Road, Ipswich IP1 5DJ Tel: 01473 740494

Diamond Mills & Co, 117 Hamilton Road, Felixstowe IP11 7BL Tel: 01394 282281

Dyson & Son, The Auction Room, Church Street, Clare CO10 8PD Tel: 01787 277993
info@dyson-auctioneers.co.uk
www.dyson-auctioneers.co.uk

Lacy Scott and Knight, Fine Art Department, The Auction Centre, 10 Risbygate Street, Bury St Edmunds IP33 3AA Tel: 01284 763531

Neal Sons & Fletcher, 26 Church Street, Woodbridge IP12 1DP
Tel: 01394 382263

Olivers, Olivers Rooms, Burkitts Lane, Sudbury CO10 1HB Tel: 01787 880305
oliversauctions@btconnect.com

Vost's, Newmarket CB8 9AU
Tel: 01638 561313

Surrey
Bonhams, Millmead, Guildford GU2 4BE
Tel: 01483 504030

Clarke Gammon, The Guildford Auction Rooms, Bedford Road, Guildford GU1 4SJ Tel: 01483 880915

Ewbank Auctioneers, Burnt Common Auction Room, London Road, Send, Woking GU23 7LN Tel: 01483 223101
antiques@ewbankauctions.co.uk
www.ewbankauctions.co.uk

Lawrences Auctioneers Limited, Norfolk House, 80 High Street, Bletchingley RH1 4PA Tel: 01883 743323
sarah@lawrencesbletchigley.co.uk
www.lawrencesbletchingley.co.uk

John Nicholson, The Auction Rooms, Longfield, Midhurst Road, Fernhurst GU27 3HA Tel: 01428 653727

Richmond & Surrey Auctions Ltd, Richmond Station, Kew Road, Old Railway Parcels Depot, Richmond TW9 2NA Tel: 020 8948 6677
rsatrading.richmond@virgin.net

P. F. Windibank, The Dorking Halls, Reigate Road, Dorking RH4 1SG
Tel: 01306 884556/876280
sjw@windibank.co.uk
www.windibank.co.uk

East Sussex
Burstow & Hewett, Abbey Auction Galleries and Granary Salerooms, Lower Lake, Battle TN33 0AT Tel: 01424 772374
www.burstowandhewett.co.uk

Gorringes Auction Galleries, Terminus Road, Bexhill-on-Sea TN39 3LR
Tel: 01424 212994
bexhill@gorringes.co.uk
www.gorringes.co.uk

Gorringes inc Julian Dawson, 15 North Street, Lewes BN7 2PD
Tel: 01273 472503
auctions@gorringes.co.uk
www.gorringes.co.uk

Edgar Horns, 46–50 South Street, Eastbourne BN21 4XB Tel: 01323 410419
sales@edgarhorns.com
www.edgarhorns.com

Raymond P. Inman, 98a Coleridge Street, Hove BN3 5AA Tel: 01273 774777
www.invaluable.com/raymondinman

Rye Auction Galleries, Rock Channel, Rye TN31 7HL Tel: 01797 222124
sales@ryeauction.fsnet.co.uk

Scarborough Perry Fine Art, Hove Auction Rooms, Hove Street, Hove BN3 2GL
Tel: 01273 735266

Wallis & Wallis, West Street Auction Galleries, Lewes BN7 2NJ
Tel: 01273 480208
auctions@wallisandwallis.co.uk
grb@wallisandwallis.co.uk
www.wallisandwallis.co.uk

West Sussex

Henry Adams, Fine Art Auctioneers, Baffins Hall, Baffins Lane, Chichester PO19 1UA Tel: 01243 532223
enquiries@henryadamsfineart.co.uk
www.henryadamsfineart.co.uk

John Bellman Auctioneers, New Pound Business Park, Wisborough Green, Billingshurst RH14 0AZ
Tel: 01403 700858
jbellman@compuserve.com

Peter Cheney, Western Road Auction Rooms, Western Road, Littlehampton BN17 5NP Tel: 01903 722264 & 713418

Denham's, The Auction Galleries, Dorking Road, Nr Horsham RH12 3RZ
Tel: 01403 255699
info@denhams-auctions.com
www.denhams-auctions.com

R. H. Ellis & Sons, 44–46 High Street, Worthing BN11 1LL Tel: 01903 238999

Sotheby's Sussex, Summers Place, Billingshurst RH14 9AD
Tel: 01403 833500 www.sothebys.com

Stride & Son, Southdown House, St John's Street, Chichester PO19 1XQ
Tel: 01243 780207

Rupert Toovey & Co Ltd, Spring Gardens, Washington RH20 3BS Tel: 01903 891955
auctions@rupert-toovey.com
www.rupert-toovey.com

Worthing Auction Galleries Ltd, Fleet House, Teville Gate, Worthing BN11 1UA Tel: 01903 205565
info@worthing-auctions.co.uk
www.worthing-auctions.co.uk

Tyne & Wear

Anderson & Garland (Auctioneers), Marlborough House, Marlborough Crescent, Newcastle-upon-Tyne NE1 4EE Tel: 0191 232 6278

Boldon Auction Galleries, 24a Front Street, East Boldon NE36 0SJ
Tel: 0191 537 2630

Bonhams, 30–32 Grey Street, Newcastle Upon Tyne NE1 6AE
Tel: 0191 233 9930

Sneddons, Sunderland Auction Rooms, 30 Villiers Street, Sunderland SR1 1EJ
Tel: 0191 514 5931

Wales

Anthemion Auctions, 2 Llandough Trading Park, Penarth Road, Cardiff CF11 8RR Tel: 029 2071 2608

Bonhams, 7–8 Park Place, Cardiff CF10 3DP Tel: 029 2072 7980
cardiff@bonhams.com
www.bonhams.com

Peter Francis, Curiosity Sale Room, 19 King Street, Carmarthen SA31 1BH
Tel: 01267 233456
Peterfrancis@valuers.fsnet.co.uk
www.peterfrancis.co.uk

Morgan Evans & Co Ltd, 30 Church Street, Llangefni, Anglesey, Gwynedd LL77 7DU Tel: 01248 723303/ 421582
llangefni@morganevans.demon.co.uk
www.morganevans.com

Rogers Jones & Co, The Saleroom, 33 Abergele Road, Colwyn Bay LL29 7RU
Tel: 01492 532176
www.rogersjones.co.uk

J. Straker Chadwick & Sons, Market Street Chambers, Abergavenny, Monmouthshire NP7 5SD Tel: 01873 852624

Wingetts Auction Gallery, 29 Holt Street, Wrexham, Clwyd LL13 8DH
Tel: 01978 353553 auctions@wingetts.co.uk
www.wingetts.co.uk

Warwickshire

Bigwood Auctioneers Ltd, The Old School, Tiddington, Stratford-upon-Avon CV37 7AW Tel: 01789 269415

Locke & England, 18 Guy Street, Leamington Spa CV32 4RT
Tel: 01926 889100
www.auctionsonline.com/locke

West Midlands

Bonhams, The Old House, Station Road, Knowle, Solihull B93 0HT
Tel: 01564 776151

Fellows & Sons, Augusta House, 19 Augusta Street, Hockley, Birmingham B18 6JA Tel: 0121 212 2131
info@fellows.co.uk www.fellows.co.uk

Weller & Dufty Ltd, 141 Bromsgrove Street, Birmingham B5 6RQ
Tel: 0121 692 1414
wellerdufty@freewire.co.uk
www.welleranddufty.co.uk

Wiltshire

Henry Aldridge & Son, Unit 1, Bath Road Business Centre, Devizes SN10 1XA
Tel: 01380 729199
andrew.aldridge@virgin.net
www.henry-aldridge.co.uk

Finan & Co, The Square, Mere BA12 6DJ
Tel: 01747 861411
post@finanandco.co.uk
www.finanandco.co.uk

Kidson Trigg, Estate Office, Friars Farm, Sevenhampton, Highworth, Swindon SN6 7PZ Tel: 01793 861000

Dominic Winter Book Auctions, The Old School, Maxwell Street, Swindon SN1 5DR Tel: 01793 611340
info@dominicwinter.co.uk
www.dominicwinter.co.uk

Woolley & Wallis, Salisbury Salerooms, 51–61 Castle Street, Salisbury SP1 3SU
Tel: 01722 424524
mail@salisbury.w-w.co.uk
www.w-w.co.uk

Worcestershire

Andrew Grant, St Mark's House, St Mark's Close, Worcester WR5 3DJ
Tel: 01905 357547

Philip Laney, The Malvern Auction Centre, Portland Road, off Victoria Road, Malvern WR14 2TA Tel: 01684 893933
PhilipLaney@compuserve.com

Philip Serrell, The Malvern Saleroom, Barnards Green Road, Malvern WR14 3LW Tel: 01684 892314

Yorkshire

BBR, Elsecar Heritage Centre, Wath Road, Elsecar, Barnsley S74 8HJ
Tel: 01226 745156
sales@bbrauctions.co.uk
www.onlinebbr.com

Bonhams, 17a East Parade, Leeds LS1 2BH Tel: 0113 2448011

Boulton & Cooper, St Michael's House, Market Place, Malton YO17 7LR
Tel: 01653 696151

H. C. Chapman & Son, The Auction Mart, North Street, Scarborough YO11 1DL Tel: 01723 372424

Cundalls, 15 Market Place, Malton YO17 7LP Tel: 01653 697820

Dee, Atkinson & Harrison, The Exchange Saleroom, Driffield YO25 6LD
Tel: 01377 253151
exchange@dee-atkinson-harrison.co.uk
www.dahauctions.com

David Duggleby, The Vine St Salerooms, Scarborough YO11 1XN
Tel: 01723 507111
auctions@davidduggleby.freeserve.co.uk
www.davidduggleby.co.uk

David Duggleby, The Paddock Salerooms, Whitby YO23 3DB Tel: 01947 820033
auctions@davidduggleby.freeserve.co.uk
www.davidduggleby.com

ELR Auctions Ltd, The Nichols Building, Shalesmoor, Sheffield S3 8UJ
Tel: 0114 281 6161

Andrew Hartley, Victoria Hall Salerooms, Little Lane, Ilkley LS29 8EA
Tel: 01943 816363
info@andrewhartleyfinearts.co.uk
www.andrewhartleyfinearts.co.uk

Lithgow Sons & Partners, The Auction Houses, Station Road, Stokesley, Middlesbrough TS9 7AB
Tel: 01642 710158
info@lithgowsauctions.com
www.lithgowsauctions.com

Malcolm's No. 1 Auctioneers & Valuers
Tel: 01977 684971
info@malcolmsno1auctions.co.uk
www.malcolmsno1auctions.co.uk

Christopher Matthews, 23 Mount Street, Harrogate HG2 8DQ Tel: 01423 871756

Morphets of Harrogate, 6 Albert Street, Harrogate HG1 1JL Tel: 01423 530030

Sheffield Railwayana Auctions, 43 Little Norton Lane, Sheffield S8 8GA
Tel: 0114 274 5085
ian@sheffrail.freeserve.co.uk
www.sheffieldrailwayana.co.uk

Tennants, The Auction Centre, Harmby Road, Leyburn DL8 5SG Tel: 01969 623780
enquiry@tennants-ltd.co.uk
www.tennants.co.uk

Tennants, 34 Montpellier Parade, Harrogate HG1 2TG Tel: 01423 531661
enquiry@tennants-ltd.co.uk
www.tennants.co.uk

Wilkinson & Beighton Auctioneers, Woodhouse Green, Thurcroft, Rotherham SY3 8LA Tel: 01709 700005

Wombell's Antiques & General Auction, The Auction Gallery, Northminster Business Park, Northfield Lane, Upper Poppleton, York YO26 6QU
Tel: 01904 790777
www.invaluable.com/wombell

AUSTRIA

Dorotheum, Palais Dorotheum, A–1010 Wien, Dorotheergasse 17
Tel: 0043 1 515 60 354

AUSTRALIA

Leonard Joel Auctioneers, 333 Malvern Road, South Yarra, Victoria 3141
Tel: 03 9826 4333
decarts@ljoel.com.au or
jewellery@ljoel.com.au
www.ljoel.com.au

Shapiro Auctioneers, 162 Queen Street, Woollahra, Sydney NSW 2025
Tel: 00 612 9326 1588

BELGIUM

Bernaerts, Verlatstraat 18–22, 2000 Antwerpen/Anvers
Tel: +32 (0)3 248 19 21
edmond.bernaerts@ping.be
www.auction-bernaerts.com

CANADA

Bailey's Auctions, 467 Elmira Road, North Guelph, Ontario N1H 6J4
Tel: 001 519 823 1107
auctioneer@baileyauctions.com
www.baileyauctions.com

Robert Deveau Galleries Fine Art Auctioneers, 297–299 Queen Street, Toronto, Ontario M5A 1S7
Tel: 00 416 364 6271

Ritchies Inc, Auctioneers & Appraisers of Antiques & Fine Art, 288 King Street East, Toronto, Ontario M5A 1K4
Tel: (416) 364 1864 auction@ritchies.com
www.ritchies.com

A Touch of Class Auctions, 92 College Crescent, Barrie, Ontario L4M 5C8
Tel: 001 705 726 2120
krista.richards@rogers.com
www.atouchofclassauctions.com

Waddington's Auctions, 111 Bathurst Street, Toronto M5V 2RI Tel: 001 416 504 9100
vb@waddingtonsauctions.com
www.waddingtonsauctions.com

When the Hammer Goes Down, 440 Douglas Avenue, Toronto, Ontario M5M 1H4 Tel: 001 416 787 1700 TOLL FREE 1 (866) BIDCALR (243 2257) BIDCALR@rogers.com www.bidcalr.com

CHINA

Christie's Hong Kong, 2203–5 Alexandra House, 16–20 Chater Road, Hong Kong Tel: 00 852 2521 5396

Sotheby's, Li Po Chun Chambers, 18th Floor, 189 Des Vouex Road, Hong Kong Tel: 852 524 8121 www.sothebys.com

DENMARK

Bruun Rasmussen-Havnen, Pakhusvej 12, DK–2100, Copenhagen Tel: +45 70 27 60 80 havnen@bruun-rasmussen.dk www.bruun-rasmussen.dk

FINLAND

Bukowskis, Horhammer, Iso Roobertink, 12 Stora Robertsg, 00120 Helsinki, Helsingfors Tel: 00 358 9 668 9110 www.bukowskis.fi

Hagelstam, Bulevardi 9 A, II kerros, 00120 Helsinki Tel: 358 (0)9 680 2300 www.hagelstam.fi

FRANCE

Sotheby's France SA, 76 Rue du Faubourg, Saint Honore, 75008 Paris Tel: 00 33 147 42 22 32 www.sothebys.com

GERMANY

Auction Team Koln, Postfach 50 11 19, 50971 Koln Tel: 00 49 0221 38 70 49 auction@breker.com

Hermann Historica OHG, Postfach 201009, 80010 Munchen Tel: 00 49 89 5237296

Sotheby's Berlin, Palais anmFestungsgraben, Unter den Linden, Neue Wache D–10117 Tel: 49 (30) 2010521www.sothebys.com

Sotheby's Munich, Odeonsplatz 16, D–80539 Munchen Tel: 49 (89) 291 31 51 www.sothebys.com

ISRAEL

Sotheby's Israel, Gordon 38, Tel Aviv 63414 Tel: 972(3)522 3822 www.sothebys.com

ITALY

Christie's Rome, Palazzo Massimo, Lancellotti, Piazza Navona 114, Rome 00186 Tel: 00 396 687 2787

Sotheby's, Palazzo Broggi, Via Broggi, 19, 20129 Milano Tel: 02 295001 www.sothebys.com

Sotheby's Rome, Piazza d'Espana 90, 00187, Rome Tel: 39(6) 69941791/6781798 www.sothebys.com

MEXICO

Galeria Louis C. Morton, GLC A7073L IYS, Monte Athos 179, Col. Lomas de Chapultepec CP11000 Tel: 52 5520 5005 glmorton@prodigy.net.mx www.lmorton.com

MONACO

Christie's (Monaco), S.A.M., Park Palace, Monte Carlo 98000 Tel: 00 337 9325 1933

Sotheby's Monaco, Le Sporting d'Hiver, Place du Casino, 98001 Cedex Tel: 00 377 93 30 8880 www.sothebys.com

NETHERLANDS

Christie's Amsterdam, Cornelis Schuystraat 57, Amsterdam 107150 Tel: (3120) 57 55 255

Sotheby's Amsterdam, De Boelelaan 30, 1083 HJ, Amsterdam Tel: 00 31 20 550 22 00 www.sothebys.com

Van Sabben Poster Auctions, PO Box 2065, 1620 EB Hoorn Tel: 31 229 268203 uboersma@sabbenposterauctions.nl www.vsabbenposterauctions.nl

REPUBLIC OF IRELAND

James Adam & Sons, 26 St Stephen's Green, Dublin 2 Tel: 00 3531 676 0261 www.jamesadam.ie

Christie's Dublin, 52 Waterloo Road, Dublin 4 Tel: 00 353 1 6680 585

Hamilton Osborne King, 4 Main Street, Blackrock, Co. Dublin Tel: 00 353 1 288 5011 blackrock@hok.ie www.hok.ie

Mealy's, Chatsworth Street, Castle Comer, Co Kilkenny Tel: 00 353 56 41229 info@mealys.com www.mealys.com

Whyte's Auctioneers, 38 Molesworth Street, Dublin 2 Tel: 00 353 1 676 2888 info@whytes.ie www.whytes.ie

SINGAPORE

Christie's, Unit 3 Park Lane, Goodwood Park Hotel, 22 Scotts Road Tel: (65) 235 3828

Sotheby's (Singapore) Pte Ltd, 1 Cuscaden Road, 01–01 The Regent Tel: (65) 732 8239 www.sothebys.com

SWEDEN

Bukowskis, Arsenalsgatan 4, Stockholm-SE111 47 Tel: 00 46 (0)8 614 08 00 info@bukowskis.se www.bukowskis.se

SWITZERLAND

Christie's (International) S.A., 8 Place de la Taconnerie, 1204 Geneva Tel: 00 4122 319 1766

Phillips, Kreuzstrasse 54, 8008 Zurich Tel: 00 41 1 254 2400

Phillips Geneva, 9 rue Ami-Levrier, Geneva CH–1201 Tel: 00 41 22 738 0707

Sotheby's, 13 Quai du Mont Blanc, Geneva CH–1201 Tel: 00 41 22 908 4800 www.sothebys.com

Sotheby's Zurich, Gessneralee 1, Zurich CH–8021 Tel: 00 41 1 226 2200 www.sothebys.com

USA

Bloomington Auction Gallery, 300 East Grove St, Bloomington, Illinois 61701 Tel: 001 309 828 5533 joyluke@aol.com www.joyluke.com

Frank H. Boos Gallery, 420 Enterprise Court, Bloomfield Hills, Michigan 48302 Tel: 001 248 332 1500

Braswell Galleries, 125 West Ave, Norwalk CT06854 Tel: 001 203 899 7420

Butterfields, 220 San Bruno Avenue, San Francisco CA 94103 Tel: 00 1 415 861 7500

Butterfields, 7601 Sunset Boulevard, Los Angeles CA 90046 Tel: 00 1 323 850 7500

Butterfields, 441 W. Huron Street, Chicago IL 60610 Tel: 00 1 312 377 7500

Christie, Manson & Woods International Inc, 502 Park Avenue, (including Christie's East), New York 10022 Tel: 001 212 636 2000

Christie's East, 219 East 67th Street, New York NY10021 Tel: 001 212 606 0400

Copake Auction, Inc., PO Box H, Copake NY 12516 Tel: 518 329 1142 info@copakeauction.com www.copakeauction.com

William Doyle Galleries, 175 East 87th Street, New York 10128 Tel: 212 427 2730

Du Mouchelles, 409 East Jefferson, Detroit, Michigan 48226 Tel: 001 313 963 6255

Eldred's, Robert C Eldred Co Inc, 1475 Route 6A, East Dennis, Massachusetts 0796 02641 Tel: 00 1 508 385 3116

Freeman Fine Art Of Philadelphia Inc., 1808 Chestnut Street, Philadelphia PA 19103 Tel: 001 215 563 9275

The Great Atlantic Auction Company, 2 Harris & Main Street, Putnam CT 06260 Tel: 001 860 963 2234 www.thegreatatlanticauction.com

Gene Harris Antique Auction Center, 203 S. 18th Avenue, PO Box 476, Marshalltown, Iowa 50158 Tel: 641 752 0600 geneharris@geneharrisauctions.com geneharrisauctions.com

Hunt Auctions, 75 E. Uwchlan Avenue, Suite 130, Exton, Pennsylvania 19341 Tel: 001 610 524 0822 info@huntauctions.com www.huntauctions.com

Randy Inman Auctions Inc, PO Box 726, Waterville, Maine 04903–0726 Tel: 001 207 872 6900 inman@inmanauctions.com www.inmanauctions.com

Jackson's Auctioneers & Appraisers, 2229 Lincoln Street, Cedar Falls IA 50613 Tel: 00 1 319 277 2256

MastroNet, Inc, 1515 W.22nd Street, Suite 125, Oak Brook, Illinois 60523 Tel: 001 630 472 1200 lauraharden@mastronet.com www.mastronet.com

Paul McInnis Inc Auction Gallery, 21 Rockrimmon Road, Northampton, New Hampshire 03862–2336 Tel: 001 603 964 1301

New Orleans Auction Galleries, Inc, 801 Magazine Street, AT 510 Julia, New Orleans, Louisiana 70130 Tel: 00 1 504 566 1849

Northeast Auctions, 93 Pleasant St, Portsmouth NH 03810–4504 Tel: 001 603 433 8400 neacat@ttlc.net

Phillips New York, 406 East 79th Street, New York NY10021 Tel: 00 1 212 570 4830

R. O. Schmitt Fine Art, Box 1941, Salem, New Hampshire 03079 Tel: 603 893 5915 bob@roschmittfinearts.com www.antiqueclockauction.com

Skinner Inc, 357 Main Street, Bolton MA 01740 Tel: 00 1 978 779 6241

Skinner Inc, The Heritage On The Garden, 63 Park Plaza, Boston MA 02116 Tel: 001 617 350 5400

Sotheby's, 1334 York Avenue, New York 10021 Tel: 00 1 212 606 7000 www.sothebys.com

Sotheby's, 9665 Wilshire Boulevard, Beverly Hills, California 90212 Tel: (310) 274 0340 www.sothebys.com

Sotheby's, 215 West Ohio Street, Chicago, Illinois 60610 Tel: 00 1 312 670 0010 www.sothebys.com

Sprague Auctions, Inc., Route 5, Dummerston VT 05301 Tel: 802 254 8969 bob@spragueauctions.com www.spragueauctions.com

Swann Galleries Inc, 104 East 25th Street, New York 10010 Tel: 00 1 212 2544710

Theriault's, PO Box 151, Annapolis MD21401 Tel: 001 800 638 0422 info@theriaults.com www.theriaults.com

Treadway Gallery Inc and John Toomey Gallery, 2029 Madison Road, Cincinnati, Ohio 45208 Tel: 001 513 321 6742 www.treadwaygallery.com

TreasureQuest Auction Galleries Inc, 2581 Jupiter Park Drive, Suite E 9, Jupiter, Florida 33458 Tel: 561 741 0777 www.tqag.com

Weschler's, 909 E. Street NW, Washington. DC2004 Tel: 202 628 1281/ 800 331 14630 judy@weschlers.com www.weschlers.com

Wolfs Gallery, 1239 W. 6th Street, Cleveland OH 44113 Tel: 216 575 9653

WALES

SOUTH EAST

SOUTH WEST

DENHAM'S

THE SUSSEX AUCTIONEERS – FOUNDED 1884

Monthly Fine Art Auctions & Collectors Auctions
Also monthly Secondary Antiques and General Effects sales

☆ FREE PRE-SALE VALUATIONS ALSO VALUATIONS FOR
INSURANCE, PROBATE & FAMILY DIVISION PURPOSES
☆ TRANSPORT SUBSIDISED OVER **LONG DISTANCES**

Regular collections from Sussex, Surrey and Kent

EXCELLENT FACILITIES INCLUDING
Easy access and substantial free parking. Refreshments

THE AUCTION GALLERIES (On the A24 two miles north of Horsham)
Warnham, Nr. Horsham, Sussex Tel: 01403 255699 Tel & Fax: 253837
www.denhams-auctions.com   Email: info@denhams-auctions.com

EWBANK
FINE ART
AUCTIONEERS & VALUERS

Antiques and Fine Art
Auctioneers

Valuations for Probate,
Insurance and Family Division

House clearances arranged

Burnt Common Auction Rooms,
London Road, Send, Woking GU23 7LN
Tel: 01483 223101 · Fax: 01483 222171

www.ewbankauctions.co.uk

Out of town location fronting the A3 halfway
between Guildford and M25

CHARTERED ART AND ANTIQUES SURVEYORS

MEMBERS OF THE SOCIETY OF FINE ART AUCTIONEERS

Amersham Auction Rooms
Tel: 01494 729292   Fax: 01494 722337
www.amershamauctionrooms.co.uk

Every week
throughout the year
General Sales
of
Victorian & Later
Household Furnishings
Decorative Arts & Objects of Purpose
and
Monthly Specialist Sales
of
Antique Furniture
Works of Art & Collectable Items

— **Pretty & Ellis** —
Fine Art & Furniture Valuers & Auctioneers Since 1877

Auctioneers and valuers
of furniture and fine art

RPI
Est. 1929

RAYMOND P. INMAN
FREE AUCTION ADVICE THROUGHOUT SUSSEX

Regular Sales of Antique and Reproduction Furniture, Pictures,
Silver, Jewellery, Ceramics, Glassware, Collectors Items, etc.

PROBATE VALUATIONS AND EXECUTORS SERVICES
WRITTEN VALUATIONS FOR INSURANCE
98a COLERIDGE STREET, HOVE BN3 5AA
RICS

TEL: 01273 774777 www.invaluable.com/raymondinman

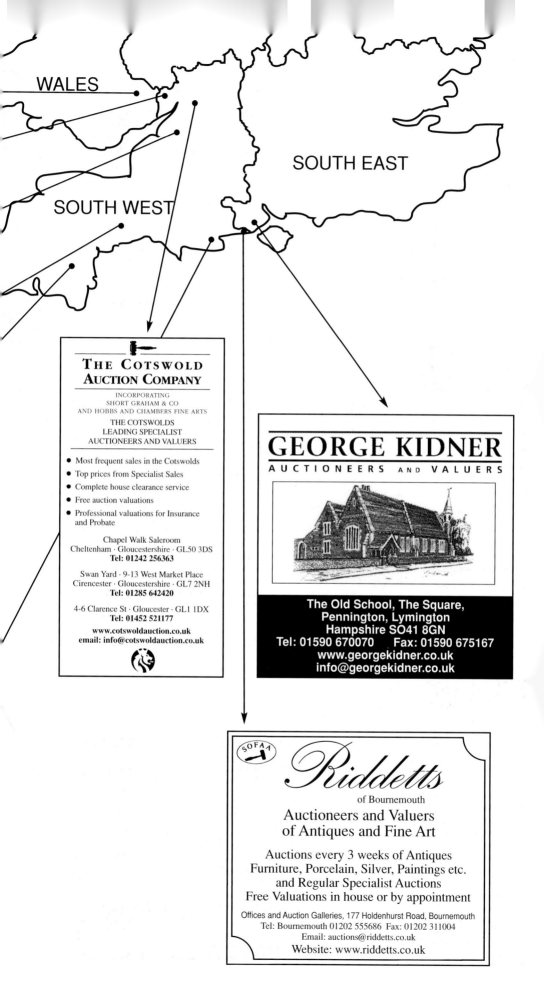

WALES

SOUTH EAST

SOUTH WEST

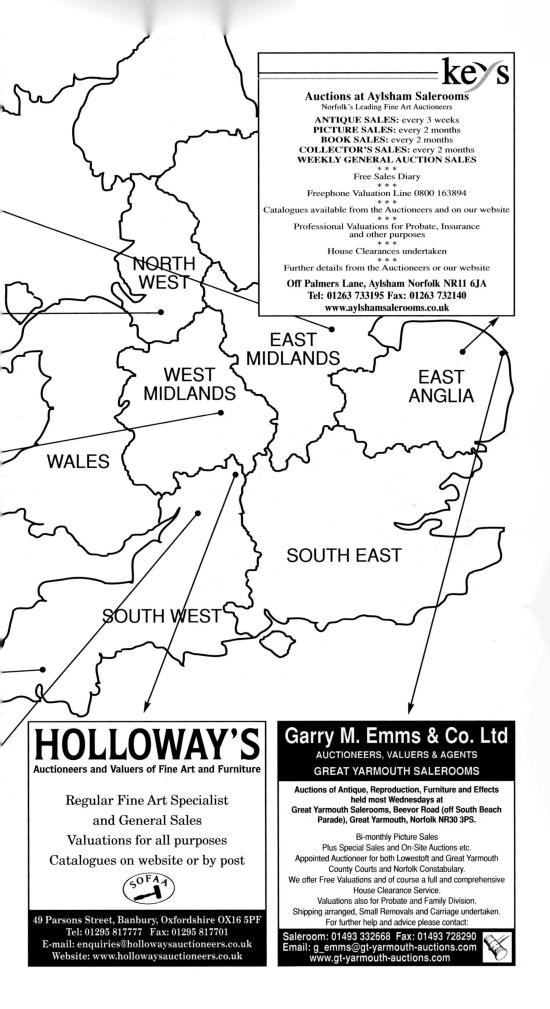

NORTH WEST

EAST MIDLANDS

WEST MIDLANDS

EAST ANGLIA

WALES

SOUTH EAST

SOUTH WEST

Key to Illustrations

Each illustration and descriptive caption is accompanied by a letter code. By referring to the following list of auctioneers (denoted by ⚒) and dealers (⊞) the source of any item may be immediately determined. Inclusion in this edition in no way constitutes or implies a contract or binding offer on the part of any of our contributors to supply or sell the goods illustrated, or similar articles, at the prices stated. Advertisers in this year's directory are denoted by †.

If you require a valuation for an item, it is advisable to check whether the dealer or specialist will carry out this service and if there is a charge. Please mention Miller's when making an enquiry. Having found a specialist who will carry out your valuation it is best to send a photograph and description of the item to the specialist together with a stamped addressed envelope for the reply. A valuation by telephone is not possible.

Most dealers are only too happy to help you with your enquiry; however, they are very busy people and consideration of the above points would be welcomed.

A&O ⊞ Ancient & Oriental Ltd Tel: 01664 812044 alex@antiquities.co.uk www.antiquities.co.uk

AB ⊞ The Antique Barometer Company, 5 The Lower Mall, 359 Upper Street, Camden Passage, London N1 0PD Tel: 020 7226 4992 sales@antiquebarometer.com www.antiquebarometer.com

ACO ⊞ Angela & Clive Oliver, 68 Watergate Street, Chester CH1 2LA Tel: 01244 312306/335157

ADD ⊞ Addyman Books, 39 Lion Street, Hay-on-Wye, Herefordshire HR3 5AD Tel: 01497 821136 www.hay-on-wyebooks.com

AEL ⊞ Argyll Etkin Ltd, 1–9 Hills Place, Oxford Circus, London W1F 7SA Tel: 020 7437 7800 philatelists@argyll-etkin.com www.argyll-etkin.com

AFD ⊞ Afford Decorative Arts Tel: 01827 330042 Mobile: 07831 114909 afforddecarts@fsmail.net

AG ⚒ Anderson & Garland (Auctioneers), Marlborough House, Marlborough Crescent, Newcastle-upon-Tyne, Tyne & Wear NE1 4EE Tel: 0191 232 6278

AGR ⊞ Anthony Green Antiques, Unit 39, The Bond Street Antique Centre, 124 New Bond Street, London W1S 1DX Tel: 020 7409 2854 vintagewatches@hotmail.com www.anthonygreen.com

AH ⚒† Andrew Hartley, Victoria Hall Salerooms, Little Lane, Ilkley, Yorkshire LS29 8EA Tel: 01943 816363 info@andrewhartleyfinearts.co.uk www.andrewhartleyfinearts.co.uk

AKS ⊞† Alan & Kathy Stacey Tel: 01963 441333 Mobile: 07810 058078 By appointment only info@antiqueboxes.uk.com www.antiqueboxes.uk.com

AL ⊞† Ann Lingard, Ropewalk Antiques, Rye, East Sussex TN31 7NA Tel: 01797 223486 ann-lingard@ropewalkantiques.freeserve.co.uk

ALiN ⊞ Andrew Lineham Fine Glass, The Mall, Camden Passage, London N1 8ED Tel: 020 7704 0195 andrew@andrewlineham.co.uk www.andrewlineham.co.uk

ALS ⊞† Allan Smith Clocks, Amity Cottage, 162 Beechcroft Road, Upper Stratton, Swindon, Wiltshire SN2 7QE Tel: 01793 822977 Mobile: 07778 834342 allansmithclocks@lineone.net www.allansmithantiqueclocks.co.uk

AMB ⚒ Ambrose, Ambrose House, Old Station Road, Loughton, Essex IG10 4PE Tel: 020 8502 3951

AMC ⊞ Amelie Caswell Tel: 0117 9077960

AMH ⊞ Amherst Antiques, Monomark House, 27 Old Gloucester Street, London WC1N 3XX Tel: 01892 725552 Mobile: 07850 350212 amherstantiques@monomark.co.uk

AMR ⊞ Art Market Research, 71 Oxford Gardens, London W10 5UJ Tel: 020 8968 9999 artmarketsearch@easynet.co.uk www.artmarketresearch.com

AMS ⊞ Andy & Margaret Shannan, 28 Plymouth Road, Buckfastleigh, Devon TQ11 0DB Tel: 01364 644624 Mobile: 07971 590395

AnAr ⊞ Ancient Art, 85 The Vale, Southgate, London N14 6AT Tel: 020 8882 1509 ancient.art@btinternet.com www.ancientart.co.uk

ANG ⊞† Ancient & Gothic, PO Box 5390, Bournemouth, Dorset BH7 6XR Tel: 01202 431721

ANO ⊞ Art Nouveau Originals Tel: 01733 244717 Mobile: 07774 718 096 cathy@artnouveauoriginals.com www.artnouveauoriginals.com

APC ⊞ Antique Photographic Company Ltd Tel: 01949 842192 alpaco47@aol.com

APO ⊞† Apollo Antiques Ltd, The Saltisford, Birmingham Road, Warwick CV34 4TD Tel: 01926 494746/494666 mynott@apolloantiques.com www.apolloantiques.com

APS ⊞ The Antique Print Shop, 11 Middle Row, East Grinstead, West Sussex RH19 3AX Tel: 01342 410501 printsandmaps@www.theantiqueprintshop.com www.theantiqueprintshop.com

ARB ⊞ Arbour Antiques Ltd, Poet's Arbour, Sheep Street, Stratford-on-Avon, Warwickshire CV37 6EF Tel: 01789 293453

ARTi ⊞ Artifactory, 641 Indiana Avenue NW, Washington DC 20004, USA Tel: 202 393 2727 artifactorydc@msn.com www.artifactorydc.com

ASA ⊞† A. S. Antique Galleries, 26 Broad Street, Pendleton, Salford, Greater Manchester M6 5BY Tel: 0161 737 5938 Mobile: 07836 368230 as@sternshine.demon.co.uk

ASB ⊞ Andrew Spencer Bottomley, The Coach House, Thongs Bridge, Holmfirth, Yorkshire HD7 2TT Tel: 01484 685234 andrewbottomley@compuserve.com

ASC ⊞ Andrew Sclanders, 32 St Paul's View, 15 Amwell Street, London EC1R 1UP Tel: 020 7278 5034 sclanders@beatbooks.com www.beatbooks.com

ASH ⊞ Adrian Ager Ltd, Great Hall, North Street, Ashburton, Devon TQ13 7QD Tel: 01364 653189 afager@tinyworld.co.uk www.adrianager.co.uk

ASP ⊞ Aspidistra Antiques, 51 High Street, Finedon, Wellingborough, Northamptonshire NN9 9JN Tel: 01933 680196 info@aspidistra-antiques.com www.aspidistra.antiques.com

AUA ⊞ Austin's Antiques, PO Box 4723, Ringwood, Hampshire BH24 2DN austinsantiques@ukonline.co.uk www.austins-antiques.co.uk

AUTO ⊞ Automatomania, M13 Grays Mews, 58 Davies Street, London W1K 5LP Tel: 020 7495 5259 Mobile: 07790 719097 magic@automatomania.com www.automatomania.com

AW ⊞† Alan Walker, Halfway Manor, Halfway, Nr Newbury, Berkshire RG20 8NR Tel: 01488 657670 Mobile: 07770 728397 www.alanwalker-barometers.com

B ⚒† Bonhams, 101 New Bond Street, London W1S 1SR Tel: 020 7629 6602 www.bonhams.com

B(Ba) ⚒ Bonhams, 10 Salem Road, Bayswater, London W2 4DL Tel: 020 7313 2700

B(Ch) ⚒ Bonhams, 65–69 Lots Road, Chelsea, London SW10 0RN Tel: 020 7393 3900

B(EA) ⚒ Bonhams, 32 Boss Hall Road, Ipswich, Suffolk IP1 5DJ Tel: 01473 740494

B(Ed) ⚒ Bonhams, 65 George Street, Edinburgh EH2 2JL, Scotland Tel: 0131 225 2266

B(Kn) ⚒ Bonhams, Montpelier Street, Knightsbridge, London SW7 1HH Tel: 020 7393 3900

B(L) ⚒ Bonhams, 17a East Parade, Leeds, Yorkshire LS1 2BH Tel: 0113 2448011

B(Nor) ⚒ Bonhams, The Market Place, Reepham, Norwich, Norfolk NR10 4JJ Tel: 01603 871443

B(NW) ⚒ Bonhams, New House, 150 Christleton Road, Chester CH3 5TD Tel: 01244 313936

B(O) ⚒ Bonhams, 39 Park End Street, Oxford OX1 1JD Tel: 01865 723524

B(Pr) ⚒ Bonhams, Cornubia Hall, Eastcliffe Road, Par, Cornwall PL24 2AQ Tel: 01726 814047

B(S) ⚒ Bonhams, 49 London Road, Sevenoaks, Kent TN13 1AR Tel: 01732 740310

B(SW) ⚒ Bonhams, 7–8 Park Place, Cardiff CF10 3DP, South Wales Tel: 029 2072 7980

B(W) ⚒ Bonhams, Dowell Street, Honiton, Devon EX14 1LX Tel: 01404 41872

B(WM) ⚒ Bonhams, The Old House, Station Road, Knowle, Solihull, West Midlands B93 0HT Tel: 01564 776151

B&L ⚒ Bonhams and Langlois, Westaway Chambers, 39 Don Street, St Helier, Jersey JE2 4TR, Channel Islands Tel: 01534 722441

B&R ⊞† Bread & Roses, Durham House Antique Centre, Sheep Street, Stow-on-the-Wold, Gloucestershire GL54 1AA Tel: 01451 870404/01926 817342

BAL ⊞ A. H. Baldwin & Sons Ltd, Numismatists, 11 Adelphi Terrace, London WC2N 6BJ Tel: 020 7930 6879

BaN ⊞ Barbara Ann Newman Tel: 07850 016729

BAu ⚒† Bloomington Auction Gallery, 300 East Grove St, Bloomington, Illinois 61701, USA Tel: 309 828 5533 joyluke@aol.com www.joyluke.com

BB(L) ⚒ Butterfields, 7601 Sunset Boulevard, Los Angeles CA 90046, USA Tel: 323 850 7500

BBA ⚒ Bloomsbury Book Auctions, 3 & 4 Hardwick Street, Off Rosebery Avenue, London EC1R 4RY Tel: 020 7833 2636/7 & 0207923 6940

info@bloomsbury-book-auct.com
www.bloomsbury-book-auct.com

BBe ⊞† Bourton Bears, Bourton-on-the-Water, Gloucestershire Tel: 01451 821466 mel@strathspey-bed-fsnet.co.uk www.bourtonbears.com

BBo ⊞ Bazaar Boxes Tel: 01992 504 454 Mobile: 07970 909 206 bazaarboxes@hotmail.com commerce.icollector.com/BazaarBoxes/

BBR ⚒ BBR, Elsecar Heritage Centre, Wath Road, Elsecar, Barnsley, Yorkshire S74 8HJ Tel: 01226 745156 sales@bbrauctions.co.uk www.onlinebbr.com

BD ⊞ Banana Dance Ltd, 16 The Mall, Camden Passage, 359 Upper St, Islington, London N1 0PD Tel: 020 8699 7728 Mobile: 07976 296987 jonathan@bananadance.com www.bananadance.com

BDA ⊞ Briar's C20th Decorative Arts, Skipton Antiques & Collectors Centre, The Old Foundry, Cavendish Street, Skipton, Yorkshire BD23 2AB Tel: 01756 798641

Bea/ ⊞ Bearnes, St Edmund's Court, Okehampton
Bea(E) Street, Exeter, Devon EX4 1DU Tel: 01392 422800 nsaintey@bearnes.co.uk www.bearnes.co.uk

Beb ⊞ Bebes et Jouets, c/o Post Office, Edinburgh EH7 6HW, Scotland Tel: 0131 332 5650 Mobile: 0771 4374995 bebesetjouets@u.genie.co.uk you.genie.co.uk/bebesetjouets

BeF ⊞ Bevan Fine Art, PO Box 60, Uckfield, East Sussex TN22 1ZD Tel: 01825 766649 Mobile: 07711 262022 bevanfineart@quista.net

BELL ⊞† Bellhouse Antiques, Chelmsford, Essex Tel: 01268 710415 Bellhouse.Antiques@virgin.net

BERA ⊞ Berry Antiques, 3 High Street, Moreton-in-Marsh, Gloucestershire GL56 0AH Tel: 01608 652929 chris@berryantiques.com berryantiques.com berryantiques.co.uk

BERN ⚒ Bernaerts, Verlatstraat 18–22, 2000 Antwerpen/Anvers, Belgium Tel: +32 (0)3 248 19 21 edmond.bernaerts@ping.be www.auction-bernaerts.com

BEV ⊞ Beverley, 30 Church Street, Marylebone, London NW8 8EP Tel: 020 7262 1576

BEX ⊞† Daniel Bexfield, 26 Burlington Arcade, London W1J 0PU Tel: 020 7491 1720 antiques@bexfield.co.uk www.bexfield.co.uk

BHa ⊞† Judy & Brian Harden Antiques, PO Box 14, Bourton-on-the-Water, Cheltenham, Gloucestershire GL54 2YR Tel: 01451 810684 Mobile: 07831 692252 harden@portraitminiatures.co.uk www.portraitminiatures.co.uk

BIB ⊞† Biblion, Grays Antique Market, 1–7 Davies Mews, London W1K 5AB Tel: 020 7629 1374 info@biblion.com www.biblion.com www.biblionmayfair.com

BIG ⚒ Bigwood Auctioneers Ltd, The Old School, Tiddington, Stratford-upon-Avon, Warwickshire CV37 7AW Tel: 01789 269415

BLm ⊞ Lyn Bloom & Jeffrey Neal, Vault 27, The London Silver Vaults, Chancery Lane, London WC2A 1QS Tel: 020 7242 6189 Mobile: 07768 533055 bloomvault@aol.com www.bloomvault.com

BMi ⊞ Bobbie Middleton, 58 Long Street, Tetbury, Gloucestershire GL8 8AQ Tel: 01666 502761 Mobile: 07774 192660 bobbiemiddleton@lineone.net

BNO ⊞ Beanos, Middle Street, Croydon, London CR0 1RE Tel: 020 8680 1202 enquiries@beanos.co.uk www.beanos.co.uk

Bns ⊞ Brittons Jewellers, 4 King Street, Clitheroe, Lancashire BB7 2EP Tel: 01200 425555 info@brittons-watches.co.uk www.brittons-watches.co.uk www.antique-jewelry.co.uk

BoC ⊞ Bounty Antiques Centre, 76 Fore Street, Topsham, Devon EX3 0HQ Tel: 01392 875007 Mobile: 07939 526504

BR ⚒† Bracketts, The Auction Hall, The Pantiles, Tunbridge Wells, Kent TN2 5QL Tel: 01892 544500 sales@bfaa.co.uk www.bfaa.co.uk

Bri ⚒ Bristol Auction Rooms, St John's Place, Apsley Road, Clifton, Bristol, Gloucestershire BS8 2ST Tel: 0117 973 7201 www.bristolauctionrooms.com

BrL ⊞ The Brighton Lanes Antique Centre, 12 Meeting House Lane, Brighton, East Sussex BN1 1HB Tel: 01273 823121 Mobile: 07785 564337 peter@brightonlanes-antiquecentre.co.uk www.brightonlanes-antiquecentre.co.uk

BROW ⊞ David Brower, 113 Kensington Church Street, London W8 7LN Tel: 0207 221 4155 David@davidbrower-antiques.com www.davidbrower-antiques.com

BrW ⊞ Brian Watson Antique Glass, Foxwarren Cottage, High Street, Marsham, Norwich, Norfolk NR10 5QA Tel: 01263 732519 By appointment only brian.h.watson@talk21.com

BUK ⚒ Bukowskis, Arsenalsgatan 4, Stockholm SE111 47, Sweden Tel: 00 46 (0)8 614 08 00 info@bukowskis.se www.bukowskis.se

BUK(F) ⚒ Bukowskis, Horhammer, Iso Roobertink, 12 Stora Robertsg, 00120 Helsinki Helsingfors, Finland Tel: 00 358 9 668 9110 www.bukowskis.fi

BWL ⚒† Brightwells Fine Art, The Fine Art Saleroom, Ryelands Road, Leominster, Herefordshire HR6 8NZ

Tel: 01568 611122 fineart@brightwells.com www.brightwells.com

ByI ⊞† Bygones of Ireland Ltd, Lodge Road, Westport, Co Mayo, Republic of Ireland Tel: 00 353 98 26132/25701 bygones@anu.ie www.bygones-of-ireland.com

C&A ⊞† Campbell & Archard Ltd, Lychgate House, Church Street, Seal, Kent TN15 0AR Tel: 01732 761153 campbellarchard@btclick.com www.campbellandarchard.co.uk

C&R ⊞† Catchpole & Rye, Saracens Dairy, Jobbs Lane, Pluckley, Ashford, Kent TN27 0SA Tel: 01233 840840 info@crye.co.uk www.crye.co.uk

CaF ⊞ Caren Fine, USA Tel: 301 854 6262 jdcicca@bellatlantic.net

CAL ⊞ Cedar Antiques Ltd, High Street, Hartley Wintney, Hampshire RG27 8NY Tel: 01252 843222 or 01189 326628

Cas ⊞ John & Barbara Gair, Castle Antiques, Essex www.castle-antiques.com

CAT ⊞ Lennox Cato, 1 The Square, Church Street, Edenbridge, Kent TN8 5BD Tel: 01732 865988 Mobile: 07836 233473 cato@lennoxcato.com www.lennoxcato.com

CAV ⊞ Rupert Cavendish Antiques, 610 King's Road, London SW6 2DX Tel: 020 7731 7041 www.rupertcavendish.co.uk

CB ⊞ Christine Bridge, 78 Castelnau, London SW13 9EX Tel: 07000 445277

CBB ⊞ Colin Baddiel, Gray's Mews, 1–7 Davies Mews, London W1Y 1AR Tel: 020 7408 1239/020 8452 7243

CBP ⚒† Comic Book Postal Auctions Ltd, 40–42 Osnaburgh Street, London NW1 3ND Tel: 020 7424 0007 comicbook@compuserve.com www.compalcomics.com

CCO ⊞ Collectable Costume, Showroom South, Gloucester Antiques Centre, 1 Severn Road, Gloucester GL1 2LE Tel: 07980 623926

CGA ⊞ Castlegate Antiques Centre, 55 Castlegate, Newark, Nottinghamshire NG24 1BE Tel: 01636 700076 Mobile: 07860 843739

CGC ⚒ Cheffins, Clifton House, Clifton Road, Cambridge CB1 7EA Tel: 01223 213343 www.cheffins.co.uk

CHAC ⊞† Church Hill Antiques Centre, 6 Station Street, Lewes, East Sussex BN7 2DA Tel: 01273 474 842 churchhilllewes@aol.com www.church-hill-antiques.co.uk

ChC ⊞ Christopher Clarke (Antiques) Ltd, The Fosseway, Stow-in-the-Wold, Gloucestershire GL54 1JS Tel: 01451 830476 cclarkeantiques@aol.com www.campaignfurniture.com

Che ⊞ Chevertons of Edenbridge Ltd, 67–73 High Street, Edenbridge, Kent TN8 5AL Tel: 01732 863196

CHI ⊞ Chinasearch, 9 Princes Drive, Kenilworth, Warwickshire CV8 2FD Tel: 01926 512402 helen@chinasearch.uk.com jackie@chinasearch.uk.com www.chinasearch.uk.com

CHT ⊞ Catherine Hunt Antique Oriental Ceramics, PO Box 743, Cheltenham, Gloucestershire GL52 5ZB Tel: 01242 227794 cathyhunt@btinternet.com

CHTR ⚒ Charterhouse, The Long Street Salerooms, Sherborne, Dorset DT9 3BS Tel: 01935 812277 enquiry@charterhouse-auctions.co.uk www.charterhouse-auctions.co.uk

CO ⚒ Cooper Owen, 10 Denmark Street, London WC2H 8LS Tel: 020 7240 4132 www.CooperOwen.com

CoA ⊞ Country Antiques (Wales), Castle Mill, Kidwelly, Carmarthenshire SA17 4UU, Wales Tel: 01554 890534

CoC ⊞ Comic Connections, 4a Parsons Street, Banbury, Oxfordshire OX16 5LW Tel: 01295 268989 comicman@freenetname.co.uk

CoCo ⊞ Country Collector, 11–12 Birdgate, Pickering, Yorkshire YO18 7AL Tel: 01751 477481

COF ⊞ Cottage Farm Antiques, Stratford Road, Aston Subedge, Chipping Campden, Gloucestershire GL55 6PZ Tel: 01386 438263 info@cottagefarmantiques.co.uk www.cottagefarmantiques.co.uk

CoH ⚒ Cooper Hirst Auctions, The Granary Saleroom, Victoria Road, Chelmsford, Essex CM2 6LH Tel: 01245 260535

CoHA ⊞† Corner House Antiques and Ffoxe Antiques, The Old Ironmongers Centre, 5 Burford Street, Lechlade, Gloucestershire GL7 3AP Tel: 01367 860078 jdhis007@btopenworld.com www.corner-house-antiques.co.uk

COPA ⚒† Copake Auction, Inc, PO Box H, Copake NY 12516, USA Tel: 518 329 1142 info@copakeauction.com www.copakeauction.com

CoS ⊞ Corrine Soffe: 01295 730317 soffe@btinternet.co.uk

CrF ⊞ Crowdfree Antiques, PO Box 395, Bury St Edmunds, Suffolk IP31 2PG Tel: 0870 444 0791 info@crowdfree.com www.crowdfree.com

CS ⊞ Christopher Sykes, The Old Parsonage, Woburn, Milton Keynes, Buckinghamshire MK17 9QM Tel: 01525 290259

CTO ⊞† Collector's Corner, PO Box 8, Congleton, Cheshire CW12 4GD Tel: 01260 270429 dave.popcorner@ukonline.co.uk

CuS ⊞ Curious Science, 319 Lillie Road, Fulham, London SW6 7LL Tel: 020 7610 1175 Mobile: 07956 834094 curioussience@medical-antiques.com

DA ⚒† Dee, Atkinson & Harrison, The Exchange Saleroom, Driffield, East Yorkshire YO25 6LD Tel: 01377 253151 exchange@dee-atkinson-harrison.co.uk www.dahauctions.com

DAC No longer trading

DAD ⊞† decorative arts@doune, Stand 26, Scottish Antique and Arts Centre, By Doune, Stirling FK16 6HD, Scotland Tel: 01786 461 439/0141 946 3571 Mobile: 07778 475 974 decorativearts.doune@btinternet.com www.decorativearts-doune.com

DAN ⊞ Andrew Dando, 34 Market Street, Bradford on Avon, Wiltshire BA15 1LL Tel: 01225 865444 www.andrewdando.co.uk

DAU ⚒ Dickins Auctioneers Ltd, The Claydon Saleroom, Calvert Road, Middle Claydon, Buckinghamshire MK18 2EZ Tel: 01296 714434 info@dickens-auctioneers.com www.dickens-auctioneers.com

DAV ⊞ Hugh Davies, The Packing Shop, 6–12 Ponton Road, London SW8 5BA Tel: 020 7498 3255

DAW ⊞ Douglas Dawson, Dawson Gallery, 222 West Huron, Chicago, Illinois 60610, USA

DD ⚒† David Duggleby, The Vine St Salerooms, Scarborough, Yorkshire YO11 1XN Tel: 01723 507111 auctions@davidduggleby.freeserve.co.uk www.davidduggleby.com

DeA ⊞ Delphi Antiques, Powerscourt Townhouse Centre, South William Street, Dublin 2, Republic of Ireland Tel: 00 353 1 679 0331

DeG ⊞ Denzil Grant, Suffolk Fine Arts, Drinkstone House, Drinkstone, Bury St. Edmunds, Suffolk IP30 9TG Tel: 01449 736576

Del ⊞ Delomosne & Son Ltd, Court Close, North Wraxall, Chippenham, Wiltshire SN14 7AD Tel: 01225 891505

DFA ⊞† Delvin Farm Antiques, Gormonston, Co Meath, Republic of Ireland Tel: 00 353 1 841 2285 john@delvinfarmpine.com www.delvinfarmpine.com

DHA ⊞ Durham House Antiques Centre, Sheep Street, Stow-on-the-Wold, Gloucestershire GL54 1AA Tel: 01451 870404

DHu ⊞ Diana Huntley Antiques, 8 Camden Passage, Islington, London N1 8ED Tel: 020 7226 4605 diana@dianahuntleyantiques.co.uk www.dianahuntleyantiques.co.uk

DIA ⊞ Mark Diamond Tel: 020 8508 4479

DID ⊞ Didier Antiques, 58–60 Kensington Church Street, London W8 4DB Tel: 020 7938 2537/07836 232634

DJH ⊞ David J. Hansord & Son, 6 & 7 Castle Hill, Lincoln LN1 3AA Tel: 01522 530044 Mobile: 07831 183511

DLP ⊞† The Dunlop Collection, PO Box 6269, Statesville NC 28687, USA Tel: (704) 871 2626 or Toll Free Telephone (800) 227 1996

DMa ⊞ David March, Abbots Leigh, Bristol, Gloucestershire BS8 Tel: 0117 937 2422

DMC ⚒ Diamond Mills & Co, 117 Hamilton Road, Felixstowe, Suffolk IP11 7BL Tel: 01394 282281

DMe ⊞ Ireland's Own Antiques, Alpine House, Carlow Road, Abbeyleix, Co Laois, Republic of Ireland Tel: 00 353 502 31348

DN ⚒† Dreweatt Neate, Donnington Priory, Donnington, Newbury, Berkshire RG14 2JE Tel: 01635 553553 fineart@dreweatt-neate.co.uk www.auctions.dreweatt-neate.co.uk

DNo ⊞ Desmond & Amanda North, The Orchard, 186 Hale Street, East Peckham, Kent TN12 5JB Tel: 01622 871353

DNW ⚒ Dix-Noonan-Webb, 1 Old Bond Street, London W1S 4PB Tel: 020 7499 5022

DOA ⊞ Dorchester Antiques, 3 High Street, Dorchester-on-Thames, Oxfordshire OX10 7HH Tel: 01865 341 373

DORO ⚒ Dorotheum, Palais Dorotheum, A–1010 Wien, Dorotheergasse. 17, 1010 Austria Tel: 0043 1 515 60 354

DSA ⊞ David Scriven Antiques, PO Box 1962, Leigh-on-Sea, Essex SS9 2YZ Mobile: 07887 716677 david@david-scriven-antiques.fsnet.co.uk

DSG ⊞† Market Street Gallery Ltd T/A Delf Stream Gallery, Bournemouth, Dorset Tel: 07974 926137 oastman@aol.com www.delfstreamgallery.com

DUK ⊞ Dukeries Antiques Centre, Thoresby Park, Budby, Newark, Nottinghamshire NG22 9EX Tel: 01623 822252

DuM/ Dum/DUM ⚒ Du Mouchelles, 409 East Jefferson, Detroit, Michigan 48226, USA Tel: 313 963 6255

DW ⚒† Dominic Winter Book Auctions, The Old School, Maxwell Street, Swindon, Wiltshire SN1 5DR Tel: 01793 611340 info@dominicwinter.co.uk www.dominicwinter.co.uk

DY ⊞ Dycheling Antiques, 34 High Street, Ditchling, Hassocks, West Sussex BN6 8TA Tel: 01273 842929 Mobile: 07785 456341 www.antiquechairmatching.com

E ⚒† Ewbank Auctioneers, Burnt Common Auction Room, London Road, Send, Woking, Surrey GU23 7LN Tel: 01483 223101 antiques@ewbankauctions.co.uk www.ewbankauctions.co.uk

EAL ⊞† The Exeter Antique Lighting Co, Cellar 15, The Quay, Exeter, Devon EX2 4AP Tel: 01392 490848 Mobile: 07702 969438 www.antiquelightingcompany.com

Ech ⊞ Echoes, 650a Halifax Road, Eastwood, Todmorden, Yorkshire OL14 6DW Tel: 01706 817505

EH ⚒† Edgar Horns, 46–50 South Street, Eastbourne, East Sussex BN21 4XB Tel: 01323 410419 sales@edgarhorns.com www.edgarhorns.com

ETO ⊞ Eric Tombs, 62a West Street, Dorking, Surrey RH4 1BS Tel: 01306 743661 ertombs@aol.com www.dorkingantiques.com

EXC ⊞ Excalibur Antiques, Taunton Antique Centre, 27–29 Silver Street, Taunton, Somerset TA13DH Tel: 01823 289327/07774 627409 pauldwright@btinternet.com www.excaliburantiques.com

F ⊞ Freshfords, High Street, Freshford, Bath, Somerset BA3 6EF Tel: 01225 722111 Mobile: 07714 362863 antiques@freshfords.com www.freshfords.com

F&C ⊞ Finan & Co, The Square, Mere, Wiltshire BA12 6DJ Tel: 01747 861411 post@finanandco.co.uk www.finanandco.co.uk

F&F ⊞ Fenwick & Fenwick, 88–90 High Street, Broadway, Worcestershire WR12 7AJ Tel: 01386 853227/841724

FAC ⊞† Fagan Arms, Inc, 22952 E Fifteen Mile Road, Clinton Township, MI 48035, USA Tel: 586 465 4637 info@faganarms.com www.faganarms.com

FEN See **RbF**

FHF ⚒† Fellows & Sons, Augusta House, 19 Augusta Street, Hockley, Birmingham, West Midlands B18 6JA Tel: 0121 212 2131 info@fellows.co.uk www.fellows.co.uk

FRY ⊞ Curiosities and Collectables, Gloucester Antiques Centre, The Historic Docks, 1 Severn Road, Gloucester GL1 2LE Tel: 01452 529716

FU ⊞ Fu Ts'ang Lung, Rotherham, Yorkshire Tel: 01709 829805 futsanglung@hotmail.com

G(B) ⚒ Gorringes Auction Galleries, Terminus Road, Bexhill-on-Sea, East Sussex TN39 3LR Tel: 01424 212994 bexhill@gorringes.co.uk www.gorringes.co.uk

G(L) ⚒ Gorringes inc Julian Dawson, 15 North Street, Lewes, East Sussex BN7 2PD Tel: 01273 472503 auctions@gorringes.co.uk www.gorringes.co.uk

G&CC ⊞† The Goss & Crested China Club & Museum, inc Milestone Publications, 62 Murray Road, Horndean, Hampshire PO8 9JL Tel: (023) 9259 7440 info@gosschinaclub.demon.co.uk www.gosscrestedchina.co.uk

G&G ⊞ Guest & Gray, 1–7 Davies Mews, London W1K 5AB Tel: 020 7408 1252 info@chinese-porcelain-art.com www.chinese-porcelain-art.com

G&H ⊞ Garret & Hazlehurst Tel: 07976 247942 garhaz.com@btopenworld.com

GAA ⊞ Gabrian Antiques Tel: 01923 859675 gabrian.antiques@virgin.net

GAK ⚒† Keys, Off Palmers Lane, Aylsham, Norfolk NR11 6JA Tel: 01263 733195 www.aylshamsalerooms.co.uk

Gam ⚒ Clarke Gammon, The Guildford Auction Rooms, Bedford Road, Guildford, Surrey GU1 4SJ Tel: 01483 880915

GBr ⊞ Geoffrey Breeze Antiques, 6 George Street, Bath, Somerset BA1 2EH Tel: 01225 466499

GD ⊞† Gilbert & Dale Antiques, The Old Chapel, Church Street, Ilchester, Nr Yeovil, Somerset BA22 8ZA Tel: 01935 840464

GDO ⊞† Gavin Douglas Fine Antiques Ltd, 75 Portobello Road, London W11 2QB Tel: 01825 723441/0207 221 1121 Mobile: 07860 680521 gavin@antique-clocks.co.uk www.antique-clocks.co.uk

GGv ⊞ G. G. van Schagen Antiquair Tel: 0031 229 275692 Mobile: 06 51 393975 g.schagen@wxs.nl

GH ⚒ Gardiner Houlgate, The Bath Auction Rooms, 9 Leafield Way, Corsham, Nr Bath, Somerset SN13 9SW Tel: 01225 812912 gardiner-houlgate.co.uk www.invaluable.com/gardiner-houlgate

GKe ⊞ Gerald Kenyon, 6 Great Strand Street, Dublin 1, Republic of Ireland Tel: 00 3531 873 0625/873 0488

GLD ⊞ Glade Antiques, PO Box 873, High Wycombe, Buckinghamshire HP14 3ZQ Tel: 01494 882818 Mobile: 07771 552 328 sonia@gladeantiques.com www.gladeantiques.com

Gle ⚒ Glendining's (A division of Bonhams specializing in coins & medals), 101 New Bond Street, London W1S 1SR Tel: 020 7493 2445

GM ⊞ Philip Knighton, Bush House, 17B South Street, Wellington, Somerset TA21 8NR Tel: 01823 661618 philip.knighton@btopenworld.com

GN ⊞† Gillian Neale Antiques, PO Box 247, Aylesbury, Buckinghamshire HP20 1JZ Tel: 01296 423754/07860 638700 gillianneale@aol.com www.gilliannealeantiques.co.uk

GoW ⊞ Gordon Watson Ltd, 50 Fulham Road, London SW3 Tel: 020 7589 3108

GRe ⊞ Greystoke Antiques, 4 Swan Yard, (off Cheap Street), Sherborne, Dorset DT9 3AX Tel: 01935 812833

GRG ⊞ Gordon Reece Galleries, Finkle Street, Knaresborough, Yorkshire HG5 8AA Tel: 01423 866219 www.gordonreecegalleries.com

GRI ⊞ Grimes House Antiques, High Street, Moreton-in-Marsh, Gloucestershire GL56 0AT Tel: 01608 651029 grimes_house@cix.co.uk www.grimeshouse.co.uk www.cranberryglass.co.uk

GS ⊞ Ged Selby Antique Glass Tel: 01756 799673
By appointment only

GTH ⌿ Greenslade Taylor Hunt Fine Art, Magdelene House,
Church Square, Taunton, Somerset TA1 1SB
Tel: 01823 332525

GTM ⊞ Gloucester Toy Mart, Ground Floor, Antique Centre,
Severn Road, Old Docks, Gloucester GL1 2LE
Tel: 07973 768452

GWe ⊞ Graham Webb, 59 Ship Street, Brighton, East Sussex
BN1 1AE Tel: 01273 321803

H&G ⊞ Hope & Glory, 131A Kensington Church Street, London
W8 7LP Tel: 020 7727 8424

HA ⊞ Hallidays, The Old College, Dorchester-on-Thames,
Oxfordshire OX10 7HL Tel: 01865 340028/68
Mobile: 07860 625917 antiques@hallidays.com
www.hallidays.com

HAA ⊞† Hampton Antiques, The Crown Arcade, 119 Portobello
Road, London W11 2DY Tel: 01604 863979
info@hamptonantiques.co.uk
www.hamptonantiques.co.uk

HAL ⊞† John & Simon Haley, 89 Northgate, Halifax, Yorkshire
HX1 1XF Tel: 01422 822148/360434
toysandbanks@aol.com

HAld ⌿† Henry Aldridge & Son, Unit 1, Bath Road Business Centre,
Devizes, Wiltshire SN10 1XA Tel: 01380 729199
andrew.aldridge@virgin.net www.henry-aldridge.co.uk

HAM ⌿ Hamptons International, Baverstock House, 93 High
Street, Godalming, Surrey GU7 1AL Tel: 01483 423567
fineartauctions@hamptons-int.com www.hamptons.co.uk

HarC ⊞ Hardy's Collectables Tel: 07970 613077

HARP ⊞ Harpers Jewellers Ltd, 2/6 Minster Gates, York YO1 7HL
Tel: 01904 632634 harpersyork@btopenworld.com
www.vintage-watches.co.uk

HCA ⊞ Hilltop Cottage Antiques, 101 Portobello Road, London
W11 Tel: 01451 844362 Mobile: 0777 365 8082
noswadp@aol.com

HCFA ⊞ Henry T. Callan, 162 Quaker Meeting House Road, East
Sandwich MA 02537–1312, USA Tel: 508 888 5372

HEG ⊞ Stuart Heggie, 14 The Borough, Northgate, Canterbury,
Kent CT1 2DR Tel: 01227 470422
heggie.cameras@virgin.net

HEL ⊞ Helios Gallery, 292 Westbourne Grove, London W11 2PS
Tel: 077 11 955 997 heliosgallery@btinternet.com
www.heliosgallery.cpm

Herm ⌿ Hermann Historica OHG, Postfach 201009, 80010
Munchen, Germany Tel: 00 49 89 5237296

HiA ⊞† Rupert Hitchcox Antiques, The Garth, Warpsgrove,
Nr Chalgrove, Oxford OX44 7RW Tel: 01865 890241
www.ruperthitchcoxantiques.co.uk

HIS ⊞† Erna Hiscock & John Shepherd, Chelsea Galleries,
69 Portobello Road, London W11 Tel: 01233 661407
Mobile: 0771 562 7273 erna@ernahiscockantiques.com
www.ernahiscockantiques.com

HL ⊞ Honiton Lace Shop, 44 High Street, Honiton, Devon
EX14 1PJ Tel: 01404 42416 shop@honitonlace.com
www.honitonlace.com

HO ⊞ Houghton Antiques, Houghton, Cambridgeshire
Tel: 01480 461887 Mobile: 07803 716842

HoG ⌿† Honiton Galleries, 205 High Street, Honiton, Devon
EX14 1LQ Tel: 01404 42404 sales@honitongalleries.com
www.honitongalleries.com

HOK ⌿ Hamilton Osborne King, 4 Main Street, Blackrock,
Co Dublin, Republic of Ireland Tel: 353 1 288 5011
blackrock@hok.ie www.hok.ie

HOLL ⌿† Holloway's, 49 Parsons Street, Banbury, Oxfordshire
OX16 5PF Tel: 01295 817777
enquiries@hollowaysauctioneers.co.uk
www.hollowaysauctioneers.co.uk

HON ⊞ Honan's Antiques, Crowe Street, Gort, County Galway,
Republic of Ireland Tel: 00 353 91 631407
www.honansantiques.com

HOW ⊞ John Howard at Heritage, 6 Market Place, Woodstock,
Oxfordshire OX20 1TA Tel: 0870 4440678
Mobile: 07831 850544 john@johnhoward.co.uk
www.johnpottery.co.uk

HRQ ⊞† Harlequin Antiques, 79–81 Mansfield Road, Daybrook,
Nottingham NG5 6BH Tel: 0115 967 4590
sales@antiquepine.net www.antiquepine.net

HUM ⊞ Humbleyard Fine Art, Unit 32 Admiral Vernon Arcade,
Portobello Road, London W11 2DY Tel: 01362 637793
Mobile: 07836 349416

HUN ⊞ The Country Seat, Huntercombe Manor Barn, Henley-
on-Thames, Oxfordshire RG9 5RY Tel: 01491 641349

HUR ⊞† Shana Dumont, Hurst Gallery, 53 Mt Auburn Street,
Cambridge, MA 02138, USA Tel: 617 491 6888
manager@hurstgallery.com www.hurstgallery.com

HYD ⌿ Hy Duke & Son, Dorchester Fine Art Salerooms,
Dorchester, Dorset DT1 1QS Tel: 01305 265080

IM ⊞† Ibbett Mosely, 125 High Street, Sevenoaks, Kent
TN13 1UT Tel: 01732 456731
auctions@ibbettmosely.co.uk www.ibbettmosely.co.uk

IS ⊞† Ian Sharp Antiques, 23 Front Street, Tynemouth,
Tyne & Wear NE30 4DX Tel: 0191 296 0656
iansharp@sharpantiques.demon.co.uk
www.sharpantiques.demon.co.uk

JAA ⌿† Jackson's Auctioneers & Appraisers, 2229 Lincoln Street,
Cedar Falls IA 50613, USA Tel: 319 277 2256

JAd ⌿ James Adam & Sons, 26 St Stephen's Green, Dublin 2,
Republic of Ireland Tel: 00 3531 676 0261
www.jamesadam.ie

JAK ⊞ Clive & Lynne Jackson Tel: 01242 254375
Mobile: 0410 239351

JAY ⊞ Jaycee Bee Antiques, Hampshire

JBL ⊞† Judi Bland Antiques Tel: 01276 857576 or 01536 724145

JC ⊞ J. Collins & Son, The Studio, 28 High Street, Bideford,
Devon EX39 2AN Tel: 01237 473103

JCH ⊞ Jocelyn Chatterton, 126 Grays, 58 Davies St, London
W1Y 2LP Tel: 020 7629 1971 Mobile: 07798 804 853
jocelyn@cixi.demon.co.uk www.cixi.demon.co.uk

JDJ ⌿† James D. Julia, Inc, PO Box 830, Rte. 201, Skowhegan
Road, Fairfield ME 04937, USA Tel: 207 453 7125
jjulia@juliaauctions.com www.juliaauctions.com

JE ⊞† Julian Eade Tel: 01491 575059 Mobile: 07973 542971

JeF ⊞† Jeffrey Formby, The Gallery, Orchard Cottage, East Street,
Moreton-in-Marsh, Gloucestershire GL56 0LQ
Tel: 01608 650558 www.formby-clocks.co.uk

JeH ⊞ Jennie Horrocks Tel: 07836 264896
gallery@aw18.fsnet.co.uk
info@artnouveaulighting.co.uk
artnouveaulighting.co.uk

JF ⊞ Julia Foster, 84 York Street, London W1H 1DP
Tel: 07973 146610 By appointment only

JHa ⊞ Jeanette Hayhurst Fine Glass, 32a Kensington Church
Street, London W8 4HA Tel: 020 7938 1539

JHo ⊞† Jonathan Horne, 66 Kensington Church Street, London,
W8 4BY Tel: 020 7221 5658 JH@jonathanhorne.co.uk
www.jonathanhorne.co.uk

JIL ⊞ Jillings Antique Clocks, Croft House, 17 Church Street,
Newent, Gloucestershire GL18 1PU Tel: 01531 822100
Mobile: 07973 830110 clocks@jillings.com
www.jillings.com

JM ⌿† Maxwells of Wilmslow inc Dockree's, 133A Woodford
Road, Woodford, Cheshire SK7 1QD Tel: 0161 439 5182

JNic ⌿ John Nicholson, The Auction Rooms, Longfield, Midhurst
Road, Fernhurst, Surrey GU27 3HA Tel: 01428 653727

JOA ⊞ Joan Gale Antiques Dealer, Tombland Antiques Centre,
14 Tombland, Norwich, Norfolk NR3 1HF
Tel: 01603 619129 joan.gale@ukgateway.net

JOL ⊞ Kaizen International Ltd, 88 The High Street, Rochester,
Kent ME1 1JT Tel: 01634 814132

JON ⊞ Jonkers, 24 Hart Street, Henley-on-Thames, Oxfordshire
RG9 2AU Tel: 01491 576427
bromlea.jonkers@bjbooks.co.uk
www.bjbooks.co.uk

JOP ⊞ Jonathan Potter Ltd Antique Maps, 125 New Bond Street,
London W1S 1DY Tel: 020 7491 3520
jpmaps@attglobal.net www.jpmaps.co.uk

JPr/ ⊞† Joanna Proops Antique Textiles & Lighting,
JPR 34 Belvedere, Lansdown Hill, Bath, Somerset BA1 5HR
Tel: 01225 310795 antiquetextiles@aol.co.uk
www.antiquetextiles.co.uk

JRe ⊞ John Read, 29 Lark Rise, Martlesham Heath, Ipswich,
Suffolk IP5 7SA Tel: 01473 624897

JSt ⊞ Jane Strickland & Daughters, 71 High Street, Honiton,
Devon EX14 1PW Tel: 01404 44221
JSandDaughtersUk@aol.com
www.janestricklanddaughters.co.uk

JuC ⊞ Julia Craig, Bartlett Street Antiques Centre,
5–10 Bartlett Street, Bath, Somerset BA1 2QZ
Tel: 01225 448202/310457 Mobile: 07771 786846

JUJ ⊞ Just Jewellery

JUN ⊞ Junktion, The Old Railway Station, New Bolingbroke,
Boston, Lincolnshire PE22 7LB Tel: 01205 480068

JUP ⊞ Jupiter Antiques, PO Box 609, Rottingdean, East Sussex
BN2 7FW Tel: 01273 302865

K&D ⊞† Kembery Antique Clocks Ltd, Bartlett Street Antiques
Centre, 5 Bartlett Street, Bath, Somerset BA1 2QZ
Tel: 0117 956 5281 Mobile: 07850 623237
kembery@kdclocks.co.uk www.kdclocks.co.uk

KES ⊞ Keystones, PO Box 387, Stafford ST16 3FG
Tel: 01785 256648

KEY ⊞† Key Antiques of Chipping Norton, 11 Horsefair, Chipping
Norton, Oxfordshire OX7 5AL Tel: 01608 644992
info@keyantiques.com www.keyantiques.com

KHW ⊞† Keith Harding's World of Mechanical Music,
The Oak House, High Street, Northleach,
Gloucestershire GL54 3ET Tel: 01451 860181
keith@musicbox10.demon.co.uk
www.mechanicalmusic.co.uk

KK ⊞ Karl Kemp & Associates, Ltd Antiques, 36 East 10th
Street, New York NY 10003, USA Tel: (212) 254 1877
info@karlkemp.com www.karlkemp.com

KMG ⊞ Karen Michelle Guido, Karen Michelle Antique Tiles,
PO Box 62, Blairsville PA 15717, USA Tel: (724) 459 6669
Karen@antiquetiles.com www.antiquetiles.com

L ⌿ Lawrence Fine Art Auctioneers, South Street, Crewkerne,
Somerset TA18 8AB Tel: 01460 73041

L&E ⌿ Locke & England, 18 Guy Street, Leamington Spa,
Warwickshire CV32 4RT Tel: 01926 889100
www.auctions-online.com/locke

L&L Linen & Lace, Shirley Tomlinson, Halifax Antiques Centre, Queens Road/Gibbet Street, Halifax, Yorkshire HX1 4LR Tel: 01422 366657 Mobile: 07711 763454

LAY David Lay ASVA, Auction House, Alverton, Penzance, Cornwall TR18 4RE Tel: 01736 361414

LBO Laura Bordignon Antiques, PO Box 6247, Finchingfield, Essex CM7 4ER Tel: 01371 811 791 Mobile: 07778 787929 laurabordignon@hotmail.com

LBr Lynda Brine, Assembly Antiques, 6 Saville Row, Bath, Somerset BA1 2QP Tel: 01225 448488 lyndabrine@yahoo.co.uk www.scentbottlesandsmalls.co.uk

LCM Galeria Louis C. Morton, GLC A7073L IYS, Monte Athos 179, Col. Lomas de Chapultepec CP11000, Mexico Tel: 52 5520 5005 glmorton@prodigy.net.mx www.lmorton.com

LDC L. & D. Collins Tel: 020 7584 0712

LFA Law Fine Art, Firs Cottage, Church Lane, Brimpton, Berkshire RG7 4TJ Tel: 0118 971 0353 info@lawfineart.co.uk www.lawfineart.co.uk

LGU Linda Gumb, Stand 123, Grays Antique Market, 58 Davies Street, London W1K 5LP Tel: 020 7629 2544 linda@lindagumb.com

LJ Leonard Joel Auctioneers, 333 Malvern Road, South Yarra, Victoria 3141, Australia Tel: 03 9826 4333 decarts@ljoel.com.au or jewellery@ljoel.com.au www.ljoel.com.au

LOP Lopburi Art & Antiques, 5/8 Saville Row, Bath, Somerset BA1 2QP Tel: 01225 322947 mail@lopburi.co.uk www.lopburi.co.uk

LU Lucia Collectables, Stalls 57–58 Admiral Vernon Antique Arcade, Portobello Road, London (open Saturdays) Tel: 01793 790607 sallie_ead@lycos.com

LUNA Luna, 23 George Street, Nottingham NG1 3BH Tel: 0115 924 3267 info@luna-online.co.uk www.luna-online.co.uk

LVS Loves Auction Rooms, 52 Canal Street, Perth PH2 8LF, Scotland Tel: 01738 633337

M Morphets of Harrogate, 6 Albert Street, Harrogate, Yorkshire HG1 1JL Tel: 01423 530030

MAA Mario's Antiques Tel: 020 7226 2426 Mobile: 07956 580772 marwan@barazi.screaming.net www.marios_antiques.com

MAG Magna Gallery, Antiques on High, 85 High Street, Oxford OX1 5BG Tel: 01285 750753 info@magna-gallery.com

MAQ Marie Miller Antique Quilts, 1489 Route 30, PO Box 983, Dorset VT 05251, USA Tel: 802 867 5969 www.antiquequilts.com www.antiquehookedrugs.com www.antiquequimper.com

MAR Frank R. Marshall & Co, Marshall House, Church Hill, Knutsford, Cheshire WA16 6DH Tel: 01565 653284

MARK 20th Century Marks, 12 Market Square, Westerham, Kent TN16 1AW Tel: 01959 562221 Mobile: 07831 778992 lambarda@btconnect.com www.20thcenturymarks.com

MB Mostly Boxes, 93 High Street, Eton, Windsor, Berkshire SL4 6AF Tel: 01753 858470

MCA Mervyn Carey, Twysden Cottage, Scullsgate, Benenden, Cranbrook, Kent TN17 4LD Tel: 01580 240283

McP R. & G. McPherson Antiques, 40 Kensington Church Street, London W8 4BX Tel: 020 7937 0812 Mobile: 07768 432 630 rmcpherson@orientalceramics.com www.orientalceramics.com

MDL Michael D. Long Ltd, 96–98 Derby Road, Nottingham NG1 5FB Tel: 0115 941 3307 sales@michaeldlong.com www.michaeldlong.com

MEA Mealy's, Chatsworth Street, Castle Comer, Co Kilkenny, Republic of Ireland Tel: 00 353 56 41229 info@mealys.com www.mealys.com

MER Mere Antiques, 13 Fore Street, Topsham, Exeter, Devon EX3 0HF Tel: 01392 874224

MFB Manor Farm Barn Antiques Tel: 01296 658941 Mobile: 07720 286607 mfbn@btinternet.com btwebworld.com/mfbantiques

MHA Merchant House Antiques, 19 High Street, Honiton, Devon EX14 1PR Tel: 01404 42694/44406 antiquesmerchant@ndirect.co.uk

MI Mitofsky Antiques, 8 Rathfarnham Road, Terenure, Dublin 6, Republic of Ireland Tel: 00 353 1 492 0033 info@mitofskyartdeco.com www.mitofskyartdeco.com

MINN Geoffrey T. Minnis, Hastings Antique Centre, 59–61 Norman Road, St Leonards-on-Sea, East Sussex TN38 0EG Tel: 01424 428561

MIR Mir Russki Tel: 01506 843973 Mobile: 07979 227779 info@russiansilver.co.uk www.russiansilver.co.uk

Mit Mitchells Auction Company, The Furniture Hall, 47 Station Road, Cockermouth, Cumbria CA13 9PZ Tel: 01900 827800

ML Memory Lane, Bartlett Street Antiques Centre, 5/10 Bartlett Street, Bath, Somerset BA1 2QZ Tel: 01225 466689

MLa Marion Langham Limited Tel: 020 7730 1002 marion@ladymarion.co.uk www.ladymarion.co.uk

MLL Millers Antiques Ltd, Netherbrook House, 86 Christchurch Road, Ringwood, Hampshire BH24 1DR Tel: 01425 472062 mail@millers-antiques.co.uk www.millers-antiques.co.uk

MPC M. C. Tel: 01244 301800 Sales@Moorcroftchester.co.uk www.Moorcroftchester.co.uk

MSB Marilynn and Sheila Brass, PO Box 380503, Cambridge MA 02238–0503, USA Tel: 617 491 6064 mpbkitty@aol.com

MSh Manfred Schotten, 109 High Street, Burford, Oxfordshire OX18 4RG Tel: 01993 822302 www.antiques@schotten.com

MTay Martin Taylor Antiques, 323 Tettenhall Road, Wolverhampton, West Midlands WV6 0JZ Tel: 01902 751166/07836 636524 enquiries@mtaylor-antiques.co.uk www.mtaylor-antiques.co.uk

MUL Mullock & Madeley, The Old Shippon, Wall-under-Heywood, Church Stretton, Shropshire SY6 7DS Tel: 01694 771771/07803 276394 auctions@mullockmadeley.co.uk www.mullockmadeley.co.uk

MUR Murray Cards (International) Ltd, 51 Watford Way, Hendon Central, London NW4 3JH Tel: 020 8202 5688 murraycards@ukbusiness.com www.murraycard.com/

NART Newel Art Galleries, Inc, 425 East 53rd Street, New York 10022, USA Tel: 212 758 1970 info@newel.com www.Newel.com

NAW Newark Antiques Warehouse Ltd, Old Kelham Road, Newark, Nottinghamshire NG24 1BX Tel: 01636 674869 Mobile: 07974 429185 enquiries@newarkantiques.co.uk www.newarkantiques.co.uk

NBL N. Bloom & Son (1912) Ltd, 12 Piccadilly Arcade, London SW1Y 6NH Tel: 020 7629 5060 nbloom@nbloom.com www.nbloom.com

NMA Noel Mercer Antiques, Aurora House, Hall Street, Long Melford, Sudbury, Suffolk CO10 9RJ Tel: 01787 311882/01206 323558

NOA New Orleans Auction Galleries, Inc, 801 Magazine Street, AT 510 Julia, New Orleans, Louisiana 70130, USA Tel: 504 566 1849

NoC No.1 Castlegate Antiques, 1–3 Castlegate, Newark, Nottinghamshire NG24 1AZ Tel: 01636 701877 Mobile: 07850 463173

NOS Nostalgia and Comics, 14–16 Smallbrook Queensway, City Centre, Birmingham, West Midlands B5 4EN Tel: 0121 643 0143

NS Nicholas Shaw Antiques, Virginia Cottage, Lombard Street, Petworth, West Sussex GU28 0AG Tel: 01798 345146/01798 345147 Mobile: 07885 643000/07817 572746 silver@nicholas-shaw.com www.nicholas-shaw.com

NW Nigel Williams Rare Books, 22 & 25 Cecil Court, London WC2N 4HE Tel: 020 7836 7757

OE Orient Expressions, Assembly Antiques Centre, 5–8 Saville Row, Bath, Somerset BA1 2QP Tel: 01225 313399 Mobile: 07747 691128

OLA Olliff's Architectural Antiques, 19–21 Lower Redland Road, Redland, Bristol, Gloucestershire BS6 6TB Tel: 0117 923 9232 marcus@olliffs.com www.olliffs.com

OLD Oldnautibits, PO Box 67, Langport, Somerset TA10 9WJ Tel: 01458 241816 geoff.pringle@oldnautibits.com www.oldnautibits.com

OND Ondines Tel: 01865 882465

ONS Onslow's Auctions Ltd, The Coach House, Manor Road, Stourpaine, Dorset DT8 8TQ Tel: 01258 488838

ORI Origin 101, Gateway Arcade, Islington High Street, London N1 Tel: 07769 686146/07747 758852 David @origin101.co.uk www.naturalmodern.com www.origin101.co.uk

OTB Old Tackle Box, PO Box 55, Cranbrook, Kent TN17 3ZU Tel: 01580 713979 Mobile: 07729 278 293 tackle.box@virgin.net

P&T Pine & Things, Portobello Farm, Campden Road, Nr Shipston-on-Stour, Warwickshire CV36 4PY Tel: 01608 663849 www.pinethings.co.uk

PaA Pastorale Antiques, 15 Malling Street, Lewes, East Sussex BN7 2RA Tel: 01273 473259 or 01435 863044 pastorale@btinternet.com

PAO P. A. Oxley Antique Clocks & Barometers, The Old Rectory, Cherhill, Calne, Wiltshire SN11 8UX Tel: 01249 816227 info@paoxley.com www.british-antiqueclocks.com

PAS Tina Pasco, Waterlock House, Wingham, Nr Canterbury, Kent CT3 1BH Tel: 01227 722151 tinapasco@tinapasco.com www.tinapasco.com

PAY Payne & Son, 131 High Street, Oxford OX1 4DH Tel: 01865 243787 silver@payneandson.co.uk www.payneandson.co.uk

PCA Patricia Cater Tel: 01451 830944 Patriciacaterorg@aol.com www.PatriciaCater-OrientalArt.com

Penn Penny Fair Antiques Tel: 07860 825456

PEx Piano-Export, Bridge Road, Kingswood, Bristol, Gloucestershire BS15 4FW Tel: 0117 956 8300

PF Peter Francis, Curiosity Sale Room, 19 King Street, Carmarthen SA31 1BH, South Wales Tel: 01267 233456 Peterfrancis@valuers.fsnet.co.uk www.peterfrancis.co.uk

PFK Penrith Farmers' & Kidd's plc, Skirsgill Salerooms, Penrith, Cumbria CA11 0DN Tel: 01768 890781 penrith.farmers@virgin.net

PGO ⊞† Pamela Goodwin, 11 The Pantiles, Royal Tunbridge Wells, Kent TN2 5TD Tel: 01892 618200 mail@goodwinantiques.co.uk www.goodwinantiques.co.uk

PHA ⊞† Paul Hopwell, 30 High Street, West Haddon, Northamptonshire NN6 7AP Tel: 01788 510636 Mobile: 07836 505950 paulhopwell@antiqueoak.co.uk www.antiqueoak.co.uk

PHo ⊞ Paul Howard Mobile: 07881 862 375 scientificantiques@hotmail.com

PIC ⊞ David & Susan Pickles Tel: 01282 707673

PICA ⊞ Piccadilly Antiques, 280 High Street, Batheaston, Bath BA1 7RA Tel: 01225 851494 Mobile: 07785 966132 piccadillyantiques@ukonline.co.uk

Pott ⚒ Potteries Specialist Auctions, 271 Waterloo Road, Cobridge, Stoke on Trent, Staffordshire ST6 3HR Tel: 01782 286622

PPC ⊞ Period Piano Company, Park Farm Oast, Hareplain Road, Biddenden, Nr Ashford, Kent TN27 8LJ Tel: 01580 291393 www.periodpiano.com

PrB ⊞ Pretty Bizarre, 170 High Street, Deal, Kent CT14 6BQ Tel: 07973 794537

PSA ⊞ Pantiles Spa Antiques, 4, 5, 6 Union House, The Pantiles, Tunbridge Wells, Kent TN4 8HE Tel: 01892 541377 Mobile: 07711 283655 psa.wells@btinternet.com www.antiques-tun-wells-kent.co.uk

PSC ⊞ Peter & Sonia Cashman, Bartlett Street Antique Centre, 5–10 Bartlett Street, Bath, Somerset BA1 2QZ Tel: 01225 469497 Mobile: 0780 8609860

PT ⊞† Pieces of Time, (1–7 Davies Mews), 26 South Molton Lane, London W1Y 2LP Tel: 020 7629 2422 info@antique-watch.com www.antique-watch.com

PTh ⊞ Antique Clocks by Patrick Thomas, 62a West Street, Dorking, Surrey RH4 1BS Tel: 01306 743661 clockman@fsmail.net www.antiqueclockshop.co.uk

PVD ⊞ Puritan Values at the Dome, St Edmunds Business Park, St Edmunds Road, Southwold, Suffolk IP18 6BZ Tel: 01502 722211 Mobile: 07966 371676 sales@puritanvalues.com www.puritanvalues.com

Q&C ⊞† Q & C Militaria, 22 Suffolk Road, Cheltenham, Gloucestershire GL50 2AQ Tel: 01242 519815 Mobile: 07778 613977 qcmilitaria@btconnect.com www.qcmilitaria.com

QM ⊞ The Quiet Man, Core One, The Gas Works, 2 Michael Road, London SW6 2AN Tel: 020 7736 3384 cullis24@hotmail.com

RAN ⊞ Ranby Hall-Antiques, Barnby Moor, Retford, Nottinghamshire DN22 8JQ Tel: 01777 860696 Mobile: 07860 463477 paul.wyatt@virgin.net www.ranbyhall.antiques-gb.com

RAP ⊞ Rapparee Antiques at Louisa Frances Fine Antiques, High Street, Brasted, Westerham, Kent TN16 1JB Tel: 01959 561222 or 020 8777 4016

RAV ⊞ Ravenwood Antiques Tel: 01886 884 456 alan@arthur81.freeserve.co.uk

RAY ⊞ Derek & Tina Rayment Antiques, Orchard House, Barton Road, Barton, Nr Farndon, Cheshire SY14 7HT Tel: 01829 270429 Mobile: 07860 666629 and 07702 922410 raymentantiques@aol.com www.antique-barometers.com

RbF ⚒† Robin A. Fenner & Co, The Stannary Gallery, Drake Road, Tavistock, Devon PL19 0AX Tel: 01822 617799 sales@rafenner.com www.rafenner.com

RdeR ⊞ Rogers de Rin, 76 Royal Hospital Road, London SW3 4HN Tel: 020 7352 9007

RdV ⊞ Roger de Ville Antiques Tel: 01629 812496 Mobile: 07798 793857 www.rogerdeville.co.uk

REF ⊞† The Refectory, 38 West Street, Dorking, Surrey RH4 1BU Tel: 01306 742111 www.therefectory.co.uk

REI ⊞ Reindeer Antiques Ltd, 43 Watling Street, Potterspury, Northamptonshire NN12 7QD Tel: 01908 542200 nicholasfuller@btconnect.com www.reindeerantiques.co.uk

RGA ⊞ Richard Gibbon, Shop 4, 34/34a Islington Green, London N1 8DU Tel: 020 7354 2852 Mobile: 07958 674447 neljeweluk@aol.com

RGa ⊞ Richard Gardner Antiques, Swanhouse Market Square, Petworth, West Sussex GU28 0AN Tel: 01798 343411

RGe ⊞ Rupert Gentle Antiques, The Manor House, Milton Lilbourne, Nr Pewsey, Wiltshire SN9 5LQ Tel: 01672 563344

RH ⊞ Rick Hubbard Art Deco, 3 Tee Court, Bell Street, Romsey, Hampshire SO51 8GY Tel: 01794 513133 Mobile: 07767 267607 rick@rickhubbard-artdeco.co.uk www.rickhubbard-artdeco.co.uk

RHa ⊞ Robert Hall, 15c Clifford Street, London W1X 1RF Tel: 020 7734 4008

RIT ⚒ Ritchies Inc, Auctioneers & Appraisers of Antiques & Fine Art, 288 King Street East, Toronto, Ontario M5A 1K4, Canada Tel: (416) 364 1864 auction@ritchies.com www.ritchies.com

RKa ⊞ Richardson & Kailas Tel: 020 7371 0491 By appointment only

RMC ⊞† Romsey Medal Centre, The Grapes Hotel,16 Douglas Square, Newcastleton, Roxburghshire TD9 0QD Tel: 013873 75245 post@romseymedals.co.uk www.romseymedals.co.uk

RMe ⊞ Jubilee Photographica, 10 Pierrepoint Row, Camden Passage, London N1 8EE Tel: 07860 793707

ROSc ⚒† R. O. Schmitt Fine Art, Box 1941, Salem, New Hampshire 03079, USA Tel: 603 893 5915 bob@roschmittfinearts.com www.antiqueclockauction.com

RPh ⊞† Phelps Antiques, 133–135 St Margaret's Road, Twickenham, Middlesex TW1 1RG Tel: 020 8892 1778/7129 antiques@phelps.co.uk www.phelps.co.uk

RTo ⚒† Rupert Toovey & Co Ltd, Spring Gardens, Washington, West Sussex RH20 3BS Tel: 01903 891955 auctions@rupert-toovey.com www.rupert-toovey.com

RTW ⊞† Richard Twort Tel: 01934 641900 Mobile: 07711 939789

RUSK ⊞ Ruskin Decorative Arts, 5 Talbot Court, Stow-on-the-Wold, Cheltenham, Gloucestershire GL54 1DP Tel: 01451 832254 william.anne@ruskindecarts.co.uk

RYA ⊞† Robert Young Antiques, 68 Battersea Bridge Road, London SW11 3AG Tel: 020 7228 7847

S ⚒ Sotheby's, 34–35 New Bond Street, London W1A 2AA Tel: 020 7293 5000 www.sothebys.com

S(Am) ⚒ Sotheby's Amsterdam, De Boelelaan 30, 1083 HJ, Amsterdam, Netherlands Tel: 00 31 20 550 22 00 www.sothebys.com

S(G) ⚒ Sotheby's, 13 Quai du Mont Blanc, Geneva, Switzerland CH–1201 Tel: 00 41 22 908 4800 www.sothebys.com

S(HK) ⚒ Sotheby's, Li Po Chun Chambers, 18th Floor, 189 Des Vouex Road, Hong Kong, China Tel: 852 524 8121 www.sothebys.com

S(NY) ⚒ Sotheby's, 1334 York Avenue, New York NY 10021, USA Tel: 212 606 7000 www.sothebys.com

S(O) ⚒ Sotheby's Olympia, Hammersmith Road, London W14 8UX Tel: 020 7293 5000 www.sothebys.com

S(P) ⚒ Sotheby's France SA, 76 Rue du Faubourg, Saint Honore, 75008 Paris, France Tel: 00 33 147 42 22 32 www.sothebys.com

S(S) ⚒ Sotheby's Sussex, Summers Place, Billingshurst, West Sussex RH14 9AD Tel: 01403 833500 www.sothebys.com

S&D ⊞ S. & D. Postcards, Bartlett Street Antique Centre, 5–10 Bartlett Street, Bath, Somerset BA1 2QZ winstampok@netscapeonline.co.uk

SA ⊞ Sporting Antiques, St Ives, Cambridgeshire Tel: 01480 463891 john.lambden@virgin.net

SAM ⊞ Samarkand Galleries, 7–8 Brewery Yard, Sheep Street, Stow-on-the-Wold, Gloucestershire GL54 1AA Tel: 01451 832322 mac@samarkand.co.uk www.samarkand.co.uk

SAM ⊞ Samarkand Galleries, 16 Howe Street, Edinburgh EH3 6TD, Scotland Tel: 0131 225 2010 howe@samarkand.co.uk www.samarkand.co.uk

SAS ⚒† Special Auction Services, Kennetholme, Midgham, Reading, Berkshire RG7 5UX Tel: 0118 971 2949 www.invaluable.com/sas/

SAT ⊞ The Swan at Tetsworth, High Street, Tetsworth, Nr Thame, Oxfordshire OX9 7AB Tel: 01844 281777 antiques@theswan.co.uk www.theswan.co.uk

SAW ⊞ Salisbury Antiques Warehouse Ltd, 94 Wilton Road, Salisbury, Wiltshire SP2 7JJ Tel: 01722 410634 Mobile: 07703 211151 kevin@salisbury-antiques.co.uk

SAY ⊞ Charlotte Sayers, 360 Grays Antique Market, 58 Davies St, London W1K 5LP Tel: 020 7499 5478

SBL ⊞ Twentieth Century Style Tel: 01822 614831

SCO ⊞ Peter Scott Tel: 0117 986 8468 Mobile: 07850 639770

SDA ⊞ Stephanie Davison Antiques, Bakewell Antiques Centre, King Street, Bakewell, Derbyshire DE45 1DZ Tel: 01629 812496 Mobile: 07771 564 993 bacc@chappells-antiques.co.uk www.chappells-antiques.co.uk

SEA ⊞† Mark Seabrook Antiques, PO Box 396, Huntingdon, Cambridgeshire PE28 0ZA Tel: 01480 861935 Mobile: 07770 721931 enquiries@markseabrook.com www.markseabrook.com

SeH ⊞† Seventh Heaven, Chirk Mill, Chirk, Wrexham, County Borough LL14 5BU, Wales Tel: 01691 777622/773563 requests@seventh-heaven.co.uk www.seventh-heaven.co.uk

SER ⊞ Serendipity, 125 High Street, Deal, Kent CT14 6BB Tel: 01304 369165/01304 366536 dipityantiques@aol.com

SET ⊞† Setnik's In Time Again, 815 Sutter Street, Suite 2, Folsom, California 95630, USA Tel: 916 985 2390 Toll Free 888 333 1715 setniks@pacbell.net setniksintimeagain.com

SGr ⊞ Sarah Groombridge, Stand 335, Grays Market, 58 Davies Street, London W1K 5LP Tel: 020 7629 0225 Mobile: 07770 920277 sarah.groombridge@totalise.co.uk

SHa ⊞† Shapiro & Co, Stand 380, Gray's Antique Market, 58 Davies Street, London W1K 5LP Tel: 020 7491 2710

SIE ⊞ Sieff, 49 Long Street, Tetbury, Gloucestershire GL8 8AA Tel: 01666 504477 sieff@sieff.co.uk www.sieff.co.uk

SJH ⚒ S. J. Hales, 87 Fore Street, Bovey Tracey, Devon TQ13 9AB Tel: 01626 836684

SK   Skinner Inc, The Heritage On The Garden, 63 Park Plaza, Boston MA 02116, USA Tel: 001 617 350 5400

SK(B)   Skinner Inc, 357 Main Street, Bolton MA 01740, USA Tel: 978 779 6241

SMI   Skip & Janie Smithson Antiques Tel: 01754 810265 Mobile: 07831 399180

Som   Somervale Antiques, 6 Radstock Road, Midsomer Norton, Bath, Somerset BA3 2AJ Tel: 01761 412686 Mobile: 07885 088022 ronthomas@somervaleantiquesglass.co.uk www.somervaleantiquesglass.co.uk

SPA   Sporting Antiques, 10 Union Square, The Pantiles, Tunbridge Wells, Kent TN4 8HE Tel: 01892 522661

SPF   Scarborough Perry Fine Art, Hove Auction Rooms, Hove Street, Hove, East Sussex BN3 2GL Tel: 01273 735266

SPG   Sprague Auctions, Inc, Route 5, Dummerston, VT 05301, USA Tel: 802 254 8969 bob@spragueauctions.com www.spragueauctions.com

SPT   Sporting Times Gone By, Warehouse (Clubhouse) Tel: 01903 885656 Mobile: 07976 942059 www.sportingtimes.co.uk

SSW   Spencer Swaffer, 30 High Street, Arundel, West Sussex BN18 9AB Tel: 01903 882132

STA   Michelina & George Stacpoole, Main St, Adare, Co Limerick, Republic of Ireland Tel: 00 353 61 396 409 stacpool@iol.ie

SuA   Suffolk House Antiques, High Street, Yoxford, Suffolk IP17 3EP Tel: 01728 668122 Mobile: 07860 521583

SWA   S. W. Antiques, Newlands (road), Pershore, Worcestershire WR10 1BP Tel: 01386 555580 sw-antiques@talk21.com www.sw-antiques.co.uk

SWB   Sweetbriar Gallery Paperweights Ltd, Sweetbriar House, Robin Hood Lane, Helsby, Cheshire WA6 9NH Tel: 01928 723851 Mobile: 07860 907532 sales@sweetbriar.co.uk www.sweetbriar.co.uk

SWN   Swan Antiques, Stone Street, Cranbrook, Kent TN17 3HF Tel: 01580 712720

SWO   Sworders, 14 Cambridge Road, Stansted Mountfitchet, Essex CM24 8BZ Tel: 01279 817778 www.sworder.co.uk

TDG   The Design Gallery 1850–1950, 5 The Green, Westerham, Kent TN16 1AS Tel: 01959 561234 Mobile: 07974 322858 sales@thedesigngallery.uk.com www.thedesigngallery.uk.com

TDS   The Decorator Source, 39a Long Street, Tetbury, Gloucestershire GL8 8AA Tel: 01666 505358

TeG   The Temple Gallery, 6 Clarendon Cross, Holland Park, London W11 4AP Tel: 020 7727 3809 info@templegallery.com www.templegallery.com

TEM   Tempus, Tunbridge Wells Antique Centre, Union Square, The Pantiles, Tunbridge Wells, Kent Tel: 01932 828936 tempus.watches@tinyonline.co.uk www.tempus-watches.co.uk

TEN   Tennants, The Auction Centre, Harmby Road, Leyburn, Yorkshire DL8 5SG Tel: 01969 623780 enquiry@tennants-ltd.co.uk www.tennants-ltd.co.uk

TEN   Tennants, 34 Montpellier Parade, Harrogate, Yorkshire HG1 2TG Tel: 01423 531661 enquiry@tennants-ltd.co.uk www.tennants.co.uk

TF   Tayler & Fletcher, London House, High Street, Bourton-on-the-Water, Cheltenham, Gloucestershire GL54 2AP Tel: 01451 821666 bourton@taylerfletcher.com www.taylerfletcher.com

TH   Tony Horsley, PO Box 3127, Brighton, East Sussex BN1 5SS Tel: 01273 550770

THE   Theriault's, PO Box 151, Annapolis MD21404, USA Tel: 410 224 3655 info@theriaults.com www.theriaults.com

TLG   The Lamp Gallery, Talbot Walk Antiques Centre, The Talbot Hotel, High Street, Ripley, Surrey GU23 6BB Tel: 01483 211724

TMA   Tring Market Auctions, The Market Premises, Brook Street, Tring, Hertfordshire HP23 5EF Tel: 01442 826446 sales@tringmarketauctions.co.uk www.tringmarketauctions.co.uk

TML   Timothy Millett Ltd, Historic Medals and Works of Art, PO Box 20851, London SE22 0YN Tel: 020 8693 1111 Mobile: 07778 637 898 tim@timothymillett.demon.co.uk

TOM   Charles Tomlinson, Chester Tel: 01244 318395 charles.tomlinson@lineone.net www.lineone.net/~charles.tomlinson

TPC   Pine Cellars, 39 Jewry Street, Winchester, Hampshire SO23 8RY Tel: 01962 777546/867014

TQA   Treasure Quest Auction Galleries, Inc, 2581 Jupiter Park Drive, Suite E9, Jupiter, Florida 33458, USA Tel: 561 741 0777 www.tqag.com

TRA   Tramps, Tuxford Hall, Lincoln Road, Tuxford, Newark, Nottinghamshire NG22 0HR Tel: 01777 872 543 info@trampsuk.com

TREA   Treadway Gallery, Inc, 2029 Madison Road, Cincinnati, Ohio 45208, USA Tel: 513 321 6742 www.treadwaygallery.com

TRI   Trident Antiques, 2 Foundry House, Hall Street, Long Melford, Suffolk CO10 9JR Tel: 01787 883388 Mobile: 07860 221402 tridentoak@aol.com

Trib   Tribal Gathering, No. 1 Westbourne Grove Mews, Notting Hill, London W11 2RU Tel: 020 7221 6650 bryan@tribalgathering.com www.tribalgatheringlondon.com

TRL   Thomson, Roddick & Medcalf Ltd, Coleridge House, Shaddongate, Carlisle, Cumbria CA2 5TU Tel: 01228 528939

TRM   Thomson, Roddick & Medcalf Ltd, 60 Whitesands, Dumfries, Scotland DG1 2RS Tel: 01387 279879

TRM   Thomson, Roddick & Medcalf Ltd, 20 Murray Street, Annan, Scotland DG12 6EG Tel: 01461 202575

TRM   Thomson, Roddick & Medcalf Ltd, 43/4 Hardengreen Business Park, Eskbank, Edinburgh EH22 3NX, Scotland Tel: 0131 454 9090

TRO   The Troika Man Tel: 01535 273088 thetroikaman@aol.com www.troikapottery.org

TSC   The Silver Collection Ltd Tel: 01442 890954 Mobile: 07802 447813

TUN   Tunbridge Wells Antiques, 12 Union Square, The Pantiles, Tunbridge Wells, Kent TN4 8HE Tel: 01892 533708

TWh   Tim Wharton, 24 High Street, Redbourn, Nr St Albans, Hertfordshire AL3 7LL Tel: 01582 794371 Mobile: 07850 622880

TWI   Twinkled, High St Antiques Centre, 39 High Street, Hastings, East Sussex TN34 Tel: 01424 460068 info@twinkled.net www.twinkled.net

UCO   Unique Collections, 52 Greenwich Church Street, London SE10 9BL Tel: 020 8305 0867 glen@uniquecollections.co.uk www.uniquecollections.co.uk

US   Ulla Stafford Tel: 0118 934 3208 Mobile: 07944 815104

VB   Variety Box, 16 Chapel Place, Tunbridge Wells, Kent TN1 1YQ Tel: 01892 531868

VCL   Vintage Cameras Ltd, 256 Kirkdale, Sydenham, London SE26 4NL Tel: 020 8778 5416 info@vintagecameras.co.uk www.vintagecameras.co.uk

VEC   Vectis Auctions Ltd, Fleck Way, Thornaby, Stockton-on-Tees, Cleveland TS17 9JZ Tel: 01642 750616 admin@vectis.co.uk www.vectis.co.uk

VJ   Ventnor Junction, 48 High Street, Ventnor, Isle of Wight PO38 1LT Tel: 01983 853996 shop@ventjunc.freeserve.co.uk

VS   T. Vennett-Smith, 11 Nottingham Road, Gotham, Nottinghamshire NG11 0HE Tel: 0115 983 0541 info@vennett-smith.com www.vennett-smith.com

VSP   Van Sabben Poster Auctions, PO Box 2065, 1620 EB Hoorn, Netherlands Tel: 31 229 268203 uboersma@sabbenposterauctions.nl www.vsabbenposterauctions.nl

W&C   Westland & Co, St Michael's Church, Leonard Street (off Great Eastern Street), London EC2A 4ER Tel: 020 77398094 westland@westland.co.uk www.westland.co.uk

WAC   Worcester Antiques Centre, Reindeer Court, Mealcheapen Street, Worcester WR1 4DF Tel: 01905 610680 WorcsAntiques@aol.com

WAL   Wallis & Wallis, West Street Auction Galleries, Lewes, East Sussex BN7 2NJ Tel: 01273 480208 auctions@wallisandwallis.co.uk grb@wallisandwallis.co.uk www.wallisandwallis.co.uk

WAW   Warwick Antiques Warehouse, Unit 7, Cape Road Industrial Estate, Cattell Road, Warwick CV34 4JN Tel: 01926 498849 aboylin1@tiscali.uk

WBB   William Bentley Billiards, Standen Manor Farm, Hungerford, Berkshire RG17 0RB Tel: 01488 861711 www.billiards.co.uk

WD   Weller & Dufty Ltd, 141 Bromsgrove Street, Birmingham, West Midlands B5 6RQ Tel: 0121 692 1414 wellerdufty@freewire.co.uk www.welleranddufty.co.uk

WeA   Wenderton Antiques Tel: 01227 720295 By appointment only

WEL   Wells Reclamation & Co, Coxley, Nr Wells, Somerset BA5 1RQ Tel: 01749 677087

WELD   J. W. Weldon, 55 Clarendon Street, Dublin 2, Republic of Ireland Tel: 00 353 1 677 1638

WELL   Anthony Welling, Broadway Barn, High Street, Ripley, Surrey GU23 6AQ Tel: 01483 225384 ant@awelling.freeserve.co.uk

WiB   Wish Barn Antiques, Wish Street, Rye, East Sussex TN31 7DA Tel: 01797 226797

WilP/ WilP   W. & H. Peacock, 26 Newnham Street, Bedford MK40 3JR Tel: 01234 266366

WIM   Wimpole Antiques, Stand 349, Grays Antique Market, 58 Davies Street, London W1K 5LP Tel: 020 7499 2889 WimpoleAntiques@compuserve.com

WL   Wintertons Ltd, Lichfield Auction Centre, Fradley Park, Lichfield, Staffordshire WS13 8NF Tel: 01543 263256 enquiries@wintertons.co.uk www.wintertons.co.uk

WMa   William Macadam, Edinburgh, Scotland Tel: 0131 466 0343

WOS   Wheels of Steel, Grays Antique Market, Stand A12–13, Unit B10 Basement, 1–7 Davies Mews, London W1Y 2LP Tel: 020 7629 2813

WRe   Walcot Reclamations, 108 Walcot Street, Bath, Somerset BA1 5BG Tel: 01225 444404

WRi   Linda Wrigglesworth, 34 Brook Street, London W1K 5DN Tel: 020 7408 0177 linda@wrigglesworth.demon.co.uk www.artnet.com/chinesetextileswrigglesworth.html

WSA   West Street Antiques, 63 West Street, Dorking, Surrey RH4 1BS Tel: 01306 883487 weststant@aol.com www.antiquearmsandarmour.com

WW   Woolley & Wallis, Salisbury Salerooms, 51–61 Castle Street, Salisbury, Wiltshire SP1 3SU Tel: 01722 424524 mail@salisbury.w-w-c.com www.w-w-c.com

WWo   Woman's Work Tel: 020 8940 2589 Mobile: 07971 691748

WWW   WW Warner, The Forge, The Green, Brasted, Kent TN16 1JL Tel: 01959 563698

YC   Yesterday Child, Angel Arcade, 118 Islington High Street, London N1 8EG Tel: 020 7354 1601

Index to Advertisers

Index

Bold numbers refer to information and pointer boxes

INDEX

INDEX